INTRODUCTION TO LAW
FOR PARALEGALS

The West Legal Studies Series

Your options keep growing with West Legal Studies

Each year our list continues to offer you more options for every area of the law to meet your course or on-the-job reference requirements. We now have over 140 titles from which to choose in the following areas:

Administrative Law	Family Law
Alternative Dispute Resolution	Federal Taxation
Bankruptcy	Intellectual Property
Business Organizations/Corporations	Introduction to Law
Civil Litigation and Procedure	Introduction to Paralegalism
CLA Exam Preparation	Law Office Management
Client Accounting	Law Office Procedures
Computer in the Law Office	Legal Research, Writing, and Analysis
Constitutional Law	Legal Terminology
Contract Law	Paralegal Employment
Criminal Law and Procedure	Real Estate Law
Document Preparation	Reference Materials
Environmental Law	Torts and Personal Injury Law
Ethics	Will, Trusts, and Estate Administration

You will find unparalleled, practical support

Each book is augmented by instructor and student supplements to ensure the best learning experience possible. We also offer custom publishing and other benefits such as West's Student Achievement Award. In addition, our sales representatives are ready to provide you with dependable service.

We want to hear from you

Our best contributions for improving the quality of our books and instructional materials is feedback from the people who use them. If you have a question, concern, or observation about any of our materials, or you have a product proposal or manuscript, we want to hear from you. Please contact your local representative or write us at the following address:

West Legal Studies, 3 Columbia Circle, P.O. Box 15015, Albany, NY 12212-5015

For additional information point your browser at
www.westlegalstudies.com

WEST
TM
THOMSON LEARNING

INTRODUCTION TO LAW
FOR PARALEGALS

Beth Walston-Dunham

WEST

THOMSON LEARNING™

Australia Canada Mexico Singapore Spain United Kingdom United States

WEST

™
THOMSON LEARNING

WEST LEGAL STUDIES

Introduction to Law for Paralegals
Beth Walston-Dunham

Business Unit Director:
Susan L. Simpfenderfer

Executive Editor:
Marlene McHugh Pratt

Senior Acquisitions Editor:
Joan M. Gill

Developmental Editor:
Rhonda Dearborn

Editorial Assistant:
Lisa Flatley

Executive Production Manager:
Wendy A. Troeger

Production Manager:
Carolyn Miller

Production Editor:
Betty L. Dickson

Technology Project Manager:
James Considine

Executive Marketing Manager:
Donna J. Lewis

Channel Manager:
Nigar Hale

For permission to use material from this text or product, contact us by Tel   (800) 730-2214
        Fax (800) 730-2215
        www.thomsonrights.com

Library of Congress Cataloging-in-Publication Data
Walston-Dunham, Beth
    Introduction to law for paralegals/Beth Walston-Dunham
        p. cm.—(The West Legal Studies series)
    Includes index
    ISBN 0-7668-1693-1
        1. Law—United States. 2. Legal assistants—United States—Handbooks, manuals, etc. I. Title. II. Series

KF386 W33 2001
349.73—dc21   2001052608

NOTICE TO THE READER

Dedication

For Ben, Sam, Bobby, and my parents.

Thank you for showing me the light at the end of the tunnel and standing by me while I made the journey.

B.

PREFACE

This text was developed to acquaint the reader with an interest in paralegal training to the profession and also as a basic introduction to the most prominent subjects of law. Hopefully the text will generate additional interest in the law and the profession. Secondly, the goal of the text is to create an awareness of the impact that law and the law-related professions have on virtually every aspect of American culture and society. The chapters dedicated to the structure and function of the American government as it has developed over time and exists today should enable the student to more fully understand the system as it concerns individual citizens, and the adaptability of our government to a culture that is in a constant state of change.

The text is directed toward the student who is studying law for the first time. Chapters are designed to introduce the student to fundamental legal concepts and principles. Early chapters introduce the American legal system and the legal professionals who deal with it on a daily basis. There is also attention to the development and specific functions of the paralegal profession as well as ethical concerns that are an integral part of law-related fields. Additionally, ethical notes at the conclusion of each chapter identify specific points that are relative to the particular subject. Subsequent chapters concentrate on different areas of law by exploring basic principles and terminology. The areas covered include property, business law, estates, tort, domestic relations, contract, and criminal law/procedure. Chapter applications and actual cases provide realistic examples of the materials presented in the text. Written and Internet assignments are designed to reinforce the concepts presented. Each substantive law chapter concludes with a brief discussion of the types of things a working paralegal would encounter if employed in that particular area of law. At the conclusion of the text, the student should have a clearer perspective on the paralegal profession and opportunities as well as a basic understanding of the function of the paralegal in each major area of law.

ANCILLARY MATERIALS

- The **Instructor's Manual** is available both in print and on-line at *www.westlegalstudies.com* in the Instructor's Lounge under Resource .
- **Computerized Test Bank**—The Test Bank found in the Instructor's Manual is also available in a computerized format on CD-ROM. The platforms supported include Windows™ 3.1 and 95, Windows™ NT, and Macintosh. Features include:

  - Multiple methods of question selection
  - Multiple outputs—that is, print, ASCII, and RTF

- • Graphic support (black and white)
- • Random questioning output
  - • Special character support
- **Web page**—Come visit our site at *www.westlegalstudies.com*, where you will find valuable information specific to this book such as hot links and sample materials to download, as well as other West Legal Studies products.
- **WESTLAW®**—West's on-line computerized legal research system offers students "hands-on" experience with a system commonly used in law offices. Qualified adopters can receive ten free house of WESTLAW®. WESTLAW® can be accessed with Macintosh and IBM PC and compatibles. A modem is required.
- **Citation-At-A-Glance**—This handy reference card provides a quick, portable reference to the basic rules of citation for the most commonly cited legal sources, including judicial opinions, statutes, and secondary sources. *Citation-At-A-Glance* uses the rules set forth in *The Bluebook: A Uniform System of Citation*. A free copy of this valuable supplement is included with every student text.
- **Strategies and Tips for Paralegal Educators,** a pamphlet by Anita Tebbe of Johnson County Community College, provides teaching strategies specifically designed for paralegal educators. A copy of this pamphlet is available to each adopter. Quantities for distribution to adjunct instructors are available for purchase at a minimal price. A coupon in the pamphlet provides ordering information.
- **Survival Guide for Paralegal Students,** a pamphlet by Kathleen Mercer Reed and Bradene Moore covers practical and basic information to help students make the most of their paralegal courses. Topics covered include choosing courses of study and note-taking skills.
- **West's Paralegal Video Library**—West Legal Studies is pleased to offer the following videos at no charge to qualified adopters:
  - • *The Drama of the Law II: Paralegal Issues Video* ISBN 0-314-07088-5
  - • *I Never Said I Was a Lawyer Paralegal Ethics Video* ISBN 0-314-08049-X
  - • The Making of a Case Video ISBN 0-314-07300-0
  - • Mock Trial Video—Anatomy of a Trial: A Contracts Case ISBN 0-314-07343-4
  - • Mock Trial Video—Trial Techniques: A Products Liability Case ISBN 0-314-07342-6
  - • Arguments to the United States Supreme Court ISBN 0-314-07070-2
- **Court TV Videos**—West Legal Studies is pleased to offer the following videos from Court TV available for a minimal fee:
  - • New York v. Ferguson—Murder on the 5:33: The Trial of Colin Ferguson ISBN 0-7668-1098-4
  - • Fentress v. Eli Lilly & Co., et al—Prozac n Trial ISBN 0-7668-1095-X
  - • Ohio v. Alfieri—Road Rage ISBN 0-7668-1099-2
  - • Flynn v. Goldman Sachs—Fired on Wall Street: A Case of Sex Discrimination? ISBN 0-7668-1096-8
  - • Dodd v. Dodd—Religion and Child Custody in Conflict ISBN 0-76681094-1
  - • In Re Custody of Baby Girl Clausen—Child of Mine: The Fight for Baby Jessica ISBN 0-7668-1097-6

- Garacia v. Garcia ISBN 0-7668-0264-7
- Northside Partners v. Page and New Kids on the Block (Intellectual Property) ISBN 0-7668-0426-7
- Maglica v. Maglica (Contract Law) ISBN 0-7668-0867-X
- Hall v. Hall (Family Law) ISBN 0-7668-0196-9

ACKNOWLEDGEMENTS

Thanks and appreciation are extended to the manuscript reviewers, instructors, and others who provided invaluable suggestions and support in the preparation of the third edition:

Linda Anderson
Woodbury College, VT

Elaine Brown
Victoria College, TX

Holly Enterline
*State Technical Institute
at Memphis, TN*

Patricia Greer
Berkely College, NJ

Richard Hughes
California State University, CA

Cassy Kent,
Finger Lakes Community College, NY

Brian McCully,
Fresno City College, CA

Kathryn Myers,
St. Mary of the Woods College, IN

Linda Potter,
Delta College, MI

Melody Schroer,
Maryville University, MO

Catherine Stevens,
College of Southern Maryland, MD

The author wishes to thank William P. Statsky for the use of material from *Legal Thesaurus/Dictionary*.

Thanks, also, to Joan Gill, of Delmar Publishing, for her tremendous support and patience as I undertook this project under what was often less than ideal circumstances.

Beth Walston-Dunham

TABLE OF CASES

TABLE OF ILLUSTRATIONS

CONTENTS

10 The Law of Agency, Business Organizations, and Bankruptcy 263

Chapter 1

THE DEVELOPMENT OF THE AMERICAN LEGAL SYSTEM

CHAPTER OBJECTIVES

Upon completion of this chapter you should be able to do the following:

- Trace the chronological history of documents used to establish American independence.

- Identify the three philosophical theories that primarily impacted the development of the American legal system.

- Explain the traditional balance.

- Explain the modern balance.

- Diagram the structure of the current American legal system.

- Distinguish the three branches of the federal government in the American legal system.

- Discuss and distinguish the various roles of law-related professions.

A. FOUNDATION OF THE CURRENT LEGAL SYSTEM

While the American legal system has been in place for well over 200 years, it is quite different from the original plans of those first individuals to cross the Atlantic ocean. In fact, the current structure of the American legal system is quite different from the first government established at the time of the Declaration of Independence. However, the ideals and principles of those early citizens are still evident in the laws that govern American society today.

1. Origins of the American Legal System

When settlers first came to the North American continent, the goal was religious freedom. They had no grand plan to establish a new and powerful nation or even to seek independence from the governments of Europe (especially England) from which they came. In fact, for more than 100 years many settlers were more or less resigned to the fact of the sovereignty of the crown. However, as these people learned to function on their own, largely independent of any formal presence of government, they came to resent attempts by authorities thousands of miles away to influence them. This resentment increased exponentially when the English government attempted to extract taxes from the settlers on their goods. These people perceived little or no benefit from the government across the Atlantic. Yet, they were expected to pay taxes as if they still resided in England and lived under the protection of the English crown. It was readily apparent to the settlers that the same rules of conduct, including those that had originally caused them to flee with respect to religious freedoms, would soon follow.

This resentment was met with stepped-up efforts by the British government to firmly colonize the settlers and establish a military presence to enforce British government here. Although the settlers (known as colonists) were willing to adopt many legal principles from England, they were not interested in adopting a governmental structure that they felt was not responsive to the will of the people. After all, this was exactly what they had sought to avoid by coming to America.

During the revolutionary era, the colonists realized they had to establish some form of permanent and independent governmental structure if they were to avoid rule by another country. The present-day structure derives from a combination of factors that influenced those responsible for establishing the American government. The incredible thought and foresight of these individuals in their attempt to establish a solid foundation is most clearly evidenced by the basic structure of government that is still functional and strong well over two centuries later.

The first official step taken by the colonists toward an independent government was a declaration to England, and the world, that the citizens in the new colony intended to reject colonization and function as an independent nation. Already there had been military skirmishes, but this was the first formal act by an organized group. Representatives of each of the colonies signed the Declaration of Independence and forwarded it to England. In the meantime, these representatives drafted the framework for a new national government in a document known as the Articles of Confederation. It served as the basis for the government of the United States until 1787. Yet, almost from their inception, the Articles were fraught with flaws and resulting problems. Under the original Articles of Confederation, the national government was more of a theory than an actuality. The delegates of each state committed their colony to contribute monies toward the support of a government and army. But the states functioned on a largely independent basis and no provisions were made to enforce support from each of the states' citizens and local governments for a national army and a central government to deal with foreign nations. As the British continued to attempt control, the need for a unified front was painfully evident. A more comprehensive form of government had to be developed.

The goal of a unified nation was not met through the Articles, which had no tools to ensure that the colonies acted more collectively rather than independently. So, as the representatives convened periodically to address issues of the nation and the ongoing fight for independence, they began to form ideas for a more solid national government structure that could withstand attack by other governments. A government was needed that could bring together colonies with vastly different interests and could adapt to changes and growth of population, geographical area, and societal standards of the people as they occurred. The result was the U.S. Constitution, passed in September 1787, that has steered the United States well in excess of 200 years. But the Constitution was not written or agreed upon overnight.

The initial decision facing the delegates of the various states to the constitutional convention was whether to abolish independent states and operate under a single government or attempt a national government for national issues and local state government for issues affecting citizens within their respective colonies. Due to the lingering concerns about a government that was unresponsive to individuals, popular support fell behind the local/national system of government. This allowed states to respond effectively and quickly to the needs of citizens and their individual economies. The national government would then protect the fundamental rights of all citizens with respect to foreign interests and ensure that the state governments did not interfere with these fundamental rights. By having such a combination of governmental systems, the colonists were able to satisfy the needs they had seen largely ignored by the national governments of Britain and other European countries. In September 1787, after 11 years of debate and drafting and reviewing the various provisions with colonists, the delegates of the newly formed United States of America adopted the U.S. Constitution. The first 10 Amendments, known as the Bill of Rights, were adopted in 1789 and ratified in 1791 (Appendix A). The U.S. Constitution establishes the framework and policies for the function of the national government. The Bill of Rights sets forth the inalienable rights guaranteed to all citizens of the nation. The factors that brought about the final document were not only the product of political change, but also of changing philosophies of the society that had developed in the United States, away from the traditional and cultural influences of Great Britain and Europe.

Once the issue of statehood versus a single national government was decided, the Congress set out to create the structure of the national government. The Constitution clearly delineated the powers and limitations of national and state governments with respect to each other and individual citizens. Three distinct branches of government were created with legislative, judiciary, and executive (administrative) powers. Each had a separate purpose and duties and the ability to influence the other branches to ensure that no one branch obtained too much power. In this way, another safeguard was put in place to protect the individual freedoms that were so important to the citizens of the newly formed government as the laws were administered.

The Bill of Rights protects what are considered to be the essential fundamental human freedoms. It protects all citizens from government infringement on those matters presumed to be inherently personal and a matter of choice for all human beings.

Following is a summary of the guarantees established in these initial 10 amendments. Over time, they have been interpreted more broadly to encompass current applications and definitions given the evolution of American society at any given point.

- Freedom of speech, religion, and press; peaceable assembly; petitions for governmental change
- Right to bear arms
- Freedom from unreasonable invasion of home by the government for purposes of search and seizure of persons or property
- Right to have an independent judicial magistrate determine if probable cause exists before a search or arrest warrant can be issued
- Right not to be tried twice for the same crime (freedom from double jeopardy)
- Right to due process before seizure of person or property
- Right to a speedy and public trial
- Right to an impartial jury in the jurisdiction where the alleged crime occurred
- Right to be free from forced self-incrimination
- Right to counsel in criminal prosecutions
- Right of the accused to know what crime is alleged
- Right of the accused to confront the witnesses for the prosecution
- Right not to be subjected to excessive bail
- Right to be free from cruel or unusual punishment
- Right of the states to govern on matters not addressed in the Constitution or its amendments

Assignment 1.1

> Referring to the list above, describe five present-day circumstances in which a citizen exercises a freedom based in the Bill of Rights.

The Bill of Rights establishes the standards of fundamental fairness by which the government must deal with its citizens. These standards of fairness have been and continue to be protected by the U.S. Supreme Court. Each year the Court interprets cases that allege some type of interference with basic freedoms guaranteed under the Bill of Rights. While societal standards and technological advancements have altered the circumstances affecting citizens, the Court still functions to ensure that the basic freedoms under the Constitution remain intact.

2. Sociological Influences

Naturalist Theory
Philosophy that all persons know inherently the difference between right and wrong.

The original system of justice and the foundation for government in America was a simplistic theory of right and wrong. For some time, the colonists saw no need for written statutes. This belief, also known as the **naturalist theory,** was based on the belief that all persons inherently knew the difference between right and wrong and should conduct themselves accordingly. However, as the population increased and industry advanced and expanded, vast numbers of individuals with differing opinions of right and wrong made simple aristocratic beliefs obsolete. The people required a more detailed legal system that included written legal principles applicable to the entire population.

The functioning of the branches of government and the manner in which issues between government and citizens are decided are the product of several distinct philosophies that have influenced the American legal system since its inception. As Congress structured the new government, the naturalist theory became inadequate to deal with the complexity of legal issues that arose. As a result, other theories regarding the establishment of an orderly society were incorporated into the U.S. system of government and law. One influential philosophy was the **positivist theory,** which proposes that a government should have a single entity to determine what is right and wrong as a matter of law. The law cannot be questioned or challenged. If a law is violated, punishment will automatically follow. Some elements of this theory are evident in the court of last resort—the U.S. Supreme Court. Short of a constitutional amendment, the decisions of the Supreme Court are not subject to any other authority. When the Supreme Court issues a mandate, it must be adhered to unless the Congress acts collectively in the form of an amendment to state an alternative view representing the will of the people.

Another political theory of law that has become an integral part of American law is rooted in social consciousness. This sociological view suggests that people as a group determine what is and is not acceptable, based on the needs of society at the time. **Sociological theory** holds that society and the law are in a constant state of change and that laws adjust according to the needs and demands of society. Society as a whole decides what is acceptable and what is unacceptable conduct. In conjunction with the naturalist theory, the positivist and sociological theories provide the components for a successful and durable government. Today, the majority of law is created by representatives elected to Congress by the population. If citizens believe a law is wrong, they can lobby to have it changed. If they believe their elected representatives are not enacting laws that embody the beliefs of the people, they can elect new legislators. If the legislature passes a law that appears to violate the Constitution, citizens can challenge the law in the courts that have the power to resolve the issue by upholding the statute or invalidating it as unconstitutional.

In some respects, the American legal system is a product of each of the three philosophies. The naturalist theory is reflected in the language of the Constitution and especially in the Bill of Rights, which state what was and continues to be considered fundamentally acceptable or unacceptable governmental conduct. The Constitution and the Bill of Rights also contain statements indicative of the positivist idea of law and the ultimate authority that interprets the laws and decides in what circumstances they apply and how they should be enforced. The ultimate rule has been embodied in the judiciary. Although laws can be challenged in such cases, the Supreme Court is generally the final authority on legal issues. A decision by this Court can be affected only by a congressional constitutional enactment or by a decision wherein the Court reverses a previous position. Both are relatively rare occurrences. The Supreme Court helps ensure that the laws are applied consistently to all people. The duty of the Court is to guarantee that each individual's rights will be protected against government, persons, or entities that might violate those rights.

The sociological theory plays an important role in our governmental structure, because society can influence the government and laws in a number of ways. The people have the right to periodically elect representatives to Congress and to select a president. They even have the right to approve or reject constitutional amendments and certain other laws. If society's needs change, the flexible system of government allows

Positivist Theory
Doctrine that there should be one government entity which is not subject to question and which is responsible for the final resolution of all disputes.

Sociological Theory
Doctrine that follows the principle that government should adapt laws to reflect the current needs and beliefs of society.

passage of laws, election of representatives who will enact laws suited to the changing times, or both. Evidence of this can be seen in any governmental election. Senators and representatives are elected by a majority who share similar political beliefs. Theoretically, the members of Congress elected by the majority represent the beliefs of the people with regard to the law.

3. An Issue of Balance

As a practical matter, citizens have more frequent personal contact with the judicial branch than with any other branch of government. Judges hear everything from traffic cases to domestic disputes to claims that the state or federal legislature has exceeded the limits of its authority by passing laws that are in violation of the Constitution. Since the beginning of the current system of government, courts have continually faced the task of balancing competing interests. These interests might be called the **traditional balance** and the **modern balance,** both of which are employed by all branches of government when considering the establishment and interpretation of legal principles.

Traditional Balance
Goal of the judiciary to allow maximum personal freedom without detracting from the welfare of the general public.

Modern Balance
Goal of lawmaking authorities to balance the need for consistency and stability against the need for a flexible and adaptive government.

The traditional balance arose from the very inception of our governmental system. The people no longer wanted strictly positivist rule from a single source but wanted to have input into the laws they had to live by (sociological theory). However, not everyone agrees as to what the law should be in a given situation (naturalist theory). Under majority rule, laws are enacted based on what the majority thinks is necessary to protect the rights of the public as a whole. Some individuals may maintain, however, that they have a valid right to disobey a particular law or that the law as written does not apply to their particular situation. In that case, the judiciary must examine the broadly written laws and apply them to individual circumstances. The challenge facing every judge is to enforce the laws to the extent necessary to protect the rights of the public while permitting the greatest amount of personal freedom possible for the individual. Simply stated, the traditional balance equals the rights of the people versus the rights of the individual.

Initially, judges had only to balance individual freedoms against the good of the nation as a whole, but, over the course of time, American society became increasingly complex. People from many different cultures, races, and religions came to this country in large numbers. The industrial revolution reached full force, followed by the age of advanced technology. The impact of the Civil War, two world wars, numerous conflicts with other countries, and the cold war created an even stronger demand for rapid development of technology and adaptation of societal standards. Despite these tremendous stresses and a state of constant change, the American governmental system did not falter. The longevity of the American legal system is largely the result of the willingness of the judiciary and the other branches of government to develop and employ the modern balance in conjunction with the traditional balance.

The modern balance is a very delicate one. In essence, it is the need to enforce existing legal principles based on the Constitution versus the need to adopt legal principles more reflective of current society. To write laws that would envision all the potential situations and changes in society for hundreds of years to come is an impossible task. Thus, the judiciary, with the help of the executive branch and Congress, must be able to recognize those situations where modifications in the existing system were perceived as warranted. This balance has been accomplished without ever disturbing the fundamental structure set forth in the Constitution. Indeed, the modern balance is the ability to enforce law consistently while retaining enough flexibility to adapt to changes in societal standards.

APPLICATION 1.1

Lawrence went out with friends and drank several beers. As he exited the bar he felt too intoxicated to safely drive home. It was very cold outside, so he got into his parked car and turned on the ignition to run the heater while he waited for the effects of the alcohol to wear off. He fell asleep and was awakened by a police officer who charged him with driving under the influence. The applicable statutory law indicates that anyone with a blood alcohol level above the legal limit and in control of a vehicle is guilty of the offense. In the present case, while Lawrence was in violation of the letter of the law, his intent and actions clearly demonstrate an attempt to avoid such a violation and the very harm the statute was intended to protect. While a judge would not have the authority to disregard the statute, an attempt to balance the needs of society with the needs of the individual could possibly result in a more lenient sentence.

Point for Discussion: Why should Lawrence receive a more lenient sentence if he violated the terms of the statute?

B. THE CURRENT LEGAL SYSTEM—ITS BASIC STRUCTURE AND FUNCTIONS

1. The Branches of Federal Government

The present system of government and law in America is far more sophisticated and much larger than the first government that took effect under the Constitution in 1787. That government consisted of the Congress with representatives and senators from each of the 13 states that then formed the United States of America, a president who had only a basic outline of duties under the Constitution, and a single court that served as the judicial system for the entire nation.

Today, that same Congress includes senators and representatives elected by the population of each of the 50 states. The presidency has developed into a complicated office that not only represents this country in foreign affairs but also oversees the administrative agencies of government and approves or rejects all acts of Congress. The federal judiciary has grown to include three separate levels: the Supreme Court, 13 U.S. Circuit Courts of Appeals, and more than 90 U.S. District Courts. Interestingly, all three branches still follow the same basic purposes outlined in the Constitution.

The three branches of government created in the Constitution were developed to meet the needs of the citizens, and also to protect the general population from one person or group of persons gaining too much control over the majority. The first branch of government, the legislative branch, was called Congress and was split into two elected bodies. The Senate was comprised of two popularly elected representatives from each state. This gave all states, regardless of size, an equal voice. The House of Representatives was based on population, giving more heavily populated areas more representatives to ensure a fair representation of all citizens.

Congress retained the sole authority to make statutory law. In this way, the people as a whole would always have significant influence in making the laws that all persons were required to follow. As delegated by the Constitution, only Congress, and no other

Delegation Doctrine
Policy that Congress does not have the power to delegate or assign its original law making authority to any other body of government.

branch, has the power to create statutory law. In the past, when any other governmental source attempted to create statutory law, the law was struck down as being in violation of what is known as the **delegation doctrine.** The delegation doctrine is based on the legal principle that under the Constitution Congress cannot delegate, give away, or allow another entity the authority to make statutory law. The doctrine has been applied most often in the creation of regulatory law by administrative agencies under the executive branch. Administrative agencies have the responsibility to define and clarify statutory law through administrative regulations and rules. But when these exceed the parameters of a statute, they violate the doctrine. The delegation doctrine is addressed more fully in Chapter 2, which addresses administrative law and the executive branch.

The second branch of government to be created was the executive branch. The president heads the executive branch at the national level, and each state executive branch is headed by a governor. Under the Constitution, the president is elected indirectly by the people through the electoral college. Each state is entitled to appoint a number of electors equal to the state's total number of senators and representatives to Congress. A person cannot serve as both a member of Congress and an elector. Each state legislature determines the manner in which the electors are appointed. The electors vote and elect the president by a majority. Generally, the electoral vote reflects the popular vote. In the event there is no one person with a majority, the House of Representatives is responsible for electing the president. The details of the electoral process can be found in Article II of the Constitution.

The president has the power to approve or reject acts of Congress; however, the power is not absolute, and the president cannot deny the authority of Congress to enact law if it is in fact the will of the majority that such law be enacted. Rejection by the president of a law enacted by Congress is known as the veto power and can be overridden by a significant majority of Congress. The president also has several important functions with respect to foreign affairs and has the ultimate duty to enforce the laws of the United States. Consequently, federal law enforcement agencies are considered to be part of the executive branch. A similar structure is in place at the state level between the governor and state law enforcement personnel. Executive authority is addressed more fully in Chapter 2, which examines the executive branch and administrative law.

A third and separate branch of government was created to serve as mediator of disputes between states and disputes involving citizens who are challenging the application of federal laws. Thus, the judicial branch was established. The judiciary has the authority to interpret laws and protect the Constitution from violation by Congress, the president, or the states. Although the Constitution vests the ultimate authority to enforce laws in the president, in practice, the judiciary also assists in enforcement when the courts apply law to specific cases.

CASE IN POINT
Sante Fe Ind. School Dist. v. Doe, 530 U.S. 290, 120 S.C. 2266, 147 L.2d.2d 295 (2000).

____ *S.Ct.* ____ *(2000).*

Justice STEVENS delivered the opinion of the Court.

Prior to 1995, the Santa Fe High School student who occupied the school's elective office of student council chaplain delivered a prayer over the public address system before each varsity football game for the entire season. This practice, along with others, was challenged in District Court as a violation of the Establishment Clause of the First Amendment. While these proceedings were pending in the District Court, the school district adopted a different policy that permits, but does not require, prayer initiated and led by a student at all home games. The District Court entered an order modifying that policy to permit only nonsectarian, nonproselytizing prayer. The Court of Appeals held that, even as modified by the District Court, the football prayer policy was invalid. We granted the school district's petition for certiorari to review that holding.

I

The Santa Fe Independent School District (District) is a political subdivision of the State of Texas, responsible for the education of more than 4,000 students in a small community in the southern part of the State. Respondents are two sets of current or former students and their respective mothers. One family is Mormon and the other is Catholic. The District Court permitted respondents (Does) to litigate anonymously to protect them from intimidation or harassment.

Respondents commenced this action in April 1995 and moved for a temporary restraining order to prevent the District from violating the Establishment Clause at the imminent graduation exercises. In their complaint the Does alleged that the District had engaged in several proselytizing practices, such as promoting attendance at a Baptist revival meeting, encouraging membership in religious clubs, chastising children who held minority religious beliefs, and distributing Gideon Bibles on school premises. They also alleged that the District allowed students to read Christian invocations and benedictions from the stage at graduation ceremonies, and to deliver overtly Christian prayers over the public address system at home football games.

On May 10, 1995, the District Court entered an interim order addressing a number of different issues. With respect to the impending graduation, the order provided that "non-denominational prayer" consisting of "an invocation and/or benediction" could be presented by a senior student or students selected by members of the graduating class. The text of the prayer was to be determined by the students, without scrutiny or preapproval by school officials. References to particular religious figures "such as Mohammed, Jesus, Buddha, or the like" would be permitted "as long as the general thrust of the prayer is non-proselytizing."

In response to that portion of the order, the District adopted a series of policies over several months

dealing with prayer at school functions. The policies enacted in May and July for graduation ceremonies provided the format for the August and October policies for football games. The May policy provided:

" 'The board has chosen to permit the graduating senior class, with the advice and counsel of the senior class principal or designee, to elect by secret ballot to choose whether an invocation and benediction shall be part of the graduation exercise. If so chosen the class shall elect by secret ballot, from a list of student volunteers, students to deliver nonsectarian, nonproselytizing invocations and benedictions for the purpose of solemnizing their graduation ceremonies.' " 168 F.3d 806, 811 (C.A.5 1999) (emphasis deleted).

The parties stipulated that after this policy was adopted, "the senior class held an election to determine whether to have an invocation and benediction at the commencement [and that the] class voted, by secret ballot, to include prayer at the high school graduation." In a second vote the class elected two seniors to deliver the invocation and benediction.

In July, the District enacted another policy eliminating the requirement that invocations and benedictions be "nonsectarian and nonproselytising," but also providing that if the District were to be enjoined from enforcing that policy, the May policy would automatically become effective.

The August policy, which was titled "Prayer at Football Games," was similar to the July policy for graduations. It also authorized two student elections, the first to determine whether "invocations" should be delivered, and the second to select the spokesperson to deliver them. Like the July policy, it contained two parts, an initial statement that omitted any requirement that the content of the invocation be "nonsectarian and nonproselytising," and a fallback provision that automatically added that limitation if the preferred policy should be enjoined. On August 31, 1995, according to the parties' stipulation, "the district's high school students voted to determine whether a student would deliver prayer at varsity football games. . . . The students chose to allow a student to say a prayer at football games." A week later, in a separate election, they selected a student "to deliver the prayer at varsity football games."

The final policy (October policy) is essentially the same as the August policy, though it omits the word "prayer" from its title, and refers to "messages" and "statements" as well as "invocations." It is the validity of that policy that is before us.

The District Court did enter an order precluding enforcement of the first, open-ended policy. Relying on our decision in Lee v. Weisman, 505 U.S. 577, 112 S.Ct. 2649, 120 L.Ed.2d 467 (1992), it held that the school's "action must not 'coerce anyone to support or participate in' a religious exercise." Applying that test, it concluded that the graduation prayers appealed "to distinctively Christian beliefs," and that delivering a prayer "over the school's public address system prior to each football and baseball game coerces student participation in religious events." Both parties appealed, the District contending that the enjoined portion of the October policy was permissible and the Does contending that both alternatives violated the Establishment Clause. The Court of Appeals majority agreed with the Does.

The decision of the Court of Appeals followed Fifth Circuit precedent that had announced two rules. In Jones v. Clear Creek Independent School Dist., 977 F.2d 963 (1992), that court held that student-led prayer that was approved by a vote of the students and was nonsectarian and nonproselytizing was permissible at high school graduation ceremonies. On the other hand, in later cases the Fifth Circuit made it clear that the Clear Creek rule applied only to high school graduations and that school-encouraged prayer was constitutionally impermissible at school-related sporting events. Thus, in Doe v. Duncanville Independent School Dist., 70 F.3d 402 (1995), it had described a high school graduation as "a significant, once in-a-lifetime event" to be contrasted with athletic events in "a setting that is far less solemn and extraordinary." Id., at 406–407.

In its opinion in this case, the Court of Appeals explained:

"The controlling feature here is the same as in Duncanville: The prayers are to be delivered at football games—hardly the sober type of annual event that can be appropriately solemnized with prayer. The distinction to which [the District] points is simply one without difference. Regardless of whether the prayers are selected by vote or spontaneously initiated at these frequently-recurring, informal, school-sponsored events, school officials are present and have the authority to stop the prayers. Thus, as we indicated in Duncanville, our decision in Clear Creek II hinged on the singular context and singularly serious nature of a graduation ceremony. Outside that nurturing context, a Clear Creek Prayer Policy cannot survive. We therefore reverse the district court's holding that [the District's] alternative Clear Creek Prayer Policy can be extended to football games, irrespective of the presence of the nonsectarian, nonproselytizing restrictions."

We granted the District's petition for certiorari, limited to the following question: "Whether petitioner's policy permitting student-led, student-initiated prayer at football games violates the Establishment Clause." 528 U.S. 1002 (1999). We conclude, as did the Court of Appeals, that it does.

II

The first Clause in the First Amendment to the Federal Constitution provides that "Congress shall make no law respecting an establishment of religion, or prohibiting the free exercise thereof." The Fourteenth Amendment imposes those substantive limitations on the legislative power of the States and their political subdivisions. Wallace v. Jaffree, 472 U.S. 38, 49-50, 105 S.Ct. 2479, 86 L.Ed.2d 29 (1985). In Lee v. Weisman, 505 U.S. 577, 112 S.Ct. 2649, 120 L.Ed.2d 467 (1992), we held that a prayer delivered by a rabbi at a middle school graduation ceremony violated that Clause. Although this case involves student prayer at a different type of school function, our analysis is properly guided by the principles that we endorsed in Lee.

As we held in that case:

"The principle that government may accommodate the free exercise of religion does not supersede the fundamental limitations imposed by the Establishment Clause. It is beyond dispute that, at a minimum, the Constitution guarantees that government may not coerce anyone to support or participate in religion or its exercise, or otherwise act in a way which 'establishes a [state] religion or religious faith, or tends to do so.' " Id., at 587 (citations omitted) (quoting Lynch v. Donnelly, 465 U.S. 668, 678, 104 S.Ct. 1355, 79 L.Ed.2d 604 (1984)).

Moreover, the District has failed to divorce itself from the religious content in the invocations. It has not succeeded in doing so, either by claiming that its policy is " 'one of neutrality rather than endorsement' " or by characterizing the individual student as the "circuit-breaker" in the process. Contrary to the District's repeated assertions that it has adopted a "hands-off" approach to the pregame invocation, the realities of the situation plainly reveal that its policy involves both perceived and actual endorsement of religion. In this case, as we found in Lee, the "degree of school involvement" makes it clear that the pregame prayers bear "the imprint of the State and thus put school-age children who objected in an untenable position." 505 U.S., at 590.

The District has attempted to disentangle itself from the religious messages by developing the two-step student election process. The text of the October policy, however, exposes the extent of the school's entanglement. The elections take place at all only because the school "board has chosen to permit students to deliver a brief invocation and/or message." App. 104 (emphasis added). The elections thus "shall" be conducted "by the high school student council" and "[u]pon advice and direction of the high school principal." Id., at 104-105. The decision whether to deliver a message is first made by majority vote of the entire student body, followed by a choice of the speaker in a separate, similar majority election. Even though the particular words used by the speaker are not determined by those votes, the policy mandates that the "statement or invocation" be "consistent with the goals and purposes of this policy," which are "to solemnize the event, to promote good sportsmanship and student safety, and to establish the appropriate environment for the competition." Ibid.

In addition to involving the school in the selection of the speaker, the policy, by its terms, invites and encourages religious messages. The policy itself states that the purpose of the message is "to solemnize the event." A religious message is the most obvious method of solemnizing an event. Moreover, the requirements that the message "promote good citizenship" and "establish the appropriate environment for competition" further narrow the types of message deemed appropriate, suggesting that a solemn, yet nonreligious, message, such as commentary on United States foreign policy, would be prohibited. Indeed, the only type of message that is expressly endorsed in the text is an "invocation"—a term that primarily describes an appeal for divine assistance. In fact, as used in the past at Santa Fe High School, an "invocation" has always entailed a focused religious message. Thus, the expressed purposes of the policy encourage the selection of a religious message, and that is precisely how the students understand the policy. The results of the elections described in the parties' stipulation make it clear that the students understood that the central question before them was whether prayer should be a part of the pregame cere-

mony. We recognize the important role that public worship plays in many communities, as well as the sincere desire to include public prayer as a part of various occasions so as to mark those occasions' significance. But such religious activity in public schools, as elsewhere, must comport with the First Amendment.

The actual or perceived endorsement of the message, moreover, is established by factors beyond just the text of the policy. Once the student speaker is selected and the message composed, the invocation is then delivered to a large audience assembled as part of a regularly scheduled, school-sponsored function conducted on school property. The message is broadcast over the school's public address system, which remains subject to the control of school officials. It is fair to assume that the pregame ceremony is clothed in the traditional indicia of school sporting events, which generally include not just the team, but also cheerleaders and band members dressed in uniforms sporting the school name and mascot. The school's name is likely written in large print across the field and on banners and flags. The crowd will certainly include many who display the school colors and insignia on their school T-shirts, jackets, or hats and who may also be waving signs displaying the school name. It is in a setting such as this that "[t]he board has chosen to permit" the elected student to rise and give the "statement or invocation."

In this context the members of the listening audience must perceive the pregame message as a public expression of the views of the majority of the student body delivered with the approval of the school administration. In cases involving state participation in a religious activity, one of the relevant questions is "whether an objective observer, acquainted with the text, legislative history, and implementation of the statute, would perceive it as a state endorsement of prayer in public schools." Wallace, 472 U.S., at 73, 76. Regardless of the listener's support for, or objection to, the message, an objective Santa Fe High School student will unquestionably perceive the inevitable pregame prayer as stamped with her school's seal of approval.

The text and history of this policy, moreover, reinforce our objective student's perception that the prayer is, in actuality, encouraged by the school. When a governmental entity professes a secular purpose for an arguably religious policy, the government's characterization is, of course, entitled to some deference. But it is nonetheless the duty of the courts to "distinguis[h] a sham secular purpose from a sincere one." Wallace, 472 U.S., at 75.

According to the District, the secular purposes of the policy are to "foste[r] free expression of private persons . . . as well [as to] solemniz[e] sporting events, promot[e] good sportsmanship and student safety, and establis[h] an appropriate environment for competition." Brief for Petitioner 14. We note, however, that the District's approval of only one specific kind of message, an "invocation," is not necessary to further any of these purposes. Additionally, the fact that only one student is permitted to give a content-limited message suggests that this policy does little to "foste[r] free expression." Furthermore, regardless of whether one considers a sporting event an appropriate occasion for solemnity, the use of an invocation to foster such solemnity is impermissible when, in actuality, it constitutes prayer sponsored by the school. And it is unclear what type of message would be both appropriately "solemnizing" under the District's policy and yet non-religious.

Most striking to us is the evolution of the current policy from the long-sanctioned office of "Student Chaplain" to the candidly titled "Prayer at Football Games" regulation. This history indicates that the District intended to preserve the practice of prayer before football games. The conclusion that the District viewed the October policy simply as a continuation of the previous policies is dramatically illustrated by the fact that the school did not conduct a new election, pursuant to the current policy, to replace the results of the previous election, which occurred under the former policy. Given these observations, and in light of the school's history of regular delivery of a student-led prayer at athletic events, it is reasonable to infer that the specific purpose of the policy was to preserve a popular "state-sponsored religious practice." Lee, 505 U.S., at 596.

School sponsorship of a religious message is impermissible because it sends the ancillary message to members of the audience who are nonadherants "that they are outsiders, not full members of the political community, and an accompanying message to adherants that they are insiders, favored members of the political community." Lynch v. Donnelly, 465 U.S., at 688 (1984). The delivery of such a message—over the school's public address system, by a speaker representing the student body, under the supervision of school faculty, and pursuant to a school policy that explicitly and implicitly encourages public prayer—is not properly characterized as "private" speech.

The District next argues that its football policy is distinguishable from the graduation prayer in Lee because it does not coerce students to participate in religious observances. Its argument has two parts: first, that there is no impermissible government coercion because the pregame messages are the product of student choices; and second, that there is really no coercion at all because attendance at an extracurricular event, unlike a graduation ceremony, is voluntary.

The reasons just discussed explaining why the alleged "circuit-breaker" mechanism of the dual elections and student speaker do not turn public speech into private speech also demonstrate why these mechanisms do not insulate the school from the coercive element of the final message. In fact, this aspect of the District's argument exposes anew the concerns that are created by the majoritarian election system. The parties' stipulation clearly states that the issue resolved in the first election was "whether a student would deliver prayer at varsity football games," App. 65, and the controversy in this case demonstrates that the views of the students are not unanimous on that issue.

The District further argues that attendance at the commencement ceremonies at issue in Lee "differs dramatically" from attendance at high school football games, which it contends "are of no more than passing interest to many students" and are "decidedly extracurricular," thus dissipating any coercion. Attendance at a high school football game, unlike showing up for class, is certainly not required in order to receive a diploma. Moreover, we may assume that the District is correct in arguing that the informal pressure to attend an athletic event is not as strong as a senior's desire to attend her own graduation ceremony.

There are some students, however, such as cheerleaders, members of the band, and, of course, the team members themselves, for whom seasonal commitments mandate their attendance, sometimes for class credit. The District also minimizes the importance to many students of attending and participating in extracurricular activities as part of a complete educational experience. As we noted in Lee, "[l]aw reaches past formalism." 505 U.S., at 595. To assert that high school students do not feel immense social pressure, or have a truly genuine desire, to be involved in the extracurricular event that is American high school football is "formalistic in the extreme." Ibid. We stressed in Lee the obvious observation that "adolescents are often susceptible to pressure from their peers towards conformity, and that the influence is strongest in matters of social convention." Id., at 593. High school home football games are traditional gatherings of a school community; they bring together students and faculty as well as friends and family from years present and past to root for a common cause. Undoubtedly, the games are not important to some students, and they voluntarily choose not to attend. For many others, however, the choice between whether to attend these games or to risk facing a personally offensive religious ritual is in no practical sense an easy one. The Constitution, moreover, demands that the school may not force this difficult choice upon these students for "[i]t is a tenet of the First Amendment that the State cannot require one of its citizens to forfeit his or her rights and benefits as the price of resisting conformance to state-sponsored religious practice." Id., at 596.

Even if we regard every high school student's decision to attend a home football game as purely voluntary, we are nevertheless persuaded that the delivery of a pregame prayer has the improper effect of coercing those present to participate in an act of religious worship. For "the government may no more use social pressure to enforce orthodoxy than it may use more direct means." Id., at 594. As in Lee, "[w]hat to most believers may seem nothing more than a reasonable request that the nonbeliever respect their religious practices, in a school context may appear to the nonbeliever or dissenter to be an attempt to employ the machinery of the State to enforce a religious orthodoxy." Id., at 592. The constitutional command will not permit the District "to exact religious conformity from a student as the price" of joining her classmates at a varsity football game.

Therefore, the simple enactment of this policy, with the purpose and perception of school endorsement of student prayer, was a constitutional violation. We need not wait for the inevitable to confirm and magnify the constitutional injury. In Wallace, for example, we invalidated Alabama's as yet unimplemented and voluntary "moment of silence" statute based on our conclusion that it was enacted "for the sole purpose of expressing the State's endorsement of prayer activities for one minute at the beginning of each school day." 472 U.S., at 60; see also Church of Lukumi Babalu Aye, Inc. v. Hialeah, 508 U.S. 520, 532, 113 S.Ct. 2217, 124 L.Ed.2d 472 (1993). Therefore, even if no Santa Fe High School student were ever to offer a religious message, the October policy fails a facial challenge because the attempt by the District to encourage prayer is also at issue. Government efforts to endorse religion cannot evade constitutional reproach based solely on the remote possibility that those attempts may fail.

To properly examine this policy on its face, we "must be deemed aware of the history and context of the community and forum," Pinette, 515 U.S., at 780 (O'CONNOR, J., concurring in part and concurring in judgment). Our examination of those circumstances above leads to the conclusion that this policy does not provide the District with the constitutional safe harbor it sought. The policy is invalid on its face because it establishes an improper majoritarian election on religion, and unquestionably has the purpose and creates the perception of encouraging the delivery of prayer at a series of important school events.

The judgment of the Court of Appeals is, accordingly, affirmed.

It is so ordered.

Case Review Question: Why is the policy to allow a majority vote on whether to include prayer at school functions still a violation of the First Amendment?

2. State Government

From the initial 13 states to the present 50, as each state government evolved, a structure similar to that of the federal government was put in place to administer the laws of each state within its own boundaries. All 50 states have a similar trio of governmental branches—an executive branch with a governor as its head, a judicial branch, and a legislative body. However, there are nuances in the internal structure of these branches reflective of the individual nature of the citizens of the various states. For example, the Nebraska state legislature consists of only one body of senators, known as the unicameral, as opposed to the federal system and the majority of state systems, that have a two-body legislature comprised of senators in one house and representatives in another. Similarly, the judicial branch of the various states are composed of courts and are arranged to be most effective and efficient in meeting the specific needs of particular states. For example, some states may not cover much geographical area but may contain a dense population. This requires many courts to meet concurrently (some even at night) in one general location. This is in contrast to a sparsely populated state covering a large geographical area wherein the judiciary may only have scheduled hearings in various parts of the state on a monthly basis with other hearings as necessary. The offices of the executive and judicial branches of government may also differ from state to state depending upon the state's resources, forms of industry, population, and general socioeconomic status. However, the ultimate governmental goal mirrors that of the federal government and the U.S. Constitution and its amendments—to provide maximum personal freedom, with only the essential governmental involvement necessary to maintain order and protect individual rights.

Assignment 1.2

> 1. Identify state and federal legislators and representatives of your state/district.
> 2. Determine how many different federal, state, and local courts are located in your county.

C. CURRENT LAW-RELATED PROFESSIONS AND THEIR ROLES WITHIN THE LEGAL SYSTEM

As our society and culture increase in complexity, so does the legal system designed to maintain order among the population. The growth of the structure of the American legal system has resulted in the evolution of various law-related professions. Initially, the legal professions consisted primarily of judges and lawyers, established with the beginning of a civilized society and the first forms of government. Over time, a clerical role developed to assist the lawyers and judges in maintaining records of legal events. However, in the last 200 years, the various roles of individuals concerned with governmental operations and the administration of law in the United States and the world has led to an explosion of professionals and paraprofessionals who make their careers in law-related settings. Today, they consist of several types of judges, court clerks, law clerks, court officers, lawyers, paralegals/legal assistants, legal investigators, legal secretaries, general accounting and clerical staff, and others. Most of these positions have developed during the 20th century as a result of the great increases in population, technology, transportation, and communications systems and the complexity of government. To illustrate some of these changes, take the example of filing a court document. In 1850, the lawyer handwrote the document using a fountain pen and ink. He then carried it to the courthouse and often presented it personally to the judge. Today, that same document may be discussed by the lawyer and paralegal; researched by the lawyer, paralegal, or law clerk; and dictated by machine or perhaps even spoken directly into the computer. The clerical staff would then prepare the final document, inserting proper format details such as the caption (title) for the case and attorney identification. The document may then be transmitted electronically to the parties to suit and the court or sent/taken in hard copy form to the court and appropriate parties. At the court, the document is registered by a clerk and may be recorded on computer before being placed in the file for the particular case. The clerk or an assistant to the judge would then establish a time for a hearing and notify all parties by telephone, mail, or electronic transmission such as a fax or e-mail.

It seems as though the method of 1850 was simpler and more efficient. Given the status of the legal system at the time, perhaps it was. However, with the phenomenal technological developments that respond to the ever-increasing number of cases on file in the courts, the current system is incredibly efficient. The following discussion examines the various roles of the legal professionals and supporting careers now essential to the American legal system.

1. Judges

Jurists—commonly called **judges**—are individuals who resolve disputes between parties who have different interpretations of the law. It is the duty of a judge to objectively evaluate the circumstances of the parties and to determine which legal standards are most appropriate. In the absence of a jury (bench trial or appellate review), the judge applies the law to the facts of the case and issues a ruling. In a jury trial, the judge presides over the proceedings to ensure that the law is applied properly and that the evidence is presented in accordance with rules of evidence and procedure. Before and sometimes during a trial, a judge issues rulings on various procedural issues such as discovery of evidence, motions of parties, selection of a jury, and how the jury is to be instructed about the case that must be dealt with. The judge must also determine which laws will be applied to the facts of the case presented.

The present-day legal system has many different kinds of judges: federal and state appellate judges, trial judges, and magistrates; municipal judges and various levels of hearing officers; and administrative law judges. All have the essential duty to interpret and apply the law within the boundaries of their particular role as an officer of the court. However, significant differences in the function and authority of judges lie in the distinction between appellate, trial, and administrative judges.

a. Trial Judges To properly perform their duties, trial judges must maintain current knowledge of the law at all times. Because of the large volume of litigation, many courts assign trial judges to specific categories of cases, such as domestic relations, probate, or criminal. This not only creates a more organized and efficient court system, it also allows the trial judge the opportunity to develop expertise in certain areas of law. However, many less congested courts still have judges in courts of general jurisdiction who hear cases of all types.

Changes in case law begin with the trial judge. At some point, a judge will take the position that an existing legal standard, relied upon in the past as a rule of law, is no longer appropriate. The judge may follow new statutory or administrative legal standards or indicate that societal standards dictate a change in the legal standards applicable to a situation. The judge has the option of applying existing precedent. When the case reaches conclusion, and possibly earlier in certain situations, a party dissatisfied

Judge/Jurist
Judicial officer who presides over cases in litigation within a court system.

with the result may challenge the trial court judgment before an appellate court. In some jurisdictions, including federal, a series of appeals can be taken before increasingly powerful courts. On appeal, the higher court affirms or reverses the position of the trial court and establishes the rule of law to be followed in the future. Consequently, the trial judge plays a crucial role in the establishment of legal standards.

b. Appellate Judges   Appellate judges review cases that have been previously ruled on in a trial court. The goal of an appellate judge is to ensure that the correct law was applied properly, fairly, and consistently. If it is the opinion of the appellate court that the lower court exceeded or improperly used its authority (abuse of discretion), the court issues a ruling as to what should occur next in the case to correct the error. The case then returns to the lower court for corrective action. If, however, the court finds that the actions in the trial court were appropriate, the result in the lower court is affirmed. In many cases and in many jurisdictions there are a series of courts that one can follow with subsequent appeals.

The likelihood of a reversal declines as each subsequent judge(s) considers a case and agrees with those who have previously considered the appeal. Usually, several appellate judges review a case together as a panel in an appellate court. This collective wisdom reduces the possibility of error or personal bias on a legal issue. Because it is the duty of appellate judges to ensure proper, fair, and consistent application of law for a jurisdiction, the position of appellate judges requires a great deal of knowledge of legal principles. As with other legal professionals, appellate judges often have the assistance of law clerks, which are discussed later in the chapter.

Typically, the appellate panel will issue a written opinion after consideration of a case and possibly after hearing a short argument by each party. The opinion not only will give the rationale for the judgment but will also indicate the support or nonsupport by each judge. If the entire membership of an appellate court—rather than a panel of a few members—issues a joint decision, such decision is known as an *en banc* opinion. Typically, joint decisions are reserved for issues of great significance. A judge who agrees with the result but not with the reasoning of the other appellate judges may issue a *concurring* opinion. A judge who disagrees with the result but is in the minority may issue a *dissenting* opinion. Concurring and dissenting opinions are valuable for the light they may shed on dealing with future cases, but the majority opinion is the controlling precedent that lower courts generally look to for guidance in future cases. The majority opinion also dictates the outcome of the particular case on appeal.

c. Administrative Law Judges   The administrative law judge functions in a totally different arena from that of the appellate or trial judge. The duties of administrative law judges are confined to hearing cases involving the conduct of administrative agencies and the effects of that conduct on the individual or entity who challenges the agency action.

The administrative law judge (A.L.J.) is presumed to be an objective judicial authority who rules exclusively on issues of administrative law. The A.L.J. determines such issues as whether a party is subject to the authority of the agency and whether a party's conduct is in accordance with administrative rules and regulations. Typically, administrative cases are initially filed with the agency rather than in the courts. Appeals of an administrative decision are generally made to the trial court level in the judicial system. This is a limited instance when the trial court exercises appellate rather than original authority.

Each type of judicial officer plays an extremely important role in the American legal system. Whether hearing evidence at trial or reviewing another judge's application of law, the input of a judge as an objective observer with knowledge of legal standards is necessary to the effective operation of the American system of government.

2. Lawyers

Because of the increasing complexity of the American legal system, **lawyers (attorneys)** function not only as advocates for clients but also as counselors and liaisons between the lay public and the courts, legislatures, and executive branches of state and federal governments. To become a lawyer, certain graduate level coursework must be completed and standards for licensure in the state or federal area of practice must be met. Most states require that prior to licensure, the lawyer must graduate from an accredited law school following completion of an undergraduate degree and pass a bar exam in the licensing state or in another state. The exam tests the legal knowledge and the analytical ability of the lawyer.

While, historically, states often granted licenses to practice to those who demonstrated licensure in another state, known as reciprocity, the trend has been to require licensure by examination in each state of practice. This is due, at least in part, to the fact that as laws become more complex in each jurisdiction, the likelihood of variance in legal procedures and standards increases. Consequently, many states require a lawyer to demonstrate a working knowledge of the laws of that particular state prior to licensure.

Although the definition of the practice of law varies from state to state, certain components of the definition are fairly standard. Most jurisdictions give the lawyer, when licensed to practice law, the generally exclusive privilege to give legal advice and to advocate with third parties on the behalf of a client's legal rights.

Attorney/Lawyer
Individual who has completed the necessary requirements of education and training to apply for a license to practice law in a jurisdiction.

a. Legal Advice and Analysis   Giving legal advice requires a special analytical ability by a lawyer. A lawyer is responsible for examining the law applicable to a situation, informing a client as to the likely outcome of the case, and often recommending the next course of action. Based on the information received, the client can choose to accept the analysis and recommendation or reject it.

A licensed attorney must use analytical ability to locate all relevant legal principles in a given circumstance, to recognize the significant facts of the case, and to determine the impact of the principles on those facts. To do this, the lawyer must be able to take each of the applicable legal principles, break them down into the necessary components, and compare them to the specific elements of the client's circumstance. Then, based on the similarities and differences identified in this analysis, the lawyer must make a determination of the likely outcome of the client's case if these legal principles were to be applied by a court. Such analytical ability by a lawyer is a valued and respected skill and, because clients often determine future conduct affecting their rights based on the lawyer's recommendation, the process of giving legal advice is licensed by the state and prohibited for anyone not having a proper license.

b. Advocacy   The second function of a licensed attorney is advocacy—the process of representing the legal rights and interests of another person within the confines of legal proceedings in one of the branches of government. In business, it is not uncommon to have an agent represent one's interests in such areas as negotiations, sales, and purchases, but a license to practice law is required to represent the interests of another person in court and other legal proceedings. However, many times attorneys are used in nonlegal proceedings if the effect is on the legal rights of the parties, such as in contractual matters. This is because in the event a dispute arises, a party wishes their legal rights to be well protected. Because advocacy frequently has a long-term effect on a person's legal rights, it is monitored by the government through licensure and law practice requirements. Failure to represent one's client zealously and with the degree of competence required by law can result in an action for malpractice as well as disciplinary action by a state bar association.

c. Practicing Law Without a License   When an individual undertakes the practice of law without a license, a statutory violation occurs and criminal proceedings may be instituted. In recent years, there has been an increasing awareness of this issue as a gray area has developed among lawyers and some other professions. This will be further discussed later. However, the real controversy has been in drawing the line within the lawyer's own office. At what point does a subordinate staff member such as a legal assistant, legal secretary, or even law clerk stop providing support and start practicing law. Secondly, what of the freelance individuals who prepare legal forms, provide paralegal services, and assist individuals in meeting the procedural requirements of the legal system? There has been litigation across the United States in the last decade over issues such as these. Essentially, the courts have maintained their original position. If the conduct of the individual extends in any way to giving advice affecting another person's legal rights or advocacy on behalf of another's legal rights, the practice of law has occurred. If the individual is not properly licensed, then a criminal prosecution may follow. Additionally, if the individual was in the employ of a licensed attorney, a suit for malpractice may be brought and disciplinary action can be taken against the lawyer in some circumstances.

3. Paralegals

Paralegal/Legal Assistant
One who has legal training and education and performs tasks in the law office that have traditionally been performed by the attorney, with the exception of client advocacy and giving of legal advice. In some geographical areas, these terms are used interchangeably while in others they imply distinct levels of professional ability.

The concept of the **paralegal,** or **legal assistant,** has been recognized as a formal profession in this country only during the past few decades and the development of this career path has been rapid. While no uniformly accepted definition of a paralegal exists, certain standards have been developed and gained wide acceptance in the United States. In recent years, a number of states have issued definitions of paralegals or legal assistants, or recognized duties for which services may be billed. Essentially, a paralegal is someone with training and knowledge in the law who should be able to perform all functions historically performed by an attorney with the exception of giving legal advice and advocacy. In some jurisdictions, even limited advocacy may be permitted. While the typical perception of an attorney is someone who is in court all of the time, the reality is quite different. Attorneys have traditionally performed many daily functions that are now also within the parameters of the paralegal job description. The evolving standards of competence of the paralegal clearly identifies a growing place for this paraprofessional within the American legal system.

Many paralegals are still employed to conduct, in addition to true paralegal duties, a degree of work that is clerical in nature. This is waning, however, because of the economic benefits of having a trained paralegal perform paralegal functions. Because the tasks performed by a paralegal are traditionally those performed by attorneys, it has been established that a paralegal's services may be billed to clients. This principle was a major achievement in establishing paralegals as legal professionals in their own right. However, a key element that remains in paralegal functions and billing is that billed paralegal work must be performed under the supervision of a licensed attorney. Nevertheless, the paralegal continues to evolve and gain respect as a valuable member of the team comprising those who contribute to the functioning of the American legal system. Much greater detail is given in subsequent chapters as to the role and opportunities of today's qualified paralegal.

In addition to the paralegal, a number of support personnel have become recognized as integral parts of today's law office or legal department. Each position represents the performance of duties key to the orderly and efficient progression of legal matters. While the degree of training and education necessary for the positions may vary dramatically, the role played by each is of equal importance. Much like a team on an assembly line, the legal team works together to move a case or law-related matter from inception to conclusion in such a way as to maximize efficiency, produce the best possible result, and adhere to the necessary parameters, such as procedural rules. Following is a brief description of the types of personnel often found within law offices and legal departments providing necessary support services to attorneys. The role of the paralegal will be addressed in much greater depth in subsequent chapters.

4. Law Office Administrator

This individual manages the day-to-day operations of the law office or legal department as a business entity. Included in a typical administrator's duties are hiring, evaluation, and termination of staff; scheduling; overseeing billing and accounting issues; delegation of work to appropriate personnel; coordination of attorneys and support staff; and supervision of risk management issues such as conflict of interest files, court and deposition schedules, and deadlines.

5. Law Clerk

Often, but not always, a law clerk is a law school student who performs basic functions such as legal research and document/correspondence drafting under the supervision of an attorney. In the court system, law clerks to judges are quite often recent law school graduates who assist the judge by performing legal research and providing a synopsis of the results in preparation of written judicial opinions.

6. Legal Investigator

This is a dramatically growing field. Originally, legal investigators were most often found in law firms specializing in personal injury. Their primary task was to locate witnesses and evidence in support of the client's case. However, as the complexity of laws and the basis for lawsuits increases, many firms and corporate legal departments now employ legal investigators or contract with legal/private investigation firms. Their primary function is still to collect evidence of all types in support of and opposition to a client's case to enable the attorney to assess and follow through appropriately on the case.

7. Law Librarian

In the first three quarters of the 20th century, the number of legal publications and regular updates required many larger law firms and corporate legal departments to employ individuals to maintain the constantly growing body of information. The publications had to be placed in an organized fashion, and updates frequently needed to be incorporated into the existing collection. However, as more and more legal research is performed by computer, the job of the law librarian may change somewhat from primarily manual record keeping to maintaining a current working knowledge of computer programs, updates, and research techniques. The role of the law librarian is still essential in the large firm or corporate legal department to facilitate the work of those performing legal research.

8. Legal Secretary

Historically, the clerical staff in a law firm spent most of the workday typing legal documents. That duty is still a fundamental part of the job; however, the traditional role of the legal secretary has expanded to include a great deal more. Clerical staff is often expected to have exceptional computer skills, to coordinate schedules of attorneys from various firms for depositions and hearings, and to act as the primary contact person between the attorney and other staff members as well as clients and professionals outside the firm. The legal secretary may see that documents are properly and timely filed with the courts and provide all forms of general clerical support to the attorney, legal investigator, law clerks, and paralegals.

9. Filing Clerk

Even with the advent of computer transference of information, the legal profession still ultimately relies on hard copy of all pertinent information. The legal documents, correspondence, research, memos, notices, and documentary evidence all must be maintained. Even the smallest law firm processes hundreds, perhaps thousands, of pieces of paper on a monthly basis. As a result, it is imperative that the files be maintained in a predictably organized manner and kept current as well. For this reason, an integral position within any law firm or legal department is an individual who is responsible for managing the documents within the files. The person(s) with this responsibility must be extremely organized and attentive to detail. It is also important that this individual, and all members of the staff, understand the importance of maintaining the confidentiality of the files he or she is handling.

10. Billing Personnel

Aside from the practice of law, the ultimate truth is that a law firm or legal department is a business that operates on incoming funds. In order to do this, it is important to track the time spent by the attorneys and other staff members who bill their time on each client file. This information must then be integrated into the proper accounts and tracked for billing and collection. The billing clerk may also manage incoming and outgoing funds, but in large firms or corporate legal departments this position may be expanded to a complete accounting department. Smaller firms often coordinate with an independent accountant for monthly accounting statements and tax issues.

11. Receptionist

One of the most important people in the law firm is the receptionist. While this person does not have the authority of an attorney or administrator, the receptionist is often the first and last contact the client has with the law firm. As a result, the attitude, professionalism, and general appearance of the firm may be judged by the presentation of the receptionist. With respect to duties, the receptionist may schedule appointments and screen and route phone calls and appointments with clients and others who come into contact with the firm.

These are a few of the people necessary to make the legal profession operate in an organized and efficient manner. All work is considered to be done under the ultimate supervision of the attorney, and it is the legal responsibility of the lawyer to see that each works within the constraints of the ethical standards imposed on all licensed attorneys. As discussed in the chapter on ethics, the failure of any staff member to adhere to appropriate ethical standards can result in liability of the attorney. Also, the absence of any of these individuals can cause the most organized law firm to falter and even allow for mistakes that might ultimately result in liability for malpractice. Unlike many businesses, the law firm depends on support staff not only for day-to-day operations, but for the future viability of the practice.

Assignment 1.3

Prepare a diagram demonstrating the placement of each of the positions in a law office structure.

12. Professions with Semi-Legal Authority

In recent years, as technology and business have developed rapidly, so has the reality that some other licensed professions engage in practices that might be considered the practice of law. For example, a certified professional accountant (CPA) might advise a client on tax matters involving federal, state, and local tax laws. A licensed real estate agent or broker might advise a client about certain laws or regulations relevant to a transfer of property. Thus far, the courts have by and large dealt with such situations on a case-by-case basis. They examine the law involved, the other subject area affected (such as accounting or property), the expectations of the party receiving information, and the extent of the advice given by the professional. Typically, if the conduct of the professional was well within the accepted industry standards of that profession and did not unreasonably affect the legal rights of the individual, a very limited ability to practice law is inferred from the professional license of the individual.

CHAPTER SUMMARY

The focus of this chapter has been on the development of the American legal system from its inception to its present-day status. Our system of government has progressed from a small group of representatives of a few thousand colonists, to a multifaceted government that serves hundreds of millions of people and acts as one of the most powerful nations in the world. The operation of this government still turns on the Constitution that was enacted more than 200 years ago and on its principles of basic fairness and fundamental freedoms that all persons should be entitled to. This system of government is the product of a number of theories of government and the underlying concept that no one entity should gain so much control that it is no longer responsive to the will of the majority. As the population has grown, the government has evolved and grown commensurately. In direct consequence to this, the legal profession that assists the citizens in working within the framework of the government has also evolved into a sophisticated network of individual professions. Each of these roles is an integral part of the working government that is known as the American legal system.

ETHICAL NOTE

A fundamental basis of the American legal system is morality. The absolute requirements of the Constitution and amendments that respect be given to individuals and to their inherent rights comes from a belief that all persons should act and be treated with honor. This belief in moral and honorable conduct is evident throughout the legal system and in the code of conduct imposed on legal professionals. Throughout the remainder of the text and in addition to a chapter dedicated to the discussion of legal ethics, there are chapter notes on ethical aspects relevant to the particular subject matter of each chapter.

Relevant Internet Sites

Internet Legal Resource Guide	www.ilrg.com
U.S. Government	www.governmentguide.com
U.S. Government	www.firstgov.gov

Internet Assignment 1.1

Locate Internet addresses for the following governmental offices within your state:
Governor

Legislature

Highest Appellate Court

KEY TERMS

Attorney/Lawyer	Modern Balance	Positivist Theory
Delegation Doctrine	Naturalist Theory	Sociological Theory
Judge/Jurist	Paralegal/Legal Assistant	Traditional Balance

ENDNOTE

1. *Sante Fe Independent School District v. Doe*, 530 U.S. 290, 120 S.C. 2266, 147 L.2d.2d 295 (2000).

Chapter 2

THE CREATION OF LEGAL PRINCIPLES

CHAPTER OBJECTIVES

Upon completion of this chapter you should be able to do the following:

- Define and discuss terminology relevant to rules of law.

- Describe the manner in which each branch of government creates legal standards.

- Explain the function and purpose that underlie the various types of legal standards.

- Briefly describe the manner in which published legal standards are organized.

- Distinguish statutory, judicial, and administrative law.

- Discuss the hierarchy of the various forms of law.

- Distinguish criminal and civil law.

- Explain the function and nature of substantive and procedural law.

The entire American legal system hinges upon established rules of law that all persons are expected to follow. These rules were present even before the Constitution and have continued to increase and develop as the foundation of an ordered society. This chapter explores how those rules come into being and how the legal system attempts to employ them.

A. RELEVANT TERMS

As with any profession, there is a body of terminology that develops peculiar to the matters encountered within the profession. In the American legal system there is such a collection of terms often jokingly referred to as "legalese." In truth, there is a rationale for the terminology used within the legal system. Whether it be a purely Latin term or an ordinary language term with a different meaning in a legal context, much of the terminology can be traced back hundreds of years. While the trend for many years has been to make the legal system and its terminology more "user friendly," some antiquated terms remain in use because their meaning is so well established and to replace them with alternative contemporary terms would open them to new and different interpretations. This would in turn create the possibility of confusion or even inequity in the application of laws. For that reason, certain terms have persisted either in their legal definition or even in their original Latin form.

Some terms in legal documents may have one meaning in everyday language but have a different effect when used in a legal context. For example, the phrase *reasonable person* has a common English meaning. Most individuals would define it as average, fair minded, ordinary. This meaning might also be minimally acceptable in a legal context. However, the legal definition of the *reasonable person* may require that this person be observant and considerate of the surrounding environment. In essence, in a legal context, the reasonable person is not only ordinary and fair minded but, in addition, considers all possible outcomes of his or her conduct and chooses the most prudent or careful course of action. For purposes of clarification, terms introduced will be defined as they apply in the legal context. Another example might be the term *judgment*. While the lay definition includes an exercise of reason, the legal definition includes an order of court with the effect of enforceable law.

Law can be referred to in a number of ways. Anything with the effect of law can be considered a **legal standard** or a legal principle. Based upon the origin, legal standards can also be identified as cases or case law (emanating from the judicial branch), legislation or statute (emanating from a legislative body), or regulatory or administrative law (rules and regulations emanating from the administrative branch of government). As can be seen, any number of terms can be used to refer to a guideline that has a binding effect on citizens, that is, law. Because each branch of government has the capability of issuing mandates with the effect of law, each branch also has terms that are unique to the type of law it creates.

The judicial branch creates legal standards through judicial opinions. These principles are commonly referred to as **case law.** Most often, case law interprets and/or applies other established standards such as statutes, administrative regulations, or previous judicial opinions. If a judicial standard is based on a principle that does not have its ultimate basis in administrative or legislative law, but rather within the courts, the term used for the judicial legal standard is **common law.** The legislature is responsible for creating law that protects the population in accordance with the standards of the Constitution and its amendments. Further, laws are created to maintain public safety and order. This law is known as **statutory law.** Finally, the administrative branch issues legal principles that clarify and define the objectives of certain statutory law, which is often broadly written. These legal principles are commonly referred to as **administrative law** and consist generally of administrative rules, regulations, and decisions.

When a governmental body with the authority to establish legal standards relies upon an existing standard and affirms its validity, the existing standard is referred to as **precedent.** Specifically, when a court relies on a prior judicial opinion, the application

Legal Standard
Law created by one of the three sources of government: the legislature, executive branch, or the judiciary.

Case law
Law that is created judicially when a legal principle of common law is extended to a similar situation.

Common Law
Judicially created legal principles or standards. The judiciary has the authority to create law in situations where none currently exists.

Statutory Law
A statute. Law that is created by the legislature.

Administrative Law
Regulations and decisions issued by administrative agencies that explain and detail statutes.

Precedent
Existing legal standards that courts look to for guidance when making a determination of a legal issue.

is called **stare decisis.** This Latin term quite literally means *let the decision stand.* Most often courts will strive to follow precedent from all sources unless there is a compelling legal argument why the precedent should be distinguished from a current situation. In the subsequent discussion, the manner in which each of these standards is created will be explained. Additionally, it will be demonstrated how such legal principles are placed into actual practice in the everyday functioning of the American legal system and how these legal standards from the various sources of government interrelate.

Stare Decisis
"Let the decision stand." Method used by the judiciary when applying precedent to current situations.

APPLICATION 2.1

Micah was raised in the heart of a large city with mass transportation. As a result, he never learned to drive and had virtually no experience around engines of any kind. When he was 18, he went away to college in a rural Midwestern community. To make extra money he took a job at a service station. Micah's employer instructed him to clean the service bays each night with gasoline to cut through the oil and grease that accumulated on the floor each day. One evening during his first week on the job, Micah was mopping the floors with gasoline as instructed. The door to the mechanical room was ajar and the fumes from the gas connected with the pilot light on the water heater. The entire station exploded. Micah was severely burned and ultimately died from his injuries. OSHA (a government agency overseen by the executive branch) cited the service station owner for unsafe work practices according to their regulations. Micah's parents sued the owner claiming various violations of state law. The service station owner claimed that Micah was an employee and therefore subject to workers' compensation laws and that, as a result he, the employer, could not be sued in civil court for Micah's death. Micah's parents responded citing prior cases in which the courts had allowed the workers' compensation laws to be disregarded in favor of a civil suit with unlimited recovery of funds when the employer intentionally subjected the employee to ultra-hazardous activities and inherently unsafe work conditions. The court agreed with Micah's parents and permitted them to sue in civil court.

Point for Discussion: Which branches of government are involved in this situation?

Assignment 2.1

Referring to Application 2.1, identify an example of each of the highlighted terms discussed in section A of the chapter.

B. HOW VARIOUS TYPES OF LEGAL STANDARDS ARE CREATED

1. Statutory Law

Perhaps the most familiar law is statutory (legislative) laws. Such laws are enacted by a state legislature or by the U.S. Congress. If a state legislature enacts a law, all persons and entities present or interacting with persons and entities within the state must obey it. If Congress enacts a federal law, all persons and entities present or interacting with persons or entities in the nation are required to follow it. Once approved by the legislature, a statute will generally continue indefinitely as law until either the legislature repeals (deactivates) it or the high court of the state or federal government rules it unconstitutional. Federal laws must be consistent with the U.S. Constitution, whereas state laws must be in accordance with both the state and the federal constitutions. Similarly, no state constitution can conflict with the U.S. Constitution.[1] The provision of the U.S. Constitution declaring that federal laws take precedence over conflicting state laws is known as the supremacy clause. States do have authority to grant greater or additional rights to those given in the U.S. Constitution as long as they do not conflict or in any way limit those granted expressly or by interpretation of the U.S. Constitution.

The language of statutes is fairly broad. Such open language is necessary because the legislature wants to include as many potential situations as possible when it sets down a legal standard of what is permissible conduct. However, if a court determines that a law is written so broadly that it is vague, and citizens cannot determine exactly what is and is not acceptable conduct, the law will be declared invalid. The Constitution guarantees the right to fair notice of what is considered illegal conduct. Thus, courts have stricken statutes for being unconstitutional because of overly broad language.[2] The legislature has a particularly difficult but necessary task in establishing laws that apply to all intended persons and situations but that are also specific enough to warn an individual of what is required in a particular situation.

APPLICATION 2.2

Virginia Statutes Annotated s. 18.2-158 (1950).
Driving, etc., Animal On Track to Recover Damages

If any person with a view to the recovery of damages against a railroad company willfully ride, drive, or lead an animal or otherwise contrive for an animal to go on the railroad track of such company and such animal is by reason thereof killed or injured, he shall be guilty of a Class 3 misdemeanor.

Point for Discussion: Why would the legal standard above be an appropriate subject for statutory law?

---

a. The Purpose of Statutory Law   All legislation serves one or more of three basic purposes. The particular purpose a statute serves strongly influences the statute's content and scope. These purposes are commonly referred to as protective, remedial, and procedural. A primary purpose of the American democratic system of government is to provide laws that will protect society from what is considered to be unsafe or socially and/or morally unacceptable to the majority of citizens. Generally, statutes serve to protect the citizens as a whole from unnecessary physical, social, and financial dangers. Law as a protective measure began with the original 10 amendments to the Constitution, known as the Bill of Rights. From the very start, specific laws were established to protect the people from unnecessary governmental influence or intrusion into their private lives. With the passage of time, additional constitutional amendments and statutes have been designed to provide protection from dangers that would interfere with all fundamental personal rights.

Many other types of laws also serve a type of protective purpose. Any statute that sets out the type of conduct required or prohibited protects the public from harmful behavior by others. For example, something as simple as the statutes that govern motor vehicles serves an invaluable protective purpose. Without such laws, persons could drive as they pleased, and untold injuries and deaths could occur. Protective laws do exactly what their name implies: they protect what are considered to be the rights of the people to a safe and reasonable environment in which to live and work.

Legislative standards (statutes) can also serve a remedial purpose. A remedial statute has been defined as one that "provides a remedy or a means to enforce a right; a statute designed to correct an existing law or to redress an existing grievance." As this definition indicates, remedial statutes are designed to cure something that has already gone wrong or caused injury. Occasionally, a remedial statute is used to supersede a previous statute that was unfair or poorly drafted and resulted in injury or invasion of personal rights or property interests. One example of an extremely important remedial law is the Thirteenth Amendment, which states in part:

> AMENDMENT XIII, Section 1. Neither slavery nor involuntary servitude, except as a punishment for crime whereof the party shall have been duly convicted, shall exist within the United States, or any place subject to their jurisdiction.

With the ratification of this amendment to the Constitution, all previous decisions of courts and state and federal legislatures that permitted slavery were overruled. The amendment corrected laws that the majority of the people believed were wrong, unfair, and injurious to a large element of our society.

Remedial law is not always in the form of a constitutional amendment. More often, remedial laws are federal or state statutes that are used to adjust law to the changing needs of the society. These laws come about as the result of technological advancements, changing values of society on a particular topic, and identified inequities in the current system of laws.

A third purpose that legislation serves is to ensure that protective and remedial statutes are available and applied to all citizens in the same way.[3] Such legal standards are commonly known as procedural laws. If it were not for procedural laws, citizens would have no effective way of enforcing the rights to which they are entitled. Procedural laws give specific directions on everything from how to initiate a lawsuit to how a trial is to be conducted. They even explain how to get a bill introduced to the legislature for consideration as law. Occasionally, people complain that the procedural laws are too numerous and that the legal system is more concerned with procedures than with resolving issues. In reality, our legal system guarantees all citizens the right to be heard. Hundreds of thousands of lawsuits are filed every year. The procedural laws provide a consistent and predictable course from the start of a legal proceeding to its conclusion for all those in contact with the American legal system. Given the size of this task, the procedural laws are extremely efficient.

Procedural laws are not designed solely to deal with great numbers of people. Rather, their true purpose is to ensure that everyone can enjoy the same basic rights in the legal system. All persons are entitled to voice their opinions to elected delegates in the legislature and those affected by a particular law are entitled to dispute that law. The procedural laws make it possible for the orderly expression of rights to occur in a fair setting and provide for the fair treatment of all parties in a dispute. Without procedural laws, there would be no clear, consistent, and fair method of seeking assistance from or input to the legal system.

b. The Creation of Statutory Law   Each state varies somewhat on the procedures used for enacting statutes, but most are loosely modeled after the federal procedures for creating statutory law. The federal system follows the method described in Article I, Section 7, of the U.S. Constitution. Since the enactment of the Constitution a number of supplemental procedures have been employed to facilitate the handling of the growing Congress and the number of proposed statutes introduced each year for consideration. However, the basic process has remained the same for more than 200 years.

Bill
Proposed law presented to the legislature for consideration.

When a proposed law is introduced to the legislature, it is called a **bill.** The legislature (Congress) consists of two bodies: the House of Representatives and the Senate. A bill will be initiated in one of these two houses. The Constitution requires that revenue-raising bills initially be introduced in the House of Representatives, but other bills may be initiated in either house of Congress. A bill is sponsored by a legislator who introduces it. When a bill is formally proposed as legislation, it is registered and assigned a number. Often, the bill is also known by the name of the legislators who introduce it; for example, the Gramm-Rudman Act. Officially, however, the statute is referenced in publications by its assigned number. As the bill progresses through the legislative process, it carries the same number for identification until it is either voted into law or defeated, or the session of Congress ends without action on the bill.

After a bill has been introduced, it is assigned to the appropriate committee of legislators for consideration of its contents and its potential ramifications as law. Congress has created a number of such continuing committees to study the need for legislation and proposed laws in specific areas of government, commerce, and other appropriate legislative subjects. At times, the bill will be revised while in committee with necessary additions or deletions to make it a complete and effective statute. After committee hearings, the bill is presented to the originating body of Congress, either the House of Representatives or the Senate, for a vote by the legislators. The bill must pass by a majority vote before it can be sent to the corresponding body for consideration. Prior to a vote, the bill is discussed and debated by Congress. At that time, changes may be made in the language of the bill. Often such changes are necessary to gain the approval of a sufficient number of legislators to pass the bill. If a bill succeeds by a majority vote in the house of Congress where it began, it moves on to the corresponding body. For example, if a bill is introduced in the House of Representatives and passes by a majority vote, the final version is then submitted to the Senate. If the bill passes by a majority in the corresponding body of Congress, it is forwarded to the president for approval or disapproval.

Veto
Presidential power to invalidate law passed by a majority of Congress (2/3 majority of each house needed to override.)

Once a bill has been submitted to the president, the **veto** power of the president may be exercised. The veto is a key element in the system of checks and balances. As mentioned in Chapter 1, each branch of government has a method to influence the other branches. Such a mechanism is designed to prevent one branch from obtaining too much power or acting in a way that is inconsistent with the Constitution. According to Article I of the U.S. Constitution, each bill that has received a majority vote in both houses of Congress shall be presented to the president. After the president receives a bill, under the Constitution, the bill must be acted upon within 10 days, excluding Sundays.[4] If nothing is done during this time and Congress is still in session, the bill automatically becomes law. If Congress is not in session, it becomes a pocket veto. If the president signs the bill, it becomes law on the date indicated by Congress. If the president returns the bill with objections to the house where it originated, the bill is vetoed (rejected). Once a bill has been vetoed, a second vote can be taken. If each body of Congress approves the bill by at least a two-thirds majority (rather than by the

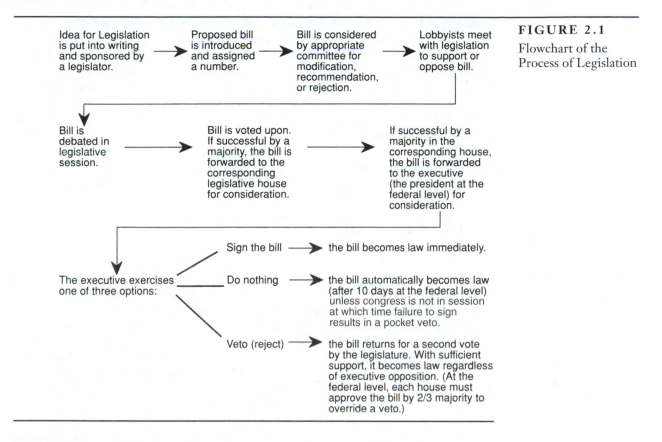

FIGURE 2.1

Flowchart of the Process of Legislation

originally required simple majority), the bill becomes law regardless of the presidential veto. Figure 2.1 is a diagram of the legislative process.

This method for passing laws employs a number of safeguards to ensure that the proposed law is in the best interest of the people and not a product of the control or personal agenda of the executive branch or one of the houses of Congress. The Congress is elected by the public and its members must account to the public in future elections if they do not vote on laws in a way that is generally consistent with the opinions and best interests of the public. Similarly, the president acts almost as a backstop to intervene when it is believed that Congress has not acted in the best interest of the public when passing a law. However, if a two-thirds majority of the Congress thinks the president was misguided in the exercise of the veto, then the veto can be overridden.

When a number of bills addressing the various aspects of a single subject are introduced, the package of bills is referred to as an act. This may include entirely new legislation as well as amendments to previously passed legislation. The idea is to comprehensively address an area of law that is in need of legislation with separate laws that focus on each aspect of the subject. The act may or not be passed in total. Congress also has the option to modify or delete sections of the bill that do not meet the necessary majority vote requirement as submitted.

Statutes for each jurisdiction are published collectively and are typically arranged by subject in what is commonly referred to as a **code.** Once the subjects are established, they are most often arranged alphabetically and assigned consecutive numbers. Frequently, these are referred to as *chapter* or *title* numbers, for example, Agriculture—Title 1, Banking—Title 2, and so on. Each existing law is then assigned a particular statute

Code

Published collection of statutes within a jurisdiction.

number to identify it from all other laws of the jurisdiction. Codification is the process of incorporating a new statute, order of repeal, or amendment to a law into the existing code. During this process the new statute follows a procedure similar to that used when the first statutes were initially codified. When a bill is passed by a legislative body and becomes law, the new statute is first delegated to the appropriate subject area. Next, it is given a statute number to distinguish it from all other past and present statutes within the same subject area. Consequently, if you are looking for statute number 53-456 in a particular jurisdiction, you would go to subject area 53 and statute number 456 within that subject. Once a statute is repealed, that is, withdrawn from the body of effective law for a jurisdiction, its number is not used again for another statute. A more detailed discussion of researching statutory law will be presented in Chapter 8 of the text.

2. The Creation of Administrative Law

The legislature attempts to arrive at legal principles that apply to all persons while the judiciary deals with individual circumstances. During the 20th century, however, it became increasingly clear that an additional source of law that could tailor rules for targeted groups of citizens or subjects was necessary. In many sectors of our society and economy, large numbers of people or areas of commerce needed more specific guidelines. But, while legal standards were called for, the need was not common to the entire population. Therefore, it did not warrant an inordinate amount of time and attention from the legislature, which might interfere with law making for the rest of the society. This situation caused the advent and development of an entire body of legal principles known as administrative law. One example is the transport of products throughout the United States via the interstate highway system. Trucking in this country is a massive industry and transport among different states calls into question various laws with regard to over-the-road transport. The Interstate Commerce Commission (ICC) is an administrative agency dedicated primarily to this area of law. It can address relevant issues more effectively, consistently, and efficiently than the Congress or the courts. Similar fields include the Federal Aviation Administration (FAA) for air transportation and the National Railway Labor Administration (NRLA). Agencies that create administrative law can focus on a particular area of concern identified by the legislature and carry out legislative objectives more efficiently than a legislative body.

While developed largely in the 20th century, in actuality administrative agencies have been a part of the American legal system since the 1800s. Agencies can perform many legal functions that Congress, for practical reasons, cannot effectively accomplish. Administrative agencies offer several advantages, including the following:

1. They can deal with large groups of citizens or entire industries.
2. They have the ability to respond quickly to rapidly changing needs of industries or citizens.
3. Their staff members are more knowledgeable about the specifics of an industry or a group of citizens than the legislature or the judiciary.
4. They can provide consistent and fair standards for citizens and industries.

The Constitution gives the duty for enforcement of law to the executive branch, which has the primary responsibility to determine when a law has been violated or whether the law is even applicable to a particular situation. Administrative agencies are overseen by the executive branch with direct influence by the Congress and the judiciary. At the federal level, the president is assisted by administrative agencies in carrying out the law enacted by Congress.

Administrative law is primarily made up of two elements: administrative regulations (sometimes called rules) and administrative decisions. Administrative agencies issue regulations or rules that more specifically define the broadly written statutes. Administrative decisions are issued for individual cases, and these applications of regulations have the same effect of law as judicial or legislative law. These cases usually involve persons or entities that challenge the authority of the agency to issue or enforce a particular regulation. Administrative law is an extension of statutory law established by the Congress. Failure to obey it can result in penalties or even criminal prosecution. See Figure 2.2.

Before an agency comes into existence, Congress must pass a resolution stating that an agency is necessary to carry out the goals of certain legislation. The resolution must show that no more effective way exists to implement the goals of the legislation, and that there is a need for specific enforcement by a dedicated source. Congress then passes what is commonly referred to as an **enabling act.** This is a statute(s) that expresses the goals of Congress on a particular subject of legislation. For example, in the first half of the 20th century electronic communications began with simple telegraph lines and grew to include telephones, radio, television, satellites, and various other forms of electronic transmission of information. As this industry exploded in terms of technology and capabilities, Congress identified the need for a specific governing body to oversee fair and proper use of the evolving technologies. The response was the passage of a resolution and enabling act, and ultimately the creation of the Federal Communications Commission (FCC). The FCC issues regulations for the various affected industries and interprets the individual applications of regulations in administrative decisions.

When the enabling act is passed into law, the executive branch (at the federal level, the president) has the authority to issue an executive order for the creation and staffing of an administrative agency. Article II of the Constitution gives the president the authority to appoint government officers. These are individuals who oversee the various offices that enforce the law consistent with the constitutional duty of the executive branch. With respect to administrative agencies, the officers of the agencies cannot be concurrently employed or have a business interest in any profession or industry that the agency oversees, since that would not constitute an arena for the fair and unbiased administration of the law. This potential conflict of interests was settled by the U.S. Supreme Court early on in the 1936 decision of *Carter v. Carter Coal Company.*[5] In that case, it was exposed that many regulations for the coal industry were created by the very persons who had senior interests in the industry. This does not mean that someone who has been employed in the industry cannot leave the private sector and come to work in an administrative agency. In reality, the expertise of such persons is a valuable tool in the creation and enforcement of agency standards over a particular subject area. However, individuals may not be involved on both sides of the equation—employed by the agency at the same time they have business interests within the industry governed by the agency.

Once an agency is staffed, its employees are responsible for organizing its administration and addressing the subject or industry that the statutes affect. An agency is permitted a virtual free rein in its methods of internal organization, operations, and management as long as it is well organized and efficient. Often the structure of organization and management is guided by the needs of the industry or subject area the agency oversees. For example, an agency that oversees public air travel such as the FAA does not operate in the same way as the Internal Revenue Service (IRS).

Enabling Act
Congressional enactment that creates the authority in the executive to organize and oversee an administrative agency.

FIGURE 2.2
Sample Regulation

ARIZONA ADMINISTRATIVE CODE
TITLE 20. COMMERCE, BANKING, AND INSURANCE
CHAPTER 5. THE INDUSTRIAL COMMISSION OF ARIZONA
ARTICLE 1. RULES OF PROCEDURE FOR WORKERS' COMPENSATION HEARINGS BE-
FORE THE INDUSTRIAL COMMISSION OF ARIZONA
Current through June 30, 2000

R20-5-164. Human Immunodeficiency Virus Significant Exposure: Employee Notification;
Reporting; Documentation; Forms

A. Employers subject to the provisions of Title 23, Chapter 6, Arizona Revised Statutes, shall
notify their employees of the requirements of A.R.S. 23-1043.02 by posting the Commission
notice entitled "Work Exposure to Bodily Fluids." This notice shall be conspicuously posted immediately adjacent to the Notice to Employees required by A.R.S. 23-906(D). The notice, when
posted, shall constitute sufficient notice to employees of the requirements of a prima facie
case under A.R.S. 23-1043.02(B) The insurance carrier or claims processor shall provide the
notice to the employer. This notice is also available from the Commission upon request.
B. Employers shall make readily available a supply of Commission forms entitled "Report of
Significant Work Exposure to Bodily Fluids", the content of which is described in subsection
(D). The insurance carrier or claims processor shall provide these forms to the employer.
These forms are also available from the Commission upon request.
C. In the event of a significant exposure as defined in A.R.S. 23-1043.02(G), the "Report of
Significant Work Exposure to Bodily Fluids" form shall be completed, dated, signed and given
to the employer by the employee or the employee's authorized representative. The employer
shall return 1 copy of the completed form to the employee or to the employee's authorized rep-
resentative. Nothing in this subsection shall be construed to limit the requirements of reporting
an injury or filing a claim pursuant to Title 23, Chapter 6, Arizona Revised Statutes.
D. In addition to stating the requirements of A.R.S. 23-1043.02(B), the "Report of Significant
Work Exposure to Bodily Fluids" requires the following information:

1. Employee identification;
2. Employer identification;
3. Details of the Exposure: Date, time, and place of exposure, how exposure occurred, type of
   bodily fluid(s), source of bodily fluid(s), part(s) of body exposed to bodily fluid(s), presence
   of break/rupture in skin or mucous membrane and witnesses (if known).

**Administrative
Procedures Act**
Congressional
enactment applied to
all federal
administrative agencies
requiring them to
follow certain
procedures in the
issuance of
administrative law.

**Code of Federal
Regulations (CFR)**
Publication that
contains all current
U.S. administrative
regulations.

One organization focuses on safety issues while the other focuses on enforcement of
tax laws.

There is one federal act however, that is designed to provide consistency by all
agencies in the delivery, enforcement, and appeal of administrative legal standards.
This is the **Administrative Procedures Act,** passed in 1946. It includes all the basic
elements that must be followed by administrative agencies to prevent violation of the
delegation doctrine or failure to provide adequate input and consideration of the public in the creation and enforcement of administrative legal standards. Many states also
have a similar comprehensive statutory act that requires certain standards by state administrative agencies. This promotes the global governmental objective of consistency,
fairness, and equal access to the agency and public voice in agency actions.

All administrative law at the federal level is first published in the federal register.
Subsequently, it is incorporated into the **Code of Federal Regulations (CFR),** where
all existing regulations are located. Each agency is assigned a title, similar to the titles
in a statutory code. Each regulation is assigned a specific section number and is placed

with the other regulations of that agency under its proper title. A subject index for each title is included and the code is updated regularly to incorporate new, amended, and repealed regulations.

a. Identify five specific groups or subject areas in which administrative law is currently a primary method used to govern.
b. Identify an area where you see the potential need for an administrative agency to govern.

3. The Creation of Judicial Law

The creation of judicial law is much more traditional and straightforward than statutory or administrative law. Perhaps this is because a judicial standard generally interprets and applies existing legal principles to a singular situation. However, when a case follows the route of appeals, that individual opinion may become the precedent for all similar cases in the future and thus the responsibility of the judiciary is just as immense as that of the other branches of government.

Typically, judicial law is an extension of other forms of law. The basis for most lawsuits is a dispute between parties over the meaning or application of an existing legal standard. This standard may be a statute, administrative rule or regulation, or even a prior judicial opinion. When the lawsuit is filed and ultimately determined, the objective of the court is to apply the law to the particular facts of the present circumstance of the parties. If one or more of the parties take exception to the ruling of the trial court, they may appeal. Generally appellate courts are comprised of a panel of judges who review the trial court actions and determine whether they fall within the boundaries of the authority of the court and within the definition of the legal standard applied.

On rare occasions, the parties will present a case where no applicable legal standard exists. In such a case, the court is left to examine the situation and create a legal standard, which is known as common law. In the past, the creation of common law legal standards was a fairly routine occurrence. However, as the body of law from all branches of government increases, the opportunity for a unique occurrence goes down proportionately. Decisions that interpret and apply, or do not apply, existing legal standards to new or similar situations as those encountered in the past are commonly referred to as case law.

Case law significantly benefits the general public. Individuals can look at existing case law in relation to their own situations. By comparing established precedents, persons involved in lawsuits can often predict with some certainty the likely outcome of their case. In so doing, through a process known as legal analysis, they can make intelligent decisions about whether to pursue, settle, or dismiss a dispute. It is also a very useful method for determining the best course of action for avoiding a legal dispute altogether.

The process for the actual creation of judicial law is similar throughout the federal and state judicial systems. While each jurisdiction follows its own procedural rules, the general method used to establish judicial legal standards is basically the same. Once a lawsuit is filed and goes through the various pretrial stages, the case is heard and decisions are ultimately rendered. A detailed analysis of this process appears in Chapter 4. As mentioned, if a party or parties are dissatisfied with the result and they can identify some alleged error in the application of law, there may be an appeal for review to a series of higher courts. An affirmation by the higher court firmly establishes the applicability of the legal standards used and strengthens them as precedent for future similar cases. Likewise, a case reversed on appeal is in effect a rejection by a higher court of the trial court's interpretation or application of legal standards. It distinguishes the manner in which the law was applied as inappropriate for reasons stated by the court. That distinction establishes limits for the legal standard, which can then be used as a guidepost by future litigants.

Judicial law is published in a variety of formats. However, the official reference system is a publication of judicial opinions by jurisdiction. State opinions are published for each state. In some instances, intermediate level appellate court decisions and state high court decisions are published separately. At the federal level, the opinions are published by the level or type of federal court from which the decision came. For example, cases from the bankruptcy courts are published in one collection, while cases from the circuit courts of appeals are published in another. The U.S. Supreme Court cases are also published in a separate collection. A detailed index and very brief case summaries in the form of a digest are updated constantly to provide a current database that allows research into the most recent and most remote judicial opinions.

CASE IN POINT

Hedges v. Musco, 204 F.2d 109 (3rd Cir. 2000)

OPINION OF THE COURT

STAPLETON, Circuit Judge:

Parents of a high school student commenced this action against a teacher, school officials, and members of the school board ("the NHRHS defendants"), alleging that, by requiring her to submit to a blood test and urinalysis, their child was subjected to an unconstitutional search and that, by disclosing the results of those tests, the defendants violated the child's right to privacy. In addition, plaintiffs argue that the school's drug policy is unconstitutionally vague and assert a state-law claim for assault and battery against the health care provider and nurse ("the medical defendants") who administered the blood test. The District Court granted the defendants' motion for summary judgment and denied plaintiffs' cross-motion for summary judgment. Accordingly, in our review, we view all of the evidence, and draw all inferences therefrom, in the light most favorable to the plaintiffs. See Wicker v. Consolidated Rail Corp., 142 F.3d 690, 696 (3d Cir.1998). We will affirm.

At approximately 9:18 a.m. on April 8, 1996, Tara Hedges was entering her third-period class, Defendant Greg McDonald's math class, at Northern Highlands Regional High School ("NHRHS"). As she entered the classroom, McDonald observed that she seemed uncharacteristically talkative and outgoing. In addition, her face was flushed; her eyes were glassy and red; and her pupils were dilated. It is likewise undisputed, however, that Tara's speech was not slurred, McDonald did not smell anything on her breath, and she did not smell of marijuana.

During the math class, Tara asked permission to leave the room to get a drink from the water fountain, which is located within view of McDonald's classroom door. Instead of getting a drink of water, however, Tara went in the opposite direction from the water fountain and disappeared around the corner of the hallway. Tara was gone for approximately ten minutes. McDonald testified that it was not consistent with Tara's normal behavior to ask permission to go someplace and then leave the room to go elsewhere. Based on Tara's appearance and uncharacteristic behavior, McDonald suspected that Tara was under the influence of alcohol or some other drug.

The NHRHS Board of Education's Revised Drug, Alcohol and Tobacco Policy ("NHRHS Policy" or "Policy") provides that:

Any staff member to whom it appears that a pupil may be under the influence of alcoholic beverages or other drugs on school property or at a school function shall report the matter as soon as possible to the Principal or his/her designee. The substance abuse counselor and nurse shall be notified by the Principal/designee.

In accordance with this Policy, McDonald contacted a school administrator and reported his suspicion that Tara was "high."

Whenever a school official suspects that a student is under the influence of drugs or alcohol, school policy dictates that the student "shall be escorted to the school nurse for an examination of any dangerous vital signs."

Id. Pursuant to that Policy, at the end of the class period, a school security guard escorted Tara from Mr. McDonald's classroom to the nurse's office. The school nurse, Defendant Cathy Kiely, testified that her first impression of Tara when she saw her that day was "oh, my God, she looked so high. . . . She just looked totally out of it. She just didn't know where she was. Her eyes were red, they were glassy, she looked stuporous, she looked high. . . . [She had a] [b]lank look, staring into space, looking right through me, just out of it." Nurse Kiely informed Tara that she was suspected of being under the influence of drugs or alcohol and that her vital signs would have to be checked. Nurse Kiely checked Tara's vital signs and found that her blood pressure was elevated but her pulse and respirations were normal. Although Tara's eyes were bloodshot, her pupils were normal. At no point during the examination did Tara offer an explanation for her uncharacteristic appearance.

"For students suspected of being under the influence of alcohol/drugs," the NHRHS Policy provides that, "if there is reasonable suspicion, the Principal/designee may conduct a search, including lockers and bookbags, luggage, etc. . . ." In accordance with the Policy, a school security guard searched Tara's locker but found nothing incriminating. The guard also searched Tara's bookbag in Tara's and Nurse Kiely's presence. The search revealed an old, worn, plastic bottle containing some small white pills and a large brown pill. Tara told Nurse Kiely that they

were diet pills. NHRHS students are prohibited from possessing medication of any kind, including prescription and over-the-counter medications.

Finally, the NHRHS Policy directs that, when a student is suspected of being under the influence of drugs or alcohol, "[t]he Principal/designee shall immediately notify a parent or guardian and the Superintendent and arrange for an immediate medical examination of the student." When Nurse Kiely asked Tara for a phone number where her parents could be reached, however, Tara was unable to remember the relevant numbers. After retrieving the phone numbers, and in accordance with the NHRHS Policy, Nurse Kiely called Tara's father, Plaintiff George Hedges, and asked him to come to her office. When Mr. Hedges arrived, Nurse Kiely informed him that Tara was suspected of being under the influence of drugs or alcohol. The school principal, Defendant Ralph Musco, showed Mr. Hedges the pills that were found in Tara's bookbag. When it was suggested that the pills might be diet pills, Mr. Hedges responded: "I know for a fact that she's not on a diet." Mr. Hedges took the pills, stating that he would find out what they were.

Either Nurse Kiely or Mr. Musco told Mr. Hedges that Tara would have to be tested for drug and alcohol use before she would be permitted to return to school. The NHRHS Policy provides that "[t]he examination may be performed by a physician selected by the parent or guardian, or by the school doctor if she s/he is immediately available. . . . If, at the request of the parent or guardian, the medical examination is conducted by a physician other than the school doctor, such an examination shall be at the expense of the parent and not the school district." Either Mr. Musco or Nurse Kiely told Mr. Hedges that the school generally used Urgent Care, and Mr. Hedges took Tara there.

Shortly after Mr. Hedges and Tara arrived at Urgent Care, an Urgent Care doctor, Dr. Foley, who has not been named as a defendant, examined Tara. Based on the physical examination, Dr. Foley concluded that Tara did "not appear to be under the influence of any illicit substance or alcohol" and there was "no evidence of any chronic use of illicit substances or alcohol." Tara then provided Urgent Care with a urine specimen.

Nurse Barbara Neumann attempted to draw blood from Tara's right arm but was unsuccessful. She then attempted to draw blood from Tara's left arm but was also unsuccessful. The parties dispute what happened next. According to Ms. Neumann, after the two unsuccessful attempts, she left the room and summoned Dr. Foley. Tara testified, however, that Ms. Neumann inserted a needle in her arms five times unsuccessfully before asking for Dr. Foley's help. Tara also testified that, when Ms. Neumann left the room to get Dr. Foley, she left the tourniquet on Tara's arm. Ms. Neumann denies doing so. Dr. Foley was able to draw blood from Tara's arm on his first attempt. Plaintiffs allege that Tara suffered hematoma in both arms as a result of Ms. Neumann's actions.

Later that day, Mr. Hedges contacted his attorney, Warren Clark. The next day, April 9, 1996, the Hedges and Mr. Clark met with Principal Musco at 7:20 a.m. Nurse Kiely called Urgent Care at approximately 7:30 a.m. that same morning for the results of Tara's drug and alcohol tests. The test results were negative for drugs and alcohol, and NHRHS readmitted Tara in time for her second period class on April 9th.

When Tara returned to school that day, a student approached her and told her that he had overheard Nurse Kiely on the phone when she was obtaining Tara's results. The student told Tara that he heard Nurse Kiely say, "Negative? Are you sure? You are kidding. I am shocked." (Tara Hedges Deposition). By the end of the school day, many students knew that Tara had been tested for drugs and alcohol. Thirty to forty students asked Tara what had happened and asked to see the bruises on her arms; they asked if she had been caught using drugs. Tara perceived that the students believed that she had actually done something wrong. Tara further testified that she has lost friends as a result of the incident and also has lost a number of babysitting jobs.

The plaintiffs filed this civil rights action under 42 U.S.C. § 1983. They allege that the NHRHS Defendants subjected their daughter to an intrusive search, including the testing of bodily fluids, without reasonable suspicion, in violation of the Fourth and Fourteenth Amendments' protection against unreasonable searches and seizures and in violation of the New Jersey Constitution. Plaintiffs further allege that defendants disclosed the results of the search to NHRHS students in violation of their daughter's right to privacy under the Ninth and Fourteenth Amendments. Plaintiffs' third claim is that the NHRHS drug testing policy is unconstitutionally vague. Finally, plaintiffs assert a pendant state-law claim for assault and battery against the medical defendants.

The defendants moved for summary judgment on all counts, and the plaintiffs made a cross-motion for summary judgment with respect to their claims that the search violated both the United States and New Jersey Constitutions. The District Court granted the defendants' motion for summary judgment and denied the plaintiffs' cross-motion for summary judgment. See Hedges v. Musco, 33 F.Supp.2d 369 (D.N.J.1999). This appeal followed.

The New Jersey legislature has promulgated a statutory scheme designed to combat the problems of drug and alcohol abuse in New Jersey schools. See N.J.S.A. § 18A:40A-8 et seq. As a part of that scheme, the following provision was enacted:

The statute provides in relevant part:

Whenever it shall appear to any teaching staff member, school nurse or other educational personnel of any public school in this State that a pupil may be under the influence of substances as defined pursuant to section 2 of this act, other than anabolic steroids, that teaching staff member, school nurse or other educational personnel shall report the matter as soon as possible to the school nurse or medical inspector, as the case may be, or to a substance awareness coordinator, and to the principal or, in his absence, to his designee. The principal or his designee, shall immediately notify the parent or guardian and the superintendent of schools, if there be one, or the administrative principal and shall arrange for an immediate examination of the pupil by a doctor selected by the parent or guardian, or if that doctor is not immediately available, by the medical inspector, if he is available. . . . The pupil shall be examined as soon as possible for the purpose of diagnosing whether or not the pupil is under such influence. A written report of that examination shall be furnished within 24 hours by the examining physician to the parent or guardian of the pupil and to the superintendent of schools or administrative principal.

N.J.S.A. 18A:40A-12. The regulations enacted pursuant to that title require that the "[d]istrict board of education . . . adopt and implement policies and procedures for the evaluation . . . of pupils . . . who on reasonable grounds are suspected of being under the influence." N.J.A.C. § 6:29-6.3. The NHRHS Policy is an effort to comply with this mandate.

No action of any kind in any court of competent jurisdiction shall lie against any teaching staff member, including a substance awareness coordinator, any school nurse or other educational personnel, medical inspector, examining physician or any other officer, agent or any employee of the board of education or personnel of the emergency room of a hospital because of any action taken by virtue of the provisions of this act, provided the skill and care given is that ordinarily required and exercised by other teaching staff members, nurses, educational personnel, medical inspectors, physicians or other officers, agents, or any employees of the board of education or emergency room personnel.

N.J.S.A. § 18A:40A-13. The District Court, relying on that provision, held that Mr. McDonald, Nurse Kiely, and Mr. Musco, as school officials within the meaning of the statute, were immune from the plaintiffs' suit.

In Good v. Dauphin Co. Social Serv. for Children and Youth, 891 F.2d 1087, 1091 (3d Cir.1989), however, we held that "state law cannot immunize government employees from liability resulting from their violation of federal law." We explained:

[A state] immunity statute, although effective against a state tort claim, has no force when applied to suits under the Civil Rights Acts. The supremacy clause of the Constitution prevents a state from immunizing entities or individuals alleged to have violated federal law. This result follows whether the suit to redress federal rights is brought in state or federal court. Were the rule otherwise, a state legislature would be able to frustrate the objectives of a federal statute.

The District Court, therefore, erred in holding that the school officials were immunized from plaintiffs' federal claims by the New Jersey statute. Because we may affirm a district court's grant of summary judgment on any ground that appears in the record, however, we will proceed to consider the merits of plaintiffs' case.

In New Jersey v. T.L.O., the Supreme Court recognized that "[i]t is now beyond dispute that 'the Federal Constitution, by virtue of the Fourteenth Amendment, prohibits unreasonable searches and seizures by state officers.' Equally indisputable is the proposition that the Fourteenth Amendment protects the rights of students against encroachment by public school officials." 469 U.S. 325, 334, 105 S.Ct. 733, 83 L.Ed.2d 720 (1985) (quoting Elkins v. United States, 364 U.S. 206, 213, 80 S.Ct. 1437, 4 L.Ed.2d 1669 (1960)).

The Supreme Court has recently said that "[a]rticulating precisely what 'reasonable suspicion' . . . mean[s] is not possible." Ornelas v. United States,

517 U.S. 690, 695, 116 S.Ct. 1657, 134 L.Ed.2d 911 (1996). It is a "commonsense, nontechnical conception[ ] that deal[s] with the factual and practical considerations of everyday life on which reasonable and prudent men, not legal technicians, act." Id. (internal quotation omitted); see also Karnes v. Skrutski, 62 F.3d 485, 495 (3d Cir. 1995) ("The test for reasonable suspicion is a totality of the circumstances inquiry.").

Applying those legal principles to the facts of this case, we hold that defendants McDonald, Kiely, and Musco's suspicion that Tara was "high" was reasonable. In addition, we believe that the searches were reasonable in scope and not excessively intrusive.

A. Mr. McDonald, Nurse Kiely and the School Search
As we have explained, when Tara entered Mr. McDonald's class on the morning of April 8, 1996, she was behaving in an uncharacteristically gregarious manner. In addition, her face was flushed; her eyes were glassy and red; and her pupils were dilated. Then during class, Tara, after obtaining permission to leave the room to get a drink of water, proceeded in the opposite direction, disappeared around the corner of the hallway, and did not return for approximately ten minutes. All of this was inconsistent with Tara's normal behavior and appearance. In our view, these facts gave Mr. McDonald a sufficiently "particularized and objective basis" for suggesting that Tara be examined by the school nurse. United States v. Cortez, 449 U.S. 411, 417-18, 101 S.Ct. 690, 66 L.Ed.2d 621 (1981). While, as plaintiffs point out, Tara's speech was not slurred, McDonald did not smell anything on her breath, and she did not smell of marijuana, those facts do not undermine the reasonableness of McDonald's suspicion. Tara may not have possessed every characteristic that may be exhibited by a person who has consumed alcohol or other drugs, but the symptoms she did manifest created a reasonable suspicion that she had consumed some quantity of alcohol or other drugs. McDonald had reasonable grounds for suspecting that a further and more comprehensive evaluation of Tara might produce evidence of such consumption.

It bears noting that McDonald did not immediately order Tara to submit to a blood test and urinalysis. Rather, pursuant to school policy, he had her escorted to Nurse Kiely's office for further examination. Because Nurse Kiely's examination only involved observing Tara and checking her vital signs, we hold that the scope of the search at this point was reasonably related to its objectives and not excessively intrusive given the age and sex of the student and the nature of the infraction. Because requiring Tara to submit to Nurse Kiely's examination represents the full extent of McDonald's participation in the relevant events, McDonald's conduct did not amount to a Fourth Amendment violation.

Before Nurse Kiely conducted her "vital signs" examination, her own observations in her office led her to conclude that Tara's behavior and appearance were abnormal and consistent with her having consumed alcohol or another drug. Given those observations and McDonald's report, Nurse Kiely's ensuing, limited examination did not, in our view, constitute an unreasonable search.

The analysis conducted by the Seventh Circuit Court of Appeals suggests that, where a teacher's suspicion is based on objective facts that suggest that a student may be under the influence of drugs or alcohol, an examination of the kind here performed by Nurse Kiely will be permissible.

B. Principal Musco and the Urgent Care Search

In T.L.O., the Supreme Court, after concluding that it was reasonable for a teacher to search a student's purse for cigarettes after being informed that the student was smoking in the lavatory, further held that additional information secured in the course of the search warranted more intrusive, follow-up searches. See 469 U.S. at 347, 105 S.Ct. 733.

Here, too, the information learned as the investigation progressed provided additional justification for the decision to require a blood test and urinalysis. After Tara arrived at Nurse Kiely's office and before she went to the Urgent Care for the blood test and urinalysis, Principal Musco learned that her blood pressure was above normal, and that she was unable to remember her parents' day-time phone numbers. In addition, at some point during this process, Tara's book bag was searched. An old pill bottle, containing two different types of unidentified pills, was discovered there. As Tara had not registered any medications with the Nurse, her possession of those pills—whether they were illegal drugs or not—was a violation of school policy. Tara's explanation for the pills was that they were diet pills, but her father informed Principal Musco that he was confident Tara was not on a diet.

Based on the combination of Mr. McDonald's observations (which were confirmed, except for the di-

lated pupils, by the Nurse) and this newly gathered evidence, it simply cannot be said that Principal Musco lacked reasonable grounds for concluding that a further search would produce additional evidence of drug consumption.

Accordingly, we turn to the issue of whether the search ordered by Principal Musco was reasonably related to its objectives and not excessively intrusive given the age and sex of the student and the nature of the infraction. Certainly a drug test is reasonably related to the objective of determining whether a student is under the influence; the issue then is whether a urinalysis and blood test were excessively intrusive given the nature of the suspected infraction.

The Supreme Court has recognized that "collecting samples for urinalysis intrudes upon 'an excretory function traditionally shielded by great privacy.' " Vernonia School Dist. 47J v. Acton, 515 U.S. 646, 658, 115 S.Ct. 2386, 132 L.Ed.2d 564 (1995) (quoting Skinner v. Railway Labor Executives' Ass'n, 489 U.S. 602, 626, 109 S.Ct. 1402, 103 L.Ed.2d 639 (1989)). The Court cautioned, however, that "the degree of intrusion depends upon the manner in which production of the urine sample is monitored."

Under the District's Policy, male students produce samples at a urinal along a wall. They remain fully clothed and are only observed from behind, if at all. Female students produce samples in an enclosed stall, with a female monitor standing outside listening only for sounds of tampering. These conditions are nearly identical to those typically encountered in public restrooms, which men, women, and especially school children use daily. Under such conditions, privacy interests compromised by the process of obtaining urine samples are in our view negligible.

In this case, Tara's urinalysis was performed at a private medical clinic. Nurse Neumann described the urinalysis procedure as follows:

The patient would be sent to the lavatory, where the water has previously been turned off. . . . The patient takes the large container and goes into the restroom and fills it up. . . . They bring it back into the room. . . . I check the temperature on it, then they pour it into the containers. . . . The patient goes into the bathroom with the cup by themselves. We don't go in with him—with them.

Based on Vernonia, we hold that the urinalysis performed on Tara Hedges was not excessively intrusive given the age and sex of the student and the nature of the infraction.

In addition to the urinalysis, Principal Musco ordered that a blood-alcohol test be performed. Plaintiffs assert that "either a saliva strip or the breathalyser are more effective tools to determine alcohol use . . . and are less intrusive than a blood test." Brief for Appellant at 44. Plaintiffs misconceive T.L.O.'s standard, however. T.L.O. did not hold that the search must be the least intrusive way of achieving its objectives; it held that the search must not be excessively intrusive. See T.L.O., 469 U.S. at 342, 105 S.Ct. 733. Therefore, the mere fact that there are less intrusive means of ascertaining whether a student has consumed alcohol, though perhaps probative, is not dispositive of the reasonableness of the search.

The Supreme Court has upheld the use of blood-alcohol tests in a multitude of cases. In Schmerber v. California, the Court explained:

"Extraction of blood samples for testing is a highly effective means of determining the degree to which a person is under the influence of alcohol. . . . Such tests are a[sic] commonplace in these days of periodic physical examination and experience with them teaches that the quantity of blood extracted is minimal, and that for most people the procedure involves virtually no risk, trauma, or pain."

In summary, we conclude that the searches of Tara Hedges were reasonable under all the circumstances. See T.L.O., 469 U.S. at 341, 105 S.Ct. 733. Each was justified at its inception and reasonably related in scope to the circumstances which justified the interference in the first place. See id. at 341-42, 105 S.Ct. 733. Summary judgment in favor of the NHRHS defendants on the unreasonable search claims was therefore appropriate.

Case Review Question: What one change in the facts could render the case one of unreasonable search and seizure?

Assignment 2.3

From the list below identify whether the subject would be more appropriately addressed by the judiciary, legislature, or an administrative agency. Explain your response.

a. Sale and transmission of computer programs from companies to communities for the operation and control of traffic lights.
b. Standards for obtaining a driver's license at an earlier than standard age for the purpose of operating farm trucks on a family-owned farm.
c. Whether an individual is in control of a vehicle for the purposes of drunk driving statutes if he or she starts a vehicle while inebriated but goes into the back seat to sleep until sober.

C. THE EFFECT OF VARIOUS LEGAL STANDARDS IN RELATION TO ONE ANOTHER

In the preceding materials, the various methods of creating legal standards was discussed. However, what happens when more than one legal standard from more than one source appears to apply to a situation, but the different standards indicate different results? The immense number of legal standards in existence and constant additions and amendments combined with an infinite number of possible circumstances cause this issue to arise on a fairly regular basis. If the sources of law were completely independent of one another, the potential for deadlock would exist when such conflicts occurred. This in turn would result in the exercise of personal discretion on the part of judges and juries. The end result would be no consistent pattern of law and therefore no means to guide one's conduct by looking to established principles of law.

American law is governed by a distinct hierarchy. First in the hierarchy is the U.S. Constitution. Although technically the Constitution and its amendments are statutory law, they are considered superior to all other law, since they established the governmental structure and the process for creating all other law. One concept that has remained consistent throughout the legal history of this country is that all branches of state and federal government and all persons in the United States must function within the parameters of the U.S. Constitution. If at any time the will of the people is in conflict with the Constitution, the Constitution can be amended through the proper process, which is designed to guarantee that the amendment does in fact reflect the will of the majority. Chapter 3 discusses in more detail the process for amending the Constitution.

Next in the hierarchy of laws are the legislative (statutory) acts of Congress. Statutes have greater weight than judicial or administrative law since statutes are enacted by Congress and state legislatures, which are composed of people elected by the people. Thus, statutes are most likely to represent the laws intended for and desired by the majority.

The judiciary has the authority to interpret legislation and to fill in gray areas where law is unclear or nonexistent. This is when case law is established. However, the judiciary is also obligated to ensure that statutory law is consistent with the Constitution. We might think of the judiciary as the protectors of the Constitution. In any case, when the judiciary determines that the law does not meet the requirements of the Constitution, it has the authority to declare the law invalid and thereby supersede the ordinarily superior statutory law. Constitutionality is the only reason a judiciary may control an issue subject to statutory law. If the court finds that the law violates constitutional standards, the judiciary may strike down the law on that basis and declare it inapplicable. A prime example of this would be a law that is vague or overbroad. Such a law is unconstitutional because it would not provide fair and clear notice to persons of what is illegal conduct. Such notice is a requirement of the Constitution and its amendments. Thus, the court would have the authority to strike down the statute and dismiss charges against anyone who is alleged to have violated the statute. Such an action by a court is an uncommon occurrence but not unheard of at both the state and federal levels.

Last in the hierarchy is administrative law. Administrative agencies assist Congress by issuing regulations and decisions that clarify and aid in the enforcement of statutes. However, Congress has the right to eliminate an agency or regulations that are inconsistent with legislative objectives. The judiciary also has the authority to overrule actions of an agency when such actions are unconstitutional or inconsistent with legislative objectives. The authority of the judiciary to overrule and invalidate law is not exercised lightly or frequently. The courts generally defer to Congress and administrative agencies unless there is a clear constitutional violation.

APPLICATION 2.3

Max was a truck driver who contracted with meat packers to bring in loads of animals ready for butcher. He also contracted with farmers' groups to bring the animals to market. On one such occasion, a group of farmers contacted Max and hired him to take a load of pigs to market in an adjoining state. Max operated his own truck and trailer. Early in the morning he picked up the load of animals. Late that afternoon he stopped for dinner and also consumed a large quantity of alcohol. He got back on the road and had only traveled a short distance when his truck collided with another vehicle carrying several passengers. All those in the vehicle were killed. Max was not injured. The families of the passengers sued Max, the farmers, and the meat packers for causing the deaths of their family members. In the suit, federal trucking regulations issued by the ICC, state laws, and federal laws all came into question regarding the employment status of Max in relation to the other two defendants.

Point for Discussion: In this situation, how would conflicts of the laws described be resolved?

Assignment 2.4

Using the situation in Application 2.3, assume the following conflicts of laws developed. Arrange the laws in the order the conflicts would be resolved and explain why each legal standard would be applied in favor of the conflicting standard.

a. Federal regulation versus state law
b. Federal law versus federal regulation
c. Federal judicial opinion versus state law

D. PROCEDURAL AND SUBSTANTIVE LAW IN CIVIL AND CRIMINAL CASES

The body of law that has developed in this country is organized in a number of ways. Law is arranged by jurisdiction, by its source (legislative, judicial, administrative), by subject matter, and so forth. Each method serves a common function—to distinguish one area of law from another in a way that makes it accessible to researchers from a variety of viewpoints. However, regardless of the subject matter, the jurisdiction, the source of law, or how these are arranged, certain characteristics can be applied to all law. First, all legal standards are either criminal or civil. Secondly, all legal standards are either substantive or procedural. The distinction in the criminal and civil standard, addressed briefly here, will be further explored in later chapters. The differences between substantive and procedural law will be discussed later in this chapter.

1. Criminal Versus Civil Law

Criminal Law
Law created and
enforced by the
legislature for the
health, welfare, safety,
and general good of
the public.

Civil Law
Law that governs the
private rights of
individuals, legal
entities, and
government.

Criminal and civil law serve very different functions in our legal system and in society as a whole. While **criminal law** was the first law to be applied in the American legal system, **civil law** was equally necessary and followed almost immediately thereafter. All criminal law has a common purpose—to protect society from those who would injure the standards of an orderly society. While crimes are often committed against specific persons or entities, the criminal law is intended to protect the public as a whole as well as its individual components. Consequently, all criminal prosecutions are brought in the name of the jurisdiction rather than the name of the victim, for example, *The People of the State of Utah vs. Sherrets* rather than *Smith vs. Sherrets*. A crime committed against a person or entity is considered injurious to the public as a whole because it threatens the order of our society and those rights to which we are all entitled in this country.

Criminal law varies from parking violations to capital murder. It includes all legal standards designed by the legislature to maintain order and safety within our borders. Criminal law carries penalties that may include monetary fines, community service, or imprisonment. It may also include restitution to a victim, but in general penalties are paid or served to the government. This is quite different from civil law, which leaves issue resolution and penalty, if any, to the parties themselves that is, the injured and the alleged violator of civil legal standards.

APPLICATION 2.4

Mary Ann is a charter pilot. On one occasion, she was hired by two hunters to fly them to a remote area of Montana where they intended to hunt elk. Mary Ann's pilot license had been recently suspended as the result of former incidents of reckless conduct while operating aircraft. She did not inform the hunters of this. During the flight, she made several errors in judgment that resulted in a crash landing in which the hunters were both seriously injured. Criminal charges were brought against Mary Ann for operating a plane without a license and thereby endangering public safety, specifically the hunters. The hunters also brought civil suits against Mary Ann seeking compensation for their injuries.

Point for Discussion: Why would compensation for the injuries not be part of the criminal penalty?

Civil law governs the issues that arise between parties over private rights. Thus, a citizen who sues another for an invasion of personal rights has grounds for a civil case. An example of a civil case is an individual suing the government for invasion of private rights. Another is the government suing an individual for damage to public property, such as a stop sign. Still another example is a suit by one citizen against another for property damage or physical injury caused by an automobile accident. While the person responsible for the accident may also be subject to criminal charges, these are separate and distinct from claims for injury to the other persons involved or their property. A civil case is brought by the injured party for damage to his or her personal rights, as opposed to the rights of society as a whole. The injured party seeks some sort of compensation (usually monetary) for the injury or damage to the person or property.

In a civil case, penalties are quite different from those in a criminal case. There is no threat of imprisonment. In addition, any judgment that awards money benefits the individual whose rights were invaded and injured. Awards of money are generally intended to compensate the injured party for the reasonable cost of the injuries, thus the term **compensatory damages.** Additionally, in cases where money cannot adequately compensate but some action could, the defendant may be ordered to act or refrain from acting in a certain way. This is called an injunction or **injunctive relief,** or in some cases specific performance (particular court-ordered conduct). This type of relief is limited and not routinely granted by courts unless there is a clear and present danger of further damage to a person's safety or legal rights, or there is no adequate means to establish damages. Some jurisdictions also permit the recovery of **punitive damages,** also known as exemplary damages. These are additional monies that the defendant is ordered to pay as a form of punishment. The rationale of punitive damages is that some conduct is so grossly improper and shows such a total disregard for others that the defendant should be punished in a way that will not only compensate the injured party but will also serve as an example to others who might contemplate similar grossly wrongful conduct. Punitive damages are awarded only in cases of very serious misconduct that typically demonstrate wanton recklessness.

Compensatory Damages
Award of money payable to the injured party for the reasonable cost of the injuries.

Injunctive Relief
Court-ordered action or nonaction to legally limit or enforce specific conduct.

Punitive Damages
Award of money payable to the injured party as punishment and act as a deterrent to the defendant and others for wanton and reckless conduct. Also referred to as exemplary damages.

APPLICATION 2.5

Joseph was a building contractor who was hired to build a summer cabin for the Chimes family. Joseph cut a lot of corners and installed substandard materials in the cabin. As a result, during a heavy rainstorm, the roof collapsed and the cabin was destroyed. The Chimes family brought suit against Joseph for the loss of their cabin due to his actions, and they also sought punitive damages. The theory was that Joseph installed the substandard materials and workmanship knowing the likely ultimate effect. According to the Chimes complaint, this showed a reckless disregard for the Chimes property rights and their safety.

Point for Discussion: What distinguishes this case to support a claim for punitive damages?

Assignment 2.5

Determine whether the following cases would be criminal or civil actions. Explain your answers.

a. A man is injured when a ladder he is on collapses beneath him due to faulty design.
b. A woman is driving 40 m.p.h. in a 30 m.p.h. zone during a rainstorm and her car slides off the road causing her serious injury.
c. A guest at a dude ranch is given a horse to ride that has a history of unpredictable behavior. Without warning, the guest is thrown from the horse and suffers a broken leg.
d. In the same circumstances as c, rather than being thrown, an employee who has been drinking deliberately runs into the horse with a car. The guest is remarkably uninjured.

2. Substantive Versus Procedural Law

Substantive Law
Law that creates and resolves the issue between the parties. Legal standard that guides conduct and is applied to determine whether or not conduct was legally appropriate.

Substantive law actually determines the legal rights of parties. Legal standards of substantive law are relied upon to establish whether a party acted appropriately in a given circumstance. In real practice, substantive law creates, defines, and regulates rights. It is exactly what its name implies: the body, essence, and substance that guides the conduct of citizens. It encompasses principles of right and wrong as well as the principle that wrong will result in penalty. It includes the rights and duties of citizens, and it provides the basis to resolve issues involving those rights. Every citizen has the right to live and enjoy his or her own property and person free from intrusion by other citizens in most instances. The exception is when the action or nonaction of one citizen infringes on the same basic freedoms of another citizen. An old phrase, "your rights end where someone else's begin," is the basic definition of substantive law. The American legal system dictates that all members of society are obligated to respect and not to interfere with the rights of others. Substantive law is the basis for establishing and enforcing this mandate.

Legal standards of substantive law have been developed over centuries. Substantive and procedural law are essentially subclasses of both the areas of civil and criminal law. However, this discussion is confined to civil law. Early on, the principles were primarily confined to protection of one's property rights. If one individual interfered with another's property, the courts offered some redress. As society has advanced and developed, so has the body of law to address the myriad of rights that merit protection. In an application of substantive law, the court examines the circumstance in which the parties are at issue. Typically, one party will advance the claim that another party has acted in such a way as to cause injury or damage to the rights, person, or property of the complaining party. Consequently, a claim is made for damages, which generally consists of a monetary award to compensate the injured party for the assessed value of the injury. The court's function is to consider the facts of the case and render a decision, by a judge or jury, as to whether the accused party's conduct was improper and also the cause of the injuries. If this is found to be the case, then an award of damages is typically made. In some jurisdictions and instances, punitive damages may also be awarded in cases of gross misconduct.

As mentioned, the body of substantive law has grown over time and continues to evolve in direct response to a changing and developing society. Consequently, what was once a few established principles has become tens of thousands of standards to govern virtually every conceivable circumstance. And when it does not, a new standard is created. The sheer size of the body of law, and the ever-increasing population require a complex system of organization in order to make the law and courts accessible. This role is fulfilled by procedural law.

APPLICATION 2.6

Acme Company owns a fleet of over-the-road trucks that haul lumber from the northeast to lumber companies around the midwest. On May 1, an Acme driver started out with a loaded truck heading toward Ohio. In the early morning hours of May 2, the driver encountered a severe storm and, unable to see the road clearly, crossed the center line hitting an oncoming car.

Point for Discussion: What would be the substantive issue of law in this situation?

Procedural law is a unique set of legal principles designed for a particular legal system. Each legal system, whether it is a state judicial system, the federal courts, an administrative agency, or a legislature, has a set of operating rules. Quite simply put, procedural law is more or less an owner's manual. Just as the manual for a new car explains all the attributes of a particular vehicle and how to operate it most efficiently, procedural law guides citizens through all the necessary steps to maneuver most efficiently through the various aspects of a legal system. Regardless of the branch of government, or whether the system is state or federal, all procedural law has a common goal: to ensure that the laws are applied fairly and consistently to all. Ideally, the amount of influence or money or social position a party has should not in any way impact how they are treated by the American legal system. Injustices do occur and some officials are corrupt, as in any society and form of government. Given the size of the task, however, the American procedural laws are remarkably effective in the administration of law and justice.

Criminal procedure will be covered more thoroughly in a subsequent chapter. The focus of the following discussion will be confined to that of civil procedure. The majority of citizens encounter procedural law in the court systems. Civil procedure can be likened to a large piece of machinery that assembles a product. It is devoid of emotion or personal opinion. The function is to provide the route for the orderly assembly of a product, in this instance, the completion of a lawsuit. The parties to the suit and the courts provide the pieces to the product at the appropriate times and in the appropriate order. The completed product that is delivered from the machine is the decision that resolves the dispute. This decision is the result of the pieces of information (substantive legal principles and facts of the case) that have been fed into the machine and assembled by the judge or jury.

Assume in the situation described in Application 2.6 that the trucking company and driver of the car became involved in litigation. The principles of law that were applied in their case to determine who should prevail, based on the most reasonable explanation of the facts, is substantive law. Procedural law also plays a part in the litigation and includes the following:

1. The time limit for filing a lawsuit
2. The manner in which the lawsuit is begun (e.g., by filing a complaint of petition)
3. The proper way to inform the defendant that a lawsuit has been filed
4. The types of information that each party must release to the other party
5. The procedure at trial
6. The evidence that can be introduced at trial
7. The method for appealing the decision if the losing party feels the decision was the result of an error in the application of law

Procedural Law
Law used to guide parties fairly and efficiently through the legal system.

Assignment 2.6

After the collision between the truck and car described in Application 2.6, the parties were both taken to an area hospital. Mr. Gonzeles (driver of the truck) was not seriously injured and was treated and released. Mr. Washington (driver of the car) was very seriously injured and required multiple surgeries and months of rehabilitation. Ultimately, he was left without the use of his left arm. Mr. Washington was a resident of the state of Indiana. Shortly after release from the hospital, Mr. Washington sought the advice of an Indiana attorney. The lawyer explained that he would need to obtain permission from the Ohio courts to represent Mr. Washington if suit was filed there, as he did not possess an Ohio license to practice law. He further explained that there were a number of courts where suit could be filed, including the states of Ohio, Indiana, and New Hampshire where Acme Trucking was incorporated and did business. The case could also be filed in federal courts in any of these jurisdictions. Once the jurisdiction was determined, it would be necessary to determine the time available to bring this type of suit. Next, the case would need to be filed, stating why Acme was alleged to be at fault for Mr. Washington's injuries and disability. They would need proof of the fault and the appropriate amount needed to compensate Mr. Washington for his injuries and disability as well as any related expenses, such as lost time from work, medical bills, future losses, and so forth. Once Acme was properly put on notice of the suit, the case could move toward trial following procedural rules for evidence and trial preparations.

3. When Substantive and Procedural Issues Become Blended

There are times when one's substantive rights may be affected by procedural laws. For example, in a case where more than one court system may have authority to hear a case, the substantive law in one system may be more favorable to a party than the substantive law in another. Procedural law may dictate which court should hear the case. When more than one court has authority, the procedural law may be more favorable to a party, for example, by providing a longer time in which suit may be brought. A number of circumstances can occur in which procedural law impacts the substantive rights of the parties to a dispute. Such conflicts of procedural and substantive law are dealt with differently by the various court systems. However, a basic rule, which is usually followed, is that a court should attempt to apply its own procedural rules and the most appropriate substantive law even if it emanates from a different jurisdiction.

APPLICATION 2.7

Shakur is at an ice skating rink in Omaha, Nebraska. He lives in neighboring Council Bluffs, Iowa. The equipment for the ice rink malfunctions leaving a number of irregularities in the ice that are not readily visible. Shakur falls when skating over such an irregularity and suffers a compound fracture. Shakur files suit in the U.S. District Court of Iowa. The court applies its own procedural law, but applies the substantive law of the state of Nebraska where the alleged negligent conduct of the skating rink and Shakur's injuries occurred.

Point for Discussion: Why would the court not apply the law of Iowa where it is located?

As stated, the issue of conflicting procedural and substantive standards from varying jurisdictions arises when more than one jurisdiction (area within a court's authority) could serve as the site for a lawsuit. The party bringing the action will no doubt select the jurisdiction whose laws most favor the claim. An example is a choice between two states based on the statute-of-limitations laws. The statute of limitations (also known as limitation of actions) is a procedural law in a jurisdiction that indicates the maximum amount of time in which a lawsuit can be commenced. For example, in some states, the limit is one year. Therefore, if a plaintiff in one of these states with a personal injury claim decides to file a suit two years after the injury, the suit could be brought only in a state with a three-year statute of limitations. In a jurisdiction with a one-year statute of limitations, the suit would be barred after one year had passed. Because the circumstances that produce a lawsuit sometimes occur in more than one jurisdiction, there is more than one place where suit can be brought.

CHAPTER SUMMARY

A detailed system of legal standards is necessary to address the size and complexity of the American society. As structured, it has the capability to address the population in its entirety, targeted groups, and individual circumstances. The various branches interrelate within an established hierarchy that promotes consistency throughout the American legal system and, at the same time, serves the dual function of preventing overly broad exercises of power by any one branch of government. The system is able to grow and evolve with society and to adapt to changing standards and technology.

The legislature bears the ultimate responsibility for establishing the legal standards that are the guideposts for conduct by all members of society. These standards are then interpreted by the judiciary as they apply to the specific circumstances of individuals. When an area of law, technology, or society develops to the point that a detailed analysis of legal standards and a formal system of enforcement is warranted, an administrative agency can help to clarify and enforce the objectives of the legislature. Each source of law has a connection to the other two. A distinct hierarchy prevents any branch of government from obtaining too much authority or exercising authority beyond its own boundaries. Ultimately, the system is designed to be reflective of the current needs and standards of an ever-changing society. Regardless of the source, law can usually be categorized as criminal or civil, and substantive or procedural. While criminal addresses the rights of the public as a whole, civil is focused on more personal and private issues. Similarly, while substantive legal standards dictate the required conduct in a given situation, procedural addresses how that conduct should be examined and dealt with.

ETHICAL NOTE

Ethical considerations are the very core of legal standards in the American legal system. Every legal standard is created and enforced in an attempt to promote fairness by the government and by citizens toward one another. This is evident in both the purposes of the various types of legal principles and in the methods employed to create them by the different branches of government in order to fully and efficiently address legal issues and related ethical concerns. And even though the system may not always appear to function smoothly, quickly, or fairly, given the size of the task and the enormous variance among the general population in the definition of what is and is not acceptable, the system performs amazingly well.

Relevant Internet Sites

White House Offices/Agencies	http://infoplease.lycos.com/ipa/A0197404
United States Congress	www. Congress.com
United States Supreme Court	www.supremecourtus.gov

Internet Assignment 2.1

Locate Internet addresses for 10 different state (U.S. Government) administrative agencies.

KEY TERMS

Administrative Law	Common Law	Punitive Damages
Administrative Procedures Act	Compensatory Damages	Stare Decisis
Bill	Criminal Law	Statutory Law
Case Law	Enabling Act	Substantive Law
Civil Law	Injunctive Relief	Veto
Code	Legal Standard	
Code of Federal Regulations	Precedent	
(CFR)	Procedural Law	

ENDNOTES

1. *Gonzalez v. Automatic Emp. Credit Union*, 419 U.S. 90, 95 S.Ct. 289, 42 L.Ed.2d. 249 (1974).
2. *Schware v. Board of Bar Examiners*, 353 U.S. 232, 77 S.Ct. 752, 1 L.Ed. 2d 796 (1957).
3. *Litsinger Sign Co. v. American Sign Co.*, 11 Ohio St. 2d, 227 N.E.2d 609 (1967).
4. Article I, U.S. Constitution
5. *Carter v. Carter Coal Company*, 298 U.S. 238, 56 S.Ct. 855, 80 L.Ed.2d 796 (1957).
6. *Hedges v. Musco*, 204 F.2d 109 (3rd Cir. 2000).

Chapter 3

LEGAL ANALYSIS AND APPLICATION OF LEGAL PRINCIPLES

CHAPTER OBJECTIVES

Upon completion of this chapter you should be able to do the following:

- Define legal analysis.
- Discuss the importance and value of legal analysis for legal professionals and others.
- Distinguish legal analysis of statutory and administrative law from case law.
- Explain the steps of legal analysis and the significance of each.
- Discuss how the product of legal analysis can be applied to a current situation.
- Discuss the basic components of a legal citation.

A. WHAT IS LEGAL ANALYSIS?

1. Legal Analysis Defined

Legal Analysis
Process of examining precedent in detail to predict its effect on future similar circumstances.

In earlier chapters, the role of an attorney was distinguished from that of other legal professionals. The lawyer must demonstrate a proficiency sufficient to warrant a statutorily granted license that permits giving legal advice and representing the legal rights of others. The training and experience that is required for a lawyer to effectively give legal advice and represent the rights of others is grounded in **legal analysis.** Analytical ability is present in every facet of life. It is the skill of applying past experiences to current or foreseen circumstances to determine the probable outcome. This skill begins to develop in children. For example, if a child refuses to wear a coat to school on a chilly day and is cold on the way to and from school, in the future the child will know that the experience was unpleasant and on the next cold day a coat will prevent it from happening again. As knowledge accumulates, this ability to examine how situations developed and were resolved in the past becomes more refined and guides our present and future conduct. For attorneys, the skill lies in the ability to analyze past similar situations that were dealt with in the legal system and use them to predict the likely outcome of a present case. Because no two situations are exactly alike and legal issues are not as simplistic as what to wear for a given type of weather, legal analysis is performed at a much more complex level. It is necessary to identify all of the relevant similarities and differences of facts, the law of the jurisdiction, the parties, and the apparent attitude of the judge and jury. Each of these must be evaluated in terms of their significance and impact on the likelihood of a similar result in the present case. Also the attorney's analytical skill is directly supported by the training and skill required to locate and identify all relevant facts and law in a particular case.

It is rare that legal research and investigation/discovery of facts produces little or no result. On the contrary, it is more often the case that a great wealth of information must be sifted through and either retained as significant or discarded as unimportant or inapplicable. This, in and of itself, is legal analysis at the base level. Next, the more complicated task of evaluation (analysis) of the applicability and significance of what remains becomes the focus. Finally comes the crucial point when the lawyer determines what the likely outcome of the case will be when the existing legal principles, now analyzed in terms of the present case, are applied. This determination guides the case in terms of settlement, trial tactics and strategies, and even whether to appeal an unsatisfactory result.

Legal analysis is the cornerstone of the American judicial system. It allows the judge to resolve a dispute consistent with established legal principles and allows the lawyer to advise and represent the client as to the appropriate course of conduct. It enables the paralegal to know what information will be necessary to interview a client and properly prepare legal documents. Legal analysis is performed with respect to statutes, administrative law, and cases. The process of analyzing different types of law varies somewhat because the format between law generated for the general public and legal standards applied to specific parties is different. However, the desired effect is the same, to determine the applicability or nonapplicability of the legal standard to the case at hand.

Legal analysis is predominantly the domain of legal professionals, and lawyers in particular. The paralegals, legal investigators, and entire support staff of the attorney also routinely engage in some level of legal analysis. The nonprofessional also derives significant benefit from the process of legal analysis in the application of legal standards through contact with attorneys and even the media.

By looking to established legal precedents, the paralegal and support staff can develop a sense of how various types of cases typically proceed. This also enables them to anticipate and deal with common procedural issues. In knowing what was and was not acceptable when engaged in discovery and investigation based on past cases, the legal support professional can perform these tasks much more efficiently and effectively. Human beings are basically analytical creatures who learn by experience and example. While traditional methods of education are necessary, lessons are truly learned and then applied in a variety of other circumstances when they are experienced or, at the very least, observed in a realistic setting. It is one thing to read a principle of law such as the definition of negligence, but that principle becomes much clearer when a judicial opinion is read that demonstrates how negligence occurs in a real-life situation. As the legal support professional gains more and more knowledge of legal principles through practice, the skills of the professional can become more well developed.

APPLICATION 3.1

Leon is a recent graduate from an accredited paralegal studies program. In his first job he is required to prepare many discovery documents and interview witnesses. At first, Leon spends a great deal of time on each case as he learns how to obtain information, what kinds of data to look for, and how to prepare the various required documents. After several months, Leon is still proceeding rather slowly with his assignments as a result of his efforts to do a thorough job. A senior paralegal asks Leon if he would like to observe and assist her as she begins the discovery and investigation for a very large case the firm has just accepted. Leon jumps at this chance. As he works alongside the senior paralegal, he asks questions about why things are done a certain way. By observing and assisting, he is able to identify a number of things he has been doing that do not provide significant benefit to the case and that cause delay in completing his assignments. When Leon returns a few weeks later to his regular job duties he is better able to prepare documents that are effective and rarely challenged by opposition. He also spends much less time interviewing witnesses, yet obtains just as much or more of the necessary information.

Point for Discussion: What other things could Leon do to improve his effectiveness?

Assignment 3.1

Explain in the following situations how legal analysis could help.

a. A new client comes to see an attorney. The client complains that the computer program responsible for the timing of stoplights malfunctioned and caused an accident involving the client. Is there a case? The attorney has never heard of a case like this before and is not even sure who to sue—the city, the programmer, the driver of the other vehicle, or a combination.

b. A paralegal accepts a position with a local law firm. The paralegal has several years experience working in the trust department of a bank. The new position is with a firm that does primarily divorce and custody cases. The paralegal is first assigned to investigate in a custody case. The assignment is to collect all the facts and information that are relevant in this type of case.

2. Legal Analysis of Judicial Opinions

Case Analysis
Function of evaluating
and synthesizing a
judicial opinion.

Judicial Opinion
Legal document stating
the finding and
rationale for an order
of court.

Of the various methods of legal analysis, **case analysis** is the specific means to examine past **judicial opinions** and their impact on a current situation. The similarities and differences between the past cases and the current situation give insight with regard to whether the outcome should be similar in the present case. Because case analysis is used so extensively, an organized system for publishing and arranging the cases has become necessary so that cases on specific topics or from particular courts can be easily accessed. While this is discussed in greater detail in Chapter Seven, a brief introduction will be given here for the purposes of illustration.

Published cases are predominantly appellate for quite practical reasons. First, since trial courts are generally the lowest level of judicial authority (there are no subordinate courts), a trial court opinion does not have to be followed by a judge in a subsequent case. Appellate court opinions on the other hand must be followed by trial courts that are subordinate to the authority of the appellate court that issued the opinion. Also, appellate decisions are usually rendered by a panel of appellate judges using their collective wisdom in the review of how the law was applied in the trial court. Such opinions are infrequently overturned by higher level appellate courts and thus provide a stable basis for comparison of the state legal standard to a present situation. A second reason for the limited number of published trial court opinions is cost effectiveness. Literally hundreds of thousands of trials take place annually in this country. It would not be reasonable to publish all of the opinions supporting the outcome of these cases when they are of such limited authority.

Judicial opinions are published chronologically, as they are handed down by the courts, in a series of books. That is to say that the published opinions of a jurisdiction, and sometimes more than one, are published in the same book series as they are issued. Each new volume in the publication is numbered consecutively and contains the most recently issued opinions. When there is a change in how the information is presented, such as introductory materials in advance of each case, the changes are signaled by a new *series* of the same publication, for example Pacific Reporter, Pacific Reporter 2nd series, Pacific Reporter 3rd Series. With each new series, the numbering of volumes starts over as well. For example, the last book of the first series may be volume 311. If a new series is begun at this point, the next volume published will be volume 1 of the 2nd series of the same publication. Volume 1 is not Volume 312 because a change in the regular format within the publication has been implemented and, therefore, a new series and new numbering sequence begins.

The usefulness of published cases is immeasurable. By having access to opinions the courts have issued in past similar cases, an intelligent assessment can be made of the likely outcome of a current or potential dispute. Judges look to published cases to determine the appropriate legal standards and the manner in which the standards should be applied in pending cases. In addition, it is not uncommon for parties or their lawyers to examine the published cases before taking any action whatsoever. Such examination often guides the conduct of an individual or business in matters that do not involve imminent legal action. Rather, these legal standards may be consulted in an attempt to avoid finding oneself in the very circumstances that have prompted lawsuits in the past.

When reading judicial opinions for the first time, they may appear to be long and drawn out with many difficult terms and obscure references, and they may not even seem to make clear sense. However, with some basic skills and practice, reading and analyzing a case may become second nature. It is possible to read an opinion and mentally analyze it simultaneously. Throughout this text a number of cases are included for illustration of the various legal principles under discussion. Although these cases are edited somewhat to facilitate ease of comprehension, all of the essential elements of the original opinion are represented. Reading the judicial opinions in the text serves two functions. Obviously, they are real-life demonstrations of the subject matter of the various chapters. In addition, reading them provides the opportunity to develop basic legal analytical skills. Even those who do not anticipate a career in the legal profession can benefit from the ability to read and understand legal principles as law impacts all facets of personal and professional life.

Regardless of the judge or jurisdiction from which an opinion is derived, nearly all complete judicial opinions contain the same essential elements. This consistency allows not only a thorough understanding of the opinion and reasoning behind it, but also allows for easy comparison to other similar legal issues that arise. Because the process of legal analysis allows consistency in the application of legal standards in similar cases, it is necessary that a regular pattern of information and reasoning be included. See Figure 3.1.

The initial step in case analysis is to know and understand the various elements of the judicial opinion. Note that various methods are available for analyzing a case and that the elements are sometimes broken down differently and given different titles. This is not to confuse. Rather, it is more often a matter of style and semantics than an indication of any meaningful difference in the way an opinion is composed. No matter what titles are used for the elements or the number of elements into which a case is broken down, the analysis contains the same basic information. It is simply packaged differently. The analytical method used in this text is straightforward and succinct. The ultimate analysis can be renamed, reorganized, or even broken into additional elements, but it will still be made up of the same basic components of information.

FIGURE 3.1
Sample Judicial
Opinion

SMITH V. GETSCHOW,
235 WIS.2D 278, 616 NW2 526 (WIS.APP. 2000)

Phillips Getschow Co. (PGC) appeals from a judgment awarding Franklin and Patricia Smith $6,000 in compensatory damages and $130,000 in punitive damages for their intentional tort claim against PGC. PGC argues that the trial court erred by allowing the punitive damages issue to go to the jury. In the alternative, PGC contends that although the trial court correctly determined that the jury's punitive damages award was excessive, the court nevertheless erred by offering the Smiths the option of remittitur and, further, failed to apply the appropriate criteria in remitting the punitive damages.

The Smiths cross-appeal from that part of the judgment remitting their punitive damages award. The Smiths argue that the jury's punitive damages award was not excessive as a matter of law and that the trial court therefore erred by requiring a remittitur. In the alternative, the Smiths contend that the trial court erroneously exercised its discretion when it failed to apply the appropriate criteria in determining the amount of the remittitur. We reject both parties' arguments and affirm the judgment.

BACKGROUND

This case arises from a claim alleging that Kurt Getschow, PGC's chief executive officer, intentionally battered Franklin Smith, a former PGC employee. At trial, Franklin testified that in October of 1995, Getschow told Franklin that he had worked in a circus guessing people's weight and that during work break, he would guess Franklin's weight. Franklin followed Getschow to PGC's shop area for the "weighing in ceremony." As several employees watched, Getschow, carrying a four-foot-long carpenter's level, circled Franklin as if to measure him. Getschow then asked

(continued)

FIGURE 3.1

Sample Judicial
Opinion—(*continued*)

another employee, Vincent Hanson, to stand in front of Franklin with his back toward him. Getschow instructed Franklin to place his hands over Hanson's shoulders, at which point Hanson grabbed Franklin's hands and bent forward, thus draping Franklin over his back.

Franklin testified that when he was lifted off the ground, he feared that Getschow was going to pull his pants down, but as he looked back over his shoulder, he saw Getschow draw back the carpenter's level as if to hit a baseball. Franklin stated: "I closed my eyes. He hit me. I tightened up and I felt him hit me again, and then I just waited for it to be over." Franklin further stated that it felt like Getschow had hit him a dozen times, though he had not kept count after the first two hits.

Sandy Garland, a former switchboard operator at PGC, testified that she saw the "weighing in ceremony" and heard a crack as Getschow struck Franklin. Garland stated that she left after seeing only one strike. Brian Donlevy, a former job coordinator at PGC, also testified that he saw the "weighing in ceremony." He observed Getschow strike Franklin twice and heard a loud crack both times. He testified that although the employees who had gathered to watch were laughing, Franklin had a grimace on his face.

Franklin testified that when Hanson eventually released him, Getschow laughed, put the carpenter's level down, put his arm around Franklin and said, "now you're one of us." Franklin claimed that as a result of being struck, his buttocks were tender and it was uncomfortable for him to sit. Franklin's wife, Patricia, a registered nurse, testified that when Franklin arrived home on the evening of the "weighing in ceremony," he had "four or five marks on his buttocks that were purple in the center with red rings around them." Franklin testified that the pain lasted at least two days, and the bruising remained for seven to ten days.

Getschow testified that the "weighing in ceremony" was a "ritual right of passing" at PGC, and that he had been on the receiving end of this "ceremony" when he was sixteen years old. Getschow stated, however, that the ceremony had not happened in years. He repeatedly denied striking Franklin or even being present at any "weighing in ceremony" involving Franklin.

Dale Leifker, PGC's chief financial officer, testified that he was not present at a "weighing in ceremony" involving Franklin. He noted, however, that he had heard generally about these ceremonies and, sometime prior to the alleged incident with Franklin, Leifker had advised Getschow that the ceremonies should stop. Leifker additionally testified that PGC's net worth was $5,578,015.

After hearing the evidence, the jury returned a verdict finding that PGC, through Getschow, had committed a battery on Franklin and that the battery was a cause of his damages. It awarded Franklin $5,000 in compensable damages for his pain and suffering and awarded Patricia $1,000 for her loss of consortium. The jury further awarded the Smiths $1,000,000 in punitive damages.

On motions after verdict, the trial court determined, pursuant to WIS. STAT. § 805.15(6), that the jury's punitive damages award was excessive and offered the option of remittitur to the Smiths. They opted to accept the committed amount of $130,000 over having a new trial on punitive damages. The trial court denied PGC's motion for reconsideration. This appeal and cross-appeal followed.

ANALYSIS

PGC argues that the trial court erred by allowing the punitive damages issue to go to the jury. Punitive damages are designed to punish and deter conduct that is malicious or "wanton, willful and in reckless disregard of the plaintiff's rights." Sharp ex rel. Gordon v. Case Corp., 227 Wis.2d 1, 21, 595 W.2d 380 (1999); see also WIS. STAT. § 895.85. Our supreme court has used the shorthand designation "outrageous" to describe this type of conduct. . . . Before a punitive damages question may be submitted to a jury, the trial court must determine, as a matter of law, "that evidence was presented at trial that would support an award of punitive damages." Id. at 20-21, 595 N.W.2d 380. The issue of punitive damages should not be submitted to a jury "in the absence of evidence warranting a conclusion to a reasonable certainty that the party against whom punitive damages may be awarded acted with the requisite outrageous' conduct." Id. at 21, 595 N.W.2d 380.

When determining whether, as a matter of law, the question of punitive damages should have been submitted to the jury, an appellate court independently reviews the record. PGC argues that the evidence established that the "weighing in ceremony" was light-hearted and that Getschow

FIGURE 3.1

Sample Judicial
Opinion—(*continued*)

did not intend to harm Franklin. However, a person's conduct is wanton, willful and in reckless disregard of the plaintiff's rights "when it demonstrates an indifference on the person's part to the consequences of his or her actions, even though he or she may not intend insult or injury." Id. at 21, 95 N.W.2d 380. Our review of the record convinces us that there was clear and convincing evidence that Getschow effectively tricked Franklin into participating in the "weighing in ceremony" and battered him in front of a number of laughing co-workers—this after Leifker advised him that these ceremonies should stop. There was also evidence that Getschow's conduct resulted in Franklin's injuries. Accordingly, we agree with the trial court's conclusion that the evidence was sufficient to submit the question of punitive damages to the jury.

Contrary to PGC's assertions, the trial court did not "find" that the jury's punitive damages award was based on prejudice. Rather, the court, while using the term "prejudice," merely opined that the jury just did not like Getschow because it believed he lied. The court explained that it did not use the term "prejudice" as contemplated by Wis. Stat. § 805.15(6). We conclude that the jury received a proper instruction on punitive damages, see Wis JI—Civil 1707.1, and that there was sufficient evidence to sustain an award for punitive damages under those instructions. Accordingly, we conclude that the jury's punitive damages award was not based on prejudice within the meaning of § 805.15(6) and that the trial court, therefore, was not precluded from offering the option of remittitur to the Smiths.

On cross-appeal, the Smiths argue that the jury's punitive damages award was not excessive as a matter of law, and that the trial court therefore erred by requiring a remittitur. With respect to the amount of the remittitur, both PGC and the Smiths contend that the trial court did not apply the appropriate criteria in remitting the punitive damages award to $130,000. We disagree.

Where a trial court "states its reasons for finding the jury's award of damages excessive and for reducing the award, we will reverse the trial court's determination only if we conclude there has been an abuse of discretion." Oahrenberg v. Tengel, 96 Wis.2d 211, 229-30, 291 N.W.2d 516 (1980). Under this standard, there are two questions on review: "Was the trial court's determination that the jury award was excessive an abuse of discretion and was the trial court's fixing of a reduced amount an abuse of discretion?" Id. at 230, 291 N.W.2d 516. An appellate court will not find an erroneous exercise of discretion "if the record shows that discretion was in fact exercised and there exists a reasonable basis for the [trial] court's determination after resolving any direct conflicts in the testimony in favor of the prevailing party, even if the reviewing court would have reached a different conclusion than the [trial] court." Management Computer Servs., Inc. v. Hawkins, Ash, Baptie & Co., 206 Wis.2d 158, 191, 557 N.W.2d 67 (1996).

However, where a trial court "fails to analyze the evidence or set forth the reasons supporting its decision, the reviewing court should give no reference to the [trial] court's decision." Id. In making its determination, the reviewing court must view the evidence in the light most favorable to the jury verdict. Id. at 192, 557 N.W.2d 67. In addition to the factors noted above, "a reviewing court must consider the reasonableness of punitive damages on a case-by-case basis, considering the relevant circumstances in each particular case." Id. at 194, 557 N.W.2d 67.

In Management Computer, our supreme court held:

[I]n determining whether an award of punitive damages is excessive, courts should consider the grievousness of the acts, the degree of malicious intent, whether the award bears a reasonable relationship to the award of compensatory damages, the potential damage that might have been caused by the acts, the ratio of the award to civil or criminal penalties that could be imposed for comparable misconduct, and the wealth of the wrongdoer.

Id. at 194, 557 N.W.2d 67. The court added that "if an award is determined to be excessive, courts should consider these factors in determining the proper amount to be awarded as punitive damages." Id.

Here, the trial court found that the jury's $1,000,000 punitive damages award was excessive. This court has recognized that "the test of excessiveness [of punitive damages] does not necessarily depend upon some arbitrary proportion [and a] [p]unitive damage [award] ought to serve its purpose." Fahrenberg, 96 Wis.2d at 233, 291 N.W.2d 516. "An award which is more than necessary to serve its purposes (punishment and deterrence) or which inflicts a penalty or burden on the defendant which is disproportionate to the wrongdoing is excessive and is contrary to public policy." Id. at 234, 291 N.W.2d 516.

In finding the punitive damages award excessive, the trial court stated: "I find that it inflicts a burden on the defendant that is disproportionate to the wrong that it did, and what I am doing is

FIGURE 3.1

Sample Judicial
Opinion—(*continued*)

following [WIS. STAT. § 805.15(6)]." The court recognized that although PGC had net assets of $5.7 million, not all assets were readily convertible into cash to pay a judgment and further noted that "to take a million dollars from a corporation that took over a hundred years to get to its present financial status just is not right." Because the trial court set forth evidence and rational reasons supporting its finding of excessiveness, we conclude it properly exercised its discretion.

Both PGC and the Smiths nevertheless contend that the trial court did not apply the appropriate criteria in remitting the punitive damages award to $130,000. Specifically, the parties assert that the trial court was required to address all of the factors delineated by Management Computer. We disagree. Although the Management Computer court listed various factors that a court "should" look at in determining both whether a punitive damages award is excessive and what a proper amount should be, the court did not indicate that a court's discussion of each factor is mandatory. Management Computer, 206 Wis.2d 194, 557 N.W.2d 67.

Here, the trial court found the $1,000,000 punitive damages award to be excessive and offered the Smiths the option of accepting an award remitted to $130,000. The court stated:

Now, why do I come to the determination that I did of $130,000? If these same acts had been charged criminally, the maximum fine would have been $10,000. That would have been top dollar that could have been assessed against that corporation. $130,000 is approximately the same cost as the yearly salary for a top company executive of the defendant, so the company obviously determines that $130,000 is a substantial chunk of money. That is the amount that they believe is a fair compensation for one of their top executives.

As mentioned above, the court also considered that not all of PGC's $5.7 million in net assets were readily convertible into cash to pay a judgment. The court consequently recognized that "[r]equiring the defendant to come up with $130,000 cash is a punishment, but it is not so much as to be confiscatory." The trial court here, consistent with Management Computer, considered the ratio of the award to criminal penalties that could be imposed for comparable misconduct and the wealth of the wrongdoer. See id. Both PGC and the Smiths argue that the trial court improperly considered an executive's salary in remitting the punitive damages award. We disagree. "Punitive damages are properly denominated 'smart money' and are designed to hurt in order to punish and to deter." Fahrenberg, 96 Wis.2d at 234, 291 N.W.2d 516. The trial court concluded that $130,000—the salary of one of PGC's top executives—constituted a substantial amount of money to PGC and determined the amount of the remittitur accordingly. Because the trial court set forth evidence and rational reasons supporting its determination, we conclude it properly exercised its discretion in remitting the punitive damages award to $130,000.

By the Court.—Judgment affirmed. Costs denied to both parties.

Case Review Question: *Smith v. Getschow,* 235 Wis.2d 278, 616 N.W.2d 526 (Wis.App. 2000). Why is the fact that the individual lied about striking the defendant important?

Case Brief
Synopsis of a judicial
opinion that identifies
pivotal facts, primary
issues, applicable legal
standards, and
rationale for decision.

Virtually everyone who performs case analysis consistently uses the term **case brief.** In law-related professions, the term *brief* usually refers to some type of document containing legal analysis. A case brief is the analysis of a single judicial opinion. The much more complex appellate brief is the analysis and persuasive argument of all applicable legal standards to a case before the appellate courts. Other types of briefs contain varying degrees of depth and scope of legal analysis. The discussion at this stage is confined to the case brief. A common purpose of a case brief is to determine the effects of a previously issued judicial opinion on a current situation. To accurately make such a determination, one must examine each aspect of the case and decide whether the case is sufficiently similar to the present situation to create a likelihood that the same legal standards would be applied in the same way today. While judicial opinions may be very lengthy, the case brief is usually not. A brief is a synopsis that identifies only those points that were pivotal in the decision and consequently would be considered in a similar case. Therefore, when analyzing a case, no matter what element is being examined, the focus should be on those statements that directly affect the final decision.

a. The Facts   Since case law is the application of a prior judicial determination to a similar situation, the first step in preparing a case brief is to identify the key facts. In many situations, such identification will control whether the legal principles of a previous case would be applicable to another situation.

A case brief contains two types of facts: occurrence facts and legal (sometimes called procedural) facts. Both of these are important to the brief for different reasons. Both are generally present in the opinion in full detail, and both should be edited in the case brief to include only those facts, either occurrence or legal, that had a direct impact on the result in the case. Facts to be excluded from the case brief include those that provide a backdrop for the case and help to fill in details of the occurrence and legal procedings but do not directly impact the outcome.

Occurrence facts are all the details of the circumstances that initially gave rise to the lawsuit. The amount of such information that is included in the opinion depends largely on the particular writing style of the judge, who is the author. However, most opinions contain a substantial amount of factual information based on what has been disclosed by the parties, which creates a clear representation of the setting of the case, development of legal issues, and circumstances of the various parties to the suit.

While background information is helpful to thoroughly understand the intricacies of a judicial opinion, it is not necessary to include all factual details in a case brief. When editing an opinion for the composition of a brief, keep in mind that only the most essential facts should be included. Two questions can be asked about each fact when deciding whether to include that fact in a brief. First, will exclusion of the fact from the brief prevent the reader from understanding the general premise of the case? Second, was the fact pivotal in the outcome of the case?

APPLICATION 3.2

A lawsuit that ultimately produced an appeal and published judicial opinion arose from the following facts reported in the opinion:

On July 14, 1999, plaintiff and defendant were involved in a head-on collision at 2 A.M. The accident occurred at approximately mile marker 3 on Highway 890. At the time of the accident the roads were clear and dry. The defendant was found to have a blood alcohol of .01 below the legal limit. Evidence showed the defendant had consumed alcohol in the two hours prior to driving the vehicle at the time of the accident. The plaintiff was a professional truck driver who was driving home in his own vehicle following the end of his regular eight-hour work shift in which he had made a number of local deliveries. The accident occurred when a deer crossed the highway, first in the path of plaintiff and then in the path of defendant. The defendant, swerving to avoid the deer, turned into the oncoming path of the plaintiff where the cars subsequently collided.

Facts to include in the case brief based on the information provided thus far:

Plaintiff and defendant were involved in a head-on collision at night when defendant swerved to avoid a deer in the path of his vehicle. Evidence showed that while not legally drunk, the defendant had consumed alcohol prior to driving and had a blood alcohol content of .01 below the legal limit.

Point for Discussion: Why would the fact that plaintiff is a professional driver be left out?

The legal facts consist of what took place once litigation began and then chronicle the progression of the lawsuit. A number of these facts may be recited in the actual opinion to show case development. However, the only real legal facts necessary in the case brief are those that tie directly into the basis for the appeal, which ultimately prompted the ruling and consequent judicial opinion. When first learning to read and analyze judicial opinions, there is a temptation to assume that the appeal is based on an allegedly improper finding of liability or innocence. Appeals are almost never so simply stated. Rather, there must be a legally objectionable basis for how the improper result came about. Examples include exclusion or inclusion of evidence objected to by one of the parties, improper jury instructions, and so forth. When preparing a case brief, the important legal facts to include are those surrounding the alleged error that created the basis for the appeal.

APPLICATION 3.3

Following the facts in the previous application, the additional legal facts were established. The plaintiff filed an action against the defendant for negligence in leaving his lane of traffic and entering that of plaintiff. In his response to the complaint, the defendant alleged that the plaintiff had the last clear chance to avoid the accident on the basis that the deer first crossed the path of the plaintiff and thus plaintiff was already on notice of the dangerous condition prior to defendant coming upon the deer. Defendant further alleged that the deer appeared so suddenly and immediately in front of his vehicle that he reacted by turning the vehicle away from the animal. Subsequently, the vehicle veered into the path of plaintiff's vehicle. The jury found sufficient evidence to support the defense that was raised and returned a judgment in favor of the defendant. The plaintiff filed an appeal stating that there was insufficient evidence to support the jury's application of the theory of last clear chance and that the verdict should have been in favor of the plaintiff.

Legal facts in a case brief might include the following: The jury returned a verdict in support of the defendant's assertion that plaintiff had the last clear chance to avoid the incident. The plaintiff appealed on the basis that evidence was insufficient to support the legal defense of last clear chance.

Point for Discussion: Why not include information about the response to the complaint?

There are, of course, exceptions to the rule as to when less than absolutely vital information should be included. Such cases occur when otherwise ordinary information has an impact as the result of the particular circumstances of the case. With occurrence facts, an example might be the time of day in a case involving an auto accident, whether visibility is an issue, or a date in a contract case. Similarly, a pretrial motion might be a relevant legal fact to include if the subject of the motion ultimately becomes an issue at trial or causes the case to be dismissed before trial. While such information is more often than not a backdrop for the case, if it might influence other facts or legal issues, then it should be included.

b. The Legal Issue   Identifying the issue in the opinion is quite often one of the most difficult tasks for someone just beginning legal analysis. As with legal facts, the assumption tends to be that the legal issue is the question of guilt or liability of the defendant. In the case of a published judicial opinion, this is almost never the issue. As discussed in earlier chapters, the appellate courts that publish the vast majority of judicial opinions do not serve the same function as trial courts. While the ultimate legal issue in a trial court is usually one of guilt or innocence, in the appellate court, and consequently the published opinion, the issue is almost always whether something inappropriate occurred in the trial court that in turn prevented the proper finding on the issue of guilt or innocence. Most often the question turns on whether the trial court judge or jury properly applied one or more legal principle to the evidence before the court.

The authority of a trial court is not one with clearly defined boundaries. This is because the law itself is not black and white, but instead considers all the relevant factors in an individual circumstance. Because no two cases are exactly alike, there must be some room for the court to consider and apply the law it interprets for a given situation. Likewise, no two juries are identical in makeup or in the way they interpret evidence. Because the American legal system places such high value on the ability to have questions decided by one's fellow citizens, a significant respect is also afforded the reasoning of a jury as to why a particular verdict is reached. Consequently, both judges and juries are given a certain degree of discretion in their roles. The appellate court examines whether this grant of discretion has been abused in such a way that the result in the case is clearly and unequivocally contrary to the existing principles of law and whether any justification exists for the deviation. Therefore, when conducting legal analysis of a judicial opinion, the task is to identify what serious breach of discretion is asserted by the appellant, that is, the party seeking to have the trial court action reviewed and changed.

The goal of case analysis is to identify why the appellate court ultimately agreed or disagreed with the trial court. This result rests on the question considered by the appellate court. One method that can be helpful to the less experienced in the identification of the legal issue is to read the opinion and then complete the following statement:

The appellant alleges the trial court erred (abused its discretion) when _____ .

or

The question before the court is _____ .

Very often, one of these statements, or a similar one will appear in the opinion itself. Without exception, the judicial opinion will make some reference to the legal issue either as part of the recitation of legal facts or in a discussion of the task before the appellate court. It might read, for example, "The defendant sought a new trial and subsequently filed this appeal asserting the jury ignored the manifest weight of the evidence;" or "The question that lies before this court is whether the trial court abused its discretion when it granted summary judgment on the finding that no reasonable issue existed as to the defendant's liability."

c. The Law Another essential part of legal analysis is the identification of the legal authorities used to decide the primary issue. This includes both the principle of law and its citation (reference to the publication source of the principle). When a judicial opinion is issued, the court will generally rest its decision on existing legal authorities addressing similar issues. This may include applicable statutes, former judicial opinions in like cases, administrative regulations, or even the Constitution. In substance, the entire judicial opinion is an example of legal analysis. The reviewing court analyzes the present case and compares it to the current applicable precedents. The opinion generally explains why a particular precedent(s) applies and the indicated result.

The inclusion within the brief of the legal standards used in an opinion are important to clarify the reasoning of the court. It is also essential when attempting to determine if the current case is similar or should be distinguished from the case described in the opinion that is briefed. The opinion may include a wide variety of legal citations. The brief should include those that bear directly on the issue that is stated within the brief. If an opinion contains more than one relevant issue, the issues and the corresponding legal standards should be stated separately, for example, issue 1,2, etc.; law applied to issue 1,2, and so on. Always report both the synopsis of the basic legal principle and the citation because further research may require consultation of the full legal standard and not just the portion excerpted within the opinion. In lengthy recitations from the standard, it may be simpler and more concise to summarize the legal standard. However, take great care when doing so not to change the meaning of the precedent.

d. The Ruling (Holding, Reasoning)   The final essential element of the case brief is the rationale of the court (usually appellate) that issued the opinion. This includes much more than the statement of whether the action of the trial court in the case on appeal was affirmed, reversed, or remanded with instructions. It is important to provide a brief explanation of how the precedent was applied and why the indicated result was achieved. This requires a summary of the reasoning by the court that is the core of the judicial opinion. Again, when summarizing the action of a court, caution should be used to avoid altering the context or meaning of the opinion as originally issued by the court. The ruling essentially compiles the previous elements of facts, issue, law, and rule into a single comprehensive summary of the opinion that is briefed.

CASE IN POINT

Torres v. Wis. Dept. of Health and Social Services,
859 F.2d 1523 (7th Cir. 1988).

Ripple, Circuit Judge.

Defendant Nona J. Switala is the superintendent of defendant Taycheedah Correctional Institution (TCI), the only women's maximum security prison in Wisconsin. TCI is operated by the Wisconsin Department of Health and Social Services (DHSS), also a defendant here. Ms. Switala, an experienced prison administrator, determined that the rehabilitation of TCI's inmates would be enhanced by employing only female correctional officers in TCI's living units. The plaintiffs Raymond Torres, Franklin Utz, and Gerald Schmit were reassigned to other positions at TCI, with no loss in pay, because of this plan. Unhappy with this reassignment, the plaintiffs brought this action alleging sex discrimination by the defendants in violation of Title VII of the Civil Rights Act of 1964. 42 U.S.C. §§ 2000e to 2000e-17. The defendants responded that sex was a bona fide occupational qualification (BFOQ), 42 U.S.C. § 2000e-2(e)(1), for the positions formerly held by the plaintiffs. The district court determined that the defendants had not established a valid BFOQ because the defendants had not offered "objective evidence, either from empirical studies or otherwise," proving that the BFOQ would further inmate rehabilitation, and because prison security and inmate privacy were not materially advanced by the plan. We reverse and remand.

Facts

TCI has three buildings for housing inmates. Each building has three residence floors, and the inmates live in single, double, or multiple occupancy rooms. The rooms are not cells with bars, but are more akin to college dormitory rooms. Each room has a solid door with a clear glass window at eye level that is approximately four inches by six inches. The rooms have one bed per inmate, a desk, chair, light, toilet, and wash basin. In two buildings, privacy curtains have been installed around the toilets. When an inmate is behind the curtain, only her feet are visible. At the time of trial, TCI had plans to install privacy curtains in the other residence building soon.

From 6 a.m. until 9 p.m., inmates may place "privacy cards" inside the door windows so that they can use the toilet or change their clothes without being observed. TCI's rules allow the privacy cards to be up for only ten minutes per day per inmate. In multiple inmate rooms, this means that the cards can be up permissibly for as much as thirty or forty minutes. However, the testimony offered at trial suggests that correctional officers are not able to keep careful track of the time that a privacy card has been in place, and that inmates sometimes leave their cards up for more than ten minutes per inmate. On one occasion, two inmates used their privacy card to facilitate an escape, and on another occasion an inmate beat up her roommate while the privacy card covered the window.

From 9 p.m. until 6 a.m., inmates may not place their privacy card on the inside of their window, but they may place their card outside the window all night long in order to prevent light from entering the room. Correctional officers then lift up the card for body counts and inspections. The guards are required to see the inmates' skin or hair during nighttime body counts.

Each floor of the residence buildings has a shower room. Inmates must sign up with their floor officer before taking a shower, and they are required to wear some sort of clothing when walking to the shower room. Testimony at trial suggested that guards normally do not enter the shower rooms when occupied. The doors to the shower rooms are solid, although some contain windows that have been rendered opaque. The shower rooms have one to three shower stalls, one to three toilets, and some have one or more bathtubs. The showers and toilets have privacy curtains or privacy doors. Only one inmate may occupy the shower room at a time, except that roommates may enter together. TCI allows each inmate fifteen minutes in the shower room.

The Wisconsin Administrative Code allows prison officials to perform four types of inmate searches. Wis.Admin.Code § HSS 306.16 (1987). Correctional officers may perform pat searches at any time. During a pat search, inmates empty their pockets and the officer runs his or her hands over the inmates' entire body. The custom at TCI is that only female guards perform pat searches. The second type of allowable search is the strip search. Strip searches must be authorized by a supervisor and performed in private by an officer of the same sex, except during emergencies. § HSS 306.16(b). The third type of search is the body cavity search. Body cavity searches are only performed by medical personnel in special circumstances. § HSS 306.16(c). The fourth permissible search is a body content search, such as urinalysis or blood analysis. § HSS 306.16(d). Under this regulation, body content searches are permitted only in extreme circumstances. In addition, correctional officers are expected to search occasionally inmates' rooms and the shower rooms when they are unoccupied.

Ms. Switala became superintendent of TCI in 1978. She previously had worked for three years as treatment director at TCI and for eight years as a probation and parole agent with the Wisconsin Division of Corrections. Ms. Switala, her superiors at the DHSS, and her personnel at TCI, soon began discussions regarding TCI's staffing needs. It ultimately was decided, principally by Ms. Switala, that certain positions at TCI should be staffed only by female correctional officers. It is clear from Ms. Switala's testimony at trial that the principal reason for this decision was her concern for inmate rehabilitation and security. TCI's administrators then advised all correctional officers in 1980 that a BFOQ program would be implemented gradually in the next two years.

TCI has three different ranks for its correctional officers. The lowest position is a correctional officer 1 (CO-1), followed by correctional officer 2 (CO-2) and correctional officer 3 (CO-3). The CO-3 in charge of a living unit is a "sergeant." The positions to be affected by the BFOQ plan were nineteen of the twenty-seven correctional officer positions in the living units, including all of the CO-3 posts in the living units. As a result of the plan, only three CO-3 positions at TCI would be open to men. The three plaintiffs, Mr. Torres, Mr. Utz, and Mr. Schmit, were all CO-3's prior to implementation of the BFOQ plan. Because of the limited number of available CO-3 positions, the three plaintiffs were required to accept CO-2 positions, although this demotion resulted in no loss of pay. The plaintiffs presently work under female CO-3's who have less seniority and experience.

The District Court Opinion

The district court first determined that the BFOQ is a narrow exception to Title VII's prohibition of discrimination in employment. The court noted that "administrative convenience is insufficient to justify a BFOQ exception," and that discrimination based on sex is permissible only " 'when the essence of the business operation would be undermined.' " Torres v. Wisconsin Dep't of Health and Social Servs., 639 F.Supp. 271, 277 (E.D.Wis.1986) (quoting Diaz v. Pan Am. World Airways, 442 F.2d 385, 388 (5th Cir.), cert. denied, 404 U.S. 950, 92 S.Ct. 275, 30 L.Ed.2d 267 (1971)). The burden of establishing a BFOQ is a "heavy one," according to the court, and is "justified only in rare, appropriate circumstances." Id. at 278.

The court then analyzed the BFOQ under each of the defendants' proposed justifications: security, rehabilitation, and inmate privacy. Regarding security, the court found that male correctional officers had filled all of the BFOQ positions from 1975 until 1982 "without any contention that TCI suffered from a lack of security." Id. Moreover, the court noted that TCI continued to allow inmates to use privacy cards even after the BFOQ program had been installed, thus rebutting the argument that the presence of male guards reduced observation of the inmates. Although the court acknowledged that staffing problems at TCI might have been reduced by the BFOQ, since all guards then could perform all tasks, the court found that this justification merely constituted administrative convenience and not a genuine justification for sex discrimination. Thus, since the defendants had not presented evidence of any decline in inmate escapes or violence as a result of the BFOQ, the court found "that defendants have failed to justify the Plan based on security reasons." Id. at 279.

The court next analyzed the BFOQ under the defendants' rehabilitation justification. The court acknowledged that the defendants had "presented various witnesses familiar with the field of corrections who testified in support of this theory." Id. at 280. However, the court said that the plaintiffs also had presented witnesses who testified that male guards can enhance

rehabilitation by "normaliz[ing]" the prison environment. Id. at 280 & n. 9. Thus, the court determined that the defendants had offered only a "theory of rehabilitation as a justification for the BFOQ Plan. They offered no objective evidence, either from empirical studies or otherwise, displaying the validity of their theory." Id. at 280 (emphasis in original). Having concluded that the rehabilitation theory was unproven, the court refused to justify the BFOQ based on the theory.

The court concluded its analysis by reviewing the BFOQ under the justification of inmate privacy. The court ruled that inmates do have a constitutional right to be free from unwarranted privacy intrusions, but that this right necessarily was limited. Id. at 280-81. The court then determined that any intrusions of privacy occasioned by male guards were not unwarranted nor unreasonable because of other precautions taken by the prison administration. For example, the court noted that toilet facilities have privacy curtains, that correctional officers do not observe inmates while they are showering, and that guards do not see inmates unclothed except during an emergency or when the inmate voluntarily allows it to happen. Therefore, the court found that privacy concerns did not justify the defendants' BFOQ plan.

Because the defendants had overtly discriminated against the plaintiffs on account of their sex, and since, in its view, there was no valid BFOQ, the court found that the defendants had violated Title VII. However, the court did not find that the plaintiffs were entitled to monetary damages. The court determined that the plaintiffs' reassignment had not caused any reduction in salary or overtime hours, and that therefore the plaintiffs had not established any monetary damages. For that reason, the plaintiffs' only remedy was an order abolishing the BFOQ plan and reinstating the plaintiffs in their prior assignments.

Analysis

A. Title VII and the BFOQ

We begin by reiterating several basic propositions, long established in the precedent, that must guide our decision today. "Title VII prohibits employment discrimination, which is 'one of the most deplorable forms of discrimination known to our society, for it deals not with just an individual's sharing in the "outer benefits" of being an American citizen, but rather the ability to provide decently for one's family in a job or profession for which he qualifies or chooses.' " Hardin

v. Stynchcomb, 691 F.2d 1364, 1369 (11th Cir.1982). The statute forbids both overt discrimination and practices that are " 'fair in form, but discriminatory in operation.' " Pullman-Standard v. Swint, 456 U.S. 273, 276, 102 S.Ct. 1781, 1784, 72 L.Ed.2d 66 (1982) (quoting Griggs v. Duke Power Co., 401 U.S. 424, 431, 91 S.Ct. 849, 853, 28 L.Ed.2d 158 (1971)).

This case involves overt sex discrimination. It presents one issue—whether the district court correctly determined that sex was not a BFOQ for correctional officer positions at TCI. Section 703(e) of Title VII only permits classifications based on sex "where . . . sex . . . is a bona fide occupational qualification reasonably necessary to the normal operation of that particular business or enterprise." 42 U.S.C. § 2000e-2(e)(1) (emphasis supplied). " '[D]iscrimination based on sex is valid only when the essence of the business operation would be undermined by not hiring members of one sex exclusively.' " Id. (quoting Diaz v. Pan Am. World Airways, 442 F.2d 385, 388 (5th Cir.), cert. denied, 404 U.S. 950, 92 S.Ct. 275, 30 L.Ed.2d 267 (1971). As an alternative formulation, noted the Supreme Court, it has been held that "an employer could rely on the BFOQ exception only by proving 'that he had reasonable cause to believe, that is, a factual basis for believing, that all or substantially all women would be unable to perform safely and efficiently the duties of the job involved.' " Id. (quoting Weeks v. Southern Bell Tel. & Tel. Co., 408 F.2d 228, 235 (5th Cir.1969)).

It is also well established that a BFOQ may not be based on "stereotyped characterizations of the sexes." Dothard, 433 U.S. at 333, 97 S.Ct. at 2729. "Myths and purely habitual assumptions about a woman's [or a man's] inability to perform certain kinds of work are no longer acceptable reasons for refusing to employ qualified individuals, or for paying them less." City of Los Angeles Dep't of Water & Power v. Manhart, 435 U.S. 702, 707, 98 S.Ct. 1370, 1375, 55 L.Ed.2d 657 (1978). ("[T]he different treatment of men and women . . . reflects, not archaic and overbroad generalizations, but, instead, the demonstrable fact that male and female line officers in the Navy are not similarly situated with respect to opportunities for professional service." This same principle has been recognized in the Title VII area. See, e.g., Backus v. Baptist Medical Center, 510 F.Supp. 1191, 1195 (E.D.Ark.1981), (recognizing the need to have female registered nurses care for obstetrical patients); see also I A. Larson & L. Larson, Employment Discrimination—Sex § 14.30 (1987) ("[G]iving respect to deep-seated feelings of personal privacy involving one's own genital area is quite a different matter from catering to the desire of some male airline passengers to have . . . an attractive stewardess.").

Nevertheless, while recognizing that sex-based differences may justify a limited number of distinctions between men and women, we must discipline our inquiry to ensure that our tolerance for such distinctions is not widened artificially by—as the district court aptly put it—our "own culturally induced proclivities." Torres, 639 F.Supp. at 278. Nor, of course, can we tolerate the same preconceptions or predilections on the part of employers. Rather, we must ask whether, given the reasonable objectives of the employer, the very womanhood or very manhood of the employee undermines his or her capacity to perform a job satisfactorily. Dothard, 433 U.S. at 336, 97 S.Ct. at 2730.

One of the most important means by which an appellate court disciplines its inquiry is by keeping in mind the appropriate standard of review. The district court's "[f]indings of fact shall not be set aside unless clearly erroneous, and due regard shall be given to the opportunity of the trial court to judge of the credibility of the witnesses." Fed.R.Civ.P. 52(a). Of course, this deferential standard of review presumes that the district court has applied correct legal standards—decisions of law are reviewed de novo.

B. The "Business" of the Employer

With the foregoing propositions reaffirmed, we turn to the case before us. In our view, the decision of the district court that the defendants' BFOQ plan cannot be justified by concerns for prison security or for the basic privacy rights of the inmates is correct in law and fact. Thus, we turn to the only remaining question: whether the district court properly rejected defendants' contention that the BFOQ was necessary to further their goal of inmate rehabilitation.

The validity of a BFOQ can only be ascertained when it is assessed in relationship to the business of the employer. Our first step, therefore, must be to come to an understanding of the employer's business—its mission and the methodologies necessary to fulfill that mission. In accomplishing this task, we cannot deal in generalities. See Trans World Airlines v. Thurston, 469 U.S. 111, 122, 105 S.Ct. 613, 622, 83 L.Ed.2d 523 (1985). Rather, we must focus on the "particular business" of the employer in which the protected employee worked. Id. Oftentimes, this task requires that a court recognize factors that make a particular operation of an employer unique or at least substantially different from other operations in the same general business or profession. See Pime v. Loyola Univ., 803 F.2d 351, 353-54 (7th Cir. 1986) (upholding the maintenance of a Jesuit "presence" as "important to the successful operation of the University," when there was evidence that it was "significant to the educational tradition and character of the institution that students be assured a degree of contact with teachers who have received the training and accepted the obligations which are essential to membership in the Society of Jesus").

Here, of course, the broadest description of the "business" of the defendants is to say that they are in the business of governance at the state level. This general description, standing alone, gives them no special license with respect to Title VII. In Dothard v. Rawlinson, 433 U.S. 321, 332 n. 14, 97 S.Ct. 2720, 2728, 53 L.Ed.2d 786 (1977), the Supreme Court said that "Congress expressly indicated the intent that the same Title VII principles be applied to governmental and private employers alike." A more precise definition of the "business" of the defendants is to recognize that they are in the business of administering a penal institution. Few tasks are more challenging. As the Supreme Court has explained:

Prison administrators are responsible for maintaining internal order and discipline, for securing their institutions against unauthorized access or escape, and for rehabilitating, to the extent that human nature and inadequate resources allow, the inmates placed in their custody. The Herculean obstacles to effective discharge of these duties are too apparent to warrant explication. Suffice it to say that the problems of prisons in America are complex and intractable. . . .

Procunier v. Martinez, 416 U.S. 396, 404-05, 94 S.Ct. 1800, 1807, 40 L.Ed.2d 224 (1974). Those who assume the responsibility of administering any prison must grapple with the "perplexing sociological problems of how best to achieve the goals of the penal function in the criminal justice system: to punish justly, to deter future crime, and to return imprisoned persons to society with an improved chance of being useful, law-abiding citizens." Rhodes v. Chapman, 452 U.S. 337, 352, 101 S.Ct. 2392, 2402, 69 L.Ed.2d 59 (1981); see also Bell v. Wolfish, 441 U.S. 520, 547-48, 99 S.Ct. 1861, 2402, 60 L.Ed.2d 447 (1979). See generally Jones v. North Carolina Prisoners' Labor Union, 433 U.S. 119, 127-29, 97 S.Ct. 2532, 2538-40, 53 L.Ed.2d 629 (1977). In fulfilling these responsibilities, prison administrators always have been expected

to innovate and experiment. See Turner v. Safley, 482 U.S. 78, 107 S.Ct. 2254, 2262, 96 L.Ed.2d 64 (1987) (prison administrators must be allowed "to adopt innovative solutions to the intractable problems of prison administration"). Unless prison administrators try new approaches, the "intractable problems" will remain and the lot of the incarcerated individual will not improve. Indeed, it probably will deteriorate.

This general description of the task of prison administrators is still too general to permit us to assess accurately the claims of the parties. In Dothard, the Supreme Court focused not on maximum security institutions as a generic class but rather on the environment then existing in Alabama's penitentiaries—"a peculiarly inhospitable one for human beings of whatever sex." 433 U.S. at 334, 97 S.Ct. at 2729. In conformity to the mandate of the Supreme Court in Dothard, we must therefore refine further our focus. The defendants here are charged with the administration of a distinct type of penal institution—a women's maximum security facility. As the district court and one of the plaintiffs' own witnesses quite candidly acknowledged, the same historical and empirical evidence that might guide the administrator of a similar institution for males simply is not available with respect to this environment. Therefore, the administrators of TCI were obliged, to a greater degree than their counterparts in male institutions, to innovate in achieving one of the tasks mandated by the Wisconsin legislature—rehabilitation. The defendants' "business" explicitly included—by legislative mandate—the task of rehabilitation. See Wis.Admin.Code §§ HSS 303.01(3)(c), HSS 306.01 (1987). One of the plaintiffs' expert witnesses testified that this goal was not considered, in modern penological theory, a high priority or, by some, even a realistic goal. Tr. 6 at 160 (testimony of Dr. David Kalinich). Wisconsin has made a contrary decision and rehabilitation, no matter how elusive, must be attempted. Wisconsin's goal is clearly a reasonable course, see Rhodes, 452 U.S. at 352, 101 S.Ct. at 2402, and we must accept it as part of the "business" of the defendants.

C. Rehabilitation: The TCI Approach

Ms. Switala, the superintendent of TCI, made a professional judgment that giving women prisoners a living environment free from the presence of males in a position of authority was necessary to foster the goal of rehabilitation. This decision was based on

Ms. Switala's professional expertise and on her interviews and daily contact with female prisoners. Tr. 10 at 110-11. She also based her decision on the fact that a high percentage of female inmates has been physically and sexually abused by males. Indeed, she noted that sixty percent of TCI's inmates have been so abused. Tr. 9 at 39.

1.

There can be no question that the proposed BFOQ is directly related to the "essence" of the "business"—the rehabilitation of females incarcerated in a maximum security institution. See Dothard, 433 U.S. at 333, 97 S.Ct. at 2728-29 (quoting Diaz v. Pan Am. World Airways, 442 F.2d 385, 388 (5th Cir.), cert. denied, 404 U.S. 950, 92 S.Ct. 275, 30 L.Ed.2d 267 (1971)). As we already have noted, the Wisconsin legislature has mandated that rehabilitation is one of the objectives of that state's prison system. See Wis.Admin.Code §§ HSS 303.01(3)(c), HSS 306.01 (1987). Therefore, we stress that this is not a case where the interest of the plaintiffs in their continued employment simply conflicts with the basic privacy rights of the inmates. Here, the interest of the plaintiffs conflicts with the task of the administrators to rehabilitate the inmates for whom they are responsible. Forts v. Ward, 621 F.2d 1210 (2d Cir.1980), involved a female penitentiary. However, in that case, the suit was brought by prisoners against prison administrators. The prisoners sought to enjoin the administrators from assigning male guards to duties in the housing units of the prison. Forts therefore involved a straightforward conflict between the prisoner's right to privacy and the guards' rights, secured by Title VII, to employment security. Rehabilitation was not an issue in the case; the administrators made no claim that the presence of male personnel interfered with the performance of their duty. By contrast, this case involves just such a claim. Consequently, we are not dealing here with a mere matter of "consumer preference." See Fernandez v. Wynn Oil Co., 653 F.2d 1273 (9th Cir. 1981); Diaz v. Pan Am. World Airways, 442 F.2d 385, 389 (5th Cir.), cert. denied, 404 U.S. 950, 92 S.Ct. 275, 30 L.Ed.2d 267 (1971). See generally Schlei & Grossman, Employment Discrimination Law 341 (2d ed. 1983). The issue here is not what the prisoners want or believe is beneficial or appropriate. Rather, the issue is whether the state, charged with the responsibility of rehabilitation—a responsibility not only to the inmate but to the public—may pursue that goal in the manner at issue here.

2.

The more difficult question is whether the proposed BFOQ was "reasonably necessary" to furthering the objective of rehabilitation. The defendants can establish that the BFOQ was reasonably necessary only if they "had reasonable cause to believe, that is, a factual basis for believing, that all or substantially all [men] would be unable to perform safely and efficiently the duties of the job involved." Dothard, 433 U.S. at 333, 97 S.Ct. at 2729 (quoting Weeks v. Southern Bell Tel. & Tel. Co., 408 F.2d 228, 235 (5th Cir.1969)).

The district court determined that the defendants had not met this hurdle because "[t]hey offered no objective evidence, either from empirical studies or otherwise, displaying the validity of their theory." Torres, 639 F.Supp. at 280. We respectfully differ with our colleague in the district court as to the legal appropriateness of this standard. Certainly, there is no general requirement that the necessity of a BFOQ be established by this type of evidence. In Dothard, the Supreme Court determined that Alabama prison officials were justified in removing female guards from the state's "peculiarly inhospitable" penitentiaries. 433 U.S. at 334, 97 S.Ct. at 2729. The Court said that "[t]here is a basis in fact for expecting that sex offenders who have criminally assaulted women in the past would be moved to do so again if access to women were established within the prison." Id. at 335, 97 S.Ct. at 2730. The Court also said that there would "be a real risk that other inmates, deprived of a normal heterosexual environment, would assault women guards because they were women." Id. (footnote omitted). These appraisals were not based on objective, empirical evidence, but instead on a common-sense understanding of penal conditions, and, implicitly, on a limited degree of judicial deference to prison administrators. As noted earlier, in Pime v. Loyola University, 803 F.2d 351 (7th Cir. 1986), this court held that a Jesuit university could discriminate permissibly in favor of Jesuit instructors even though it had "not been shown that Jesuit training is a superior academic qualification, applying objective criteria, to teach the particular courses." Id. at 354. Similarly, in Chambers v. Omaha Girls Club, 834 F.2d 697 (8th

Cir.1987), the Eighth Circuit held that a BFOQ need not always be supported by objective evidence. The Omaha Girls Club had discharged an unmarried pregnant staff member. The Club expected its staff members "to act as role models for the girls, with the intent that the girls will seek to emulate their behavior." Id. at 699. The court concluded that the Club's "role model rule" was justified by business necessity even though the plaintiff contended that "the role model rule is based only on speculation by the Club and has not been validated by any studies showing that it prevents pregnancy among the Club's members." Id. at 702. The court said:

> Although validation studies can be helpful in evaluating such questions, they are not required to maintain a successful business necessity defense. Indeed, we are uncertain whether the role model rule by its nature is suited to validation by an empirical study. Consequently, the court's conclusion in Hawkins [v. Anheuser-Busch, Inc., 697 F.2d 810 (8th Cir.1983)] is apt in this case: "We cannot say . . . that validation studies are always required and we are not willing to hold under the facts of this case that such evidence was required here."

Id. (footnote and citations omitted). Certainly, it is hardly a "[m]yth or purely habitual assumption, " Los Angeles Dep't of Water & Power v. Manhart, 435 U.S. 702, 707, 98 S.Ct. 1370, 1375, 55 L.Ed.2d 657 (1978), that the presence of unrelated males in living spaces where intimate bodily functions take place is a cause of stress to females. See, e.g., EEOC v. Mercy Health Center, 29 FEP 159, 163 (W.D.Okla.1982) [available on WESTLAW, 1982 WL 3108] (employment of male nurses in labor and delivery area would cause medically undesired tension); Backus v. Baptist Medical Center, 510 F.Supp. 1191, 1194 (E.D.Ark.1981) (same); Norwood v. Dale Maintenance System, 590 F.Supp. 1410, 1422-23 (N.D.Ill.1984) (stress when attendant in office washroom is of opposite sex).

There is, it would seem, a substantial question as to whether the sort of problem that the defendants' BFOQ plan was designed to resolve ever "is suited to validation by an empirical study." Chambers, 834 F.2d at 702. We need not resolve this matter definitively here. In this case, there was general agreement among the parties and the district court that such material simply did not exist. One of the plaintiffs' own witnesses, Dr. David Kalinich, testified that there is little scholarship in the area of rehabilitation of the female felon. Tr. 6 at 138, 142. The plaintiffs emphasized this point by failing to introduce any witness with substantial experience or who had done scholarly work in the field of rehabilitation within female institutions. The plaintiffs' case was, to a very great extent, based on experts who had experience in male, not female, institutions. Indeed, the district judge, in accepting the credentials of Dr. Kalinich despite his lack of background in female institutions, specifically noted that comparable information about female institutions—and comparable experts—simply were not available. Tr. 6 at 143.

We believe, therefore, that the defendants were required to meet an unrealistic, and therefore unfair, burden when they were required to produce "objective evidence, either from empirical studies or otherwise, displaying the validity of their theory." Torres, 639 F.Supp. at 280. Given the nature of their "business"—administering a prison for female felons—the defendants, of necessity, had to innovate. Therefore, their efforts ought to be evaluated on the basis of the totality of the circumstances as contained in the entire record. In the Title VII context, the decision of penal administrators need not be given as much deference as accorded their decisions in constitutional cases. Whitley v. Albers, 475 U.S. 312, 321-22, 106 S.Ct. 1078, 1085-86, 89 L.Ed.2d 251 (1986); Rhodes v. Chapman, 452 U.S. 337, 351-52, 101 S.Ct. 2392, 2401-02, 69 L.Ed.2d 59 (1981); Bell v. Wolfish, 441 U.S. 520, 547, 99 S.Ct. 1861, 1878, 60 L.Ed.2d 447 (1979). However, their judgments still are entitled to substantial weight when they are the product of a reasoned decision-making process, based on available information and experience. The fact that the program is considered a reasonable approach by other professional penologists also is a factor to be given significant consideration. In an area where the questions are so many and the answers so few, the range of reasonable options must necessarily be more extensive. Certainly, the court ought not require unanimity of opinion and ought not to substitute completely its own judgment for that of the administration.

Conclusion

Because the district court resolved the issue before it on the ground that there was a lack of "objective evidence, either from empirical studies or otherwise," 639 F.Supp. at 280, it had no occasion to evaluate the entire record, according the decision of the administrator the appropriate weight. Accordingly, we believe that this matter ought to be remanded to the district court for further consideration. After the parties have had an opportunity to submit additional evidence, the court may redetermine the issue in accordance with the standard set forth in this opinion.

Finally, we emphasize that it would be a mistake to read our decision today as a signal that we are willing to allow employers to elude Title VII's requirements simply by arguing that they were "innovating." Rare is the employment situation in which an employer could argue that gender-based distinctions are a "reasonably necessary" approach to innovation in one's business. We hold only that, given the very special responsibilities of these defendants and the obvious lack of guideposts for them to follow, it was error to require that they adopt only a course that was subject to objective validation. Accordingly, the judgment of the district court is reversed and the case is remanded for proceedings consistent with this opinion. Circuit Rule 36 shall not apply.

REVERSED AND REMANDED.

Case Review Question: Would the case be likely to turn out differently if female officers were excluded from a male correctional institution?

Assignment 3.2

> Prepare a case brief for the preceding case beginning on page 60.

3. Statutory and Administrative Analysis

Statutory Analysis
Function of evaluating and synthesizing statutory law.

Unlike the case brief, which requires the synopsis of a factual occurrence as well as legal issues, the **statutory analysis** and administrative legal analysis procedure is much more straightforward. Statutes and administrative regulations are more broadly written and do not generally provide detailed discussions of exact case scenarios. A statute will only be applied when its various conditions or elements are satisfied. Because statutes are written to apply to the entire public rather than specific individuals, the language and description of legal standards is generally quite different from the judicial opinion.

When examining a statute, the first step is to break it down into each specific element. Great care should be used in evaluating the effect of each word in a statute. For example, the mere difference between using the word *and* rather than *or* can dictate whether all conditions must be met, as opposed to whether different ones can satisfy the statute alternatively. See Figure 3.2.

The specific elements of a statute are rarely listed in a laundry-list format. Rather, they are written most often in a narrative form. Often a single sentence includes multiple elements that must be satisfied for the statute to apply and to indicate a result. Consequently, great care must be taken in reading the statute and identifying the exact meaning of each statutory requirement based on the language used.

FIGURE 3.2

Sample Statute

PURDON'S PENNSYLVANIA STATUTES AND CONSOLIDATED STATUTES ANNOTATED
PURDON'S PENNSYLVANIA CONSOLIDATED STATUTES ANNOTATED

TITLE 75. VEHICLES

PART III. OPERATION OF VEHICLES
CHAPTER 37. MISCELLANEOUS PROVISIONS
SUBCHAPTER B. SERIOUS TRAFFIC OFFENSES

Copr. © West Group 2000. All rights reserved.
Current through Act 2000-86
3731. Driving under influence of alcohol or controlled substance

(a) Offense defined.—A person shall not drive, operate or be in actual physical control of the movement of a vehicle in any of the following circumstances:

(1) While under the influence of alcohol to a degree which renders the person incapable of safe driving.

(2) While under the influence of any controlled substance, as defined in the Act of April 14, 1972 (P.L. 233, No. 64), [FN1] known as The Controlled Substance, Drug, Device and Cosmetic Act, to a degree which renders the person incapable of safe driving.

(3) While under the combined influence of alcohol and any controlled substance to a degree which renders the person incapable of safe driving.

(4) While the amount of alcohol by weight in the blood of:

(i) an adult is 0.10% or greater; or

(ii) a minor is 0.02% or greater.

(a.1) Prima facie evidence.—

(1) It is prima facie evidence that:

(i) an adult had 0.10% or more by weight of alcohol in his or her blood at the time of driving, operating or being in actual physical control of the movement of any vehicle if the amount of alcohol by weight in the blood of the person is equal to or greater than 0.10% at the time a chemical test is performed on a sample of the person's breath, blood or urine;

(ii) a minor had 0.02% or more by weight of alcohol in his or her blood at the time of driving, operating or being in actual physical control of the movement of any vehicle if the amount of alcohol by weight in the blood of the minor is equal to or greater than 0.02% at the time a chemical test is performed on a sample of the person's breath, blood or urine; and

(iii) a person operating a commercial vehicle had 0.04% or more by weight of alcohol in his or her blood at the time of driving, operating or being in actual physical control of the movement of the commercial vehicle if the amount of alcohol by weight in the blood of a person operating a commercial vehicle is equal to or greater than 0.04% at the time a chemical test is performed on a sample of the person's breath, blood or urine.

Copr. © West 2001 No Claim to Orig. U.S. Govt. Works

Once the language has been synthesized into basic elements, each element must be considered as it applies to the facts of the present case. Each statutory element that is not satisfied by the case must be considered in terms of whether such an absence will render the statute inapplicable or whether it will direct a particular result.

Assignment 3.3

Examine and evaluate the statute in Figure 3.3 and break into the applicable components.

VA ST s 18.2-158
Code 1950, s 18.2-158

TEXT

CODE OF VIRGINIA
TITLE 18.2. CRIMES AND OFFENSES GENERALLY.
CHAPTER 5. CRIMES AGAINST PROPERTY.
ARTICLE 8. OFFENSES RELATING TO RAILROADS AND OTHER
UTILITIES.
Copyright © 1949-1998 by Michie, a division of Reed
Elsevier Inc. and Reed
Elsevier Properties Inc. All rights reserved.
Current through End of 1998 Reg. Sess.

s 18.2-158 Driving, etc., animal on track to recover damages.
    If any person, with a view to the recovery of damages against a railroad company, willfully ride, drive, or lead any animal, or otherwise contrive for any animal to go, on the railroad track of such company, and such animal is by reason thereof killed or injured, he shall be guilty of a Class 3 misdemeanor.
CREDIT

(Code 1950, s 18.1-154; 1960, c. 358; 1975, cc. 14, 15.)

NOTES, REFERENCES, AND ANNOTATIONS

    Cross references.—As to trespassing on railroad track generally, see s 18.2-159.

Code 1950, s 18.2-158
VA ST s 18.2-158
END OF DOCUMENT

FIGURE 3.3

Sample Statute

4. Application of Legal Analysis

The evaluation of legal authorities is only one part of the process of legal analysis. Once authorities have been considered and summarized appropriately, the second stage can begin. This involves the comparison of the legal precedent and the current case. The effective legal professional considers not only those authorities that support the position taken, but those that discount it as well. The latter can be useful in predicting and preparing for the opposition.

    When considering applicable authorities, the key is to compare and distinguish. With respect to judicial opinions, the information contained within the case brief should be closely compared with the current facts and issues. A similarity in legal issues is obviously necessary, but equally important is the fact comparison. A case that is too dissimilar in facts can be easily distinguished as inapplicable. While no two cases are exactly alike, it is important to seek out those cases involving similar fact patterns with respect to the pivotal facts of the current situation. Any facts that are not present or mentioned, or that are dissimilar need to be considered in terms of the importance they played or might play in affecting the outcome of the present case. Legal standards should also be compared in terms of their applicability to the present case and the degree of influence the authority, the precedent, and its cited legal standards would have on the court in the current lawsuit if one is pending or anticipated. Ultimately, a decision must be reached as to whether the present case is likely to have a similar or different outcome.

As mentioned above, statutory analysis also requires more than synthesizing the language of the statute. It is very important to closely examine all the facts of the present case to determine whether they are addressed in the current statute. If they are not, a determination must be made as to the overall applicability of the statute to the case. If it does apply, what result does the analysis indicate? If it does not appear to apply due to the absence of facts that satisfy the elements, then be prepared to explain how the statute can be distinguished from the present case.

5. Citation of Legal Standards

The discussion here is by no means an exhaustive treatment of legal citations. Further discussion is provided in Chapter Seven. At this point, the focus is to provide a basic understanding of common legal citations and their meanings. For a more comprehensive approach to legal research and interpretation or preparation of citations, the appropriate authorities should be consulted.

A legal citation is a reference to the name and information that indicates the location of a legal document in a legal publication. This reference may be to a single paper or multiple volumes of books within an ongoing series. Although there are thousands of publications in a library containing legal authorities, locating them through a systematic method of arranging information makes the process quite user friendly.

Nearly all published legal authorities are indexed by subject in one or more resources. The most familiar to the novice researcher might be a subject index similar to that found in any kind of library. However, many legal publications have extensive subject indexes. In fact, many of the publications in the typical law library are nothing more than extensively cross-referenced subject indexes to other legal publications. By understanding a uniform system for referencing all legal authorities, the subject indexes can be used more effectively to locate the authorities sought. Typically, a publication will contain primarily one type of authority. For example, a reporter publishes judicial opinions from a specific jurisdiction(s), while a code publishes the statutes from a particular legislative body. In some jurisdictions, there is more than one publication of an authority. In this case, one of the publications is designated as the *official* statement for the jurisdiction. The official publication should always be the first one listed in a citation. Traditionally, each jurisdiction published its own report for judicial opinions and code for statutes, however, commercial publishing houses have begun to publish them as well. More than 100 years ago, the West Publishing Company undertook to publish the judicial opinions for every jurisdiction, with a common subject index that was extensive and contained brief summaries of the major findings in the opinions. By using the very same index, terms, and arrangement of opinions, research among several jurisdictions became so much easier that it became the preferred publication of most subscribers (primarily attorneys and libraries). Other commercial publications also sought to focus on improved accessibility of information. This made research so much easier that in many instances the various government authorities have adopted the commercial publication as the official site and ceased their own publication.

PARALEGALS IN THE WORKPLACE

An extremely valuable paralegal skill is the ability to perform legal analysis. Paralegals, in virtually any type of employment, must be able to read and understand legal principles. Where the paralegal is employed—in a litigation firm, government agency, corporate legal department, or other setting—will largely dictate the kind of legal principles the paralegal will come into contact with most frequently. But the essential skill is the same. The qualified paralegal will be able to read a statute, administrative regulation, or judicial opinion and make sense of it as it applies to a current situation. The form and language of legal principles is such that this skill often takes time to develop, but it is one that is well worth the investment. A paralegal who can efficiently and accurately analyze legal principles on the job can be worth his or her weight in gold to an attorney.

CHAPTER SUMMARY

A key element in the success of the American legal system is legal analysis. Review of existing legal standards guides individuals in their conduct, allows insight to parties in litigation, and provides the foundation for courts to extend legal principles to real situations. Published appellate decisions allow easy access to established legal standards. This, in turn, promotes consistency in how the law is applied throughout a jurisdiction. Because legal standards are often lengthy statements of law and because a large number might apply in a given situation, it is beneficial to analyze the standard before considering its application to a present case. In judicial opinions this process is commonly known as briefing, but whether briefing a case or analyzed statutory or administrative law, the goal is the same. That is to identify all information that is relevant and may impact the present case.

ETHICAL NOTE

In legal analysis as in research, it is incumbent on the party considering law to discuss and reveal both positive and adverse authorities. In this way, a deciding court is empowered to make a fair decision and apply law properly so that the outcome is not influenced by the party with the best legal research or analysis product.

Relevant Internet Sites

Legal Research and Citation Style in the USA	www.rbs0.com/lawcite.htm
Legal Citation	http://www.legalcitation.com
Legal Research Guide	www.west.net/~smith/research.htm

Internet Assignment 3.1

Locate the statutory law publication for your state on the Internet.

KEY TERMS

Case Analysis

Case Brief

Judicial Opinion

Legal Analysis

Statutory Analysis

ENDNOTE

1. *Smith v. Getschow Co.*, 235 Wis.2d 278, 616 N.W.2d 526 (Wis.App. 2000).

Chapter 4

ANATOMY OF A CIVIL LAWSUIT

CHAPTER OBJECTIVES

Upon completion of this chapter you should be able to do the following:

- Discuss the general concept of jurisdiction.
- Distinguish among the various types of jurisdiction.
- Explain the types and bases of federal jurisdiction.
- Describe the progression of the various steps of pretrial procedure.
- Explain the stages of trial.
- Discuss the alternatives upon the conclusion of trial.
- Define the various types of motions.
- Distinguish relevance and materiality.
- Discuss the differences between a judicial branch trial and administrative hearing.

While a number of differences exist between criminal and civil cases, there are many similarities as well in the general progression of a case once trial has begun. However, the method by which a court achieves authority over a case and the parties involved in a civil action is quite distinct. Also, a number of pretrial procedures are unique to the civil process. The goal of reaching settlement between parties is different from the criminal process goal of determining whether criminal conduct has been committed and by whom. In the discussion that follows, the progress of civil cases will be examined from the source of court authority to posttrial issues.

A. JURISDICTIONAL ISSUES

1. Basic Principles of Civil Jurisdiction

Jurisdiction
(1) Authority of a court over parties and subject of a dispute.
(2) Geographical boundaries of the area and citizens over which a court has authority.

Early chapters provided some discussion of the concept of legal jurisdiction. Essentially, **jurisdiction** can be defined in one of two ways:

1. The power of a court to decide a matter in controversy.
2. The geographic area over which a particular court has authority.

The first definition of jurisdiction can be quite complex. It is based on the principle that a court should not have authority to pass and enforce judgment over persons or issues with which the court has absolutely no connection. The court has the duty to uphold the rights of those within its geographic boundaries and not to spend time interpreting cases that do not affect the citizens or property within those boundaries. Because the authority of the court is related to all of the parties to the lawsuit and all the incidents that ultimately produced the suit, the decision of exactly which court has jurisdiction can be a complicated process.

The judiciary and the legislatures have created various rules to help courts determine when they have sufficient connection and, consequently, proper authority over persons and issues associated with a particular lawsuit. Jurisdiction has been broken down into several categories, each of which represents subtypes of the general concept of court authority. Each type of jurisdiction addresses a particular aspect of the court's authority over a case given its particular circumstances. For example, if a case involves parties from different states, that aspect must be considered when determining which court(s) have authority. The following discussion examines a number of these subtypes of jurisdiction.

Subject Matter Jurisdiction
Authority of a court to determine the actual issue between the parties.

Subject matter jurisdiction is just what its name implies. It is the authority of a court over the actual dispute between the parties. This type of jurisdiction is concerned with the relationship of the court to the basis for the dispute.[1] Persons cannot create this type of jurisdiction by an agreement as to which court will have authority to hear their case. Nor can this type of jurisdiction be created because a party fails to object if a case is improperly brought in a particular court. Rather, subject matter jurisdiction is an issue that each court should identify before any case proceeds beyond the initial filing of documents.

The citizens of a jurisdiction as a whole must have some interest in the issues of a lawsuit before any court within the geographical boundaries will have subject matter

APPLICATION 4.1

Suzzane and Daniel decide to divorce. They agree on most of the terms and are amicable. They decide to combine the expense of the divorce with a final family vacation. Together with their children they fly to Hawaii, where they file for divorce. The marriage did not occur in Hawaii, and neither party has a domicile there.

The courts of Hawaii would have to decline to consider the dissolution of marriage action because it had no connection to the marriage or the parties that would provide a basis for jurisdiction over the case.

Point for Discussion: Would the situation be different if the parties had been married in Hawaii? Why or why not?

jurisdiction (authority) to hear the case. The purpose of this is to ensure that the resources of the legal system are used to promote and benefit the interests of the persons who support the legal system and who are most affected by its actions. Therefore, applying laws of one locale to citizens from another jurisdiction regarding issues that arose elsewhere would be a misuse and waste of the court's authority and the legal system for the jurisdiction in general.

In addition to the broad notion of subject matter jurisdiction, there is a more particular application. State and federal court systems have numerous judges located throughout many different courts across the jurisdictional area. The purpose is to have courts that are accessible to all of the citizens and, by using different courts, to hear different types of cases. Also, court systems with heavy docket loads often subdivide courts to hear specific types of cases in order to move the cases through the system more efficiently. One common denominator is that all of these courts at the trial level are considered courts of **original jurisdiction.** A court of original jurisdiction is one that can determine the rights of the parties initially, as opposed to the appellate courts, which review the actions of a trial or other subordinate level court. See Figure 4.1.

An obvious added benefit of subdivided courts is that the judges become quite familiar with a particular area of law and can develop a range of knowledge and experience that helps them to apply the law more fairly and consistently. The long-range effect of this is that attorneys can develop a sense of how the law is likely to be applied by a particular court in various situations and can better consider settlement possibilities that would eliminate the need for costly trials.

When a court is subdivided such as by areas of law (e.g., domestic relations, probate, criminal, etc.), the court system also subdivides the subject matter authority of the court. Consequently, a judge in the domestic relations division would not ordinarily have subject matter authority to hear a criminal case. This would generally be true even though the case technically met the basic requirements for subject matter jurisdiction. This prevents parties from shopping for what they consider to be the best judges for their case. Further, it promotes the underlying rationale for such subdivisions which is to increase the efficiency of the court system. This extended type of specialization of the courts is based on the idea of organization of the courts rather than on the original purpose of subject matter jurisdiction. Therefore, it is not considered

Original Jurisdiction
Authority of a court to rule in a lawsuit from commencement through the conclusion of trial.

FIGURE 4.1

Diagram of Court
Structure

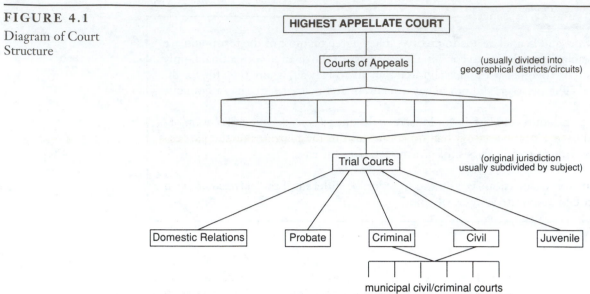

A two-tier court system is the same as the system pictured above, but with the intermediate level court of appeals deleted.

to be a true form of jurisdiction by definition. Rather, it facilitates the best method for application of subject matter jurisdiction.

Assignment 4.1

Consider the following situations, then determine and explain why the specific court in which the case is filed does or does not have (1) actual subject matter jurisdiction, and (2) extended subject matter jurisdiction of the specific court.

a. Tamika has filed a lawsuit against her business partner for fraud and deception. Tamika is a resident of state X. The partner is a resident of state Y. The business is located in state C. The suit is filed in the probate court, where Tamika's cousin is a judge, of state Y.

b. Bill files for divorce in state M from his wife Gina. The couple was married in state M. Both Gina and Bill are currently domiciled in State N. The court system in State M is not subdivided by class of case.

c. Monroe and Neville are contesting the last will and testament of their deceased mother who disinherited them by executing the will three days before her death and leaving her one million dollar estate in trust for the care of her cat. At the time of her death, Mother was visiting New York. Her cat and estate assets are located in California. Monroe lives in Connecticut and Neville lives in California. The case is filed in domestic relations division of the circuit court in New York. The other possible divisions are criminal, civil cases greater than $75,000 in value, civil cases less than $50,000 in value and probate and estates division.

Occasionally, a dispute between two parties is not confined to a single issue. When several claims arise from the same occurrence, a court that has subject matter jurisdiction over some of the issues will also usually be considered to have **ancillary jurisdiction.** This is the authority to hear closely related claims that the court generally would not have the power to hear. Similar to this is **pendent jurisdiction.** When a case is in a federal court, the court may also have authority to hear claims founded on state law that arose out of the same set of circumstances that produced the jurisdiction for the federal court's authority. By allowing courts to hear closely related issues in addition to those over which they have authority, duplicate trials and expense are avoided. Again, this is an attempt to achieve efficiency and organization within the court system.

In addition to the requirement of subject matter jurisdiction, which gives the court the authority to determine the issues in a case, there must also be authority to enforce the decision with respect to the parties involved. This type of authority is known as **personal jurisdiction.** Depending on the subtype, it creates authority in a court to enforce a decision with respect to an individual, the individual's ownership interest in property, or actual authority over the property.

The most commonly employed form of personal jurisdiction is known as **jurisdiction in personam.** This type of authority gives the court the power to compel the person to appear in court and answer questions or claims of a party to the lawsuit. It also includes the power to seize any or all assets of the person or even to impose a jail sentence.

A court may obtain in personam jurisdiction in a number of ways. Generally the **domicile** method is used. A domicile is the place where one intends to make a permanent residence and has actual residence, even if it is periodic. A person is presumed to be subject to the authority of the court in the geographical jurisdiction where that person lives. The key to domicile is intent. Although a person may have residences in many states, the domicile is considered to be the primary residence. The domicile may be shown by examples of a strong personal connection to a particular jurisdiction, such as paying income taxes in a particular state, being registered to vote there, having a driver's license for that state, or living in that residence more than any other place during the year. The greater the number of connections, the more likely it is that a certain jurisdiction will be considered one's domicile. A natural person can have only one domicile, as opposed to a corporation, which is discussed later.

A second method of obtaining in personam jurisdiction is by consent. Unlike subject matter jurisdiction, a party can agree to vest a court with personal jurisdiction by waiving any objections. An example of this might be a party who is separated from his or her spouse, and no longer resides in the state where the parties were married and the other spouse is domiciled. The party from out of state can agree to the jurisdiction of the court since subject matter jurisdiction already exists. When a person fails to object to a court's authority over him or her at the beginning of a lawsuit, it is presumed that the person agrees to the exercise of court authority. When authority is achieved this way it is considered jurisdiction by waiver.

Finally, all states have statutes that grant long arm jurisdiction, which refers to the authority of a court over someone because of his or her contacts within a state. Under these laws, the person need not live in the jurisdiction or consent to court authority. Rather, the person's acts are considered to be implied consent. The theory is that if a person accepts the benefits of a jurisdiction and that person subsequently injures a party within the jurisdiction, the courts have the right to impose responsibility for the wrongdoing. Thus, the court has a "long arm" that reaches beyond the geographical boundaries and into other jurisdictions to draw the party back for accountability.

Ancillary Jurisdiction
Authority of a court over issues in a case subject to the court's authority on grounds unrelated to the issues.

Pendent Jurisdiction
Occurs when a case involves multiple issues and the court in which the case is filed has actual authority over some but not all of the issues, in which case, the court has the option to exercise authority over those issues it could not ordinarily decide, thus exercising pendant jurisdiction.

Personal (In personam) Jurisdiction
Authority of a court over an individual and all of his/her assets.

Domicile
The intended permanent place of residence of an individual. Corporations are domiciled in the state of incorporation and where the nerve center of corporate operations are located.

The circumstances that will trigger long arm jurisdiction are based on state law. Each state has identified the specific acts that will subject non-citizens to jurisdiction. However, they must be acts that are in some way connected to the state in order to justify extending a court's authority beyond its boundaries and imposing on the boundaries of another jurisdiction. The legal theory that supports the concept of long arm jurisdiction and causes courts of varying jurisdictions to honor the long arm laws of sister states is basic. If a person accepts the benefits of a jurisdiction, such as by doing business for profit in that jurisdiction, the courts of the jurisdiction have the right to impose responsibility for any wrongdoing that occurs as a result. Typically long arm laws apply to individuals who conduct business (by the statutory definition) within a jurisdiction or with citizens of the jurisdiction, those who travel through the jurisdiction if an action arises from something that occurred during their presence, contracts that affect citizens or property within the jurisdiction, owning or possessing property within the state, or entering into or living in marriage within the state, but issues are typically confined to those connected to the marital relationship. While these are the most common grounds adopted by states in long arm jurisdiction statutes, each state determines what it considers to be actions or omissions sufficient to create extraordinary personal jurisdiction by the courts over individuals.

FIGURE 4.2

Sample Long Arm Statute

> ### INDIANA RULES OF TRIAL PROCEDURE
> ### II. COMMENCEMENT OF ACTION; SERVICE OF PROCESS, PLEADINGS, MOTIONS AND ORDERS
>
> **TRIAL RULE 4.4 SERVICE UPON PERSONS IN ACTIONS FOR ACTS DONE IN THIS STATE OR HAVING AN EFFECT IN THIS STATE**
>
> (A) Acts Serving as a Basis for JURISDICTION. Any person or organization that is a nonresident of this state, a resident of this state who has left the state, or a person whose residence is unknown, submits to the JURISDICTION of the courts of this state as to any action arising from the following acts committed by him or his agent.
>
> (1) doing any business in this state;
>
> (2) causing personal injury or property damage by an act or omission done within this state;
>
> (3) causing personal injury or property damage in this state by an occurrence, act or omission done outside this state if he regularly does or solicits business or engages in any other persistent course of conduct, or derives substantial revenue or benefit from goods, materials, or SERVICES used, consumed, or rendered in this state;
>
> (4) having supplied or contracted to supply SERVICES rendered or to be rendered or goods or materials furnished or to be furnished in this state;
>
> (5) owning, using, or possessing any real property or an interest in real property within this state;
>
> (6) contracting to insure or act as surety for or on behalf of any person, property or risk located within this state at the time the contract was made; or
>
> (7) living in the marital relationship within the state notwithstanding subsequent departure from the state, as to all obligations for alimony, custody, child support, or property settlement, if the other party to the marital relationship continues to reside in the state.
>
> (B) Manner of SERVICE. A person subject to the JURISDICTION of the courts of this state under this RULE may be served with summons:
>
> (1) As provided by RULES 4.1 (SERVICE on individuals), 4.5 (SERVICE upon resident who cannot be found or served within the state), 4.6 (SERVICE upon organizations), 4.9 (in rem actions); or
>
> (2) The person shall be deemed to have appointed the Secretary of State as his agent upon whom SERVICE of summons may be made as provided in RULE 4.10. . . .

Assignment 4.2

Examine the following circumstances and, based on the long arm statute in Figure 4.2, determine whether the court has personal jurisdiction over the out-of-state party.

Marnie ordered a weight loss product over the Internet. She used her home computer and the product was delivered to her house from a company located in another state. The company has no offices within Marnie's state of domicile. After taking the product for approximately three days, Marnie developed severe high blood pressure and consequently suffered a massive stroke. Her guardian wants to file suit against the company who makes and sells the product over the Internet.

In addition to jurisdiction in personam, there are also various types of authority with respect to property. Historically, this authority was limited to the actual property. Today that definition has been broadened somewhat. Inanimate property actually could, and still can, be named as a party in a lawsuit. It would be the responsibility of anyone with a vested interest in the property to defend the property. If the property is not defended, the court has authority to seize the property and award it to the opposition. This is known as an action **in rem,** wherein anyone and everyone claiming an interest in a property is affected by the suit and is therefore obligated to defend that interest.

In an action based on **quasi in rem,** only the property interests of the person or persons named in the suit are affected. Unlike jurisdiction in personam, any judgments on an action brought qausi in rem are limited to the person's interest in the property identified in the suit. In personam judgments can affect virtually any and all assets and property interests of an individual.

Quasi in rem may be a way to obtain jurisdiction over the property interests of a person when in personam jurisdiction cannot be achieved. Assume, for example, that a person is subject to the court's authority but cannot be located. Or perhaps the person appears at trial and a judgment is rendered against the person, but the person seemingly has no assets in that state. In the first instance, the plaintiff can file an action on the basis of quasi in rem jurisdiction to attach any of the property of the missing person in the state where the property is located. In the latter situation, a suit that claims quasi in rem jurisdiction can be brought in any state where assets exist for the purpose of satisfying the judgment rendered in another jurisdiction.

In rem and quasi in rem actions are brought much less frequently than actions based on in personam jurisdiction. The primary reason is that if a suit is brought in personam and is won, virtually all of the assets of the defendant can be used to satisfy the judgment. In an action based on property, no matter how great a judgment, only the value of the property named or the degree of interest in the property can be used to satisfy the judgment. Therefore, if the injuries or rights one seeks to protect are greater than the value of the property, it is wiser to seek in personam jurisdiction.

In Rem Jurisdiction
Authority of a court over a person's real or personal property.

Quasi in Rem Jurisdiction
Authority of a court to alter a person's interest and/or ownership in real or personal property.

APPLICATION 4.2

In 1999, four good friends in Illinois purchase a condominium in Florida together in equal shares from another friend, A. The property is listed in name A at the time of the purchase but B, C, D, and E each have deeds conveying a 1/5 interest. Shortly after buying the property, owner A has a party at the property and a guest falls through a weakened balcony railing and is seriously injured. A few months later, owner A supposedly moves to New Mexico and the others completely lose touch with him. However, each files their deed with the county clerk to record their claim in the property.

The guest files an action against A property owner who was occupying the property at the time of the injury and obtains a $250,000 judgment. To collect, the action can be filed in personam for the entire judgment against only the property owner originally sued, but his whereabouts are unknown. Alternatively, the action can be filed quasi in rem for a judgment up to the value of the property interest of owner A, assuming the value of the interest is not greater than $250,000. The other option is to file an action in rem against the property and thereby attempt to recover the entire value of the property. In order to prevent this, the other four owners would have to appear and defend their interests in the property.

Point for Discussion: Why would the injured guest not want to file an action in personam against property owner A?

2. Federal Jurisdictional Issues

As discussed in earlier chapters, the federal system of courts is wholly independent of the state court systems. The opportunity to present a case in a federal court is generally limited to those situations where (1) a federal law or the Constitution is involved, (2) the United States is a party, or (3) there is complete diversity of citizenship and the amount in controversy is valued in excess of $75,000. The following sections describe these three situations.

Even if federal jurisdiction exists, the particular federal court where the case is filed must have subject matter jurisdiction. If it does not, the case must be transferred to the federal court where such jurisdiction exists. If the suit is brought against a citizen of the United States, automatic in personam jurisdiction exists since U.S. citizenship implies domicile in the United States.

Federal Question
Method of achieving jurisdiction of the federal courts over a dispute between parties. It is necessary that a significant part of the dispute arise from the Constitution or a federal law.

a. Federal Question   One type of federal jurisdiction is known as a **federal question.** This occurs when a primary issue in the dispute is based on the application of a statute passed by the U.S. Congress, a federal administrative regulation, or the U.S. Constitution or its amendments. For this type of jurisdiction to exist, the issue that arises out of federal law must be considered by the court to be a substantial issue in the case.

If it appears that a party has created a federal question merely by adding an issue of federal law to the suit when it was unnecessary, unconnected to the true nature of the claim, or otherwise inappropriate as an inherent issue in the dispute between the parties, the court will refuse to consider the case. Even if the opposing party fails to object because they also want a federal court to hear the case, this is considered to be conspiratorial and is referred to as collusion. Collusion is basis in and of itself to dismiss a case from the federal courts.

APPLICATION 4.3

Parties A and B are business partners in a dispute over the value of the business. The local state courts have a backlog of cases creating more than a two-year wait for a trial date. The attorneys for the parties agree that the case will be brought on grounds of diversity by alleging party B's vacation home in a neighboring state is his domicile. By doing so, the case can be brought in federal court, which has a trial log of only six months. If the federal court becomes aware of this, the case will be dismissed from federal court for collusion.

Point for Discussion: Why would the federal courts care if the parties agree to its jurisdiction?

As mentioned earlier in the text, a pendent claim exists when there are separate issues based on federal and state law filed in the same lawsuit within the federal courts. In such a situation, the federal court will usually not order that the case be split into two separate trials (one in state and one in federal court) but rather may exercise pendent jurisdiction and hear both the federal and the state issues. When this is done, the federal court will follow principles of state law in determining the state issues and will apply federal law when determining the federal issues.

The case of pendent jurisdiction occurs frequently in federal courts. As legal disputes in our society become more and more complex and many issues must be decided, the likelihood increases that some of the issues will arise out of state law and others from federal law. It would be far too expensive and time consuming for the parties and the courts to try all of the issues separately. Exercising pendent jurisdiction has become the solution to this problem. However, if the state and federal issues are totally distinct and appear to have been deliberately combined, the court may order that the claims be severed and tried in separate courts.

Distinguished from pendent authority is **concurrent jurisdiction.** This occurs when more than one federal court, or a combination of federal and state courts, all have subject matter jurisdiction over a case based on its facts. The case may have solely federal or state issues, but because of the domicile of the parties or because the occurrence that gave rise to the suit is located in one or more jurisdictions, more than one court finds itself with the authority to determine the issues. This type of situation is expected to occur more often as electronic communications become more and more commonplace through the use of the Internet and computers. When multiple courts have authority over one case, the suit may be filed by the plaintiff in any court with subject matter jurisdiction. However, the defendant may change the location of the suit if various criteria are met under the statutes permitting removal from state to federal courts, or under the doctrine of forum non convenient, which will be addressed later.

b. The United States as a Party   One obvious basis for federal jurisdiction is when the federal government, a federal elected official, a federal employee in an official capacity, or an office or agency of the federal government is sued. This type of suit must

Concurrent Jurisdiction
When more than one court has authority to hear a case.

be filed in the federal courts from its inception. Traditionally, the U.S. government did not permit actions to be filed against it, claiming sovereign immunity. This was a long-standing English precedent based on the positivist theory. Over time, however, the United States has made some exceptions to this rule to encourage accountability by government officials. A small number of federal statutes have been enacted that set forth specific instances and procedures in which the government may be liable for certain physical or financial injuries to a citizen. If a suit is brought against the United States, it must be done in accordance with these statutes.[2] Each requirement of the statutes must be precisely met for the action to proceed. Depending on the nature of the claim, this may include first making a claim to the appropriate administrative agency and then following through all proper agency channels to seek redress. Ultimately, if the party is still not satisfied with the result, the case may be filed in the courts. This requirement of first attempting reconciliation through the agency is known as **exhaustion of remedies.**

c. Diversity of Citizenship   Perhaps the most common method used by individual parties to establish federal jurisdiction is **diversity of citizenship.** This basis for jurisdiction requires no determination of an interest by the court in the issues of the case. Rather, the objective of diversity of citizenship jurisdiction was to place parties from other jurisdictions in equal standing with those who were domiciled where the suit was brought. There was a question as to whether state judges and juries might be biased in favor of a resident citizen and, as a result, an outsider bringing an action might not receive equal treatment. Federal juries are often drawn from a broader geographical area, and federal judges are recommended by the U.S. Congress for presidential appointment rather than being subject to local appointment or election. In today's mobile society, the possibility of disparate treatment is less of a threat than it was 200 years ago when there was much rivalry among the states. However, as a safeguard, the federal courts still accept cases of substantial value that involve parties from different states.

There is a two-pronged test to establish grounds for diversity of citizenship jurisdiction. First, all opposing parties must have domiciles in diverse (different) jurisdictions. This means that no plaintiff can be domiciled in the same state as any defendant in an action. If the case involves a single plaintiff and defendant, this is relatively easy to determine. If, however, a case involves multiple parties, the domicile of each must be taken into consideration. It does not matter if two or more plaintiffs share the same state of domicile or two or more defendants share the same state of domicile. The key is whether parties with opposing interests in the suit share a state of domicile.

Generally, individuals are considered to have only one domicile regardless of the number of personal residences they may occupy. However, a different rule applies for corporations. Ordinarily, the law treats the corporation as a person, but unlike a person, a corporation may have an ongoing occupation and intent to reside permanently in several states simultaneously. As a result, special rules have been developed to determine the domicile of a corporation.

The state in which a corporation has filed its articles of incorporation is presumed to be the corporation's domicile. If the corporation does regular and ongoing business in a state or states other than that of incorporation, the court will consider where the central operating point for the corporation is located. This is the place from which the primary directives for the corporate operations emanate. Often this will be the corporate headquarters. Additionally, a corporation is required to register and supply a person and place for service of process in each state where it conducts business. Once the domiciles of a corporation are identified, that is, a place of incorporation and central

Exhaustion of Remedies
Requirement that anyone having a dispute with an administrative agency must first follow all available procedures to resolve the dispute within the agency before taking the issue before the judiciary.

Diversity of Citizenship
Method of achieving federal jurisdiction over a matter. It is necessary that all parties be diverse in domicile; that is, no plaintiff and defendant may be domiciled in the same state.

business location, a determination can be made as to whether diversity exists with the opposing parties in a suit.

APPLICATION 4.4

Gina is employed by Smack Shoe Sales, Inc. She is terminated from her job and wants to file an action against Smack Shoe Sales, Inc. for wrongful discharge. Gina is a resident of state Q. Smack Shoe Sales has retail outlets in all 50 states. It manufactures shoes in states P, R, and S. The board of directors meetings, senior officers of the company, and marketing division are all located in state T. Smack is incorporated in state G. The domicile of Smack Shoes is in states G and T. Federal jurisdiction exists on the basis of diversity regardless of the fact that Smack Shoes, Inc. has a retail outlet in state Q, where Gina is domiciled.

Point for Discussion: Why is there diversity of citizenship even though Smack has a place of business in State Q?

The second requirement to establish diversity of citizenship is the amount in controversy, meaning that the total value must exceed the minimum statutory value. Currently, the amount is $75,000, so an amount greater than $75,000 must be at issue between the parties. However, the same type of rule applies to the amount in controversy as to the domicile. If the court finds that the amount or amounts sued over are arbitrary and that the case is not reasonably worth $75,000, the federal court will dismiss the case. If a jury returns a verdict of less than $75,000, the federal jurisdiction is not defeated or affected. Many factors can affect a jury verdict. The only requirement is that the party or parties were reasonable in the assertion that the claim could be worth more than the statutorily required amount and that diversity was complete.

There are two exceptions that do not permit the use of the diversity of citizenship method of establishing federal jurisdiction. These are cases involving probate and domestic relations. Each state has very specific laws concerning these areas, which affect extremely personal rights in cases such as divorce, adoption, custody, support, alimony, administration of wills and estates, guardianships. The federal courts will not determine the personal rights of parties in cases such as these. Rather, only after a state court has entered judgment may diversity of citizenship be used to establish federal jurisdiction to ask that a federal court enforce the ruling of the state court.

When there is concurrent jurisdiction among state and federal courts, the plaintiff has the option to file suit in either location. However, when a sound basis for federal jurisdiction exists, the defendant has the right to have the case brought through the federal courts even if the plaintiff filed originally in state court. When the defendant in an action elects to this, the procedure is known as **removal.**

The U.S. Congress passed the following statute to enable removal:

Title 28 United States Code Section 1441: Actions Removable Generally.
(a) Except as otherwise expressly provided by Act of Congress, any civil action brought in a State court of which the district courts of the United States have original jurisdiction, may be removed by the defendant or the defendants, to the district court of the United States for the district and division embracing the place where such action is pending.

Removal
Transfer of a case to federal court that was originally filed in state court.

(b) Any civil action of which the district courts have original jurisdiction founded on a claim or right arising under the Constitution, treaties or laws of the United States shall be removable without regard to the citizenship or residence of the parties. Any other such action shall be removable only if none of the parties in interest properly joined and served as defendants is a citizen of the State in which such action is brought.

(c) Whenever a separate and independent claim or cause of action which would be removable if sued upon alone is joined with one or more otherwise nonremovable claims or causes of action, the entire case may be removed and the district court may determine all issues therein, or in its discretion, may remand all matters not otherwise within its original jurisdiction.

Constructive Knowledge
That which one knew or should have known under the circumstances.

The actual process for removing a case from state to federal court is quite specific and is prescribed in exact detail by statute. First, a defendant has only 30 days from the date of constructive knowledge of the existence of federal jurisdiction. **Constructive knowledge** occurs when the defendant knew, or should have known, of the basis for federal jurisdiction. If federal jurisdiction exists at the time the suit is originally filed in the state court, then the defendant must seek removal within thirty days of being formally notified of the suit through service of process according to one of the approved methods for service. If something occurs while the suit is pending that creates a valid basis for federal jurisdiction, the defendant has 30 days from knowledge of that event to seek removal. An example of the latter would be if a party moved his or her domicile and there was diversity of citizenship.

To start the removal proceedings, the defendant must file a petition for removal in the federal court. The petition must be filed in the federal court whose geographical boundaries include the location of the state court. It must provide the facts of the case that support the claim of federal jurisdiction. The petition must then be verified. A verified pleading requires the party submitting the document to sign a sworn statement, known as an affidavit, indicating that all the information in the petition is true and accurate to the best of his or her belief and knowledge. This is not usually a requirement for most pleadings in most jurisdictions. The intent is to provide added assurance to the courts that the petition is sound in its basis before incurring the time and expense needed to close a case out in one legal system and open it in another. If a court determines that the moving party did not have a reasonable basis for the petition for removal, penalties may be assessed against the petitioner. Because a petitioner must file a bond, one of the penalties may be the enforcement of the bond. A bond is like an insurance policy indicating that the removal of the case to federal court is appropriate. The petitioner makes a promise of a fee as bond. If the petition is denied and the case is sent back to state court, the petitioner may be ordered to pay the fee. The petition for removal is also required to have a copy of all pleadings filed in the state court to date attached. This enables the federal court to examine the case immediately rather than delaying the suit while the state court file is copied and transferred to the clerk of the federal court for filing.

Once the petition for removal is filed, a "stay" takes effect, which means that all actions in the state court stop immediately. All future hearings, motions, and trial will be conducted in the federal court. At the moment the stay takes effect, the state court loses authority over all matters in the case. Removal is automatic with the filing of the petition. No hearing is required, and it cannot be prevented from happening by objections a plaintiff may voice.

The only remedy for a plaintiff who believes removal has been improper is to submit a motion to the federal court to send the case back to state court. This is done through a motion to **remand.** In this type of motion, the plaintiff asks the federal court to review the facts of the case and make a formal determination of whether federal jurisdiction actually exists. If the court finds that it does not, the case will be remanded back to the state court. Similar to removal, once remand has been granted, the federal court will take no further action on the case other than possibly to enforce penalties against the party who removed the case originally. If the motion to remand fails, the case continues in federal court. There are some very specific situations in which federal jurisdiction exists, but the plaintiff's right to have the case heard in state court supersedes the defendant's right to removal. Only a handful of situations are specifically prescribed by federal statute.[3] However, in the vast majority of cases, the traditional rules of removal and remand apply. See Figure 4.3, 4.4.

Remand
Action of one court that returns a case to the court where it originated, such as following a reversal or improper transfer.

FIGURE 4.3
Petition for Removal

IN THE UNITED STATES DISTRICT COURT
DISTRICT OF MONTE VISTA

MATHIAS SNYDER,   ]
Plaintiff   ]
vs.   ]   Docket No. 94-321
                         ]   Judge David Madde
BILL BOON,   ]
Defendant   ]

PETITION TO REMOVE

Comes now the Defendant, Bill Boon, by and through his attorneys, Smart, Steel, and Harper, and petitions this court to remove the above-captioned case from the state court where it is pending and to accept said case into this court for further proceedings. In support of his petition, the Defendant states as follows:

1. On or about June 1, 1993, the Plaintiff instituted an action against Defendant in the District Court of Diamond County, State A, which case is assigned state Docket number 93-1010.

2. Since the commencement of Plaintiff's action against Defendant, diversity of citizenship has occurred when Plaintiff's domicile changed on or about August 31, 1993, from State A to State B.

3. Plaintiff's complaint alleges damages due from Defendant in an amount in excess of $50,000.

4. The current circumstances of the pending case satisfy all requirements of diversity of citizenship, and consequently, this court is vested with the authority to remove said case pursuant to the Federal Rules of Civil Procedure.

WHEREFORE, Defendant prays that this court will grant said petition and cause the aforementioned case to be removed from the state court where it is currently pending and to be filed in this court for further proceedings.

Respectfully submitted,

Sam Harper
Attorney for Defendant Bill Boon
Smart, Steel, and Harper
1 Empire Drive
Union City, UN 11190

FIGURE 4.4

Petition for Remand

IN THE UNITED STATES DISTRICT COURT
DISTRICT OF MONTE VISTA

MATHIAS SNYDER,   ]
Plaintiff   ]
vs.   ]   Docket No. 94-321
                                   ]   Judge David Madden
BILL BOON,   ]
Defendant   ]

PETITION TO REMAND

Comes now the Plaintiff, Mathias Snyder, by and through his attorneys, Hayford, Stanley, and Jackson and petitions this court to remand the above-captioned case to the state court where it was originally filed, for all further proceedings. In support of his petition, the Plaintiff states as follows:

1. On or about September 30, 1993, the Defendant filed a Petition to Remove the above-captioned case on the basis of diversity of citizenship and subject to the Federal Rules of Civil Procedure.

2. In said petition, the Defendant represented to this Court that the Plaintiff's domicile had changed to State B.

3. The Plaintiff has a temporary residence in State B for the purpose of attending State University during the months of August through May 1994.

4. At no time has the Plaintiff had the intent to adopt State B as his domicile and further has maintained all domiciliary ties with State A.

5. Defendant's petition is unfounded as both Plaintiff and Defendant continue to reside in State A. Therefore, diversity of citizenship does not exist between the parties to this action.

WHEREFORE, the Plaintiff prays that his petition to Remand be granted and that the above-captioned action be permitted to resume proceedings in the District Court where it originated.

Respectfully submitted,

Michael J. George
Attorney for Plaintiff Mathias Snyder
Firm of Hayford, Stanley, and Jackson
311 Lagoon Lane
Harristown, UN 11115

CASE IN POINT

Tylka v. Gerber Products Co., 211 F.3rd 445
(7th Cir. 2000).

COFFEY, Circuit Judge.

In February and March of 1996, Pamela Jean Tylka, H. Joshua Chaet, Cheryl Keller, Jeanette DeLeon, Toni Cainkar, Elaine T. Hyneck, and Barbara F. Berg filed almost identical class-action lawsuits against Gerber Products in the Circuit Court of Cook County, Illinois. In their complaints, the plaintiffs alleged that Gerber engaged in a pattern of false and deceptive advertising concerning the nutritional value and content of its baby food products, in violation of the Illinois Consumer Fraud and Deceptive Business Practices Act, 815 Ill. Comp. Stats. 505/1, the Uniform Deceptive Trade Practices Act, 815 Ill. Comp. Stats. 51 0/1, and Illinois common law fraud. Pursuant to 28 U.S.C. § 1446, Gerber removed these cases to the United States District Court for the Northern District of Illinois, alleging that diversity jurisdiction existed.

Obviously unhappy with their lawsuits being removed to federal court, the plaintiffs moved to remand their cases back to the state court system, arguing that the amount in controversy requirement of 28 U.S.C. § 1332 ($50,000 at the time the suit was filed) was not met. The district court judge denied the plaintiffs' motion for a remand to the state courts because, according to the court, the injunctive relief sought by at least one plaintiff would cost Gerber more than $50,000, and therefore diversity jurisdiction existed. Subsequently, the judge entered summary judgment in favor of Gerber. Plaintiffs appeal the trial court's determination of subject matter jurisdiction; that is, the judge's conclusion that the requirements for diversity jurisdiction were met. Because Gerber has failed to take the steps necessary to ensure federal jurisdiction, a surprising failure given this court's direction at oral argument, we VACATE the district court's opinion and REMAND this case with instructions to REMAND these lawsuits back to Illinois state court.

Because the basis for the resolution of this appeal lies in Gerber's failure to perfect subject matter jurisdiction as directed by the court, only the facts relevant to that issue will be addressed in this opinion and we will leave it up to the Illinois courts to determine the precise nature of the plaintiffs' claims.

In February and March 1996, seven plaintiffs filed six virtually identical lawsuits against Gerber in the Circuit Court of Cook County, Illinois, in which they claimed that Gerber's advertising describing its baby food products as nutritious and of high quality was false and misleading. All six complaints sought compensatory damages, punitive damages, injunctive relief, and attorney's fees. But, as mentioned earlier, the complaint filed by Tylka and the one jointly filed by Chaet and Keller requested, in addition to the relief sought by the other plaintiffs, that Gerber "run corrective marketing, publicity, and advertising for an appropriate period of time."

Gerber removed the actions to federal court in the Northern District of Illinois. See 28 U.S.C. § 1441(a). However, in its notice of removal Gerber referred to the residence of the individual plaintiffs, not their citizenship as required by 28 U.S.C. § 1332(a)(1). Despite this obvious shortcoming, none of the parties brought this to the trial judge's attention and the cases were allowed to proceed in federal court.

Instead of focusing on the obvious deficiency of Gerber's notice of removal, the parties (and the district court) directed their attention to the question of whether the jurisdictional minimum for diversity jurisdiction was satisfied. Given that determinations as

to the exact nature of the plaintiffs' claims are now better left to the sound discretion of the Illinois state courts, it is enough to say that the judge was of the opinion that the demand for corrective advertising made by three of the named plaintiffs satisfied the jurisdictional minimum of $50,000 and thus the court had subject matter jurisdiction. The trial judge then granted summary judgment in favor of Gerber.

We review the propriety of the removal of a state action to federal court de novo, see Chase v. Shop 'N Save Warehouse Foods, Inc., 110 F.3d 424, 427 (7th Cir. 1997) (citing Seinfeld v. Austen, 39 F.3d 761, 763 (7th Cir. 1994)), keeping in mind that federal courts are always "obliged to inquire sua sponte whenever a doubt arises as to the existence of federal jurisdiction." Mt. Healthy City Board of Educ. v. Doyle, 429 U.S. 274, 278, 97 S.Ct. 568, 50 L.Ed.2d 471 (1977) (emphasis added) (citations omitted).

We begin with the well-known rule that removal is proper over any action that could have been filed originally in federal court. See 28 U.S.C. § 1441; Grubbs v. General Elec. Credit Corp., 405 U.S. 699, 702, 92 S.Ct. 1344, 31 L.Ed.2d 612 (1972). Here, Gerber removed the case on diversity grounds, and as the party seeking to invoke federal diversity jurisdiction, Gerber bears the burden of demonstrating that the complete diversity and amount in controversy requirements were met at the time of removal. See In re County Collector, 96 F.3d 890, 895 (7th Cir. 1996); NLFC, Inc. v. Devcom Mid-America, Inc., 45 F.3d 231, 237 (7th Cir. 1995). As stated before, the parties have ignored the fact that the notice of removal was ineffective in terms of properly alleging diversity because allegations of residence are insufficient to establish diversity jurisdiction. See Guaranty National Title Co. v. J.E.G. Associates, 101 F.3d 57, 58 (7th Cir. 1996) (It is well-settled that "[w]hen the parties allege residence but not citizenship, the court must dismiss the suit."); see also Steigleder v. McQuesten, 198 U.S. 141, 25 S.Ct. 616, 49 L.Ed. 986 (1905); Denny v. Pironi, 141 U.S. 121, 11 S.Ct. 966, 35 L.Ed. 657 (1891); Robertson v. Cease, 97 U.S. (7 Otto) 646, 24 L.Ed. 1057 (1878).

While it is surprising that a counsel would fail to follow the simple step of alleging citizenship, what is even more surprising is Gerber's counsel's failure to follow the invitation and direction given to it at oral argument.

At oral argument, this court advised the parties that "28 U.S.C. § 1653 permits the allegations of jurisdiction to be amended even in the Court of Appeals. . . . But until that happens we certainly don't have [jurisdiction] on the allegations in this record." After Gerber assured the court that there was diversity of citizenship, counsel was informed that: "You may then be able to amend the complaints under section 1653, and should count your lucky stars because this case should have been remanded instantly."

Surprisingly to say the least, Gerber has yet to file a section 1653 amendment of pleadings addressing the jurisdictional problem despite the fact that this court has given Gerber approximately two months to do so.

On a number of occasions we have dismissed actions where litigants fail to make section 1653 amendments to correct deficient allegations of diversity of citizenship after being instructed to do so. For example, during oral argument in America's Best Inns, Inc. v. Best Inns of Abilene, L.P., 980 F.2d 1072, 1073 (7th Cir. 1992), as in this case, "the court reminded the parties of the need to establish complete diversity of citizenship." But "[d]espite receiving express directions about what they had to do, counsel did not do it. At some point the train of opportunities ends." Id. at 1074. Consequently, we vacated the district court's judgment on the merits and remanded with instructions to dismiss for lack of subject matter jurisdiction. See id.; see also Guaranty, 101 F.3d at 59; see, e.g., Held v. Held, 137 F.3d 998,

1000 (7th Cir. 1998); Dausch v. Rykse, 9 F.3d 1244, 1245 (7th Cir. 1993); Chicago Stadium Corp. v. State of Indiana, 220 F.2d 797, 799 (7th Cir. 1955).

As we have stated in the past, these lawyers knew what they had to do, and they did not do it. Failure in one round of supplemental filings leads us to doubt that a second would be any more successful. Anyway, it is not the court's obligation to lead counsel through a jurisdictional paint-by-numbers scheme. Litigants who call on the resources of a federal court must establish that the tribunal has jurisdiction, and when after multiple opportunities they do not demonstrate that jurisdiction is present, the appropriate response is clear. Counsel have only themselves to blame if they must now litigate this case from scratch in state court. Guaranty, 101 F.3d at 59.

Gerber, in this case, has neglected to file the necessary documents with the court despite our warning at oral argument that "we certainly don't have [jurisdiction] on the allegations in this record." Consequently, the judgement of the district court is VACATED, and this case is REMANDED to the district court with instructions to REMAND the plaintiffs' lawsuits back to the Illinois state court system.

Case Review Question: Why should the entire case fail because documents weren't properly filed?

Assignment 4.3

In the following situations (a) determine whether federal jurisdiction exists and (b) if a petition to remove, motion for remand, or no action would be most appropriate.

1. Plaintiff A and defendant B are residents of the same state. The plaintiff files an action in state court against B seeking $68,000 in damages. During the pendency of the suit, B moves to another state.
2. Plaintiffs C, D, E, and F all reside in the same state. They bring an action together in state court against a corporation domiciled entirely within the adjoining state. During the action, plaintiff C adds a count to her portion of the complaint based on an alleged violation of a federal law by the corporation.
3. Plaintiff G sues defendant H for dissolution of marriage in federal court. Both parties are private citizens domiciled in different states. The value of their combined property to be divided in the divorce is well in excess of $100,000.
4. Plaintiff I brings an action in state court against the state of J alleging that a statute is in violation of plaintiff I's constitutional rights under the terms of the state's constitution.

B. STEPS OF PROCEDURE IN A CIVIL CASE

The basic function of civil procedural law is to facilitate the movement of a lawsuit through the legal system, whether in the state or federal courts. Procedural laws are created to ensure that each party will be afforded fair and impartial treatment. Further, the goal of procedural law is that judges and juries will receive only evidence that will allow them to make a fair and impartial decision.

Civil procedure can be likened to a large piece of machinery that assembles a product. It does not feel or possess opinions. The function of procedural law is to assemble all of the pieces into a complete product. The parties to the suit provide the pieces to the product at appropriate times and in the appropriate manner. The completed product delivered from the machine is the decision that resolves the dispute. This decision is based on the pieces of information (substantive law and facts of the case) that have been fed into the machine and assembled. Procedural laws include, but are not limited to, the following in a typical civil case:

1. The time limit for bringing a particular type of lawsuit (also known as statute of limitations or limitation of actions)
2. The manner is which the lawsuit is begun (e.g., by filing a complaint or petition, and providing any necessary information)
3. The acceptable methods to formally provide notice to the defendant that a lawsuit has been initiated
4. The types of information that each party must release to the other during the preparations for trial
5. The procedure to be followed at trial
6. The evidence that is admissible at trial
7. The methods for filing an appeal to the outcome of the case if a party feels the decision or result was improper according to the law as it applies to the facts presented

Rules of civil procedure become relevant at the time a lawsuit is begun. In fact, the very first rule of the Federal Rules of Civil Procedure states: "A civil suit is commenced by the filing of an action."[4] Each state also has a published collection of statutory laws and, in some cases, supplemental court rules that set out the requirements for procedure. With some variances concerning terminology, time limits, and administrative matters, for the most part they mirror the Federal Rules of Civil Procedure, which were passed by Congress and are used by the federal courts. For the sake of convenience, these rules will be discussed here as the basic progression of litigation is examined.

1. Commencement of an Action

An action is a lawsuit predicated upon a recognized legal theory that states a required conduct. If this conduct is not adhered to and as a result someone is injured personally or financially, then they may seek relief in the courts by filing an action against the party who allegedly failed to follow the law. The party bringing the action is referred to as the plaintiff or petitioner. The document used to submit the action to the court is the complaint or petition, which was discussed earlier in the chapter. The complaint (usually including at least one copy) is filed with the clerk of court along with appropriate fees and any information required to provide notice of the suit that has been filed to the defendant. The complaint is organized into what are usually single statements that are numbered and referred to as paragraphs. Each statement is either an allegation of a particular act that occurred in relation to the claim or an assertion of the specific theory of law that was violated, such as negligence. Finally, there is a section commonly referred to as the prayer in which the plaintiff states what type of redress is sought as restitution for the injuries. When read in its entirety, the complaint should clearly state which legal principles have allegedly been breached and which facts of the current situation demonstrate how the violated principle resulted in injury of some type to the plaintiff. There should also be an indication of the redress being sought for the injuries. It is not necessary to include every single fact of the case. For example, a case predicated on negligence requires the plaintiff to prove that specific events have occurred before the defendant will be held accountable for the plaintiff's injuries. Each theory of law contains such specific elements or conditions. The facts in the complaint must include those that identify the parties, the basis for court jurisdiction, and how the various conditions of the legal principle were breached.

Venue
Proper individual court within a jurisdiction to determine a dispute between parties.

Because there are many different courts within a jurisdiction, it is important to establish which is the proper one to hear a case. The specific court to hear a case filed within a particular legal system, whether it is federal or state, is known as an issue of **venue.** This is the court where the case should be tried according to the laws of procedure. Although each type of jurisdiction has its own rules regarding what constitutes proper venue, it is safe to say that proper venue will always have some relationship to the domicile of the parties or the subject of the lawsuit. Typically, the proper venue is the court within whose geographical boundaries all defendants, and/or sometimes all plaintiffs, are domiciled or where the lawsuit arose. In state systems, the proper venue would be the trial court at the county level. In the federal system it would be the U.S. District Court within whose boundaries one of the jurisdictional elements exists.

Frequently, the media will feature a news story about a request for a change of venue in a much publicized case. While the courts have the authority to hear cases over which there is proper jurisdiction and venue, they also have the discretion to decline venue when a case could not be fairly heard. This discretion also extends to cases where there is concurrent jurisdiction with other courts and another court would be more suitable. The process of declining jurisdiction in such a case is known as forum non convenions.

When more than one jurisdiction has authority to hear a case (concurrent), the plaintiff is usually given the choice of where the lawsuit will be conducted. Literally translated, the term *forum non conveniens* means an "inconvenient forum" and refers to the situation in which a court, for all practical purposes, is dramatically more inconvenient to the parties when compared with other courts that also have jurisdiction to hear a case. In such a situation, the court has the power to use its own judgment and determine whether the plaintiff's choice of jurisdiction should be ignored and the case transferred or dismissed with leave to refile in another jurisdiction.

As a general rule, courts are extremely hesitant to disturb the right of a plaintiff to choose the forum. However, if it appears that another court is in a much better position to decide the case, the first court may decline to exercise its jurisdiction based on the forum non conveniens doctrine. The issue is most often brought to the attention of the court by the defendant. Many times, this will be done on the premise that the plaintiff filed suit in a less convenient forum in hopes of obtaining a more favorable result. An example would be filing in a jurisdiction with a strong history of high dollar judgments for plaintiffs. Whatever the plaintiff's reason for filing suit in a jurisdiction, the court will not question it. However, the court may consider a series of factors that, when weighted manifestly in favor of another jurisdiction, may result in a decline to exercise jurisdiction to hear the case. The factors typically considered include the following:

1. Residence of each of the parties
2. Domicile of witnesses and whether they are subject to subpoena power of a particular court
3. Location of evidence
4. Site of the occurrence giving rise to the suit, in cases where a jury might be taken to the site to view it
5. Docket backlog of the two courts (where the suit can reach trial first)
6. Interest of the citizens of the jurisdiction where the case was originally filed in having the suit heard there (will the case help settle an issue of undecided law in the jurisdiction and venue)
7. Differences in law to be applied in each of the concurrent jurisdictions

Once the lawsuit has been filed, the wheels of the judicial system begin to turn. A summons is the document used to formally notify a party that he or she is a named defendant in a lawsuit. It is typically issued along with a copy of the complaint. The method for notice of an action to a defendant is also prescribed by procedural law. The summons is usually delivered in person to the defendant or the defendant's representative and in certain cases by mail. This may be referred to as service of process. In some instances, notice may be given through publication in a newspaper where the action is filed or where the last known residence of the defendant is located. As the technology of communications expands, so most likely will the methods of service allowed by law. The summons/notice will specify how long a party has to respond to the allegations of the complaint. If the defendant does not respond to the complaint within the allotted time period, the court may accept everything alleged in the complaint as true and grant a decision in favor of the plaintiff without any additional prior notice to the defendant. This is known as a default judgment. If it is not properly appealed or challenged within a stated time, the order takes effect; the defendant has no further recourse and must satisfy the judgment as rendered by the court.

2. Response

A defendant may respond to the complaint in a number of ways. Responsive pleadings have different names in different states, but the basic methods of responding to a complaint are the same. These were briefly addressed earlier, but will be examined in more detail here. One method of response is by answer, in which the defendant responds specifically to each allegation of the complaint. While it is possible to issue a blanket denial of all allegations, more often they will be addressed individually. Commonly, the defendant will respond by admitting, denying, or pleading the inability to admit or deny based on a lack of sufficient information in the complaint. The latter claim is given in response to an allegation that is perceived as vague or cannot be answered with an admission or denial unless more information is provided by the plaintiff. Claiming a lack of knowledge is generally treated as a denial to protect the defendant from having to admit or deny claims about which too little is known at the time. Once an answer has been filed, the parties move into pretrial proceedings.

At the time the answer is filed, the defendant may also include any alleged **affirmative defenses.** Ordinarily, the plaintiff alleges facts and is responsible for proving them in order to prevail over a defendant in a lawsuit. The task of the defendant is to submit evidence of facts that show the plaintiff's version of the case is incorrect or that shed further light on the case and demonstrate why the defendant's conduct was not a

Affirmative Defenses
Allegation by a defendant that conduct by the plaintiff legally precludes plaintiff from recovery.

violation of legal standards. However, in some cases, the defendant may also assert facts that demonstrate the plaintiff was in actuality responsible for all or part of the alleged injuries regardless of the defendant's actions. This type of allegation by a defendant is known as an affirmative defense. As stated, legal theories prescribe certain conduct, the breach of which can result in liability for injury to another. There are also legal theories that impose conduct on individuals requiring them to be responsible to some extent for their own well-being. The failure to properly do so may prevent them from recovery from another. When such a theory is advanced by a defendant alleged to have caused injury, it is known as an affirmative defense.

Another possible response to a complaint is a motion for a bill of particulars. This is a claim by the defendant that the complaint cannot be answered in its current form. This type of motion requests the court to order the plaintiff to clarify one or more allegations of the complaint by explaining or adding information. If the motion is granted, the plaintiff will be required to provide the defendant with additional information. If it is denied, the defendant will be ordered to answer the complaint as it was originally filed.

If the complaint is procedurally deficient in some way, a motion to dismiss (also sometimes referred to as a demurrer) may be filed. This simply states that the complaint does not contain the facts that warrant any type of lawsuit, that the facts stated do not state an actual breach of a recognized legal theory, or that the complaint is improperly stated according to procedural rules. If granted, this type of motion can result in permanent dismissal of the lawsuit, known as dismissal with prejudice or dismissal without prejudice. When dismissed without prejudice, the plaintiff may be given the opportunity to amend (correct) and refile the complaint. Often, leave to amend is granted and if it is done within a specified period of time, the court accepts the amended complaint directly and does not require the filing process to start completely over. This is important because if the time limit for filing the action expired after the case was initiated, refiling could be objected to by the defendant on grounds of timeliness. See Figure 4.5.

Whether a case is dismissed with or without prejudice often depends upon the basis for the dismissal. If the reason is that the stated facts do not support a legal action, the suit may be dismissed with prejudice unless the plaintiff can demonstrate to the court that additional facts could be added to the complaint that would then support a foundation for the lawsuit.

The failure to properly serve the summons or complaint on the defendant can also result in an action being dismissed. For example, if the summons and complaint was served on someone other than the defendant or on an inappropriate representative, such as a small child in the household, the defendant could file a motion to dismiss. Each jurisdiction has its own procedural rules concerning service of process and these must be followed exactly in order to avoid objections by a defendant. See Figure 4.6.

Finally, once the complaint has been addressed, the defendant has an opportunity to file counter-claims and third party pleadings. The counter-claim is filed when the defendant asserts the allegation that the plaintiff has in fact violated legal standards, which consequently resulted in injury to the defendant. Thus, both parties advance claims of violation of principles and resultant injury. The law requires that all related claims be tried together as a means of facilitating a comprehensive resolution to the disputes among parties. Thus, if the defendant intends to file a claim against the plaintiff for matters arising out of the same basic relationship that precipitated the initial lawsuit, it must generally be filed as a counter-claim or it is waived.

In addition to counter-claims, the defendant may also file third-party pleadings. These are filed when the defendant claims that it was a third party who is ultimately responsible for the plaintiff's injuries. This is seen in various types of actions. One ex-

Comes now the Defendant, Pauline McPaul, by and through her attorneys, Winter, Somers, and Snow, and moves the Court to enter an order dismissing the Complaint of Defendant. In support thereof, the Defendant states as follows:

1. On or about August 19, 1993, the Plaintiff instituted an action against the Defendant in the above-captioned court.
2. The Complaint of Plaintiff fails to state a cause of action upon which relief can be granted.
   Further, Plaintiff's allegations are legal conclusions and unsupported by any allegations of fact.

WHEREFORE, the Defendant prays that the Court enter an order dismissing the Plaintiff's complaint, awarding Defendant costs and such other and further relief as the Court deems necessary and proper.

Respectfully submitted,

Marvin Henry, atty.
Winter, Somers and Snow, P.C.
Suite 260 Park Place
Canoga, State 000000

FIGURE 4.5
Motion for Bill of Particulars

Comes now the Defendant, Pauline McPaul, by and through her attorneys, Winter, Somers, and Snow, and moves the Court to enter an order requiring Plaintiff to additional facts to support the allegations of his Complaint. In support thereof, the Defendant states as follows:

1. On October 31, 1993, Plaintiff instituted an action against the Defendant alleging breach of contract with respect to an agreement to which both Plaintiff and Defendant were parties.
2. That during the period 1990–1994, Plaintiff and Defendant had an ongoing business relationship, the product of which was no fewer than 70 separate contracts.
3. That Defendant is without information as to the specifics of the alleged breach and as a result is unable to frame a proper answer to the allegations of Plaintiff.

WHEREFORE, the Defendant prays that the Court will enter an order requiring the Plaintiff to more particularly describe the specifics of the facts supporting the allegations of Plaintiff's Complaint.

Respectfully submitted,

Marvin Henry, atty.
Winter, Somers and Snow, P.C.
Suite 260 Park Place
Canoga, State 000000

FIGURE 4.6
Motion to Dismiss

---

ample is an action for breach of contract where the defendant asserts that the actions of another were the legal cause for the injuries of the plaintiff; for example, a building contractor cannot fulfill the terms of a contract due to the delays of a supplier. The builder could then file a third-party complaint against the supplier for indemnity for liability to the plaintiff.

3. Investigation and Discovery

From the time a case is undertaken, the process of investigation begins and continues until the conclusion of the suit. In order to successfully bring an action or defend one, the key is evidence. First, it is essential that all evidence collected meet the criteria for admissibility. Unless the evidence can be admitted at trial according to the statutory rules of evidence, it is of little use regardless of how powerful it may seem. There are numerous rules that apply to various types of evidence such as business records, testimony, and photographs. However, all evidence must satisfy two preliminary rules—relevance and materiality—to even be considered.

Relevant
Tends to establish an essential fact in a dispute.

    Relevant evidence is that which tends to establish or refute some basic element of the legal action.[5] Recall that an action consists of elements and that breach of those elements resulting in injury gives rise to the basis for the lawsuit. At trial, it is necessary to present evidence supporting or defending the presence of each element and indicating whether it was breached or satisfied. Each party presents evidence that supports their version of the facts as they pertain to the cause of action. Other evidence, such as information about one of the parties that is perhaps interesting, but unrelated to the present circumstance, is not relevant and should not be admitted.

Material
Necessary to a fair and informed decision.

    To be admissible, all evidence must also be **material** to the case at hand. Material evidence is that which is considered necessary to a fair and informed determination of the dispute.[6] It is not effective to overwhelm the judge or jury with evidence of the same individual fact from a multitude of sources. One or two credible sources are usually considered, which keep the focus on the case rather than a single point. Additionally, evidence that may inform the court but is so extreme that it might prevent a jury from being fair and objective could be considered immaterial. An example would be graphic and grotesque photographs of an injury. Although a clear understanding of the nature and extent of the injury may be necessary, often jurors can be more fair if they consider detailed medical reports or testimony rather than evidence so graphic as to offend one's sensibilities and generate an emotional or physical response. Consequently, great care should be taken when considering any type of graphic materials for use as evidence, because they may well end up being excluded entirely.

    Throughout preparation for trial, the legal team collects and considers possible evidence to support or defend the claims in the complaint. This may include gathering documents, visiting a location relevant to the suit for photographs, taking measurements, or videotaping. Often, an important part of investigation is interviewing the client and any potential witnesses that are not parties to the suit. Anyone who is directly connected to the opposition must be contacted in accordance with the standard rules of discovery.

    Discovery begins after the answer has been filed in the suit. At this stage, the parties exchange information under strict guidelines and close supervision of the courts. A primary goal of discovery is to foster the fair exchange of information to enable the parties to clearly evaluate the strength of their positions.[7] Often, discovery results in settlement of the case, once the parties become aware of all the pertinent information, since they may not have had access to certain facts that would influence the outcome of the case in a trial. Discovery is sort of a show and tell process where both parties ask to see the evidence of the other. However, it is the responsibility of the party to ask properly for the right information at the right times. It is not incumbent on the producing party to simply offer up everything they have in support of their position. Discovery encourages the objective assessment of the strengths and weaknesses of each side, thereby encouraging settlement. The parties may use several different methods of discovery, which are detailed later. A party may object to answering a discovery request that is irrelevant, immaterial, invades the attorney-client or some other recognized privilege, or allegedly violates a procedural or evidentiary rule. Privileged information is that which is conveyed within the context of a legally recognized confidential relationship such as attorney-client, doctor-patient, or clergy-parishioner. When an objection is raised, it may be taken to a judge who determines whether the party must respond.

Interrogatories. Frequently, the first step in discovery is the submission of interrogatories—written questions submitted to the opposing party in the case. The party who receives the questions must answer them under oath (verified) and in writing unless an objection is made and sustained (granted) by a court. Many jurisdictions limit the number of interrogatories that may be submitted to the opposition. See Figure 4.7.

Request for Production. It is fairly commonplace for interrogatories to be accompanied by a request for production, which is another form of discovery. This is a written request to produce documents or copies of documents. Because many of the functions of our society depend upon written records, it is often very helpful to review documents for insight into what actually occurred. In this sense, documents may include records in the form of paper, photographs, videos, or even electronically stored information. See Figure 4.8.

Deposition. One method of discovery—the deposition—applies not only to the parties in the lawsuit but also to all persons with relevant information about the facts of the case. In a deposition, the attorneys ask a party or witness in the suit to respond to

---

FIGURE 4.7
Sample Interrogatory

In the District Court
45th Judicial District
State of Tucammawa

Buzzy Jamison,
Plaintiff
vs.
Malcolm Smythe,
Defendant.

INTERROGATORIES

Comes now the Plaintiff Buzzy Jamison by his attorneys Marjoram, Coburn, and McEachern and with respect to the above-named case submit the following interrogatories pursuant to Court Rule 606. Pursuant to said rule, the interrogatories below are to be answered in writing and under oath within 28 days of the date submitted.

1. With respect to the Defendant please state:
   a) All names by which the Defendant has been known.
   b) All addresses at which the Defendant has claimed residence since 1970.
   c) The names and current address of any current or former spouse.
   d) The address, of Defendant's current employment, position held, and current wage rate.
   e) The Defendant's social security number.
2. State the whereabouts of the Defendant between the hours of 3:00 p.m. March 16, 1990, and 3:00 a.m. March 17, 1990.
3. With respect to the time and dates listed in interrogatory number 2, state the name and address of each person, business, or other entity which provided alcohol or other drugs, by gift or sale, to the Defendant.
4. State all prescription medications and the prescribing physician's name and address for all drugs the Defendant was taking March 16–17, 1990.

Buzzy Jamison
Attorneys Marjoram, Coburn, & McEachern
7719 Hamilton
Sequoia, Tucammawa 00000

Submitted to Defendant by placing the above-stated interrogatories, postage paid, in the United States Mail, on the 31st day of April 1991.

FIGURE 4.8
Sample Request to
Produce

Comes now the Defendant, in the above-captioned action, and pursuant to applicable rules of civil procedure, requests that the plaintiff produce for examination, testing, sampling or copying by the defendant or agents of the defendant the following items:

1. All photographs, recordings, reports, records, documents, videotapes, notes, memoranda, accounts, books, papers, and other recorded, written, photographic or transcribed information that represent, are pertinent or related to in any manner, the allegations of the plaintiff against the defendant. The only exception to such request are the working papers and/or notes of plaintiff's attorney which would be characterized as work product of said attorney.

Marvin Henry, atty.
Winter, Somers and Snow, P.C.
Suite 260 Park Place
Canoga, State 000000

---

questions about his or her knowledge of the case. Usually, depositions are taken in person and in the presence of attorneys for each party. The entire proceeding is taken down by a stenographer who is also a notary public and asks the person deposed to swear to tell the truth. As long as the questions remain pertinent to the case, there is usually no limit to how many may be asked.

More often, depositions are taken on videotape. In another type of deposition, the party requesting the deposition sends written questions and the deposee is asked to answer the questions under oath and to provide a notarized statement that the responses are true and accurate to the best of his or her knowledge.

If it is anticipated that the witness will not be present at trial, the deposition may be taken for evidentiary purposes as well as discovery. The procedure is basically the same, but in addition to the discovery party asking questions, the other attorneys may ask questions in the same manner as they would in a trial. Both direct examination and cross-examination are conducted. If objections are made, the questions are later presented to a judge. If it is determined that the witness should respond, the answers are given and presented to the jury. See Figure 4.9

Physical Evidence. In some cases, physical evidence is an integral part of the lawsuit. For example, if a person is injured by a tool or on private property, the condition of the tool or the property may become paramount in the lawsuit. When such physical evidence is owned or controlled by another party to the suit, the discovering party may file a request for inspection. This type of discovery allows a party to inspect, photograph, measure, and evaluate a particular item or place. If the party wants custody of an item or wants to subject the item to any procedures that might affect it, court approval may be required. Otherwise, in most cases, plaintiffs and defendants are entitled to a reasonable inspection of the items that may be produced as evidence in a trial. See Figure 4.10.

Examination. A party may also request physical or mental examination of an opposing party if such examination is relevant to the lawsuit. An example is a plaintiff who is claiming injuries as the result of alleged negligence by the defendant. In such a case, the defendant may very well be allowed to select a physician to examine the plaintiff and give an opinion as to the extent of the injuries. Another example might be a dispute over child custody between two parents. If the child or one of the parents has a history of what might be considered abnormal behavior, the court may allow a mental examination by a qualified specialist to determine whether the behavior has had an adverse effect on the child. However, the court may also enforce limits on the extent or nature of the examination.

Pursuant to the rules of civil procedure applicable to this proceeding, the oral deposition of Defendant shall be taken before a notary public on December 12, 1994, commencing at 1:00 p.m. and continuing thereafter until such time as completed. The aforementioned deposition will be conducted at place of business of the Defendant, 401 East 1st St., Knobbe, IK 030303.

Marvin Henry, atty.
Winter, Somers and Snow, P.C.
Suite 260 Park Place
Canoga, State 000000

FIGURE 4.9
Notice of Deposition

Comes now the Plaintiff, Mortimer Vance, by and through his attorneys, Winter, Somers, and Snow, and moves the Court to enter an order permitting Plaintiff to inspect the premises under control of the Defendant. In support thereof, the Plaintiff states as follows:

1. On or about July 5, 1993, Plaintiff instituted an action in this Court against the Defendant alleging injury as the result of negligent conduct of Defendant.
2. Said allegations of neglect arose from an explosion that occurred on Defendant's property in which Plaintiff was seriously injured.
3. It is necessary for Plaintiff to inspect the aforementioned property of Defendant and site of Plaintiff's injuries for the proper preparation of Plaintiff's case.
4. Said inspection is appropriate pursuant to applicable rules of procedure.

WHEREFORE, the Plaintiff prays the Court will enter an order permitting Plaintiff to inspect the aforementioned property of Defendant upon reasonable notice and circumstances for the purposes of discovery in the above-captioned action.

Respectfully submitted,

Marvin Henry, atty.
Winter, Somers and Snow, P.C.
Suite 260 Park Place
Canoga, State 000000

FIGURE 4.10
Request for Inspection

Genuineness of documents. An extremely important discovery tool is the request or motion to admit genuineness of documents or facts. In some jurisdictions this is referred to as a request for admissions. Although this may not be included as a common form of discovery, it is directly related to information discovered or found through investigation. This document asks the opposing party to review the facts or information attached and to specifically admit or deny the truthfulness of their content. If admitted completely or verified (admitted to the best of the party's knowledge and belief), then the party who filed the document may seek an early end to the lawsuit with a motion for summary judgment. Usually, a motion to admit genuineness of documents or facts is not submitted unless the evidence identified directly contradicts the core basis of the admitting party's position in the lawsuit. Because most parties believe and have supporting evidence for their position, these documents are not seen in the majority of lawsuits. See Figure 4.11.

4. Motion Practice

Throughout any lawsuit, the parties communicate with the court largely through motions. A **motion** is a request by a party for assistance or a specific ruling by the court on a particular issue between the parties to the suit. Motions can result in something

Motion
Formal request by a party to a lawsuit for court-ordered action.

FIGURE 4.11

Request to Admit
Genuineness

Comes now the Plaintiff, by and through her attorneys as requests that the Defendant admit the
genuineness and truthfulness of content of the attached document for the purposes of the above-
captioned action, and further to stipulate the admission of said document into evidence in the
above-captioned action.

Marvin Henry, atty.
Winter, Somers and Snow, P.C.
Suite 260 Park Place
Canoga, State 000000

---

as serious as permanent dismissal of the lawsuit. The following discussion examines
some of the more common motions in terms of what they request and the effect they
have if granted. We have seen that motions can be used to request dismissal of suit
when the complaint is deficient in some way. Motions also have many other uses
throughout pretrial, trial, and even posttrial proceedings. While the reasons for motions are virtually limitless, some of the more commonly sought motions are briefly
discussed here.

Motion to Dismiss. This motion is used when a party believes that the facts of the
case do not support a viable legal claim or that the complaint is improperly stated and
does not conform to legal requirements as outlined by the rules of procedure.

Motion to Make More Definite and Certain. Also called a bill of particulars, this document is filed by the defendant and asks that the plaintiff be required to provide more
detailed information than that contained in the complaint.

Motion to Quash Service of Process. This motion is filed when a plaintiff allegedly
does not follow the rules of procedure for proper service of process of the summons
and complaint on the defendant. If the rules are violated, the service will be quashed
(rejected) and the plaintiff must generally attempt to serve the defendant properly. In
some instances, the wrong defendant is served and the appropriate one must be located
and served with process.

Motion to Inspect. This motion is used to gain access to property, including land and
specific items, that is privately owned and controlled. If granted or agreed to, the party
requesting access is permitted to inspect the property as it pertains to evidence in the lawsuit. This may include examination by an expert in an area relevant to the issues of the
suit including photographs, videotapes, measurements, and possibly even pre-approved
testing of some type. Examples might be a product that was allegedly defective and
caused injury as a result, or the location of an injury that occurred on private property.

Motion for Mental/Physical Exam. Whenever the mental or physical condition of a
party or a witness is raised as an issue and is found to be relevant to the basis for the
lawsuit or the credibility of evidence (including testimony), the opposition may seek
the opportunity to have their own witness give an opinion. When granted, the physician or expert of the requesting party is allowed to examine the party or witness in
question and give a report as to that person's mental or physical condition.

Motion to Compel. Each jurisdiction imposes procedural limits on discovery. This
often includes time limits in which a party must respond in some way to a discovery request such as interrogatories. When these time limits are not adhered to by the receiving party, the party seeking the information may request that the court order
compliance immediately or within a specified time to avoid penalty. See Figure 4.12.

Motion for Sanctions. At any time during a legal proceeding, including discovery,
pretrial, and trial, if a party willfully disregards procedural rules or specific court or-

Comes now the Plaintiff, Mortimer Vance, by and through his attorneys, Winter, Somers, and Snow, and moves the Court to enter an order compelling Defendant to respond to Plaintiff's discovery. In support thereof, Plaintiff states as follows:

1. On or about January 13, 1993, Plaintiff submitted interrogatories to Defendant in accordance with applicable rules of civil procedure.
2. Response from Defendant to said interrogatories was due on or about February 13, 1993.
3. Said date for response has passed, and Plaintiff has made further written requests to Defendant for compliance with this discovery. As of March 29, 1993, Defendant has failed to respond to the aforementioned interrogatories.
4. Defendant is in violation of the rules of discovery and is thwarting Plaintiff's attempts to proceed with this litigation.

WHEREFORE, the Plaintiff prays the Court to enter an order compelling the Defendant to respond to Plaintiff's interrogatories within 7 days and to order such other further and necessary relief as the Court deems proper.

Respectfully submitted,

Marvin Henry, atty.
Winter, Somers and Snow, P.C.
Suite 260 Park Place
Canoga, State 000000

FIGURE 4.12

Sample Motions

ders, the opposing party may request that the court impose sanctions. This is a penalty and, depending upon the seriousness of the offensive conduct, may range from an order of immediate compliance with the rules or an order to monetary fines, findings in favor of the opposing party, dismissal of the suit, and even time in jail for a party, witness, or attorney.

Motion for Rule/Reason to Show Cause. Similar to the motion for sanctions, this motion is typically filed when a party has failed to comply with a specific order of court. Often, this motion is filed after conclusion of a case if a party does not comply with the terms stated in the dismissal. An example might be in a dissolution of marriage action wherein a party is ordered to pay child support to the other spouse and then fails to do so as ordered. If granted, the penalties have a wide range based on the court's findings with respect to intent to disobey a court order, any special circumstances or conditions, and the seriousness of the failure to honor the court order.

Motion for Summary Judgment. This is not a routinely filed motion. The basis of the motion is that the evidence is so overwhelmingly in favor of one party that no reasonable judge or jury could find in favor of the other party. Consequently, the party seeking the motion contends that there is no basis for a trial and the case should be determined without a trial and in favor of the requesting party. The motion for summary judgment is one of the most serious motions that can be filed in any lawsuit. It asks that the judge make a final decision on the issues of the suit without a trial, based solely on the evidence that exists at the time of the motion. The effect of such a motion is that the judge removes the case from the hands of the jury before it ever reaches them. Because our system of government places so much importance on the jury system, this is a very serious step for any judge to take.

When a motion for summary judgment is sought, the judge must make a serious evaluation of the evidence. If the evidence is so strongly in favor of one party that a judge determines a jury could reasonably reach only one decision, and there is no substantial question left to be determined regarding the facts that occurred, a motion for summary judgment may be granted. However, if there is any way that the jurors could reach a different conclusion as to whose version of the story is more probable, the motion must be denied, and the case must be left to the trier of fact.[8]

Because the effect of a successful motion for summary judgment is that there will be no trial in the case, such a motion must be filed before trial begins. Other than that requirement, when or if the motion is filed is entirely up to the party submitting it. Usually such a motion is made only when it appears that the evidence on one side overwhelmingly defeats the opposition, but the parties are unable to reach a settlement. In most cases, each side has at least some credible evidence that would tend to prove or disprove the case. Consequently, these motions are filed less often than other types of motions and it is rare for a court to make such a serious finding with respect to the weight of the evidence and grant the motion.

If a motion for summary judgment is made by a defendant and is successful, then the case is dismissed with prejudice. The issues between the parties are permanently settled. If the motion is brought by a plaintiff, the defendant is not entitled to an opportunity to present evidence at trial. If the plaintiff sought a specific dollar amount in the complaint, then the defendant is ordered to pay that amount. If the request was for damages but it was nonspecific, a trial may be held to determine exactly how much the defendant should pay. See Figure 4.13.

Motion in Limine (Motion to Limit or Exclude). When evidence that is otherwise admissible may be considered immaterial, a motion to limit or even preclude its admissibility may be filed. This is based on the contention that the evidence at issue would interfere with an informed and fair decision by the jury. Most often this is filed when there are graphic depictions of physical injuries to humans or animals, or when infor-

---

FIGURE 4.13
Sample Motion

Comes now the Defendant, Pauline McPaul, by and through her attorneys, Winter, Somers, and Snow, and moves the Court to enter an order of Summary Judgment in favor of Defendant and against Plaintiff. In support thereof, the Defendant states as follows:

1. On or about August 31, 1993, Plaintiff filed an Amended Complaint against Defendant alleging that the Defendant negligently caused Plaintiff's financial injury and ultimate bankruptcy as the result of a breach of contract. Defendant filed an answer denying the allegations of the Plaintiff.

2. The parties have subsequently engaged in discovery, and the information discovered indicates that no genuine issue of fact exists to support Plaintiff's allegations.

3. Attached in support of Defendant's motion is the affidavit of Plaintiff's former employee, Alexander Grant. Said affidavit states, inter alia, that as general manager of Plaintiff's business, Mr. Grant had full knowledge of Plaintiff's financial status at the time of the alleged breach of contract.

4. Affiant further states that at the time of the alleged breach of contract by Defendant, the Plaintiff was insolvent and consulting attorneys with respect to filing bankruptcy. Shortly following the alleged breach, Plaintiff did in fact file for bankruptcy.

5. Affiant avers that if called to testify, he would affirmatively state that Plaintiff suffered no financial injury by Defendant's breach and that said breach had no bearing on Plaintiff's subsequent bankruptcy.

WHEREFORE, the Defendant prays that the Court enter a finding that no genuine issue of facts exists with respect to Plaintiff's allegations of damage proximately caused by Defendant, and further that the Court enter an order of Summary Judgment in favor of the Defendant and against the Plaintiff and such other and necessary relief as the Court deems necessary and proper.

Respectfully submitted,

Marvin Henry, atty.
Winter, Somers and Snow, P.C.
Suite 260 Park Place
Canoga, State 000000

mation unnecessarily duplicates other evidence. Because a court is hesitant to interfere with a party's right to present the most effective case through its strongest admissible evidence, such motions are not considered lightly. It is granted only when the information would almost certainly lead any reasonable juror to an unfair conclusion based on emotion or lead the juror to give undue weight or consideration to the evidence. If granted, there must generally be another less imposing or offensive method to present the general nature of the evidence. See Figure 4.14.

Motion for Directed Verdict. Not to be confused with the summary judgment motion, this motion is filed only after evidence has been presented to a jury in trial, rather than prior to the beginning of the trial as with the motion for summary judgment. However, similar to the other motion, the motion for directed verdict asks that the judge make a determination that there is only one reasonable outcome to the suit based on the evidence presented and, because of this, further presentation of the case and consideration of it by a jury is unnecessary. The moving party asks the court to instruct the jury as to what its finding should be. This is a routine motion that is often made by each side in a case at some point or points in a trial. For the same reasons as those discussed with regard to the motion for summary judgment, this motion also is rarely granted. See Figure 4.15.

Motion for Judgment Notwithstanding the Verdict (Non Obstante Verdicto or Judgment NOV). This request is made after the verdict has been delivered by the jury and a party contends that the jury misconstrued the evidence and reached a result that is in conflict with the totality of the evidence. If the motion is granted, the judge will substitute his or her own verdict for that of the jury. Judges are also reluctant to grant this motion because it usurps the jury's function, which is to interpret the evidence. If granted the judge may grant it in whole or in part. What this means is that

---

FIGURE 4.14
Sample Motion

Comes now the Defendant, Pauline McPaul, by and through her attorneys, Winter, Somers, and Snow, and moves the Court to enter an order excluding certain evidence that Plaintiff has indicated it intends to submit in the trial of the above-captioned action. In support thereof, the Defendant states as follows:

1. This action involves allegations of personal injury to the Plaintiff as the result of claimed negligence of the Defendant.
2. Through discovery, Defendant has ascertained that Plaintiff intends to submit into evidence certain graphic photographs depicting Plaintiff's injuries.
3. Said photographs are immaterial in that they are not necessary to a fair and informed determination by the jury. Further, said photographs are of a nature that could inflame and prejudice the jury and prohibit the jury from making an objective finding.
4. Other suitable evidence of Plaintiff's injuries exist that would adequately and accurately depict the injuries for the jury's consideration.
5. Attached for the Court's consideration are copies of the aforementioned photographs and the alternative forms of evidence.

WHEREFORE, the Defendant prays that the Court enter an order excluding from evidence the aforementioned photographs and further that the Court order Plaintiff, Plaintiff's attorneys, witnesses, and all others from any direct or indirect reference to said photographs during the proceedings of the above-captioned action.

Respectfully submitted,

Marvin Henry, atty.
Winter, Somers and Snow, P.C.
Suite 260 Park Place
Canoga, State 000000

FIGURE 4.15
Sample Motion

Comes now the Defendant, Pauline McPaul, by and through her attorneys, Winter, Somers, and Snow, and moves the Court to enter a Directed Verdict in favor of Defendant and against Plaintiff. In support thereof, the Defendant states as follows:

1. Plaintiff has concluded the presentation of her case in chief and in doing so has failed to present a prima facie case that would reasonably allow a jury to find in Plaintiff's favor based on a preponderance of the evidence.
2. "Where the plaintiff fails to present any significant evidence in support of the elements of the alleged cause of action, a directed verdict is appropriate." *Walston v. Dunham,* 111 E.W.2d 444 (CS App. 1987).

WHEREFORE, the Defendant prays that the Court will direct the jury in the above-captioned action to enter a verdict in favor of Defendant and against Plaintiff and such other relief as the Court deems necessary and proper.

Respectfully submitted,

Marvin Henry, atty.
Winter, Somers and Snow, P.C.
Suite 260 Park Place
Canoga, State 000000

the judge may grant the motion with respect to the entire verdict or only with respect to certain elements of the verdict such as the amount of damages awarded. For example, the judge may find the jury was correct in a finding of liability of the defendant. However, the judge may find that the jury did not properly consider the amount of damages incurred by the plaintiff and that the jury award was insufficient or even excessive. In this case, the judge may substitute an amount or order a special hearing just on the issue of damages.

Motion for a New Trial. This motion is sought after a verdict is rendered and when a party contends that something occurred during the trial that prevented the legally correct result of the lawsuit. It may be the exclusion of certain evidence, improper testimony or conduct by a witness, improper argument by the attorneys, or even a procedural error by the judge. Anything a party can point to that had a significant impact on the case can provide the basis for the motion, but it must be established that the irregularity was objected to at or about the time it occurred and was not corrected. The party may argue that while the judge did not perceive the irregularity at the time as significant, it can now be shown in some way to have altered the outcome of the case and the only remedy is to set aside the verdict and order a new trial.

C. STAGES OF TRIAL

Procedural rules helped to guide the parties in assembling their evidence and presenting it at trial. Like the pretrial proceedings of discovery and motion practice, the steps in a trial are well established in each jurisdiction and follow a distinct set of rules. In addition to the statutory procedural rules, a particular court and even a specific judge may supplement the rules with additional requirements tailored to the particular court and courtroom. These are known as local rules. The basic stages of trial, however, are essentially the same throughout the federal and state court systems with only a few changes or variations.

1. Voir Dire

The first stage of trial is generally the **voir dire** at which time the members of the jury are selected. If the case is a bench trial, the judge rules on both the law to be applied and its effect on the facts of the case. Bench trials have no jury and therefore the voir dire stage is eliminated. But if the parties seek a jury trial, voir dire is an extremely important phase of the process.

Voir dire generally begins with a fairly large pool of potential jurors. The attorneys/parties—and sometimes the judge—ask each potential juror a number of questions, the goal of which is to determine whether a potential juror has any biases regarding the parties, attorneys, or circumstances of the case. There is very little limitation on the type of questions asked as long as they support the search for biases that would prove relevant. The questions may be quite general and directed to the group, or they may be very specific toward particular individuals. For example, an attorney may ask if any of the jurors have ever been a party in a lawsuit. Anyone in the group who responds positively may be questioned on an individual basis regarding the lawsuit. Many times, the attorneys will question smaller groups of three or four and after each side has completed its questions, the attorneys will offer to accept or reject each of the members of the group as members of the final jury panel that will hear the case.

When a potential juror is rejected, it is known as a challenge. There are two types of challenges in voir dire. These are known as peremptory challenges and challenges for cause. Each party to a lawsuit is allowed a set number of peremptory challenges. The number varies with the jurisdiction. An attorney exercising a peremptory challenge does not have to give a reason to the court for rejecting the potential juror. The right to exercise the peremptory challenge is absolute and cannot be challenged regardless of how much the opposition may want the juror on the panel. The only exception to this is when it can be established that a peremptory challenge is used to exclude a juror on the basis of membership in a federally protected class such as race, religion, nationality, or any other identified and protected group.

Each side is also given the opportunity to challenge for cause. In that situation, an attorney asks that a juror be excused from serving on the basis of a particular prejudice or bias that was clearly evident from the juror's answers to the questions previously asked. In a challenge for cause, the opposition may object to use of the challenge. It is incumbent upon the party exercising the challenge to persuade the judge that the juror could not render an objective opinion in the case and that the impartiality would be so unfair as to endanger a result that was not based on an application of the law to the facts. It is the responsibility of the judge to consider the arguments of both sides, the responses previously made by the juror, and the answers to any questions the judge might ask of the juror. The judge then renders a decision of whether the juror will serve or be excused.

This process of questioning and challenge continues until the number of jurors and alternates required for the particular type of case has been accepted. At this point, voir dire is concluded. The accepted jurors are sworn in and given preliminary instructions by the judge. The excused jurors are permitted to go. Depending on the rules of the jurisdiction they may either be released from jury duty or required to serve on another panel of potential jurors. Traditionally, juries are composed of twelve persons and one or two alternates who serve in the event a juror cannot complete the trial process for some reason. Some states also use petit juries composed of fewer people, such as six jurors. Petit juries are generally used in cases of a less serious nature that nevertheless warrant the right to a trial by a jury of one's peers under state or federal

Voir Dire
Process of selecting jurors for trial of an action.

law. In some states, if loss of liberty is not at stake the case is considered minor and the right to a jury is not granted.

Because the selection of a jury ultimately guides the outcome of a lawsuit, voir dire justifies a great deal of time and attention in addition to thorough and adequate preparation. There are even individuals who do nothing but consult with attorneys on jury selection. In a multi-million dollar lawsuit, the services of an expert in jury selection can be well worth the expense. The questions and considerations given potential jurors include the evaluation of every available aspect of the juror's answers, appearance, general demeanor, and known background. Because many people are reluctant to offer up a great deal of personal information, the ability to ferret out these details is of tremendous importance and value.

2. Opening Statements

Following voir dire and the impaneling of the jury, the trial proceedings begin. In most trials, the first step is the opening statement by the plaintiff's attorney. In the American legal system, the accused in civil as well as criminal cases, is presumed innocent of the actions alleged until there is sufficient proof to the contrary. Thus, the plaintiff has the burden of proof and generally offers their case first. This also extends to the order in which opening statements are given. The defendant's attorney has the option of presenting an opening statement immediately thereafter, or reserving the opening statement until just prior to the presentation of the evidence of the defense.

Opening statements are unlike the rest of the case. A fair amount of lenience is granted to the parties as they attempt to persuade the jury to accept their version of the facts and how the law should be applied. Generally enforced rules of procedure require that the opening statements be nonargumentative. The purpose of the opening statement is simply to acquaint the jury with the facts of the case and the evidence a party expects to be presented. It more or less provides an outline for the jury of what to expect and how the party expects the evidence to develop under the applicable legal standards they must apply. Opening statements are not evidence and their content is not to be considered by a jury in reaching a decision, other than to the extent the actual evidence presented deviates from what the attorney indicated it would be during the opening. If an attorney makes argumentative statements, draws conclusions about what the law or verdict ought to be, or pleads for a particular verdict, the comments are considered improper. If the opposing party objects and that objection is sustained (granted), the comments may be stricken from the record and the jury instructed to disregard them. If the comments are so inflammatory as to be considered having an irreversible effect on the jury, a mistrial may be declared and the entire proceeding ended. In that case, another trial with a new jury may be set (scheduled).

As a practical matter, attorneys will tread as nearly to the line of being argumentative as possible without crossing over. There are only a few opportunities in a trial to communicate directly with a jury and the opening statement is seen by some as the most influential. This is the first time the jury is introduced to any of the facts of the case. Obviously, if those facts can be presented in a fashion that is favorable to the party making the opening statement, a first impression can be made that the opposition must combat in addition to the evidence. Thus, opening statements are often carefully constructed by an attorney and sometimes even rehearsed before actually being delivered to the jury. While the purpose may be to inform the jury, no opportunity can be missed to establish a picture in their mind of how the party wants the jury to perceive the information conveyed.

3. Case in Chief

The case in chief is the stage of a trial during which the party with the **burden of proof** presents evidence to support its claim(s). What constitutes meeting the burden of proof is determined by the standard of proof applied. Different types of cases and different jurisdictions have different standards of proof. The burden of proof is the amount of evidence required to meet the standard and justify a verdict. Typical burdens of proof include preponderance, clear and convincing, and beyond a reasonable doubt.

Burden (Standard) of Proof
Extent of evidence required for plaintiff to prevail in trial of an action.

Evidence by a Preponderance   This is sufficient evidence that a reasonable juror would be more likely than not to support the claim of the party offering the evidence versus the party opposing it.[9]

Clear and Convincing Evidence. This requires that the bulk of the evidence presented weighs obviously in favor of one party to the suit over another.[10]

Evidence Beyond a Reasonable Doubt. In this instance, evidence is so heavily in favor of one party over another that the only reasonable conclusion that can be drawn is for the party whose position the evidence supports.[11]

Most jurisdictions impose a standard of evidence of beyond a reasonable doubt only in criminal cases. The majority of civil cases are subject to the standard of evidence by a preponderance, which is a much lighter burden. Clear and convincing evidence is a standard used in specific types of civil and criminal cases that are usually identified by statute in each jurisdiction.

In addition to providing enough evidence to meet the standard of proof, the burden of proof on a party also includes the requirement that the plaintiffs establish a prima facia case. Literally translated the Latin term prima facia means *on its face*. As discussed earlier in the chapter, each cause of action (recognized legal theory) consists of certain elements or conditions that must be proven in order to recover any damages or other relief for injuries received. Every plaintiff must submit at least some proof facts that demonstrate each element. If they do not, then a prima facie case has not been made and the court would be proper in granting a motion for a directed verdict in favor of a defendant.

APPLICATION 4.5

K brings an action against M for negligence. The standard of proof is a preponderance. At trial, K must produce evidence that demonstrates to the jury how each of the four parts of the definition of negligence occurred in this case. That establishes the prima facie case. Additionally, the evidence K produces must, when compared to the evidence of M in defense, be convincing to the point that the jury would consider K's version of what took place as more likely than not to be the most accurate one.

Point for Discussion: Why is a prima facie case not sufficient to prevail?

Most parties with the burden of proof attempt to establish a much stronger case than one that is marginal with merely enough evidence to pass the test of a prima facie case. The evidence presented must withstand contradictory evidence presented by the defense and still prevail as the most likely explanation of the circumstances that created the dispute. Realistically, simple evidence of a prima facie case is probably not enough to win the suit.

The rules of relevance and materiality that apply to all evidence have already been discussed. In addition to these considerations, other broad rules include those of hearsay and privilege. Hearsay is a rule of evidence that is disputed in nearly every trial. In fact, entire volumes have been written about the hearsay rule and its application. Hearsay is defined as follows:

An out-of-court statement offered to prove the truth of the matter asserted.[12]

Hearsay evidence is testimony by a witness who repeats something that was communicated outside the trial by someone not under oath. Hearsay follows the reasoning that everything said, written, or otherwise communicated in everyday life is not necessarily true. Therefore, such information should usually not be admitted as evidence in a trial where all other evidence is considered to be reliable and true. To be hearsay, the content of the communication must be offered as evidence of the truth. If it is offered only to show the ability to communicate, it would not be considered hearsay.

Because some statements are made under circumstances that are very reliable and promote only truthful communication, there are exceptions to the hearsay rule. Such information, which would otherwise be considered hearsay, is reliable enough in its truthfulness to warrant introduction as evidence in the trial. An example is a statement that is directly contrary to the person's own best interest, such as an admission of guilt. Ordinarily, individuals do not confess to acts for which they are not responsible. If there is evidence that a party or a witness made such a statement, the information may be admitted as an exception to hearsay.

When someone has an experience and makes an immediate statement about it, the statement may be considered an exception to hearsay. Statements made in circumstances where there was not time to formulate the best legal answer are highly reliable. Thus, spontaneous statements may be admitted.

Other exceptions include regularly maintained business records, statements made to physicians during care or treatment, and original documents. While there are many additional exceptions, it is important to remember that evidence of communication made out of court must have a high degree of reliability for truth before it will be admitted as an exception to hearsay.

Another important aspect of evidentiary law involves privilege. As a general rule, the theory of privilege states a person cannot be required to testify about confidential communications, including communications between physician and patient, attorney and client, clergy and parishioner, husband and wife, or any other relationship that the court determines should be protected. The underlying idea is that society encourages certain relationships and, by their nature, development of these relationships hinge on trust. Therefore, the American legal system honors these relationships by generally refusing to compromise the development of that trust with the danger that at some point a court may force its breach. However, with respect to the husband-wife privilege, some exceptions have been made in recent years, especially in the area of criminal law. The overriding analysis is that in a spousal relationship the trust is already developed and this should not be misused in order to protect the other spouse from responsibility for his or her actions. Other exceptions to privilege occur when the same party who claims that information is privileged and thereby inaccessible, has made the very content of the communication an issue in the lawsuit. For example, one claiming physical injuries is not permitted to use the physician-patient privilege to prevent the opposition from examining medical records to assess the true origin, nature, and extent of the injuries.

In addition, there are many rules that apply to various types of evidence, such as information about past criminal conduct of a witness or party, expert opinions on scientific matters, and the personal background of a rape victim. Even when evidence is relevant and material, it may still be objected to on the basis of one of the more specific rules. Assembling and presenting admissible evidence is one of the most crucial elements of trial. Working at any stage of legal proceedings requires a full awareness of the rules. Presentation of evidence within the trial setting requires an ability to argue why the rules of evidence do or do not apply in a specific circumstance.

4. Defense

Once the plaintiff has presented all of the evidence in support of the complaint, the defense is given the opportunity to refute that evidence by presenting their own. If the defense did not make an opening statement at the beginning of the trial, the opportunity to make one at this time is available. The opening statement is followed by the presentation of the defendant's evidence.

In the presentation of evidence, the defendant has no initial burden to meet. Rather, a burden occurs only if the plaintiff establishes a prima facie case. At this point, the burden shifts, and the defendant must present enough evidence in response to the plaintiff's evidence to create a question in the minds of the jury as to whether the plaintiff's version is the most likely version of the facts.

This is also when the defendant must produce evidence of any affirmative defenses that have been alleged. Like the cause of action, an affirmative defense is legally recognized as a theory of law and contains specific elements that must be proven. If the defendant is successful in doing this, the plaintiff's claim and therefore the plaintiff's case is defeated and defendant is not held liable for his or her own damage. In such an occurrence, the defendant could file a motion for directed verdict. However, in most cases the evidence is not this clear. Rather, the jury is required to balance the cause of action and affirmative defense and then to assign degrees of responsibility among the parties.

After the defendant has concluded the presentation of evidence, the plaintiff may request permission to reopen his or her case and submit rebuttal evidence. This may be allowed when the plaintiff has evidence, previously unsubmitted, that is relevant and responds to some or all of the evidence introduced by the defendant. However, it is not permissible to present entirely new evidence that the plaintiff may have forgotten or otherwise failed to include in the original case in chief presentation of evidence. The plaintiff is permitted only to respond to the evidence of the defendant. An example might be a witness who testifies that a defendant's witness is not credible for some reason. The defendant may then be permitted to introduce rebuttal evidence.

5. Closing Argument

After both parties have completed their presentation of evidence, each party attempts to persuade the jury as to what the verdict should be when the evidence is viewed collectively. This closing argument is also commonly referred to as the summation by a party. The order of presentations among parties varies from jurisdiction to jurisdiction and depends on whether more than two parties are involved in the suit. However, typically each party is given a set amount of time to summarize the case and the recommended verdict. Usually, the side going first is also given a brief time to rebut at the end of the opposition's summation. The rebuttal may not revisit or address anything that was not raised in the opposition's summation or it could produce an unfair advantage by allowing summation of the same facts twice by the same party.

During the closing argument, the attorneys employ their advocacy skills perhaps more than at any other time in the practice of law. While attorneys frequently argue motions on specific points, attempt to bring witnesses around to a particular view, and negotiate settlements, the closing argument is different. In a summation, the attorney must address all the significant evidence that has been introduced, both for and against their position. That evidence must be discussed and characterized in such a way that the majority (and in some jurisdiction the totality) of the jurors are convinced that the account given in the summation is the most plausible explanation for the course of events that led to the lawsuit. The strengths of the evidence must be emphasized in a way that persuades the particular individuals on the jury panel. Any weakness must be explained and the jury must be convinced that they would not prevent a decision in favor of the attorney's client. This is the final opportunity for the parties to address the jury and leave them with any impressions of the case before the verdict is deliberated and reached. Closing argument is the only time that the attorneys can openly attempt to sway the jury's opinion and ultimately their verdict.

6. Jury Instructions

After the closing arguments, the judge instructs the jury as to how the deliberation process works. The specific instructions given in a case vary based on the causes of action and the defenses that are pled in a case, the jurisdiction, and the relief sought. The jury instructions explain the law that applies to the case, the burden of proof, and the types of things the jury can consider as evidence in support of its final verdict. As a general rule, each of the parties submits a complete set of the instructions they would like to have read to the jury. Obviously, these instructions are ones that tend to be more favorable to party's position in the way the law is interpreted and defined for the jury. The judge will rule on which instructions from each party are to be read and may also add instructions. The final set is then read to the jury and the deliberation process begins. The jury is sequestered and is not permitted to discuss the case with anyone. Any questions must be submitted to the judge who will decide whether to answer the question, and if so, what the response will be. Depending on the rules of the particular jurisdiction, the jury is required to continue deliberations until they reach a verdict or they become convinced that there is a hopeless deadlock among the jurors as to what the final outcome of the case should be.

7. Verdict and Posttrial Motions

Each jurisdiction determines whether jury verdicts in civil cases must be unanimous or by a majority. If the requirement cannot be met in favor of a verdict for the plaintiff, the jury may reach the verdict that the burden of proof was not established and therefore the defendant is not liable. However, there may be such a division among jurors that neither party receives a verdict. When this happens, the jury is considered deadlocked. This is also commonly known as a hung jury. In this situation, no verdict is returned, and motion for directed verdict or motion for new trial may be granted. In either event, the jury is excused. The parties may be given the opportunity to retry the case with a different jury at another time. When the jury does return with a verdict, the verdict is read to the parties. If a party requests, the judge may poll the jury by asking each individual juror whether the verdict reflects his or her opinion in the case. This is used as a safeguard to assist the court in discovering situations where jurors have been coerced by other members of the jury to change their vote in order to reach a final verdict. If the judge discovers that a juror does not feel their vote was properly considered and that a different vote would produce a different final result in the case, a motion for directed verdict or motion for new trial may be granted.

At the conclusion of the trial, motions for new trial and/or motions for judgment notwithstanding the verdict are made by one or both parties. The motion for a new trial verdict may be made in the case of a hung jury as described earlier, or in a number of other circumstances as well. Essentially, any time a party believes the verdict or amount of damages was improperly affected by something that occurred (and was objected to) during trial, they may attempt to persuade the judge that the verdict should be set aside and a new trial granted with a new jury. For the reasons discussed in the section on motion practice, these are rarely granted.

The motion for judgment notwithstanding the verdict (judgment non obstante verdicto or judgment NOV) is used when the party does not seek a new trial but rather a different judgment. If it can be clearly established that the jury disregarded the manifest weight of the evidence in its totality or misapplied the law, then the judge has the right to substitute a different verdict or amount of damages than what the jury awarded. This situation is most appropriate when it can be shown that the jury functioned improperly as opposed to there being an error in the actual trial process.

D. POSTTRIAL MATTERS

When a case concludes at trial, it may be far from over. The parties have the opportunity for appeals through the appellate level courts of the jurisdiction. Even when there is no appeal, there is still the matter of collection in the event of a judgment for the plaintiff. Defendants do not always willingly and promptly offer up the judgment even when it has been ordered by a court. Some defendants simply ignore the orders. Others may allege that they do not have the resources to satisfy the judgment. The situations of appeal and enforcement require additional time and resources of the legal professionals.

Appellate procedure is largely governed by the appellate system in a jurisdiction. There are specific rules of appellate procedure tailored to the structure of each system, whether it consists of one or more levels of appellate courts, subdivided courts by type of case, or state or federal in its origin. The common thread of appellate courts is that the primary function remains the same. Most often appellate courts review only what has occurred procedurally in the lower courts. Such review may encompass what took place before, during, or after the trial. Most often, appellate courts refuse to hear or consider any new evidence in a case. This does not mean that the court will only hear what was admitted at trial. Rather, it will hear all evidence that was offered, irrespective of whether the trial court admitted or refused the evidence. The appellate court will not hear evidence that was available but not presented for admission to the trial court.[13] Appellate court decisions are usually confined to the issue of whether an error was made in the trial court. Further, the error must be serious enough to warrant intervention by the appellate court. Consequently, an appellate court will not exchange its opinion of right or wrong or guilt or innocence for that of the trier of fact (usually the jury). It will only consider whether the opinion of the trier of fact was based upon a fair presentation of the case according to the requirements of substantive and procedural law.

The appeals process is generally started by a notice to the courts and all other parties from the appealing party (known as the appellant), who claims that something improper has taken place. The party who defends against the appeal and claims that the procedure has been proper is the appellee.

Once the courts and other parties have been given notice, several events must occur. The order and time for these events may vary from jurisdiction to jurisdiction. Generally, the appellant is responsible for having the trial court records of the case prepared and sent to the appellate court. These records enable the appellate court to review the entire history of the case including the alleged error by the trial court. The records consist of all pleadings and motions filed with the court by the parties. Also included will be all court orders in the case and the transcribed statements of the parties, attorneys, witnesses, and the judge during court hearings.

In addition to submitting the court records, the appellant and the appellee may submit appellate briefs—detailed explanations of the case, applicable law, and written arguments—to the reviewing court. In many appellate cases, the courts permit attorneys for the parties to present oral arguments of the briefs. At this stage, each attorney presents the brief and answers questions by the appellate court about the brief's content. The court may ask the attorneys to explain why they think a particular point of law is applicable to the present case. In addition, the attorneys may be given time to argue their brief and respond to points raised in their adversary's brief.

The appellate court considers the case and renders a written opinion. Possible results include that the trial court judgment is affirmed (approved) or reversed. If the judgment is reversed, the appellate court will give instructions as to what further action, if any, should occur in the lower court. This could be something as significant as a new trial.

In some situations, the court will enter an order during the pretrial phase that is considered immediately appealable. These appeals are commonly referred to as interlocutory. This type of appeal is only allowed when the lower court order is such that, if followed, it will likely change the entire outcome of the suit. When this occurs the party can file an interlocutory appeal in which the appellate court confines its review only to the single issue of the court order. The case then returns to the lower court and proceeds in a manner consistent with the appellate court decision on the issue and any specific instructions.

If a party does not comply with the final order in a case, then the opposing party may seek enforcement. This may include contempt proceedings in which the defendant is required to justify why there should not be a finding of contempt for the court order and consequent punishment. Also, the plaintiff may seek information about all of the defendant's assets and ask that some or all be applied to payment of the judgment. There can be a proceeding for garnishment of bank accounts, present and future wages, and even inheritances. Often, collecting a judgment is an exercise of diligence on the part of the plaintiff. But the law recognizes the plaintiff's right to recover an award and, in response, has developed a number of procedures to assist the plaintiff.

Although great attention has been given by the legal system to appropriate procedures for litigation of claims, the reality is that the vast majority of claims are settled without trial. The settlement of a claim between parties can be reached at any point in a legal proceeding. Parties can agree to settle before the action has been filed, or they may agree to settle during appeal and thus eliminate the expense associated with an appeal. All that is necessary is for the parties to come to a meeting of the minds. This may include monetary settlements or agreements by each party to drop claims/defenses against the other. If the action has been formally initiated, a court order is required to end it when a settlement is reached. In some instances, the court may require that the settlement be approved first. Such an occurrence is frequent when the case involves a minor or a person who has been adjudicated as legally incompetent.

Another method in which parties may avoid the traditional trial process is through arbitration and mediation. In this case, the parties agree to have an objective and independent party review all the information in the case and mediate (act as a facilitator) for each side as they attempt to resolve the issues and settle the matter. Another option is for the parties to agree on a third party to arbitrate (rule) on the matter. In either case, the expense and delay of a trial is avoided, but the parties also give up important rights such as right to a jury and appeal. However, the expense of litigation in recent years including attorney's fees, expert witness, court reporters, collection of evidence, and so forth, has become so great and the delays in the courts so long that more and more parties are moving toward mediation and arbitration as a means to resolve their disputes.

It is now fairly common for complex contracts to include an agreement by the parties to mediation or arbitration in the event of a conflict over contract performance or terms. This greatly shortens the time and expense for both sides in resolving issues that arise. Arbitration and mediation are used in virtually all types of civil cases to some extent. As the number of lawsuits continues to grow, arbitration and mediation are valuable methods of alternative dispute resolution.

PARALEGALS IN THE WORKPLACE

The paralegal is used heavily in the field of litigation. Much of the work previously done by the attorney can be performed by a qualified paralegal under attorney supervision. A litigation paralegal may be expected to interview clients and witness, collect and organize evidence, draft pleadings and documents, and in some instances conduct legal research. While all of this does not constitute the practice of law per se, the use of this information and these materials in a case would likely be considered part of advocacy and therefore attorney supervision would be important. Also, a competent attorney would supervise the work that he or she is going to incorporate into the process of representing clients. Even so, attorneys have discovered the tremendous advantage and efficiency of performing their own duties and simultaneously supervising others' work as opposed to doing all of it themselves. Consequently, litigation has become a very lucrative field for qualified paralegals.

In addition to litigations support, a license to practice law is usually not necessary to act as an independent arbitrator or mediator. This is an area of real potential for the qualified paralegal. Usually a course of study in arbitration/mediation and subsequent credentialing requirements can prepare a paralegal for a variety of employment opportunities either independently or as part of an organization.

CHAPTER SUMMARY

The various types of procedural law address the various stages of litigation. Rules of civil procedure often deal with the pretrial phase of a lawsuit, including the important stage of discovery. Rules of evidence give the court and the parties direction as to what types of information would be appropriate for a jury to reach a fair and intelligent verdict. Rules of appellate procedure guide the party through the appellate process to have a case properly reviewed by a higher court.

In any lawsuit, once the procedural concerns have been dealt with, the court is free to address the heart of the issue between the parties in dispute. The substantive law guides the judiciary in doing so. The facts are examined, the true issue is identified, and the law is applied to the circumstances to make the determination of which party should prevail. In fact, if more persons would look to these legal standards before taking action, the results would be apparent, and a great number of legal disputes could be avoided. But as long as people fail to inquire as to the law or disagree as to its meaning, disputes will continue and procedural law will facilitate the application of substantive law in the determination of these disputes.

As a case proceeds through the steps of trial, a jury is selected through a process called voir dire. Next, the attorneys make opening statements, which describe the evidence they intend to present. The plaintiff presents evidence first in a stage known as the case in chief. The defendant responds with evidence that weakens or contradicts the case of the plaintiff. After all the evidence has been introduced, the attorneys summarize the case and present it in a light most favorable to their clients. Following this, the jury is instructed on the law and deliberates until it reaches a verdict.

Throughout the litigation process, the attorneys communicate requests to the court in the form of motions. These formal requests seek everything from information about the evidence of the opposing party to a dismissal of the case in their favor or even a new trial. The process of motion practice provides an efficient and effective method of resolving issues that arise during litigation and cannot be resolved by the parties. In recent years mediation and arbitration of cases have developed as alternatives to traditional litigation, as the expense of time and money connected to litigation have soared.

ETHICAL NOTE

Although it may receive little direct attention in terms of ethics during general discussion, the trial process is one in which the adherence to ethical standards is paramount. If a member of the legal team acts in a manner that would be considered in violation of rules of ethics the consequences may be severe. If, for example, it is discovered in a civil case that a witness was coached in what to say, that an opposing party was contacted personally without notice to his or her counsel, that documents were altered, or that any other impropriety took place, a court has the discretion to affect the outcome of the case and pursue disciplinary action against the attorney responsible for the conduct or for supervision of the party who committed the conduct. The core of the judicial system is predicated on fairness and consistency whenever possible in the application of the law. The ethical standards imposed on members of the legal team support this as well and are inherent in the success of the judicial system. It is a common statement by attorneys when speaking to clients who complain about the system that it is not the system that is flawed, but rather those few who would attempt to manipulate it.

Relevant Internet Sites

Findlaw for Legal Professionals	www.lawcrawler.com
Findlaw:Case Law: U.S. Circuit Court Directories	www.findlaw.com/casecode/dir/cofa.html

---

Internet Assignment

Locate the Internet site for local, state, and federal courts. Specifically determine what information you can obtain about pending cases via the Internet.

KEY TERMS

Affirmative defenses	In Rem Jurisdiction	Quasi in Rem
Ancillary Jurisdiction	Jurisdiction	Relevant
Burden (Standard) of Proof	Jurisdiction in Personam	Remand
Concurrent Jurisdiction	Material	Removal
Constructive Knowledge	Motion	Subject Matter Jurisdiction
Diversity of Citizenship	Original Jurisdiction	Venue
Domicile	Pendent Jurisdiction	Voir Dire
Exhaustion of Remedies	Personal (In Personam)	
Federal Question	Jurisdiction	

ENDNOTES

1. *Lowry v. Semke*, 571 P.2d 858 (Colo. 1977).
2. Federal Rules of Civil Procedure, 28 U.S.C.
3. 28 U.S.C. 1441.
4. Federal Rules of Civil Procedure, Rule 1.
5. Federal Rules of Evidence, 28 U.S.C.
6. Id.
7. *Stastny v. Tachovsky*, 178 Neb. 109, 132 N.W. 2d 317 (1964).
8. Federal Rules of Civil Procedure, Rule 56.
9. Federal Rules of Evidence, 28 U.S.C.A.
10. Id.
11. *In re Edinger's Estate*, 136 N.W.2d 114 (N.D. 1965).
12. Federal Rules of Evidence.
13. Id.

Chapter 5

THE DEVELOPMENT AND ROLE OF TODAY'S PARALEGAL

CHAPTER OBJECTIVES

Upon completion of this chapter you should be able to:

- Explain the role of the paralegal.

- Discuss how the legal profession developed to include the paralegal.

- Explain what factors influenced the increased demand for legal services.

- Explain the types of duties paralegals may perform.

- Distinguish the practice of law from the work done by paralegals.

- Discuss the ways in which paralegals are trained/educated.

- List the types of employment in which paralegals are commonly found.

- Discuss the methods available to evaluate paralegal skills and conduct.

- Explain why paralegals are responsible for the same ethical standards as attorneys.

- Identify several paralegal-affiliated organizations and their functions.

A. HOW THE PROFESSION OF PARALEGAL DEVELOPED IN THE UNITED STATES

"A legal assistant or paralegal is a person, qualified by education, training or work experience or retained by a lawyer, law office, corporation, governmental agency, or other entity and who performs specifically delegated substantive legal work for which a lawyer is responsible"[1]

1. The Evolution of a New Profession

Paralegal
One who has legal training and education and performs tasks in the law office traditionally performed by the attorney, with the exception of advocacy and giving of legal advice.

The term **paralegal** or legal assistant is now firmly entrenched in the vocabulary of the legal profession. Similarly, the general public seems to have a basic awareness of the existence of paralegals. However, as recently as the early 1980s, the profession was still largely unknown to the public and their role and function in today's American legal system was often misunderstood. Today, while great strides have been made, it is still common to find paralegals whose skills are underutilized. However, as understanding increases along with demand for competent legal services at a reasonable cost, this should improve. In this chapter, the advent of the profession and its progression to date will be explored as well as the direction in which the profession seems to be moving.

The legal profession has existed for thousands of years. Even ancient Roman history makes reference to lawyers. It is probably safe to say that as long as there have been laws, there have been lawyers to present interpretations of the meaning and proper application of those laws. For centuries, there was relatively little change in the profession of lawyers. Each government had judges in one form or another to state affirmatively how laws were to be applied or enforced. The lawyers were advisors and advocates on these laws, giving explanation and opinion as to the proper use of laws. They represented the interests of those who could not as effectively represent themselves before judges and provided counsel to the law-making authorities. The lawyers were an integral and necessary part of the legal system of virtually every form of civilization. This includes the American legal system from its inception.

For nearly 200 years, the legal profession operated within the American legal system in much the same fashion as it had for centuries in Great Britain and Europe. Lawyers represented the rights of individuals before various tribunals and gave the individuals advice regarding the applicability of laws to specific situations. In fact, this is still the fundamental function of lawyers in the American legal system. However, like many other careers, the legal profession as a whole underwent dramatic changes in the 20th century which, for the first time, rendered it in need of significant adaptations.

Beginning in the late 19th century, automation and communication technology were used and/or planned for widespread use. We saw the first controlled electricity, assembly lines, motorized transportation, and telephone systems. As these developments progressed, there was a ripple effect throughout all facets of American culture. By the 1950s the American business world was hardly recognizable from a mere 50 years prior. Mail was processed more quickly with new machinery and rapid delivery of important documents and correspondence became an easy task. Business equipment such as typewriters, copy machines, and adding machines, operated with unprecedented accuracy and speed. Multiline telephone systems allowed several individuals in one office to communicate with several people in other offices simultaneously.

Dictaphones and transcription equipment cut in half the time necessary to dictate and prepare correspondence. In an isolated context, all of these features should in fact have increased the overall efficiency of business, including the legal profession. However, there was an unexpected series of events that taxed this modern system and demanded even more technological development for the legal profession, American business, and the world as a whole.

Various changes in American culture during the 20th century, specifically after 1929, caused a domino effect that kept a steady and astounding pressure on technological development for the remainder of the century and beyond. During the economic depression of the 1930s, the nation was forced to restructure business, banking, employment, and commercial activities. Throughout the 1930s, as the country attempted to recover, the workforce was largely reorganized into areas of mass employment. This was facilitated by the technological development of the business of manufacturing. As more people went to work in large scale businesses, many moved away from the more isolated and traditional "mom and pop" operations and farming. Simultaneous with the increase of people in the industrial workforce was the almost explosive dramatic development of the transportation industry. New and improved engines increased the speed, availability, and efficiency of rail and river carriers; the new federal interstate system enabled over-the-road trucking on a wide scale; the advent of air transportation totally changed the speed of movement of goods and widened the scope of potential customers for businesses all over the United States and the world. But, this was only the beginning.

On the heels of the depression came World War II. A whole new element entered the workforce in mass. As young healthy men went to war, they were replaced in the factories with women, who had almost exclusively worked in the home for centuries. The demand for military supplies and equipment on an immediate basis taxed the existing system and required constant development and innovation. Throughout the second World War, those left behind developed American business and technology and gained a new sense of their ability to contribute their talents outside the home. At the end of the war, many women were no longer willing to return to the home as their only source of productivity. The country was optimistic and businesses flourished. The workforce nearly doubled, yet there was no shortage of jobs to speak of. And then came the inevitable, the baby boom.

While every war is followed by an increase in population, World War II set new precedent. The population grew dramatically over the five-to-ten years following the war. This increased the demand for services, goods, transportation, and all aspects of society. The increase in population, development of technology, and large-scale business growth placed tremendous demands on the legal profession in virtually every area of law. This brought about some of the following changes in demand for services in various fields of law:

- People were buying homes—property law
- People were traveling, interacting, and broadening their scope both professionally and personally on an unprecedented scale—tort law, contract, business, and commercial law
- Traditional family roles were changing—domestic relations law
- Families increased and aged increasing the need for estate planning—probate and estate law
- New technology and population growth brought an increase in criminal conduct —criminal law and procedure

All of these developments in such a short time required more legal expertise than the profession had to give. An additional factor was the need for efficiency and the ability to offer legal services at a cost the general population could afford. By the 1960s it was dramatically evident that a better way to deliver the services of the legal profession had to be found.

The legal system was not isolated in the onslaught of demand for personal services at a reasonable cost. All service industries were similarly affected and all responded in various ways. Because of certain common issues, the legal profession followed the same path as the health care industry of physicians, dentists, hospitals, and so forth. The creation of the role of a paraprofessional seemed to be the perfect answer. Paraprofessionals were not intended to be as extensively trained, but they could deliver a number of the less involved services that were previously the responsibility of licensed professionals. Appropriate supervision of the paraprofessional could be used to ensure the quality of service and contain the scope of the service to appropriate levels.

Attorney
Individual who has completed the necessary requirements of education and training to apply for a license to practice law in a jurisdiction.

For the **attorney,** this paraprofessional role came about in an almost incidental way. There was no great awakening of lawyers, no drive by universities or bar associations. Rather, the role of paralegal was a natural evolution that became more focused and accelerated by the demands on the legal profession. For many years, probably hundreds, the legal secretary had performed nonclerical roles to some extent. When clients called or came in and the attorney was not available, it was the legal secretary who answered basic questions about scheduled hearings, status of documents filed with the courts, and so on. While it was never permissible for the legal secretary to give legal advice or advocate the clients' interests with third parties, the rules of conduct were much cloudier for other tasks that were formerly the exclusive domain of the lawyer. As the demand for legal services grew, the need for assistance in routine but time-consuming tasks grew as well. This included such things as interviewing clients and witnesses, preparing documents, gathering information, organizing collected evidence, and even carrying out basic research assignments. As the demands grew, secretaries who had the confidence of their attorney employers were delegated tasks in addition to the basic clerical role of their employment. This had already been in place to some extent, however it became a more formal arrangement for many attorneys in the 1960s. As many legal secretaries began to demonstrate an aptitude for this type of work, attorneys similarly identified the potential value. Additionally, while an attorney could not legally charge for legal services performed by a clerical person, it was conceivable that such services performed by a trained paraprofessional were billable at a rate commensurate with the level of training.

As the use of legal paraprofessionals spread, a number of developments began to occur. The dramatic increase in firms and businesses who employed paralegals demonstrated a broad concensus that there was a valuable role to be served by them within the legal system. The value was both monetary and as a support to the profession of attorneys. In terms of serving the public, the concept was very popular. The paralegal made the services of the legal profession more accessible and the cost more reasonable. In the relatively short time of approximately thirty years, an entirely new profession developed that came to be widely known as paralegal or legal assistant. Today, the U.S. Bureau of Labor Statistics recognizes paralegal as one of the fastest growing professions with expected growth of 68% between 1998 and 2006. It is predicted that by 2006 there will be in excess of 150,000 paralegal positions in the United States.

> a. Explain why producing more attorneys would not be as suitable a choice as producing a new level of paraprofessional.
> b. Identify four other professions in which paraprofessionals are used to assist licensed professionals.

2. The Development of Accepted Standards of Competence

While attorneys embraced the concept of paralegal, the problem of adequate training and validation of skills continued. As a rule, attorneys had little time to spend on quality training of their legal assistants. Most often, the paralegal learned how to perform certain tasks from watching or mimicking the work of the attorney. But, this did not provide the paralegal with the necessary understanding of why certain tasks were performed as they were. Consequently, the paralegal often did not have the knowledge base that enabled him or her to adapt to various situations that arose. Also, because the practice of law is heavily influenced by the personal style of an attorney, the range and extent of training for paralegals was vast. There was no measuring stick, so to speak, of the basic skills that a qualified paralegal should possess. When a paralegal left one job and applied for others, the skills may or may not have been present to perform effectively as a paralegal with another firm. This problem made things difficult for both the paralegals and the attorneys, and it exposed the need for more formal methods of education as well as a means to police this new profession.

By the 1970s a number of programs were appearing around the United States with the specific objective of providing training for paralegals. Within 10 years there were accredited academic degree programs throughout the United States. Today, there are a number of alternatives to train paralegals. The original method of on-the-job training is certainly used to train paralegals in many communities. However the trend has been to rely on more formal methods. These include a variety of formats. There are intensive courses of study in which one studies for a set period of time in an accelerated program and completes a certificate of training. Typically, these courses of study are confined exclusively to the area of paralegal training and do not offer other support areas such as English or math. Therefore, the paralegal should have adequate skills in these areas before undertaking such a program. There are also many associate and baccalaureate degrees, post-baccalaureate certificates, and even master's degrees available at colleges and universities throughout the United States that focus on paralegal and law office administration. These programs are geared toward a more comprehensive college education with focus in paralegal and related skills. In the United States, hundreds of training and education programs for paralegals are in place. It is also not uncommon to find individuals who have trained in other fields, or even former lawyers, serving in the role of the paralegal. The type and extent of training one pursues depends in large part on the background of the paralegal, the kind of legal support the paralegal wishes to provide in the workplace, and the setting in which the paralegal seeks employment. Paralegals are employed in many areas beyond the traditional law firm as will be discussed in subsequent sections.

While the methods and extent of paralegal training and education vary widely, some standards have been established to assist attorneys, paralegals, and the public in developing reasonable expectations of what job skills the qualified paralegal should possess. In reality, a number of factors influenced the need for an established set of standards and, while the standards and tools of measurement are still evolving, there are now widely accepted criteria for a qualified paralegal. There is still no standardized method of validation of skills that is accepted universally and, without such standards, virtually anyone can call him or herself a paralegal. Thus, the responsibility is on the one who hires a paralegal to fully investigate the true nature and level of his or her skill. The strategies employed to establish competence vary as widely as the methods of training, from attempts for uniform standards of competence all the way to legal liability for damage caused by malfeasance. It should be noted that many jurisdictions do provide some sort of definition of the term either in statute or court rules or even through caselaw. However, this varies by state and in some instances is considered on a case-by-case basis.

One natural method of regulation is the extension of the rules used to protect the public from incompetence and/or malfeasance by attorneys. This is commonly known as tort liability. The subject of tort law will be expanded upon in much greater detail in a later chapter. However, it is important to understand at this juncture that the law provides a remedy for those injured in some way by the unacceptable acts or omissions by their attorney. Rules of ethics, standards for licensure as an attorney, and well-established legal principles handed down by the courts all present a very clear picture of what is expected of attorneys with regard to level of skill in the various areas of law and in meeting the duty to serve their clients.

When an attorney accepts an individual as a client, an obligation is created to represent that client within the requirements of accepted legal standards of conduct and competence. If the attorney fails to meet any of those standards, a violation of the duty toward the client occurs. If that violation is the primary cause of injury to the client, then the attorney may be held liable for the value associated with the injury. In the event a subordinate of the attorney, such as a paralegal, is actually responsible for the violation, as the employer, the attorney may still be held accountable under the theory that he or she did not properly supervise the work of the employee.[2] For example, an attorney has an obligation to keep information provided by a client confidential. This responsibility extends to those employed by the attorney as well. The employee may also be held personally liable for any damage caused. This is true of a paralegal working under the direction of an attorney. If a paralegal is independently employed or employed on a per job basis by an attorney, such as one employed on a freelance basis, the liability could be directly assigned to the paralegal. In either situation, realistically speaking, the ultimate responsibility for performing work in a competent manner ends with the paralegal. Even if liability is assigned to the supervising attorney, the future career for a paralegal is not too promising if he or she is the ultimate cause of that liability. While the theory is that the attorney is to supervise, the reality is that even the most conscientious attorney cannot be omnipotent with regard to everything a paralegal does and says. There has to be an earned degree of trust between the attorney and the paralegal. That trust must include the paralegal's skills as well as the paralegal's knowledge of the limits between assisting an attorney and the actual practice of law.[3]

Generally speaking, the paralegal cannot give legal advice or advocate the legal rights of a client with respect to third parties. These two tasks require a licensed attorney. This is important because legal advice and advocacy can cause a client or third party to act or not act in a way that directly impacts the rights of the client. Therefore, only a licensed attorney, that is, one who has demonstrated comprehensive proficiency at understanding the law and its applicability to given situations, may perform these duties. There is an exception to this rule in that some regulatory agencies permit nonattorneys to represent individuals in agency matters. However, this is very limited in scope and in the number of agencies that permit it. In the event a paralegal, or anyone else, undertakes to engage in the practice of law, such as by advocating the rights of another or giving legal advice, then two possibilities arise. First, the individual may be prosecuted by the government for practicing law without a license. Second, the individual may be sued for any damage caused by the attempted practice of law. In most jurisdictions, the requirement is that the individual must have acted as a competent attorney would have under the same circumstances. The failure to do so would then result in civil liability. In essence, if one performs the practice of law, he or she is held accountable to possess and exercise the skills of a licensed attorney. Because the line drawn between professional services and those that constitute the **unauthorized practice of law** is not always clearly discernible, it is advisable to use great caution when approaching it.

Unauthorized Practice of Law
One who provides advocacy to third parties or gives legal advice or representation to others without proper jurisdictional licensure/certification.

Case in Point

Ore. State Bar Assn v. Smith, et. al.,
149 Or. App. 171, 942 P. 2d 793 (1999).

Defendants, People's Paralegal Service, Inc., and its president, Robin Smith, appeal from a judgment declaring them to have engaged in activities that constitute the unauthorized practice of law, ORS 9.160, and enjoining them from those activities. ORS 9.166. They argue that the injunction violated rights of free expression under the Oregon Constitution, Article I, section 8, and due process under the First and Fourteenth Amendments to the United States Constitution. We affirm.

From 1987 until 1995, when the injunction issued, defendants operated a business providing "legal technician" services for a fee. The services included providing consumers with various legal forms available to the public through such sources as Stevens Ness Publishing Company, NOLO PRESS, bankruptcy courts, and the Oregon State Bar, and advising them with respect to their individual legal concerns. Defendants never attempted to represent consumers in court, nor did they sign any documents as attorneys. Moreover, People's Paralegal posted signs at its place of business advising consumers that its employees were not attorneys, and its intake sheets, which were signed by the consumers, included the following statement:

"WE ARE NOT ATTORNEYS. WE ARE LEGAL TECHNICIANS. OUR SERVICE PROVIDES PREPARATION OF THE PAPERS INCLUDING TYPING, NOTARY SERVICE, AND PROCEDURAL INFORMATION. * * * IF YOU REQUIRE LEGAL ADVICE PLEASE SEE AN ATTORNEY."

Nevertheless, defendants did provide legal advice to consumers, and some of those persons relied on defendants' advice in resolving their legal problems.

Plaintiff Oregon State Bar brought this action in April 1995, alleging that defendants were engaged in the unlawful practice of law under ORS 9.160 and seeking injunctive relief under ORS 9.166. Defendants answered and asserted, inter alia, affirmative defenses that ORS 9.160, either facially or as applied, violated rights of free expression under Article I, section 8, of the Oregon Constitution and also violated constitutional due process guarantees. The trial court disagreed and granted the injunction, which provided, in part:

[Defendants] . . . are . . . enjoined from practicing law including:

"1. Enjoined from any personal contact with any persons in the nature of consultation, explanation, recommendation, or advice regarding their legal matters.

"2. Enjoined from meeting with any persons to discuss their individual facts and circumstances relating to their need or desire for legal forms, legal services or legal assistance.

"3. Enjoined from obtaining information orally, in writing, or in any other manner relating to individual facts and circumstances so as to assist any persons with their legal matters.

"4. Enjoined from advising any persons regarding their eligibility for or advisability of legal remedies to address any person's particular legal matters.

"5. Enjoined from advising any persons regarding procedural functions of the court system as it relates to any person's particular legal matters including advice regarding jurisdiction or venue.

"6. Enjoined from assisting in selecting particular forms, documents or pleadings for any persons to address their legal matters.

"7. Enjoined from assisting in any way with the preparation or filling out of legal forms, or any parts of such forms, documents or pleadings for any persons.

"8. Enjoined from assisting, suggesting or advising any persons how forms, documents or pleadings should be used to address or to solve particular legal problems.

"9. Nothing included in this Judgment and Decree precludes Defendant Smith from working for someone authorized to practice law so long as she is acting within the course of her duties and under the direction and supervision of an individual authorized to practice law."

On appeal, defendants renew and reiterate their constitutional challenges to ORS 9.160, both on its face and as applied. We begin with defendants' free expression arguments under Article I, section 8. Article I, section 8, provides:

"No law shall be passed restraining the free expression of opinion, or restricting the right to speak, write, or print freely on any subject whatever; but every person shall be responsible for the abuse of this right."

Defendants' principal argument is that, because the practice of law necessarily involves the "exchange of legal information," ORS 9.160 impermissibly prohibits, or impairs, constitutionally protected expression. Plaintiff responds that the statute does not explicitly refer to expression or to the content of expression. Rather, plaintiff argues, the statute is merely directed to regulating the practice of a profession, which, like many other professions, involves expression. Thus, plaintiff reasons, ORS 9.160 does not embody an impermissibly "content-driven" restriction of expression. Before addressing those arguments, it is useful—indeed, essential—to briefly review the history of the regulation of law practice in Oregon.

The only pre-statehood regulation of law practice we have located is a rule that the Supreme Court of the Oregon Territory published in 1852, which addressed practice in that court:

"1. Attorneys and counsellors at law, and solicitors in chancery, of the several District Courts of this territory, shall on notice in open court, be admitted to practice in the Supreme Court; but all the preliminary steps necessary to bring a cause to this court, and prepare the same for trial, may be taken by any attorney, solicitor or counsellor of any of the District Courts." Rules Adopted at the Supreme Court of Oregon Territory (December Term 1952).

In 1862, Oregon enacted legislation that provided that "no person shall be allowed to participate as an attorney or appear as counsel in any court of justice" unless admitted to practice by the State Supreme Court. At the same time, the legislature enacted a statutory definition of "attorney":

In 1919, the legislature enacted Oregon's first statute addressing the unlawful practice of law:

"It shall be unlawful for any person, firm, association of persons or corporation to engage in the practice of law within the state of Oregon after the taking effect of this act, without first having been duly admitted and licensed as an attorney at law in the courts of this state." Oregon Laws 1920, ch. V, § 1093-1, p. 949 (Spec.Sess.).

The legislature concomitantly enacted a definition of the "practice of law":

"Any person, firm, association of persons or corporation shall be regarded as engaging in the practice of law within the meaning of this act who shall undertake to represent or who shall represent parties litigant in courts of justice other than courts of justices of the peace, or district courts, or who shall, for a fee, prepare or undertake to prepare pleadings or other papers incident to actions, suits or special proceedings, or manage or undertake to manage such actions, suits or proceedings on behalf of clients before judges or courts, or in any manner act professionally in legal formalities, negotiations or proceedings, by warrant or authority of clients or otherwise [.]" Oregon Laws 1920, ch. V, § 1093-2, p. 949 (Spec.Sess.).

That definition encompassed litigation practice, which was the focus of earlier definitions of "attorney," as well as broader matters of client representation, i.e., "act[ing] professionally in legal formalities, negotiations or proceedings by warrant or authority of clients or otherwise[.]" However, it did not refer to, much less purport to regulate, the rendition of general, nonlitigation-related advice.

In 1937, the legislature deleted the definition of the "practice of law" from the unlawful practice statutes. Or. Laws 1937, ch. 343, § 2. Thereafter, the law simply provided:

"Reserving to litigants the rights . . . to prosecute or defend a cause in person, it shall be unlawful for any person to practice law or to represent himself as qualified to practice law after the taking effect of this act, unless he shall be an active member of the Oregon state bar. . . . Any person who is an active member of the Oregon state bar, . . . or who hereafter shall become such active member, hereby is authorized to engage in the practice of law." Or.Laws 1937, ch. 343, § 1.

That open-ended—and, arguably, amorphous—approach was characteristic of contemporaneous unauthorized practice statutes enacted in other jurisdictions. See The Unauthorized Practice of Law at 192. In Oregon, as in many other jurisdictions, the particularized definition of the "practice of law" was committed to case-by-case development by the courts.

The first Oregon decision to address that question was State ex rel. Oregon State Bar v. Johnston, 158 Or. 52, 74 P.2d 395 (1937). In Johnston, a disbarred attorney was fined for continuing to practice law. The court noted that the defendant "continued to occupy an office in the city of Portland, on the door of which appeared a sign reading, 'Harold W. Johnston, Attorney at Law'; . . . accepted employment from one Frances Peecher to secure a divorce for her; prepared a complaint for her to sign; and procured another attorney to sign the complaint as attorney for plaintiff." Id. at 53, 74 P.2d 395.

The defendant had also effected a compromise with a client's creditors. The court concluded: "It may be doubted whether effecting a compromise with creditors constitutes practicing law. The other transaction, however, did constitute practicing law[.]" Id. at 54, 74 P.2d 395. Thus, although the "practice of law" circa 1937 clearly included appearing in court and drafting court documents, it was unsettled whether that concept encompassed engaging an out-of-court negotiations on a "client's" behalf or other nonlitigation-based advice and activity.

Some of that uncertainty was dispelled in State Bar v. Security Escrows, Inc., 233 Or. 80, 377 P.2d 334 (1962). There, an escrow company appealed from a judgment enjoining it, pursuant to ORS 9.166, from drafting a range of documents, including contracts, deeds, mortgages, satisfactions, leases, and options. In reviewing the injunction, the court identified the essence of the "practice of law," as being the informed application of legal principles to address a particular person's individual circumstances and needs:

"Turning . . . to the specific matter of documents vesting property rights, the exercise of discretion concerning property rights of another should be entrusted only to those learned in the law. There are, of course, matters in which persons who are not trained in the law can give perfectly sound business advice. However, when laymen select and prepare instruments creating rights in land for other members of the public there is always the danger that they may do the job badly. In the exceptional case the routine procedure may be grossly wrong. . . . We are justified in taking judicial notice of the fact that badly drawn instruments create not only needless litigation but needless loss and liability. A little of this mischief may flow from the carelessness of lawyers, but by far the most of it is the work product of laymen. In either case the injured party may have a cause of action for damages, but it is in the public interest to keep these difficulties to a minimum."

* * * * *

"For the purposes of this case, we hold that the practice of law includes the drafting or selection of documents and the giving of advice in regard thereto any time an informed or trained discretion must be exercised in the selection or drafting of a document to meet the needs of the persons being served. The knowledge of the customer's needs obviously cannot be had by one who has no knowledge of the relevant law. One must know what questions to ask.

Accordingly, any exercise of an intelligent choice, or an informed discretion in advising another of his legal rights and duties, will bring the activity within the practice of the profession." Id. at 87, 89, 377 P.2d 334 (some emphasis supplied).

Applying that analysis, the court sustained the injunction to the extent that it restrained the defendants' selection and preparation of documents where that conduct required "an intelligent choice between alternative methods," 233 Or. at 91, 377 P.2d 334, but concluded that the injunction was overbroad to the extent that it barred the defendants from acting as "mere scriveners" who did nothing more than fill in documents at their customers' direction. Id. at 91–92, 377 P.2d 334.

In State Bar v. Miller & Co., 235 Or. 341, 385 P.2d 181 (1963), the court affirmed an injunction against a nonlawyer who, as part of his insurance business, provided advice on estate planning. The court held that, when a client receives advice from a nonlawyer and the advice "involves the application of legal principles[,] [t]his constitutes the practice of law." Id. at 344, 385 P.2d 181. The court further explained:

"It must be conceded that frequently advice given in the course of carrying on a business is shaped by a knowledge of the applicable law. But the giving of such advice is not in every instance regarded as the practice of law. The legal ingredient in the advice may be so insubstantial as to call for the application of the principle of de minimis non curat lex. This is not to say that we adopt the view permitting the practice of law where the legal element is merely incidental to the business activity being carried on. To fall outside the proscription of the statute the legal element must not only be incidental, it must be insubstantial. It cannot be said that one who plans another person's estate employs the law only in an insubstantial way." Id. at 344–45, 385 P.2d 181 (footnote omitted).

The final, and most recent, pertinent "unauthorized practice" decision is Oregon State Bar v. Gilchrist, 272 Or. 552, 538 P.2d 913 (1975). There, the court held that the advertising and sale of generic, noncustomized do-it-yourself divorce kits did not, without more, constitute the practice of law:

"We find persuasive the holding in New York County Lawyers' Association v. Dacey, 28 A.D.2d 161, 283 N.Y.S.2d 984, [rev. 21 N.Y.2d 694, 287 N.Y.S.2d 422, 234 N.E.2d 459 (1967)]. There it was held that the publication, distribution and selling of Norman F. Dacey's book 'How to Avoid Probate' did not constitute the practice of law since the publication was directed to the general public and not to a specific individual. The dissenting opinion in the Appellate Division, which was adopted by the Court of Appeals, stated in pertinent part:

'. . . It cannot be claimed that the publication of a legal text which purports to say what the law is amounts to legal practice. And the mere fact that the principles or rules stated in the text may be accepted by a particular reader as a solution to his problem, does not affect this. . . . " 'Dacey's book is sold to the public at large. There is no personal contact or relationship with a particular individual. Nor does there exist that relation of confidence and trust so necessary to the status of attorney and client. This is the essential of legal practice—the representation and the advising of a particular person in a particular situation.' "

* * * * *

"We conclude that in the advertising and selling of their divorce kits the defendants are not engaged in the practice of law and may not be enjoined from engaging in that part of their business." 272 Or. at 558–59, 563, 538 P.2d 913 (emphasis supplied).

Thus, the mere general dissemination of legal information by nonlawyers does not constitute the unauthorized practice of law. The court proceeded, however, to conclude that other, more personalized contact and advice was properly enjoined:

"[A]ll personal contact between defendants and their customers in the nature of consultation, explanation, recommendation or advice or other assistance in selecting particular forms, in filling out any part of the forms, or suggesting or advising how the forms should be used in solving the particular customer's marital problems does constitute the practice of law and must be and is strictly enjoined." Id. at 563–64, 538 P.2d 913.

There have been no notable post-Gilchrist decisions amplifying or refining the meaning of "practice of law."

"The reason for the statutes relating to all of these professions and occupations is to protect the public from the consequences resulting from attempts to engage in such professions and occupations by persons who are not properly trained and qualified to do so." Id. at 697–98, 573 P.2d 283 (footnote omitted).

We cannot, and will not, purport to derive an omnibus definition of "practice of law" from Johnston, Security Escrows, Miller, and Gilchrist. Indeed, Security Escrows cautions that a determination of unauthorized practice may depend on case-specific circumstances. 233 Or. at 85–89, 377 P.2d 334. Nevertheless, regardless of any uncertainty at the margins, certain core criteria are well settled. Most significantly, for present purposes, the "practice of law" means the exercise of professional judgment in applying legal principles to address another person's individualized needs through analysis, advice, or other assistance.

We return, then, to defendants' arguments that ORS 9.160 violates Article I, section 8. In City of Eugene v. Miller, 318 Or. 480, 871 P.2d 454 (1994), the court summarized the controlling analysis, enunciated in State v. Robertson, 293 Or. 402, 649 P.2d 569

(1982), and State v. Plowman, 314 Or. 157, 838 P.2d 558 (1992), cert. den. 508 U.S. 974, 113 S.Ct. 2967, 125 L.Ed.2d 666 (1993), which delineates three types of statutes implicating expression:

"The first Robertson category consists of laws that 'focus on the content of speech or writing' or are ' "written in terms directed to the substance of any 'opinion' or any 'subject' of communication." ' Laws within that category violate Article I, section 8, 'unless the scope of the restraint is wholly confined within some exception that was well established when the first American guarantees of freedom of expression were adopted and that the guarantees then or in 1859 demonstrably were not intended to reach.' The second Robertson category consists of laws that 'focus[ ] on forbidden effects, but expressly prohibit[ ] expression used to achieve those effects.' Laws in that category 'are analyzed for overbreadth.' Finally, the third Robertson category consists of laws that 'focus[ ] on forbidden effects, but without referring to expression at all.' Laws within the third category are analyzed to determine whether they violate Article I, section 8, as applied." City of Eugene, 318 Or. at 488, 871 P.2d 454 (citations omitted; emphasis in original).

That analysis, as framed and applied by the Supreme Court and our court, assumes that all statutes must fall into one of the three enumerated categories, no matter how awkward the fit. The Robertson/ Plowman taxonomy seems somewhat ill-suited in assessing the constitutionality of a general professional licensing and regulatory scheme, in that virtually every profession—e.g., medicine, psychiatry, teaching, accounting—involves some element of expression, albeit in the context of the broader rendition of professional services. The name could be said of such licensed vocations as securities, insurance, or real estate brokerage. Nevertheless, the Robertson/Plowman methodology purports to describe the applicable universe, and we proceed to apply it.

[3] Defendants first argue that ORS 9.160 is facially unconstitutional, as calling within the first Robertson/Plowman category, because it burdens a type of expression, viz, "out-of-court legal speech," that did not fall within any historical exception recognized at the time of statehood. Whatever the merits of defendants' arguments about the historical status of nonlitigation-related speech, their argument fails in its first premise: ORS 9.160 is not written in terms directed to the substance of any 'opinion' or any 'sub-

ject' of communication." Robertson, 293 Or. at 412, 649 P.2d 569.

As noted in Gilchrist, ORS 9.160 does not proscribe the mere generalized exchange of legal information or discussion of legal issues. 272 Or. at 558–59, 563, 538 P.2d 913. Rather, the statute is expressly directed to limiting the conduct of a profession—the practice of law—to those who possess certain qualifications. It cannot be gainsaid that some part of the practice of law involves expression—and, indeed, that expression is an indispensable component of some aspects of legal practice. However, as described above, the practice of law involves conduct, processes, and relationships that transcend mere expression. In that respect, ORS 9.160 and the corollary legal licensing statutes are no different from other professional licensing and regulatory schemes. Defendants' analysis, if extended in principle, would compel the invalidation of many, and perhaps all, of those analogous statutes. See, e.g., ORS 677.080; ORS 677.085 (prohibiting unauthorized practice of medicine); ORS 575.020 (prohibiting unauthorized practice of psychology); ORS 673.615 (prohibiting unauthorized practice of tax consulting). ORS 9.160 does not fall within the first Robertson/Plowman category.

The closer question is whether the statute is more properly consigned to the second Robertson/ Plowman category, or to the third. See, e.g., State v. Chakerian, 135 Or.App. 368, 373–75, 900 P.2d 511, aff'd 325 Or. 370, 938 P.2d 756 (1997).

An initial difficulty with assigning the statute to either category is that both assume that the statute, either by its terms or by reference to context, "focuses on" some discrete "forbidden effect," Plowman, 314 Or. at 164, 838 P.2d 558. See State v. Stoneman, 323 Or. 536, 546, 920 P.2d 535 (1996) ("An examination of the context of a statute, as well as its wording, is necessary to an understanding of the policy that the legislative choice embodies." (Emphasis in original.)). The problem, however, is that, just as ORS 9.160 does not, by its terms, refer to "the substance of any 'opinion' or any 'subject' of communication," Robertson, 293 Or. at 412, 649 P.2d 569, the statute also does not expressly refer to any targeted harmful effect of the unauthorized practice of law. Nor is the targeted harm obvious from statutory context, including particularly other laws pertaining to licensing and regulation of attorneys. See, e.g., ORS 9.241 (regulating appearances in court by attorneys licensed in other jurisdictions); ORS 9.280 (regulating immigration consulting to members of Oregon State Bar); ORS 9.500 (prohibiting some forms of solicitation by attorneys).

To be sure, ORS 9.160 and other related statutes could reasonably be, and have been, viewed as consumer-protective measures. Conversely, those statutes could be read, just as plausibly and less benignly, as perpetuating a professional "monopoly." Our point is not to give credence to the latter reading, and certainly not to take issue with the former. Our concern, rather, is that neither an examination of the unadorned "context of the statute [nor] of its wording" yields a clear "understanding of the policy that the legislative choice embodied." Stoneman, 323 Or. at 536, 920 P.2d 535. It is tempting in such circumstances to carve out a fourth category, beyond the Robertson/Plowman three, consisting of statutes that neither expressly prohibit expression nor are directed against some textually or contextually verifiable evil, but whose application may, nevertheless, collaterally burden expression. Unfortunately, the prevailing methodology seems to foreclose that possibility.

So constrained, we consign ORS 9.160 to the third Robertson/Plowman category. To fall within the second, a statute must "expressly prohibit expression." Plowman, 314 Or. at 164, 838 P.2d 558. See Stoneman, 323 Or. at 543, 920 P.2d 535 ("If such a statute expressly prohibits certain forms of expression, it must survive an overbreadth challenge [.]"). In Chakerian, we considered the content of that requirement:

"[W]hat does it mean that a statute 'expressly prohibits expression'?

"We perceive in Robertson's progeny two classes of statutes that fall within the second Robertson category. The first includes statutes that explicitly identify communicative conduct as a proscribed means of achieving a forbidden effect. . . .

"The second class of statutes is less obvious. It includes statues that, although they do not explicitly refer to communicative conduct, can be violated only by means of expression. In other words, regardless of the statute's particular language, a person cannot violate the statute without engaging in communicative conduct. That class acknowledges the dictates of substance over form. Regardless of the precision—or, perhaps the studied imprecision—of statutory language, when expression is the only possible means of violating the statute, the statute, necessarily, expressly proscribes expression." 135 Or.App. at 375, 900 P.2d 511. (emphasis in original; footnote omitted).

Here, as noted, ORS 9.160 does not "explicitly identify communicative conduct as a proscribed means of achieving a forbidden effect." 135 Or.App. at 375, 900 P.2d 511. The statute does not explicitly refer to expression at all.

Nor can ORS 9.160 be "violated only by means of expression." Chakerian, 135 Or.App. at 375, 900 P.2d 511. Our conclusion in that regard flows from the essence of the "practice of law"—and, thus, of the unauthorized practice of law—described above. That essential element is the rendition of legal services that required the exercise of informed discretion in applying legal principles to address a particular "client's" individual needs. 149 Or.App. at 183, 942 P.2d at 800. Some of those services are intrinsically communicative or expressive—e.g., advice, negotiation, or drafting. But others, for which attorneys routinely bill their clients, are not—including, most significantly, research and analysis. Indeed, even advice, negotiation, and drafting, are only the final, articulated products of the skills and processes that form the core of the lawyer's craft, the exercise of professional judgment. In a related sense, the consumer-protective policies that underlie ORS 9.160 may be offended not merely by what is expressed, but also by what is not—by advice not given and by actions not taken. Because ORS 9.160 can be violated by means other than expression, it falls, albeit somewhat unsatisfactorily, into the third Robertson/Plowman category.

Statutes in the third category "are analyzed to determine whether they violate Article I, section 8, as applied." Miller, 318 Or. at 488, 871 P. 2d 454. Such statutes "are subject to challenge * * * on vagueness grounds or on the ground that the statute's reach, as applied to defendant, extends to privileged expression." Stoneman, 323 Or. at 543, 920 P. 2d 535. In Oregon State Bar v. (Cite as: 149 Or.App. 171, 942 P. 2d 793) Wright, 180 Or. 693, 700–701, 573 P.2d 283 (1977), the court concluded that ORS 9.160 was not unconstitutionally vague for purposes of the Fourteenth Amendment to the United States Constitution, and plaintiff here advances no persuasive reason for reaching a different conclusion under Article I, section 8. Nor was the statute's application to defendant's activities impermissibly overbroad. The injunction, issued pursuant to ORS 9.160 and ORS 9.166, carefully limits the breadth of its prohibition to conduct, including communication, that pertains to representing and counseling persons with regard to their particular legal matters. Such a prohibition does not impermissibly burden protected expression for purposes of Article I, section 8.

Defendants' second assignment of error asserts, primarily, that the injunction itself is overbroad under the First and Fourteenth Amendments to the United States Constitution. Defendants argue:

"The trial court's injunction banned Ms. Smith from all law practice including all forms of federal and state sanctioned nonlawyer law practice. In doing so, the trial court's injunction order violates Ms. Smith's rights to free speech and association guaranteed by the First and Fourteenth Amendments . . ., as well as by the Oregon Constitution."

* * * * *

"In short, while certain areas of law practice are proscribed, large areas of nonlawyer law practice are state and federally sanctioned. Yet the trial court's injunction prospectively bans Ms. Smith and her company from all forms of law practice, whether authorized or not. State and federally sanctioned legal advice is educational speech and cannot be banned absent a compelling state interest and means narrowly tailored to further the state's interest while protecting the speakers right to speak freely."

That argument fails. As we have explained, the injunction does not ban speech qua speech; it restrains speech in the context of a putatively professional relationship. As significantly, defendants have not demonstrated that they actually engage in practices within the supposed areas of overbreadth. Finally, and in all events, defendants' argument assumes, without apt authority or analysis, that the First Amendment somehow generally preempts state law-based restraints on unauthorized legal practice of law. The only authority defendants invoke, United Transportation Union v. State Bar of Michigan, 401 U.S. 576, 91 S.Ct. 1076, 28 L.Ed.2d 339 (1971), and Brotherhood of Railroad Trainmen v. Virginia, 377 U.S. 1, 84 S.Ct. 1113, 12 L.Ed.2d 89 (1964), involved injunctions actually burdening the continuing exercise of rights of labor organization and representation. Here, defendants have not shown any such impairment.

We reject defendants' remaining arguments without further discussion. Affirmed.[4]

Case Review Question Why was the case dismissed in favor of the school if the court found it was not immune from suit?

APPLICATION 5.1

Mandy is a paralegal with the firm of Johnson and Hernandez. Attorney Johnson represents a client in a case of breach of contract. The statute of limitations (time limit to file suit following the breach) will expire on May 1 of this year. The case is a solid one and Ms. Johnson is convinced they will win a judgment for the value of the contract, which is $25,000. The pleadings are drafted and Mandy is instructed to file the petition in the lawsuit with the courts no later than April 30. An additional regular job duty of Mandy is to keep the firm calendar and check that all documents are timely filed. Mandy is generally a competent paralegal but somewhat disorganized. On June 19 she discovers the petition under a stack of papers on her desk. She files the petition that day, but the suit is dismissed with prejudice (it cannot be refiled) due to failure to file within the statute of limitations. The client files suit against attorney Johnson and receives a judgment for $25,000.

Point for Discussion: Why should the attorney be held liable if the responsibility was totally within Mandy's control?

APPLICATION 5.2

Ora is hired as a paralegal with the firm of Weiner and Vaughn. She has moved to a city from a distance of 2000 miles. Ora presents herself as a qualified paralegal with extensive training and experience in the firm where she was previously employed for seven years. Once on the job, Ora's first few weeks are spent interviewing family members in a bitter custody battle. Her interviews produce a fairly large amount of very personal information about both sides of the family. One Sunday after church, a number of people in Ora's congregation go to a local restaurant to eat. During lunch, Ora discloses much of the information gained as the result of her interviews. What Ora does not realize is that the waitress is the best friend of one of the parents in the custody battle. Subsequently, the firm is sued for breach of confidentiality and judgment is granted in favor of the parent of the child and against the firm in the amount of $40,000.

Points for Discussion: (1) What should the firm have done to minimize the risk of such an exposure of confidential information by Ora or other staff members? (2) Why would the attorney-client privilege of confidentiality extend to someone other than the attorney representing the client?

The obvious problem with tort liability as a sole means of policing the qualifications and delivery of services by the paralegal is that control is put in place after the harm is done. Consequently, while tort liability can be an effective method of compensating the victims of incompetence and misconduct, it does nothing proactively to prevent these behaviors. Thus, early on in the profession of paralegal, the need was clear for some method by which attorneys and the public could identify competent and responsible paralegals.

One method used throughout the United States is approval of paralegal programs by the American Bar Association (ABA). Because attorneys are ultimately liable for the work and conduct of the paralegals they employ, the legal profession has a strong interest in creating standards by which paralegals are trained and educated. Consequently, an arm of the ABA was delegated the task of defining standards of education and applying them to the various types of formal paralegal training programs. This group also monitors adherence to the standards by those programs. ABA approval is a voluntary process and not required for any program of education. Programs may also have other types of approval by organizations that survey and rate or approve various types of educational programs and institutions at the post-secondary level. Currently, fewer than one half of the existing paralegal programs have ABA approval, however such approval is highly regarded by the legal profession. Approval by the ABA is a rigorous process and once achieved is subject to regular review. Programs must demonstrate comprehensive training by qualified instructors. They must show an established program with definite goals, methods of achievement, and accurate measurement of student progress. The program directors are required to stay abreast of developments in the profession and to incorporate them into the programs when appropriate. Other organizations provide similar credentialization or endorsement of qualified education and training programs. Such approvals offer the legal profession and the aspiring paralegal objective standards by which to measure the quality of education and level of skill to be expected from individuals graduating from these programs.

Assignment 5.2

> Identify whether there is a chapter in your locality or state of a national paralegal or legal assistant organization and the requirements for membership.

The types of subject matter addressed in approved paralegal training/educational programs are those in which the paralegal can expect to be called upon in a supportive role to the attorney. This includes a clear understanding of the American legal system, and its function and form. There is also an expectation of practical knowledge and skills. The ideal paralegal is able to perform all the tasks formerly and currently performed by attorneys that do not include elements exclusive to the practice of law. The various supportive tasks that a qualified paralegal should be trained in include legal writing, basic legal research, drafting documents, interviewing clients and witnesses, investigative techniques, and any other routine matters that arise within the procession of a case. In Figure 5–1, the chart depicts duties traditionally performed by the attorney that a qualified paralegal can now undertake within the scope of the profession. Note that there is some variation in the standards and limits from jurisdiction to jurisdiction and in some states the paralegal is permitted an even more active role.

Many practices today specialize by confining their practice to particular topics of law such as real property, estate planning, or tort law (personal injury). A great deal of overlap occurs, though, and the qualified paralegal needs at least an introductory knowledge of most basic subjects of law. This would include a command of relevant terminology, current legal principles, common procedures, and relevant forms and documents. The paralegal is then in a position to appreciate the potential impact of certain occurrences within a case, rather than being limited to a knowledge of how to complete a form and file it with the appropriate court/agency. A fundamental concept supporting paralegal training/education and the profession as a whole is that in order to provide a valuable system of support, the paralegal should have the ability to not

DUTY/SKILL	Attorney	Paralegal
Legal advice and representation (client contract, settlement negotiation, depositions, trial, and all situations involving advisement or advocacy)	X	
Client interview and subsequent meetings	X	X
Legal research	X	X
Draft pleadings/motions	X	X
Obtain evidence	X	X
Interview witnesses	X	X
Draft demand letters and settlement documents	X	X
Select and prepare jury instructions	X	X
Abstract depositions	X	X
Trial notebook and general case management	X	X
Draft contracts and corporate documents	X	X

FIGURE 5.1

Comparison of Duties of Attorneys and Paralegals*

*With proper attorney supervision, the qualified paralegal can perform all of the functions indicated in the table and all other tasks required in the law office that do not involve legal advice or advocacy. Some paralegals also make excellent law office administrators, especially helpful in firms that do not employ a full-time administrator.

only perform routine tasks, but to understand the underlying reasons for them, and to know when the various tasks are appropriate and why.

In addition to the tort (retroactive) and educational (proactive) forms of monitoring the quality of skill and service delivered by paralegals, methods have also developed by which practicing paralegals can measure their ability and achieve a level of acceptance within their profession. As the profession has evolved, paralegal organizations have developed as well. One such organization is the National Association of Legal Assistants (NALA). This is one of the oldest formalized bodies that supports the paralegal profession. In addition to the local chapters throughout the United States that offer support, continuing education, and communication for paralegals, NALA also offers a rigorous and respected examination to test one's paralegal skills. To be eligible for the exam, the candidate must demonstrate a background that would establish a basic knowledge of paralegal skills. These skills are then measured by the examination and the successful candidate receives a certificate from NALA that allows use of the designation certified legal assistant (CLA). Throughout the United States, the exam and the certificate are considered authentication by many attorneys with respect to the level of skill a paralegal professes to have. However, the organization and certification are purely voluntary and only a small minority of the paralegals in the United States have pursued it. There is a distinction to be made between a person with the CLA designation and one who has received a certificate of completion from a paralegal education or training program. While both are indicative of a certain level of demonstrated skill, they are by no means interchangeable titles. Several national, state, and local organizations exist with similar functions related to the promotion of professional standards of competence and acceptance for paralegals. At the end of the chapter is a partial list of some national organizations and their web site addresses.

Another support organization is the National Federation of Paralegal Associations (NFPA). An original objective of NFPA, formed in 1974, was to bring together various local paralegal organizations and form a cohesive group with a collective ability to advance the paralegal career and professional standards on a national level. The organization has as members more than 60 paralegal organizations throughout the United States and more than 17,500 individual members. In 1994 the organization elected to create a comprehensive exam to validate the skills of paralegals. NFPA recommends a four-year degree with a minimum recommendation of a two-year degree. The Paralegal Advanced Competency Examination (PACE) is available to paralegals with a college degree and significant experience as a paralegal. Successful candidates can use the title registered paralegal (RP). Like NALA, the NFPA organization enjoys a positive reputation in the legal community, and one who has passed the rigorous standards to achieve the title of registered paralegal is considered to have proven skills as a legal professional.

Through the years, many states have sought to establish guidelines and standards for paralegal skills, but as yet no comprehensive legislation is in place to test, regulate, and monitor this profession.[5] However, as most service professions have developed during the last century, the government has identified a strong public interest in regulating such professions to protect an unwitting public from those who would act with less than a necessary degree of competence or integrity. Some states have enacted or modified legislation with respect to the definition of the unauthorized practice of law and placed limitations on law-related services by nonlawyers such as the preparation and sale of generic legal documents including kits to prepare wills and noncontested divorces. There is no comprehensive legislation at this stage, however, to address licensure or regulation of paralegals. In this respect, the profession is still quite young. Consequently, it is highly likely that paralegals will see a great deal of legislation concerning the profession in the years to come.

Issues that have arisen with regard to government regulation are serious. Paralegals and attorneys alike recognize the need for some sort of recognizable standard by which to measure and monitor paralegal skills and abilities. The problem lies in the wide array of backgrounds that exist in the profession. Universally an attorney is required to meet minimum educational requirements and demonstrate a basic level of knowledge, but there are no such uniform standards for paralegals. In addition to those formally educated, there are thousands of job-trained paralegals and a large number of laterally trained paralegals. These are individuals who entered the profession because of their technical knowledge and skill in another field. For example, a medical professional or engineer can be of invaluable assistance to an attorney involved in complex litigation concerning those subject areas. However, the legal knowledge of such persons may be limited or nonexistent. Yet these individuals, along with formally educated, degreed paralegals, are all within the same field of employment. The task of creating a system to evaluate skills relevant to the particular employment of such a wide variety of professionals has led to great difficulty for governing bodies. Because the need for regulation is clearly identified and is generally seen to outweigh the obstacles, it can likely be expected in the coming years.

B. THE CURRENT POSITION OF THE PARALEGAL

1. An Overview of the Types of Positions Commonly Held by Paralegals

The primary evolution of the paralegal profession clearly came out of the traditional law office, but the growth of the profession was not confined to that environment. The need for legal professionals and paraprofessionals extends far beyond the law firm. In nearly every setting where there is a lawyer, there is an opportunity to use the skills of a competent paralegal. Additionally, many business settings lend themselves to the use of paralegal-type skills without the necessity of an in-house attorney. It should always be remembered however that a definite line exists with regard to paralegal duties and the practice of law. To cross this line, in any setting, is to risk liability from a number of sources.

The most commonly known setting for the paralegal is perhaps the law office, where the paralegal works primarily as an extension of the licensed attorney. The paralegal may assist in interviewing clients and witnesses, scheduling various meetings such as depositions, preparing basic legal documents, and doing legal research and writing. In many offices, especially smaller firms, the paralegal also serves in a quasi clerical role. However, this is usually not the most efficient use of the paralegal's time or the attorney's resources as an employer.

Other areas where the paralegal may be employed are virtually limitless. The position is recognized in the federal government and in most states. Paralegals work everywhere from the offices of the legislature to administrative agencies. Many are employed by the courts to assist judges, clerks of court, and other court officers. Administrative agencies make particularly extensive use of paralegals since much of the work performed requires basic legal knowledge but not the advocacy and analytical skills of a licensed attorney. Throughout the various levels of government, the paralegal has come to be viewed as a valuable member of the staffing that carries out the objectives of the legal system. In the past, these roles were largely filled by attorneys, but the training and experience of a qualified paralegal is equally suitable for these positions in the majority of instances. More often than not the team of attorneys has been replaced with a team of paralegals under the supervision of one or more attorneys.

This increasing use of paralegals in what were traditionally attorney roles has not been lost on corporate America. In the past decade, as companies fought to stay current with ever-changing legal standards while keeping costs from escalating, many former corporate attorneys were replaced with paralegals. The logic is much the same as that used by the government. Much of what is accomplished on a day-to-day basis in a corporate legal department does not require extensive legal analysis or advocacy. Corporate paralegals (under the supervision of an attorney) can prepare documents and correspondence, investigate legal issues, and perform legal research. By hiring an individual who has comparable skills in most of the necessary areas but does not have the expertise required for the practice of law, the corporate employer reaps a significant savings in overhead. This translates to the ability to hire more people for less money and thereby increases efficiency while controlling rising overhead costs.

There are also a myriad of opportunities for employment of paralegals beyond the law office, government, and large corporations. Virtually every industry in existence encounters legal issues on a daily basis. Manufacturers must comply with environmental regulations, service industries ranging from health care to real estate risk liability for failure to properly follow all the requirements of their profession, banks deal with various legal documents in the form of loans, trusts, and so forth on a daily basis. And all entities who have subordinate employees must adhere to applicable labor laws and regulations. As the complexity of the legal system and American society increases, so does the need for individuals who can assist in coping with the interaction of law and society.[6]

Assignment 5.3

> Identify five different areas of business, industry, or service professions where a paralegal might be employed, and describe what benefit such a position would offer.

2. Common Skills and Duties of Today's Paralegal

The skills demanded of a qualified paralegal vary as much as those of an attorney. Law has become a relatively subspecialized field. Because the legal system is so complex and the body of law increases virtually on a daily basis, the trend in the past few decades has been for attorneys to more or less confine their practice to a limited number of areas. It is not feasible to maintain a current and competent knowledge of all areas of law, and the risk of error far exceeds the benefit of offering a full array of services by a single individual. Thus, many attorneys, and firms for that matter, have narrowed their focus to offer legal services of a comprehensive quality within a particular area of law or geographical location. Similarly, corporate legal departments, government offices, and businesses are usually most concerned with a particular area of law. The primary training for attorneys is broad based to develop the basic skills needed to then focus on a specific area of practice. Paralegal training is much the same. While a paralegal may have extensive knowledge in real estate law, property transfers, and so forth, he or she may know relatively little about pension plans, domestic relations, or other areas of law. As more and more paralegals seek out formal training as the basis for their professional advancement, programs strive to offer much the same curriculum as those seen in law schools. The focus however is changing. In law schools the emphasis is on analytical training and how to approach and manage a legal issue. For paralegal education, the trend is more toward the practical aspects of the legal issue as it is normally dealt with in business or the courts. Both require a basic knowledge of legal principles and terminology, which are secondary to the primary emphasis. As more paralegal training programs seek out ABA approval, they are molding the curriculum to complement their law school counterparts. Much like attorneys who a century ago had a somewhat disorganized system of education and licensure standards, the paralegal profession is slowly coming into a more standardized perception among legal professionals around the country.

Today's paralegal is required to have a number of basic skills to be competitive in the national job market. As mentioned, a basic understanding of legal principles and terminology in a variety of areas of law is essential. But it is the ability to self-educate that will enable the paralegal to adapt to a variety of employment settings as well as remain current in the field. A sound educational basis is important, and this is most effectively and efficiently achieved through formal education. However, many qualified job-trained paralegals exist and excel in the field. Those who exist and thrive do so because of their ability to learn quickly by example and adapt as circumstances and standards change. Yet, the law is in a constant state of change. The paralegal profession is young and still evolving. Anyone who wishes to pursue a long-term career in this field must have the basic skills to perform legal research and to interpret that research in order to maintain a current state of knowledge. It is true that many continuing legal education programs are offered to lawyers and paralegals alike. These programs are important to polish skills and stay abreast of the most current and notable developments, but in the every day practice of law changes come far more frequently than do seminars. A paralegal who can research changes in the law, the profession, and technology is a paralegal who can survive the evolution of the career.

In addition to legal research, the paralegal requires extraordinary organizational skills. Quite often, the paralegal is responsible for ensuring that all aspects of a case or project continue to move forward and that legal standards are satisfied. This includes everything from documentation, to ethical requirements such as confidentiality, to making sure statutory requirements are satisfied. A paralegal with poor organizational skills can quite easily cause the most certain of cases to fail and even to result in legal liability for the supervising attorney and the paralegal. The responsibility is significant and often a paralegal must establish these skills as a subordinate before being placed in a position of authority with respect to case or project management.

The paralegal must also be a good communicator because he or she is often the primary contact person for clients, opposing counsel, other corporate offices, and so on. The need to have polished written and verbal communication skills can largely impact future success. This is often the most obvious way to judge the effectiveness of a paralegal because it is the most visible aspect of a paralegal's work. One who cannot compose correspondence, speak intelligently and coherently, or coordinate information from several sources will have great difficulty regardless of his or her degree of skill in other areas. For example, a paralegal can have a photographic memory and know the entire collection of laws of procedure for the courts, but if the paralegal cannot effectively and professionally communicate that information when necessary, the opportunity to use the knowledge will probably be lost.

Finally, the paralegal profession has also become a career path for managers. Historically, lawyers delegated many of the office management decisions to a clerical person. As firms and corporate legal departments grew, some hired formal managers with training in business. Because of the peculiarities of the legal profession, such as statutory deadlines and ethical requirements, those trained clerically or in business did not always have the knowledge necessary to effectively manage risk and simultaneously delegate paralegals or other subordinate staff in the most effective manner. However, a paralegal with management skills can not only act as a leader in the business setting, but also take into account the impact of legal issues on projects. This minimizes the risk for liability and, in turn, causes the work to be produced in the most efficient manner. Consequently, the paralegal who can demonstrate strong management capability in addition to the standard paralegal competencies has a distinct edge in professional advancement.

CASE IN POINT

Doe v. Condon, 532 S.E. 2d 879 (2000).

Proposed Findings and Recommendations of the Referee

This is a declaratory judgment action in the Supreme Court's original jurisdiction. The Court referred this matter to me as Referee. Petitioner, a paralegal, has submitted a generalized list of tasks he wishes to perform and has inquired whether performing them constitutes the unauthorized practice of law. Petitioner also seeks a determination of the propriety of his proposed fee splitting arrangement with his attorney-employer. Despite my repeated offers for an evidentiary hearing, neither party requested a hearing. The record before me is sufficient to address and resolve whether the activities in question constitute the unauthorized practice of law.

I find that a paralegal conducting unsupervised legal presentations for the public and answering legal questions from the audience engages in the unauthorized practice of law. Further, I find that a paralegal meeting individually with clients to answer estate planning questions engages in the unauthorized practice of law. Finally, I find the proposed fee arrangement is improper and violates the ethical prohibition against fee splitting.

Background

Petitioner submitted the following questions to the Court:

(1) Is it the unauthorized practice of law for a paralegal employed by an attorney to conduct educational seminars for the general public, to disseminate general information about wills and trusts, including specifically a fair and balanced emphasis on living trusts, including answering general questions, without the attorney being present at the seminar as long as the seminar is sponsored by the attorney's law firm and the attorney has reviewed and approved the format, materials and presentation to be made for content, truthfulness and fairness?

(2) Is it the unauthorized practice of law for a paralegal employed by an attorney to meet with clients privately in the law office for the purpose of answering general questions about wills, trusts, including specifically living trusts, and estate planning in general, and to gather basic information from said clients for such purposes as long as it is done under the attorney's direction, and the clients have a follow-up interview and meeting with the attorney who would have primary responsibility for legal decisions?

(3) Can a paralegal receive compensation from the law firm he is employed by, through a profit-sharing arrangement, which would be based upon the volume and type of cases the paralegal handled?

Discussion

To protect the public from unsound legal advice and incompetent representation, South Carolina, like other jurisdictions, limits the practice of law to licensed attorneys. S.C. Code Ann. § 40-5-310 (1976).

While case law provides general guidelines as to what constitutes the practice of law, courts are hesitant to define its exact boundaries. Thus, the analysis in 'practice of law' cases is necessarily fact-driven. The Supreme Court has specifically avoided addressing hypothetical situations, preferring instead to determine what constitutes the unauthorized practice of law on a case by case basis. In Re Unauthorized Practice of Law Rules Proposed by the South Carolina Bar, 309 S.C. 304, 422 S.E.2d 123 (S.C. 1992). I find that Petitioner's proposed actions constitute the unauthorized practice of law and that the proposed fee agreement violates the ethical prohibition against fee splitting.

Our Supreme Court has set forth a succinct standard of the proper role of paralegals:

The activities of a paralegal do not constitute the practice of law as long as they are limited to work of a preparatory nature, such as legal research, investigation, or the composition of legal documents, which enable the licensed attorney-employer to carry a given matter to a conclusion through his own examination, approval or additional effort. Matter of Easler, 275 S.C. 400, 272 S.E.2d 32, 33 (S.C. 1980).

While the important support function of paralegals has increased through the years, the Easler guidelines stand the test of time. As envisioned in Easler, the paralegal plays a supporting role to the supervising attorney. Here, the roles are reversed. The attorney would support the paralegal. Petitioner would play the lead role, with no meaningful attorney supervision and the attorney's presence and involvement only surfaces on the back end. Meaningful attorney supervision must be present throughout the process. The line between what is and what is not permissible conduct by a non-attorney is oftentimes "unclear" and is a potential trap for the unsuspecting client. State v. Buyers Service Co., Inc., 292 S.C. 426, 357 S.E.2d 15, 17. The conduct of the paralegal contemplated here clearly crosses the line into the unauthorized practice of law. It is well settled that a paralegal may not give legal advice, consult, offer legal explanations, or make legal recommendations. State v. Despain, 319 S.C. 317, 460 S.E.2d 576 S.C. 1995).

A. Educational Seminars

Petitioner intends to conduct unsupervised "wills and trusts" seminars for the public, "emphasizing" living trusts during the course of his presentation. Petitioner also plans to answer estate planning questions from the audience. I find Petitioner's proposed conduct constitutes the unauthorized practice of law. I find, as other courts have, that the very structure of such "educational" legal seminars suggests that the presenter will actually be giving legal advice in legal matters. See, In Re Mid-America Living Trust Assoc. Inc., 927 S.W. 2d 755 (Mo. banc 1996). At the very least. Petitioner will implicitly advise participants that they require estate planning services. Whether a will or trust is appropriate in any given situation is a function of legal judgment. To be sure, advising a potential client on his or her need for a living trust (or other particular estate planning instrument or device) fits squarely within the practice of law. These matters cry out for the exercise of professional judgment by a licensed attorney. Thus, in conducting these informational seminars, Petitioner would engage in the unauthorized practice of law as a non-attorney offering legal advice.

Petitioner plans to answer "general" questions during his presentation. I have reviewed the Estate Planning Summary submitted by Petitioner and his attorney-employer. This summary sets forth the subject matter to be covered by the paralegal. Petitioner would present information on, among other things, revocable trusts, irrevocable living trusts, credit shelter trusts, qualified terminable interest property trusts, charitable remainder trusts, qualified personal residence trusts, grantor retained annuity trusts, grantor retained unitrusts and charitable lead trusts. It is difficult to imagine such specific state planning devices eliciting "general" questions or a scenario in which the exercise of legal judgment would not be involved. It is, after all, a legal seminar, apparently for the purpose of soliciting business. To suggest that some "plan" would anticipate all possible questions with predetermined non-legal responses is specious. And so complex is this area of law that many states, including South Carolina, have established stringent standards for an attorney to receive the designation of "specialist" in Estate Planning and Probate Law. SCACR, Part IV, Appendices D and E. This is the practice of law.

I fully recognize the prevailing popularity of 'financial planners' and others jump[ing] on the estate planning bandwagon." (Estate Planning Summary submitted by Petitioner's attorney-employer, p. 1). This trend in no way affects the decision before the Court. This paralegal would not be presenting the estate planning seminar as a financial planner. This seminar would be conspicuously sponsored by the paralegal's attorney-employer. The attorney's law firm is prominently displayed in the brochure submitted, e.g., name, address, telephone number and "Firm Profile." In promoting the law firm and representing to the public the 'legal' nature of the seminar, neither the paralegal nor his attorney-employer can escape the prohibition against the unauthorized practice of law.

B. Initial Client Interview

Petitioner intends to gather client information and answer general estate planning questions during his proposed "initial client interviews." While Petitioner may properly compile client information, Petitioner may not answer estate planning questions. See Matter of Easler, supra. Petitioner's answering legal questions would constitute the unauthorized practice of law for the reasons stated above. While the law firm in which Petitioner is employed plans to direct clients to an attorney for "follow-up" consultations, a paralegal may not give legal advice in any event. Moreover, permissible preparatory tasks must be performed while under the attorney's supervision. The proposed after the fact attorney review comes too late.

C. Compensation

Petitioner's law firm intends to compensate him based upon the volume and types of cases he "handles." A paralegal, of course, may not "handle" any case. This fee arrangement directly violates Rule 5.4 of the Rules of professional conduct, SCACR 407. This limitation serves to "discourage the unauthorized practice of law by lay persons and to prevent a non-lawyer from acquiring a vested pecuniary interest in an attorney's disposition of a case that could possibly take preeminence over a client's best interest." Matter of Anonymous Member of the S.C. Bar, 295 S.C. 25, 26, 367 S.E.2d 17, 18 (S.C.1998 [1988]). This compensation proposal arrangement coupled with Petitioner's desire to market the law firm's services via the educational seminars and meet individually with clients creates a situation ripe for abuse. Indeed, the proposal by Petitioner presents the very evil Rule 5.4 was designed to avoid. Accordingly, I find Petitioner's proposed compensation plan violates both the letter and the spirit of Rule 5.4 prohibiting fee splitting with non-attorneys.

Recommendations

1. Offering legal presentations for the general public constitutes the practice of law.

2. Answering estate planning questions in the context of legal seminars or in private client interviews constitutes the practice of law.

3. Fee sharing arrangements with non-attorneys based on volume and cases "handled" by a paralegal violates Rule 5.4, Rules of Professional Conduct, SCACR 407.

RESPECTFULLY SUBMITTED.[7]

Case Review Question Would the entire result change if there were attorneys present at the seminars?

Assignment 5.4

In the following situation, explain how paralegal skills could produce a better result.

Jane, Joe, Jim, and Julie are lawyers. They have a busy practice and employ three secretaries, a bookkeeper, a filing clerk, and an office manager. None of the support staff have more than a high school education, but each has several years of experience in their job. One Friday, all four attorneys are absent at various trials and depositions. The file clerk comes across a file that was inadvertently left in the copy room. A note on the file indicates that the case must be filed no later than December 24 and, in fact, it is Friday December 24. Nothing in the file indicates the suit was ever filed. None of the attorneys are available by phone and none are expected back before the end of the day. The office manager knows the client and decides that he would probably not sue the firm for failing to file this case since they represent him in several other matters. A secretary offers to prepare a petition by copying one from a similar type of suit and changing the names. Ultimately, the staff decided to do nothing and leave the case for the attorneys to handle when they return to work on Tuesday, December 28.

C. THE FUTURE DIRECTION OF THE PARALEGAL PROFESSION

It is clear that the paralegal profession is still growing and developing. Dramatic strides have been made in the last 30 years. But, the answers are not all in place yet. It is true that many believe that in the future paralegals will be regulated to place some boundaries and accountability within the ranks of the profession. This would protect an unwitting public and attorneys from those with less than acceptable skill from portraying themselves as competent professionals. Other changes will be largely the product of a changing market. Paralegal services can be billed, though at a lesser rate than their lawyer counterparts, which makes them desirable from the standpoint of offering services to the consumer. However, employers of legal professionals, like any other employer in business, will always be faced with the issue of keeping overhead to a minimum in order to maximize profits. As a result, paralegals will need to demonstrate skills that are indispensable. The more flexible a paralegal is in terms of expertise in more than one area, the greater the likelihood for success and advancement. Additionally the ability to act in a managerial role to delegate work to the lowest competent level and at the same time optimize efficiency of staff will become an increasingly valuable commodity.

The need for professional avenues of advancement will likely cause a tier of paralegal professionals to develop even further. Currently, corporate legal departments and large law firms offer levels of advancement and responsibility for paralegals based upon their level of education, skill, and achievement. These types of internal structures will likely continue and even grow. Further, the current trend to offer additional testing and certification for paralegals in specialized areas will also continue to develop as a method for paralegals to establish themselves as being above the ordinary within their profession.

These demands will require that the paralegal of the future be intelligent and professional, have strong verbal and written skills and the ability to organize and lead, and most important, have the ability to adapt. Such skills will certainly serve the paralegal in the traditional law office setting. However, as the legal system becomes more and more complex, and American business looks for ways to increase its legal knowledge without increasing its attorney's fees, many businesses will look to the paralegal to fill in the gray area between no representation and a corporate legal staff. The paralegals who succeed will need to have knowledge not only of their profession, but of the business and individuals they serve. To do this the paralegal will have to become increasingly specialized but flexible enough to adapt to an ever-changing job market.

CHAPTER SUMMARY

The paralegal profession has developed in the 20th century from nonexistence to a common and fixed presence within the American legal profession. Paralegals offer services that are traditionally offered by attorneys but do not require the practice of law. Their use has increased efficiency and lowered the cost for the delivery of legal services in the United States. This profession came about in large part as a response to a rapidly increasing demand for legal representation at a reasonable expense to the consumer. The profession has grown laterally as well, expanding beyond the traditional law firm into corporate legal departments and various businesses with regular legal concerns and issues.

The development of the profession has resulted in formalized training programs and educational curriculum dedicated solely to the preparation of the paralegal as a recognized legal professional. There have also been continuing attempts to establish standards of competence by which the profession can be measured and policed. In the alternative, paralegals are held to certain standards of competence and ethics by the courts and may be held accountable for any damage they cause as the result of professional malfeasance.

Already, paralegals are expected to have a working knowledge of basic legal terminology and principles; common aspects of practical legal skills such as document preparation and research; good communication skills; and the ability to organize and manage work as well as individuals. These trends will likely continue and even develop further as the profession fine tunes its role in the American legal system.

ETHICAL NOTE

The importance of ethics permeates the entire legal profession. Individuals entrust their legal rights to legal professionals at great risk and must feel confident that the professionals will do nothing to endanger these rights or cause harm as a result of the knowledge they have been entrusted with. Because the paralegal performs work and delivers legal services that were once the exclusive domain of the attorney and engenders the same trust, then the same ethical requirements apply.

Relevant Internet Sites

National Association for Legal Assistants (NALA)	www.nala.org
American Association for Paralegal Education	www.aafpe.org
American Bar Association Standing Committee On Legal Assistants	www.abanet.org/legalassts/home.html
Association of Legal Administrators	www. alanet.org
National Federation of Paralegal Associations	www.paralegals.org
Legal Assistant Management Association	www.lamanet.org
American Corporate Legal Assistants Association	www.aclaa.org
Association of Trial Lawyers of America—Paralegal Membership	www.atlanet.org/members/parabro.ht

NOTE: These Internet sites are links to national paralegal organizations that often have the most current information available on the paralegal profession, training, regulation, and licensing issues. Many state organizations also have websites to provide information on a local level.

Internet Assignment 5.1

Contact one of the Internet sites listed and identify the requirements for membership by a legal assistant.

Internet Assignment 5.2

Search the Internet for a directory of paralegal training and educational programs.

Key Terms

Attorney   Paralegal   Unauthorized Practice of Law

Endnotes

1. ABA definition of Legal Assistant/Paralegal, adopted by the ABA House of Delegates, August 1997.
2. "Conflicts and Confidences," 82 A.B.A. J. (June 1996).
3. Id.
4. *Ore State Bar Assn. v. Smith, et. al.*, 149 Or.App. 171, 942 P.2d 793 (1999).
5. "Defining the Role of Paralegals," 71 Dec. Wisc. L. 10 (1998).
6. "Paralegals in the 1990s: Fewer Jobs, More Specialists, Innovative Training," 11 Of Counsel 9 (April 1992).
7. *Doe v. Condon*, 532 S.E. 2d 879 (2000).

Chapter 6

Today's Paralegal in the Workplace: Communication Skills as a Core Element

CHAPTER OBJECTIVES

Upon completion of this chapter you should be able to do the following:

- Explain the importance of communication in the legal profession as a whole and in paralegal functions in particular.

- Explain why some language has a different meaning in a legal context.

- Discuss how the level of verbal or written language should be established in a legal communication.

- Define the common forms of legal written communications.

- Distinguish between leading and direct forms of questioning.

- Discuss the important elements of a legal interview.

- Distinguish a pleading from a motion.

- Distinguish an internal memorandum from an external memorandum.

A. THE IMPORTANCE OF WRITTEN AND VERBAL COMMUNICATION SKILLS

Something that should be understood at the outset for anyone considering a law-related profession is that communication skills are the ultimate basis for any measure of success. While the charismatic television lawyer may dramatize the ability of attorneys to sway a jury or court, nonetheless the principle rings true. Effective lawyers and their support staff, including especially the paralegal, must have exceptional verbal and written communication skills. These skills enable cases to move forward with a minimum of confusion. In a lawsuit, such skills enable the relay of essential information. They also facilitate the collection of evidence; interviewing, preparing, and deposing witnesses; and ultimately persuading a jury and/or judge. Without the ability to effectively present a case both in written documents and verbally in a concise and appropriate manner, fewer cases would be settled, more would be tried, and the legal system would become increasingly less efficient.

In the law, an extremely important element is accurate but effective presentation of information. This requires more than the ability to simply locate information or disseminate copies of researched law. Rather, being able to communicate information completely, concisely and, in some situations, in the light most advantageous to one's position is an absolute must. This ability is needed for the simplest of correspondence to the most complex of legal documents.

B. VERBAL COMMUNICATION

1. Exchanging Ideas

It is not uncommon for members of a legal team and/or a client to periodically meet to exchange ideas about a particular issue at hand. It is extremely important that one is able to convey ideas in a fashion that is understandable to all. This minimizes the opportunity for misinterpretation and encourages the open exchange of information. For paralegals, this is especially important because of the heavy contact paralegals often have with clients and witnesses. For example, the written legal language used in an appellate brief may be quite sophisticated, because one would expect the judge to have the ability to understand and appreciate the meaning of the terminology used. However, while it may seem impressive to use a lot of *legalese* with a client, it typically does not aid in the gathering of information nor does it encourage open communication. A good rule of thumb to follow when communicating verbally, or in writing, is to address the least sophisticated member of the listening/reading audience. Simply put, speak in terms that the person with the least amount of legal knowledge can understand. The interviewer should always consider the level of education of the witness, the age, and any other personal characteristics that might affect the ability of the witness to communicate. After all, the goal is not to impress the witness with a command of terminology, but rather to approach each case comprehensively. This requires maximization of all opportunities to gain information.

One pitfall to be avoided when communicating with clients or witnesses is to assume the answers to questions. By doing so, it is easy to direct or lead the individual and imply the appropriate answers. If this happens, the conversation is no longer an exchange of ideas. The obvious problem is that valuable information may not be brought out when needed. The same risk may occur when members of the legal team converse. The assumption can usually be made that the attorney has a greater degree of knowledge of the law. However, each individual may have a different perspective on a situation. As a result, it is essential to communicate with one another about the various aspects of a case to ensure that all relevant issues are identified and dealt with. Shyness or introversion are qualities that do not lend themselves to law-related professions. One must be willing and able to effectively communicate thoughts with regard to the issues at hand.

2. Interviewing

An important part of any lawyer, paralegal, or legal investigator's work is the legal interview. Often the paralegal is responsible for conducting many of the initial and follow-up interviews in a case. The ability to effectively interview clients and witnesses is a skill that can ultimately make or break a case. A number of factors contribute to the successful interview. Contrary to first appearance, the effective interviewer does not simply sit down with a list of questions and obtain answers. Rather, the gathering of information must be the product of a carefully orchestrated procedure that gleans all the relevant information the interviewee has to offer.

a. Physical Setting   One of the first considerations in the interview is the physical arrangement of the room where the interview is to take place. It is important that clients or witnesses feel comfortable, at ease, and free to be open, in their responses. This requires a setting that protects the confidentiality of the interview but is not intimidating to the interviewee. Interviews should always be conducted in a closed space such as an office, law library, or other room with clear barriers to the presence or intrusion of others. Once in the room, furniture arrangement should be such that the interviewee feels a professional presence but is at ease and open.

There are a number of schools of thought as to the most effective arrangement of furniture in an interview situation. While some consider a desk between the interviewer and interviewee to be a barrier to open communication, others state that it lends the interviewer a perception of authority over the interviewee that requires compliance when responding to questions. One possible compromise is to place the interviewee in a chair to the side of the desk, thereby eliminating the obvious barrier but maintaining a perception of authority.

It is important to note that in American culture, each person requires a certain degree of actual physical space to maintain a sense of comfort and to avoid a feeling of intrusion. In a business environment, when a person places him or herself too physically close to another it can be quite intimidating and can thwart the purpose of the meeting. A reasonable space of a few feet between individuals should always be respected to maximize the sense of security and to open the lines for communication.

The proper physical setting for an interview requires consideration of the type of interview that is most often conducted, taking into account typical clients, their expectations, and what arrangement will be most conducive to meeting those expectations. For example, business clients may expect a more formal setting than nonbusiness clients. Clients who are elderly may have a more professional perception than more casual younger clientele. One thing is certain — if clients are uncomfortable in the physical setting of the interview, they will be less focused on the purpose of the interview, which is to gain information.

Assignment 6.1

> Create a diagram of an office setting that you believe would be conducive to effective interviewing for each of the following situations. Explain why the setting changes or does not change for the various circumstances described.
>
> a. The president of a large corporation is coming to discuss a possible suit against a competitor.
> b. An elderly client is coming in to discuss preparation of a will and related documents.
> c. A young couple is coming in to discuss a possible suit for malpractice against the doctor who was responsible for the care of their child who died in the hospital.

Another consideration in the physical setting for the legal interview is the protection of confidentiality. The interviewee should never feel that comments might be heard by passersby regardless of who they might be. This includes other members of the office staff or anyone else. The person who is the subject of a legal interview is often hypersensitive to the nature of the communication. This, in and of itself, presents a barrier to communication. The thought that someone might hear part of the communication and possibly even take it out of context may inhibit the interview process. As a result, it is important to avoid conducting interviews in casual settings and surroundings where others are coming and going and generally milling about. A secondary effect of such interference is its adverse effects on the ability of the interviewer and the interviewee to stay focused on the content and direction of the interview.

APPLICATION 6.1

K, a paralegal, is preparing to interview witnesses to a multicar accident. She has scheduled the interviews individually. K's desk is located in the center of a large work area in the office in a three-sided cubicle. She has scheduled the use of a conference room in the office for the interviews. The walls of the conference room are glass and open to the central work area of the office. K wants the witnesses to feel relaxed and at ease so for the first interview she leaves the curtains and door open to the conference room. She is seated immediately next to the witness at a conference table. During the interview, she often has to repeat questions to the witness. The answers given are usually very short, and the witness keeps looking out the door and windows. For the second interview, K draws the curtains across the glass walls and closes the door. This interview goes somewhat better, however the witness still seems quite fidgety throughout the interview. K assumes it is just the nature of the witness's personality.

Point for Discussion: Why did the change in the physical setting affect the interview? What could K do to improve the interview setting further?

Finally, the interviewer must be aware of the nonverbal communication that is taking place in a legal interview both by the interviewee and the witness. It is important to always use facial expressions, eye contact, and body language that encourage the interviewee to communicate. Turning one's back or side to the interviewee, folding one's arms decisively across the chest, or slumping over a stack of papers on a desk are all signs of challenge or disinterest to the interviewee and should be avoided. Similarly, the failure to look at the witness frequently may convey similar messages. On the return, these and other gestures by the interviewee may be quite telling with respect to whether the witness is being open, forthright, and honest with respect to the information supplied.

Another important factor is the tone of voice. While the interviewer should convey a sense of confidence, the tone should not be accusatory or strongly authoritative. Both tend to trigger a defensive posture and in turn inhibit the exchange of information. The tone of the interviewee should also be carefully followed, along with any repetitive behaviors or phrases. For example, one who hesitates before providing an answer to a quite basic question may be searching for a way around the question if he or she does not want to provide a forthright response for some reason.

b. The New Client Interview   In addition to the physical setting, there are other factors to consider when conducting a legal interview. Proper preparation for the interview is essential. Because the information obtained in an interview can potentially impact the outcome of a case, it is not something that should be done casually and without forethought. To prepare for a legal interview, one should gather any available information that is relevant to the case at hand. Relevance is often dictated by whether the interview is a first meeting with a client, a follow-up meeting, or the questioning of a potential witness. Each should be approached in a somewhat different manner.

In the initial interview, a number of topics must be explored. Because a professional relationship is being created, it is important to collect all of the information needed to set up a file for the client, including some personal information such as methods of contact and billing data. With respect to the actual nature of representation, it is important to collect objective information such as important times, places, and people, including witnesses. A key element is to listen thoroughly to the client's version of events. Even though this is subjective (biased by the client's own opinions) it is often when the most relevant information comes out.

The exact information needed in an initial interview varies of course with the type of case. For example, the information required from a client coming in about a dissolution of marriage is somewhat different from that of a client who was involved in a car accident or a client interested in starting up a corporation. For this reason, many firms use standard intake forms that are focused on the particular type of file being opened.

Intake forms or checklists often include personal demographics used for a variety of purposes including billing, references for client contact, and information necessary to communicate with the opposing party. In addition, the intake form is often tailored to a type of case in order to obtain information that is commonly needed to prepare the appropriate legal documents. For example, in a dissolution of marriage case, it would be necessary to know such things as the date and location where the marriage took place, whether either of the parties is in the military, and the names and ages of any children of the parties. In a personal injury case, the interviewer would need to know the specifics of the incident that produced the injury and all persons who were involved or who witnessed the incident. In a case of bankruptcy, it would be important to know the creditors and types of assets and debt the client had. As stated, most law firms keep forms on file to help guide the initial interview with the client in a particular type of case.

However, it is important to keep these forms updated to accommodate changes in the law and to keep in mind that the forms are not all-inclusive of the information that needs to be obtained in the interview. Forms are an excellent way to initiate the collection of information in the interview process and serve as a basic guide for those areas to be more fully explored. In many firms, the paralegal is assigned to keep intake forms current. Therefore, it is a commensurate responsibility to keep abreast of changes in the law that may in turn indicate the need for a change in the forms. Another essential element of the primary interview is to confer with the supervisor to determine if there is any specific area of information to be gathered or focused upon in addition to that on a checklist or intake form.

Assignment 6.2

> Create a list of 20 separate items of information that you think would be appropriate for the intake form. Be prepared to explain your answers.

An additional key element of the initial interview is to ensure that the client understands the role of each member of the legal team including him or herself. If the client understands what each person, such as the attorney, paralegal, clerical person, and client, should be expected to do as the case progresses, many misunderstandings and much wasted time can be avoided. Never assume that the new client has a clear understanding of these matters even if he or she has had legal representation in the past. Firms function differently in terms of their hierarchy and delegation of duties and in some instances the type of case dictates what types of tasks are performed by the various members of the legal team. By establishing the roles of each person clearly with the client, not only is the efficiency of the movement of the case increased, but this open communication helps to increase the confidence of the client in the firm's representation.

In addition to collecting the essential intake information and explaining the roles of the members of the legal team, an effective tool to open the lines of communication is to reassure the client that the staff members who assist the attorney are bound by the same ethical standards, such as confidentiality. Many clients may not be aware of this and may be hesitant to open up to anyone other than the attorney. By clarifying the ethical issues, the client may feel more at ease and provide more relevant information. Also, questions the client may have should either be addressed directly or, in matters involving legal advice, they should be submitted to the attorney in person or in the form of a memorandum, and followed up to ensure the client's questions are answered satisfactorily. By doing what may appear to be small tasks at the outset, a strong foundation for client satisfaction is established.

c. Guiding the Interview   The ability to effectively conduct a legal interview requires preparation, thought, and insight. Any interview should be given careful thought in advance as to the goals to be accomplished. In addition to a physical setting conducive to the interview format, the questions to be answered fully by the person conducting the interview include the following:

   i. What is the reason for the interview(s)?
  ii. What information am I trying to obtain in the interview?
 iii. Who is the most likely to have the information I need?

iv. How is interviewee likely to respond emotionally to the interview?

v. What are the possible problems with conducting the interview?

i. What is the reason for the interview?   After the initial intake interview, other reasons for interviewing include updating information from a client, obtaining background information from persons connected to the case, and gathering evidence. In these interviews, the type of information sought may be quite different depending on the current state of progress of the case and the kind of case. It is very true in the law that time is money. The more time wasted on unnecessary efforts, the more money the case will cost, and the less profitable it may be.

Before an interview is ever scheduled, certain decisions should be made. For example, it should be determined whether the interview is the most effective means to gain the information sought. An interview is one of the more costly forms of gathering information because it requires the time of two or more people for scheduling, for transcribing the information obtained, and for review of the information as it impacts the case. If the interview is the most effective means or the only means of obtaining the necessary information, then it should be as thorough and well thought out as possible.

ii. What information am I trying to obtain in the interview?   Being a good interviewer requires focus. If one has a natural ability to get people to talk about things, there may also be a predisposition toward just letting the person talk. It is important to go into any type of interview with a very clear idea of what information is being sought and to maintain that focus throughout the interview. To do this, it is helpful to start any interview with a detailed written outline of the course one expects the interview to follow. Very specific objectives should also be detailed in the form of written questions designed to obtain specific answers. But always remain open to the importance of information that is not specifically requested but comes out in the course of the interview, if it is relevant to legal representation.

There are basically two types of questions. Those that seek a narrative answer with detailed explanation, and those that affirm or deny a statement. The former are known as **direct questions.** These open-ended questions allow the person being interviewed to express their knowledge and possibly their opinions on the subject matter under discussion. These open-ended questions should be carefully framed so they are not so confined that relevant information is left out of the response, and not so broad that a great deal of unnecessary information is proffered. The questions that affirm or deny a statement are often referred to as **leading questions.** As the term implies, the question actually leads the respondent to the answer. As a general rule, the leading question will imply an answer of either yes or no or very specific facts such as a date, time, address, number, or name. It does not lend itself to discussion. In the event the person being interviewed is one that tends to talk a lot about irrelevant information, leading questions can be effective in controlling the interview. However, caution should be used because if leading questions are overused, valuable information may not be discovered.

Ultimately, preparing for the interview with written outlines and specific questions should be combined with a balance of direct and leading questions. The interviewer should also be always open to the idea that necessary information may exist that the interviewer is totally unaware of. This requires a willingness to guide the interview with some degree of control while allowing information to flow freely to the extent it produces relevant information.

Direct Question
Open-ended question that seeks a narrative answer.

Leading Question
Closed question that implies a specific answer.

iii. Who is the most likely to have the information I need? Much valuable time can be wasted looking in the wrong or less-effective places for information. It should never be assumed that there is only one source for the answer to a question. Rather, the preliminary question should be who and what are all the possible sources for information on a particular question. Second, examine the ease and expense of obtaining the information from the various sources. Third, before scheduling and conducting an interview, determine whether this individual can offer information on any other aspects of the case. This consolidation of efforts minimizes the time and money spent on the interview process. Often needed information can be just as easily and perhaps even more quickly obtained from other sources, such as public records or other accessible documents.

iv. How is the interviewee likely to respond emotionally to the interview? Not all individuals are anxious to take part in a legal interview. Most are hesitant to become involved in a legal dispute. This may even include clients. There are also many misconceptions about the progression of lawsuits and how witnesses are treated in general. As a result, many potential witnesses will hesitate to subject themselves to the possibility of appearing in a trial to give testimony and then being cross-examined. Because the object of cross-examination is to identify flaws in testimony, it is no surprise that people are not anxious to subject themselves to this type of attack. This is especially true if the witness is not a party to the suit and/or has no vested interest in its outcome. However, it is just as important for the interviewer to go into the meeting without preconceived notions about the client or case and with a professional attitude.

Because it is not uncommon for witnesses to be reluctant, the interviewer must be keenly aware of this and adept at extracting information. While the task is not a simple one, it can be quite challenging and rewarding when success is achieved. Think of the task of interviewing a reluctant witness as being much like that of finding the way through a complicated maze. There is no map and there are numerous dead ends but ultimately, the willingness to persevere in a consistent and calculated manner will result in finding the way out.

What many inexperienced interviewers may not realize is that the witness who is anxious to provide information can be just as difficult in the interview process as the one who is reluctant. One lawyer reported that the worst witness he ever had was a client who was a sweet and outgoing kindergarten teacher. He said all he needed to do was ask for her full name and she could talk animatedly for 45 minutes. In order to conduct an effective interview, focus is the key. This requires the interviewer to frame questions very carefully and to know when to move the witness on to the next question. While it is always important to gain all relevant information, when a witness begins to veer off into topics that are unrelated or irrelevant to the legal issues, the interviewer must gently take control of the interview and move forward.

Hostile Witness
One who is predisposed to the opposition or who is an unwilling participant in a legal action.

Finally there is the overtly **hostile witness.** This is the individual who is not a party to the suit but who openly supports the opposition. This interviewee, whether in a witness setting or under subpoena in a deposition, is not going to want to volunteer any information that may prove helpful. Special care must be taken when preparing for such an interview. Very specific areas of interest should be identified in advance. This may even go so far as to require the advance preparation of a very particular series of questions. The interviewer must be adept at determining what attitude toward the witness will be most effective. For example, some hostile witnesses might respond better to one who clearly presents a position of authority by tone and physical posture and an air of expected compliance. Another witness might respond better to one who approaches the interview as a friend who is just trying to get at the truth of the matter. Still another tactic might be to approach the interview in a seemingly disorganized and distracted fashion to give the interviewee a false sense of control or comfort about the information he or she does not want to volunteer. Whatever the case, the hostile witness can be the most challenging but also the most important. There is rarely more than one opportunity to meet with such witnesses and they are often in the unique position of exposing the weaknesses of the opposition's case.

v. What are the possible problems with conducting the interview? Much like the leader of an orchestra, when conducting a legal interview it is important to keep a number of elements functioning at once and under the supervision and control of the interviewer. The physical setting most conducive to the purpose of the interview must be maintained; the necessary information should be gathered; the attitude of the interviewee should be considered; any relevant but unanticipated information must be adequately drawn out; the control of the flow and content of information must be monitored; and the interviewer must know when the interview has produced the maximum possible result. The potential for difficulty with these has been discussed; additional pitfalls to be avoided include misintention or misunderstanding.

One of the keys to good interviewing is to confirm the information provided. The interviewer asks for information. Following the response, the interviewer should verbally summarize the interviewee's response to confirm that it was properly understood. If there is any doubt as to the witness's meaning, more questions should be asked to clarify the issue. Also, when discussing behavior it is always important to explore the interviewee's intentions or motives with respect to their actions. While the interviewer might respond to a situation in a particular way, the interviewee is from a different background and might have specific reasons for responding in the same or a different manner. This is not the type of information one wants to become aware of for the first time in the presence of opposing counsel or in open court. Always identify any personal biases or sensitivities at the interview stage.

When conducting a legal interview, it is always important to maintain a careful observation of the witness. This includes body language, attitude, tone of voice, and any other characteristics that might give insight as to how committed the witness is to the accuracy and truthfulness of the information provided. If a witness does not communicate easily, fumbles for answers, or appears openly nervous, these can be impediments to a comprehensive interview and also act as an indicator of how well the witness is likely to function under the stresses of testifying in open court, under oath, and subject to cross-examination. Some witnesses may be uncomfortable having the interview recorded or videotaped. Depending on the circumstances and how necessary such documentation is for the interview, it may be preferable to dispose with the recording devices and proceed verbally and with notes.

One common pitfall for interviewers is the personal need to be accepted by the witness. Everyone wants to be liked and accepted by the people with whom they come into contact. This also holds true for the legal interviewer. However, it is very easy to allow the desire for the interviewee to be comfortable and at ease to be translated into a performance by the interviewer intended to gain the admiration and/or respect of the witness. The interviewer should be cognizant of spending too much time making polite conversation and monopolizing the interviewee with personal comments. The goal of the interview is to gain information rather than to disclose it.

What happens when the witness appears to be lying? This is a very delicate situation in the legal interview. It is important not to place a barrier between the interviewer and witness by making broad accusations. However, to get at the truth, it is essential to explore the areas where there appears to be deception. It is also important to determine whether the interviewee actually intends to deceive or whether it is simply an attempt to put forth a good front so that the interviewee will be seen in a positive light. When there is reasonable suspicion that the witness is not being wholly truthful about the amount and content of knowledge concerning the facts of the case, the interviewer must carefully probe for additional information surrounding the suspected deceptive remarks. The interviewer should examine how the witness reacts both verbally and physically when tactfully asked about conflicting information. Are the questions met with additional fictitious information, rationalizations as to why there is a conflict, a defensive attitude and posture, a reluctance to continue with the subject, or an acceptable explanation? From a series of questions like this and observation of the response, the interviewer can better establish the productiveness of continuing the interview and the potential problems of using the witness in court. Ultimately however, it is important to preserve, whenever possible, a positive relationship between the interviewer and witness. One never knows when this witness may be needed again or may be called by the opposition. Consequently, an air of cooperation and respect should always be maintained, regardless of the personal opinion or feelings of the interviewer toward the witness.

3. Recording the Results

There are a number of ways to preserve the product of the interview — the information. These methods increase and change each year as technology changes. The methods used to preserve information range from handwritten notes to voice responsive computer systems. However, regardless of the method employed, the objective is constant, to record all the essential information of the interview in an organized fashion using a method that is the least intrusive to the interview process. For example, while handwritten notes of an interview are the traditional method, the result can be an incorrect or incomplete collection of facts, a distraction between the parties to the interview since handwriting inhibits eye contact and thorough observation, and a considerable slow down of the interview process.

If the witness is comfortable with an electronic method of recording the meeting, the distraction of stopping to write notes can be eliminated. However, it is important to periodically check that the equipment is functioning properly and that it is adequately recording the content of the conversation. This includes volume and clarity. In circumstances where the witness does not speak very clearly or audibly, it may be appropriate to supplement with handwritten notes. Another option is videotaping the interview process. While these interviews give a much broader basis for interpretation of the interview, there are also disadvantages. Often, individuals who are unaccustomed to being videotaped become nervous during such a recording. Because the legal interview, by its very nature and implications, can cause a witness to be uncomfortable, the added component of videotaping may not allow a true assessment of the individual as a potential witness in court and may even interfere with the witness's ability to cooperate fully and comfortably. Also, such tapes are generally more difficult and time-consuming to transcribe to a written form for use in the case. As a result, the most effective method of safeguarding the results of the interview may be a combination of note-taking and voice recording. However the unique circumstances of each interview should ultimately dictate how the content is to be preserved.

Assignment 6.3

In the following situations, explain what method would be most appropriate for recording an interview and the potential problems.

a. Witness Jones is a very elderly lady who is Amish. She is not accustomed to machinery of any type. She speaks clearly and distinctly, but she is very abrupt and forthright. She will only speak when looking directly into the eyes of the listener.

b. Witness Ramirez was one of several people injured in a terrible chain reaction automobile accident. Ramirez was the passenger in a car hit by a tractor trailer truck. He suffered a number of serious injuries, and it is questionable whether he will even survive them. However, at this point he is alert and oriented and able to communicate. The party requesting the interview is the insurance company of the truck driver.

C. WRITTEN COMMUNICATION

A daily part of the existence of all legal professionals is practicing the art of written communication. This includes but is not limited to correspondence, memoranda, pleadings, and motions. An old adage for all those involved in legal issues is, "If it isn't in the record, it didn't happen." Simply put, when a business record is a routine matter of a particular business, the failure to include vital information in that record creates the presumption that the event never occurred. For example, if a physician explains the risk of a medical procedure to a patient, yet fails to note that in the patient's medical record, there is a presumption that the patient was never informed. The same holds true for legal records. The failure to voice an objection over a piece of evidence at trial and to have that objection noted in the record results in waiver of raising the same objection on appeal. All representations made to clients should be recorded in writing. All witness statements should be preserved for future reference or use. All communications with the opposition should be recorded to track progress toward settlement. Ultimately, in addition to court pleadings, it is absolutely essential that all terms of settlement of a case are recorded to prevent any confusion as to the meaning or interpretation of the terms.

Without an accurate and complete record of the progression of a lawsuit, terms of contracts to be carried out, and correspondence that addresses one's legal rights, there would be a virtual flood of litigation, much greater than is seen in the courts today. Also, the potential for unfair and inappropriate results would increase dramatically as judges and juries attempted to step back in time and decipher what the parties to suit originally intended based solely on what each party says took place. Clearly, the written record is necessary. As a result, the ability to effectively and concisely draft written documents that affect and recite legal rights is equally important whether it is in the form of correspondence, pretrial preparations, memoranda, or pleadings.

1. Correspondence

As with any business, correspondence is an integral and daily part of operations. For the legal professional there are several basic types of correspondence. There is notice correspondence, which is used to relay information about specific events such as an upcoming hearing, trial, deposition, or meeting. These documents are generally brief and to the point. As a general rule, a simple statement giving the particulars of the scheduled event and any related information, such as items to bring along, is sufficient. Nevertheless, attention should always be given to professional and clear statements and proper language. It is important to remember that all communications emanating from an office help to form the opinions of others about the competence of the persons employed within that office.

APPLICATION 6.2

Following are samples of notice correspondence. The first is an example of how a notice document should not be prepared. The second is a corrected version.

Example A

Dear Morris,

Your deposition is set for next week. We'll see you about 3 on Thursday. Appearance is important.

Madeline

Example B

November 1, 2002

Mr. Morris Washington
1234 Beauregard Lane
Kenosha, WI 52897

Re: Deposition of Morris Washington

Dear Mr. Washington,

Please be advised that your deposition has been scheduled for 5 p.m. on Thursday, November 9, 2000. The deposition will be conducted at our offices in the New American Bank building, 500 Center Court Drive, Kenosha. It will be necessary for you to meet with us in advance to prepare for the deposition. At this time you are scheduled for deposition preparation at 3 p.m. on the day of the scheduled deposition. Please note that your personal appearance is also important and should be professional. If you have any questions about the time or nature of the deposition preparation and/or the actual deposition, please do not hesitate to contact my paralegal Lars at 555-9250. I look forward to meeting with you on November 9th.

Sincerely,

Madeline Smits,
Attorney at Law

Point for Discussion: Why is it important to include the contact name and number for the paralegal?

Other common types of correspondence that emanate from the law office or legal department include letters that state the intentions of the attorney(s) involved. One such letter might be to notify a potential defendant that legal action is imminent. Another type may be to notify a client, or proposed client, that legal representation will either not be undertaken or will be terminated. In either case, the terminology of the letter is very important. In the first instance, the letter should not threaten or communicate a threatening tone in any way. Rather, the intent of the letter is to inform the recipient that the plaintiff believes there is a sound basis for legal action to protect the plaintiff's rights as they are affected by the proposed defendant. Often such letters will provoke a response by the potential defendant to settle the matter without the expense and delay of a lawsuit. Obviously such a result is far preferable to all parties involved.

It is critical that a letter to terminate or decline legal representation be written properly. Failure to do so could have disastrous results, including a subsequent action for malpractice. Whenever there is even a remote possibility that a client could reasonably perceive that there is legal representation, the attorney must be quite clear in the intent to cease or decline such representation and to inform the client of the action that must be taken in order to further protect his or her legal rights. This often includes identifying the effective statute of limitations, which is the last date a case can be filed; allowing a specific amount of time to seek alternative counsel; informing the individual of any upcoming scheduled hearings if the case is already on file with the courts, and giving the reason for not offering further representation. By failing to do any of the above, the client could argue that there was a perception of continued representation. Failure to actually represent the client could in turn be considered malfeasance.

APPLICATION 6.3

Notice of Proposed Legal Action

January 3, 2003

Mr. Irving Agar
P.O. 447
Grand Island, NH 00218

Re: Klienschmidt v. Agar

Dear Mr. Agar,

My firm represents the legal interests of Ms. Johanna Klienschmidt. As you are aware, an automobile accident occurred on or about September 30, 2002 involving yourself and Ms. Klienschmidt. In the incident our client suffered serious and permanent personal injuries as well as significant damage to her vehicle. After thorough investigation, it is our position that these injuries and damage were the direct and proximate result of your negligent operation of the vehicle you were driving at the time of the accident. Please contact me or a member of my firm within 30 days to discuss compensation of our client for her injuries and damage. Failure to do so will leave us no alternative but to fully pursue Ms. Klienschmidt's legal remedies in an action filed within the appropriate courts.

Your prompt attention to this matter is appreciated and we look forward to settling it in a fair manner and without delay.

Sincerely,

Maxwell Hopkins, atty.

(continued)

APPLICATION 6.3 (*Continued*)

Notice of Intent to Terminate Legal Representation

June 21, 2002

Mr. Eldred Toffery
Toffery Construction Inc.
68 Forest Drive
New Braunfels, CA 95612

Re: Toffery Construction Inc.

Dear Mr. Toffery:

As you are aware through past conversations and correspondence, your firm is seriously past due in its payment on accounts with our firm. Although we have made numerous attempts to work with you on resolving these issues, there has been a consistent failure on your part to carry through with agreements to make regular payments for services rendered by our firm. At this time we feel that we have no choice but to discontinue further representation of your corporation in all matters. Currently, there are four pending cases in which we are listed as the attorneys of record for your firm. A copy of these and any pending legal proceedings is attached hereto. As of this date we have filed our withdrawal as your counsel with all appropriate courts and opposing parties in the mentioned legal actions. This withdrawal is effective immediately. However, we have requested and been granted 30 days by the courts in which you may seek alternative legal counsel before the pending actions will proceed further. A copy of the order granting this is also attached. We are disappointed that the issues between us could not be resolved and wish you the best with securing other legal counsel. However, your debt to us remains and is expected to be satisfied in full.

Sincerely,

Roman Stiller
Attorney at Law

Notice to Decline Legal Representation

May 30, 2002

Ms. Samantha Twining
Apt. 340C
404 5th Ave.
Dallas, TX 71555

Re: Twining v. Smith

Dear Ms. Twining,

First let me thank you for the opportunity to review your proposed legal action against Dr. J. Smith for alleged medical malpractice. Upon careful review of the facts as you presented them and preliminary research, I have come to the conclusion that at this time the firm will not be able to assist you with legal representation in this matter. This does not mean that another attorney may not find merit in your case and be willing to pursue it on your behalf. I would encourage you to consult other counsel for an opinion regarding this matter. Please be aware that any legal action in the matter

APPLICATION 6.3 (*Continued*)

must be taken no later than September 1, 2003 in order to meet the statutory procedural requirements of the courts and to enable you to pursue such legal action. I wish you the very best and hope that you will consider us in the future should you need legal assistance on other matters.

Sincerely,

Beverly Newcastle
Attorney at Law

Point for Discussion: Why is it not just as effective to communicate by phone or in person in matters such as those in the application?

Assignment 6.4

a. Prepare a letter declining representation on the following facts: Jessica Worten wants to sue her ex-boyfriend for the value of a watch she gave him two days before he unexpectedly broke their engagement. The watch was a birthday gift. Your research shows that the watch could not be recovered as a gift and is not part of any contractual relationship.
b. Prepare a letter terminating legal representation of Jim Jones based on the fact that you have discovered he has repeatedly lied to you and your staff regarding the facts of his case and has misrepresented issues so as to create a totally unfounded case against his former business partner. The case is set to go to trial in 90 days.
c. Prepare a letter notifying client Marylou Deerdles that the final hearing in her action for dissolution of marriage against her husband Donald is set for March 31, 2002 at 2 PM in the Dodge County Courthouse, Courtroom 22.

2. Memoranda

In the legal profession, as in other types of business, legal memoranda are often a daily function. A legal memorandum may be as simple as notice or confirmation of a meeting, or it may be as complex as a written report of extensive research known as a **Memorandum of Law.** In the legal setting, memoranda can be divided into two broad categories—internal memoranda used for communication among members of the same staff and external memoranda used primarily as persuasive documents and directed toward the opposition and/or the courts. The type of memoranda prepared usually dictates the degree of formality, the tone, and the extent of information disclosed.

The **internal memorandum** is often written objectively. Simply stated, this means that the content of the document is without a particular opinion or slant. Rather, the goal is to look at the subject of the memorandum from all sides in order to facilitate a clear view of the strengths and weaknesses associated with the issues that are addressed. The internal memorandum could be something as simple as the results of an interview or meeting, or a case brief, or it could be as complicated as a summary of extensive research

Memorandum of Law
Document containing legal analysis of issues. May be objectively (internal memorandum) or subjectively (external memorandum) written, depending upon the purpose of the document.

Internal Memorandum
Document of objective tone prepared to communicate information about a client, case, or issue to other members of the legal team.

and analysis of a client's case. Irrespective of the amount of depth of the document, organization is key. This includes clear headings as to the intended recipient and nature of the memo, as well as subheadings for various aspects of the more in-depth memorandum.

Many novices of legal writing are advised early on to "tell them what you are going to tell them, tell them, and then tell them what you told them." This statement is not as ridiculous as it may first seem. The point is simply this: a well-written document will first introduce the topic and its purpose. Secondly, the document will give a detailed analysis of the subject matter. Finally, it will summarize the true focus and objective of the document as a whole. By approaching the legal memorandum in this way, the reader is first prepared for the topic to be addressed. Then, the discussion progresses into more depth. Finally, the highlights are repeated to firmly embed the focus points of the document in the reader's mind. This method has been found to be an effective communication tool and as a result is often used as a foundation when teaching legal writing to lawyers and paralegals alike.

One pitfall to avoid in legal writing is the use of ineffective or faulty logic. The objective is always to make a direct connection between the supporting facts and the objective of the document, such as to support a particular legal position. Ineffective or faulty logic weakens the purpose of the document and distracts the reader. Examples of ineffective or faulty logic include the insertion of personal opinions or bias in the discussion of the topic or adding statements about the individuals involved rather than the objective facts. For example, a statement of personal bias in a legal memorandum might refer to a particular individual's professional experience. The reader is not typically concerned with the experience of one person but rather with the state of the law on a topic throughout a jurisdiction. Similarly, an attack on the opposition that implies incompetence, even indirectly, accomplishes nothing toward the goal of the document. If the position of the opposition is faulty as a matter of law, then that should be established by identifying the contradictory authorities. This is an objective examination of legal principles and the failure of the opposition to address applicable law will become self-evident.

APPLICATION 6.4

A. Interoffice Memorandum

From: Opal Calens, paralegal
To: Jose Columbus, Atty.
Date: July 18, 2002
Re: Flaming v. Wesley

I recently completed the interviews of our client James Flaming and the passenger Denise Shimkus, who was in his vehicle at the time of the accident with John Wesley. While Mr. Flaming insists that the light at the intersection was green and further, that he was traveling well within the posted speed limit, his passenger Denise Shimkus is not as committed to this recitation of facts.

Mr. Flaming states that he clearly remembers approaching the intersection with caution as he's witnessed 2–3 accidents there in the past. He states he always reduces his speed and looks carefully for any vehicles that might be approaching the intersection from a cross direction. On this date, Mr. Flaming states that he was looking at the road ahead of him and not talking or doing anything other than concentrating on his driving when he came toward the intersection. He says he looked at his

APPLICATION 6.4 (*Continued*)

speedometer as he entered the intersection and noted his speed at 30 m.p.h. The posted speed limit is 35 m.p.h. Mr. Flaming says he looked at the light. It was green. He attempted to look left and right but his view on the right was somewhat obscured by bright afternoon sun. Nevertheless, he saw cars in the area but they appeared to be stopped or slowing for the red light in their direction of traffic. As he proceeded into the intersection he says that he was unexpectedly hit by the Wesley vehicle approaching at a high rate of speed from the right.

When I interviewed Ms. Shimkus, her account of the events was somewhat different. Ms. Shimkus was seated in the right front passenger seat of Mr. Flaming's car. She says that just before the accident Mr. Flaming had told a very funny story and that they were both laughing very hard. She distinctly recalls Mr. Flaming taking at least one hand off the steering wheel and pounding the dash, he was laughing so hard. She does not recall Mr. Flaming braking or a reduction in the speed of the car. She states that she was looking ahead and is certain the light turned yellow well in advance of their entry into the intersection. She recalls this because she also remembers thinking that Mr. Flaming must be planning to "push the light." She also remembers thinking that it "wasn't such a smart move since traffic was so heavy." Ms. Shimkus was looking out the passenger window at the oncoming car at the moment of the accident. She remembers no bright sunlight. Rather, she recalled cloudy conditions. The impact was just behind her seat and she remembers thinking to herself, "he's going to get me killed!" just as the accident occurred.

While both of these people would make credible witnesses in general, I am very concerned about the discrepancies in their stories. Mr. Flaming obviously has much to lose if it is shown that the light was yellow or had turned red. Further, if the defense demonstrates that the car did not slow down and that there was no obscuring of the visual field, the case could fall apart completely. I wanted you to be well aware of these facts given that Ms. Shimkus would be a primary witness in this case. I will wait for further instructions as to how to proceed.

Respectfully Submitted.

Unlike the internal memorandum, the **external memorandum** is rarely written from an objective viewpoint. External memoranda are usually prepared for submission to a court and/or the opposition in a case. Consequently, they are typically approached in a light most favorable to the author's client. One cannot assume the reader will have a significant amount of knowledge about the particulars of the case and therefore it is helpful to include a brief recitation of the facts of the case and to use appropriate subheadings to create a more organized document. Also, in the external memorandum, any principle of law that is advanced in a case should be supported with reference to a citation of law in an applicable precedent. The failure to do so will immediately invite attack from the opposition and give the general appearance of a weak legal argument.

It is important however to remember that whenever legal argument is made and in whatever context, including memoranda, the argument should be logical in its basis. An illogical argument might be one that attacks the opposition or their counsel personally as opposed to the merits of the case. Another would be to attempt to elicit an emotional response to the case as opposed to a well-reasoned discussion. While the external memorandum is typically written from a subjective or slanted viewpoint, this does not mean that overuse of adjectives and personal affronts can be effectively used in place of sound legal argument.

A key to a well-written external legal memorandum is the ability to identify not only the strengths of one's case, but also the weaknesses, and to adequately explain why

External Memorandum
Document of subjective tone prepared in support of a legal position and intended for members outside the legal team, for example, the court or opposing counsel.

those weakness do not defeat one's position. The result in the vast majority of lawsuits is the product of balance. Cases that are so heavily weighted on one side as to be considered *open and shut* are rarely pursued to the point of legal argument and trial. Rather, most cases that proceed through the entire legal process have strengths and weaknesses on both sides of the argument. The key to success is to create the opinion in those with the authority to decide, or to perhaps offer settlement, in the case that the strengths on one side are significantly greater than its weaknesses or the strengths of the opposition.

APPLICATION 6.5

MEMORANDUM OF LAW IN SUPPORT
OF MOTION FOR CUSTODY OF PERSONAL PROPERTY

Comes now Beatrice Lincoln, by and through her attorney Anthony Judeal, and in support of her Motion for Custody of Personal Property offers the following Memorandum of Law.

Introduction of Issues

At present the court has taken under consideration the Motion for Possession of Personal Property by Respondent in this case, Beatrice Lincoln (hereinafter "Respondent"). At issue is the control and possession of the pet dog belonging to Respondent in the related Dissolution of Marriage action with Petitioner Lee Lincoln. The Respondent seeks to have sole control and possession of the dog (hereinafter "Chevas") on the premise that he is the sole and personal property of the Respondent and further that the Petitioner has no ownership rights or interest in the dog. Petitioner contends that the dog Chevas is a family pet and not personal property in the nature of an inanimate object and further, that Petitioner should be awarded joint custody and in the alternative, sole custody of Chevas.

Relevant Facts

The Petitioner and Respondent were married on or about October 6, 1995 in Dade County, Florida. On October 6, 2001, Petitioner filed a Dissolution of Marriage action in this court naming Respondent, and seeking the dissolution of marriage and distribution of all joint assets and debts of the parties. During the marriage of the parties the Respondent and Petitioner maintained totally separate bank accounts and all joint assets were acquired through equal contributions by each party from their respective income/assets. On or about April 1997, the Respondent in this action removed $400.00 from her solely held personal checking account and purchased a pedigreed puppy, which she named "Chevas" and which puppy is now the subject of this motion. Throughout the remainder of the marriage between Respondent and Petitioner, it was the Respondent who paid from her personal funds all costs associated with routine veterinary care for Chevas including annual shots, neutering, and annual teeth cleaning under anesthesia. At the time of the parties' separation and filing for Dissolution of Marriage by Petitioner, the dog Chevas was removed along with other personal possessions of the Respondent to the new residence of the Respondent. Since that time, the Petitioner has repeatedly demanded that the dog be returned to the former marital residence and to his care, control, and custody. The demands have been a constant issue between the parties and interfering with the settlement of other property issues. As a consequence, the Respondent has moved that the Court resolve the issue of possessory rights with regard to the dog Chevas.

APPLICATION 6.5 (*Continued*)

Argument

It is undisputed by the parties that in no way did the Petitioner contribute to the purchase of the dog Chevas by Respondent for the sum of $400.00. Further, in the more than four years since the purchase of the dog, the Petitioner contributed nothing toward the ongoing medical care, treatment, and services for the dog, which are now in excess of $2,000. The pedigree papers filed with the American Kennel Association list the owner of the dog Chevas solely in the name of the Respondent. The only argument advanced by the Petitioner in opposition to the Respondent's Motion is that he spent more actual hours with the dog than Respondent and as such has a personal bond and relationship with the dog that he claims should be honored. The Petitioner fails to mention or address or acknowledge the personal property issue in his response. The reason for the increased time with the dog is that Petitioner has been employed only on a part-time basis for more than six years without seeking any other employment, and the Respondent has been necessarily employed on a full-time basis in order to satisfy the financial demands on the couple for basic living expenses such as rent, food, medical care, etc. In any event, the precedent on the issue of pet custody in previous similar cases renders the arguments of the Petitioner as ineffective and an insufficient basis to successfully oppose the motion of the Respondent.

The Appellate Courts of this state in the 1st District established in 1995 that animals, regardless of the personal bond associated with them, are not to be given the same consideration as children in a Dissolution of Marriage action. Rather, they are to be treated legally as personal property in a like manner as inanimate personal property to be equitably distributed among the parties. In its opinion the court stated, "While a dog may be considered by many to be a member of the family, under Florida law, animals are considered to be personal property. *County of Pasco v. Riehl,* 620 So. 2d 229 (Fla. 2d DCA 1993); *Levine v. Knowles,* 197 So. 2d 329 (Fla. 3d DCA 1967). There is no authority which provides for a trial court to grant custody or visitation pertaining to personal property." *Bennet v. Bennet,* 655 So. 2d (Fla 1st DCA 1995). The present case is not distinguished. The dog Chevas was purchased and provided for financially by the Respondent. The Petitioner did not contribute in any way to the maintenance of this property, and as such it should be regarded as any property personal to the Respondent such as clothing or other personal effects.

Conclusion

It is readily apparent from the precedent that complete possession and control of the dog Chevas should be awarded as personal property. The facts of the instant case clearly establish that the property is exclusively that of the Respondent. That the Petitioner spent time with the dog is no more legally relevant than if the Petitioner spent time admiring a particular dress of the Respondent. The personal property i.e., the dog, was purchased and maintained by the Respondent and as such should be awarded to her without interference by the Petitioner.

WHEREFORE, the Respondent prays that her motion be granted.

Respectfully Submitted

Anthony Judeal
Attorney for Respondent

As shown in the previous examples, the tone and general approach to internal versus external memoranda differ significantly. However, the keys to an effective document remain the same:

1. Identify the purpose of the document.
2. Identify and communicate in the appropriate manner to the intended audience.
3. Include information that is necessary and relevant to accomplish the purpose of the document.
4. Adhere to the proper form for the document.

If these steps are followed and attention is given to general rules of proper written communication, such as grammar, spelling, and use of terminology, the preparation of legal memoranda is not an overwhelming task and in many instances can be the most effective method of communication in a legal action, either internally or with courts and opposing parties/counsel.

Assignment 6.5

For each of the following situations, prepare the proper type of memorandum.

a. Paralegal K needs to inform his attorney supervisor M that he suspects their client A of working odd jobs for cash while claiming to his attorneys and in a lawsuit they have filed on his behalf, that he is permanently and totally disabled from working. A is a client who claims total disability from injuries received while working with a product that allegedly contained inadequate instructions for use. During an interview, a witness in the case alluded to A's alleged working for cash and bragging about it to friends.

b. Your supervising attorney has asked you to research the rights of the parties in a pending divorce action. In the current case, the client/petitioner has filed a motion for full custody without visitation by respondent G of her son J. J is a son from a prior relationship and is not the legal son of respondent G. G claims that he has been the primary caregiver for J from the time J was six months old until his current age of eight and that S's employment has always consisted of extensive travel obligations. As such, G claims he has the right to primary custody and, in the alternative, extensive visitation with J. Your research shows in the case of *Ghonster v. Gohnster*, 334 Mich. 628 (Mich.App. 1997) that anyone other than a parent must first establish a legal relationship with the child prior to establishing any rights with respect to custody. The present case is also filed in Michigan.

3. Pleadings and Motions

Pleadings
Initial documents in a lawsuit that apprise the parties and the court of the legal position of plaintiff and defendant. Typically these are the complaint/petition and answer/response.

In any legal action, the documents typically found within the court files are pleadings and motions. While definitions of **pleadings** vary, most often they are considered to be the original complaint or petition initiating the action, any subsequent amendments, and any answers or responses. Traditionally, a complaint was an action seeking monetary compensation of some type, and a petition sought some action in equity such as the end of a legal relationship, return of property, or even court-ordered conduct or cessation of conduct of some kind. The answer was the document filed by the defendant to a complaint, and a response was filed by the respondent to a petition.

However, for a number of reasons, over time the terms have become largely a matter of practice in any given jurisdiction. While some states prefer the terminology complaint and answer, others have adopted petition and response without regard to the nature of the legal action. And, some jurisdictions still distinguish the terminology by the nature of the action.

Regardless of the title of the document, the nature of pleadings is the same. The petition or complaint is the document used to initiate a lawsuit seeking a court-enforced action. The document identifies the parties to the suit, the legal basis for seeking a judgment from a court, and usually facts necessary to support the legal action. At the close of the document, the result, known as *relief*, sought by the plaintiff or petitioner (party who files the suit) is stated. The document is filed with the appropriate court and the other party or parties to the suit are notified. Each jurisdiction has specific rules for notification and failure to follow these rules can result in the action being dismissed entirely. In some jurisdictions, the courts have approved fill-in forms for routine matters. This is part of a continuing attempt to make the courts more accessible to individual citizens.

If the responding party alleges some fatal flaw in the substance or form of the petition/complaint, or in the manner of notification, a motion to dismiss or demurrer (equivalent document) may be filed asking that the action be dismissed on its face without further required action by the defendant. However, if notification is proper, the appropriate party is named and notified in the suit, and the form and substance of the petition/complaint are proper, the next step is for the defendant/respondent to reply. The document in which the party sued acknowledges and states their reply to the allegations is the response or answer. In most jurisdictions, the party responding must reply to each of the allegations of the complaint in one of three ways. They can deny the allegation, admit the allegation, or state that it is not possible to admit or deny based on the information provided in the allegation. At this time, it is also appropriate to state any counter-claims against the plaintiff/petitioner or any affirmative defenses. In an affirmative defense, the party admits the allegation but claims that the alleged conduct was proper because of some overriding legal right to act in the manner alleged.

APPLICATION 6.6

A. Allegation excerpt from a complaint:

13) On or about June 1, 2001 the defendant recklessly and negligently ejected the plaintiff from his plane at an altitude of 4000 feet after providing insufficient training and education in skydiving.

B. Excerpt of Response and affirmative defense to allegation from complaint:

1) Defendant neither admits nor denies the allegations of Plaintiff in Paragraph 13 of the complaint based on a lack of information provided in the Complaint.

2) The Defendant alleges that the affirmative defense of assumption of risk applies and prevents recovery by the plaintiff against defendant, in that the plaintiff had knowledge of the dangers of skydiving, appreciated said dangers, and thereafter voluntarily encountered said dangers.

Point for Discussion: Why should it be permissible to not respond by either admitting or denying the allegations?

After the answer and complaint have been filed, the parties proceed with preparations for trial. Among the various steps undertaken by each party, a common occurrence is a motion. Specifically, a motion is made at any time after the lawsuit is initiated when a party wants a ruling on a particular point of contention. Some of the earliest motions may be with respect to the complaint/petition itself. A defending party may file a motion to quash, wherein they complain that there was an impropriety in the way notification of the suit was achieved. There may be a motion to dismiss if the defending party alleges that the complaint/petition was filed improperly or in the incorrect form or jurisdiction. Other motions filed deal with the discovery and exchange of evidence, matters relating to how the case will progress at trial, and any other issues that may arise between the parties. Once a case is in trial, there are also a number of motions that may be made with respect to the trial process. Most often, trial motions are made verbally and recorded by a court reporter, because all parties are present and able to argue their positions. However, pretrial motions are usually made in writing to the court. The form for motion is generally quite brief. A statement is made as to the issue between the parties and the result sought by the party filing the motion. Any supporting argument, documents, and discussion are most often presented at a hearing and/or in the form of attachments. While the court file may also contain various transcripts of court hearings, depositions, and such, its primary content and that relied upon by the judges when making determinations, consist of the complaint/petition, answer/response, and motions with supporting documentation.

APPLICATION 6.7

Sample Complaint

COMPLAINT

Comes now Flora S. Banks, "hereinafter Plaintiff," by and through her attorney James Busey, and for her cause of action against the Defendant Michael N. Epcot, states as follows:

1. On or about January 3, 1999, the parties entered into a general partnership in order to conduct the business of a restaurant.
2. Said partnership provided for equal shares of profit and loss among the parties.
3. Each party contributed cash amounts of $25000.00 to the bank account of the partnership.
4. Throughout the partnership, Plaintiff was to contribute her time and abilities to the running of daily operations of the partnership including cooking and supervision of personnel.
5. Throughout the partnership Defendant was to contribute his time and abilities to overseeing all financial matters of the partnership including daily receipts, accounts payable, payroll, taxes, and general accounting.
6. That said partnership and the subject restaurant continued until approximately March 31, 2001, when business was ceased and liquidation of assets of the parties began.
7. That on or about May 15, 2001, the Defendant represented to the Plaintiff that all assets were liquidated, debts were paid, and that Plaintiff was entitled to a share of remaining proceeds in the amount of $6452.00
8. That on or about May 30, 2001 Plaintiff discovered that Defendant had taken out proceeds from the final accounting of the partnership in the amount of $47,000.

APPLICATION 6.7 (*Continued*)

9. Defendant failed in his obligation to distribute equally the final proceeds of the partnership assets.
10. Defendant failed upon demand by plaintiff to equally distribute the final proceeds of the partnership assets.
11. Defendant breached his duty as a partner to Plaintiff.

Wherefore, the Plaintiff prays that the Defendant be ordered to return to the Plaintiff that which is due her under the original partnership agreement and all monies and such interest and penalties for Defendant's conduct as the law allows.

Respectfully Submitted,

James Busey

Attorney for Plaintiff

Sample Answer

ANSWER

Comes now Michael N. Epcot, hereinafter "Defendant," by and through his attorney Susan G. Savannah, and in response to each corresponding paragraph of the Complaint of Plaintiff Flora S. Banks, states as follows:

1. Admit
2. Neither admit nor deny based on lack of information.
3. Admit
4. Admit
5. Admit
6. Admit
7. Admit
8. Admit
9. Deny
10. Deny
11. Deny

Wherefore, the Defendant prays that the action brought against him by Plaintiff be dismissed with prejudice and costs to Plaintiff.

Respectfully Submitted,

Susan G. Savannah, atty. for Defendant

(*continued*)

APPLICATION 6.7 (*Continued*)

Sample Motion

MOTION TO COMPEL DISCOVERY

Comes now the Plaintiff Flora S. Banks, by and through her attorney, James Busey, and moves the court as follows:

1. Rule 341.A28 of the New Hampshire Rules of Civil Procedure require that parties respond to requests for written discovery within a period of 28 days from the date of filing of such discovery request.
2. On or about April 1, 2002, the Plaintiff filed with Defendant's Counsel a series of written interrogatories.
3. Said interrogatories were not answered on April 29, and to date have not been answered.
4. Plaintiff's counsel has made written demand on two separate occasions for said interrogatory answers, to no avail (see attached).

   Wherefore, Plaintiff prays that the court will compel Defendant to supply said interrogatory answers within 10 days, and to assess all costs associated with this Motion to Defendant.

Respectfully Submitted,

James Busey,

Attorney for Plaintiff

Point for Discussion: Why should parties be required to state all of their supporting evidence in the complaint/answer?

PARALEGALS IN THE WORKPLACE

As mentioned in earlier chapters, a qualified paralegal can play an essential role in the drafting of legal documents and communication with clients, witnesses, and others. Written and verbal communcation skills are necessary in virtually all paralegal employment settings. Because of this, the paralegal who has the ability to speak and write clearly and effectively will have a tremendous advantage over those who cannot adequately communicate with ease. In fact, a significant portion of the time of many paralegals may be spent on verbal and written communication-oriented tasks. As seen in the various examples throughout the chapter, virtually every step in a case must be documented in some way and it often falls to the paralegal to prepare such documentation.

CHAPTER SUMMARY

The communication skills of the legal professional have a tremendous impact on the degree to which legal issues are dealt with effectively, efficiently, and in a professional manner. These skills require much more than just good grammar and punctuation in writing. The legal professional must be adept at gathering relevant information, and assessing the value of witness testimony and the ability of the witness to provide it. Additionally, being able to write to a variety of different individuals in the appropriate tone, and including sufficient information without inundating or confusing the reader often has an impact on the outcome of the case. The knowledge of proper form for legal documents is essential for a case to move forward at each stage of a legal proceeding. Both verbal and nonverbal skills are cornerstones of the successful legal professional's career.

ETHICAL NOTE

While all of the ethical requirements for a paralegal are important, perhaps one of the most significant conditions with respect to communication is confidentiality. The relationship with a client is one of trust. Inherent within this trust is the understanding that the client is free to be totally open and honest about what are often very personal issues and can do so without fear that the information will be disseminated without the client's knowledge or consent. The condition of confidentiality is paramount and must be maintained by the paralegal at all times. This is irrespective of the fact that some information obtained is interesting or of potential conversational value. The rule of confidentiality is so heavily protected by the courts that the violation in and of itself is considered an injury and no further damage need be shown by one whose trust was breached.

Relevant Internet Sites

Legal & General Writing Resources	http://lib.law.washington.edu/ref/writing.htm
Legal Writing and Citation Resources	www.netlizard.com/yourlaw/1 writing.htm

Internet Assignment

Search for an Internet site that offers assistance in preparing legal correspondence.

KEY TERMS

Direct Question	Internal Memorandum	Memorandum of Law
External Memorandum	Leading Question	Pleadings
Hostile Witness		

Chapter 7

THE PROCESS OF LEGAL RESEARCH

CHAPTER OBJECTIVES

Upon completion of this chapter you should be able to do the following:

- Distinguish legal research from ordinary research.

- Explain the various elements represented by the components of a legal citation.

- List the steps of legal research.

- Explain the difference between finding tools and sources of legal standards.

- Identify the types of publications that contain legal standards from the various branches of government.

- Define and distinguish primary and secondary authority.

- Define and distinguish mandatory and persuasive authority.

- Explain how to validate research.

- Explain how to prioritize products of research.

A. SOURCES OF LAW

As seen in the previous chapters, the ability to locate and identify applicable precedents is crucial in virtually all aspects of law-related professions. The search may vary from something as easy as finding a sample document to follow as a model, to something as complex as locating and analyzing interpretations of the U.S. Constitution as it applies to a specific circumstance. Regardless, locating references in a law library can be challenging and frustrating. However, being exposed to the tools and methods of research and the products available, and gaining experience clearly increases one's efficiency and skill at locating the most appropriate sources to consider in any given situation.

Legal research involves maneuvering through a very complex web of the various types of law, legal authorities, and commentary, and some unique characteristics. For example, when a theory is proven in the field of science, it is established as a rule and remains as such. It may be expanded upon, but the basic proven rule typically remains constant. In law, changes in culture, society, and technological advancement, and a myriad of other variables can and have many times produced a complete turnaround of an established legal principle.

APPLICATION 7.1

In the mid-nineteenth century there was a general rule that if someone caused injury to another person as the result of negligence, the injured party could file suit for damages (costs associated with the injury) and recover them. However, if the defendant in the case could prove that the injured person contributed in any way, however small, to the cause of their own injury through their own carelessness, no recovery of any kind was permitted.

Through the latter part of the 20th century a different rule was adopted across much of the United States. The conduct of the alleged negligent party and any alleged negligence of the injured party were compared and percentages of fault for the injury were assigned. The injured party could then recover the percentage of damages that was specifically due to the actions of the defendant.

Point for Discussion: What is the potential problem with assigning percentages of fault to the parties?

As can be seen, the law is changeable. This is due not only to major cultural, societal, and technological changes, but also to the progression of legal issues through the court system. While a lower court may render a ruling on a case, a higher court or a court in another jurisdiction may render an entirely different ruling. With all of these factors to consider, the key in legal research is not only to locate the most applicable legal standard, but to locate the one that carries the greatest weight and has not been overturned or revised. The legal principle may be quite old or very recent. That is not the key. The answer lies in whether the principle has withstood challenge and whether its source is one that controls or merely influences the current situation. This additional facet associated with legal research is one not to be ignored as it carries just as much, if not more, weight than the content of the precedent itself. After all, if the authority comes from a noncontrolling source, the content of the authority is immaterial in light of authority from a controlling source such as the legislature of the jurisdiction where the case is pending.

1. Types of Authority

There are four basic categories in which essentially all legal principles and their sources can be categorized. Every legal authority can be classified as **primary** or **secondary** and as **mandatory** or **persuasive.** The type of authority indicates either the source of a legal standard or its particular degree of influence in a specific situation. The titles used to identify the general source of authority as law or non-law does not change. The terminology used to indicate the degree of weight a particular authority is accorded is governed by the context in which the authority is considered.

a. Primary Authority   To be considered primary (of legal origin and effect), the authority must be some form of law—constitutional, statutory, administrative, or judicial. Mandatory and persuasive authority indicate the degree of influence a legal standard has on a deciding court. As the name implies, mandatory authority is a legal standard that the court is required to follow. Sources of mandatory authority for all courts in the American legal system include the U.S. Constitution and decisions of the U.S. Supreme Court. Another source is a statute from the same state in which the state court in a case is located. Because the court must follow mandatory authority, it is logical to assume that all mandatory authority must be some form of law (primary authority). Additionally, mandatory authority must be law that comes from a source superior to the deciding court. Hence, mandatory authority is law that is created by a superior primary authority. Examples of mandatory primary authority for all courts would include the U.S. Congress, state legislatures and administrative agencies of the state whose law is being applied by the deciding court, federal administrative agencies, and the U.S. Supreme Court. Depending upon the status of the deciding court, there may also be other courts that issue law that a lower court must follow. That is, a state trial court would have to follow the law set down by the highest appellate court of the same state. For example, the courts of Tennessee must follow the statutory law of the Tennessee legislature. This statutory law would be mandatory on the courts of Tennessee. The statutory law of Kentucky would not, however, be mandatory because the law of Kentucky does not have to be applied in Tennessee. Persuasive authority is that which the court has no obligation to follow but which may have a logical reasoning that the court is persuaded to follow. An example of persuasive authority is primary authority from other jurisdictions or from equal and subordinate level courts. These other jurisdictions or lower courts cannot dictate to the deciding court how to rule in a given case. However, in the absence of mandatory primary authority, if the deciding court is convinced that a secondary authority, the law of another jurisdiction or a lower court ruling, is logical, the deciding court may be persuaded to issue a similar ruling.

b. Secondary Authority   This type of authority is generated by a private source, such as a legal dictionary or reference book about a basic subject of law. Secondary authority is not law, but it is sometimes helpful when clarifying the meaning of a legal term relevant to the issue between the parties. Because it is not law, all secondary authority is considered persuasive and never mandatory.

The four methods of classifying authority can be summarized in the following way:

Primary Authority

Legal authority that may or may not be binding/controlling, depending on the source and the application.

Secondary Authority

Discussion of relevant principles issued by a private source.

Mandatory Authority

A legal standard that the court is required to follow.

Persuasive Authority

Relevant legal principle or secondary authority that is not legally binding/controlling.

Primary Authority — always law
Secondary Authority — always private opinion
Mandatory Authority—always law (primary authority); the court *must* apply this to the issue before it.
Persuasive Authority—may be law or private opinion; the court may choose to apply this to the issue before it.

APPLICATION 7.2

The Alton, Tennessee, school district has stated affirmatively that they have the right to forbid students to wear certain colors and types of clothing associated with known gangs. If they do, students may be subject to permanent expulsion. A statute in Kentucky has explicitly given schools this authority. No laws have been passed in Tennessee on the subject other than one that generally states that schools may expel students known to be associated with established gangs that have a history of violence. A leading professor of law at a nationally known law school has published a lengthy article concerning a study of students at 500 schools. The students reported that those who openly wear known "gang colors" are associated with established gangs approximately 81% of the time.

When a group of students files a lawsuit against the school district in Tennessee, the court is required to follow the Tennessee statute. It may also apply the Kentucky statute to the extent it does not conflict with Tennessee law, and it may include consideration of the law journal article. However, if the court decides in favor of the school district and the case is appealed, the higher court may or may not choose to follow the same reasoning of the court with regard to the Kentucky statute and the article, as they are only primary and secondary, respectively, persuasive authority used to support the reasoning of the lower court's opinion. The only controlling authority that must be applied to reach a decision is primary mandatory authority, which is the Tennessee statute.

Point for Discussion: If the Kentucky statute is applicable, why would the courts of Tennessee not be required to follow it?

Assignment 7.1

Categorize the legal authorities listed below as primary, secondary, mandatory, or persuasive in a case involving federal law that is pending in the U.S. District Court (trial court level) in Louisiana. For each authority state (1) the type of authority it represents, and (2) whether the authority must be applied by the court.

a. U. S. Code
b. *Smith v. Doe*, 233 Supreme Court Reporter 1096 (1999). (publication of U.S. Supreme Court Opinions)
c. University of Louisiana School of Law, Law Review
d. Statutory Code of Louisiana

c. Reference Authority/Finding Tools   Finally, reference authority generally has no value in terms of impacting the decision of a court. Rather, these are publications prepared to assist in the process of legal research. Also known as finding tools, the reference authority includes those publications that make reference to primary and secondary authorities by grouping citations on a particular topic and/or within a particular jurisdiction to enable the researcher to quickly identify the location of relevant authorities. An example would be a subject indexing publication for a particular jurisdiction. This might include citations to relevant statutes, cases, and administrative rules or regulations. Sometimes finding tools are published in the form of comprehensive subject indexes. Other publications may include case summaries or brief discussions of relevant topics with references to legal standards that deal with the topic specifically.

B. INTERPRETING THE CITATION

For persons beginning legal research the first stumbling block is often understanding the numbers and abbreviations that represent the location of a legal principle. Whether the research is done by computer or in a traditional library setting, it is necessary to identify the location and source of the authority in order to determine whether it is primary, secondary, mandatory, or persuasive. This in turn impacts what authorities are actually considered in the research process. For example, if there are sufficient mandatory authorities in a given research question, it may not be necessary to consult persuasive secondary authorities. Each component of a citation (reference) to a legal authority provides information essential to these objectives.

There are as many and varied books and papers in a library containing legal authorities as there are in any other type of library. Locating the correct authorities through a systematic method of arranging information about the authority requires a basic familiarity with the system and with typical methods of organization in legal publications. Almost all are arranged or indexed by subject. These indexes may consist of a single volume, or they may be so detailed and heavily cross-referenced as to consist of multiple volumes containing nothing more than an alphabetical subject index.

Generally a uniform method is used to cite a particular type of authority such as judicial, legislative, administrative, or secondary in origin. By using the same format for a particular type of authority, such as judicial opinions, it is easier to identify and locate authorities from various jurisdictions. For example, judicial opinions from various courts in various states and the federal system follow the same citation format. The citations for the different types of authority, such as judicial or legislative, vary somewhat because the method of publication of these authorities is different. Judicial opinions are published chronologically as courts decide cases among specific parties and issue written decisions explaining the decision. However, the most frequently researched legislative publications are issued in collections arranged by subject and containing laws passed during various sessions of a legislative body. And, administrative law is issued periodically in the form of rules and regulations by the various administrative agencies within a jurisdiction. Usually they are published in some form by each agency and then collectively for all the administrative agencies within a jurisdiction. Some citations include reference to more than one publication of the same legal principle, such as a case. These are called parallel citations and indicate the same authority has been published by more than one source.

1. Judicial Citations

Citation
Identifying information
with regard to the
source and specific
location of a legal
principle.

Reporter
Chronological
publication of case law.

In a **citation** of a judicial authority, the reader is usually given the official location (report) followed by a secondary (unofficial) location (**reporter**) of the opinion, if the opinion is published at more than one location. Additional information that may be included is a reference to the source (court that delivered the opinion), year of the opinion, and the last names of the first plaintiff and first defendant listed in the case. It is not uncommon for there to be multiple plaintiffs or defendants in a suit. A typical case citation might appear as follows:

James v. Carrollton, 730 Mo.App. 1014, 775 S.W.2d 342 (1959).
A breakdown of the citation above would render the following information:

Last names of the parties to the suit: (1) James, *(2)* Carrollton.
Official publication: Missouri Appellate Reports
Volume number (number of the book in a published series of books): 730
Page number (within the volume): 1014
Unofficial publication: SouthWestern Reporter Second Series
Volume and page in the unofficial location: 775, 342
Year of the decision: 1959 (not necessarily the year of publication)
Court rendering the decision: Missouri Appellate Court (indicated by the publication of the opinion in the official report for this court)

When a report(er) contains the opinions of more than one court, it is appropriate to include the abbreviation for the court preceding the year within the parentheses. For example, if the opinions of the Missouri Supreme Court and Missouri Appellate Courts were included in the same reporter, the citation would be changed within the parentheses as follows: (Mo.App. 1959) to signify the Missouri Appellate Court as opposed to the (MO 1959), which would signify the Missouri Supreme Court. If a jurisdiction has subdivided its appellate level courts into districts or circuits to cover specific subject or geographical areas, then the appropriate district or circuit number should also be included with the court abbreviation.

Periodically, a publisher may decide to change the general format (arrangement) of the information contained within its report(er). When this occurs, a new series is started and the numbered volumes start over. As a result, it is important, when analyzing a citation, to note the series of the publication if there is more than one; for example 239 F3rd (Federal Reporter 3rd Series). Otherwise, it would be impossible to know whether the case was reported in that volume number for the first, second, third, or however many series existed for the publication. This is unlike a subsequent edition, which is merely an update of the previous material but with essentially the same content. The series is part of a continuing publication of entirely new material added with the issuance of each subsequent volume.

It is important to note that citations do not always appear in complete and proper form. Generally, however, enough information is given to enable the location of the opinion. Upon finding the case, the information that may have been omitted can usually be found at the beginning of the opinion. For example, when a judicial opinion refers to an earlier decision (precedent), the year or court of the decision may have been omitted by the citing court. However, armed with the names of the parties and the volume, page, and report(er) numbers, it is simple enough to locate the case and obtain the other necessary information to complete a proper case citation.

2. Statutory Citations

Legislative law citations generally contain the same locating information as judicial opinions. Although there are some slight variations in the arrangement, they are not so great as to prevent one from locating an unfamiliar authority. Statutes for a jurisdiction are typically organized using a designated list of subjects. While each jurisdiction determines which subject headings will be used, the methodology remains virtually identical. All the statutes are grouped under general subject headings, which are arranged alphabetically and numbered consecutively. Usually the first heading (often one beginning with the letter *A* such as Agriculture) will be assigned number one. This numbering continues on in sequence until each of the headings (in alphabetical order) have been assigned numbers. Typically each number and corresponding heading is referred to as a title or chapter, for example, "Title 1, Agriculture."

The next step in organizing the statutes is to assign a specific number to each individual law under the various subject headings. If a law is repealed, the number of that statute is never used again because of the potential for confusion between a repealed law and a new law. Because statutes of each jurisdiction are frequently modified in some form, the process of organizing is ongoing. New statute numbers are continually added, and occasionally even new subject headings are used. Because of the prohibitive cost of completely reprinting the statutes each year, the repealed, amended, and new statutes are usually placed in cumulative annual pocket parts or supplements. These are paperback books or pamphlets that are placed next to or inside the cover of the book where the subject heading is located. The changes are printed each year and included with the prior year(s) supplements until such time as new volumes of the statutes are printed and the supplements are incorporated into them. The process of supplementation then begins again.

When attempting to locate a statute by its citation, certain information should always be present: the name of the statutory publication, the number representing the subject, and the number representing the specific statute. Proper form dictates that the year of the publication should also be included, but the year is sometimes omitted in everyday practice. The symbol S represents Section and in statutory citations it is used to signify the numbers representing the section of the statute. Multiple sections are signified by a double symbol SS. If more than one series of numbers appear together but are separated by a hyphen, (e.g., S23-4446), the first number represents the subject number and the following number represents the specific statute. Breakdown of the citation Ill.Rev.Stat. S 26-1040 (1990) would render the following information:

Statutory publication: Illinois Revised Statutes
Subject: 26
Specific statute number: 1040
Year of publication of statute cited: 1990

Note that this is not necessarily the year the statute was passed. Rather, it refers to the form of the statute consulted in a 1990 publication, which may include amendments to the original text. Sometimes the subject number appears before the name of the statutory publication rather than separated from the specific statute number by a hyphen, as in 55 U.S.C. 331(a) (1998). This is a form issue only and does not change the information represented in the citation.

Within the text of some judicial opinions, reference will be made to a particular statute by using terms such as chapter, section, or paragraph rather than a formal citation using subject and statute numbers. When this occurs, if the words or terms are followed in descending order, they will produce the same information. For example, if the citation includes three terms such as chapter, section, and paragraph, it makes sense that the broader term chapter would refer to the subject, section would refer to the statute, and the narrower term paragraph would refer to a specific part of the statute.

Some jurisdictions actually arrange their statutory publication into separate smaller collections of groups of statutes related to a particular subject. For example, the Code of Procedure might contain the individual procedural laws arranged by rules of civil procedure, criminal procedure, evidence, and appellate procedure. On the other hand, a code of substantive law, such as the Code of Labor Law, contains laws that are not generally procedural in nature. This method is just one variation on the basic theme of arranging statutes by subject. If you have the proper citation, you should be able to decipher from it the name of the publication, the number representing the general subject, the number representing the specific statute, and the year of publication. Any additional information in the citation is usually present to make this task even simpler by giving more specific descriptions of the location, such as R. Civ. Pro., which indicates that the statute is within the Rules of Civil Procedure.

The year of the statutory publication, while sometimes omitted, is actually very important. As a rule, a compilation of statutes for a jurisdiction is only published every several years. Even supplements are published only annually as a general rule. Because the same statute may be modified (amended), it is important to locate the version that is the subject of discussion. The statute in effect at the time of the incident that resulted in a lawsuit may not be the same as the statute at the time the suit goes to trial. Generally, the law in effect at the time of the incident is controlling and, consequently, locating the correct version of the statute is crucial. Additionally, it is very frustrating to go to the correct subject and statutory number only to find no sign of the statute's existence. A quick reference to the year of publication, which is either on the binding, inside the front cover, or the copyright year, will eliminate this problem. You may be looking at a publication that preceded the statute, that was printed after the statute was repealed, or that moved to a different subject and consequently a different location. When looking for current law, it is important to always check any subsequent publications and supplements for any changes. When conducting formal legal research, updating services should be consulted for any changes in the law since the last publication date. For the purpose of this discussion, however, your objective is confined to locating the opinion or statute by referring to the citation.

3. Administrative Citations

The publication method and format of administrative law varies widely from state to state. At the federal level, each agency publishes its own regulations. Additionally, all federal administrative regulations are published together in compiled collections. The comprehensive and official publication is the Code of Federal Regulations. While there are some minor variances, the methods for interpretation of citations of administrative regulations and administrative decisions follow the same basic rules as those for legislation and judicial opinions respectively.

For each of the following citations, identify the significance of the numbers, the type of publication represented by the abbreviation, and the meaning of the year given in the citation.

1. *Butler Mfg. Co. v. Hughes*, 292 Ark. 198, 289 S.W.2d. 242 (1987).
2. Ind. Code 29-156 (1975).
3. *Dover v. J.C. Penney*, 307 Md. 432, 569 A.2d. 207 (1996).
4. 236 Co.Rev.Stat. 1992 (1990).
5. *West Haven Sound Development Corporation v. West Haven*, 201 Conn. 305, 514 A.2d 734 (1986).

C. FINDING TOOLS

As already mentioned, subject indexes are the opening key to all legal research. Because there is such a wealth of information available, including ever-increasing numbers and types of publications and various levels of authority, the need for effective research tools to locate specific legal principles is extremely important. To consider the hundreds of thousands of statutes, judicial opinions, administrative regulations and decisions, and secondary authorities for the federal legal system as well as all the states is overwhelming. Even more overwhelming at first is the thought of working one's way through all of these to locate an exact legal principle that is not only applicable to the facts of the current case but influential on the deciding authority as well. Yet, armed with a basic understanding of citations and how to use finding tools of the legal research system, the task can be relatively quick and painless.

The answer to virtually any legal research question can be found by using one or more subject indexes. Every jurisdiction indexes statutes, judicial opinions, and administrative regulations and decisions by subject. Additionally, there are a number of publications of indexes that compile the law from several or even all jurisdictions. Subject indexes are used heavily in virtually all publications of primary authority and many reference publications. Often the problem is not the inability to find answers to the questions, but rather finding so many answers that consulting each and every one of them is not reasonable. The key, therefore, is to know which publication to consult and to understand how the indices for the various publications are arranged to make the most effective use of the proper index.

1. Statutory and Administrative Code Indexes

Each jurisdiction authorizes an official publication of all statutory law. Earlier chapters explained how laws are passed, amended, and repealed and how that is codified (incorporated) into the existing arrangement of published law. Each publication has a subject index. When beginning research, it is helpful to become familiar with the list of topics that make up the main subject headings for the statutory publication. Quite often this will guide the researcher into the first level of the subject index.

After locating the title(s) that addresses the general topic of the applicable statute, it is simply a matter of narrowing one's focus within the topic to determine whether there are statutes in place that address the research question. The references in the topical index are almost always to the statutory citation, that is, the subject heading and specific statute number. When beginning legal research, a very useful tool is the legal thesaurus, which provides synonyms for the terms chosen by the researcher. In this way, the scope of the research can be broadened by using additional terms that may indicate statutes in locations other than those originally considered.

Publications of administrative law follow the same basic pattern as that of statutory law. However, rules vary among jurisdictions as to the required method of publication of some administrative law. Consequently, until one is familiar with the administrative law publication process of a particular jurisdiction, it may be helpful to consult the agency directly for information on publications and how to access them.

2. Locating Judicial Law

Perhaps the most-researched type of law is judicial. Judicial opinions are the product of very specific legal issues based on precise circumstances that have been considered and resolved in the courts. These considerations of exact facts and issues are based on prevailing legal principles. When no legal standards exist that control the outcome of the situation, the courts create them through case law. If research on a particular point, given certain facts, produces no statutory or administrative authority to render definitive answers, judicial opinions rendered in similar cases can give guidance as to the likely posture a court will assume should the case currently under question result in litigation and trial. Case law is much more prevalent. Unlike statutory and administrative law where relatively broad legal standards are issued periodically for the benefit of the entire population of a jurisdiction, every jurisdiction has many courts that daily hand down one or many individual decisions that result in tens of thousands of opinions per year. While not all result in widespread publication, many do and thereby provide a continuously expanding pool of legal standards as they apply in various types of situations.

Published cases are predominantly appellate. The reasons for this are practical. First, trial courts are generally the lowest level of judicial authority. Consequently, a trial court opinion does not have to be followed by a judge in a subsequent case because there are usually no courts below or subordinate to the trial court. However, appellate court opinions must be followed by trial courts that are subordinate to the authority of the appellate court that issued the opinion. Also, appellate decisions are usually rendered by a panel of several appellate judges whose collective wisdom is respected by the legal community. Such opinions are infrequently overturned by a higher appellate court and thus provide a stable basis for comparison of the stated legal standard to a present situation. A second reason for the limited number of published trial court opinions is cost. There are literally hundreds of thousands of cases heard per year in this country. It would not be reasonable to publish all the opinions supporting the outcome of these cases when they are of such limited authority. Judicial opinions are published in what are known as case reporters. New volumes of these books are published continuously and contain the judicial opinions as they are handed down by the courts. Therefore, case reporters are published chronologically. Recall that publications of statutes are organized by subject and are periodically reviewed to contain changes and additions to the law. In contrast, once a judicial opinion is handed down, it remains virtually unchanged. If the verdict is altered by a higher court, that will be explained in a separate and new judicial opinion from the higher court, which will be published in a report at the time the opinion is given. For this reason, it is always important to check the subsequent status of judicial opinions. Changes will not appear with the original, but rather with the publication of subsequent opinions.

The usefulness of published cases is immeasurable. By having access to the opinions that courts have issued in the past, the outcome of pending disputes can often be predicted by the parties with great accuracy. Judges look to the cases to decide what the appropriate legal standards are and how they should be applied. The attorneys for the parties to disputes in similar cases also examine these precedents as an indicator of their chances of winning the lawsuit. In addition, it is not uncommon for parties or their lawyers to examine the cases before taking any action whatsoever. This often will guide the conduct of an individual or a business. One of the main reasons that the vast majority of cases settle prior to an enforced judgment is the availablity of information about how similar cases have fared in the past.

One common thread that connects all reporters, whether first or second series, state or federal judicial opinions, is the indexing system. While many jurisdictions still publish an official report of their own judicial opinions, and while other commercial reporters exist, West has the distinction of coordinating all published judicial opinions in the United States with a common format for indexing both in library and computer research.

This indexing system, known as the key number system, is quite similar to the organization of the statutory code. The key number system is published in various digests that annotate (summarize) case law on national, regional, and state levels. A single established list of topics (periodically updated) is arranged alphabetically in each digest. All subtopics are assigned numbers within the topic area. As necessary, these subtopics are broken down even further with additional numbers and letters being assigned to create an extremely specific subject index. After each heading (e.g., topic and subtopic) are annotations commonly referred to as headnotes. These are very brief summaries, often a single sentence, of relevant points in a case. What makes this system unique is that the very same topics, subtopics, and so on, are used for every jurisdictional publication. For example, if you were doing legal research in West Virginia on a particular topic, you could use the exact same topic and subtopic number to locate law on the same legal principle in the West Virginia Digest as in any other U.S. jurisdiction, such as Alaska or the federal courts. In today's mobile society, cases and the practice of law frequently are not confined to one jurisdiction. The result is the need and the ability to do efficient research in a number of locations.

Even with this system, however, there is so much case law—and it continues to grow—that a simple index would be too cumbersome to manage efficient research. Consequently, the digest consists of more than a basic subject index. Part of each digest collection, which consists of multiple volumes, is called a descriptive word index. The descriptive word index contains a variety of terms that lead to particular information within the digest. However, in place of page numbers, key topics and numbers are given. Also, many terms are cross-referenced to make research easier. For example, if a term is not in the West table of topics, it might be referenced under a West topic or topics that are closely related to that term.

Once the topic and key numbers that appear to address the research query are determined, the topics can be found in the alphabetized group of topics in the remaining volumes of the digest. The topics included in each volume appear on the cover and the binding. Once located, it is necessary only to move through the consecutive numbers until the key numbers are found. At the key numbers are headnotes (annotations) of cases and/or specific references to other West publications, such as Corpus Juris Secundum. If no headnotes are given, then as of the date of publication, no cases were published under that key number. This does not mean that no cases exist concerning your query. Your search may include other topics and key numbers not consulted, which is one reason it is necessary to have as many relevant terms as possible to use in your research. Also, as with all research, check supplemental publications. West regularly publishes pocket parts for inclusion in digests that cite the more recent decisions. West also has other finding tools, such as case name tables listed by plaintiff and defendant. Case law should always be validated by using a citator for any new case law, and to ensure that the cases you have found are still effective.

The citator is a publication organized by citations for a particular jurisdiction or reporter. By consulting the citation for a particular legal principle, such as a case, it is possible to identify other authorities that have made reference to the citation. An additional function of the citator is to provide a subsequent history for the legal principle. If a principle is considered on appeal or by a subsequent authority such as a legislature, this should appear in the citator. Like other publications, the citator is frequently updated using pocket parts and pamphlets.

3. Locating Secondary and Reference Authorities

Because the law is so varied and complex, it is impossible to have a thorough knowledge of all subject areas and jurisdictions. Even the most experienced researcher may be presented with a research question for which he or she lacks a detailed and current knowledge of the terminology or issues involved. For this reason, there are numerous secondary reference authorities to provide assistance. Typical reference authorities include legal dictionaries and thesauri that provide definitions within a legal context and similar relevant terms. Also of great help are reference authorities that provide information about the nature of a particular area of law. These may be as simple as a brief article or as complex as an entire treatise in one or a series of volumes. The amount of information needed depends on the complexity of the issue under research and the depth of knowledge required by the researcher.

Some of the less-detailed reference authorities include legal periodicals, usually published by law schools, bar associations, and other associations connected to the legal profession. The articles often address changing or developing areas of law. Other sources for a less-detailed approach are legal encyclopedias and restatements. Legal encyclopedias are much like ordinary encyclopedias in that they provide a brief description of legal principles and how they are generally applied. Typically, they also provide several citations of authority that demonstrate the actual application of the principles. Restatements of the law consist of several collections of books concerning the various major subject areas of law. Each collection publishes volumes containing numerous and fairly detailed explanations on changing and developing areas of law. Because these topics change fairly often, there is no particular pattern to what articles are included in the series as is the case with the subject arrangement of statutes. Consequently, the subject index to the restatements is essential to locating articles on a particular point. The restatements also provide sample citations of cases and statutes that show the real-life application of a legal principle. However, it is important to remain aware that the citations provided are samples. They do not represent an exhaustive search of all applicable principles. More importantly, the content of the restatement articles and the citations provided may or may not be indicative of the current law in a specific jurisdiction. As stated, these are focused on reporting the developing and changing areas of law at the time the article is published. The purpose of the restatements is to provide an overview of a legal principle and its foundations. It is not to be used as a primary authority or the sole authority consulted to locate primary authority on a point of law.

The most detailed examinations of legal subjects are found in treatises. The term is used to describe a thorough and complete analysis of a subject of law and how it has developed over time to the present. Some noted authors of treatises are considered to be the consummate authority on a subject and their opinion is often accorded great weight by courts even though the publication is actually secondary authority. However, regardless of the importance of a treatise, it remains secondary and is not equivalent to mandatory primary authority. When faced with extensive legal research on a particular subject, or what appears to be a long-standing pattern of research within a subject area in the foreseeable future, it may be very useful to read through one or more treatises on the subject at hand to develop a thorough and working knowledge of the law and how it is likely to apply in more specific circumstances. However, as with restatements, law journals, and other secondary authorities, it is important to always consider the actual law of the jurisdiction on the topic before assuming it will be applied according to the interpretation by a private author.

D. THE FUNDAMENTAL RESEARCH PROCESS

Conducting legal research is unlike virtually any other type of research. If, for example, the research was about the Industrial Revolution, the subject index at the library would provide a listing of texts containing relevant information. When doing research on current medical developments on a particular disease or condition, the information obtained would be applicable in all localities. However, in legal research the task is generally much more involved. In addition to locating applicable legal standards, the following points should be considered in determining which authorities are most valuable:

- The source jurisdiction
- The current validity of the standard, i.e., has it been amended, repealed, reversed, or in some way altered since it was created
- Whether the authority is primary or secondary, mandatory or persuasive

The fact that many terms have a different meaning in a legal context and that many terms in legal documents are not commonly used in everyday language may require preliminary research into relevant terminology to enable successful legal research. Something that few people like to admit is just how limited the ordinary person's vocabulary can be. Often research is fruitless because of the lack of familiarity with the relevant terms or the habit of using the same terminology repeatedly and ignoring terminology that will assist in the research process. Throughout research, it is necessary to search for additional terms that will assist in finding the desired information. Of course, assembling the necessary information is contingent on properly constructing the research question.

1. Identifying the Research Question

The first step in conducting any research may seem obvious; before the answer can be found, the question must be formed. In legal research, proper completion of this step is crucial. By incorrectly stating the research issue in a question, many hours can be wasted on useless reading. For example, in a case of negligence, the issue is not merely whether someone acted carelessly and someone was injured. There are a number of elements to negligence and each has to be proven specifically. Also, any applicable defenses that could prevent recovery by the injured person must be considered.

APPLICATION 7.3

Jeremy Smith attended a stock car race at a local raceway. During the race the driver of a car lost control and crashed into the stands. Jeremy was sitting in the front row and was killed instantly. The family wants to sue the raceway for negligence in having insufficient barriers between the spectators and the racetrack.

Possible questions to consider: (1) Did the raceway have an obligation to spectators to have certain types of barriers between the stands and the track? (2) Did the raceway's failure to have stronger barriers between the track and the spectator stands constitute an action that a reasonable raceway owner would have done? (3) Did the failure to have stronger barriers cause Jeremy's death or would it have likely happened anyway. (4) Did Jeremy assume any of the risk for his death by placing himself in proximity to cars traveling in a confined space at a high rate of speed?

These questions represent the elements of negligence and the defense of assumption of risk. These are the things that would have to be addressed in a lawsuit.

Research Question:
Did the conduct/omission of the raceway with respect to the construction of the spectator stands constitute negligence? If it did, is that affected in all or part by Jeremy's conduct, such as assumption of risk?

Point for Discussion: What questions should be asked with respect to the race-car and driver?

An important step in stating the research question to encourage successful research is to identify appropriate terminology. A strong command of legal terminology is certainly helpful but not essential. Legal dictionaries and a good legal thesaurus can provide synonyms, antonyms, and related terms. Whenever possible, a list of several terms should be the starting point. This enables one to approach research from a variety of vantage points increasing the likelihood of locating relevant legal standards that respond to the research question and any other questions that may arise during the research process.

Based on the following, state the research question.

James Dow broke into an elderly woman's home. He assaulted her and stole a sum of money. As a result of her injuries, the woman required hospitalization and subsequent skilled nursing home care. Prior to the assault, the woman had been totally independent and capable of meeting all her own needs. Four months after the assault, the elderly woman died from a virus that swept through the nursing home where she had lived since her discharge from the hospital. Can Dow, now awaiting trial for charges of assault, be charged with murder?

2. Determination of Likely Sources of Authority

Once the issue is stated in the form of a research question and sufficient research terms are identified, the next step is to locate authority that will have the greatest impact on the case. In doing so, it is necessary to answer several questions:

1. Is the case in (or likely to be) state or federal court?
2. In which state or federal court is the case located?
3. Which appellate (intermediate and supreme) courts have authority (state and/or federal) if the case is ultimately appealed by one of the parties?
4. Is the issue likely to be governed by statute (commonly encountered situations), judicial law (very specific circumstances), or administrative law (at least one party a person, activity, or organization subject to government regulation)? Or is the issue likely to be addressed by all three? Quite often this is the case.
5. Is the subject matter familiar enough that no background research is required on the general topic of law involved in the case?

The answer to these questions in advance of the research can save a great deal of time that would otherwise be spent uselessly moving among authorities in an attempt to locate elusive information. Legal research is often time-consuming, even when done effectively and efficiently. Consequently, a logical and straightforward approach is essential to minimize the amount of time spent that is unproductive.

After the previously stated questions are answered, it is possible to approach the research with the right terminology and within the resources that are most likely to produce results that are applicable and bear authority on the deciding court. The next step is to carry the research question and relevant terms into the subject indexes of the appropriate resources and start locating authorities.

3. Knowing When to Stop

Because there is so much legal authority available, a question of "how much is enough?" always presents itself. Occasionally, research will produce few or no answers to the research question. But much more often, the equation is tilted in the other direction. The decision of how much research is sufficient to adequately respond to the research question is guided by a number of factors. These include, but are not limited to, the following:

1. How critical is the research question to the progression of the case?
2. How likely is the research question to be litigated?
3. Thus far, how current are the answers found to the research question?
4. How significant is the authority found thus far in response to the research question?
5. How much authority is there that would support the likely position of the opposition and what is its significance?

After considering these, and any other relevant factors, the final decision comes down to a basic standard. When it can be said that no stronger authorities that are currently valid and applicable to the facts of the case are likely to be found, and when there is sufficient research available to effectively rebut the probable position of the opposition, further research is likely to be redundant or of little impact. For example, when the question under research is fully understood, and when each of the various sources of mandatory primary authority have been thoroughly researched, any additional information is necessary only to the extent the research requires support. In different kinds of cases, this may or may not be of measurable help. In a case where the law is currently undergoing change or change is proposed, additional research may be quite helpful to further clarify the reasoning behind the change or demonstrate a trend of change in other jurisdictions. When the mandatory primary authority of a jurisdiction offers little guidance on the research question, other primary and secondary authorities can be quite useful to justify the desired result. Similarly, if the law is in a state of change or development, and the trend in other jurisdictions supports the likely position of the opposition, this should not be ignored and research should continue in order to address this. While no simple answer exists as to when research should stop, by considering the factors above, it is usually not difficult to reach an informed decision.

4. Analysis and Prioritization of Products of Research

Once sufficient legal authority has been found that is responsive to the research question, it must be determined which of the authorities are most significant in terms of weight with the court and with respect to answering the fundamental research question. This requires close legal analysis and prioritization. Many beginning research students find this step to be the most difficult—even more so than actually locating the information. Until a degree of confidence has been established in evaluating the significance of the products of research, there may be a nagging doubt as to whether an authority identified as less important may at some point reappear in the form of a controlling authority presented to the court by the opposition. Fortunately, prioritization skills are based upon certain established principles and a hierarchy of law that, if followed, should relieve most of these doubts.

The first step is legal analysis, which was addressed in detail in earlier chapters. This is an element of research that should never be overlooked or hurried through. For example, even if a case with very similar facts turns out in a way that would be favorable to the current case, it may or may not be applicable for a variety of reasons. The reasoning of the prior court must be examined and understood before it can be proposed as applicable and controlling in the current case.

APPLICATION 7.4

The current case involves an action for negligence in the state of Nebraska. The research question is whether a partner in a 30-year monogamous homosexual relationship can recover for emotional distress after observing the other partner killed as the result of negligence by a third party.

The products of research include the following:

a. A 1991 statute from the state of Nebraska that generally states bystander recovery may be considered in cases of negligence, but such actions must be brought within one year of the incident alleged to have caused the injury

b. A case decided in 1972 from the state of Nebraska Supreme Court that disallows "bystander recovery completely"

c. A case decided in 1988 by the Nebraska Supreme Court that permits "bystander recovery" for persons related to the injury victim

d. A case decided in 1990 by the Missouri Supreme Court that allows "bystander recovery" for persons with a "close relationship" to the injury victim

e. An excerpt from a leading authority on torts (including negligence) that explains why bystander recovery should be permitted in appropriate circumstances

Point for Discussion: What would be an additional key question to research given the information located at this point?

Assignment 7.4

Based on the information provided, prioritize the products of the research and explain the reasoning for the order in which the authorities are ranked.

---

5. Confirmation of Search Results

The final step in research is to confirm the validity of the results. This confirmation is absolutely imperative to good and thorough research. Authorities must be selected that are relevant, but each must be verified as sound statements of the applicable law. Publications and electronics services, known as citators, provide this information. Armed with the citation of a primary authority, a search can quickly be conducted in a citator that provides information as to whether the authority has been altered, amended, reversed, appealed, or affected in any way by a subsequent primary authority. The citator provides a listing of all subsequent published primary authorities such as judicial opinions, that make a reference to the citation. The reference may be to affirm and agree with one or more of the legal standards of the authority cited, or it may be to disagree, distinguish, or reject the authority. A strong history of approval or dissent with respect to a cited authority is something to consider when using the authority as a product of research in a current case. While long-standing and frequently cited approval may be helpful and even render the citation as a "landmark" authority, disapproval may indicate an underlying trend toward impending change.

If an authority has been consistently disagreed with or distinguished as inapplicable for some reason, consider that a trial court or even an appellate court, might not continue to uphold the position. If that result would harm the current case, it may be wise to look for alternative authorities to support the position and to seek ways to distinguish the potentially negative effects of the cited authority from the current case. While confirmation is typically a final step in research, in some cases it can be a catalyst for reopening the research question.

E. COMPUTERS AND LEGAL RESEARCH

Until the fairly recent past, the vast majority of legal research was conducted in the traditional law library, just as it had been done for decades before. However, during the 1980s computer-assisted research began to appear first in law libraries and then in law offices and corporate legal departments. By the late 1990s a large percentage of research was being done with the assistance of a computer.

A major expense of the practice of law is maintaining a law library in terms of keeping publications current and affording space to accommodate them. For some, the expense was too great to be justified and the alternative of sharing a library or traveling to a law library at a courthouse or law school had to be considered. However, with the advent of computer-assisted research, the work could be done in the office, little or no additional space was needed, and often the cost of subscribing to a computer-research service (database or CD ROM) was, and still is, less than that of subscribing to bound publications. Also, no one is required to update material through placement of pocket parts, supplements, and loose-leaf pages; maintain the library, copy cases and statutes, and so forth. The computer and legal research are essentially a perfect marriage, given one crucial condition: the researcher must have adequate computer research skills, or the necessary information may exist but never be found.

While other databases for legal research are on the market, WESTLAW and Lexis are the two original and current moving forces in the field of electronic legal research. Both offer access to virtually all authorities found in a comprehensive law library via computer modem, Internet resources, or CD ROM. WESTLAW has the added feature of making computer legal research queries available in the same format as traditional research by using its KEY system. In this way, even those trained in the traditional methods of legal research can adapt with relative ease to the computer-research process. For someone with no computer-research background, tutorials are readily available to walk the researcher through the various methods of research that are available with a particular computer-research service. It may be helpful to go through the tutorial program a number of times until a level of skill is developed that allows the focus to stay on the research as opposed to the process.

As with any type of research, it is important to concentrate on the jurisdiction whose authority is most relevant. In computer research, the law of the various jurisdictions is divided into different databases (collections of information by source).

Then, within the database, the various types of primary authority are further divided. For example, to research an issue in Connecticut, the first step would be to select Connecticut as a database. Second would be to select the type of authority to be consulted—first, statutory, judicial, or administrative. This is just the same as the traditional method of researching in a law library.

Because on-line computer research is often charged on a time increment basis and because research needs to be efficient for this and other practical reasons, the research question or query and list of relevant terms should be adequately prepared before accessing the computer-research system. As with other research, several specific queries should be prepared. It can always be broadened or narrowed as dictated by the results of the research. However, as the Internet becomes more and more a part of daily life in the legal profession, the cost is less of a concern as most primary authorities are accessible directly through the jurisdiction's Websites or through an Internet connection to a research service such as WESTLAW or Lexis.

Computer research programs are constantly being modified to make them more user friendly. In the early days, the researcher supplied a list of relevant terms and the computer searched for authorities containing the terms exactly as stated in the query. Today, computer research programs are much more adaptive and can respond to actual questions. This is especially helpful since the relevant authorities, while addressing the same issue, may not use precisely the same terminology. Under the original method, failure to use identical terminology would result in a response by the computer service that no relevant authorities exist. They do exist, but include different terminology.

Most computer research programs also provide a number of symbols that allow the scope of a research question to be narrowed. These symbols can be used to look for certain terms or phrases in close proximity to one another and thereby increase the likelihood that the research results will have discussion issues relevant to the research question. For example, while two or three terms may appear throughout an authority in varying contexts, by using symbols to locate only those authorities in which the terms appear within the same sentence, paragraph, or specified number of words, the search can be narrowed significantly. Also, symbols can be used to search for terms either alternatively or inclusively. The effective use of symbols in computer-assisted research can have a tremendous impact on its likelihood of success.

Another popular method of computer-assisted research is the citations method. By providing the citation of a specific relevant authority, the computer research service can locate the authority and other related authorities. With WESTLAW, the key numbers can be used to locate all authorities identified within the West Digest system having the same key numbers or topics addressed. Computer-assisted research programs also offer citation services for confirming authorities. As with the traditional publication, all subsequent references to the citation are given, as well as any notable changes, approval, or objection to the cited authority.

An alternative to the popular and virtually unlimited on-line research services available is the CD ROM method. The concept is a simple one. Compact discs containing research materials for a particular subject of law or jurisdiction can be loaded into the CD ROM player on a computer. Similar to on-line research, queries and terms can be entered and the relevant authorities on the disc can be retrieved. This method eliminates the cost associated with telephone lines and access to the computer research service, which may include specific charges for the time spent on-line. The disadvantage is that the discs are limited in scope and must be continually updated to maintain a current library. Also, numerous discs are required, including regular updates, to maintain even a moderate collection of authorities and resources.

PARALEGALS IN THE WORKPLACE

Legal research is an essential element of the practice of law in that precedents are what guide lawyers in their ability to advise and represent clients effectively. Thus, the paralegal who can conduct legal research under the supervision of an attorney possesses an incredibly strong job skill. Also, it is important to be at ease with the process of incorporating citations of authority into legal writing. The paralegal who can locate and reference legal authorities can be an invaluable member of the legal team. Typical job duties might include researching possible causes of action for a new client, authorities to support or oppose a motion filed in a case, legal memoranda and even appellate briefs. The extent of this work performed by the paralegal is dependent upon the sophistication of the research skills. But it is entirely conceivable that the qualified paralegal could perform virtually all legal research that was previously the sole responsibility of the attorney.

CHAPTER SUMMARY

The process of legal research is a complex one because of the variables that must be considered in addition to the basic task of locating relevant information. Things to consider include the types of authorities, the most relevant sources of authorities, applicable terminology, balancing the authorities against one another, and of course validation of an authority's continued effectiveness. Yet, with the comprehensive indexing system in place for all types of legal research resources, the job of legal research is challenging, but one that can be accomplished quite effectively. The advent of computer-assisted research has made the process of searching out answers to legal issues both more affordable and efficient when the proper research techniques are employed.

ETHICAL NOTE

Just as in all other aspects of the legal profession, there are ethical standards imposed on the legal researcher as well. Anyone who submits the products of legal research to a court in support of a particular position must submit any clearly adverse authority as well. At first glance, this may seem unfair in that one is required to submit authority against their position even if the opposition fails to locate and submit the authority. However, it must be remembered that the legal system is based on distributing equity and is not a contest or game to be won at all costs. If it is determined that a party had constructive knowledge of adverse authority and withheld it from a court, the attorney in the case may be subject to disciplinary action for the failure to assist the court in making the most fair and informed decision possible.

Revelant Internet Sites	
Legal Research Guide	www.virtualchase.com
Legal Research on the Internet	www.law.onu.edu/internet

Internet Assignment 7.1

Locate a legal research service such as Lexis or WESTLAW and determine all that is necessary to access the service in order to conduct legal research.

Internet Assignment 7.2

Identify what research finding tools can be accessed through the Internet for primary authorities of your jurisdiction.

KEY TERMS

Citation
Mandatory Authority

Persuasive Authority
Primary Authority

Reporter
Secondary Authority

Chapter 8

LEGAL ETHICS FOR THE LEGAL PROFESSIONAL

CHAPTER OBJECTIVES

Upon completion of this chapter you should be able to do the following:

- Explain the role of ethical standards in the American legal system.

- Discuss the attitude of the legal profession toward ethical standards.

- Describe the ethical standards applicable to various components of the legal profession.

- Distinguish between ethical canons and ethical standards.

- Explain the rationale for requiring subordinates to follow the same ethical standards as attorneys.

- Explain the rationale for holding attorneys accountable for the ethical conduct of subordinates.

- Discuss major ethical requirements that are universal to all legal professionals.

A. LEGAL ETHICS: AN OXYMORON?

1. The Purpose and Function of Ethical Standards

Bottom feeder, ambulance chaser, shyster, license to steal, carp of the law, mouth with a life support system, shylock. All of these are derogatory terms somewhat jokingly used to refer to lawyers. As with any profession, there exists a small percentage of members who, on occasion, act without integrity. Unlike most other professions, the work of legal professionals is often discussed in the media and is the subject of publication. It draws a great deal of attention because nearly the entire general population is affected by it at some level. However, the fact that the courts are busier than ever and the law as a profession continues to thrive is evidence that public opinion of the legal profession and the American legal system continues, in large part, to be one of respect and trust.

Ethical Standards
Defined course of conduct imposed to satisfy ethical requirements.

Something *not* often mentioned in the media are the rigorous **ethical standards** imposed on law-related professions by its own members, the courts, and the legislatures. For hundreds of years there have been clearly stated ethical standards for the conduct of attorneys. In recent years these standards have been called upon many times for guidance as the legal system and the profession have evolved. The states and professional associations have developed committees and disciplinary bodies to review the conduct of legal professionals and to exercise discipline when appropriate. As the paralegal profession has matured, similar rules and authoritative bodies have been generated to advance professional standards for those who act so closely with attorneys.

Despite the jokes and media attention focused on the negative conduct of a few legal professionals, the law profession is one of the very few to voluntarily maintain a comprehensive set of legal and ethical standards for attorneys that can result in professional discipline and, occasionally, criminal prosecution under state law if violated. In addition to being required to take a multi-day exam on basic legal principles to obtain a license to practice law, attorneys are also required to pass a separate exam on legal ethics. A similar exam is often required of those seeking certification by associations of paralegals and legal assistants such as the National Association of Legal Assistants (NALA) and the National Federation of Paralegal Associations (NFPA), although membership and certification are voluntary. Every state has an office where ethical violations of lawyers, those holding themselves out as qualified legal professionals, and those who engage in the unauthorized practice of law can be reported and duly investigated. When warranted, these offices have the authority to impose discipline with respect to licensure/certification and/or to refer the information to government authorities for possible criminal prosecution.

The question might be asked, why so much emphasis on ethics? The answer is simple. While the remarks at the opening of the chapter are usually used in a humorous sense, most legal professionals are quite aware of their responsibility to the public. They know that individuals often place their legal rights, and possibly a tremendous impact on their own future, entirely into the hands of legal professionals. This relationship of trust is a significant one. In some cases, the result has minimal effects; in others it can mean the difference between prosperity and bankruptcy, freedom or prison. Often the stakes in a client's case are very high. In an increasingly complicated legal system, with a plethora of legal standards, a litigation explosion, and constantly changing technology, legal professionals have an overwhelming task to effectively represent the best interests of their clients. Rules of ethics help to ensure that this responsibility is met to the very best of the ability of the legal professional and subject to minimum standards of competence and integrity.

2. Legal Ethical Standards Defined

So what exactly is an ethical standard for an attorney or paralegal? Essentially, these standards are accepted rules that form the framework of the fiduciary relationship between the legal professional and client. While historically the formalized rules were promulgated for lawyers, paralegal associations have adopted similar rules that correspond to the duties of paralegals and their ethical component.

Fiduciary—A person or institution that manages money or property for another; someone in whom another has a right to place great trust and to expect great loyalty.

The lawyer-client relationship is one that is based on trust. The client places, in the lawyer or support staff, trust in ability, trust in commitment to competently perform the required duties, and trust to act in the best interest of the client to the exclusion of all others.

Ethics—Principles, moral principles, code of conduct, right and wrong, values, conscience, moral philosophy, mores, criteria.

Ethical—Legitimate, proper, aboveboard, correct, unimpeachable, principled, honorable, decent, upright, respectable.

As can be seen from the definitions above, the foundation for legal ethics is quite similar to the general interpretation of ethical behavior. The American legal system, and society in general, places a high value on behavior that is considered moral, truthful, and concerned about its effects on others. The legal professional's ethical obligations have the same underlying theme, however, for the legal professional, certain acts with respect to the client have been specifically identified and a definition has been given to what actually constitutes ethical behavior. By doing this, whenever a situation is presented that may be somewhat questionable in terms of what the ethical duty of the legal professional might be, the stated ethical rules can provide guidance.

Fiduciary
Person or institution that manages money or property for another, someone in whom another has a right to place great trust and to expect great loyalty.

Ethics
Principles, moral principles, code of conduct, right and wrong, values, conscience, moral philosophy, mores, criteria.

Ethical
Legitimate, proper, aboveboard, correct, unimpeachable, principled, honorable, decent, upright, respectable.

APPLICATION 8.1

Michael is a paralegal in a very busy law firm. The firm has undertaken the representation of Mr. James in a dispute over some business dealings with Mrs. Delaney in which she claims that Mr. James defrauded her out of a large sum of money. Michael is assigned to work with the attorney on the case. Michael has personal knowledge of Mr. James. He knows for a fact that he has been involved in a number of questionable business dealings in the past, and that he has a reputation in parts of the community for dishonesty and unfair dealings. Michael also knows Mrs. Delaney personally as an acquaintance and is aware that her reputation for business dealings in the community is well respected and that she is known for her honesty and forthrightness. Michael has a legal ethical obligation to act with the best of his ability to assist the attorney in advancing the position of the client. However, he finds it very difficult given his perceptions of the two parties.

Point for Discussion: What should Michael do?

As can be seen from the example, the right thing to do is not always crystal clear. In the application, the paralegal must consider a number of factors including his obligation to a client of the firm, how much personal knowledge he has about the parties, and what the ramifications could be if he refused to accept an assignment from his superiors. Often ethical questions fall into a gray area and require close examination and a logical resolution. This can be difficult, because ethical standards inherently have an emotional quality. One's sense of right and wrong is based on personal beliefs rather than knowledge of facts. It is not a mathematical or scientific equation that can be answered with absolute certainty. Rather, it is a qualitative problem that must be transferred somehow into a quantitative sum. This requires a careful balance of all known facts and a disregard of any information that is based in pure emotion.

Assignment 8.1

Consider the following situation and explain whether there appears to be an ethical issue for the legal professional involved.

Suzanna and Neil have decided to divorce after nine years of marriage and two children. To save money, they decide to let one attorney handle the divorce. Suzanna and Neil each meet individually with the attorney and state what they want to get out of the divorce in terms of financial settlement, custody, child support, and visitation. The attorney then prepares a compromise settlement agreement and urges each to sign in order to move the divorce proceeding more quickly through the courts.

3. The Impact of Legal Ethics on the Profession and the Public

The effect of established legal ethical standards has a tremendous effect on the legal profession and the public as a whole. Without such standards, legal professionals would have no guideposts for those questionable situations that arise in the ordinary course of business. Because each person brings the culmination of their own experience and values to a situation, today's society is far too complex to expect that a uniform standard of conduct would develop if the entire system were to operate on an honor system. After all, who would be the authority to give definition to the term honor? In addition, any protection for the public would come in the form of remedial law. That is to say, that there would be no assistance available to citizens until after an injury by unethical conduct had occurred. Clearly, it is preferable to have established standards that provide a relatively clear course of conduct for legal professionals and a measurement of appropriate conduct upon which expectations of the public can be based.

APPLICATION 8.2

Assume for the purposes of discussion that Attorney Grant practices law in a jurisdiction that has not yet adopted ethical standards or other legal principles with respect to the duty owed to one's client. In one particular case, Attorney Grant loses a crucial piece of evidence. The case is ultimately dismissed in favor of the opposition. Without ethical standards, Grant has done no more than act carelessly with regard to this client, and there is no requirement to the contrary. However, the end result is that the client loses a valuable claim worth hundreds of thousands of dollars. If the client were to sue Grant for negligence, the best that could be hoped for is a monetary judgment. However, Grant may or may not have the resources to pay. Such a judgment would also be difficult to obtain because of the speculative nature of the issue as to whether the lost evidence would have won the client's case and how much of an award the client could have expected to obtain in the event of such a win.

Point for Discussion: How would an appropriate legal ethical standard applicable in this situation be useful?

B. FORMAL ETHICAL STANDARDS

1. Ethical Canons and Rules

Initially, rules of ethical conduct were established only for attorneys, however, similar types of rules have been established for other legal professionals, including members of the judiciary and paralegals. By becoming a member of a certain component of a law-related profession, such as a licensed attorney, there is an underlying acceptance to be bound by the formal requirements established for ethical conduct that protect the integrity of the profession and the interests of those who are served by the profession. Failure to honor these rules can result in a variety of consequences from a formal statement of reprimand to revocation of licensure. For attorneys, the root of ethical considerations are in the form of rules promulgated by the American Bar Association (ABA). Most jurisdictions have adopted these or very similar standards as conditions of licensure for attorneys. The ethical standards for attorneys consist of canons that include traits that all attorneys should aspire to include in their work when serving clients. These are more or less the qualities of the consummate legal professional with the highest degree of integrity. Disciplinary rules are those basic requirements of conduct that, when violated, can result in formal discipline as well as civil actions for damages by parties injured as a result of the conduct. Consequently, the conduct of all legal professionals should fall within a range between the minimum requirements of the disciplinary standards and the ultimate goals of the canons. The professional career of a licensed attorney should reflect a constant compliance with disciplinary rules and evidence of a continuing effort to exemplify the ethical canons. While the appendices of this text contain a more complete publication of common standards, a few of the most relevant to the everyday function of lawyers and paralegals will be addressed within the context of this chapter.

2. Major Ethical Standards

Four of the most common issues for attorneys and paralegals alike are competence, conflict of interest, confidentiality, and commitment to zealous representation. Each of these is of extreme importance and has served as the basis for many lawsuits when lawyers or their staff have failed to meet the required standards. There are other standards as well, but these four affect virtually every type of legal professional and every client relationship. Each support part of the fiduciary relationship between attorney and client that is so protected in the American legal system. The ABA Model Rules of Professional Conduct of 2001 states:

> "Rule 1.1: A lawyer shall provide competent representation to the client. Competent representation requires the legal knowledge, skill, thoroughness and preparation reasonably necessary for the representation."

The question of competence is more involved than one might first surmise. Every lawyer who is licensed today must pass an examination that tests basic knowledge of legal principles. However, this does not ensure that the attorney will keep abreast of changes in the law and always apply that knowledge in client representation. That is an ethical responsibility placed on the attorney as part of the privilege of the license. Many jurisdictions have continuing education requirements to assist in this objective, but this is by no means a guarantee that competence will be exercised in every situation.

To act competently, an attorney should meet one of three basic requirements. He or she must (1) possess an adequate and current knowledge of the subject matter of the representation, (2) obtain such knowledge prior to undertaking representation, or (3) refer the matter to an attorney who has adequate and current knowledge of the subject matter. Because the law is so varied and complex, and in a constant state of change, maintaining full and current knowledge of one, much less many, areas of law can be a daunting task. Yet, this is the requirement imposed on legal professionals to ensure that the client, who places his or her trust in the attorney, is protected.

While in theory it is quite easy for the requirement of competence to be met, in practice it is quite a different thing. After all, the practice of law is a business. A business only profits from serving its customers. If too many clients are referred to other attorneys, there will not be a practice sufficient to support the attorney and staff. On the other hand, the more cases that are accepted by an attorney increases the hours needed to represent them. This may leave precious little time for education and keeping abreast of changes. Then too, what of the subordinate staff? The attorneys and paralegals who are employed by a firm or legal department are paid to get the work done. Frequent refusals to take on assignments on the grounds of lack of competence does not create a promising future for any professional. The obligation is present and serious, but as shown the burden is significant to balance the responsibilities associated with it and client representation in general.

CASE IN POINT

Clinard v. Blackwood, 1999 WL 976582
(Tenn. Ct. App. 1999).

I.

In the late 1960s, Maclin P. Davis, Jr., then a partner in the Nashville law firm of Waller, Lansden, Dortch & Davis, represented C. Roger Blackwood in a divorce proceeding. Thereafter, Mr. Davis represented Mr. Blackwood in other matters. After Mr. Blackwood married Nancy Dods Blackwood in 1973, Mr. Davis represented Ms. Blackwood as well. In 1988, Mr. Davis joined the Nashville office of Baker, Donelson, Bearman & Caldwell, a large law firm with offices in six cities in Tennessee. As far as this record shows, Mr. Davis continued to represent the Blackwoods in various matters following his lateral move between firms.

The Blackwoods own a farm in Robertson County that adjoins property owned by John M. and Edward Clinard. For many years, the Clinards leased their property to various companies that quarried limestone on the site. Two disputes arose between the neighbors after the Blackwoods began building a new home on their farm. First, Mr. Blackwood and John Clinard disagreed about the location of their boundary line. Second, the Blackwoods asserted that blasting at the quarry had damaged their new house and stable. According to Mr. Blackwood, American Limestone Company, Inc. ("American Limestone") moderated the blasting and performed some clearing and excavation work for the Blackwoods after he complained about the blasting. However, the Blackwoods later asserted that the blasting at the quarry caused extensive damage to their house.

In February 1996, Mr. Blackwood repaired portions of the fence along Pepper Branch Creek that had sparked his earlier disagreement with John Clinard over the location of the boundary line. Two months later, the Clinards filed a declaratory judgment action against Mr. Blackwood in the Chancery Court for Robertson County seeking to establish the disputed boundary line. Mr. Blackwood retained Mr. Davis to represent him in the lawsuit.

On May 16, 1996, Mr. Davis formally entered an appearance in the case on behalf of Mr. Blackwood. Later, on June 24, 1996, Mr. Davis filed an answer and counterclaim against the Clinards asserting that the fence was the proper boundary line and requesting that the Clinards be enjoined from removing or damaging the fence. Mr. Blackwood and Mr. Davis also discussed filing a counterclaim and third-party claim against the Clinards and American Limestone for blasting damage to their property. However, Mr. Davis eventually informed Mr. Blackwood that he could not file a claim against American Limestone because the Baker, Donelson firm represented American Limestone in an unrelated environmental matter and because American Limestone had declined to permit Mr. Davis to represent interests adverse to the company's. Accordingly, on August 4, 1996, Mr. Davis withdrew as Mr. Blackwood's lawyer and was replaced by Winston S. Evans.

On September 30, 1996, Mr. Evans filed an amended counterclaim and third-party claim on behalf of the Blackwoods against the Clinards and American Limestone. In this pleading, the Blackwoods sought damages from both the Clinards and American Limestone for negligent blasting, dumping a large amount of contaminated fill material on their farm, and polluting the air with dust from the quarry operations. On October 29, 1996, Ames Davis and Waller, Lansden, Dortch & Davis entered an appearance on behalf of American Limestone. Approximately one month later, Ames Davis and Waller, Lansden, Dortch & Davis replaced the lawyer who had represented the Clinards from the outset of the litigation.

In June 1997, Mr. Davis left the Baker, Donelson firm and returned to Waller, Lansden, Dortch & Davis as a non-equity member of the firm. By that time, the Waller firm had grown to approximately one hundred lawyers. Upon Mr. Davis's return, the Waller firm implemented its "Conflict of Interest Screening procedures" to prevent Mr. Davis and his secretary from communicating information concerning the Blackwoods' case to the other lawyers and staff of Waller, Lansden, Dortch & Davis.

On August 12, 1997, soon after discovering that Mr. Davis had returned to the Waller firm, the Blackwoods' lawyer mailed a letter to Ames Davis stating that the Blackwoods did not assent to the Waller firm's representation of either the Clinards or American Limestone and requesting the Waller firm to withdraw from the pending lawsuit. Thereafter, on

September 22, 1997, the Blackwoods filed a motion in the Circuit Court for Robertson County seeking to disqualify Waller, Lansden, Dortch & Davis from continuing to represent the Clinards and American Limestone. The Waller firm opposed the motion. The trial court considered the motion based on affidavits without conducting an evidentiary hearing. On December 16, 1997, the trial court declined to disqualify the Waller firm but authorized the Blackwoods to seek an interlocutory appeal. On January 4, 1998, this court granted the Blackwoods' Tenn.R.App.P. 9 application.

II.

The practice of law has changed dramatically during the last half of the twentieth century. Greater numbers of lawyers practice in firms rather than as sole practitioners or in small associations. The number and size of these Law firms have grown at an accelerating pace, and much of this growth has been accomplished through mergers and the lateral hiring of experienced lawyers. In this environment, the generation of revenue and the maximization of profit have become important, if not primary, drivers of the law firm's culture.

At the same time that the structure and size of firms have been changing, so have the career goals and attitudes of lawyers themselves. As late as twenty years ago, it was not uncommon for lawyers to spend their entire career with the law firm that hired them right out of law school. Today, there is increased mobility among lawyers, and it is not uncommon for associates and even partners to change firms several times during their career because of mergers or firm restructuring or because they desire to increase their personal income by treating new firms. It is also becoming common for law firms to hire temporary lawyers to work a particular piece of business with no expectation of continued employment once the business is completed.

The changes in the legal profession have also been accompanied by changes in the relationships between law firms and their clients. In today's competitive, cost-conscious environment, clients wield more power than they once did. Clients are now more conscious of the cost of legal services. Rather than remaining with a single lawyer or law firm as they once did, clients today will frequently shop around for legal services or will look to in-house attorneys to provide these services. Because of the increased complexity of the legal matters facing clients and the growing spe-

cialization among lawyers, it is also quite common for clients to be represented by more than one lawyer or law firm at any given time.

These changes in the legal landscape, whether they be lamented or welcomed, have had a tendency to generate more conflict of interest problems than ever before. These problems have placed a strain on the ethics rules governing the conduct of lawyers. The bench and the bar have realized that the traditional rules must be adapted to provide practical solutions for the problems currently facing lawyers and clients. The profession is now engaged in the process of formulating functional rules that give proper weight to the differing, and sometimes competing, interests of all parties concerned. Thus, the traditional more professional values of client loyalty, the preservation of a client's confidences and secrets, and the avoidance of the appearance of professional impropriety are being re-examined in light of prospective clients' interest in retaining a lawyer of their choice and the legitimate prerogative of lawyers to enhance their ability to earn a livelihood in their chosen profession. Agreement concerning the proper way to balance these potentially competing interests has proven to be elusive, and, even today, the legal profession has yet to reach a consensus on many important issues.

Among the most intransigent ethics issues currently confronting the profession involves the use of screening arrangements to avoid the imputed disqualification of an entire law firm because of a single member's conflict of interest with a former client. For the past twenty-five years, lawyers and judges have debated whether and in what circumstances screening arrangements should be allowed. This case requires us to revisit this issue at a time when the organized bar in Tennessee is exerting increasing pressure on the courts to permit the use of screening arrangements to avoid the seemingly harsh effects of imputed disqualification.

The propriety of using screening arrangements has precipitated a pointed debate among practicing lawyers, judges, and academicians. Those favoring the use of screening arrangements insist that they are an appropriate way to protect clients' free access to lawyers of their choice and to facilitate lawyer mobility without sacrificing client confidentiality. Those opposing the use of screening arrangements insist that the profession's ancient obligation to protect a former client's confidences should not be diluted by lawyers' pragmatic business interests. Even the most cursory examination of the literature on the subject reveals that the debate over the use of screening arrangements by lawyers in private practice is far from settled and that the prospects of an early consensus are guarded.

Based on the facts of this case, we have determined that the screening arrangement employed by Waller, Lansden, Dortch & Davis for Mr. Davis and his secretary cannot prevent the disqualification of the entire firm. Mr. Davis became deeply involved in the facts of this case when he served as the Blackwoods' primary lawyer. Accordingly, it is virtually certain that Mr. Davis obtained significant confidential information from the Blackwoods while he was representing them and that this information could, if divulged either purposefully or accidentally, cause material adverse effects on the Blackwoods in the present litigation.

III.

We recognize at the outset that the most authoritative sources for the principles needed to decide this case are the rules and opinions of the Tennessee Supreme Court. The Court has the exclusive power to regulate the conduct of lawyers in Tennessee. See In re Petition of Burson, 909 S.W.2d 768, 73 (Tenn. 1995).

Early in our history, the courts fashioned the rules governing both the practice of law and the conduct of lawyers from common-law principles and from their own understanding of the practice of law and the role of lawyers in litigation. In the early part of this century, however, the organized bar, motivated to some degree by self-interest began to play a more active role in regulating the conduct of lawyers by adopting ethics codes for the profession. These codes, for the most part, reflected the rules and principles that had been fashioned by the courts over the years. Accordingly, the rules in the organized bar's early ethics codes virtually mirrored the judicial decisions regarding lawyer conduct.

Ethics codes were never intended to supplant the court-created principles of professional conduct or to prevent the courts from continuing to refine and apply these principles. For the good of the profession, the courts have a continuing obligation to safeguard the attorney-client relationship and to maintain the public's confidence in the integrity of the legal system. See Panduit Corp. v. All States Plastic Mfg. Co., 744 F.2d 1564, 1576 (Fed.Cir.1984).

The Code of Professional Responsibility, as adopted by the Tennessee Supreme Court, has the force and effect of law. See Gracey v. Maddin, 769 S.W.2d 497, (Tenn. Ct. App.1989) However, the Code of Professional responsibility is itself divided into Canons, Ethical Considerations, and Disciplinary Rules, and each of these divisions has different authoritative weight. The Canons are "statements of axiomatic norms" that "embody the general concepts from which the Ethical Considerations and the Disciplinary Rules are derived." The Ethical Considerations are "aspirational in character and represent objectives toward which every member of the profession should strive." Finally, the Disciplinary Rules are "mandatory in character" and state "the minimum level of conduct below which no lawyer can fall without being subject to diciplinary action." See Tenn.S.Ct.R. 8, Preamble.

However, in 1981, the court reluctantly empowered the Board of Professional Responsibility and its disciplinary counsel to issue formal and informal advisory ethics opinions construing the Court's own ethics rules. See Tenn.S.Ct.R. 9, § 26, West Publishing Co., Tennessee Decisions 609–614 S.W.2d. The formal ethics opinions, which only the Board may issue, "constitute a body of principles and objectives upon which members of the bar can rely for guidance in many specific situations." Tenn.S.Ct.R. 9, § 26.4(a). However, even though formal ethics opinions are binding on the Board and the person requesting the opinion, they are not binding on the courts. See In re Youngblood, 895 S.W.2d 322, 325 (Tenn.1995); State v. Jones, 726 S.W.2d at 519–20. Nonetheless, formal ethics opinions can provide guidance to the courts because they reflect the legal profession's considered opinions regarding the appropriate standards of practice. See King v. King, 1989 WL 122981, (Koch, J., concurring).

IV.

The parties have presented starkly different portrayals of the legal profession's current attitude regarding screening arrangements. On one hand, caller, Lansden, Dortch & Davis asserts that screening arrangements in the private sector have become generally accepted and are currently being widely used; while the Blackwoods assert that screening arrangements have fallen into disfavor. Both parties are, at least in part, correct. There is, however, currently no consensus among the members of the legal profession concerning the necessary ingredients of screening arrangements or the circumstances in which a screening arrangement may be used to avoid the consequences of the imputed disqualification doctrine.

The Conflict of Interest Rules

The fiduciary relationship between a lawyer and a client requires the lawyer to exercise the utmost good faith to protect the client's interests. See Alexander v. Inman, 974 S.W.2d 689, 693–94 (Tenn.1998); Lawyers must preserve their client's confidences and secrets, exercise independent judgment on their client's behalf, and represent their client zealously within the bounds of the law. See Tenn.S.Ct.R. 8, Canons 4, 5 & 7; Dyer v. Farley, No. A01-9506-CH-00229, 1995 WL 638542, (Tenn. Ct. App. Nov.17, 1995) (No Tenn.R.App.P. 11 application filed). They must also avoid serving two clients whose interests are adverse to each other. See State v. Locust, 914 S.W.2d 554, 557 (Tenn.Crim.App.1995).

The prohibition against serving two masters is enforced using conflict of interest rules developed by the courts long before the organized bar began adopting ethics codes.

A conflict of interest arises whenever a lawyer is placed in a position of divided loyalties—a circumstance in which a lawyer's regard for the duty owed to one client tends to lead to disregard of the duty owed to another client. See State v. Tate, 925 S.W.2d at 552. To avoid conflicts of interest, lawyers are prohibited from undertaking to represent a client whose interests are adverse to those of one of the lawyer's other clients. See State v. Phillips, 672 S.W.2d 27, 430–31 (Tenn.Crim.App.1984); Tenn.Crim.App. 95.

These conflict of interest prohibitions continue to govern a lawyer's conduct after he or she is no longer representing a client. See Mills v. Crane, No. 66, 987 WL 9165, (Tenn. Ct. App. Apr.10, 1987). In fact, they continue after the death of a client or former client. Therefore, a lawyer may not represent interests materially adverse to those of a former client if the subject matter of the new representation is substantially related to the subject matter of the previous representation. See State v. Hoggett, No. 1C01-9003-CR-00073, 1990 WL 172632, (Tenn.Crim.App. Nov. 9, 1990).

The application of the conflict of interest prohibitions to individual lawyers is relatively straightforward. A lawyer must not simultaneously represent two or more persons who have adverse interests in the same subject matter. See Tenn.S.Ct.R. 8, DR 5-105(A),

EC 5–15; State v. Tate, 925 S.W.2d at 52. Likewise, a lawyer must not switch sides during an ongoing dispute. See Henriksen v. Great Am. Sav. & Loan, 14 Cal.Rptr.2d at 187; Finally, a lawyer cannot undertake to represent a client with interests adverse to those of a former client. See Mills v. Crane, 1987 WL 9165.

The Imputed Disqualification Doctrine

The growth in the number and size of law firms and the increased career mobility of lawyers have created new dimensions to conflict of interest problems. In addition to the primary disqualification rules applicable to individual lawyers, secondary or imputed disqualification rules became necessary to deal with lawyers practicing in a firm setting. Developing and refining the principles for imputed disqualification has not been an easy task.

Simply stated, the doctrine of imputed disqualification provides that if the conflict of interest rules require the disqualification of an individual lawyer, then all that lawyer's professional colleagues are likewise disqualified. See askey Bros. of W. Va., Inc. v. Warner Bros. Pictures, Inc., 224 F.2d 824, 826 (2d Cir.1955). This principle is based on common sense assumptions concerning the way lawyers work in a firm setting, including the personal and financial relationships among members of a law firm and the motivations for firm members to share information and to support each other's efforts. It is also premised on the common-law rule that partners are deemed to be agents of one another.

The essential component of the imputed disqualification doctrine is the presumption that lawyers associated in a law practice, as agents of one another, know what the other lawyers in the firm know. Thus, it is presumed that information regarding a client that has been imparted to one member of a law firm has been shared with, and is known by, the other members of the firm. See State v. Claybrook, 1992 WL 17546, at *8. When a client's confidence and secrets are involved, this presumption is commonly referred to as the presumption of shared confidences.

By 1969, the doctrine of imputed disqualification had become so widely accepted that the American Bar Association included it in the Code of Professional Responsibility. See Model Code of Professional Responsibility DR 5-105(D) (1969). The American Bar Association broadened the 1969 version of

DR 5-105(D) in 1974 to require imputed disqualification of affiliated lawyers whenever an individual lawyer becomes disqualified under any disciplinary rule. See Model Code of Professional Responsibility DR 5-105 (1974). The 1974 version of DR 5-105(D) is currently part of Tennessee's code of Professional Responsibility. See Tenn.S.Ct.R. 8, DR 5-105(D).

The Courts' Response to the Imputed Disqualification Doctrine and to Screening Arrangements

Most courts currently employ a three-step approach to imputed disqualification issues. The first step involves determining whether a substantial relationship exists between the subject matter of the former representation and the subject matter of the subsequent adverse representation. The second step involves determining whether the lawyer who has changed firms is personally disqualified under the applicable conflict of interest rules. The third step involves determining whether the lawyer's new firm must also be disqualified from representing the party with an interest adverse to the interests of the personally conflicted lawyer's former client.

The "substantial relationship" inquiry is universally accepted as the starting point for the disqualification analysis. While it has several formulations, the inquiry examines (1) the scope of the former representation, (2) whether it is reasonable to infer that confidential information would have been given to a lawyer representing a client in such matters, and (3) whether the information is relevant to the issues being raised in the litigation pending against the former client. See LaSalle Nat'l Bank v. County of Lake, 703 F.2d 252, 255–56 (7th Cir.1983). If the court finds that there is no substantial relationship between the subject matter of the former and present representations, the inquiry ends because there can be no conflict of interest between the lawyer and his or her former client or between the former client and the lawyer's new law firm. If, however, the court finds that a substantial relationship exists, then the court must determine whether the lawyer should be disqualified.

There are two bases for disqualifying the lawyer if the court finds a substantial relationship between the subject matter of the present and former representations. First, the lawyer could be disqualified if he or she has a primary conflict of interest resulting from the lawyer's direct exposure to the former client's confidential information. Second, the lawyer, like the rest of the lawyer's former firm, could be disqualified if he or she has a secondary conflict of interest arising from the presumption of shared confidences.

A majority of courts hold that the presumption of shared confidences with regard to the information received by the lawyer's former firm is irrebuttable once a substantial relationship between the present and former representations has been established. See Arkansas v. Dean Foods Prods. Corp., 605 F.2d 380, 384–85 (8th Cir.1979). Other courts have held that the presumption can be rebutted if the lawyer shows that he or she was not privy to any confidential information. This approach is not widely accepted and has generally been followed only in cases involving associates of large firms who performed minor tasks such as researching points of law. See Silver Chrysler Plymouth, Inc. v. Chrysler Motors Corp., 518 F.2d 751, 756–57 (2d Cir.1975) differentiating between lawyers who become heavily involved in the facts of a particular matter and those who enter briefly on the periphery); Ann. Model Rules of Conduct, supra note 45, at 157–59; Bateman, supra note 8, at 253.

Once the party seeking disqualification establishes a prima facie case, the burden of proof shifts to the lawyer and the firm whose disqualification is sought to demonstrate why they should not be disqualified. See SLC Ltd. v. Radford Group West, Inc., 999 F.2d 464, 468 (10th Cir.1993); Norman v. Norman, 623 Ark. 644, 970 S.W.2d 270, 274 (Ark.1998). This rebuttal effort should not force either party to reveal the former client's confidential information. Any doubts regarding the existence of an asserted conflict of interest should be resolved in favor of disqualification.

If there is a substantial relationship between the former and present representations and if the lawyer who has changed firms is personally disqualified from representing the present client because of a conflict of interest regarding the former client, then the final step of the analysis is to determine whether the lawyer's new firm should be disqualified by implication. For those courts following the traditional view that the presumption of shared confidences is irrebuttable, imputed disqualification of the new firm is mandatory. Other courts, believing that mandatory imputed disqualification casts an unnecessarily wide shadow, are reluctant to invoke the doctrine to disqualify the new law firm except as a last resort. For these courts, the presumption of shared confidences among the lawyer and his or her associates at the new firm is rebuttable. See Freeman v. Chicago Musical Instrument Co., 689 F.2d 715, 722–23 (7th Cir.1982).

Courts viewing the presumption of shared confidences as rebuttable must balance the former client's legitimate right to be free from apprehension that its confidential information will be revealed with the party's interest in choosing his or her own lawyer and with the former lawyer's interest in following his or her career path to its best advantage.

The use of screening arrangements for lawyers moving from one private firm to another remains highly controversial, see Hamilton & Coan, supra note 20, and has not been approved by a majority of the courts that have been squarely presented with the issue. Currently, United States Courts of Appeals for four circuits, five United States District Courts, and courts in six states have approved the private sector use of screening arrangements. At the same time, United States Courts of Appeal in five circuits have declined to approve screening arrangements. Likewise, United States Court of Appeals in two circuits, eight United States District Courts, and courts in ten states have rejected the use of screening arrangements for lawyers in private practice. Two state courts have declined to approve screening arrangements.

Case Review Question: Would the result change if the attorney had represented the plaintiff in the past but not in the pending case?

"Rule 1.6 Confidentiality of Information

(a) A lawyer shall not reveal information relating to representation of a client unless the client consents after consultation, except for disclosures that are impliedly authorized in order to carry out the representation, and except as stated in paragraph (b)

(b) A lawyer may reveal such information to the extent the lawyer reasonably believes necessary:

(1) to prevent the client from committing a criminal act that the lawyer believes is likely to result in imminent death or substantial bodily harm; or

(2) to establish a claim or defense on behalf of the lawyer in a controversy between the lawyer and the client, to establish a defense to a criminal charge or civil claim against the lawyer based upon conduct in which the client was involved, or to respond to allegations in any proceeding concerning the lawyer's representation of a client." 1999 American Bar Association Model Rules of Professional Conduct.

The ethical requirement that is vigorously enforced is the duty to maintain client confidentiality. There are only a handful of relationships in which the courts will protect private communications with total commitment. One of those is the attorney-client relationship. The benefits of protecting the confidentiality of such communications is seen as essential to the protection of the fundamental freedoms associated with the American legal system. Other such relationships include minister-parishioner, physician-patient, and in many cases husband-wife. These are relationships that, by their nature, often involve private matters. They also are seen as positive relationships that should be promoted. The refusal of the government to intrude on these relationships and expose their communications to compulsory disclosure is an obvious example of the original intent of the framers of the Constitution to protect individuals from unnecessary and unfair government intrusion into private life. The added benefit is to encourage full disclosure in highly personal relationships that can affect legal rights of the individual.

The privilege of confidential communications belongs exclusively to the party who is disclosing private information. In the attorney-client relationship, this party is the client. The privilege cannot be waived or in any way compromised by the attorney. The only exceptions occur when the client personally waives the privilege, when breach of the privilege is necessary to prevent a death or serious bodily harm, or when the client places the substance of the communication in issue and/or disclosure is necessary pursuant to court order. These exceptions are uncommon and highly scrutinized by the courts.

To qualify as an attorney-client communication, there must be a statement made verbally, nonverbally, or in a documentary form from a party who reasonably believes her or himself to be represented by the attorney and further reasonably believes the communication to be subject to the protection of the privilege. For example, the fact that one is a friend of an attorney does not create a professional relationship. Communications that take place as the product of social interaction are usually not considered privileged. Also, communications that take place prior to the establishment of a formal legal relationship would not be considered privileged unless those communications were made with the intent that such a relationship be formed as the result, that is, an initial consultation followed by an agreement for representation.

It is not necessary that a statement be made directly to an attorney to receive protected status as confidential. If the relationship exists, then statements made to an employee or other representative of the attorney, such as a paralegal, clerical staff, legal investigator, or another attorney connected with the primary attorney on the case are also considered privileged. The ethical rules for attorneys require also that the attorneys take reasonable steps to see that their subordinates and associates maintain the same standards with respect to client communications. The failure to do this can have a number of negative effects. Of course the attorney can be disciplined for inappropriate conduct that occurred with respect to a matter under his/her supervision. Another significant risk is that of a civil action for malfeasance by the client and against the attorney and/or the paralegal. In such a case, the client need only prove that confidentiality was breached. This breach, in and of itself, is considered to be damaging. There is no requirement to establish that the client suffered some personal or financial harm as the result of the breach.

It is impractical to think an attorney could or should oversee every word spoken and action taken by paralegals and other support staff. Each must monitor his or her own behavior and ensure that it meets the ethical requirements of the attorney. For this reason, it is essential that attorneys educate and impress upon their staff the importance of ethical conduct and make such behavior a key element of continued employment. When it comes to ethical behavior, the law grants little or no tolerance for laziness or neglect.

APPLICATION 8.3

John is a paralegal employed by Ramirez and Associates. Frequently, after work on Fridays a number of the staff of the firm go to a local bar for happy hour. On one such Friday, several of the members and staff, including John, are seated around a table in the bar. They are discussing the prior week and laughing about the facts of a particular client's case. John repeatedly uses the client's name and goes into great detail about the various assets the client stands to lose if the case is lost, as he thinks it will be. John also recaps the opinion of the attorney about the various weaknesses and few strengths of the case. Unknown to John and the others, the client's sister is seated at a nearby table and hears the entire conversation.

Point for Discussion: Is it ever appropriate to discuss the details of a client's case in a public place?

Assignment 8.2

In the foregoing application, identify specifically what the grounds for the ethical violation would be.

"Rule 1.7 Conflict of Interest: General Rule

(a) A lawyer shall not represent a client if the representation of that client will be directly adverse to another client unless:

(1) the lawyer reasonably believes the representation will not adversely affect the relationship with the other client: and

(2) each client consents after consultation.

(b) A lawyer shall not represent a client if the representation of that client may be materially limited by the lawyer's responsibilities to another client or to a third person, or by the lawyer's own interests, unless:

(1) the lawyer reasonably believes the representation will not be adversely affected; and

(2) the client consents after consultation. When representation of multiple clients in a single matter is undertaken, the consultation shall include explanation of the implications of the common representation and the advantages and risks involved." American Bar Association Model Rules of Professional Conduct, 1999.

The issue of conflict of interest is a particularly difficult one for attorneys. Unlike other professions, the legal profession is based on an adversarial system. There are conflicting sides to a lawsuit and each has strategies and information that is not available to the other. Also, unlike the physician-patient or minister-parishioner relationship, the attorney may also have personal interests that could potentially conflict with those of the client and the duty to put the client's interests first. There are a wide variety of situations that can present conflict of interest questions. They range from a current or former professional relationship with an opposing party to a business opportunity in which the attorney as well as the client might be involved.

In law, as in any other profession, there is a certain percentage of turnover. It is unusual in the present day for someone to accept a position and keep that same job for the remainder of their career. As opportunities arise, interests change, or conflicts develop, people change jobs. Because legal training is relatively specific, the majority of these changes take place within the same employment area, both as to type of work and geography. The potential for problems is enormous. What happens when a person leaves a job with one local firm and accepts a position with another firm that represents the opposition in a number of cases? If the first job was of long duration, the individual could have dealt with literally thousands of cases. Working at a firm with clients who are adversaries in any of these cases creates a conflict of interest. The client of the former firm may be at a disadvantage because the legal professional had access to his or her file and is now employed by the opposition. Presumably, the knowledge gained as part of a fiduciary relationship could now be used against the client. To avoid this type of occurrence, rules have been established to require certain safeguards to protect the interests of a client.

By definition, a fiduciary relationship is one of trust. The relationship between a lawyer and a client is fiduciary. As a result, the client is entitled to certain expectations of loyalty. This includes not only confidentiality, but also that their interests will be put first. Thus, when legal professionals change employment, they are not permitted to have any type of conduct or to disclose any information with respect to cases that involve either the former client or their adversaries. This is commonly known as building an ethical wall. To accomplish this, firms typically maintain a cross-referenced index of clients. Essentially, they maintain an index of all their own clients and a separate index of all opposing parties. Any new employee should identify all opposing parties who are or were represented by their former employer. Each of these files should be earmarked in some way that indicates the new employee is to have no contact with the case in any capacity. Even if the employee (lawyer, paralegal, etc.) did not have contact with the client's case at the former employer, there is a presumption that the accessibility to the file creates a situation that is dangerous to the client. The best way to avoid problems is to avoid the file of the client at the new employer.

Another safeguard used regularly is for a legal professional to maintain an ongoing list of all client files, including names of opposition, with which there is contact. Clients may change lawyers during the pendency of a lawsuit and it is unreasonable to expect one to remember the name of every case ever worked on. A list of client files allows an easier matching of potential conflicts when there is a change in employment. Whatever method is used, the key is to maintain a clear separation from any file with which there has ever been the opportunity for access to the opposing position's case.

There are exceptions to the rule on conflicts with regard to client files. For example, a client may have more than one lawsuit pending or completed in the past for which there could be a conflicting interest. However, if there is absolutely no connection with the present case, then it may be permissible for an attorney, paralegal, or other legal personnel to assist on the present case. Even in this situation, though, there should be a full disclosure to both sides of the case and consent before any action is taken.

APPLICATION 8.4

Lisa is a paralegal employed at the same firm for 11 years. Recently, she accepted a position with another local firm. After identifying all potential conflicts of interest, she considered each case. In several of the cases, the clients of the former firm were represented on unrelated matters several years ago. She is now asked to work on several cases involving these former clients as opposing parties. A letter of disclosure is prepared and sent to the opposition in each case along with a written release to be signed by the former client. In three of the four cases, the releases are signed because the old cases involved matters such as divorce and probate of estates of family members. However, in the fourth case the client refuses to sign the release allowing Lisa to work on the case because the former case involved the same two businesses as the present case, although the issues were distinct. Nevertheless, Lisa cannot work on the present case without risking ethical discipline and possibly legal ramifications for her employer and herself.

Point for Discussion: Why should she be prevented from contact if the old cases were unrelated to the new one?

Other issues that can bring about questions of conflict of interest are when a client and lawyer or other legal professional have common business interests. Because it is presumed that the legal professional may have expertise and/or skills superior to that of the client, such relationships are to be avoided. This includes entering into business relationships with clients other than as attorney-client, for example, co-investors, and entering into competitive business opportunities in which the client would be considered a competitor. If such an opportunity is presented, the legal professional has the obligation to pass on it until such time as it becomes clear that the client has considered and decided to pass on the opportunity. This approach ensures that the legal professional will not employ his or her professional skill to the detriment of the client. Similarly, a legal professional should not generally represent a client in any matter that will result in additional benefits to the legal professional. An example of this might be when a client asks an attorney to draw a will that names the attorney as the sole beneficiary. A case such as this would be ripe for attack on the grounds that undue influence was exercised on the client. An exception, however, might be found if the attorney was the only surviving relative of the client and if other facts would make him or her by all indications the most likely beneficiary of the estate.

There are as many possibilities for conflict of interest as there are clients and attorneys. For this reason the rules are broadly written. However, the basic rule of thumb to follow is quite simple. No action should be taken that could, in any way, be perceived as putting the interests of oneself or another ahead of those of the client, or that could be considered as disloyal or a breach of trust in any fashion.

> "Rule 1.3
> A lawyer shall act with reasonable diligence and promptness in representing a client."
> ABA Model Rules of Professional Conduct, 1999.

Once a professional relationship with a client has been established, there is a duty to represent the client with complete professionalism. This requires that the best efforts of the legal professional be used in all aspects of the case. What constitutes zeal and professionalism is a somewhat open-ended question because every case is unique. However, certain steps can be taken to create and maintain a professional relationship with the client. Important considerations in any professional legal relationship include the following:

1. Communicate with clients on a regular basis to keep them abreast of the status or changes in the matters of representation.
2. Meet all deadlines in a timely manner with respect to communications with the opposition, courts, and all legal proceedings.
3. Make sure the client understands the typical steps in the matter of representation and the time frames generally associated with each step.
4. Respond promptly and completely to all inquiries of the client, no matter how trivial they seem.
5. Provide a thorough explanation of all billing and expenditures made on behalf of the client and for which the client is responsible.
6. Consult the client in advance on all matters that affect the cost and/or potential outcome of the case.
7. Document the time, date, and nature of all communications with the client and concerning matters of representation.
8. Demonstrate an ongoing interest in the matters of representation.

All of the items listed above take time and in the profession of law, time is money. However, each of these items also lead to ethical and effective representation and client relations. The general attitude reflected in the manner and actions of the legal professional has a direct impact on future referrals and client satisfaction. Thus, such behaviors as those listed are not only professional, ethical, and supportive of the duties of the legal professional, they are ultimately good public relations and marketing.

Assignment 8.3

Speak to 10 different people who have been represented by a lawyer at one time and ask their opinion of the best and worst aspects of the representation they received. Explain how each could affect future referrals to the attorney and what could be done, if anything, to improve the chance for referrals by the person you spoke with.

C. WHEN A VIOLATION OF AN ETHICAL STANDARD INJURES THE PUBLIC

1. Remedies for the Injured Party

The license to practice law, the certification granted by NALA, and the validation by NFPA are essentially earned privileges. When someone demonstrates the requisite ability and qualifications to receive the license or certification, it is done subject to certain conditions. Failure to abide by these conditions can have a variety of results.

As mentioned earlier in the chapter, a lawyer can be the subject of disciplinary action by the professional body. A lawyer or paralegal may also be the subject of legal action within the courts. These remedies are not mutually exclusive in any way. The professional discipline of an attorney and a lawsuit against a lawyer or paralegal are seen as separate and distinct. The disciplinary action is designed to protect an unwitting public by taking action against the licensure/certification of someone who negligently or deliberately acts unethically in violation of his or her license/certification requirements. The focus of the lawsuit is to compensate a specifically injured party for damage caused as the result of another's unethical conduct.

In the first circumstance, anyone can lodge a complaint with the appropriate administrative body stating the facts of the alleged unethical behavior. The allegations of the complaint are investigated and a determination made as to whether action is warranted. In some circumstances a hearing may be held to give the alleged wrongdoer the opportunity to present their response to the complaint in person. Once the merits of the complaint have been evaluated, there are a number of possible outcomes. While each state has its own specific rules and disciplinary procedures, a number of common outcomes are often used. It is possible that the authoritative body will find that the complaint is unfounded or that the conduct was not sufficient to constitute a clear violation. On the other hand, if a violation has occurred, then based on the severity, willfulness, previous history of violations, and damage to the client a variety of forms of discipline may be imposed. These include everything from a formal reprimand to suspension or total revocation of licensure. In some instances the individual who was complained about may be required to attend educational programs to raise his or her level of awareness of ethical duties.

In addition to disciplinary action, the party allegedly injured by the unethical conduct can, in many cases, file an action for malfeasance against the attorney responsible for the wrongful action or the party who committed it, such as a subordinate. The procedure would be the same as for any other type of personal injury lawsuit including a statement of the allegedly wrongful conduct by the defendant and the consequent injury to the party filing suit (plaintiff). The possible outcome would range from dismissal of the action to a monetary judgment against the defendant, payable to the plaintiff. The party or parties named as defendants could include the party who is accused of having acted unethically and, in some instances, the employer if it is a subordinate employee or attorney of a larger firm.

2. Sources of Impact on the Legal Professional

The potential professional impact on someone accused of unethical behavior can be much more far reaching than a disciplinary action or lawsuit. In either instance, such matters are typically popular with the media and often reported in the news. In turn, this notoriety can adversely affect the trust and confidence of current and potential clients. There is also the professional impact. It can be difficult to maintain or secure employment when there is a reputation for unethical conduct. Depending on the severity of the breach and the general regard for one's abilities, the impact of a claim of unethical conduct on employment can range from virtually nothing to professional devastation in a particular community or field of employment. The risk for long-term effects is so great that it is one more reason to take great care when it comes to ethical responsibilities.

PARALEGALS IN THE WORKPLACE

The impact of legal ethics on the paralegal profession is perhaps stronger than for any other employment in the field with the exception of attorneys. The qualified paralegal now takes on many of the duties traditionally performed exclusively by attorneys. As such, the responsibility to meet the ethical standards imposed on attorneys is extended to the paralegal. While other members of the legal team have an obligation to perform their duties within ethical bounds, it is the paralegal and attorney who are perhaps most at risk, as they are the most deeply enmeshed in case preparation and the trial/appeal process. Therefore, the paralegal is obligated to remain abreast of not only paralegal, but attorney ethical standards as well.

CHAPTER SUMMARY

The duties and obligations associated with legal ethics are present in every area of law and at every level of the law-related professions. For this reason, it should be a constant presence in the minds of legal professionals and should guide the manner in which they do their work. Keys to ethical behavior consist of acting at all times with honesty, integrity, and the client's best interest at the forefront. Because the legal relationship to a client is a fiduciary one, the duty to honor the client's trust in matters of confidence is paramount. The privilege of confidentiality belongs to the client and typically can only be waived by the client unless a court order or planned criminal conduct is involved. In addition to confidentiality, all legal professionals, associates, and support staff are required to avoid situations in which a conflict of interest might occur. This requires that the interests of the client come first in matters of business opportunities as well as matters involving employment of the legal professional. At no time may an attorney or other legal professional place him or herself in a position that might create an occasion for the breach of any other ethical duty, such as confidentiality, or result in benefit to the professional at the expense of the client. In line with this is the obligation to undertake to perform only those duties for which the legal professional has achieved an adequate level of competence. If this cannot be accomplished then there is an obligation to decline the representation or assistance. This level of competence requires not only training but current knowledge in the area of concern. Thus, legal professionals are under a continuing obligation to maintain their skills and knowledge of the law. Finally, the legal professional is required to act at all times with a degree of professionalism that constitutes zealous representation of their clients. While attorneys are bound by the ABA Code of Ethics, the NALA has adopted its own code, which incorporates the ABA Code of Ethics by reference. All subordinate staff members and those associated with the delivery of legal services are similarly bound as a matter of reality even if not as a condition of licensure. The failure to honor legal ethical standards can result in formal disciplinary action, legal action in civil court, and long-term effects on professional employment and advancement.

Revelent Internet Sites

NFPA Model Code of Ethics	www.paralegals.org/Development/modelcode.html
NALA Code of Ethics and Professional Responsibility	www.nala.org/stand.htm

Internet Assignment 8.1

Locate the Internet addresses for the licensure and disciplinary offices for attorneys in your jurisdiction.

KEY TERMS

Ethical	Ethics	Fiduciary
Ethical Standards		

Chapter 9

TORT LAW IN AMERICA

CHAPTER OBJECTIVES

Upon completion of this chapter you should be able to do the following:

- Explain the difference between an action in tort and other types of legal actions.
- Discuss the general development of American tort law.
- Define negligence.
- Distinguish comparative and contributory negligence.
- Explain the purpose of the theory of res ipsa loquiter.
- Distinguish gross negligence and intentional torts.
- Explain the rationale for strict liability and when it should be applied.
- Discuss general defenses to torts.

A. THE EVOLUTION OF AMERICAN TORT LAW

From the very inception of the American legal system, there has been a recognized need for legal alternatives when issues arise involving injury to one's person or property as the result of improper conduct by another. Tort law is the area of law that provides such alternatives. Originally, the English system dealt with issues of property and contracts. However, as far back as the middle ages, the need for redress in less formal circumstances and between parties without any legal relationship was apparent. The English system of law created two types of lawsuits for injuries to persons and property that did not involve contract or real property transactions. These lawsuits were known as *forms of action*. They consisted of legal actions permitted for injury to a person as the direct result of improper conduct known as *trespass*, and injury as the result of an indirect action known as *trespass on the case*. These early legal actions were somewhat vague and primitive with respect to requirements to establish a case and obtain damages. Nevertheless, they served as the foundation for the early recognition by governmental authorities that individuals should be held accountable for the results of their conduct even if the act did not constitute a crime. These first forms of action were the first recognized torts.

1. Early Influences

The torts of trespass and trespass on the case were intended to assist people injured in some way by the careless conduct of others. At the time these legal remedies were developed, the word *trespass* was defined as something that would be considered wrong. This of course is quite different from the common interpretation today, which ties the term trespass to an unlawful entry onto land. In the original cases of trespass, the alleged wrongdoer acted in such a way that the near immediate result would be an injury to a person or their property. This is distinguished from trespass on the case in which someone created a condition that subsequently caused injury.

APPLICATION 9.1

A tort of trespass according to the original definition:

ACME contractors is a construction company that saves costs by using inexperienced workers. One such worker accidentally cuts a natural gas line when digging a trench to lay phone lines between two buildings. The worker is smoking and tosses the end of a lit cigarette onto the ground. Within seconds, there is an explosion and both buildings are leveled.

A tort of trespass on the case according to the original definition:

Assume the previous scenario except for the cigarette being thrown. Instead, assume the worker leaves the area after the trench work is completed without reporting the cut in the gas line. Later that day the building owner smells gas and calls the local gas company.

They confirm there is a leak and proceed to look for it. While doing this, the leak ignites and the buildings are leveled in an explosion.

Point for Discussion: What would have been the court's basis for distinguishing the two scenarios into different types of torts?

In the first example, there was a direct chain of events that caused the explosion. In the second scenario, the stage was set and conditions created that ultimately resulted in an explosion. Both actions produced damage. Over the centuries, trespass and trespass on the case were developed into a much more sophisticated set of rules. Unlike the original actions, more and more attention has been given to the degree of knowledge or intention by the alleged wrongdoer and any inherent dangers of the allegedly wrongful conduct. From these origins, the modern collection of legal principles has evolved that make up a large body of tort law in the current American legal system encompassing many distinct causes of action.

2. Changes and Adaptations

The law of torts is *one* of the most, if not *the* most, litigated areas of law in the United States. It began as a catch-all for cases that were not criminal, contract, or property in origin. That broad scope has continued and, even today, there is not a universally accepted definition of a tort. Rather, there is more of a consensus as to what a tort is not.

- A tort is not a criminal action.
- A tort is not a breach of contract action.
- A tort is not an action with respect to a dispute over property ownership rights, either real or personal.

By this definition, and in practice, a tort is a civil action and includes disputes between individual citizens, businesses, and even governmental bodies with respect to personal rights. In some situations, a circumstance may give rise to both a criminal and a tort action. In criminal matters, the government acts against a party charged with a crime because criminal statutes are designed to address injuries to the general concept of public good, safety, and welfare. This does not typically provide a personal remedy for any damage to individuals or property that occurs as the result of conduct that is also criminal.

A tort does not include breach of contract. Although contract actions are included in the definition of civil law, the elements of a lawsuit in tort are different from the elements of a lawsuit in contract. Contract actions occur when two or more parties voluntarily enter into a legal relationship with certain specified rights and obligations, and a subsequent dispute arises as to the nature or extent of those rights or obligations. In contrast, a tort arises when a party infringes on the rights of another person or government when there was no permission or agreement to do so, and the infringement causes some type of measurable harm.

APPLICATION 9.2

K is a shop owner who becomes involved in a confrontation over a sales contract to X. X then leaves the shop and returns later, driving his car through the shop window of K. A number of customers are injured as a result. X may be arrested and criminally prosecuted on a variety of charges. However, K and the injured customers may also file civil tort against X for the damage and injuries they received in the incident.

Point for Discussion: Why would K and the injured customers not be compensated in the criminal action against X?

By definition, a tort must involve an element of harm or damage. No matter how seriously one party may violate the personal rights of another, unless there is verifiable and measurable harm by societal standards that can be compensated, there is no action in tort. This means that the injury must be of a nature that is recognized as harmful by generally accepted standards and can be assessed in some way as to the appropriate amount of compensation. While property damage is usually fairly simple to measure in terms of value, certain actions for violation of personal rights, for example injury to one's reputation, may be more difficult to assign a dollar amount to. Nevertheless, one's reputation is recognized by society as having value and impact on various personal and business opportunities. Therefore the law will even attempt to place a discernible value on this intangible right.

APPLICATION 9.3

Sam was employed by Ty and together they ran a successful investment company. However Sam decided to open a competing business that he would own. He systematically removed various supplies over a period of several months and made plans to open the new business. At the same time, Sam commenced a campaign to undermine Ty's reputation as an honest businessman in the community and started rumors about concern for Ty's well-being as he had begun a pattern of erratic behavior resulting in several bad business decisions. Then Sam opened his own business and many of Ty's longtime customers followed him. A percentage of these customers had never even done business with Sam during his tenure as Ty's employee. Ty may report the theft to law enforcement for possible prosecution. He would also have an action in tort for the value of the theft and property damage with regard to supplies, but also for the damage to his goodwill and reputation as evidenced by the dramatic decline of business.

Point for Discussion: Why should Ty be able to sue Sam for things Sam said about him if they were not true?

While the basic components of the definition of tort have been present for hundreds of years, other societal changes have caused the law of torts to develop much more fully. In the early to mid-1800s a number of occurrences precipitated many of the modern-day tort principles. At first the law made certain persons who did business with the general public liable for injuries caused by the business pursuits. Some business owners were presumed to be in a contractual relationship with customers regardless of whether a formal agreement existed. This included such individuals as doctors and blacksmiths. These people were deemed to have knowledge and skill that the ordinary person did not and as such owed a certain duty to perform competently in exchange for payment received for their services. Several states passed legislation that put a statutory burden on operators of public transportation and public lodging, such as stagecoaches and innkeepers, to provide for the reasonable safety of their passengers and lodgers. As the population increased at a faster pace than roads and buildings could be properly developed, accidents causing injury rose dramatically. In the

1820s the American courts began to recognize the concept of liability for negligence or failure to act in a reasonably safe manner under the circumstances. Negligence was then applied to all persons, including the parties not previously included by means of contract or statutory law. Essentially, a broad scope of liability was imposed for issues involving injuries received as the result of a person's failure to act carefully in the interest of others.

Within a short time, the concept of negligence was developed much more fully to include essential elements and degrees of wantonness with respect to the defendant's conduct and regard for the safety of others. Thus, the action for gross negligence evolved. Also advanced during this time was an action for intentional tort, which required more proof but also imposed greater liability when it was shown that the actor should have known that the conduct complained of was virtually certain to cause injury. Of course in response to these developing legal theories came the outgrowth of accepted legal defenses that excused conduct that, in most circumstances, would be considered improper.

During the latter half of the 20th century a catch phrase emerged—*litigation explosion*. This was not due to any aggressive action on the part of the legal profession. Rather, it was the end result of a long chain of events put into motion during the previous 75 to 100 years. During this time technology, industry, and population saw dramatic increases. As a result, there was more and more interaction among individuals as well as newly developed products, tools, equipment, and such. The legal system saw a distinct increase in cases over property and contract law principles. But much of the focus was on the velocity with which the number of tort cases filed increased throughout the United States. A primary reason for the wide media attention given to the growth of these types of claims is that they have an impact on the economy as a whole. Many actions in tort are defended by insurance companies who have provided an insurance policy to the defendant, whether for automobile, homeowners, professional liability, or something else. The chain reaction has been that as costs for the insurance company increased due to legal defense and payment of claims and judgments against the insured individuals, the expense was passed along to the entire customer base in the form of increased premiums. In turn, business raised their own prices to help cover the increased cost of insurance. For example, the cost of health-care rose due in part to the increased cost of insuring health care providers and facilities. As increases are passed on in costs to consumers, they contribute to overall inflation. Some make the argument, and can support it to an extent, that often the increases were greater than the legal expenses. They say that companies increased profits and passed the fault on to members of the legal professions for representing so many clients in legal actions.

Nevertheless, the massive influx of cases did occur and, in response, many legislatures have adopted laws that place restrictions on the amounts that can be awarded in certain types of claims. In some subject areas limitations have been put on the method for filing tort actions and the specific procedures for doing so. Additionally, a growing number of jurisdictions have established penalties for lawyers and their clients for advancing cases that are essentially unfounded and considered to be frivolous claims attempting to gain some type of financial settlement. These recent occurrences in the legal system show more clearly than ever that the law is in a constant state of refinement to meet the standards expected by society at large.

3. Modern Tort Terminology

Before undertaking a more detailed discussion of present day legal principles concerning torts, it is necessary to discuss some of the terminology that is an integral part of modern day tort law. While the following list is by no means exhaustive, it does provide an initial and brief explanation of some of the more commonly employed terms. The terms described here are actions and some terms of art that are frequently employed in discussions of tort law. As terms of art, they may have a meaning different than what you might ordinarily expect if they were encountered in everyday language.

Negligence

Act or failure to act toward another when (1) a duty was owed to the other person, (2) the act or failure to act was less than a reasonable person would have done under the circumstances, (3) the act or failure to act was the direct cause of injury to the other person, and (4) the injury caused measurable financial, physical, or emotional damage to the other person.

Negligence. The word negligence in ordinary language is often interpreted as carelessness. In very loose terms, this may be somewhat equivalent to the legal interpretation. In actual practice however, the legal term negligence is much more detailed and precise in describing a particular action. In a legal context, to be negligent one must (1) owe a duty of care with respect to another person or their property, (2) fail to act in accordance with that duty when the party knew or should have known that such failure might produce an injury to the other person or property, (3) fail to meet the duty of care and that failure is the proximate (direct) cause of injury and, (4) produce an injury sufficient to warrant compensable damages. Thus, in any successful legal action for negligence of another party, it is necessary to produce sufficient evidence to establish the following:

1. Existence of a duty by the defendant toward the plaintiff.
2. The extent of the duty, that is, the standard of care that was required to meet the duty and evidence that it was breached.
3. Injury as the proximate result of the breach of the standard of duty of care.
4. Injury that is sufficient to warrant an award of damages.

Reasonable Conduct

Action or nonaction that is appropriate under the circumstances when all risks and benefits are taken into account.

Reasonable Conduct. Throughout the law of negligence, conduct of the alleged wrongdoer is measured against the standard of reasonableness. Typically this is considered to be what would be appropriate in the circumstances. While in common language reasonable has a definition more consistent with fairness or what would be considered average behavior, in legal contexts the term is more demanding. Most often, the actions or omissions of a party accused of negligence are measured by the courts against what the conduct of a *reasonable person* would have been in the same situation. The conduct of what is reasonably obvious varies with each case. However, this person is always presumed to be one who would act with care and attention to every detail of behavior that might affect the situation and, thus, the other party. Reasonable conduct requires the actor to evaluate the surroundings, all benefits and all risks, and to respond in the most careful manner. This measurement of the reasonableness of the alleged liable person does not usually take into account the mental state of the actor. It does, however, take into account the intelligence, age, experience, and physical conditions over which the actor has no control.

Foreseeable

Those facts of which a party was or should have been aware under the circumstances.

Foreseeability. An important element of any tort action is foreseeability. Whatever conduct the defendant engages in, one thing that must be considered is the likely or certain results of that conduct. In the case of negligence, the actor is required to consider all reasonably foreseeable effects of a particular course of conduct. In strict liability cases (to be discussed later), the actor is imposed upon to know that the conduct is so inherently dangerous that he or she will be held accountable for any injuries produced as the result of it. The risk of the injury must be of a nature that was, or should have been, apparent. Foreseeability is determined by a legal finding of whether the risk of harm was known as a matter of constructive knowledge. Constructive knowledge is what one knew or, under the circumstances should have known, as a reasonable person would have. Foreseeability, thus, is a key element in the determination of what the reasonable standard of care should have been. A person must be able to foresee an occurrence before he or she can be held responsible for it.

Proximate Cause. Tort law hinges on the concept that one party's conduct is inappropriate to the extent that it results in injury to another. The necessary relationship between a breach of a duty and claimed damage in a negligence action is commonly referred to as proximate cause. To sustain an action for negligence, the injured party must prove that injuries occurred as a consequence of the breach of duty by the actor both as a matter of fact and as a matter of law.

Intentional Tort. In addition to negligence, other types of torts have been established to place greater focus and responsibility on the awareness of the party whose actions are responsible for an injury. Negligence imposes on the defendant constructive knowledge of the possibility of injury resulting from his or her actions. As indicated by its name, an intentional tort requires actual intent, not to cause damage, but to engage in the harmful activity despite the fact that the actor knew or should have known that the activity was all but certain to cause damage.

Strict Liability. An older theory of recovery that saw phenomenal growth in the latter part of the 1900s and still today is the action based on strict liability. This type of tort has no consideration of intent or knowledge per se. Rather, it is a liability that one automatically assumes for any injuries caused by an activity that is overwhelmingly and inherently dangerous to others who have no influence or control or reasonable means of protection from the activity. The reasoning behind strict liability is that one who benefits from such a dangerous activity should shoulder the responsibility for injuries to innocent persons or property caused by it, regardless of how carefully the actor tries to conduct the activity.

While each of these terms will be explored more thoroughly within the chapter, an introduction is important at the outset to gain a perspective of how they correspond to form the general areas of tort law. Additional subordinate terms will be explained throughout the chapter as well. It is important to note at this juncture that while these terms have generally accepted meanings, some states have employed variations or limitations on these definitions in the development of the body of law for the particular jurisdiction and that the definitions are not universally accepted.

Proximate Cause
Direct cause sufficient to produce a result. No other intervening force can occur independently and prior to the result that is also sufficient to produce the result.

Intentional Tort
Act that the actor knows or should know with substantial certainty will cause harm to another.

Strict Liability
Liability without fault. Applied in situations where the intention or neglect of the party is immaterial. The mere performance of the act or omission will result in liability.

B. THE CONCEPT OF NEGLIGENCE

As the introductory materials pointed out, negligence was the first true tort developed in the United States. While the types of situations in which negligence is recognized has expanded greatly, the elements identified early on are essentially the same. In an action for negligence, the injured party must plead, and ultimately be able to prove at trial, facts of an occurrence showing that each of the necessary elements existed. Only after such proof will the defendant (the party who is alleged to be at fault) be required to compensate the plaintiff for the injuries. The following elements must be proven specifically:[1]

1. The actor (defendant) owed a duty to the injured party (plaintiff) to refrain from conduct that would likely cause injury.

2. By failing to exercise a degree of care based on the standard of what a reasonable person would do in a like circumstance, the actor breached his or her duty.
3. The breach of the duty proximately caused an injury to the plaintiff.
4. The plaintiff's injuries are significant enough to warrant compensation from the actor.

1. The Elements of Negligence

a. The Concept of Duty   The first element that must be proven in any negligence action is that of duty. Specifically, the injured party (plaintiff) must demonstrate that the actor (defendant) owed a duty of acting with the care of the plaintiff's safety or well being in mind. It is commonly accepted that all persons have a general duty not to act negligently and thereby to harm others around them. This general duty also includes the responsibility to act carefully for one's own safety under the circumstances. It is not necessary that the plaintiff and defendant have some special relationship to one another. There is not even a requirement that they know one another or, for that matter, be aware of the existence of the other. What is required is that the defendant be aware of the potential impact of an action on anyone within a reasonable distance that could reasonably be expected to be present. It is important to note that there are occasions when the duty is to refrain from acting rather than to act. Therefore, failing to act—an omission—can also be a violation of a person's duty. An example of such an omission is a situation in which danger to another is within a person's control, and the person fails to exercise that control even though he or she has the opportunity to do so.

APPLICATION 9.4

Nicky rented a booth in a craft mall. She was not at work on Friday when the building manager came through the mall and informed all booth operators that on the weekend, the building would be treated for rodents and that no one was to be in the building on the weekend as noxious and dangerous fumes would need sufficient time to dissipate. No attempt was made to inform Nicky and on Sunday morning she came to work on the displays in her booth. The building had been fumigated and the workers gone by the time she arrived. She noticed the smell immediately and planned to question the building manager when he arrived at work. In a very short time she became extremely ill and was subsequently hospitalized. Nicky brought an action in negligence against the mall owners for the failure to take reasonable steps to notify the occupants of the mall of the dangerous condition that they planned to create. Most courts would consider that the mall owners had a duty to take reasonable steps to inform known occupants who had access to the building of its temporarily unsafe condition. They would probably not consider a casual conversation with the occupants who were present in the building on one occasion the day before the fumigation was planned as meeting that duty.

Point for Discussion: What would have been considered reasonable notice?

To prove the element of duty in an action for negligence, several things must be shown. The first is that the defendant owed a duty to the plaintiff who was injured. It is not necessary to show that the defendant owed a duty to this particular individual. Rather, it must be shown that the defendant knew or should have known that others within a certain range, which included the plaintiff, could be affected by his or her actions.

Two primary schools of thought exist as to the area this range should include. One theory is frequently referred to as the "zone of danger,"[2] which refers to the area that the defendant should reasonably expect or foresee his or her actions to affect. Consequently, no duty is owed and no negligence can be proven for injuries that occur beyond the zone of danger. This means that usually there can be no recovery for injuries that are the result of remote or bizarre chain reaction events. Whether something is remote or not is generally determined by whether the defendant's conduct was the direct product through an uninterrupted chain of events and in the absence of additional and/or intervening causal factors.

The second theory used to determine boundaries within which the defendant owes a duty is the "world-at-large" approach,[3] which takes into account a much wider range. It requires the defendant to foresee more remote possibilities of harm to persons not in the immediate area and injuries not as readily foreseeable to occur as a result from his or her conduct. The defendant is expected to identify all persons in the surrounding area who could reasonably be subjected to danger of injury as the result of the defendant's actions. The extent of this range also turns on a question of whether the conduct proximately caused the injury, but it allows a more indirect chain of events to be included as to what composes proximate cause.

Each state has adopted a theory upon which to try cases of negligence. The zone of danger is more limited and would likely better contain the number of allegations of negligence filed. However, as society becomes more and more crowded and daily life more complex, there is an increasing concern that individuals take care toward all others that might be negatively impacted by their conduct. One way to enforce this is to recognize liability for one's actions on a wider scale. That line of reasoning would support the world-at-large approach. Consequently, it is important not only to check the position of a particular jurisdiction when considering an action for negligence, but it is necessary to remain abreast of any changes in the law that either expand or place greater limitations on the boundaries of duty.

Once it has been established that the plaintiff was within the area that the defendant should have expected to be affected by his or her conduct, it is necessary to prove the more precise nature and extent of duty that is relative to the degree of risk of injury. The defendant's actions will expose the plaintiff to certain risks in the range where risk exists. The defendant is responsible for risks that foreseeably could cause significant harm. This means that when a party engages in conduct that may affect others in the surrounding area, the actor must act carefully so as not to allow that conduct to injure persons in ways that can be reasonably foreseen. As a result, as the risk of significant injury decreases so does the extent of the duty to protect the potential plaintiffs from the risk. This is not to say the duty is extinguished or less important. Rather, the steps necessary to meet the duty are diminished in terms of what must be done to see that injury is avoided.

APPLICATION 9.5

A. ABC Corp. owns a small amusement park. Among the attractions is a roller coaster. The duty of ABC toward customers of the park would include regular maintenance of the roller coaster and safety guards on each car of the roller coaster. Additionally they may impose certain height/weight requirements to permit only those who fit properly into the safety guards within the cars. This is because the roller coaster cars carry passengers high above the ground in open cars at a high rate of speed. The risk of injury without these precautions would be significant as would the likely extent of the injuries received.

B. G owns an apple orchard that is open to the public for apple picking. One of the services in the orchard is a very brief hay wagon ride from the parking lot to the orchards through a flat and level pasture. The wagon is completely enclosed with a 2-foot-high wood rail. The risk of injury to the customers during the hay ride is much less than during a roller coaster ride if no safety precautions are taken. Nevertheless, there would be some safety steps required to meet the duty, such as instructing passengers to keep arms and legs within the wagon and to remain seated at all times when the wagon is moving. Although there is still a duty to be met, it would probably not be so great as to require individual seat belts or guards for each passenger.

Point for Discussion: Would the extent of duty in the latter situation change if the wagon ride was up and down hills in a flatbed open wagon for a significantly longer duration? How would the duty change and why?

b. Breach of the Standard of Care   Once the existence of any duty whatsoever is established between a plaintiff and a defendant, the plaintiff's next obstacle is to provide proof of how the duty was violated, specifically, what activity or omission by the defendant constituted a violation of the duty. Because every circumstance is unique in some way, it is not always easy to determine every step that would constitute the only appropriate way to meet a duty. Therefore, it is equally difficult sometimes to determine whether a defendant's actions constituted a breach. In most situations, the defendant takes some steps toward meeting a duty. It is then a determination of whether they were sufficient.

The usual test applied in negligence actions is whether the defendant, under all the circumstances, exercised ordinary (reasonable) care.[4] Whether the defendant acted with ordinary care or not is determined by measuring his or her conduct against what the reasonable person would have done in a similar situation. On the one hand, no two situations are alike and each must be judged in light of its own particular setting. On the other hand, most occurrences do bear some resemblance to others. By comparing similarities and differences of past like events there is generally some basis for determining what the reasonable person would have done in the situation presently under consideration.

It is important to note that when the reasonable or ordinary standard is applied to determine what the defendant should have done, the reasonable person will have the same characteristics of age, intelligence, experience, and physical ability (or disability) as the defendant.[5] A number of additional factors are also taken into consideration. The first factor is the underlying reason or necessity for the defendant's conduct. Was the defendant acting for a reason that was self-serving, such as driving his or her vehicle to work? Or was the defendant engaged in some activity or omission that had social value, such as attempting to help someone in trouble or danger. The second consideration is the physical surroundings and conditions at the time of the alleged negligence. Anything that might impair or improve the defendant's ability to formulate the proper scope, nature, and extent of duty must be added to the equation. This would include the tangible physical surroundings, weather, conditions such as lighting, and any activities that were taking place in the vicinity concurrently that may have influenced the defendant in any way. Finally, what kind of people were in the area? For example, were children, elderly, handicapped, or others with special needs likely to be present? All these external factors could influence the actions of a reasonable person in a given situation.

The particular mental ability or disability of the defendant as a general rule is not considered.[6] This is especially true when any disability is the result of a voluntary act such as intoxication. Liability for one's actions cannot be escaped as the result of an individual's willful reduction of capacity. Also, to consider the individual intellectual ability of each defendant and its potential impact on a given situation would be speculative at best. As a result, the defendant is usually presumed to be of average intelligence and experience unless some extreme variation can be established. Given this, the defendant is charged with considering, as a person of average intelligence and experience, whether his or her conduct generates a duty and if so the scope, nature, and extent of that duty. Keep in mind that the courts can moderate the general rule by considering age, experience, intelligence, and physical condition, which may affect the overall mental ability factor. For example, someone who is mentally challenged to the extent that they are unable to function as an ordinary person, might be compared to a reasonable person of similar disability. Conversely, one who purports to have specialized knowledge or who has acted as a specialist or licensed professional will be considered responsible to act properly as such, regardless of whether they actually have the special ability.

Once the determination is made as to what the reasonable person would be like in a given situation, taking into account the nature of the true defendant, the next step is to determine how that person would have acted in the same circumstance as the defendant. This is done while keeping in mind that the reasonable person takes into account all details of the surroundings, appreciates all foreseeable risks, and acts in the most prudent and careful manner to avoid damage or injury to others or their property. This culmination of considerations results in the more precise definition of the appropriate standard of care against which the defendant's conduct will be measured.

There are rare exceptions when a standard greater than ordinary care is applied. These situations are usually identified by statute and are used when the persons situated as potential plaintiffs within the foreseeable area and subject to the actions of the defendant are limited or nonexistent in their capacity to protect themselves from the defendant's actions.[7] Common examples include those who provide mass transportation that the average person is unable to assess as safe or not, such as planes, trains, and other commercial carriers. Many jurisdictions require such common carriers to act with extraordinary care for the safety of their passengers who have virtually entrusted their lives to the carrier.

Slight care is the most basic of all duties and requires only the most minimal action to prevent injuries to those in the surrounding area.[8] When this most basic and minimal duty is violated, many jurisdictions permit an action for gross negligence as an alternative to one for negligence. If there is a standard of ordinary care in place, the plaintiff may also be permitted to sue for punitive damages for the failure to exercise even slight care. Punitive damages are used in some jurisdictions in addition to compensatory damages. Punitives—or exemplary damages, as they are sometimes called,—punish the defendant and are designed to deter others from such gross carelessness.

Circumstances that impose only a duty of slight care include situations such as the duty of a landowner to trespassers. Although there is not a duty to obey a standard of ordinary care to persons invading another person's property, neither can a person willingly expose others to substantial risks of danger.

c. Proximate Cause   The duty to take reasonable care for those likely to be affected by one's actions is a primary element of negligence. Just as important is that the injury complained of be the direct result of the breach of duty. The injured party must establish a causal link between the breach of duty and the subsequent injury in a way that would be considered by legal definitions a direct link.

Proximate cause is a major element of any negligence action. The plaintiff must demonstrate that the defendant's conduct proximately caused the plaintiff's injuries.[9] While in ordinary language a direct connection between action and injury may be somewhat broadly defined, in legal terms there are specific tests that must be passed before the proximate cause element is proven. The legal standard to establish proximate cause is a two-pronged test. First, it must be shown that the injuries were the result of the conduct as a matter of factual occurrence (known as cause in fact). Second, it must be shown that the injuries were caused by the conduct as a matter of law commonly called the legal or proximate cause.

One of the most long-standing and foremost recognized authorities on tort law, Prosser, has said that proximate cause is the "reasonable connection between the act or omission of the defendant and the damage which the plaintiff has suffered. . . Legal responsibility must be limited to those causes which are so closely connected with the result and of such significance that the law is justified in imposing liability."[10]

In the test to establish whether proximate cause is present, the cause in fact is typically the easiest to prove. The plaintiff needs only to trace a chain of events, short or long, that leads directly from the defendant's allegedly wrongful conduct to the plaintiff's injuries. This is influenced somewhat by the extent of the duty of the defendant, as discussed earlier, to reasonably foresee those affected by his or her actions. In simple situations, where there are no intervening forces or remote circumstances, cause in fact and legal cause may be established by the same evidence.

While it is accepted that there must be a factual and legal connection between the defendant's conduct and plaintiff's injuries, most commonly these are determined by one of two popularly accepted methods. The first is often referred to as the "but for" test.[11] In the jurisdictions that apply this method of establishing proximate cause, the judge or jury is asked to consider the facts of the case and answer the following question: "But for the defendant's actions, would the plaintiff's injuries still have occurred?" As society and technology become more complex, circumstances are fewer and fewer that lend themselves to such a simplistic view. Quite often someone's actions may impact another, but as a contributing factor rather than a sole producing cause. The view that one must be totally responsible or not at all in producing an injury is used less and less because it would permit too many to avoid responsibility for conduct that plays a significant role in producing an injury.

In place of the decreasing use of the but for test, has been the increased application of a test that is much more equitable. This increasingly popular method of establishing proximate cause is commonly known as the "substantial factor analysis."[12] Under this test, the defendant's conduct is considered in light of all relevant facts in the situation, and it is determined whether or not the defendant's conduct was a substantial factor in producing the plaintiff's injury.[13] Irrespective of other factors that may have contributed to the injury, if the defendant's conduct was a substantially producing factor, then cause in fact has been established. Given the complexity of most cases to-day, the substantial factor analysis seems to be a fairer method of determining cause than the but for test.

APPLICATION 9.6

Corrina is pushing her toddler in a shopping cart through a grocery store. As they move through the aisle, the toddler reaches out and pulls a jar from a shelf, which crashes to the floor and breaks. Corrina moves quickly to the next aisle and does not report the spill. About 20 minutes later, the store manager notices the spill. A half hour after that, he tells a checker to clean up the mess after finishing lunch break. In the meantime, two other children in the store with their parents are racing through the aisles. The mother is chasing them to get them to stop. As she rounds the corner she steps in the spill and falls, severely fracturing her arm. The injured woman sues the store for the dangerous condition in the store as the cause of her injuries.

Under the but for test, the contributing factor of the children and mother racing through the store as well as Corrina, who allowed the spill to occur and then did not report it, are also contributing factors. As a result, the store would very possibly not be considered liable in spite of the fact that it allowed a known dangerous condition to remain without attempts to clean it up or warn other customers. Under the substantial factor analysis, the store would be held accountable for its role in allowing the dangerous condition to continue for such a long time.

Point for Discussion: Would the result be any different if the store manager testified that he was unaware of the spill until almost two hours after it occurred and cleaned it up immediately upon finding it?

When proximate cause becomes an issue, it can be the most disputed point in the case. Proximate cause is heavily influenced by the extent of the duty imposed by the court: the larger the area to which a defendant owes a duty, the greater the chance of a remote occurrence causing an injury to someone within that area. Consequently, such situations present a greater likelihood for an issue of proximate cause.

Sometimes an injury occurs and the cause is not easily foreseeable. In that situation, causation is much more difficult to prove. It may be easy to trace a chain of events from an action/nonaction to an injury. But in a case of negligence, the injury has to be traced backward to an action or omission that the defendant should have foreseen as a possible cause of injury to another (i.e., breach of duty). Proximate cause can be established in fairly remote situations, even when other forces come into play producing the injury. However, when these remote situations become so removed and convoluted with other facts that the occurrence is bizarre or something that would ordinarily be considered a freak accident, the direct connection and significance of the defendant's conduct may be difficult to prove. Similarly, when an intervening force capable of producing the injury independently occurs between the moment of the conduct of the defendant and the moment of injury, the proximate cause is very difficult to prove in terms of the original defendant. Again, the courts often apply the "but for" test or "substantial factor" analysis to determine legal causation.

d. Damage   After the duty, standard, breach, and causal links are established, it remains necessary to establish damage. A defendant's conduct can be utterly reprehensible, but if no compensable damage has occurred, there is no basis for an action at law in negligence. The plaintiff must prove that he or she suffered some type of compensable injury, that is, that something happened to the plaintiff or the plaintiff's property as the proximate result of the defendant's breach of the standard of care that warrants compensation by the defendant to the plaintiff. Damage comes in many forms. It can be monetary, physical, mental, and emotional. It can affect a person or the person's property. However, in a negligence action it must be something the courts recognize as compensable and must be significant enough under the circumstances to warrant a monetary award as compensation.

APPLICATION 9.7

Kim is the father of Lou. One day as Kim is mowing the grass, Lou, aged 5, is riding his bike along the sidewalk in front of their home. As Kim watches helplessly, a drunken driver careens from the road to the sidewalk and runs down Lou. Kim holds Lou in his arms waiting for the ambulance and watches as the child slowly suffers and dies before the ambulance arrives. In some jurisdictions, the only action against the driver would be for Lou's injuries, suffering, and death. There would be no recovery permitted for the emotional suffering of Kim who witnessed the accident and subsequent death of his child.

Point for Discussion: Why do you think the trend has begun to allow actions and recognition of this type of occurrence as compensable damage?

Assignment 9.1

Consider the following situation and identify the specific facts that would represent each element of an action in negligence.

Janelle decides to open up her own greenhouse and nursery business. Her start-up funds are somewhat limited and the cost to pave the long drive from the street is more than she can afford. Janelle rents a large truck and goes to a local quarry where she purchases several tons of large-grade gravel/rock, which is less expensive than that which is finely crushed. Janelle uses her tractor with a blade to spread the rock along the dirt driveway so that it will not be so muddy during rainy periods. On Mother's Day weekend the business is bustling and the very small parking area is full. Individuals begin parking along the drive and walking to the nursery. An elderly woman trips and falls while walking through the large rocks. She badly breaks her hip and ultimately ends up in a nursing home.

2. Hidden Elements of Negligence: Res Ipsa Loquitur

A traditional concept of negligence has found new applications in modern society. The Latin term res ipsa loquitur is translated to "the thing speaks for itself." Originally developed shortly after the formal acceptance of the negligence doctrine, res ipsa loquitur is used under very special circumstances in cases involving negligence as a means to aid disadvantaged plaintiffs. A plaintiff claiming negligence may also seek to have the theory of res ipsa loquitur applied in certain cases where the defendant has an unfair advantage with respect to access to essential evidence. A plaintiff may only claim the doctrine under very special circumstances where the following can be proven:

1. The occurrence was of a type that would not happen without negligence.
2. The instrument producing the injury during the occurrence was within the exclusive control of the defendant at all relevant times.
3. The plaintiff in no way contributed to the injury.

Res ipsa loquitur was developed for cases where a plaintiff was injured but unable to prove the chain of events required in proximate cause because the defendant controlled the evidence that depicted the occurrence. To prevent unwarranted claims of negligence, however, the three elements must be proven in place of proof of the exact way in which the duty was breached and in lieu of the missing elements of the proximate cause issue. As a result, res ipsa loquitur is no easier to establish than straight negligence and is applicable only in limited circumstances. Nevertheless, it does provide a much-needed remedy for plaintiffs who would otherwise be unable to prove a case successfully as the result of a defendant's ability to conceal the necessary evidence or prevent the plaintiff from gaining it.

In the latter part of the 20th century a whole new arena for res ipsa loquitur opened up. Advancements in technology gave negligent defendants a distinct upper hand in the control of evidence. Manufacturers produced defective products, and plaintiffs were injured by these products as a result of negligent production. However, plaintiffs had no means of knowing or discovering the exact acts of negligence. When all the elements were present, res ipsa loquitur could provide an avenue of legal recourse for the injured plaintiffs. Similarly, with tremendous advancements in medicine came a large increase in the number of procedures performed by physicians. Often these were performed while the plaintiff was under anesthesia or the influence of medications that altered his or her normal state of consciousness. The availability of the doctrine of res ipsa loquitur to plaintiffs injured during such procedures revolutionized the methods and conditions under which all medical procedures are performed. It placed the general safety of the patient on an equal level with the specific medical condition that was the subject or cause of the procedure performed. However, as awareness of the broader duty toward consumers and patients has been recognized, safety conscious practices and procedures have been identified as priorities, and rules of discovery have become more broad, the use of res ipsa loquitur has begun to decline again.

CASE IN POINT

Cain v. Johnson, 146 Ed.Law.Rep. 259, 755 A.2d 156 (R.I. 2000).

WEISBERGER, Chief Justice.

This case comes before us on the plaintiffs' appeal from a summary judgment entered in the Superior Court in favor of the defendants. For the reasons that follow, we affirm.

The facts of this case are not in dispute. At approximately 2 a.m. on August 1991, Michael T. Cain (the decedent) and two friends went for a walk along a section of Newport's Cliff Walk. While walking along an area of the Cliff Walk that winds through Salve

Regina University's (the university) campus, the decedent stepped from the paved walk onto a grassy area on the ocean side of the walk. He fell from the cliff to his death after the ground beneath his feet gave way.

On July 25, 1994, plaintiffs, William G. Cain and Mary H. Cain (plaintiffs or the Cains), filed a wrongful death action individually and on the part of the estate of Michael T. Cain against defendants, the City of Newport (city), the state of Rhode Island (state), and the university. The plaintiffs alleged that defendants' negligence caused the decedent's death because defendants failed to properly inspect, maintain, and repair the Cliff Walk. In September 1997, the city moved for summary judgment, arguing that the decedent was a trespasser because the Cliff Walk had closed at 9 p.m. The state and the university joined in the city's motion. On November 7, 1997, the motion justice granted summary judgment in favor of all defendants, ruling that summary judgment was required based on this Court's decision in Brindamour v. City of Warwick, 697 A.2d 1075 (R.I.1997) (holding that a landowner owes a trespasser only the duty to refrain from willful and wanton conduct). On November 21, 1997, the motion justice reconsidered the matter, and allowed the summary judgment to stand.

The plaintiffs then appealed the grant of summary judgment. The case was heard on the show cause calendar on March 3, 1999. After argument, the case was placed on the regular calendar with directions to the parties to provide the court with authorities and guidance on the following issues:

"1. Would the conduct of the defendants or any of them amount to willful and wanton conduct under the facts that were presented to the motion justice in this case?

"2. Would willful and wanton conduct include reckless indifference to the safety of the plaintiffs' decedent whether or not the defendants were aware of his presence on the premises?

"3. Would the alleged conduct of the defendants or any of them rise to the level of reckless indifference to the safety of the plaintiffs' decedent in light of the nature of the defective condition which caused him to fall to his death?

"4. In the event that it was determined that the defendants or any of them directly or indirectly invited or permitted the plaintiffs' decedent to use the subject property for recreational purposes, would the duty toward him differ in any respect from that owed to a trespasser? See G.L. § 32–6–1 et seq. and particularly § 32–6–3 and § 32–6–5.

"5. In the circumstances of this case, should the question of whether the defendants' conduct amounted to willful or wanton acts or ordinary negligence be determined by the court on motion for summary judgment or should it be determined by a trier of fact?"

These issues will be discussed as they are presented, beginning with a short discussion of the Brindamour case on which the motion justice's ruling was based. Further facts will be supplied as may be necessary to deal with these issues.

Brindamour v. City of Warwick, 697 A.2d 1075 (R.I.1997)

Colleen Marie Brindamour was killed at approximately midnight on a midsummer evening in 1993 when a car in which she was a passenger skidded off a road located within a city-owned park and slammed into a tree head-on. See Brindamour, 697 A.2d at 1076. Brindamour's mother, Rose Brindamour, filed suit against the City of Warwick, alleging that the city was negligent in failing to maintain the park and its roadways in a safe manner. The park was closed at the time of the accident. See id. We held that because Brindamour was in the park after hours, she was a trespasser, and that the city owed to trespassers only the duty to refrain from wanton or willful conduct. See id. at 1077.

For purposes of this opinion, we shall assume without deciding that all three defendants had the same relationship to the decedent and that there was no distinction among them with respect to the duty owed him. We make this assumption even though counsel for the university has argued vigorously that its duty concerning the Cliff Walk was superseded by the authority exercised over the pathway by the City of Newport and by the state. We also recognize that the state has argued that its duty varied from that of the city. We do not believe that it is necessary in this context to resolve those contentions.

I
Was the decedent a trespasser?

Initially, plaintiffs argue that Brindamour does not apply, and that there is a genuine issue of material fact about whether the decedent was a trespasser at the time of the accident. Pursuant to Newport City Ordinance § 12.32.010(C), the Cliff Walk is "closed for public use between nine p.m. and six a.m. of the following day, daily, and no person shall go upon such public areas during the hours of closing . . . except that the Cliff Walk shall remain open for the purpose of access to the water for fishing." The plaintiffs argue that in Brindamour, it was an uncontested fact that the plaintiff was a trespasser. The plaintiffs argue, however, that in the instant case, the decedent had no way of knowing that the walk closed at a particular time every night. The plaintiffs argue that despite the fact that a city ordinance prohibits people from being on the walk after hours, unless for the purpose of fishing, only two signs posted on either end of the walk notify people of the hours that the walk is open to the public. The plaintiffs argue that such notice is insufficient, as there are numerous other unrestricted entrance points along the walk, which stretches approximately 18,000 feet along the Atlantic Ocean.

However, we recently rejected a similar argument in Bennett v. Napolitano, 746 A.2d 138 (R.I.2000). In Bennett, we held that an individual who, in violation of a city ordinance, entered a park after closing was a trespasser. Id. at 141. There, the plaintiff, Donald Bennett (Bennett), was walking his dogs at about 2 a.m., along a path in Roger Williams Park in Providence that he had used for about ten years, when a tree limb fell on him. Bennett filed suit against the City of Providence, alleging that the city was negligent in maintaining the park. The city filed a motion for summary judgment, arguing that Bennett was a trespasser because he was in the park after it had closed and that therefore the city owed him only the duty to refrain from willful and wanton conduct. The motion justice granted the motion and entered judgment accordingly.

On appeal, Bennett argued that he had the implied consent of the city to use the park after hours because he had done so for a period of ten years and because he had been observed on numerous occasions by park rangers and Providence police officers, who had never asked him to leave. See id. We rejected plaintiff's argument. We noted that the park was closed from 9 p.m. to 7 a.m. pursuant to city ordinance, and that an "individual who enters a city park after closing is a trespasser." Bennett, 746 A.2d at 141. We held that local police and park rangers did not have the authority to waive the provisions of that ordinance by affirmatively or impliedly inviting people

into the park after closing. To conclude otherwise would be equivalent to holding that a "landowner who does not aggressively exclude a trespasser thereby assumes an enhanced duty of care towards the trespasser or that a driver who regularly exceeds the authorized highway speed limit while observed by law enforcement officials can claim an implied permission to speed." Id. at 142.

A strict adherence to this Court's decision in Bennett leads one to conclude that the decedent was a trespasser even though the Cliff Walk was not to intensively posted as to notify all possible visitors of the hours of operation. The holding in Bennett suggests that the existence of a city ordinance closing a park establishes as a fact that any person in the park after hours is a trespasser, even if the person is completely unaware of the ordinance. Brindamour and Bennett both clearly establish that a person in a park after it has closed is a trespasser. Because the decedent was on the Cliff Walk at about 2 a.m., he was a trespasser as a matter of law. We shall now turn to the questions raised by the Court.

II
The willful and wanton standard

The first and the second questions posed by the Court are interrelated, and, therefore, will be discussed together. These questions ask whether defendants' conduct rises to the level of willful and wanton conduct (question 1), and whether the duty to refrain from willful and wanton conduct arises before or after the trespasser is discovered (question 2).

Under Rhode Island law, it is well settled that a landowner owes a trespasser no duty except to refrain from willful or wanton conduct. See Bennett, 746 A.2d at 142. It is also well settled that such a duty arises only after a trespasser is discovered in a position of danger. See Wolf v. National Railroad Passenger Corp., 697 A.2d 082, 1086 (R.I.1997). . . .

In Wolf, 697 A.2d at 1084, a young boy suffered fatal injuries when he was struck by a train as he was attempting to cross a trestle that spanned an inlet of the Narragansett Bay. The plaintiff, Warren Wolf, the administrator of the young boy's estate, filed a wrongful-death action against the railroad and its engineer, alleging negligent design and maintenance of the railroad trestle and its surrounding areas. The railroad moved for summary judgment, arguing that the boy was a trespasser, and accordingly, the railroad owed him only a duty to refrain from willful and wanton injury. A Superior Court justice granted the railroad's motion and entered a final judgment in its favor. We affirmed the judgment, holding that because the boy was a trespasser, the railroad owed him no duty except to refrain from willful or wanton injury after his trespass was discovered.

Accordingly, the duty to refrain from willful and wanton conduct did not arise until the boy was discovered by the railroad engineer; by that time, however, "there was simply not enough time for the train to stop and thereby prevent this catastrophe." Id.

The plaintiffs argue, however, that the holding of the cases above should not be extended to the case at bar. Rather, plaintiffs urge the Court to accept the rule set forth in the Restatement (Second) Torts, § 334 (1965), which provides as follows:

"A possessor of land who knows, or from facts within his knowledge should know, that trespassers constantly intrude upon a limited area thereof, is subject to liability for bodily harm there caused to them by his failure to carry on an activity involving a risk of death or serious bodily harm with reasonable care for their safety."

Under plaintiffs' definition, the decedent's status as a discovered trespasser, versus an undiscovered trespasser, would be irrelevant.

Section 334 of the Restatement is analogous to the "beaten path exception" available under the common law. "The defendant in such instances is liable to a trespasser injured while using a limited area containing an unreasonable risk of harm." Mariorenzi v. Joseph DiPonte, Inc., 114 R.I. 294, 302 n. 2, 333 A.2d 127, 131 n. 2 (1975). This theory, which turns on a landowner's knowledge of the use of his land by trespassers, however, has not been accepted by this Court. In Mariorenzi, this Court eliminated the distinction that the common law drew among invitees, licensees, and trespassers. Id. at 307, 333 A.2d at 133. Nineteen years later, we rejected the holding of Mariorenzi and restored the distinction between invitees and trespassers. See Tantimonico, 637 A.2d at 1061. Save for the aberration of Mariorenzi, this Court has steadfastly held that a landowner owes a trespasser no duty until he or she is actually discovered in a position of peril. See Wolf, 697 A.2d at 1086; Zoubra, 89 . . . I. at 44, 150 A.2d at 644–45; Previte v. Wanskuck Co., 80 R.I. 1, 3, 90 A.2d 769, 770 (1952); New England Pretzel Co., 75 R.I. at 394, 67 A.2d at 43.

For example, in Zoubra, the plaintiff alleged that "her presence on [the railroad] tracks in the exercise of due care on her part raised a duty on [the railroad's] part not to willfully or wantonly injure her if it 'knew or in the exercise of reasonable care would have known' of her presence." Zoubra, 89 R.I. at 45, 150 A.2d at 645. The majority held, however, in sustaining the trial court, which found the declaration insufficient as a matter of law, that the law does not impose upon a landowner any duty toward a trespasser unless it has first discovered him or her in a position of peril, even though there was an allegation that the defendant knew or should have known of the presence of people on the crossing. We held that a landowner is " 'under no duty to keep a cookout for trespassers. Their probable presence on the tracks is not such a circumstance which the law requires a railroad to anticipate and reasonably guard against.' " 150 A.2d at 645. . . .

The plaintiffs also argue that the holdings of the cases cited above are specific to railroad trespassers, and that they do not apply to the instant case. This argument, however, cannot be accepted. We are not persuaded that this Court should promulgate special rules for different types of landowners. Such fragmentation of duties would create chaos in the attempted application of rules wherein consistency is essential.

Furthermore, although the above cases relate specifically to railroad properties, support for extending the proposition beyond railroad cases exists on G.L.1956 § 32-6-5 and in previous decisions of this Court. Section 32-6-5, provision of the Public Use of Private Lands statute, provides in pertinent part as follows:

"(a) Nothing in this chapter limits in any way any liability which, but for this chapter, otherwise exists:

"(1) For the willful or malicious failure to guard or warn against a dangerous condition, use, structure, or activity after discovering the user's peril. . . ." (Emphasis added.)

Under Rhode Island statutory law, a landowner owes no duty to a trespasser unless the trespasser first is discovered in a position of peril. Even though this statute may not apply to the public entities involved in the case at bar, it represents a considered policy adopted by our legislature and applies to all types of recreational property.

This Court also has specifically applied the holding of the railroad cases outside of the railroad context. See Tantimonico, 637 A.2d at 1057; Previte, 80 R.I. at 3, 90 A.2d at 770. In Previte, for example, a wrongful-death action brought by the parents of a young boy who drowned in a pond in Providence, this Court held that "no duty is owed a trespasser by a landowner except to refrain from injuring him wantonly or wilfully after discovering his peril. . . . [W]e see no legal duty imposed on defendant to anticipate the presence of plaintiffs' son as a trespasser on its property." Id. at 3–4, 90 A.2d at 770. Based on the foregoing authorities, it is clear that a landowner does not owe a trespasser any duty until after the trespasser is discovered in a position of peril. Once the trespasser is discovered, the landowner owes the trespasser a duty to refrain from willfully or wantonly injuring the trespasser. Because the decedent in the instant case never was discovered in a position of peril, we need not consider whether defendants' conduct rose to the level of willful and wanton conduct. The defendants did not owe the decedent any duty.

III
The nature of the defective condition of the land

The third question posed by the Court asks whether liability arises in light of the nature of the defective condition of the land. The plaintiffs argue that the overall condition that led to the decedent's death was the paved nature of the Cliff Walk. Therefore, plaintiffs argue that even though the precise area of the ground from which the decedent fell was a "natural condition" of the land, the paved nature of the walk rendered it an artificial condition, thereby imposing liability pursuant to the Restatement (Second) Torts § 337, which provides:

"A possessor of land who maintains on the land an artificial condition which involves a risk of death or serious bodily harm to persons coming in contact with it, is subject to liability for bodily harm caused to trespassers by his failure to exercise reasonable care to warn them of the condition if

"(a) the possessor knows or has reason to know of their presence in dangerous proximity to the condition, and

"(b) the condition is of such a nature that he has reason to believe that the trespasser will not discover it or realize the risk involved."

The plaintiffs' argument with respect to this provision, however, must fail for two reasons—(1) because the precise area from which the decedent fell was a natural condition for which defendants could not be held liable, even if this court were to adopt the foregoing rule, which we have hitherto declined to do, and (2) even if it were considered an artificial condition, it was a condition of such a nature that a trespasser would discover or realize the risk involved.

The area from which the decedent fell is just northeast of McCauley Hall, the university's former library. In a police report following the accident, the Newport police described the area as follows:

"I noticed there was a patch of mud measuring approx. 5' square with numerous sneaker and footprints embedded in the mud, a cement slab which rose approx. 8" above the mud, approx. 10" wide on the top surface and then de[s]cended the cliff approx. 6'. The slab appeared to be approx. 7' in length. To the immediate right (south) of the slab there was a hole in the grass which measured approx. 8" square which appeared to be due to erosion which may have also been a factor in this incident. Judging from where the bloodstain on the rock below where the victim landed, it is possible the victim stepped in to this small hole which would have placed him in the logical trajectory to land where the bloodstain appeared."

The report was accompanied by photographs of the cliff, taken from both the top of the cliff and from the water. Those photographs clearly show a muddy area of earth distinct from the paved path. Further investigation revealed that there had been heavy rains during the preceding weekend that had made the area muddy and slippery.

The area from which the decedent fell is clearly a natural condition of the land. With respect to the duty of care owed by a landowner for natural conditions on the land, we have held that

"the possessor of land owed a trespasser 'no duty to discover, remedy, or warn of dangerous natural conditions. Perhaps if the possessor sees a trespasser about to encounter extreme danger from such a source, which is known to the possessor and perceptibly not known to the trespasser, there may be a duty to warn (as by shouting). That is about as far as the bystander's duty to a highway traveler would traditionally go, if indeed it would go that far.' " Tantimonico, 637 A.2d at 1057 (quoting 4 Harper, James & Gray, The Law of Torts § 27.3 at 139 (2d ed.1986)).

Upon leaving the paved portion of the path, the decedent in the instant case had to walk an additional five feet or so to reach the edge of the cliff. It is from this edge of the cliff where the decedent fell. That area was clearly a natural condition of the land, and liability for it could not be imposed upon defendants, even pursuant to § 337 of the Restatement (Second) Torts.

Even if the area was considered an artificial condition of the land, plaintiffs' argument must fail because the conditions of § 337 cannot be met. Specifically, a visitor to the Cliff Walk certainly should be aware of and appreciate the risks that exist along the edge of a cliff that rises approximately sixty to seventy feet from the ocean. The top of the portion of the Cliff Walk from which the decedent fell is approximately fifty-three feet from the rock on which he was fatally struck. The rock itself is five feet from the water's edge. The plaintiffs argue in the instant case that the decedent, as well as other visitors, would not be aware of the risk because the Cliff Walk is open during parts of the year when it would be dark, and, specifically, because it was dark when the decedent visited the cliff. This fact, however, should increase one's awareness of the risks associated with the cliff. Indeed, any visitor along the walk in the dark should be that much more cautious, given the height of the cliff and the inability to see adequately where one is stepping.

Accordingly, no liability arises because of the defective condition of the land.

The fourth question posed by the Court concerns the effect of chapter 6 of title 32, particularly § 32-6-3 and § 32-6-5, on the duty owed to the decedent. Chapter 6 of title 32 sets forth liability limitations for the public use of private lands. Section 32-6-3, entitled "Liability of Landowner," provides that:

"Except as specifically recognized by or provided in § 32-6-5, an owner of land who either directly or indirectly invites or permits without charge any person to use that property for recreational purposes does not thereby:

"(1) Extend any assurance that the premises are safe for any purpose;

"(2) Confer upon that person the legal status of an invitee or licensee to whom a duty of care is owed; nor

"(3) Assume responsibility for or incur liability for any injury to any person or property caused by an act of [sic] omission of that person."

Section 32-6-5 provides in pertinent part "(a) Nothing in this chapter limits in any way any liability which, but for this chapter, otherwise exists: (1) For the willful or malicious failure to guard or warn against a dangerous condition, use, structure, or activity after discovering the user's peril. . . ."

The plaintiffs and the state have taken the position that the above provisions do not apply in the instant case because the statute is designed to encourage private property owners to allow the public to use their land for recreational purposes. The plaintiffs argue that even though § 32-6-2 has been amended to include the state and municipalities as "owners," the statute in force at the time of the accident did not include such entities. The city argues that the statute was applicable to the state and municipalities before the 1996 amendment pursuant to this Court's holding in O'Brien v. State, 555 A.2d 334, 338–39 (R.I.1989) (state and/or municipality responsible as a private landowner in certain circumstances).

Regardless of whether the statute is applicable, the duty owed to decedent under the statute would not change in this case. Even under the statute, a landowner owes no duty to a trespasser unless the trespasser is first discovered in a position of peril. See § 32-6-5. Section 32-6-5 provides that liability still exists "(1) [f]or the willful or malicious failure to guard or warn against a dangerous condition, use, structure, or activity after discovering the user's peril. . . ." (Emphasis added.) Therefore, as has been stated, no duty could arise toward the decedent until he had been discovered in a position of peril. It is undisputed that he had not been discovered. This rule is simply legislative codification of the common law that is enunciated in our cases.

Was summary judgment appropriate?

The final question posed by the Court is whether summary judgment was appropriate in the instant case, or whether the issue of willful and wanton conduct should have been determined by the trier of fact.

Summary judgment is appropriate if upon "examination of all the pleadings, affidavits, admissions, answers to interrogatories, and other materials viewed in the light most favorable to the party opposing the motion reveals no genuine issue of material fact and that the moving party is entitled to judgment as a matter of law." Sullivan v. Town of Coventry, 707 A.2d 257, 259 (R.I.1998). In the instant case, it is clear that a landowner owes a trespasser no duty except to refrain from willful and wanton conduct after the trespasser has been discovered in a position of peril. Absolutely no evidence has been presented to suggest that the defendants or any of them were aware of the decedent's position of peril. Accordingly, summary judgment was properly entered.

Conclusion

For the foregoing reasons, we conclude that the decedent was an undiscovered trespasser to whom the defendants owed no duty. Accordingly, we deny and dismiss the plaintiffs' appeal and affirm the judgment of the Superior Court, to which the papers in the case may be remanded.

Case Review Question: Would the park be liable if the accident had occurred during the day and the park had knowledge of the muddy conditions surrounding the path?

APPLICATION 9.8

Chloe purchases a new car. On the same day, she is driving down the highway when suddenly a tire blows out and she crashes the car. In the accident investigation, it is determined that the tire had a defect in that there was a very thin area on one portion of the tire. When the weight of the car combined with the heat generated by driving the vehicle on hot dry pavement at speeds over 50 miles per hour, the weakened area gave way and split. The investigation of the accident also showed that the car was traveling at approximately 55 m.p.h. in a 55 m.p.h. zone at the time the brakes were applied. In this situation, Chloe could claim res ipsa loquitur against the tire manufacturer, as well as other possible actions. Each of the elements were satisfied. The tire had been under the control of the manufacturer at the time the defect was created. Tires do not ordinarily fail under normal highway conditions. Chloe was operating the vehicle at a legal speed on the highway at the time of the incident. Because the tire was new and there was no evidence of other causes, there is no indication any other factors contributed to the cause of the accident other than the defective tire. A defendant is not likely to volunteer access to information of a defect in the manufacturing process to an injured party. By claiming res ipsa loquitur, the plaintiff could successfully prove the case or, in the alternative, force access to the needed evidence through formal discovery proceedings during the lawsuit.

Point for Discussion: Why would information that showed Chloe was driving at speeds well above the limit be relevant if the cause of the wreck was still the defective tire?

Occasionally, an action will be brought claiming *gross negligence.* In this situation all of the elements typically required in ordinary negligence must still be proven. However, to establish the higher level of gross negligence, it must be shown that the risk of injury of which the defendant should have been aware was not only possible, it was probable. Most often these cases are filed in jurisdictions that permit punitive damages. A supplemental action is filed with the primary counts of the complaint to seek exemplary (punitive) damages in addition to compensatory damages as punishment for the defendant's reckless disregard for the welfare of the forseeable plaintiff. Essentially, in actions for gross negligence the plaintiff claims that the defendant's conduct was more than mere carelessness and that it demonstrated a willful disregard for the safety of others and/or their property.

APPLICATION 9.9

Paul worked approximately 25 miles from his home. The road between the two locations was very winding and hilly and heavily traveled. Paul routinely stopped at a bar next to his workplace on Friday evenings and had several drinks before heading home. Twice in a period of three years, Paul had wrecked his car on Friday nights when he had been drinking. Finally, one Friday night Paul went to the bar and had four drinks in less than two hours before heading home. On the way he crossed the center line and hit another vehicle head-on, killing all of its occupants. The action against Paul may be brought alleging gross negligence because of the overwhelming evidence that Paul not only should have known of the dangers to others as the result of his drinking and driving, but that the history of previous accidents under those conditions showed an additional basis for knowledge that his driving was impaired when drinking and a consequent willful disregard for the safety of other motorists on the roadway between his home and work.

Point for Discussion: Why would the other incidents be relevant if they did not involve injury to others?

C. INTENTIONAL TORTS

1. Distinguished from Other Torts

An actor engaged in conduct is subject to constructive knowledge, that is, knew or should have known, that injury to another or another's property was possible as a direct result of the conduct. This is pivotal in the theory of negligence. The legal actions for what have become known as intentional torts have a different approach and, when proven, often result in more serious consequences for the defendant. A common misconception by those without knowledge of this area of law is that an intentional tort describes an action toward another with the intent to cause injury. This is not at all the case. Such conduct as that would likely be more appropriately addressed in a criminal action. Rather, an intentional tort does have an essential element of intent, but it is the intent to act as opposed to the intent to injure. More specifically, the intentional tort requires proof that the defendant acted voluntarily, even with the knowledge that the act would almost certainly bring about the injury. Thus, unlike negligence where only an awareness of the possibility is needed, the intentional tort imposes much greater knowledge on the actor.

Another distinguishing factor between negligence and intentional torts is one of specificity with respect to the factual situations. The elements of negligence remain the same regardless of how the case arose, such as a case involving an automobile accident or a case of negligent infliction of emotional distress. In a case claiming intentional tort, there are specific types of intentional tort actions for specific types of occurrences. Each action has distinct elements that must be proven by the plaintiff and typically only established types of actions for intentional tort may be brought. Therefore, if a circumstance is not addressed by a recognized form of intentional tort, it must be brought under a different legal theory such as negligence.

Intentional tort differs from the degree of duty concept in negligence because in an intentional tort, the risk is so great that it can be counted upon to produce the injury. If the actor commits the action despite this knowledge, then the action may constitute an intentional tort against the injured party. A major distinction between gross negligence and an intentional tort is that mere knowledge and appreciation of a danger are insufficient in an intentional tort. As stated, there must be evidence of voluntary conduct in light of the knowledge and appreciation of the danger. In addition, the risk of harm must be a near certainty rather than a probability.

There are many intentional torts and the elements of each tort are somewhat broadly stated to accommodate a variety of factual situations that all result in a common type of injury. The discussion that follows explores some of the more common intentional torts and their elements. See Figure 9.1

2. Common Actions for Intentional Torts

a. Assault   The most popular interpretation of an assault has a criminal connotation. While it certainly is a criminal act, there is also a civil action for assault that is entirely separate and distinct. While both criminal and civil assault typically involve an affront to another person, the criminal occurrence often requires physical contact. This is distinguished from the usual definition of a civil assault. To prove an act of the intentional tort of assault, the following elements must be proven:

- Physical conduct that may or may not be accompanied by words
- As a result of the conduct the plaintiff is placed in apprehension of immediate and harmful physical contact[14]

By definition, the tort of assault involves no physical contact (unlike the criminal counterpart) but rather the immediate threat of such contact. Further, an assault cannot be claimed based on the mere spoken word threatening a future injury. The basis for an assault action is that threat of immediate physical harm produces such fear and/or other reaction that it actually injures the plaintiff.

APPLICATION 9.10

Desiree becomes embroiled in a heated argument with her boyfriend. During the argument he begins making verbal threats of physical harm. Desiree goes into the bathroom and locks the door. Shortly thereafter she realizes that her boyfriend is removing the door from the hinges and at the same time he is yelling that he has a knife and is going to stop her from ever arguing with him or anyone else again. As Desiree hears the first hinge pin removed from the door she climbs out the bathroom window and falls to the ground below breaking both legs.

In an action for assault, Desiree experienced verbal as well as physical action that demonstrated to her an intent to carry out the threats. In fear of her life, she jumped out a window and was seriously injured. Under these facts, the elements of civil assault are present.

Point for Discussion: At what point in the factual scenario did the civil assault take place?

FIGURE 9.1   Torts and Related Causes of Action*: The Elements

The Cause of Action	Its Elements
1. Abuse of Process	i. Use of civil or criminal proceedings ii. Improper or ulterior purpose iii. Actual damage
2. Alienation of Affections	i. Intent to diminish the marital relationship between spouses ii. Affirmative conduct iii. Affections between spouses are in fact alienated iv. Causation of the alienation

3. Assault (Civil)	i. Act
	ii. Intent either
	      a. to cause a harmful or offensive contact or
	      b. to cause an apprehension of a harmful or offensive contact
	iii. Apprehension of an imminent harmful or offensive contact to the plaintiff's own person
	iv. Causation of the apprehension

4. Battery (Civil)	i. Act ii. Intent to cause harmful or offensive contact iii. Harmful or offensive contact with the plaintiff's person iv. Causation of the harmful or offensive contact
5. Civil Rights Violation	i. A person acting under color of law ii. Deprives a citizen of federal constitutional or federal statutory rights
6. Conversion	i. Personal property (chattel) ii. Plaintiff is in possession of the chattel or is entitled to immediate possession iii. Intent to exercise dominion or control over the chattel iv. Serious interference with plaintiffs' possession v. Causation of the serious interference
7. Criminal Conversation	Defendant has sexual relations with the plaintiffs' spouse (adultery)

8. Deceit	i. a. Statement of past or present fact or
	      b. Concealment of past or present fact or
	      c. Nondisclosure of past or present fact when there is a duty to disclose or
	      d. A statement of opinion (only some opinions qualify)
	ii. The statement is false
	iii. Scienter (intent to mislead) (some states say negligence in misleading is enough)
	iv. Intent to have the plaintiffs rely on the statement or a reason to believe the plaintiff will rely
	v. Causation in fact (actual reliance)
	vi. Justifiable reliance
	vii. Actual damages

Defamation (two torts)
 9. Libel
	i. Defamatory statement by the defendant (written)
	ii. Of and concerning the plaintiff
	iii. Publication of the statement
	iv. Damages:
	      a. In some states, special damages never have to be proven in any libel case
	      b. In other states, only libel on its face does not require special damages. In these states, libel per quod requires special damages
	v. Causation

*With the exception of negligence and strict liability torts, the causes of action identified here constitute intentional torts.
Statsky Torts: Personal Injury Litigation p2–6 1991.

FIGURE 9.1 (*Continued*)

The Cause of Action	Its Elements

10. Slander	i. Defamatory statement by the defendant (spoken)
	ii. Of and concerning the plaintiff
	iii. Publication of the statement
	iv. Damages:
	  a. Special damages are not required if the slander is slander per se
	  b. Special damages must be proven if the slander is not slander per se
	v. Causation

11. Disparagement	i. False statement of fact ii. Disparaging the plaintiff's business or property iii. Publication of the statement iv. Intent v. Special damages vi. Causation

12. Enticement of a Child or Abduction of a Child	i. Intent to interfere with a parent's custody over his or her child
	ii. Affirmative conduct by defendant:
	  a. to abduct or force child from the parent's custody or
	  b. to entice or encourage the child to leave the parent or
	  c. to harbor the child and encourage him/her to stay away from the parent's custody
	iii. The child leaves the custody of the parent
	iv. Defendant caused child to leave or to stay away

13. Enticement of Spouse	i. Intent to diminish the marital relationship between the spouses
	ii. Affirmative conduct by the defendant:
	  a. to entice or encourage the spouse to leave the plaintiff's home or
	  b. to harbor the spouse and encourage him/her to stay away from the plaintiff's home
	iii. The spouse leaves the plaintiff's home
	iv. Causation

14. False Imprisonment	i. An act that completely confines the plaintiff within fixed boundaries set by the defendant ii. Intent to confine plaintiff or a third person iii. Causation of the confinement iv. Plaintiff either was conscious of the confinement or was harmed by it
15. Intentional Infliction of Emotional Distress	i. An act of extreme or outrageous conduct ii. Intent to cause severe emotional distress iii. Severe emotional distress is suffered iv. Causation of this distress
16. Interference with Contract Relations	i. An existing contract ii. Interference with the contract by defendants iii. Intent iv. Damages v. Causation
17. Interference with Prospective Advantage	i. Reasonable expectation of an economic advantage ii. Interference with this expectation iii. Intent iv. Damages v. Causation
Invasion of Privacy (four torts) 18. Appropriation	i. The use of the plaintiff's name, likeness, or personality ii. For the benefit of the defendant

(continued)

FIGURE 9.1 (*Continued*)

The Cause of Action	Its Elements
19. False Light	i. Publicity ii. Placing the plaintiff in a false light iii. Highly offensive to a reasonable person
20. Intrusion	i. An act of intrusion into someone's private affairs or concerns ii. Highly offensive to a reasonable person
21. Public Disclosure of a Private Fact	i. Publicity ii. Concerning the private life of the plaintiff iii. Highly offensive to a reasonable person
22. Malicious Prosecution	i. Initiate or procure the initiation of legal proceedings ii. Without probable cause iii. With malice iv. The legal proceedings terminate in favor of the accused
23. Negligence	i. Duty ii. Breach of duty iii. Proximate cause iv. Damages
Nuisance	
24. Private Nuisance	An unreasonable interference with the use and enjoyment of land
25. Public Nuisance	An interference with a right that is common to the public
26. Prima Facie Tort	i. Infliction of harm ii. Intent to do harm (malice) iii. Special damages iv. Causation
27. Seduction	The defendant has sexual relations with the plaintiff's daughter with or without consent
28. Strict Liability for Harm Caused by Animals	Domestic Animals i. The owner had reason to know the animal has a specific propensity to harm others ii. Harm is caused by the animal by that specific propensity Wild Animals i. Keeping a wild animal ii. Causes damage
29. Strict Liability for Abnormally Dangerous Conditions or Activities	i. The existence of an abnormally dangerous condition or activity ii. Knowledge of the condition or activity iii. Damages iv. Causation
30. Strict Liability in Tort	i. Seller ii. A defective product that is unreasonably dangerous to person or property iii. User or consumer iv. Physical harm v. Causation
31. Trespass to Chattels	i. Personal property (chattel) ii. Plaintiff is in possession of the chattel or is entitled to immediate possession iii. Intent to dispossess or to intermeddle with the chattel iv. Dispossession, impairment, or deprivation of use for a substantial time v. Causation of element (iv)
32. Trespass to Land	i. An act ii. Intrusion on land iii. In possession of another

b. Battery   In discussions of criminal conduct it is not uncommon to hear assault and battery described as a single event. However, in the context of intentional torts, battery is a totally distinct tort from that of assault. They may occur in the same case but will always occur at different moments by definition. Battery is perhaps the most litigated intentional tort, because it includes all unpermitted physical contact that results in harm. This may or may not involve a violent confrontation. Battery encompasses physical attacks certainly, but it also includes medical treatment without proper consent and every other conceivable act that results in physical contact between two parties as long as the following elements are present:

- Intent to make physical contact
- No consent to such contact
- Contact occurs to the person or something so closely identified with the person that it would be considered part of the person such as clothing
- Contact results in some form of injury (not necessarily physical)[15]

As mentioned, the civil tort of battery has a much broader perspective than a violent confrontation between two persons and, in fact, those circumstances probably make up the minority of cases filed for civil battery. Battery is a very common basis for actions of medical malpractice. For example, if a patient undergoes a procedure and something is left inside the patient's body such a sponge or instrument, a battery has occurred. Similarly, if a patient consents to one procedure and an additional or different procedure is performed without the informed consent of the patient, there has been a battery. These types of lawsuits have revolutionized the methods by which medicine is practiced in the United States, prompting numerous safeguards to be implemented for patient safety and ultimately to reduce the risk of expensive lawsuits against the health care providers and facilities. Other types of situations that may give rise to a claim for the civil action of battery include unpermitted sexual contact, acts of violence, and any other situation that satisfies the necessary elements.

There is an exception or defense to an action for battery that is known as the emergency rule.[16] Under special circumstances, such as a true medical emergency, an unpermitted physical contact will not ordinarily give rise to an action for battery if the conduct is an attempt to help the plaintiff and the plaintiff is (1) unable to give consent, and (2) has not previously denied consent. For example, if someone is unconscious, there is not carte blanche to do whatever the person offering assistance pleases. Rather, the only physical contact permitted is that which is reasonably necessary to offer assistance, and certainly no conduct that is not directly related to helping the individual is excused by the emergency rule. Also, any assistance should be within the capability of the person offering help. For example, it would not be ordinarily permissible for any citizen on the street to perform exploratory surgery on an unconscious individual found by the roadside. Secondly, some assistance may still be actionable despite the emergency rule if the denial of consent has been expressed previously. An example might be the resuscitation of a terminally ill patient who has previously made it known that no resuscitation efforts were to be made. Many states have enacted statutes known as *Good Samaritan* rules that excuse one from liability when offering assistance to someone in real distress. This protection encourages individuals among the general public to help one another rather than to alienate them and cause further harm because of a fear of legal action.

c. False Imprisonment   An action that is not heard of much in ordinary conversation, but is still quite actively used in litigation is that of false imprisonment. There are very specific elements; therefore, it is applicable in a limited number of cases. Nevertheless, the action for false imprisonment still appears in the courts when the following can be shown:

- A party (who may or may not be law enforcement personnel) creates boundaries of some kind with the intent that the other party be confined within those boundaries.
- The confined party must be aware of the confinement and must not give consent to the same.
- The confined party must perceive no reasonable means of escape.
- The circumstances giving rise to the confinement must be unreasonable.[17]

False imprisonment has been the basis for lawsuits ranging from false arrests by law enforcement officers to kidnapping to unwarranted detention in stores by store security and personnel.

In a case of false imprisonment, it is not necessary to create actual physical barriers to confine the plaintiff. Rather, it is only necessary to show that through physical barriers, conduct, or words, the injured party was reasonable in the belief that the ability to leave was restricted.[18] For example, a security guard who is armed tells an individual that he or she cannot leave a particular area. While not limited to a locked room or building, the fear of being shot for most people would be sufficient to create the perception of confinement.

One of the most unusual aspects of the tort of false imprisonment is the definition of damage. Unlike most torts, false imprisonment does not require an additional showing of some type of injury. The unreasonable interference with and loss of liberty is considered to be a sufficient and compensable injury in and of itself. This does not mean the damages must be confined to the loss of liberty. There may also be additional elements such as loss of income if someone was kept from their employment, emotional distress if the circumstances were unduly embarrassing or stressful, and even physical damages if there is injury to the person or their property.

There is a limit on the applicability of actions for false imprisonment regarding those who are reasonably exercising authority of law when detaining individuals suspected of criminal conduct. To place severe restrictions on this would hinder the capture of criminals. The general public interest requires there be sufficient latitude to take steps to investigate reasonable suspicions. However, this discretion is not without limits. If the plaintiff can establish that the detention or the steps taken during the investigation were unreasonable, the privilege may not be applied. This discourages overreaching by those with the authority to detain and/or arrest.

APPLICATION 9.11

Guy was shopping in a department store. He made his purchases and left the store. As he neared his car, he was approached by two armed security guards who accused him of stealing and asked him to return to the store. He did so and was taken to a windowless room with no furnishings except a wooden stool. His packages were examined and he was interrogated for the next six hours as the security guards attempted to get him to confess to where he had hidden the package of white socks they had seen him carrying in the store. He was not allowed to leave the room for any reason or communicate in any way with anyone other than the guards. Ultimately, the guards determined the $1.99 package of socks were not in Guy's possession and released him. An action for false imprisonment was brought and under the circumstances would be likely to prevail against the store and its employee security guards.

Point for Discussion: What part of the situation caused the case to go from a reasonable investigation to a case of false imprisonment?

d. Trespass   Early in the chapter, the historical torts of trespass and trespass on the case were discussed. The modern day tort of trespass is quite different from the expansive cause of action first recognized as a tort. Today, the tort of trespass is confined to an invasion of property rights. Most jurisdictions have a corresponding criminal action for an unlawful entry or presence on private property. But as with any civil and criminal action arising from the same incident, the cases are filed separately in civil and criminal courts, respectively. By the current definition, trespass occurs when one of the following conditions are met:

- A party personally or through an instrument under his or her control enters the land of another.
- Permits such a presence to continue even though the party has turned control of the property over to another.

Under trespass principles, there is no need to prove an intent to interfere with property rights or even the knowledge that the invasion is occurring. Rather, it need only be established that the intent existed with respect to the activity that constituted the trespass. The injury in a case of trespass is the interference with the right of quiet enjoyment—to use one's land without interference by others. There is no need to establish that any physical or financial damage occurred as the result of the trespass. However, if such is the case, these damages can be pled as well in the trespass action.

APPLICATION 9.12

Quantrell was driving her car on an icy road when she lost control and the car skidded off the road and through a fence. This would not constitute trespassing because she had no intent to drive the vehicle onto the private property. Rather, the vehicle was no longer under her control or intent at the time of the trespass.

Ross was a hunter walking through a wooded area. He inadvertently crossed the boundary line of the property where he had permission to hunt and entered the private property of another. This would constitute a trespass even though Ross did not have the intent to enter the other owner's property.

Point for Discussion: What distinguishes the latter scenario to create an act of trespass?

---

e. Fraud   Actions for fraud are found in a number of areas of law in addition to tort law. Fraudulent conduct is recognized as actionable in nearly every subject of civil law and criminal law as well as tort law. It is one of the most commonly filed tort actions for business dealings that do not involve formal or enforceable contracts, which would be addressed by fraud-in-contract actions. The tort of fraud is not easily proven, however, because the law places an obligation on individuals to be reasonably diligent in their dealings with others and in most cases an attempt at fraud would be discovered. However if the elements are properly satisfied, the tort action is applied and damages may be recovered. Specifically, the necessary elements include the following:

- Defendant made a material (significant) misrepresentation to plaintiff
- The representation was false
- The defendant had knowledge that the statement was false or at the very least was reckless in not determining whether it was true or false

- Defendant did or said something that demonstrates the intent that the plaintiff rely on the statement
- Plaintiff reasonably relied on the statement
- Plaintiff's reliance resulted in some form of compensable injury
- Plaintiff did not have a reasonable opportunity to discover the representation was false[19]

As seen from the restrictive elements of the tort of fraud, it is not an action brought simply because someone is dissatisfied with a noncontract business dealing. Unless shown otherwise, all persons are presumed to have adequate capacity and are expected to act responsibly toward protecting their own best interests. However, if the tort of fraud does occur and the elements are proven, damages may be awarded for the harm suffered as the result of fraud. Also, because fraud is typically successful in the most blatant circumstances of intentional tort, it is also often a basis for seeking punitive damages in jurisdictions where they are allowed.

f. Defamation   Tort law also provides remedy for actions against intangibles such as injury to one's reputation and position within their community. Defamation is a broader term used to describe two kinds of intentional torts for this type of action—libel and slander. Libel is an action for injuries that occur as the result of a false written communication to a third party, whereas slander is the appropriate action when the injuries occur as the result of a false oral communication to a third party. In either case, the damage is the same. The distinction is the way in which the tort was accomplished.

In both cases, the following elements must to be proven:

- Defendant made a communication to a third party about the plaintiff
- Defendant knew or should have known the content of the communication was untrue
- Defendant intended that the communication be directed to the attention of the third party or that the third party perceived it as directed to him or herself
- The content of the communication caused the third party to have a lowered opinion of the plaintiff or be discouraged from association with the plaintiff

A different standard of defamation requirements exists with respect to public figures. Persons who place themselves in the public light are considered by the courts to invite comment and publicity, and this right to comment is protected by the constitutional right of free speech. Because public figures place themselves up for notice by the media and general public, the courts are quite generous in the latitude allowed as to what may be said about such figures before a comment is considered injurious. Nevertheless, there are limits to what can be said publicly and in recent years a number of celebrities have prevailed in actions against tabloid magazines for what have been determined to be outrageously false statements. Essentially, a public figure must show that a statement was made with actual malice. This requires showing that the statement was made by the defendant with actual (versus constructive) knowledge that the statement was false, or that the defendant showed a total disregard with respect to the truth or falsity of the statement. In cases such as this, even public figures can recover damages in a defamation action.

Unlike many intentional torts, the action of defamation has defenses that are specific to that action. First, the truth is always a defense. If a truthful statement is made about another, no matter how damaging, no action for defamation can be successfully maintained. Another defense is known as privilege. Since certain communications are deemed to serve the public interest, they are encouraged and, as a result, opinions provided to government agencies may be considered privileged and exempt from an action for defamation. Privilege applies whenever public policy requires communication between the private sector and the government. While such statements are presumed to be true, the government accepts the responsibility in these situations to sort out what is true, what is false, and what is perhaps an innocent misperception. The benefit gained from allowing citizens to speak quite freely and openly to government officials about others who may be engaged in misconduct outweighs the risk of defamation. Additionally, the government, while made up of individuals, is considered to be an objective entity as a whole and thereby not subject to something as personal and specific as opinions regarding the reputation of citizens.

g. Intentional Infliction of Emotional Distress   Often called the *catchall tort,* intentional infliction of emotional distress is perhaps the most broadly defined intentional tort. Frequently, when it is difficult to prove the necessary elements of a more specific intentional tort, emotional distress is used as an alternative cause of action. It can also be brought as an independent cause of action along with an action for any other kind of tort.

The jurisdictions are divided on the issue of whether some type of physical contact must accompany an emotional injury. But to prove an action for intentional infliction of emotional distress, the basic elements to establish are these:

- Defendant was engaged in outrageous conduct
- Defendant knew or should have known the conduct would have so great an impact on the plaintiff as to cause mental or emotional disturbance
- The upset to plaintiff is so great it is likely to produce a resulting physical injury

When the conduct of the defendant is less outrageous or carried out with near certain knowledge of its effects, the courts have recognized an action for negligent infliction of emotional distress. This requires proof of the elements of negligence accompanied by the damage element of emotional distress as previously defined. This is used most often in cases where the conduct was without a doubt unreasonable, but proving the intent element is difficult. Yet, at the very least, extreme recklessness is supported by the evidence.

Assignment 9.2

Describe the intentional tort most likely to apply and determine whether the necessary elements are present for each of the following situations:

a. Joe and Laura are riding their bikes through a rural area. They see a path down a steep hill and decide to race. At the bottom of the hill they are unable to stop and instead crash through a fence.

b. Same situation as A only the plan is to gain speed going down the hill and jump the fence. However, neither make it and crash through instead.

c. Drew is using a snowblower on his driveway and walk. He is listening to headphones while he works and does not hear cars approach or pass. Just as a car passes by, Drew changes the position of the blower without looking up or pausing and a large amount of snow covers the windshield of the passing car and blocks the driver's view. The car swerves into the path of an oncoming car and caused an accident with property damage and personal injuries.

D. STRICT LIABILITY

By far, negligence is the most commonly employed tort action. This is primarily due to the fact that it has application in such a broad variety of circumstances. Next is intentional torts because, collectively, the various types of intentional torts address most other circumstances that arise regarding injury to individuals resulting from civilly actionable conduct other than breach of contract. Another method of tort action that has been developed, though in more limited situations, is strict liability. Traditionally, strict liability was applied rarely and only in cases of extremely dangerous activators. This area of law grew out of the law of negligence for use in very special circumstances. Strict liability was developed for use in cases of persons who obtained some personal or financial benefit from an activity that could not be made safe and from which the innocent public had no means to protect itself. Originally, strict liability was limited to cases involving those who kept dangerous wild animals or those involved in activities that had the capacity to cause great injury to helpless members of the public. Typically these included persons using explosives, such as construction or demolition crews.

The unique characteristic of strict liability is that there is no consideration given to the relative fault or intent or steps taken to meet any sort of duty. The concept of strict liability includes the premise that no matter how carefully an activity might be conducted or how closely an animal might be guarded, it is a near certainty that if the danger escapes into a public area, innocent bystanders will be harmed. It is further reasoned that the persons in control of the activity or animal benefit from it and it is only reasonable that they should bear the costs of harm.

Through the latter part of the 20th century to the present, strict liability has been expanded to address a variety of situations that describe the same type of danger as the original definition. Specifically, as science and technology advanced, individuals became less and less knowledgeable about the world in which they lived. More and more, the average person must depend on those who create the products that are part of daily life and trust that they will be produced in a safe manner. Those who profit from the creation, manufacture, and delivery of highly skilled services and products also bear a responsibility to consumers who cannot protect themselves from dangers for which they have no means of knowledge.

In recent history, strict liability has been one of the leading causes of action against manufacturers of consumer products. The users of these products typically have no knowledge of or way of determining product design and the potentially dangerous aspects of the product. However, the manufacturer producing the design and ultimately the product has every opportunity to know of any defects or extremely hazardous properties. Without sufficient warning of dangers to consumers, the manufacturer has placed into commerce a dangerous instrument that is likely to injure innocent persons. This is a basis for liability of the manufacturer who ultimately benefits most from the sale of such products. However, despite the expansion of application, the foundation of the theory of strict liability remains constant. It is only applicable in cases where those engaged in, and benefiting from, ultrahazardous activity will certainly sustain injury should the activity exceed the control and safeguards of the manufacturer. That injury will be caused to innocent individuals who have no reasonable means to protect themselves.

Consider each of the following situations and explain whether one or both would be appropriate for a successful strict liability claim.

a. Xavier opens his own blasting business as a blaster for areas of bedrock to make way for roads, home foundations, and so forth. His inventory of necessary equipment and supplies includes various explosive devices. On July 17, an earthquake strikes the area and many of the explosives ignite and cause extensive property damage to adjacent neighbors.

b. Nancy owns a local business. Her building is heated by a furnace using natural gas. The system is quite old but in good working condition. For the first time in history, a flash flood moves through the area after a record rainfall. The floodwaters cause the pipes to tear away from the furnace and burst, causing a large explosion and damaging adjacent properties by fire even in parts of the properties that weren't affected by the flood, such as upper stories of buildings.

E. PRODUCTS LIABILITY

An area of law that gets a great deal of media attention and which has revolutionized the manufacturing industry standards is typically referred to as products liability law. Unlike the other categories of tort law, which each have substantial and recognized legal theories, products liability is not a specific body of law with its own distinct causes of action and elements necessary to prove for recovery. Rather, it describes the subject matter of a tort action that may be based on any one of the major tort theories discussed thus far. The common denominator is that the action involves a product that has been placed in commerce. The number and variety of commercial products has grown to such proportions that an entire area of law has been developed to establish precedent for disputes that arise out of the sale and use of products. Each year, several million injuries result from using manufactured products. It is not surprising that the number of lawsuits in this area has grown accordingly.

Some of the legal standards that have been established in the broad field of products cases include recognized and applicable causes of action and standards of care. The most commonly found causes of action in present day products liability actions include, but are not limited to, the following:

- Breach of express warranty
- Breach of implied warranty of fitness for a particular purpose
- Breach of implied warranty of merchantability
- Negligence
- Deceit
- Strict liability

Many of these causes of action are brought in the same manner as an ordinary tort such as negligence. In fact, all actions specific to products liability, such as breach of warranty actions, are derived from the basic principles of tort law and, most often, the particular law of intentional torts. However, unlike most other tort actions, the manufacturer and consumer are in a unique quasi-contractual relationship with exchange of consideration and so forth. However, there are often parties in the middle, such as retailers, and distributors, and in most consumer transactions, there is not a formalized contract. Additionally, the product may be in commerce for some time and even pass through more than one consumer before a defect causes injury. All of these things have contributed to the development of products liability actions that are tailored to this unique situation.

One trait in particular that is common to products liability actions in most states is statutes of repose. Each state has statutes that define the time for which an action must be brought in a particular type of case. In actions for tort, the time that the clock starts to run on the limitation is typically the date of the alleged damage. However, in products actions, the injury from a defect may not occur right away. It would be unfair to hold a manufacturer accountable for injuries that occur some 20 or 30 years, for example, after the product left its control. That would put a nearly impossible burden on the manufacturer to defend itself, because of the cost of maintaining records, the loss of employees who would be witnesses, and so forth. Consequently, statutes of repose have been enacted to supplement the ordinary limitation of actions statutes and to place a cap on the length of time between the manufacture and sale of a product and any products liability action brought alleging damage caused by the product.

Res ipsa loquitur is a commonly employed alternative in actions based on products liability because so often the consumer is unable to determine exactly how the product was defective or how the defective design was created. This information is most often within the exclusive control of the manufacturer. As a result, the plaintiff must rely on the doctrine to establish the liability of the defendant and to rule out other possible causes of the injury. Yet, as with ordinary tort actions, the expansion of the rules of discovery often render the doctrine unnecessary once the information of the defendant is made available to the plaintiff.

Specific legal standards regarding the standard of care in product liability cases include the idea that a manufacturer is presumed to be an expert on the product and therefore must manufacture the product with the same care as someone with extensive knowledge about the product and its potential dangers. Part of the standard of care required to meet the duty to the consumer also includes adequate warnings of any dangers associated with the product. A manufacturer who should have such knowledge or who does not use it to make reasonably sure that the product is safe and that adequate warnings are given, may be held responsible for injuries caused by the product.

The same defenses apply in products liability actions as in other similar tort actions. Additionally, a manufacturer may also claim as a defense extreme misuse of the product. It is established that manufacturers must foresee a certain degree of misuse of a product and take reasonable steps to prevent the misuse or warn of its dangers. This includes such things as placing safety guards over moving parts that could cause injury. However, if the consumer significantly modifies the product or uses it in a manner that the manufacturer could not have been reasonably expected to foresee, the manufacturer will not be held liable for any injuries.

APPLICATION 9.13

XYZ corporation manufactures hair dryers. On their portable models of hand-held dryers, the wattage goes as high as 1250, when not in use. Rachel purchased one such hair dryer and came up with the idea of using it to assist in the grooming of her prize-winning Persian cat. She first bathed the cat and then locked it in a plastic kennel with only a small screen door at the front. She then used wires and various other items from around her house to create a makeshift stand for the dryer. She tied the dryer to the stand, placed it against the wire mesh of the door to the kennel and turned it on. The cat's hair dried but the cat was overcome by the heat and died. Rachel sued XYZ as the manufacturer of the dryer. The manufacturer claimed the defense of significant misuse. If the manufacturer had issued no warnings with the dryer such as extended use, use in seriously confined spaces, or use with animals, it may be that this extent of misuse could be considered foreseeable and the manufacturer held liable. However, it is more likely that all the steps taken by R to modify the use of the dryer with the stand and kennel would be considered a significant misuse.

Point for Discussion: Would the situation turn out differently if the manufacturer also provided a stand for the dryer with the stated purpose that it was to hold it when not in use?

F. TORTS IN THE WORK PLACE

The area of labor law was primarily created during the 20th century. During the 1800s and prior to that employees were offered no protection in terms of safety, training, limitation on hours worked, and so on. But along with the Industrial Revolution came assembly-line manufacturing and mass employment. In addition to creating standards for working conditions, a broad area of tort law developed concerning the responsibility of employers toward employees and toward third parties who were affected by the employee's actions while in the service of the employer. All states now have certain statutes and case law governing the employment relationship and indicating when actions for tort arising out of that relationship are appropriate. Also, limited exceptions to these statutes may further open the door to actions in tort.

1. Injured Third Parties

All jurisdictions in the United States have long accepted and upheld the legal standard known as respondeat superior. The theory holds that when one is acting within the scope of their employment, the employer should be held accountable for the acts of the employee with respect to third parties. Generally, an injured third party has the right to sue either the employer or the employee if it can be proven that the defendant who was responsible for the injury was an employee and not an independent contractor.

The independent contractor is one who works on a per job basis and is not subject to the direct supervision and control of the employer with respect to how the work is carried out. It must also be shown that the employee was acting within the scope of employment and/or under the direction, supervision, or control of the employer. Simply stated, the employee must be acting subject to the ultimate supervision of the employer at the time of the alleged tortious conduct. The employee does not need to be engaged in a regular job duty as long as he or she is engaged in a task that benefits the employer in some direct manner. Generally employers are not responsible for occurrences while the employee is going to or from work. However, a different rule would apply if the employee were running an errand for the employer (even though it may not be a part of his or her regular duties to do so).

Ordinarily, employers will not be held responsible for intentional torts committed by an employee. An intentional tort requires that the actor knew or should have known with substantial certainty that the act would produce the injury. An employer cannot be held responsible for such intentional acts over which he or she has no control. If this were permitted, employees could escape responsibility for acts that the employer neither benefited from nor condoned. The exception to this rule takes place when the intentional tort is considered to be within the scope of the employee's duties. Security guards are a common example. Often, such personnel are required to restrain customers physically or compel them to leave the premises. In such a situation, the actions of the employee are presumed to be directed by the employer. Therefore, any injuries resulting from the guard's conduct with respect to how they perform their job duties could result in liability of the employer.

APPLICATION 9.14

Gigi is a civil engineer employed by ABC Company. One day during her lunch hour she is involved in an accident as the result of her failing to obey a red light. Her employer would not be liable for the injuries caused by Gigi's actions because she was not engaged in job duties at the time.

Point for Discussion: Would the result change if Gigi was on the way back from picking up lunch for a noon meeting at the office when the accident occurred?

2. Development of Laws to Protect Workers/Workplace

As mentioned previously, each state has enacted specific statutes to address certain areas of employment law. A number of federal laws and regulations also exist with respect to matters between the employer and employee, such as discriminatory practices and safety in the workplace. State statutes cover a much broader spectrum of employment-related legal actions. One of the most heavily legislated and regulated areas pertains to employee injuries.

In the late 18th and early 19th centuries mass production and the growth of machinery in the workplace resulted in large numbers of individuals going to work in factories rather than the traditional small craftsman's shops and farming. Many of these individuals were untrained, and working conditions were sometimes brutal. The result was a significant number of injuries in the workplace. With disabling injuries, many workers had little alternative but to file tort actions against their own employers for damages. The length of time for such a process was often significant, and the hardship on the families of these employees was immense. At the same time, employers were suffering the blows of large jury awards for employee injuries. Insurance was usually available but often cost-prohibitive. Also, once an employee sued the employer, the animosity created effectively ended any chance of returning to work. Both sides were losing and the legislatures responded with workers' compensation laws during the mid 1900s.

Although the details of workers' compensation laws vary from state to state, the underlying principle is the same. The statutes provide a basis for compensation to employees who are injured while performing job-related duties. But the statutes also place limitations on the extent to which an employer may be held financially liable. Workers' compensation laws in each state have fairly well-defined methods to calculate limits of compensation for various injuries. This, in turn, enables employers to predict with some degree of certainty what their liability will be in the event of injury. With such limits, insurers are then able to provide insurance to employers at a more reasonable cost without risking huge monetary awards by juries.

A second and major benefit of workers' compensation laws is that they typically are not based on findings of fault or negligence by the employer. This aids the injured employee who could not recover without proof of tortious conduct of the employer. The employer is presumed to have the benefit of the employee's presence on the job and contribution toward the making of profits. To bear the cost of injuries on the job, even accidental ones, seemed only fair.

One major development in the latter half of the 20th century with respect to workers' compensation statutes had to do with job security. Employer's quickly discovered that the fewer the claims against them, the lower the cost of workers' compensation insurance. Many employers subsequently engaged in a kind of subversive tactic to inhibit injured employees from filing actions for workers' compensation benefits. Some employers fired employees who filed claims. Others simply did not have a job available for the injured employees when they were ready to return to work. This quickly gained the attention of the courts and the legislatures and was condemned. The employers were found to be *chilling* the rights of employees to pursue the rights given to them as a matter of law. As a matter of public policy, the right to pursue statutory rights has always been protected. Now states have statutes that make it illegal to fire an injured employee for filing a workers' compensation claim. If such an employee is in fact terminated, the employer must be able to establish totally independent grounds for the termination or be subject to a tort action by the employee for wrongful discharge. This provides the injured employees the opportunity to seek reasonable compensation for their injuries and for wages lost from time not worked without fear of losing employment. Ultimately, the workers' compensation laws have reduced the number and expense of lawsuits between employers and employees, have encouraged employers to provide a safer working environment, and have directly contributed to the flow of industry and commerce in this country.

APPLICATION 9.15

Darwin was injured while working and subsequently filed a workers' compensation claim. Ultimately Darwin returned to work while the workers' compensation claim was pending. Within one month of returning to work, Darwin was fired and consequently brought an action against the employer claiming wrongful discharge on the basis that he had a pending workers' compensation claim against the employer. At the trial in the wrongful discharge case, it came out that Darwin had a lengthy employment file showing repeated instances of below-satisfactory job performance and a high incidence of absenteeism. On the day before Darwin's injury, he was warned that if there were another unexcused absence from work, he would be terminated. One month after Darwin's return to his job following the injury, he did not show up for work and was terminated the next day. In this case, the well-documented problems with Darwin's employment would likely prevent a judgment against the employer as they were only carrying out a policy put in place prior to his injury.

Point for Discussion: Would the result be different if Darwin were able to establish that several other employees of many years were also terminated for similar reasons found in the employee file after a workers' compensation claim?

There are some circumstances, however, that are exempt from otherwise applicable workers' compensation laws. For example, if an employer places an employee in a position of great danger and this action demonstrates a clear disregard for the safety of the employee, many states permit an avoidance of the workers' compensation laws in favor of an unlimited action for tort. In addition, certain types of employment that have been historically considered to be extremely dangerous with a high probability of serious injury or death during one's worklife are subject to federal employer liability laws. These laws preceded workers' compensation laws and are limited primarily to the railroad and maritime industries.

Although each law has specific provisions, an employer liability law will generally permit a civil action by an employee against an employer for injuries received within the scope of employment. However, it must be shown that both parties are subject to the statute and that the employer was somehow negligent. This differs from the no-fault standard of workers' compensation laws. In addition to federal employer liability laws, a number of states also have state employer liability laws for specified areas of employment. The federal laws do not necessarily apply to employees of the federal government. Rather, they are laws passed by the national government that apply to an entire industry that operates on an interstate basis.

Originally, employer liability laws were enacted to provide protection to a class of workers who were engaged in a hazardous occupation where serious injuries or fatalities were frequent, and where the workers were often disadvantaged economically and educationally. The reasoning behind such laws was to provide protection to employees whose education and ability to seek other types of employment were frequently limited—even more so after a serious injury. The injuries that commonly occurred in these industries were so serious that the employees were often prevented, through this combination of factors, from ever working again, leaving them and their families with no means of support other than government assistance. Consequently, legislatures enacted statutes to ease somewhat the burden of proving civil suits against employers and at the same time to remove the limitations of recovery under the workers' compensation statutes. Although the statutes usually require the proof of negligence, the statutes make the proof easier to establish.

3. Employment Discrimination

It has only been during the past 100 years or so that employers have been charged with the responsibility to be fair to all persons in the manner in which they are hired, supervised, and terminated. Employers have long been subject to liability for injuries to employees or third parties that arose incident to employment. But in the more recent past, the focus has been just as great on the injuries that affect psychosocial and economic aspects of employment. Today, state and federal government legislatures and agencies have established minimum legal standards for employers regarding hiring, termination, and providing a suitable work environment. While there is some common-law liability, the majority of actions are based in alleged statutory violations of legislation designed to make the workplace more fair and appropriate to all employees.

While a few major strides were made from 1850 to 1950 for minorities and women, such as the constitutional amendments granting the right to vote, these were more or less the foundation for the sweeping changes that were to come in the second half of the 20th century. With the social movements of the 1960s, a greater awareness began to develop about the rights of minorities, women, handicapped individuals, and other Americans who received disparate treatment in the workplace. Case after case established that many employers would not hire individuals with certain characteristics or would treat them differently from other employees. As a result, legislation and regulations were passed to protect various classes of people. These laws were designed to keep employers from discriminating against employees for possessing characteristics that had nothing to do with their ability to adequately perform the duties of employment. Such characteristics include gender, race, religion, and in many cases age. Similar restrictions apply for handicapped individuals. If an employer is found to treat an employee differently, refuse to hire someone, or use as a cause for termination one or more of the characteristics of the protected classes, the employer is subject to scrutiny under federal law. If it is determined that the employer violated the legal standards by using improper reasons for hiring, termination, or discipline, then the employer may be subject to a variety of penalties.

APPLICATION 9.16

QRS Corporation was a local business with a workforce of approximately 200 individuals. While the regular staff of approximately 160 included a diverse population of all races and both men and women, a difference was apparent in management. Of 40 individuals in management positions with the corporation, none were women, handicapped, or Asian; only one was black; and no other minorities were represented. Because a representation of 99.5 percent is a much higher than average percentage of the general population, QRS may be subject to scrutiny in its hiring and promotion practices.

Point for Discussion: If QRS can establish that the nature of its business is such that relatively few of the protected classes are adequately trained/educated for the positions and therefore these persons can demand much higher salaries than QRS can reasonably afford to pay, would its conduct still be considered discriminatory?

Another area of employment law that has seen dramatic growth and that continues to develop is the safety of the work environment. Just as federal agencies such as OSHA strive to protect the employee from physical dangers on the job, the branches of state and federal government are now focused on protecting the employee from unnecessary psychological and emotional dangers on the job as well. One such example is sexual harassment. If an employee can demonstrate that an employer participated or acquiesced in a course of conduct that subjected the employee to an environment that was reasonably perceived as hostile because of differential treatment based on the gender or sexual preference of the employee, the employee may have a basis for legal action against the employer. This imposes on the employer the responsibility to monitor the conduct of all employees and to be responsive to complaints in a continuing effort to maintain a workplace that encourages fair and professional treatment of each employee by the employer and co-workers alike.

Case in Point

Jones v. Chicago HMO Ltd. of IL, 191 Ill.2d 278, 730 N.E.2d. 1119 (IL 2000).

Justice BILANDIC delivered the opinion of the court:

Facts

In reviewing an award of summary judgment, we must view the facts in the light most favorable to the non-moving party. Petrovich v. Share Health Plan of Illinois, Inc., 188 Ill.2d 17, 30-31, 241 Ill.Dec. 627, 719 N.E.2d 756 (1999). The following facts thus emerge.

On January 18, 1991, Jones' three-month-old daughter Shawndale was ill. Jones called Dr. Jordan's office, as she had been instructed to do by Chicago HMO. Jones related Shawndale's symptoms, specifically that she was sick, was constipated, was crying a lot and felt very warm. An assistant advised Jones to give Shawndale some castor oil. When Jones insisted on speaking with Dr. Jordan, the assistant stated that Dr. Jordan was not available but would return her call. Dr. Jordan returned Jones' call late that evening. After Jones described the same symptoms to Dr. Jordan, he also advised Jones to give castor oil to Shawndale.

On January 19, 1991, Jones took Shawndale to a hospital emergency room because her condition had not improved. Chicago HMO authorized Shawndale's admission. Shawndale was diagnosed with bacterial meningitis, secondary to bilateral otitis media, an ear infection. As a result of the meningitis, Shawndale is permanently disabled.

The medical expert for the plaintiff, Dr. Richard Pawl, stated in his affidavit and deposition testimony that Dr. Jordan had deviated from the standard of care. In Dr. Pawl's opinion, upon being advised of a three-month-old infant who is warm, irritable and constipated, the standard of care requires a physician to schedule an immediate appointment to see the infant or, alternatively, to instruct the parent to obtain immediate medical care for the infant through another physician. Dr. Pawl gave no opinion regarding whether Chicago HMO was negligent.

Although Jones filed this action against Chicago HMO, Dr. Jordan and another party, this appeal concerns only counts I and III of Jones' second amended complaint, which are directed against Chicago HMO. Count I charges Chicago HMO with institutional negligence for, inter alia, (1) negligently assigning Dr. Jordan as Shawndale's primary care physician while he was serving an overloaded patient population, and (2) negligently adopting procedures that required Jones to call first for an appointment before visiting the doctor's office or obtaining emergency care. Count III charges Chicago HMO with breach of contract and is based solely on Chicago HMO's contract with the Department of Public Aid. Chicago HMO moved for summary judgment on both counts. Jones and Chicago HMO submitted various depositions, affidavits and exhibits in support of their positions.

In her deposition testimony, Jones described how she first enrolled in Chicago HMO while living in Park Forest. A Chicago HMO representative visited her home. According to Jones, he "was telling me what it was all about, that HMO is better than a regular medical card and everything so I am just listening to him and signing my name and stuff on the papers. . . . I asked him what kind of benefits you get out of it and stuff, and he was telling me that it is better than a regular card."

The "HMO ENROLLMENT UNDERSTANDING" form signed by Jones in 1987 stated: "I understand that all my medical care will be provided through the Health Plan once my application becomes effective." Jones remembered that, at the time she signed this form, the Chicago HMO representative told her "you have got to call your doctor and stuff before you see your doctor; and before you go to the hospital, you have got to call."

When Jones moved to Chicago Heights, she did not select Dr. Jordan as Shawndale's primary care physician. Rather, Chicago HMO assigned Dr. Jordan to her. Jones explained:

"They gave me . . . Dr. Jordan. They didn't ask me if I wanted a doctor. They gave me him.

* * *

. . . They told me that he was a good doctor . . . for the kids because I didn't know what doctor to take my kids to because I was staying in Chicago Heights so they gave me him so I started taking my kids there to him."

Dr. Trubitt stated that, before Chicago HMO and Dr. Jordan executed the Chicago Heights service agreement, another physician serviced that area. Chicago HMO terminated that physician for failing to provide covered immunizations. At the time that Chicago HMO terminated that physician, Dr. Jordan agreed "to go into the [Chicago Heights] area and serve the patients." Chicago HMO then assigned to Dr. Jordan all of the patients of that physician. Dr. Trubitt explained:

"Q. So then with the elimination of [the other physician], Dr. Jordan then- were the members notified that Dr. Jordan would be their [primary care physician] from that point on?

A. Yes.

Q. They weren't given a choice?

A. At that point in the area there was no choice.

Q. So they weren't given a choice?

A. They were directed to Dr. Jordan."

Dr. Trubitt also explained that Dr. Jordan was Chicago HMO's only physician who was willing to serve the public aid membership in Chicago Heights.

Dr. Trubitt characterized this lack of physicians as "a problem" for Chicago HMO.

Dr. Jordan testified at his deposition that, in January of 1991, he was a solo practitioner. He divided his time equally between his offices in Homewood and Chicago Heights. Dr. Jordan was under contract with Chicago HMO for both sites. In addition, Dr. Jordan was under contract with 20 other HMOs, and he maintained his own private practice of non-HMO patients. Dr. Jordan estimated that he was designated the primary care physician of 3,000 Chicago HMO members and 1,500 members of other HMOs. In contrast to Dr. Jordan's estimate, Chicago HMO's own "Provider Capitation Summary Reports" listed Dr. Jordan as being the primary care provider of 4,527 Chicago HMO patients as of December 1, 1990.

Jones' legal counsel and Dr. Trubitt engaged in the following colloquy concerning patient load:

"Q. In entering into an agreement with a provider, is any consideration given to the number of patients to be designated as the primary provider for?

A. Yes, there is consideration given to that element in terms of volume of patients that he is capable of handling.

Q. And who determines the volume of patients he is capable of handling? The Chicago HMO or the provider or-

A. There is some guidelines that HCFA provides.

Q. Who provides?

A. HCFA. The Health [Care Finance Administration], the governmental health and welfare.

Q. Do you happen to know what those limits are with respect to pediatricians?

A. I am going to say I believe they are 3,500 patients to a primary care physician. The number can be expanded depending on the number of physicians in the office and the number of hours of operation.

Q. So you can't tell me whether or not if Dr. Jordan had 6,000 or 6,500 that would be an unusually large number?

A. If he himself had it.

Q. It would be unusually large?

A. It would.

Q. And that would be of some concern to the Chicago HMO, right?

A. Well, yes, if he had those."

In January of 1991, Dr. Jordan employed four part-time physicians, in addition to himself. This included an obstetrician/gynecologist, an internist, a family practitioner and a pediatrician. Dr. Jordan, however, did not explain in what capacities these physicians served. The record contains no further information regarding these physicians.

The record also contains evidence concerning Chicago HMO procedures for obtaining health care. Chicago HMO's "Member Handbook" told members in need of medical care to "Call your Chicago HMO doctor first when you experience an emergency or begin to feel sick." Also, Chicago HMO gave its contract physicians a "Provider Manual." The manual contains certain provisions with which the providers are expected to comply. The manual contains a section entitled, "The Appointment System/Afterhours Care," which states that all HMO sites are statutorily required to maintain an appointment system for their patients.

Dr. Trubitt testified that Chicago HMO encouraged its providers to maintain an appointment system and also "to retain open spaces on their schedules so that patients who came in as walk-ins could be seen." Retaining space on the schedule for walk-ins was recommended because it offers quicker access to care, keeping patients out of the emergency room with its increased costs, and because, historically, the Medicaid patient population often did not make or keep appointments.

Dr. Jordan related that his office worked on an appointment system and had its own written procedures and forms for handling patient calls and appointments. When a patient called and Dr. Jordan was not in the office, written forms were used by his staff or his answering service to relay the information to him. If Dr. Jordan was in the office, the procedure was as follows:

"Q. . . . [I]f it was a routine appointment for the purpose of having a routine shot or checkup, [the office staff] could make the appointment themselves?

A. Yes.

Q. But if the caller calls and says there is some problem, then they would take the temperature and find out the complaints and refer that call to you; is that correct?

A. That's correct.

Q. And you were the one who would make the determination as to whether or not to schedule an appointment, is that correct?

A. Medical decision, yes.

Q. Medical decision. And I assume there were times when people would call and after you reviewed the information and talked to them that you decided that they didn't need the appointment; is that correct?

A. Of course.

Q. In other words, you would perform some type of triage over the telephone; is that correct?

A. Yes."

Three agreements appear in the record. First, Chicago HMO and the Department of Public Aid entered into a 1990 "AGREEMENT FOR FURNISHING HEALTH SERVICES." This agreement was "for the delivery of medical services to Medicaid recipients on a prepaid capitation basis." Jones and her children, Medicaid recipients, fall within the agreement's definition of beneficiaries.

The preamble to the agreement stated that Chicago HMO "is organized primarily for the purpose of providing health care services." It continued: "[Chicago HMO] warrants that it is able to provide the medical care and services required under this Agreement in accordance with prevailing community standards, and is able to provide these services promptly, efficiently, and economically."

Article V of the agreement described various duties of Chicago HMO, as follows. Chicago HMO "shall provide or arrange to have provided all covered services to all Beneficiaries under this Agreement." Chicago HMO "shall provide all Beneficiaries with medical care consistent with prevailing community standards." In addition, a section entitled "Choice of Physicians" provided in relevant part:

"[Chicago HMO] shall afford to each Beneficiary a health professional who will supervise and coordinate his care, and, to the extent feasible within appropriate limits established by [Chicago HMO] and approved by the Department, shall afford the Beneficiary a choice of a physician.

There shall be at least one full-time equivalent, board eligible physician to every 1,200 enrollees, including one full-time equivalent, board certified primary care physician for each 2,000 enrollees. . . . There shall be . . . one pediatrician for each 2,000 enrollees under age 17."

Another article V duty stated that, although Chicago HMO may furnish the services required by the agreement by means of subcontractors, Chicago HMO "shall remain responsible for the performance of the subcontractors."

Regarding appointments, this agreement stated that Chicago HMO "shall encourage members to be seen by appointment, except in emergencies." The agreement also stated that "[m]embers with more serious or urgent problems not deemed emergencies shall be triaged and provided same day service, if necessary," and that "emergency treatment shall be available on an immediate basis, seven days a week, 24-hours a day." Finally, the agreement directed that Chicago HMO "shall have an established policy that scheduled patients shall not routinely wait for more than one hour to be seen by a provider and no more than six appointments shall be made for each primary care physician per hour."

The record also contains a second agreement, a 1990 "MEDICAL GROUP SERVICE AGREEMENT" between Chicago HMO and Dr. Jordan, that lists a Chicago Heights office address for Dr. Jordan. This agreement described numerous duties of Dr. Jordan. Pertinent here, Dr. Jordan would provide to Chicago HMO subscribers specified medical services "of good quality and in accordance with accepted medical and hospital standards of the community." Pursuant to a "PUBLIC AID AMENDMENT TO THE MEDICAL GROUP SERVICE AGREEMENT," Dr. Jordan agreed to "abide by any conditions imposed by [Chicago HMO] as part of [Chicago HMO's] agreement with [the Department]."

The third agreement appearing of record is a second "MEDICAL GROUP SERVICE AGREEMENT" between Chicago HMO and Dr. Jordan. This agreement was entered into in 1987 and lists a Homewood office address for Dr. Jordan.

Both agreements between Chicago HMO and Dr. Jordan provided for a capitation method of compensation. Under capitation, Chicago HMO paid Dr. Jordan a fixed amount of money for each member who selected Dr. Jordan as the member's primary care provider. In exchange, Dr. Jordan agreed to render health care to his enrolled Chicago HMO members in accordance with the Chicago HMO health plan. Dr. Jordan was paid the same monthly capitation fee per member regardless of the services he rendered. For example, for each female patient under two years old, Chicago HMO paid Dr. Jordan $34.19 per month regardless of whether he treated that patient. In addition, Chicago HMO utilized an incentive fund for Dr. Jordan. Certain costs such as inpatient hospital costs were paid from this fund. Chicago HMO would then pay Dr. Jordan 60% of any remaining, unused balance of the fund at the end of each year.

As earlier noted, the appellate court affirmed the circuit court's grant of summary judgment in favor of Chicago HMO as to count I, institutional negligence, and as to count III, breach of contract. 301 Ill.App.3d

103, 234 Ill.Dec. 641, 703 N.E.2d 502. We are asked to decide whether Chicago HMO was properly awarded summary judgment on these two counts.

Analysis

This court first addressed a question of whether an HMO could be held liable for medical malpractice in Petrovich v. Share Health Plan of Illinois, Inc., 188 Ill.2d 17, 29, 241 Ill.Dec. 627, 719 N.E.2d 756 (1999). Petrovich, however, involved different legal theories of liability than those presented here. Petrovich held that an HMO may be held vicariously liable for the medical malpractice of its independent-contractor physicians under both the doctrines of apparent authority and implied authority. Petrovich, 188 Ill.2d 17, 241 Ill.Dec. 627, 719 N.E.2d 756. In contrast, this appeal focuses on whether an HMO may be held liable under the theory of institutional negligence.

I.
Institutional Negligence

Institutional negligence is also known as direct corporate negligence. Since the landmark decision of Darling v. Charleston Community Memorial Hospital, 33 Ill.2d 326, 211 N.E.2d 253 (1965), Illinois has recognized that hospitals may be held liable for institutional negligence. Darling acknowledged an independent duty of hospitals to assume responsibility for the care of their patients. Ordinarily, this duty is administrative or managerial in character. Advincula v. United Blood Services, 176 Ill.2d 1, 28, 223 Ill.Dec. 1, 678 N.E.2d 1009 (1996) (and authorities cited therein). To fulfill this duty, a hospital must act as would a "reasonably careful hospital" under the circumstances. Advincula, 176 Ill.2d at 29, 223 Ill.Dec. 1, 678 N.E.2d 1009. Liability is predicated on the hospital's own negligence, not the negligence of the physician.

In accordance with the preceding rationale, we now hold that the doctrine of institutional negligence may be applied to HMOs. This court in Petrovich acknowledged the potential for applying this theory to HMOs. See Petrovich, 188 Ill.2d at 30, 241 Ill.Dec. 627, 719 N.E.2d 756 (and authorities cited therein). A court in another jurisdiction has likewise extended the theory of hospital institutional negligence to HMOs. Shannon v. McNulty, 718 A.2d 828 (Pa.Super.Ct.1998). It did so out of a recognition that HMOs, like hospitals, consist of an amalgam of many individuals who play various roles in order to provide comprehensive health care services to their members. Shannon, 718 A.2d at 835–36. Moreover, because HMOs undertake an expansive role in arranging for and providing health care services to their members, they have corresponding corporate responsibilities as well. Shannon, 718 A.2d at 835–36; see Petrovich, 188 Ill.2d at 28, 33–40, 241 Ill.Dec. 627, 719 N.E.2d 756 (recognizing that HMOs act as health care providers and attempt to contain the costs of health care); 215 ILCS 125/1-2(9) (West 1998) (defining an HMO as "any organization formed . . . to provide or arrange for one or more health care plans under a system which causes any part of the risk of health care delivery to be borne by the organization or its providers". . . .

Having determined that institutional negligence is a valid claim against HMOs, we turn to the parties' arguments in this case. Jones contends that Chicago HMO is not entitled to summary judgment on her claim of institutional negligence. She asserts that genuine issues of material fact exist as to whether Chicago HMO (1) negligently assigned more enrollees to Dr. Jordan than he was capable of serving, and (2) negligently adopted procedures requiring Jones to call first for an appointment before visiting the doctor's office.

Chicago HMO argues that Jones' claim of institutional negligence cannot proceed because she failed to provide sufficient evidence delineating the standard of care required of an HMO in these circumstances. In particular, Chicago HMO contends that Jones should have presented expert testimony on the standard of care required of an HMO.

Jones responds that she has provided sufficient evidence showing the standard of care required of an HMO in these circumstances. She argues further that her claim does not require expert testimony on this point. In support, Jones relies on Darling, where a claim of institutional negligence was allowed against a hospital without expert testimony because other evidence established the hospital's standard of care. Darling, 33 Ill.2d 326, 211 N.E.2d 253.

Given that the parties' dispute centers on standard of care evidence and the need for expert testimony, we briefly review the roles of the standard of care and expert testimony in negligence cases. We then discuss Darling and its progeny.

The elements of a negligence cause of action are a duty owed by the defendant to the plaintiff, a breach of that duty, and an injury proximately caused by the breach. Cunis v. Brennan, 56 Ill.2d 372, 374, 308 N.E.2d 617 (1974). The standard of care, also known as the standard of conduct, falls within the duty element.

In an ordinary negligence case, the standard of care required of a defendant is to act as would an " 'ordinarily careful person' " or a " 'reasonably prudent' person." Advincula v. United Blood Services, 176 Ill.2d 1, 22, 223 Ill.Dec. 1, 678 N.E.2d 1009 (1996), quoting Cunis, 56 Ill.2d at 376, 308 N.E.2d 617. No expert testimony is required in a case of ordinary negligence. See Advincula, 176 Ill.2d at 24, 223 Ill.Dec. 1, 678 N.E.2d 1009.

In contrast, in a professional negligence case, the standard of care required of a defendant is to act as would an "ordinarily careful professional." Advincula, 176 Ill.2d at 23, 223 Ill.Dec. 1, 678 N.E.2d 1009. Pursuant to this standard of care, professionals are expected to use the same degree of knowledge, skill and ability as an ordinarily careful professional would exercise under similar circumstances. Advincula, 176 Ill.2d at 23–24, 223 Ill.Dec. 1, 678 N.E.2d 1009.

The foregoing principles of law establish that the crucial difference between ordinary negligence and professional malpractice actions is the necessity of expert testimony to establish the standard of care and that its breach was the cause of the plaintiff's injury. Although not applicable to this case, there are exceptions to the requirement of expert testimony in professional negligence cases. For example, in instances where the professional's conduct is so grossly negligent or the treatment so common that a lay juror could readily appraise it, no expert testimony or other such relevant evidence is required. Advincula, 176 Ill.2d at 24, 223 Ill.Dec. 1, 678 N.E.2d 1009 (and cases cited therein). . . .

As earlier noted, this court in Darling recognized an independent duty of hospitals to assume responsibility for the care of their patients. Relevant here, Darling also held that the hospital bylaws, licensing regulations, and standards for hospital accreditation were sufficient evidence with which to establish the hospital's standard of care. Darling likened this evidence to evidence of custom, which may also be used to determine a hospital's standard of care. The jury was therefore entitled to conclude from the plaintiff's evidence that the hospital had breached its duty to the plaintiff. Darling, 33 Ill.2d at 330–33, 211 N.E.2d 253.

In Greenberg v. Michael Reese Hospital, 83 Ill.2d 282, 47 Ill.Dec. 385, 415 N.E.2d 390 (1980), a group of plaintiffs sued the hospital for injuries that they sustained as a result of being X-rayed without a protective shield. As standard of care evidence, the plaintiffs presented an expert witness who was a health physicist specializing in the effects of radiation. The hospital challenged the qualifications of plaintiffs' expert, claiming that, since he was not a physician practicing in any school of medicine, he could not testify concerning conduct that involves a medical judgment. This court held that the affidavit of the plaintiffs' nonphysician expert was sufficient to withstand the hospital's motion for summary judgment. Greenberg, 83 Ill.2d at 293–94, 47 Ill.Dec. 385, 415 N.E.2d 390. Although the expert was not a medical practitioner, he was highly qualified and familiar with radiation therapy in hospitals. This court deemed "it appropriate to the diversity inherent in hospital administration that a broad range of evidence be available to establish the applicable standard of care." Greenberg, 83 Ill.2d at 293, 47 Ill.Dec. 385, 415 N.E.2d 390.

Darling and its progeny have firmly established that, in an action for institutional negligence against a hospital, the standard of care applicable to a hospital may be proved via a number of evidentiary sources, and expert testimony is not always required. Advincula, 176 Ill.2d at 29–34, 223 Ill.Dec. 1, 678 N.E.2d 1009. . . . We likewise conclude that, in an action for institutional negligence against an HMO, the standard of care applicable to an HMO may be proved through a number of evidentiary sources, and expert testimony is not necessarily required. Accordingly, expert testimony concerning the standard of care required of an HMO is not a prerequisite to Jones' claim. Nonetheless, Jones, as the plaintiff here, still bears the burden of establishing the standard of care required of an HMO through other, proper evidentiary sources. We must therefore evaluate the evidence presented on this point to determine whether Jones' claim withstands Chicago HMO's motion for summary judgment. In deciding whether Jones' standard of care evidence is sufficient, we look to whether that evidence can equip a lay juror to determine what constitutes the standard of care required of a "reasonably careful HMO" under the circumstances of this case.

A. Patient Load

We first consider Jones' assertion that Chicago HMO negligently assigned more patients to Dr. Jordan than he was capable of serving. Parenthetically, we note that this assertion involves an administrative or managerial action by Chicago HMO, not the professional conduct of its physicians. Therefore, this claim properly falls within the purview of HMO institutional negligence. Jones argues that the standard of care evidence in the record is sufficient to support her claim. She points to Dr. Trubitt's testimony, as well as the contract between Chicago HMO and the Department of Public Aid.

Dr. Trubitt was the medical director for Chicago HMO. He testified that, when Chicago HMO entered into agreements with primary care physicians, it considered the number of patients that the physician is capable of handling. The HMO would look to federal "guidelines" in making this determination. Based on those guidelines, Dr. Trubitt expressed 3,500 as the maximum number of patients that should be assigned to any one primary care physician. He stated that, if Dr. Jordan himself had 6,000 or more patients, then that would be an unusually large number and of concern to Chicago HMO.

We agree with Jones that Dr. Trubitt's testimony is proper and sufficient evidence of the standard of care on this issue. According to Dr. Trubitt, an HMO should not assign more than 3,500 patients to any single primary care physician. Chicago HMO even concedes in its brief that the maximum patient load to which Dr. Trubitt testified "represent[s] a 'standard of care' whose violation could affect the quality of patient care." This particular standard of care evidence, setting forth a limit of 3,500 patients per primary care physician, is adequate to equip a lay juror to determine what constitutes the standard of care required of a "reasonably careful HMO" under the circumstances of this case. Whether Dr. Trubitt relied on an unidentified federal regulation or some other source in arriving at a maximum patient load of 3,500 is of no consequence. It is enough that Chicago HMO, through its medical director, admitted that it used the 3,500 limit as a guide in assigning patient loads. See Darling, 33 Ill.2d at 330–33, 211 N.E.2d 253 (holding that the hospital's own bylaws may be used to establish the hospital's standard of care).

Chicago HMO, however, submits that there is no evidence in the record that Dr. Jordan's patient load exceeded 3,500. We disagree. Chicago HMO's "Provider Capitation Summary Reports" listed Dr. Jordan as being the primary care provider of 4,527

Chicago HMO members as of December 1, 1990. Thus, Chicago HMO's own records show Dr. Jordan's patient load as exceeding the 3,500 limit by more than 1,000 patients. In addition, Dr. Jordan estimated that he himself was designated the primary care physician for an additional 1,500 members of other HMOs. He also maintained his own private practice of non-HMO patients. This evidence supports Jones' theory that Dr. Jordan had more than 6,000 HMO patients.

Chicago HMO, in support of its position, points to Dr. Jordan's testimony that he employed four part-time physicians in his office. We disagree with Chicago HMO concerning the significance of this testimony. Although Dr. Jordan testified that he employed four part-time physicians, he never explained in what capacities these physicians served. In fact, the record contains no further information regarding these physicians. Notably, the agreements between Chicago HMO and Dr. Jordan do not refer to any physicians other than Dr. Jordan himself. The evidence in the record, therefore, supports Jones' theory that Chicago HMO negligently assigned more than 3,500 patients to Dr. Jordan himself. At best, the testimony regarding the four part-time physicians creates a genuine issue of material fact as to how many patients Dr. Jordan actually served himself. Consequently, this limited information in the record about part-time physicians does not entitle Chicago HMO to summary judgment. As earlier noted, it is well established that summary judgment is a drastic remedy and should be awarded only where the right of the moving party is clear and free from doubt.

Chicago HMO also submits that Jones' claim of patient overload must fail because there is no evidence of a causal connection between the number of patients that Dr. Jordan was serving and his failure to schedule an appointment to see Shawndale. We disagree. We can easily infer from this record that Dr. Jordan's failure to see Shawndale resulted from an inability to serve an overloaded patient population. A lay juror can discern that a physician who has thousands more patients than he should will not have time to service them all in an appropriate manner.

We note, moreover, that additional evidence in the record supports Jones' claim. The record indicates that Chicago HMO was actively soliciting new members door-to-door around the same time that it lacked the physicians willing to serve those members. Jones described how she first enrolled in Chicago HMO while living in Park Forest. A Chicago HMO representative visited her home and persuaded her to become a member, telling her that Chicago HMO "is better than a regular medical card." When Jones later moved to Chicago Heights, another Chicago HMO representative visited her home. Jones explained that this meeting was not arranged in advance. Rather, the representative was "in the building knocking from door to door." Jones also testified that, when she moved to Chicago Heights, Chicago HMO assigned Dr. Jordan to her and did not give her a choice of primary care physicians.

The latter aspect of Jones' testimony was supported by Dr. Trubitt. He explained that, before Chicago HMO and Dr. Jordan executed the Chicago Heights service agreement, another physician serviced that area. When Chicago HMO terminated that other physician, Dr. Jordan agreed "to go into the [Chicago Heights] area and serve the patients." Chicago HMO then assigned to Dr. Jordan all of the patients of that physician. Chicago HMO directed its members to Dr. Jordan; they had no other choice of a physician because "[a]t that point in the area there was no choice." According to Dr. Trubitt, Dr. Jordan was Chicago HMO's only physician who was willing to serve the public aid membership in Chicago Heights. Dr. Trubitt stated that this lack of physicians was "a problem" for Chicago HMO.

The record further reflects that Chicago HMO directed its Chicago Heights members to Dr. Jordan, even though it knew that Dr. Jordan worked at that location only half the time. Chicago HMO entered into two service agreements with Dr. Jordan, the first for a Homewood site in 1987, and the second for the Chicago Heights site in 1990. Dr. Trubitt indicated that Chicago HMO and Dr. Jordan executed the Chicago Heights service agreement at the time that Chicago HMO terminated the other physician. Dr. Jordan confirmed that, in January of 1991, he was dividing his time equally between his two offices. All of the foregoing evidence supports Jones' theory that Chicago HMO acted negligently in assigning more enrollees to Dr. Jordan than he was capable of handling.

Jones also relies on the contract between Chicago HMO and the Department of Public Aid as standard of care evidence. That contract stated that

Chicago HMO shall have one full-time equivalent primary care physician for every 2,000 enrollees. We need not address in this appeal whether this contractual provision may serve as standard of care evidence. Our role here is to determine whether Chicago HMO is entitled to summary judgment on the patient overload aspect of the institutional negligence claim. Even if this contractual provision is removed from consideration, Chicago HMO is not entitled to summary judgment. Accordingly, we express no opinion on whether this provision may properly serve as standard of care evidence.

One final matter with respect to patient load remains to be considered. Chicago HMO contends that imposing a duty on HMOs to ascertain how many patients their doctors are serving would be unreasonably burdensome. Chicago HMO asserts that only physicians, and not HMOs, should have the duty to determine if the physician has too many patients.

To determine whether a duty exists in a certain instance, a court considers the following factors: (1) the reasonable foreseeability of injury, (2) the likelihood of injury, (3) the magnitude of the burden of guarding against the injury, and (4) the consequences of placing that burden upon the defendant. Deibert v. Bauer Brothers Construction Co., 141 Ill.2d 430, 437–38, 152 Ill.Dec. 552, 566 N.E.2d 239 (1990); Kirk v. Michael Reese Hospital & Medical Center, 117 Ill.2d 507, 526, 111 Ill.Dec. 944, 513 N.E.2d 387 (1987). Lastly, the existence of a duty turns in large part on public policy considerations. Ward v. Kmart Corp., 136 Ill.2d 132, 151, 143 Ill.Dec. 288, 554 N.E.2d 223 (1990); see Mieher v. Brown, 54 Ill.2d 539, 545, 301 N.E.2d 307 (1973). Whether a duty exists is a question of law to be determined by the court. Cunis, 56 Ill.2d at 374, 308 N.E.2d 617.

Here, given the circumstances of this case, we hold that Chicago HMO had a duty to its enrollees to refrain from assigning an excessive number of patients to Dr. Jordan. HMOs contract with primary care physicians in order to provide and arrange for medical care for their enrollees. It is thus reasonably foreseeable that assigning an excessive number of patients to a primary care physician could result in injury, as that care may not be provided. For the same reason, the likelihood of injury is great. Nor would imposing this duty on HMOs be overly burdensome. Here, for example, Chicago HMO

needed only to review its "Provider Capitation Summary Reports" to obtain the number of patients that it had assigned to Dr. Jordan. This information is likely to be available to all HMOs, as they must know the number of patients that a physician is serving in order to compute the physician's monthly capitation payments. The HMO may also simply ask the physician how many patients the physician is serving. Finally, the remaining factors favor placing this burden on HMOs as well. Public policy would not be well served by allowing HMOs to assign an excessive number of patients to a primary care physician and then "wash their hands" of the matter. The central consequence of placing this burden on HMOs is HMO accountability for their own actions. This court in Petrovich recognized that HMO accountability is needed to counterbalance the HMO goal of cost containment and, where applicable, the inherent drive of an HMO to achieve profits. Petrovich, 188 Ill.2d at 29, 241 Ill.Dec. 627, 719 N.E.2d 756.

In conclusion, Chicago HMO is not entitled to summary judgment on Jones' claim of institutional negligence for assigning too many patients to Dr. Jordan.

Conclusion

An HMO may be held liable for institutional negligence. Chicago HMO is not entitled to summary judgment on Jones' claim charging Chicago HMO with institutional negligence for assigning more enrollees to Dr. Jordan than he was capable of serving. We therefore reverse the award of summary judgment to Chicago HMO on count I of Jones' second amended complaint and remand that claim to the circuit court for further proceedings.

The judgments of the appellate and circuit courts are affirmed in part and reversed in part and the cause is remanded to the circuit court.

Judgments affirmed in part and reversed in part; cause remanded.

Case Review Question: Why would the physician be a defendant as well if the HMO was the one who assigned too many patients?

G. DEFENSES TO ACTIONS IN TORT

While the most obvious defense in any legal action is to establish that the essential elements of the legal theory advanced by the plaintiff have not been proven, there are other specific responses to a legal action that neutralize the claims of the plaintiff regardless of the plaintiff's evidence. A number of tort defenses are applicable in various circumstances as a means to justify the defendant's actions or to expose the plaintiff's own part in the occurrence that produced the injury. As with all legal theories, they are constantly developing and changing to accommodate changes in society, technology, and the world as a whole. Yet, even with these changes and slight variances among the jurisdictions, the underlying principles remain substantially the same.

1. Contributory and Comparative Negligence

Unlike the name might imply, the allegations of contributory or comparative negligence are actually defenses to the plaintiff's claims of negligence and/or gross negligence. Contributory negligence was the first tort defense to be developed and widely recognized. It was used in all jurisdictions for nearly a century but has lost much of its support by the legal system in more recent history. In the past, the courts would apply this defense to prevent recovery by a plaintiff when a defendant could prove that the plaintiff contributed to the injury by some form of negligent conduct of his or her own. When a court applies the defense of contributory negligence, the plaintiff cannot recover any damages from the defendant. The rationale is that one should not ultimately receive compensation for injuries caused in part by their own wrongdoing.

APPLICATION 9.17

Fran owned a fitness club. The facilities included a racquetball court with polished wood floors. Vincent was a customer at the club and one day was injured while playing racquetball. Vincent filed an action in negligence stating the floors were not properly maintained and caused him to slip and fall when he stepped in a place where a spilled drink had not been properly cleaned up. It had caused a sticky area on the ordinarily smooth surface. Fran responded that Vincent wore strong prescription lenses and that on the day of the incident was not wearing them and otherwise would have seen the area on the floor. In a contributory negligence jurisdiction, it is very possible Vincent would be denied recovery because of the failure to wear glasses needed to see normally.

Point for Discussion: Would the result change if Vincent forgot his regular sport glasses and instead wore prescription sunglasses since they were more breakage resistant than his regular glass lenses?

As the law of negligence developed and as society became increasingly liberal in its attitudes generally, contributory negligence seemed more and more a harsh response to claims of negligence. This was especially true when the negligence of a plaintiff was minor in comparison to that of the defendant. The result was one of inequity. The defendant could escape liability entirely for clearly negligent conduct if even the slightest percentage of fault could be found with the plaintiff's own conduct. In addition, the causes of injuries are no longer as straightforward. They have become increasingly complex in the methods and sources that produce them. A growing body of thought reasoned and succeeded in changing the views of a majority of jurisdictions. The basis for the change was that, although plaintiffs should not recover for their own misconduct, neither should defendants be relieved of liability for theirs. Accordingly, the theory of comparative negligence was developed.

Under the theory of comparative negligence, the fault of the parties in producing the injury is balanced. The jury determines the value of the damages suffered by the plaintiff as the result of negligence. Then, they determine the degree of negligent conduct of the plaintiff and of the defendant in producing the injuries. This is then converted into percentages of fault. The percentage of the plaintiff's fault is applied to the damage amount and the verdict is reduced by that amount. A majority of jurisdictions have now adopted some form of comparative negligence as the standard defense in favor of contributory negligence. The various forms range from an unrestricted application of comparative negligence to a modified version in which the standard switches to contributory negligence if it is determined that the plaintiff played a significant role in producing the injury, for example, greater than 50%. In other jurisdictions a combination is used, such as comparative negligence, unless there is evidence that the plaintiff was grossly negligent and showed reckless disregard for his or her own safety of person and property.

Comparative negligence responds to negligence of the plaintiff without relieving the defendant of liability for his or her own misconduct. A steady trend by jurisdictions in the American legal system has been to adopt the theory of comparative negligence in some form and to abandon the traditional theory of contributory negligence as the sole means of weighing the conduct of the parties.

APPLICATION 9.18

Following the same fact situation as in Application 9.17, in a comparative negligence application, it is likely that the fitness club would be held accountable for a percentage of the injuries but that a total recovery would be reduced by the percentage of fault attributed the plaintiff's not wearing prescribed glasses that might have enabled him to see the defect in the floor surface and prevent the fall entirely.

Point for Discussion: Would the result be different if the fitness club advertised that it was fully accessible for handicapped individuals and catered to individuals with special physical needs by offering a variety of special classes and specially designed equipment?

---

2. Assumption of Risk

A long-standing and general defense in tort litigation is assumption of risk, although it has also seen some decline in recent years as comparative negligence has gained acceptance. Traditionally, a defendant could prevent recovery by a plaintiff if the defendant could prove that the plaintiff met three criteria:

- Awareness of the risk of danger by placing oneself in proximity to the activities of the defendant
- Appreciation of the seriousness of the risk and the potential for injuries
- Voluntarily placing oneself in the zone of danger

If the elements of assumption of risk were established, the court took the position that the plaintiff understood the possibility of harm and willingly exposed him or herself to that harm, thereby relieving the defendant of any duty. The more common present-day application of this defense is accepted in a modified version. Many jurisdictions allow the defendant to establish the degree to which the plaintiff was responsible for his or her own injury, either through personal negligence or assumption of risk. Unlike the traditional method that barred recovery by the plaintiff entirely, today the court looks more precisely at how much risk was perceived, appreciated, and voluntarily encountered.

APPLICATION 9.19

Isaac goes to a dude ranch in Colorado. As part of the week-long stay, he goes on daily horseback rides. One morning as the guests are getting onto the horses in the corral, Isaac is standing next to the horse he intends to ride. Some of the horses begin moving around and one kicks at another horse. Instead of the horse, the kick lands on Isaac's right leg, breaking it. Isaac subsequently sues the ranch for negligence in the way the horses were handled. The ranch responds, claiming assumption of risk, and presents evidence that upon arrival at the ranch, guests were given a lecture on safety matters and the inherent dangers of being around horses given the percentage of unpredictability and the inexperience of the riders. Each guest then signed a form stating that they had been informed of the dangers and accepted them. Isaac's position is that he understood the dangers associated with falling from horses, etc. but not that one might attack another and injure him in the process when he was not even riding yet. Under traditional assumption of risk, Isaac would likely be unable to recover on the basis of the blanket acceptance of danger in the signed form. Under a modified version, a closer look would be taken at how the horses were handled by the ranch in the corral area at the time of the incident, and whether the dangers of that situation were some that Isaac could have been reasonably expected to foresee as part of the "inherent dangers" of horseback riding.

Point for Discussion: Is it significant that the plaintiff was not physically on the horse at the time of the injury? Why or why not?

---

3. Last Clear Chance

Unlike the other defenses employed by defendants, the doctrine of last clear chance is a rebuttal by the plaintiff to claimed defenses by the defendant. In essence, it is a defense to a defense. When a plaintiff makes allegations of negligence and a defendant raises a defense that could bar or reduce recovery by the plaintiff, the plaintiff may respond with the claim of last clear chance. The doctrine states that even though a plaintiff may have contributed to the injury or assumed some degree of risk, the defendant ultimately had the last distinct opportunity to avoid the occurrence and prevent the plaintiff's injury, but failed to do so.

APPLICATION 9.20

Mike was riding a motorcycle on a busy highway. As he approached an intersection, he did not slow down as the light turned yellow and, in fact, passed through the intersection as the light was turning to red. Orion was approaching the same intersection in the cross-traffic lane and began across without slowing as the light turned from red to green. Orion collided with Mike and Orion was seriously injured. Orion sued Mike for negligence claiming Mike should not have entered the intersection at a high speed when the light was yellow to red. Mike claimed contributory/comparative negligence of Orion for entering the intersection at a high speed when the light was turning green only as he entered it. Orion responded alleging that Mike had the caution light that gave last warning and gave him the last clear chance to avoid the accident had he stopped. In this case, if in fact Orion did have the green light at the time he entered the intersection and he was not exceeding the speed limit, an application of the doctrine of last clear chance would probably conclude that Mike did have the last distinct opportunity to heed the caution light and avoid the accident.

Point for Discussion: Should the result be different if Orion had been speeding?

---

4. Defenses to Intentional Torts

The traditional defenses in tort primarily address the actions based in negligence. Defenses to intentional torts most often charge that one or more of the essential elements were not proven. This is more common in the area of intentional torts because the elements are more detailed and, as such, require more specific proof. Additional common defenses to intentional torts include those of consent, privilege, and immunity, and various procedural defenses.

The defenses of consent, privilege, immunity, and involuntary conduct are seen most often in intentional tort suits. The defense of consent requires the defendant to establish that the plaintiff, in fact, consented to or agreed, either expressly or by implication, to the defendant's action. This defense is often raised when the plaintiff and defendant are known to one another, and the defendant has the consent to do certain acts and the plaintiff claims the extent of the consent was exceeded.

The defense of privilege is quite different from that of consent. Whereas in consent, the focus is on the conduct of the plaintiff toward the defendant, in privilege, the view is taken that regardless of the plaintiff's agreement or protestations, the defendant had a special legal right to act. A variety of situations exist in which a party has a privileged relationship, and any tortious activity resulting from that privileged relationship cannot be prosecuted by a plaintiff. In addition to privilege that serves a public interest or protects a special relationship, another common privilege is that of self-defense. Depending on the circumstances, a person has the right to use reasonable or necessary

---

APPLICATION 9.21

The plaintiff went to a tattoo establishment for the purpose of having a tattoo of a small, light-blue butterfly placed on the back of her right shoulder. The pattern she selected was approximately the size of a quarter. She had no experience with the process and had no idea how long it took or what it would involve. After selecting the pattern, she signed the consent form and proceeded to have the tattoo applied. At the end of the session she discovered the tattoo artist had placed a tattoo of a butterfly approximately 5×7 inches on her back. The plaintiff sued for battery. The tattoo artist raised the defense of consent and produced the signed consent form that stated across the bottom in small print: The tattoos in the pattern book are smaller than the finished product. With this signed consent of the plaintiff, regardless of whether she read it or not, the defense could likely establish consent.

Point for Discussion: Would the result be likely to change if the tattoo artist had a usual practice of drawing out the tattoo in actual size on paper for clients but failed to do so in this situation?

---

force to defend him or herself, and can even use force to defend another if that person would have been entitled to use self-defense under the circumstances. Limited force can also be used to defend property, but not if it would result in a breach of the peace. The privilege does not extend to the use of deadly force to defend property. Rather, it must be shown that the defendant was in fear for his or her immediate safety or that of another.

Immunity is similar to privilege in that it is a defense viewed from the position of the defendant rather than the conduct of the plaintiff. It gives protection to defendants who, in other circumstances, might be guilty of the tort alleged and be liable for damages. One of the more common examples of immunity concerns government offices and officials. Historically, no lawsuit of any kind could be brought against the government for the torts committed by government servants while acting within the scope of their duties. This has been modified over the years at both the state and federal levels to allow suits against the government in limited circumstances and in accordance with strict procedural rules. In this way, the government is accountable for its torts but is not at risk of being victimized by a litigation explosion of its own.

PARALEGALS IN THE WORKPLACE

One of the most common areas of employment for paralegals is with firms engaged in tort law practice. The very nature of the law lends itself to paralegal employment. Because tort cases hinge so heavily on the actual facts of each case, clear and effective evidence is crucial. This may be in the form of photographs and other documentary evidence, witnesses, and tangible items. The paralegal can be an essential part of the legal team collecting, evaluating, and organizing evidence as part of the discovery/investigation process. The typical tasks of the paralegal may include interviewing clients/witnesses, gathering necessary background information, such as researching environmental conditions, evaluating and recording the scene of an incident, and locating expert witnesses. Unlike other areas of the law that may require much more legal expertise, much of what a jury considers in a tort case is often what occurs in common surroundings. Therefore, the paralegal who is trained in tort and understands what kinds of evidence are necessary to prove or defend the alleged cause of action/defense can perform a significant portion of case preparation.

CHAPTER SUMMARY

In comparison to other areas of law, such as property and contract, tort law is perhaps the most recently developed field of law. It is most certainly one of the areas that was most developed within the American legal system, rather than through the adoption of other principles from other governments. The law continues to develop as societal standards change and technology advances. However, these are now usually variations on established theories of law. The defenses to tort have also undergone dramatic development as the courts have searched for more equitable ways to balance the conduct of the parties rather than using the traditional method of all or none with respect to responsibility for actions and subsequent damages.

Theories that have remained intact and have only been further refined in definition and expanded in application include negligence, intentional torts, and strict liability. Each addresses a different type of circumstance with regard to the knowledge and action of defendants. The extent of the intent to act and the likelihood of injury is often correspondent to a more specific burden of proof on the plaintiff and greater potential damage liability for the defendant when found responsible.

The defenses to tort actions have only changed to the extent that they are applied in a more measured way under the particular circumstances of a case. In all areas, the courts consider the facts more liberally than in the past and are more and more willing to make exceptions to the formerly hard and fast rules when fairness dictates that it be so.

ETHICAL NOTE

A major area of ethical concern in tort law has been centered on the validity of claims filed. Tort claims often succeed and damages are awarded based on a jury's subjective perceptions rather than on more concrete facts such as relied upon in contracts and property cases. There may then be the temptation to proceed with a case in which there is serious question as to the validity of the claim or the damage as claimed by the plaintiff. In response, many states now have frivolous lawsuit actions that penalize both parties and attorneys who bring actions that are determined to be unfounded or are not in the good faith belief that there is legal liability on the part of the defendant for the injuries.

Relevant Internet Sites	
American Tort Reform Association	www.atra.org
Tort Law at Megalaw.com	www.megalaw.com

Internet Assignment 9.1

Search the Internet and locate three new journal articles regarding litigation explosion.

Internet Assignment 9.2

Search the Internet sites relevant to your jurisdiction and determine whether a frivolous lawsuit statute has been enacted.

KEY TERMS

Foreseeable
Intentional Tort

Negligence
Proximate Cause

Reasonable Conduct
Strict Liability

ENDNOTES

1. Prosser, Handbook on Torts (West 1971).
2. *Palsgraf v. Long Island R.R. Co.* 248 N.Y. 339, 162 N.E. 99 (N.Y. 1928).
3. Id.
4. 65 C.J.S. Negligence, Section 11 (1955); (1998 Supp.).
5. Id.
6. See note 5, Supra.
7. See note 5, Supra.
8. Id.
9. Id.
10. Prosser, Handbook on Torts, Chapter 5, Section 31 (West 1987).
11. Id.
12. Id.
13. Id.
14. *Guin v. City of Riviera Beach Fla.*, 388 So.2d 604 (Fla.App. 1980).
15. American Law Institute, Restatement of the Law on Torts II 1976.
16. Id.
17. Annot., 32 A.L.R.4th 1221.
18. Annot. 96 A.L.R. 3rd 1064.
19. *New York Times v. Sullivan*, 376 U.S. 254 (1964).

Chapter 10

The Law of Agency, Business Organizations, and Bankruptcy

CHAPTER OBJECTIVES

Upon completion of this chapter you should be able to do the following:

- Explain the concept of agency and distinguish the various types.

- Identify and distinguish the various forms of business.

- Explain the concept of stock ownership.

- Identify the various types of stock and the rights associated with them.

- Discuss partnership rights and obligations.

- Explain the procedures for ending a partnership or corporation.

- Identify the various forms of bankruptcy and the type of relief they provide.

A. FORMS OF BUSINESS, AGENCY, AND UNIFORM LAW—AN OVERVIEW

Commerce is the very foundation of the United States and nearly all other cultures of the world. Even early explorers to the new world came in search of new lands and new resources to increase the power of their home country in the economic world. Still today our entire social, governmental, and even religious structures are supported and facilitated by the stream of commerce that permeates every aspect of American life. Early on in America, businesses were predominantly small local operations owned by an individual or family, but a few businesses were set up here as satellites of businesses based in England and Europe. At the same time the population was growing, the number and size of businesses increased. Territories also began to establish local, state, and ultimately a federal government. These governments, in turn, began to mediate disputes among citizens and businesses, and to issue judicial opinions, ordinances, regulations, and laws to guide businesses and citizens in their operations as a means to promote fairness and consistency. As a result of all of these factors a number of different forms of businesses evolved and continue to develop today. However, three forms of business encompass all the variations of the different types of business objectives of the owners. They are the sole proprietorship, the partnership, and the corporation/company.

The sole proprietorship is by far the simplest of the business forms and remains the most common. This type of business has an individual owner and no formal steps need to be taken to qualify as a business. To create a sole proprietorship, it is necessary only to commence doing business of some kind with the public. The sole proprietor ranges from the successful business entrepreneur with his or her own flourishing and established business in a commercial setting to the individual who sells products or services out of his or her home or by mail or phone. The partnership business organization is not terribly different from the sole proprietorship except that it involves more than one person as owner. There are certain obligations among the partners that are defined by law and by whether the partnership is general or limited. While not necessary, documentation with respect to these rights and obligations are best put into writing. Finally, the corporation is the most formal and organized of the business entities. It is a statutorily created entity that must adhere to specific statutory requirements to be legally recognized as in existence. There are many ways to classify corporations, but most often they are either general corporations that conduct various types of commerce or professional corporations that deliver professionally licensed/regulated services of some kind. Each of these organizations will be addressed in much greater detail later. However, at this point it is helpful to gain at least a basic understanding of their similarities and differences.

The way a business entity is organized will dictate who receives the income of the business, who or what resources can be reached for debts or judgments against the business, and who in the business has the authority to make decisions regarding the operation of the business. In addition, the law of agency is frequently used in the area of business law with respect to the authority and responsibility of the business and its owners for the acts of subordinates and/or the acts of individual owners concerning third parties. See Figure 10.1.

Throughout the chapter references will be made to various models and uniform acts. These are collections of laws on a particular subject, such as partnerships, that have been adopted in a number of jurisdictions. They are designed for adoption by all the states to promote interstate commerce and business growth through a consistency of laws and a similarity in the application of laws in all states. With these interstate

Characteristic	Sole Proprietorship	General Partnership	Limited Partnership	Corporation
Number of Owners	1	2 +	2 +	1 +
Life	Limited	Limited	Limited	Unlimited
Liability	Unlimited personal	Unlimited personal	General— Unlimited personal Limited— Limited personal	Limited personal
Control	Complete	Shared	General— Shared Limited— None of day-to-day	Limited to policy changes
Income	All personal	All personal	All personal	Only dividends personal
Legal Status	None	Very limited	Very limited	Separate entity

FIGURE 10.1

Chart of Business Entities

transactions becoming more and more frequent, these laws provide for fair and consistent treatment of businesses and consumers regardless of where the transaction occurred. In turn, this reduces forum shopping by parties and the number of disputes with respect to where an action is most appropriately heard.

These acts (collection of related topic) have become more and more popular as the general mobility of society has increased. While they are not unique to the law of business and are also found in areas such as probate and domestic relations, it seems that the law of business is particularly appropriate for uniform laws. As a result, they exist for a number of different areas.

One of the first uniform laws to gain wide acceptance was the Uniform Commercial Code, which addresses the proper methods for handling the different types of business transactions. Others, such as the Model Business Corporation Act, Uniform Partnership Act, and Revised Uniform Limited Partnership Act deal with the formation, operation, and ending of these types of business organizations. While a majority of states have adopted part or all of these acts, it is still the prerogative of each state legislature to amend or supplement the language of any statutory law that is adopted. For this reason, it is important to read the exact language of the state statute in question rather than count upon the language of the original uniform act.

B. CONCEPT OF AGENCY

Agency is present in the vast majority of business transactions in the United States today. Although agency can exist in a variety of settings, including those unrelated to business, the law of agency was developed largely within the area of business law, and it is there that most agency relationships are found. Simply stated, an agency exists any time one party acts in a binding way on behalf of another.

Agency relationships have a distinct beginning and ending, and they occur as the result of an act or words of intent by the party who is granting the authority to another

Agency
Relationship in which one party, known as the agent, acts on behalf of another party, known as the principal. In a valid agency relationship, the agent can legally bind the principal; for example, an agent can enter into a contract on behalf of a principal.

to act in their behalf. The person who grants this authority is referred to as the principal. The corresponding party who receives the authority is known as the agent. When a co-owner, employee, or other party granted authority by a business entity acts in its behalf, an agency takes place.

Before an agency can be created, the principal must have the legal capacity to authorize such a relationship. Because an agency involves the granting of legally binding authority by the principal to the agent, the principal must have contractual capacity. If the principal did not have contractual capacity, it would be impossible for the agent to act in the principal's behalf in a legally binding contract, because the agency simply allows the agent to temporarily stand in the place of the principal for the purpose of entering the agreement. Specifically, the principal must be over the age of majority in the jurisdiction, usually 18 or 21, and must be legally competent. A declaration of legal incompetence means that the court has found the person to be incapable of managing his or her own affairs. If the principal is a business entity such as a corporation or partnership, it should be organized so that it is recognized as that by the laws of the state.

Conversely, it is not necessary for an agent to have contractual authority.[1] Conceivably, a principal could appoint a minor or a person who has been declared legally incompetent to act as an agent. In agency, it is still possible for such a person to have authority to deal in the affairs of a principal, because one with true agency authority is not binding themselves but rather the principal; they are more or less a conduit. However, most jurisdictions do impose some minimum levels of competence for an agent. This prevents cases of principals claiming avoidance of obligations because the agent exceeded authority due to incompetence, and a resultant inability to discern proper authority. Generally, lunatics or persons who are significantly deficient in mental ability will not be considered part of a valid principal-agent relationship.

APPLICATION 10.1

Jim is a mentally handicapped 16 year old with the intellectual development of a child who is about 10 years old. He is employed part time at a local fast food restaurant and helps with stocking inventory and cleaning around the restaurant. One day while working in the stockroom a supplier delivers a number of regularly ordered items. The supplier has several cases of hamburger buns that will go out of date soon. The supplier tells Jim that if he will sign for the extra buns, the next time he comes in he will bring him a terrific surprise. Jim eagerly agrees and signs the invoice on behalf of the restaurant. There are many more buns than are typically used by the restaurant, and the owner refuses to pay the invoice claiming that Jim was an employee but did not have authority as such to sign for deliveries that were in excess of the items previously ordered. Under the circumstances, it is likely that although Jim may have regularly signed for delivery of pre-ordered items, his lack of mental ability and immaturity may have been unduly taken advantage of, as evidenced by the promise of a surprise as enticement to sign for the additional supplies. The actions of the supplier would support the evidence that Jim did not have the ability, without the enticement, to discern the appropriate course of action.

Point for Discussion: Should the situation change if Jim were 18 and of normal ability and was promised some personal incentive for acting in behalf of the owner and accepting the additional order?

1. Types of Authority

There are four general types of authority in recognized agency relationships: actual authority, apparent authority, inherent authority, and authority by ratification. Each type of authority is distinguished by the kind of authority given to the agent and the manner in which it is created. Each type of agency comes about in a different way and imposes different degrees of responsibility on the parties involved.

a. Actual Authority   This is the most straightforward type of agency and requires express consent to agency by the principal.[2] The principal and the agent must both speak or act in a way that manifests agreement to the relationship. It is sufficient that the principal and the agent both speak or act in a way that similarly positioned individuals would perceive as an agreement to the relationship. Of course, as with any agency, the principal must have capacity. It is not necessary that the agency serve some mutually beneficial purpose for both agent and principal. An agency can exist in a setting where the agent receives no consideration in exchange for acting as an agent.

   In most circumstances short of a complex contractual agreement, a written document is not necessary to establish the existence of an agency. Words or actions of the two parties are usually enough to prove an agency exists. Some states, however, have an exception to this. That exception occurs if the purpose of the agency is to grant authority to the agent to enter into written contracts on behalf of the principal. In this situation, the agent must have written evidence of authority from the principal. This rule is known as the equal dignities rule.[3] If a contract must be in writing under the statute of frauds, according to the statute of the jurisdiction, it is only logical that the grant of authority to enter into the contract on behalf of one of the parties to the contract also be in writing.

   An agency based on actual authority is created solely by the principal and agent through agreement and is not based on what a third party perceives as the relationship between the principal and the agent. Actual authority includes two subcategories that indicate more precisely the manner in which the agency was created and to some extent the degree of the agent's authority.

i. Actual Express Authority   This authority occurs when the principal gives the agent an overt verbal or written communication stating the nature of the authority.[4] The principal is not required to place specific limits on the authority such as time, value, or extent of authority, although these are certainly helpful in terms of clarifying agency limits. If no such limits are given, the agent is presumed to have the same extent of agency that other similar types of agents would have under the circumstances.[5]

ii. Actual Implied Authority   When the principal acts in such a way that the agent is reasonable in the perception that authority to act for the principal has been granted, an actual implied authority agency is created.[6] In limited situations, implied authority can occur in conjunction with express authority. The agent who has express authority to accomplish specific objectives for the principal also has the principal's implied authority to do that which is reasonably necessary to accomplish the objectives of the agency. For example, in the situation described in the previous application, it is implied that the agent would have authority to visit the customers of the principal and make the necessary contacts with suppliers or the appropriate departments within the business to see that the orders are processed appropriately.

APPLICATION 10.2

A salesman works in the field taking orders for office supplies from various businesses in his sales territory. The salesman/agent routinely negotiates discounts on bulk purchases from the retail catalogue of his employer. On one occasion, the salesman negotiates a discount on a variety of items that actually results in a loss for his employer/principal. The principal attempts to avoid the agreed terms and increase the price. Because, typically, a salesman in this line of work has this type of authority, most courts would not consider the buyer responsible to ascertain the limits of the authority and, because the salesman was acting in the usual and customary manner, the original sales contract would probably be enforced.

Point for Discussion: How would the result likely be affected if the customary bulk discounts ranged from 5% to 20% and the salesman, on this occasion, offered a 75% discount across the board?

It is also reasonable and accepted that an agent with express authority would employ customs and methods generally used in that type of business, regardless of whether the express authority specifically identifies the right to do so. Consider Application 10.2 involving the office supply salesman. If the customs or methods used in that type of sales include giving away promotional items, then the agent would have reasonable authority to use such tactics to obtain the business of customers.

Another type of actual implied authority that is technically independent from actual express authority is implied authority by acquiescence. It takes place when the principal has not given an agent the express authority to do certain acts on behalf of the principal.[7] Nevertheless, the agent does act and the principal does not interfere or object and accepts any benefit that results from the agent's actions. When this type of conduct occurs, the agent is presumed to have implied authority to continue acting on behalf of the principal, and the principal is bound by the acts of the agent that are consistent with previous actions agreed to or acquiesced to by the principal.

The principal and agent alike have authority to terminate actual authority regardless of whether it is express or implied. The simplest means of terminating an agency is to make the termination part of the original agency agreement. When the agency is created, the principal states when it will end. Often this is a certain date or a specified event. For example, if the agent is hired to locate investors willing to join in funding a $100,000 business venture, the agency will end when the investors have been secured.

Assignment 10.1

> Identify 10 different situations in business that represent an agency relationship.

A more complicated issue arises when agencies end due to unforeseen circumstances. If something occurs that effectively prevents the purposes of the agency from being fulfilled, a court may find the agency terminated at that point. If the agent continues on after the occurrence, and with knowledge of it, the agent may be held entirely responsible for any obligations incurred rather than passing them on to the principal. Circumstances that automatically terminate an agency include loss or destruction of items necessary to the purpose of the agency; a drastic change in business conditions; a change in relevant laws; the potential bankruptcy of the principal, or agent if that is relevant to the purpose of the agency; the death of the principal or agent; the total loss of capacity of the principal or agent; dissolution, if the principal is a business entity; or action by the agent that is adverse or in competition with the interests of the principal or the principal's purpose in hiring the agent.

APPLICATION 10.3

George is an agent of CBS Fitness Club. The club is under construction and George is selling memberships to businesses as a benefit for their employees. He is allowed to keep 10% of all pre-paid memberships and the rest goes to the owners of the club. The club burns down, but George continues to sell memberships claiming that the club is going to open at another location. In reality, while the owners (principals) considered this, they never made this commitment and in the end decide to abandon the venture entirely. The club owners return the 90% of the collected membership fees and the additional 10% of those fees collected prior to the fire. George, however, would probably be held accountable for the 10% in membership fees that he kept from sales that occurred after the club burned, when he had no basis for the representations he made that the club would open at another location.

Point for Discussion: Why do the owners have to pay the 10% of fees collected prior to the fire, if that money was retained by George at the time of the sale? Why should George not have to pay that as well?

---

2. Apparent Authority

Originally, this type of authority was referred to as ostensible authority. However, in recent times the term *apparent authority* has gained wide acceptance. This type of authority requires the presence of a third party for its creation. When a third party reasonably perceives the actions of the party who will become the principal as the actions of one conferring authority on an agent, an agency by apparent authority is established.[8] Generally, a third party cannot conclude that an agency agreement exists based solely upon the acts and assertions of the agent. The general rule regarding apparent authority is that if a principal behaves in such a way that third parties would reasonably believe an agency relationship exists, the third parties can rely on and deal with the agent, and the principal will be bound by such dealings.[9]

First, assume an agent represents to a third party that he or she has the authority to act for the principal. If the principal knows of this and does not tell the third party differently, the third party is justified in believing the agent has the authority. Apparent authority can also be created if the principal acts in such a way or makes statements that would reasonably lead the third party to believe the agent has authority. In that situation, if the third party and the agent make an agreement, regardless of whether the agent in fact has authority, the principal will be bound to the terms of the agreement.

APPLICATION 10.4

Max owns a construction business. For about a year, Max is always accompanied by Brad who is introduced as his project manager. Bids submitted for jobs on Max's stationary are usually signed by Max. Most bids for smaller jobs are given orally by Brad. The following year, Brad signs a number of bids on jobs. Many of these bids are accepted. It is discovered later that Max was unaware of the bids and had not given Brad express authority to sign them. Many of the bids are too low to generate a profit, and Max wants to avoid the contracts. It is very likely that a court would find Max's representations to third parties of Brad being the project manager and allowing Max to submit oral bids for more than a year, would be a reasonable foundation for third parties to perceive Brad had the authority to submit written bids.

Point for Discussion: Would the result likely remain the same if Max were able to produce evidence that the third parties knew the bids were far below any others and not consistent with Max's history of bids?

When an agency is terminated, the principal is obligated to notify any third parties that the principal could reasonably foresee might have dealings with the former agent. If the principal does not make the termination known to those who have a history of doing business with the agent, the principal may be held responsible for the acts of the agent. This is because in most circumstances of a continuing agency, the third parties would be reasonable in their perception that the agency was ongoing. Exceptions to this rule would include death or sudden incompetence of the principal, or an agency that would be considered limited in duration under the circumstances.

3. Inherent Authority

Earlier discussion of agency indicated that a principal would be responsible for actions necessary or incident to a valid agency. There may also be liability for the principal in certain limited circumstances when an agent acts outside the scope of the agency. In these situations, the courts have balanced the interest of the principal who does receive some benefit from the agency against innocent third parties who are adversely affected by the agent's actions at a time when the agent is, or is reasonably perceived to be, subject to the authority of the principal. The two circumstances that can produce such liability for nonagency acts are respondeat superior and similar conduct.

Respondeat superior is a theory in tort law and is discussed in greater detail in the chapter on torts. Simply stated, a principal is considered to be responsible for the acts of an employee acting within the scope of employment even if the specific act complained of was not authorized or incident to employment. The rationale is that the principal is the primary beneficiary of the employee's (agent's) performance of job duties. If, while on the job, the agent also conducts him or herself in a manner that causes injury to an unsuspecting and innocent third party as the result of negligence, the prin-

APPLICATION 10.5

A. Kelly is hired by ABC company to sell shares of ownership in a proposed new subsidiary corporation. Kelly has official documents from ABC with respect to the offering. Five hundred shares are available. M, P, Q, and R are brothers who each purchase 1/4 of the shares. Six months later, Kelly approaches M offering an additional 100 shares. Kelly says these are in addition to the original offering, but she has no supporting documentation. M purchases the shares only to find out later that Kelly has taken the money and left town. ABC would probably not be held accountable. Under the circumstances, M would not likely be reasonable in the perception that Kelly still had authority to sell stock in a corporation once 100% ownership was established and without documentation of expansion or new shares issued by ABC or the subsidiary corporation.

B. Renee hires Gordon to work in his florist shop. One of Gordon's duties is to order inventory for the store. Renee subsequently fires Gordon and does not inform suppliers of this. Disgruntled, Gordon calls in large orders of flowers from every supplier. Because the flowers are perishable, they cannot be returned. The suppliers demand payment by Renee. Because Renee did not inform them that Gordon no longer had authority, Renee would likely be held accountable for the flowers.

Point for Discussion: Would the situation change if the orders were for nonperishable inventory for the store?

cipal is a proper party to bear the cost of the injury, more so than the third party. The agent is not excluded from responsibility. However, as a purely practical matter, the ability to pay such costs of injury is often more available to the principal than the agent.

When an action is based on an agency under the theory of respondeat superior, the necessary elements to prove are essentially the same as for an employee who was acting within the scope of employment as directed by the employer.[10] First, it must be shown that there was a master-servant relationship, that is, a relationship that had a clearly defined authority figure and a person to carry out the directions of that authority figure. This may be an employer-employee, principal-agent, or both. A partner in a partnership is a principal-agent relationship that does not involve an employer and an employee. The partnership as a business entity has the authority to give direction, and the partners as individuals carry out these directions. Thus, the partnership would be the principal, and the partners would be the agents. Partners are not considered employees of the partnership, however.

The second requirement of respondeat superior is that the agent acts within the scope of the agency. This means that the act of the agent that causes injury to a third party must be committed while the agent is engaged in performing the purpose of the agency. Even though the exact conduct that caused the injury may not be directed by the principal, if it occurred while subject to the authority of the agency, it would be considered within the scope.

Exceptions to a principal's responsibility for an agent under respondeat superior occur when the agent deviates substantially from the instructions of the principal or when the agent is engaged in conduct that ultimately serves the agent rather than the principal.[11] In most jurisdictions, the doctrine does not apply to incidents that result from personal acts of the agent that ultimately serve the benefit of the agent, such as smoking. An additional exception would be for intentional torts committed by the agent, that is, conduct, unrelated to the agency, that the agent knows or should know will almost certainly result in injury to another. For example, if a security officer in a night club starts a fight with a patron, the principal would probably not be responsible for injuries caused by the guard, unless the fight was the result of the guard attempting to lawfully remove the patron from the premises.

APPLICATION 10.6

Frank is retiring from the company after 40 years of service. On his last day, the staff throws a big party during the last two hours of work. During this time, alcohol is served. Ned, another employee, attends the party. After about an hour Ned decides to go to the store for more liquor. He takes the company car that he normally drives and heads to the store. During the trip Ned runs a red light and causes an accident, seriously injuring another motorist. The injured motorist sues the company. Even though Ned was not engaged in regular job duties, he was on the job at the time of the accident. In all likelihood, the company will be held liable for injuries caused by Ned under the theory of respondeat superior.

Point for Discussion: Should the result be any different if Ned was in his own car rather than a company car?

The other situation in which a principal is frequently considered responsible for the acts of an agent, even though they are outside the scope of the agency, is known as similar conduct. This theory is based on the concept that a principal should be held responsible for actions that are so similar to the authorized acts that third parties would not be expected to know the difference. If the agent is represented to have certain types of authority, then absent specific statements by the principal or industry standards to the contrary, a third party would ordinarily be justified in believing the agent had authority to conduct transactions that differ only slightly. Consequently, if a principal wants precise limitations on the authority of an agent, such limitations should be clearly conveyed to any third parties.

APPLICATION 10.7

Tom is the office manager for a busy medical practice. Included in Tom's job duties is payment of various expenses of the business. Tom has check writing authority and is listed on the signature at the local bank. Over a period of six months, Tom systematically writes a series of four checks to himself totaling more than $20,000. When the embezzlement is discovered, the owners of the practice confront the bank and insist that the checks and their amounts should have been questioned. The only probable legal recourse for the owners of the practice would have been a limitation on the amounts of checks Tom could write and/or on checks both made out to Tom and signed by him.

Point for Discussion: Should the result be different if the business were a small operation in a small community and Tom did not have authority to sign payroll checks?

4. Ratification

Finally, it is possible for an agency to be created after the fact, that is, after the agent acts on the principal's behalf without authority. This is known as an agency by ratification. If someone represents agency authority to a third party who, in reliance on the representation, transacts with the agent, the principal can only be bound if he or she elects to do so. However, if the principal does become aware of the transaction after the fact and subsequently agrees to be bound, an agency by ratification is created.[12]

This theory is distinct from the other types of agency. If the principal ratifies the actions of the agent, the authority is retroactive rather than proactive. But a principal cannot ratify only some of the agent's actions. If the principal accepts any part of the agent's actions, all of the actions must be accepted under agency by ratification. To do otherwise would be unfair to the third party who is already in peril because he or she relied on an agent who did not have true authority at the time of the transaction. Once an agency is ratified, unless there is an agreement to the contrary by the parties, any contractual obligations are considered to have begun on the date of the agent's representation and the transaction with the third party, rather than the date of the ratification.

A final requirement of an agency by ratification is that the principal must have access to knowledge of all material facts prior to the ratification. This is necessary to prevent subsequent claims of fraud by a principal who becomes fully aware of obligations created by the agency by ratification after the fact.

C. FORMS OF BUSINESS ENTITIES

1. Sole Proprietorships

The simplest and most common form of business organization in the United States is the sole proprietorship. This was one of, if not the first type of business to be established in the United States and despite the many changes and developments in society, law, technology, and general culture, it remains the most popular. In fact, after a trend of nearly 100 years toward partnerships and then large corporate conglomerates, recent trends have shown an increasing desire by the American population to regain some sense of control over their careers and employment. This is evidenced by a strong resurgence in the establishment of small businesses. Many times these are operated by a single individual out of the home or a location near one's home.

To qualify as a sole proprietorship, the entire ownership interest of the business must be vested in a single individual. There is no need for legal documents to establish the business, define its structure or purpose, or delegate responsibilities. There is no need to set forth in writing how the business is to be funded, how profits and losses are to be shared, or liability for debts or judgments. These are all the responsibility of the individual who owns the business. It is entirely possible, however, for a sole proprietorship to employ other persons. In fact, there is no limit to the number of persons a sole proprietor may employ. As a practical matter, though, when a business grows to a certain size, other forms of business such as incorporation may be a more suitable alternative. The key element with employees in a sole proprietorship is not the number, but rather that they are not allowed to take part in ownership decisions and do not have the right or obligation to share in profits and losses. The business must remain individually owned to remain as a sole proprietorship.

Similarly, if ownership changes, the sole proprietorship ends and a new one begins. This may occur without much notice to casual observers. The name and manner of doing business may remain essentially the same. However, the change in owners signals a legal change in the form of the business. The prior owner was the party in control of and responsible for all legal matters associated with his or her sole proprietorship. When a new owner takes over, an entirely new business begins and with it new control and responsibilities. A key concern of sole proprietors when selling their businesses is whether the new owner accepts as part of the purchase all known and unknown liabilities of the business. For example, someone may have been injured on the premises but at the time of the sale neither the original nor the new owner were aware of this. If a subsequent lawsuit is filed for damages as the result of the injury, it should be made clear who will be responsible for dealing with the issue.

The reasons many sole proprietorships ultimately convert to some other form of business entity, such as a corporation, is twofold. In some instances, a sole proprietorship has fewer tax advantages than a corporation. Historically, corporations are taxed at a higher rate than the average individual. However, the rules for what deductions may be used to offset income and what income must be declared as individual may make the corporate form more appealing. This is especially true when an individual has several sources of income. An especially high profit year in the sole proprietorship might increase the individual's income to a level that is taxed at a much higher rate.

Another reason for the decline of sole proprietorships is judgment liability. When an outside party sues a sole proprietorship and wins, the judgment can be enforced against the individual owner, including all of the owner's personal assets. However, some forms of corporations provide a shield of liability for the owners and limit any recovery against a corporation to the assets of the company and not to the individual assets of owners. Many sole proprietors who are engaged in businesses where the risk of litigation is high, opt for the protection of the corporate entity.

However, sole proprietorships remain a popular form of business. This is especially true for the single entrepreneur just starting out in a business with a low risk of litigation resulting from injuries to third parties. Many home-based businesses are begun as sole proprietorship to determine whether the business is viable. The business can be started informally and ended just as easily. The only record often is a special form attached to the owner's tax returns showing what business deductions are claimed for the particular enterprise. This informality is appealing to the business owner who is more properly trained to conduct the nature of the business than to act in an administrative role. It is important that anyone who undertakes to establish a sole proprietorship seeks competent advice from professionals in these matters, such as lawyers and accountants, to ensure that all applicable laws and regulations are properly complied with. This becomes especially important when employees are added to the business operation.

As the business grows and develops into an operation involving the owner, employees, and a widening customer base, the legal requirements concerning compliance with government regulations and laws increase. Tax laws and rate structures for business income and deductions become more relevant. The greater the number of employees and their interaction with customers, the greater the potential for legal issues and potential litigation. All of these factors cause an increasing complexity that is often more than the original concept of sole proprietorship was envisioned to accommodate. Consequently, there is a trend for growing businesses to start or convert to a more formalized legal entity, such as the corporation.

APPLICATION 10.8

Eric started a snow removal business out of his home. He lined up a number of customers who agreed to pay him according to a set fee schedule for snow removal each time it snowed. At first, Eric had no difficulty keeping up with the work. However, his dependability and reasonable rates made him very popular with local businesses and after about two years he had to hire someone to help. That same year he also began a mowing service for the same customer base during the summer months. In about fifteen years, Eric had a staff of 15 employees year round and a fleet of equipment to provide snow removal and lawn and garden care for an ever-growing number of businesses in and around the community. Eric's proceeds from the business had grown from providing part-time employment for himself, to supporting a full-time workforce of 16. At the same time, Eric had a number of other investments that had developed into a significant source of personal income. Along with the growth of the business came increasing liability. It was not unusual for customers to claim property damage from Eric's equipment, and the inherent danger in using equipment in snowy conditions during winter and mowing equipment on hillsides and such in summer, created potential for injury to bystanders, customers, and employees. The increased profits of the business, when combined with his other income, propelled Eric into a much higher tax bracket than he would have incurred on a salary and investments. Also, the increasing liability of the business caused Eric some concern as his personal standard of living increased and assets accumulated. These factors motivated Eric to incorporate the business, thereby establishing a tax rate for the profits of the business that was separate from his income and to protect his personal assets from any judgments that might be granted against the business.

Point for Discussion: Why does the fact that Eric had lucrative investments outside the business support his decision to incorporate?

---

2. Partnerships and Limited Partnerships

Partnerships are the counterpart to sole proprietorships. While the sole proprietorship is an entity owned by an individual, the partnership is an entity shared in ownership by more than one individual. Partnerships have been recognized as forms of business from the very beginning of the American legal system.

A partnership requires an interaction of individuals who act on behalf of the common objectives. This establishes partners as agents of the collective partnership, which is in turn the principal. Because the partnership itself is the product of a contract, legal issues that arise among partners are usually resolved by the application of the legal standards of contract and agency law. Within these areas, and in the law of business organizations generally, a number of legal standards peculiar to the issues of partnerships have been developed. With respect to the creation, operation, and end of partnerships,

Partnership
Agreement of two or more parties to engage in business or enterprise, with profits and losses shared among all parties.

common issues are addressed specifically by statutes in each state. In an effort to promote consistency, since many partnerships do business and have members in more than one jurisdiction, a majority of states have adopted all or part of the Uniform Partnership Act and the Revised Uniform Limited Partnership Act as the text for statutory law regarding partnerships. However, as with any uniform law, the adoption is voluntary and each state has the option to substitute its own law or statutory language. Consequently, when examining the law of a particular jurisdiction, even if it has adopted the uniform laws, it is essential to consult the laws of the specific state to ensure that all relevant statutory language is considered.

The Uniform Partnership Act and the Revised Uniform Limited Partnership Act are model laws that have embodied the most commonly employed legal principles, with respect to partnership law, into suggested statutory language. The Uniform Partnership Act addresses the business form of general partnerships. The Revised Uniform Limited Partnership Act addresses the related form of business known as the limited partnership. The uniform laws address such issues as how to effectively create the partnership; general rules of operation, such as profit and loss sharing; rights and obligations of partners; and ultimately termination and winding up of the business of a partnership. The majority of states have adopted these uniform laws in whole or in part as most states already adhered to the standards through a combination of statutory and case law.

a. Types of Partnership   The two basic forms of partnership are general partnership and limited partnership. Each has distinct characteristics making it readily distinguishable. In a general partnership, there are two or more general partners and personal liability is unlimited. This means that in the event of a judgment against the partnership for a debt or other type of civil liability, the assets of the partnership as well as the personal assets of the individual partners may be reached and, if necessary, seized or sold to satisfy the judgment. In addition, the general rule of law regarding a partner's liability is that the partners are jointly and severally liable, meaning that a creditor, having exhausted partnership assets, can move against the assets of one, all, or any combination of partners. The liability is not necessarily shared equally. If one partner had a great deal of cash available, while another partner had real estate but little cash, under joint and several liability a creditor could collect the entire debt from the partner with available cash. It is possible then that the partner could seek reimbursement from the other partner, but that would depend on the terms of the partnership agreement and could also take a much longer time to recover. In the event the remaining partner(s) do not have adequate resources, it is possible that a partner could bear the loss of the partnership entirely alone. These considerations make it very important for partners to have a full understanding of the potential for liability and a clear understanding of the financial solvency of any potential partners.

Each partner is considered to be the agent of the partnership, which gives each partner the authority to legally bind the partnership in contractual agreements. In most instances, the consent of the other partners is not needed to enter into contracts on behalf of the partnership. Even if the partners agreed to other terms, any third parties who might be affected would have to be informed about the conditions as with any other limited agency authority.

Because the partner can bind the partnership, it is entirely possible that, in the event the partnership was sued for breach and lost, the assets of the partnership and the personal assets of the partners could be at risk. Once again, it is important to establish the financial stability of potential partners to have a detailed agreement with respect to agency authority, and to communicate with third parties whenever possible. Each state has specific rules of procedure with respect to the manner in which a partnership is sued. Some states require that the name of the partnership be included on the complaint/petition, while others require the names of the individual partners, or both.

APPLICATION 10.9

Bob and Tim decided to create a partnership and open a used car lot. Bob agreed to put approximately $50,000 into the start-up expenses and work 40 hours per week. Tim agreed to put $25,000 into the startup expenses and to work 60 hours per week. After approximately six months the car dealership was sued by a customer who purchased a vehicle that was represented to be in good working order. In reality, the car was in poor working order and broke down on the highway, causing a multi-car accident. Based on the warranty given, a judgment was rendered against the dealership for an amount of $500,000. The partners had no insurance to cover the judgment. At the time of collection, the assets of the dealership were approximately $75,000. Bob's personal assets subject to the judgment were in excess of $750,000 and Tim's were approximately $2,000. The judgment creditors collected the entire amount by attaching the assets of the partnership and Bob's assets, in the amount of $425,000. Under partnership principles, joint and several liability would allow the creditor to collect entirely from Tim. In turn, under partnership principles of sharing losses, Bob could seek reimbursement by Tim for a portion of the judgment. However, realistically, Tim does not have the assets and Bob would probably be faced with bearing the brunt of the judgment.

Point for Discussion: How would the result be likely to differ if the assets of the partnership were $400,000 as the result of a recent contribution by Tim of $250,000?

As a general rule, there is a presumption that profits and loss within a partnership are to be shared equally by all partners. However, it is permissible for partners to have a written agreement that provides for a different distribution, such as 70/30. This might come about if one partner is more heavily invested and/or has more personal exposure in terms of liability. But in the absence of a written agreement, courts will generally assume the posture that the partners intended to share profits and losses equally.

Partnerships are required to file federal tax returns but not to pay federal taxes. Essentially, the return is used to cross check the income the individual alleges to have received from the partnership on the individual return, against the amount claimed to have been distributed on the partnership return. Because partnership income and loss is considered personal to the partners, any tax paid on income is paid on the personal return. Similarly, if the partnership has an annual financial loss, the partners can claim their proportionate share of the loss against their total annual income on their personal returns in accordance with federal and state tax laws.

b. The Limited Partnership   A special type of partnership, known as a **limited partnership,** can be used to protect the personal assets of a partner from judgment and debt liability to some extent and to provide other benefits with respect to investments and taxes. The Revised Uniform Limited Partnership Act, is a model law adopted by a

Limited Partnership
Partnership of two or more persons in which the limited partner can be held liable for partnership debts only to the extent of his or her investment and cannot take part in general management and operation of the partnership business.

majority of the states as statutory law to govern most aspects of limited partnerships. Specifically, the Act defines the rights, liabilities, methods of creating and dissolving a limited partnership. Generally, in a limited partnership, a party who is a limited partner can be held liable only to the extent of his or her investment or promised investment in the partnership.[13] In this sense, a limited partner is similar to a corporate shareholder, but the cost of protection to a limited partner is significant. A limited partner can have no direct control or influence into the regular operation of the partnership.

A limited partner invests in the partnership as capital venture and not as a participant in an operating business. He or she is allowed no input into the operation of the business of the partnership and cannot be employed by or contract with the partnership for profit. Finally, the limited partner cannot be openly associated with the partnership through inclusion of his or her name in the partnership name. This is where the term *silent partner* originated. The limited partner is entitled to share in profits as agreed upon by the partners, and the losses cannot exceed the investment. Because the limited partner cannot contribute services to the partnership, there must be at least one general partner to operate the business of the partnership. The general partners have the risk of personal liability just as if they were members of an ordinary partnership. In turn, they also have control over how the partnership operates and the continuing business of the partnership.

There have been many cases in which a limited partnership has been sued and attempts have been made to obtain judgment against the limited partner as well as the general partner(s). Obviously, for the party suing the partnership, holding more partners liable increases the chances of actually recovering a judgment because there are more assets to attach. In order to obtain judgment against a limited partner beyond their level of investment, it must be proven that the limited partner was such in name only. The court will look at the type of business the partnership is engaged in, and such things as the involvement of the limited partner in day-to-day operations of the business, management decisions, and authority to recommend or demand changes. The presence of any of these may result in a finding of a general partnership despite the intention to create a limited partnership. If this occurs, the limited partner will be treated no differently from general partners in the manner in which judgments are enforced.

APPLICATION 10.10

Gwen and Henry form a limited partnership. Gwen is a landscape architect and Henry invests in Gwen's new business of designing and installing landscaping. On a new project, Gwen applies the incorrect chemicals to a customer's lawn and kills several trees considered to be more than 100 years old. The customer sues Gwen and Henry. Gwen has few assets, while Henry is financially independent. Through the discovery process and investigation the customer is able to establish that Henry took part in developing the initial marketing plan for the business and in fact prepared company tax returns and quarterly reports in an attempt to save the cost of hiring an accountant. These activities, while not directly involved in the business of landscaping, are regular and necessary elements of doing business and would probably be viewed by a court as active participation. Consequently, Henry would more than likely be treated as a general rather than a limited partner.

Point for Discussion: Would the result be likely to change if Henry did not take part in the marketing plan development and only reviewed the returns that were prepared by an accountant?

c. The Relationship of Partners   In addition to the agency relationship that partners have with the partnership as an entity, the partners also have other traits incident to their participation in the partnership. First and foremost, partners have a fiduciary obligation to one another. A fiduciary relationship is one in which there is a presumption of trust between the parties. In a partnership, each partner is obligated and presumed to honor the obligation of trust to place the interest of the partnership above personal interest or gain. If a partner is presented with a situation in which he or she must choose to incur benefit to the partnership or personal benefit to the exclusion of the partnership, the obligation is to place the interest of the partnership first. Any partner who makes a profit in a business venture that would have been an appropriate venture for the partnership would be considered to engage in what is known as self-dealing and would be expected to turn the profit over to the partnership.

APPLICATION 10.11

Ralph is a member of a partnership that purchases and sells rare coins. On a buying trip Ralph comes across a coin that is extremely valuable. However, the seller is completely unaware and has it included with a mediocre collection that is moderately priced. Ralph purchases the collection on behalf of the partnership, but he holds out the rare coin and sells it himself. The buyer represents a museum and issues a press release about the acquisition. When the partners find out that Ralph sold the coin to the museum, they bring an action against Ralph for breach of fiduciary duty through self-dealing. In this type of situation, the court would probably find that Ralph did breach the duty and award a judgment equal to the share of profits the other partners would have received had the coin been sold by the partnership.

Point for Discussion: Would the situation change if the rare piece was something other than a coin that Ralph encountered while on business for the partnership?

General partners should always decide in advance whether a partner is to be compensated for work done in the partnership other than through a share of profits. A partner is not usually entitled to payment for services rendered as an employee but is only entitled to a share of the profits or losses, as are the other partners. The exception to this rule is when a partner or partners agree to payment or are in the process of closing down the partnership and winding up business as the result of the death of one of the partners. In the case of winding up after death of a partner, the surviving partners are presumably entitled to reasonable compensation for their services in the closing of partnership accounts.

Aside from compensation, partners are generally entitled to receive reimbursement for monies expended outside of the investment and in the pursuit of the ordinary business of the partnership.[14] Because of the agency relationship between a partner and partnership, it is not necessary for a partner to obtain approval for payment of every expense incurred on behalf of the partnership. As with ordinary agency relationships, if the expense is one that would be reasonably incurred in the operation of the business, a partner generally has the right to either obligate the partnership for payment or to receive reimbursement if he or she makes payment personally on the partnership's behalf.

In some instances, disputes arise among the partners with respect to the conduct of other partners. In limited instances, the courts recognize a legal right of partners to a full accounting of partnership assets and liabilities.[15] Suits by partners regarding partnership activity is limited for obvious reasons. Because a partner is a member of the partnership, the individual partner bringing the action would essentially be suing him or herself. The law does not ordinarily permit dual capacity in a lawsuit in adversarial positions, for example a partner suing a partnership. The exceptions in which a partner is permitted to sue a partnership are essentially threefold:

1. The partnership is ending and in the process of winding up business.
2. A partner has been improperly excluded by the other partners from activity, participation, or knowledge of partnership activity (in the event of a limited partner).
3. There is a reasonable basis to suspect a partner has made personal profit at the expense of the partnership.

In these instances, the partnership is ending or in danger of ending and a partner may not have access to the information necessary to properly assign any final profit, return of investment, or responsibility for debt. At such a time, full disclosure is essential and the courts have permitted such actions in an attempt to achieve fairness for each of the partners.

d. Partnership Assets   One of the more unusual aspects of a partnership is ownership of assets. As discussed above, partnership income and debt is considered to flow through the partnership directly to the individual partners and is considered personal income and debt. However, partnership property is treated differently. Property may be owned in the name of the partnership rather than the individuals. This makes transactions easier for those doing business with the partnership and also clearly identifies property as that of a formal partnership and not jointly owned property by a number of individuals. However, some creditors may require financing for purchases of personal property to be in the names of the partners or at least include both the names of partners and the partnership. This eliminates any confusion if collection of the debt becomes an issue as each partner voluntarily accepts the debt jointly and severally as an individual and as a partner.

Partnership property that is held in the name of the partnership is the property of the partnership as a whole and not the individual property of the partners. While it is true that any income of the partnership is automatically considered the personal income of the individual partners, the property owned by the partnership is not considered the personal asset of the individual partners. Occasionally, some confusion or conflict arises as to whether property belongs to the partnership or to a particular partner. This may be the result of a number of facts such as property loaned to the partnership, property given as investment, or property that becomes inadvertently intermingled with partnership property. When such an issue arises, the courts often consider the following factors in determining the rightful owner of the property:

1. Was the property acquired with partnership funds?
2. Has the partnership made use of the property?
3. Does the partnership have legal title to the property?
4. Is the property of a type that would be used in the business of the partnership?
5. Has the partnership taken any steps to maintain or improve the condition of the property?
6. Is the property recorded in the books of the partnership as an asset?

APPLICATION 10.12

Sam, Amy, and Todd create a partnership. They purchase a computer system and finance it in the name of the partnership. When Sam goes to finalize the purchase, he agrees to the planned purchase for the partnership, but also includes a remote system that will allow him to access the business accounts from home. The various changes more than double the cost of the originally planned purchase. The partnership business never really gets off the ground and in six months closes. The computer sales company attempts to collect on the finance agreement that was breached when the partnership stopped making payments. The computer company sues the individual partners. Amy and Todd attempt to avoid liability on the basis that Sam exceeded his agency authority and in fact purchased property for himself in the name of the partnership when he ordered the home computer system. Under the laws of agency, the partnership would still likely be held liable for the debt. However, there could be a valid issue as to the portion representing the home system Sam purchased for himself and whether the computer company should have considered that part of the business of the partnership. If the computer company had required all of the partners individually to assume the entire debt in addition to Sam accepting the debt on behalf of the partnership, the partners could not later claim they were not responsible for all or part of the debt.

Point for Discussion: Would the same issues exist if Sam had purchased additional items for the business rather than the home system?

While any one of these factors will not typically determine if property is owned by the partnership, a consideration of them collectively will establish with much more certainty what the intent of the partners was in the acquisition of the property. If the answers to the considerations strongly indicate that the partnership was the rightful owner of the property, all partners will be held responsible for any obligations with respect to the property. Similarly, if the property should suddenly increase in value, the partners will be joint owners of the property for that purpose as well.

e. The Duration of a Partnership   While a sole proprietorship begins when the entrepreneur commences business activities and ceases when business activities end, a partnership has a more formal and distinct lifespan. A partnership is an entity that must be created by agreement of each of those who are partners and who are ultimately responsible for the existence of the partnership. Because it is created by an agreement that establishes the business and the legal rights of the partners, it is governed by the law of contracts. Therefore, all the requirements of a valid contract must typically be present for a valid partnership to be created. This includes the requirements of capacity, manifestation of assent, consideration, and so forth. Not all states require that partnership agreements be in writing, but it is always advisable. In the absence of a written agreement, the courts look to the conduct exhibited by the parties and determine whether it implies that an agreement existed.

Even if a court determines that the parties intended to create a partnership, there must still be the determination of whether that intent was achieved in the actual formation of a legally recognizable entity. When considering the existence of a valid partnership, several

APPLICATION 10.13

Oswald and Rachel create a partnership and together open a commercial greenhouse. As part of the business, they also have a fresh flower and vegetable market and raise much of the produce themselves. When the partnership was starting, Oswald brought his tractor to the property and used it on the outdoor gardens. Periodically it was taken home but generally was kept at the business. The partnership also paid for all gas, maintenance, and repairs on the tractor. After a period of three years the partners decided to dissolve the partnership and distribute its assets. Oswald claimed that the tractor belonged to him and should not be included in the partnership assets. Rachel claimed that Oswald had contributed the tractor to the partnership and that it should be considered an asset.

When considering the factors to establish whether property belongs to a partnership, a court would most likely determine the property was not part of the partnership assets because it was not acquired with partnership funds, was not in the exclusive use of the partnership, was not titled in the name of the partnership, and was not recorded in partnership books as an asset. While the partnership did use the property and take steps to maintain and improve its condition, these factors alone would appear more like a rental than ownership.

Point for Discussion: Would the result be different if Oswald, who lived in an adjacent state, did not claim the tractor as personal property when paying the personal property tax in his home state for those three years and claimed the maintenance/repairs on the tractor as a deduction for care of partnership equipment on the partnership tax return?

factors must be applied to the circumstances. Those most often contemplated include the following:

1. Do the alleged partners have some type of joint title to real or personal property?
2. Do the alleged partners operate under a single name?
3. Do the alleged partners all share in profits and losses of the business?
4. How much money and time does each alleged partner invest in the business?

Similar to the considerations of what constitutes partnership property, none of the above factors alone will independently establish a partnership. When considered together, though, they create a much clearer view of whether a valid partnership existed and whether third parties would be reasonable in the perception of a partnership among the alleged partners.[16]

A nontraditional partnership may also be established under a legal theory known as partnership by estoppel. This is applied when one party allows a second party to represent him or herself as a partnership to outsiders. If the outsider relies on the representation, the original party may be held responsible for the acts of the second party. The first party is precluded from denying the existence of a partnership after allowing another to represent to outsiders that such a relationship, in fact, existed.[17] This is similar to the agency principals that also apply to partnerships as discussed previously. The theory is that innocent third parties should not be required to suffer loss as the result of the actions or omissions of others. While everyone has a basic duty to inquire into the parties with whom they do business, it is still incumbent on the corresponding parties to act responsibly with respect to who they authorize or permit to do business in their behalf.

f. Termination or Dissolution   A partnership has a definite life span. Sole proprietorships can be started, ended, restarted, or continued indefinitely without much, if any, formality. A partnership however must take into account the equity of each of the partners in the business and the proper methods of bringing the business to a close or changing its status. Any change in the identity of the partners in a partnership results in a technical, if not formal, dissolution of the partnership.[18] The business itself may continue without notice by outsiders, but the legal status of the partners undergoes a distinct change. When a partner dies, declares personal bankruptcy, sells his or her interest in the partnership, or withdraws as a partner, the existing partnership agreement is ended and the partnership must be dissolved. This does not mean that the business must cease to operate. In a case where by agreement or order of the court the partnership ends permanently with no intent by any of the partners to continue, the business is brought to a close. But when one or more original partners remain and/or a new partner joins the original partner(s), a new partnership may continue the business uninterrupted. One other instance in which a partnership ends is by operation of law. This is when the business of the partnership becomes illegal and the partnership is dissolved automatically. In this instance, business must cease immediately.

When a partnership is voluntarily dissolved, third parties who have done business with the partnership are entitled to notice. This prevents partners from wrongfully representing apparent authority and binding the members of a dissolved partnership through the application of partnership by estoppel. The only continued authority of partners after a dissolution takes effect is that which is necessary to conclude the business obligations and concerns existing at the time of the dissolution and any activities necessary to the dissolution, such as the sale or distribution of assets in the event the business does not continue under a new partnership. However, a partner who has declared personal bankruptcy is no longer considered to be an active partner as of the time of the bankruptcy and cannot act on behalf of the partnership even in dissolution proceedings. Further, the dissolving partnership cannot engage in any new business. This includes taking or filling orders, or continuing ordinary business operations. All of these, if done at all, must be done under the new partnership.

In the case of a partnership that is dissolved and the business of the partnership ended, there is a specific process for bringing the entire partnership business to a close. After the dissolution is effected, existing obligations and concerns of the business are addressed and creditors are paid. In some instances, this requires selling off assets. After all creditors are paid in full, the investment of the partners is repaid and any excess is distributed according to a specific procedure. The partnership agreement may set forth the exact method and proportions of distribution but, in the absence of an enforceable agreement, there are well-established methods. First, any partner who has made loans over and above investment in the partnership will be repaid as the partner, in that capacity, is considered to be a creditor just as any other would be. Second, each partner is repaid the amount of his or her contribution or investment in the partnership. This is the equivalent of cash and fair market value of property turned over to the partnership business. Any remaining assets are distributed on a pro rata basis, that is, in a percentage equivalent to the investment of the partner. This is considered the most fair rather than a distribution of equal shares because the partners who invested more also placed more at risk. Therefore, it is appropriate that in the event the partnership ended with an excess the partners with more at risk should receive a greater return on the investment.

APPLICATION 10.14

Partners K, L, and M decide to dissolve their partnership. Over the life of the partnership, K has invested $60,000, L has invested $30,000, and M has invested $15,000. At the conclusion of the partnership after all debts are paid, there is a surplus of $150,000. Each of the partners receives their initial investment back. A surplus of $45,000 still remains. K is entitled to $25,715.00, L is entitled to $12,857.00 and M is entitled to $6,428.00 of the surplus amount.

Point for Discussion: If the partners L and M put in additional hours working in the partnership in order to equalize the investment, what should have occurred to cause an adjustment in the manner in which the surplus was distributed?

Much more often in the event of a dissolved partnership, the final assets are insufficient to repay all of the partners for their investment. In such cases, the shortage is also distributed on a pro rata basis. To follow the preceding example, the larger contributor would be responsible for a portion of the debt commensurate with the percentage of total investment. The other two partners would also be responsible for a pro rata share of the debt. However, keep in mind that should any partner fail to repay the percentage of debt for which they were responsible, the joint and several liability concept applies for as long as debt of the partnership exists.

Assignment 10.2

In each of the following situations, determine how much each partner would be entitled to or responsible for in a dissolution of the partnership.

a. D, E, and F dissolve an equal partnership. At the conclusion of all business and winding up, debt remains in the amount of $48,000. Assets remain in the amount of $20,000, and $6,000 of the debt is a loan made by D to the partnership.

b. M and N dissolve their partnership. M has $75,000 invested in the partnership. N invested $25,000 and 150 hours of time at the rate of $10.00 per hour over and above that of M without pay. There was no written agreement as to the terms of the partnership. At the conclusion of winding up of business, the partnership has $150,000 in assets after all debt has been paid.

Corporation
Entity legally recognized as independent of its owners, known as shareholders. A corporation can sue or be sued in its own name regarding its own rights and liabilities.

3. Corporations

Legal advantages and new subtypes make the **corporation** one of the most common forms of business in America today. Unlike sole proprietorships and partnerships that have existed as business entities for as long as there have been entrepreneurs, corporations are a legal entity created by statute. The concept of a corporation was advanced through legislation as a clearly defined entity separate from its owners and with distinct rights, capabilities, obligations, and duration. Because a corporation is created purely by statute, the legislatures have been free to create different subtypes of corporations to suit the needs of different types of businesses. Nevertheless, most corporations share standard characteristics, many of which have been embodied in the Model Business Corporation Act (see Appendix).

a. Corporate Characteristics   What makes a corporation different from a sole proprietorship or a partnership? The corporation is a purely fictional entity in that it is not personally associated with an individual entity, as a proprietorship or partnership would be. Under the law, a corporation is recognized as a distinct entity or person for the purposes of holding property, initiating or defending legal actions, paying taxes on its income, and so on. Generally, in the past, a corporation was not considered to be capable of committing crimes. When criminal conduct occurred, the individuals representing the corporation who actually committed the crimes were held responsible.[19] This attitude has been changing in recent years and more often legislatures are enacting laws that permit the corporate entity, as well as the agents, to be convicted of criminal acts and punished accordingly. This is because large numbers of persons are often involved, sometimes innocently, in the criminal conduct, and it is often engaged in as an attempt to gain some type of benefit for the corporation. Thus, it would be illogical to punish the individuals for the criminal conduct and still permit the corporation to reap the benefits of that conduct. Although a corporation cannot be imprisoned, it can be fined or even forced to dissolve, as penalty of illegal conduct. Corporations may also be required to carry out certain acts of restitution to individuals or communities as a consequence of criminal conduct. In addition, the acting individuals may be held criminally responsible and prosecuted for their conduct.

CASE IN POINT

State v. D.J. Master Clean Inc, 123 Ohio App.3d 388, 704 N.E.2d 301 (1997).

Corporation which was engaged in carpet-cleaning business was found guilty in the Municipal Court, Franklin County, Environmental Division, of one count of placing industrial waste in location where it caused pollution of waters of the state. Corporation appealed. The Court of Appeals, Petree, J., held that: (1) witness' testimony regarding prior incident in which corporation's vans discharged liquid into storm sewer drain was admissible to show that corporation had plan or scheme for disposing of waste water; (2) there was sufficient evidence that liquid discharged by corporation's vans into storm sewer was "industrial waste"; and (3) there was sufficient evidence to impose criminal liability upon corporation for acts of its employees.

Affirmed.

David C. Winters, Columbus, for appellant.
PETREE, Judge.

Defendant, D.J. Master Clean, Inc., appeals from a judgment of the Franklin County Municipal Court, Environmental Division, finding it guilty of one count of placing industrial waste in a location where it caused pollution of the waters of the state in violation of R.C. 6111.04.

   Master Clean is a closely held corporation which specializes in commercial janitorial services and residential carpet-cleaning services. In its carpet-cleaning business, Master Clean uses GMC vans equipped with specialized carpet-cleaning equipment. When this equipment is used to clean a carpet, clean water from a one-hundred-twenty-five-gallon storage tank is forced into the carpet as steam and then extracted from the carpet by a powerful vacuum. The wastewater extracted from the carpet is then stored in a one-hundred-fifty-gallon holding tank. When the wastewater holding tank is full, it must be emptied before further carpet cleaning can be performed.

According to the state's evidence, during the early morning hours of Monday, October 23, 1995, Edward Klos was behind his place of business in the industrial park at 6663 Huntley Road loading his van in preparation for the day's work. At approximately 5:30 a.m., Klos noticed two red GMC vans with the words "MASTER CLEAN" painted on their sides stopped, one in front of the other, a few doors down from where he was working. The van in front was parked over a parking lot storm drain and was discharging some sort of liquid into the storm sewer, while the second van appeared to be waiting to repeat the procedure when the first van had finished. Klos immediately went and telephoned the Worthington Police Department to report what he had witnessed.

In response to Klos's report, Officer Michael Gibson of the Worthington Police Department was dispatched to 6663 Huntley Road. Officer Gibson arrived at 6663 Huntley Road at approximately 6:20 a.m., whereupon he was met by Klos, who told him what he had witnessed. Officer Gibson then inspected the area around the storm drain in question. According to Officer Gibson, the area around the drain was damp and he detected what appeared to be a soap or chemical residue in the area.

Officer Gibson then proceeded to Master Clean's place of business, which is located at 527 Schrock Road, just across the street from where the vans were seen discharging into the storm sewer. Officer Gibson exited his cruiser and walked up to Master Clean's building. As Officer Gibson approached the building, he could see several people working around a red van inside the building through an open overhead door. Officer Gibson walked up to the open door and asked the persons inside who was in charge. According to Officer Gibson, David Lee May came forward, introduced himself as the general manager, and indicated that he was in charge. Officer Gibson explained the situation to May, and inquired as to what the substance was that the vans had discharged into the storm sewer. In response, May explained that Master Clean's policy was to get permission to discharge the wastewater onto the lawns of its carpet-cleaning customers and, if unable to obtain

such permission, to dispose of the wastewater through the sanitary sewer at the company's place of business. Before returning to his regular duties, Officer Gibson asked his radio dispatcher to notify Captain William Fields, the hazardous materials coordinator for the Worthington Fire Department, of the situation.

Captain Fields arrived at 6663 Huntley Road at approximately 10:50 a.m. and commenced an investigation of the reported discharge into the storm sewer. He examined the storm drain where the dumping was alleged to have occurred and traced the drain to where it empties into Rush Creek a short distance away. Captain Fields observed fibers of some sort in and around the drain grate, in the bottom of the drain, and where the drain empties into the creek. Fields then photographed these areas. Following his investigation, Captain Fields referred the matter to the Franklin County Sheriff's environmental enforcement officer, Rick Klema.

Klema and Christopher Bonner, an official from the Ohio Environmental Protection Agency ("OEPA"), investigated the scene of the alleged discharge on October 27, 1995. Upon finding "a large amount of hair, fiber and dirt" around the drain opening and where the drain empties into the creek and photographing these areas, Klema and Bonner proceeded to Master Clean's place of business. Upon their arrival, they were met by Master Clean's president and CEO, Donald Kessler. Kessler was informed of the complaint which had been lodged against Master Clean and was presented with an OEPA notice of violation, which charged Master Clean with illegally disposing of wastewater from carpet cleaning into a storm sewer leading to waters of the state, and ordered the company to immediately clean up around the storm drain and where the sewer line empties into Rush Creek.

The case against Master Clean was tried to a jury in the Franklin County Municipal Court, Environmental Division, beginning on December 2, 1996. At the close of the state's case, Master Clean moved for a judgment of acquittal pursuant to Crim.R. 29(A). The trial court overruled the motion. At the close of its own case, Master Clean renewed its motion for acquittal. The trial court reserved its decision on the motion until after the jury returned its verdict. On December 6, 1996, the jury returned a guilty verdict. The trial court then overruled Master Clean's motion for acquittal and imposed sentence.

Master Clean appeals from the judgment of the trial court, assigning the following errors:

The trial court's unreasonable admission into evidence of inflammatory and unfairly prejudicial character testimony in the prosecution's case-in-chief constitutes an abuse of discretion and a denial of fair trial guarantees secured by the Fifth and Fourteenth Amendments to the Unites States Constitution and by Article I, Sections 10 and 16 of the Ohio Constitution.

The trial court erred to the substantial prejudice of appellant when it failed to enter a judgment of acquittal where no rational trier of fact could have found the essential elements of the crime proven beyond a reasonable doubt and when it failed to reject a jury verdict overwhelmingly against the weight of the evidence.

Master Clean's first assignment of error challenges the trial court's decision to allow, over objection, Laura Staten to testify that between 7:00 and 8:00 p.m. on October 12, 1993, she witnessed two red vans with the words "Master Clean Carpet Cleaning" painted on the side pull up and park over a storm sewer drain located in the rear parking lot of 6663 Huntley Road and discharge some type of liquid into the drain. Master Clean argues that the admission of Staten's testimony violated Evid.R 404(B), which provides as follows:

"Evidence of other crimes, wrongs, or acts is not admissible to prove the character of a person in order to show that he acted in conformity therewith. It may, however, be admissible for other purposes, such as proof of motive, opportunity, intent, preparation, plan, knowledge, identity, or absence of mistake or accident."

The first sentence of Evid.R. 404(B) forbids the admission of evidence of other bad acts committed by a defendant for the purpose of proving that the character of the defendant makes it likely that he committed the crime charged. 1980 Staff Note to Evid.R. 404(B). However, the rule's second sentence provides that evidence of such other acts is admissible for other purposes to which it may be relevant. Staff Note, supra.

Master Clean contends that Staten's testimony was improperly admitted to show that the company was of a character which was consistent with the crime charged. We disagree. The incident described by Staten occurred in exactly the same manner and location as the crime with which Master Clean is charged. As a result, Staten's testimony was relevant to show that Master Clean had a plan or scheme for disposing of the wastewater generated by its carpet-cleaning vans by discharging that water into the storm sewer behind the industrial complex located at 6663 Huntley Road. State v. Davis (Apr. 6, 1995), Franklin App. No. 94APA08-1206, unreported, 1995 WL 170320.

Master Clean argues, however, that, even if Staten's testimony was relevant to one of the permissible purposes enumerated in the second sentence of Evid.R. 404(B), the testimony should have been excluded under Evid.R. 403(A), as its probative value for those purposes was "substantially outweighed by the danger of unfair prejudice." "In reaching a decision involving admissibility under Evid.R. 403(A), a trial court must engage in a balancing test to ascertain whether the probative value of the offered evidence outweighs its prejudicial effect." State v. Steele (Sept. 21, 1995), Franklin App. No. 95APA01-124, unreported, 1995 WL 559930. In order for the evidence to be deemed inadmissible, its probative value must be minimal and its prejudicial effect great. State v. Morales (1987), 32 Ohio St.3d 252, 258, 513 N.E.2d 267, 273–274. Furthermore, relevant evidence that is challenged as having probative value that is substantially outweighed by its prejudicial effects "should be viewed in a light most favorable to the proponent of the evidence, maximizing its probative value and minimizing any prejudicial effect" to the party opposing its admission. State v. Maurer (1984), 15 Ohio St.3d 239, 265, 15 OBR 379, 402, 473 N.E.2d 768, 792. Finally, a trial court's admissibility determination under Evid.R. 403(A) may be reversed only upon a showing that the court abused its discretion. State v. Hurt (Mar. 29, 1996), Franklin App. No. 95APA06-786, unreported, 1996 WL 145486; Steele, supra.

It is self-evident that Staten's testimony created a considerable risk of unfair prejudice to Master Clean. However, immediately after Staten testified, the trial court carefully instructed the jury as follows:

"And I emphasize, you may not, under any circumstances, consider [Staten's testimony] to be proof of the character of Master Clean, to suggest that Master Clean acted in conformity with such character on October 23, 1995. That would be very unfair; because the law does not allow you, even if you believe this evidence were true, to punish Master Clean because you believe it may have done another act not charged as a crime in this case."

The trial court's clear and exacting limiting instruction severely reduced the danger of unfair prejudice presented by the admission of Staten's testimony. Given this fact, and the relevance of the testimony to show the existence of a plan on Master Clean's part, we cannot say that the trial court abused its discretion in admitting her testimony. Master Clean's first assignment of error is overruled.

In its second assignment of error, Master Clean alleges that the trial court erred in refusing to grant its Crim.R. 29 motions for acquittal. Pursuant to Crim.R. 29(A), the trial court is authorized to enter a judgment of acquittal if the evidence presented is insufficient to sustain a conviction on the offense charged. However, a trial court shall not order an entry of judgment of acquittal if the evidence is such that reasonable minds can reach different conclusions as to whether a material element of the crime has been proven beyond a reasonable doubt. State v. Bridgeman (1978), 55 Ohio St.2d 261, 9 O.O.3d 401, 381 N.E.2d 184, syllabus. Furthermore, in reviewing a ruling on a motion for judgment of acquittal, a reviewing court must construe the evidence in a light most favorable to the prosecution. State v. Wolfe (1988), 51 Ohio App.3d 215, 216, 555 N.E.2d 689, 690–691.

Master Clean first argues that the state failed to present sufficient evidence to allow a jury to conclude that the liquid discharged from its vans on October 23, 1995 was "industrial waste" within the meaning of R.C. 6111.04. In making this argument, Master Clean does not contend that the wastewater which results from the process of cleaning carpets is not "industrial waste" for purposes of R.C. 6111.04. Instead, Master Clean argues that there was insufficient evidence to allow the jury to conclude that the liquid discharged from its vans on October 23, 1995 was wastewater rather than clean water.

Officer Gibson testified that he found a soapy residue at the drain into which the Master Clean vans were reported to have discharged liquid on October 23, 1995. Further, both Captain Fields of the Worthington Fire Department and Officer Klema of the Franklin County Sheriff's Department testified that they found fibers and other debris at the site of the discharge which looked as though they had come from carpet cleaning. Finally, the jury was shown pictures of this scene taken by Captain Fields and Officer Klema which plainly show what appears to be a large quantity of soggy carpet fibers around the drain in question. This evidence was sufficient to permit a jury to conclude that the liquid which Klos saw being dis-

charged from Master Clean's vans was wastewater resulting from the carpet-cleaning process rather than clean water.

Master Clean also argues that the state failed to present sufficient evidence to impose liability upon the corporation for its employees acts of discharging wastewater into the waters of the state. R.C. 2901.23 sets forth the circumstances in which a business entity may be held criminally liable for the acts of its employees. In the present case, the state charged Master Clean under R.C. 2901.23(A)(4), which provides as follows:

"(A) An organization may be convicted of an offense under any of the following circumstances:

* * *

"(4) If, acting with the kind of culpability otherwise required for the commission of the offense, its commission was authorized, requested, commanded, tolerated, or performed by the board of directors, trustees, partners, or by a high managerial officer, agent, or employee acting in behalf of the organization and within the scope of his office or employment."

The Ohio Supreme Court has interpreted this provision to mean that a corporation may be found guilty of a criminal offense only if the criminal act or omission was authorized, requested, commanded, tolerated, or performed by a high managerial officer, a high managerial agent, or a high managerial employee of the corporation who has policy-making authority over the area at issue. State v. CECOS Internatl., Inc. (1988), 38 Ohio St.3d 120, 123, 124, 526 N.E.2d 807, 810–811, 811–812. "High managerial personnel are those who make basic corporate policies." Id. at paragraph one of the syllabus.

In the present case, Master Clean was prosecuted on the theory that the corporation's high managerial personnel recklessly tolerated the practice of discharging wastewater from the carpet-cleaning process into the storm sewers. Master Clean contends that the state failed to present any evidence from which a jury could find that a high managerial official of the corporation tolerated the practice.

At trial, Master Clean's sales manager, Van Wilcox, testified that, on September 12, 1995, he received a telephone call from OEPA regarding a complaint that a Master Clean van had been seen discharging liquid down a storm sewer earlier in the day. Wilcox testified that he informed Kessler of the complaint. In addition, the state admitted a letter addressed to Wilcox at Master Clean and dated September 18, 1995, in which OEPA followed up on its earlier telephone call. The letter again notified Master Clean of the report of an illegal discharge by one of its vans on September 12, 1995, and suggested several possible alternatives for disposing of wastewater. Kessler testified that he read this letter when he opened the mail before passing it on to Wilcox.

In addition, the evidence revealed that at the time of the incident in question, Master Clean's drivers had three legal options for disposing of carpet-cleaning wastewater: they could discharge it onto a customer's lawn with the customer's permission; they could discharge it at the Columbus wastewater receiving station; or they could discharge it into the sanitary sewer, via the single toilet located in Master Clean's shop. Kessler testified that only forty to fifty percent of Master Clean's residential customers allow wastewater to be discharged onto their lawns, and that he was not aware of his employees ever having used the Columbus wastewater receiving station. Wilcox, however, testified that approximately ninety percent of the carpet-cleaning vans returned to the shop at the end of the day with their wastewater holding tanks empty.

Finally, Kessler testified that after he learned of the reported illegal discharge of October 23, 1995, the company created a written addendum to the company's policy handbook which listed the acceptable alternatives for disposing of carpet-cleaning wastewater, as follows:

"1. With permission of clients, waste water can be discharged into a toilet or floor drain connecting to a sanitary sewer.

"2. Waste water can be brought back to the company to be discharge in the sanitary sewer.

"3. With permission of clients, waste water can be discharged over the client's lawn, without causing runoff to storm sewers or bodies of water."

Master Clean distributed this addendum to each of its carpet cleaners and required them to sign and return it.

The above evidence is sufficient to support a finding that Kessler knew or should have known that Master Clean's employees were regularly discharging carpet-cleaning wastewater into the storm sewers, and that he nonetheless failed to take meaningful steps to prevent the practice until after he learned that Master Clean was being charged with a crime. Based thereon, a jury could reasonably conclude that Kessler recklessly tolerated the discharge of October 23, 1995. Master Clean's second assignment of error is overruled.

Having overruled Master Clean's assignments of error, we hereby affirm the judgment of the Franklin County Municipal Court, Environmental Division.

Judgment affirmed.

TYACK, P.J., and LAZARUS, J., concur.

Case Review Question: Would the result likely change if the company could show it took extensive measures to stop the illegal discharges after it was charged with criminal conduct?

The life of a corporation typically begins when the statutory requirements to establish legal corporate status are satisfied. There are other instances in which a corporation not in compliance will still be held accountable as a corporation, but these are rare and will be addressed later in the chapter. In addition to statutes outlining the steps to create a corporation, there are also requirements to maintain corporate status. As long as the statutory requirements continue to be met, the corporation will continue. This is unlike sole proprietorships or partnerships that end anytime there is a change of ownership. For a corporation, a change of owners has no real effect on the corporate status as a legal entity. Rather, as long as the statutory mandates are met, such as paying an annual fee for continued registration with the state as an active corporation, maintaining a registered agent to accept service of process in legal actions, compiling an annual report or other documentation necessary to establish that the corporation is a functioning legal entity, the corporation will continue to exist in the eyes of the law.

Typically, a corporation will cease to be recognized as a legal entity when it either fails to comply with statutory requirements or commences corporation dissolution proceedings. These will be discussed in greater detail later in the chapter. At this point it is significant to note that the end of a corporation occurs most often by acts that demonstrate the intent to cease corporate status rather than as the byproduct of another event such as death, resignation, or change of ownership.

Perhaps the greatest advantage of a corporation is that individuals who invest in the corporation by purchasing shares of ownership typically have limited exposure for losses. Ordinarily, a person who invests in a corporation is called a shareholder. In return for investment, a shareholder receives shares of stock in the corporation that represent a percentage of ownership. The greater the amount of the investment, the greater the percentage of ownership. Some corporations are *closely held* meaning that only a few persons have ownership (often members of a family but not necessarily so) and that the ownership is limited to a specific group. In this case, the shareholders would typically hold large percentages of the corporation. Publicly held corporations sell shares of ownership to virtually anyone. In a close corporation, ownership is closed to the general public as the name implies.[20] A further discussion of the common types of close corporations such as S corporations and limited liability companies will be provided later in the chapter. At this point, the discussion will focus on the original form, which is the general corporation. In a general corporation the number of owners is limited only by the number of shares and even then some corporations sell fractions of shares. Thus, it is possible for a business to be owned (not managed) by literally millions of people. Obviously, to permit liability of all owners would be unrealistic.

When a shareholder purchases shares of stock or a percentage of ownership in a corporation, that purchase is an investment. The shareholder gambles that the company will profit and the owners will in turn receive a portion of those profits. On the other hand, if the company fails, the shareholder stands to lose his or her investment. Typically shareholders stand only to lose the amount of their investment and not more.[21] Thus, the corporation is distinct from most other types of business entities in which the owners are personally liable for a judgment against the business irrespective of whether it exceeds their investment.

Assignment 10.3

Consider the following situation. Determine the potential financial liability, in addition to amounts previously invested, of each owner for a judgment against it of $250,000.

a. JKL Corporation has five shareholders, each with an existing investment of $50,000 in the business. The assets of the business are valued at $200,000.
b. X is a sole proprietor with a business valued at $10,000.
c. R, L, and Z are partners. R has invested $150,000 in the business. L and Z have invested time but no money in the business. The business has assets of approximately $150,000. R has personal assets exceeding 1 million dollars. L and Z have virtually no personal assets.
d. Same situation as C, however R is a limited partner.

As mentioned, corporations may have an unlimited number of owners, known as shareholders. Often, the persons who are in a position to invest are not the persons who are best qualified to run the corporation. Because of the sheer impracticality of having too many owners to let each have a role in day-to-day operation and management of corporate issues and for many other practical reasons, another unique characteristic of corporations is that management of the business is typically kept separate from ownership. When a corporation is created, a board of directors is appointed to oversee the general operation of the corporation, and the officers of the corporation supervise day-to-day issues and activities. This method of separating the management from ownership protects the interests of shareholders who are not involved in the management of the corporation. It is often desirable for at least a percentage of the board not to have an ownership interest in the corporation. In this way, they can act objectively and in the best interests of all shareholders when making decisions about the direction of the corporation's business. Also, because a corporation is operated by the directors and officers, changes in ownership do not often have a significant impact unless the corporation ownership is closely held.

Unlike other types of businesses, ownership (represented by shares of stock) in a corporation can be freely transferred by sale or gift with virtually no effect on the corporation. This allows the investors the opportunity to profit from their investments and have some control over how their money is invested. This is unlike a sole proprietorship or partnership, which ends with the sale of ownership. To create a new partnership to continue the business, the remaining partners must agree to accept the party to whom the ownership interest is sold. In a corporation, an owner may sell the ownership interest to anyone without limitation. Because management and ownership are separate considerations, the corporation can ordinarily continue operating without interruption. The exception to this, obviously, is if the new owner purchased a controlling percentage of ownership and used it to institute changes. However, this is not often the case.

b. Creating a Corporation

Because a corporation is a fictional legal entity or *person* created by statute, much more is required to start a business than to just begin operations. A number of statutory requirements must be established before a currently operating or newly proposed business will be considered a corporation. The failure to follow the requirements properly can result in a failure to recognize the corporation and ultimately lead to personal liability for the owners in any judgments or debts of the corporation.

When a corporation is formed, state statutes require that the purpose of the corporation be set forth as well as the general manner in which the purpose will be achieved. This information, along with other basic facts such as the original incorporators, are put in a document called the **articles of incorporation.** This is sometimes referred to as a corporate charter. These documents generally contain the name and purpose of the corporation; the number and classes of shares, which determine the division of ownership percentages to be issued; the value per share assigned by the corporation; the voting rights or limitations on voting by the various classes (types) of shareholders; and the provisions for the election, removal, or appointment of board members or officers. The basic rules of operation and the methods to be used in carrying out the corporate purpose and in governing the corporation are set forth in a document known as the **bylaws.**

Articles of Incorporation
Document filed with the state at the time of incorporation to state the purpose of the corporation and define the corporate structure.

Bylaws
Document of a corporation that details the methods of operation, such as officers and duties, chain of command, and general corporate procedures.

While the articles of incorporation define the basic structure and purpose of the corporation, the bylaws are more detailed in terms of how the business of the corporation will operate. It defines the officers and their duties, the chain of command, the decision-making power, and so on. The bylaws are not meant to serve as an operating manual for every single issue that arises in the day-to-day business. Rather, the bylaws more or less detail the authority and limitations of those in charge of seeing that the purpose of the corporation is carried out. Typically, any amendments to the articles of incorporation or the bylaws, must be approved by a majority of shareholders. Also, the corporation is legally prevented from deviating significantly from the articles of incorporation and bylaws without obtaining prior approval of the shareholders and passing a formal amendment.

Assignment 10.4

Identify which of the following items would be appropriate for inclusion in the articles of incorporation, the bylaws, or neither.

a. Number of members of the board of directors
b. Duties of the treasurer of the corporation
c. Location of the primary place of business of the corporation
d. General nature of the business of the corporation
e. Names of each department within the corporation
f. Amount the corporation would be required to pay investors to repurchase stock in the event of a dissolution of the corporation
g. Term of office of the members of the board of directors
h. Term of office of the officers
i. Salary of the president of the corporation
j. Number of shareholders required to be present before a vote can be taken on amendments to the bylaws or articles of incorporation

Promoter
One who is hired as a fiduciary to recruit investors in a proposed corporation.

For some businesses, a corporation is formed using **promoters.** These persons are often the initial incorporators and shareholders, but in some instances, they are professionals who are hired by prospective incorporators/shareholders. A promoter's primary duty is to obtain sufficient funding (capitalization) for the corporation by obtaining commitments to purchase stock. The promoters also typically ensure that all the formalities required by the statute for incorporation are satisfied. In some jurisdictions, promoters are personally liable for the contracts they make on behalf of the corporation unless and until the corporation agrees to substitute itself for the promoter in the contract. This is known as a *novation.* If more than one promoter is involved in forming a corporation, each has a fiduciary duty to the other and cannot act in his or her own self-interest if it will harm the interests of the other promoters.

The promoters also have a fiduciary duty to the corporation and its shareholders.[22] They cannot use secret corporate information for their personal benefit or gain. If a promoter does use secret information for self-profit, the corporation and its shareholders can file suit to reclaim that profit. If, however, the promoter fully discloses the information to the corporation and if the corporation or interested shareholders who would be affected approve, the promoter may use the information to obtain all possible profits.

APPLICATION 10.15

A promoter is one of several potential incorporators seeking funding for a new Internet-based business. While researching potential shareholders, the promoter becomes aware of an individual who has tremendous capabilities in this area of business. The promoter hires the individual to create an Internet-based business of his own and does not tell the other prospective incorporators. The corporation that the promoter was initially seeking to establish with his fellow incorporators is created and has a lackluster performance, while the secretly established corporation rapidly increases in size, volume, and profits. The other incorporators hear of this and bring suit against the promoter/fellow incorporator for all profits since the only significant difference between the two businesses was the creative input of the individual hired to get the business off the ground. In this type of situation, it is likely that a court would award some or all of the profits to the plaintiff incorporators based on a breach of fiduciary duty. Had the incorporator not started a competing business or at the very least had he disclosed the availability of the Internet wizard he discovered, he would have met the duty. But keeping such information secret breached his obligation of trust.

Point for Discussion: If the facts were exactly the same but the promoter disclosed the availability of the individual and deliberately downplayed his skills, would the result change?

All states have some type of statutory law to prescribe the methods for creation, statutory maintenance of records, and dissolution of corporate entities. A majority of the states have adopted a uniform law known as the Model Business Corporation Act (MBCA) (see Appendix) as all or part of their corporate statutes. This act is a collection of individual statutes that address all the legal aspects of corporate existence from incorporation to reporting requirements to dissolution. It includes provisions for everything from establishing and protecting a corporate name or logo to the proper steps to effectively dissolve a corporate entity. By establishing the same basic statutory provisions in most states, the process of handling legal disputes over corporate status is much easier. Also, with the ever-increasing amount of interstate commerce, this commonality of standards reduces the complexity that has occurred in the past when corporations would form in one state, which had beneficial corporate laws, and conduct operations in another state where the business was more likely to thrive. While this still occurs and is not a major hurdle, the simpler a business organization can be, the better it is for all who are in contact with it.

Some of the most important statutory requirements of the MBCA or any statutory law concerning corporations are those that provide for the creation of a corporation. Typically, this is accomplished through a number of steps, including the drafting of certain documents. The articles of incorporation and bylaws must be drafted and signed by the incorporators. Necessary documents and fees must be submitted to the secretary of the state or other designated person where the business is incorporated. When the incorporators have complied with these formalities, the secretary of state will grant a certificate of incorporation.

The mere drafting of these documents does not establish a corporation. All other statutory requirements of the particular state must be met for the corporation to be recognized by the state as a corporation doing business in that state. Until these requirements are met, the corporation will not be entitled to the benefits generally afforded to corporations, such as limited liability. However, when an outside party makes a claim against an alleged corporation in court, it may be found that the corporation exists for the purposes of the dispute even though the state has not previously recognized it in a formal manner.

c. Types of Corporate Status   A de jure corporation (corporation by law) is created by meeting each requirement of relevant statutes that provide for corporation formation and maintenance. These statutes usually require that incorporators have legal capacity and submit articles of incorporation and bylaws. When all the provisions for incorporation have been satisfied, the state issues a certificate of incorporation that generally remains valid for as long as the corporation continues to satisfy the statutes.

On occasion, incorporators attempt to satisfy the statutes but are not successful. In some cases, the law will recognize the organization as a de facto corporation (corporation by fact or actions). The shareholders of a business that is recognized as a de facto corporation are protected in liability, the same as de jure corporation shareholders would be.

To establish a de facto corporation, there must be evidence that the incorporators made a good-faith attempt to comply with the state laws regarding incorporation and continuance of the corporations, and that the business has been conducted as if it were a corporation at all times. It must also be shown that the corporation was represented as such and not as another type of business entity and that outside persons dealt with the business as if it were a corporation.[23] When all such evidence exists, the court may recognize the entity as a de facto corporation and allow it to claim all the privileges of a de jure corporation. But if all the tests for a de facto corporation are not met satisfactorily, the corporation will be treated as a partnership or sole proprietorship, liability for judgments against the business will become personal, and the assets of the individual owners will become available to creditors if necessary to satisfy the debts.

Finally, corporation by estoppel (preclusion from denying corporate existence) is the opposite of the other types, in which a noncompliant company seeks recognition as a corporation. Corporation by estoppel occurs by one of two methods. In the first, a person or persons hold a business out to be a corporation to the public and deal with the public as a corporation but later attempt to deny that the corporation ever existed.[24] The second occurs when outsiders deal with a business as a corporation with the knowledge that it is not a proper corporation. Then, when a dispute arises between the two, the outsiders attempt to deny that a corporation exists and claim that the owners should be personally liable.[25] In either instance, the courts will often treat the business as a corporation by estoppel and apply the law as if it were a real corporation. The rationale is that people should not be able to derive the benefits of corporation status but at the same time avoid the obligations.

d. Piercing the Corporate Veil   A court will sometimes ignore the corporate structure of a de jure corporation and hold all or some of the shareholders, officers, and directors responsible for the acts of the corporation. Thus, the court ignores the wall of protection from exposure to liability that shareholders usually enjoy as owners of a corporation. This is called piercing the corporate veil, and it happens when a court finds that a corporation has improperly used corporate status.

Generally, a corporation may be subject to piercing the corporate veil in three instances: (1) when it is necessary to prevent fraud, (2) when there is inadequate capitalization, and (3) when the corporation refuses to recognize the formalities necessary to a de jure corporation.

i. Prevention of Fraud   In the case of the prevention of attempted fraud, the veil will be pierced only when it can be shown that a person or persons formed the corporation in a direct attempt to avoid legal obligations to creditors or others with legal rights. Usually, such debts were incurred through the corporation but the funds were used to benefit the shareholders personally. This is not the same as protecting the shareholders from obligations that were incurred as the result of the ordinary business of the corporation. If the obligations were originally intended to benefit the business of the corporation or were the result of doing the business of the corporation, the corporation will be responsible for the obligations, and the shareholders will continue to receive protection from personal liability.

ii. Inadequate Capitalization   In the case of inadequate capitalization, the point at which the corporate veil will be pierced is not as clear. It is true that shareholders are generally responsible only for the amount invested in the corporation. It is also true that the original corporate structure must provide for investment that is adequate to allow the corporate purpose to be achieved. If the investment in a business is so slight that even the minimal requirements to establish a going concern in a business of the type begun are not met, the court may consider that there was no sincere intent to form a corporation. In addition, there must be a pattern of reinvestment of sufficient profits to enable the corporation to continue until such time as the shareholders agree to formally dissolve the entity. Failure to do these things is considered a lack of true intent to form a legal corporation for the purpose of doing legitimate business.

iii. Failure to Recognize Corporate Formalities   Finally, the corporate status of a corporation is ignored if evidence shows that it refused or willfully failed to recognize corporate formalities. In this case, the shareholders are held individually responsible as if they were partners in an ordinary business venture. One basis for piercing the corporate veil because of lack of corporate formality is to claim that the corporation was nothing more than an alter ego or front for another business. Specifically, this means that the corporation has no true purpose of its own but is simply a shell used as a tool by another corporation to limit the liability of the other business. For example, if a very large and profitable corporation undertakes a risky venture or one that is often involved in litigation, it may attempt to create a new and separate corporation for that business. Then, if there is litigation and ultimately a judgment, or the business fails and there is significant debt, any liability is limited to the value of the newer and smaller corporation and not the responsibility of the large profitable corporation. This is considered an attempt to misuse corporate status and when proven, results in the liability of the parent business. When faced with this type of issue, the courts consider such things as how much control the parent company had over the corporation; whether it owned assets, such as equipment, or whether they were rented or borrowed; whether the assets and employees were under the exclusive control of the business or whether they were also in some ways managed and used by the parent company, and so forth.

One type of alter ego corporation involves very small or close corporations that generally consist of only a few shareholders, all of whom are often active in the business of the corporation. The problem arises when the shareholders begin to treat the property of the corporation as personal property. For example, the shareholders may use corporate funds to pay private debts or fail to keep separate corporate accounting records. They may take or use corporate funds or property without following proper procedures for removing the funds or property from the corporation and transferring them to personal possession. If the shareholders engage in such activities, a court is likely to find that the corporation did not have a true corporate existence.[26]

Another situation in which the alter ego theory may be applied involves parent and subsidiary corporations. It is entirely legal for one corporation to totally own and control another corporation. However, unless both corporations operate independently, comply separately with the legal corporate formalities, and represent themselves to the public as separate and distinct, the courts may consider them to be a single corporation, with one corporation acting as the alter ego of the other.[27] In that event, the parent or owning company, which usually has the greater assets, can be held liable for the debts of the subsidiary.

A situation that is encountered less frequently, but is also a basis for the alter ego theory is that of joint ownership. If a shareholder has a major interest in more than one corporation and strongly influences the policies and actions of the various corporations so that they become mere common tools for the manipulation of the business of this shareholder, the corporations may be considered alter ego corporations and be held liable for the actions of one another.

When a corporation, regardless of size, consistently engages in a pattern of conduct that demonstrates an intent to use the corporate entity for other than a valid legal purpose, rather than to carry on the business as the corporate structure was intended by statute, the corporation's limited liability of shareholders may be lifted. This disregard of corporate status by the courts forces the shareholders to be individually responsible to injured outsiders for the damage that resulted from the injuries.

When the court does ignore the corporate structure and holds the shareholders liable, it does not necessarily follow that all shareholders will have to bear the losses of the business. If a corporation consists of many shareholders, only those who actively engaged or acquiesced in the wrongful conduct will ordinarily be held responsible.[28] Innocent shareholders who did not take part in the management of the corporation and were not in a position to be aware of the conduct or to stop it will not generally be held accountable for the acts of the persons who were in control.

Piercing of the corporate veil is not a routine occurrence. The situations presented are generally the only types of circumstances that will prompt a court to pierce the veil. Certain types of plaintiff's claims are more common when a court determines that piercing the corporate veil and imposing personal liability is appropriate. One such claim is made by persons whose person or property has been seriously injured as the result of a negligent or intentional act of the corporation. It is not necessary that the person(s) have a business relationship with the corporation. Courts may resort to piercing the veil in these cases because if the injured party were confined to suing the corporation for its wrongful conduct and the corporation was nothing more than a shell, the shareholders could avoid liability for clearly improper conduct.

APPLICATION 10.16

Brock rents a small backhoe from an equipment rental company. The company has removed the roll cage from the backhoe to provide greater visibility for the less-experienced operators who typically rent the backhoe. While Brock is operating the backhoe on a small incline it rolls over. Brock falls out and is trapped beneath the equipment, ultimately resulting in the loss of his leg. He brings suit against the rental company for the removal of the cage, which would have prevented his falling beneath the backhoe. The equipment company is a wholly owned subsidiary of a large construction company. The equipment company's assets consist of one month's operating capital of $2,000 and various items of used equipment donated by the parent company with a total value of approximately $20,000. Every three months all profits (less one month's operating capital) are removed from the rental company accounts. The construction company has a regular habit of using rental company equipment for its own projects. In this situation, it is likely that the court would find the rental company as a mere shell used to avoid liability of the parent corporation. To limit recovery by the plaintiff to $22,000 for the loss of his leg when it occurred as the result of a deliberate removal of a safety device by the rental company would probably be considered an unjust result.

Point for Discussion: Would the result be different if the rental company was a newly started business by three investors rather than a subsidiary of a large corporation that bled the company of money and intermingled assets, even if it meant recovery would be severely limited?

Another instance of piercing the corporate veil occurs in contract claims. In such situations, a party has business dealings with the corporation, only to find out later that the corporation was a sham. In most cases, the courts will find that the outsider had an opportunity to investigate the credibility of the corporation before doing business with it. If the situation did not lend itself to this, however, and would have appeared proper to reasonable persons, the corporate veil will be pierced.

Assignment 10.5

Create a detailed factual situation that would warrant piercing of the corporate veil. Next change one or two facts that would result in a court's refusal to pierce the veil.

e. Corporate Stock Already stated is that a shareholder is a person who invests in a corporation and owns a percentage of the corporation represented by shares of stock. The articles of incorporation for each company state specifically how many shares are to be issued. Additional issuances require an amendment, so that current shareholders cannot have their percentage of ownership diluted without notice. The total number of shares represents the total ownership of the corporation. The corporation may hold some of the shares in a reserve.

At the time a corporation issues stock, it assigns specific values to the stock. This is commonly referred to as par value. As the demand for ownership in a particular company grows or declines, the price people are willing to pay may vary on the open market. Normally, the greater the investment, the greater the number of shares one possesses, and the greater the number of shares possessed, the greater the percentage of ownership or control over the business. Therefore, in times of great profitability and earnings by the corporation, the demand for shares and, consequently, the price the buyers are willing to pay for available shares increases. The investor hopes, of course, that the shares will increase even more in value so they can be sold to the next investor at a profit. The corporation, however, continues to value the shares at the stated amount in the articles and should the corporation dissolve, this is the amount they would pay to redeem the stock. Therefore, if a business is doing poorly in terms of earnings and profits, investors may rush to sell their shares ahead of other shareholders and get the maximum price. As more shares become available on the market, the price declines. The worst-case scenario is when an investor buys stock at a premium price and is left to sell it below its stated value because the assets of the corporation are no longer sufficient to even pay the stated par value.

Corporations have different classes of stock. All corporations have common stock, which is the most basic, and many corporations only issue common stock. Corporations may also choose to issue preferred stock, which is usually entitled to more benefits and, thus, may be more marketable. Finally, some corporations issue what is called cumulative preferred stock. With this type of stock, in years when earnings are low and no profits are distributed, the right to dividends carries over and accumulates until a year of better profits. Then these shares are entitled to multiple awards of profits as opposed to common stock, which is only entitled to a percentage of profit for the year in which the profit is earned. For example, assume a company issues 70 shares of common stock and 30 shares of cumulative stock. For two years there is no profit. In the third year, the company does very well and declares a dividend (profit distribution to stockholders). The total amount available might be divided into 160 units, 90 for the three years of accumulated rights of the 30 cumulative stock shareholders and one year of profit distribution for the common stock shareholders. The exact formula for determining dividend rights is typically specified by the corporation.

Certain rights are acquired along with some types of stock. If, for example, a shareholder purchases stock that has voting rights attached, in addition to having ownership interests in the financial status of the corporation, the shareholder receives the right to cast one vote or percentage thereof for each corresponding share or portion of a share owned. Voting is usually done annually to elect new directors to replace those whose terms are about to expire and to approve any major changes, such as an amendment to the articles of incorporation.

Some shares also have certain provisions regarding the dividends. When the board of directors determines that a corporation is profitable, it may declare a dividend after reinvesting a reasonable amount of the profits. When a dividend is declared, the money assigned to the dividend is split among the shareholders, based on the type and number of shares owned. Preferred stock usually has a higher value than the common stock and is entitled to dividends first. If sufficient funds left, a dividend may then be paid on common stock. Ordinarily, the dividends are paid in cash, but it is also possible to grant dividends in the form of product or even additional stock.

A significant right to be considered with stock is that of liquidation. This refers to the rights of shareholders to receive the value of assets of the corporation in the event of a dissolution. Preferred shareholders may have the first right to receive assets up to the value of their stock after creditor shares have been paid. Common shareholders are apportioned the remaining assets toward their investment. Regardless of how much a shareholder may have paid for stock, only the par or stated value is paid, and this is only if enough assets remain after creditors and all stock for each of the types of preferred stock shareholders have been redeemed.

Some corporations will sell stock with preemptive rights. This means that when a corporation decides to issue additional stock, the shareholders with preemptive rights are given an opportunity to purchase the shares of new stock based on their percentage of ownership before the shares are offered for sale to the public. Such rights are not only a reward for investors who have previously shown confidence in the corporation by purchasing stock, but more importantly, it allows an investor the opportunity to maintain the same percentage of ownership.

A corporation may sell subscriptions to stock when it is formed or after its formation when approved by the directors. Generally, a stock subscription is an agreement between the corporation and a subscriber for the stock to purchase a certain number of shares at a certain price. A corporation that has not yet been formed accepts such agreements at the time of incorporation when shares are authorized and issued. Generally, persons who offer to purchase subscriptions do not have a contract with the corporation until the board of directors accepts the subscription; instead, the subscribers have an option that the board may accept or reject.[29]

If a corporation's board of directors elects to accept a stock subscription and the subscriber defaults by not paying for the stock, the corporation would have all the remedies available under breach of contract principles, including an action against the subscriber for the value of the stock under the subscription agreement.[30]

Stock subscriptions are especially helpful to promising new corporations. The corporation receives adequate capitalization from the investors and, in return, the investors have the opportunity to purchase large amounts of stock at a price that is usually lower than the cost on the open market. Thus, if the prospects for a new corporation are hopeful, subscribers have an opportunity to buy more shares.

f. The Securities and Exchange Commission   The courts have addressed issues such as improper profits and other illegal behavior by corporations, but significant issues with respect to the buying, selling, and trading of stock resulted in the creation of the Securities and Exchange Commission (SEC). Following the stock market crash of 1929, the Securities and Exchange Act of 1934 established the SEC to oversee the stock market system in the United States. The SEC administers laws of Congress and issues regulations with respect to major transactions of stock, corporate ownership, and management. The goal of the SEC is to see that corporations and major corporate shareholders do not take advantage of unwary minor shareholders or vulnerable corporations.

As mentioned earlier, a person who owns a controlling interest in a corporation has certain influence in corporate operations and opportunities. Under SEC rules, a shareholder who possesses 10% or more of the corporate stock is considered to have certain responsibilities.[31] The SEC further considers a 10% or more shareholder to owe a fiduciary duty to the corporation and its shareholders. Officers and directors have an even greater fiduciary duty to the shareholders.[32]

When a controlling shareholder sells the controlling interest in a corporation, the fiduciary duty requires that the stock not be transferred to someone who would injure the corporation. Therefore, before selling a controlling interest, the shareholder has the duty to investigate the interested purchaser. If this is not done, or if the interest is sold to someone the shareholder knows or should know will injure the corporation to obtain personal gain, the shareholder may be held personally liable for any damage to the corporation or shareholders.[33]

In addition, a controlling shareholder, officer, or director who purchases controlling stock and sells that stock within a six-month period must disclose and return any profits to the corporation. This prevents the use of inside information, which is not available to other prospective purchasers, for personal gain that may injure the corporation and affect its stability through frequent and major changes in the ownership. The minority shareholders and the public are thus placed on an equal footing with large investors. This promotes investment in business and ultimately the economy through business growth. It would be unfair to allow persons with access to secret information that might affect the value of the stock to avoid losses or obtain a huge advantage in profits, while other shareholders and members of the public who lack access to the information lose or at least do not have the same opportunity to improve their own position. The key to legal stock transactions is disclosure. If major toeholds fully disclose their actions and adhere to the other requirements of the SEC, the corporation, its shareholders, the public, and ultimately the American economy are protected.

g. Corporate Operations   The first board of directors (sometimes with the assistance of the promoter) of a corporation is responsible for seeing that all of the statutory formalities are complied with, including the preparation of the articles of incorporation and bylaws. Generally, the officers of the corporation will be responsible for daily management and administrative decisions, while long-range decisions about the policies of the corporation are made by the board.

Shareholders also have limited input into the operations of the corporation. They usually vote on major changes in the direction of the corporation and elect new board members when a term ends or a vacancy occurs. Shareholders also generally have the right to remove a director with or without reason. Examples of justifications for removal include mismanagement of the corporation or negligent risking of the shareholder's investments.

In smaller corporations, such as close corporations, the officers, board of directors, and shareholders are often all the same people. In large corporations however, many shareholders never even meet the board members or officers. Voting at annual meetings may even be conducted by mail or across the Internet, and the shareholders make decisions on the basis of published annual reports of the progress of the business and other published materials provided by the corporation and through the media.

Shareholders who are dissatisfied with the job a particular director, or directors, is doing may vote against the reelection of the director or vote to remove the director during a term of office. Each state has statutes that indicate when and how this may be accomplished. Each state's statutes also contain provisions that dictate the minimum number of meetings each corporation must have with shareholders annually. Statutes also provide for the type, timing, and method of notice that must be given to each shareholder before a meeting, and the procedure for voting by mail or via other means if a shareholder cannot attend a meeting.

Fixed rules exist with regard to which shareholders are entitled to vote on a corporate matter. Because stocks are continually sold and transferred on the stock market, a corporation's shareholders may change every day. Statutes specify and require the calculation of a record date for a corporation with respect to upcoming meetings and voting. A record date is the date by which one must own stock in a corporation prior to a shareholder's meeting in order to be eligible to vote on corporate changes. The board of directors then includes this time frame, or an even longer one, in the bylaws of the corporation when stating how much notice of a meeting shareholders will be given. Only persons whose names appear as shareholders in corporate records on the record date are entitled to vote at the annual meeting.[34]

If a shareholder cannot attend a meeting or does not vote by mail, the vote may be made by proxy, the written consent of one person to vote on behalf of another. It is also legal for a group of persons to request other shareholders to give their proxies so that votes can be accumulated on a certain issue. With public corporations, this is strictly controlled by the SEC and must follow very specific guidelines. A proxy can be solicited only if the shareholders are given an accurate description of the matter to be voted on and are allowed to vote for or against the issue on appropriate proxy forms. This enables the persons soliciting the proxies to determine in advance how many votes they have secured in favor of a given issue. Statutes require that at least a majority of the issued shares be voted. An amendment to the articles of incorporation may require more than a mere majority. Generally, every share is entitled to at least one vote. However, the articles of incorporation may allow for the issuance of shares without the right to vote such as some preferred sharers.

In a corporation with a very large number of shareholders, persons owning only one or a few shares would not have much influence over decisions, because other persons own a great many shares. Under the method of cumulative voting, each share is entitled to one vote, and when several different issues are to be decided, each shareholder will cast one vote for every share on every issue.

APPLICATION 10.17

Three new directors are to be elected. A person owns one share of stock. That person will have three votes to cast (1 share × 3 issues). If cumulative voting is permitted, the shareholder can apportion the votes in any way he or she chooses. For example, all three votes may be cast in support of one director, and no votes cast on the elections of the other two. This allows shareholders to maximize the value of their vote on issues most important to them. However, when cumulative voting is permitted and employed, a shareholder also gives up voting power on other issues. In the situation described, absent cumulative voting power, the shareholder would be permitted to cast one vote in each of the director's elections.

Point for Discussion: If a shareholder possessed 20 votes and there were three directors to be elected and three proposed amendments to the articles of incorporation, what is the maximum number of votes the shareholder could cast in favor of a particular issue with cumulative voting?

Some states allow what are commonly called voting trusts and pooling agreements. In a voting trust, several shareholders give their proxies to one person, known as the trustee, who votes on the issues. The advantage of a voting trust is that the weight of the shares on a single issue is greater.[35] The disadvantage is that the trustee votes on all issues in the manner most advantageous to an individual.

A pooling agreement is somewhat similar to a voting trust. The goal here is to concentrate the votes on an issue. In a pooling agreement, the members of the pool agree that each will vote the way the majority of the members of the pool indicate. Generally, in a pooling agreement, a vote per share will be cast against each issue, rather than employing cumulative voting. Also, a written contract states who is involved in the agreement and its terms.

Assignment 10.6

> Examine the stock descriptions below and identify which of the following characteristics apply:
>
> | | |
> |---|---|
> | cumulative voting | pooling agreement |
> | cumulative stock | preferred stock |
> | voting stock | preemptive rights |
>
> a. Shareholder A is entitled to dividends for the year paid and may preserve the percentage of ownership in the event of future stock issuances. Shareholder A also belongs to a legally bound group of shareholders with respect to influencing matters before the ownership of the corporation at annual meetings.
> b. Shareholder B is entitled to the return of the par value of her stock in a liquidation if the company has sufficient assets to redeem all stock.
> c. Shareholder C is permitted to have input into issues of election and amendments to the articles of incorporation.
> d. Shareholder D is entitled to vote the total of his shares collectively on one or more issues and is entitled to dividends for years they were not issued in the event a dividend is declared in a subsequent year.
> e. Shareholder E is entitled to redemption of the par value of her stock prior to some other shareholders in the event of a dissolution.

In most states, all shareholders, by virtue of their ownership interests in the corporation incorporated there, are entitled to certain rights with respect to the corporation in addition to those rights associated with their stock. Shareholders ordinarily have the right to inspect the corporate records upon reasonable notice and at a reasonable time.[36] Although shareholders in a large corporation do not ordinarily have input into the daily management and operations of the corporation, they are entitled to observe them to the extent it does not interfere with the business of the corporation. The rationale is that shareholders are better informed about their investment and thus better able to make intelligent decisions when voting on corporate issues or selling their stock. In addition, limited inspection is not seen as unnecessary interference with the business of the corporation. Historically, shareholders were given the right to inspect only if they could show a proper purpose. In response, most states have now enacted statutes that do away with the requirement of proper purpose.

The right to inspect corporate records is subject to limitation. Generally, inspection must be done during a time and subject to conditions set out in the corporate bylaws. This permits shareholders to inspect but also allows the corporation to avoid unreasonable interruptions of its operations. If a state statute permits such inspections and a corporation refuses or through its bylaws makes it virtually impossible to inspect, the corporation and the other officers who refuse inspection may be subject to legal penalties in the event the shareholder sues the corporation. In addition, a shareholder has the alternative of bringing an action against the corporation.

In addition to right of inspection, shareholders have other privileges that are specified in the articles of incorporation for the particular type of stock they own. As stated earlier, these privileges may be liquidation, voting, and dividends. Finally, shareholders have the right to sue persons involved with the corporation when they have mismanaged the corporation.

h. Legal Actions by the Corporation and Shareholders Two types of actions can be brought against persons who have a fiduciary relationship with the corporation. The first is a direct action by the shareholders, generally brought against officers of the corporation. If it becomes apparent that an officer or director has acted in their personal best interest or in the interests of a third party over and above the interest of the corporation in business dealings, the fiduciary duty has been breached. If this breach results in direct injury to the shareholders, such as the loss of their investment, the shareholders may maintain a direct suit against the officer or director. It is only necessary for the shareholders who bring the suit to have been damaged, and not for them to have been shareholders at the time of the alleged wrongful conduct. This is because the ownership may change between the time of the conduct and the time its impact is felt by ownership. If the shareholders are successful in such a suit, they may be awarded damages personally.

The second type of action is known as a derivative action. This can be brought only by persons who were shareholders at the time both of the wrongful conduct and its ultimate impact. Such shareholders act on behalf of the corporation against officers or others who allegedly breached a fiduciary duty to the corporation. The shareholders must establish that the duty was breached and that as a result the business of the corporation was damaged.[37] Any damages awarded in a derivative action are paid directly to the corporation.

i. Corporate Dissolution As stated at the outset of this discussion, the life of a corporation is created by statute. It ends in the same manner. As long as the corporation complies with the statutory requirements, the secretary of state where the business is incorporated will continue to recognize the business as a corporate entity. A corporation may dissolve, however, on grounds that include failure to comply with legal requirements or with the action of shareholders or creditors. It may also dissolve by voluntary assent of the board of directors and, when necessary, of the shareholders. Although each state has specific requirements for dissolution, the following items are generally common to all state statutes.

When a corporation decides to dissolve voluntarily, several things must be accomplished prior to the dissolution. Before a formal voluntary dissolution takes effect, the following are generally required:[38]

1. The shareholders consent to the dissolution.
2. Notice is given to creditors and to interested third parties affected by agency relationships the corporation has with others.
3. All assets are sold.

4. No suits are pending against the corporation.
5. Debts are paid, and the remaining cash is distributed to shareholders.

Although court proceedings are usually not required in a voluntary dissolution, the corporation is usually required by statute to file documents that indicate the intent to dissolve the corporation. With the exception of that required for the sale of assets and payment of debts, the corporation must stop doing business. After all business is completed, articles of liquidation are filed with the secretary of state. If all requirements have been complied with, a certificate of dissolution is issued.[39]

The process of liquidation can take place over a long period of time depending upon the size and nature of the business. The existing legal obligations of the corporation must be satisfied or otherwise resolved. Therefore, if a corporation has pending contracts to perform work or supply goods and services, these contracts are still binding on the corporation and the notice of dissolution does not relieve the corporation of its duties. However, the notice of dissolution does require the cessation of business with respect to accepting or offering any new contracts that are not directly related to the liquidation of assets. During this process, it may be necessary for the corporation to engage in its regular business as part of the liquidation. For example, a retail business may need to continue to sell products to customers as a means of depleting inventory. This would not be considered doing new business as long as the retailer does not bring new inventory in to replace that which was sold. Once the assets have been liquidated to the extent that continuing business would exceed the value of the remaining assets, the liquidation may cease. Once creditors are satisfied, any remaining assets are used to redeem the stock from shareholders at the par value. On the rare occasion that there is a surplus, this too is distributed among the shareholders in a manner consistent with the rights of the various types of stock issued. After all business is completed, articles of liquidation are filed with the secretary of state. If all requirements are complied with, a certification of dissolution is issued by the secretary of state. This formally ends the legal entity and any further obligations. However, the corporation may still be held accountable for actions that arose prior to the certificate of dissolution. Because there are no longer any assets, as a practical matter actions brought would be confined generally to issues for which there had been insurance or actions to pierce the corporate veil.

The involuntary dissolution of a corporation occurs against the wishes of the ownership and/or board of directors. It may come about in one of several ways. Persons who have legal authority to request an involuntary dissolution through the legal system include the attorney general of the state of incorporation, shareholders, and creditors. When a party other than the board of directors proposes dissolution, the grounds and procedures are quite limited and specific, and are prescribed by statute.

The attorney general of the state may bring an action to dissolve a corporation when the corporation fails to appoint a registered agent to accept service of process (delivery of legal documents), when the corporation exceeds or abuses its authority as stated in the articles of incorporation, or when the corporation was created with the intent to accomplish fraud.[40] Frequently, statutes provide that the attorney general must file a complaint in the courts requesting an order of involuntary dissolution. The corporation may then respond to the complaint and an objective court will make a determination as to the validity of the allegations.

Shareholders are entitled to bring an action to dissolve the corporation when the conduct of the directors seriously threatens the shareholder's well-being. This includes such things as fiscal mismanagement, fraud, deadlock on pivotal corporate decisions, wasting corporate assets, and illegal conduct. Generally, the courts will consider the actions of the directors and, in some cases, officers and controlling shareholders to determine whether the conduct is likely to cause irreparable injury to the shareholders. The court can then remove directors or officers, enjoin them from further harmful conduct, or order that the corporation be formally dissolved.

Creditors are the most limited of all in the ability to cause the involuntary dissolution of a corporation. In most cases, statutes require a creditor, and in some cases more than one, to have actual judgments against the corporation that are in danger of recovery if the corporation is permitted to continue. The other option is when there is not yet a judgment, but the corporation admits liability for the debt, and the court makes a determination that continued operations would prevent the corporation from any chance to satisfy the debt.

CASE IN POINT

Manning v. K.P. Adjusters, Inc., 2000 WL 502874
(Ohio App.8thDist. 2000)

Character of Proceeding: Civil appeal from the Court of Common Pleas Case No. CP-CV-357711. Affirmed.

David J. Ingersoll, Esq., Cleveland, for Plaintiff-Appellant.

Michael Westerhaus, Esq., North Royalton, David R. Mayo, Esq., Cleveland, Philip Pavarini, Sr., Kathryn H. Krinek, Strongsville, for Defendants-Appellees.

JOURNAL ENTRY AND OPINION

DYKE, A.J.

Plaintiff Robert Manning appeals from the judgment of the trial court which refused to permit him to attach the corporate assets of K.P. Adjusters, Inc. in order to satisfy a judgment which he obtained against Philip Pavarini. For the reason set forth below, we affirm.

On December 24, 1997, Manning was awarded judgment in the amount of $15,000 against Pavarini in an unrelated matter. On June 19, 1998, Manning filed a complaint for a creditor's bill against K.P. Adjusters, Inc., Pavarini, Katherine Krinek Pavarini, and Credit Acceptance Corp. alleging that Pavarini has a one-third interest in K.P. Adjusters, Inc. ("K.P. Adjusters"), that corporate formalities were not maintained with respect to this corporation, and that it has no separate corporate existence. Manning therefore asked that the trial court permit him to satisfy the judgment obtained against Pavarini with assets from K.P. Adjusters.

The matter proceeded to trial on August 3, 1999. On August 27, 1999, the trial court issued findings of fact and conclusions of law which provided in relevant part as follows:

3. Defendant Philip Pavarini is the Vice President and Secretary of K.P. Adjusters, Inc., and owns five (5) shares of common, voting stock in the corporation.

4. K.P. Adjusters, Inc., is an ongoing concern, with both money owing on account, and money owed to others in the course of its operation.

5. K.P. Adjusters, Inc. does not, in all respects, observe corporate formalities, such as the conduct of formal corporate meetings and the maintenance of a corporate record book.

6. In conducting business for K.P. Adjusters, Inc., Katherine Pavarini holds herself out to the public as an officer of K.P. Adjusters, Inc. and satisfies corporate debt through the use of a corporate checking account in the name of K.P. Adjusters, Inc.

7. Physical stock certificates evidencing the issuance of stock in K.P. Adjusters, Inc. were never prepared.

8. Since the inception of K.P. Adjusters, Inc., no corporate taxes have been paid, with an extension having been obtained each year.

9. For approximately thirteen (13) months pre-ceding trial, Defendant, Philip Pavarini has been paid no salary by K.P. Adjusters, Inc., and is owed approximately $16,000. . . .

* * *

Defendant Philip Pavarini was not subpoenaed for trial and was not called as a witness for the Defense. No testimony was elicited, or evidence introduced, to show that Defendant Philip Pavarini is using corporate assets for personal gain. (Emphasis added).

The trial court therefore denied Manning's request to attach the assets of K.P. Adjusters. Manning now appeals and assigns two errors for our review.

Manning's assignments of error are interrelated and state:

THE TRIAL COURT ERRED IN FAILING TO GRANT PLAINTIFF-APPELLANT'S MOTION FOR SUMMARY JUDGMENT.

THE TRIAL COURT ERRED IN ITS FINDINGS OF FACT AND CONCLUSIONS OF LAW, AND THEREFORE, ERRED IN ITS FINAL JUDGMENT.

Within these assignments of error, Manning asserts that the trial court erred in refusing to permit him to reach the assets of K.P. Adjusters in order to satisfy his judgment against Pavarini.

A corporation is a distinct legal entity, separate and apart from the natural individuals who formed it. Janos v. Murduck (1996), 109 Ohio App.3d 583, 587, citing Ohio Bur. of Workers' Comp. v. Widenmeyer Elec. Co. (1991), 72 Ohio App.3d 100, 105.

However, in Ameritech Ohio v. Pub. Util. Comm. (1999), 86 Ohio St.3d 78, 82 the Supreme Court observed, "Ohio law does recognize that a corporation which is the mere alter ego of an affiliate or is established for the sole purpose of circumventing the law will not be recognized as an independent entity." When a corporation is found to be the alter ego of the shareholders, the corporate forms are disregarded and the shareholder and the corporation are treated as one and the same. Tessler v. Ayer (1995), 108 Ohio App.3d 54–55; Dirksing v. Blue Chip Architectural Products, Inc. (1994), 100 Ohio App.3d 213, 228.

In Belvedere Condominium Unit Owners' Assn. v. R.E. Roark Cos., Inc. (1993), 67 Ohio St.3d 274, 288, the Ohio Supreme Court explained:

The plaintiff must show that the corporation is so dominated by the shareholder that it has no separate mind, will, or existence of its own, and that injury or unjust loss resulted from the shareholder's control of the corporation. . . . The first element is a concise statement of the alter ego doctrine; to succeed a plaintiff must show that the individual and the corporation are fundamentally indistinguishable. The second element is the requirement that the shareholder's control of the corporation proximately caused the plaintiff's injury or loss. Both are fairly obvious, but necessary, preconditions to recovery under the alter ego doctrine.

The Belvedere Court then delineated the elements necessary to pierce the corporate veil as follows:

(1) Control over the corporation by those to be held liable was so complete that the corporation has no separate mind, will, or existence of its own, (2) control over the corporation by those to be held liable was exercised in such a manner as to commit fraud or an illegal act against the person seeking to disregard the corporate entity; and (3) injury or unjust loss resulted to the plaintiff from such control or wrong.

Id. at 289.

In the instant case, Manning asserted that K.P. Adjusters was Pavarini's alter ego and asked the trial court for reverse piercing of the corporate veil in order to use corporate assets to satisfy a judgment which he had obtained against Pavarini. Manning demonstrated that K.P. Adjusters failed to comply with various corporate formalities. Manning failed to demonstrate, however, that Pavarini's control over the corporation was so complete that the corporation has no separate mind, will, or existence of its own, that Pavarini's control over the corporation was exercised in such a manner as to commit fraud or an illegal act against Manning; and that he suffered injury or unjust loss as the result of such control or wrong. We are therefore unable to conclude that the judgment of the trial court was erroneous.

Affirmed.

It is ordered that appellees recover of appellant their costs herein taxed.

Case Review Question: Could the plaintiff have done anything at trial given the facts adduced, to strengthen the case against the corporation?

j. Personal and Close Corporations   There are sub-types of corporations in addition to the most commonly known general corporation, also known as a C-corporation—a designation given by the Internal Revenue Service (IRS). The most common forms of small corporations are the S-corporations, professional corporations, and limited liability companies. Each of these provides some degree of limitation on liability for corporate acts, but each allows the income of the corporation to flow through directly to the owners. With a general corporation, profits are taxed at a corporate rate. Any distribution of profits to the owner shareholders is in the form of dividends. These are then considered income for the purpose of income tax at the federal and state level. The smaller personal corporations only pay tax once as all income of the corporation is considered income of the owners. Depending on the nature of the business, its size, its profitability, the number of owners, and their own personal tax status, the most attractive corporate form may be general or personal.

The more personal and close corporations are totally created and overseen through statutory law just as the general corporation. Specific statutes prescribe the necessary steps to create, maintain, and dissolve such corporations. Historically, the S-corporations were used for small operations of several individuals in virtually any type of legal business who sought to limit the exposure to liability they might have in a partnership. The professional corporation was created for licensed professionals whose business was to provide services rather than ordinary types of commercial business. This corporate form continues to be common among physicians, attorneys, accountants, and other similarly situated professionals. However, the limitation of liability will not protect the professional for his or her own personal malfeasance in the delivery of professional services. The newest corporate form is the limited liability company (LLC). This is rapidly growing in acceptance and has been recognized by statute in a majority of jurisdictions. Typically the professional corporation statutes required all shareholders to be members of a common profession. Under the LLC, individuals who are not members of the profession that is the basis for the business may be owners. For example, a physician may enter into an LLC with an attorney in which the physician provides medical services as the primary business of the corporation, and the attorney is responsible for the management of the business. In this type of company, most often the shareholders are subject to liability only for their own personal conduct. Thus, in this example, the attorney would not ordinarily be held accountable for the medical malpractice of the physician.

D. BANKRUPTCY

Every business venture is not a success. Neither is every personal financial situation. Sometimes the debt-to-profit or income ratio becomes so extreme that the only reasonable alternative is to abandon the current endeavor. Congress created a method for the proper management of such situations that seeks to assist the failing business or individual and to protect, as much as possible, the rights of creditors. Over the years, the bankruptcy laws have been developed to provide a variety of options that give the debtor the opportunity to avoid total liquidation of assets. When that cannot be avoided, a method is in place to provide maximum fairness to all who are involved, including the debtor.

A common misconception is that when bankruptcy is declared, the creditors lose all hope of collection. In reality, the effect of bankruptcy in many respects can be positive. Several different forms of bankruptcy will be discussed in this section. The forms of bankruptcy depend on the nature of the entity or the person seeking relief, and on the type of relief sought. However a few characteristics are common to all forms.

Initially, when a petition is filed by a debtor with the bankruptcy courts for relief, an immediate *stay* is granted. The stay prohibits further attempts at collection and effectively freezes the financial activity of the debtor. To ensure fairness, the debtor is required to list all creditors with the court and provide notice of the filing of the bankruptcy petition to those creditors. By doing so, not only is the debtor protected from further collection attempts, but the creditors are also protected because they are advised of the financial situation of the debtor and have the opportunity to discontinue extending credit.

Generally, following the filing of a bankruptcy petition, a series of hearings are conducted to allow input by the debtor and creditors so the court may make an informed finding regarding whether the bankruptcy petition field is an appropriate form of relief for the debtor and creditors. Ultimately, an order is rendered by the court that details the rights of the debtor and creditors with respect to repayment or discharge of debts.

The two primary forms of bankruptcy are reorganization and liquidation. Reorganization allows an entity or person to be granted protection from collection while a plan for repayment of all debts is developed and implemented. Sometimes the amount and time of payment is different from that originally agreed upon by the debtor and creditor. However, the creditor does receive repayment of either the total debt or an accepted amount. The law also imposes limits as to how long repayment under the plan may take.

Liquidation is the absolute discharge of debt. In this type of bankruptcy, the assets of the debtor (subject to some exceptions) are liquidated or converted to cash. The court prioritizes the debts and begins the process of repayment. Secured debts have the highest priority. Secured debts are those for which there is a written pledge of collateral, such as a car or house. If the amount of liquidated assets is not sufficient to cover the total amount of the debt, the creditors at the bottom of the priority list are discharged. This means that they will never receive payment for the amount owed, and that they must write it off as a bad debt. Just as certain assets cannot be seized and liquidated in a bankruptcy, there are certain debts that cannot ordinarily be discharged. These are listed in the statutes and are only included in the discharged debts in extreme circumstances, and in some cases not at all.

When discussing the different types of bankruptcy, various references are made to the term *chapter*. The term refers to the chapter in the bankruptcy statutes that deals with the particular type of entity or person in bankruptcy or the specific type of relief sought— reorganization or liquidation. For example, Chapter 7 of the federal bankruptcy statutes provides for the liquidation of assets and discharge of debts. Chapter 13 provides for a reorganization plan by the individual, and Chapter 11 provides for a reorganization by most types of corporations and partnerships. Various other chapters provide specific relief to farmers and highly regulated industries such as insurance companies.

When the individual or company wants to avoid bankruptcy and its inevitable effect on their credit standing, creditors may seek to force a bankruptcy, known as involuntary bankruptcy. This occurs when a number of creditors of a single debtor cooperatively and jointly file a petition asking the court to declare a stay and impose bankruptcy. At first the question may arise as to why a creditor would seek bankruptcy by one of its debtors and possibly foreclose the chance of full repayment under what is often a more stringent payment plan than what a court might order? The answer is quite simple: If the debtor shows an established pattern of accumulating debt beyond the value of assets and/or mismanagement of funds, the creditors may want to put a halt to the increasing debt and thereby protect their chances of at least a partial repayment.

Bankruptcy has been a part of American law for well over 100 years. It is more heavily called upon than ever as the economy continues to grow. In response, the laws continue to evolve in an attempt to provide fairness to both creditors and debtors. As a result, bankruptcy is an area of law that is subject to frequent changes and variations.

CASE IN POINT

Kapinos v. Graduate Loan Center, 243 B.R. 271 (2000).

In 1995 and 1996, Kapinos obtained five student loans for the purpose of financing her law school education at Nova Southeastern University in Florida. Kapinos obtained two student loans from Key Bank, which were guaranteed by The Educational Resource Institute ("TERI") and have a current principal balance of $25,269.60; two loans guaranteed by the Pennsylvania Higher Education Assistance Authority ("PHEAA") with a current principal balance of $19,768.10; and one loan from EDUCAP (trading as Concern Education) with a current principal balance of $3,767.14. The Graduate Loan Center is the guarantor and servicer of Kapinos' PHEAA and TERI loans. The total balance of the student loans with interest is approximately $48,000.

Kapinos left law school short of graduation, completing only one and one-half years of study. She is currently employed at BB & T as a customer sales representative, earning $8.00 per hour and working approximately forty hours per week. Kapinos earned a B.A. degree in hotel management, but has been unable to find employment in her educational field. Kapinos is married, but separated, has no dependants, and there is no evidence of any medical or physical conditions that would prevent her from remaining employed.

According to her schedules, Kapinos earns $1,156.78 per month and incurs $2,028 per month in expenses. The bankruptcy court concluded after reviewing her schedules that Kapinos could reduce a portion of her expenses, though the court did not specifically identify which expenses Kapinos could reduce or the sum of the reducible expenses. Kapinos made no effort to repay her loans after leaving law school, and made no request for deferment. Kapinos filed for bankruptcy approximately five months after leaving law school.

The issue presented in this case is governed by 11 U.S.C. § 523, which provides in relevant part that:

(a) A discharge under section 727, 1141, 1228(a), 1228(b), or 1328(b) of this title does not discharge an individual debtor from any debt—

* * *

(8) for an educational benefit overpayment or loan made, insured, or guaranteed by a governmental unit or nonprofit institution, or for an obligation to repay funds received as an educational benefit, scholarship, or stipend,

* * *

(B) unless excepting such debt from discharge under this paragraph will impose an undue hardship on the debtor and the debtor's dependents. . . .

Congress did not define "undue hardship" in the Bankruptcy Code, preferring to leave the construction of that phrase to the courts. One judge in this district has adopted the three-part test for determining "undue hardship" set forth by the Second Circuit in Brunner v. New York State Higher Educ. Servs. Corp., 831 F. 2d 395, 396 (2d Cir. 1987), and this court will follow that analysis. See In re Dillon, 189 B.R. at 384 (adopting Brunner). Under the Brunner test, a debtor seeking to establish a case of "undue hardship" must show:

(1) that the debtor cannot maintain, based on current income and expenses, a minimal standard of living for herself and her dependents if forced to repay the loans; (2) that additional circumstances exist indicating that this state of affairs is likely to persist for a significant portion of the repayment period of the student loans; and (3) that the debtor has made good faith efforts to repay the loans. Brunner, 831 F.2d at 396.

The bankruptcy court applied Brunner and concluded that Kapinos could take reasonable steps to reduce her monthly expenses and that it would not create an undue hardship on Kapinos to repay a portion of the student loan. The court then issued an order providing that Kapinos pay, without interest, part of her loan obligation, over a five-year period, and discharging the rest. Both parties agree that Brunner constitutes the appropriate analysis. The creditors appeal, however, on the ground that the bankruptcy court committed legal error in discharging a portion of Kapinos' burden. Section 523(a)(8), in their view, constitutes an all or nothing proposition: a court must discharge the entire debt if a condition of "undue hardship" would follow from requiring payment of the debt, or require payment of the entire debt if "undue hardship" is not found. The Fourth Circuit has not yet addressed the issue of partial discharge of student loans.

However, the wide majority of courts that have considered the question, including bankruptcy courts, have concluded that § 523(a)(8) permits partial discharge. This court finds the majority view persuasive and holds that § 523(a)(8) authorizes a bankruptcy judge to partially discharge a debtor's student loan obligation.

The language of § 523(a)(8) does not explicitly authorize partial discharge. The courts that have adopted the minority position conclude from the absence of an affirmative statutory authorization that § 523(a)(8) unambiguously precludes partial discharge. See In re Taylor, 223 B.R. at 752; In re Hawkins, 187 B.R. at 301. These courts refer to §§ 523(a)(2), (a)(5), and (a)(7), which authorize partial discharge by inclusion of the phrase "to the extent," and conclude from this that "where Congress has failed to include language in statutes, it is presumed to be intentional where the phrase is used elsewhere in the Code." In re Taylor, 223 B.R. at 753; see 11 U.S.C. §§ 523(a)(2), (a)(5), (a)(7).

This court finds unpersuasive the plain language position set forth in In re Taylor and In re Hawkins. As the Southern District of California noted in In re Brown,

"the phrase 'to the extent' in section 523(a)(2), (a)(5), and (a)(7) serves a different purpose than it would if used to allow partial discharge under section 523(a)(8). . . . Specifically, it separates debts into categories which may or may not be dischargeable. For example, section 523(a)(2) states that money, property, or services are not dischargeable 'to the extent' they are obtained by false pretenses or fraud. . . . The phrase 'to the extent' thus describes the type of debt

dischargeable rather than referring to the amount of debt to be discharged. . . . [T]he intentional omission of the phrase in section 523(a)(8) does not support the interpretation of dischargeability under this section."

In re Brown, 239 B.R. at 211. The weakness of the plain language position is reinforced by the legislative history of § 523. Originally, the Bankruptcy Code included no prohibition on the discharge of student loans. See Thad Collins, Forging Middle Ground: Revision of Student Loan Debts in Bankruptcy As an Impetus to Amend 11 U.S.C. § 523(a)(8), 75 Iowa L.Rev. 733, 740 (1990) ("Because neither the old Bankruptcy Act nor the laws governing the student loan programs expressly prohibited the discharge of loans in bankruptcy, they were presumed to present no impediment to discharge."). Subsequent amendments limited discharge to persons who had a five-year period pass since their loans first came due, and to persons who could show that undue hardship would result if they were forced to repay their student loans. See 11 U.S.C. § 523(a)(8) (Historical and Statutory Notes). In 1990, Congress increased the discharge limitation period in § 523(a)(8) from five to seven years. See id. Finally, Congress amended § 523(a)(8) in 1998 by removing the limitation period altogether, thus permitting discharge only when a person establishes undue hardship. See id.

Congress changed section 523(a)(8) because of an increase in bankruptcy proceedings by former students trying to avoid repaying their student loans. See Report of the Commission on the Bankruptcy Laws of the United States, House Doc. No. 93-137, Pt. I, 93d Cong., 1st Sess. (1973) at 140 n. 14 (recognizing a "rising incidence of consumer bankruptcies of former students motivated primarily to avoid payment of education loan debts."). This pattern of amendment represents an obvious tendency on the part of Congress to tighten the gaps through which students could avoid loan repayment. To use an all-or-nothing approach "has the effect of rendering large debt more likely of discharge, and rewarding irresponsible borrowing, neither of which can be presumed to be part of congressional intent." In re Brown, 239 B.R. at 211. The fact that § 523(a)(8) does not, on its face, provide for partial discharge does not render the court powerless to interpret § 523 in a manner which comports with the over-riding intent of Congress. See United States v. Ron Pair Enter., Inc., 489 U.S. 235, 242, 109 S.Ct. 1026, 103 L.Ed.2d 290 (1989) (noting that when a "literal application of a statute will produce a result demonstrably at odds with the intentions of its drafters, . . . [then] [i]n such cases, the intention of the drafters, rather than the strict language, controls.").

A majority of courts have held that bankruptcy courts are empowered to partially discharge a debtor's student loan by virtue of 11 U.S.C. § 105. See, e.g., In re Hornsby, 144 F.3d at 440. Section 105 provides that:

(a) The court may issue any order, process, or judgment that is necessary or appropriate to carry out the provisions of this title. No provision of this title providing for the raising of an issue by a party in interest shall be construed to preclude the court from, sua sponte, taking any action or making any determination necessary or appropriate to enforce or implement court orders or rules, or to prevent an abuse of process.

11 U.S.C. § 105(a). This "statutory directive [is] consistent with the traditional understanding that bankruptcy courts, as courts of equity, have broad authority to modify creditor-debtor relationships." United States v. Energy Resources Co., 495 U.S. 545, 549, 110 S.Ct. 2139, 109 L.Ed.2d 580 (1990). Section 105(a) essentially allows a bankruptcy court to tailor an equitable solution around the facts of a particular case. The precise scope of a bankruptcy court's equitable power "is as yet undefined," In re Hornsby, 144 F.3d at 439, and is limited where there are clear statutory directives that speak to the court's power. As indicated above, this court finds no statutory directive that prohibits the bankruptcy court from ordering partial repayment of student loans. In addition, this court can identify no policy rationale for ignoring the flexibility of § 105 and requiring an all-or-nothing approach to § 523(a)(8). Such a rule would operate to either relieve a debtor from any obligation to repay a loan, though the debtor is capable of making some repayment, or force a debtor to repay the entirety of a loan and therefore fail to satisfy the Bankruptcy Code's objective of relieving "the honest debtor from the weight of oppressive indebtedness and permit[ting] him to start afresh." Local Loan Co. v. Hunt, 292 U.S. 234, 244, 54 S.Ct. The court recognizes the breadth and diversity of remedies available to a bankruptcy court under § 105 to ensure that the dual policies of § 523(a)(8)—ensuring the solvency of student loan programs while providing relief to debtors, in appropriate cases, from oppressive financial circumstances—are accomplished. The court therefore concludes that § 523(a)(8), understood in combination with § 105, authorizes partial discharge of student loans. If the bankruptcy court finds that the Brunner standard has been met, it may, in exercise of its equitable power, discharge all of Kapinos' loans or only a portion of them. Likewise, the bankruptcy court may exercise its equitable power under § 105 to discharge a portion of Kapinos' student loans even if it finds that the Brunner standard has not been satisfied.

Applying Brunner, the bankruptcy court found, first, that Kapinos' expenses currently outweigh her monthly income but that it was possible that she could reduce a portion of her monthly expenses. The court did not, however, specify which expenses Kapinos could reduce or the total monthly sum of these reductions. Second, the bankruptcy court found that Kapinos' financial condition was likely to continue in the future, noting that Kapinos is precluded from her failure to complete law school from taking any bar exam, and that she has been unable to procure employment in the field of hotel management, where she received her undergraduate degree. The bankruptcy court did not address the "good faith" prong of Brunner, other than to note that Kapinos has made no attempts to repay that loan and has made no requests for deferments.

The bankruptcy court's findings of fact were insufficient to determine whether the first or third prongs of Brunner—inability to maintain a minimal standard of living and good faith—have been met. This court therefore remands the matter to the bankruptcy court for additional findings of fact. On remand, the bankruptcy court should identify the particular monthly expenses that Kapinos could reduce and the total amount of reducible expenses, and determine whether Kapinos has satisfied the "good faith" standard of Brunner. After making these determinations, the court should exercise its authority under §§ 105 and 523(a)(8) as indicated above.

For the reasons stated above, the case is remanded to the U.S. Bankruptcy Court for proceedings consistent with this opinion.

Case Review Question: Given the facts in the opinion, is it likely that the test of *Brunner* can be met even on reconsideration by the court?

PARALEGALS IN THE WORKPLACE

One of the largest areas of employment for paralegals in terms of volume is, surprisingly, not in private law firms. Rather, it is within a variety of business settings. Many large corporations have one or more legal departments in their various offices throughout the country and even the world. Corporations were one of the first to identify the value of paralegals and many have replaced what were traditionally positions reserved only for attorneys with qualified paralegals. Other types of businesses that are known to heavily utilize paralegals are investment firms, banks, and title companies. Virtually any entity that deals with a regular stream of legal documents and legal proceedings as part of the course of business, or businesses for which compliance with statutes and regulatory law is important can be fertile ground for paralegal employment. Paralegals can be used to draft or review documents, retrieve information from governmental sources, and communicate information about these. As long as anything that results in advocacy or giving of legal advice is performed by an attorney, all other work can be done by attorney-supervised paralegals. Therefore, paralegals with a background and/or interest in business have a promising future in terms of career opportunities in corporate America.

CHAPTER SUMMARY

Even though business entities have existed for as long as people have interacted on an economic basis, the development of legal standards has advanced rapidly in the past 100 years. There has been tremendous refinement of accepted policies for sole proprietorships and partnerships, in terms of the rights and liabilities of the partners, the ownership of property, taxation, and the transfer of assets. In addition, a fictional person was created by the legislatures to encompass many of these principles and to support new ones as the nature of business as a whole began to evolve from small and limited operations to multi-billion dollar interstate and even intercontinental operations. As a practical matter, the corporation was necessary to organize the growing business in a manner that required fair treatment of and by the company as it dealt with large numbers of owners as well as those with whom it did business.

Common to all forms of business is the legal concept of agency. More often present in partnerships and corporations, all those acting on behalf of the business in any capacity are bound by the laws of agency, as is the business organization that is represented. The principal business has a fiduciary relationship to the agent and that duty is mutual on the part of the agent. This requires loyalty and avoidance of self-dealing. Depending upon whether the agency is created by actual authority, apparent authority, or authority by ratification, the duties toward third parties may change in terms of the commencement and termination of the agent's authority and the rights of the third party with respect to the principal. However, when properly authorized, an agent has the power to act on behalf of the principal and enter legally binding agreements with third parties.

Finally, even though businesses are typically entered into with high expectations of a profitable future, in some instances unforeseen circumstances cause the financial status of a business and even individuals to reach a point of irreversible debt. At this stage, the protection of the bankruptcy laws may be employed to either suspend creditor's demands while an appropriate plan for repayment is devised or, in the extreme case, discharge the debts of creditors allowing the individual or business permanent relief from repayment of the debts incurred. Because the effects on future credit are so detrimental for business and individuals, bankruptcy protection is generally seen as a last resort.

ETHICAL NOTE

While matters of business may seem less personal than other areas of law, such as probate and domestic relations, it should be kept in mind that the ethical standards remain the same. Additionally, adherence to strong ethical principles increases the quality of business as a whole and serves to protect those who are affected personally but are perhaps unable to have a direct influence on the business, such as shareholders in a publicly held corporation. It was the lack of ethical standards in large part that prompted the creation of the SEC more than 60 years ago in an attempt to protect those very shareholders from future abuses. Any legal professional involved in business dealings either as the result of the client relationship or on behalf of a client with third parties should remain vigilant at all times with respect to the ethical obligations associated with the legal work performed.

Revelant Internet Sites

LawTalk—Business Law and Personal Finance	www.law.indiana.edu/law/bizlaw.html
American Bankruptcy Institute	www.abiworld.org
Bankruptcy in Brief	www.bankruptcy-expert.com
Bankruptcy Laws Resource Center	www.bankruptcyresource.com
Small Business Administration-Getting Out of Business	www.sba.gov/regions/states/wa/seattle/selegalintro.html

Internet Assignment 10.1

Create a business name and conduct an Internet search to determine if it is a registered name in your state or if it is available for use in a new corporation.

KEY TERMS

Agency	Corporation	Promoter
Articles of Incorporation	Limited Partnership	
Bylaws	Partnership	

ENDNOTES

1. 3 Am.Jur.2d, Agency, Sections 9–16.
2. Id.
3. *Sim v. Edenborn*, 242 U.S. 131 (1916).
4. See note 2, Section 222–224.
5. Id., Section 218.
6. *Consolidated Oil & Gas, Inc. v. Roberts*, 162 Colo. 149, 425 P.2d 282 (1989).
7. *Lauderdale v. Peace Baptist Church*, 246 Ala. 178, 19 So.2d 538 (1944).
8. See note 6 supra, Section 73.

9. *McGirr v. Gulf Oil Corp.*, 41 Cal.App.3d 246 (1991).

10. *Elliott v. Mutual Life Insurance Co.*, 185 Okl. 289, 91 P.2d 746 (1939).

11. See note 6 supra, Section 77.

12. *Bronson's Ex-r v. Chappell*, 79 U.S. (12 Wall.) 681, 20 L.Ed. 436 (1871).

13. *Cavic v. Grand Bahama Dev. Co.* 701 F2d. 8879 (11th Cir. 1983).

14. Id.

15. *Pfliger v. Peavey Co.* 310 N.W.2d 742 (N.D. 1981).

16. *Shafer v. Bull*, 233 Md.68, 194 A.2d 788 (1963).

17. See note 6, supra. Section 185.

18. Id., Section 280.

19. Id.

20. 18 Am. Jur. 2d, Corporations, Section 104.

21. Id.

22. *Lamkin v. Baldwin & Lamkin Mfg. Co.* 72 Conn. 57, 43 A. 593 (1899).

23. 18 Am. Jur. 2d, Corporations 2804.

24. Id., Section 45, 51.

25. Id., Section 49.

26. Id., Section 55, 61.

27. *Jefferson v. Holder*, 195 Ga. 346, 24 S.E.2d 198 (1943).

28. *Lettinga v. Agristor Credit Corp.*, 686 F.23d 442 (6th Cir. 1982).

29. *Fitzpatrick v. Rutter*, 160 Ill. 282, 43 N.E. 292 (1896).

30. *Guthrie v. Harkness*, 199 U.S. 148 (1905).

31. Id.

32. Id.

33. Id.

34. Id.

35. Id.

36. See note 28, Supra Section 94–98.

37. Id.

38. Id.

39. Id.

40. Id.

Chapter 11

THE LAW OF PROBATE AND ESTATES

CHAPTER OBJECTIVES

Upon completion of this chapter you should be able to do the following:

- Explain the purpose of estate law and the function of probate courts.

- Distinguish between testate and intestate estates.

- Describe the process of probating an estate.

- Discuss various methods of intestate distribution of assets.

- Discuss the requirements of a valid will.

- Explain the concept of a will contest.

A. WHAT IS PROBATE AND ESTATE LAW?

Probate
Process of paying creditors and distributing the estate of one who is deceased. Probate courts also often administer the estates of living persons who are incapable of managing their own affairs.

Guardianship
Legally appointed individual to manage the estate of one who has been declared legally incompetent.

An area of law that affects perhaps as many or more lives than any other is that of **probate** and estates. Many people, but not all, are at some point involved in the law of domestic relations, property, and business, as well as other subject areas. In today's society, very few citizens die with no assets, no debt, and no legal heirs. Even one who dies without debt incurs costs for burial or cremation unless they donate their body to science, and rarely does someone die without a final medical expense, even if it is confined to ambulance transportation of the body. Anyone who is an heir or who wishes to dictate how their estate will be handled after their death will be affected by the law of probate. This area of law affects every facet of society. In addition to those who stand to inherit, nearly every person or entity with whom the deceased was in some form of financial contact prior to death is affected. A popular misconception is that, when someone dies, the person's possessions are immediately divided up among the surviving family. In reality, the legal process is much more complicated. Similarly, anyone involved in some way with **guardianship** of a minor in need of supervision or an incapacitated adult will likely encounter the probate division of the courts as well. When an adult is unable to manage his or her own affairs because of severely limited mental capacity, there is a need to take proper legal steps to appoint someone to manage the disabled individual's affairs. The following discussion addresses such topics as the distribution of an estate when there is no will and when there is a valid will. The probate process is also explained. Although probate administration of estates is governed by state law, many of the procedures are similar in most states. This discussion is limited to those general procedures observed in most jurisdictions.

B. THE FUNCTION OF THE PROBATE COURTS

The probate division of the legal system is assigned the task of administrating the estates of those who are deceased, and those who are under legal guardianship. In either instance, the party can no longer be responsible for their own legal issues and, as a result, the probate courts oversee these matters. The probate courts follow specific rules of procedure and well-established substantive law with respect to the processing of these cases. Unlike the typical civil litigation, a case in the probate court may or may not have adversarial parties represented by attorneys. Indeed, a case may be handled entirely by a single attorney, or there may be a large number of attorneys making appearances in the case.

In processing the estate of someone who is deceased, typically there is an attorney for the estate. Any parties who wish to contest the manner in which the estate is considered and depleted also may be represented by counsel. This might include potential heirs, creditors, or persons who wish to contest the validity of a will or the jurisdiction of the court to process the estate. In short, anyone who stands to be affected by the final accounting and distribution of the estate, may elect to have an attorney enter an appearance in the case to protect their interests.

APPLICATION 11.1

Candy McIntosh was 34 years old when she was struck by a bus and killed instantly. At the time of her unexpected death, she had a large number of creditors, a home, a vehicle, and several bank accounts in addition to her personal possessions. She had one son from a previous relationship and a spouse from whom she was separated, but not divorced. In the probate of Candy's estate, a question arose as to whether some of the alleged creditors were valid debt holders of Candy at the time of her death. Her parents and siblings are concerned that Candy's estate will be entirely depleted by creditors and that nothing will be left for the care and support of her five-year-old son. The identity of the father of Candy's son is completely unknown. Attorneys who filed appearances in the case included an attorney representing the interests of Candy's son, an attorney for Candy's estate, an attorney for her husband and attorneys for several of the creditors. A separate case is brought to establish legal guardianship for her son.

Point for Discussion: Why would there need to be different attorneys for Candy's son and for the estate?

The probate courts are also responsible for acting in a supervisory role for incapacitated adults and minors without parents who have full parental rights and responsibilities. At first, one might think of this as being confined primarily to orphans and persons in a physical condition so severe as to constitute a vegetative state. In fact, this makes up only a very small percentage of the persons for whom the probate court appoints and oversees guardianships. Countless situations occur in the present day society that render an individual legally or physical unable to make his or her own legally binding decisions in a manner consistent with the individual's best interest. In many such cases, the courts will assume a supervisory role for the individual through the guardianship (conservator) process. Although some jurisdictions use different terminology, the fundamental concept of helping those not in a position to help themselves remains the same.

In the case of minors, quite often the courts will intervene on a temporary or permanent basis to protect the interests of minors. Obviously, when someone is orphaned while still a minor, the courts are obliged to step in until such time as an adoption, the age of majority, or legal emancipation occurs. The same situation arises when the parental rights over a minor are superseded by the courts, either temporarily or permanently. This most often occurs when a child is removed from the home by a government agency for reasons such as abuse or neglect. In any event, when the government intervenes on behalf of a minor, it may supersede the rights of the parent or parents and assume responsibility for making decisions in the best interest of the minor child.

In the case of incapacitated adults, guardianship may occur in a wide variety of situations. An example is when a mentally disabled youth reaches the age of majority. If the young person is not declared legally incompetent and then proceeds to enter into legally binding agreements or situations, the young person may be considered liable for the terms of the agreement.

APPLICATION 11.2

Cindy is a moderately retarded 20-year-old woman. She lives in a group home and is employed at a workshop for the mentally challenged. She is unable to live independently or work in a routine job setting. Cindy's parents did not seek to have a guardianship established for her when she reached the age of majority (18 in the state where she lives). Cindy recently signed an agreement to join a video club wherein she received 20 videos of her choice in exchange for agreeing to buy 20 additional videos over the next three years at a cost of $20.00 per video plus $5.00 shipping and handling. Cindy received the free videos and passed them out on the city bus that she rides to work each day. Her parents wrote to the company, but the company refuses to disregard the agreement. They threaten collection action if the terms of the contract are not honored by Cindy.

Point for Discussion: How would the situation differ if Cindy was 14 years old?

An adult might also require assistance from the courts if he or she is temporarily or permanently incapacitated due to illness or injury and did not have adequate documents in place at the time it occurred to give someone else authority in the event of incapacitation.

When the court is presented with a minor or an adult in need of legal supervision due to a physical and/or mental condition, a petition is filed and the court establishes a form of guardianship for the individual. The terms and extent of this guardianship depend largely on the circumstances of the incapacitated individual. The court appoints a person or entity, such as a bank, to act on behalf of the incapacitated person. Additionally, if there is any dispute about who the guardian should be, or about the terms of the guardianship, an attorney may be appointed as a guardian ad litem. The guardian ad litem is supposed to be objective to the dispute and review the circumstances in terms of the best interest of the individual at issue. The guardian ad litem then makes recommendations to the court on what he or she considers to be in the best interest of the disabled person. Issues may involve everything from physical custody and living arrangements to health care alternatives and managing the assets of the one who is incapacitated.

Once a guardianship has been established, the guardian is required to periodically report to the courts with respect to the guardianship and the status of the incapacitated person. The frequency of reports often depends on the age and condition of the individual and the size of the estate, if any, that is being overseen. In some instances, the disability may resolve or, in the case of a minor returned to the full care and custody of the parents, the guardianship is discontinued. In other circumstances, the guardianship may continue under the court's supervision for the remainder of the disabled person's natural life.

C. THE ESTATES OF DECEASED INDIVIDUALS

When an individual dies, it is rarely without legal impact. Especially in the case of adults, there are almost always possessions and other assets, legal relationships, debts, and creditors that must be resolved. The estate, which is made up of the entirety of the assets of the deceased, is subject to claims of inheritance and creditors. A primary function of the probate courts is to settle and distribute the estates of those who have died. Estates are processed in one of two ways, testate or intestate.

1. Intestate Succession

When someone dies **intestate,** it means that the person died without leaving a known valid will. Often persons with substantial assets do not make provisions for the distribution of those assets after death. The obvious disadvantage of not leaving a valid will is that distribution by the state may not be at all what the deceased would have wished. Nevertheless, it is such a frequent occurrence that the states have designed various standards to distribute the assets of an intestate deceased person. The manner in which this is done is called intestate succession. Literally, this means that the state decides who will succeed to the assets of a person who dies without a valid will.

One method that is now seldom applied in laws on the distribution of estates, but which was once the most common, is called per capita distribution. It is discussed here for purposes of background and comparison. Per capita is a rather simple method. The initial task is to identify all living relatives of the deceased. The assets of the deceased that remain after probate of the estate are divided equally among the number of survivors.[1] For example, assume that there are 14 known living blood relatives of a deceased individual ranging from siblings to fourth cousins. Under per capita distribution, no regard would be given to the proximity of the relationships. The estate would be divided into 14 shares with a fourth cousin receiving the same amount as a brother.

The second method, and the one generally employed under state statute, is known as **per stirpes** distribution. Under this method, as with per capita, all surviving relatives are identified. However, entitlement to receive any of the estate whatsoever and the percentage received depends upon the proximity of the relationship.[2] For example, if children and cousins of the deceased are living, but no spouse survives, under a per stirpes statute the children would be entitled to the entire estate, irrespective of the fact that there may be other collateral (rather than descendant) relatives still living. The per stirpes method is the favored rule because it is equitable in nature. In a per stirpes jurisdiction, all members of a specific degree of relationship inherit or do not inherit equally, for example all grandchildren entitled to inherit, would inherit the same amount. However, the closer the blood connection of the relative to the deceased, the larger the percentage of inheritance he or she is likely to be assigned. See Figure 11.1.

Each state that uses the per stirpes method has particular methods for determining exactly how the estate will be distributed. The common thread is that whether a person inherits depends upon the person's relationship to the deceased and how many other persons have the same relationship. Generally, the estate is distributed to descendants. If there are none, it is distributed to ascendants, such as parents, and across to siblings (brothers and sisters) and then to the descendants of the siblings. If there are no living relatives at these levels, it proceeds to ascendants such as aunts and uncles and their descendants, that is, cousins. Depending on the limit set by the state statute, this may continue on for several degrees of family relation. Following are some of the more common rules among the states that are employed based on the survivors. The entire estate goes to the first level heirs of spouse and/or descendants. In the event this combination does not exist among the heirs, then the second level is applied and so on

Intestate
Method of distributing the estate of one who died without a valid will.

Per Stirpes
Distribution in equal shares to one level or class of persons; if a member of this level or class is deceased, the member's heirs divide the share.

FIGURE 11.1   Sample Intestate Statute

Wisconsin Statutes Annotated Chapter 852—Intestate Succession

852.01. Basic rules for intestate succession

(1) Who are heirs. The net estate of a decedent which he has not disposed of by will, whether he dies without a will, or with a will which does not completely dispose of his estate, passes to his surviving heirs as follows:

(a) To the spouse:

  1. If there are no surviving issue of the decedent, or if the surviving issue are all issue of the surviving spouse and the decedent, the entire estate.
  2. If there are surviving issue one or more of whom are not issue of the surviving spouse, one-half of that portion of the decedent's net estate not disposed of by will consisting of decedent's property other than marital property and other than property described under 861.02(1).

(b) To the issue, the share of the estate not passing to the spouse under part (a), or the entire estate if there is no surviving spouse; if the issue are all in the same degree of kinship to the decedent they take equally, but if they are of unequal degree then those of more remote degrees take by representation.

(c) If there is no surviving spouse or issue, to the parents.

(d) If there is no surviving spouse, issue or parent, to the brothers and sisters and the issue of any deceased brother or sister by representation.

(e) If there is no surviving spouse, issue, parent or brother or sister, to the issue of brothers and sisters; if such issue are all in the same degree of kinship to the decedent they take equally, but if they are of unequal degree then those of more remote degrees take by representation.

(f) If there is no surviving spouse, issue, parent or issue of a parent, to the grandparents.

(g) If there is no surviving spouse, issue, parent, issue of a parent, or grandparent, to the intestate's next of kin in equal degree.

(2) Requirement that heir survive decedent for a certain time. If any person who would otherwise be an heir under sub. (1) dies within 72 hours of the time of death of the decedent, the net estate not disposed of by will passes under this section as if that person had predeceased the decedent. If the time of death of the decedent or of the person who would otherwise be an heir, or the times of death of both, cannot be determined, and it cannot be established that the person who would otherwise be an heir has survived the decedent by at least 72 hours, it is presumed that the person died within 72 hours of the decedent's death. In computing time for purposes of this subsection, local standard time at the place of death of the decedent is used.

(2m) Requirement that heir not have intentionally killed the deceased. (a) If any person who would otherwise be an heir under sub. (1) has unlawfully and intentionally killed the decedent, the net estate not disposed of by will passes as if the killer had predeceased the decedent.

(b) A final judgment of conviction of unlawful and intentional killing is conclusive for purposes of this subsection.

(bg) A final adjudication of delinquency on the basis of unlawfully and intentionally killing the decedent is conclusive for purposes of this subsection.

(br) In the absence of a conviction under par. (b) or an adjudication under par. (bg), the court, on the basis of clear and convincing evidence, may determine whether the killing was unlawful and intentional for purposes of this subsection.

(c) This subsection does not affect the rights of any person who, before rights under this subsection have been adjudicated, purchases for value and without notice from the killer property that the killer would have acquired except for this subsection; but the killer is liable for the amount of the proceeds. No insurance company, bank or other obligor paying according to the terms of its policy or obligation is liable because of this subsection unless before payment it has received at its home office or principal address written notice of a claim under this subsection.

(3) Escheat. If there are no heirs of the decedent under subs. (1) and (2), the net estate escheats to the state to be added to the capital of the school fund.

Assignment 11.1

> a. Identify all living relatives of your own estate reaching as far as first cousins (children of aunts/uncles). Specify if any siblings are half-blood relationships (share only one parent by blood).
> b. Based on the statute in Figure 11.1 identify how your own estate would proceed by intestate succession.

reaching more and more remote degrees of proximity of relationship until the statutory limit of relationship is reached.

1. A surviving spouse and children all born to the surviving spouse and deceased: The spouse receives a lump sum of money and an additional percentage of the estate. The children receive the entire remaining percentage to be distributed equally.
2. A surviving spouse and children, some or all of whom are not the children of the surviving spouse: Spouse and children receive one half of the estate each. If there is more than one child, the one half will be divided equally among the number of children.
3. A surviving spouse, no children, surviving parents and/or siblings or children of siblings: Surviving spouse is entitled to a lump sum of cash and one half of the remaining estate. Parents and siblings each take an equal share of the remaining one half of the estate. If a sibling is deceased but leaves children, the children each take an equal share of what would have been the sibling's share.
4. Surviving parents, siblings, and children of siblings: The entire estate would be distributed on the same basis as indicated in 3.

As shown, under per stirpes, the shares are divided based on categories of living relatives. Thus, if siblings are alive, the shares are divided among the number of living siblings, and the siblings' children are entitled only to split a deceased siblings share. This is different from per capita, which gives no attention to the level of the relationship but rather distributes according to the number of relations.

The per stirpes method does not search out relatives to an infinite degree to receive the estate. Rather, most states have a maximum level of relationship, such as a fifth cousin, who can inherit the estate.[3] If there are no sufficiently close relatives left surviving, the estate of the deceased goes into what is called escheat, a process by which the assets are taken over by the state. When this occurs, the state receives ownership of the assets of the estate to do with as it chooses. All personal claims of individuals are disregarded, and it is as if the state were the sole heir. In today's society, with the extended family rapidly disappearing and individuals moving and living around the country and the world, escheat is no longer an extreme or rare occurrence. The only notice of an estate seeking to locate heirs may be in a legal newspaper or the legal section of the classifieds in the local paper where the decedent resided. Relatives who stand to inherit but are not in contact with the decedent prior to death, and do not monitor these publications may easily lose their rights of inheritance by failing to step forward while the case is in the process of probate. With no will to identify intended beneficiaries, the courts have no obligation to take further measures to locate potential heirs. Consequently, it is obvious that these windfalls to the state through escheat stand to increase with regard to intestate estates.

What of persons who have a partial blood relationship or relationship created by law to the deceased? As previously indicated, a spouse is considered to be a blood relative for purposes of inheritance, even though the relationship is a legal one. But what is the status of adopted children? The relationship is recognized by law. Generally, when a parent adopts a child, for all purposes of intestate succession, the child is treated as a natural child of the parent.[4] The states are divided on the status of any remaining testamentary relationship between the adopted child and the biological parent to inherit from the intestate adopted child in the event the parent survives the child. Any permitted inheritance in such a situation would, of course, require knowledge of the identity of the parties involved.

Siblings of half-blood relationships share only one parent with the deceased. In most states, a half-blood sibling is entitled to inherit by intestate succession at least

APPLICATION 11.3

Richard Smith was born and raised in State X. Both parents and two siblings are still living in his hometown. Many years ago, Richard moved to State Y. Other than infrequent visits home every few years, he has virtually no contact with his family. It is not unusual for a year to pass without speaking or writing to family members. He returns from one such visit on December 30. On New Year's Eve, Richard is killed in a car accident. He has significant assets in the form of an art collection that is valued in excess of $250,000. There is also a $100,000 mortgage on his condominium valued at $300,000, as well as various other smaller assets and debts. Creditors file a petition to probate Richard's estate in order to collect their debts. Richard never spoke much of his family to friends, and they assume that the court will notify any living family. After the steps of probate are completed, including notices in the newspaper, and assets are liquidated, no one steps forward to claim as an heir. Approximately nine months after his death, Richard's estate of cash in the amount of $450,000 escheats to the state. Approximately 1-1/2 years after his death, Richard's brother attempts to contact him and learns of his death. Under the law of the state of Richard's domicile, state Y, the family has lost any rights to claim as heirs to the estate.

Point for Discussion: What could Richard have done to avoid the state receiving his entire estate other than execute a will?

some portion of the estate.[5] But, unlike the per stirpes rule of equal inheritance for equal degrees of relationship, some states do not recognize the half-blood sibling as a true full sibling and, as a result, reduce the percentage of inheritance from what a full blood brother or sister would receive. Other states do not distinguish between half and full-blood siblings.[6]

If a child is born out of wedlock and subsequently makes a claim of inheritance against the father's estate, it has traditionally been required that some formal acknowledgment of the child be made during the father's lifetime.[7] This can be demonstrated by a legal finding of paternity in a court or by action of the father that would indicate the father believed and accepted the child to be his. However, with the advancement of scientific technology and posthumous DNA matching, soon proving paternity as evidence to claim inheritance will be possible after the death of the father.

Another consideration is the posthumous heir. This is a child born after the death of the parent. Most states have a specific statutory time limit on such cases. For example, many states require that a child be born within 10 months of the death of the father in order to make a claim for paternity.[8] However, increasing technology may cause changes in this rule, although the situation presents more complications. No longer is it unheard of for frozen sperm or embryos to be used to produce children of a man who is deceased. This may take place months or even years after the death of the individual. A case that received much notoriety in the 1990s did hold that the artificially conceived posthumous child could not receive social security survivor's benefits. But what of rights of inheritance? An obvious problem is that the greater the time between the death of the father and the birth of the child, the more difficult it could become to process an estate in a timely manner. Consequently, even if the rule on posthumous heirs changes, it is unlikely that the time limit for claims will be significantly changed or abandoned.

CASE IN POINT

Estate of O'Handlen, 213 Ill.App.3d 160,
571 N.E.2d 482, 156 Ill.Dec. 698 (1991).

Justice *SLATER* delivered the opinion of the court:

Craton O'Handlen was married twice, to Matte Karr and to Lena Brewer. Offspring were produced from both unions. Esther O'Handlen, a grandchild of Craton and Lena, died intestate and it is the distribution of her estate which is in question. The descendants of Craton and Matte, who are related by half blood to the decedent, object to the distribution of the intestate estate. They contend that the trial court erred by creating two moieties for distribution of the estate, one for descendants of the Craton/Matte union and one for the descendants of the the Craton/Lena union. We affirm. The record shows that Esther O'Handlen died intestate in 1988. She left no surviving spouse, descendant, parent, brother, sister, or descendant of a brother or sister. Her only living relatives were the descendants of her paternal and maternal grandparents. The parties to this case are the only heirs of the paternal grandparents and at issue is the distribution of the paternal half of the estate. The relationship between the parties to this appeal is as follows:

Craton/Matte Karr*	Craton/Lena Brewer*
(First Marriage)	(Second Marriage)

Otto O'Handlen*   Nina Bradford* John O'Handlen* Metta
                  O'Handlen Richert

Crayton O'Handlen* Corinne   John Bradford* Esther O'Handlen
     O'Handlen Frazier   (Decedent)

Corrine O'Handlen Soderberg Thomas   Deeann Bradford
     O'Handlen   Krieg

The decedent's property was to be distributed under the Probate Act of 1975 (Ill.Rev.Stat.1989, ch. 110 1/2, par. 1-1 *et seq.*) which states as follows:

"If there is no surviving spouse, descendant, parent, brother, sister or descendant of a brother or sister of the decedent but a grandparent or descendant of a grandparent of the decedent: . . . 1/2 of the entire estate [goes] to the decedent's paternal grandparents in equal parts or to the survivor of them, or if there is none surviving, to their descendants *per stirpes.*

* * * * * *

In no case is there any distinction between the kindred of the whole and the half blood." Ill.Rev.Stat.1989, ch. 110 1/2, par. 2-1(e), (h).

In the trial court, Metta moved for distribution of the property passing to the heirs of the paternal grandparents. She contended that the property should be divided into two moieties. One moiety was to pass completely to her through the paternal grandmother, and the second was to pass through the paternal grandfather to then be divided among herself and the other heirs *per stirpes.* She concluded that the heirs should receive the following fractions of the total estate: 1/3 to Metta; 1/12 to Deeann Krieg; 1/24 to Corinne Frazier; 1/48 to Corinne Soderberg; and 1/48 to Thomas O'Handlen. The appellants objected, contending that the proposed distribution improperly drew a distinction between kindred of the whole blood and kindred of the half blood. They also argued that the statute only required that the property be divided into two moieties if both paternal grandparents had survived the intestate. In the appellants' view, all of the children of the paternal grandfather were entitled to equal shares. They therefore concluded that the heirs should receive the following fractions of the total estate: 1/6 to Metta; 1/6 to Deeann Krieg; 1/12 to Corinne Frazier; 1/24 to Corinne Soderberg; and 1/24 to Thomas O'Handlen.

The trial judge granted Metta's motion and divided the estate as she suggested. On appeal, the appellants argue that the court erred.

We agree with the trial court's decision. In Illinois, the right to inherit property is controlled by statute. (*Eckland v. Jankowski (1950), 407 Ill. 263, 95 N.E.2d 342.*) Here, the statute provides that if the paternal grandparents do not survive the decedent, the property should pass *per stirpes* to their descendants. Since Metta was related to both paternal grandparents, she should inherit through each of them. Such a distribution does not violate the prohibition against favoring kindred of the whole blood over those of the half blood. That prohibition was not meant to create a new class of heirs, but only to prohibit discrimination within a class. (*In re Estate of Paus (1944), 324 Ill.App. 58, 57 N.E.2d 212.*) Since the appellants belong only to the class of those inheriting through the grandfather and they have received the proper share for those in that class, their rights have not been violated. The judgment of the circuit court of Peoria County is affirmed.

Affirmed.

BARRY and GORMAN, JJ., concur.
Ill.App. 3 Dist.,1991.

Another matter than can affect both intestate and testate (distribution by will) succession arises when the deceased is murdered. Anyone who is found by the probate court (a civil as opposed to criminal court) to be responsible for the death of the decedent as the result of foul play generally cannot inherit.[9] Many states do not even require a criminal prosecution and conviction. Rather, it need only be established in probate court that the person was criminally charged with and prosecuted for the murder. At this point, the probate court makes its own findings with respect to responsibility for the death. Even if one suspected or charged with homicide is not ultimately convicted of criminal charges, a civil (not probate) court may on its own hearing find one liable for the death of the decedent. Most states have procedures for a formal hearing in the probate court to determine whether, by probate standards, a murder occurred if the one alleged to have caused the death stands to inherit. Because the probate court is civil in nature, the standards of proof may well be significantly less than the traditional criminal standard, which is proof beyond a reasonable doubt. Consequently, much less evidence may be required to cause a disinheritance based on a finding of responsibility for the death than what is required to achieve a conviction for murder in the criminal court.

It is also possible to lose rights of intestate inheritance by committing acts other than causing the death of the decedent. Some states have statutes on file that terminate a spouse's rights of inheritance for adulterous conduct, for an extended period of abandonment of the marriage, and for various other acts that demonstrate a disregard by the surviving spouse of the marital relationship. This disinheritance by intestate succession also applies to spouses who have legally divorced or annulled the marriage to the decedent.

Because so many people die intestate, statutes and case law have combined to create a clearly defined area of law to answer questions of intestacy in the traditional family. The laws attempt to dispose of an estate by assuming traditional family relationships and the method by which such relationships are often dealt with in testate estates. However, because so often today the family unit is defined differently than in the past, these laws may become obsolete. But always, the law favors and encourages individuals not to leave these questions to the courts to answer, but rather to create a valid testamentary document that states precisely what the individual desires are in terms of estate distribution.

Testate
Method of distributing the estate of a deceased person in accordance with the terms of a valid will.

2. Testate Succession

Before a will can be used as the instrument to distribute an estate under principles of **testate** law, it must be declared a valid will by proving that a number of requirements have been met. Contrary to what may be depicted in the movies and on television, dying declarations and hastily written notes rarely meet the requisites of a valid will to serve as the basis for distribution of an estate. Every state has statutes that explicitly dictate the exact procedure for the preparation of a will. If the procedure is not followed, or if any significant irregularities are present, the will may be declared invalid and the estate distributed by intestate succession regardless of the existence of a will.

A majority of states now require that a will be in writing. Although oral wills are still permitted in some states, it generally must be shown by convincing evidence that at the time of the oral will a number of factors existed. First, the deceased believed death to be imminent and, second, the terms of the will were declared to witnesses who would not stand to inherit or be beneficially affected by another's inheritance; in other words, totally disinterested parties.[10] The rationale for upholding oral wills by states that still honor them is that such circumstances would lend credence to the terms of the testator's oral will and, thus, would be truly indicative of the deceased's intent.

Oral wills are an increasingly rare occurrence. Rather, the bulk of the statutes pertain to the requirements for a valid written will. It is required that a testator sign the will with knowledge that the instrument being signed is a declaration of intent for distribution of assets upon death. Thus, if it is established that someone was tricked into signing a document without knowledge that it was a will, the document will be invalid. If the testator knows the document is a will but because of some limitation is unable to sign it, the testator can direct another to affix the signature so long as it is accomplished in the presence of the testator.[11]

It is also required that the testator have testamentary capacity to issue the will. There are various kinds of capacity discussed in law. Testimonial capacity describes the requirements necessary before one is considered capable of offering sworn testimony in court. Legal capacity describes the ability to enter legally binding agreements. Testamentary capacity are the personal characteristics necessary to create a valid will. A testator (person making the will) is not required to have testimonial or even legal capacity to issue a valid statement of their intent with respect to their estate at the time of death.

Testamentary capacity has two essential requirements. First, the testator must have a clear understanding of the relative value and extent of the estate. This does not mean that the testator must have a thorough understanding of the entire inventory and fair market value of every single item in the estate. Rather, the testator must appreciate the size of the estate, however large or small, and its value relative to other items. For example, assume that Jay executed a will and stated the intent to split his estate equally between his two great-grandsons. He then devised one million dollars in cash to one great-grandson and his collection of his own college diplomas and family snapshots to the other. It is probably fair to say that the latter gift does not approximate one million dollars in value to the majority of those who consider the two gifts in comparison. This could be evidence that Jay did not fully appreciate the nature and extent of his estate.

The second requirement is that the testator appreciate the effect of his or her actions. That is to say that the testator understood that the effect of executing the will would be to distribute the assets of the estate in the will following the death of the testator. For example, assume Jay is 94 years old. He executes a will. The next day he tells a close friend that he has done this so that his great grandson who is 18 and is in college will have enough money to pay for his education. Jay further explains that when this is accomplished he plans to put the remainder of the one million dollars in a trust fund for the education of his 10-year-old great-grandson but, in the interim he thought the child would enjoy the diploma and photo collection more. It is clear that Jay did not understand the full effect of his act of executing the will. In the case of very large estates, it is not uncommon for the testator to seek out an independent evaluation of mental capacity at the time of the execution of the will in an attempt to avoid challenges to the will by persons who are dissatisfied with its contents. Also, videotaped wills that demonstrate the state of mind better than a written document have become popular when the testator foresees a challenge to his or her capacity or when allegations of improper influence are a risk. However, these are typically supported by a written document as well.

If it is established that the testator prepared the will under some mental impairment that would prevent a full comprehension of the will's effects, the testator may be considered not to have had the required capacity. Additionally, if the testator prepares the terms of the will based on false information, undue influence, fraud, or some other factor that would impede the ability to exercise a voluntary testamentary document, the testator would be considered to have lacked capacity. Either circumstance will result in an invalid will, and the estate will be distributed by the law of intestate succession.

Witnesses are a necessary element to any valid will.[12] It is usually not required that they know the contents of what they are signing. Rather, the purpose of witnesses is to establish that the document was voluntarily signed by the testator. If the testator signs the document in the presence of the witnesses and the witnesses then affix their signatures, the requirement has been met. Witnesses generally do not have to sign in the presence of one another, so long as they each were present when the testator signed the document or acknowledge the signature as his or her own. Thus, witnesses can sign the document at a later time and the requirement of witnesses to the signature is still satisfied.

One significant issue that arises in many will contests is the intention behind the specific terms of the will. Often a will cannot be entirely stated on a single page of paper. When there are several pages, there is the opportunity for unscrupulous individuals to insert additional terms in the will. Therefore, any will of multiple pages should indicate on each page the page number and the total number of pages. Also, any changes by crosscut, apparent deletion, or changes in type should be initialed by the testator and witnesses. Many courts prefer, and it adds to the authenticity, for the testator and witnesses to initial each page of the will and any attachments, for example, page 6 of 14 pages, and to actually sign the final page of the will.

It is not uncommon for a will to make reference to another document. Often, the will even includes the content of the other document. This is known as incorporation by reference.[13] If the will makes reference to a specific document as an attachment and specifies that the content of the document is to be treated as if it were part of the will itself, then an incorporation by reference has been made. The effect is to treat the language in the document as if it were an original part of the language of the will. For incorporation by reference to be effective, the document must be in existence at the time the will is formally executed. One cannot incorporate by reference a document that is intended to be created and added later. This would enable the incorporated document to be altered and the risk would be too great of it not reflecting the intent of the testator at the time the will was executed.

While most persons think of a will as merely passing out assets among the named beneficiaries, it is not always quite that simple. A testator has the right, with very few limits, to place conditions on bequests received under a will. The testator may indicate an intent to grant the bequest only if the recipient performs certain conditions. If these conditions are not met, that portion of the will is considered ineffective and the inheritance will not occur.[14] An example of a failed bequest might be land donated to a city for use as a park at a very specific location. If, for some reason, the city is unable or unwilling to meet the condition of using the land as a park at the specified location, the bequest would fail.

When the intended disposition of assets in a will fails for any reason, the asset falls into the estate residuary. The residuary portion of an estate is the place for consideration of all assets that are not addressed in the will or those that are addressed and fail. Failure to make a successful disposition may be due to wrongdoing on the part of the recipient, such as in the case of murder; the failure to meet a condition; a recipient who predeceases the testator, and any other circumstance that legally prevents the terms of the will from being carried out. To avoid this, it has become standard procedure in drafting wills to create alternatives for the various terms of the will. Also, the typical will contains a residuary clause that identifies to whom the assets in the residuary portion of the estate should go. If no one is identified, then state statute will dictate whether the residual assets are distributed per stirpes or directly by escheat to the state.

A common question that arises with respect to wills is the concept of disinheritance. Essentially, the issue that arises is whether someone can disinherit a blood relative. With one exception, the answer is absolutely. The assets of the estate presumably belong to the testator and generally he or she can dispose of them as desired. However, if someone is specifically excluded, it is generally sound logic to state this clearly and offer some type of explanation. This often diffuses any claims that the disinherited individual was inadvertently forgotten or that the testator was improperly influenced, resulting in the exclusion. The only regular exception to the right to disinherit is that of the spouse at the time of the testator's death. If the parties are married, then there is a presumption that the spouse also has an ownership interest in part of the assets of the estate. Each state has a statute providing a fixed percentage of the estate for the disinherited spouse. This is known as a forced share election. Even if the spouse is not disinherited, if the amount of money or assets bequest is questionable, the spouse may elect to inherit under the forced share statute. This protects the rights of the spouse to what are presumably marital assets. The only way to avoid the forced share election is if a valid prenuptial or postnuptial agreement between the parties to waive inheritance rights is executed and upheld in court. While these are addressed more fully in Chapter 14: Domestic Relations Law, it is sufficient here to note that such an agreement must be fair in nature and contain full disclosure of assets of the parties at the time the document is signed. Also, the document should reasonably represent the condition of the estate of the testator. If there have been dramatic positive changes between the time of the agreement and the testator's death, a court may be reluctant to enforce the agreement as a document that is fair to the rights of the surviving spouse.

Often a person continues to live for many years after an initial will has been executed. During such time, circumstances may take place that alter the intent of the person with respect to the estate after death. Such factors as death of other family members, or of unrelated but intended beneficiaries; divorce; birth; marriage; remarriage; and changed financial status all influence testamentary intent. At some point it may become necessary to alter the contents of one's will. This can be accomplished through a codicil or the execution of a new will and revocation of the old one. Which is more appropriate depends upon the extent and type of changes to be made.

A **codicil** is an addition to an existing will.[15] As recently as the 1980s these documents were fairly common. This is because execution of a new will required that the entire document which was sometimes quite lengthy, be totally redone to incorporate what might be a single and minor change. However, with the advent of computers, it is possible to execute a new will incorporating changes within a matter of minutes. This advance in technology alone has eliminated much of the need for and benefit of

Codicil
Amendment to a will. A codicil incorporates by reference non-conflicting terms of the will and republishes the date of the entire will.

codicils. Nevertheless, they are recognized and honored by the courts if properly executed. Whether a new will or a codicil is more appropriate depends upon the extent and type of changes to be made and the wishes of the testator. It should be noted that a codicil incorporates the pre-existing will by reference and should only contain additions. If the terms of the will and the codicil terms conflict, then a new will should be executed. The most common functions of a codicil are either to provide for additional individuals to inherit under the will, and/or to provide for the distribution of assets acquired following the execution of the will that need to be specifically addressed.

All of the requirements necessary for a valid will are also required of a codicil because the terms in the codicil actually become part of the will for all legal purposes. When a codicil is executed and signed, the incorporation by reference serves as a sort of reaffirmation of the terms of the original will. As a result, the date of the original will is revised and considered to be the same date as that of the codicil.[16] This is known as republication.

Will revocation becomes necessary when the intent of the testator changes with respect to the distribution of assets upon death. Whenever a new will is executed, all prior wills are considered to be revoked and invalid, as they no longer reflect the intent of the testator.[17] Nevertheless, it is always prudent to clearly state the intent to revoke former wills, and usually to state the dates of those wills, to avoid any confusion with respect to the intent and testamentary capacity of the testator. Even if a testator does not execute a new will, the old will can still be revoked. If the will is not revoked by a written document, it may be required that the intent to revoke be so clearly demonstrated that the testator is intent on the revocation. The attempt to revoke or physical destruction of the former will may be necessary. The condition of the will and the acts of the testator toward it must show the revocation by destruction as intentional.

In some instances, after revocation a testator will seek to have the prior will made valid again. This can occur in one of several ways. When a new will is executed, it can contain a statement that if it is declared invalid, the old will should be reinstated. This prevents an automatic intestate succession if the new will is defective. Another method is for the testator to say and do acts in the presence of witnesses that clearly establish the intent that the former will be revived. A condition of this method is usually that the original will is still in existence. Assuming that a will is located and presented to the court for probate (the legal process of the distribution of the estate), parties still have the opportunity to challenge the contents of the will. This occurs during probate and can be based on several different grounds in the form of a will contest.

3. Will Contests

Most often, any publicity about the estate of someone deceased is centered around a dispute over the validity of the will presented to the court for probate. There are three common grounds for a will contest: mistake, duress or improper influence, and fraud.[18] Generally, one who contests a will has the burden of proof to establish by clear and convincing evidence that the will is not a valid testamentary instrument that was properly executed by the decedent prior to his or her death.

When a will is challenged on the basis of mistake, the challenger must allege and subsequently prove that the testator either did not know that the document being signed was a final will or was not aware of all of the terms and the effects of what had been included in the will.[19] When mistake is proven as to any part of a will, most courts will declare the entire instrument to be invalid and refuse to probate the estate according to its terms. The reasoning for this practice is that if it can be shown that the testator made a significant mistake with respect to one part of the will, who is to say that other mistakes were not made as well? When the entire will is declared invalid, the estate generally passes under the laws of intestate succession.

Another means by which to challenge a will is that the testator did not execute the will independently and voluntarily. In most cases, the contestant must prove that the

---

APPLICATION 11.4

Sarah executed a will with the assistance of an attorney. At the time, she appeared to the attorney and witnesses to have testamentary capacity. However, after her death a few years later of an Alzheimer's related illness, it came out that when Sarah identified those she wished to bequeath assets, she had identified a number of individuals who were not living at the time of the will execution. Among them were her sister and one of her own children who had died quite young. She also provided her own address in the will, but the address she had given had not been her address for more than 40 years. A will contest was filed challenging the validity based on Sarah's testamentary capacity. Given the additional evidence that Sarah suffered from Alzheimer's and the nature of the inaccuracies in her will, it is quite possible that a probate court would find her lacking appropriate capacity and declare the entire will invalid.

Point for Discussion: If Sarah had not been declared incompetent or diagnosed with Alzheimer's at the time of the will execution, why should the will be declared invalid?

---

testator was convinced there was no real intent to execute the will that is the subject of the probate proceeding. Rather, there must be clear and convincing evidence that the testator was so impaired, that the contents of the will reflect the desires of another and that the testator would not have executed the terms of the will but for the existence of improper influences.[20]

Generally, the burden of proof falls on the party who challenges the validity and subsequent probate of the estate according to the terms of the will. There is, however, an exception to this rule. Whenever the will is drawn up or witnessed by someone who is a fiduciary—one in a position of personal trust to the testator—or who stands to inherit significantly under the terms of the will, the burden may shift automatically to the other party. In many states, if such a person draws the will or acts as a witness, there is a presumption of undue influence. In that case, the will is considered ineffective unless it can be shown by clear and convincing evidence that there was no improper influence and that the actions of the testator in drawing the terms were reasonable and justified under the circumstances. Because attorneys are fiduciaries, they should avoid drafting or witnessing wills in which they are beneficiaries. Most states will make an exception, though, if the will is for a close or immediate family member when surrounding circumstances appear proper and reasonable.

Persons who may not draft or witness a will without the presumption of improper influence are specified in the statutes of each state. Similarly, the burden of proof (amount of evidence) needed to show that the will was properly executed is also dictated by statute. The preceding are common rules, but variations may also exist in some states. Consequently, before relying on these propositions, always consult the existing statutes in the state where the case is subject to probate.

The final reason for challenging a will is an allegation of fraud. The contestant must prove several elements before a will is considered to be ineffective on the grounds of fraud. Specifically, the following must be demonstrated:

1. An identifiable person made false statements to the testator.
2. Such person did so with the intent of misleading the testator by the statements.
3. The testator was, in fact, misled and executed a will based on the false statements.
4. The testator would not have executed the terms of the will in the absence of reliance on the false allegations.[21]

CASE IN POINT

Estate of Morris, 2000 WL 707284 (Neb.App. 2000).

Morris died on February 1, 1998, at the age of 86. Thereafter, on February 12, Ruth M. Kramer filed an application for informal probate of Morris' 1994 will. In the 1994 will, Morris devised her estate in three equal shares to George Shubert and/or Helen Shubert, Kramer and/or John Vokoun or Rose Vokoun, and Evelyn Covalciuc and/or George Covalciuc (the appellees). The record shows that the persons named in the 1994 will were Morris' closest living relatives.

On June 2, 1998, the appellants filed a petition for formal probate of the 1989 will. In their petition, the appellants alleged that the original of the 1989 will had not been located but that they were devisees under the 1989 will, that the 1989 will had not been revoked, that Morris was without testamentary capacity when the 1994 will was executed, and that Morris was the subject of undue influence. It appears that the appellants were longtime neighbors of Morris and that while Morris resided in her home, they regularly helped her with chores around her house and took her to run her errands. In the 1989 will, Morris devised her estate in five equal shares to the appellants, the Covalciucs, the Shuberts, and Kramer, if Kramer survived Morris by more than 60 days, and if Kramer did not, then to John Vokoun, Kramer's son.

A trial was conducted on August 18 and 20 and December 4, 1998. Numerous witnesses testified and various exhibits were received. The testimony generally shows as follows:

After the death of Morris' husband in the 1980's, Morris continued to reside at her home until March 1994. In March, Morris was hospitalized at Methodist Hospital as a result of several falls and the onset of

some confusion. While Morris was at Methodist Hospital, numerous tests were done. It was determined that Morris was suffering from renal dysfunction and was dehydrated. A neurologist also diagnosed her with Alzheimer's-type senile dementia. Senile dementia was described at trial as a progressive loss of intellectual or cognitive functioning over time. The progressive effect of the disease varies with each individual.

According to the neurologist, Morris' recall was "very poor." and her general cognition and ability to think properly were impaired. The neurologist did not believe that Morris was capable of handling her own personal affairs from that day forward. According to Morris' attending physician, on March 8, 1994, Morris did not know the name of the president or the mayor, or the day, month, or year.

On March 15, 1994, Kramer filed a "Petition for Appointment of Temporary and Permanent Conservator/Guardian for an Incapacitated Person." Kramer alleged that Morris was impaired by reason of advanced age, possible senility, lack of proper care and poor health to the extent that she lacks sufficient understanding or capacity to make or communicate responsible decisions concerning her person and that the appointment of a conservator/guardian is necessary or desirable as a means of providing continuing care and supervision of the person and property of the above-captioned person. Kramer was appointed Morris' conservator and guardian on May 3.

After Morris' discharge from the hospital, she was admitted into the Hillcrest Care Center (Hillcrest) in Bellevue, where she remained until her death. According to the certified social worker at Hillcrest who saw Morris more than five times per week, Morris' mental state improved after approximately 6 weeks, during which time she became rehydrated. While Morris initially had problems with forgetfulness and confusion, after about 6 weeks, Morris knew people, was aware of time, and could find her room and other rooms in Hillcrest, read the newspaper, and converse intelligently. Morris' attending physician at Methodist Hospital testified that to the contrary, Morris' memory did not improve when her renal function was returned to a safe level.

The evidence showed that according to Kramer, in the summer of 1994, Morris sent Kramer to retrieve from Morris' safety deposit box everything but her jewelry in an attempt to find some insurance policies. One of the documents retrieved was Morris' 1989 will. After reading the will, Kramer laughed and told Morris, "Well, shows how much I mean to ya." According to Kramer, Morris did not recall signing the 1989 will and asked to see a lawyer. After Kramer consulted with Evelyn Covalciuc, her sister, Kramer contacted attorney Dean Hascall on Morris' behalf. Kramer testified that Morris kept the 1989 will in her possession and that Kramer never saw it again. There was no evidence that anyone else ever again saw the 1989 will.

According to Hascall, he met with Morris at Hillcrest. It appears that Kramer and Evelyn Covalciuc were present but did not participate in the meeting. Although Hascall did not have an independent memory of the meeting, he testified that his usual practice was to interview a client to determine if he or she was competent to execute a will. He also would go over any previous will with the person and discuss the changes sought and the reasons for the changes. If, after the interview, Hascall was uncertain of the person's competence, his usual practice was to make further inquiries. Hascall testified that he did not make further inquiries in this case. Hascall did recall that Morris discussed a particular piece of personal property that she wanted to leave to a particular person.

When Hascall completed the first draft of the will, he forwarded it to Kramer, who then took it to Morris for her review. According to Kramer, Morris examined the will and discovered that the Covalciucs had been left out. The will was returned to Hascall for revision. The will was executed on August 16, 1994, in Morris' room at Hillcrest.

The following evidence was received regarding Morris' state of mind: The majority of the witnesses described Morris as a strong-willed, eccentric individual who was not easily persuaded by others. Morris was described as an individual who did not want to inconvenience others and was appreciative of the help her neighbors and family provided her. JoAnn Pechar testified that she began to visit Morris with less frequency in 1995 because Morris seemed less aware of who she was. The Vokouns, who were Morris' second cousins, testified that when visiting with Morris at Hillcrest and when taking Morris to family gatherings, they did not notice any loss of memory until Morris was hospitalized in August 1995. According to Kramer, Kramer visited Morris at least weekly at Hillcrest and did not notice any memory deficiencies in Morris until after the August 1995 hospitalization. According to Kramer, Kramer became Morris' conservator and guardian due to Morris' physical restrictions, not her mental state. According to Kramer, Kramer and Morris regularly discussed Morris' financial affairs and Morris was aware until at least August 1995 of who her heirs were and of what her property consisted. According to the Hillcrest social worker, Morris began to experience some confusion and loss of memory in the year prior to her death.

The appellants offered the testimony of Morris' treating physicians that Morris suffered from Alzheimer's-type senile dementia from at least March 1994 and that, in their opinion, Morris was unable to conduct her own business affairs from that date forward.

A psychiatrist who testified for the appellees reviewed Morris' medical records. He opined that the relatively sudden onset of Morris' confusion prior to her 1994 hospitalization and the improvement of her condition after her arrival at Hillcrest were consistent with delirium, which is a temporary state of confusion, rather than dementia. Testimony showed that a person with a chronic dementia may experience a delirium on top of the dementia due to physical illness. Such a delirium will worsen the degree of confusion already present and should improve over a few months after the physical illness has been treated.

After taking the matter under advisement, the county court entered judgment on December 16, 1998. The county court concluded that the 1989 will was presumed destroyed because the original had been in Morris' possession and was not proferred, that Morris possessed testamentary capacity at the time the 1994 will was executed, and that there was no evidence of the appellants' claim of undue influence. Therefore, the county court admitted the 1994 will to probate. From this order, the appellants timely appealed.

III. Assignments of Error

On appeal, the appellants contend that the county court erred in finding that the 1989 will was presumed destroyed, in finding that Morris possessed testamentary capacity to execute the 1994 will, and in failing to find undue influence.

IV. Analysis
1. Standard of Review

Appeals of matters arising under the Nebraska Probate Code, Neb.Rev.Stat. §§ 30-2201 through 30-2902 (Reissue 1995 & Cum.Supp.1998), are reviewed for error on the record. In re Guardianship of Zyla, 251 Neb. 163, 555 N.W.2d 768 (1996); In re Conservatorship of Estate of Martin, 228 Neb. 103, 421 N.W.2d 463 (1988); In re Estate of Rolenc, 7 Neb.App. 833, 585 N.W.2d 526, (1998). When reviewing an order for errors appearing on the record, the inquiry is whether the decision conforms to the law, is supported by competent evidence, and is neither arbitrary, capricious, nor unreasonable. Nebraska Pub. Serv. Comm. v. Nebraska Pub. Power Dist, 256 Neb. 479, 590 N.W.2d 840 (1999). On questions of law, an appellate court has an obligation to reach its own conclusions independent of those reached by the lower courts. In re Guardianship of Zyla, supra.

2. Status of 1989 Will

The appellants contend that the county court erred in finding that the 1989 will was presumed destroyed. It is well established that a will which is left in the custody of the testator, and which cannot be found after his or her death, is presumed to have been destroyed by the testator with the intention of revoking it. Hober v. McArdle, 173 Neb. 510, 113 N.W.2d 625 (1962). The presumption is one of fact and may be overcome by evidence, circumstantial or otherwise, to the contrary. Id. The evidence required to overcome the presumption of revocation of a lost will must be clear, unequivocal, and convincing. Id.

In the case before us, Kramer's testimony established that she had left the 1989 will in the possession of Morris. No evidence suggests that the 1989 will was seen again by anyone. Therefore, the presumption exists that the will was destroyed by Morris with the intention of revoking it. There was no evidence presented to overcome the presumption of destruction. Therefore, this assigned error is without merit.

3. Admission of 1994 Will to Probate

The appellants generally contend that the county court erred in admitting the 1994 will to probate. They contend that at the time the 1994 will was executed, Morris lacked testamentary capacity and was the subject of the undue influence of Kramer.

In order to prevail, the personal representative as proponent of the will is required to prove by a preponderance of the evidence not only the lawful execution of the will, but also the testamentary capacity of the testator at the time when the will was made. If the proponent makes a prima facie case in chief as to both, then it devolves upon a contestant to proceed and adduce sufficient competent evidence to overcome the presumption arising therefrom. In re Estate of Camin, 212 Neb. 490, 323 N.W.2d 827 (1982). The contestants of a will have the burden of establishing lack of testamentary intent or capacity, undue influence, fraud, duress, mistake, or revocation. Id.

(a) Testamentary Capacity

We first address whether the county court erred in concluding that the evidence established that Morris possessed the testamentary capacity to execute the 1994 will. One possesses testamentary capacity if he or she understands the nature of his or her act in making a will or codicil thereto, knows the extent and character of his or her property, knows and understands the proposed disposition of his or her property, and knows the natural objects of his or her bounty. In re Estate of Peterson, 232 Neb. 105, 439 N.W. 2d 516 (1989); In re Estate of Villwok, 226 Neb. 693, 413 N.W. 2d 921 (1987). Testamentary capacity is tested by the state of the testator's mind at the time the will or codicil is executed. In re Estate of Peterson, supra; In re Estate of Villwok, supra.

Prima facie proof of a testator's testamentary capacity is established by the introduction of a self-proved will. In re Estate of Wagner, 246 Neb. 625, 522 N.W. 2d 159 (1994); In re Estate of Camin, supra. See, also, § 30- 2430(b). Such prima facie proof is rebuttable with competent evidence to the contrary. In re Estate of Camin, supra.

The 1994 will before us is a self-proved will as described in § 30-2329. Therefore, a rebuttable presumption arises that Morris possessed testamentary capacity at the time of its execution. The appellants had the burden to present evidence to rebut this presumption. The appellants argue that because Kramer had been appointed Morris' conservator and guardian and Morris had been diagnosed with Alzheimer's-type senile dementia prior to the execution of the 1994 will,

Morris was necessarily incapable of executing a will. The law does not support this argument.

We first address the appointment of a conservator and guardian. The Nebraska Supreme Court has recognized that the determination of mental capacity for the purposes of a conservatorship proceeding is different from a determination of testamentary capacity. See In re Estate of Wagner, supra. The general rule is that the mere fact that an adult is under guardianship does not deprive him or her of the power to make a will or to revoke a will. 79 Am.Jur.2d Wills § 58 (1975).

One's mental powers may be so far impaired as to incapacitate him from the active conduct of his estate, and to justify the appointment of a guardian for that purpose, and yet he may have such capacity as will enable him to direct a just and fair disposition of his property by will.

Id. at 320. Therefore, the fact that a conservator and guardian was appointed to protect Morris, without more, is insufficient to rebut the presumption of testamentary capacity.

Next, we address the effect of senile dementia on testamentary capacity. In In re Estate of Bose, 136 Neb. 156, 285 N.W. 319 (1939), the Nebraska Supreme Court concluded that the decedent had possessed testamentary capacity at the time of the execution of his will despite suffering from senile dementia. The court quoted with approval the following from Corpus Juris:

"Senile dementia, often a result from old age, does not necessarily result in mental incapacity to make a will, but there must be such a failure of mind as will deprive the testator of intelligent action. The disease is progressive in nature, and it must be determined whether its progress has so impaired the faculties of the testator that they fall below the mark of legal capacity. This must be determined not alone by the nature and tendency of the disease, but by its effect in the particular case."

136 Neb. at 168, 285 N.W. at 327, quoting 68 C.J. Wills § 39 (1934). The court further stated that it was committed to the view that when the testamentary capacity of a testator is challenged on grounds of alleged senile dementia, this fact should be determined according to the rules applicable to other forms of insanity. The accepted view is that the mental capacity of a testator is tested by the state of his or her mind at the time he or she executed his or her will. The court further noted that in respect to capacity to make a will, it is not medical soundness of mind that governs, but testamentary capacity as defined in law, and that "a high degree of mentality is not required." Id. at 169, 285 N.W. at 327.

Based upon our review of the record, we conclude that there is competent evidence to support the county court's determination that the appellants failed to rebut the presumption that Morris possessed testamentary capacity. The appellants failed to present any evidence showing that at the time Morris executed the 1994 will, she did not know and understand the nature of her act, the extent and character of her property, the proposed disposition of her property, or the natural objects of her bounty. See In re Estate of Peterson, 232 Neb. 105, 439 N.W. 2d 516 (1989). At most, the appellants' evidence established that perhaps in March 1994, Morris probably lacked the capacity to execute a will. They provided no evidence regarding Morris' state in August 1994.

The evidence before us shows that those who regularly visited Morris did not see a mental deterioration of Morris until after her August 1995 hospitalization. The evidence also shows that Hascall, the attorney who met with Morris and thereafter prepared the 1994 will, did not recall any doubts as to her competency to execute a will. In addition, the devises made in Morris' 1994 will are certainly reasonable, as they were to her closest living relatives.

For these reasons, we find no error on the record. The conclusion of the county court conforms to the law, is supported by competent evidence, and is neither arbitrary, capricious, nor unreasonable. See Nebraska Pub. Serv. Comm. v. Nebraska Pub. Power Dist., 256 Neb. 479, 590 N.W. 2d 840 (1999).

(b) Undue Influence

We next address whether the county court erred in finding no evidence of undue influence. The appellants argue that Morris was susceptible to undue influence as a result of her Alzheimer's-type senile dementia and that Kramer had the opportunity to exercise and did exert undue influence on Morris.

Undue influence such as to defeat a will is such manipulation as destroys the free agency of the testator and substitutes another's purpose for that of the testator. In re Estate of Wagner, 246 Neb. 625, 522 N.W. 2d 159 (1994). Mere suspicion, surmise, or conjecture does not warrant a finding of undue influence; there must be a solid foundation of established facts on which to rest the inference of its existence. Id. To establish undue influence, the party asserting that theory has the burden to prove that the person who executed the challenged instrument was subject to undue influence, that there was an opportunity to exercise undue influence, that there was an intent to exercise undue influence for an improper purpose, and that the result was clearly a product of the undue influence. Pruss v. Pruss, 245 Neb. 521, 514 N.W. 2d 335 (1994).

Based upon a review of the evidence, we cannot conclude that the appellants met their burden of proving undue influence. There was competent evidence that Morris was not subject to undue influence. Numerous witnesses testified that Morris was a strong-willed individual who was not easily persuaded. Although Kramer may have had the opportunity to influence Morris, the evidence does not establish an intent on the part of Kramer to exercise undue influence over Morris. In addition, the result in this case, the 1994 will, is not clearly the product of any undue influence. In the 1994 will, Morris leaves her estate to her closest relatives. These relatives, the appellees, regularly visited her at Hillcrest and helped care for her. In contrast, the appellants were no longer Morris' neighbors and were no longer helping her with her daily activities. For these reasons, we find no error in this regard.

Case Review Question: Would the result be likely to change if the family had not produced evidence of how strong willed and independent the decedent was? Why or why not?

4. Probate of Estates

Throughout this chapter, there has been frequent mention of the process of probate. Early on, it was explained that probate is the method by which the estate of a decedent is legally distributed. Each jurisdiction has clearly defined statutes used in the administration of probate. Every jurisdiction has statutes tailored to the specific manner in which the courts are organized and function. In addition, a uniform probate code has been adopted in all or part as law by most states, which results in a similarity of probate procedures and underlying principles. With today's very mobile society, many persons have personal and business interests in more than one jurisdiction. This uniformity of laws is of tremendous help to those dealing with the probate courts in jurisdictions other than their own. It also facilitates enforcement of the orders of probate courts by courts of other jurisdictions. Under the uniform code the probate procedures and standards in each adopting state are nearly identical. In the past, state laws concerning the rights of inheritance could vary dramatically, but with the uniform code, inheritance rights are determined in the same manner irrespective of where the property of the estate is located. However, even in jurisdictions where the uniform code has not been adopted, the steps in probate are relatively similar.

APPLICATION 11.5

Sam died in state X. At the time of his death, he owned real estate in state X where he was domiciled. He also owned a partnership interest in a business in state Y. He had debts to creditors and assets located in state Z. The estate was probated in state X. The probate court issued orders with respect to the business partnership interest, and the creditors and assets in state Z. The business partners registered the order pertaining to the business in the courts of state Y, and the creditors registered the order pertaining to repayment of debt with the courts of state Z. The courts of states Y and Z then had authority to honor the terms of the orders. The similarity of laws between the three states made enforcement of the terms much easier because there was no issue of a conflict of laws between the state where the order was issued and the states where the orders were to be carried out.

Point for Discussion: Why should probate not be determined for the assets in each location rather than in a jurisdiction where some of the assets are not located?

The process of probate is a relatively straightforward one. See Figure 11.2. The estate is evaluated in terms of content, claims of creditors, and rights of inheritance. Other than during the beginning stages, probate is quite similar for both testate and intestate estates. When an individual dies, state law often requires that all assets be frozen. Typically, though, businesses in which the decedent had an ownership interest may continue. All bank accounts, stocks, bonds, and other financial transactions in the name of the deceased must stop. These assets are frozen until such a time as the court has finally determined the status of the deceased's estate (assets and liabilities).

The first step in any probate case is to notify the court of the decedent's estate by filing appropriate documents. In a testate estate, this is accomplished by filing the proposed will—the original as opposed to a copy, affidavits of witnesses that the document was properly witnessed and executed, and a petition for the probate of the estate to be opened and for the will to be accepted by the court. In the event of an intestate estate, a petition to open probate of the estate is filed. Generally, probate of an estate is initiated by the next of kin, as they usually stand to inherit and cannot do so until the estate has completed probate. However, probate may be initiated by anyone—creditors, attorney, or one appointed to the task by the decedent before his or her death. The petition is usually a fairly short document that identifies the decedent, the date of death, the jurisdiction of domicile, and any attachments such as a will and affidavits.

Upon filing the petition, a hearing is typically scheduled to address whether the will, in testate cases, should be admitted to probate, and to appoint a person to be responsible for the estate during probate. The exception to the hearing phase and many of the other steps of probate is when a case of limited value is presented. The laws of the jurisdiction define what is considered limited, but essentially the reasoning is that costs associated with full probate could possibly deplete the entire estate. In that circumstance, the petition for a shortened probate is filed, including affidavits of the value of the estate. The process is both limited and, in some aspects, accelerated to minimize expense.

In testate estates, any challenges to the will are typically made at the initial hearing. This eliminates the time and expense associated with probating a will that ultimately may not be recognized. Many jurisdictions impose a time limit for contesting a will's validity. Additionally, failure to do so at the time the will is considered for probate may require evidence of what reasonably caused the delay. If a will is challenged, the estate remains frozen, with the possible exception of business interests and living

Testate	Intestate	FIGURE 11-2
1. Filing of petition* (to admit will and appointment of personal representative).	1. Filing of petition (to open estate and appointment of personal representative).	Typical Steps in Probate
2. Notification of heirs/beneficiaries.	2. Notification of heirs.	
3. Notice to creditors.	3. Notice to creditors.	
4. Inventory of estate.	4. Inventory of estate.	
5. Hearing on creditors' claims/payment of creditors.	5. Hearing on creditors' claims/payment of creditors.	
6. Final accounting of estate.	6. Final accounting of estate.	
7. Distribution of estate to beneficiaries in accordance w/terms of will.**	7. Distribution of estate in accordance w/laws of intestate succession.	
8. Hearing on creditors' claims/payment.		

*Law varies by state regarding when a hearing on a will contest occurs.
**In some cases, bequests cannot be honored because the property did not exist in the estate or the property was sold or otherwise used to satisfy creditors or the spouse's statutory rights.

allowances for dependents, until such time as the validity of the will can be fully evaluated. Once determined, the court decides whether to probate the estate testate (with a will) or intestate (without a will) according to the procedures of state law for each type of estate. For all practical purposes the estates are probated in the same manner until such time as it becomes necessary to distribute the assets of the estate.

After the form of the estate (testate or intestate) has been established, the individual responsible for the estate is appointed. Traditionally, an executor (male) or executrix (female) was appointed to oversee a testate estate. In the case of the intestate estate, the titles used were administrator or administratrix. Today, the term commonly used in either type of estate is that of personal representative. The function is essentially the same as all of the other titles. However, this term is more universal in that it can be used for both testate and intestate estates and does not denote gender of the individual, which has no relevance anyway. The proper terminology to be used is dictated by the law of the jurisdiction and should be adhered to in all documents and proceedings. The duty of the personal representative is to manage the estate during probate. They are responsible to inventory the assets; pay creditors whose debts are approved by the court; collect any debts due to the decedent; take reasonable steps to protect the assets of the estate; for example, paying insurance premiums that are due, and generally protect the estate until the final distribution. The personal representative is a fiduciary of the estate and is required to make periodic reports to the court with regard to the duties performed. As a fiduciary, the personal representative has a legally binding obligation to care for the assets of the estate and not to convert them to personal use or to waste them. Any breach of the duty as a fiduciary can result in criminal charges as well as a civil judgment for damages.

If the deceased is survived by a spouse, or children, or others who were dependents of the decedent at the time of death, then claims can be made at the outset of probate, or later, for reasonable living allowances. These are sums of money from the estate that provide for the basic living expenses of the dependents until such time as the estate is probated and assets distributed.[22] Statutes give some insight and judges also have a fair amount of discretion as to what is a suitable allowance based upon such facts as the size of the estate, the needs of the dependents, and the type of lifestyle the decedent had previously provided for the dependents.

In addition to allowance, certain property in which the deceased may have had an interest is exempt from probate.[23] Generally, such property includes the primary residence of the deceased, if the surviving spouses and/or minor children reside there; an automobile; apparel; home furnishings; and other personal items specified by statute. The idea is to protect the family residing with the decedent prior to his or her death, from claims against the property by creditors. Again, these allowances are generally effective only when there is a surviving spouse, minor children, or other dependents and the state statutes list exactly what may be considered exempt from the estate of the deceased.

After a personal representative is appointed, inventory of the estate is completed, and allowances to the spouse and children are dealt with, it is necessary to process the claims of creditors. In modern times, it is seldom that a person dies totally free of obligations. Therefore, each state has procedures for notifying creditors of the person's death. Such procedures include publication in the local papers' legal section of the classified ads and other methods designed to reasonably alert potential creditors of the pending probate of the deceased's estate.[24]

Creditors are generally given a specific length of time to come forward with claims against the estate. Often, the time limit is a period of several months after several publications to provide every opportunity for claims. Many larger business entities maintain a vigilant watch over legal notices and legal publications where they have customers, in order to make timely claims on estates for amounts owed. Creditors who seek to have obligations paid by the estate must file the appropriate forms with the court that document the amount and nature of the claim. If the personal representative challenges the validity of the claim, a hearing is needed to determine whether it should be paid by the estate in whole or in part.

After the deadline has passed for making claims, the court considers all requests by creditors. Recommendations are made by the personal representative as to what claims should be paid and what claims should be challenged. If a claim is challenged as to payment or amount, a hearing is scheduled and the court then makes a determination of whether the claim and amount are valid. Each state has a statute listing a specific order in which types of debts are to be paid. This prioritizes debts in the event the estate is not large enough to cover all money owed by the creditor at the time of death, and any debts incurred and associated with the final illness or injury and funeral related expenses. Arrangements are made for the payment of the claims from the assets of the estate. Occasionally, it is necessary to sell some or all of the property of the estate to obtain enough money to pay all the creditors, even if the sale of assets depletes items that were bequeathed specifically in the will. Usually the court will approve an order of items to be sold for this purpose. If a bequeathed asset is sold and the proceeds used to satisfy debts, then the bequest is usually extinguished. The same is true for a bequest in a will that was disposed of by the testator prior to death. The proper term to describe this occurrence is ademption.

Once all creditor's claims have been considered and satisfied or rejected, the court is free to distribute the estate. In the testate case, the remaining inventory of the estate is used to satisfy the specific bequests and devises. A devise differs from a bequest only in the respect that it is the term used to describe a gift of real property of land and any improvements. If there is a surviving spouse in a testate case, as discussed previously, he or she is given the option of accepting what he or she is entitled to under the will or claiming a forced share election. Every state has statutory law that grants an absolute minimum to a surviving spouse. This forced share is generally a significant portion of the estate. The only exception to such a case might be if the spouse had previously waived the right to claim a forced share by signing an enforceable agreement. Each state also has a rule as to rights of intestate inheritance or forced share election or will bequest in the event there is a pending divorce between the parties at the time of death of one of them.

The personal representative generally presents a proposed distribution of the remaining estate to the court. Once approved, the assets are distributed. In intestate cases, they will be distributed according to applicable rules of law, such as the per stirpes method. In testate estates, the specific bequests and devises of property within the estate are made, and any remaining assets are distributed according to the residual clause of the will or laws applying to unassigned residuary. In a testate case, the residual estate can be quite large if a person who was bequeathed property pre-deceases the testator and no alternate is named, or if property unspecified in the will is acquired after the will is executed. For these reasons, it is important that once executed, a will be kept up to date to reflect changes in either the estate or the persons who stand to inherit.

In the case of intestate estates, the common practice is to liquidate the estate. This consists of selling all noncash assets and reducing them to a cash value. Then, the total amount is distributed according to the laws of intestacy in the jurisdiction where the testator was domiciled.

PARALEGALS IN THE WORKPLACE

Probate and estate law is a lucrative area of employment for paralegals in a variety of settings. Of course in the traditional law firm, the probate paralegal can be effectively used to collect necessary information and even draft documents such as wills under the supervision of the attorney. However, there are also other arenas of employment. Many banks have trust departments that offer the service of probate administration to clients who are legally incompetent and administration of estates of deceased parties. There is no legal requirement that an estate administrator be an attorney. In fact, most administrators are not lawyers. A paralegal who is well versed in probate law could prove to be an invaluable asset to the trust department of any bank or investment house that provides such services. The paralegal would, as would any administrator, be responsible for tracking the estate and moving it through the required steps. Key abilities would include attention to detail, dates, and documentation. In the case of a legally incompetent client, the paralegal might be responsible for seeing that the income and expenses of the client are properly managed and regularly required reports are submitted to the courts. In the case of a deceased client, the paralegal would be responsible for seeing that the steps of probate are followed in a timely and well-documented fashion.

CHAPTER SUMMARY

The probate courts are multifaceted and serve a large percentage of the population. In addition to the traditional concept of processing the estates of persons who have died, the probate courts also supervise the care, custody, and estates of persons who are unable to legally manage their own affairs. This includes both minors and legally incapacitated adults. The supervision generally involves appointment of a guardian or representative and periodic review of the individual's capacity and well-being under the guardianship. The probate court continues to oversee the incapacitated individual until such time as the incapacity is terminated by age, return to appropriate health, or death.

In the event of decedent's estates, the cases fall into one of two categories. Estates are considered testate, with a valid will to govern distribution, or intestate. When a person leaves a will, the document must be properly written and executed under fair and reliable circumstances. When irregularities exist in a will or no will is left, the law of intestate succession takes effect. The intestate succession provides an equitable distribution of the estate to the heirs who are presumed to be the most likely candidates for bequest or devise had there been a valid will. The only way to truly control one's estate after death is to leave a validly executed will. Any changes in the estate that are significant or changes in the beneficiaries under the will should be addressed in a codicil (addition) or a new will.

Regardless of whether a person dies testate or intestate, the probate courts serve the function of ensuring that the debts of the estate are paid and that the remaining assets of the estate are properly distributed. This is also accomplished with the assistance of an administrator in an intestate case and an executor in a testate estate. In either case, this personal representative, as they are sometimes called, keeps the estate organized and intact until the final order of the probate court is issued to dissolve and close the estate.

ETHICAL NOTE

While ethical conduct is required in every situation, when it comes to matters of probate and estates there is an increased emphasis on avoiding so much as the appearance of impropriety. Because this area of law deals with individuals who ultimately cannot protect themselves, either through incompetence or because of death, every reasonable step must be taken to ensure that all matters are dealt with objectively and by not subjecting the testator or incompetent individual to any inappropriate influences. Objectivity and fair dealing are perhaps more crucial in this area than any other as an individual's entire estate of worldly possessions and income are at stake. And because these individuals are ultimately at a disadvantage to continue acting in their own best interest, the courts assume the role of protector and are quite intolerant of those who would act unethically in an attempt to take unfair advantage.

Revelant Internet Sites

Estate Planning Page	www.estateattorney.com
EstatePlanBasics.com	www.estateplanbasics.com
Estate Planning.com	www.estateplanning.com/new/homepage.shtml

---

Internet Assignment 11.1

Consult the law of your jurisdiction and determine the rights under intestate succession for adopted individuals with regard to natural parents and relatives through adoption.

KEY TERMS

Codicil	Intestate	Probate
Guardianship	Per Stirpes	Testate

ENDNOTES

1. *Martin v. Beatty*, 253 Iowa 137, 115 N.W.2d 706 (1962).
2. Id.
3. 26 C.J.S. Descent and Distribution, Section 25.
4. *Debus v. Cook*, 198 Ind. 675, 154 N.E. 484 (1962).
5. *Lofton v. Lofton*, 26 N.C.App. 2103 (1975).
6. *McLendon v. McLendon*, 277 Ala. 323, 169 So.2d 767 (1964).
7. 79 Am.Jur. 2d Wills, Section 289.
8. Id., Section 321
9. Id.
10. Id.
11. Id.
12. 79 Am.Jur.2d, Wills, Section 289.
13. Id., Section 321.
14. *In re Bernatzki's Estate*, 204 Kan. 1341 (1969).
15. 71 A.L.R.3d. 877.
16. *In re Erbach's Estate*, 41 Wis.2d 335, 164 N.W2d 238 (1969).
17. *Wright v. Benttinen*, 352 Mass. 495, 226 N.E.2d 194 (1967).
18. *Solomon v. Dunlap*, 372 So. 2d 218 (Fla. App. 1st Dist. 1979).
19. *Remon v. American Sec. & Trust Co.*, 110 U.S.App.D.C. 37, 288 F2d. 849 (1961).
20. *Estate of Krukenberg*, 77 Nev. 226, 361 P.2d 537 (1961).
21. *Crosby v. Alton Ochsner Medical Foundation*, 276 So.2d 661 (Miss. 1973).
22. 79 Am.Jur.2d, Wills, Sections 415–418.
23. 36 Am.Jur.2d, Proof of Facts, Section 109.
24. Id.

Chapter 12

THE LAW OF CONTRACTS

CHAPTER OBJECTIVES

Upon completion of this chapter you should be able to do the following:

- Define a contract.
- Discuss the essential elements of a contract.
- Identify the elements of an offer to contract.
- Explain the accepted legal standards for acceptance of a contract.
- Define a third-party contract.
- Distinguish assignment and delegation.
- Discuss accepted defenses for claims of breach of contract.
- Explain the applicability of specific performance in contracts.

A. CONTRACTUAL ELEMENTS

Regardless of the type of profession one enters, or whether a profession is undertaken at all, contracts permeate virtually all aspects of American society. With electronic communications influencing payroll, credit, and just about every kind of business transaction, contracts have become necessary to formally establish the agreements for the terms of these transactions. No longer do settlers grow and hunt their own food and build their own homes with materials they harvest from the forest. Today's society is one of supply and demand, one of high technology, one of material acquisitions. All of these things require individuals to deal with each other and with businesses on a large scale and on a long-term basis. Home loans last for decades, and service agreements support the maintenance of complex equipment and appliances. Utilities for power, water, heat, and phone all require agreements for the ongoing delivery of service in exchange for payment. Agreements are present in almost every part of a typical American's life in today's society.

However, contracts are not new to the American culture or the rest of the world. After all, one of the earliest reported dialogues involved an agreement about tenants not eating the apples in the landlord's garden. Many of the early recorded legal actions involved disputes over agreements that had previously been entered into willingly and optimistically by both parties. As circumstances arise, plans change, and different interpretations of the duties and obligations of an agreement are exposed, it is sometimes necessary for a third party to intervene and resolve the conflict. For this reason, the area of contract law has evolved over the past several hundred years into one of the most detailed areas of law. But with the constant advancement of technology and societal changes, there always seems to be new twists in the law of contracts that require a review and occasionally a revision of the established standards.

Contract law is ultimately founded in a basic principle of the expectation of honor. That is, if two parties agree to an exchange of goods or services, each should be secure in the knowledge that the other party will uphold their promise and follow through as agreed. If a party fails to honor his or her commitment, then logically there should be some recourse for the party who did fulfill the agreement. What then constitutes a legally enforceable agreement?

Contract
A legally binding agreement that obligates two or more parties to do something they were not already obligated to do or refrain from doing something to which they were legally entitled.

Contractual Agreement
A promise or set of promises for the breach of which the law provides a remedy and the performance of which the law recognizes a duty.

> **Contract:** A legally binding agreement that obligates two or more parties to do something they were not already obligated to do or to refrain from doing something to which they were legally entitled.
>
> **Contractual Agreement:** A promise or set of promises for the breach of which the law provides a remedy and the performance of which the law recognizes a duty.

More simply stated, if two or more distinct parties make a promise or promises to one another, those parties are obligated to perform (complete) the terms of the promise(s). If one party fails to complete the terms as promised, the party who did not receive that to which they were entitled would have a legal remedy.

1. Unilateral and Bilateral Contracts

Before any court will enforce a contract, certain facts must be established. First, it must be determined what kind of contract existed, and second, whether all of the essential elements of an enforceable contract were present and identifiable. There are a number of ways to characterize contracts based on the number of parties involved, the subject matter, and so

APPLICATION 12.1

Sam and Tim enter into an agreement to build a house. Tim owns two parcels of land. Sam agrees to build a house valued at $100,000 on parcel A. In exchange, Tim will pay Sam for all materials and will deed over the ownership of parcel B. Sam builds the house. Tim deeds over the ownership of parcel B. However, Tim refuses to pay the approximately $50,000 in materials costs because he claims that the value of the finished house is nowhere near $100,000. Sam has the right to pursue a legal action against Tim for breach of contract for Tim's failure to pay for the cost of the materials.

Point for Discussion: Could Tim file suit against Sam? If so, on what basis?

forth. However, all contracts can be classified as either bilateral or unilateral agreements. The difference lies primarily in how the contract is entered into. If one party creates a valid offer for a contract by communicating a promise to the receiving party, and that promise induces the receiving party to accept the contract by performing the desired benefit for the promising party, a **unilateral contract** has been created. The more obvious contract is the **bilateral contract.** This occurs when, prior to any performance, each of the parties state their intentions to create a contract through the exchange of mutual promises.

APPLICATION 12.2

Unilateral Contract

Dear Maria,

I am writing to let you know that my trip to visit my elderly father has been extended due to his poor health. Because I am not returning as planned, I need to find someone to help with the care of my pets. A friend's daughter has been caring for them, but she will be returning to college this week and cannot continue. If you would take care of them for me, I will pay you the rate of $20.00 per day beginning Monday the 25th of this month for each day I am gone. I would ask that you feed and water them daily, clean their kennels weekly, and walk each one for approximately 20 minutes twice each day. The food is stored in the shed behind the house and the keys to the kennel are there as well. I plan to return the 15th of next month at which time I will pay you in full. Please let me know if you cannot do this and I will make other arrangements.

   Upon receipt of the letter, Maria began caring for the animals on the 25th and continued to do so until the 15th of the following month.

Bilateral Contract

Kim planned to visit her father in Korea and was not exactly sure how long she would be gone. She asked her friend Maria to care for her prize-winning show dogs. Kim promised to pay Maria $20.00 per day to feed, water, and exercise the dogs and to clean their kennels weekly. Maria agrees to do this for three weeks. They agreed that at that time Kim would pay Maria for the three weeks and if she still had not returned, then Kim would continue under the same terms as before.

Point for Discussion: What type of contract would exist if the agreement was for three weeks? After three weeks Kim did not return but instead E-mailed Maria asking her to continue as before and Maria did not respond but did continue to care for the dogs.

Unilateral Contract
A contractual agreement in which one party makes a promise to perform upon the actual performance of another.

Bilateral Contract
An agreement between two or more persons in which each party promises to deliver a performance in exchange for the performance of the other.

In a unilateral contract a promise is made in exchange for an actual performance without first making a promise of that performance.

The question arises as to just what is necessary to create a valid and enforceable contract? Prior to creating the actual terms, there are a number of prerequisites for any contract. They include the following:

- At least two parties
- Legal capacity of all parties
- Manifestation of assent by all parties
- Consideration
- Enforceable promise

2. At Least Two Parties with Capacity

Typically, this is the easiest element to satisfy. In most situations, there are two or more distinct parties who wish to enter into a contract. A century ago, the same party being on both sides was almost unheard of. But today, there are multi-faceted corporations with subcorporations, subsidiaries, and so forth. There are also individuals who operate more than one business and individuals who are both partners and individual business owners. With these variations, there are infinite possibilities for conflict when contracts occur that involve common interests or parties.

The rule traditionally has been that a person with an ownership interest in a business cannot contract to render services independently to that business when those services are part of the primary purpose and focus of the business. For example, a doctor/lawyer cannot establish a medical practice and then contract with himself as both employer and employee for the delivery of medical services. He might, however, contract to provide other professional services, such as those of a lawyer. Legal services to a medical practice are not an ordinary part of the business and service that the medical practice would be expected to deliver. Consequently, the two separate entities element would exist.

When two or more related corporations are dealing with each other, it must be clear that the corporations have separate and distinct identities and a dissimilarity of purpose. This line is sometimes blurred so it becomes necessary to conduct a detailed examination of all aspects of the corporations and the businesses they engage in to make a determination if the businesses were actually separate in origin and purpose or whether the contract is essentially a sham.

There are various types of capacity in the law. They include capacity as a competent adult—one who is subject to the laws without the excuse of minority of age or mental infirmity; testamentary capacity—the ability to execute a valid will; testimonial capacity—the ability to understand the obligation to be truthful when under oath in a court of law; and contractual capacity—the ability to legally enter into and be bound by the terms of an enforceable contract.

Contractual capacity, which is essentially the same as being a competent adult, requires that one has reached the age of majority and has not been formally adjudicated as incompetent, that is, incapable of managing his or her affairs. The law is relatively settled that only competent adults can be bound by the terms of contracts. An issue arises, then, when a party without contractual capacity enters into a contract with a party that does have capacity.

The age requirement is essentially a straightforward one. Each state has established a chronological age at which a person is deemed legally to have reached adulthood. The marker is arbitrary and does not take into consideration the vast differences in maturity and intellectual ability of individuals, but it would be impossible to do so. Instead, a minimum age has been established as a standard. The most common standard used in the state statutes is 18. However, there is a range of a few years among the states and each state also has statutes in place that allow a person to be considered a legal adult in certain circumstances even before the age of majority has been reached. If there is a reason why an individual does not have the capability to function as an adult, then steps must be taken to have that person declared legally incompetent.

Emancipation occurs when a person has not reached the statutory age of adulthood but has demonstrated that he or she is capable of functioning as an adult. One example might be a person who marries and accepts total responsibility for his or her own needs at age 16. If this person is functioning in every other capacity on a daily basis as an adult, it would not make sense to prevent him or her from entering into any contractual agreements. Each state determines the procedure for emancipation and any requirements that must be met in order for it to occur. In some instances, a hearing may be required to prove to the court that the young person is truly capable of accepting and meeting adult responsibilities.

When establishing a contract, it is only necessary to determine that the person has reached the age of majority or has been emancipated and has not been declared incompetent to meet the requirement of capacity. The question of competence is most often the basis for an issue of capacity. Legal incompetence generally requires a declaration by a court of law. The declaration states that the mental capacity of the individual has been determined to be so lacking or deficient that the person is incapable of exercising appropriate judgment to manage his or her own affairs. If someone appears to be quite obviously insane, but has not been declared incompetent, it is still unlikely the contract will be enforced. After all, who would enter into a contract in good faith, and ultimately seek its enforcement, with someone they believe to be insane and thus incompetent?

Many persons act outside what would be considered the normal range of behavior. This does not mean they are without the ability to manage their own affairs. Many famous and wealthy individuals have been notorious for odd or eccentric behavior. Yet, their behavior did not preclude them from amassing great fortunes. Conversely, some of the most notorious and vicious criminals of our time functioned in society relatively unnoticed for years. The law cannot be based on the subjective and individual perceptions of normal or abnormal behavior. Consequently, anyone whose condition has not been objectively considered by a court is responsible for any contractual agreements to which he or she is a party, regardless of his or her actual mental abilities.

The problem arises when someone is marginally competent and no formal action has been taken to establish whether the individual has adequate mental capacity. For example, what about the adult who suffers from a mental disability that impairs his or her judgment, yet functions on a relatively normal scale? Perhaps the individual is able to live independently and hold a nontechnical or lower-level job, but has the maturity and developmental levels of someone approximately 12 years old. If the onset is during adulthood, then it is not uncommon for family or medical personnel to suggest that a competency hearing be pursued to establish competence. If the condition occurs at birth or during childhood, then the matter should be considered on or before the time the individual reaches the age of majority. If a court determines there is insufficient mental capacity, then the person is declared legally incompetent and typically is relieved from enforcement of any contracts he or she might enter into.

Traditionally, if a person with capacity entered a contract with a person lacking legal capacity as a matter of law, the person without capacity could choose whether or not to complete the terms of the agreement. The other party was virtually at the mercy of the person without capacity, who could disaffirm or withdraw from the contract at any time. It did not matter that the party with capacity had already performed all obligations under the contract. The minor or incapacitated person could accept the benefits of that performance without further obligation. The reasoning behind this was that, because the party was legally incapable of being party to a contract, a contract could not be enforced against the person.

The inherent unfairness of this situation caused the courts and some legislatures to set forth legal standards that would protect parties with capacity who unknowingly entered in good faith into a contract with a minor or incapacitated person. This was done under the theory of restitution,[1] which is based on the principle of fairness. With respect to contracts, the theory basically states that if one person accepts or takes a benefit from another who was not obligated to provide that benefit, some sort of payment should be made.

In addition to enacting the law of partial or complete restitution in contracts, many states have enacted statutes, and many courts have issued decisions that follow the theory of restitution. Such legal standards provide a remedy to those who have entered contractual agreements with parties who do not have capacity. However, these legal standards often limit the recovery from the minor or incapacitated person to the amount of his or her liability. Such amount will be the reasonable value of the goods or services received rather than the amount contracted for. Additionally, the law of a number of states regarding the liability of minors and incompetents is that restitution can be claimed only for items considered to be necessary to life, such as food and shelter.[2]

As a consequence of the law of contracts and restitution, today in business, those with capacity usually require the minor or known incompetent to have an additional party enter the contract in his or her behalf. These are often referred to as suretyship contracts. For example, a competent adult might cosign or guarantee a loan to a minor. Then, if the minor breaches the contract, the contract can be enforced against the adult who cosigned. Note that competent persons may also be required to have a cosigner as a condition of the contract for other reasons, such as to guarantee good credit.

APPLICATION 12.3

Barb is 17 years old and lives with her mother. In December, Barb purchases a large quantity of steaks from a local market and has them delivered to various family members and friends as gifts. She signs a six-month installment payment agreement to pay for the $600 cost of the meat. No questions are asked with respect to Barb's age. Barb is unemployed and has no resources to pay for the meat. Her plan had been to get a job before the first payment was due, but after two months she has been unable to locate employment that coincides with her school and extracurricular activities. The market files an action against Barb and her mother as legal guardian of the minor. The court establishes that local meat prices indicate that actual fair market value of the meat averages $450 at local grocery stores. That is the amount of the judgment rendered against Barbara and her mother, which they must pay to the market.

Point for Discussion: Would the result likely be different if Barb were living away at college rather than living with her mother at the time of the occurrence?

Assignment 12.1

Identify and explain why which of the following parties could or could not be bound by contract:

a. A is 21 years old. He suffers from schizophrenia that, when controlled by medication, allows him to function well within normal limits. He does so at almost all times. However, when he misses medication, he may act irrationally and days may pass before he recovers to normal processes. On one such occasion, he goes to the Internet and signs up for multiple record, video, and book clubs with contracts requiring additional purchases in exchange for free or below-cost products. A few days later, the products arrive and he delivers them to a shelter as a donation. Once the medication is reestablished, he does not even recall his actions. Yet, the contractual obligations have been made.

b. Fourteen-year-old Deeandra went alone to the doctor for her annual school physical. She had done this the year before as well. On this visit, she asked that each of her ears be double pierced. The nurse complied. While insurance paid for the physical, Deeandra's parents received a bill for $100 for the four ear piercing. They refused to pay and the doctor's office responded with a copy of the intake form signed by the parents two years prior at her first appointment. On the form, the parents agreed to pay for all services delivered to Deeandra that were not covered by insurance. The jeweler at the local shopping mall charges $15 for each set of two ear piercings.

c. The same as in situation 2, except the signature on the same type of form signed the day of the physical and the ear piercing is Deeandra's.

d. Fourteen-year-old Juan's parents have an account at a local store. While visiting Juan's family, his grandfather takes Juan shopping. They purchase a complete computer system at a price of $3,000 and put it on the account. Juan's grandfather suffers from early Alzheimer's and sometimes uses poor judgment when making decisions, although he presents himself quite normally most of the time. They hook up the system, but damage several components in the process. Juan's parents do not think they should be required to pay for the computer since Juan is a minor and the grandfather is mentally disabled, although there has been no court action on the matter.

CASE IN POINT

Quantum Chemical Corp. v. Mobil Oil Corp., 1995
WL 610739 (Ohio App. 1st Dist. 1995)

This case arises from a contract entered into between plaintiff-appellant/cross-appellee Quantum Chemical Corporation ("Quantum") and defendant-appellee/cross-appellant Mobil Oil Corporation ("Mobil"). The contract was a toll conversion contract which stipulated that Mobil was to provide Quantum with a material called decene, and that Quantum would convert the material into a substance known as PAO for Mobil's use. Quantum would also supply some of the decene needed for conversion. The toll contract contained a clearly defined termination clause, which allowed either party to terminate the contract by giving notice 180 days prior to the end of a contract term, and required a two-year step-down period following a notice of termination in which gradually decreasing amounts of decene would be converted. The contract also included a non-assignment provision prohibiting the assignment of the contract unless both parties consented, which consent could not be unreasonably withheld.

In April of 1989, Quantum sold the division which included the PAO business ("the Emery Division") to Henkel Corporation. The sale excluded, however, the PAO business; i.e., the entire division was transferred to Henkel except the tolling of decene into PAO. All Emery Division employees, including those responsible for servicing the Mobil contract, became Henkel employees. Quantum contracted with Henkel to allow these employees to remain involved with the Mobil contract for a transition period of six months.

When Mobil learned of the sale of the Emery Division to Henkel, it objected to the continued involvement of the Emerynow-Henkel employees in the toll contract, and it protested the alleged assignment of the contract to Henkel in violation of the non-assignment provision in the contract. Quantum insisted that no assignment had taken place, but agreed to remove all Emerynow-Henkel employees from any involvement in the toll contract by August 1989. Nonetheless, Mobil suspended all performance under the contract in July of 1989. Mobil's termination letter stated that the termination would be in accordance with the terms of the contract; however, no further liftings of PAO occurred, contrary to the step-down period provided for in the contract's termination provision.

Quantum sold the PAO business to Ethyl Corporation in July 1990, and sued Mobil for breach of contract the day after. Mobil raised several affirmative defenses, and brought numerous counterclaims against Quantum. At the close of trial, the only affirmative defense left to Mobil was that its performance under the contract had been discharged when Quantum materially breached the contract by assigning it to Henkel. The only counterclaims which remained pending against Quantum were breach by short shipment, breach by assignment, and tortious interference with contract.

The jury returned four verdicts: one on Quantum's claim against Mobil for breach of contract, and three on Mobil's counterclaims against Quantum. The jury found in favor of Mobil on Quantum's claim of breach of contract through cessation of performance. The jury found in favor of Quantum on all three of Mobil's counterclaims. Both parties moved for judgment notwithstanding the verdict ("jnov"), and for a new trial. All motions were denied. Quantum appealed, and Mobil brought a cross-appeal.

Quantum raises as error the trial court's denial of its motion for jnov and a new trial. Quantum also contends that the jury's verdict in favor of Mobil on Quantum's breach-of-contract claim through cessation of performance is against the manifest weight of the evidence. Mobil asserts that the trial court erred in denying its motions for jnov on counts three (tortious interference) and five (breach of contract through assignment) of its counterclaims against Quantum.

Quantum's challenge to the jury verdict in favor of Mobil on Quantum's breach-of-contract claim is still before this court. Quantum's assertion that the verdict was against the manifest weight of the evidence is based on the proposition that Mobil failed to prove a material breach by Quantum which excused Mobil's performance under the contract. Therefore, Quantum argues, the evidence of Mobil's cessation of performance contrary to the terms of the contract can lead to only one conclusion, that Mobil breached the contract and is liable for damages. We agree.

After a thorough review of the record, we determine that Mobil failed to meet its burden of proving that Quantum materially breached the contract, thereby discharging Mobil's performance. With respect to Quantum's alleged breach of the nonassignment provision, we conclude that there was no competent, credible evidence which showed that an assignment had taken place. An assignment is defined simply as a transfer of one's rights to something to another. 6 Ohio Jurisprudence 3d (1978), Assignments, Section 1. There must be an intent on the part of the assignor to assign the rights in question, and an intent on the part of the assignee to be assigned the rights in question. 6 Ohio Jurisprudence 3d (1978), Assignments, Section 24.

Both Quantum and Henkel presented testimony that they had no intent to create an assignment. Quantum and Henkel admitted to entering into the marketing agreement described above, but maintained that the delegation of administrative duties with respect to a contract does not constitute an assignment of that contract. The law corroborates this conclusion. By definition, a delegation of some duties incident to a contract, without a delegation of all the duties or the transfer of the rights under the contract, does not constitute an assignment under the law. 6 Ohio Jurisprudence 3d (1978), Assignments, Sections 1-24; see, also, Arnold Productions v. Favorite Films Corp. (C.A.2, 1962), 298 F.2d 540, for an excellent discussion of partial delegation as not constituting a breach of a non-assignment provision.

The evidence shows that after Quantum sold the Emery Division to Henkel, it retained the PAO plant in Texas where the decene was tolled. Quality control, product specifications, shipment, and all other facets of production were performed in Texas by Quantum. There was no evidence adduced which supported the position that Quantum had abandoned its responsibility for the contract. On the contrary, Henkel had no rights to the profits from the toll contract, and no involvement with its manufacturing. Therefore, we hold that Quantum did not materially breach its contract with Mobil through assignment to Henkel. Our holding applies to the issue of assignment raised as both an affirmative defense in Quantum's case against Mobil, and as a counterclaim in Mobil's case against Quantum. Mobil's first assignment of error regarding the jury verdict on its counterclaim for breach of contract through assignment is thus overruled.

It follows from our holding that a violation of the nonassignment provision in the toll contract cannot provide a legal justification for Mobil's failure to perform under the contract. Furthermore, we are unable to determine any other legal justification for Mobil's admitted non-performance of its contractual duties. Evidence was submitted to the trial court which showed that Quantum occasionally failed to ship the full amount of PAO requested by Mobil. However, this breach of the shipment requirements was waived by Mobil, and if not waived, it did not constitute a material breach which discharged Mobil's performance under the contract. See Software Clearing House, Inc. v. Intrak, Inc. (1990), 66 Ohio App.3d 163, 583 N.E.2d 1056 ("a breach of a portion of the terms of a contract does not discharge the obligations of the parties to the contract, unless performance of those terms is essential to the purpose of the agreement," citing to Kersh v. Montgomery Developmental Ctr. [1987], 35 Ohio App.3d 61, 519 N.E.2d 665); Reynolds &

Associates, Inc. v. Feeks (Feb. 6, 1991), Hamilton App. No. C-890695, unreported; Restatement of the Law 2d, Contracts (1981) 237, Section 241 (discussion of five factors relevant to determining materiality of a breach).

Having concluded that Mobil failed to prove its affirmative defense of assignment, and discerning no other legal justification for Mobil's cessation of performance, we are left with the uncontroverted evidence in the record that Mobil did not complete its performance under the contract with Quantum. We hold that reasonable minds could not have concluded that Mobil did not breach its contract with Quantum, and a verdict in favor of Mobil on Quantum's claim was therefore against the manifest weight of the evidence. Quantum's first assignment of error is sustained.

In the appeal numbered C-940357, that part of the trial court's judgment finding in Mobil's favor on Quantum's claim for breach of contract is reversed, and the balance of the judgment entered on the jury's verdicts in favor of Quantum on Mobil's counterclaims is affirmed. The cause is remanded to the trial court with instructions to enter judgment as a matter of law in favor of Quantum on the issue of liability with respect to Quantum's breach-of-contract claim, and to hold a new trial confined solely to the amount of damages to be awarded on that claim.

DOAN, P.J., and HILDEBRANDT, J., concur.[3]

Case Review Question: Would the result be different if Quantum had turned over production to the buyer with the proviso that the Mobil product be processed in exactly the same manner as it had been during Quantum's ownership of the business?

3. Manifestation of Assent

In all contracts, each party to the agreement must signify acceptance of the terms in some way. This requirement to manifest or demonstrate a willingness to be bound by the contract is essential. Otherwise, it would be possible for persons to claim a contract exists where one party did not even have notice of a contract or the intention to enter one. There are a number of common issues that arise relevant to the manifestation of assent including the following: (1) the objective standard that must be met to prove there was assent, (2) circumstances that may affect the termination of the assent, and (3) methods of creating a situation for assent to a contract by the parties.

As with competence, it is far too risky to leave the question of whether someone intended to enter into a contract up to the perceptions of the other party to the agreement. Also, when a dispute arises, they are unlikely to recall events leading up to the contract with clarity. As a result, whether or not someone has manifested assent to a contract is measured by an objective standard. There is a great difference between objectivity and subjectivity. When one is objective, no personal bias plays a role in one's thoughts. However, when one is subjective, personal bias greatly influences perceptions. For example, if someone was denied a job they wanted very badly and felt well qualified for, they might have strong feelings about the perceived injustice done to them. However, if someone totally uninvolved in the situation were to consider all the applicants and choose someone else, they probably would not perceive it as an injustice at all but simply a business decision. The unsuccessful job applicant would have the subjective perception; the person considering the applicants would have the objective perception.

In a number of areas of law, the importance of objectivity plays a role. The entire concept of a jury system is based on the belief that a group of peers who can examine a situation objectively can see it more clearly than the participants and reach a fairer conclusion. Judges also are required to consider the matters before them and objectively apply the law to the facts. This supports the old saying that "Justice is blind." In contract law, as a fundamental part of determining whether all the elements of a contract are present, the judge and jury have the duty to determine whether there was mutual assent by all parties to the agreement.

The objective standard requires that a third person observing the transaction would perceive that the parties agreed to the terms of the contract and intended to be legally bound by those terms. The parties do not need to say or do any particular thing. Rather, their conduct alone is enough to indicate agreement to the terms of the contract.[4] The existence of subjective intent claimed or denied by a party is not relevant for the purposes of determining whether a contract existed. For example, the jury will not consider the claim of a party that his or her conduct, even though it might appear to have indicated intent, was not what the party meant.

APPLICATION 12.4

Kerry operated a small gift shop. She often took consignments from local artisans. When she took items on consignment, she kept 20% of the purchase price of any items sold and, quarterly, issued a check for the remainder of the sale price to the artisan. Well aware of this arrangement, Kerry's best friend Joy asked if she could display items in the shop that she had crafted and take orders from customers for additional items. Kerry agreed. Over the course of the next few months, Kerry took numerous orders for Joy's work and passed them on to Joy. Joy would then fill the order and make the sale directly to the customer, but she did not pay the 20% consignment fee to Kerry. Joy's knowledge of Kerry's standing terms for display and sale of products would indicate that she knew Kerry did not perform this service free of charge. Her placing items in the store and taking orders through the store from customers was essentially the same process as other artisans and doing so would indicate she accepted Kerry's terms for consignments.

Point for Discussion: Does the fact that Kerry took orders and conveyed them to Joy rather than completing the financial transaction in the store make a significant difference in whether Joy understood and accepted the terms?

In applying an objective standard, the circumstances surrounding the supposed creation of the contract are taken into consideration. When the situation that existed at the time the contract was allegedly entered supports a finding that one of the parties lacked true intent to be bound, the court may find that a reasonable person would not have perceived a contract to have been created. Some of these situations include the following:

- Agreements made in jest or as jokes
- Negotiations prior to the creation of an actual contract
- Promises or indications of future gifts in exchange for another's promise or performance
- Promises for what a person is already legally obligated to do

Agreements made in jest. With respect to the first situation, persons cannot be held to agreements that have been made in jest. If such agreements were enforced, everyone would have to be on guard against saying things in conversations that could later be construed as a contractual promise. A frequent obstacle to enforcing contracts where circumstances indicate jest is the inability to prove the party never meant to be bound by the agreement. Normally, persons talking in jest have no real intent to form a contract. Therefore, when attempting to enforce a contract under such circumstances, it would be necessary to show that an objective observer would conclude that the parties actually intended to be bound by their statements or conduct regardless of the jovial manner of their discussion.

APPLICATION 12.5

Jake and Madison are getting a divorce. At a barbecue, after a few drinks, Madison laughingly tells a neighbor, "If I had a taker, when I came back from visiting my parents, all of Jake's tools that he left behind would be gone and a hundred dollar bill left in its place." When Madison returns from her trip, the tools worth approximately $3000 are gone and $100 is left on the tool bench. The neighbor refuses to return the tools claiming a valid contract. The court finds that the tone used by Madison, the lack of any serious discussion, and the casual environment were all circumstances to indicate Madison was not making a serious offer to sell the tools.

Point for Discussion: Would the result be different if the comment was made during a neighborhood garage sale in which Madison had the tools placed out for sale?

Negotiations. For many of the same reasons as those that apply to statements made in jest, negotiations do not constitute contractual agreements. During the negotiation, there is no real intent to make a firm commitment. Rather, the intent of the parties during the negotiation is to investigate whether they have objectives that would allow them to meet on a common ground and assist one another in the achievement of those objectives. If this common ground cannot be clearly defined in acceptable terms to all concerned, then no contract will have been entered, and both parties are left as they were when the negotiations began. If parties could be bound by mere negotiations, the incentive would be to avoid even a discussion of a possible agreement and, consequently, it would be virtually impossible to create contracts with any degree of depth or complexity or compromise.

APPLICATION 12.6

Law firm X and law firm Y are attempting to agree on terms for the settlement of a lawsuit in which each represents one of the parties. Both have written authorization to act on behalf of the parties in settlement of the claims. The day of trial, X suggests payment to Y's client of an amount of $85,000 in exchange for dropping the lawsuit. Y responds that the money would need to be increased to an amount of $100,000 and paid in one lump sum. In response, X suggests a payment of $100,000 payable in installments of $10,000 over 10 years. Y indicates the client should agree to this but wants to confirm it. Y then does not respond further. No formal settlement agreement is reached and the case proceeds to trial, where the client of X is ordered to pay the sum of $150,000 to the client of Y.

Point for Discussion: If negotiations could be considered binding, what could the possible outcome be? Why would this be a problem and for whom?

Future gifts. With respect to the third circumstance, it may at first seem illogical to refuse enforcement of contracts for future gifts. It is certainly possible to contract for a future performance of some act. It is also necessary in every contract that a person promise something he or she is not otherwise legally obligated to do. So why is it not legal to contract for a future gift? The answer is quite simple. By definition, a gift is something that one is never *required* to grant. In a contract, however, if something becomes the basis of a contractual agreement, it loses its gift quality and must be delivered. If not delivered, there are legal consequences. As a result, it is a contradiction in terms to promise a gift—something one is not required to do—as a part of a contractual obligation to do the very same thing.

Performance of a legal obligation. A contract cannot be created in which one party's obligation is to do that for which they already had a prior legal obligation. The basis of any contract must be a voluntary act by each of the parties that in some way benefits the other. To allow one to satisfy a contract by performing an existing legal duty, that person has given the receiving party only that to which he or she was already entitled. There is no exchange of benefits, which forms the reasoning for the very existence of contracts.

APPLICATION 12.7

Tyrone and Joanna are divorced. The parties currently have a written agreement that requires Tyrone to pay Joanna the sum of $300 each month for support of their two children. Tyrone is chronically late and occasionally misses payments completely. To remedy the situation, he offers a contractual agreement to Joanna that would require her to accept $200 per month as full payment of the child support. In exchange, Tyrone agrees to make the payments on time and in full. Under current laws, Tyrone's current requirement to pay child support is that it be done in a timely and complete manner. The fact that he has not met that obligation in the past does not diminish it in the future. Joanna is already entitled to full and timely payment of the child support. Therefore, she receives no real benefit from a contract that requires Tyrone to do so now.

Point for Discussion: Would a valid contract exist if Tyrone instead offered a late fee of $25 for each of the support payments that was not timely?

4. Consideration That Supports an Enforceable Promise

As stated earlier, to constitute an offer to contract, all material terms must be present. One of these terms is consideration—the benefit received by a party in exchange for the party's promise or performance. Essentially, consideration is the element that induces a person to enter a contract.[5] A person promises or performs an act that he or she is not otherwise obligated to do in exchange for a promise or performance he or she is not otherwise entitled to receive.

It must be possible to determine and assess the specific value of the consideration for a specific contract to the offeree. This guarantees that a party is able to obtain something of value to them in exchange for the promise or performance and, essentially, is required to prevent deception of innocent parties. The courts will not recognize and enforce a contract where the description of the consideration is vague or where there is no clear opportunity to assess its value. This is not to say that the promises/performances exchanged must be of significant or even equal value. A particular performance valued by one person may not be of value at all to another. And often the nature of the consideration exchanged is quite dissimilar and not easily compared for the sake of determining equivalent value even on an objective basis, much less the subjective positions of the individual parties. Whether the parties receive adequate value is generally left to them to negotiate. The law does require, however, that a party to a contract be able to reasonably determine the value, quantity, and quality of the consideration to be received. This allows the party to make an informed decision of whether or not to enter the contract. In addition, the consideration must be something that is genuine. It does not matter that one party's consideration is seemingly inadequate when compared with the other party's offered consideration. The law does not concern itself with the adequacy of consideration.[6] The only exception to this would be if the consideration was represented as a genuine or real article but was actually a fake or reproduction. If the consideration is a promise that turns out to be a sham in an attempt to deceive another party, it may not be treated as a valid consideration, and then the contract would not be enforced. Again though, the court would evaluate the circumstances to determine whether there was intent to deceive and whether the other party had a reasonable opportunity to discover the misrepresentation.

For a consideration to be legally enforceable, it must be something that the law recognizes as a proper basis for a contract. Generally, this means that the consideration cannot be something that would be illegal or that would force the party to engage in illegal conduct. If, for example, one party promised another party $50 in exchange for stealing a typewriter, there would not be a valid contract. Because one party's consideration is an illegal act, the element of a legally enforceable promise would not be met.

B. CREATION OF A VALID CONTRACT

1. Offers

Before there can be acceptance and formation of a contract, the parties must come to a meeting of the minds about all the essential terms of the contract. Frequently, an offer to enter a contract does not occur until after various types of negotiation have taken place. When one party has actually made an offer, the other party can accept or reject the offer for as long as it is in effect. A number of occurrences can affect whether an offer is created and its duration.

> Offer: [the] manifestation of willingness to enter a bargain, so made as to justify another person in understanding that his assent to that bargain is invited and will conclude it.[7]

The terms offer and acceptance are commonly employed in reference to the assent by each party. The party who creates the opportunity to be bound by a contract, as opposed to negotiation, is the offeror. The party who accepts the offer is the offeree. The acceptance is the last step in the formation of a valid contract; assuming the duties and obligations undertaken by each party constitutes the appropriate consideration. An integral part of any offer and acceptance to a contract is the consideration.

An offer can be made to enter either a bilateral or a unilateral contract. When negotiations precede the contract, it is sometimes difficult to distinguish the offeror from the offeree. Usually, both parties suggest terms for the contract. When negotiations take place, the point must be determined at which they cease to be mere negotiations and one party makes an offer that can become the basis for a contract. Identifying when negotiations end, as well as the identity of the offeror and the offeree, is necessary to separate the terms of the contract from the terms of the negotiations. Only the terms of the contract will be enforceable.

The question to be asked is, would a reasonable objective observer perceive the actions of a person to be those of one who is creating the opportunity for a second person to enter into a contractual relationship by doing nothing more than accepting the terms that are already clearly set forth by the first person? If so, the last person to have offered terms during the negotiations would be the offeror. The offeror is the person who identifies all significant terms of the actual contract and then promises or performs. All that needs to follow is the assent by promise or performance of the second person, who is the offeree. Additionally, the time for acceptance by the offeree must be reasonably ascertainable.[8] It is not important who initiated the discussion or opportunity for contractual terms to develop. What is significant is who the last person was to present all the essential elements for a clearly defined agreement to exist.

a. Advertisements   Much of the general public shares the belief that all advertisements are offers to enter contractual agreements for the sale of goods or services. Conversely, much of the legal community believes that such advertisements do not create an offer, because certain terms of the agreement are lacking. In reality, both are true to a limited extent. Whether or not an advertisement constitutes an offer must be determined on a case-by-case basis by a finding of whether all the essential contractual elements are present within the advertisement.

As a consequence of the requirements of identity of the offeror, time for acceptance, and clearly defined consideration, most advertisements do not contain sufficient specificity to constitute an offer. Rather, they are an invitation to a buyer to make an offer after selecting specific goods or services. If, however, an advertisement indicates a particular good or service whose value can be reasonably ascertained by one who sees or hears the advertisement, the time for the contract to be accepted is clear, and the offeree is clearly identified (e.g., the first ten customers), the advertisement may be treated as an offer, and offerees have the opportunity to accept it and form a contract.

b. Indefinite Promises   Similar to the advertisement is the indefinite promise. Even if all the terms necessary to a contract are technically present, an indefinite promise is not an offer and cannot be accepted to create a valid and enforceable contract. A promise is indefinite if the benefit offered by the promise (the consideration) is vague or if its value cannot be reasonably determined.[9] The ambiguity can concern the nature or extent of the consideration. For example, assume A knows B is looking for a puppy for a Christmas gift. A tells B that he can provide an AKC registered puppy with royal bloodlines in exchange for $750. There is no way for this to constitute an offer because there is no specificity as to what type of puppy is involved, and there is no such thing as dog royalty. The information provided does not enable B to make an informed decision about the value of the contract. If vague language in contracts were enforceable, persons could take advantage of others who had different expectations. Much of the determination of whether a promise is indefinite is based on the circumstances and whether the other party could, in fact, identify with specificity the value of the consideration to be received.

c. Auctions   It is possible for an auctioneer to stand in the role of offeror, but there are additional requirements, called reserve. In an auction, all elements of the offer are usually present. The item is specific, it can be inspected and valued, and the time for acceptance is set (while the item is being bid upon). The only thing that will affect the party who makes the offer is a sale with or without reserve. If an auction is conducted with reserve, the auctioneer can reserve in advance the right to refuse a bid prior to the final sale of the particular item. In effect, this makes the auctioneer an offeree with the right to refuse an offer (bid). Therefore, until an auctioneer announces whether a bid will be accepted, the contract is not formed. In an auction without reserve, the auctioneer is an offeror calling for bids (acceptance) of the promise of any amount on an item. When a bid is received, the contract is established.[10] The actual value or the amount of the bid is not a matter of legal concern as, the parties have the opportunity to inform themselves on these matters in advance.

d. Illusory Promises   An illusory promise is one in which the promisor retains the ability to withdraw or negate the promise.[11] When this occurs, there exists nothing of real or ascertainable value to induce the promise or performance by the other party. For example in the statement, "If you paint my house, I'll probably sell it to you for $5,000 less than I have it advertised in the paper," the homeowner has, in reality, promised nothing. The other party could perform but has no way to legally enforce a promise by the other side since nothing affirmative was promised, only a possibility. One of the keys to a valid contract is a legally enforceable promise. When any significant element of the agreement is vague or uncertain, it becomes impossible to determine the intent of the parties at the time the agreement was created. Courts are very reluctant to speculate as to the intent of parties entering agreements and thus require that virtually all elements be clearly stated, including the intent to offer a particular promise or performance and to be legally bound by that offer.

e. Termination of the Offer   Ordinarily, the party who extends the offer to enter a contract has the right to withdraw or cancel the offer at any time prior to its acceptance. The exception to this rule is known as an option contract, which is, essentially, a contract in and of itself that affects another potential contract. An option contract is an enforceable agreement much like any other valid contract. However, the promises are quite specific. In an option contract, one party promises to pay a certain sum of money or provide a certain type of consideration. In exchange, the other party agrees to leave an offer for a separate contract open for a set period of time and not to dispose of or alter the subject matter of that separate contract. For example, A has a champion bloodline racehorse valued on the open market at $100,000. B wants to purchase the horse but needs to arrange financing from other investors. B offers A $2,500 to hold the horse from sale to anyone else for a period of 60 days. A agrees that the horse will be cared for and not sold or otherwise disposed of or altered in any way for 60 days and further agrees to sell the horse to B for the sum of $100,000 at any point within that time frame in exchange for the nonrefundable sum of $2,500. This contract holds the other contractual offer open for a period of 60 days only to B. Option contracts such as this consist of a bilateral promise agreement and are relatively straightforward. However, there is also a type of option contract that applies to unilateral agreements.

When a party offers a promise in exchange for a performance, the offer is for a unilateral contract. Ordinarily, a unilateral contract is not accepted and enforceable until such time as the performance is rendered. However, once performance has begun, it is only fair that the party be given a reasonable opportunity to complete the performance. For example, assume J promises to pay K $1500 to complete body work on his car and K immediately undertakes the repairs. When K has the repairs nearly complete, J informs K that he has changed his mind and is not willing to pay $1500 for the repairs. To allow J the benefit of the repairs and not obligate him to compensate K as promised would be inherently unfair. In such situations the law implies an option for the performing party and keeps the offer open until such time as there is a reasonable opportunity to complete performance and thereby accept the offer.

In the absence of an option contract, there are a number of ways for an offer to end prior to establishment of an agreement. An offer that is open for a specified time and is not accepted during that time will cease to be an offer. If no exact time for acceptance is stated, the law implies a reasonable time for that type of offer. Note, however, that if several such elements are missing, it may be found that no offer really existed and that, rather, it was only an invitation to the other party to make an offer. If the offeree rejects the offer, then it is no longer effective and the opportunity to contract based on that offer is terminated. In some instances, the offeree may respond not by acceptance or rejection but by issuing a counteroffer. A counteroffer by an offeree is considered to be a rejection of the offer and is treated as an entirely new and different offer, thereby making the initial offeree the offeror. Finally, if the offeror or the offeree should die or lose legal capacity prior to acceptance, the offer is terminated automatically.[12] In addition, an offeror has the right to notify the offeree of a retraction of the offer at any point prior to acceptance. The question then becomes, at what point does acceptance take effect? Does it occur when issued or received?

2. Acceptance

The ultimate step in creating any contract is an acceptance of the terms of the offer by the offeree. What constitutes a valid and enforceable acceptance is at least in part dictated by the type of offer and contract. In a bilateral contract—a promise for a promise—before the contract becomes binding, the offeree must give a promise in exchange and as consideration for the offeror's promise. At that point, both parties are obligated to fulfill their promises according to their terms.

To solidify a unilateral contract, the offeree must begin performance in response to the offeror's promise. The contract is not actually accepted until the offeree has substantially performed what was asked by the offeror. At that time, however, the offeror cannot withdraw the offer that induced the offeree to perform and is obligated to allow the offeree to finish the job. This prevents an offeror from accepting the benefits of a performance and withdrawing the offer before the performance is complete. If the offeree completes the task, the offeror must provide the promised consideration. When an offeree does not complete performance of a unilateral contract, the offeror may have to pay partial consideration for the work done if the offeree substantially performed.

The offeree must have knowledge of an offer. Acceptance cannot be the result of coincidence. If by chance or for some other reason the offeree promises or performs what the offeror seeks, there will be no contract. For a contract to exist, the offeree must be induced by the offeror's promise to give a specific promise or performance in exchange. Similarly, the consideration for each party must be something the receiving party would not otherwise be entitled to receive. If it is not, consideration would not act as an inducement to enter the contract.

As a general rule, an offeree cannot alter, delete, or add terms to the contract when accepting. This would effectively create a counteroffer. The contract offer must be accepted or rejected *as is*. If such changes were allowed, there would really be no offer at all. Rather, the discussion would be nothing more than negotiations in advance of a valid offer capable of being transformed into a binding contract. More importantly, in unilateral contracts, where acceptance is established by a completed performance, allowing changes in the terms could cause the offeror to receive something very different from what he or she sought. The performance by the offeree would no longer be of the type of consideration that would encourage the offeror to honor the original promise contained in the offer.

There is to some extent an exception to the rule with respect to commercial transactions between persons engaged in the sale of goods. Merchants are governed by the laws of the states designed especially for transactions and contractual agreements between parties regularly engaged in commerce. Each state has adopted all or part of a uniform set of laws for this type of transaction known as the Uniform Commercial Code (UCC). This is a collection of laws regarding commercial transactions that addresses various accepted practices of sales and financing by commercial businesses, with one another and the general public. The intent is to establish a fundamentally fair set of rules to guide business transactions and encourage business and commercial trade on the premise that fairness will prevail over unprincipled business owners. By adopting a uniform law in all states, interstate commerce and widely accepted fair business practices are encouraged. A variety of related subjects, such as bank transactions and bulk transfers, are included in the code as well. Each subject is addressed under a separate heading known as an article. Article 2 of the UCC sets forth the provisions for commercial transactions involving the public sale of goods by merchants. Under Article 2, it is permissible for an offeree to include additional or varied terms when accepting a written contract. However, even in such situations as that, if the contract states that such changes must be expressly approved by the original offeror in advance, no acceptance is valid and no contract exists until the offeror has approved the varied terms. Additionally, any substitution must be of items of a similar nature and value.

APPLICATION 12. 8

XYZ Retail sends an order to ACME manufacturing corporation. XYZ states that if they receive 2000 of the rare and hard to find green widgets before December 1, from ACME, XYZ will pay the manufacturer's listed price plus a 10% bonus. The objective of XYZ is to have enough widgets to sell for the pre-Christmas rush. ACME responds by sending 2000 widgets; however, they are of the common red variety. Because the market is already flooded with red widgets; they are of little or no value to XYZ. ACME cannot be allowed legally to change the terms in this manner and enforce the payment plus bonus because its performance did not constitute a valid acceptance. If it were permitted to change the terms of the offer in this way, XYZ would be required to honor a contract offer that it never issued.

Point for Discussion: Would XYZ be likely to be bound by contract if they received the green widgets on December 10 and sold them all by December 31?

To summarize, the offer must contain the following elements:

- Be communicated to the offeree in advance of promise or beginning of performance by the offeree
- Clearly identify consideration in a way that allows it to be evaluated by the offeree
- Clearly identify the consideration sought in the return promise or performance
- State or imply the reasonable duration of the offer
- Contain consideration on both sides of the proposed agreement that is not illusory or illegal in nature

The acceptance must have the following elements:

- Be for the exact terms offered, except for commercial transactions, which are governed by the UCC
- Be within the time stated, and if not, within a reasonable time under the circumstances
- In a unilateral contract performance constituting acceptance, be completed within a reasonable time based on the subject and nature of the offer

Generally, acceptance is effective at the time it is tendered. The exception, of course, occurs in a unilateral contract. Acceptance by the tender of performance is sufficient to create an option to continue until the performance and, consequently, the acceptance are complete, or when it is reasonable to conclude by an objective third party that there is no intent to fully perform and thereby accept. If the offer is made to a specific individual or type of individual, for example, the first 10 customers, no one else may respond and create a binding contract. If it is made with sufficient specificity but to the general public, all who become aware of the offer are offerees and have the right to accept and create a contract.

In face-to-face confrontations, there is usually little doubt about when an acceptance takes effect. At the moment an objective observer would perceive the offeree as tendering an acceptance of the contract terms, the contract would become a legally enforceable agreement, assuming all other requirements were met. More and more often though, contracts are not created through face-to-face encounters, but are communicated through a medium other than personal conversation.

More commonly, offerees accept terms of an offer by a written or electronic transmission. This may be through mail, telegram, telephone, or computer-generated messaging. For any of these methods to constitute a valid acceptance, all necessary steps must be taken to ensure prompt and proper delivery of the acceptance. This includes proper address and identification of the offeree, payment of any necessary fees, and authorization, when necessary, for the transmission to be sent. In the case of a unilateral contract, appropriate notice of the initiation of accepting performance should be made in such a way that the offeror has a reasonable basis to discover that performance has begun.

3. Rescinding the Offer

As previously mentioned, at any time prior to acceptance the offeror has the right to revoke the offer, with the exception of option contract situations. While an acceptance is considered effective at the time it is dispatched, a revocation is typically not considered effective until such time as it is received. This is especially important in unilateral contracts because a performance may have begun and the offeree have contributed toward the acceptance without knowledge that a revocation had been issued. This would produce an unfair result unless the revocation was ineffective and the offer still subject to acceptance until such time as the offeree was reasonably made aware of the termination of the offer.

There is an exception to the rules regarding acceptance by methods other than direct and personal communication. The exception is that the means of communicating an acceptance or revocation must be reasonable under the circumstances. This requires a case-by-case evaluation to determine what the most reasonable methods of acceptance would be in a particular case. If, for example, the parties had communicated exclusively by electronic transmissions on the Internet in the past, acceptance by regular U.S. mail might be considered inappropriate as the only means of notice of acceptance. If however, an electronic transmission were sent informing the offeror of acceptance and indicating that a written acceptance would be coming by mail, then such a transaction might be considered reasonable.

Assignment 12.2

Consider the following and determine if acceptance is likely to be effective. If so, when would it take effect?

Jose and Lee work together every day. Over time they discuss Lee's purchase of Jose's boat and come to an agreement on all of the essential terms. However, Lee must apply for a bank loan before he can formalize the agreement. When the loan is approved, Lee mails a written acceptance to Jose but does not mention it at work. Jose receives the acceptance two days later. During that two day period, Jose received a much higher offer on the boat and wants to accept it instead of the acceptance by Lee.

C. ENFORCEMENT OF CONTRACTS

Ideally, all contracts would be entered into with a full understanding of the terms and expectations of the opposite party and with full intent and ability to complete those terms. However for every possible term in a contract, there are multiple possibilities for misunderstanding and unforeseen circumstances that prevent the contract from being carried to completion as originally intended by all those concerned. When it becomes apparent that the parties understood the terms differently from one another at the time the contract was created, there are established legal principles to resolve the disputed terms.

Generally, in the case of an innocent mistake, the court will examine each side of the contract and make a determination as to what a reasonable person would perceive the terms and the offeror's intention to be under the circumstances. This is the use of the objective standard to determine intent. If these are the same terms alleged to have been perceived by the offeree, then they will be applied as the actual terms of the contract. The same rule applies to the offeree and the consideration presented to the offeror. In the absence of very specific language, what was a reasonable interpretation is what will be applied.

APPLICATION 12.9

On the Internet, X makes an offer to Y to sell two "show-quality registered toy poodles for $1,000." Y accepts. X ships the poodles to Y and Y responds with a check to X for $1,000. X now claims that the agreed amount was for $1,000 per poodle. The court finds that because the language of the offer discussed two poodles and only one amount without a distinction such as "each" or "per poodle" that Y was reasonable in the perception that the amount covered the cost of both dogs.

Point for Discussion: Would it cause a different result if X could establish that dogs such as these are virtually never sold for an amount as low as $500 per animal?

Ordinarily, an application of a "reasonable" standard will be done with ordinary language. This is referred to as the plain-meaning rule.[13] This means that technical language will not generally be implied in a contract unless the terms of the agreement are part of a technical subject. In most cases, the court will assume that the offeror or offeree should have used ordinary meanings and definitions when interpreting the terms of the contract. The court will, however, deviate from this rule when terms of art—terms of technical terminology or terms used in a particular trade—are used in the contract and a regular part of the communication between the parties to the contract. If all parties to the contract are members of the profession or trade that uses this type of terminology, the common meaning of the term by members of the profession or trade will be used to determine what the offeror and offeree should have interpreted the term to mean.[14]

As technology increases and the level of education and literacy climbs, people are better able in many respects to protect themselves from being taken advantage of, or so it would seem. However, there are always those who are less than honorable among us who would seek to get something for nothing, or search out a way to manipulate and take advantage of those who are trusting and in a weaker bargaining position. Consequently, while the methods to obtain them may have been upgraded, unconscionable and fraudulent contracts still occur and find their way into the courts for resolution.

1. Unconscionable Contracts

There are two basic types of unconscionable contracts. The first is the classic unconscionable contract, in which the innocent party had no real bargaining power or opportunity to decline. This is often based on a lack of knowledge of the true terms of the contract. The innocent party is given the terms of the contract without an opportunity to discover their real meaning and extent prior to acceptance. For example, a large group of tourists are left without shelter when they are caught in a hurricane on a Hawaiian island and their hotel is destroyed and all power and phone to the island is knocked out. An individual appears and offers lodging for the remainder of their stay in exchange for a written contract agreeing to pay an exorbitant price. A more realistic example might be a vacationing motorist whose car breaks down in the desert or mountains many miles from the nearest home or business. A passerby offers a ride to the nearest phone in exchange for all of the motorist's cash on hand and a written agreement for $1000 to be paid within 30 days. In either case, the vulnerable party is not in a position to bargain but, rather, has little choice but to accept the terms offered in order to obtain immediate assistance. Effectively, they are in an untenable position. In such cases as this, the contract may be considered unconscionable if the terms are found to be so far outside of what would be considered reasonable under ordinary circumstances that they offend notions of fairness and sensibility.

Another type of unconscionable contract is known as an adhesion contract. This is induced by duress imposed directly on the offeree by the offeror in an attempt to force acceptance of the terms. This differs from the situation above in which the offeror takes advantage of an existing vulnerability. Adhesion contracts employ force or the threat of force.[15] The threat may include physical injury, financial injury, injury to reputation, or anything else that might cause significant harm to the innocent party. An example might be to take photos of a celebrity in a private setting and then threaten to publish them unless a specific sum of money is paid. If a court finds that a reasonable and similarly situated person would have no choice but to agree to the terms of the contract as a means of protecting their reputation and credibility, the agreement would be considered an adhesion contract and unconscionable.

Unconscionability is extremely difficult to prove and to prevail upon in court for a variety of reasons. Courts are reluctant, and understandably so, to take the objective standard too far into a subjective area such as that of personal experiences and their effect on intent. Each individual is a product of their unique life experiences and perceives personal situations differently. The more personal a decision, the more difficult it becomes to establish an objective standard of what should or should not have influenced the motivation to accept or decline a contract offer. Because unconscionability by its very nature alleges that a personal vulnerability was preyed upon, the courts tend to have a fairly broad view of what constitutes acceptable, if not desirable, conduct by offerors.

Second, there is a presumption that no one should enter a legally binding agreement without fully investigating its total ramifications. As a result, there is generally an expectation that parties with full capacity at least demonstrate an attempt to fully inform themselves about the contract terms before a court will consider issues such as unconscionability or other circumstances that might render the contract invalid. Obviously, in the case of duress or overt attempts by the other party to conceal information about contract terms, a different issue is presented.

2. Fraud in Contracts

Fraud is the basis for a legal action that can be brought in a variety of situations including contract law. Specifically, two types of actions for fraud can be brought to invalidate a contract: fraud in fact and fraud in the inducement. Different circumstances support each and, if proven, each produces somewhat different results for the parties involved. Ultimately, though, the party who is the victim of a fraudulent contract is offered some type of relief by the courts.

Fraud in fact occurs when one party tricks another into signing a contract by leading the other party to believe the contract is something entirely different and there is not a reasonable opportunity to discover the fraud.[16]

APPLICATION 12.10

On his 18th birthday Sam goes to a car dealership to purchase his first car. Sam decides on a vehicle and agrees on a price. He goes into the sales office to complete the paperwork. There he is asked to sign a large number of documents. The salesman assures him that each document has to do with the purchase of the car and the financing agreement for the monthly payments to the dealership. The salesman reminds Sam repeatedly that it is near closing time and while Sam glances over the papers, the figures seem to be in order and he quickly signs all of the documents. The salesman gives Sam the keys to the car and tells him that when the owner of the business comes in the next day, he will sign on behalf of the dealership and that copies of all the papers will be sent to Sam by mail. After a week Sam calls and is assured the papers will be mailed that day. He then leaves on a two-week vacation. Upon his return, Sam opens the envelope containing the paperwork on his car and as he goes through it, he is stunned to find that he has signed a contract for an additional $2,000 car-care service and cleaning package in which he is billed monthly for two years and in exchange has the option to bring the car in once each month to be washed and quarterly to have the oil changed. This agreement was never even mentioned to Sam and he signed it under the impression that it was part of the various other documents necessary to complete the sale of the car.

Point for Discussion: If Sam were older and more experienced in purchasing automobiles would he be more or less likely to be able to establish fraud?

For the same reasons as discussed previously, fraud in fact is difficult to prove because parties generally have a duty to examine a document before affixing their signature. However, if it can be shown that the terms were not obvious or were added later, or that some other circumstance existed that prevented the party from ascertaining that he or she was actually signing a contract, the court may find fraud in fact. In the situation described above, Sam may have a case because of his young age and inexperience, the lateness of the hour, and the assurances of the salesman that all of the documents signed pertained to the sale of the car. However, the defense would likely argue that regardless of those factors Sam had an obligation to read each document fully before signing it. Very possibly the argument would also be made that the salesman in fact did tell Sam about the car-care agreement and that he willingly entered into it. As can be seen, the court must consider each side and impose certain responsibilities on the parties. If it is still apparent after meeting those responsibilities that a party could not reasonably have discovered that he or she was entering a contract, a finding of fraud in fact may be rendered by the court.

When there is a finding of fraud in fact, the result of such a case is rescission of the contract, in other words, the contract is void. A void contract or rescission is a finding that a contractual agreement never really existed. In this case, it would be due to the missing element of manifestation of assent to the contract terms. In the situation where a contract is found to be void, the court rescinds the contract, which places the parties in the positions they held prior to signing the agreement. If the innocent party has in any way incurred a negative change in circumstances because of the contract, the court attempts to restore the party to his or her original position. For example, if an innocent party has incurred obligations because of the contract, or damage such as a bad credit rating based on a refusal to comply with the contract, the court may require the party responsible for the fraud to pay or do whatever is necessary to satisfy any obligation or to eliminate or correct any damage.

The other type of fraudulent contract is known as fraud in the inducement and is quite different. In this type of case, both parties knowingly and willingly enter into a contractual agreement. Fraud in the inducement generally occurs when one party intentionally misrepresents the amount or quality of the consideration the opposing party is to receive under the contract. This is even stronger when the innocent party takes steps to evaluate the proposed consideration prior to entering the contract but the deception prevails. In such a case, fraud in the inducement has occurred.

APPLICATION 12.11

Manuel searches the Internet frequently for collectible items. He comes across an advertisement for a one of a kind vintage vase providing a very specific description and price, and information about the offeror. Manuel researches the Internet to determine the reputation of the seller and finds no negative comments. He asks for an appraisal of the vase that would support the asking price and one is faxed to him. Manuel agrees to purchase the vase and it arrives following his payment of 10% of the purchase price. He takes it to an art dealer who informs him that the vase is a very good reproduction but not an original piece. The dealer even confirms that an appraiser not heavily experienced in this area could mistake it for an original. The purchase price on the vase was $16,000. The value of the reproduction is approximately $1350. Manuel sues the seller claiming he is the victim of fraud in the inducement. Under the circumstances, the conditions of fraud are probably satisfied and he would likely prevail.

Point for Discussion: Would the result change without the original appraisal?

When an action for fraud in the inducement is successful, a court does not consider the contract void but rather voidable. In a void contract, the innocent party is restored to his or her original position and the contract is rescinded and treated as if it never existed. A voidable contract is recognized as a valid and intended agreement, however the court does not enforce the continuation of terms. An attempt may also be made by the court to achieve a level of fairness based on the true value of the consideration that was misrepresented. But the parties are not restored to their original positions. This is because the parties did intend to enter a contractual agreement and a rule of law such as this encourages parties to take every reasonable measure to fully evaluate proposed consideration before entering a contractual agreement.

3. The Statute of Frauds

Statute of Frauds
Statutory law that specifies what contracts must be in writing before they will be enforced.

The term **statute of frauds** is somewhat misleading. It dates back hundreds of years but has carried over as the term used to describe the law that defines what types of contracts must be in writing before they will be enforced by a court.[17] The term statute of frauds does have some relevance however. It was created to establish a requirement for written contracts in matters of significance and thereby reduce the opportunity for fraudulent misrepresentations. That theory still carries through today as a foundation of basic contract law. While all states recognize both oral and written agreements, courts and legislatures established long ago that certain agreements should be in writing to minimize any misunderstandings, doubt, or difficulty in completing the terms of the agreement by the parties involved. Every state has passed legislation that clearly defines the types of agreements that must be reduced to writing and acknowledged by the parties before they will be considered enforceable contracts. Similar to the historic tradition, the types of agreements that must be written are those which involve substantial rights, property, or transactions and whose terms should be clearly stated to minimize the opportunity for mistake or misinterpretation.[18] There are some variations from state to state on the types of contracts required to be written, but most commonly they follow the same pattern as those used for hundreds of years and include some or all of the following types of agreements:

- Promise by executor or administrator of an estate to answer personally for the debts or obligations of the deceased
- Promise by one party to answer for the debts or obligations of another
- Promise given in exchange for a promise of marriage
- Promise to sell, transfer, or convey an interest in land, may include ownership, possession, control, or any other interest
- Promise for the sale of commercial goods by a merchant in which the price exceeds a statutory amount such as $500
- Promise that, according to its own terms, will require more than one year for completion

Ordinarily, if a contract is oral and the subject matter falls within the statute of fraud, a court will not recognize the existence of a contract and consequently will not enforce its terms. However, if a party acts in the belief that a valid contract exists but the opposing party seeks to retain the benefit without providing the consideration he or she had promised, by alleging under the statute of frauds that there was never a contract, a court may be inclined to treat the case differently. The requirement that a contract be in writing if it is of the type described in the statute of frauds may be disregarded if a party acts in good faith that a valid contract exists and another party attempts to avoid his or her duty by then alleging that the statute of frauds voids any agreement. The court will determine whether any other adequate and available legal remedy exists. If the finding is that the most adequate remedy would be to recognize a contract, the court may then do so to prevent injustice.[19] This enforcement and refusal to abandon the contract is known as estoppel.

D. BREACH OF CONTRACT AND DEFENSES TO CLAIMS OF BREACH OF CONTRACT

Even when both parties initially enter into a contractual agreement with honorable intentions, circumstances may arise that prevent the contract from being completed as originally planned. When one or both parties does not complete the contract terms, claims of breach may be raised. When an action for breach of contract is brought, several defenses are available that may prevent a judgment against the defendant. Many were discussed previously as defects or irregularities in the steps of creating a contract. The following paragraphs discuss these and other defenses in the context of defenses.

Some of the most common defenses include the following:

- Absence of one or more essential elements to create a contract
- Unconscionable contract
- Fraud
- Statute of frauds
- Accord and satisfaction
- Justifiable breach
- Impossibility or impracticability
- Frustration of purpose or terminated duty

A party may allege one, several, or all of the defenses alternatively. Thus, while a jury may not find sufficient evidence to support one defense, it might be persuaded that another applies, and the plaintiff's case will fail. In any event, there are a number of reasons that a contract may not end with the exchange of consideration as originally intended. In some instances, a party does not carry out the contract terms as the result of conduct by the other party. In others, there are external forces that make the completion of the contract an unreasonable task, or a party may simply refuse to honor the contract, in which case the other party is left only the alternatives of doing nothing or pursuing legal action.

The defenses of fraud, unconscionability, and statute of frauds are typically raised when a party is sued for breach upon a refusal to complete the terms of a contract, or when the innocent party files suit for breach on the basis that he or she suffered damage or loss as the result of another's fraudulent or unconscionable act. Other grounds for suits involving breach are those just listed. One such basis is commonly referred to as accord and satisfaction. Under this theory, the defendant claims to have satisfied the requirement of consideration by the performance of a new and different consideration, which the parties agreed to in place of the original consideration. The *accord* is the amendment to the original agreement with a substitution and the *satisfaction* is the performance of the more recent consideration. If however, it can be shown that the new consideration was not rendered, suit can be brought on either of the promises.

Assignment 12.3

> Consider the following circumstances and answer this question: If A paid the original amount and got the party as originally planned, why should B have the option to sue on the second promise?
>
> A contracts with B to cater a wedding reception in exchange for $2,500. Later, A contacts B and asks to change the reception to an outdoor event complete with tents and live music. B agrees to provide everything for an additional $2,500, making a total cost of $5,000. A agrees and makes a $2,500 down payment. However, the day before the scheduled event there is a hurricane-force storm and A changes the party back to an indoor event. B has already expended over $2,500 on preparations, much of which was for the outdoor event. A refuses to pay the balance of $2,500 and B sues on the basis of the second promise.

Another type of defense often raised in breach of contract cases is a justified breach of contract. When one party breaches a contract, the second party is excused from the completion of performance. The reasoning is that the second party did not receive the consideration that originally induced his or her own promise or performance. Therefore, if consideration fails, there is no basis for requiring the contractual agreement to continue. Additionally, some circumstances force the involuntary breach of contract. When this occurs, the party who fails to perform as required by the contract will not be held liable. Most commonly, such situations are referred to as impossibility or impracticability of performance and include situations where the contract cannot be completed through no fault of the parties.[20]

APPLICATION 12.12

J lived in an apartment in a large city. He bought a boat and contracted to pay $1500 for one year of rent at a marina outside the city. After three months, there was a flood and the docks at the marina were badly damaged, making them virtually unusable for four months. J took his boat to a different marina and contracted to store the boat there. The second marina would only accept one-year leases. When the first marina reopened, they informed J that he was committed for an additional five months and demanded that he continue to pay according to his contract. In this situation, J was left with no alternative but to find a location for his boat as the result of the damage to the first marina. Therefore, he was justified in his ending the first contract and would probably not be held liable for the remaining rent.

Point for Discussion: Would the outcome be different if J lived on the river-front and had a dock himself but used the marina because of its social club for members?

Similar to the impossibility or impracticability rule are the defenses of frustration of performance and terminated duty. These occur when, through no action by the parties, the purpose of the contract is destroyed. Consequently, the duty to perform ends.[21]

APPLICATION 12.13

A company that manufactures ski equipment contracts with a small ski shop in a mountainous area to provide several thousand dollars worth of custom-made skis with the shop logo imprinted on them. Two weeks before the scheduled shipment there is an enormous avalanche and the shop is destroyed under tons of snow. The owner sends a notice to the manufacturer to stop production. The manufacturer holds to the contract, produces the skis, and demands payment. When the business was destroyed and the manufacturer given notice of this prior to making the skis, the owner would have the right to claim justified breach as the result of frustration of purpose.

Point for Discussion: Should the result be different if the skis had already been received but the contract not yet paid?

E. REMEDIES FOR BREACH OF CONTRACT

1. Damages

As the examples clearly illustrate, numerous circumstances arise that prevent contracts from reaching completion, and many defenses can be offered against the charge of breach of contract. But what happens when the defenses fail and there is a judgment finding that a contract was wrongfully breached by one of the parties involved? When the finding is that a breach did occur and was not justified in any way, the plaintiff is then entitled to some type of remedy for the damage incurred as a result of the breach.

There are typically three remedies available for breach of contract cases. They include (a) compensatory or liquidated, (b) exemplary damages, and, on rare occasions, (c) specific performance. Each is distinct and the latter two only apply in particular situations of breach and when the law of the particular jurisdiction allows.

The most common remedy is compensatory damages to a plaintiff who has suffered from a breach of contract. This is the typical remedy in nearly all lawsuits seeking damages. The purpose of compensatory damages is exactly as the name implies. It is to award a sufficient amount of money to place the plaintiff in the same position he should be in if the contract had been fulfilled. The exception would be in the case of a contract that was found to be void, in which case the court would attempt to restore the injured party to the position he or she occupied prior to the contract being entered. In this way, the plaintiff is compensated for any loss or injury. Even if the injury or loss did not actually involve money, the purpose of the remedy is to enable the plaintiff to repair the damage.

Liquidated damage clauses are often included in contracts that address subjects in which it is difficult for laypersons to establish loss with any degree of specificity. An example is a production contract for a subject or item that is affected by seasonal fluctuations. Such a case might be in a construction contract, when the failure to complete parts of the process in a timely manner can have a significant effect in an area subject to harsh winter weather that may slow or halt further work. Another example might be the production of seasonal items such as those produced for a specific holiday, for example, paper plates with a Christmas motif. In these types of contracts, the damage due to indeterminable delays or possible lost sales are difficult to determine with great accuracy. As a result, such contracts may indicate a pre-established amount of damage in the event that the contract is breached. In this situation, the court determines if the terms of the liquidation clause are fair and reasonable to the parties who entered the contract. If so, the only issue in the lawsuit is whether the contract was breached. If it was, then the court applies the terms of the liquidated damage clause that was included in the contract.

In some cases, a liquidated damage clause will not be enforced by a court. This occurs when, upon consideration, the court finds that the language of the clause will have more of an effect of imposing a penalty on the breaching party than of compensating the party who suffered damage. This is likely if the amount is extraordinarily high given the extent of the breach. Liquidated damage clauses are intended to replace the element of compensatory damages and not to act as penalty clauses. The goal is the same as that of compensatory damage, which is to fairly offset any actual or likely loss. If a liquidated damage clause is found to be more penal in nature, then the court will assess what is considered to be a reasonable amount of compensatory damages. The reasoning behind the refusal to enforce penalty clauses is quite simple. In some situations, a party does not have a true defense to the breach and the breach was not intentional. Rather, it may be the result of unforeseen circumstances that cause the breaching party to cease or delay performance. In such instances, it would not be fair to allow parties to penalize one another in excess of what would be reasonable compensation for the breach. The courts prefer to retain authority to determine appropriate circumstances for penalizing persons who breach a contract and in some jurisdictions, such penalties are not even permitted.

As mentioned earlier, some jurisdictions do permit damage awards in addition to compensatory damages that are for the sole purpose of punishing the defendant for their conduct. Such damages are commonly referred to as exemplary or punitive damages. When these are allowed, they are typically awarded only in extreme cases. Punitive damages are most often awarded when it can be shown that the defendant—the breaching party in a contract case—did so with full knowledge and intention and with total disregard for the effects of the breach on the injured party. These types of damages may also be awarded in other types of lawsuits when they are permitted by the law of a jurisdiction. Because the function of the civil, as opposed to criminal, courts is to repair injury, the focus on punishment in civil cases is usually reserved for those who act with total disregard for both the rights of others and the law.

Another type of remedy available in limited situations in contract law is specific performance. This is not often sought out and is even more rarely granted.

2. Specific Performance

The remedy of specific performance is an order by the court that a party complete all the terms of the contract. When the relationship between the parties has deteriorated to the point of litigation, it is not usually productive to force the parties to continue to

APPLICATION 12.14

Two business partners contract to have a new building constructed for an ice cream shop they plan to open on May 25, which is the start of the Memorial Day weekend of the coming year. In the construction contract they want to ensure that the building is ready for occupancy by May 15 so they can take full advantage of the summer business in the resort community where the building is located. The contract includes a liquidated damage clause that states for each day beyond May 15 that the building is not completed, the contractor will reduce the cost of the building by $1,000. As the result of a record winter for snow, the contractor falls behind and does not complete the work until June 15. The business opens on June 18. The owners allege the final price should be reduced by $31,000 due to the 31 days during which the building was not completed. The contractor claims that the average income from the business, without considering expenses, is $200 to 400 per day and even during the holiday weekend of July 4th the business income was only an average of $600 per day for three days. The contractor also claims that the business was not even scheduled to open until May 25 and required only three days of preparation prior to opening rather than the originally scheduled 10 days (May 15 to 25). The court finds that the lost profits as the result of the delay to be dramatically less than the liquidated damage clause of $1,000 per day and finds the clause to be unenforceable to the extent it penalizes the contractor. The court reduces the award to an amount more reflective of the actual damages suffered by the delay.

Point for Discussion: In the situation above, should any other factors be considered beyond the expected profits of the business? Would the result be different if the business were in an established neighborhood with repeat customers rather than a tourist area?

work together. However, in a very limited set of circumstances, specific performance may be the only way to truly correct the breach in a manner that adequately compensates the party injured by the breach.

When specific performance is awarded, the party who has breached the contractual terms, in all or in part, is ordered to continue performance under the contract to the best of his or her ability. Traditionally, under the old English system, cases were brought either at law or equity. Cases at law usually involved monetary disputes and sought a fair resolution. Cases in courts of equity involved disputes over a party's legal duty or relationship to another and sought the fairest possible result. Cases in equity are based on the principle that money is an insufficient remedy and fairness warrants court-ordered action or nonaction of some kind. In the case of contract law, it would usually be specific performance. Over the years and through the evolution of the American legal system, the separate courts of law and equity for most purposes have been combined, but the principles still apply. The key to obtaining a court-ordered performance of contract terms is to clearly prove that because the performance is unique, it can only be satisfied through the actual performance. Before the court will award specific performance, the plaintiff must show that he or she has fully satisfied all obligations under the contract and that he or she has not acted in any way that contributed to or encouraged the breach by the defendant, including intervention or lack of cooperation. This is commonly referred to as the requirement of *clean hands*. An additional obligation is that the claim for breach and requested remedy must not be delayed so long that it causes an impairment or significant additional burden on the defendant's ability to render a specific performance. Because there are so few instances in which the courts cannot award a reasonable sum to compensate a party injured by a contractual breach, specific performance is seldom granted. Often it is confined to situations in which a unique subject or talent is part of the consideration that cannot be reasonably assessed in terms of dollars and cents. Even then, the courts are reluctant because determination must be made as to whether the specific performance was completed to the best of the defendant's ability in a situation where an unwilling defendant was literally forced to comply with the contractual obligations.

Assignment 12.4

> Describe a contractual situation in which a breach occurs and specific performance would be appropriate. Explain fully why compensatory damages would be inadequate as a remedy.

F. WHEN CONTRACTS AFFECT OR INVOLVE THIRD PARTIES

Typically, a contract is entered into by all affected parties at the same time with a mutual exchange of consideration. However, it is possible to enter a contract with the intent to deliver or receive consideration from one who is not party to the contract or to subsequently alter contract terms to deliver or receive consideration from one who is not originally party to the agreement. Such situations are called third-party contracts and have special requirements and circumstances to be determined enforceable. There are several different kinds of third-party contracts depending upon the status of the third parties in their relationship to the contractors and whether the third party is to receive or deliver the consideration that was the subject of the original agreement.

Essentially, there are three types of third-party contracts that involve receipt of consideration by a third party rather than the original party to the contract. These third parties benefit from receiving this consideration and, thus, are referred to as **third-party beneficiaries.** The three types of third-party beneficiaries are donee beneficiaries, creditor beneficiaries, and incidental beneficiaries. The rights of each to receive consideration are the direct result of their relationship to the contractor whose consideration they are to receive.

In the case of the donee beneficiary, a party to contract fully intends and wants the beneficiary to receive the performance in the form of a gift from the donor contractor. This is a quite common occurrence. For example, assume someone calls a florist and offers payment by credit card in exchange for the florist's delivery of a flower arrangement to a third party. The contract donor wants to make a gift of flowers to the donee beneficiary and does so by contracting with the florist for the delivery of flowers in exchange for payment. The donee did nothing and was not obligated in any way by the contract. Rather, he or she received the benefit of the consideration to which the contract donor was entitled—a delivery of flowers—in place of the donor. However, once

Third-Party Beneficiary
One who, as the result of gift or collateral agreement, is entitled to the contractual performance owed another.

the donee beneficiary relationship has been completely established, the donee or the contract party can pursue a remedy if a breach occurs.

The creditor beneficiary is quite different from the donee beneficiary. Here, a party to a contract has a legal obligation as a debtor of some type to a third party who acts as a creditor. The contract party can ask that the consideration to be received under the contract be given instead to the creditor in the form of payment on the debt. For example, a student might take out student loans to pay for educational expenses. Later, the student accepts a job with a local business. The student has a contractual arrangement in which he or she works in exchange for periodic payment at a set rate. If the student asks that once each month a certain amount of the entitled pay be deposited directly into the account of the creditor who issued the student loans until they are repaid, the creditor becomes a third-party beneficiary of the student's contractual arrangement with the employer. The creditor beneficiary, unlike the donee beneficiary, is in fact entitled to something from the debtor/contract party. This entitlement is satisfied through the receipt of consideration that the student would otherwise be receiving from the employer. Like the donee beneficiary, either the contract party or the creditor beneficiary who has been clearly identified as such, can pursue action against the other party to the contract in the event of breach. In addition, if the creditor does not receive the consideration, he or she may also be able to pursue legal remedies against the contractor who promised them the benefit because the original debt existed between them.

Finally, there is the incidental beneficiary. This is the simplest of all because the incidental beneficiary is not contemplated by either party to the contract as an intended recipient of any benefit and has no legal relationship to either party. As a result, if the contract is not fulfilled, the incidental beneficiary has no rights. For example, assume an elderly woman in a small community contracts to have her home made handicap accessible in all respects. The job is extensive and requires a great deal of lumber and related supplies. The local builder with whom she contracts, purchases all of the goods needed at the local hardware company. The hardware company is an incidental beneficiary. Assume the woman dies before the work is completed. The builder who had been receiving periodic payments ceases work and effectively breaches the contract. The woman's estate representative does nothing to force completion of the work. The incidental beneficiary who would have continued to benefit from the purchase of the goods to complete the work has no rights as neither party ever had actual intent to benefit him or her in the first place. Rather, the incidental beneficiary is created through fortuitous circumstance and is just as easily denied by the occurrence of circumstances that bring an end to the contract.

Any time a third party is brought into a contract, whether it is to receive or give performance, there is an issue of assignment and delegation. An assignment or delegation takes place when one or more parties to a contract assign rights or delegate duties under the terms of the contract to a third party. Generally, assignment or delegation is acceptable *unless* (1) the parties have stipulated in the contract that it is not permissible or (2) the assignment or delegation would significantly alter the duty or rights of the other party to the contract.

In an assignment, a promisor under the contract assigns the rights or benefits of the consideration they are entitled to receive under the terms of the contract to a third party. The promisor in the contract is known as the assignor and the receiving third party—also known as a third-party beneficiary, creditor, or donee—is the assignee. If there is a complete assignment, the assignee steps into the shoes of the assignor and can enforce the contract against the remaining party to the contract. In a partial assignment, the enforcement, if necessary, would come from the assignor.

In the case of a delegation of duty, a promisor in a contract receives consideration but delegates his or her own duty to perform and provide consideration under the contract to a third party. In such a case, the delagatee (party accepting the duty) must be able to provide an equivalent performance. In addition, the party delegating the duty as the original party to the contract (delegator) remains liable for performance until the duties are performed satisfactorily by the delagatee.

PARALEGALS IN THE WORKPLACE

The employment of paralegals in the area of contract law can occur in a multitude of settings. Of course in the traditional law firm, paralegals may be used to collect information, communicate with clients, and in some instances even draft simple contracts under the supervision of an attorney. But many paralegals also find employment in the corporate world processing contracts, monitoring compliance, and so forth for businesses who regularly use standard contracts in the daily course of business. The settings for this vary from the legal department of a hospital to manufacturing. The reality is that most businesses have contractual relationships with other businesses for goods or services and processing these documents requires a basic knowledge of contract principles. However, most do not involve interpretation and legal advice or advocacy, so contract law can be a lucrative opportunity for paralegals both within the law firm and outside that traditional setting.

Chapter Summary

While it is one of the oldest established areas of law, contract law continues to be a major component of the American legal system. With every change and development in society and technology, a plethora of situations arise in which contracts and their fulfillment come into question. While the established principles remain the same, each unique situation requires a different application. Because clear principles are so well thought out and tried over the centuries, there is a sound and adequate fund of knowledge that can be used to create valid contracts that anticipate difficulties and resolve differences without litigation.

First and foremost, the basic elements of contracts must be satisfied. That is, the parties must have capacity, intent shown through a manifestation of assent, and an exchange of adequate consideration. When an offer is extended, it must contain all the essential elements for an acceptance for it to constitute a valid and enforceable agreement. Any conditions that exist at the time of the agreement that would affect appropriate disclosure, fairness, or voluntary action by either of the parties can result in the contract being treated as void or voidable. Further, the extended offer is good until such time as it expires, is properly rescinded, or is accepted or denied by the offeree. The point in time at which this occurs depends on the circumstances of the parties and the terms under which the offer was extended.

If an agreement to contract is reached, both parties are obligated to render their performance or complete the performance promised, depending on whether the agreement is a bilateral or unilateral contract. When a party fails to perform or complete a promised performance, the party entitled to that consideration may bring an action for breach. While there are limited situations when a defense for breach can be effectively raised, if none apply, the court may impose penalties that include compensatory, liquidated, and possibly even exemplary damages, or specific performance.

In some situations, third parties benefit from or accept duties under a contractual agreement. In this case, the assignment of benefit or delegation of duty must not significantly alter the terms of the agreement, nor may it be allowed if the parties previously agreed to prohibit it. When it does occur, the contracting parties still may be considered responsible until the assignment or delegation and ultimately the contract terms are successfully concluded.

ETHICAL NOTE

The standard ethical obligations for legal professionals apply in the practice area of contract law just as they would in any field. However, the lawyer is considered to be in a contractual relationship with the client as well as representing the client with respect to contractual matters. For this reason, it is perhaps even more incumbent on the legal professional to ensure that ethical obligations are fully satisfied with respect to the client and in support of that contractual relationship.

Relevant Internet Sites

World Wide Web Virtual Law Library	www.law.indiana.edu/v-lib/
Employment Court	www.nzir.dol.govt.nz/oldsite/court.html
Encyclopedia.com	www.encyclopedia.com/articles/03110.html
WWW Multimedia Law	www.oikoumene.com

Internet Assignment 12.1

Locate two resources for form contracts on the Internet.

KEY TERMS

Bilateral Contract	Contractual Agreement	Third-Party Beneficiary
Contract	Statute of Frauds	Unilateral Contract

ENDNOTES

1. Restatement (Second), Second 24 of Contracts.
2. Chilfres and Spritz, Status in the Law of Contracts, 47 New York Law Review 1 (April 1972).
3. *Quantum Chemical Corp. v. Mobil Oil Corp.*, 1995 WL 610739 (Ohio App. 1st. Dist. 1995).
4. *Kilroe v. Troast*, 117 N.H. 598, 376 A.2d 131 (1977).
5. *Flemington National Bank & Trust Co. (N.A.) v. Domler Leasing Corp.*, 65 A.D.2d 29, 410 N.Y.S.2d 75 (1978).
6. Restatement of Contracts, (Second), Section 12.
7. Restatement (Second) of Contracts, Section 12.
8. 17 Am.Jur. 2d. Contracts, Section 31.
9. *European-American Banking Corp. v. Chock Full O'Nuts Corp.*, 109 Misc.2d 615, 442 N.Y.S.2d 715 (1981).
10. 7A C.J.S., Auctions and Auctioneers, Section 11.
11. *Schmidt v. Foster*, 380 p.2d 124 (Wyo. 1963).
12. *Mobil Oil Corp. v. Wroten*, 303 A.2d 698 aff'd 315 A.2d 728 (Del. 1973).
13. 17A. C.J.S., Contracts, Section 586.

14. Id.
15. *Mitchell v. Aetna Casualty & Surety Co.*, 579 F.2d 342 (5th Cir. 1978).
16. *Christian v. Christian*, 42 N.Y.2d 63, 396 N.Y.S.2d 817, 365 N.E.2d 849 (1977).
17. 17 AmJur.2d, Contracts.
18. Id.
19. Restatement of Contracts 2nd, Section 139(2).
20. Id.
21. 17 Am.Jur. 2d Contracts, Section 400.

Chapter 13

THE LAW OF REAL AND PERSONAL PROPERTY

CHAPTER OBJECTIVES

Upon completion of this chapter you should be able to do the following:

- Define the terms real property and personal property.
- Discuss the various forms of property ownership.
- Explain the right of quiet enjoyment.
- Identify a situation in which the elements of adverse possession are satisfied.
- Define and distinguish fixtures and trade fixtures.
- Discuss the nature and purpose of easements.
- Define and distinguish the various ways in which personal property can be separated from the owner.
- Discuss the warranty of habitability.
- Define and distinguish latent and patent defects.

A. THE DEVELOPMENT OF PROPERTY LAW

Much like contract law, legal principles that pertain to the ownership and possessory rights of property are some of the oldest on record. However, as societal and cultural changes have occurred, property law has evolved into a much different state than it was originally. Property law principles date back thousands of years, but most of the principles that have carried through the fabric of the developing American legal system have their roots in medieval England, as does much of the history supporting American legal standards. While many of the fundamental goals of fairness in ownership rights, transfers, and inheritances are still present, the types of ownership have developed significantly. Under the original English system, most of the land was held by a relatively small number of men and most land was rented to the less-wealthy farming community. Women could not own property. Today, anyone with capacity to contract can own property although rental and leases are also still popular. Inheritance of a relative's property is no longer a foregone conclusion and depends upon the type of ownership interest in the property that the decedent had. In addition, there are now ownership/lease property interest combinations. Each of these will be discussed as they currently exist in the American legal system.

1. What Is Property?

Early in the text the point was made that in legal terminology sometimes words that have one meaning in ordinary language have an entirely different effect when used in a legal context. The term *property* is one such term. While virtually anyone who speaks English would understand the word property to describe a physical thing or location, its meaning in a legal discussion is quite different. The legal definition of property is the right to possess or control something. Consequently, when discussing an interest in property in legal terms, the focus is on the right to possess, control, own, or transfer an interest in the item in question rather than on the item itself.

a. Real versus Personal Property   The first distinction to be made is the difference between the two basic forms of property: real and personal. There are a number of other ways to categorize property that will be discussed as well but the basic distinction between real and personal property underlies most other classifications. **Real property** is the term used to refer to land or that which is attached to land in such a way that it is considered permanent, fixed, and immovable. This definition applies to what is typically considered immovable even though the possibility might exist. Essentially the requirement is that the item must be attached to the land in such a way that it is clear the original intent was to permanently affix it to the land, such as a house. The law of real property governs all that is part of the land naturally or as a result of being artificially incorporated into the land in a permanent way. Real property includes houses, buildings, and other structures that are affixed to the property by some permanent means. An example of something that would not ordinarily be considered real property might be a mobile home that has not been permanently affixed to the ground. This type of structure is considered to be movable, even though it is a residential dwelling, so it would not be considered real property.

The converse of real property is **personal property.** While this will be discussed in greater detail later in the chapter, at this point it will be distinguished from matters of real property. Personal property describes the interest in movable items that are not

Real Property
Land or anything permanently affixed to land and no longer movable.

Personal Property
Movable items that are not land or permanently affixed to land. Personal property includes tangible (physical) and intangible items, such as rights of ownership in property held by others, such as bank accounts or rights of ownership in legal entities.

land or items permanently affixed to land. Personal property includes both tangible and intangible items. It includes money, goods, and movable, tangible items. Legally, personal property can be sold, lent, given, lost, stolen, mislaid, confused, abandoned, or altered. Generally speaking, personal property is not an interest in land or items permanently attached to land. Nor does it ordinarily include personal rights to certain intangible interests such as the right to bring a lawsuit; for example, you cannot sell your right to sue someone for property damage. However, some personal rights that are considered to be personal property would include patents and goodwill of a business, which are treated as personal property because they are rights directly associated with movables. Another significant difference in property interests are those that are owned versus those that are leased or rented. The rights and duties associated with each can vary dramatically, as seen in the discussion that follows.

b. Forms of Ownership   One's ownership interest in real property can be affected by such things as the method in which it is acquired, whether it is acquired alone or with others, marriage, inheritance, or terms of possession or ownership specified at the time the property is transferred. The right to control or own property can be obtained in a variety of ways depending on the factors mentioned. While some of those ways date back hundreds of years, other old standards have become obsolete and new ones developed. Most often, ownership interests are classified as **freehold estates,**[1] whereas interests in real property arising from lease or rental agreements are termed **nonfreehold estates.**[2]

Freehold estates involve the rights of a property owner and the conditions or limitations that might be imposed on the interest, based upon the type of freehold estate that is held. In fact, it is even possible to have a freehold estate property that is not owned. That is, there may be rights of control or use of real property without ownership rights of that property. But the most common freehold estate property interest involves ownership and the rights associated with it.

i. Fee Simple Estates   Fee simple is the most common type of real property interest in the United States. Under English common law, when a man obtained property in fee simple, it meant that the man owned the property for the duration of his lifetime. He could not transfer, sell, or give away the interest and upon his death the property interest automatically reverted back to the original owner. This is quite similar to the present day principle of a life estate discussed later.

Historically, to own property outright on a permanent basis and without limitation, the property had to be owned in a title known as fee simple absolute. To obtain such ownership, the transfer document, usually a deed, was required to include special language that clearly stated the intent of the original owner, the transferor, to give up the right of reversion. The right of reversion is when a property interest reverts back to the former owner upon the death of the current owner. It limits the ability to further transfer the property by the current owner during life, so the process of giving up such a right made the property more valuable. In the United States today, fee simple has the interpretation of the traditional transfer of fee simple absolute. In fact, for a right of reversion to exist in a modern transaction, it must be spelled out in the deed unlike the old English requirement that it was present unless excluded. This promotes the best use and freedom of ownership that was a basic tenet of the original homesteaders in the United States. Today, all transfers in fee simple are considered to be a sale of total and absolute rights over the property unless a limitation is clearly specified in certain terms on the transferring document, which is most often the deed.

Freehold Estate
Interest in real property that involves certain rights of ownership.

Nonfreehold Estates
Interest in real property that is limited in duration and involves the right of possession but not ownership.

ii. Life Estates   The holder of a life estate in real property has an ownership interest that is more focused on possessory rights than on those of ownership. One who receives a life estate has the right to totally control the property during the lifetime identified in the transferring document, such as a deed, generally without interference. The life estate tenant may prevent the sale or any other form of transfer in fee simple of the property if such a transaction would in any way impact the life estate interest. The life estate interest includes the right to do all the things an owner in fee simple could do, with one exception. The property cannot be disposed of or transferred or treated in such a way as to ruin it for its usual and customary purpose or purposes. This is known as wasting. If it is found that the life estate tenant is causing the property to be destroyed for its usual and customary purposes, the party with the original ownership interest can seek to have the life estate legally terminated. If this does not occur, the life estate continues until the death of the tenant of the life estate or until the life estate is voluntarily relinquished. When the life estate ends, possessory rights revert to the party who has the ownership interest or to the person designated by the owner to receive the possessory rights.[3]

APPLICATION 13.1

The Hutchins family owns several thousand acres of land. The land is used for recreational and agricultural purposes and includes a number of small vacation residences. They have divided the land into multiple parcels and sold life estate interests in many of these. One of the life estate holders is found to have been dumping toxic wastes collected in his trash hauling business on the parcel property to which he holds a life estate. Tests have established the property to be so contaminated that it is unfit for residential, agricultural, or recreational use. The Hutchins family sues to terminate the life estate and the court grants the action and returns the possessory rights to the Hutchins family.

Point for Discussion: Should the Hutchins have any other actions against the life estate holder? What would they be and why?

A life estate is considered to be a type of freehold estate in and of itself, even though it does not contain the basic element of transferability of ownership. A person with a life estate is responsible for the property and all duties otherwise associated with property ownership during the term of the life estate. This would include upkeep of the property and payment of real estate taxes, any insurance, and other costs associated with the property. The life estate holder cannot transfer ownership to someone else, but can transfer part or all of the life estate interest in the property, if this is allowed by the holder of the ownership rights in the property. This means that a life estate tenant could lease the property during the course of his or her lifetime, but such lease would expire when the life estate ended. Thus, with the exception of limitations on transferability and the condition of not wasting the property, the life estate holder has all the rights otherwise associated with ownership. One common situation of a life estate occurs when a spouse dies and leaves a life estate in solely owned property to the surviving spouse. When the surviving spouse dies, the estate passes completely and automatically to the one named in the transferring document, such as the will of the spouse who held the ownership interest. This is a more common occurrence as parties enter second and third marriages but wish to retain ultimate ownership of their real property to pass on to their descendants.

> Describe a situation in which a life estate holder might voluntarily relinquish the rights of the interest when wasting of the property is not involved.

iii. Other Freehold Estates Various other types of conveyances in fee simple exist as well. Conveyances of interests in real property associated with ownership but subject to a transfer back to a former holder of the interest under certain conditions is known as a reversionary interest. This is similar to the old English definition of fee simple but occurs under different circumstances that must be clearly stated when the property is transferred. For example, if one buys property by making installment payments to the owner directly, the contract may state that if the buyer dies before a certain percentage of the principal purchase price has been paid, the property will automatically revert to the seller.

Another interest in real property is known as a defeasible fee, which causes any rights associated with ownership to end when a certain event occurs. At that time the property rights pass to the party named in the document that specifies the terminating event. This pending condition might cause a change in the use of the property or even something totally arbitrary and out of the control of the owners such as a change in zoning of permitted uses of the property. Historically, the various fees had a tremendous effect on property rights, but today they are rarely used and even less often become an issue. Most land is owned predominantly in fee simple or, at most, fee simple subject to a life estate.

One interest that has survived the changes in types of real property rights is the remainder interest, which is created automatically upon the end of another. Giving one's surviving spouse, or anyone for that matter, a life estate or even ownership in property to which the spouse had no prior interest would be a remainder interest. Unless the remainder interest is indicated on the document used to transfer the property, such as a deed or will, any conveyance of property ownership is presumed to be in fee simple (historically fee simple absolute), with total control and ownership vested in the receiving party.

Among the most significant developments in the law of property are those concerning who may own, bequest, or inherit rights of ownership. Today the law is much more equitable. Under original property law principles, women could not own property. Even property inheritances from a woman's family would be passed over her and given to her spouse and/or male children. Similarly, persons of color in many jurisdictions were not permitted to own real property until much later, in 19th century America. Currently, anyone with capacity can own property. Even persons without capacity may have property held in trust for them by appointed guardians. There is no distinction between men and women on the issue of property ownership and inheritance. In the event that a spouse does not provide what would be considered fair for the surviving spouse by will, a statutory provision for what is commonly known as a forced (elected) share permits a surviving spouse to claim or elect a certain percentage of the property (real and personal) of the deceased. This claim is superior to all other heirs and prevails even if it decreases or eliminates amounts that would have otherwise been received by persons designated in a will. While it is permissible to totally disinherit one's children or anyone else, the spouse is presumed to have certain marital rights that supersede the wishes of the decedent. The law makes no distinction as to whether the surviving spouse is husband or wife. The interest received is in fee simple, rather than a life estate, and surviving children are not necessary for the interest to be received.

2. When Similar Real Property Interests Are Held by More Than One Person

Today, it is very common for more than one party to hold the title to (own) a particular parcel of real property. The relationships of these persons and reasons for multiple ownership vary widely and may be for business or personal reasons. As a result, certain types of multiple ownership have evolved to clarify such issues as what portion of the property is possessed by each, who has the right to sell or dispose of the property, and what should happen in the event one of the owners dies. The most commonly employed types of multiple ownership are tenancy in common, joint tenancy, and tenancy by the entirety.

Tenancy in Common

Form of multiple ownership of property in which each tenant (owner) shares with the other(s) an undivided interest in the property.

a. Tenancy in Common   The most frequently used type of multiple property ownership interest in the United States is **tenancy in common.** In fact, unless there is language to the contrary in the transferring document, such as the deed, the creation of ownership property interests of two or more persons is presumed to be by tenancy in common. With this type of ownership, each owner has an undivided interest in the property.[4] An undivided interest is different from having equal shares. If parties simply have equal shares in something, then conceivably the item could be split evenly among them. In the situation of an equal and undivided interest, each party has an equal share in every aspect of the property. The undivided interest concept is truly a collective interest and guarantees that no one owner has a better portion of the property. Each owner has a balanced interest in both the positive and negative aspects of the property as a whole. The percentage of undivided interest is equal to one's percentage of ownership. For example, if one tenant in common owns 40% of the property and three additional tenants in common each have a 20% interest in the property, then the first would have a 40% undivided interest in all of the property and the other partners an undivided 20% interest in the total property. Without the undivided interest, there would essentially be four owners of four parcels of property. This would defeat the concept of multiple ownership and would encourage the breaking up of parcels of land into much smaller parcels. The undivided interest encourages multiple ownership and encourages parties to work together for the best use of the property.

APPLICATION 13.2

A mother and father own 1000 acres of land. In their wills, the property is to be given to their surviving four sons in joint ownership with each son having an equal percentage of ownership. The will further provides that in the event a son predeceases his parents, the children of that son would receive his interest. If the parents die and are survived by all four sons then each would have a 25% ownership interest in each one of the 1000 acres of the property. If one of the sons had predeceased the parents but was survived by five children, then each of the children would have a 5% undivided interest in each of the 1000 acres with the surviving sons each given a 25% undivided interest in the 1000 acres.

Point for Discussion: How would the property be divided if three sons survived the parents and the son who predeceased them left no surviving children?

Although a tenant in common shares ownership of an undivided interest in the property, tenants in common may do all things with their interest as if they owned the property alone. This is, of course, subject to the exception that they cannot exclude or interfere with the use by the other tenants in common and vice versa. Essentially, a tenant in common cannot make use of the property in a way that is inconsistent with the other tenants, nor can the tenant waste the property. A tenant who does either of these things with any part of the property is doing it with a portion of the property controlled by the other tenants.

When tenants in common (or any other type of multiple ownership tenants) cannot agree on the rights and use of the property and cannot resolve the issue to the extent that joint ownership can continue effectively, they may resort to the courts for resolution. The most common suit in this situation is an action for partition. In a partition action, the court considers all the attributes of the property and then sells the property or in some cases, subdivides it into individual parcels that are then owned solely by each tenant in common. The purpose is to attempt an equitable distribution of the interests, extinguish the tenancy in common, and create in its place several individual fee simple tenancies. Such actions are relatively uncommon. Instead, one of the tenants in common will usually buy out the interest of the other tenant in common and end the multiple tenancy in that manner. In some circumstances, partition is not a viable alternative due to zoning restrictions and ordinances or laws that control the subdivision of property.

APPLICATION 13.3

Recall the previous example in which the sons inherit the property. Assume that after the parents die and each of the four sons inherits the tenancy in common property interest, they set about to make the most of their inheritance. One son begins farming approximately 25% of the property, which has been put to this use in the past. Two of the sons begin selling guided hunting trips through a wooded portion of the property covering approximately 50% of the property. The remaining son takes what was once pasture land and installs a golf driving range on the remaining 25% of the property. However, the fourth son has a great deal of difficulty in developing his business because of the constant sound of gunfire and frequent occurrence of birds being shot above and falling onto the driving range. Also, the son who farms is duly concerned for his own safety when operating his machinery near the area where the farmland meets the woods. In this situation, dividing the land is not going to resolve the issues because, although each may obtain their own interests, the activities of two of the sons would continue to interfere with the ownership rights of the other two sons. For this reason, although a partition might be legally possible, the better option would be for two of the sons to buy out the interests of two of the other sons.

Point for Discussion: If none of the sons were willing to sell their interest, how should the matter be resolved?

Tenancies in common do not always start and end with the same individuals or even start or end at the same time. A tenant in common can sell, give, or in some manner convey the interest in the property on an individual basis. When this occurs, the new owner becomes a tenant in common with the existing tenants in common, but without the one who transferred interest to the new owner. Similarly, when a tenant in common dies, the heirs of the estate or specifically identified heir in a will assume the role of the new tenant in common with the prior tenants in common. The exception to this rule is when the tenancy in common is owned by a recognized and legal partnership. In that case, the ownership may pass to the heirs, however they do not become part of the partnership. Additionally, as the partnership is dissolved and property/assets distributed, the surviving partners may have a claim against the property to the extent it would provide them with an equitable portion of the partnership value.

Joint Tenancy
Form of multiple-property ownership in which the property owners have fee simple and share four unities. Each owner shares in the unity of right of survivorship.

b. Joint Tenancy   In very specific circumstances, another type of multiple ownership tenancy can be created, known as a **joint tenancy.** One of the unique characteristics of a joint tenancy is what has come to be known as the right of survivorship. In this type of multiple ownership, if a joint tenant dies, the interest passes at the moment of death to the surviving joint tenants. The interest is not considered part of the estate of the deceased joint tenant and is not subject to the claims of the joint tenant's creditors or heirs. Because a joint tenancy defeats the claims and rights of one's natural or appointed heirs, and circumvents the claims of creditors of one who dies, there is a strict requirement that the creation of a joint tenancy reflect an intent by each of the tenants to create a joint tenancy and consequent right of survivorship. In this way, the heirs are protected from losing an interest in property when it was not the desire of the deceased for them to do so.

Before a joint tenancy will be legally recognized, four conditions must be satisfied that the joint tenants have in common and that together clearly establish the intent to create a joint tenancy rather than the ordinary tenancy in common. These four items are called *unities*, because they are shared by the tenants. They include the following:

1. Each tenant must receive his or her other interest in the property at the same time (unity of time).
2. Each tenant must receive his or her interest from the same source, namely, the previous owner (unity of title).
3. Each tenant must share identical rights regarding the property such as an equal share or percentage of ownership (unity of interest).
4. Each tenant must have an undivided ownership interest in the property itself (unity of possession).

Thus, the only way to have a joint tenancy is for the multiple owners to agree to it with the intent of right of survivorship among themselves. They must then purchase the entire property at the same time, from the same owner, in equal shares, and with an undivided right of possession that is not subject to a superior right of possession, such as a life estate, by another. If all of the preceding occur and a state statute does not indicate otherwise, the parties also automatically receive the right of survivorship. However, in some states, the right of survivorship must also be clearly stated in the conveying instrument (usually the deed) to further demonstrate the understanding and the intent of the parties to create this interest. If no such statute exists, the right is usually presumed from the words joint tenancy in the deed.

A joint tenancy and the consequent right of survivorship are extinguished when one or more of the parties transfers their interest in the property to another. What remains is a joint tenancy between two or more of the remaining original tenants (assuming there are at least two remaining) and a tenancy in common between them and the new tenant. The important effect of this is that the new owner is a tenant in common and will receive nothing upon the death of one of the original joint tenants. This failure to inherit is reciprocal. However, if one of the joint tenants dies, the remaining joint tenant(s) will receive that tenant's interest.

APPLICATION 13.4

A group of six investors purchase property as a joint tenancy with rights of survivorship. They intend to hold the property for investment purposes. After some time, investors five and six want to commercially develop the property. Investors one through four refuse. Investor five sells his interest to new investor A. Investor 6 sells his interest to new investor B. Investors one through four remain joint tenants with one another. Investors A and B are tenants in common with respect to their interest with each other and the first four investors. If Investor three dies, then 1/6 of the interest in the property will be equally divided among investors one, two, and four. If investor B dies, 1/6 of the interest will pass according to the terms of B's estate to the heirs and nothing will go to investors one, two, three, four, or A.

Point for Discussion: How would the situation change if investor five sold his interest to investor three? What type of interest would investor three have?

The basic rights of joint tenants are similar to those of tenancy in common. The joint tenant can use and possess the property in any way that does not waste or interfere with the rights of the other joint tenants. However, a joint tenant cannot successfully devise (give) his or her interest to heirs in a will. Such a conveyance would take place after the owner's death, which would be ineffective since the right of survivorship is complete at the moment of death. At the moment a joint tenant dies, the interest passes to the other joint tenant(s) so there is nothing to transfer as part of the estate. Consequently, if a joint tenant wants to sever a joint tenancy or to pass a property interest to another, it must be completed prior to death by legal conveyance of one or more of the unity interests to the receiving party.

c. Tenancy by the Entirety   The last and least common type of multiple ownership interest is known as tenancy by the entirety. This has been largely abandoned and many states no longer recognize it as distinct from joint tenancy. Those that do, often require the instrument of conveyance, such as the deed, to use the specific language for such a tenancy to be created. Tenancy by the entireties requires all of the same four unities as a joint tenancy and also includes a right of survivorship. In addition, there is the requirement that the owners of the property interest be husband and wife. When one spouse dies, the property passes at the moment of death (rather than through the estate) to the surviving spouse, who then takes title to the property in fee simple as an individual owner. Because the only distinction is that the parties be married, the reasoning of many jurisdictions is that the same thing is accomplished when the parties take the property interests as joint tenants. As with any transfer of property to multiple owners, the presumption is that the interests transferred are as tenants in common unless the instrument of conveyance specifically identifies a different type of tenancy and the requirements of that type of tenancy are satisfied.

A tenancy by the entirety is one that cannot be conveyed in its same form. This is because of the requirement of unity of person (marriage). Any conveyance by one spouse would result in a tenancy in common between the remaining spouse and the recipient of the other spouse's interest. The interest of a tenant by the entirety cannot be conveyed by a will to another person, nor is the interest of one of the tenants subject to claims of nonjoint creditors. In the same progression as a joint tenancy interest, the right of survivorship causes the interest to pass automatically by operation of law at the moment of death. Thus, a will would be an incomplete conveyance prior to the death and, because the property interest passes at the moment of death, it is not part of the estate to be claimed by heirs and creditors.

Assignment 13.2

> In the following situations, describe the type of interest of each party, if any, at the conclusion of the occurrences.
>
> a. A and B have a tenancy in common. B dies and is survived by C, his spouse.
> b. A and B have a joint tenancy. B dies and is survived by C, his spouse.
> c. A and B are partners and have property in joint tenancy. B dies and is survived by C, his spouse.
> d. A and B have a joint tenancy and are married. B dies and is survived by C, his son from a former marriage.
> e. A and B have a tenancy in common and are divorced. B dies and is survived by C, his son from a former marriage.
> f. A and B have a joint tenancy and are divorced. B dies and is survived by C, his son from a former marriage.
> g. A and B have a tenancy by the entireties and obtain a divorce. On the same day, B dies and is survived by C, his son from a former marriage.

3. Air and Subsurface Rights

Since the early days of property principles in common law, it has been established that the ownership of property extends below the property to the center of the earth and above the property to the top of the sky.[5] With respect to natural bodies of moving waters, when a nonnavigable stream flows on property, the owner possesses the bed of the stream but not the water flowing on it. This is because the water is not a permanent part of the land. Navigable streams are part of the public domain and ownership of property adjacent to them generally extends to the shore.[6] When these concepts were originally established as legal principles, they were simplistic yet effective and answered any questions of control, ownership, use, and possession that might arise. However, over time, modifications have become necessary.

As population and technology have grown, the concepts have been altered slightly to adapt to new questions associated with property interests. But, remarkably, the basic principles have stood the test of time in their general approach toward fairness and equity among those with competing interests in property. The fee simple property owner still typically has the right to possess all of the property to the very heights but is subject to some minor limitations. The public necessity of access to the air for air travel is considered more important and of greater public benefit than the right to control the air above one's land to infinite space. Consequently, the public interest overrides the private rights to control the entire sky above one's property. Similarly, while an owner is entitled to control a stream bed on his or her property, the course of the bed cannot be changed so as to substantially alter the flow of water as it enters another's property, because such a change could flood the land or deprive the owners of the use of the water. These types of principles continue to be developed as changes in technology and culture occur. The common thread is that the individual's rights to control the property are honored and left intact to the greatest extent possible and are only affected when the public interest or the rights of another are jeopardized or are waived through a formalized limitation, transfer, or sharing of rights.

In general, the owner has the right to all aspects of the property on, above, and below the land except that which has been somehow limited, as was shown in the examples concerning air travel and moving waters. The same is true of mineral rights. It is possible to own property and yet lease or sell the rights to mine below the surface to the extent the mining does not affect surrounding properties. Also, it is possible to obtain a limited space of property interest such as in the case of a condominium. In a situation where many individual units are contained within a building on one parcel of property, the owner obtains a property interest over the limited space occupied by the particular unit. In that circumstance, the ownership by voluntary waiver, does not extend above and below the property, and often may not include the land at all except to the extent it supports the unit in the building. Rather, the unit is owned individually. The ownership interest in the land and below, as well as the air above is something that may be held in a multiple-type tenancy and shared among the owners of the various units located on the property. The key is that ownership interests allow total and unlimited use of a property unless the natural boundaries of the property are subject to a voluntary limitation or one imposed for what is considered the greater public good.

4. Incorporeal Interests

In the law of property, the term incorporeal interests describes the rights or privileges associated with ownership of real property. One such right that is highly protected is the right of quiet enjoyment. It is presumed that the right to possess real property automatically includes the right to such possession and the right to use it free from interference by others. When someone invades another's property, he or she is, in effect, invading the right of quiet enjoyment. A corresponding area of incorporeal interests deals with the the law of easements—rights of nonowners to affect the use of an owner's real property. The law of easements is fairly complex and is only briefly introduced here.

Easements   An **easement** is the right of one other than the owner to affect another's property interest and rights. What this means in real terms is that it is possible to obtain a limited legal right to influence the use, control, or possession of a property owner.[7] When an easement exists, the property interest that is subjected to control is referred to as the servient tenement. The person or entity who exercises the limitation is the dominant tenement. An easement is not a lease or other relinquishment of control over an entire property interest, but rather, it affects a limited portion of the property in a limited way. An easement may be a limited right to use property or to control the manner in which the property is used by its owner and others.

Easement
Legal right of one to interfere with property use by owner or one in legal possession of property due to a superseding interest.

Easements, like other property interests, are recorded in government records. This is to provide formal notice for all with real or potential interests in property that limitations have been legally exercised. If an easement is titled *in gross*, then the party who has the dominant tenement interests cannot transfer the rights to the easement. When that party's interest in the subject that created the easement ends, the easement is extinguished. If an easement is considered to be *appurtenant*, then it is an ongoing limitation and the control by the dominant tenement can be passed on to others indefinitely.

APPLICATION 13.5

(1) Landowner X has a parcel of land that is surround on three sides by water. The only land access is across the property of landowner Y. Landowner X is granted an easement appurtenant to create a road along a specific portion of Landowner Y's property to provide access to the otherwise landlocked property. Landowner Y cannot interfere with the creation, maintenance, or use of the road in any way that would inhibit X's right of access. This is an easement appurtenant because the need for the easement would continue even if Landowner X sold his own property interest to someone else.

(2) Landowner A and B own adjacent farmland. The only accessible water for livestock is a stream crossing through the property of Landowner B. Landowner A purchases an easement from Landowner B to allow his livestock to enter the fenced pasture area where the stream is located for water. The easement is granted for as long as A continues to own his property and use it for livestock production. The limited duration of the easement and the inability of A to sell his easement to the property of B is an easement in gross.

Point for Discussion: Why is situation A considered appurtenant and B is not?

An easement is an interest associated with property and, therefore, is subject to the statute of frauds. As discussed in the chapter on contract law, any matter dealing with an interest in real property must generally be in writing before it is considered legally enforceable. This includes the transfer of any interest, partial or whole, limited or unlimited, in real property. If real property or an easement affecting it is created or conveyed voluntarily, the conveyance must be in writing to be effective and enforceable. However, some easements are not the result of a voluntary transaction of purchase and grant of rights.

An easement can be created in several ways. Two common methods are easement by conveyance and easement by necessity. An easement by conveyance grants another an easement over existing property rights. Such a conveyance can be for an easement in gross or an easement appurtenant. An easement of necessity, which is implied by circumstances, can be created when no other reasonable alternative exists to satisfy the rights of others affected by the property and the grantor does not voluntarily grant the easement. Because all property is adjacent to other property, it is somewhat common for the use of one's property to interfere with the use of another's property. An easement created by necessity may be without the consent of the owner, but it must be legally established in court before it will be recognized and enforced. A less common type is the easement by prescription. In this case, there is no formal creation of the easement either through conveyance or necessity but a landowner acquiesces in another's limited use of some aspect of the property without permission for a period of time. Easements can occur between private parties or between individuals and governmental bodies. For example, the easements described in the previous application involved private property owners. However, a very common form of easement occurs when the government obtains easement rights to allow utilities to cross the property of others to establish a network of service.

In addition to the various descriptive terms for how easements are created and their elements, they can also be classified in two other ways. The first is known as an affirmative easement. This occurs when the party holding the dominant tenement has the right to enter onto the servient tenement for a particular purpose.[8] An example would be to use the property for access to another property. The other type of easement is known as a negative easement. As implied by its name, the negative easement is the right to prevent the use of property in a particular manner because the use would adversely affect the rights of the dominant tenement. An example would be that a utility company can prohibit the laying of a concrete patio on an area of ground that covers submerged utility lines, because it would interfere with necessary access to the lines for repairs. Most easements for purposes of running utility or phone lines also include negative easements with respect to actions that might interfere with them.

CASE IN POINT

Pender v. Matranga, 123 Ohio App. 3d 307,
704 N.E.2d 58 (1998)

The trial court found the following facts. The plaintiffs own certain lots on the west shore of Candlewood Lake in New Fairfield. The Matrangas own a ten acre undeveloped parcel that abuts the plaintiffs' smaller lots and overlooks Candlewood Lake. The boundaries of the parties' parcels are stated on a property map, titled, "MAP SHOWING SUBDIVISION OF PROPERTY OF BURTON F. SHERWOOD LOCATED ON THE WEST SHORE OF LAKE CANDLEWOOD IN THE TOWN OF NEW FAIRFIELD, FAIRFIELD COUNTY CONNECTICUT." (Rapp map). The Rapp map was prepared and certified as being substantially correct by Sydney Rapp, and was recorded in the New Fairfield land records on December 7, 1953.

Both the plaintiffs and the Matrangas trace title to a common grantor, Burton F. Sherwood, who was a seasoned real estate developer in the area. On October 23, 1944, Sherwood and a group of landowners known as the Kellogg Point residents signed an agreement. The agreement gave those residents access to a nearby thoroughfare through a "private road" across Sherwood's land. The agreement gave Sherwood "the

right to pass and repass for all purposes whatsoever over the existing roadway 14 feet in width from a point marking the common bound of land of the Estate of Stanley T. Kellogg, land formerly of Rosalind D. Martel, now of said Sherwood, and the 440 foot contour line of The Connecticut Light & Power Company's Rocky River Datum, over and across land of the Kellogg Point Residents to a point of land of Louise F. Taylor, and thence in a Northerly direction in a course marked by iron pipes to other land of said Sherwood at a point approximately 100 feet Southerly of land of Neil G. Hayes." The defendant Chris Wallace constructed a road on behalf of the Matrangas, which bisects the property owned by the plaintiffs, following the "wood road" as noted on the Rapp map. The plaintiffs brought an action seeking to enjoin the defendants from using or improving this wood road, which runs through the rear of the plaintiffs' property and provides access to the Matrangas' lot. The Matrangas wanted to construct a dwelling on their property. The plaintiffs have admitted that the Matrangas have "the right to pass and repass over a right-of-way traversing [the plaintiffs'] . . . property," but challenge the width of the right-of-way and whether the Matrangas have a right to construct, maintain or use the road on the right-of-way located on the plaintiffs' property.

David Ryan, a licensed land surveyor, was called by the defendants to testify at trial as an expert witness. He explained the meaning of double dotted lines that signify the presence of the wood road on the Rapp map. Ryan stated that the double dotted lines on the Rapp map signify a traveled way or road, while a single dotted line indicates a path. Ryan noted that in 1991 he observed the wood road to be between seven feet and ten feet wide, but that the double dotted lines scale to eight feet wide on the Rapp map.

Ryan also examined the agreement with the Kellogg Point residents and compared that agreement with the Rapp map. While performing field work, Ryan located an iron pipe where the wood road begins a generally northerly path toward the Matrangas' lot Ryan concluded that the road referred to in the Rapp map creating the right-of-way is the same wood road that passes over the property of the plaintiffs.

The court found that a fourteen foot express easement, a twelve foot easement of necessity and an eight foot easement by implication existed over the plaintiffs' property in favor of the Matrangas. The court further found that the Matrangas may maintain, construct and repair those easements when necessary.

I

The plaintiffs first contend that the court improperly found that the Matrangas hold certain easements over the subject property. We agree with the trial court that there is an express easement of fourteen feet in width.

The determination of the scope of an easement is a question of fact. Strollo v. Iannantuoni, 53 Conn.App. 658, 659, 734 A.2d 144, cert. denied, 250 Conn. 924, 738 A.2d 662 (1999). The court's factual findings are "binding upon this court unless they are clearly erroneous in light of the evidence and the pleadings in the record as a whole. . . . We cannot retry the facts or pass on the credibility of the witnesses. . . . A finding of fact is clearly erroneous when there is no evidence in the record to support it . . . or when although there is evidence to support it, the reviewing court on the entire evidence is left with the definite and firm conviction that a mistake has been commit-

ted." (Internal quotation marks omitted.) Food Studio, Inc. v. Fabiola's, 56 Conn.App. 858, 862, 747 A.2d 7 (2000); see Powers v. Olson, 252 Conn. 98, 104–105, 742 A.2d 799 (2000). The plaintiffs have admitted that an express easement exists in favor of the Matrangas over the plaintiffs' land. The issue remaining in dispute is the width of that express easement and the presence of any nonexpress easements.

A

The court concluded that a fourteen foot easement exists over the plaintiffs' land pursuant to the October, 1944 agreement. The court reasoned in part. "Here, we are presented with a general grant of authority to pass and repass 'for all purposes whatsoever.' . . . [The Matrangas' land] is almost inaccessible by any other means, and contains ten acres overlooking Candlewood Lake. The testimony of both David Ryan and Christina Matranga affirmed that a steep grade renders access . . . unfeasible. Since the actual road was approximately eight feet in width in 1952, according to reliable testimony, one must conclude that either Burton F. Sherwood had the foresight to reserve fourteen feet as an easement in the event access to this ten acre parcel was necessary for development or he grossly miscalculated the width of the existing road by a full six feet prior to signing the agreement with the Kellogg Point residents." The court concluded that the plaintiffs' deed to the property and the mortgage instrument executed on the property referenced the easement. The court concluded that the plaintiffs took title to their property subject to the agreement between Sherwood and the Kellogg Point residents. We agree.

The phrase "for all purposes whatsoever" is a broad one, without any restrictions as to the use of the right to pass or repass. See Birdsey v. Kosienski, 140 Conn. 403, 412–13, 101 A.2d 274 (1953); Lichteig v. Churinetz, 9 Conn.App. 406, 410, 519 A.2d 99 (1986). The phrase permits any use reasonably connected to the reasonable use of the land. Lichteig v. Churinetz, supra, 9 Conn.App. at 410, 519 A.2d 99.

The agreement uses the phrase "over the existing roadway 14 feet in width," even though no testimony indicated that the wood road actually was fourteen feet at any recorded time. This indicates the intention to develop the parcel at a later time and to reserve sufficient width in the travel spaces for the development to occur. As the defendants rightly note in their brief, it is very unlikely that Sherwood, an experienced real estate developer, would intentionally fail to provide access to ten acres overlooking Candlewood Lake and render them essentially useless for development. See Kelly v. Ivler, 187 Conn. 31, 39, 450 A.2d 817 (1982) (effect of deed considered in light of surrounding circumstances).

We also look to the intent of the parties when interpreting the meaning of the easement. Birdsey v. Kosienski, supra, 140 Conn. at 410, 101 A.2d 274. The intention of the parties, as shown by the language of the 1944 agreement, further supports the court's conclusion. The "whereas" clauses in the agreement, as set forth by the parties, reveal that "the Kellogg Point Residents desire to have free access from their land to the public highway," "Sherwood owns other land . . . to which access is difficult without passing through land of the Kellogg Point Residents" and "the parties hereto feel that it would be mutually beneficial to exchange rights of way." In essence, the Kellogg Point residents received access to a nearby highway in exchange for Sherwood's gaining access to his property over the wood road. The fact that a fourteen foot easement over the plaintiffs' land has significant value to the dominant tenement is a relevant factor in determining the easement's scope. See id, 410–11, 101 A.2d 274.

"A court will not torture words to import ambiguity where the ordinary meaning leaves no room for ambiguity. . . ." HLO Land Ownership Associates Ltd. Partnership v. Hartford, 248 Conn. 350, 357, 727 A.2d 1260 (1999). The plain meaning of the easement grants an express right-of-way of fourteen feet over a specified route, which includes the plaintiffs' property. The court so found, and we conclude that sufficient evidence exists in the record to support this conclusion.

B

Since we agree with the trial court that an express easement exists over the subject property, any implied easements or easements of necessity that may have existed over the same right-of-way are extinguished. An easement of necessity may occur when a parcel has become landlocked from outside access such that the owner would have no reasonable means of ingress or egress except over lands promised by another and a right-of-way is necessary for the enjoyment of the parcel. Hollywyle Assn., Inc. v. Hollister, 164 Conn. 389, 398–99, 324 A.2d 247 (1973); Collins v. Prentice, 15 Conn. 39, 43–44 (1842); Friedman v. Westport, 50 Conn.App. 209, 214, 717 A.2d 797, cert. denied, 247 Conn. 937,

722 A.2d 1216 (1998). The inverse also is true; that is, a common-law right-of-way based on necessity expires when the owner of a dominant estate acquires access to a public or private road through another means. See R. Powell & P. Rohan, Powell on Real Property (1999) § 34.07, p. 34–67 n.29, citing Parham v. Reddick, 537 So.2d 132, 135 (Fla.Dist.Ct.App.1988) (right-of-way based on necessity expires when owner of dominant estate acquires adjoining lands that provide access to public or private road).

Similarly, an easement by implication does not arise by mere convenience or economy, but exists because of some significant or unreasonable burden as to access that demands the easement's presence. "In this state, the law regarding easements by implication arising out of the severance of title of two adjoining or commonly owned properties is well settled. Where, during the unity of title, an apparently permanent and obvious servitude is imposed on one part of an estate in favor of another, which at the time of the severance is in use, and is reasonably necessary for the fair enjoyment of the other, then, upon a severance of such ownership . . . there arises by implication of law a . . . reservation of the right to continue such use. . . . [I]n so far as necessity is significant it is sufficient if the easement is highly convenient and beneficial for the enjoyment of the dominant estate." (Internal quotation marks omitted.) Schultz v. Barker, 15 Conn.App. 696, 700–701, 546 A.2d 324 (1988).

Here, the Matrangas possess an express easement of fourteen feet in width by which to access and develop the parcel. No reason exists to retain an implied easement or easement of necessity over the exact same tract of land. We therefore conclude that because the fourteen foot express easement exists along the wood road in the Rapp map, no implied easement or easement of necessity can be found.

The judgment is reversed only as to the trial court's findings that the defendants have a twelve foot easement of necessity and an eight foot easement by implication over the plaintiffs' property and the case is remanded with direction to vacate those findings. The judgment is affirmed in all other respects.

In this opinion the other judges concurred.[9]

Case Review Question: What is the importance of whether the original document used single or dotted lines to indicate paths or roads for the easement?

5. Sales and Purchase of Real Property Interests

While the focus thus far has been on the various types of property ownership interests, only brief references have been made to the most common transaction to produce these interests, which is the sale and purchase of property. First-time buyers of real property are often astounded at the many issues and subsequent documents that are generally involved in the transfer of a property interest from buyer to seller. Also surprising is the number of people who are involved in the sale. A typical sale of real property includes not only the buyer and seller, but also a broker, attorney, title company, mortgagor, financier, and possibly others who each play a role in completing the necessary steps for the transaction.

Obviously, the seller is the party who is conveying the property interest in exchange for money or some other consideration, and the buyer is the party who is providing the consideration in exchange for the property interest. The broker either acts as the real estate agent or supervises the agent who brings the parties together and facilitates the documentation necessary to complete the transaction. The attorney prepares and/or reviews the documents of the sale. However, with the advent of computerized forms, attorneys are not always actively involved with simple transactions. Yet, consultation on even minor questions can save significant problems in the future. The title company searches the history of the real property in question and reports all claims of rights over the property in the past and any that are currently pending. The mortgagor/financier is the party who loans the purchase money to the buyer. Typically this is in exchange for a right to the property that is superior to the rights of the buyer until such time as the loan is repaid.

In addition to the various parties involved, there are also usually a number of documents that must be prepared and signed before the transaction is complete and can be recorded. Some of the more common documents in a real property transaction include the following:

1. *Purchase Agreement.* This is a contract in which the seller agrees to sell property to the buyer for a set price upon the completion of specified conditions. The buyer agrees to pay a specified amount or convey a specified type of consideration upon the completion of the conditions. Each party is obligated to take reasonable steps to see that the conditions are satisfied according to the terms of the agreement. This may include an inspection of the property and terms for correction of any items found in need of repair, the condition of the property at the time of the transfer, an appraisal of the property that determines the value to be in accordance with the purchase price, application and receipt of certain terms of financing, and any other conditions the parties might wish to include and agree to.

2. *Mortgage or Financing Agreement.* This is the contract between the buyer and the party who supplies the purchase money to the seller. Typically, the agreement will identify the parties bound by the contract, the property that is the basis for the loan, the terms of repayment such as interest rate terms, the amount and time of periodic payments, and the rights of the mortgagor to the property until the loan is repaid.

3. *Deed.* This is the document used to formally transfer the title to the property from one party to another. It specifies the type of interest being conveyed and the type of interest being received (for example, fee simple from one party to fee simple by tenancy in common to two persons). There are various types of deeds such as quitclaim, which simply conveys whatever interest the transferor has, and warranty, which guarantees that the transferor does in fact have the ownership rights represented. The warranty deed is the most common in sale/purchase transfers of real property. The deed

is typically recorded with the local governmental entity such as the county clerk's office or county recorder.

4. *Required Government Forms.* Most states require certain information to be reported when there is a transfer of ownership of real property. These forms are distributed to the proper authorities for purposes of record keeping, tax assessments, and so forth. Most states also charge a processing fee for such forms among the various agencies that keep records concerning property transfers. These fees are paid at the conclusion of the transaction, which is commonly referred to as a closing.

5. *Required Inspection Reports.* Most jurisdictions require certain types of inspections on property each time it is transferred. This is for the general public benefit and also to encourage fair and open transactions. Commonly required inspections are for such things as termites or a history of termite damage or treatment. The inspector produces a report that is filed with the other documents at the closing.

6. *Escrow Agreement.* Typically, a prospective buyer will offer a percentage of the purchase price with the offer to purchase. Because a purchase agreement typically prevents the seller from selling the property to anyone else for the same or less money, the deposit offered by the buyer (usually called earnest money) is a sign of good faith that the buyer intends to consummate the sale. The deposit is subject to forfeiture if the buyer willfully does not complete the sale. The money is often held by a third party who is independent of the two. While the sale is pending and the ultimate recipient of the money is unknown, it is held in escrow. The escrow agreement is simply a contract to hold the money and to distribute it according to the terms of the purchase agreement between the parties.

7. *Buyer and Seller Agreements.* These can be called purchase contracts, contract for deed, or land contracts. The primary difference in this type of purchase agreement for the sale of a real property interest is the absence of a mortgagor/financier. In this type of agreement the buyer enters into an installment contract with the seller and makes payments directly to the seller. The actual conveyance usually does not take place until the payments are completed. However, the document is recorded and the other steps typical in the transaction may occur as well with the exception of the actual recording of the new deed and government documents. If the purchase takes place over a very long period of time, the buyer may obtain a growing percentage of ownership as the total of the payments increase and the balance due goes down.

8. *Title Policy.* This is, in essence, an insurance policy. The title company researches the history of the property and any recorded claims of interest or rights to the property that currently affect it. These are prepared in a title report and provided to the buyer and seller. The company also issues an insurance policy stating that the report is complete and accurate. If it turns out, after the completion of the transaction, that there was an error and the buyer purchased property subject to the claims and ownership of others, the buyer's recourse is against the title company on the basis of their representations and not against the seller. If it is determined that the title company was in error, then the value of the policy must be paid to the buyer who purchased the property on the basis of the title company's representations.

Although it is generally true that conveyances of title to real property must be in writing in accordance with the statute of frauds, an exception is recognized in some jurisdictions. Under the doctrine of part performance, if a substantial portion of the purchase price has been paid and actual possession of the property has been turned over, the transaction will usually be enforced.[10] The court infers from the actions of the parties that the parties intended the conveyance of the property to be completed. Thus, the court will usually require the parties to complete the balance of the transaction. However, courts have some division on this issue and in many states a written agreement must be presented before there will be completion of a real property transaction. The argument is whether the basic fairness of the specific situation should be sought out, or whether the fairness principle that is the foundation of the statute of frauds theory should be supported.

Even when a written agreement exists, the problem often arises as to who bears responsibility for the property during the completion of the purchase requirements. The numerous documents associated with the purchase of property are not prepared instantaneously even with the advent of computer generated forms. Time is required for the application and approval of financing, the title search, necessary inspections, and so forth. Often, a sale of property takes from two to six months depending on the terms of the purchase agreement and their complexity. During this time, what happens if the property is partially damaged or even totally destroyed? What if the property is discovered to have a claim of right against it that the seller did not disclose? What if the seller causes wasting to the property? What if the buyer disappears or fails to meet the conditions of the agreement in a reasonable fashion? These are all issues that arise periodically and must be addressed.

While there is some variation among the jurisdictions, general principles have developed for the most common questions that arise during the interim between the signing of the purchase agreement and the final conveyance of the deed. As a rule, if something occurs during a pending sale that partially or totally destroys the property through no fault of the seller, the buyer cannot refuse completion of the transaction. However, the buyer is entitled to any insurance payments received against the loss if the seller was the party who carried the insurance.[11] Thus, the purchase agreement should always clearly indicate which party should bear the cost of and provide insurance for the property during the pendency of the agreement.

APPLICATION 13.6

X travels to the North Carolina coast for a vacation. He likes it so much he decides to buy a vacation home that is under construction. The sale is due to close upon the completion of the construction in approximately five months. During that time the entire area is devastated by a hurricane. Without provisions to the contrary, the seller may require the buyer to complete the sale.

Point for Discussion: Why should the buyer be required to complete the purchase of a home that no longer exists?

If the property is only damaged and not destroyed, the seller would have a reasonable amount of time to adequately repair the property and the buyer might still be held to the terms of the purchase agreement. However, questions of whether the damage is too substantial, how much delay is reasonable, and whether the repairs would restore the property adequately to its former condition must all be considered on a case-by-case basis. While a court is not likely to excuse a buyer from a sale in a minor occurrence, something that would substantially alter the terms of the agreement either in the condition of the property or the time for performance may be considered an excuse for breach and the buyer may be allowed to avoid completion of the transaction.

A minority of jurisdictions place the cost of loss due to unforeseen casualty on the seller. However, the most common occurrence and the most appropriate is that the purchase agreement specifies who bears the risk of loss and that the parties agree to this. If it is the buyer, and even though the buyer has not yet obtained an ownership interest, it is possible to insure the impending interest based on the purchase agreement.

If something is discovered during the pendency of the sale, such as a defect or irregularity in the property, that is contrary to what is specified in the contract or a claim against the title, the seller is allowed a reasonable amount of time to cure the defect and is generally permitted to use part of the purchase price to do so.[12] A frequent example is when the title is subject to the claim of a mortgagor of the seller. The seller cannot convey clear title until the mortgage is paid. However, the mortgage cannot be paid and title transferred without claims until the seller receives the purchase money. In this situation, the amount necessary to pay the seller's mortgage is withheld from the seller at closing and paid directly to the mortgagor in exchange for the release of the claim to the title. Flaws discovered on the property that are in need of repair are typically the responsibility of the seller (unless the purchase agreement contains different terms) and the seller is responsible for completing the repairs necessary to transfer the property in the condition that is described.

All sellers are under a general duty to continue to care for the property and prevent it from waste or damage beyond ordinary wear and tear during the time necessary to complete the sale. In the sale of real property with dwellings on it, a seller is also under a duty to convey the property in habitable condition. This will be discussed further at a later point but at this stage it is sufficient to state that this is generally interpreted to mean safe for occupancy and accessible to local utilities.

Not all duties, however, are on the seller. The courts still apply an ancient theory known as *caveat emptor*—let the buyer beware. Under this theory, a purchaser of property has the limited duty to reasonably investigate and discover defects in the property. Failure to do so can result in the court's refusal to rescind the purchase agreement or require the seller to repair the defect. This includes anything that one knows or should know through a reasonable examination of the property in its entirety. What would be considered a reasonable examination varies somewhat with the geographical area, the standard practices regarding inspection of land and buildings, and the type of property involved. For example, what should be inspected on the sale of an office building might vary dramatically from what should be inspected on property offered as a single family dwelling. One thing the courts have made clear is that the buyer cannot assume that the structure and its component are sound and in good working order. A buyer is usually obligated to inquire about such things as the condition of roofs, structures, leaks, appliances, and the electrical system.

While the rule of caveat emptor still applies generally, some changes have come about in recent years to assist the buyer. As technology increases, so have the complexity of structures and their supporting components, such as heating and cooling systems, insulation, and structural materials. It has become increasingly difficult for the buyer to have sufficient knowledge to ask all the right questions when making a purchase decision. Many buyers enlist professionals to inspect the property on their behalf and expose any questionable items or defects. Also, many jurisdictions now require a government form containing a series of questions about the property to be filled out and signed by the seller. The buyer is often required to sign upon acceptance of a copy of the form and prior to signing the purchase agreement. This eliminates the issue of whether the buyer inquired appropriately or the seller hid defects in the property. While consultants and disclosure statements are certainly helpful, they do not relieve the buyer entirely of the obligation to make sufficient inquiries about the property. The failure to do so may well result in the buyer paying more for the property than he or she would have paid had the defect been discovered. However, if the buyer does make inquiry and the seller makes representations that turn out to be false, the buyer may have recourse in actions for breach of an express warranty or fraud.[13] Any of the generally accepted duties of buyer and seller can be altered by agreement between the parties as long as there has been fair disclosure of any relevant facts. Following are a series of sample documents that are representative of those commonly found in a real estate transaction.

CASE IN POINT

Outdoor Systems Advertising, Inc. v. Korth, 238 Mich.App. 664, 607 N.W.2d 729 (1999).

October 1996, defendant became the new owner of the building where plaintiff's signs are located. On January 17, 1997, defendant wrote to plaintiff and stated that his ownership of the building included ownership of the billboards. Defendant also demanded that the advertisements, or panel boards, attached to the billboard structures be removed by February 1, 1997. Plaintiff thereafter provided defendant with copies of its lease agreements and with copies of canceled rent checks, but defendant continued to assert ownership over the billboards.

To preserve its interest in the billboards, plaintiff brought this action on the ground that defendant sought to wrongfully evict plaintiff. Plaintiff also styled its action as one for claim and delivery. In response, defendant averred that the original lease agreements "manifested an intention that any structures placed on the property were to become permanent fixtures simulated to the real estate and annexed thereto." Both parties moved for summary disposition. The trial court partially granted summary disposition to plaintiff by ruling that the panel boards (a component of the billboards) were plaintiff's personal property. However, the trial court partially granted summary disposition to defendant by ruling that the billboard structures themselves were part of defendant's realty. Apparently, the trial court's decision was based on evidence that though the panel boards could be removed, the billboard structures either could not be removed or removed only with great difficulty. Plaintiff now appeals.

Plaintiff maintains that the billboards were trade fixtures and therefore plaintiff's personal property as a matter of law. We agree. This Court has defined "trade fixtures" as follows:

A trade fixture is merely a fixture which has been annexed to leased realty by a lessee for the purpose of enabling him to engage in a business. The trade fixture doctrine permits the lessee, upon the termination of the lease, to remove such a fixture from the lessor's real property. [Michigan Nat'l Bank, Lansing v. Lansing, 96 Mich.App. 551, 555, 293 N.W.2d 626 (1980).]

A trade fixture is considered to be the personal property of the lessee. Wentworth v. Process Installations, Inc., 122 Mich.App. 452, 465, 333 N.W.2d 78 (1983). A chattel is a trade fixture if devoted to a trade purpose, regardless of its form or size. Id., see also Waverly Park Amusement Co. v. Michigan United Traction Co., 197 Mich. 92, 163 N.W. 917 (1917). The question if a given object is a trade fixture is a mixed question of law and fact, which we review de novo on appeal as issues of law. 35 Am. Jur. 2d, Fixtures, § 40, p. 731; Johnson v. Harnischfeger Corp., 414 Mich. 102, 121, 323 N.W.2d 912 (1982).

The Supreme Court long ago addressed the policy behind allowing a tenant to remove trade fixtures installed in furtherance of the tenant's business:

The right of the tenant to remove the erections made by him in furtherance of the purpose for which the premises were leased is one founded upon public policy and has its foundation in the interest which society has that every person shall be encouraged to make the most beneficial use of his property the circumstances will admit. . . .

The reason property of this kind is personal, rather than real, is based upon the rule the law implies [that the parties made] an agreement that it shall remain personal property from the fact the lessor contributes nothing thereto and should not be enriched at the expense of his tenant when it was placed upon the real estate of the landlord with his consent. There is no unity of title between the owner of the land and the owner of the structures, and the buildings were not erected as permanent improvements to the real estate, but to aid the lessee or licensee in the use of his interest in the premises. [Cameron v. Oakland Co. Gas & Oil Co., 277 Mich. 442, 452, 269 N.W. 227 (1936).]

In Wentworth, supra at 467, 333 N.W.2d 78, this Court held that trade fixtures remain the personal property of the lessee as long as the lessee remains in legitimate possession of the property unless: 1) it is expressed or clearly implied in a second lease, executed after the term in which the fixtures were erected, that the fixtures belong to the leasehold, or 2) such a fundamental change in the nature of the tenancy has occurred that it would not unjustly enrich the lessor to include the fixtures as a permanent part of his real property.

Here, plaintiff presented evidence that the billboards were erected by the original lessee and that there was continuous possession by its predecessors in interest without any period of abandonment. Defendant presented no competent evidence in rebuttal. Furthermore, defendant does not argue that the lease entitled defendant to keep plaintiff's trade fixtures at the expiration of the lease. Rather, defendant contends that the billboards are not trade fixtures as a matter of law.

In In re Acquisition of Billboard Leases & Easements, 205 Mich.App. 659, 661–662, 517 N.W.2d 872 (1994), involving just compensation for a local government's eminent domain taking of certain leaseholds that included billboards, this Court noted that there was "no dispute that all the billboards in question are trade fixtures." Id., 661–662, 517 N.W.2d 872. However, this statement does not settle the issue before us. It appears that the parties there did not dispute the issue, obviating the need for the Court to decide the issue as a matter of law. Lacking Michigan case law on this matter, we consider how our sister states have resolved the issue.

We found several cases that addressed this issue. In each case, the court had to decide if a billboard was personal or real property for purposes of determining just compensation in condemnation proceedings. In Rite Media, Inc. v. Secretary of Massachusetts Hwy. Dep't, 429 Mass. 814, 712 N.E.2d 60 (1999), the court held that a billboard was a trade fixture and therefore personal property for eminent domain purposes. The court concluded that because the owner had the right

to remove the billboard, the billboard had not been taken by eminent domain. Id., 817, 712 N.E.2d 60. Likewise, in State ex rel. Comm'r, Dep't of Transportation v. Teasley, 913 S.W.2d 175 (Tenn.App., 1995), the court held that the billboard in question was a trade fixture, and therefore not compensable in eminent domain. Id., 177–178.

In Lamar Corp. v. State Hwy. Comm., 684 So.2d 601 (Miss., 1996), contrary to Rite Media and Teasley, the court held that billboards were realty for purposes of eminent domain and that the owner was entitled to just compensation. Id., 604. However, the court's remarks in dicta firmly support the conclusion that the billboards at issue here should be treated as trade fixtures:

[T]he property here involved does not become "personal property" [for eminent domain purposes] . . . simply because it may be classified as a "trade fixture" and therefore treated as personal property for ownership purposes as between lessor and lessee. [Id.]

Thus, while the Lamar court declined to hold that billboards were noncompensable personal property in eminent domain cases, it expressly commented that billboards are trade fixtures for purposes of establishing ownership between lessor and lessee.

The case In re Condemnation by the Commonwealth of Pennsylvania, Dep't of Transportation, of Right of Way for State Route 0060, Section A01, 720 A.2d 154 (Pa. Cmwlth., 1998) presented the trade fixture personalty/realty issue in a slightly different context. Although the parties acknowledged that the billboard owner was entitled to compensation for the taking, they disputed whether the owner of condemned billboards should be compensated according to the "sales comparison approach" used for valuation of realty, or the "reproduction cost less depreciation" approach used for personalty. Id., 156. The Court held that the billboards were trade fixtures and should therefore be valued as personalty. Id., 158–159.

In sum, the jurisdictions that have specifically addressed the question—whether billboards are trade fixtures clearly hold that billboards are trade fixtures. The majority has drawn this conclusion in the context of eminent domain cases; even the minority jurisdiction has stated that billboards are trade fixtures in the context of lessor-lessee relations. We join these states in holding that billboards are properly characterized as trade fixtures and personal property rather than as realty.

Defendant erroneously argues that the billboards cannot be trade fixtures because they were large and could only be removed with a crane. The cases defendant cites all involve nontrade fixtures. This Court has held that form and size are not determinative of whether a chattel is a trade fixture. Wentworth, supra at 465, 333 N.W.2d 78.

Whatever is affixed to the land by the lessee for the purpose of trade, whether it be made of brick or wood, is removable at the end of the term. Indeed, it is difficult to conceive that any fixture, however solid, permanent, and closely attached to the realty, placed there for the sole purpose of trade, may not be removed at the end of the term. [Cameron, supra at 459–460, 269 N.W. 227, quoting Wiggins Ferry Co. v. Ohio & M R Co., 142 U.S. 396, 416, 12 S.Ct. 188, 35 L.Ed. 1055 (1892).]

The documentary evidence established plaintiff's ownership of the billboards and the billboard struc-tures. Therefore, we find that plaintiff owned the billboards, that the billboards were trade fixtures and, consequently, were the personal property of plaintiff subject to removal by plaintiff in accordance with the terms of the billboard lease agreements. We affirm that portion of the trial court's decision ruling that plaintiff owned and could remove the billboard panels. We reverse that portion of the trial court's decision ruling that the billboard structures were permanently attached to the building and could not be removed by plaintiff.[14]

Case Review Question: Would the outcome of this case be likely to change if the defendant could establish that the billboards were constructed at the time of the construction of the building and incorporated into the side of the building in a permanent fashion?

6. Adverse Possession

Adverse Possession
When title to real property is acquired without purchase or voluntary transfer of title. Ordinarily, one who obtains title by adverse possession must openly and continuously exercise possession and control over the entire property inconsistent with the interest of the current owner and all others who claim rights to the property for a period of time specified by statute.

Thus far, the discussion of transfer of real property interests has been confined to those transfers accomplished by sale or gift/devise. To be sure, these are by far the most common. But a legal principle dating back to very early property law also enables one to obtain an ownership interest without purchasing the property, or receiving a voluntary gift of the property. The principle is that of **adverse possession,** and it has remained a supported and effective method of gaining ownership throughout the history of the American legal system. The reasoning behind the theory of adverse possession is that the government encourages the productive use of land owned by private citizens. If the owner does not make productive use of the land and does not protect the right of possession of owned property, the law may recognize ownership in one who will. What is considered productive use is left entirely to the discretion of the property owner as long as it is consistent with applicable laws and regulations. This may include allowing the property to remain unused for aesthetic purposes. The key, however, is that the property not be abandoned entirely. To do so is not considered productive in any fashion. This does not mean that anyone can merely assume ownership of an uninhabited parcel of property and through that obtain legal rights. Rather, each state has specific requirements that must be satisfied before a court will employ the theory of adverse possession and transfer the rights of ownership. However, most state requirements are, in substance, the same as the requirements of the original common-law theory that preceded the statutes. The elements that must usually be established to prove the right to title of ownership by adverse possession include the following:[15]

- Open and notorious possession
- Continuous possession
- Exclusive possession
- Adequate duration of possession

Open and notorious possession is established when the person who seeks title by adverse possession actually takes steps that would indicate to observers that the person has taken the property under his or her control. This does not mean the party is required to inhabit the property or patrol it day and night. What it does mean is that an objective observer would perceive the actions of the person as someone who has possession of the property. This might include such things as undertaking general maintenance of the land and any improvements, placing personal property there, or installing improvements to the property. The actions may be minimal but must be such that others, including an alert property owner, would perceive them as those of one exercising control over the property.

Continuous possession is designed to prevent transients and squatters from claiming title to the property. The law does not propose to take away property from one party and vest title in anyone who expresses an interest. Rather, the theory supports granting title by adverse possession only to those who demonstrate an ongoing concern for the property. This requires that the actions of the adverse possessor not be intermittent or periodic. Whatever the party does to establish control over the property must be done in a manner that is essentially uninterrupted. Any abandonment for a significant time will cause this requirement to be defeated and further attempts at adverse possession would require that each of the elements be established all over again.

Exclusive possession is necessary to show that the person claiming title by adverse possession would act as a typical property owner and exclude others from possessing the property. Until all the elements are sufficiently established, the adverse possessor is not entitled to exercise exclusive possession toward the true owner of the property. If one becomes aware that another has begun actions that could result in a transfer of title by adverse possession, he or she has the right to retrieve the property. However, each state has established a statutory period of time that the elements of adverse possession must continue. Once the statutory time has been reached, the adverse possessor can petition the court for title to the property and, if granted, the adverse possessor becomes the owner in fee simple and has the right to exclude all others from the property, including the previous owner from whom title was obtained.

The final element of adequate duration of possession refers to the statutory requirement previously mentioned. While statutes vary from state to state on the length of time, it typically involves a significant period. Many of the statutes state a period somewhere between 5 and 20 years. Because the law does not deprive someone of ownership interest lightly, the requirement that the elements of adverse possession be demonstrated over many years ensures not only that the adverse possessor is committed to productive use of the land, but also that the original owner has truly abandoned the intent to exercise the rights of ownership. The law gives every chance to the original owner to reclaim the rights of title to property. However, when there is a total failure to use property for a significant period of time and another party exists who would make beneficial use of the property, adverse possession may take effect.

Most states and the federal government do not permit claims of adverse possession over government-owned property. Those that do permit such claims only do so in very specific areas. Originally this was done through homesteading. When the United States was going through westward expansion, settlers were encouraged to stake out, figuratively and literally, a parcel of government-owned land and make use of it. By doing so, they could essentially earn the right of ownership. Today, however, as space becomes more and more limited, so do the opportunities to obtain land in this manner. Also, as a practical matter, the government oversees large areas of land to protect animal habitat and wilderness. Because it would be virtually impossible to inspect all areas at all times, as an owner of a smaller parcel might be expected to do, these areas have been excluded from the option of title by adverse possession to serve the greater public interest of preservation.

When adverse possession of privately held property is pursued, it is possible to do so through a series of connected persons. The entire burden of proof of the elements over many years is not placed entirely on one person. When this occurs, it is called tacking, and it is allowed only under certain circumstances. The theory does not permit a series of unrelated transient individuals to periodically control the property and thus meet the statutory time requirement and vest ownership in the last settler. Rather, it must be permitted by statute and in accordance with the established requirements. Frequently this requires the succeeding adverse possessors to be descendants/heirs, spouse, or someone who was intentionally, specifically, and voluntarily granted possession during the life of the first adverse possessor.[16]

CASE IN POINT

Birkholz v. Wells, 2000 WL 539393 (N.Y.A.D. 3 Dept.)

Appeal from a judgment of the Supreme Court (Viscardi, J.), entered April 28, 1999 in Warren County, upon a decision of the court in favor of defendants.

Defendant Susan J. Wells and defendants Kenneth E. Gussow and Rochelle B. Gussow (hereinafter collectively referred to as defendants) own adjoining parcels of real property fronting on Monte Vista Drive in the Town of Warrensburg, Warren County. Their rear (east) property lines abut a parcel of land owned by plaintiffs. It is undisputed that for a number of years, defendants and the Gussows' predecessors in title treated a portion of plaintiffs' property, i.e., a strip of land approximately 50 to 100 feet deep extending from defendants' rear lines to a steep ravine on plaintiffs' property (hereinafter the disputed property), as a part of their own backyards. In 1996, plaintiffs brought this action pursuant to RPAPL article 15 to clear title to the disputed property, and defendants each counterclaimed for a determination that they owned their respective portions by adverse possession. Following a nonjury trial, Supreme Court rendered a verdict dismissing the complaint and granting judgment in favor of defendants on their counterclaims for title by adverse possession. Plaintiffs appeal.

We affirm. In order to sustain their claims of ownership by adverse possession, defendants were required to establish by clear and convincing evidence that their possession of the disputed property was hostile and under a claim of right, actual, open and notorious, exclusive and continuous for 10 years (see, Brand v. Prince, 35 N.Y.2d 634, 636, 364 N.Y.S.2d 826, 324 N.E.2d 314). In addition, because defendants' claim is not founded upon a written instrument

or judgment or decree, only so much of the disputed property as was usually cultivated or improved or protected by a substantial inclosure (see, RPAPL 522) will be deemed to have been possessed by them.

The essential premise underlying the appeal is that, because defendants were aware during the statutory 10-year period that they did not own the disputed property, they failed to establish the essential element of possession that was hostile and under claim of right (see, Van Gorder v. Masterplanned Inc., 78 N.Y.2d 1106, 578 N.Y.S.2d 126, 585 N.E.2d 375; Belotti v. Bickhardt, 228 N.Y. 296, 302, 127 N.E. 239; City of Tonawanda v. Ellicott Cr. Homeowners Assn., 86 A.D.2d 118, 123–124, 449 N.Y.S.2d 116, appeal dismissed 58 N.Y.2d 824). In our view, plaintiffs' analysis focuses far too much on defendants' state of mind, i.e., what they knew or reasonably should have known by virtue of deed descriptions, survey maps and title insurance policies that were available for their review, and far too little on their actions. As stated in the landmark Connecticut case of French v. Pearce (8 Conn. 439):

> Into the recesses of [the adverse claimant's] mind, his motives or purposes, his guilt or innocence, no enquiry is made. It is for this obvious reason; that it is the visible and adverse possession, with an intention to possess, that constitutes its adverse character, and not the remote views or belief of the possessor (id., at 443).

In fact, "[t]he object of the statute defining the acts essential to constitute an adverse possession is that the real owner may, by unequivocal acts of the usurper, have notice of the hostile claim and be thereby called upon to assert his legal title" (Monnot v. Murphy, 207

N.Y. 240, 245, 100 N.E. 742). "Thus, the actual possession and improvement of premises, as owners are accustomed to possess and improve their estates, without any payment of rent, or recognition of title in another, or disavowal of title in oneself, will, unless rebutted by other evidence, establish the fact of a claim of title" (2 N.Y. Jur. 2d, Adverse Possession, § 40, at 488; see, Monnot v. Murphy, supra, at 244, 100 N.E. 742; Barnes v. Light, 116 N.Y. 34, 39–40, 22 N.E. 441).

Consistent with that view, New York courts have consistently held that hostility will be presumed if the use is open, notorious and continuous for the full 10-year statutory period (see, Robarge v. Willett, 224 A.D.2d 746, 747, 636 N.Y.S.2d 938; Sinicropi v. Town of Indian Lake, 148 A.D.2d 799, 800, 538 N.Y.S.2d 380). Moreover, the element of "hostility" need not be supported by proof of enmity or literally hostile acts (see, Sinicropi v. Town of Indian Lake, supra). All that is required is a showing that the possession actually infringes upon the owner's rights (see, id.), such as to give the owner a cause of action in ejectment against the occupier throughout the requisite period (see, Brand v. Prince, supra, at 636, 364 N.Y.S.2d 826, 324 N.E.2d 314). "Indeed, hostility may be found even though the possession occurred inadvertently or by mistake" (Kappes v. Ruscio, 170 A.D.2d 743, 744, 565 N.Y.S.2d 596; see, Sinicropi v. Town of Indian Lake, supra; Bradt v. Giovannone, 35 A.D.2d 322, 325–326, 315 N.Y.S.2d 961; West v. Tilley, 33 A.D.2d 228, 231, 306 N.Y.S.2d 591, lv. denied 27 N.Y.2d 481, 312 N.Y.S.2d 1025, 260 N.E.2d 874).

Viewed in the light of the controlling legal standards, the trial evidence by no means requires a finding that, during the 10-year statutory period, defendants or their predecessors in title recognized or acknowledged any superior claim to the disputed property (see, Van Gorder v. Masterplanned Inc., supra; MAG Assocs. v. SDR Realty, 247 A.D.2d 516, 520, 669 N.Y.S.2d 314; City of Tonawanda v Ellicott Cr. Homeowners Assn., supra, at 123–124, 449 N.Y.S.2d 116). We similarly conclude that the Gussows' claim of tacking was not defeated by their failure to produce one of the prior owners. In our view, it was not necessary to look into that owner's mind to determine her subjective intent at the time she transferred title, and other witnesses were qualified to provide evidence of her outward acts of ownership. Further, given the ample trial evidence supporting Supreme Court's findings of fact, we are not persuaded by plaintiffs' citation to contrary evidence which, if credited, may have supported a judgment in their favor (see, Esposito v. Stackler, 160 A.D.2d 1154, 1156, 554 N.Y.S.2d 361).

"As a final matter, we conclude that Supreme Court did not abuse its discretion in denying plaintiffs' motion for a mistrial or in awarding costs to defendants. Plaintiffs' additional contentions have been considered and found to be also unavailing.

ORDERED that the judgment is affirmed, with one bill of costs."[17]

Case Review Question: Can someone obtain property by adverse possession if they are under the mistaken impression that the property is their own from the start?

Assignment 13.3

Explain why the following situations describe either an easement or adverse possession.

a. Beverly and Nancy are best friends. They live in houses next door to one another. Beverly decides to install a fence around her yard. In obtaining her permit she has the lot surveyed and finds that Nancy's driveway, poured approximately 20 years ago, extends 18 inches onto Beverly's property. However, if the driveway were not that wide it would not accommodate the turn in it that is necessary to get into Nancy's garage, which faces the side of the lot rather than the street.

b. Mike works at a marina on the river. He buys a house on an island in the river, however, the location of his house is in an area where the water is very shallow and does not accommodate a boat. Mike wants to use the boat dock on the adjacent property where the water is much deeper and does so for a long period of time until that property is purchased by a new owner who objects to Mike's use of the dock.

7. Rights and Duties of Ownership

An ownership interest in property generally includes the right of possession and control, free from the interference or influence of third parties. These benefits of property ownership are collectively referred to as the right to quiet enjoyment. This right protects the right to make use of property however the owner wishes. The right of quiet enjoyment is strongly protected by law and considered inherent in property ownership, but it is not without limitation. Anyone with an ownership interest in property accepts it subject to certain obligations.

a. Public or Private Nuisance   A primary obligation associated with property ownership is the prohibition against using property in such a way that it becomes a public or private nuisance to surrounding areas. A private nuisance is a use that has a direct adverse effect on specific persons.[18] A public nuisance is something that has a more widespread negative impact on the surrounding population. The potential in either situation is essentially the same—to force the nuisance behavior to cease. Nuisance behavior that is ongoing and/or causes some type of personal or financial harm can also result in an action for damages.

In a case of private nuisance, the effects of the conduct are limited and the impact is personal on specific persons. If the conduct is such that it interferes with another person's quiet enjoyment of their own property or other personal rights, the court will consider the nature of the conduct and try to balance the rights of the parties, that is, the right of one person to quiet enjoyment versus the rights of another. However, if the activity is found to be damaging, a court will not only order it to cease, but may also award damages to the individual.

A public nuisance is one that generally has a continuing adverse effect on the public good, welfare, or safety.[19] Conduct, even though it takes place entirely on privately owned property, can be considered a public nuisance if the effects of that conduct extend beyond the property and has a negative impact on other persons or their property. If the conduct has broad-reaching effects, then public authorities may institute an action to force the property owner to cease the conduct and possibly to pay damages to the government for the injury to the public and in some instances to facilitate repairs or restoration to damaged public property or domain. Generally, a private party cannot bring an action for public nuisance unless it is accompanied by an action on behalf of the private individual for injuries that are different from those to the general public.

b. Maintenance of Property Condition   The right of those outside the property not to be adversely affected by one's exercise of the right of quiet enjoyment is understandable. However, it is also important to note that there are basic obligations placed upon real property owners with respect to the condition in which the property is kept. Such obligations serve the public interest of safety. The property must be maintained in an appropriately safe condition for anyone who enters it, with or without permission. The failure to do so may result in injury to someone who has entered the property and the owner may be held accountable for damages associated with the injury. The degree of protection provided to entrants and, consequently, the level of obligation to maintain the property in a safe condition varies with the purpose or nature of the entrants' presence on the property. However, some grade of protection from dangerous conditions is given to all, even those who are present without the knowledge and/or consent of the property owner.

APPLICATION 13.7

Property owner A has a factory on land adjacent to property owner B. The factory emits fumes as a result of certain manufacturing processes. The fumes, while not harmful, are so offensive that the community is suffering economically because people have started moving to other nearby communities and new growth of homes is at a standstill. The problem has been reported in the news and on television and has had a devastating effect.

Additionally, the fumes are so bad at the factory site that the workers must wear special ventilation masks. This is also necessary for property owner B's family whenever they are outdoors. In addition, they are unable to open any windows that might allow the fumes within the house. Property owner B has decided to move but after six months on the market, no one has even been willing to look at the house. Property owner B and the city bring an action against A for abatement of the processing that is causing the fumes and damages that will be used to publicize the fact and renew interest in the community. B seeks damages to compensate him for injury to his property values and the inability to use his property without interference.

Point for Discussion: What would be the proper result if the only way to keep the factory in operation was to continue the processing, and to order it to cease would effectively put A out of business and render the property worthless, assuming the factory could not be converted to another use?

A trespasser is one who enters onto another's property without permission or acquiescence of any kind by the owner. This unpermitted entry is a violation of the property owner's right to quiet enjoyment and may result in an action by the property owner toward the trespasser. Regardless, the landowner still has a fundamental duty to keep the property free from unreasonable dangers that could cause injury, even to a trespasser. The extent of the obligation is to protect all entrants from dangers that they could reasonably be expected to discover. There is not a general duty to warn or to take action to protect. Rather, there is only the duty to correct conditions that would cause injury or to give notice of these conditions.[20]

APPLICATION 13.8

A owns property in a run-down area of the city. Located on the property is an empty 100-year-old building that has been abandoned for several years. B, thinking the property is abandoned, enters the property in order to go upstairs and take photographs from a third floor window that gives a panoramic view of the city. A staircase is blocked by a stack of boxes. B moves the boxes in order to gain access to the third floor. While going up the stairs the staircase collapses and B is seriously injured. B sues A for the injuries. A makes the argument that the boxes were intended to keep people from using the stairs. A court would probably find that a reasonable person, even though trespassing, would not perceive the stack of boxes as a sufficient warning or notice of a dangerous condition.

Point for Discussion: Should the result be different if A had a no trespassing sign posted and a board nailed across the entrance to the stairs?

Another class of individuals who enter property are licensees. The licensee does so with the knowledge and permission of the owner but does so socially and not for any purpose associated with the owner's regular business. This would include guests or others who are requested to enter the property or who are on it subject to the owner's knowledge and acquiescence. The landowner owes a general duty to warn of dangers that are present on the property. These include both latent (hidden) and patent (readily discoverable) dangers. This is slightly greater duty than that owed to a trespasser of latent dangers. This duty is broader and more extensive because, by having full knowledge and permitting others to enter the property, the landowner has a somewhat greater duty to see to the safety of these persons.

APPLICATION 13.9

Consider the same situation as in the previous application. However, in this case, B is a neighbor of A and requests permission to enter the building. A would have a duty to warn B of the specific dangerous condition of the stairs. It is doubtful that merely blocking the staircase, even with heavy objects, would be sufficient since A knew B wanted access to the upper floors and could reasonably expect B to attempt using the staircase.

Point for Discussion: Would this situation have a different result if the stairs were barricaded with boards nailed across the entry rather than boxes or other heavy objects blocking the entrance?

The final category of individuals who enter the property of another are invitees. These individuals are invited (expressly or impliedly) to the property of the owner for business purposes—either for obtaining benefit for the business or for reasons of providing employment to others. Consequently, shopkeepers and landowners have a duty to actively inspect their premises to protect their invitees from harm.[21] The obligation includes reasonable maintenance of the property to eliminate dangerous conditions or active steps to clearly inform the invitee of the nature of any specific hazards.

APPLICATION 13.10

Consider the previous two examples. Assume A decides to rehabilitate the property for resale and hires a number of individuals to come and assist with the work. A must take special care to make sure each employee is aware of the specific dangers located on the property. A has a further duty to take steps to correct or at least adequately warn any potential buyers of any existing dangers if they enter the property.

Point for Discussion: Does an advertisement that states the property is for sale in "as is" condition and that various elements do not satisfy current code standards for commercial buildings meet the duty?

The right of quiet enjoyment is paramount and is resolutely protected by the American legal system. However, it is also recognized that there are those who would abuse the privilege. Also, there are any number of reasons for one person to enter the property of another—by invitation, mistake, or for some specific yet innocent purpose, as well as those who willfully and wrongfully trespass. In addition to the laws of a jurisdiction regarding property uses, the basic duties with respect to avoidance of nuisance behavior and fundamental maintenance of property to avoid or warn of dangerous conditions are considered a minimal imposition on the property owner in exchange for the otherwise unlimited rights to use, control, and possess property.

8. Condominiums

As previously discussed, ownership of a condominium is a freehold real property interest just as a parcel of land would be. However, the description of the property owned may be indirectly attached to the land. For example, in a high-rise building, the actual unit an individual owns may be many feet above the ground, but it is inextricably attached to the building, which is in turn attached to the ground. However, condominiums typically have some characteristics that are unlike the typical fee simple. The concept of condominium ownership wherein a single tenancy exists for part of the real property estate and multiple tenancy ownership for other elements of the property, dates back several hundred years to Europe. However, it is only in the relatively recent past that condominium ownership has become popular in the United States as urban growth and the demand for property in specific areas has increased so dramatically.

A condominium is in fact a fee simple freehold interest in land as opposed to a lease or rental type interest, but there are some non-freehold traits as well. Condominium ownership usually involves collateral obligations to abide by certain rules regarding the use of the property, payment of fees for maintenance of surrounding areas, and restrictions on the sale of the property. These restrictions on a typical real property ownership might be considered a violation of the right to quiet enjoyment. However, because the condominium typically involves sharing of some space among the adjoined units, concessions must be made in order to respect the rights of each of the owners equally. In this respect, condominium owners are required to treat the property to some extent as if it were leased or rented and subject to conditions of a landlord.

As stated previously, the various owners of condominiums on a specific property are owners as tenancy in common of the air and subsurface rights. They are also typically tenants in common in any areas that are open and not the subject of individual ownership. This includes such areas as grounds, access, parking, and utility maintenance. Because the tenancy in common is typically held among strangers whose only common interest is the location of their ownership, all fifty states have enacted laws to govern the establishment and running of condominium complexes.

The laws require a fair and organized plan to operate the common areas of the property, to establish guidelines for use of the portion of the properties held as individual units, and to enforce such rules and guidelines. While it is permissible to impose restrictions on owners regarding the sale and purchase of their condominium units, the restrictions cannot be unconditional or even unreasonable so as to significantly limit the ability to transfer the interest at will. Also, as with any other type of transaction, there are laws to protect certain classes from discriminatory acts. For example, the law is clear that restrictions based either directly or indirectly on race, religion, sex, handicap, or nationality are impermissible.[22]

In addition to all the rights and duties, although somewhat limited, of the fee simple ownership interest over the individual property, and the rights with respect to the areas held by tenancy in common, the same obligations apply as to any other type of real property ownership interests. Therefore, if a trespasser, licensee, or invitee is injured on a common area through negligence or through some other fault basis of the owners, then all owners of that part of the property are equally liable for the damages. This is one of the reasons that the courts allow some restrictions, so that owners can take steps to maximize the possibility that they will become tenants in common and share the rights and duties of property ownership with responsible persons.

CASE IN POINT

Ridgely Condominium Assoc., Inc. v. Smyrnioudis, Jr. et al. 343 Md. 357, 681 A.2d 494 (1996).

MURPHY, Chief Judge.

This case involves a judgment enjoining the Ridgely Condominium Association, Inc. (Association) from enforcing a bylaw amendment which prohibited clients of the condominium's seven first-floor commercial unit owners from entering and leaving the commercial units via the condominium lobby.

I

A condominium is a "communal form of estate in property consisting of individually owned units which are supported by collectively held facilities and areas." Andrews v. City of Greenbelt, 293 Md. 69, 71, 441 A.2d 1064 (1982).

The term condominium may be defined generally as a system for providing separate ownership of individual units in multiple-unit developments. In addition to the interest acquired in a particular apartment, each unit owner also is a tenant in common in the underlying fee and in the spaces and building parts used in common by all the unit owners.

Richard R. Powell, Powell on Real Property ¶ 632.1 (1996). A condominium owner, therefore, holds a hybrid property interest consisting of an exclusive ownership of a particular unit or apartment and a tenancy in common with the other co-owners in the common elements. Andrews, supra, 293 Md. at 73–74, 441 A.2d 1064; see also Starfish Condo. v. Yorkridge Serv., 295 Md. 693, 703, 458 A.2d 805 (1983); Black's Law Dictionary 295 (6th ed. 1990).

In exchange for the benefits of owning property in common, condominium owners agree to be bound by rules governing the administration, maintenance, and use of the property. Andrews, supra, 293 Md. at 73, 441 A.2d 1064. Upholding a rule prohibiting the consumption of alcohol in a condominium's clubhouse, a Florida court observed.

It appears to us that inherent in the condominium concept is the principle that to promote the health, happiness, and peace of mind of the majority of the unit owners since they are living in such close proximity and using facilities in common, each unit owner must give up a certain degree of freedom of choice which he might otherwise enjoy in separate, privately owned property. Condominium unit owners comprise a little democratic sub society of necessity more restrictive as it pertains to use of condominium property than may be existent outside the condominium organization. Hidden Harbour Estates, Inc. v. Norman, 309 So.2d 180, 181–82 (Fla.Dist.Ct.App.1975); see also Nahrstedt v. Lakeside Village Condo., 8 Cal.4th 361, 33 Cal.Rptr.2d 63, 878 P.2d 1275, 1281 (1994) ("Use restrictions are an inherent part of any common interest development and are crucial to the stable, planned environment of any shared ownership arrangement."); Dulaney Towers v. O'Brey, 46 Md.App. 464, 466, 418 A.2d 1233 (1980) ("The courts stress that communal living requires that fair consideration must be given to the rights and privileges of all owners and occupants of the condominium so as to provide a harmonious residential atmosphere.").

The Maryland Condominium Act (the Act), Maryland Code (1996 Repl.Vol.) §§ 11-101 et seq. of the Real Property Article, regulates the formation, management, and termination of condominiums in Maryland. The Act was originally enacted by Ch. 387 of the Acts of 1963, as the Horizontal Property Act in response to § 104 of the Federal Housing Act of 1961, Pub.L. No. 87-70, 75 Stat. 149, which made federal mortgage insurance available to condominiums in states where title and ownership were established for such units. The Act was based on the Federal Housing Administration's Model Horizontal Property Act of 1961. 66 Op.Atty.Gen. 50, 52 (1981). The legislature amended and recodified the Act by Ch. 641 of the Acts of 1974.

Under the Act, property becomes a condominium upon the recording of a declaration, bylaws, and a condominium plat. § 11-102. The declaration must include the name of the condominium; a description of the entire project, the units, and the common elements; and the percentage interests in the common elements and votes appurtenant to each unit. § 11-103(a). The declaration may be amended with the written consent of at least 80% of the unit owners, except that unanimous consent of the owners is required for some amendments, such as altering percentage interests in common elements, changing the use of units from residential to nonresidential and vice versa, and redesignating general common elements as limited common elements. §§ 11-103(b); 11-107(c).

The bylaws govern the administration of the condominium and must include the form of the condominium administration and its powers, meeting procedures, and fee collection procedures. § 11-104(a), (b). The former § 11-111(f) also required the bylaws to include restrictions on the use of units and common elements. The 1974 amendments made inclusion of such use restrictions in the bylaws optional. Section 11-104(c) now provides: "The bylaws may also contain any other provision regarding (appellees) filed suit in the Circuit Court for Baltimore County against the Association seeking to enjoin the enactment or enforcement of rules restricting the use of the lobby by the appellees' clients.

On or about October 1, 1991, the members of the Association voted to amend the bylaws. Originally, Article XV, § 1 of the bylaws provided: "All units shall be used as a single family residence, except that up to a maximum of seven (7) units on the first floor may be used as professional offices." The amendment added:

provided however, that all clients of, or visitors to, professional office owners or their tenants shall be required to use the exterior entrances of each such professional office for ingress and egress.

No visitor or clients of any owner of a professional office or tenant thereof, shall be permitted in any other area of the building, unless accompanied by the owner of the office unit or the tenant of such office unit. For the purpose of this section, the terms "clients" or "visitor" of professional office owner or tenant, shall include the clients or visitor and all person(s) who may accompany such client or visitor to such professional office.

The appellees do not challenge the procedures used to adopt the resolution or amend the bylaws.

The appellees filed an amended complaint on September 27, 1991. Pending trial, the parties reached an agreement which allowed commercial visitors to use the lobby, but required them to sign in and wait at the front desk for an escort.

After a trial, Judge John F. Fader, II, on April 18, 1994, enjoined the Association from enforcing the bylaw. In his opinion, Judge Fader determined that "the proper standard of review is whether the Condominium's rule is reasonable." The restriction, he said, "is unenforceable for failure to reasonably relate to the health, happiness and enjoyment of unit owners." Safety concerns, he noted, had prompted the adoption of the restriction, but there was no evidence that any commercial visitors had threatened the building's security. Judge Fader added:

"There was no indication that the prohibition of all access by commercial tenants and their clients/patients was the only method, the least intrusive method, or the best means available to lessen the possibility of unauthorized persons entering the building, or of authorized individuals causing trouble. In prohibiting commercial access via the main lobby, the Board reacted to a situation, which objectively was not dire, and which did not require the stringent regulation initiated by the Board.

Judge Fader also held that the restriction "fails the reasonableness test since it has a discriminatory impact on commercial unit owners."

On appeal, the Court of Special Appeals affirmed. Ridgely Condo. v. Smyrnioudis, 105 Md.App. 404, 660 A.2d 942 (1995). At the outset, it said that "our review of the record convinces us that this case actually concerns an access restriction that has diluted appellees' respective percentage interests in the Condominium lobby." Id. at 409, 660 A.2d 942. In a footnote, the court said that, "To deny the use of the lobby to clients of the commercial unit owners constitutes an ultra vires taking of a portion of their percentage interest in the common areas in derogation of the Ridgely Condominium declaration as well as certain provisions of the Maryland Condominium Act." Id. at 409 n. 2, 660 A.2d 942. Nonetheless, the court declined to base its decision on that issue since it was not argued by the parties in the circuit court. Id. at 410, 660 A.2d 942.

The court held that the reasonableness test is the proper standard of review for evaluating restrictions contained in a bylaw amendment. Id. at 422, 660 A.2d 942. Courts apply a more deferential standard of review to recorded use restrictions, the court said, because unit owners have notice of the restrictions when they purchase their units. Id. at 417, 660 A.2d 942. In contrast, the court concluded that the more restrictive reasonableness standard is appropriate in this case, because owners did not have notice of the restriction when they purchased their units. Id. at 418, 660 A.2d 942.

The court emphasized the disparate impact of the restriction on the commercial unit owners, id. at 421, 660 A.2d 942, and indicated that § 11-108 may require any use restriction that does not apply equally to all unit owners to be stated in the declaration. Id. at 420, 660 A.2d 942. Thus, the court held that application of a deferential standard of review is particularly inappropriate where the use restriction has a discriminatory impact. Id. at 421, 422, 660 A.2d 942.

III

The Association filed a petition for a Writ of Certiorari, which we granted, and which presented this question: "Did the trial court and the Court of Special Appeals apply the appropriate standard of review for evaluating the propriety of a condominium bylaw amendment?" In their brief and before the lower courts, the appellees argued that courts should apply a reasonableness test in reviewing the validity of condominium bylaw amendments. At oral argument before us, however, they argued in addition that the bylaw amendment at issue violated both the declaration and the Act by "taking" a property right. Such changes in property interests, they maintained, may only be accomplished by amending the declaration with the unanimous consent of the unit owners. Although this point was not briefed by the parties and was only briefly alluded to in the opinion of the Court of Special Appeals, the appellees urge this Court to reach the issue.

Under Rule 8-131(b), we "ordinarily will consider only an issue that has been raised in the petition for certiorari or any cross-petition and that has been preserved for review by the Court of Appeals." Appellees' argument is directly responsive to the question in the petition for certiorari. They assert that the test for evaluating the

propriety of the bylaw amendment is whether it deprives a unit owner of a property right. Consequently, in our view, the argument is encompassed within the question presented in the certiorari petition.

IV

In reviewing the validity of a rule, a court must determine whether the Board of Directors or Council of Unit Owners had the authority to promulgate the rule at issue under the Act, declaration, and bylaws. Dulaney Towers, supra, 46 Md.App. at 466, 418 A.2d 1233; Johnson v. Hobson, 505 A.2d 1313, 1317 (D.C.App.1986); Juno by the Sea North Condominium v. Manfredonia, 397 So.2d 297 (Fla.Dist.Ct.App.1981); 68 Op.Atty.Gen. 112, 119 (1983). Since we find that the Association did not have the authority to enact the rule at issue here by amending the bylaws, we do not reach the question briefed by the parties.

The Association contends that the rule is merely a use restriction which the Council of Unit Owners may enact by amending the bylaws with a 2/3 vote of the unit owners. Cases addressing the propriety of use restrictions fall generally into two categories. In the first class of cases, which we will refer to as "exclusive use" cases, some courts rule that granting exclusive use of common elements to one or few unit owners changes the percentage interest of the excluded unit owners in the common elements. E.g., Kaplan v. Boudreaux, 410 Mass. 435, 573 N.E.2d 495 (1991). In the second class of cases, which we will refer to as "equality" cases, some courts rule that if a restriction applies equally to all the unit owners, it does not change their respective percentage interests in the common elements. E.g., Jarvis v. Stage Neck Owners Ass'n, 464 A.2d 952 (Me.1983).

The Supreme Judicial Court of Massachusetts, in Kaplan, supra, 573 N.E.2d at 497, reviewed a bylaw amendment granting exclusive use of a path, which was part of the condominium's common elements, to one unit. The statute required consent of all the unit owners to alter the percentage interests in the common elements. Id. The court found that it was not necessary to "transfer . . . the sum total of a unit owner's interests in a portion of the common area" in order to "affect [the] percentage interest in the common area." Rather, "[t]ransfer of an interest that is smaller than an 'ownership' interest would suffice to alter the percentage interest held by each [owner]." Id. 573 N.E.2d at 498-99. The court held that the amendment affected an interest in land because it resembled an easement and concluded that the amendment changed the relative percentage interests of the unit owners in the common elements. Therefore, consent of all the unit owners was required to enact the amendment. Id. at 500; see also Makeever v. Lyle, 125 Ariz. 384, 609 P.2d 1084, 1089 (Ariz.Ct.App.1980) (converting general common elements to exclusive use of one owner constitutes taking of other owners' property without authority); Preston v. Bass, 13 Ark.App. 94, 680 S.W.2d 115, 116 (1984) (Board approval of carport in common area created limited common element requiring 100% vote of unit owners); Penney v. Association of Apt. Owners, 70 Haw. 469, 776 P.2d 393, 395 (1989) (change from general to limited common element altered unit owners' percentage interests); Carney v. Donley, 261 Ill.App.3d 1002, 199 Ill.Dec. 219, 224, 633 N.E.2d 1015, 1020 (1994) (board did not have authority to approve balcony extensions into common area); Sawko v. Dominion Plaza One Condo. Ass'n, 218 Ill.App.3d 521, 161 Ill.Dec. 263, 269, 578 N.E.2d 621, 627 (1991) (assigning parking spaces to some units diminished other owners' interests in common elements); Stuewe v. Lauletta, 93 Ill.App.3d 1029, 49 Ill.Dec. 494, 496, 418 N.E.2d 138, 140 (1981) (developer's grant of parking space to one unit gave exclusive easement and diminished other owners' interests in common elements); Strauss v. Oyster River Condominium Trust, 417 Mass. 442, 631 N.E.2d 979, 981 (1994) (additions built in common area changed percentage interests of unit owners); Grimes v. Moreland, 41 Ohio Misc. 69, 322 N.E.2d 699, 702 (1974) ("placing fences and [air conditioner] compressors on condominium common areas constitutes a taking of property and an ouster of co-tenants from common areas"); cf. Alpert v. Le'Lisa Condominium, 107 Md.App. 239, 247, 667 A.2d 947 (1995) (parking spaces assigned to 20 of 32 unit owners did not become limited common elements because they would not be conveyed with the unit); Juno by the Sea, supra, 397 So.2d 297, 303 (assigning parking spaces to 50 of 70 unit owners did not convert general into limited common elements because spaces would not be conveyed with the unit). Compare Parrillo v. 1300 Lake Shore Drive Condo., 103 Ill.App.3d 810, 59 Ill.Dec. 464, 466, 431 N.E.2d 1221, 1223 (1981) (enclosing limited common element would not change unit owners' percentage interests in common elements because use was already exclusive) with Gaffny v. Reid, 628 A.2d 155, 157 (Me.1993) (cottage encroaching on limited common area violated other owners' property rights despite prior exclusivity of use).

In contrast, the Supreme Judicial Court of Maine, in Jarvis, supra, 464 A.2d at 954, reviewed an agreement approved by 80% of the unit owners which granted an adjacent resort hotel use of the condominium's pool, tennis courts, and parking area. The court discussed Stuewe, supra, 93 Ill.App.3d 1029, 49 Ill.Dec. 494, 418 N.E.2d 138, and Makeever, supra, 125 Ariz 384, 609 P.2d 1084, and said:

"There is a distinct difference between these cases, in which exclusive use, control and/or ownership of the common areas is taken from some or all of the unit owners and cases in which some reasonable restrictions or regulation of the common areas is imposed on all owners. In the first instance, each owner's percentage interest in the common area is altered. In the second instance, the percentage ownership interest is unaffected. Jarvis, supra, 464 A.2d at 956."

Since the agreement did not increase or decrease the common elements and did not grant any owner exclusive use, it did not alter the percentage interests of the unit owners. Id. at 957; see also Schaumburg State Bank v. Bank of Wheaton, 197 Ill.App.3d 713, 144 Ill.Dec. 151, 555 N.E.2d 48, 52-53, cert. denied, 133 Ill.2d 573, 149 Ill.Dec. 337, 561 N.E.2d 707 (1990) (declaration amendment granting nonexclusive easement over driveway to neighbor did not change unit owners' percentage interests in common element); Bd. of Dir. of By the Sea Council v. Sondock, 644 S.W.2d 774, 781 (Tex.App.-Corpus Christi 1982) (declaration amendment allowing removal of carports did not change unit owners' percentage interests in common element because applied equally to all unit owners); cf. Coventry Square Condominium Ass'n v. Halpern, 181 N.J.Super. 93, 436 A.2d 580, 582 (1981) (bylaw amendment requiring security deposit from rented units only created "a special class of owners" and was unreasonable, arbitrary, and unnecessary).

Here, the rule at issue affected an "interest" in property. The bylaw amendment revoked the commercial unit owners' right to have their clients use the lobby. That right resembles an easement, which is an interest in property. In Condry v. Laurie, 184 Md. 317, 320, 41 A.2d 66 (1945), we discussed the difference between a license and an easement:

While an easement implies an interest in land, a license is merely a personal privilege to do some particular act or series of acts on land without possessing any estate or interest therein. In De Haro v. United States, 5 Wall. 599, 627, 18 L.Ed. 681, 688. Justice Davis spoke of the incidents of a license as follows: "It is an authority to do a lawful act, which, without it, would be unlawful, and while it remains unrevoked is a justification for the acts which it authorizes to be done. It ceases with the death of either party, and cannot be transferred or alienated by the licensee, because it is a personal matter, and is limited to the original parties to it."

The right which the bylaw amendment revoked was not "a mere personal privilege," Griffith v. Montgomery County, 57 Md.App. 472, 485, 470 A.2d 840 (1984), cert. denied, 469 U.S. 1191, 105 S.Ct. 965, 83 L.Ed.2d 970 (1985), but was appurtenant to the condominium unit and would be conveyed with the unit. Since the right resembles an easement, we hold that the bylaw amendment affected an interest in the appellees' property. See Kaplan, supra, 573 N.E.2d at 500.

Here, however, and unlike the exclusive use cases, such as Kaplan, supra, 410 Mass. 435, 573 N.E.2d 495, the bylaw amendment did not grant one or few unit owners exclusive use of a common area. Nonetheless, unlike the equality cases, such as Jarvis, supra, 464 A.2d 952, the bylaw amendment disparately affected a portion of the unit owners by revoking a property interest they acquired when they purchased their units, without affecting the rights of the other unit owners.

In terms of the Maryland Condominium Act the lobby was a general common element, the use of which all of the tenants enjoyed equally. This was consistent with § 11-108(a) requiring that, "except as provided in the declaration, the common elements shall be subject to mutual rights of . . . access, use, and enjoyment by all unit owners." By bylaw amendment, the Association has attempted to deny that mutuality of use of a general common element. Further, under § 11-106(a), "[e]ach unit in a condominium has all of the incidents of real property." By bylaw amendment, the Association has attempted to reduce the "easement" that the professional office units enjoyed in the lobby, and that "easement" is one of the incidents of the ownership of a professional office unit.

For these reasons, we hold that it was beyond the power of the Association by bylaw amendment to purport to deprive the owners of the professional office units of their rights under the declaration and under the Maryland Condominium Act to the enjoyment of the lobby for the ingress and egress of their business invitees.

JUDGMENT AFFIRMED WITH COSTS.[23]

Case Review Question: Would the result be different if the restriction were in place at the time the condominium owners of commercial units purchased them?

9. Non-freehold Estates

Not all property is occupied or controlled by persons with an ownership interest. In addition to interests associated with freehold estates of ownership, numerous non-freehold estate interests are present in American property law. A non-freehold estate includes the specific right to possess property, exercise primary control, and even exclude the true owner to a great extent. These proprietary interests are generally by agreement, for a fixed time, and do not include the rights that are incident to true ownership, such as the right to transfer title to the property. A freehold estate prevents the holder from engaging in any conduct that would result in wasting of the property, and the holder must return the property to the true owner at the agreed time or upon legal proceedings that result in a formal termination of the non-freehold interest. In many ways, the non-freehold interest represents a life estate. However, it is more limited. One with a non-freehold estate does not have the right to totally exercise control over the property. The owner may include a variety of limitations on the use of the property as long as they are not unlawful or discriminatory. The estate typically is not one defined in time by the natural life of the estate holder. In a life estate, wasting is essentially the only way that the property can be retrieved prematurely. In a non-freehold estate, a variety of infractions or violations of conditions of possession may result in proceedings to terminate the possessory interest and return it to the owner. Finally, in a life estate, the holder may exclude the true owner completely from the property. However, in a non-freehold estate, the owner has limited rights to inspect the property and to make entrance for repairs and other necessary tasks to maintain the property. Most often the relationship between the person with a property ownership interest and the non-freehold estate holder is that of landlord and tenant and is governed in part by property law principles and in part by the established standards for contract law. Because the non-freehold estate is so common, each state has laws that specifically address the rights and obligations in the landlord–tenant relationship.

a. The Landlord–Tenant Relationship: Rights and Obligations   A non-freehold estate is commonly called a leasehold. The parties are referred to as landlord (ownership interest) and tenant (possessory interest). A leasehold agreement may or may not be in writing, depending upon the specific nature of the arrangement. The contract statute of frauds principle dictates that agreements that cannot be completed within one year must be in writing. This is to ensure that the parties do not forget or confuse the terms of the agreement as time passes. Whenever an owner turns over control of property for any length of time to another, the terms of possession should be clear and recorded for any future issues that arise. The same rules for such written agreements apply as in any contractual setting, including such things as capacity and the requisite elements of a valid contract. An important factor is a specific description of the property to be transferred and the rights and limitations, if any, on possession.

The terms of the agreement should be thoroughly understood by both parties. If the agreement contains an option to renew and that option is not formally executed according to its terms, a tenant who remains in possession past the original contract term may become a tenant at will and be subject to eviction proceedings. The various types of possessory tenancies will be discussed in great length later. It is first important, however, to understand the rights and obligations associated with any type of tenancy.

The landlord and tenant each have certain duties and privileges related to their interest in the property. The landlord has an initial duty to turn over the property free from latent defects or dangers and to see that the property is habitable. A latent defect or danger is one that is not obvious or readily discoverable. The defect must be one that substantially affects the condition or safety of the property. While the specific definition of habitability varies among jurisdictions, there are some elements that are included or inferred by most statutory definitions. In order for a property to be habitable, the structure upon the premises must be in such condition that tenants can be reasonably expected to occupy the property for its primary purpose. For example, an apartment must be suitable within certain standards for residential use. Typically, conditions of habitability include access to utilities and hot water, and protection of persons and property from elements of weather by a sound roof. The exact elements of habitability may vary with geographical regions and climate conditions. For example, in the south the access to heat may not be considered nearly as essential as in a northern state. If the landlord fails to provide a habitable structure as agreed upon, or fails to maintain the property in a habitable condition during the tenure of the agreement, then the landlord's warranty of habitability is violated and the landlord is presumed to have breached the agreement.

APPLICATION 13.11

G rented a commercial building from H for the express purpose of operating a restaurant. Two months after taking possession of the property, a central pipe burst and the water had to be shut off. The restaurant had to be closed until repairs could be made. H made repeated promises to have the problem fixed but did not do so. G brought an action against H for breach of contract on the basis of H's breach of warranty of habitability.

Point for Discussion: Should the result be different if the property became uninhabitable as the result of an act by G?

In contrast, the tenant is responsible to prevent waste from occurring on the property, to discover patent defects or dangers, and to make ordinary repairs.[24] A patent defect is that which is readily apparent or discoverable. An example of the difference between a latent and patent defect might be dangerous electrical wiring located within the walls versus a broken stair. If a significant patent defect exists or occurs, the tenant is obligated to notify the landlord and to give the landlord a reasonable opportunity to repair it. If the defect does not affect habitability, the tenant is generally responsible for the repair unless the agreement contains terms to the contrary. The responsibility to make repairs also typically includes the obligation to pay for those same repairs.

Assignment 13.4

Consider the following items and identify whether they would be considered latent or patent defects and, further, whether they would violate the warranty of habitability.

a. Electrical wires running under carpet and creating an uneven floor surface.
b. Broken garbage disposal, a condition that existed at the time the property was turned over to the tenant.
c. A cracked window.
d. Floorboards in a porch that are supported by timber that has incurred water damage and subsequently has begun to rot.
e. The same as number 4 except that the porch is the only access to a third-story apartment.
f. The air conditioning in a rented house stops working.
g. The only sink in a rented commercial property used as a pet grooming salon becomes clogged and the attempts of the tenant to clear the clog have only made it worse.
h. Moles have left the ground of a rented property deeply rutted. The property is rented during the winter when the ground is under a deep blanket of snow. The property was rented for use as soccer fields for a local soccer club.

An additional obligation of the landlord is to provide complete possession of the property described in the agreement to the tenant and to provide the tenant with quiet enjoyment of the property. In other words, unless specifically proscribed by the agreement or law, or conduct that would cause wasting is engaged in, the landlord cannot dictate the manner in which the tenant uses the property. The landlord may only enter the property with reasonable notice and upon reasonable terms, including time and day of entry.

The tenant is bound by all of the terms of the agreement and applicable laws, and must take care not to permit or cause wasting of the property. In addition, the tenant must pay the agreed-upon consideration (usually rent) and give reasonable notice when vacating the property. This is commonly known as quitting the property. When possession of the property is returned, the tenant is obligated to see that it is in essentially the same condition as when it was received.

If either party substantially fails to meet his or her responsibilities, such failure may be treated as a breach, and the innocent party has the right to terminate the agreement. A landlord's failure to meet the required obligations is termed constructive eviction.[25] In other words, the tenant is left with no other reasonable alternative but to vacate the premises. It is not required that the landlord intentionally fail to meet his or her legal responsibilities. Any occurrence, whether caused or exacerbated by the landlord, or by something unrelated such as fire or weather that causes such significant damage that the property becomes uninhabitable, may result in constructive eviction. In many instances, the lease agreement allows the landlord a reasonable length of time to make repairs before the lease agreement is terminated for constructive eviction that is not the fault of the landlord. In that event, the terms of the agreement will dictate such issues as payment of rent during the term of uninhabitability, recovery of deposits, and so forth. For this and other reasons, it is very important to carefully go through all terms of a landlord–tenant agreement.

Regardless of who initially breached the agreement, many states impose on both parties a duty to mitigate any damage caused by the premature end of the landlord–tenant relationship. Mitigation of damages is the term used when one is required to lessen or minimize the damage when possible. This prevents persons from adding to their damages to increase the amount of monetary recovery in a lawsuit. In the event the property is significantly damaged, the landlord is often under the obligation to make every reasonable effort to repair the premises and restore a condition of habitability. Further, if a tenant vacates or abandons the property, the landlord must make reasonable attempts to rent the property. The landlord cannot merely let the property stand empty and seek to collect the balance of the rent from the tenant.

The tenant also is responsible for mitigating damages. A tenant who is forced to move on grounds of constructive eviction must make reasonable efforts to minimize the cost of the move and the damage to any personal property before recovering compensation from the landlord. The tenant who played a role in creating the condition that forced the constructive eviction probably has no recourse against the landlord.

b. Leasehold Agreements   As mentioned previously in this chapter, there are a variety of leasehold arrangements. Each has a specific duration and basis for termination. The term of the lease will dictate whether it must be in writing to be enforceable under the statute of frauds, although it is always advisable to have any type of leasehold agreement in writing. Generally, leases that extend beyond the period of one year are required to be in writing. Shorter and more casual arrangements may be based on an oral agreement, but these too can give rise to disputes over terms and ultimately litigation if the terms are not clearly stated and agreed to by the parties in written form.

The shortest type of regular leasehold agreement is the month-to-month tenancy. These are also sometimes referred to as periodic tenancies. They are the least restrictive of the common and formal agreements. The agreement between the parties is effective for one month. Unless otherwise stated, the month is presumed to begin on the first calendar day and to end on the last calendar day of the same month. This type of agreement is considered to automatically renew, unless otherwise stated in the terms, each month thereafter until one of the parties chooses to terminate it. Termination, other than for wrongful conduct by one of the parties, requires reasonable notice. In most states this is considered to be the equivalent of at least one full term or one calendar month or more. If a party breaches other terms of the agreement such as by nonpayment of rent, each state has statutes that prescribe the time and methods for ending the tenancy.

A very common type of tenancy in residential leaseholds is the year-to-year tenancy. This type of agreement has a term of one year. Like month to month, the term may automatically renew each year. However, in leaseholds that extend this long, most written leases require some type of notice to renew or cancel the agreement by either party. If the original agreement extends beyond one calendar year, then the agreement must be written to be enforceable under the statute of frauds. Unlike the month-to-month tenancy, the year-to-year tenancy does not typically require a full term's advance notice of the intent not to renew or to quit the lease. If a written agreement does not state a reasonable period for notice regarding renewal, state statutes will provide a specific amount of time that is necessary. The objective is to provide the other party with a reasonable amount of time to make other arrangements in the event the lease will be coming to an end. A common length of time is three months for year-to-year or multi-year tenancies. Many states, however, have laws that limit leases from extending so long that development of the property is unreasonably impeded. But since the limitation is often as much as 100 years, it is usually not a problem for landlords and tenants.

A tenant who remains in possession of the property beyond the agreed term without exercising an option to do so or without automatic renewal has no legal right to remain on the premises. When a tenant does this, the former tenancy is converted to a tenancy at sufferance. Unlike other tenancies, which require proper notice, a tenant at sufferance can be sued for immediate eviction without notice. This does not mean that the landlord can enter the property and forcibly remove the former tenant or have police do so, as if the tenant were a trespasser. Once a tenancy is established, and even if it converts to a tenancy at sufferance, certain statutory procedures for eviction must be followed. Typically this includes written notices to vacate the premises immediately. If this is not done within the prescribed period, the landlord may seek a court order and ultimately forcibly remove the tenant from the premises with the assistance of law enforcement.

Finally, the most casual form of leasehold is the tenancy at will. A tenant at will is one who enters or remains on the property with no certain terms of agreement; consent of the owner is sufficient. Tenancy at will continues indefinitely and has no fixed time at which it will end. The amount of notice needed to end such a tenancy is usually set by statute. Often reasonable notice is considered to be one month. However, the reasonable period may be largely influenced by the length of time the tenant has occupied the property and any evidence of the previous understanding of the parties. This type of tenancy and tenancy at sufferance are the least desirable for the tenant because he or she may be required to vacate with very little or no notice. For the landlord who uses the property for income purposes, such a tenancy provides little security of continued income, either. Yet, in some circumstances the situation may be desirable to one or both parties when portability of the use of the property is the desired objective.

10. Fixtures: Real or Personal Property?

While real property consists of land or things permanently affixed to land, such as buildings, personal property readily movable although it may require some mechanical assistance to accomplish the movement. There are certain instances when property may begin as personal property and then be attached to real property in such a way that it does not become a part of the real property, but is not readily movable either. These items are characterized as fixtures. A fixture is an article of personal property that has been so attached to the real property that it cannot be removed without substantially altering or damaging the real property. Fixtures are not such things as houses and permanent buildings, but fixtures are often included with real property because they have lost the characteristics of personal property. They are items that have been physically incorporated into the structure but are removable, such as lighting and bathroom fixtures, and ceiling fans. Unlike the roof or windows whose removal would substantially alter the structure, a fixture can be removed and the location of the attachment repaired with comparative ease. Because fixtures are semi-permanently attached, they are generally conveyed with the interest in the real property unless the agreement states to the contrary.

There are limitless possibilities as to what might constitute a fixture, and when something is semi-attached or permanently attached to the real property, thus converting the personal property into a fixture. In the past, disputes have been frequent among buyers and sellers as to what is and is not a fixture when both want the personal property/fixture that is at issue. Because of the many kinds of personal property that exist and the countless ways they can be attached, the courts have developed a four-prong test to resolve whether an item is a fixture that should be transferred with the real property interest, or whether it is personal property that should remain in the possession of the previous estate holder. The factors taken into consideration by the courts include the following:

1. Evidence of intent that the item was to be considered personal property or a fixture
2. Mode of annexation
3. Adaptation
4. Extent of damage, if any, that will result if the object is removed from the property

The element of intent refers to the original intent of the party who first attached the personal property to the real property.[26] If there is evidence that the property was placed with the idea that it would become a permanent attachment, this would support a finding that the item is a fixture and should convey with the property. The term *mode of annexation* is often used to describe the method and steps taken to attach the fixture to the real property. Typically, the more extensive the process of attachment was, the more likely the property was considered to be a fixture and intended to be treated as such. Adaptation refers to the function of the item that has been attached. If the personal property has become attached in a way that it serves to consistently benefit or facilitate the use of the property, then it may very well be considered to be an integral part of the property as a fixture. Finally, the issue of damage supports the other elements. If the property is attached and in some way incorporated into the use of the real property, it may be evidenced by how significant the physical damage or loss of benefit/use would be if the property were to be removed.

APPLICATION 13.12

A builds a house and throughout the house installs ceiling fans with the light fixtures. Each of the fixtures is attached in a typical manner by making a simple connection to wires extending out of the ceiling. When A sells the house, the fans and lights are removed and replaced with ordinary lights. B, the purchaser, claims that the fan/light combinations were an integral part of the property as fixtures and should have been left in place. Under the four-pronged test, while lights are certainly an integral part of the property, specific fixtures that can be easily removed and replaced with minimal effort and without damage to the property probably would not show sufficient intent that the original fans and lights would legally be considered permanent fixtures.

Point for Discussion: What if the property were in a climate such as that of Montana, and the fans were used in lieu of an air conditioning system to circulate air flow on warm days? Would the result be different?

There is a subcategory of fixtures that receive slightly different treatment from those found in standard buildings and homes. This type of incorporated personal property is commonly known as a trade fixture. The trade fixture originates as personal property but is annexed to the property for use in the business or trade conducted on the premises by the owner of the personal property. Very often, businesses lease the real estate where they conduct their business objectives and install any nec-

APPLICATION 13.13

Acme Hardware rents a commercial space in a local retail center for the purpose of operating a home tool repair shop. The various pieces of equipment used to repair the items brought into the shop are quite heavy and oddly configured and as a result must be attached to the floors and walls for stability. The attachments are substantial and require various holes to be drilled in the building's concrete foundation and walls. Also, braces are installed in the ceiling for a lifting device that is used to raise and lower heavy items such as riding mowers. After approximately one year, the real property is sold by the owner to a new owner. When the lease term ends and Acme vacates the property, they are obligated to remove all the equipment and to make repairs that restore the property to its condition at the time the tenancy was created. This must be done at Acme's own expense. Neither the former nor the new real property owners have any interest in or right to Acme's equipment regardless of the fact that it was incorporated into the real property in such a way that in other circumstances it might be considered a fixture.

Point for Discussion: Should the result change if the equipment was installed in the garage of a home and could not be removed without irreparable damage to the integrity of the structure?

essary equipment. In some types of commerce, the tools and equipment used in a business require that they be installed or attached in a relatively permanent way to the property in order to be fully functional. When this occurs, the courts consider the trade fixture to remain the property of the installer and not subject to any conveyance of the real property interest unless otherwise agreed upon. However, the owner of the trade fixtures does have an obligation to restore the property to its former condition and to repair any damage caused by the installation or the removal. The owner of the personal property is also obligated to remove it when the possessory interest is transferred.

B. PERSONAL PROPERTY

1. Bailments Generally

Unlike real property, personal property may consist not only of tangible items, but also of intangibles, such as a patent or copyright. These are legal rights over something that is essentially a complete creative idea, a concept, or even a perception. However, very specific rules apply and usually require appropriate documentation before something intangible would be considered personal property according to legal definitions. Most legal issues with respect to personal property arise when the possessory and/or ownership rights to a particular item come into question. There are a number of ways to transfer such rights other than by sale or gift. Each method is accomplished in a slightly different way and gives rise to different rights with respect to the former and present owner/possessor.

A very commonplace transfer of possession of personal property occurs in the form of bailments. A **bailment** occurs when a party known as the bailor temporarily delivers possession of the property to another party known as the bailee. The delivery is made for a specific purpose and/or as part of a contract with the understanding that the property will be cared for and returned to the original party upon demand.[27] Certain conditions must be satisfied for a bailment to occur and to attain the legal rights of the parties associated with bailments. Specifically, it must be established that the transfer demonstrated the following elements:

Bailment
Temporary relinquishment of control over one's personal property to a third party.

1. Personal property was transferred.
2. The bailor was a party with a legal right to possession of the property.
3. The bailee received possession of the property for a specific purpose and/or as part of the terms of a contract.
4. The bailee voluntarily accepted the obligation to protect the property.
5. The bailor retained the right to reclaim the property.
6. Certain bailments also require compensation in return for some act pertaining to the property.

It is common to find state statutes that address certain types of bailments. These often include bailments that involve personal property of substantial value, and bailments among persons who may not be well known to one another. Examples include safe deposit boxes and vehicle parking services, such as garages or valet parking. However, in the absence of a state statute that speaks to an issue involving a bailment, common law principles prevail.

2. Forms of Bailment

As a general rule, there are two basic categories of bailments. The rights and duties undertaken by the bailee influence which type of bailment exists. The obligations of the bailor will be determined to be consistent with the rights and obligations of the bailee under the particular type of bailment.

When the bailment occurs more or less as a favor, it is considered to be a gratuitous bailment. This is when either the bailor or bailee is benefited by the bailment without any obligation to provide a commensurate benefit to the other. This might be a situation of lending personal property by one party to another. Another circumstance might be offering to maintain or hold personal property for someone. For example, many businesses offer bailment type services to certain customers as a means of establishing good will and enhancing public relations. A large depositor at a bank might be offered the use of a safe deposit box with waiver of the usual fee. Whether the property is loaned to or held by another gratuitously does not matter. In either situation, the bailee (party receiving the property) has the duty to exercise ordinary care to protect the bailed property. What constitutes ordinary care obviously depends in large part on the nature of the property itself. Essentially, though, the duty would include reasonable precautions under the circumstances to protect the property from damage or theft.

The other type of bailment is mutual benefit bailment. This bailment is more formal in nature and imposes certain rights and obligations on both the bailor and the bailee. Such bailments encompass all occurrences of a temporary nature where the bailor promises to provide some sort of compensation in return for safekeeping of the property and possibly for additional agreed-upon duties by the bailee. The bailee accepts the obligation to care for the property, to return it upon demand or at a specified time, and to perform any additional agreed-upon duties with respect to the property.

APPLICATION 13.14

Gratuitous Bailment: A is assigned to a temporary job post in New York City for six months. B offers to let A keep his car in her garage while he is gone.

Mutual Benefit Bailment: The same as above, however A offers to pay a set dollar amount for the use of the garage and B (the owner of a service station) agrees to store the car and to service the car prior to A's return.

Point for Discussion: What type of bailment would exist if B does not have the obligation to service the vehicle?

Whether or not property has been bailed is based upon the actions of the bailor and whether that conduct demonstrates the intent to divide the rights of possession, control, and ownership.[28] For example, leaving a vehicle in a commercial garage would not be considered a bailment unless the keys were turned over to the garage operator/owner as well, since without the keys to the vehicle, the receiving party could not exercise control over the car. Instead, the car owner would have created a lease or license relationship depending on the terms and duration of the parking arrangement. Essentially, the owner would lease or have a license to use the space but would retain possession of the car at all times by retaining possession of the keys. In a bailment, the owner (bailor) keeps the title and right to ownership of the property but temporarily gives up the right to exercise control over its possession.

To determine the existence and nature of a bailment relationship, the court considers whether the elements of a bailment are evidenced by the actions of the parties and the relationship between the parties, if any, and what the parties' reasonable expectations should have been under the circumstances. Issues in cases involving bailments arise for a variety of reasons. They often turn on whether the release of the property by the bailor to bailee was done with the intent and right to reclaim, and/or the degree of duty the bailee had to protect the property as well as perform any additional duties agreed upon.

As a general rule, the duty of a bailee is only to possess and take basic steps to protect the personal property from damage unless other conditions are specified by an agreement between bailor and bailee. The agreement may be expressly stated in written or oral form, or it may be implied from the surrounding circumstances. For example, if someone brings a VCR to a VCR repair shop, explains the problem, hands the VCR to the owner of the shop and leaves after the owner states that the VCR will be ready in four days, it is probably not necessary to have a written document to establish that a bailment was created. However, if the bailment takes place between friends, it is quite possible that the court would infer a gratuitous bailment in ordinary circumstances and, thus, there would be no duty beyond that of ordinary care.

A compensated bailee who is party to a mutual benefit bailment has a greater duty to care for the personal property that is the subject of the bailment. The reasoning is that the compensation paid by the bailor is, at least in part, for the ensured well-being of the property. Thus, while the bailee may not be expected to risk life or limb for the property, it may be necessary to take further steps. For example, if the VCR is repaired by one friend for another, the court may infer a gratuitous bailment and require no additional degree of care. But if the VCR is repaired for a customer by a commercial business, that business is expected to take greater care to protect the property. Such care might include steps to prevent a theft at the store or casualty insurance on the bailed property within the shop.

Bailment is a voluntary and temporary division of ownership and possession of personal property. There are other instances as well when ownership and possession are divided. However, such a separation is not always voluntary and in some instances may become permanent with a loss of ownership rights as well. This generally depends on how the separation of ownership and possession occurred and the roles played by the parties involved.

3. Property That Is Lost or Mislaid

The key distinction between bailed property and that which is lost or mislaid is intent. When property is lost or mislaid, the owner does not plan to give up possession. There is a further distinction between property that is lost and property that is mislaid. If property is lost, it becomes separated from the owner involuntarily and accidentally.[29] In fact, the owner is often unaware at the time it occurs. Mislaid property occurs when the owner deliberately places it in a given spot and subsequently forgets the location. The majority of states have enacted statutes to deal with situations where lost or mislaid property is found by another and the rights, if any, of the finder as well as the original owner. In the absence of such statutes, common law principles that often served as the framework and foundation for subsequent statutory law are applied.

Many jurisdictions take the position that the finder of lost or mislaid property is the constructive bailee for the benefit of the bailor.[30] The bailee, by accepting possession, accepts the duty to care for the property until it is reclaimed by the original owner. Statutes may or may not require the bailor to provide compensation for these acts. But if statutory provisions provide for compensation, then the duty to care for the property arises according to a mutual benefit bailment. After a reasonable time, if the property is not reclaimed, the finder may be entitled to retain possession and assume ownership in accordance with the statutory provisions.

A number of jurisdictions, however, do not imply found property as a type of bailment. In these states, the finder has the right to claim possession and ownership from the outset. This, of course, assumes that the personal property was not found on or around the real property or other personal property held by the original owner. If the property is truly lost, the finder may exercise ownership even if it was found on the premises of yet a third party. However, mislaid property is considered to belong to the owner of the premises where the property is located. The circumstances surrounding the personal property are used to determine whether the owner intended to place it there or whether it was lost.

There is an exception to these rules under common-law principles that has also been adopted in a number of state statutes. The exception follows the traditional rule of what is called *treasure trove*. If the jurisdiction recognizes the finder of property as someone entitled to assume ownership, and if the property is considered to be highly valuable, then the finder is entitled to the property regardless of whose property it is found on (with the exception of course of the true owner). In these cases, no distinction is made between lost or mislaid property or the location where it is found. For treasure trove to apply the item must usually be cash or its equivalent. Because there is such a variation in law and how it applies depending on the nature of the personal property found, it is essential to consult the law of a jurisdiction to determine the rights and obligations with respect to property that is found.

APPLICATION 13.15

1. Z finds a small silver bracelet lying on a bench in a city park. The property would likely be considered lost since ordinarily someone would not place such an item in a public place and intentionally leave it there. Because the location is a public place, Z would have the right to claim the property.

2. Z finds a small silver bracelet lying on a seat in a movie theater. Z would still be entitled to claim the bracelet over the rights of the theater owner as circumstances indicate it was lost.

3. Z rents a locker in a bus station and inside at the very back, finds a small silver bracelet. In this case, the circumstances might lean toward the property having been mislaid by the previous owner, perhaps mistakenly not retrieved when the rest of the articles were removed from the locker. In this case, the owner of the bus station may have a claim to the property if it is determined that the bracelet was, in fact, mislaid.

Point for Discussion: Would the situations change if Z found a wallet with $500 rather than a bracelet?

4. When Personal Property Is Abandoned

Sometimes, the owner of personal property will cast it aside with full intent to give up all rights of possession and ownership. When this occurs, the law considers the property to have been abandoned.[31] When one finds abandoned property, that property can be claimed and ownership assumed for as long as possession and intent to own is demonstrated. However, if the finder subsequently ceases to exercise rights associated with ownership, he or she cannot later reconsider and reclaim it upon a change of heart if the property has since come into the possession/ownership of yet a third party.

APPLICATION 13.16

J is on vacation in the southwest. During a tour of an old mining town and nearby abandoned mines, J comes across something on a hillside that appears to be shiny. J assumes the area has been thoroughly mined and considers the shiny stone to be fool's gold and without value. Nevertheless it is a large piece. J keeps the piece for a few days but, at the end of the vacation, gives the stone to a tour guide who states the intent to use it as a decorative piece in one of the buildings in town. Two weeks later J sees a large piece in the national news that shows the tour guide holding the stone and the headline "Rich New Vein of Gold Discovered. This individual piece valued at $100,000!"

Originally, the owners of the mine had ownership of the gold located in it. Subsequently, J could have been considered to be the owner. But, once J gave up the rights of ownership, the tour guide would be the new owner and J would have lost all rights.

Point for Discussion: If J gave the piece to the guide after being told by the guide that it was valueless fool's gold, should the result be any different?

---

5. When the Properties of More Than One Person Are Blended

It is possible for someone to know the location of their property but be unable to clearly identify it as such. This is known as *confused* property and occurs when the personal property of one person is somehow combined with other similar personal property. When this occurs, and there is insufficient evidence available to distinguish the property items, the value of the property is considered to be shared equally by each party who can affirmatively establish that they are entitled to any share.

6. When the True Owner Seeks the Return of Property in the Possession of Another

Many legal disputes arise when there is disagreement over the rights of possession or ownership of personal property. As a result, a large body of law has developed to deal with these situations that range from recovery of lost or mislaid property to

APPLICATION 13.17

Four college roommates have a habit of each buying his or her own lottery ticket on Saturdays before the weekly drawing. One Saturday morning the tickets are purchased as usual while the roommates do their weekly shopping. During the day the tickets are laid down around the kitchen by the various roommates. On Saturday night, one of the tickets has the correct combination and the owner wins $37 million dollars. Each of the roommates claims the ticket to have been theirs. Because there is no firm evidence as to who purchased the winning ticket, the $37 million is split equally into four shares rather than being awarded to the individual purchaser.

Point for Discussion: Should the result be different if the tickets were purchased weekly by one of the roommates and then given to the others as gifts?

compensation for damage or theft of property left in the care of another. In cases dealing with persons who claim to have involuntarily lost permanent possession of their property, a variety of legal alternatives exist to seek the return of the property or the cash equivalent of its fair market value. In the event the property was stolen, criminal laws may apply. However, as discussed in the chapter on criminal law and procedure, typically any penalty upon a finding of guilt involves penalties for the injury to the public by such behavior and may not include any form of restitution to the injured individual. As a result, the individual may need to also pursue a civil action with respect to the personal injury of the loss of property and/or its value. Following is a discussion of the various civil actions that may be brought for one who seeks to regain lost personal property or the fair market value of such.

a. Actions for Conversion   If a party obtains possession of another's personal property and refuses to return it either on demand or according to agreed-upon terms, the proper action to obtain the physical return of the property is an action for conversion. The property may have been taken without permission or it may have been the subject of a previous bailment. If possession of the property was transferred as the result of a contract, there may also be an action for breach of contract. However these actions, as well as other legal alternatives, often result in an award of monetary damages rather than the actual return of the property.

   To prove an action for conversion, the property owner must establish the following elements:

1. The right of ownership to the property
2. Wrongful possession of the property by another party
3. Intent by the party in possession to exercise total control over the property as an owner and to exclude the owner from the rights associated with ownership and possession

   If the elements are proven, and the property is in substantially the same condition as when it was converted to the use of the second party, the court may order the return of the property as well as a monetary award sufficient to compensate for the lost use of the property (if any) during the period of conversion. If the property has been altered, damaged, or disposed of, the court may award monetary damages for an amount equal to the fair market value of the property as well as any incidental expenses incurred during the period of time the property was unavailable to the owner as the result of the conversion.

APPLICATION 13.18

P and Q are friends. P owns some property in the country with several outbuildings. P stores various items of personal property there and allows Q to do the same. P decides to sell the property and when it comes time to remove the personal items, Q offers to do so for P and to bring it to a specified location. P agrees. However, instead of returning P's property, Q takes the property along with his own to another storage area. P and Q subsequently have a falling out and Q refuses to turn the property over to P. P files an action in conversion for several items of personal property. In the judgment, P is awarded damages for property that was virtually destroyed when it was left out of doors for several months, a court order for the return of other items, and an additional damage award to compensate P for lost use of some items, since P had to rent similar items when he could not gain access to his own.

Point for Discussion: Would the result be different if P had asked Q to store the property at his own location in exchange for rent and then refused to pay the rent when the damaged property was discovered?

---

b. Trespass to Personal Property   Even if possession is not seized, there may still be an action in the case of one who substantially interferes with another party's possession or ownership of property. The primary difference between conversion and trespass to property, or trespass to chattels as it is sometimes known, is that in the latter it is not necessary to establish that the defendant ever intended to possess or actually possessed the property or exercised control over it. It need only be established that the owner was dispossessed of the property, either permanently or for a substantial period of time, and that damage was suffered as a result. The owner of the property in an action for trespass can claim damages for the fair market value of the use of the property during the period of interference by the defendant.

c. Actions for Replevin   A number of jurisdictions have done away with this aged legal theory carried over from the English system because the issues are considered to be covered adequately by other theories such as conversion. However, a number of states still recognize actions in replevin as a method to regain possession of the actual property that was wrongfully taken. Unlike conversion, monetary compensation will not be substituted in an action for replevin. Rather, the sole remedy is return of the property. The historical foundation of the action is that a monetary award of damages would be insufficient to remedy the wrong. This is quite similar to the breach of contract action for specific performance, which is also based on equity rather than equality.

APPLICATION 13.19

G owned a champion stallion and received large sums of money for the services of the horse in various breeding programs with race horse owners around the southwest. The commonly accepted practice was to transport the horse to the location of the mare. G owned a specially equipped and heavily padded horse trailer designed to safely transport the stallion, who did not tolerate transport well and frequently engaged in behavior in the trailer that was potentially harmful to himself. G's trailer was in need of repair before it could be used again and G turned the trailer over to a company that specialized in livestock trailer repairs. The repairs, however, took several months instead of the promised 10 day because the company ran behind on a number of jobs. As a result, G lost numerous appointments for the horse and subsequently lost earnings in excess of $100,000. G sued the trailer company for trespass to property because the unavailability of the trailer prevented him from gaining the benefits of selling the services of his stallion. If G could establish there was no other reasonable alternative available to him for safe transport of the stallion, a trespass to property may well prevail.

Point for Discussion: Should G also be allowed to recover for lost future earnings as the result of customers going to other stallion owners after the unavailability of G's horse as had been promised them?

APPLICATION 13.20

Mitchell is a wealthy entrepreneur and the father of one adult daughter. When the daughter was quite young, Mitchell engaged a well-known artist to paint the daughter's portrait. Over time the portrait became quite valuable and was even placed on loan to several museums periodically. In later years Mitchell was widowed and remarried Noreen. Upon Mitchell's death, his will proposed that he bequeathed his real property and all contents to his wife. He further bequeathed to his daughter the real property and contents of his commercial building.

At the time of the will, the portrait was hanging in Mitchell's office in his commercial building. During Mitchell's last illness, his wife brought a number of items to the house, including the portrait. Mitchell was unconscious at the time and unaware of this. The daughter filed an action in replevin for the return of the property after Noreen refused to turn it over to her. Noreen has offered to pay a reasonable sum for the portrait. If the court determines that the daughter is the rightful owner of the property, the daughter may succeed in the replevin action. The action for replevin and actual return of the portrait is supported over an action for monetary compensation due to the personal nature of the painting and its meaning to the daughter, which has nothing to do with the investment value.

Point for Discussion: Why should the daughter receive the portrait in a replevin action if she did not own it at the time it was removed from the commercial building to the residence?

An action for replevin has three essential elements that must be proven before a court will order the transfer of personal property.

1. The plaintiff alone has the right to immediate possession of the property and does not share that right with the defendant, such as in the case of jointly owned property.
2. The property in issue must be personal property by definition and not part of real property or a fixture.
3. The property must be unlawfully in the possession of the defendant and detained as such at the time the action is commenced. It is not necessary to show that the defendant initially gained possession unlawfully.

In some instances, it may also be required to establish the inadequacy of monetary damages.

CASE IN POINT

Estep v. Johnson, 123 Ohio App. 3d 307,
704 N.E.2d 58 (1998).

Deshler, Presiding Judge.

Plaintiff-appellant, Marcia B. Estep, appeals from a judgment of the Ohio Court of Claims dismissing appellant's claims against defendants- appellees, Kevin L. Johnson, Lisa M. Johnson, and the Ohio State Highway Patrol, stemming from the sale of appellant's impounded vehicle.

Appellant was arrested on September 17, 1993, for operating a motor vehicle while under the influence of alcohol, driving under suspension (imposed following a previous DUI conviction), carrying a concealed weapon, and giving false statements. Because appellant had a previous DUI conviction, the arresting trooper seized appellant's 1983 Nissan Sentra, as was required under the then-applicable version of R.C. 4507.38.

The trooper contacted appellees Kevin L. Johnson and Lisa M. Johnson (d.b.a. and hereinafter referred to as "Best Towing") to tow and store appellant's vehicle. When Mr. Johnson arrived at the scene, the arresting trooper informed him that the vehicle could not be released to appellant without a court order and execution of an Ohio State Highway Patrol ("OSHP") document known as a form HP-60. Mr. Johnson had no contact with appellant at the scene of the arrest and discussed the tow and impoundment only with the arresting trooper.

On December 23, 1993, the Chillicothe Municipal Court sanctioned the state in appellant's case for failure to provide timely discovery to appellant's counsel under Crim.R. 16. The court ordered certain evidence barred

from admission, resulting in the state's dismissal of all charges against appellant. Appellant filed a motion on December 30, 1993, to have the court order the release of her vehicle, pursuant to R.C. 4507.38(D)(1)(c), which mandates the release of a vehicle seized under the same circumstances as appellant's, when the DUI charge is subsequently dismissed:

"If the charge that the arrested person violated division (B)(1) or (D)(2) of section 4507.02 of the Revised Code, a substantially equivalent municipal ordinance, or section 4507.33 of the Revised Code is dismissed for any reason, the court shall order that the vehicle and its identification license plates immediately be returned or released to the vehicle owner or a person acting on his behalf." Former R.C. 4507.38(D)(1)(c), Sub. S.B. No. 62, 145 Ohio Laws, Part I, 534.

The Chillicothe Municipal Court denied appellant's motion, and she then appealed to the Fourth District Court of Appeals. In the interim, the OSHP refused to execute a form HP-60 without a court order ordering release of appellant's vehicle, and Best Towing refused to release the vehicle without payment of towing and storage charges and an HP-60 form.

The Fourth District Court of Appeals subsequently issued its decision in State v. Estep (June 26, 1995), Ross App. No. 94CA2007, unreported, 1995 WL 392878. The court found that appellant was statutorily entitled to an order of the Chillicothe Municipal Court releasing her vehicle without liability for the towing and storage expenses.

The court initially noted that the plain language of R.C. 4507.38(D)(1)(c) clearly mandated that the municipal court order release of appellant's vehicle upon dismissal of charges against her. The court then examined appellant's assertion not only that her vehicle must be released, but that she should not be required to pay any accumulated towing and storage charges.

The court held that appellant should not be required to pay any expenses as a condition for release of her vehicle. The court noted that then-applicable R.C. 4507.38(D)(1)(c) itself made no provision for payment of towing fees and that the state could point to no other section so providing. The court then examined the legislative history of the statute, particularly subsequent amendments enacted in 1994 pursuant to Sub.H.B. No. 236, which for the first time allocated impoundment expenses to the defendant vehicle owner. The court thus concluded that appellant could not be required, in the absence of statutory authority, to pay impoundment costs to obtain release of her vehicle. The court went on to state, although the issues were not specifically before it, that liability for payment of the expenses of towing and storage were a matter of contract law between the OSHP and Best Towing, and that "some level of state government would be liable" for the accruing charges.

In compliance with the court of appeals' decision, the Chillicothe Municipal Court subsequently entered an order pursuant to R.C. 4507.38(D)(1)(c) that appellant's vehicle held by Best Towing and her license plates held by the OSHP be returned and released to appellant and that appellant not be required to pay towing, storage, or impoundment costs as a prerequisite to return of the vehicle. In the interim, however, Best Towing had on May 20, 1994, sold appellant's vehicle to recover the cost of towing and storage. The vehicle was sold by purportedly following procedures outlined in R.C. 4505.101 for the sale of "unclaimed" motor vehicles by repair or storage garages.

Appellant was thus left with an order of the municipal court which could not be given effect, and filed an action in the Ohio Court of Claims against the OSHP seeking damages resulting from the loss of her automobile. Appellant filed a companion action in the Chillicothe Municipal Court against Best Towing. Best Towing then filed a third-party complaint against the Ohio Department of Public Safety, and a simultaneous petition for removal to the Court of Claims, which was granted. The matters were consolidated for trial on issues of liability and tried to the court on June 2, 1997.

On August 21, 1997, the Court of Claims entered its decision in favor of both the OSHP and Best Towing.

The Court of Claims also dismissed appellant's claim against Best Towing, again finding that appellant had failed to establish the elements of conversion, and further finding that Best Towing had made sufficient efforts to contact her regarding the pending sale of her vehicle and had sold her vehicle in the belief that it had been abandoned. The Court of Claims further found that Best Towing's third-party complaint against OSHP was accordingly mooted, but, even were it not mooted, Best Towing had failed to show a right of relief against the OSHP for the same reasons that appellant failed to demonstrate a right to relief.

Appellant has timely appealed and brings the following assignments of error:

"I. The trial court erred by finding appellant had shown no right to relief on the claims of violation of bailment.

"II. The trial court erred by finding appellant failed to prove conversion by the Ohio State Highway Patrol by a preponderance of evidence.

"III. The trial court erred by finding appellant failed to prove conversion by Best Towing by a preponderance of evidence.

"IV. The trial court erred by finding appellant had shown no right to relief on her claims against the OSHP for an uncompensated taking of her property.

"V. The trial court erred by finding appellant had shown no right to relief on her claims against the OSHP for violation of her due process rights.

"VI. The trial court erred by finding appellant failed to show a right to relief against Best Towing for violations of the Ohio Consumer Sales Practices Act."

We will first address the Court of Claim's disposition of appellant's claims against the OSHP. These claims are based on bailment, alleging conversion, denial of due process, and violation of the bar against uncompensated takings under Section 19, Article I of the Ohio Constitution.

Appellant's first assignment of error encompasses claims against both the OSHP and Best Towing for violation of their respective duties as bailees. We will initially address only those arguments raised under this assignment of error pertaining to the OSHP.

"A bailment exists where one person delivers personal property to another to be held for a specific purpose with a contract, express or implied, that the property shall be returned or accounted for when this special purpose is accomplished or retained until the bailor reclaims the property. The duty of the bailee is to hold the property in accordance with the terms of the bailment. Bailment involves the transfer of a possessory interest only and not an ownership interest in property. A bailment may be for the benefit of only bailor or the bailee, or for the mutual benefit of both. . . . If the bailee causes or permits the property to be destroyed or damaged, this constitutes a conversion of the property to the bailee's own use." Tomas v. Nationwide Mut. Ins. Co. (1992), 79 Ohio App.3d 624, 628–629, 607 N.E.2d 944, 946–947. A bailee cannot avoid its duties to the bailor by subsequently transferring the property to a further bailee. Id. at 629, 607 N.E.2d at 947.

Appellant argues that the impoundment of appellant's vehicle made the OSHP the bailee of the vehicle, and that the subsequent transfer to a further bailee, Best Towing, did not release OSHP from its duty of care to preserve the bailed property. While this initial contention has merit, it does not follow that the OSHP necessarily breached its duty of care simply by entrusting the vehicle to Best Towing.

Impoundment of a vehicle has been held to create a bailment relationship between the owner of the vehicle and the impounding authority. Bader v. Cleveland (Feb. 18, 1982), Cuyahoga App. No. 44118, unreported, 1982 WL 2354. Subsequent transfer to a private towing or storage lot has been similarly held to create a bailment between the vehicle owner and the subsequent bailee. Lykins v. Wilson (Oct. 21, 1997), Richland App.No. 96CA106, unreported. The cases on this point have not been clear, however, on the nature of the bailment so created. This is significant in the present case because the question whether a bailment is made for the benefit of the bailee or bailor, or the mutual benefit of both parties affects the duty of care imposed upon the bailee. It can be argued on the present facts that the bailment was for the benefit of appellant as the vehicle owner, because, being lawfully prevented from further operating her vehicle in the state of intoxication and under license suspension, she was compelled to abandon it at the point of the arrest, and removal of the vehicle to a lot placed it in a situation of reasonable security from which she was more likely to recover the vehicle intact. Conversely, it may be argued that the bailment is for the benefit of the state because it serves the state's interest in maintaining the roadways free of abandoned vehicles, and in pursuing an eventual vehicle forfeiture under the DUI statutes. Similarly, the bailment may be taken as for the benefit of the bailee in the case of the private towing service and impounding lot, Best Towing, because it was undertaken with the expectation of recovering towing and storage fees from the vehicle owner. Considering all these circumstances, we find that the bailment is best described as one made for the mutual benefit of the parties, in consideration of the various interests outlined above. If a bailment is made for the mutual benefit of the parties, then the bailee has the common-law duty to exercise ordinary care in protecting and keeping the bailed property safe. Midwestern Indem. Co. v. Winkhaus (1987), 42 Ohio App.3d 235, 238, 538 N.E.2d 415, 418–419.

We find that, on the facts in the record, appellant has not established a breach by the OSHP of its duty of ordinary care. There is no indication that Best Towing, to whom the vehicle was entrusted by the OSHP, had on any previous occasion been involved in any controversy over its towing and storage practices for vehicles impounded under the direction of the OSHP. There is nothing to indicate that the OSHP was in any way unreasonable in placing Best Towing upon the "rotation list" for towing services on call, or summoning Best Towing to tow the vehicle on the night of appellant's arrest for DUI and driving under suspension. Nor is there any indication in the record that the OSHP was negligent in declining to order the release of the vehicle without the requisite court order. We therefore find that the Court of Claims did not err in holding that the OSHP could not be held liable to appellant for breaching its duties as bailee of the vehicle. Appellant's first assignment of error is therefore overruled to the extent that it addresses issues concerning the OSHP.

Appellant's second assignment of error asserts that the trial court erred in finding that appellant had failed to prove conversion of appellant's automobile by the OSHP. Conversion has been described as "any exercise of dominion or control wrongfully exerted over the personal property of another." Ohio Tel. Equip. & Sales, Inc. v. Hadler Realty Co. (1985), 24 Ohio App.3d 91, 93, 24 OBR 160, 162, 493 N.E.2d 289, 292. Appellant has not established that the OSHP's seizure and impound of her car were wrongful; in fact, as set forth above, the OSHP acted under a statutory duty to do so once appellant was stopped and found to be driving without a valid license and while intoxicated. At the time of appellant's arrest in 1993, R.C. 4511.195 provided that law enforcement officers, when arresting a person for driving under the influence of alcohol who had been convicted within the five previous years of a similar offense, seize the vehicle the person was operating at the time of the alleged offense and its license plates. R.C. 4511.195(B)(1). Similarly, R.C. 4507.38 provided that an officer arresting a person for driving without a valid license seize the vehicle and plates. R.C. 4507.38(B)(1). The seizure of appellant's vehicle and subsequent conveyance to a private towing service was therefore not a wrongful exercise of dominion or control over appellant's personal property. In the same vein, the OSHP was unable to order the subsequent release of appellant's vehicle after charges against her had been dismissed because the municipal court had declined to issue the necessary order. A refusal by OSHP to release appellant's license plates and order Best Towing to release the vehicle was also not a wrongful exercise of dominion or control over her property. The OSHP had no power to either impose towing and storage expenses on appellant or to waive them when charges against her were dismissed. All the OSHP could do was act in accordance with statute and await the order of the municipal court. When the municipal court refused to issue such an order, the OSHP was in no position to override such a refusal, until the Fourth District Court of Appeals reversed and directed the municipal court to issue the appropriate order.

Appellant having failed to establish one of the necessary elements of conversion, the Court of Claims did not err in finding that the OSHP had not converted appellant's property. Appellant's second assignment of error is accordingly overruled.

We next address appellant's assignments of error related to the Court of Claim's dismissal of her action against Best Towing. Appellant's first assignment of error, as with appellee OSHP, asserts that Best Towing breached its duty as bailee when it sold appellant's vehicle and thus deprived her of her statutory right to have the vehicle returned to her without charge upon dismissal of the charges against her in Chillicothe Municipal Court.

Best Towing asserts that no bailment claim can be asserted because Best Towing was never in legal con-

trol of the vehicle, which could not be released without an order of the Chillicothe Municipal Court. While this may justify the initial refusal to return appellant's vehicle without the appropriate court order, that is not the basis for appellant's claims in this case. It is undisputed that Best Towing had physical possession of the vehicle following impoundment and ultimately sold the vehicle to cover the towing and storage costs. Best Towing cannot simultaneously argue the irreconcilable propositions that it did not have legal control over the vehicle and yet was able to legally sell the vehicle. The gravamen of appellant's claim is that Best Towing deprived her of the benefit of the eventual order from Chillicothe Municipal Court to have the vehicle released without cost, because Best Towing had sold the vehicle and retained the proceeds. It is this sale, and not the initial retention of the vehicle by Best Towing, that gave rise to a claim of breach of Best Towing's duty as bailee to return appellant's vehicle.

Best Towing asserts that it properly sold the vehicle pursuant to R.C. 4505.101, which provided at relevant times as follows:

"(A) The owner of any repair garage or place of storage in which a motor vehicle with a value of less than three hundred dollars has been left for fifteen days may send by certified mail, return receipt requested, to the last known address of the owner a notice to remove said vehicle. If the motor vehicle remains unclaimed by the owner for fifteen days after the mailing of such notice, the person on whose property the vehicle has been abandoned shall obtain a certificate of title to such motor vehicle in his name in the manner provided in this section." Am.S.B. No. 10, 142 Ohio Laws, Part I, 64.

This statute appears inapposite for several reasons. First, although it is not necessary to disturb the conclusion of the finder of fact on this issue, it appears unlikely the vehicle could be considered "abandoned" when its owner was diligently pursuing judicial relief, first in the Chillicothe Municipal Court, and then in the Fourth District Court of Appeals, and claimed to have informed Best Towing of this activity. Second, R.C. 4505.101 applied at the time in question only to vehicles with a value of less than $300. While Best Towing attempted to reduce the "value" of the vehicle beneath this amount by setting off accumulated towing and storage fees against the $1,300 book value of the vehicle once title had been obtained, this is not a permissible way of computing the "value" of an abandoned vehicle. Finally, the abandoned-vehicle statute should not be read to allow the sale of an unclaimed motor vehicle to collect towing and storage charges which Best Towing was specifically not entitled to receive from appellant as held in the Fourth Appellate District's prior decision.

We therefore conclude that appellee Best Towing was a bailee with respect to appellant's vehicle, and breached its duty as bailee to return the property when it improperly obtained title to the vehicle and sold it prior to the issuance of the order from the Chillicothe Municipal Court ordering the vehicle returned to appellant. Appellant's first assignment of error therefore has merit insofar as it addresses a claim of a breach of bailment duties by appellee Best Towing, and to this extent is sustained.

Appellant's third assignment of error asserts that the trial court erred in finding that appellant had failed to prove conversion by Best Towing. As stated above, the tort of conversion involves any exercise of dominion or control wrongfully exerted over the personal property of another. It is uncontroverted in the present case that Best Towing required payment from appellant of towing and storage charges before releasing the vehicle, and ultimately sold the vehicle to recover such charges. It is also uncontroverted that, at the time in question, R.C. 4507.38(D)(1)(c) mandated the return of appellant's vehicle. While the circumstances of this case were undoubtedly muddled by the initial refusal of the Chillicothe Municipal Court to enter the appropriate order providing for the release of appellant's vehicle, any exercise of dominion and control by Best Towing over the vehicle

beyond the bare retention of the vehicle on the storage lot was inconsistent with appellant's statutory right to reclaim her vehicle without cost. Since it is uncontroverted that Best Towing sold the vehicle in May 1994, the inescapable conclusion is that Best Towing wrongfully exercised dominion and control over appellant's vehicle in a manner inconsistent with her rights. We therefore hold that the trial court erred in finding that appellant had failed to prove conversion by Best Towing by a preponderance of the evidence. Appellant's assignment of error is therefore sustained.

The matter is remanded to the Court of Claims for a determination of damages based upon appellee Best Towing's conversion of appellant's vehicle and consequent breach of its duty as bailee. While our disposition of this case raises some question whether appellee Best Towing's claim in contract against the OSHP was properly dismissed by the trial court, that determination was not raised as a conditional cross-appeal by Best Towing in this appeal. Therefore, the determination of the trial court in this respect will not be disturbed. The dismissal of appellant's claims against the OSHP by the trial court is affirmed in all respects.[32]

Case Review Question: Would the result change at all if plaintiff were convicted of the drunk driving charges and subsequently went to obtain release of her vehicle with an offer to pay storage only to find it had been sold?

PARALEGALS IN THE WORKPLACE

While the first thought of paralegal employment tends to be the traditional law firm, there are many other excellent resources. This is particularly true in the area of property law. Some law firms specialize in litigation and transactions involving property law. The paralegal may find employment there in the typical aspects of litigation as well as preparation and handling of documents relating to property transactions. However, another wide arena for employment of paralegals lies in the real estate industry. Many large real estate and title companies can effectively use paralegal skills in the management of property transactions ranging from landlord/tenant to property management to sales proceedings. Property is a document-intensive area and the ability to prepare and handle such documents throughout all stages of a process is a valuable skill. Because no two properties are identical, no two transactions are likely to be identical in nature. Therefore, what might at first glance seem dull can be an interesting and even exciting area of employment.

Chapter Summary

Clearly, the law of property, both real and personal, is well developed in the American legal system. Yet, in spite of the age-old traditional legal principles transported from the English system of common law, new issues have continued to develop as property uses have changed and technology has increased. While there are a variety of property ownership interests, the unrestricted and unlimited fee simple remains by far the most common. In multiple tenancies, the key is an undivided interest in all aspects of the property. This is true whether a tenancy in common exists that permits the free change of ownership and limits the rights of the tenants to the lifetime of one another, or whether a joint tenancy exists with the required four unities and the right of survivorship that reserves the ownership interest in the other tenants rather than in the estate of a joint tenant who dies.

Although the goal of the law is to provide the right of quiet enjoyment to all landowners giving them the maximum degree of freedom in the manner in which the property is used and/or developed, the right is not boundless. The public interest will prevail in a conflict whether it is a matter of public nuisance as the result of an owner's action or nonaction, or the right of easement by a party or government entity whose interest supersedes the right of quiet enjoyment on a limited basis. Hybrid forms of ownership also affect quiet enjoyment such as the mixed ownership of a condominium owner whose rights are partly in individual fee simple and partly in tenancy in common with other parties occupying the same parcel of land. The objective is to balance maximum personal freedom in the enjoyment of one's property with serving the public interest. However, when it is established that a property has been effectively abandoned, the theory of adverse possession may permit one who will make beneficial use of the property to assume ownership and deprive the original owner of all rights, including those associated with the right of quiet enjoyment.

The owner of a freehold estate in real property has certain minimum obligations to those who enter the property with or without permission. The landlord always has a duty to take reasonable steps to protect entrants of any type from latent dangers and defects on the property. The degree of interest the landlord has in the party entering the property determines the level of care owed. Entrants who are present with the knowledge and consent of the landlord are provided a greater standard of care and those invitees on the property for business purposes are owed the highest standard.

In addition to the defined real property, any time personal property has become semi-permanently attached in such a way that it could not be removed without damaging the physical structure of the property or the usefulness of the property, then those items are considered fixtures and ordinarily convey when the property is conveyed as to possession and/or ownership. The exceptions are trade fixtures, which remain with their owner as part of the tools of the trade of the owner. However, there is an obligation to take all measures necessary to repair any damage and restore the property upon their removal.

In addition to freehold estates of real property ownership, there are also split estates known as non-freehold estates. These occur when the rights associated with possession and ownership are split. Commonly known in the American legal system as landlord–tenant law, these estates provide real property rights to those who cannot have or do not want ownership of the real property they occupy. The landlord has an obligation to provide a habitable environment for the tenant while the tenant has the obligation to not waste the property and to pay the agreed-upon compensation. The agreed-upon length of tenancy also guides the rules for proper notice of ending the agreement when not otherwise agreed upon in the lease agreement. If the property suffers damage to the extent it becomes uninhabitable, the tenant may in certain circumstances end the tenancy prematurely. If either party materially breaches the agreement or violates the basic duties of a landlord or tenant, the tenancy may also be terminated. However, appropriate procedures in accordance with state statutes must be followed when doing this.

Finally, personal property is also the subject of a large body of law. Primarily, issues with respect to personal property most often arise when the rights of ownership and possession are divided and not readily restored at the appropriate time. This may be in the situation of a bailment (either gratuitous or mutual benefit), or lost, mislaid, abandoned, or confused property. The outcome is determined most often by the manner in which the owner was dispossessed of the property and the circumstances under which the current possessor obtained the property. If someone wrongfully holds the personal property, legal actions of conversion, trespass, and, in some jurisdictions, replevin may be brought to either restore the possession to the rightful owner or to provide compensation for the time period of the loss and/or the fair market value of the property itself.

ETHICAL NOTE

With regard to actions involving property law, ethical standards are just as important as in any type of professional legal representation. However, as respects property law, the obligation to keep a client reasonably informed and zealously represented are of paramount importance. First, it is essential that a client fully understand each of his or her rights and obligations with respect to the property issues involved. There are many misconceptions with respect to rights associated with co-ownership of property as well as those rights and obligations in the landlord–tenant relationship. If a client is represented in such matters and does not understand the applicable law, the person may later claim that a member or members of the legal team failed in their ethical duties to assist him or her in understanding such things.

Relevant Internet Sites

Real Property, Probate and Trust Law Journal	www.abanet.org/rppt/journal.html
RentLaw.com	www.rentlaw.com

Internet Assignment 13.1

Consult the Internet and determine the statutory period for adverse possession in your jurisdiction.

KEY TERMS

Adverse Possession	Freehold Estate	Personal Property
Bailment	Joint Tenancy	Real Property
Easement	Nonfreehold Estates	Tenancy in Common

ENDNOTES

1. Boyer, *Survey of the Law of Property*, 3rd ed. (West, 1981).
2. Id.
3. Id.
4. Id.
5. Id.
6. Id.
7. *Bouska v. Bouska*, 159 Kan. 276, 153 P.2d 923 (1944).
8. *Daniel v. Wright*, 352 F.Supp. 1, (D.D.C. 1972).
9. *Pender v. Matranga*, 2000 WL 668973 (Conn.App. 2000).
10. 63 Am.Jur.2d Property.
11. *Sneed v. Weber*, 307 S.W.2d 681, 690 (Mo.App. 1958).
12. Powell & Rohan, *Powell on Property* (Bender, 1968).
13. *Putnam v. Dickinson*, 142 N.W.2d 111, 124 (N.D. 1966).

14. *Outdoor Systems Advertising, Inc. v. Korth*, 238 Mich.App. 664, 607 N.W.2d 729 (1999).

15. *Huggins v. Castle Estates, Inc.*, 36 N.Y.2d 427 (1975).

16. 40 Annot., 27 A.L.R. 2d 444.

17. *Birkholz v. Wells*, 2000 WL 539393 (N.Y.A.D. 3 Dept.).

18. Annot., 36 A.L.R. 4th 544.

19. 8 Am.Jur.Sec. 2, Bailments.

20. Id.

21. Annot. A.L.R. 2d 1294.

22. See note 34, Sec. 1014(2) Annot. 96 A.L.R. 3d Sec. 1014(2).

23. *Ridgely Condominium Association, Inc. v Smyrnioudis*, 343 Md. 357, 681 A.2d 494 (1996).

24. *Thomas v. Mrkonich*, 247 Minn. 481, 78 N.W.2d 386 (1956).

25. Annot. 96 A.L.R. 3d Sec. 1014(2).

26. Id.

27. Id.

28. *Thacker v. J.C. Penney Co.*, 2545 F2d 672 (8th Cir. 1958).

29. Id.

30. *Paul v. Taders & General Ins. Co.*, 127 So.2d 801 (La.App. 1962).

31. See note 23, supra.

32. *Estep v. Johnson*, 123 Ohio App.3d 307, 704 N.E.2d 58 (1998).

Chapter 14

THE LAW OF DOMESTIC RELATIONSHIPS

CHAPTER OBJECTIVES

Upon completion of this chapter you should be able to do the following:

- State the requirements for a valid marriage.

- Explain the appropriate circumstances for annulment.

- Distinguish annulment from dissolution of marriage.

- Explain the types of property distribution applied in dissolution of marriage cases.

- Discuss the considerations in a child custody issue.

- Explain the nature and purpose of child support and child visitation.

- Discuss current issues in reproductive law.

A. THE MARRIAGE RELATIONSHIP

Perhaps the most recently and broadly expanded area in the American legal system is the law of domestic relations. The radical changes in American culture and society during the 20th century has resulted in a very different view of what is popularly accepted as the American family unit. These changes, in turn, have required the legislatures to respond accordingly with guidance and procedures to accommodate the changes in societal standards.

Before the latter half of the 20th century, divorce was a rare occurrence. In addition, a woman's role was perceived to be primarily that of caretaker of the home and children, not a worker in the public workplace. In the event of divorce, there was no question but that the husband would be solely responsible for the material needs of his wife and children. Additionally, the societal pressures not to divorce and the negative view of those who did, caused many to handle the matter as quickly and quietly as possible. Little, if any, consideration was given to challenging court decisions or doing anything else to call attention to the situation. The relatively few divorces, social pressures, and the fact that the public was largely uneducated in matters of law resulted in few challenges to the fairness of court orders in matters of divorce.

Over the years, the role of women changed, due in large part to technological developments, the opening of the job market, and the growth of educational opportunities. Gradually, women began to live more and more independently. This trend increased markedly during World War II when, for the first time, large numbers of women entered the nation's work force. In addition, society became more mobile as families relocated away from the traditional extended family to find jobs—a trend that had begun during the depression of the 1930s. These societal changes were accompanied by an increased awareness of legal rights. For example, the first specific laws were put into place that protected the rights of victims of domestic violence. As a consequence of all theses developments, the option of dissolving a marriage became a more realistic choice for many. Multiple marriages in one lifetime became more likely and, as a result, more detailed laws on the total marriage relationship became necessary.

The changes in family law have ranged from defining and, in many states, abolishing common-law marriage to regulating custody and visitation rights when parents live in different states. Aside from the fact that virtually everyone has some contact with family law during his or her lifetime, this area of law is having an increasing effect on the workplace. For example, some employers have the duty to report and withhold wages for payment of child support or maintenance (alimony), and job transfers or changes may be delayed while a divorced parent seeks changes in the visitation schedule or obtains court permission to remove a child from the state.

This chapter addresses the creation and dissolution of marriages and the relationships that result from terminated marriages. Its emphasis will be on the dissolution of marriages and the resulting relationships, since during a marriage the parties are generally in accord with respect to marital concerns, such as child care and education. It is when discord occurs and cannot be resolved that the parties seek intermediary help from the legal system.

Antenuptial Agreements
Agreement between parties prior to a marriage that states the terms for distribution of assets and liabilities in the event the marriage relationship ends.

1. Antenuptial (Prenuptial) Agreements

Antenuptial Agreements (sometimes referred to as prenuptial agreements when entered into prior to marriage) are contracts entered into by parties who are going to be married and in some cases after the marriage has already occurred. These are contracts that provide for the equitable division of property rights at the time the marital relationship between the parties comes to an end. Historically, antenuptial agreements dealt only with property division upon the death of a spouse and typically only in situations where one party entering the marriage had a great deal more wealth than the other. Under state statute, one spouse cannot entirely disinherit another spouse. If no provisions are made by will, either intentionally or in the absence of a will, the surviving spouse can elect under a special statute that exists in each state to receive a percentage of the estate. This is commonly referred to as a forced share because the spouse forces a portion of the property from the estate of the deceased spouse. In a traditional antenuptial agreement, however, each of the spouses could agree by contract not to challenge the provisions of the other spouse's will. The provisions of the will in effect at the time of the agreement must be disclosed and cannot change substantially in value for the antenuptial agreement to remain effective. This is often done when one spouse has a great deal more wealth and/or when a spouse has children by someone other than the surviving spouse and seeks to protect the inheritance of the children.

More recently, antenuptial agreements have taken on an entirely new meaning. As divorce became more commonplace, so did antenuptial agreements that were intended to be applied if a marriage ended by divorce as well as death. For a time, there were few legal standards for this situation and, as a result, many agreements were held to be invalid when the courts considered them unfair to one or both parties for any number of reasons. However, as more and more cases have been considered and more precedents established, the standards for valid agreements in the event of divorce or dissolution have become more clear. Consequently, properly drafted agreements are being upheld increasingly by the courts. No longer are these agreements reserved only for the wealthy. Rather, they are often a reasonable alternative for spouses who each have a career and the ability to contribute financially to the relationship. Many such couples have minor children from previous relationships whose interests must be protected. For these and other reasons, an antenuptial agreement often resolves the concerns that may prevent parties from getting married at all. The agreement allows the parties to continue their relationship with one less concern. The agreement may never be used, but if it is, there is some reassurance in knowing that reasonable terms were arranged when each of the parties was acting logically rather than emotionally and with fairness to the other in mind.

It has taken some time for the courts and legislature to settle on standards for antenuptial agreements that are considered to be fair to all concerned and enforceable. Part of the problem has been that the contract is written in anticipation of a future event with little or no guarantees as to what the status of the parties will be at the time of the event, if it should in fact occur. Because contract law hinges on the ability to accurately assess the value of the consideration of the agreement by all parties, this speculativeness has posed a real dilemma. Yet, the demand for standards by which to create enforceable antenuptial agreements has remained. Ultimately, standards have been developed, and today it is much more likely that a well-drafted agreement will be upheld.

Because the agreement is a contract, it must contain the necessary elements of any contract.[1] Most states also require the agreement to be in writing pursuant to the statute of frauds. While there is no known time for the terms of the contract to be carried out, it will probably be greater than one year. Also, when done prior to a marriage the agreement would also be part of an agreement made in contemplation of marriage. Based on these traditional foundations for the statute of frauds and the serious nature and potentially far-reaching effects of the agreement, it is widely accepted that such an agreement be in writing. An exception to the requirement of a written agreement may be recognized when a party can demonstrate that he or she has significantly altered his or her position in a detrimental manner as a direct result of reliance on the other party's promises in an oral antenuptial agreement.[2]

APPLICATION 14.1

An accountant falls in love with the receptionist in his office. After dating for some time, he encourages her to continue her education. Together they arrive at an agreement that he will pay her educational expenses for a bachelor's degree and all additional requirements to become a certified public accountant. They agree to be married and also agree that, in the event of a divorce or death of the parties, she will not be required to repay any of the monies expended for her education. In exchange, she agrees to waive any claim to his investment portfolio, which he plans to use for the education of his children as they mature. The agreement is not put into writing. The parties marry and as promised, the education of the woman is fully funded by the husband. She does not work or contribute financially in any way to her education or the household. Domestic help is employed to prepare meals, clean house, and do laundry so that the wife's full attention can be given to her studies. However, upon receiving notice that she has passed the exam to become a certified public accountant, she also serves notice to her husband that she is seeking a divorce and half of all his current assets. The husband claims, as a defense, the agreement made by the parties. If the husband can successfully produce credible evidence that the agreement existed and was voluntarily entered into by both parties, a court is likely to uphold it even in the absence of a written agreement, based on the fact that the husband had so altered his financial position in reliance on the agreement.

Point for Discussion: Would the result be likely to change if the woman had continued to work in the office with the husband, without salary, during the time of her education?

In addition to the requirement of writing, identifiable consideration must be given for the promises of each party in the antenuptial agreement. As with all consideration, this must be a legal performance that is not otherwise obligated by the party giving it. Traditionally, the promise of marriage by each party has served as consideration for the other party's agreement to the terms of the antenuptial contract. In a case where the parties are already married, there must be some other identified promise of performance that would not be considered part of the obligation of marriage. Finally, and perhaps most importantly, a valid antenuptial agreement must be made with the free will of both parties without duress or coercion, not unconscionably either when made or implemented, and based upon a full disclosure of all relevant information by the parties.

The requirement of disclosure applies to assets as well as liabilities. The failure to do so would negate the element of mutual assent. In this way, antenuptial agreements are somewhat more stringent than the ordinary contract. Under general contract law each party must be capable of determining the value of the consideration. In an antenuptial agreement, because the parties share their entire lives rather than a single contract, the burden is one of disclosure rather than availability of information to the other party. Also, in addition to the valuation of the consideration, the corresponding party is entitled to knowledge about the entire economic position of the party he or she intends to marry. The courts and legislatures are concerned that unscrupulous persons would take advantage of the position of another and persuade the other to enter an agreement that, in the event of divorce or death, would be inherently unfair. This is known in legal terms as overreaching.

APPLICATION 14.2

Darby and Collin agree to be married and enter an antenuptial agreement. In the agreement Darby, who is independently wealthy with assets of approximately $20 million agrees to pay a specified dollar amount and to be solely responsible for all accumulated debts of either of the parties in the event of a divorce. Collin has no substantial assets other than some inherited land valued at approximately $750,000 and no real professional earning power. He agrees to maintain the homes, oversee the household operations, and act as host at various social events that benefit Darby's business interests, and to retain ownership of his (Collin's) inherited property solely in his name. After five years of marriage, Collin files for divorce. At that time, it is disclosed that Collin has invested in the development of the land owned solely in his name and has debts on the property exceeding $12 million. The property is now valued at approximately $25 million. It is also discovered that Collin has been involved with Darby's accountant for almost eight years with plans to develop the property. In this type of situation, a court could likely be persuaded that the marriage and the antenuptial agreement was no more than a scheme to get Darby to fund development of a property and not one entered into in good faith and in support of a marriage commitment.

Point for Discussion: Would the result be likely to change if the plans to develop the property with the accountant did not come about until after the marriage and antenuptial agreement?

In addition to full disclosure, the agreement should contain provisions for some sort of fair and reasonable economic settlement. The parties do not usually expect divorce and cannot anticipate what the accumulation of wealth will be at the time of a divorce. However, they can assume that each will contribute to the marriage, and assets should be divided in a manner that is fair to each based on that contribution regardless of a change in assets or wealth.

A difficulty in dealing with the settlement provisions is that the courts often refuse to recognize an agreement that provides for a specific financial award. Ordinarily, the more specific a contract's terms are, the easier it is to enforce. However, in this instance, set dollar amounts are seen as encouraging dissolution of the marriage in an attempt to obtain a monetary settlement.[3] The courts will, however, uphold agreements that provide for a fair distribution of assets to be determined by an objective third party, such as a court, in the event the parties should cease to share marital assets. This reassures the parties that they are not being taken advantage of. Such an agreement also does not include any anticipation of divorce that the court might see as encouraging the end of a marriage. To ensure an enforceable and fair agreement, each party should seek independent legal counsel before entering into an antenuptial agreement.

Consider the following situation and explain why you think it should be upheld and enforced, or invalidated.

Ben is widowed and, as a result, receives the benefits of a large insurance policy. Shelly, is an acquaintance of the family who became quite close before Ben's spouse's death. She becomes romantically involved with Ben after the death of his spouse. Ben is under the impression, based on Shelly's statements and actions that she has numerous financial assets of her own. The parties agree to marry and enter an antenuptial agreement. Under the terms of the agreement, the parties state that in the event they cease to be married, Ben will retain all monies in his brokerage account, and Shelly will retain all interests in properties she owned at the time of the marriage. Each party waives the right to claim an interest in these items that belong to the other party. During the next two years, Shelly persuades Ben to invest in her various financial interests on the basis that they are building their retirement wealth potential. After approximately three years of marriage, Ben and Shelly divorce. Ben is left with virtually nothing in his brokerage accounts having invested over 95% in Shelly's interests. Shelly's interests have tripled in value and her debt on them has been reduced by nearly 75%. The parties had no other significant assets.

2. Requirements for Marriage

The process of getting married has become quite complex in the legal sense. In many states, two people wishing to marry cannot simply obtain a license at the justice of the peace and be married at the same time. Because marriage so deeply affects the lives of those involved, because many marriages do not succeed, and for reasons of public health and various other concerns linked to citizen welfare, laws have been created to establish the best possible environment for the marriage. Every state has legislation that sets forth certain fundamental requirements that must be met before a legally recognized marriage will exist.

a. Capacity and Consent For a marriage to be valid, there must be capacity and consent.[4] As previously noted, capacity requires that the party be of legal age and not be declared legally incompetent. The party must be capable of making the decision to enter into such an agreement. Many states also have provisions for parental or court-granted consent, or withholding of consent if a party to the marriage is not of legal age or has been previously declared legally incompetent, which would presume them to be incapable of appreciating the consequences and responsibilities of marriage. If there is capacity, it is also necessary that each party openly and voluntarily consent to the marriage.

b. Marriage License Each state has a licensure provision for marriages. Before a legal marriage exists, the parties are required to make application of a marriage license. It is generally granted unless some factor exists that would prevent the marriage from being legally recognized according to state law. While the language varies from state to state, most of these factors are fairly common among the states. Examples of factors that prohibit marriage include the following:

* The parties to the marriage are family members with a close blood relationship (each state indicates the degree of kinship that will prevent a valid marriage)

- The parties are persons of the same sex (although attempts are being made to change this in many states)
- One or both parties lack legal capacity
- One or both of the parties is already in a valid legal marriage

Blood tests and a waiting period between issuance of the license and validation of the license through a ceremony are also sometimes required before a license is issued and/or validated. There are a number of reasons for the blood test requirement. Traditionally, the tests were required so that the parties would be informed if there was a potential conflict in their blood types that could endanger or cause any physical complications for offspring from the marriage because of the combination of the two parents' blood types. However, medicine has now advanced to the point that most problems can be treated effectively. Nevertheless, in many jurisdictions the parties are still presumed to be entitled to this information. In more recent years, the blood tests have taken on a new and important role: to inform the parties of any diseases present in the other party that are likely to be transmitted as the result of the marriage relationship. This includes sexually transmitted diseases, and in some states notice is given of a positive HIV status.

Statutes that require a waiting period—usually a matter of a few days—discourage marriages that are entered into without sufficient thought to the consequences. Requiring a brief delay between the issuance of the license and the time when it can be validated by a judge or minister encourages the parties to consider the ramifications of their action.

c. Marriage Vows   Finally, the parties are required to solemnize the marriage. This involves an exchange of vows (an agreement to marry) in the presence of one who is permitted to legally acknowledge such an exchange and thereby validate it.[5] Usually this is a minister, judge, or other duly authorized individual who will then validate the license by certifying that the parties have indeed agreed to be married. At that time, the official and the parties will sign the license. Often, additional witnesses are required to sign the license. If citizens of one state wish to marry, but would not be permitted to under the law of their own state, they cannot simply go to another state to get married. Many states now have laws that declare a marriage invalid if it was entered into in another state for the purpose of avoiding the laws of the first state. In the event this becomes an issue, parties typically must be able to show that they had valid reasons for conducting the marriage outside their state of domicile, other than to circumvent state law.

3. Annulment

A legal **annulment** is a judicial declaration that a marriage never actually existed because the legal requirements of a valid marriage were not met.[6] This is to be clearly distinguished from a religious annulment, in which parties in some churches seek the dispensation of church authorities nullifying a marriage relationship. This is totally separate from a legal annulment. A religious annulment has no legal effect, and it is pursued totally independent of the courts and of any end of the marriage legally by dissolution of marriage or legal annulment. Accordingly, a legal annulment has no religious significance.

Annulment
Legal relationship declared invalid in which the parties to the relationship are treated as if the relationship never existed, for example, marriage.

Legal annulments can be obtained for a variety of reasons. Whatever the basis for the annulment, one requirement is common to all. The reason that the marriage should be declared invalid, as opposed to a valid marriage ended through divorce, must have been in existence at the time the parties took the steps to accomplish the marriage through license and ceremony.[7] Therefore, if an annulment is sought on the basis that one or both of the parties was under the legal age or without sufficient mental capacity, the incapacity must have existed at the time the parties attempted to marry. Other common reasons for annulment include close blood relationships, incest, bigamy, or polygamy. The general rule is that an annulment may be granted if the reason supporting the annulment would have prevented the parties from legally marrying had it been previously disclosed.

If the party seeking the annulment has capacity and has taken steps toward accepting and acknowledging the marriage relationship, his or her request may be denied. The theory is that one who attempts to solemnize a marriage cannot then take the position that the marriage never existed. This is very similar to the contractual defense of unclean hands, which holds that a party who assisted in the creation or accepted benefit from the circumstances for a breach of contract cannot then turn around and allege that he or she has been injured because of the breach. Nevertheless, the courts may still grant an annulment if the reason is a serious one, such as bigamy or incest.

Less-frequently encountered actions for annulment are based on frolic, duress, or fraud. If the parties married as some sort of joke or game and never truly intended a binding marriage, the court will grant an annulment. As with most contractual agreements, intent is required for a valid marriage to exist. For example, a marriage by parties who were intoxicated at the time of the marriage and did not intend to actually marry would be invalid.

If a party believes that he or she has no choice but to marry or, alternatively, suffer serious physical, financial, or other harm, a marriage of duress has taken place. Effectively, the party had no real choice in the matter as they perceived it, and the courts will likely find no real intent to marry. As a result, an annulment is a very real possibility in such situations.

Annulment on the basis of fraud is one of the most difficult to establish. The party seeking the annulment must prove all of the necessary elements of fraud. In the case of marriage, the elements are that (1) a misrepresentation of a fact essential to the marriage relationship must have been made, and (2) the party claiming fraud must have reasonably relied on the misrepresentation as truth when making the decision to marry. Examples of such misrepresentations include, but are not limited to, imposition of religious beliefs or the ability to biologically parent children when the party committing fraud knows this to be untrue.

Although an annulment is a declaration that the marriage relationship never existed in the eyes of the law, it does not mean that no relationship existed. Therefore, the courts may apportion rights and duties regarding property, assets, debts, and even children as if the annulment were an action for dissolution of marriage (divorce).[8] However, it is unlikely that this will be done in a manner that would provide greater benefit to the one who obtained the marriage through fraud. The purpose of annulment is to do whatever possible to return the parties to their original position before the marriage. Therefore, if a party would benefit much more through a dissolution of marriage from a spouse who was in a much better financial position at the time of the marriage, than through an annulment, it is easy to see why the party would oppose an annulment versus a dissolution. If the parties have contributed anything to the relationship or if there are children, the court will consider the rights under the same equitable grounds as are used in dissolving a marital relationship in that particular jurisdiction. See Figure 14.1

FIGURE 14.1   Annulment Statute

McKINNEY'S CONSOLIDATED LAWS OF NEW YORK
ANNOTATED DOMESTIC RELATIONS LAW
CHATER 14 OF THE CONSOLIDATED LAWS
ARTICLE 9—ACTION TO ANNUL A MARRIAGE OR DECLARE IT VOID

§ 140. Action for judgment declaring nullity of void marriages or annulling voidable marriage

(a) Former husband or wife living. An action to declare the nullity of a void marriage upon the ground that the former husband or wife of one of the parties was living, the former marriage being in force, may be maintained by either of the parties during the life-time of the other, or by the former husband or wife.

(b) Party under age of consent. An action to annul a marriage on the ground that one or both of the parties had not attained the age of legal consent may be maintained by the infant, or by either parent of the infant, or by the guardian of the infant's person; or the court may allow the action to be maintained by any person as the next friend of the infant. But a marriage shall not be annulled under this subdivision at the suit of a party who was of the age of legal consent when it was contracted, or by a party who for any time after he or she attained that age freely cohabited with the other party as husband or wife.

(c) Party a mentally retarded person or mentally ill person. An action to annul a marriage on the ground that one of the parties thereto was a mentally retarded person may be maintained at any time during the life-time of either party by any relative of a mentally retarded person, who has an interest to avoid the marriage. An action to annul a marriage on the ground that one of the parties thereto was a mentally ill person may be maintained at any time during the continuance of the mental illness, or, after the death of the mentally ill person in that condition, and during the life of the other party to the marriage, by any relative of the mentally ill person who has an interest to avoid the marriage. Such an action may also be maintained by the mentally ill person at any time after restoration to a sound mind; but in that case, the marriage should not be annulled if it appears that the parties freely cohabited as husband and wife after the mentally ill person was restored to a sound mind. Where one of the parties to a marriage was a mentally ill person at the time of the marriage, an action may also be maintained by the other party at any time during the continuance of the mental illness, provided the plaintiff did not know of the mental illness at the time of the marriage. Where no relative of the mentally retarded person or mentally ill person brings an action to annul the marriage and the mentally ill person is not restored to sound mind, the court may allow an action for that purpose to be maintained at any time during the life-time of both the parties to the marriage, by any person as the next friend of the mentally retarded person or mentally ill person.

(d) Physical incapacity. An action to annul a marriage on the ground that one of the parties was physically incapable of entering into the marriage state may be maintained by the injured party against the party whose incapacity is alleged; or such an action may be maintained by the party who was incapable against the other party, provided the incapable party was unaware of the incapacity at the time of marriage, or if aware of such incapacity, did not know it was incurable. Such an action can be maintained only where an incapacity continues and is incurable, and must be commenced before five years have expired since the marriage.

(e) Consent by force, duress or fraud. An action to annul a marriage on the ground that the consent of one of the parties thereto was obtained by force or duress may be maintained at any time by the party whose consent was so obtained. An action to annul a marriage on the ground that the consent of one of the parties thereto was obtained by fraud may be maintained by the party whose consent was so obtained within the limitations of time for enforcing a civil remedy of the civil practice law and rules. Any such action may also be maintained during the life-time of the other party by the parent, or the guardian of the person of the party whose consent was so obtained, or by any relative of that party who has an interest to avoid the marriage, provided that in an action to annul a marriage on the ground of fraud the limitation prescribed in the civil practice law and rules has not run. But a marriage shall not be annulled on the ground of force or duress if it appears that, at any time before the commencement of the action, the parties thereto voluntarily cohabited as husband and wife; or on the ground of fraud, if it appears that, at any time before the commencement thereof, the parties voluntarily cohabited as husband and wife, with a full knowledge of the facts constituting the fraud.

(f) Incurable mental illness for five years. An action to annul a marriage upon the ground that one of the parties has been incurably mentally ill for a period of five years or more may be maintained by or on behalf of either of the parties to such marriage.

4. Common-Law Marriage

Only a few states still allow an older form of recognized marriage known as common-law marriage. Known for centuries, the common-law marriage came about as the result of parties who agreed to marry but did not have access to the methods of formal marriage ceremonies such as an authorized officiant. Over time, even parties who had access to the formal procedures did not always undertake them, and the law still recognized the marriage as one by common-law in an attempt to achieve fairness to the parties who had obviously demonstrated the intent to act as married individuals accepting both its benefits and obligations. However, during the 20th century, as divorce became more prevalent, questions arose more and more often as to what exactly would be necessary to create a common-law marriage and, in turn, what would be needed to have the separation of the parties by death or divorce determined according to standards for married persons. Additionally, all states initially rejected same-sex marriages in all legal matters. To accept marriages created by common-law and to legally recognize the marital relationship without proven satisfaction of marital requirements by statute, put the states in an awkward position with regard to the rights of those in same-sex committed relationships. Consequently, the vast majority of states have now either abolished common-law marriages from legal recognition and/or enacted statutes preventing legal recognition of same-sex marriages. However, if a common-law marriage is validly established in a state where it was created, even a state not permitting common-law marriages will honor it as a valid marriage. This is based on the constitutional requirements that whenever possible the states give full faith and credit, and honor the laws of sister states.

Generally, no public record of a common-law marriage is made. Contrary to popular belief, a common-law marriage is not based on the length of time two parties live together. Rather the courts usually examine a number of factors in determining whether such a marriage exists. Some of the more common considerations include the following:

- Did the parties hold themselves out to the public as married to one another?
- Did the parties cohabit?
- Did the parties file joint tax returns?
- Does the conduct of the parties indicate an intent to be married?

If the evidence of the above questions and anything else relevant is insufficient to establish the intent to create a common-law marriage or if the relationship was created in a jurisdiction that does not recognize the creation of common-law marriage, the parties still may have valid legal rights under principles developed to address agreements of parties who cohabit in an ongoing reciprocal relationship. These nonmarital relationships are discussed in greater detail later in the chapter.

Assignment 14.2

Use the subject index to your state statutes or code to locate the appropriate laws that will answer the following questions. Then locate the answers and respond to the questions.

a. Is there a state statute that addresses common-law marriage?
b. What are the grounds for a valid and legally formalized marriage?
c. What are the grounds for an annulment?

5. Legal Obligations in the Marriage Relationship

It is important to recognize that issues of marriage and divorce are dealt with in a variety of ways from state to state. The discussion in the following sections applies general trends, however one should always examine the laws of a jurisdiction to answer specific questions. Today, most states have statutes that impose an equal duty on each spouse to aid and financially support the other spouse during the marriage. No longer is it the sole duty of the husband to provide financial support for the wife, as in times prior to the latter part of the 20th century. The practical result is that in the event of a dissolution, the husband may also be entitled to financial support and, in most cases, maintenance (alimony) is no longer awarded for life unless special circumstances exist. These specifics are discussed in a later section that addresses questions of spousal support.

During the marriage, the spouses have an ongoing mutual duty to provide support of at least that which is necessary to meet the needs of the parties. Such necessities include food, shelter, and clothing. If one party has agreed to work outside the home while the other remains at home, the party at home also has a duty to contribute toward maintaining the existence of the marriage relationship. Often what is considered necessary is largely influenced by the income of the parties, the demands of their respective professions or occupations, and what their income enables them to realistically provide.

During the marriage, most states recognize the principle of *marital debt.* This presumes that a debt incurred by one spouse is binding on both, irrespective of consent to the incurring of debt or whether the basis for the debt benefitted both parties to the marriage.[9] This becomes particularly important if the parties subsequently terminate the marital relationship. In that case, marital debts must be apportioned fairly while also taking into account the ability of each party to satisfy claims of creditors. The subject of apportionment is addressed in the subsequent section on property and debt division in a dissolution of marriage action.

The primary rule regarding the approach of the courts toward intact marriages is one of nonintervention. Generally, the courts refuse to become involved in settling marital disputes regarding the duties of the parties.[10] When third parties such as creditors become involved and debts are going unpaid, the court may issue a declaration that both parties are jointly liable. Beyond this, the courts presume that the parties are meeting their obligations of support for one another as long as they continue to maintain the marriage relationship and do not enter into a legal separation or proceedings for dissolution of marriage.

If the parties cease living together and abandon the marital relationship, the courts may become involved in dictating the legal rights of each party before and after a formal dissolution of the marriage. Most states have enacted statutes that permit awards of support during a legal separation or while a divorce is pending. Because divorces can sometimes become quite drawn out, it may be necessary to provide for the well-being of the parties, and possibly any children, during the interim.

6. Effects of Tort and Criminal Law on the Marriage Relationship

An additional factor to be considered regarding the marital relationship is the effect of a marriage on tort and criminal law. Historically, one spouse was not permitted to bring a legal action against the other spouse for injuries inflicted during the marriage. The reasoning was that marital harmony would be disturbed if the courts entertained lawsuits by spouses against one another. Slowly the realization came about that if injuries by one spouse to another were so serious as to warrant a lawsuit, marital disharmony more than likely already existed. Further, it seemed unfair that gross negligence or intentional misconduct would be excused on the basis that it injured a family member. Therefore, most states have now abolished the doctrine of interspousal tort immunity. No longer are parties who cause injury to their spouses immune from legal action. Rather, such individuals are being held accountable in an attempt to combat the pervasive problem of domestic violence in American society.

7. Actions of Third Parties Against Married Persons

Other legal matters that may affect the marital relationship include actions against third parties for tortious conduct against the marriage relationship. Such actions are typically quite difficult to prove, and most persons are reluctant to raise the issue due to the notoriety they often generate. One such action is criminal conversation, which is an action by one spouse against a third party for adulterous conduct with the other spouse. Another is alienation of affection, which requires proof that a third party induced the other spouse to transfer his or her affections away from the plaintiff spouse and to the third party.[11] In the past, these actions have sometimes been used as a means to threaten and as virtual extortion, that is, blackmail on a threat of public embarrassment. Additionally, the individual today is seen as much more sophisticated and informed than those in centuries past when manipulation was more easily accomplished. For these reasons, some states have abolished the statutes that permit these types of actions. Even in states where they exist, they are becoming increasingly rare occurrences due to the media attention they incur and the difficulty to prove. More often than not, the courts assume the posture that the spouse engaged in the behavior with the third party as an independent and willing participant.

8. Domestic Violence

Unfortunately, the occurrence of domestic violence, defined as violence perpetrated by one member of a household on another member of the household, is all too prevalent in American society and law. In the early 1990s, one study cited 1.13 million reported cases of domestic violence. This does not even reflect the immeasurable number of unreported incidents. However, one benefit of the growing knowledge of individuals regarding their personal legal rights is the increased willingness of individuals to step forward in such matters. As a result, a body of law has been developed and continues to evolve in the area of domestic violence.

State legislatures, courts, and law enforcement agencies have began to develop, implement, and enforce laws—although some still consider them to be in the formative stages—designed to protect individuals against domestic violence. These agencies, along with social service agencies, offer counseling, reporting assistance, and training to overcome tendencies toward violent behavior in an attempt to stem the increasing problem. A majority of states now impose a requirement on those interacting with children, such as health care personnel and teachers, to report suspected abuse or incidents of violence without fear of reprisal. In fact, many statutes carry penalties for the failure to report. It is hoped that the latter will influence those who are tempted to look the other way and avoid getting involved when they are suspicious, but unsure whether violence is occurring in the life of a child. Many jurisdictions also have similar laws pending or in place to protect older citizens as elder abuse becomes an increasing area of concern.

9. Marital Violence

A rapidly changing area of criminal and civil law affecting the family involves marital violence. More than half the states now have statutes that permit an action of a wife for marital rape by her husband. For the first time in history, a distinction has been made between sexual contact as part of the marriage relationship and sexual contact as an act of violence. However, many of these statutes require the parties to have been living apart at the time of the incident. Additionally, because of the doctrine of nonintervention in the marital relationship, there has been little if any alternative for the abused spouse but to leave the marital home or force the other spouse to leave by court order as part of a pending dissolution proceeding. But there are now statutes in place permitting special intervention by police and, subsequently, by the courts where a reasonable belief exists that a spouse has committed a felony against his or her partner.

The statute in the following Figure 14.2 is one example of an attempt to deal with the domestic violence issue through the legal system. In addition, many community and charitable organizations have established shelters, crisis intervention centers, hotlines, counseling, and other methods to effectively deal with the domestic violence that occurs in our society. As more cases are reported and the guilt often felt by victims of domestic violence is exposed as unfounded, this area of law and community support can be expected to grow dramatically in coming years.

In criminal law, certain principles affect the marriage relationship. A primary example is the testimonial privilege. Traditionally, a person could not testify against his or her spouse during a criminal prosecution. But over time, the law has been modified, and most states now permit but cannot compel a spouse to testify against his or her partner. Because the spouse has the right to protect the confidentiality of the marriage relationship, testimony cannot be forced or ordered.

Assignment 14.3

Locate the name, address, phone number, and website (if any) of organizations other than police that respond to domestic violence issues for children, women, and the elderly. If none exist locally, expand the search to county and state levels.

FIGURE14.2   Domestic Violence Statute

CONNECTICUT GENERAL STATUTES
ANNOTATED TITLE 46B
FAMILY LAW CHAPTER 815 E. MARRIAGE

§ 46b-38a: Family violence prevention and response: Definitions

For the purposes of sections 46b-38a to 46b-38f, inclusive:

(1) "Family violence" means an incident resulting in physical harm, bodily injury or assault, or an act of threatened violence that constitutes fear of imminent physical harm, bodily injury or assault between family or household members. Verbal abuse or argument shall not constitute family violence unless there is present danger and the likelihood that physical violence will occur.

(2) "Family or household member" means (A) spouses, former spouses; (B) parents and their children; (C) persons eighteen years of age or older related by blood or marriage; (D) persons sixteen years of age or older other than those persons in sub-paragraph (C) presently residing together or who have resided together; and (E) persons who have a child in common regardless of whether they are or have been married or have lived together at any time.

(3) "Family violence crime" means a crime as defined in section 53a-24 which, in addition to its other elements, contains as an element thereof an act of family violence to a family member and shall not include acts by parents or guardians disciplining minor children unless such acts constitute abuse.

(4) "Institutions and services" means peace officers, service providers, mandated reporters of abuse, agencies and departments that provide services to victims and families and services designed to assist victims and families. § 46b-38b. Investigation of family violence crime by peace officer. Arrest, when. Assistance to victim. Guidelines. Education and training program.

(a) Whenever a peace officer determines upon speedy information that a family violence crime, as defined in subdivision (3) of section 46b-38a, has been committed within his jurisdiction, he shall arrest the person or persons suspected of its commission and charge such person or persons with the appropriate crime. The decision to arrest and charge shall not (1) be dependent on the specific consent of the victim, (2) consider the relationship of the parties or (3) be based solely on a request by the victim.

(b) No peace officer investigating an incident of family violence shall threaten, suggest or otherwise indicate the arrest of all parties for the purpose of discouraging requests for law enforcement intervention by any party. Where complaints are received from two or more opposing parties, the officer shall evaluate each complaint separately to determine whether he should seek a warrant for an arrest.

(c) No peace officer shall be held liable in any civil action regarding personal injury or injury to property brought by any party to a family violence incident for an arrest based on probable cause.

(d) It shall be the responsibility of the peace officer at the scene of a family violence incident to provide immediate assistance to the victim. Such assistance shall include but not be limited to: (1) Assisting the victim to obtain medical treatment if such is required; (2) notifying the victim of the right to file an affidavit or warrant for arrest; and (3) informing the victim of services available and referring the victim to the commission on victim services. In cases where the officer has determined that no cause exists for an arrest, assistance shall include: (A) Assistance included in subdivisions (1) to (3), inclusive, of this subsection; and (B) remaining at the scene for a reasonable time until in the reasonable judgment of the officer the likelihood of further imminent violence has been eliminated.

(e) On or before October 1, 1986, each law enforcement agency shall develop, in conjunction with the division of criminal justice, and implement specific operational guidelines for arrest policies in family violence incidents. Such guidelines shall include but not be limited to: (1) Procedures for the conduct of a criminal investigation; (2) procedures for arrest and for victim assistance by peace officers; (3) education as to what constitutes speedy information in a family violence incident; (4) procedures with respect to the provision of services to victims; and (5) such other criteria or guidelines as may be applicable to carry out the purposes of subsection (e) of section 17-38a and sections 17-38g, 46b-1, 46b-15, 46b-38a to 46b-38f, inclusive, and 54-1g.

(f) The municipal police training council, in conjunction with the division of criminal justice, shall establish an education and training program for law enforcement officers, supervisors and state's attorneys on the handling of family violence incidents. Such training shall: (1) Stress the enforcement of criminal law in family violence cases and the use of community resources and include training for peace officers at both recruit and in-service levels; (2) include: (A) The nature, extent and causes of family violence; (B) legal rights of and remedies available to victims of family violence and persons accused of family violence; (C) services and facilities available to victims and batterers; (D) legal duties imposed on police officers to make arrests and to offer protection and assistance; (E) techniques for handling incidents of family violence that minimize the likelihood of injury to the officer and promote safety of the victim.

B. ENDING THE MARITAL RELATIONSHIP

1. Jurisdiction

When one or both of the parties to a marital relationship decide to end the marriage, a judicial declaration must be made before the marriage and its associated rights and duties will be terminated. The declaration must come from a court that has authority over the parties to the suit. Again, this is an area in which the law varies greatly from state to state. However, some fundamentals are generally recognized in a majority of states. Procedural rules in each state specify when the courts will accept jurisdiction over a marital dissolution action.

One of the most common requirements for seeking an action for dissolution is that of residency. The length of residence varies, but generally states require the party commencing the action to have been a resident of the state for a specified period of time. In a majority of states parties may also obtain jurisdiction in a court if the marriage was formalized there or if the grounds for divorce occurred while the parties maintained their residence in the state, regardless of whether the time requirement has been met.[12]

When a party obtains a decree, but the court does not have jurisdiction to decide matters involving the settlement of the marital estate (e.g., assets are located in other jurisdictions), the decree may be registered with a court that has jurisdiction over both the parties and their property. That court may then determine the rights and obligations of each party. Under the U.S. Constitution, each state is obligated to give full faith and credit to the judgment of another state's decree. This means a state should honor and enforce the judgments of a court from another state. Most often, however, the decree and distribution of debts and assets will all be rendered in the same court.

A major jurisdictional issue in dissolution actions pertains to the authority of a court over the rights and duties concerning children of a marriage. Initially, the court that has jurisdiction to determine the rights, duties, and division of the assets of the marital estate also has authority to make findings regarding custody, visitation, and support of minor children. However, later adjustments to these findings, commonly termed modifications, may raise serious issues as to which court has authority. Fortunately, these issues have been settled in large part by the Uniform Reciprocal Enforcement of Support Act (URESA). Most states adhere to the act, which states quite specifically what courts have jurisdiction over matters concerning children of divorced parties.

2. Legal Separation

Many times a divorce is a long and complicated process. Also, it is not uncommon to go through a period of separation before making the decision to end the marriage permanently through divorce. This may be for religious reasons, or because the parties want time to consider the possibility of reconciliation or at least the potential for agreement to the terms of the divorce. During this period, the parties remain legally obligated to each other as well as for the support of their children. As a consequence, a special area of law has developed by statute and by judicial decision that governs the rights of the parties during this period of **legal separation.**

As discussed previously, courts are reluctant to recognize antenuptial agreements that provide specifically for divorce. However, when a physical separation has occurred

Legal Separation
Legal document that establishes the property rights of the parties without effecting a dissolution of the marriage relationship.

or is about to occur, the courts will consider an antenuptial or separation agreement between the parties that discusses the parties' rights and duties, prior to the divorce when the marriage still exists legally but marital assets and liabilities are no longer shared. The courts will generally examine the agreement for fairness, full disclosure, and availability of legal counsel to each party.[13]

Separation agreements include such issues as custody, visitation, and support of minor children; possession of the marital residence; responsibility for payments due on marital debts; and maintenance (alimony), where appropriate. If the terms are agreeable to the parties, they may also serve as the basis for the terms in the final divorce decree for matters of convenience to the parties. However, it is important to note that legal separations have no direct connection to dissolution proceedings, and each may take place without the other.

3. Grounds for Dissolution of a Marriage

Historically, very distinct grounds had to be proven in order to justify an order of dissolution of marriage. It was insufficient by American societal standards to agree to disagree. Rather, the institution of marriage was considered a fundamental component of ordered society and only in extreme cases was a divorce granted. During the 20th century attitudes changed dramatically. Divorce became more common and the legislatures became increasingly less involved with the reasons supporting a divorce and more focused on the equitable settlement of issues arising from the end of the marriage. Prior to this time, though, a party had to establish behavior of the other spouse that would be considered so extreme and/or reprehensible by societal standards that it warranted release of the innocent party from the marriage. The specific grounds for a *fault* divorce are still found on the books in a majority of states and are still used to some extent. They commonly include but are not limited to the following:

- Habitual drunkenness or substance abuse
- Adultery
- Physical cruelty
- Mental and emotional cruelty
- Abandonment
- Insanity

Traditionally, the party who suffered because of the existence of one or more of these grounds brought an action for divorce. He or she would be required to give evidence of the grounds and on that basis the divorce would be granted.

More recently adopted has been the concept of no-fault divorce, the grounds for which are often referred to as irreconcilable differences. This has been in response to changing societal standards. Also, it has been recognized for many years that the parties would agree in advance to plead and accept a specific grounds for a divorce as a means to expedite the end of the legal relationship when the marriage itself had to come to an end sometime before. Many times, parties who no longer want to continue the marriage have a variety of reasons other than statutorily stated grounds. In addition, the time and expense associated with divorce to the individuals and courts alike have increased significantly. As a result, over the past few decades every state has adopted a no-fault statute in some form. Although the requirements of proof of a broken marriage may differ from state to state, the premise remains the same. It is unnecessary to claim that one party unilaterally caused the break in the marital bond. Rather, the premise is that the parties have reached a point where they are no longer interested in maintaining the marital relationship. For this reason the bond is broken, and the legality of the relationship can be dissolved.

In an attempt to prevent parties from entering into a no-fault divorce when reconciliation could still be achieved, many statutes impose requirements of proof that the marital bond is irreparably broken. Such requirements include lengthy separations before a no-fault divorce will be granted. Parties should be given every opportunity to evaluate the situation carefully and be sure of their decision. However, those parties who have firmly made a decision to end the marriage may evade these requirements by returning to the former method of privately agreeing to one or more grounds based on fault of a party so that the divorce may be granted more quickly. Thus, although the statutes have assisted many in obtaining a divorce without laying blame, abuse of statutes by giving grounds of fault continues in those jurisdictions where it is still more time-consuming to obtain a divorce on grounds of no-fault.

4. Temporary Orders

It is a rare occurrence for two individuals to appear before a court ready for a dissolution of their marriage with all issues between them resolved equitably and without need of further mediation or court intervention. Rather, the much more likely scenario is that one or both individuals present themselves to legal counsel knowing only that a dissolution of marriage is necessary. However, they need assistance in the actual accomplishment of the dissolution, the separation of assets and liabilities and often in working out issues of custody, support, and visitation of children. Often, the relationship between the marital partners at this stage is strained, making the possibility of working the various issues out amicably less than hopeful. In some instances, domestic violence, custody and visitation, and wasting of asssets is an immediate issue that requires intervention prior to the time of the final order of the court.

In instances where the parties are unwilling or unable to reach an agreement regarding property or other rights during the pendency of the proceedings, state statutes give the courts authority to make temporary provisions during the period after dissolution proceedings have begun but before a final decree is issued. These temporary orders provide terms that the parties must follow with respect to the marital obligations previously discussed.

In addition to issuing temporary orders, courts are often requested to issue **temporary restraining orders** and **preliminary injunctions,** which are granted in circumstances where the court is convinced that one spouse will injure the partner, or will harm, destroy, or dispose of marital property.[14] If the threat of harm is immediate, the spouse who is in danger of injury or harm can appear in court *ex parte*. An *ex parte* proceeding is conducted without giving the other party to the action the opportunity to be present and voice his or her position. Because these orders are based on one person's version of the story, the court will usually issue the order only in compelling circumstances. Such orders are usually effective for only a short period of time as an emergency measure.

Temporary Restraining Orders
Court order that requires a party to act or refrain from acting in a particular manner for a short time until the court has the opportunity to consider a more permanent ruling.

Preliminary Injunctions
Court order that orders a party to act or refrain from acting in a particular manner for a specified period of time.

APPLICATION 14.3

Diane and Ed have been married for several years. For some time Ed has wanted a divorce. However, Diane is the primary earner and has threatened repeatedly to take the children out of state and to hide all of their liquid assets if Ed files for divorce. On one occasion, Ed came home to find that Diane had taken the children and left for two weeks. She also changed banks, transferring virtually all funds to accounts solely in her name in another town. Ed fears that if he files for dissolution, Diane will take the children out of state and take all of their assets with her. In a circumstance like this, where there is a history of behavior against the interests of one party to the marriage, particularly involving the children of the marriage, a court is likely to grant temporary orders that would freeze accounts and require specific guidelines for the custody and visitation of the children.

Point for Discussion: Should the court require a past history of such behavior before entering an order or should testimony of threats be sufficient?

After a temporary restraining order has been issued, it is served on the party who is restrained. Even if the restrained party cannot be located, the order is effective and if it is violated, the party can be arrested. Without such a rule, parties could simply avoid being served and in the interim destroy marital property or perhaps seriously injure their spouse. Given the alternatives, the safer course seems to be to give the order effect from the time it is issued. As a practical matter, anyone likely to be affected by the order should also be given notice. For example, in the case of children, schools and caretakers should receive a copy of the order. If an order is issued to leave assets intact, the bank where funds are maintained should be apprised.

Temporary restraining orders are usually issued for a very short period of time. Thus, a party who can show evidence that such an order was improperly issued can have the order revoked at the earliest opportunity. When a hearing is held, however, if sufficient evidence is presented to warrant continuance of the order, a preliminary injunction may be issued that remains in effect during the pendency of the dissolution proceedings.

A preliminary injunction often contains provisions similar to a temporary restraining order, however, the injunction will be effective until the final divorce decree is entered or for a stated period of time. At that time, if the marital property will continue to be held jointly or if the physical danger still exists, a **permanent injunction** may be issued that will remain effective until an order of the court removes it. Many times, these orders are left in force forever.

Permanent Injunction
Court order that permanently orders a party to act or refrain from acting in a particular manner.

APPLICATION 14.4

In the previous application, assume the court issued temporary orders freezing the accounts of the parties and granting temporary custody of the children to Ed. The court would also schedule a hearing within a matter of days to enable Diane to present her side. At that time, the court would issue preliminary orders with respect to custody, visitation, and access to assets for living expenses. The court may also issue preliminary orders with respect to child support and/or maintenance.

Point for Discussion: Why should the court not issue the permanent orders at this time?

5. Custody

Charge over minor children is perhaps one of the most litigated areas of family law. Unfortunately, it is also one of the most misunderstood areas in terms of popular misconceptions about legal standards and the likely actions of a court in a given area. For example, one popular misconception is that whichever parent has the children at the time the action for dissolution is filed will receive custody. In reality, the court is not bound by the timing of filing or the geographical location of a child at any given moment. Rather, the courts will consider the best interest of the child when determining custody. **Custody** is the legal term used to describe the care, control, and responsibility for education of a minor child. It is effective as long as the child is a minor or is still in high school. A synonymous term used in some jurisdictions is parental rights. For purposes of this discussion, the term custody will be used here. When the child reaches the age of majority under statute in the state where the child is domiciled, custody ends, and the child is considered to be an adult. Domicile is determined by the child's intended permanent dwelling and not by where the child attends school or where the other parent lives whom the child may visit, even extensively. Generally, the state of domicile of the custodial parent is the state of domicile of the child. In the event of joint custody by parents domiciled in different states, the court typically issues a determination of which jurisdiction is controlling.

Custody does not always end at the age of majority, however. In special circumstances, such as when a child is mentally disabled or otherwise unable to accept responsibility for his or her actions, a custodial parent may be appointed as a permanent custodian. This status would continue until, if, and when the court made a determination that the disability of the child had been removed.

In the event of the death of the custodial parent, the presumption is that custody will be transferred to the other parent. The exception to this is if the surviving parent is not able to provide an acceptable environment for the child. In such circumstances, stepparents, grandparents, or other interested parties who can provide a suitable environment for the child may be appointed temporary or permanent guardian.

Fortunately, the courts rarely have to deal with such cases. However, there are quite often decisions to be made by the courts when both parents are living and willing to provide a home for the child or children. Formerly, the mother almost always received custody of the children. No longer is this the case. Courts now consider numerous factors to determine who is best able to care for and attend to the needs of the children. This enlightened and broadened view has come about as the traditional family structure has changed. It is no longer the general rule that the father is the only one to work outside the home, and the mother serves the role of primary caretaker and nurturer of children. Rather, in today's society, the roles of parents are seen as much more equal in terms of responsibilities to meet both the financial and emotional needs of the children. In the past, the only chance a father had to rebut the presumption that the mother should have custody of minor children was to produce overwhelming evidence that the mother was unfit to act in the role of mother and parent, or at the very least, that the father was far more fit to serve in this role.

Under what is known as the *tender years* doctrine, followed for decades but now rapidly declining in this country, the mother was presumed to be the best alternative for custody of young children, otherwise known as children of tender years. These were usually children who had not reached their teens. In recent years, however, many fathers have taken an increasingly active role in the upbringing of their children. In

Custody
Legal right for primary care, education, and parenting of minor children.

some families, it is the father who acts as the primary nurturer and caregiver. In others, the more traditional circumstance of mother in this role continues, and in yet other families, the obligations of parenting are shared equally. As the number of dissolutions of marriage increased, various movements and organizations sprang up to support men in their quest for continued and increased parenting roles with their minor children, regardless of the fact that the marriage to the mother no longer existed. This has been supported by the change in societal roles of women as well. Many mothers have jobs and are away from the home just as fathers would have been in more traditional settings. For all of these reasons, many courts have struck down the tender years doctrine in favor of a more personal case-by-case evaluation of who will best serve as primary caretaker. This more recent approach is known as the best interest of the child doctrine.[15]

What is the standard that must be proven then to obtain custody of a child? Contrary to popular belief, it is not necessary to prove that the other party is unfit as parent. Although the evidence may establish this in some cases as a byproduct, it is not the standard used by most courts. Rather, the courts look at what will be in the best interest of the child. Thus, instead of encouraging the parties to look for the negatives they can bring out about the other parent, the incentive it to put one's own best foot forward as the potential custodian. Divorce is extremely difficult for children of all ages to deal with. That is not to say that it may not be a better alternative than to continue the marriage. But divorce does mean that a child's world goes through dramatic changes that require adjustment. Consequently, the court examines several areas that affect the child's life and looks to the child's particular needs. The court then looks at the environment that each parent would offer the child. The environment that is most compatible with the child's need is the one that is in the child's best interests. Each parent may offer a suitable environment, but the parent that is better suited to meet the needs of the child should prevail. The factors that a court considers in making this determination may include, but are not limited to, the following:[16]

- The ability of the parent to care for the child personally, as opposed to extensive use of child-care services
- The religion of the parent
- The ability of the parent to attend to any special needs of the child because of young age or disability
- Immoral conduct that would have a direct effect on the child such as substance abuse or criminal behavior (otherwise this is considered to be irrelevant)
- Ability to give continuity to the child's current environment, such as home, school, and friends
- The availability of contact with members of the child's extended family

None of the preceding factors is individually controlling, and the court will usually consider the factors that are peculiar to each case when making its determination. The U.S. Supreme Court has determined that race or ethnic background cannot be used as a singular determining factor in a custody case, although a court may consider race or ethnicity along with other factors in a custody decision when it is relevant.

An additional factor that is not controlling but may be given some weight is the desire of the child. The general rule is that a child may not be able to determine objectively what is in his or her best interests. However, as a child matures, courts are often more willing to consider his or her opinion. Many states have statutory provisions that expressly permit the judge to give weight to this factor after a child reaches a certain age. In absence of this, it is left to each judge's own discretion as to whether to consider the opinion of the child. Because the child is still a minor and is deemed legally incompetent to make such significant decisions, a court will rarely accept the child's wishes as the sole determining factor.

a. Joint Custody   Thus far, the discussion has been confined to the issue of single-parent custody, in which one parent has the primary responsibility for the care, control, and education of the child. The noncustodial parent has visitation rights but no legal right to take an active part in the decisions regarding the child's rearing.

Because the limitation on such input was unacceptable to many parents, the concept of joint custody was developed. A common misconception is that joint custody involves only shared physical custody of the child or children. Although this sometimes occurs in joint custody, it is not the primary purpose. The child may very well live permanently with one parent. Joint custody gives each parent the right to take an active part in the rearing of the child. The parents are expected to discuss and come to agreement on all significant issues of education and religious upbringing, and, in general, all major decisions that affect the child's life.[17]

A majority of states have enacted statutes that permit the courts to award joint custody. It is left to the discretion of the judges to determine on a case-by-case basis whether the circumstances are appropriate for joint custody or whether the child's interests would be better served by an award of individual custody to one parent and significant contact with the other parent.

In the best of circumstances, joint custody allows both parents to have input into all aspects of a child's upbringing. As a practical matter, however, it is often an untenable situation. Because of this, judges are frequently reluctant to grant joint custody unless the circumstances appear overwhelmingly in favor of it. For example, if parties battle throughout the pendency of the divorce over issues of support, maintenance, visitation, and property division, it may be virtually impossible to convince a court that they will suddenly be able to work things out among themselves when it comes to the day-to-day rearing of children.

The problem that arises with joint custody is that in many situations it is contradictory to the objectives sought by the divorce. The parties have sought a dissolution of marriage because the relationship has reached a point of irreconcilable differences. There are significant matters that the parties simply cannot come to agreement on, yet in joint custody, the parties seek to have the legal right to determine important matters of child rearing together in a cooperative attitude. Often these are the same parties who were so opposed to each other that they were not willing to work together in the best interests of the child in the past. Also, the parties typically seek to end their relationship and their need for future contact in virtually every area. Once the true definition of joint custody is understood, many parties determine on their own that it is not likely to work. When the concept first developed it was popularly received until judges, lawyers, and parties found themselves resolving issues in court time and time again. When this occurs, the purpose of joint custody to serve the best interest of the child is not achieved, the parents incur additional legal expenses, and the child is subjected to more disruption than ever. Therefore, unless the parties seem to be genuinely interested and capable of working with each other for the duration of the child's minority, many courts are very reluctant to grant joint custody today.

b. Enforcement of Custody Orders   An increasingly common issue in child custody cases is that of court jurisdiction. With the expanding mobility of American society, it is no longer uncommon for parents to live in different states. Consequently, enforcement of child custody orders can rapidly develop into a costly and time-consuming battle for parents in conflict. In response, the Uniform Child Custody Jurisdiction Act (UCCJA) has been adopted by the states. It sets up guidelines for determining jurisdiction and establishing cooperation among the states in the enforcement of custody orders. While not a cure, this uniform law has eliminated a great many of the problems and concerns that parents might otherwise face when they live in separate jurisdictions.

Assignment 14.4

> Examine the UCCJA in Figure 14.3 and determine the proper steps that a parent must take to register a custody order in a jurisdiction other than where it was originally granted.

Assignment 14.5

> Examine the UCCJA and summarize the requirements for a court to exercise jurisdiction in a custody matter that was originally determined in another court.

6. Child Support

Although the obligation to provide support to a spouse may end with the dissolution of the marital relationship, support of children of the marriage continues as long as the court determines it is necessary. Generally, this is for the remainder of the child's minority or until high school graduation. The theory is that the child of divorced parents should be in a position similar to what they would have been in with respect to lifestyle and opportunities had the divorce not occurred. Additionally, support may be extended beyond a child's majority if the child has some physical or mental incapacity that prevents the child from becoming responsible for filling his or her own needs. A growing area of law, and one of some controversy and varying results, is whether support should be continued to offset expenses of college.

If a child marries or becomes legally emancipated before the age of majority, the child will become fully independent. As a result, the parents will no longer be legally responsible for providing support for the child. On the other hand, if a parent dies and leaves no provision for the support of the minor child, he or she is still entitled to a share of the parent's estate for support. If the parent specifically disinherits the child, most states will still require support to be paid. However, there are jurisdictions in which a deliberate disinheritance will be respected and support may be terminated, in which case the child becomes the sole responsibility of the surviving parent. Therefore, as with all legal issues including those of domestic relations, the law of the particular state in question should be examined before reaching any conclusions.

There is usually little contest over the obligation to provide support. Most parties accept that they are obligated to support their natural or adopted children. The real turmoil begins when the parties attempt to determine the amount of support to be contributed. If financially able, the noncustodial parent, whether the mother or the father,

FIGURE 14.3   Uniform Child Custody Jurisdiction Act

§ 1. Purposes of Act; Construction of Provisions.—

(a) The general purposes of this Act are to:

(1) avoid jurisdictional competition and conflict with courts of other states in matters of child custody which have in the past resulted in the shifting of children from state to state with harmful effects on their well-being;

(2) promote cooperation with the courts of other states to the end that a custody decree is rendered in that state which can best decide the case in the interest of the child;

(3) assure that litigation concerning the custody of a child take place ordinarily in the state with which the child and his family have the closest connection and where significant evidence concerning his care, protection, training, and personal relationships is most readily available, and that courts of this state decline the exercise of jurisdiction when the child and his family have a closer connection with another state;

(4) discourage continuing controversies over child custody in the interest of greater stability of home environment and of secure family relationships for the child;

(5) deter abductions and other unilateral removals of children undertaken to obtain custody awards;

(6) avoid re-litigation of custody decisions of other states in this state insofar as feasible;

(7) facilitate the enforcement of custody decrees of other states;

(8) promote and expand the exchange of information and other forms of mutual assistance between the courts of this state and those of other states concerned with the same child; and

(9) make uniform the law of those states which enact it.

(b) This Act shall be construed to promote the general purposes stated in this section.

§ 2. Definitions.—As used in this Act:

(1) "contestant" means a person, including a parent, who claims a right to custody or visitation rights with respect to a child;

(2) "custody determination" means a court decision and court orders and instructions providing for the custody of a child, including visitation rights; it does not include a decision relating to child support or any other monetary obligation of any person;

(3) "custody proceeding" includes proceedings in which a custody determination is one of several issues, such as an action for divorce or separation, and includes child neglect and dependency proceedings;

(4) "decree" or "custody decree" means a custody determination contained in a judicial decree or order made in a custody proceeding, and includes an initial decree and a modification decree;

(5) "home state" means the state in which the child immediately preceding the time involved lived with his parents, a parent, or a person acting as parent, for at least 6 consecutive months, and in the case of a child less than 6 months old the state in which the child lived from birth with any of the persons mentioned. Periods of temporary absence of any of the named persons are counted as part of the 6-month or other period;

(6) "initial decree" means the first custody decree concerning a particular child;

(7) "modification decree" means a custody decree which modifies or replaces a prior decree, whether made by the court which rendered the prior decree or by another court;

(8) "physical custody" means actual possession and control of a child;

(9) "person acting as parent" means a person, other than a parent, who has physical custody of a child and who has either been awarded custody by a court or claims a right to custody; and

(10) "state" means any state, territory, or possession of the United States, the Commonwealth of Puerto Rico, and the District of Columbia.

§ 3. Jurisdiction.—

(a) A court of this State which is competent to decide child custody matters has jurisdiction to make a child custody determination by initial or modification decree if:

(1) this State (i) is the home state of the child at the time of commencement of the proceeding, or (ii) had been the child's home state within 6 months before commencement of the proceeding and the child is absent from this State because of his removal or retention by a person claiming his custody or for other reasons, and a parent or person acting as parent continues to live in this State; or

(2) it is in the best interest of the child that a court of this State assume jurisdiction because (i) the child and his parents, or the child and at least one contestant, have a significant connection with this State, and (ii) there is available in this State substantial evidence concerning the child's present or future care, protection, training, and personal relationships; or

(3) the child is physically present in this State and (i) the child has been abandoned or (ii) it is necessary in an emergency to protect the child because he has been subjected to or threatened with mistreatment or abuse or is otherwise neglected [or dependent]; or

(Continued)

FIGURE 14.3   *(Continued)*

(4)(i) it appears that no other state would have jurisdiction under prerequisites substantially in accordance with paragraphs (1), (2), or (3), or another state has declined to exercise jurisdiction on the ground that this State is the more appropriate forum to determine the custody of the child, and (ii) it is in the best interest of the child that this court assume jurisdiction.

(b) Except under paragraphs (3) and (4) of subsection (a), physical presence in this State of the child, or of the child and one of the contestants, is not alone sufficient to confer jurisdiction on a court of this State to make a child custody determination.

(c) Physical presence of the child, while desirable, is not a prerequisite for jurisdiction to determine his custody.

§ 4. Notice and Opportunity to be Heard.—Before making a decree under this Act, reasonable notice and opportunity to be heard shall be given to the contestants, any parent whose parental rights have not been previously terminated, and any person who has physical custody of the child. If any of these persons is outside this State, notice and opportunity to be heard shall be given pursuant to section 5.

§ 5. Notice to Persons Outside this State; Submission to Jurisdiction.—

(a) Notice required for the exercise of jurisdiction over a person outside this State shall be given in a manner reasonably calculated to give actual notice, and may be:

(1) by personal delivery outside this State in the manner prescribed for service of process within this State;

(2) in the manner prescribed by the law of the place in which the service is made for service of process in that place in an action in any of its courts of general jurisdiction;

(3) by any form of mail addressed to the person to be served and requesting a receipt; or

(4) as directed by the court [including publication, if other means of notification are ineffective].

(b) Notice under this section shall be served, mailed, or delivered, [or last published] at least [10, 20] days before any hearing in this State.

(c) Proof of service outside this State may be made by affidavit of the individual who made the service, or in the manner prescribed by the law of this State, the order pursuant to which the service is made, or the law of the place in which the service is made. If service is made by mail, proof may be a receipt signed by the addressee or other evidence of delivery to the addressee.

(d) Notice is not required if a person submits to the jurisdiction of the court.

§ 6. Simultaneous Proceedings in Other States.—

(a) A court of this State shall not exercise its jurisdiction under this Act if at the time of filing the petition a proceeding concerning the custody of the child was pending in a court of another state exercising jurisdiction substantially in conformity with this Act, unless the proceeding is stayed by the court of the other state because this State is a more appropriate forum or for other reasons.

(b) Before hearing the petition in a custody proceeding the court shall examine the pleadings and other information supplied by the parties under section 9 and shall consult the child custody registry established under section 16 concerning the pendency of proceedings with respect to the child in other states. If the court has reason to believe that proceedings may be pending in another state it shall direct an inquiry to the state court administrator or other appropriate official of the other state.

(c) If the court is informed during the course of the proceeding that a proceeding concerning the custody of the child was pending in another state before the court assumed jurisdiction it shall stay the proceeding and communicate with the court in which the other proceeding is pending to the end that the issue may be litigated in the more appropriate forum and that information be exchanged in accordance with sections 19 through 22. If a court of this State has made a custody decree before being informed of a pending proceeding in a court of another state it shall immediately inform that court of the fact. If the court is informed that a proceeding was commenced in another state after it assumed jurisdiction it shall likewise inform the other court to the end that the issues may be litigated in the more appropriate forum.

§ 7. Inconvenient Forum.—

(a) A court which has jurisdiction under this Act to make an initial or modification decree may decline to exercise its jurisdiction any time before making a decree if it finds that it is an inconvenient forum to make a custody determination under the circumstances of the case and that a court of another state is a more appropriate forum.

(b) A finding of inconvenient forum may be made upon the court's own motion or upon motion of a party or a guardian ad litem or other representative of the child.

(c) In determining if it is an inconvenient forum, the court shall consider if it is in the interest of the child that another state assume jurisdiction. For this purpose it may take into account the following factors, among others:

(1) if another state is or recently was the child's home state;

(2) if another state has a closer connection with the child and his family or with the child and one or more of the contestants;

FIGURE 14.3 *(Continued)*

(3) if substantial evidence concerning the child's present or future care, protection, training, and personal relationships is more readily available in another state;

(4) if the parties have agreed on another forum which is no less appropriate; and

(5) if the exercise of jurisdiction by a court of this State would contravene any of the purposes stated in section 1.

(d) Before determining whether to decline or retain jurisdiction the court may communicate with a court of another state and exchange information pertinent to the assumption of jurisdiction by either court with a view to assuring that jurisdiction will be exercised by the more appropriate court and that a forum will be available to the parties.

(e) If the court finds that it is an inconvenient forum and that a court of another state is a more appropriate forum, it may dismiss the proceedings, or it may stay the proceedings upon condition that a custody proceeding be promptly commenced in another named state or upon any other conditions which may be just and proper, including the condition that a moving party stipulate his consent and submission to the jurisdiction of the other forum.

(f) The court may decline to exercise its jurisdiction under this Act if a custody determination is incidental to an action for divorce or another proceeding while retaining jurisdiction over the divorce or other proceeding.

(g) If it appears to the court that it is clearly an inappropriate forum it may require the party who commenced the proceedings to pay, in addition to the costs of the proceedings in this State, necessary travel and other expenses, including attorneys' fees, incurred by other parties or their witnesses. Payment is to be made to the clerk of the court for remittance to the proper party.

(h) Upon dismissal or stay of proceedings under this section the court shall inform the court found to be the more appropriate forum of this fact, or if the court which would have jurisdiction in the other state is not certainly known, shall transmit the information to the court administrator or other appropriate official for forwarding to the appropriate court.

(i) Any communication received from another state informing this State of a finding of inconvenient forum because a court of this State is the more appropriate forum shall be filed in the custody registry of the appropriate court. Upon assuming jurisdiction the court of this State shall inform the original court of this fact.

§ 8. Jurisdiction Declined by Reason of Conduct.—

(a) If the petitioner for an initial decree has wrongfully taken the child from another state or has engaged in similar reprehensible conduct the court may decline to exercise jurisdiction if this is just and proper under the circumstances.

(b) Unless required in the interest of the child, the court shall not exercise its jurisdiction to modify a custody decree of another state if the petitioner, without consent of the person entitled to custody, has improperly removed the child from the physical custody of the person entitled to custody or has improperly retained the child after a visit or other temporary relinquishment of physical custody. If the petitioner has violated any other provision of a custody decree of another state the court may decline to exercise its jurisdiction if this is just and proper under the circumstances.

(c) In appropriate cases a court dismissing a petition under this section may charge the petitioner with necessary travel and other expenses, including attorneys' fees, incurred by other parties or their witnesses.

§ 9. Information under Oath to be Submitted to the Court.—

(a) Every party in a custody proceeding in his first pleading or in an affidavit attached to that pleading shall give information under oath as to the child's present address, the places where the child has lived within the last 5 years, and the names and present addresses of the persons with whom the child has lived during that period. In this pleading or affidavit every party shall further declare under oath whether:

(1) he has participated (as a party, witness, or in any other capacity) in any other litigation concerning the custody of the same child in this or any other state;

(2) he has information of any custody proceeding concerning the child pending in a court of this or any other state; and

(3) he knows of any person not a party to the proceedings who has physical custody of the child or claims to have custody or visitation rights with respect to the child.

(b) If the declaration as to any of the above items is in the affirmative the declarant shall give additional information under oath as required by the court. The court may examine the parties under oath as to details of the information furnished and as to other matters pertinent to the court's jurisdiction and the disposition of the case.

(c) Each party has a continuing duty to inform the court of any custody proceeding concerning the child in this or any other state of which he obtained information during this proceeding.

§ 10. Additional Parties.—If the court learns from information furnished by the parties pursuant to section 9 or from other sources that a person not a party to the custody proceeding has physical custody of the child or claims to have custody or visitation rights with respect to the child, it shall order that person to be joined as a party and to be duly notified of the pendency of the proceeding and of his joinder as a party. If the person joined as a party is outside this State he shall be served with process or otherwise notified in accordance with section 5.

(Continued)

FIGURE 14.3   *(Continued)*

§ 11. Appearance of Parties and the Child.—

[(a) The court may order any party to the proceeding who is in this State to appear personally before the court. If that party has physical custody of the child the court may order that he appear personally with the child.]

(b) If a party to the proceeding whose presence is desired by the court is outside this State with or without the child the court may order that the notice given under section 5 include a statement directing that party to appear personally with or without the child and declaring that failure to appear may result in a decision adverse to that party.

(c) If a party to the proceeding who is outside this State is directed to appear under subsection (b) or desires to appear personally before the court with or without the child, the court may require another party to pay to the clerk of the court travel and other necessary expenses of the party so appearing and of the child if this is just and proper under the circumstances.

§ 12. Binding Force and Res Judicata Effect of Custody Decree.—A custody decree rendered by a court of this State which had jurisdiction under section 3 binds all parties who have been served in this State or notified in accordance with section 5 or who have submitted to the jurisdiction of the court, and who have been given an opportunity to be heard. As to these parties the custody decree is conclusive as to all issues of law and fact decided and as to the custody determination made unless and until that determination is modified pursuant to law, including the provisions of this Act.

§ 13. Recognition of Out-of-State Custody Decrees.—The courts of this State shall recognize and enforce an initial or modification decree of a court of another state which had assumed jurisdiction under statutory provisions substantially in accordance with this Act or which was made under factual circumstances meeting the jurisdictional standards of the Act, so long as this decree has not been modified in accordance with jurisdictional standards substantially similar to those of this Act.

§ 14. Modification of Custody Decree of Another State.—

(a) If a court of another state has made a custody decree, a court of this State shall not modify that decree unless (1) it appears to the court of this State that the court which rendered the decree does not now have jurisdiction under jurisdictional prerequisites substantially in accordance with this Act or has declined to assume jurisdiction to modify the decree and (2) the court of this State has jurisdiction.

(b) If a court of this State is authorized under subsection (a) and section 8 to modify a custody decree of another state it shall give due consideration to the transcript of the record and other documents of all previous proceedings submitted to it in accordance with section 22.

§ 15. Filing and Enforcement of Custody Decree of Another State.—

(a) A certified copy of a custody decree of another state may be filed in the office of the clerk of any [District Court, Family Court] of this State. The clerk shall treat the decree in the same manner as a custody decree of the [District Court, Family Court] of this State. A custody decree so filed has the same effect and shall be enforced in like manner as a custody decree rendered by a court of this State.

(b) A person violating a custody decree of another state which makes it necessary to enforce the decree in this State may be required to pay necessary travel and other expenses, including attorneys' fees, incurred by the party entitled to the custody or his witnesses.

§ 16. Registry of Out-of-State Custody Decrees and Proceedings.—The clerk of each [District Court, Family Court] shall maintain a registry in which he shall enter the following:

(1) certified copies of custody decrees of other states received for filing;

(2) communications as to the pendency of custody proceedings in other states;

(3) communications concerning a finding of inconvenient forum by a court of another state; and

(4) other communications or documents concerning custody proceedings in another state which may affect the jurisdiction of a court of this State or the disposition to be made by it in a custody proceeding.

§ 17. Certified Copies of Custody Decree.—The Clerk of the [District Court, Family Court] of this State, at the request of the court of another state or at the request of any person who is affected by or has a legitimate interest in a custody decree, shall certify and forward a copy of the decree to that court or person.

§ 18. Taking Testimony in Another State.—In addition to other procedural devices available to a party, any party to the proceeding or a guardian ad litem or other representative of the child may adduce testimony of witnesses, including parties and the child, by deposition or otherwise in another state. The court on its own motion may direct that the testimony of a person be taken in another state and may prescribe the manner in which and the terms upon which the testimony shall be taken.

(Continued)

FIGURE 14.3   (*Continued*)

§ 19. Hearings and Studies in Another State; Orders to Appear.—

(a) A court of this State may request the appropriate court of another state to hold a hearing to adduce evidence, to order a party to produce or give evidence under other procedures of that state, or to have social studies made with respect to the custody of a child involved in proceedings pending in the court of this State; and to forward to the court of this State certified copies of the transcript of the record of the hearing, the evidence otherwise adduced, or any social studies prepared in compliance with the request. The cost of the services may be assessed against the parties or, if necessary, ordered paid by the [County, State].

(b) A court of this State may request the appropriate court of another state to order a party to custody proceedings pending in the court of this State to appear in the proceedings, and if that party has physical custody of the child, to appear with the child. The request may state that travel and other necessary expenses of the party and of the child whose appearance is desired will be assessed against another party or will otherwise be paid.

§ 20. Assistance to Courts of Other States.—

(a) Upon request of the court of another state the courts of this State which are competent to hear custody matters may order a person in this State to appear at a hearing to adduce evidence or to produce or give evidence under other procedures available in this State [or may order social studies to be made for use in a custody proceeding in another state]. A certified copy of the transcript of the record of the hearing or the evidence otherwise adduced [and any social studies prepared] shall be forwarded by the clerk of the court to the requesting court.

(b) A person within this State may voluntarily give his testimony or statement in this State for use in a custody proceeding outside this State.

(c) Upon request of the court of another state a competent court of this State may order a person in this State to appear alone or with the child in a custody proceeding in another state. The court may condition compliance with the request upon assurance by the other state that state travel and other necessary expenses will be advanced or reimbursed.

§ 21. Preservation of Documents for Use in Other States.—In any custody proceeding in this State the court shall preserve the pleadings, orders and decrees, any record that has been made of its hearings, social studies, and other pertinent documents until the child reaches [18, 21] years of age. Upon appropriate request of the court of another state the court shall forward to the other court certified copies of any or all such documents.

§ 22. Request for Court Records of Another State.—If a custody decree has been rendered in another state concerning a child involved in a custody proceeding pending in a court of this State, the court of this State upon taking jurisdiction of the case shall request of the court of the other state a certified copy of the transcript of any court record and other documents mentioned in section 21.

§ 23. International Application.—The general policies of this Act extend to the international area. The provisions of this Act relating to the recognition and enforcement of custody decrees of other states apply to custody decrees and decrees involving legal institutions similar in nature to custody institutions rendered by appropriate authorities of other nations if reasonable notice and opportunity to be heard were given to all affected persons.

[§ 24. Priority.—Upon the request of a party to a custody proceeding which raises a question of existence or exercise of jurisdiction under this Act the case shall be given calendar priority and handled expeditiously.]

§ 25. Severability.—If any provision of this Act or the application thereof to any person or circumstance is held invalid, its invalidity does not affect other provisions or applications of the Act which can be given effect without the invalid provision or application, and to this end the provisions of this Act are several.

is responsible for periodically paying a specified amount to the custodial parent. The money is to be used for needs of the child such as food, shelter, clothing, and medical and educational expenses.

Unless the parties agree to an amount for support, a hearing will be held to determine the financial needs of the child based on information provided by the parties and the financial ability of the noncustodial parent to contribute toward the needs of the child. Using this information, the court will make a decision as to what an appropriate amount would be and how often the amount should be paid.[18] See Figure 14.4. It should be kept in mind also that in the case of a deceased parent, government benefits such as social security survivor's benefits may be available, as well, to minor children to aid in their support.

FIGURE 14.4 Child Support Guidelines

NEVADA REVISED STATUTES TITLE 11.
DOMESTIC RELATIONS. CHAPTER 125B.
OBLIGATION OF SUPPORT. GENERAL PROVISIONS

125B.070. Amount of payment: Definitions; review of formula by State Bar of Nevada.

1. As used in this section and NRS 125B.080, unless the context otherwise requires:

(a) "Gross monthly income" means the total amount of income from any source of a wage-earning employee or the gross income from any source of a self-employed person, after deduction of all legitimate business expenses, but without deduction for personal income taxes, contributions for retirement benefits, contributions to a pension or for any other personal expenses.

(b) "Obligation for support" means the amount determined according to the following schedule:

(1) For one child, 18 percent;

(2) For two children, 25 percent;

(3) For three children, 29 percent;

(4) For four children, 31 percent; and

(5) For each additional child, an additional 2 percent, of a parent's gross monthly income, but not more than $500 per month per child for an obligation for support determined pursuant to subparagraphs (1) to (4), inclusive, unless the court sets forth findings of fact as to the basis for a different amount pursuant to subsection 5 of NRS 125B.080.

2. On or before January 18, 1993, and on or before the third Monday in January every 4 years thereafter, the State Bar of Nevada shall review the formulas set forth in this section to determine whether any modifications are advisable and report to the legislature their findings and any proposed amendments.

125B.080. Formula for determining amount of support.

1. A court shall apply the appropriate formula set forth in paragraph (b) of subsection 1 of NRS 125B.070 to:

(a) Determine the required support in any case involving the support of children.

(b) Any request filed after July 1, 1987, to change the amount of the required support of children.

2. If the parties agree as to the amount of support required, the parties shall certify that the amount of support is consistent with the appropriate formula set forth in paragraph (b) of subsection 1 of NRS 125B.070. If the amount of support deviates from the formula, the parties must stipulate sufficient facts in accordance with subsection 9 which justify the deviation to the court, and the court shall make a written finding thereon. Any inaccuracy or falsification of financial information which results in an inappropriate award of support is grounds for a motion to modify or adjust the award.

3. If the parties disagree as to the amount of the gross monthly income of either party, the court shall determine the amount and may direct either party to furnish financial information or other records, including income tax returns for the preceding 3 years. Once a court has established an obligation for support by reference to a formula set forth in paragraph (b) of subsection 1 of NRS 125B.070, any subsequent modification or adjustment of that support must be based upon changed circumstances or as a result of a review conducted pursuant to NRS 125B.145.

4. Notwithstanding the formulas set forth in paragraph (b) of subsection 1 of NRS 125B.070, the minimum amount of support that may be awarded by a court in any case is $100 per month per child, unless the court makes a written finding that the obligor is unable to pay the minimum amount. Willful underemployment or unemployment is not a sufficient cause to deviate from the awarding of at least the minimum amount.

5. It is presumed that the basic needs of a child are met by the formulas set forth in paragraph (b) of subsection 1 of NRS 125B.070. This presumption may be rebutted by evidence proving that the needs of a particular child are not met by the applicable formula.

6. If the amount of the awarded support for a child is greater or less than the amount which would be established under the applicable formula, the court shall set forth findings of fact as to the basis for the deviation from the formula.

7. Expenses for health care which are not reimbursed, including expenses for medical, surgical, dental, orthodontic and optical expenses, must be borne equally by both parents in the absence of extraordinary circumstances.

8. If a parent who has an obligation for support is willfully underemployed or unemployed, to avoid an obligation for support of a child, that obligation must be based upon the parent's true potential earning capacity.

9. The court shall consider the following factors when adjusting the amount of support of a child upon specific findings of fact:

(a) The cost of health insurance;

(b) The cost of child care;

(c) Any special educational needs of the child;

(d) The age of the child;

(e) The responsibility of the parents for the support of others;

(f) The value of services contributed by either parent;

(g) Any public assistance paid to support the child;

(h) Any expenses reasonably related to the mother's pregnancy and confinement;

(i) The cost of transportation of the child to and from visitation if the custodial parent moved with the child from the jurisdiction of the court which ordered the support and the noncustodial parent remained;

(j) The amount of time the child spends with each parent;

(k) Any other necessary expenses for the benefit of the child; and

(l) The relative income of both parents.

a. Child Support Guidelines   When determining the amount of child support to order, the court considers many independent factors. Many states have guidelines that provide formulas for calculation or factors that should be considered including, but not limited to, the following:

- The number of children (of this marriage or others) for whom the parent is obligated to provide financial support
- Whether one of the parents provides necessary expenses through job benefits such as health insurance or daycare
- The net income of each parent
- Any special medical or educational needs of the child
- The standard of living the child would have enjoyed had the divorce not occurred

It is assumed that an equitable share is contributed by the custodial parent who physically provides the food, shelter, clothing, and attention to other needs of the child.

Historically, there was tremendous variance in the amounts awarded to the custodial parent for child support. The payment amount by the noncustodial parent was entirely within the discretion of the judge. Some courts tended to be lenient while others ordered a very large percentage of the noncustodial parent's income to be turned over for the support of the minor child. This discrepancy recently led to a wave of legislation in a majority of states that typically provides fairly rigid guidelines for judges to follow in determining a proper amount of support. Most often, a presumed percentage of the noncustodial parent's net income will be awarded based on the number of children. However, some discretion has been left to judges for cases involving special circumstances such as a custodial parent who is in a dramatically stronger financial position than the noncustodial parent, or a child with special needs. The guidelines and precise formulas used to determine child support amounts in the majority of cases have eliminated, to a very large degree, the inequity that previously existed when the issue was purely a matter of judicial discretion.

b. Modification of Support   Once support has been awarded, it is due and payable until the child reaches the age of majority or the court orders a change in the amount of support to be paid. If support is paid to a custodial parent for the care of more than one child, the amount is modified as each child reaches the age of majority. However, a common misconception is that the noncustodial parent may reduce the award by a percentage equal to that represented by the child in the total number of children. For example, if one of three children reaches majority, the support would be reduced by one third. In fact, this is not the case.

The base amount of support for a single child considers the essential elements of providing such things as food, shelter, and utilities as well as personal needs of the child such as clothing, school expenses, and so forth. Most statutory guidelines do not add an additional equal percentage for each additional child. Rather, a percentage of additional support is added to provide for the other child(ren)'s personal needs since the base amount has already been included in the initial calculation. Thus, when a child reaches majority, the amount of the reduction should be tied to the personal expenses of the child rather than the common items of expense for all of the children. If the parties cannot agree on an amount or even a change in the amount of support, then either or both can petition the court for an order of modification to legally change the required amount of support.

Modification of support may also be granted in circumstances other than that of a child reaching majority. Courts will periodically entertain petitions to modify support when there has been a substantial change in the general cost of supporting the child. If a divorce occurs when a child is very young, it may be necessary for the custodial parent to seek an increase in support at some time during the child's minority to accommodate inflation in the cost of living and additional expenses incurred on behalf of the child. As a child gets older, enters school, and becomes involved in activities, the cost of meeting the child's needs may increase significantly. On the other hand, in time the cost of child care services may decline or disappear entirely. Nevertheless, the increase in expenses is likely to exceed any decreases and as a result it may become necessary for the custodial parent to seek an upward modification of the original order of support.

Another issue to be considered is the financial status of the parents. This is something that may change dramatically over a longer period of time. If one parent meets with long-term financial difficulty or increased income, a downward or upward modification may be in order. For example, if the custodial parent enjoys tremendous financial gain, it may serve no purpose for the noncustodial parent to be required to continue contributing to the child's support, however, a relapse from this obligation for this circumstance is rare. The point is that many unforeseen circumstances could occur that would necessitate a change in the original order of support. Most states limit the frequency with which such changes may be made, though, and require that the circumstances that warrant such a change be substantial and long term.

Assignment 14.6

Examine the following situation and explain what facts you think the court would consider to be important in deciding this matter.

Quint and Ramey are divorced. They have joint custody of their two children and also share equal physical custody of the children. For this reason, neither parent sought child support. At the time of the divorce, both children were not yet of school age. Now, both are in private school with a current tuition cost of $3,000 per year, per child. Additionally, school uniforms for each child cost approximately $500 per year. Both children have been involved in organized soccer for the past four years at a cost of approximately $500 per child per year for uniforms, equipment, and fees. Both children also have taken music lessons weekly for the past four years at a cost of approximately $600 per child per year. To date, Quint has paid all of the above expenses. Quint's average annual expenditures have been well in excess of $8,000. Quint has filed a petition seeking an order for Ramey to pay one half of the amounts. Ramey takes the position that

> none of the activities are essential and that if Quint does not wish to pay for them, he can withdraw the children from the activities and place them in public school. Quint and Ramey have incomes that are roughly the same. There is no dispute that the costs of the items in question tax the limits of the standard of living of the parties. The primary issue is their necessity. All other expenses for the children such as health care, school supplies, and other routine matters have been split equally in the past.

c. When the Obligation to Pay Support Is Not Met   Despite the obvious administrative costs, the trend in recent years has been for the state governments to collect and make child support payments between parties. The reasons for this are numerous, but one common reason is to reduce the number of cases brought for nonpayment and to reduce the burden of legal expense on parties who are already disadvantaged by the corresponding party's failure to pay ordered support. In many jurisdictions, a common occurrence is an order of support that includes instruction to make payments directly to a government office who in turn forwards the funds to the custodial parent. In the past, many courts had to deal with arguments of the parties over what exactly was paid and whether the amounts were paid on time or late. By handling support in this way, arguments regarding how much was paid or not paid and when are eliminated. The amounts are recorded when received and disbursed. The obvious disadvantage, in addition to the added burden and expense for the government, is a delay in the time funds are paid by one party and received by the other. However, the courts and legislatures consider these concerns to be far outweighed by the decreased burden on the courts and on the parties who seek to have orders of support enforced.

Circumstances do arise that may justifiably prevent a party from paying the ordered amount of support. For example, if a party is injured and unable to work, or is terminated or suspended from employment, then the income used to pay the support is simply no longer there. However, in a case such as this, the party is under an obligation to notify the court as soon as possible of a change in circumstances and request a modification in the order of support. Any reduction or suspension in an obligation to pay support is usually made effective as of the date of the petition and not the date of the change in circumstances that affect the ability to pay. Therefore, it is in the payer's best interest not to delay. The failure to seek a modification and make timely payments may result in a finding of contempt of court by the court against the payor party.

If a party willfully fails to adhere to an order of support and does not seek a modification as soon as is reasonably possible after a change in circumstances, several things may take place. Usually, the first is a legal action by the custodial parent against the parent obligated to pay support. The action is generally a request to hold the noncustodial parent in contempt of court for deliberately disobeying a court order to provide support for the minor child. If the party is found to be in contempt, a variety of penalties may be imposed along with an order to pay all accumulated and owed support, as well as current payments. Penalties in the past included fines and occasionally jail time. However, both of these, while still used in some cases, interfered further with the ability to pay. As a result, there has been a trend to employ other types of penalties that have a strongly adverse effect on the payor. One common method is to suspend the driver's license of the noncompliant payor with permission only to drive to and from work. Other types of licenses may also be affected by the courts such as professional or business licenses. Most often penalties are assessed against those who are habitually late in payment despite an ability to pay ordered support.

In addition to penalties for failure to pay, there are a variety of additional repercussions associated with a finding of contempt in matters of child support nonpayment. One frequent occurrence is a wage garnishment. In this case, the employer of the payor may be informed that the payor has not made court ordered child support payments and the employer is ordered to withhold specified amounts from the income of the payor and to forward these amounts directly to either the court or the custodial parent. In addition to the negative light this casts on the payor in the eyes of the employer, it also generates increased paperwork for the employer, so most individuals do not want a garnishment of their wages if it can be avoided.

In extreme cases, usually where there has been ongoing contemptuous conduct, the penalties may be more severe. In some cases, a willful nonpayor may be sentenced to jail time either in a continuous sentence or one that is served in periodic increments. The latter is sometimes done in order to allow the payor to continue his or her employment and to produce income to pay accumulated and current support obligations. The payer serves the penalty of a jail sentence during time off work such as weekends.

Another common misconception among the general public is that support obligations and visitation privileges are somehow related issues. Many custodial parents have, in the past, withheld visitation by the noncustodial parent who failed to pay child support, only to find themselves as the one being held in contempt of court. A parent does not have the authority to deny visitation, and a court, in nearly all instances, will not deny visitation on the sole basis of a failure to pay child support. A custodial parent should never expect a court to approve of a deliberate denial of visitation rights based on a failure to pay support or for any other reason without an order of court. The right of visitation with one's children is highly protected by the courts. The view of the American legal system is that while a failure to pay support can certainly be injurious to the child, the denial of visitation between the child and the noncustodial parent for that reason could only cause additional damage and injury to the child, much more than it would serve as a deterrent to the parent who has failed to meet support obligations. The view of the courts is that a denial of visitation only increases the adversity that the child must deal with. If a court does deny visitation, it is for reasons other than nonpayment of support. Most often it occurs when there is a legal finding that the parent has abandoned all parental responsibility or has in some way endangered the child during visitation.

In the past, many actions to recover support were rendered virtually impossible because the noncustodial parent resided in another state. This made it very difficult for the court to exercise any control over the parent in terms of compelling payment of support. Further, the collection process for any court ordered support could be a very expensive proposition for the custodial parent. Not only would it be necessary to ob-

APPLICATION 14.5

Lee and Mark have been divorced for three years. They are very antagonistic toward one another and Mark frequently skips support payments to Lee or pays very late. At the current time, Mark is two months behind on payments and has informed Lee that unless she waives the owed support and agrees to a 30% reduction in future support, he will take the children out of state and seek custody in another jurisdiction. Mark also is frequently late bringing the children back from visitation by as much as a full day. Mark does not allow Lee to know the whereabouts of the children during periods of visitation and does not answer phone calls from Lee. On two occasions in the past three years Mark has taken the children out of town for a period of one week when visitation was to have been for a 48-hour weekend. Lee has never filed any action in court against Mark with respect to the past occurrences. Lee decides to withhold visitation entirely based on a fear that Mark will take the children and leave the jurisdiction permanently. Mark is a construction worker and often works on a cash basis. He has no permanent address and currently lives in a property rented on a month-to-month basis. After Lee withholds visitation on a Friday, Mark files a motion to have her held in contempt on the following Monday. Under the present circumstances, a court would probably not be very sympathetic to Lee despite Mark's prior conduct. The position of the court would most likely be that Lee should have come to the court on her own petition before withholding visitation. Lee might be able to file a counter motion for Mark's conduct, but it would not relieve Lee of responsibility for withholding visitation.

Point for Discussion: What could Lee have done if the threats were made on a Thursday and visitation was scheduled Friday?

tain an order in the jurisdiction where the child was domiciled, the custodial parent would then need to register the judgment in the jurisdiction where the noncustodial parent was domiciled. He or she would then take legal action to compel compliance, such as through a petition for contempt, and/or collection procedures, such as garnishment of wages. This often involved hiring legal counsel in both jurisdictions, travel, court costs, an so forth. Fortunately, all states have now adopted a uniform law known as the Uniform Reciprocal Enforcement of Support Act (URESA). This uniform law created a pact among all of the states to assist one another and their citizens in the enforcement of orders of child support. Each state government has created child support enforcement divisions within the offices of its prosecutors. Now, a custodial parent registers an order of support in the jurisdiction where the noncustodial parent resides. Failure to honor the order can be prosecuted as a contempt violation by the prosecutor in the jurisdiction and appropriate steps for collection may be taken. It is no longer necessary for the custodial parent to first file an action for contempt in the court where the order of support was issued, obtain an order finding the noncustodial parent in contempt, register that order with the jurisdiction where the noncustodial parent resides, and then attempt to force collection and enforcement of any ordered penalties. The system is not a perfect one. The child support enforcement offices of prosecutors are often overwhelmed with cases, and there may be a serious backlog. However, the option remains open to handle the matter pro se (on one's own behalf or through counsel), but for many who do not have the skills and/or funds to do this, URESA has provided relief where before there was none.

7. Visitation

When one parent is awarded custody of the child, the noncustodial parent is usually given specific visitation rights. In some cases, the rights are simply characterized in the final order as "reasonable" and it is left to the parties to define this term according to their own circumstances. However, this occurs less and less frequently as vague terms such as these all too often end up with the parties back in court when they are unable to agree on terms of visitation. It is much more practical as a rule to establish certain times, dates, and such for visitation even if they need to be modified from time to time as circumstances change.

Every parent is deemed to possess a constitutional right to share the companionship of his or her child.[19] This is highly protected by the courts and will not be abridged unless the parent is found to have legally abandoned the child or if the parent's conduct might endanger the child. Even then, courts will usually attempt some type of communication between parent and child and, when possible, actual visitation. Even parents with a history of abusive or illegal behavior, or even mental illness will often be granted limited visitation. Most often this includes visitation that is confined to a particular time and place and possibly with adequate supervision of a third-party adult. Only extreme situations usually result in a court's denial of visitation for a period of time or ultimate termination of parental rights, because the only right paramount to that of a parent to share companionship is the ultimate welfare of the child.

Many states have statutory guidelines that judges attempt to follow so that each parent is ensured adequate time and opportunity to share special holidays and other occasions with the child. It must be understood that a visitation schedule sets forth the minimum rights of the noncustodial parent. If the two parents jointly agree to additional or different times for visitation, this is entirely appropriate. If problems arise, however, the court will generally not enforce such agreements but will usually follow only the scheduled visitation plan.

When a custodial parent interferes with the scheduled visitation for any reason the view of the court is not a positive one. Penalties may result in cases where a visitation schedule is set forth in a court order but the custodial parent does not permit or in some way interferes with the time between the child(ren) and the noncustodial parent. Common complaints when the noncustodial parent files a petition to have the custodial parent held in contempt include such things as refusing visitation, not having the children available for visitation, either physical or by permitted phone calls, e-mail, and so forth; directly influencing the children to avoid visitation or to have a negative attitude toward the noncustodial parent, or engaging in any other conduct that interferes with the noncustodial parent's constitutional right to share companionship and develop a relationship with the child(ren).

Often the custodial parent will respond to such petitions with a myriad of reasons to justify the behavior. However, this is one instance in which, aside from fabrication of facts by the noncustodial parent in support of the petition, the court is likely to have very limited patience. The position of the courts is that they and only they have the authority to change terms of visitation by any method and if there are circumstances that warrant such a change, it is the obligation of the custodial parent to seek a modification of the existing order of visitation and not to take it upon themselves to make such determinations unilaterally. If a custodial parent interferes with visitation rights that have been previously awarded by a court, the noncustodial parent or party who is entitled to visitation may bring an action for contempt of court. The allegation is generally that the custodial parent willfully ignored or interfered with a court order of visitation. A court is not likely to be tolerant of this kind of behavior and frequently penalties are assessed when it is proven. Penalties range from monetary fines to jail sentences. In continuing and extreme cases, the court may even view the conduct as so adverse to the best interests of the child as to order a change of custody.

Prior to this point, the focus of the discussion has been on custody and visitation between the parents and the children. However, in the latter half of the 20th century, a strong trend developed to consider all of those present in the life of a child who have a vested interest in the child and from whose presence the child may benefit. As a result, a movement through the courts and ultimately through the legislatures has resulted in new legal standards that permit a court to recognize and award visitation to individuals who are nonparents but with whom the child has a special bond. Most often these include grandparents, however anyone who can establish a strong bond with the child can petition the court for visitation. Many states now have statutes in place that recognize the rights of grandparents to visit with grandchildren despite objections of the parents for whatever reason. Short of circumstances that endanger the child, most courts are of the view that the presence of a grandparent in a child's life is a positive experience and in the child's ultimate best interest. However, in June 2000, the U.S. Supreme Court considered such statutes and set down more clearly the limits for visitation by nonparents against objections of the custodial parents.

CASE IN POINT

Troxel v. Granville, 530 U.S. 57, 120 S. Ct. 2054, 147 L.E.2d. 49 (2000)

I.

Tommie Granville and Brad Troxel shared a relationship that ended in June 1991. The two never married, but they had two daughters, Isabelle and Natalie. Jenifer and Gary Troxel are Brad's parents, and thus the paternal grandparents of Isabelle and Natalie. After Tommie and Brad separated in 1991, Brad lived with his parents and regularly brought his daughters to his parents' home for weekend visitation. Brad committed suicide in May 1993. Although the Troxels at first continued to see Isabelle and Natalie on a regular basis after their son's death, Tommie Granville informed the Troxels in October 1993 that she wished to limit their visitation with her daughters to one short visit per month.

In December 1993, the Troxels commenced the present action by filing, in the Washington Superior Court for Skagit County, a petition to obtain visitation rights with Isabelle and Natalie. The Troxels filed their petition under two Washington statutes, Wash. Rev.Code §§ 26.09.240 and 26.10.160(3) (1994). Only the latter statute is at issue in this case. Section 26.10.160(3) provides: "Any person may petition the court for visitation rights at any time including, but not limited to, custody proceedings. The court may order visitation rights for any person when visitation may serve the best interest of the child whether or not there has been any change of circumstances." At trial, the Troxels requested two weekends of overnight visitation per month and two weeks of visitation each summer. Granville did not oppose visitation altogether, but instead asked the court to order one day of visitation per month with no overnight stay. 87 Wash.App., at 133–134, 940 P.2d, at 699. In 1995, the Superior Court issued an oral ruling and entered a visitation decree ordering visitation one weekend per month, one week during the summer, and four hours on both of the petitioning grandparents' birthdays. 137 Wash.2d, at 6, 969 P.2d, at 23, App. to Pet. for Cert. 76a–78a.

Granville appealed, during which time she married Kelly Wynn. Before addressing the merits of Granville's appeal, the Washington Court of Appeals remanded the case to the Superior Court for entry of written findings of fact and conclusions of law. 137 Wash.2d, at 6, 969 P.2d, at 23. On remand, the Superior Court found that visitation was in Isabelle and Natalie's best interests:

"The Petitioners [the Troxels] are part of a large, central, loving family, all located in this area, and the Petitioners can provide opportunities for the children in the areas of cousins and music.

". . . The court took into consideration all factors regarding the best interest of the children and considered all the testimony before it. The children would be benefitted from spending quality time with the Petitioners, provided that that time is balanced with time with the childrens' [sic] nuclear family. The court finds that the childrens' [sic] best interests are served by spending time with their mother and stepfather's other six children." App. 70a.

Approximately nine months after the Superior Court entered its order on remand, Granville's husband formally adopted Isabelle and Natalie. Id., at 60a–67a.

The Washington Court of Appeals reversed the lower court's visitation order and dismissed the Troxels' petition for visitation, holding that nonparents lack standing to seek visitation under § 26.10.160(3) unless a custody action is pending.

The Washington Supreme Court granted the Troxels' petition for review and, after consolidating their case with two other visitation cases, affirmed. The court disagreed with the Court of Appeals' decision on the statutory issue and found that the plain language of § 26.10.160(3) gave the Troxels standing to seek visitation, irrespective of whether a custody action was pending. 137 Wash.2d, at 12, 969 P.2d, at 26–27. The Washington Supreme Court nevertheless agreed with the Court of Appeals' ultimate conclusion that the Troxels could not obtain visitation of Isabelle and Natalie pursuant to § 26.10.160(3). The court rested its decision on the Federal Constitution, holding that § 26.10.160(3) unconstitutionally infringes on the fundamental right of parents to rear their children. In the court's view, there were at least two problems with the

nonparental visitation statute. First, according to the Washington Supreme Court, the Constitution permits a State to interfere with the right of parents to rear their children only to prevent harm or potential harm to a child. Section 26.10.160(3) fails that standard because it requires no threshold showing of harm. Id., at 15–20, 969 P.2d, at 28–30. Second, by allowing " 'any person' to petition for forced visitation of a child at 'any time' with the only requirement being that the visitation serve the best interest of the child," the Washington visitation statute sweeps too broadly. Id., at 20, 969 P.2d, at 30. "It is not within the province of the state to make significant decisions concerning the custody of children merely because it could make a 'better' decision." Ibid., 969 P.2d, at 31. The Washington Supreme Court held that "[p]arents have a right to limit visitation of their children with third persons," and that between parents and judges, "the parents should be the ones to choose whether to expose their children to certain people or ideas." Id., at 21, 969 P.2d, at 31. Four justices dissented from the Washington Supreme Court's holding on the constitutionality of the statute. Id., at 23–43, 969 P.2d 21, 969 P.2d, at 32–42.

We granted certiorari, 527 U.S. 1069, 120 S.Ct. 11, 144 L.Ed.2d 842 (1999), and now affirm the judgment.

II.

The demographic changes of the past century make it difficult to speak of an average American family. The composition of families varies greatly from household to household. While many children may have two married parents and grandparents who visit regularly, many other children are raised in single-parent households. In 1996, children living with only one parent accounted for 28 percent of all children under age 18 in the United States. U.S. Dept. of Commerce, Bureau of Census, Current Population Reports, 1997 Population Profile of the United States 27 (1998). Understandably, in these single-parent households, persons outside the nuclear family are called upon with increasing frequency to assist in the everyday tasks of child rearing. In many cases, grandparents play an important role. For example, in 1998, approximately 4 million children—or 5.6 percent of all children under age 18—lived in the household of their grandparents. U.S. Dept. of Commerce, Bureau of Census, Current Population Reports, Marital Status and Living Arrangements: March 1998 (Update), p. i (1998).

The nationwide enactment of nonparental visitation statutes is assuredly due, in some part, to the

States' recognition of these changing realities of the American family. Because grandparents and other relatives undertake duties of a parental nature in many households, States have sought to ensure the welfare of the children therein by protecting the relationships those children form with such third parties. The States' nonparental visitation statutes are further supported by a recognition, which varies from State to State, that children should have the opportunity to benefit from relationships with statutorily specified persons—for example, their grandparents. The extension of statutory rights in this area to persons other than a child's parents, however, comes with an obvious cost. For example, the State's recognition of an independent third-party interest in a child can place a substantial burden on the traditional parent-child relationship. Contrary to Justice STEVENS' accusation, our description of state nonparental visitation statutes in these terms, of course, is not meant to suggest that "children are so much chattel." Post, at —, 10 (dissenting opinion). Rather, our terminology is intended to highlight the fact that these statutes can present questions of constitutional import. In this case, we are presented with just such a question. Specifically, we are asked to decide whether § 26.10.160(3), as applied to Tommie Granville and her family, violates the Federal Constitution.

The Fourteenth Amendment provides that no State shall "deprive any person of life, liberty, or property, without due process of law." We have long recognized that the Amendment's Due Process Clause, like its Fifth Amendment counterpart, "guarantees more than fair process." Washington v. Glucksberg, 521 U.S. 702, 719, 117 S.Ct. 2258 (1997). The Clause also includes a substantive component that "provides heightened protection against government interference with certain fundamental rights and liberty interests." Id., at 720, 117 S.Ct. 2258; see also Reno v. Flores, 507 U.S. 292, 301–302, 113 S.Ct. 1439, 123 L.Ed.2d 1 (1993).

The liberty interest at issue in this case—the interest of parents in the care, custody, and control of their children—is perhaps the oldest of the fundamental liberty interests recognized by this Court. More than 75 years ago, in Meyer v. Nebraska, 262 U.S. 390, 399, 401, 43 S.Ct. 625, 67 L.Ed. 1042 (1923), we held that the "liberty" protected by the Due Process Clause includes the right of parents to "establish a home and bring up children" and "to control the education of their own." Two years later, in Pierce v. Society of Sisters, 268 U.S. 510, 534–535, 45 S.Ct. 571, 69 L.Ed. 1070 (1925), we again held that the "liberty of parents and guardians" includes the right "to direct the upbringing and education of children under their control." We explained in Pierce that "[t]he child is not the mere creature of the State; those who nurture him and direct his destiny have the right, coupled with the high duty, to recognize and prepare him for additional obligations." Id., at 535, 45 S.Ct. 571. We returned to the subject in Prince v. Massachusetts, 321 U.S. 158, 64 S.Ct. 438, 88 L.Ed. 645 (1944), and again confirmed that there is a constitutional dimension to the right of parents to direct the upbringing of their children. "It is cardinal with us that the custody, care and nurture of the child reside first in the parents, whose primary function and freedom include preparation for obligations the state can neither supply nor hinder." Id., at 166, 64 S.Ct. 438.

In subsequent cases also, we have recognized the fundamental right of parents to make decisions concerning the care, custody, and control of their children. See, e.g., Stanley v. Illinois, 405 U.S. 645, 651, 92 S.Ct. 1208, 31 L.Ed.2d 551 (1972) ("It is plain that the interest of a parent in the companionship, care, custody, and management of his or her children 'come[s] to this Court with a momentum for respect lacking when appeal is made to liberties which derive merely from shifting economic arrangements'" (citation omitted)); Wisconsin v. Yoder, 406 U.S. 205, 232, 92 S.Ct. 1526, 32 L.Ed.2d 15 (1972) ("The history and culture of Western civilization reflect a strong tradition of parental concern for the nurture and upbringing of their children. This primary role of the parents in the upbringing of their children is now established beyond debate as an enduring American tradition"); Quilloin v. Walcott, 434 U.S. 246, 255, 98 S.Ct. 549, 54 L.Ed.2d 511 (1978) ("We have recognized on numerous occasions that the relationship between parent and child is constitutionally protected"); Parham v. J. R., 442 U.S. 584, 602, 99 S.Ct. 2493, 61 L.Ed.2d 101 (1979) ("Our jurisprudence historically has reflected Western civilization concepts of the family as a unit with broad parental authority over minor children. Our cases have consistently followed that course"); Santosky v. Kramer, 455 U.S. 745, 753, 102 S.Ct. 1388, 71 L.Ed.2d 599 (1982) (discussing "[t]he fundamental liberty interest of natural parents in the care, custody, and management of their child"); Glucksberg, supra, at 720, 117 S.Ct. 2258 ("In a long line of cases, we have held that, in addition to the specific freedoms protected by the Bill of Rights, the 'liberty' specially protected by the Due Process Clause includes the righ[t] . . . to direct the education and up-bringing of one's children" (citing Meyer and Pierce)). In light of this extensive precedent, it cannot now be doubted that the Due Process Clause of the Fourteenth Amendment protects the fundamental right of parents to make decisions concerning the care, custody, and control of their children.

Section 26.10.160(3), as applied to Granville and her family in this case, unconstitutionally infringes on that fundamental parental right. The Washington non-parental visitation statute is breathtakingly broad. According to the statute's text, "[a]ny person may petition the court for visitation rights at any time," and the court may grant such visitation rights whenever "visitation may serve the best interest of the child." § 26.10.160(3) (emphases added). That language effectively permits any third party seeking visitation to subject any decision by a parent concerning visitation of the parent's children to state-court review. Once the visitation petition has been filed in court and the matter is placed before a judge, a parent's decision that visitation would not be in the child's best interest is accorded no deference. Section 26.10.160(3) contains no requirement that a court accord the parent's decision any presumption of validity or any weight whatsoever. Instead, the Washington statute places the best-interest determination solely in the hands of the judge. Should the judge disagree with the parent's estimation of the child's best interests, the judge's view necessarily prevails. Thus, in practical effect, in the State of Washington a court can disregard and overturn any decision by a fit custodial parent concerning visitation whenever a third party affected by the decision files a visitation petition, based solely on the judge's determination of the child's best interests. The Washington Supreme Court had the opportunity to give § 26.10.160(3) a narrower reading, but it declined to do so. See, e.g., 137 Wash.2d, at 5, 969 P.2d, at 23 ("[The statute] allow[s] any person, at any time, to petition for visitation without regard to relationship to the child, without regard to changed circumstances, and without regard to harm"); id., at 20, 969 P.2d, at 30 ("[The statute] allow[s] 'any person' to petition for forced visitation of a child at 'any time' with the only requirement being that the visitation serve the best interest of the child").

Turning to the facts of this case, the record reveals that the Superior Court's order was based on precisely the type of mere disagreement we have just described and nothing more. The Superior Court's order was not founded on any special factors that might justify the State's interference with Granville's fundamental right to make decisions concerning the rearing of her two daughters. To be sure, this case involves a visitation petition filed by grandparents soon after the death of their son—the father of Isabelle and Natalie—but the combination of several factors here compels our conclusion that § 26.10.160(3), as applied, exceeded the bounds of the Due Process Clause.

First, the Troxels did not allege, and no court has found, that Granville was an unfit parent. That aspect of the case is important, for there is a presumption that fit parents act in the best interests of their children. As this Court explained in Parham:

"[O]ur constitutional system long ago rejected any notion that a child is the mere creature of the State and, on the contrary, asserted that parents generally have the right, coupled with the high duty, to recognize and prepare [their children] for additional obligations. . . . The law's concept of the family rests on a presumption that parents possess what a child lacks in maturity, experience, and capacity for judgment required for making life's difficult decisions. More important, historically it has recognized that natural bonds of affection lead parents to act in the best interests of their children." 442 U.S., at 602, 99 S.Ct. 2493 (alteration in original) (internal quotation marks and citations omitted).

Accordingly, so long as a parent adequately cares for his or her children (i.e., is fit), there will normally be no reason for the State to inject itself into the private realm of the family to further question the ability of that parent to make the best decisions concerning the rearing of that parent's children. See, e.g., Flores, 507 U.S., at 304, 113 S.Ct. 1439.

The problem here is not that the Washington Superior Court intervened, but that when it did so, it gave no special weight at all to Granville's determination of her daughters' best interests. More importantly, it appears that the Superior Court applied exactly the opposite presumption. In reciting its oral ruling after the conclusion of closing arguments, the Superior Court judge explained:

"The burden is to show that it is in the best interest of the children to have some visitation and some quality time with their grandparents. I think in most situations a commonsensical approach [is that] it is normally in the best interest of the children to spend quality time with the grandparent, unless the grandparent, [sic] there are some issues or problems involved wherein the grandparents, their lifestyles are going to impact adversely upon the children. That certainly isn't the case here from what I can tell." Verbatim Report of Proceedings in In re Troxel, No. 93-3-00650-7 (Wash.Super.Ct., Dec. 14, 19, 1994), p. 213 (hereinafter Verbatim Report).

The judge's comments suggest that he presumed the grandparents' request should be granted unless the children would be "impact[ed] adversely." In effect, the judge placed on Granville, the fit custodial parent, the burden of disproving that visitation would be in the best interest of her daughters. The judge reiterated moments later. "I think [visitation with the Troxels] would be in the best interest of the children and I haven't been shown it is not in [the] best interest of the children." Id., at 214, 113 S.Ct. 1439.

The decisional framework employed by the Superior Court directly contravened the traditional presumption that a fit parent will act in the best interest of his or her child. See Parham, supra, at 602, 99 S.Ct. 2493. In that respect, the court's presumption failed to provide any protection for Granville's fundamental constitutional right to make decisions concerning the rearing of her own daughters. Cf., e.g., Cal. Fam. Code Ann. § 3104(e) (West 1994) (rebuttable presumption that grandparent visitation is not in child's best interest if parents agree that visitation rights should not be granted); Me.Rev.Stat. Ann., Tit. 19A, § 1803(3) (1998) (court may award grandparent visitation if in best interest of child and "would not significantly interfere with any parent-child relationship or with the parent's rightful authority over the child"); Minn.Stat. § 257.022(2)(a)(2) (1998) (court may award grandparent visitation if in best interest of child and "such visitation would not interfere with the parent-child relationship"); Neb.Rev.Stat. § 43-1802(2) (1998) (court must find "by clear and convincing evidence" that grandparent visitation "will not adversely interfere with the parent-child relationship"); R.I. Gen. Laws § 15-5-24.3(a)(2)(v) (Supp.1999) (grandparent must rebut, by clear and convincing evidence, presumption that parent's decision to refuse grandparent visitation was reasonable); Utah Code Ann. § 30-5-2(2)(e) (1998) (same); Hoff v. Berg, 595 N.W.2d 285, 291-292 (N.D.1999) (holding North Dakota grandparent visitation statute unconstitutional because State has no "compelling interest in presuming visitation rights of grandparents to an unmarried minor are in the child's best interests and forcing parents to accede to court-ordered grand-

parental visitation unless the parents are first able to prove such visitation is not in the best interests of their minor child"). In an ideal world, parents might always seek to cultivate the bonds between grandparents and their grandchildren. Needless to say, however, our world is far from perfect, and in it the decision whether such an intergenerational relationship would be beneficial in any specific case is for the parent to make in the first instance. And, if a fit parent's decision of the kind at issue here becomes subject to judicial review, the court must accord at least some special weight to the parent's own determination.

Finally, we note that there is no allegation that Granville ever sought to cut off visitation entirely. Rather, the present dispute originated when Granville informed the Troxels that she would prefer to restrict their visitation with Isabelle and Natalie to one short visit per month and special holidays. See 87 Wash.App., at 133, 940 P.2d, at 699; Verbatim Report 12. In the Superior Court proceedings Granville did not oppose visitation but instead asked that the duration of any visitation order be shorter than that requested by the Troxels. While the Troxels requested two weekends per month and two full weeks in the summer, Granville asked the Superior Court to order only one day of visitation per month (with no overnight stay) and participation in the Granville family's holiday celebrations. See 87 Wash.App., at 133, 940 P.2d, at 699; Verbatim Report 9 ("Right off the bat we'd like to say that our position is that grandparent visitation is in the best interest of the children. It is a matter of how much and how it is going to be structured") (opening statement by Granville's attorney). The Superior Court gave no weight to Granville's having assented to visitation even before the filing of any visitation petition or subsequent court intervention. The court instead rejected Granville's proposal and settled on a middle ground, ordering one weekend of visitation per month, one week in the summer, and time on both of the petitioning grandparents' birthdays. See 87 Wash.App., at 133-134, 940 P.2d, at 699; Verbatim Report 216-221. Significantly, many other States expressly provide by statute that courts may not award visitation unless a parent has denied (or unreasonably denied) visitation to the concerned third party. See, e.g., Miss.Code Ann. § 93-16-3(2)(a) (1994) (court must find that "the parent or custodian of the child unreasonably denied the grandparent visitation rights with the child"); Ore.Rev.Stat. § 109.121(1)(a)(B) (1997) (court may award visitation if the "custodian of the child has denied the grandparent reasonable opportunity to visit the child"); R.I. Gen. Laws § 15-5-24.3(a)(2)(iii)-(iv) (Supp.1999) (court must find that parents prevented grandparent from visiting grandchild and that "there is no other way the petitioner is able to visit his or her grandchild without court intervention").

Considered together with the Superior Court's reasons for awarding visitation to the Troxels, the combination of these factors demonstrates that the visitation order in this case was an unconstitutional infringement on Granville's fundamental right to make decisions concerning the care, custody, and control of her two daughters. The Washington Superior Court failed to accord the determination of Granville, a fit custodial parent, any material weight. In fact, the Superior Court made only two formal findings in support of its visitation order. First, the Troxels "are part of a large, central, loving family, all located in this area, and the [Troxels] can provide opportunities for the children in the areas of cousins and music." App. 70a. Second, "[t]he children would be benefitted from spending quality time with the [Troxels], provided that that time is balanced with time with the childrens' [sic] nuclear family." Ibid. These slender findings, in combination with the court's announced presumption in favor of grandparent visitation and its failure to accord significant weight to Granville's already having offered meaningful visitation to the Troxels, show that this case involves nothing more than a simple disagreement between the Washington Superior Court and Granville concerning her children's best interests. The Superior Court's announced reason for ordering one week of visitation in the summer demonstrates our conclusion well: "I look back on some personal experiences.... We always spen[t] as kids a week with one set of grandparents and another set of grandparents, [and] it happened to work out in our family that [it] turned out to be an enjoyable experience. Maybe that can, in this family, if that is how it works out." Verbatim Report 220-221. As we have explained, the Due Process Clause does not permit a State to infringe on the fundamental right of parents to make childrearing decisions simply because a state judge believes a "better" decision could be made. Neither the Washington nonparental visitation statute generally—which places no limits on either the persons who maypetition for visitation or the circumstances in which such a petition may be granted—nor the Superior Court in this specific case required anything more. Accordingly, we hold that § 26.10.160(3), as applied in this case, is unconstitutional.[20]

Case Review Question: Would the grandparents have a stronger case if the mother denied all contact with the children?

8. Property and Debt Division

Property Settlement
Agreement as to the property rights and obligations of coowners and co-debtors, such as parties to a marriage.

The various states follow two schools of thought with respect to **property settlement** in the case of a dissolution of marriage. Some states are considered to be "separate property" jurisdictions while others are "community property" states. The theory a state follows will dictate the rights of the parties seeking a divorce. The position of a particular jurisdiction may have radically different results than if the dissolution were obtained in a jurisdiction of a different legal standard. In this particular area, there is the potential for great diversity in how the same case would be approached in different states.

Ordinarily, items such as clothing and other personal effects are considered individual property regardless of when they were acquired. Other examples of individually owned property would be personal items received as gifts, even from the other spouse, such as jewelry. However, the less personal the nature of the item, the more likely it is to be considered in a distribution of marital property.

a. Separate Property   Separate property states take the position that all property individually owned prior to the marriage is individual property and not jointly owned marital property.[21] In addition, property acquired during the marriage through gift, inheritance, or personal earnings without contribution by the other spouse is individually owned property. In a divorce action, parties are awarded their individual property, and the court then determines how marital property should be equitably distributed.

In a total application of the separate property theory, a nonemployed spouse may be entitled to virtually nothing at the conclusion of the divorce. Realistically in most situations this would be considered an unfair result assuming that aside from a lack of financial contribution, the nonworking spouse would have contributed to the marital relationship in other ways such as maintenance of the marital residence, meal preparation, and other activities that provided the working spouse with greater opportunity to pursue financial endeavors. Because of the inherent unfairness in the pure application, many courts have modified the separate property rule to result in a more equitable application. While a state may still adhere to the theory of separate property, the court has the additional duty to make a fair distribution of property obtained during the marriage. Even though such property may have been purchased with the sole earnings of the working spouse, the nonfinancial contributions are also considered to have value and thus the acquired property is considered to be the result of a joint effort. In this way the court can more fairly consider certain property to be marital and make a more appropriate distribution.

b. Community Property   Community property jurisdictions have a very different approach to the disposition of the property of spouses. In these states, all property acquired during the marriage through personal earnings is presumed to be marital and joint property irrespective of who earned the funds with which it was purchased.[22] Also included in marital property is any property individually owned before the marriage that the party subsequently contributed to the joint use of the parties in the marriage. Unless a party can establish that certain property owned prior to the marriage was never commingled or otherwise shared and never benefited the other spouse as marital property would, the property is considered to be community property and subject to an equal claim by the other spouse. Usually property inherited or received by gift as a personal and specific bequest or given to a particular party will be considered separate, unless of course, it is subsequently contributed to the marital relationship.

After the court has determined what, if any, separate property exists, the next step is to equitably divide the community property. The contribution toward the marital relationship by each party is considered and based on that the court attempts a fair distribution. Ordinarily, the proper distribution is considered to be in equal shares. However, in compelling circumstances a court may use its discretion to make a significantly unbalanced distribution of the parties assets. For example, if one party left the marital residence for a very long period of time prior to the divorce and the party who remained made significant improvements to the residence greatly increasing its value, a court may consider the latter party to be entitled to a greater percentage of the owned equity in the residence.

c. Pensions and Employee Benefit Programs   This area of law has become highly specialized and very complicated in recent years. Complex retirement and benefit plans are largely a product of the latter 20th century. Such plans were developing at about the same time that dissolution of marriage become more commonplace. When the parties are married for a relatively short period of time, this subject may not be a significant issue. However, what about parties who are married for many years with one spouse unemployed during the primary earning years to care for the home and family and the other party pursuing a career? It would be unfair to allow the party who has been employed to retain the entirety of accumulated retirement benefits, while the party who also contributed to the marriage is left with none and limited ability to obtain them. Consequently, during the last half of the 20th century more and more attention was given to the valuation and award of percentages of future retirement benefits among married parties who divorced. Ultimately, federal and state statutes were passed to assist attorneys and individuals in sorting out the complexities of retirement benefits in a dissolution proceeding. Because retirement plans vary widely in the way they are structured, and because they are subject to a variety of other laws as well, it is important to obtain competent counsel when attempting to reach an agreement on how the benefits should be apportioned and distributed.

Part of the difficulty with the assignment of retirement benefits is that often the dissolution of marriage occurs years, even decades, before the benefits mature and are received by the parties. Also, it is difficult to determine what an equitable share of an earned pension or benefit program in the future would be, since the working spouse has not yet fully contributed, and it is ordinarily assumed that the spouse's future contributions are not subject to claims by a former spouse. For example, a spouse accumulates retirement benefits from a job during 10 years of marriage, at which point there is a divorce. The working spouse continues to accumulate benefits for an additional 25 years. Because the parties are no longer married, it would not be considered fair for the former spouse to have a claim on benefits accumulated during the entire 25 years. Thus, the court must determine what the value of 10 years of 35 years of accumulated benefits will be at retirement. This must be apportioned and the former spouse's share assigned. A final problem with this is that, in this respect at least, the parties remain somewhat bound to each other even through retirement. This becomes a problem when a party wants to take early retirement, borrow against retirement benefits, or do anything else that affects the future rights of the former spouse. Many courts prefer to make a valuation of each party's interests and, whenever possible, have one party buy out the other party's interest at the time of the dissolution. In this way, the parties' ties to each other can be completely and permanently severed, thus lessening the possibilities for future legal disputes.

It should be noted that to establish division of pension and retirement funds in a way that will be recognized by the Internal Revenue Service, a Qualified Domestic Relations Order (QDRO) must be issued in addition to any other legal documents associated with the dissolution, such as the decree and property settlement. This is pursuant to federal law and is required any time there is a court order in a dissolution action that affects retirement benefits.

d. Marital Debts   The manner in which individual and marital debts are determined and distributed is substantially the same as with property. The same tests are applied to determine whether debts were incurred as part of the marital relationship or on behalf of the individual. Similarly, the courts attempt an equitable distribution of responsibility of such debts. However, debts incurred during a marriage have an additional aspect that property usually does not—the claims of third parties.

While parties may agree—or a court may determine—that certain debts are individual rather than marital, this is not typically binding on the third party, who is the creditor. If a debt is incurred during the marriage, most creditors are able to rely on payment from either or both parties as it is presumed to be joint in most circumstances. For example, as long as the parties are joint owners of a credit card, any property purchased with the credit card is a joint debt. Even if a debt is taken on individually, if it is done during the marriage, there is a presumption that the debt benefited both parties. It is possible to stop joint liability from accruing further if the parties are in the process of a dissolution and one party notifies creditors that he or she will no longer be responsible for any further debts incurred by the other party. This places the creditors on notice and gives them the fair opportunity to reevaluate the extension of credit to one party as opposed to the previous two.

Another facet of this problem arises when the divorce is final and responsibility for debt has been distributed equitably between the two spouses. If one spouse fails to honor the responsibility, the third party can claim and collect the debt from the other spouse. Although this may appear unfair at first, it should be remembered that the creditor was not involved in the distribution of marital debts. However, that creditor was involved in the extension of credit and stands to lose through no fault of its own if one party fails to pay and the other is relieved of the joint liability that was assumed at the time credit was extended.

An area in which legislation has been enacted to offer relief to individuals who are held accountable for the debts and other financial responsibilities of his or her former spouse is the area of tax law. In recent years new legal standards have been put in place to allow former spouses to seek relief when they can establish that they were wholly innocent and unaware, despite reasonable vigilance, with respect to tax debts. This is commonly known as the *innocent spouse* rule. The rationale is that often a tax debt is not even discovered until well after the parties are divorced, but penalties and interest accumulate from the date of the debt. If a spouse establishes that the other spouse incurred the debt knowingly and withheld the information from him or her, the individual may have an opportunity to avoid liability for the debt. However, it should be noted that the cases in which this relief is offered are quite limited and if the tax return filed was joint, there is an obligation on each spouse to fully understand the return and associated tax liability before signing and submitting it.

APPLICATION 14.6

Yani and Zoe divorce. At the time of the dissolution, there is a hospital bill of almost $2,000 resulting from the birth of their child. Yani is assigned responsibility for that particular debt. Yani fails to make payment and the hospital attempts to collect from Zoe. Zoe refuses, claiming that Yani is the party responsible according to a court-ordered division of assets and debts. The hospital files an action against Zoe for collection. More than likely, Zoe would be held accountable for the debt since the hospital was a third party and did not have a voice in the divorce decree. However, the hospital did extend credit for its services to the parties jointly at the time their child was born. Zoe may have the option then of filing a contempt proceeding against Yani for failure to honor the terms of the decree.

Point for Discussion: Why are creditors not notified of the terms of a decree when it is issued and then confined to collection from the party assigned to pay the debt?

---

9. Maintenance (Alimony or Spousal Support)

Lifetime awards of maintenance or spousal support (formerly called alimony) are becoming an increasingly rare occurrence. In fact, if maintenance is awarded at all today, it is most often for a distinct period of time and purpose. The reasons are numerous. In the past, the majority of jurisdictions were separate property states. In pure applications, the wife often did not receive a significant share of marital assets of value. Also, traditionally one spouse did not work outside the home, relying instead on the income produced by the working spouse as the sole source of income. Today, all states whether they are community property or separate property states, attempt to provide a more fair distribution of assets. In addition, women now actively participate in the work force, pursue the same types of educational goals, and have greater opportunities than ever before to become self-sufficient in the production of income.

At present, a court might award maintenance to a spouse who is unable to secure employment sufficient to meet reasonable necessary expenses, until such reasonable time as the spouse's circumstances change. Another situation might be if child care by one other than a parent would be inappropriate due to the cost of such care versus the amount of income the parent would be able to produce if child care were provided, or other special circumstances relating to a child.[23] For example, if a spouse has never had gainful employment or has been absent from the workforce for an extended period, the court may award maintenance while the spouse trains for a type of employment that would enable him or her to meet his or her own living expenses. Another example might be if a child has special needs and cannot be placed in a routine day care setting and the cost of specialized care would exceed the income that could be earned by the parent if he or she returned to the workforce. Also, some children's needs are so specific, such as a child with severe behavioral disorders, that the most appropriate person to render care for the child is a parent. In that circumstance a parent may have developed skills unique to the management of that child's care that would be very difficult and expensive to replace.

As the examples suggest, the trend of the courts is to award maintenance only in compelling circumstances. Although many situations are not as clearly defined as those described, often a spouse requires some form of assistance before he or she can be restored to an independent earning capacity. For example, many spouses who are away from the workforce can reenter the employment arena by updating skills or receiving new training or education. Or the parties may have several very young children who will be entering school in the relatively near future. In such situations, short term maintenance would be appropriate. The court may award maintenance for a specified period of time to supplement the income of the other spouse.

Today, the goal of the court is to give a spouse sufficient time and resources to prepare for financial independence. Thus, the spouse required to pay maintenance is not burdened with lifetime support of a former spouse, as in the past, and the spouse receiving maintenance will not be suddenly thrust into the world unequipped to provide for such basic expenses as food and shelter. Maintenance is awarded on a case-by-case basis and almost always for a fixed period of time that is deemed reasonably sufficient to enable the receiving spouse to achieve financial independence.

The amount and duration of maintenance are generally left to the discretion of the court, which will consider such factors as the earning power and the reasonable needs of each party. Also considered is the amount of time needed to prepare the spouse who is receiving maintenance to successfully return to the work force.[24] If the age and education level of the spouse prevents a likely return to financial independence, permanent maintenance may be considered. The same is true when the parties have an incapacitated child, regardless of age, for whom the parties expect to be responsible indefinitely.

If either party dies, maintenance automatically terminates. If the intent is that the receiving party should continue to be entitled in the event of the death of the payor, it should be so stipulated in the court order approving maintenance.

If the financial status of either party changes significantly during the period of maintenance payments, a modification may be requested. A formal petition must be filed with the court setting forth the reasons that would justify adjustment of the maintenance order with any request for modification. It is then within the discretion of the court to determine whether the modification is warranted. Significant changes in circumstances include a substantial decrease in the earning power of the payor spouse or a substantial increase in the earning power of the recipient spouse. Remarriage or cohabitation of the recipient spouse may also be considered in some cases as sufficient grounds to terminate the maintenance.

Failure to pay maintenance is treated in the same manner as failure to pay other financial obligations under a decree. That is, through a petition seeking an order of contempt of court against the party in default. The procedure and penalties are basically the same as in other requests for such an order.

Assignment 14.7

> Examine the following situations and indicate whether a court would be likely to grant maintenance and, if so, whether it is likely to be permanent or temporary. Support your answer with an explanation.
>
> a. Ken and Barb are divorcing. Both are attorneys. However, Barb has not practiced law for the 15 years of their marriage because she has remained at home and overseen the rearing of their four children. The youngest child is now in school.
> b. Lynn and Don have been married for 35 years. Lynn has stayed at home to care for the couple's son who is physically handicapped. Lynn has never been employed and is now 58 years of age. Don has taken early retirement from his career of 40 years and is on a fixed income.

C. NONMARITAL RELATIONSHIPS

As previously indicated, most states no longer recognize the creation of a common-law marriage. Nevertheless, many couples do cohabit without satisfying the formal requisites of marriage. In many instances, these couples live in exactly the same manner as married individuals. They share in the support of a household, the acquisition of property and debt, and even in the rearing of children. However, the absence of the statutory requirements has a tremendous impact on their legal rights. Depending on the financial and personal status of each party, it is possible that an end to the relationship of one who is married and one who cohabits could be radically different. In addition to the obvious differences such as tax filing status, there are many other differences. For example, a party who cohabits is not presumed to be jointly responsible for a debt that he or she did not participate in incurring like a married person ordinarily would be. On the other hand, a party who cohabits typically has no inheritance rights as a matter of law like a married person would have. Generally, issues concerning the natural children of the parties would be treated the same regardless of the marital status of the parents because the issues essentially affect the relationship and responsibility between parent and child rather than between the two parties. Matters of maintenance, property, and debt division is most often considered based on contract and partnership law principles. However, a party may be found to have virtually no rights to property or maintenance if it is determined that the basis for the relationship was purely illicit (sexual) in nature. The courts will not encourage relationships that for all intents and purposes amount to providing property and funds in exchange for sexual services. Therefore, in cases of cohabitation, the court must first determine that the parties both contributed in some legal and substantial form to the success of the partnership before it will determine the property rights of the individuals.

Although previous courts had issued decisions addressing the various aspects of terminated cohabitation relationships, the landmark opinion was issued in *Marvin v. Marvin*[25] in which the court fully addressed the issues associated with the dissolution of a nonmarital cohabitation relationship. Courts in several other states have cited the decision with approval and have used it as persuasive authority to formally adopt and incorporate into the legal standards of their own jurisdiction, the position taken by the court in the *Marvin* decision.[26]

A few courts have rejected the *Marvin* decision on the basis that it too closely resembles the recognition of common-law marriage, and they are not willing to adopt a position that so closely parallels it. In a time when cohabitation is an increasingly frequent occurrence, however, methods may have to be developed to determine the legal rights of the parties involved.

CASE IN POINT

Salzman v. Bachrach, 996 P.2d 1263 (2000)

We granted certiorari to review the court of appeals' decision in Bachrach v. Salzman, 981 P.2d 219 (Colo.App.1999). We conclude that the Respondent, Erwin Bachrach, established a claim of unjust enrichment and is entitled to restitution of at least some of his contributions to the residence titled in the name of Petitioner Roberta F. Salzman. Accordingly, we affirm the court of appeals and remand this case to the trial court for a determination of the amount of restitution based upon the principles set out in this opinion.

Bachrach and Salzman met in 1986 when Salzman, a divorcee, responded to a personal advertisement in the Vail Trail newspaper placed by Bachrach, a widower. Bachrach and Salzman enjoyed a relationship that included dining, travel, and visiting with family and friends. The two maintained separate residences during the first several years of their relationship. Bachrach lived in a one-bedroom condominium that he owned; and Salzman resided in a townhouse. Salzman disliked her townhouse because of its small size, poor winter access, and because she had difficulty climbing the stairs.

In 1993, Bachrach and Salzman agreed to build a home together. Bachrach placed the condominium that he owned on the market late that year, and sold it in February 1994. Bachrach netted roughly $100,000

from the sale. On March 31, 1994, Bachrach and Salzman purchased a lot in Eagle, Colorado for $49,000, and titled it in both of their names. They contributed approximately equally to the price.

Bachrach, a designer and drafter of residential properties for fifty years, designed the new home. Initially, he estimated a total construction cost of $370,000. The construction crew broke ground on July 19, 1994 and substantially completed construction by April 1995, when the two moved into the home together. The home ultimately cost $520,876.50 to build. Bachrach contributed $167,528.86 and Salzman paid $353,347.64 of the total cost. In March 1995, the residence appraised for $445,000; in November 1996, it appraised for $584,000.

On April 18, 1995, Bachrach quitclaimed his interest in the property to Salzman, and Salzman closed on the sale of her townhouse. Bachrach's delivery of the deed to Salzman at that time served two functions. It facilitated Salzman's ability to obtain a favorable mortgage on the home, and offered tax advantages to Salzman. However, there was a third purpose that came to light approximately six months later.

In November 1995, Salzman's ex-husband notified her that he intended to terminate his monthly maintenance payment of $1800 because of her alleged marriage to Bachrach, cohabitation, and joint home-ownership. Bachrach replied to Salzman's ex-husband in writing that they were not married, but lived together for convenience and companionship; that they maintained separate financial accounts; that she alone owned the home; and that his contribution was in exchange for an indefinite period of free rent. After receiving the letter, Salzman's ex-spouse did not further pursue termination of maintenance. Hence, in a written document, Bachrach disavowed any interest in the home— equitable or otherwise.

During their cohabitation in the new home, Salzman made all of the mortgage payments and Bachrach paid only for some utilities and food. He did not pay rent. Initially, the parties shared a bedroom, but after about a year, they found one another intolerable and Bachrach moved into a separate bedroom. In August 1996, Salzman asked Bachrach to move out, and he refused. On January 15, 1997, Salzman changed the locks and posted a No Trespassing sign on the property, with the added phrase "This means you Erwin." Bachrach has not lived in the home since that day.

On January 17, 1997, Bachrach filed suit in the District Court in the County of Eagle, Colorado against Salzman, seeking a partition of the property under the theory that the two were joint venturers in the construction of the home. Salzman asserted counterclaims that Bachrach negligently designed the home, poorly managed its construction, misrepresented himself as an architect, and miscalculated the cost of the home, among others. The parties tried the case before the District Court in November 1997. The court denied both parties the relief that they sought.

The court of appeals reversed the order of the trial court holding that Salzman would be unjustly enriched were she allowed to keep Bachrach's contributions to the home. The court of appeals opined, however, that on remand, in determining the amount owed Bachrach, the trial court could consider the reasonable rental value Bachrach received while he resided in the house.

We begin our analysis by addressing Bachrach's argument that Salzman should reimburse him for his design work, construction management services, and his $170,000 contribution on principles of unjust enrichment. The Restatement of Restitution states "[a] person who has been unjustly enriched at the expense of another is required to make restitution to the other." Restatement of Restitution § 1 (1937). "A person obtains restitution when he is restored to the position he formerly occupied either by the return of something which he formerly had or by the receipt of its monetary equivalent." Id. § 1 cmt.a.

Unjust enrichment is a form of quasi-contract or a contract implied in law. See Dove Valley Bus. Park Assocs., Ltd. v. Board of County Comm'rs of Arapahoe County, 945 P.2d 395, 403 (Colo.1997). As such, it is an equitable remedy and does not depend on any contract, oral or written. See Cablevision of Breckenridge, Inc. v. Tannhauser Condominium Ass'n, 649 P.2d 1093, 1097 (Colo.1982). The theory does not require any promise or privity between the parties. See Wistrand v. Leach Realty Co., 147 Colo. 573, 576, 364 P.2d 396, 397 (1961). Rather, it is a judicially created remedy designed to avoid benefit to one to the unfair detriment of another. See Cablevision, 649 P.2d at 1097.

In Colorado, a plaintiff seeking recovery for unjust enrichment must prove: (1) at plaintiff's expense (2) defendant received a benefit (3) under circumstances that would make it unjust for defendant to retain the benefit without paying. See DCB Constr. Co. v. Central City Dev. Co., 965 P.2d 115, 119–20 (Colo.1998).

Applying the first element to the facts present here, we find that Bachrach's payment of nearly $170,000 and efforts in designing the home and managing the project certainly came at his expense. It is hardly arguable that Bachrach did not suffer in some way after paying for nearly one-third of the final construction cost of a home from which he has been evicted.

Considering the second prong, we conclude that Salzman benefited from Bachrach's expenditure on the construction of the home in which she now resides. Salzman owns and lives in an expensive custom home that Bachrach helped design and purchase.

The final prong then asks the dispositive question: whether it would be unjust for the defendant to retain the benefit conferred. Absent some countervailing consideration, the answer to this question is that it would be unjust to allow Salzman to keep Bachrach's entire contribution to the home.

Salzman argues that Bachrach is without a remedy because he delivered the funds to her in exchange for a cohabitation agreement. She contends that public-policy disapproves of such an arrangement and any decision in favor of Bachrach would operate to defeat that policy, citing three cases. See Houlton v. Prosser, 118 Colo. 304, 194 P.2d 911 (1948); Baker v. Sockwell, 80 Colo. 309, 251 P. 543 (1926); Baker v. Couch, 74 Colo. 380, 221 P. 1089 (1923).

In Baker v. Couch, this court declined to order the return of thirty-five promissory notes to the plaintiff, Paul Couch. Couch, a twenty-three year old man, and Alma Baker, a woman in her early thirties, lived together, in an intimate relationship. See 74 Colo. at 381-83, 221 P. at 1089-90. Couch had been married and divorced previously, and Baker had been married three times. See id. at 382, 221 P. at 1089. Couch argued that Baker obtained the notes through undue influence, and Baker contended they were a gift. The parties did execute a contract, which Couch argued was without consideration. See id. at 381, 221 P. at 1090. The contract closed with the following language: "Party to the first part [Baker] agrees to permit the party of the second part [Couch] to call at her home at reasonable hours and to continue the friendship already begun, until such time as the parties hereto agree to terminate this agreement." Id. at 383, 221 P. at 1089. The court concluded that past, present, and future sexual relations were the sole consideration for the original delivery of the promissory notes and the "so-called written contract." Id., 221 P. at 1090. Thus, the court held, because the contract was immoral, "neither law nor equity will aid either to enforce, revoke or rescind."

In Houlton, a single man and a married woman cohabited as husband and wife during a five-year period in the 1940s. See Houlton, 118 Colo. at 305, 194 P.2d at 911. Houlton purchased a home and the two took title as joint tenants. See id. When the relationship soured, Houlton sought to have the court order his female cohabitant, Prosser, to convey to him any interest she held in the home. See id. The court noted that Houlton knew that Prosser was married during most of their relationship and that he admitted that they lived together in an intimate relationship. See id. at 306, 194 P.2d at 911. The court reasoned that even though Houlton maintained that the sexual relationship was not in consideration of the deed, he was "not in a position to invoke the aid of a court of equity in his effort to obtain a conveyance of [Prosser's] interest in the property to himself." Id., 194 P.2d at 912.

Bachrach distinguishes the above cases because he contributed to the construction project in the expectation that he would live there indefinitely. Although

Bachrach highly valued Salzman's companionship, he asserts that sexual relations constituted no part of the exchange. We find Bachrach's argument persuasive.

The facts present here are distinguishable from the Baker v. Couch line of cases. The facts in Couch and Sockwell exhibited clearer evidence than present here that the sole consideration for the monetary conveyance was sexual relations. Perhaps due to the era of the decisions, the court provided very little information to suggest that Baker offered Couch anything other than an intimate relationship. In essence, the contract mirrored a contract for prostitution. Contrarily, in this case, Salzman's agreement to allow Bachrach to live in the home constituted substantial consideration for his contribution.

Although a closer case, Houlton can also be distinguished because one of the cohabitants was married during the majority of the parties' relationship. This adulterous component made Houlton considerably more culpable than Bachrach.

Even were we unable to distinguish the above line of cases, we would decline to follow them under the facts present here. Although we find the rule of law in these earlier cases persuasive to some degree, social norms and behaviors have changed to such an extent that we now join the majority of courts in other states in holding that nonmarried cohabiting couples may legally contract with each other so long as sexual relations are merely incidental to the agreement. Furthermore, such couples may ask a court for assistance, in law or in equity, to enforce such agreements.

The frequency of nonmarital cohabitation has substantially increased since the 1940s. See Bureau of the Census, Marital Status and Living Arrangements: March 1993, VII-VIII, tbl.D (May 1994) (indicating that from 1970 to 1993 alone, the number of unmarried-couple households in the U.S. increased 571%, from 523,000 to 3,510,000). As a result, courts throughout the country now face with increasing regularity the controversies arising out of the breakup of these relationships. Litigants have asked courts to establish the appropriate balance between the public policy favoring marriage, old cases explicitly disapproving any intimate contact outside of marriage, and accepted modern mores. The majority of courts have held in favor of the ability of nonmarried couples to contract with one another and to enforce those contracts in court.

In many jurisdictions, courts have examined the factual circumstances underlying unmarried cohabitating relationships, and have regularly enforced express and implied contracts between nonmarried cohabitants and provided equitable remedies. See Cook v. Cook, 142 Ariz 573, 691 P.2d 664 (1984) (determining that valid agreements supported by proper consideration between unmarried cohabitants will be enforced by the courts according to the intent of the parties); Marvin v. Marvin, 18 Cal.3d 660, 134 Cal.Rptr. 815, 557 P.2d 106 (1976) (holding, in this landmark case, that California courts must enforce express and implied agreements unless based wholly on sexual relations, and allowing the application of equitable remedies); Boland v. Catalano, 202 Conn. 333, 521 A.2d 142 (1987) (concluding that the existence of a sexual relationship between nonmarried cohabitants did not preclude enforcement of an express agreement to share equally in the assets accumulated while living together as long as the agreement was not founded upon their sexual relationship); Mason v. Rostad, 476 A.2d 662 (D.C.1984) (finding that a man could recover the reasonable value of the work contributed toward the renovation of another's house reduced by the benefits he received from the arrangement despite the fact they were unmarried and living together); Spafford v. Coats, 118 Ill.App.3d 566, 74 Ill.Dec. 211, 455 N.E.2d 241 (1983) (finding that a female unmarried cohabitant who furnished most of the money for several vehicles purchased during a cohabiting relationship was not barred by their cohabitation from bringing an unjust enrichment claim against the other cohabitant who retained control over the vehicles); Wilcox v. Trautz, 427 Mass. 326, 693 N.E.2d 141 (1998) (holding that unmarried cohabitants may lawfully contract concerning property, financial, and other relevant matters); Hudson v. DeLonjay, 732 S.W.2d 922 (Mo.Ct.App.1987) (opining that a man and woman living together without marriage may contract with each other); Western States Constr., Inc. v. Michoff, 108 Nev. 931, 840 P.2d 1220 (1992) (allowing unmarried cohabiting adults to agree to hold property that they acquire as though it were community property); Collins v. Davis, 68 N.C.App. 588, 315 S.E.2d 759 (1984) (reasoning that a married man living with a single woman was not barred from bringing a suit in equity for unjust enrichment when he contributed to the purchase of a house titled in the woman's name, if the agreement was not based exclusively on sexual intercourse); Tarry v. Stewart, 98 Ohio App.3d 533, 649 N.E.2d 1 (1994) (finding that the parties did not enter into a cohabitation agreement, and that under the facts, one party would not be unjustly enriched if allowed to keep the property in which they lived during their cohabitation); Wilbur v. DeLapp, 119 Or.App. 348, 850 P.2d 1151 (1993) (holding that the unmarried parties who lived together intended that the female cohabitant have a one-half interest in property held in the male partner's name); Lawlis v. Thompson, 137 Wis.2d 490, 405 N.W.2d 317 (1987) (holding that nonmarital cohabitation alone would not preclude a cohabitant from bringing an unjust enrichment claim against the other cohabitant). But see Long v. Marino, 212 Ga.App. 113, 441 S.E.2d 475 (1994) (suggesting that the law will not support a contract founded on the immoral consideration of unmarried cohabitation); Hewitt v. Hewitt, 77 Ill.2d 49, 31 Ill.Dec. 827, 394 N.E.2d 1204 (1979) (refusing to grant to a cohabitant one-half of the assets acquired during the cohabitation, reasoning that enforcing the contracts would grant a legal status to cohabitation), Schwegmann v. Schwegmann, 441 So.2d 316 (La.Ct.App.1983) (concluding that unmarried cohabitation does not give rise to property rights analogous to those arising from marriage, and that claims in equity are barred when sexual relations are interwoven with other tendered benefits); In re Estate of Alexander, 445 So.2d 836 (Miss. 1984) (deciding that the legislature was better suited to handle unmarried cohabitation policies and expressing concern that extending equitable principles would resurrect the abolished common-law marriage doctrine).

Legal scholars endorse the trend allowing nonmarried cohabitants to contract with one another. See Harry G. Prince, Public Policy Limitations on Cohabitation Agreements: Unruly Horse or Circus Pony?, 70 Minn. L.Rev. 163 (1985); J. Thomas Oldham & David S. Caudill, A Reconnaissance of Public Policy Restrictions Upon Enforcement of Contracts Between Cohabitants, 18 Fam. L.Q. 93 (1984); Robert C. Casad, Unmarried Couples and Unjust Enrichment: From Status to Contract and Back Again?, 77 Mich. L.Rev. 47 (1978); Herma Hill Kay & Carol Amyx, Marvin v. Marvin: Preserving the Options, 65 Calif. L.Rev. 937 (1977).

We find these authorities persuasive and agree that cohabitation and sexual relations alone do not suspend contract and equity principles. We do caution, however, that mere cohabitation does not trigger any marital rights. A court should not decline to provide relief to parties in dispute merely because their dispute arose in relationship to cohabitation. Rather, the court should determine—as with any other parties—whether general contract laws and equitable rules apply.

In this case, the evidence supports Bachrach's claim that sexual relations with Salzman were not the sole motivation for his contributions toward the construction of the home. He sold his condominium and placed all of the proceeds and other funds directly into the home in which he expected to live for the balance of his life. Both Salzman and Bachrach took title to the land on which the home was built, and according to undisputed testimony, Bachrach quitclaimed his entire interest in the home largely for the benefit of Salzman.

In consideration for Bachrach's contributions he obtained a much larger, more luxurious home in which to live and work, a cohabitant for whom he cared, and reduced living expenses. As we see it, sexual relations with Salzman constituted only a portion of the benefits received by Bachrach, and definitely were not the sole consideration. While the home purchase related to their intimate relationship because they both lived in the home, Bachrach's cause of action does not depend on their sexual relations. Thus, their cohabitation does not bar this suit in equity.

Having determined that Bachrach's claim is not barred by the parties' cohabitation, we must now remand the case to the court of appeals to be returned to the trial court for further factual determinations. Several financial issues remain to be sorted out by the trial court. For example, the trial court must determine the exact worth of Bachrach's contribution to date, and the reasonable rental value for the periods Bachrach lived in the house. As set forth above, we also direct the trial court to determine whether the unclean hands doctrine should bar any portion of Bachrach's recovery.[27]

Case Review Question: Why would the sexual relationship of the parties have any bearing if they both had made financial contributions?

D. REPRODUCTIVE LAW

1. Paternity

An entirely new area of law that has emerged in the American legal system during the latter part of the 20th century is the result of tremendous scientific advancements and a relaxation of cultural standards. Initially, this developed when the shame that was historically associated with children born out of wedlock was overshadowed by the increasing view of society that men should take responsibility for children they fathered. This was also advanced by the development of scientific means to test for paternity, which has developed significantly in recent years through DNA testing. It is now possible to trace ancestral lines back hundreds of years, as publicized in the case of the connection between descendants of Sally Hemmings and colonial President Thomas Jefferson. Today, paternity testing can virtually eliminate all but the true father of a child and, consequently, parental responsibilities can be placed on both mother and father.

Historically, there was no presumptive father for a child born out of wedlock. If a woman had the courage to initiate an action for paternity despite strong social pressures not to do so, the case often became focused on an issue of the credibility of the mother and alleged father. The cases were frequently notarized in newspapers as the two parties battled for a finding that they were telling the truth. Even if an individual is named on the birth certificate as the father, there is no legal presumption of this fact unless the man is married to the mother at the time of the birth or openly acknowledges his paternity of the child. Any other circumstance ultimately requires a court finding of paternity.

A paternity action is initiated in essentially the same manner as any other civil suit. However, many states have statutes that require specific methods of notice to the alleged father of the action. While it is rare that a court has authority to order invasive physical procedures such as blood tests, this is one instance where, unless a father admits to paternity or accepts a finding of paternity by default, a court may order blood tests to definitively determine whether the alleged father is the biological parent of the child in question. These actions are most often filed when the mother or guardian of the child is seeking financial assistance in the form of child support. An action may also be filed by the state if the child or its mother is receiving government financial assistance such as welfare benefits, and the state seeks reimbursement from the father. However, it is no longer uncommon for the action to be filed by a man who wants to resolve whether he is the father of a child as fathers have assumed an increasingly active role in the lives of their children in recent years. By establishing parenthood, the father not only accepts the responsibilities, but gains the rights associated with parenthood, such as the right of companionship of the child and the right to oppose adoption of the child by another man or by parents who wish to adopt the child from the natural mother. In accordance with this, many states even have registries created by statute that allow a man who believes himself to be a father to register his name and the pertinent information about the child and mother. This, in turn, prevents the mother from placing the child for adoption without consent until paternity is established.

APPLICATION 14.7

Victor believes he is the natural father of a child that Oma is about to give birth to. Oma has indicated to friends that she has already completed the paperwork and intends to place the baby up for adoption as soon as it is born. She further indicates that she has stated she does not know the identity of the father. Victor signs with a statutory registry and identifies himself as the father of Oma's unborn child. When the child is born, Oma places the child for adoption. However, in processing the paperwork, it is discovered that Victor has made a claim of paternity and the adoption is suspended while his paternity is confirmed or ruled out.

Point for Discussion: Why would an objection to the adoption proceeding by Victor at the time it is initiated not meet the same objective and work just as well?

---

2. Adoption

Another area of law that has seen immense growth in terms of statutory legal standards is adoption. There was a time when a child could essentially be handed over to another or to a child care facility such as an orphanage with little or no formality. However, the exposure of baby selling practices and other activities that did not place the best interest of the child first and ahead of any personal interests led to nationwide legislation by the states to carefully monitor the placement and adoption process. It is common now to require counseling and waiting periods for the natural parent or parents who seek to place their child for adoption. Adoptive parents are often required to go through a series of evaluations and even trial periods with the child before the adoption will be finalized, regardless of whether the parties unanimously consent to the adoption.

Historically, the vast majority of adoptions were private in that the adoptive and natural parents did not know one another's identity. However, a trend in the latter part of the 1900s was toward open adoptions. In these situations, the parents know of one another, they sometimes communicate, and in some cases the adoptive parents allow the natural parents to visit with the adopted child and develop some sort of relationship. Obviously, the open adoption is not something that is acceptable to all parties and the majority of adoptions are still private.

Historically, when an adoption occurred all records with respect to the child prior to the adoption were sealed. The rationale was that an adopted child should be raised in the belief that the adoptive parents were his or her family, and when one placed a child for adoption, he or she gave up all rights to further contact in any way with the child. Many times, because of emotional and societal pressures, the natural parent did not want the adoptive child to have access to the natural parent's identity as well. Even if an adoptive child or natural parent wanted this access, state statute prohibited such from occurring. However, along with all the other changes in domestic relations law in the late 20th century, this too has seen dramatic revision.

For a variety of reasons, adopted children and natural parents began seeking records about the other party in great numbers in the latter 1990s. They encountered great difficulty because of statutory prohibitions and movements began to change the laws. These movements were often supported by the medical profession as science produced more and more evidence of the importance of knowing one's genetic background and parental medical histories. As a result, in adoptions today much more medical information is required at the time of an adoption. In addition, natural parents may indicate whether they are willing to have their identity released to the adoptive child. Adoptive parents have the option of revealing their own identity and that of the adopted child to the natural parents. Once the adopted child has reached the age of majority, this decision becomes their own. Thus, while statutes still attempt to protect privacy and while many individuals who were party to adoptions that took place before these statutory changes still meet with the frustration of not being able to locate their natural relative, the laws today are much more flexible in meeting the needs and desires of the individuals with respect to continued contact among natural relatives after an adoption has occurred.

3. Fertility and Surrogacy

A relatively new area of medicine and subsequently law is reproductive medicine. As technology increased in the last half of the 20th century, methods of conception increased as well. The development of various procedures resulted in the ability to conceive children outside the womb, the insemination and fertilzation of an egg by anonymous donors, and even implantation of embryos from one woman into another for the gestational period prior to birth. The various procedures ultimately produced legal questions too numerous to mention. The most publicized cases have dealt with parental rights when more than two individuals are involved with the conception and gestation of the child, such as when a surrogate mother gives birth and then decides she wants to keep the child. In some instances, the egg is provided by the surrogate mother and the sperm is provided by the man in a married couple who wish to rear the child. In that case, the wife of the man would be an adoptive parent. Other cases involve implantation of an embryo, raising the issue of whether the maternal legal rights are attached to the egg or to the woman who carries it within her body through gestation and then gives birth. What of the anonymous sperm donor? Does he have any legal paternal rights with respect to a child produced? And what of parties who have embryos frozen? What happens when they divorce and the wife has the embryo implanted and subsequently delivers a child? Does the natural father have obligations or rights with respect to this child he never intended to have produced? It is even a question for courts in matters of divorce as to who should have custody of such frozen embryo's since they are truly the product and part of the physical being of both parties.

As can be seen, the legal questions arise as quickly as medical technology advances. This is an area of law that stands to see explosive growth in the upcoming decades.

PARALEGALS IN THE WORKPLACE

The law of domestic relations is an area that naturally lends itself to paralegal employment. Because so much of the field involves preparing documents and interviewing parties and witnesses, the paralegal can be very effective in relieving the attorney of these duties and allowing more time in the practice of law, whether it is making court appearances, negotiating settlements, or advising clients. Because domestic relations law often considers detailed areas such as financial status of the parties, the paralegal may find him or herself involved in collecting and summarizing employment and tax and bank records, and in going over these with clients for verification. Also, because this area of law is intensely personal and often results in two very different versions of the background facts, a significant amount of time in each case may be spent collecting facts by interviewing clients and witnesses. Paralegals are employed for these tasks in the traditional law firm, of course. However, additional resources include legal assistance foundations, which typically engage in a great amount of law in this area and government as well as private organizations that are focused on the family or family rights law.

Chapter Summary

The law of domestic relations in this country has undergone radical changes in the last century. It has probably changed the most from its origins, unlike areas such as contract and property law that still have many foundations in the original principles brought from England. In this century, divorce has gone from a rare and socially unacceptable occurrence, to a certainty in almost half of all marriages that occur. Dissolution of marriage and the consequent issues make up the majority of legal principles in domestic relations law.

Assuming a marriage is legally accomplished by meeting formal and statutory requisites, it can be ended by annulment in limited circumstances. Specifically a condition of marriage must not have existed at the time the marriage occurred, which in turn prevented it from having ever become valid. The other and much more common alternative is dissolution of marriage, in which a valid marriage relationship is dissolved and the assets, debts, maintenance, and other joint issues of the parties such as child custody, support, and visitation are resolved.

Some parties elect to legally separate rather than divorce, although this takes place in the minority of cases. In the event of a legal separation, the marital relationship is left intact. The parties remain married for legal purposes, but they separate their property, assets, debts, and responsibilities with respect to minor children. Historically, this was often done for parties who did not wish to continue living together but wanted to remain married due to social, cultural, or religious pressures and issues. Now, dissolution is much more accepted and parties most often opt for it in order to bring the relationship to a final conclusion and to allow them to move forward in their lives, totally independent of one another.

Parties who cohabit as if they are married are no longer considered common-law spouses in the vast majority of jurisdictions. Rather, in the event the cohabitation and relationship end, the parties are left to resolve matters themselves or to pursue the issues in the courts under contract and partnership principles. This assumes, however, that the relationship was not contingent upon sexual services, in which case the purpose is considered illegal and the courts will not enforce rights as if a contract or partnership existed.

ETHICAL NOTE

Ethical standards and adherence to them is of the utmost importance in the law of domestic relations. Unlike more objective areas of law such as property or contracts, in the law of domestic relations clients are quite often emotionally strained and vulnerable. Additionally, these cases frequently span many years when minor children are involved and periodic reviews or adjustments must be made to accommodate changes in circumstance of the parties or children. As a result, exceptional care must be taken with regard to all matters of competence, confidentiality, keeping the client informed, zealous representation, and so forth. These are clients who are often not in a position to act in their own best interests because of the emotional conditions attached to embattled issues of divorce, custody, and such. Therefore, they are more vulnerable to injury from the failure to act ethically than clients in other types of cases may be.

Relevant Internet Sites

Family Law   www.aol.com/webcenters/legal/family.adp
Family Law Resources at About.com   www.law.about.com/msub12.htm

---

Internet Assignment 14.1

Do an Internet search for your own jurisdiction and determine whether grandparents have specific statutory rights of visitation.

KEY TERMS

Annulment   Legal Separation   Property Settlement
Antenuptial Agreements   Permanent Injunction   Temporary Restraining Orders
Custody   Preliminary Injunctions

ENDNOTES

1. *In re Estate of Cummings*, 493 Pa. 11, 425 A.2d 340 (1981).
2. 81 A.L.R. 3d 453.

3. Mobilia, "Ante-nuptial agreements anticipating divorce: How effective are they?" 70 Massachusetts Law Review 82, 10 (June 1985).

4. 55 C.J.S., Marriage, Section 10.
5. Id., Section 28-31.
6. Id., Section 48.
7. Id.
8. 81 A.L.R.3d 453.
9. *Jackson v. Jackson*, 276 F2d 601 (D.C. Cir. 1960).
10. *Maschauer v. Downs*, 53 Ap.D.C. 142, 289 Fed. 540 (1923).
11. Federal Rules of Evidence, 28 U.S.C.A. Rule 501.
12. 51 A.L.R. 3d 223.
13. 24 Am.Jur. 2d, Divorce and Separation Section 29.
14. Uniform Marriage and Divorce Act, Section 304(b)(2).
15. 48 A.L.R. 4th 919.
16. Id.
17. 17 A.L.R. 4th 1013.
18. Comment, "Battling inconsistency and inadequacy: Child Support guidelines in the states," Harvard Women's Law Journal 197 (Spring 1988).
19. *In Re J.S.O.C.*, 129 N.J.Super. 486, 324 A.2d 90 (1974).
20. *Troxel v. Granville*, 2000 WL 712807 (U.S. Wash.).
21. 24 Am. Jur. 2d, Sections 321-370.
22. Id.
23. 97 A.L.R. 3d 740.
24. 75 A.L.R. 3d. 262.
25. Monroe, *Marvin v. Marvin:* Five Years Later, 65 Marquette Law Review 389 (Spring 1982).
26. Id.
27. *Salzman v. Bachrach*, 996 P.2d 1263 (2000).

Chapter 15

CRIMINAL LAW AND PROCEDURE

CHAPTER OBJECTIVES

Upon completion of this chapter you should be able to do the following:

- Identify and define criminal intent.
- Define the parties to a criminal act under principles of common law.
- Define the parties to a criminal act under the Modern Penal Code.
- Discuss the characteristics of an inchoate crime.
- Explain common defenses to criminal conduct.
- Explain the purpose of selective incorporation and the modern definition of due process.
- Discuss the rights that guarantee protection to those accused of criminal conduct.
- Explain the process of criminal prosecution from investigation to arrest and through trial.

A. CRIMINAL LAW

Criminal Law
Law created and
enforced by the
government for the
health, welfare, safety,
and general good of
the public.

As discussed previously in the text, **criminal law** applies to those situations wherein public standards are violated and the public welfare is thus injured. Consequently, the government prosecutes on behalf of the people, and penalties, with the exception of restitution, are paid or served to the public. While many crimes result in injury to specific victims, such injuries are personal and are typically dealt with in civil actions, such as those for tort or breach of contract. In addition, the government may prosecute for violation of the criminal law.

In the United States today, criminal law is statutory; that is, the legislature determines what will be criminal conduct. All crimes must be stated as such by statute before the conduct described will be considered criminal. When presented with the prosecution of a defendant based on a criminal statute, the judiciary examines the particular situation to determine whether it falls within the definition of the crime specifically charged. The legislature cannot enact a statute making certain conduct criminal and provide for punishment of persons who performed the conduct before it was declared illegal.

The process of punishing someone for conduct that occurred before it was made illegal is known as an ex post facto law, and it is prohibited by Article I, Section 9, of the U.S. Constitution. In the United States, a primary element of all criminal laws is the concept of fair warning. Under the Constitution, this means that one must be capable of determining that conduct would be considered criminal before the fact. This does not mean that persons must actually be aware of the criminality of their conduct but only that they could have discovered it in advance and altered their course of action had they so chosen. Thus comes the saying, "Ignorance of the law is no excuse."[1] All persons are presumed to be responsible for ascertaining the rightfulness of their actions in advance. Generally this is not a problem, because in everyday life, right and wrong are quite apparent to persons who act in accordance with the established societal standards.

The discussion that follows examines the basic principles of criminal law that exist today in the United States. Although criminal law encompasses offenses from the most minor traffic violation to capital murder, the focus will be on the elements of more serious crimes. Further, because a majority of the states have now adopted the Model Penal Code as the basis of their criminal statutes, reference will be made to the code when appropriate as the general standard of law. States that have not adopted the code still rely on principles and definitions created in historical common law as the basis for criminal statutes, so reference will be made to the basics of common law as well.

Felony
Serious crime
punishable by
imprisonment in excess
of one year and/or
other significant
penalties.

Misdemeanor
Criminal offense
punishable by a fine or
imprisonment of less
than one year.

1. Definitions and Categories of Crime

The two basic categories of crimes are felony and misdemeanor. A **felony** is any offense punishable by death or by imprisonment exceeding one year. A **misdemeanor** is a crime punishable by fine or by detention of one year or less in a jail or an institution other than a penitentiary. Many states have further divided felonies and misdemeanors into subclasses, usually for the purpose of sentencing. For example, crimes that are considered Class 1 misdemeanors may carry a heavier penalty than crimes considered Class 2 misdemeanors. Once the classes are established, the various crimes are placed within a class. The definition of the criminal offense itself will indicate the elements necessary for conviction of the crime. The category and subclass will indicate to the court what sentence should be imposed.

In some cases, a mandatory sentence is required, which means that the judge has no discretion to impose or suspend a sentence. The statute prescribes exactly what the sentence must be. In the absence of a mandatory sentence, the judge is usually given a range of punishment. The judge is responsible for imposing a sentence within this range that will adequately punish the defendant for the crime committed. This range allows the judge to take the circumstances of each case into account.

Crime has been defined as follows:

> A positive or negative act or omission that violates the penal law of the state or federal government; any act done in violation of those duties for which an individual offender shall make satisfaction to the public.

In more general terms, criminal conduct refers to acts that may be injurious not only to an individual but, more importantly, also to society. Under the American legal system, all persons in society should have the reasonable expectation and enjoyment of certain basic privileges, including privacy, uninterfered ownership of property, and physical safety. When one person invades the basic rights of another, then the basic rights of society are also invaded. Therefore, criminal laws have been set up to punish and deter individuals from such actions.

Criminal law differs from civil law in several respects. Perhaps the most significant is that in criminal law, the government protects and upholds society's rights. In a civil case, individuals typically bring legal actions or lawsuits to seek a remedy for their injuries. In criminal law, the government prosecutes the offender to punish the person who caused the injuries. The purpose and goals of the two are distinct although civil and criminal issues may arise from the same set of circumstances. For example, a car accident may result in a criminal prosecution for violation of driving statutes as well as a civil action for injuries to other persons or property.

Regardless of whether a jurisdiction follows criminal common-law principals or the Model Penal Code, all crimes contain two basic elements that must be satisfied before someone is considered to have committed criminal conduct. First is the physical action and second is the mental state of the actor. The physical conduct is called the **actus reus,** a Latin term meaning "the wrongful act." All crimes require an actus reus, although in some circumstances the wrongful conduct can be a failure to act or an omission. The mental conduct of the person is known as the **mens rea,** which means literally "a guilty mind or guilty purpose." The state of mind element requires a certain degree of intent to commit the wrongful act or omission.

a. Actus Reus   Under the Model Penal Code, three steps are followed in establishing the actus reus.[2] First, it must be shown that the actual conduct, either affirmative or by omission (failing to act when one should have acted) took place. If the criminal conduct is an omission, it must be shown that the accused was capable of acting and was obligated directly or indirectly by law to act. Second, if the definition of the particular crime requires a result from the criminal conduct, that result must occur to prove actus reus. For example, to charge a person with battery, the victim must have suffered some actual physical injury as the result of unpermitted physical contact. This would satisfy the requirements of prohibited conduct and of a result that proves an

Actus Reus
Element of physical conduct necessary to commit a crime.

Mens Rea
Mental state required as an element necessary to commit a criminal act.

offense of physical battery. Finally, under some statutes, certain circumstances must exist for conduct to constitute a crime. For example, by definition, the crime of burglary involves an unlawful or unpermitted entrance onto one's property. This is a required circumstance, so if someone entered the property with permission, burglary could not be established.

APPLICATION 15.1

Act: While driving a boat at a high rate of speed, Sue deliberately crossed the immediate path of a canoe, causing it to overturn and the passengers to be thrown into the water, one of whom drowned.

Omission: While driving a boat at a high rate of speed, Sue saw a canoe in her near right path and did not take evasive action. As a result, the canoe capsized and one of its occupants drowned.

The preceding scenarios both describe criminal acts. Although one was an overt act and the other was a failure to act, both resulted in the conscious infliction of injury that could have been prevented had Sue conducted herself differently. A person cannot be convicted of a crime based on physical conduct alone. The perpetrator must also have the statutorily defined requisite intent as well.

Point for Discussion: Why is physical conduct alone insufficient for criminal conduct?

---

b. Mens Rea   The definition of each crime in a statute requires a mens rea, which means "guilty purpose, wrongful purpose, criminal intent, guilty knowledge, willfulness."[3] Mens rea describes the state of mind or the degree of intent that the actor has toward accomplishing a criminal goal. Under common law, the two basic subtypes of mens rea are known as specific intent and general intent. More serious crimes typically require specific intent on the part of the actor to produce the result of the crime, whereas general intent crimes require a basic awareness of the likely consequences of one's actions. Under the Model Penal Code, the state of mind required for commission of a crime is based on degrees of knowledge that range from criminal negligence to recklessness to knowledge, with the most serious crimes requiring a criminal purpose. Figure 15.1 shows examples of intent and act under both common law and the Model Penal Code.

FIGURE 15.1	**Common Law**	
Comparison of Intent and Act Under Model Penal Code and Common Law	General Intent: Driving above the speed limit. Specific Intent: Deliberately running down a pedestrian.	
	Model Penal Code	
	Negligence:	Driving above the speed limit.
	Recklessness:	Driving while intoxicated.
	Knowledge:	Driving a car that you know has unsafe tires (pieces of tread frequently tear away at speeds over 50 mph).
	Purpose:	Deliberately running down a pedestrian.

In common-law jurisdictions, the statute for a particular crime or group of crimes will generally indicate only whether the intent required is specific or general. Specific intent requires that the actor form the actual intent to achieve the result of the crime,[4] whereas general intent only requires knowledge of the likelihood of the result of the act.[5] Similarly, a Model Penal Code jurisdiction will indicate the degree of awareness in the language of the statute.[6] Statutes with a mens rea standard of criminal negligence require only that the actor knew or should have been aware of the probability that the action would produce a criminal result. The standard of recklessness requires, in addition to a general awareness, that the actor demonstrate a disregard for the consequence of the action. More specific in nature, the criminal knowledge requirement includes an awareness that the conduct would undoubtedly produce a criminal result. Finally, the highest degree of criminal intent under the Model Penal Code, criminal purpose, requires premeditated intent to act in a manner consistent with criminal activity.

Criminal law follows a theory similar to tort law regarding transferred intent. In criminal law, if an individual intends to injure or kill one person and, in fact, injures or kills an entirely different person, the intent is transferred to the person actually injured or killed. The intent and act were present. It need not be shown that the intent and act were meant for a particular person or object.

A few excepted crimes have no requirement of mens rea. Commission of such crimes can result in conviction irrespective of general or specific intent. These unusual offenses are known as crimes of strict liability and have none of the ordinary intent requirements. Under criminal statutes that impose strict liability, an individual can be prosecuted on the basis of the act irrespective of the presence of general or specific intent.

Strict liability laws are often established to protect the general good of society. Crimes of strict liability generally do not require a preconceived intent to do or not do a particular act. Rather, they are usually applied when someone's preventive measures could greatly reduce risk of social or public harm.

An example of a strict liability crime is a violation of the statutory duty of persons with a license to sell and dispense liquor to sell only to persons over the age of 21. The licensee may not intend to break the law, but when the individual allows minors to be served liquor, he or she is endangering both the minors and the public at large. Simple monitoring of the persons served could totally prevent the serious harm that is presumed by law to result from the sale of liquor to minors. Therefore, if the duty to take preventive measures is minimal when compared to the social value of these measures, strict liability may be imposed. In other words, failure to take the preventive measures may result in conviction regardless of whether there was general or specific intent to cause the harm. Rather, the guilt is based on the failure to prevent the harm.

Assignment 15.1

For each of the following situations, indicate whether (1) the situation describes criminal intent, (2) the intent would be considered specific or general under common-law standards, and (3) the intent would be considered purpose, knowledge, recklessness, or negligence under the Model Penal Code.

a. Mark held a party for a number of friends that included several teenagers. At the party, Mark made beer freely available to all his guests. Two such teenage guests consumed alcohol and subsequently engaged in a drunken brawl, seriously injuring another guest of the party.

b. The same situation as above, but Mark is the owner of a tavern and hosting a private party.

c. Flying debris from a truck hit and cracked the windshield of John's car. After the truck owner refused to pay for a new windshield, John returned and shot out the windows of the truck.

d. Michael is an avid skateboarder. He is aware that a city ordinance prohibits skateboarding on all streets designated as commercially zoned areas due to high traffic and possibility of accidents. Michael skateboards on these streets between the hours of 11 PM and 1 AM.

e. Blair purchases an expensive evening dress. When she arrives home she discovers the zipper is defective. She attempts to return the dress but is told that no returns or exchanges on evening wear are permitted. Furious, she deposits the defective dress on the counter and carries out a new one. She is charged with theft.

2. Common-Law Parties to Crime

Usually, one thinks of a criminal as the person who actually committed the criminal act that caused injury or damage. Many times, however, persons act together to commit a crime. This may involve cooperation in the criminal act or assistance before or after the crime. In criminal law, one who assists in a crime can also be accused and convicted of criminal conduct. Since common-law principles and the Model Penal Code are somewhat different on this point, they are discussed separately. The issue of cooperation in a joint enterprise, commonly referred to as conspiracy, is discussed later.

Under common law, there are four basic categories of participants in criminal conduct. Specific terms describe the various types of involvement by the principals—persons who are actually involved in the primary criminal conduct—and the accessories—persons who aid the principals before or after the crime. Common law defines two types of principals and two types of accessories.

a. Principal in the First Degree   The principal in the first degree is the party or parties who actually take part in a criminal act. It is necessary that they perform the actus reus and that they have the adequate mens rea at the time they commit the crime. Under a variation of the definition, persons who can be charged as principals in the first degree include those who possess the mens rea but convince another to perform the actual physical conduct. This would include situations of coercion, threat, or trickery or would involve trained animals or programmed electronic devices.

b. Principal in the Second Degree   Principals in the second degree are persons who actually assist in the physical commission of a crime or persons whose conduct enables the principal in the first degree to commit the crime. If the conduct of a party is required to complete the crime successfully, either at the moment of the crime or immediately before or after, that person would be considered a principal in the second degree. An example is someone who makes deliveries for a dealer of illegal drugs. This person does not obtain, sell, or perhaps even use the drugs, but by assisting in the delivery of them, he or she is enabling the crime to be completed.

c. Accessory Before the Fact   Accessories before the fact are those persons who enable or aid the principal to prepare for a crime. Their conduct may consist of providing the principal with a place to plan or wait until the time has arrived for the actual commission of the crime. A very famous example involved the owners of a boarding house in Washington D.C. who supposedly knew the assassination of President Abraham Lincoln was being planned. These persons were convicted and subsequently hanged for their participation in the assassination.

d. Accessory After the Fact   Persons who assist in a successful escape or concealment of a criminal activity are accessories after the fact. This category includes anyone who is aware of the criminal activity and who aids the principal in successfully avoiding prosecution. Conduct of this type ranges from giving the principal a place to hide to rendering medical care or misleading authorities about the principal or facts of the crime. Persons who are closely related to the principal may be considered an exception to the rule in some jurisdictions. Under common law, it was considered detrimental to family unity to prosecute someone for aiding his or her spouse or children. Therefore, these persons could not be charged as accessories. This exception is still recognized in most states. Additionally, a person charged as a principal cannot also be charged as an accessory.

Usually, the division into principals and accessories applies to felonies. In the commission of misdemeanors, all who are involved are considered to be equally guilty. Common law also held that accessories in felony cases could not be prosecuted, convicted, and sentenced unless the principal was convicted. However, today most of the jurisdictions that apply common law, rather than the Model Penal Code, have modified it to no longer require the conviction of the principal prior to the conviction of the accessory. Another present-day change in these traditional common-law jurisdictions is that principals in the first and second degree and accessories before the fact are generally considered equal principals rather than the traditional accessory. Conduct that aids the preparations for a crime or enables a crime to be committed is considered as serious as the actual commission of the crime.

3. Parties to Crime Under the Model Penal Code

The Model Penal Code recognizes principals, accessories, and persons who commit offenses of "obstructing governmental operations."[7] The code defines principals as persons who actually possess the mens rea and who either commit the required actus reus or control the commission of the actus reus by such means as coercion, trickery, or manipulation. Accessories are persons who agree to aid or who actually aid in the completion of the crime, including actual physical assistance or mere encouragement. Persons who commit offenses of obstructing governmental operations can be prosecuted for assisting in the escape of the principal or the accessory, or for the concealment of the crime.

Under the Model Penal Code, it is not necessary that the principal be convicted before the accessory or the person who has obstructed government operations. Instead, each is judged on his or her own criminal conduct, although the seriousness of the

FIGURE 15.2

Comparison of
Elements and Parties
Under Model Penal
Code and Common
Law

	Common Law	Model Penal Code
Actus Reus	Physical conduct	Physical conduct or encouragement of physical conduct
Mens Rea	General Intent	Negligence
	Specific Intent	Recklessness
		Purpose
Parties	Principal 1st degree	Knowledge
	Principal 2nd degree	Principal
	Accessory before fact	Accessory
	Accessory after fact	Obstructing Governmental Operations

Under Modern Common Law, these are also considered equal principals.

penalty may be adjusted to reflect the amount of criminal involvement of the individual. This is done in much the same way as the trend toward grading the severity of each person's involvement under modern common law.

The primary difference between modern common law jurisdictions and the Model Penal Code jurisdictions lies in terminology. With a few adjustments, the basic concepts are the same as Figure 15.2 illustrates.

4. Elements of Serious Crimes

The following discussion explains some of the basic elements that must be present before an individual can be convicted of some of the most common crimes in our society. In addition to submitting the required proof of criminal conduct by the accused, the legal system must follow the criminal procedures established by the Constitution, statutes, and court rulings. The laws and procedures are designed to avoid conviction of innocent persons based on improper or unfair evidence of criminal conduct.

a. Inchoate Offenses   Some crimes are described as inchoate offenses, crimes that occur prior to but facilitate or enable other crimes. Inchoate crimes include conspiracy to commit, attempts to commit, and solicitation to commit criminal acts. Each is addressed individually.

i. Conspiracy to Commit Criminal Acts   The crime of conspiracy involves the cooperation of two or more people in planning and completing a crime as a joint undertaking.[8] Conspiracy in itself is a crime, distinct from the additional criminal act that is the common goal of the parties. As a result, conspiracy has its own mens rea and actus reus, and a defendant can be charged with both the completed criminal act and conspiracy to commit that act, unlike other crimes such as attempt and the actual crime which merge with the criminal act if completed.

The mens rea of conspiracy under common law requires specific intent. Each party to the conspiracy must have intent to agree with the other parties. Further, the agreement must be to accomplish something that is illegal. Regardless of whether the crime is actually committed, persons who have agreed to work toward a common goal that is illegal are guilty of conspiracy.

The actus reus is perhaps the most difficult element to establish in a prosecution for conspiracy. There is seldom any concrete evidence, such as a contract, that will establish that the persons have taken steps to agree to a common criminal goal. Generally, the jury must rely on evidence of the actions of the parties to the conspiracy. The prosecution's description of the acts of these parties must convince the jury beyond a reasonable doubt that the parties had no other purpose than to conspire to commit a criminal act. Many statutes today have extended this burden of proving actus reus beyond the common law. Today, most statutes require at least one of the parties to perform some physical act that demonstrates his or her intent to be a part of a conspiracy.

Under the Model Penal Code, the elements of conspiracy are much more specific. Proof of the actus reus can be shown in one of three ways. There must be evidence that the conspirators assisted in planning, soliciting, attempting, or committing the actual criminal offense that is the goal of the conspiracy. In contrast, the mens rea of conspiracy required in the Model Penal Code is much less stringent. There need only be evidence that each person accused entered the agreement "with the purpose of promoting or facilitating" a goal of criminal conduct.[9]

ii. Crime of Attempt   Under statutes in all states, an attempt to commit a crime is considered a criminal act in and of itself. An attempt takes place when the person has the mens rea to commit a particular crime and indicates a willingness to complete the crime, but for some reason, the actus reus is never completed. As a consequence, the person cannot be convicted of that particular crime. It is not in the best interest of society, however, to condone even attempts at crime. Moreover, sometimes injuries result from a failed attempt, for example, attempted murder. A would-be murderer should not go free simply because the victim was fortunate enough to live through a violent crime designed to produce death. Consequently, if someone takes material steps toward such a crime, attempt can be charged.

The question the courts must determine in cases of attempt is, how far must an individual go toward the commission of a crime before the individual is considered guilty of actually attempting the crime? Several tests have been employed in common law. Perhaps the most frequently applied today is that of proximity. The court considers how close the defendant was to completing the crime. The closer a defendant was, the less likely he or she would have turned away before completion. Adequate proximity to completion of the crime means that it is very likely that the defendant would have completed the crime if given the opportunity. This is the point at which an attempt can be said to occur.

In a variation on this rule, the court examines the individual and determines whether that particular individual would be likely to commit the particular crime. The court may also examine whether the defendant had control over all of the necessary elements to commit the crime. Whatever specific questions are applied, the basic issue remains the same. Given sufficient opportunity, is it likely beyond a reasonable doubt that the person would have completed the crime?

Unquestionably, a person cannot be convicted of attempt if his or her actual goal was not criminal. Even if the individual believes that his or her conduct constitutes a crime, if it does not, there can be no conviction of attempt. Similarly if a person attempts to commit a crime but his or her actions in reality do not constitute a crime, there can be no conviction of attempt. However, a defendant who takes steps toward the commission of the crime and would have committed the crime except for some intervening fact or force can be convicted of attempt.

APPLICATION 15.2

Jeremy, frustrated with his studies, has decided to do away with his law instructor. He waits outside the school. When the instructor passes by, Jeremy throws a knife still in its leather sheath at his instructor but misses. The instructor, unaware of the event, proceeds about his business. In this instance, no crime was committed, nor could one have resulted from Jeremy's action in the circumstances as described. Assume however, that the knife did strike the instructor but, unknown to Jeremy, the instructor was wearing a kevlar vest that deflected the blade. The instructor had been similarly attacked in the past. In this instance, Jeremy attempted the crime and completed all the necessary steps to kill the instructor, but because of an intervening fact, the vest, Jeremy's crime was incomplete. Nevertheless, in the latter situation, Jeremy could be convicted of attempting the crime of murder. A charge of criminal assault/battery would also be possible.

Point for Discussion: Does it matter whether Jeremy knew about the vest?

If the intended crime is completed, a person cannot be convicted of the offense of attempt as well as the actual crime. What is considered an attempt becomes part of the actual crime when it is completed. The two are merged into one crime and referred to as "lesser included offenses." That is, it is included in the greater and more serious offense of the crime. If for some reason the crime cannot be proven, a person may still be charged with and, in many cases, convicted of attempt during the same proceedings.

For the crime of attempt, the Model Penal Code requires that the actor do much more than simply prepare for criminal conduct. The actor must take what would be considered a substantial step toward the completion of the crime. This step is something that makes the crime more than a contemplation. At this point, the elements of the crime are within the control of the defendant and can be completed with the defendant's own further actions.

The mens rea required of attempt under the Model Penal Code is more complex. The prosecution must show that the defendant had the intent to attempt the crime and must also prove any requirements of mens rea for commission of the crime itself. In a trial, the jury must look to the mens rea of the crime that the defendant attempted and determine whether all of the mens rea requirements were met. Then the jury must determine whether the defendant had the specific intent to actually commit the criminal act. In some situations, this may be redundant.

The Model Penal Code is somewhat more liberal than the common law regarding charges and conviction. In common law, one must be charged with attempt or the actual crime or both. If convicted of the crime, however, one cannot be convicted of attempt, and vice versa. Although the result under the Model Penal Code is the same, the required procedure is slightly different. The code permits a person to be charged with only the crime. However, if the jury finds that the person did not complete the crime but did attempt it, the person can be convicted of attempt. There is no requirement that the individual be formally charged with attempt in addition to the charge for the actual crime.

iii. Crime of Solicitation   Solicitation has been defined as the act of enticing, inviting, requesting, urging, or ordering someone to commit a crime. It differs from conspiracy or attempt. In conspiracy, two or more persons work together to achieve a common goal of criminal conduct. The crime of attempt describes the acts under the control of an individual toward completion of a crime. Solicitation is a crime wherein an individual seeks to persuade another individual to commit a crime. The trend in common-law states is to adopt the Model Penal Code view of solicitation. The code allows conviction and punishment of one who solicits any criminal offense, no matter how minor. The traditional common-law approach was to punish only solicitation of serious offenses against society.

At common law, conviction can be had for anyone who attempts to communicate with another in such a way that the other person will be encouraged to commit a crime. It is not necessary that the other person receive the communication or commit the crime. Solicitation is based on the premise that it is wrong in and of itself to willfully encourage criminal conduct. The actus reus is any conduct that would demonstrate such encouragement.

Solicitation is considered to be a specific intent offense in common law. The person who solicits a crime by another must intend that the crime actually be committed. It is not required that the person who solicits understand that solicitation itself is considered criminal conduct. Rather, it need only be shown that the person knows that the conduct that is being encouraged is criminal.

The Model Penal Code definition of actus reus in solicitation is quite similar to the common-law interpretation. The primary difference is that under the Model Penal Code, a person must intend and demonstrate the intent to communicate the encouragement. As with common law, it is not required that the intent actually be communicated to the other person.

The mens rea for solicitation in the Model Penal Code requires that the person be aware that the encouragement is for a criminal act. Further, to prosecute for solicitation, it must be proven that a person has the intent that would be required to actually commit the offense that is encouraged.

In addition to conviction for solicitation in common-law states, the accused may also be convicted of being an accessory before the fact. Under the Model Penal Code, a person cannot be convicted as an accessory or as a conspirator in addition to being convicted for solicitation.

b. Miscellaneous Offenses   Some crimes, though categorized in some states as felonies, by definition are distinctly inchoate in character, and as such directly enable a person to commit a crime. Like the crimes previously discussed, these acts are such an integral part of creating the opportunity for other criminal conduct that they become crimes in and of themselves. Common examples include the illegal possession of weapons or the possession of such large quantities of drugs that it is probable that the drugs will be distributed illegally. Another example of such an offense is burglary. Traditionally, burglary was an offense that consisted of forcibly entering the home of another at night with the intent of committing a felony within the residence. This definition has been somewhat modified in many states under present day statutes. Today, definitions of burglary are much more general and often include any unpermitted entry (regardless of whether it requires force) into the property of another (regardless of whether it is the home, automobile, or other property) at any time of day with the intent to commit a felony within the property.[10] This sounds remarkably inchoate in its definition. Burglary is an act that creates the opportunity for felonious conduct.

In cases of burglary, it is no longer required that the intended felony actually occur, as in the past, which was the characteristic that distinguished it from inchoate crimes. Today, society discourages all unpermitted entry into the property of others with additional criminal intent. Such unpermitted entry is a necessary precursor to the commission of a felony on the property. Thus, if burglary is punished, perhaps persons will be deterred from entering private property to commit felonies. In any event, such persons can be punished for any actions they take that would enable the felonious conduct.

The Model Penal Code also recognizes these offenses and punishes them. Generally, punishment for all inchoate offenses including conspiracy, attempt, solicitation, burglary, or other offense, under the Model Penal Code includes a range of severity that approaches the penalty for the actual commission of the more serious offense. Consequently, the Model Penal Code does not recognize any offenses that are perhaps beyond the inchoate offense but are not quite a completion of the more serious offense. Some common-law states have such intermediate stages. Under the Model Penal Code, the definition of an inchoate offense includes all conduct leading to the moment the subsequent offense is actually completed.

Under common law, categories of homicide might include attempted murder, assault with intent to kill, and murder. Assault with intent to kill might describe a situation wherein a person actually inflicts deadly force on an individual, but the individual survives. For example, when a victim survives an intentional shooting, it is more than a mere attempt, but the actual murder is not achieved.

Under the Model Penal Code, a person may be charged with attempted murder or specifically with the crime of murder. The definition of attempt is broad enough and the penalties are severe enough to include the situation where the accused comes within a breath of murdering the victim.

c. Felony Crimes   As the preceding discussion indicates, the common-law jurisdictions and Model Penal Code jurisdictions regard the same basic types of conduct as criminal. The distinction between the two is generally in the way the crimes are formally defined. The following sections discuss some additional felony crimes that occur with some frequency. The definitions are based on basic principles of law, with the understanding that each state may have its own specific definitions and penalties.

i. Assault   In a civil case, assault is considered to be action threatening an unpermitted physical contact. However, in the criminal sense, assault often includes an actual physical contact and is synonymous with the civil tort offense of battery. Depending on the nature of the particular offense, assault is often a felony crime. Generally, an assault that is committed with a weapon or with the intent to do dangerous bodily harm, or one that results in serious bodily harm will be treated as a felony. When criminal laws differentiate assault from battery, assault is generally considered to be more consistent with the civil definition. Thus, criminal assault would be an act that causes fear of immediate physical harm through unpermitted physical contact.[11]

ii. Battery   Many times in criminal law, the terms assault and battery are interchangeable. When a distinction is made, battery is considered to be the unlawful contact with another person. Such contact can be direct or through an instrument such as a weapon. Like assault, the extent of the contact and the actor's intent will often dictate whether the crime will be prosecuted as a felony or a misdemeanor.

Usually the mens rea required for assault or battery is one of general intent. A person need only be aware that his or her conduct is likely to result in an unpermitted physical contact. Of course, if a more specific intent is present, that would also be sufficient, but the minimum requirement would be only a reasonable awareness.

iii. Theft, Robbery, and Larceny   In ordinary usage, many laypersons interchange the terms burglary, theft, and robbery. However, as previously indicated, burglary does not include the taking of another person's property, only the invasion of it. Similarly, theft and robbery are distinct terms, whereas theft and larceny are often synonymous in criminal law.

Theft occurs when a party unlawfully obtains the property of another with the intent to dispossess that person of the property.[12] The intent required can be merely to dispossess, to convert the property to one's own use, or to convey the property to another. As long as the intent is to deprive an owner of the use, possession, or ownership of the property, the mens rea requirement is satisfied.

In many jurisdictions, the value of the property influences the severity of the punishment. The theft of valuable property, usually in excess of a stated dollar amount, is considered grand larceny and is a felony. The theft of property that is valued below a stated dollar amount is considered to be petty (also known as petit) larceny and is usually considered to be a misdemeanor.

Robbery is the most serious offense involving the unlawful taking of property. To commit a robbery, one must deprive an owner of property by the use of force or threats of force. The robber must either use physical violence or demonstrate to the owner that unless the property is turned over, physical violence will be used to obtain the property.[13] Therefore, robbery must be committed in the presence of the owner. If the owner is absent and does not perceive the force or threats, there is no necessity for their use. Because robbery is considered to be a crime of violence, the penalties are generally more severe than those for larceny.

iv. Homicide   When a person is killed as the result of the conduct or omission by another person, a homicide has been committed. If there is no legal justification or excuse for such conduct, a criminal homicide has been committed. Only criminal homicide can result in conviction and punishment. Legal justification or excuse includes situations where the actor's conduct is considered noncriminal, generally because the required mens rea for a criminal homicide is not present. There are various types of homicide. Most often they are described as manslaughter and murder. Manslaughter is usually considered a less serious offense than murder because it is death caused without malice aforethought—a mental state that includes the intent to inflict deadly force. Manslaughter if further broken down into two categories: voluntary and involuntary.

Voluntary manslaughter is applicable in situations where the death of another was intentional but where special circumstances existed. An example of such a case is a crime of passion, where a person loses all ability to reason as the result of extreme provocation. It must be established that someone, often the deceased, did something so outrageous to provoke the defendant that it is understandable that the defendant lost the ability to think clearly and, in the heat of the moment, attacked the victim. Common situations include injury to one's family or to the marital relationship. One point is clear. The provocation must have been of a type so extraordinary that a jury could consider the defendant's conduct reasonable under the circumstances. This does not mean that charges against the defendant will be dropped. Rather, it explains why the defendant is not charged with murder and why the most serious penalties possible are not sought by the prosecution.

If the defendant has time to consider the action before it is taken and still elects to act on the emotionally charged situation, a charge of voluntary manslaughter would be inappropriate. The key element that separates voluntary manslaughter from murder is that in the former, the defendant did not have time to consider the ramifications of the actions about to be taken. In murder, there is time for someone to consider and plan the death or injury that ultimately produces the death of another. Thus, the longer the period of time that elapses between the provocation and the act of killing, the more likely the charge will be murder.

Involuntary manslaughter occurs when one person is responsible for the death of another because of gross and extreme negligence or recklessness but without the intent to kill or inflict bodily harm.[14] Such conduct is considered to show total disregard for the safety or well-being of others. In some states, death caused as the result of driving while intoxicated is considered to be involuntary manslaughter. However, many states have a separate statute for this, such as vehicular or motor vehicle homicide. Another example of conduct that might produce a charge of involuntary manslaughter is hunting in and around a populated area. When negligence and recklessness are differentiated by statute, negligence is treated as extreme carelessness, whereas recklessness involves a total disregard for others. Although both are types of involuntary manslaughter, generally, the penalties are more severe for the reckless homicide than for negligent homicide.

Reckless or negligent homicide may occur during the commission of another crime that is a misdemeanor, for example, death caused by a drunk driver or as the result of reckless driving, or it may occur as the result of some careless act not intended to be criminal. The latter often includes situations that are the result of circumstance, although created by negligence; for example, a person who target shoots in his or her backyard in a suburban area. Assume in such a case that a neighbor is hit and killed by a stray bullet. There was never any intent to commit a crime, and certainly no intent to kill the neighbor. Nevertheless, discharging deadly weapons in a populated area would be considered extremely careless.

The Model Penal Code recognizes the same basic principles regarding manslaughter. Although it does not use the terms voluntary and involuntary, it grades the degree of the offense and the severity of the penalty in accordance with situations that are reckless or negligent. The code places emphasis not on the actual provocation but rather on the actual emotional condition of the defendant at the time the death was caused. If the defendant was in such a mental state that control was impossible, the death could be considered a voluntary manslaughter. Under this application, there is no need to examine whether the defendant has time to cool off after the provocation. The entire question turns on the defendant's actual mental state at the time of the killing.

As indicated previously, murder is a premeditated act committed with specific malicious intent. Contrary to what the commonly used term "with malice aforethought" would suggest, the actor need not have thought out a careful plan to kill with hatred. Rather, the term describes the state of mind of a person who is aware that what he or she is doing can cause death and that he or she has the ability to choose not to act. Many states that apply this common-law theory of murder break up the definition by varying states of mind.

The term degree is often used to indicate various categories of murder. For example, murder in the first degree is usually the most serious felony. It often requires that the actor have the preconceived intent to kill and that the intent be carried out to fruition. This differs from murder in the second degree, which often describes a situation where a person intends to inflict serious bodily harm on the victim and instead death follows the assault. Finally, there is murder as the result of recklessness that is so great that the actor had no reasonable basis to believe that the death of another would not result from the action. For example, individuals racing cars on the highway and occupying all lanes of traffic at high rates of speed. The risk of death is more than substantial in cases of extreme recklessness.

Some states employ an additional category of murder known as the felony murder rule. This rule has two basic requirements: (1) the actor must be engaged in the commission of a dangerous felony and (2) the acts pertaining to the felony must proximately cause the death of another. Further, in some states, if the victim is injured and dies as a proximate result of those injuries at any time within one full year, the actor can be charged with murder even though other circumstances may have contributed to the death. Thus, if the actor sets into motion a series of events that injures or contributes in a significant manner to cause the victim to in some way become vulnerable to something that ultimately results in his or her death, the actor may be charged with felony murder.

APPLICATION 15.3

Charles commits an armed robbery of a convenience store. During the commission of the crime he strikes the store clerk over the head with a gun. Four months later the store clerk dies from a ruptured vessel in the brain that was undetected by doctors who examined the clerk after the robbery, but which bled slowly into Charles' brain until it ultimately caused his death. The coroner's report attributes the rupture to the blow to the head received in the robbery. The charges against Charles for robbery are amended to include felony murder because the clerk died as the proximate result of the assault by Charles.

Point for Discussion: Why should Charles be charged with murder if the doctors failure to diagnose the rupture was a significant factor in the clerk's death?

Assignment 15.2

Using the example in Application 15.3, chart the chain of events and explain why Charles is the proximate cause of death.

The Model Penal Code follows the same basic premise as common law when determining guilt in cases of murder. Murder that results from the intent to inflict fatal injuries is defined in much the same way as murder in the first degree under common law. The Model Penal Code also provides for situations of serious bodily harm or great recklessness that produces death, although these two situations are considered an offense of the same severity under the code. The primary difference is that the Model Penal Code contains no provision for the felony murder rule. The reasoning is that the person should be charged with murder or manslaughter in addition to the felony rather than be charged with a combined single charge of felony and murder. It is reasoned that the actual guilt and mens rea can be more easily and fairly determined by this method.

CASE IN POINT

Commonwealth v. Hart 403 Pa. 652,
170 A.2d 850

In order to determine whether there was sufficient evidence to establish a robbery within the meaning of the Felony-Murder Rule, it is necessary to consider the statute, the authorities, and the evidence. The Penal Code, Act of June 24, 1939, § 701 provides: 'All murder which . . . shall be committed on the perpetration of, or attempting to perpetrate any . . . robbery . . . shall be murder in the first degree.' Robbery is defined by § 704 of the Code as follows: 'Whoever robs another . . . or assaults any person with intent to rob him, or by menace or force demands any property of another, with intent to steal the same . . ..'

The following is a brief summary of what the jury could justifiably have found from the evidence: Defendant and Paricia K. lived together. He rented her out as a prostitute. Querey, the deceased victim, after his mother's death, came from North Carolina to Pennsylvania to collect her life insurance. He collected the insurance and on his way home engaged Patricia through a cab driver for purposes of intercourse. The price was $50. He paid her the $50 and also bought her some presents. Patricia remained some time and after it was over went back to the Naples Restaurant to meet defendant. She gave defendant $50. He became very angry because his price was $50 an hour and she had stayed three hours. Defendant shouted at her and said 'You are going out and see that man with me.' He said the man was trying to get something for nothing. Patricia was afraid to tell defendant that Querey had bought her presents because he had told her that if she ever let anybody buy her anything he would beat her—which he had already done on a prior occasion.

Defendant Hart was found guilty of murder in the first degree by a jury which imposed a penalty of life imprisonment. Defendant appealed from the judgment and sentence. He alleges four reasons: (1) The evidence was insufficient to establish that the killing occurred in the perpetration of a robbery within the meaning of the Felony-Murder Rule; (2) The Court erred in admitting into evidence in rebuttal of defendant's testimony, the transcribed testimony of a tape recording of defendant's pre-trial conversation with the Assistant District Attorney; (3) Defendant was denied a fair trial because of the ineffectiveness of

his counsel; and (4) Defendant's rights against self-incrimination were violated by the Assistant District Attorney when he obtained confession.

At his insistence, Patricia went to the Airport to see Querey to get the additional money to which he claimed he was entitled. They knocked on Querey's door and telephoned repeatedly but unsuccessfully. Defendant insisted they try once again and after defendant banged very loudly on Querey's door he forced Patricia to call Querey once more. Querey then opened the door slightly. Defendant pushed the door open and pushed Patricia inside. Then Querey asked: 'What's this all about?' Defendant answered 'I think you owe this girl some money.' Querey denied knowing Patricia and told defendant to get out. Patricia begged defendant to leave the room, but defendant replied he wanted that money. Querey threatened to call the police. He went to the phone and defendant followed him. They began struggling over the telephone. Patricia begged defendant to leave Querey alone. Querey started to put his leg in his trousers and at that point defendant, who was 6 feet 4 inches tall and weighed 170 pounds, started hitting Querey in the face with his fists. Patricia screamed at defendant, who repeatedly told her to be quiet and threatened to hit her too if she were not. Querey, who was about 5 feet 8 inches tall and weighed 150 pounds and was further handicapped by putting on his trousers, just stood there while defendant beat him until he fell to the floor. While he lay there defendant kicked him in the back of the head—which was later proved to be the cause of death. Then defendant bent down, and while Querey was unconscious, took the wallet out of Querey's pocket, removed four (or more) $50 bills from the wallet, and threw the wallet between Querey's legs.

Patricia at that point ran to the elevator, followed by defendant. He told her that he had gotten over $300. Defendant then concocted several lies for Patricia to tell, including a story that Querey had beaten her. Defendant soon became scared, hid, dyed his hair, and several days later fled with Patricia and another friend to New Orleans. In his confession to the district attorney (which was freely made after due admonitions and warnings) he admitted that he had gotten $200; that he had struck Querey and while Querey was unconscious but still living had taken his money.

Defendant contends that the above mentioned facts cannot amount to a felony murder because the Commonwealth failed to prove that he 'had any preconceived intention to rob' Querey when 'he went to his room; that the robbery was merely an afterthought' which was formulated after the beating occurred.

The Commonwealth's evidence to prove both robbery and murder was direct and overwhelming. Not only did Patricia see and testify to the beating, kicking and robbery by defendant, but defendant freely admitted it to the district attorney, who testified in behalf of the Commonwealth. Defendant in his testimony at the trial admitted striking Querey with his fist but denied taking any money from Querey, denied kicking him, and testified that he made up the story to protect and help Patricia. He likewise testified that he never lived with Patricia nor received any money from her (except once inadvertently), but he just liked to protect her. On cross-examination he was unable to recall or remember many of the incriminating statements he had made to the district attorney or to the assistant district attorney. A reading of the record demonstrates beyond any possible doubt that the jury could have found that he was an evasive, lying witness.

Defendant's highly technical argument amounts to this: Unless the Commonwealth proves that the intention to commit a robbery was formed before the beginning of the fatal assault, the evidence cannot amount to a murder which was committed in the perpetration of a robbery. In other words, defendant would require a televised stop-watch in every robbery or felony killing to prove that the felonious intent existed before the attack. It is rare, we repeat, that a criminal telephones or telegraphs his criminal intent and consequently such intent can be properly found by the jury from the facts and circumstances in a particular case. In the instant case the facts and circumstances, particularly defendant's belligerently expressed intent to get the money (to which he said

he was entitled) out of Querey, followed by his use of force to obtain it, were amply sufficient to justify a jury in finding the necessary criminal intent beyond a reasonable doubt. There is no authority to support defendant's proposition—indeed there are two authorities, although none are needed, to the contrary.

In Commonwealth v. Stelma, 327 Pa. 317, 192 A. 906, defendant signed a confession in which he stated that after his victim had hit him in the chest he knocked him down with his fist and then in a drunken rage picked up a stone and hit him in the head several times with the stone. As the victim lay on the ground, defendant took money from his pockets, but he claimed he never intended to do this until after the victim was lying unconscious or dead. The Court in sustaining a conviction of murder in the first degree with penalty of death, paid (327 Pa. at page 321, 192 A. at page 908):

'. . . The defendant's argument that the intention to rob originated subsequent to the assault upon the deceased need not be seriously considered in view of the verdict of the jury. Moreover, even though such were the case, it is immaterial when the design to rob was conceived, if the homicide occurred while defendant was perpetrating or attempting to perpetrate a robbery. Where the killing occurs in the perpetration of any of the crimes specifically named in the statute referred to, the intent to kill is immaterial. Such considerations do not affect the situation here presented because the circumstances leading up to the attack on Doyle indicate an assault with an intent to rob, . . .'

The law which has been in existence for many centuries in England and for ages in our Country, was enacted for the safety and protection of peaceable citizens of each community and we will not permit it to be thwarted or evaded by such a far-fetched and realistically-absurd construction of the Penal Code.[15]

Case Review Question: Why did the defendant want the court to believe the intent to rob came only after the beating incident?

---

v. Rape   In recent years, the crime of rape has received a great deal of notoriety for a variety of reasons. Although the crime of rape went largely unreported in the past, changes in the roles of women in our society, along with rape shield statutes, have contributed to an increasing number of reports of sexual assault. Previously, it was not uncommon for the entire sexual history of the victim to be disclosed at the trial of the defendant in an attempt to show that the victim somehow encouraged the defendant's conduct. However, a majority of states have enacted rape shield statutes that prevent such information from being introduced as evidence. Also, women are now coming forward with charges of acquaintance rape (date rape), which was virtually unheard of in the past. The government now recognizes that rape need not, and usually does not, occur between total strangers.

Rape, also known as a type of sexual assault in some jurisdictions, is the forcible act of sexual intercourse by one person against another without consent. It is a crime in all jurisdictions, and penalties range from a few years to life in prison, depending upon the circumstances. The act of rape or even consensual intercourse with a minor typically carries even heavier penalties. When consensual intercourse occurs between an adult and a minor, to whom the adult is not married, the crime of statutory rape has been committed. The presumption is that the minor is incapable of making a proper decision as to whether to consent to intercourse and, therefore, intercourse with a minor is criminal per se. The age at which a minor is presumed to have sufficient capacity to consent to intercourse varies among jurisdictions. Also, in some jurisdictions, the fact that the minor lied about his or her age is an adequate defense to the charge of statutory rape.

d. Punishment Common law and the Model Penal Code have similar concepts of punishment. Under each, the general rule is that a greater degree of specific intent will result in a more severe range of punishment for the convicted defendant. With respect to the most extreme punishment—death—the Model Penal Code includes it but neither advocates nor discourages it. The provision for the death penalty is included as an acknowledgment that the death penalty is part of American criminal law at this time. The position of common law has varied on the issue of capital punishment. At this time, it is considered an acceptable form of punishment by the government for certain types of crime.

Other punishments typically include imprisonment, monetary fines, community service (time spent doing activities that benefit the community at large), and restitution (repayment to a victim for injury to his or her person or property). Whatever the punishment, one constant remains: The punishment must not be cruel or unusual for the crime committed, according to the Eighth Amendment. For example, the death penalty has been determined to be cruel and unusual punishment for the crime of rape, while it is still permissible for other crimes such as murder.

e. White-Collar Crime Crime also exists in the workplace, and criminal responsibility for such crime has received increased attention in recent years. Although corporations generally are not specifically liable for criminal acts, it does not mean that liability is nonexistent. Although the corporation is considered to be a person under the law in terms of equality of rights and duties, it is still a legal fiction. Because the corporation does not possess a singular and independent mind, it is incapable of formulating the adequate mens rea to commit a criminal act. Only those who represent the corporation can do that. The law has come to recognize that the persons who represent the corporation are in fact the mind of the corporation and through them the corporation can be convicted of most criminal acts.

If a person is employed by a corporation and acts on its behalf, the corporation can be held responsible for those acts under the theory of respondeat superior. As long as the act was performed within the scope of the person's employment and related directly to the corporation, the entity as well as the individual can be held responsible.

Although a corporation cannot be imprisoned, it can be heavily fined or dissolved involuntarily by the courts.

Crimes frequently committed on behalf of corporations include tax law violations, securities law violations, burglary and theft (in the case of trade secrets), and damage to the property of competitors. All of these actions require some actual mental and physical conduct by an individual, but they directly or indirectly benefit the corporation. If it can be shown that the corporate representatives acted, encouraged these acts, or accepted the benefits of these acts, the corporation may be charged for the crime as well. In addition, the individuals may be held responsible as principals.

The Model Penal Code recognizes liability of business entities in much the same manner as the common law. The only real difference is that the Model Penal Code has a fairly narrow definition of the types of offenses for which a business entity may be held responsible. Specifically, for a business entity to be held responsible under the code, the offense must be one that the legislature clearly intended to apply to corporations or one in which the criminal actions can be proven to be consistent with the purpose of the corporation.[16] In other cases, only the individual will be held responsible for the criminal acts.

In addition to those crimes for which a corporation or business entity might be held criminally liable, crimes can be committed against the entity by its fiduciaries. For example, a bank employee who over a period of time extracts funds from the bank for personal use has committed embezzlement, which essentially is the theft of property. Other crimes include violation of securities laws to injure or destroy a competitor's business or to take unfair advantage of investors. From time to time there is a great deal of publicity concerning individuals charged with manipulating their position in the stock markets or technology industry to promote huge personal gains by violating securities and other similar laws that have been designed and passed to promote a level field among investors.

While white-collar crime often appears to be victimless because no clearly identifiable and individual injury may be caused by the act, it is nevertheless a violation of law and is dealt with in much the same manner as other criminal conduct.

f. Defenses to Charges of Criminal Conduct   For every act committed, there are explanations for why the act occurred. In cases of criminal acts, some explanations are sufficient to prevent conviction and punishment of the actor. Such explanations are known as defenses, and they are wide and varied. The following sections examine a number of defenses that accused persons frequently assert.

i. Justifiable or Excusable Conduct   Traditionally, **justifiable** or **excusable** conduct was a defense that could be applied in criminal cases. In present-day law, conduct that is justifiable or excusable is not considered criminal conduct and does not provide a basis for arrest or prosecution. Justifiable conduct is an act that takes place under special circumstances such as defense of oneself or others.[17] Excusable conduct refers to acts that would be considered criminal but for the actor's status at the time of the act.[18] For example, when law enforcement officers or military personnel intrude onto another's property or perhaps even kill in the line of duty, their conduct, which would otherwise be considered criminal, is excused because they are supposedly doing so in the interest of the public welfare. Of course, this may not apply if such persons abuse their authority and commit these acts without basis.

A defense to charges of criminal conduct always exist in situations where the actor's conduct was not voluntary. Obviously, involuntary conduct includes acts over which the actor has no physical control. Examples would include acts performed while

Justifiable
Behavior by one who, under the circumstances, is considered to be innocent of otherwise criminal behavior.

Excusable
Behavior by one who, under the color of authority, is considered to be innocent of otherwise criminal behavior.

sleeping, during seizures, or as the result of a reflex. Whether acts performed while under the influence of hypnosis or prescribed medication are voluntary is still questioned in most jurisdictions.

The key to the defense of involuntary conduct is proving that the defendant was physically incapable of forming the required mens rea prior to committing the crime. The lower the degree of requirement, such as a general intent or awareness, the more difficult it is to prove the act was involuntary. With respect to strict liability, since intent is not a consideration, involuntariness would not be a defense.

A similar defense is duress, in which a third party causes another person to act by exerting influence over that person. The actor has a mental choice between following or refusing the commands of the third person. If the situation is extreme, duress may be used as a defense on the basis that, in reality, only one choice could be made. For example, if the actor is told to act or his or her children will be killed, duress would apply. Although the actor has technically been given an option, in practical terms, he or she has no choice. The court will examine the circumstances to determine just how reasonable a refusal to act would have been.

Mistake is a common defense to accusations of criminal acts. Two types of mistake can be alleged. Mistake of fact occurs when the person commits the act while reasonably believing something that was not true.[19] Many cases have been reported of persons leaving a store or other public building and driving away in what they think is their car, but in fact, their key fits an identical car belonging to someone else. Although such persons did indeed steal the automobile, they are not guilty of auto theft. They reasonably believed they were driving their own car. Thus, they made a mistake of fact. Any mistake of fact must bear directly on the intent required for the particular crime.

Mistake of law is applied much more rarely. It is appropriate only where a person actually believed that his or her conduct was lawful under one statute, despite the existence of another statute that might indicate such conduct was unlawful. An example is persons who exercise their right to avoid a search of their property by police without a proper warrant when another law gives police the right to search property in emergencies. If these persons are not aware of the emergency and deny the police entry, they are exercising a legal right. If, for example, unknown to these people, a criminal is hiding in their basement, they have made an honest mistake of law in protecting their rights and cannot be prosecuted for something such as obstruction of government operations.

The Model Penal Code acknowledges both mistakes of fact and mistakes of law. In cases of mistake of fact, the mistake must be something that is believed and is part of the state of mind of the actor. The code, in line with common-law, generally holds that ignorance of the law is no excuse. It does, however, allow certain exceptions that are similar to the common-law exceptions that create a valid defense. Examples of these exceptions include (1) the actor did not have reasonable access to the law, (2) the actor reasonably believed the conduct was lawful, as in the previous common-law example, and (3) the actor was relying on the statement of the government or a government official. A person's lawyer's advice that conduct was permissible is not a defense. Such a statement must come from someone in a government capacity.

A defense that has gained some notoriety in recent years is entrapment, which alleges that law enforcement personnel created a situation that would lead a law-abiding citizen with no prior criminal intent into criminal activity. The police must plant the idea and lead a person into criminal conduct that the person would not otherwise be predisposed to commit. This is often used in cases of prostitution and drug dealing. It is absolutely necessary for the police to do no more than accept or enhance the criminal conduct. The opportunity and intent to complete the crime must be developed by the criminal without any significant influence by the police.

Probably the most publicized defense in criminal law is the insanity defense. While substantive as well as procedural law varies on this defense among the jurisdictions, the defense has common denominators. In all cases where insanity is raised as a defense to charges of criminal conduct, the issues are ultimately reduced to whether a mental impairment existed and whether it was sufficiently significant to play a role in the defendant's intent and conduct at the time the crime was committed.

The insanity defense standards applied in about one third of the states is the M'Naughten Rule, whose origins date back to 1843.[20] While the rule has been modified in some states, the basic tenet is that the mental impairment either (1) prevented the defendant from understanding the criminal nature and quality of the criminal act or (2) prevented the defendant from determining whether the act was legal or illegal. The difficulty with the M'Naughten Rule is that it requires a finding that the defendant was either sane or insane, with no middle ground. Consequently, a majority of states have chosen other methods to determine the question of insanity as an influence on the one charged with criminal conduct.

Some jurisdictions allow in place of or in addition to the M'Naughten Rule, the irresistible impulse theory. Under this premise, the defendant claims to have been unable to control his or her behavior as the result of mental impairment at the time of the alleged criminal conduct. The irresistible impulse theory rests on the basis that the defendant at the time of the crime was subjected to a sudden impulse that he or she did not have the capacity to control.

Finally, a number of states have adopted a defense standard similar to that used in federal prosecutions. In 1984, this defense was embodied in a statutory definition by the Congress:

> (a) Affirmative Defense: It is an affirmative defense to a prosecution under any Federal statute that, at the time of the commission of the acts constituting the offense, the defendant, as a result of a severe mental disease or defect, was unable to appreciate the nature and quality or the wrongfulness of his acts. Mental disease or defect does not otherwise constitute a defense.
>
> (b) Burden of Proof: The defendant has the burden of proving the defense of insanity by clear and convincing evidence.[21]

This recent statute has made it more difficult to prove insanity as a defense. In the past, insanity was seen as a way to avoid prosecution for the acts of an otherwise reasonable individual. The new statute requires extensive proof of mental disability. It must be shown that the disability was severe and that it prevented any ability to appreciate or understand the act itself and its consequences. An additional hurdle is that the burden is placed on the defendant. Usually, the burden is on the prosecution to show guilt beyond a reasonable doubt. Thus, any doubt created in the minds of the jury by the defense is sufficient to prevent conviction. Under the new insanity statute, however, the defendant must present clear and convincing evidence of the required elements.

The Model Penal Code is the approach the majority of the states take with regard to the insanity defense. The code permits a defendant to raise the insanity defense, but the defense must prove that the defendant did not have the ability to "appreciate the criminality of his conduct" or "conform his conduct to the requirements of law."[22] This requirement parallels and strengthens the reasoning of the common-law approach. Under this rule, the defendant has the burden of establishing that he or she had some cognitive inability to understand right from wrong and was unable to control his or her actions within legal bounds. The rule's significance is that ordinarily the prosecution has the burden of proving the defendant is guilty. However, when the insanity defense is raised, the burden is switched, and the defendant has the burden to present proof to meet the insanity defense standard of the jurisdiction.

Assignment 15.3

> Consult a state statutory subject index. Locate the appropriate statutory criminal code reference for the defense of insanity or incompetence due to mental condition. Then determine the requirements for pleading a defense of insanity in response to a charge of criminal conduct.

B. CRIMINAL PROCEDURE AND THE CONSTITUTION

Criminal procedure is one of the most volatile areas of law in the United States today. It differs significantly from civil procedure. Of course, the obvious difference is that rules of civil procedure govern civil actions and rules of criminal procedure govern criminal prosecutions. In addition, criminal procedure comes into play long before the action is formally commenced against a defendant. Criminal procedure affects the prosecution from the moment a crime is suspected.

Criminal prosecutions take place in federal and statute judicial systems, each of which has its own rules. However, all procedures are ultimately governed by constitutional requirements. Through its various amendments, the U.S. Constitution protects all persons from unfair and unequal treatment during criminal prosecutions. The courts vigorously enforce the Constitution and require that all persons be treated fairly and equally. Therefore, although the rules may differ somewhat from jurisdiction to jurisdiction, the effect of the rules must be constitutionally permissible or the rules may be invalidated by the courts.

As mentioned, various amendments to the U.S. Constitution affect criminal rights. The Bill of Rights was adopted, in part, to protect individuals from being unfairly or unnecessarily penalized by the justice system. Amendments 4, 5, 8, and 14 address virtually every aspect of criminal procedure, including but not limited to, invasion of one's property for the purpose of searching and seizure of criminal evidence, self-incrimination, and the grounds for capital offenses, where punishment can be death. The effects of these amendments on criminal procedure are discussed in subsequent sections.

1. The Fourteenth Amendment: Due Process

In recent years, the Fourteenth Amendment passed in 1868, has played a much-publicized and controversial role in criminal procedure. The obvious interpretation is that all citizens are subject to federal law and, further, that no state may pass or interpret laws that would conflict with federal law or the specific rights listed in the amendment. For many years, this was the interpretation given by the U.S. Supreme Court. In various decisions, the Court maintained that the Fourteenth Amendment guaranteed only fundamental rights necessary to justice and order. It did not interpret the amendment to mean that all states must follow with absolute certainty all other constitutional amendments when creating law. Rather, as long as their laws did not conflict with constitutional guarantees, the states were permitted to create laws in any manner they chose.

During the 1950s and 1960s the Court's approach to the Fourteenth Amendment changed. At that time, the justices who had been appointed to the Court were, as a group, more liberal than at any other time in the Court's history. In addition, there was a great deal of unrest in the United States. Many believed that the constitutional guarantees of the Bill of Rights were being ignored or violated at the state level. The result was a great many alleged discrimination claims against the state governments and, in some parts of the country, individuals protesting the alleged inequities by engaging in riots and other demonstrations of civil disobedience. Protest marches were held, sit-ins were conducted, and various other measures were taken by individuals to protect what were perceived to be fundamental rights. In the South, civil rights volunteers came from all over the country to help secure the freedom of blacks to vote, assemble, and be treated with equality in the way laws were applied. All around the United States, people began to stand up against local and state governments that they believed operated with indifference to the fundamental protections that were so important in the creation of the original Constitution and Bill of Rights.

Although the Supreme Court of the 1950s and 1960s was quite liberal in its thinking, it was unwilling to use the total integration approach.[23] This legal theory follows the premise that the Fourteenth Amendment effectively integrates the entire Constitution and its amendments into each state's laws. The actual result would be to replace the state constitutions with the federal Constitution or to at least add the federal Constitution and its amendments to all state constitutions. The states would have virtually no say in what rights would be afforded their citizens or how the citizens would be governed. All state laws would be virtually identical to federal laws.

Because the Court thought this theory invaded too deeply into the ability of state citizens to govern themselves without unnecessary federal government interference, it engaged in *selective incorporation*. Previously, the Court had followed the rule that only the rights expressly stated in the Fourteenth Amendment were required to be explicitly followed by the states including the right to **due process** (fundamental fairness) in the application of law before a person's life, liberty, or property could be seized. In simpler terms, an individual could not be sentenced to death or prison, or have real or personal property taken by any state or federal government unless the person was treated fairly by the government. In addition, all persons were to be treated equally in the way laws were applied. For a time, this was sufficient. However, it became increasingly apparent that state and local governments did not always take a liberal view as to what constituted fundamental fairness in the way accused persons were treated and prosecuted.

To remedy this, the court decided to more thoroughly and clearly define the term *due process*. In the past, it had been interpreted to mean essentially that which was fundamentally fair in a system of justice. However, the Court took the position that the states needed further clarification of the term. Because Congress had passed the Fourteenth Amendment, which required the states to give all citizens due process, the U.S. Supreme Court had the authority to interpret the meaning and intent of the amendment and, specifically, its language of due process. As noted earlier, the Court could have done this by simply stating that all rights in the Bill of Rights were included in the

Due Process
That which is necessary to fundamental fairness in the American system of justice.

definition of due process. However, since this was seen as too invasive, the Court opted instead for a case-by-case review to determine whether a certain right in the Bill of Rights should be included in the definition of due process. If the Court determined that a right was included, it would state with specificity how the right was to be protected at the state level.

Over the years, the process of selective incorporation has resulted in expansion of the definition of due process to include the Fourth, Fifth, Sixth, and Eighth Amendments. One by one, cases went to the Supreme Court, where it was determined that the circumstances of treatment of the accused did not afford the accused fundamental fairness during investigation, arrest, and prosecution.

The ultimate effect of selective incorporation is quite simple. Once the Supreme Court finds that a particular right is incorporated into the Fourteenth Amendment, any state laws that would affect this right must be fair and reasonable. The court will invalidate state laws that affect protected federal constitutional rights.

Selective incorporation has been especially relevant to laws of criminal procedure that guide criminal prosecutions and set forth what is considered to be fundamental to the criminal process. These laws ultimately affect the American theory that a person is innocent until guilt is proven beyond any reasonable doubt, by controlling the manner in which the accused is treated and evidence is obtained.

The following sections discuss the amendments to the U.S. Constitution that have been selectively incorporated into the Fourteenth Amendment. The reasoning behind the incorporation of each particular amendment and the effect the amendment's incorporation has on state laws are included. It is especially helpful to examine the cases in which the Court made these decisions, because the cases provide real-life examples.

2. The Fourth Amendment: Search and Seizure

As early as 1914, the U.S. Supreme Court held that evidence in a federal criminal prosecution that was obtained without a proper search warrant or probable cause was inadmissible in court.[24] This was the beginning of the exclusionary rule, under which improperly obtained evidence is excluded from trial. No matter how damaging, such evidence cannot be used to convict someone of a crime. The Supreme Court adopted this position with regard to the federal court system's criminal prosecutions.

The idea that the Fourth Amendment should be incorporated into the Fourteenth, thereby requiring states to apply the exclusionary rule, was first addressed in 1949. At that time, the Court examined what the states had done on their own and found that some 30 states had considered the exclusionary rule used in federal cases, but had chosen not to follow the rule in state criminal prosecutions. Rather, these states had decided to develop their own methods to discourage police from unreasonable practices in obtaining evidence.[25] In that case, the Court decided that since a majority of the states had rejected the exclusionary rule and were using means other than the exclusion of evidence to discourage unlawful searches and seizures, it should not forcibly impose the requirement on the state governments. The Court held that the states could adequately protect the rights of their citizens without a forced application of the exclusionary rule and could still guarantee rights under the Fourth Amendment. Therefore, the Fourth Amendment was not incorporated, at that time, into the Fourteenth Amendment definition of due process, and the states were not required to adopt the federal position on the exclusionary rule. The effect was that as long as the state law was followed, a person's property could be searched and seized and any evidence of criminal activity used against the individual in a prosecution.

Just 12 years after *Wolf v. Colorado*, the Supreme Court reconsidered the incorporation of the Fourth Amendment into the Fourteenth Amendment. In *Mapp v. Ohio*,[26] the Court reversed its prior holding, which is an extremely rare occurrence, and held that the federally developed exclusionary rule is the most appropriate way to protect citizens from unreasonable searches and seizures. The Court further held that for a citizen to be afforded due process in a criminal prosecution, a right guaranteed in the Fourteenth Amendment, the Fourth Amendment protections must be adhered to, including the federal method of using the exclusionary rule. Consequently, the Fourth Amendment protections should be incorporated into the definition of the Fourteenth Amendment, and the states should be required to follow the exclusionary rule, which is the method of choice to enforce the Fourth Amendment rule of no unreasonable search and seizure.

A major reason for the Court's reversal of its position was that since the *Wolf* decision, many states had tried methods other than the exclusionary rule and had failed. Many of these states then turned to the exclusionary rule on their own. The Court affirmed this as an acceptable method of protecting citizen's rights.

With this decision, the Fourteenth Amendment began its expansion to include the rights enunciated in other amendments. The results of the decisions continue even today. Since that time, the Court has reviewed many state laws to determine what is a reasonable search or seizure and what is unreasonable. Evidence obtained through the latter is prohibited under the exclusionary rule from being used as evidence at a trial.

Over the years, a great deal of concern has been expressed about the exclusionary rule, which was intended to deter or prevent law enforcement personnel from obtaining evidence by means that violate the Fourth Amendment rights. The rationale was that the individuals were not in a position to protect their rights against law enforcement agencies. Further, if these agencies were not encouraged in some way to honor the constitutional amendment against unreasonable search and seizure, our society could be reduced to a police state that, in its most extreme form, might include random invasions of people's homes and property in search of evidence that might incriminate them.

However noble the intent of the exclusionary rule, the actual result is indisputable. Whenever evidence is obtained in a questionable manner, the person who benefits is the accused. Although our government follows the doctrine that an accused is innocent until proven guilty, in many such cases, the evidence excluded is so strong that it would undoubtedly result in a verdict of guilty by a jury. As a consequence of applying the exclusionary rule to protect a defendant's Fourth Amendment rights, many criminals have gone free or plea bargained for greatly reduced charges.

The Supreme Court has been faced with a double bind. Without the exclusionary rule, the improper searches and seizures of innocent people's property may occur. With the exclusionary rule, known criminals can go free because of a technical, minor, or even innocent violation of the rule by law enforcement. In 1984, the Court considered this dilemma in *United States v. Leon*.[27] In the *Leon* decision, the Supreme Court addressed at length the difficulty with enforcing a broad application of the exclusionary rule. The court recognized that excluding evidence because of an improper search or seizure, no matter how small the infraction that caused it to be improper, resulted in preventing the jury from accurately determining innocence or guilt at a trial. When the exclusionary rule is applied, often the case is dismissed because little admissible evidence is available to support a conviction. At the very least, the jury is given only limited, properly obtained information to consider and with which to make its decision. In fact, they generally do not know that additional evidence exists and has been excluded.

In *Leon*, the Court was faced with a situation in which the police properly requested a search warrant. The judge properly reviewed the information to support the warrant and issued the warrant. The policed exercised the search warrant and found evidence that was very incriminating. Only after the search was completed was it discovered that the warrant was improperly issued. The police had requested a warrant on the basis of limited surveillance and the information of a person who had never before acted as an informant. Unless informants have a history of providing accurate information to law enforcement, their testimony usually requires much additional evidence before a judge will believe there is probable cause to suspect a crime and issue a search warrant. In this case, the defendant challenged the validity of the search warrant, and a higher judge found that it should not have been issued on such limited and uncorroborated information.

The Supreme Court used this decision to make a major exception to the exclusionary rule. Observing that the police had made every effort to follow the requirements to protect the Fourth Amendment rights of the defendant, the Court reasoned that since this was the entire goal of the exclusionary rule, it had been satisfied. The police had gone so far as to request permission of a judge to search for criminal evidence. Therefore, the goal of the rule had been met, and the citizen's rights had been protected. The Court refused to exclude the evidence—a large quantity of illegal drugs—and the defendant was prosecuted. The Court stated that the exclusionary rule is designed to deter unreasonable practices by law enforcement personnel, not to remedy poor exercises of authority by judges.

The *Leon* decision is very important in the law of criminal procedure. It signals that the Court has shifted toward a more conservative view of what is necessary to protect the rights of citizens. The Court currently regards certain areas as private and subject to the protection of a citizen's Fourteenth Amendment rights by requiring satisfaction of the guarantees under the Fourth Amendment.

Probable Cause
Legal concept of suspicion supported by facts necessary before a search or arrest can be conducted by law enforcement officers.

a. Probable Cause   What a person considers to be private is that which cannot be searched or seized without **probable cause.** The Court has established a two-step test to determine what is private property. First, it must be decided whether the person acted in such a way as to keep the property private from others. Second, it must be determined whether the person was reasonable in believing such property should be allowed to be kept private.[28]

Before law enforcement personnel can search or seize private property, they must have probable cause to believe a crime has been committed and/or that the owner of the property has been involved in criminal activity. There must also be probable cause to believe that a search of the property will result in finding evidence that will assist in proving this. Further, whenever possible, the law enforcement agency must seek approval of the search and seizure by obtaining a warrant from a judicial officer. The basis for the warrant must be probable cause. Although it is much debated, no absolute formula has ever been developed to determine what constitutes probable cause. Rather, probable cause falls within a range that, when examined by a neutral observer, would be considered "more than bare suspicion" but "less than evidence which would justify . . . conviction."[29]

If law enforcement personnel can support their suspicions and allegations of probable cause with outside information or with other evidence that would create this degree of probability that the person or property is connected with criminal activity, a search warrant may be issued by a judge. If there is not time to request a search warrant, the officers may proceed with the search if there is probable cause to conduct it. Because the officers are not considered to be as objective as a judicial officer, they are under a particularly heavy burden to show that their search was made with probable cause. To qualify as an exception to the warrant requirement, there must be an immediate danger that the property or person associated with the criminal activity will be lost unless an immediate search is conducted.

The type of property that may be searched has also been discussed specifically by the courts. As a general rule, before a private residence can be searched, a warrant must be issued. If the property has been abandoned, a citizen has no expectation of privacy; therefore, no warrant is needed.[30] In addition, if the criminal activity or evidence can be observed by persons around or above the property, then it is considered to be in view of the public, and there is no expectation of privacy. If an officer is lawfully upon another person's property for any reason and discovers criminal evidence in plain view, the property may be seized immediately. This is known as the plain view rule. Finally, if someone other than the resident has access to the residence and voluntarily allows officers entrance to the property, such entrance is treated as if permission had been given by the resident. Therefore, landlords, roommates, or guests generally have the power to admit police officers voluntarily to a residence for the purpose of searching for evidence of criminal activity. In such situations, no warrant is necessary.

Police do need a warrant to invade private property by other than ordinary means. If, for example, a wiretap is going to be used to obtain the content of conversations in a residence or on a telephone line from a residence, a search warrant must be obtained, because the public would perceive a reasonable expectation of privacy in such a situation. However, devices that merely record the numbers called from a residence are not considered private, as the telephone company has access to this information at all times. Further, tracking devices on vehicles are permissible because the purpose is to track the vehicle in public. There can be no expectation of privacy about where one goes in public.

Vehicles have created a whole new arena for questions about search and seizure. They are private property capable of concealing a great deal of other property. At the same time, they are transported in public, which means that the expectation of privacy is lower than that in a residence. The courts have held that looking into the vehicle from the outside is not a search and that if evidence of criminal activity is seen, there is no need for a warrant.[31]

If a car has been abandoned, there is no longer a reasonable expectation of privacy and no warrant is needed to examine the interior of the vehicle. The courts have also given officers the right to search those areas of a car that are within reasonable reach of the owner when a stop is made. The rationale is that the owner may be within reach of a weapon that could be used to assault the officers or to effect an escape. The recent trend has been to approve searches of vehicles even when the suspect is no longer in the car or the car has been impounded. The basic requirement seems to be not that an emergency must exist but rather that the officer must have probable cause to believe that evidence or dangerous items may be in the car or its compartments, or in containers within it or, if the car is not in the possession of the police, that it is subject to removal from the jurisdiction. The regulation of police searches of automobiles is a rapidly evolving area of the law with many distinctions between state and federal governments. Therefore, it is important to know the law specific to your jurisdiction.

This has been a brief examination of some areas that have been addressed by the courts in determining what constitutes a search under the Fourth Amendment. Because the amendment has been applied to the states, these rules must be followed by state as well as federal law enforcement officers. The theory is that these rules will afford citizens due process and fairness before their privacy is invaded or their property is searched or seized by the state government. The rules also help to ensure fairer criminal prosecutions by reducing the chances of improper convictions.

b. Arrest   The same basic warrant requirements that apply to search and seizure of property also apply to arrest. In essence, an arrest is a search and seizure of a person, and the person is entitled to the same fair treatment that his or her property would be afforded. Consequently, the courts prefer that arrest warrants be obtained upon a showing of probable cause before the arrest is made. Often criminal activity is discovered while it is occurring or immediately after it has occurred. In such cases, it is usually unreasonable to expect that the criminal would remain until a warrant is obtained. Therefore, most arrests are made on the basis of a probable cause determination by law enforcement officers, which is subject to judicial review, just as a search made without a warrant would be.

When an arrest based on probable cause has been made, the officer may search the arrested person and all areas within his or her reach.[32] The reason for this is that the arrestee may be carrying a weapon that could be used to harm the officer. If the officer recovers other evidence of criminal activity during the search, the evidence may also be seized. Even though it is not what the officer may have been searching for, it is considered to be fruits of crime. A suspect who carries evidence of criminal activity on his or her person and is subsequently lawfully arrested does not have a reasonable expectation of privacy regarding that property.

Even when a full-fledged arrest is not made, the officers are entitled to take minimum steps to protect their own safety. Occasionally, an officer will stop an individual on suspicion of some criminal activity, perhaps even a minor infraction, such as a traffic violation. Even in this case, the officer has the right to frisk the individual for a concealed weapon if the officer has a reasonable suspicion that the suspect is armed or otherwise dangerous. This is permitted to avoid disastrous circumstances that have occurred and still do from time to time when an individual stopped for a minor infraction pulls out a weapon and kills an officer.

As this far-from-exhaustive discussion illustrates, the law of search and seizure is quite complex. Further, this area of law changes continually as the Supreme Court seeks to mold specific rules regarding the expectation of privacy by individuals for themselves and their property. The Court must balance these expectations against what is necessary to promote law enforcement and the safety of the people as a whole. As long as this balancing continues, this area of criminal procedure will grow.

3. The Fifth Amendment: Double Jeopardy, Self-Incrimination

Practically speaking, the role of the Fifth Amendment in criminal procedure has been confined primarily to the issue of double jeopardy and self-incrimination, addressed individually below, since they are wholly separate rights.

Double jeopardy is the right of every citizen to be tried once, and only once, for a specific crime charged. The theory is that the government should prove guilt beyond a reasonable doubt at trial. If this cannot be accomplished, the presumption of innocence is sustained and questions of guilt are dismissed. Citizens cannot be subjected to a new trial for the same crime each time the government believes it can produce new evidence or select a more critical jury.

The rule of double jeopardy was rather easily incorporated into the Fourteenth Amendment and applied to all state laws. The Fourteenth Amendment clearly states that there can be no deprivation of life or liberty without due process of law. It seems quite logical that to force someone to be tried over and over again for the same crime until a conviction was achieved would not be an exercise of due process. The very notion of fair treatment to all citizens is contrary to the thought that a citizen could be singled out and charged repeatedly with a crime until the prosecution was successful.

The courts have clearly defined the point at which double jeopardy becomes an issue. A person is not considered to be in jeopardy of loss of life or limb (in modern terms, penalty, liberty, or life) until there is a real possibility that such a result could occur. After a person is charged with a crime and until the time of trial, there is a chance that the charges will be dropped. After the trial begins, however, it is assumed that a verdict will be reached and a penalty may ensue. Therefore, a person is not in jeopardy until such time as the jury has been sworn in.[33] In a *bench* trial before a judge, and without a jury, double jeopardy attaches when the first witness is sworn. At this point, the defendant can be subjected to a second trial for the charge only if the first trial results in a mistrial.

Once the verdict is reached, it is considered final. Following this, if the accused person is acquitted (found not guilty), he or she cannot be charged and tried again for the identical crime. In addition, the person generally cannot later be charged for other possible crimes arising out of the same incident. If the prosecution is unsuccessful in trying a person for murder, it cannot then charge the person with manslaughter or assault. If the judge dismisses the case because of a lack of evidence that would support a finding of guilty, ordinarily there can be no second prosecution.

Once a trial has commenced and jeopardy has attached, the person cannot be charged and tried again with a crime, with a few exceptions. They include a dismissal, if a mistrial is called for any reason other than a lack of evidence, or if the defendant appeals a guilty verdict; then the charges may be reinstated and the right as a means of escaping conviction on technicalities through the double jeopardy clause is eliminated. Thus, if the prosecution has sufficient evidence to uphold a conviction, the case may be retried. Further, if the defendant appeals a conviction and is granted a new trial, there is a second chance for sentencing as well. As long as the sentence is justified by the crime, the judge in a second trial may impose a stricter sentence than was given in the first trial.

The double jeopardy rule puts a burden on the prosecution to be relatively sure of its case before presenting it to a jury. However, the defendant is also faced with the decision of accepting a guilty verdict or taking a chance on a potentially more severe sentence in a new trial.

Interpretations regarding what constitutes self-incrimination are much more pervasive than interpretations of double jeopardy. The primary issue has been at what point the right to refuse to give information that may be incriminating originates. Under the Fifth Amendment, no person may be forced to give information that may

Double Jeopardy
Being placed in jeopardy of loss of life or liberty by trial for the same alleged crime more than once.

APPLICATION 15.4

John is charged with kidnapping, a capital crime for which the penalty may be death. He pleads innocent and goes on trial. At the conclusion of the trial he is found guilty and sentenced to life in prison. He appeals and succeeds. The appellate court awards a new trial. (Recall from Chapter 2 that appellate courts typically do not determine guilt or innocence. Rather, they determine the appropriateness of the conduct of the trial court and whether it precluded a fair and legal result.) At the new trial, John is again convicted and this time is given the death penalty.

Point for Discussion: Allowing a more serious penalty at a new trial seems to discourage an appeal of the first conviction. Why is this permitted?

then be used to convict that person of a crime. For nearly the first 200 years of the amendment's history, the courts merely examined whether information had been given voluntarily. But during the past few decades, the courts have begun to give more attention to the circumstances surrounding communications with persons suspected or accused of a crime. The courts began to recognize that in some cases, a suspect or defendant might be influenced by the circumstances and be compelled to give information that he or she would ordinarily withhold as his or her right not to take part in self-prosecution. A landmark decision in this area of the law came in *Miranda v. Arizona.*[34] In that decision, the Supreme Court firmly stated that every person accused of a crime must be informed at the very outset that all further communications might be used in a prosecution. The result of that decision was the adoption of the Miranda rights, now read to all persons in this country at the time of interrogation and/or arrest. All accused individuals are advised that (1) they have the right to remain silent, (2) anything they say may be used against them in a court of law, (3) they have the right to an attorney, and (4) they may have an attorney appointed if they cannot afford one.

As with double jeopardy, it was a logical step to incorporate this aspect of the Fifth Amendment into the Fourteenth Amendment and thus require the states to adhere to it in their own laws. Since it would be impossible to provide due process of law to any individuals who are forced to testify against themselves at any stage of a criminal proceeding, such individuals must be allowed the opportunity to remain silent.

At first this may appear to be contrary to the purpose of criminal justice, which is to catch and punish persons committing crimes against society However, the Constitution is designed to protect all of the people, including those persons who may be innocent but lack the ability to act in their own best interest. Persons who are not adept at giving testimony and for whom the circumstances would imply guilt should have the right to protect their claim of innocence through silence and not be penalized for it.

The *Miranda* decision clearly established that the right against self-incrimination originates at the moment an individual is held for interrogation or is placed under arrest, whichever occurs first. Therefore, all persons detained are placed on notice that any utterance can be used against them. Anything a suspected criminal says while in custody, even if it is not said to a police officer, may be used against him or her in a prosecution. The right against self-incrimination is the right to remain silent. It is not the right to make statements to some persons and not to others. A statement made to officers or within the confines of a police facility are considered to be voluntary statements, with the exception of confidential communication to one's attorney.

If the police wish to interrogate a prisoner, the questioning must be done in the fairest of circumstances. The police must either allow an attorney to be present on behalf of the accused or demonstrate that the prisoner waived the right to have an attorney present. Evidence of this waiver must be documented. It must be clear that the prisoner knew and understood the reasons for having an attorney present and intelligently chose not to have one. Further, the police cannot set up circumstances that play upon the weaknesses of the accused to the point that there is no voluntary waiver. For example, if a prisoner is known to suffer from some mental incapacity, the police may not take advantage of this to further impair the prisoner's ability to make a decision regarding counsel.

A prisoner who is willing to answer questions or to give a statement of confession may do so without the presence or advice of legal counsel. However, the courts will scrutinize the record to make sure such information was given voluntarily. Therefore, the police will generally ask prisoners to sign a written statement that they know and understand their rights. A prisoner will acknowledge in the statement that he or she waives the right to remain silent and the right to counsel. Subsequently, the Supreme Court has held that if a prisoner knows of the right to counsel, following *Miranda* warnings, and does not request counsel, the police may interrogate. Once a prisoner requests counsel, however, the police are under a heavier burden to show that any communications outside the presence of counsel were indeed voluntary.

The *Miranda* decision was actually one of several similar cases. The Court was presented with numerous appeals on the same issue—although the facts differed somewhat from case to case—but the Court applied its opinion in *Miranda* to each of the cases individually.

CASE IN POINT

State v. Loyal, 164 N.J. 418, 753 A.2d 1073 (2000).

On February 7, 1996, Amedeo Delacruz drove Wanda Colon and Carl Watson to Prince Street in Newark to purchase heroin. Watson had recently ingested methadone to reduce his craving for heroin, but his need continued. Because Watson was violently ill in the car and was apprehensive about the neighborhood, Colon volunteered to purchase heroin for him in an apartment building on Prince Street.

Colon saw Rahnzzan Johnson, Sharonda Posey and John Loyal in the hallway of that building. Colon did not know any of them prior to this encounter. Johnson asked Colon what she wanted and Colon told him that she wanted "a bag of dope." Colon paid ten dollars for the bag of heroin. The transaction took place quickly and Colon left the building without looking in the bag.

Colon returned to the car and Delacruz drove away. After Colon handed the bag to Watson, he opened it and discovered that it was empty. Watson convinced Colon and Delacruz that they should return to the building. Delacruz parked the car near the entrance to the building and Colon and Watson went inside. The same three individuals were present. Colon identified Johnson as the person who sold her the empty bag of heroin. After a brief argument between Loyal and Watson, Loyal gave Watson another bag that contained heroin. Watson then told Colon to leave the building.

As Colon exited the building, she heard Watson and Johnson talking to each other as they followed her towards the car. Loyal exited the building directly behind the two men. At that point, Johnson ordered Loyal to shoot Watson. Loyal took a gun out of his jacket and shot Watson several times, causing his death. Loyal then pointed the gun in Colon's direction and warned her to leave before he "blew [her] head off." Colon was shocked and immobilized until Johnson pushed her towards the street. Colon returned to the car to find Delacruz terrified and unable to drive. Colon managed to drive the car away from the scene although she was in the passenger seat. When Delacruz began to react, he drove to a nearby police station after Colon told him to do so.

Colon explained what had occurred to a lieutenant at the police station before going to a back room to calm down. After waiting about one-half hour, Detective Ronald Soto of the Newark Police Department interviewed Colon. Soto asked her what had happened and then asked her to look at two photo books to try to identify the shooter. Colon looked through the first book without success. On the first page of the second book, she misidentified a photo of Omar Smalls as the man who sold her the heroin. Soto, based on his street knowledge, knew that Smalls was connected to an individual nicknamed "Tank," whose name was John Loyal. Soto had been actively investigating Loyal on drug-related charges and had two warrants for his arrest. Soto decided to prepare a photographic array for Colon and took a picture of Loyal from the file on his desk relating to the drug investigation.

Colon completed her review of the second book without identifying the shooter. When Colon finished looking through the books, she stood up and walked over to Detective Soto's desk. Colon saw the picture of Loyal on Soto's desk and immediately identified Loyal as the shooter. When Soto asked her if she might be confused or still in shock, Colon insisted that Loyal was the shooter and said that she was sure.

Following jury selection, defendant's trial for murder and other lesser charges commenced on April 16, 1997. Colon testified that she "can't confuse [Loyal's] face with nobody's face," and stated that she "would never forget that face" then she identified defendant as the shooter. On the following day, Colon finished her testimony and the State then called Sharonda Posey, the other woman present at the scene, as a witness. She testified differently from the description of the incident she had provided in her sworn statement to the police. Posey then testified that her police statement was false. The trial court stopped the proceedings and excused the jury to conduct a Gross hearing, see State v. Gross, 121 N.J. 1, 17, 577 A.2d 806 (1990), a procedure designed to de-

termine whether a sworn statement given to the police is reliable and can be introduced substantively into evidence if the witness later recants the statement during his or her testimony.

During the three-day Gross hearing, both Johnson and Posey recanted the sworn statements that they gave to the police implicating Loyal as the shooter. Johnson's description of the events leading up to the shooting was similar to the facts recounted in Colon's testimony. Johnson, however, recognized the shooter as an "individual that comes in the neighborhood robbing, sticking up individuals, drug dealers." Johnson testified that he decided to tell the police "what they wanted to hear" to avoid a charge of conspiracy to commit murder because Watson had been killed after purchasing drugs from Johnson. Johnson admitted that everything else in his sworn statement was true except for the identity of the shooter. Detective Manuel Garcia, the officer who took Johnson's statement, refuted Johnson's testimony and testified that he did not threaten Johnson or promise him anything in return for his sworn statement.

Posey testified that she was selling drugs with her boyfriend, Johnson, at the time of the shooting. Posey stated that Johnson and Watson were exiting the building together when someone came from the side of the building and shot Watson approximately ten times. Posey alleged that the police threatened her with life imprisonment if she did not identify Loyal as the shooter from a photo array. Posey testified that she implicated Loyal as the shooter because she thought she otherwise would go to jail and lose her children. Kirk Schwindel, an employee of the Essex County Prosecutor's Office who was present when Posey made her statement, testified that Posey voluntarily identified Loyal as the shooter and that she was not threatened in any way.

Defense counsel argued that the Johnson and Posey statements were unreliable because they were induced by police officers who threatened potential criminal prosecutions. The State argued that Johnson and Posey testified voluntarily and that the specific testimony about the incident was substantially similar to Colon's, except for the detailed description of the shooting. The court was satisfied that the statements were sufficiently reliable to be admitted into evidence.

After making that ruling, and before the jury returned to the courtroom, the court asked Posey whether she had ever been represented previously by defendant's counsel, William Cucco, who was employed as an attorney for the Essex County Public Defender's office. Posey replied that Cucco never represented her in any prior criminal matter. The prosecutor reminded Posey about her prior guilty plea on January 23, 1995 for possession with intent to distribute a controlled dangerous substance within one thousand feet of school property, and her sentencing hearing on February 14, 1995 for that offense. She replied that she did not think that Cucco was her lawyer and recalled only that she was represented by the Public Defender's office.

The prosecutor had investigated Posey's prior convictions earlier that morning and learned that Cucco previously had represented Posey in his capacity as public defender. Cucco did not remember that representation but acknowledged that, because those events occurred over two years ago, he did not know for certain whether he had represented Posey. While investigating the Loyal case, Cucco interviewed Posey in prison and did not recognize her. Posey, likewise, did not recognize Cucco.

The trial court considered whether it should disqualify Cucco from representing Loyal. Cucco argued that the prosecutor had provided him with Posey's Judgment of Conviction on the drug charges and that that document did not indicate that Cucco had represented Posey. Cucco also noted that Posey's drug case was unrelated to the Loyal case, had been resolved years ago, and that either party remembered the prior representation. The court ordered an independent attorney to advise Posey of her rights under RPC 1.7, the general rule governing conflicts of interest. Posey continued to insist that she had not been represented previously by Cucco, but agreed to waive any potential conflict of interest. After consulting with Cucco, Loyal also waived any potential conflict of interest that might arise during the cross-examination of Posey.

The prosecutor then requested a mistrial because Cucco had represented Posey in the past. The prosecutor noted that, if convicted, defendant would be able to argue that he received ineffective assistance of counsel because there was a conflict between Cucco's current representation of the defendant and his prior representation of the State's witness. The court pointed out that both sides had waived any potential conflict, but the prosecutor did not believe that the Rules of Professional Conduct permitted the conflict to be waived. The prosecutor also contended that the jury needed to be informed of the prior representation, because it might be ger-

mane to the inconsistency between Posey's testimony and her prior sworn statement. Desiring to research the issue independently, the court reserved decision on the motion for a mistrial. The jury then reentered the courtroom, and the prosecutor conducted his direct examination of Posey for the remainder of the morning.

That afternoon the prosecution withdrew its motion for a mistrial, noting that the record indicated that defendant made an intelligent and knowledgeable waiver of any potential conflict and that Cucco did not possess any confidential information about Posey. However, the court declared a mistrial sua sponte over defendant's objection and despite the prosecutor's election not to seek a mistrial. The court determined that State v. Needham, 298 N.J. Super. 100, 688 A.2d 1135 (Law Div. 1996), mandated a mistrial, stating that that decision did not permit either party to waive a possible conflict. The court reasoned:

When an attorney's former client is the State's chief witness, it is beyond dispute that an appearance of impropriety is created requiring the attorney be disqualified. There is an appearance of impropriety.

After discharging the jury, the court restated its reasons for declaring a mistrial:

First of all, as the Court stated in Needham, this Court does not take lightly its decision to disqualify Mr. Cucco, Mr. Loyal's attorney. I do not and will not suggest or imply that Mr. Cucco did anything wrong or will do anything improper or unethical.

However, because of the very strong possibilities of the appearance of impropriety of a recanting eyewitness to a homicide being represented by defense counsel, I am satisfied that I must disqualify Mr. Cucco from continued representation of Mr. Loyal.

Cucco asked that the mistrial be declared with prejudice because Loyal's right to a speedy trial had been compromised. The court informed Cucco of the necessity of filing a motion seeking that relief.

In May 1997, the trial court held a hearing on defendant's motion for dismissal of the indictment based on a double jeopardy violation. The trial court again stated its reason for declaring the mistrial:

I did not find that Mr. Cucco was in [possession] of some specified, specific information that he learned from his representation of Miss Posey that would, one, lead him to a cross-examination based on information garnered while he was representing Miss Posey. I did not disqualify Mr. Cucco because I felt that because of that representation of Miss Posey, the cross-examination of Miss Posey while representing Mr. Loyal would be less than adequate. Less than vigorous. I specifically disqualified Mr. Cucco because of the appearance of impropriety.

Let's remember what was happening: Miss Posey was on the stand recanting, indicating that this defendant was not the shooter. Her boyfriend had already recanted and clearly, there was a jury question established as to who this jury was going to believe; or, what part of the testimony they were gonna believe. Were they going to believe Miss Colon, who identified Mr. Loyal as the shooter? Were they going to believe Miss Posey? And if so, were they going to believe the sworn statement given? Were they going to believe the testimony that she was about to proffer as to why she gave the sworn statement? That is, that she was forced to.

. . . I don't sit here in a vacuum. I'm well aware of the family of the deceased sitting in the courtroom. The justice system does not need a not guilty verdict when, in fact, there are grounds that—I mean, yes, I do not know what the jury was going to say. I do not know what the jury was going to believe. But what the State and—does not need, what the court system does not need is a not guilty verdict. Because, perhaps, the family of the victim believes that Mr. Cucco or Mr. Loyal got some special advantage because Mr. Cucco had represented both Mr. Loyal and the recanting witness.

The appearance of impropriety was such that in the interest of justice, once it was determined that the recanting witness was represented by Mr. Cucco, I was satisfied that I must declare a mistrial. So that when a jury makes a determination as to the guilt or innocence of Mr. Loyal, there is not the specter of Mr. Loyal getting an advantage if he's found not guilty because defense attorney also represented an eyewitness.

The only issue that concerned the court at the hearing was whether Cucco was provided a complete copy of Posey's Judgment of Conviction by the prosecutor. The court reserved decision on whether or not there was prosecutorial misconduct that would require defendant's indictment to be dismissed because double jeopardy had attached.

The court subsequently denied defendant's motion for dismissal of the indictment based on double jeopardy. The court again explained the reasons for declaring a mistrial:

I made a determination that the appearance of having a recanting witness now testifying in favor of defendant—in a way favorable to the defendant, who is represented by a defense attorney, gave the ap-

pearance that if, in fact, there was a not guilty verdict, I can see something—somebody saying, boy, something smelly there; something is fishy with this thing. She's now recanting. I felt that it was appropriate to declare the mistrial and have a new attorney appointed.

The court relied primarily on State v. Nappo, 185 N.J.Super. 600, 450 A.2d 604 (Law Div. 1982), and State v. Laganella, 144 N.J.Super. 268, 365 A.2d 224 (App.Div.), appeal dismissed, 74 N.J. 256, 377 A.2d 652 (1976), in holding that the prosecutor's actions or inactions did not rise to the level of bad faith or inexcusable neglect, and that the inadvertent failure to notify Cucco that he had previously represented a State's witness did not warrant the extreme sanction of dismissal of the indictment.

Loyal's second trial began in July 1997. Johnson testified that parts of his sworn statement were false and that Loyal did not shoot Watson. Johnson's testimony mirrored the testimony he gave during the Gross hearing at Loyal's initial trial. Detective Garcia testified about the investigation and the procedures used to acquire Johnson's voluntary sworn statement. Colon's testimony at the second trial described the incident and implicated Loyal as the shooter. Posey did not testify at defendant's second trial.

The jury convicted defendant of murder, aggravated assault, and related weapons offenses. Prior to being sentenced, defendant renewed his motion for dismissal of the indictment and argued that double jeopardy barred the convictions because prosecutorial misconduct created an opportunity for a mistrial, or alternatively, because there was not a manifest necessity to declare a mistrial based on the potential conflict. The trial court denied the motion and sentenced defendant to life imprisonment with a thirty-year parole ineligibility period on the murder charge, and to concurrent sentences on the remaining charges. The Appellate Division affirmed defendant's convictions and sentence in an unreported opinion. We granted certification. 162 N.J. 198, 743 A.2d 850 (1999).

A.

Attorneys who practice law in New Jersey are required to comply with strict ethical rules concerning actual or possible conflicts of interests. In the case of a former client, attorneys must comply with RPC 1.9:

(a) A lawyer who has represented a client in a matter shall not thereafter: (1) represent another client in the same or a substantially related matter in which that client's interests are materially adverse to the interests of the former client unless the former client consents after a full disclosure of the circumstances and consultation with the former client; or (2) use information relating to the representation to the disadvantage of the former client except as RPC 1.6 would permit with respect to a client or when the information has become generally known.

(b) The provisions of RPC 1.7(c) are applicable as well to situations covered by this rule.

RPC 1.7(c) is part of the general rule that prohibits an attorney from representing a client when that representation would create a conflict of interest. RPC 1.7 forbids an attorney from representing a client in a situation that would create an appearance of impropriety, even if there were no actual conflict:

(c) This rule shall not alter the effect of case law or ethics opinions to the effect that: (1) in certain cases or categories of cases involving conflicts or apparent conflicts, consent to continued representation is immaterial, and (2) in certain cases or situations creating an appearance of impropriety rather than an actual conflict, multiple representation is not permissible, that is, in those situations in which an ordinary knowledgeable citizen acquainted with the facts would conclude that the multiple representation poses substantial risk of disservice to either the public interest or the interest of one of the clients.

An appearance of impropriety must be "something more than a fanciful possibility" and "must have some reasonable basis." In re Opinion No. 653, 132 N.J. 124, 132, 623 A.2d 241 (1993). The appearance of impropriety "alone may be sufficient to present an ethical problem even though no actual impropriety exists." Higgins, supra, 73 N.J. at 129, 373 A.2d 372. The doctrine's purpose is "to bolster the public confidence in the integrity of the legal profession." State v. Catanoso, 222 N.J.Super. 641, 648, 537 A.2d 794 (Law Div. (1987). Although the doctrine's imprecision has provoked criticism and requests for its rescission as applied to private civil litigation, professional Responsibility Rules Committee, 158 N.J.L.J. 472 (1999), the doctrine's relevance in criminal matters and to issues of public-entity representation remains unchallenged. This Court recently declined to implement a recommendation to eliminate the appearance of impropriety standard from the rules of Professional Conduct. In determining whether there is a reasonable basis for finding an appearance of impropriety, we must view the conduct as would an "ordinary knowledgeable citizen acquainted with the facts." Dewey v. R.J. Reynolds Tobacco Co., 109 N.J. at 201, 216, 536 A.2d 243 (1988). That inquiry is highly fact-sensitive; it does not occur in a vacuum. Where there exists an appearance of impropriety in an attorney's representation of a client, that representation generally must cease. Once an appearance of impropriety is found, "only in extraordinary cases should a client's right to counsel of his or her choice outweigh the need to maintain the highest standards of the profession." Dewey, supra, 109 N.J. at 20, 536 A.2d 243.

When an appearance of impropriety is found in a criminal matter, disqualification of an attorney routinely is required. Defendant's counsel was disqualified because his firm represented an important prosecution witness and employed an attorney who had worked in the prosecutor's office while the defendant was being investigated. Defendant's waiver of his right to appeal a possible conviction based on a claim of ineffective assistance of counsel was found to be irrelevant. Morelli, supra, 152 N.J.Super. at 74, 377 A.2d 774.

In In re Garber, 95 N.J. 597, 598, 472 A.2d 566 (1984), this Court suspended an attorney from the practice of law for one year because he represented a murder witness who recanted a positive identification of the defendant, an individual whom the attorney had represented earlier in matters unrelated to the murder indictment. The Court held that a "recanting witness is confronted by enormous legal pitfalls and thus is particularly in need of careful, objective and sound legal advice." The Court found that the attorney's "intertwined connections" with both parties "presented an indelible appearance of impropriety that breaches ethical standards." The Court also was concerned with "the attendant public perception that, as a consequence of respondent's compromised position, professional probity has been diluted and the administration of justice preverted."

A case relied on by the trial court in the matter before us, the issue was "whether a defense attorney must be disqualified upon motion by the State when that attorney represented one of the chief prosecution witnesses in an entirely unrelated matter." 298 N.J. Super. at 102, 688 A.2d 1135. The defendant was charged with multiple offenses and Officer Warner was expected to testify against the defendant. Ibid. The defendant's counsel had represented Warner in an indictable criminal matter seven years earlier and, more recently, in an internal affairs investigation that did not culminate in formal charges. Id. at 102–03, 688 A.2d 1135. The Law Division held that that prior representation created an appearance of impropriety and warranted the disqualification of the defendant's counsel because "[w]hen an attorney's former client is the State's chief witness, it is beyond dispute that an appearance of impropriety is created." Id. at 103, 688 A.2d 1135.

The Needham court found that "[i]f the defendant is acquitted as a result of the trial, an inference of wrongdoing is created by the perception that the acquittal was the result of the relationship or influence between [the defendant's counsel] and Officer Warner." Id. at 105, 688 A.2d 1135. The court also was concerned that Warner could provide strategic information to assist his former attorney, that the defendant's counsel might not cross-examine his former client vigorously, or that the defendant's attorney night use confidential information from the prior attorney-client relationship to cross-examine his former client. Id. at 105–06, 688 A.2d 1135. The court concluded that an adequate factual basis existed for an informed citizen to perceive an appearance of impropriety and that the defendant's attempt to waive the appearance of impropriety did not cure the disqualification of his attorney. Id. at 107, 688 A.2d 1135. The court did not "intend to suggest or imply that the defendant's counsel has done, or will do, anything improper or unethical" at "because the possibilities of impropriety are so strong and because there is risk that [the] defendant will not be adequately represented," the court disqualified the defendant's attorney. Ibid.

Individuals are constitutionally protected against being tried twice for the same offense. The United States Constitution states: "[N]or shall any person be subject for the same offense to be twice put in jeopardy of life or limb." U.S. Const. amend. V. Likewise, New Jersey's Constitution provides: "No person shall, after acquittal, be tried for the same offense." N.J. Const. art. I, ¶ 11. Additionally, N.J.S.A. 2C:1–9 states:

A prosecution of a defendant for a violation of the same provision of the statutes based upon the same facts as a former prosecution is barred by such former prosecution under the following circumstances:

* * *

d. The former prosecution was improperly terminated. Except as provided in this subsection, there is an improper termination of a prosecution if the ter-

mination is for reasons not amounting to an acquittal, and it takes place after the jury was impaneled and sworn. . . . Termination under any of the following circumstances is not improper:

* * *

(3) The trial court finds that the termination is required by a sufficient legal reason and a manifest or absolute or overriding necessity.

Termination of a trial after jeopardy attaches does not automatically bar subsequent re-prosecution. State v. Lynch, 79 N.J. 327, 342, 399 A.2d 629 (1979). Only improper termination of proceedings by a trial court bars a pretrial. State v. Gallegan, 117 N.J. 345, 353, 567 A.2d 204 (1989); State v. Dunns, 266 N.J.Super. 349, 363, 629 A.2d 922 (App.Div.), certif. denied, 134 N.J. 567, 636 A.2d 524 (1993); State in the Interest of D.P., 232 N.J.Super. 8, 13, 556 A.2d 335 (App.Div.1989). Where the court finds a sufficient legal reason and manifest necessity to terminate a trial, the defendant's right to have his initial trial completed is subordinated to the public's interest in fair trials and reliable judgments. Wade v. Hunter, 336 U.S. 684, 689, 69 S.Ct. 334, 837, 93 L.Ed. 974, 978 (1949).

Whether "manifest necessity" or "the ends of public justice" require declaration of a mistrial depends on the unique facts of the case and the sound discretion of the trial court. That test was first articulated in United States v. Perez, 22 U.S. (9 Wheat.) 579, 580, 6 L.Ed. 165, 165 (1824), where the Supreme Court observed that the law has invested courts of justice with the authority to discharge a jury from giving any verdict, whenever, in their opinion, taking all the circumstances into consideration, there is a manifest necessity for the act, or the ends of public justice would otherwise be defeated. They are to exercise a sound discretion on the subject; and it is impossible to define all the circumstances which would render it proper to interfere. To be sure, the power ought to be used with the greatest caution, under urgent circumstances, and for very plain and obvious causes.

That standard has guided judges in making the discretionary decision whether particular trial conditions warrant a sua sponte mistrial declaration. Arizona Washington, 434 U.S. 497, 505–06, 98 S.Ct. 824, 830, 54 L.Ed.2d 717, 728 (1978); United States v. Jorn, 400 U.S. 470, 481, 91 S.Ct. 547, 555, 27 L.Ed.2d 435, 554 (1971); Gori v. United States, 367

U.S. 364, 367–68, 81 S.Ct. 1523, 1526, 6 L.Ed.2d 901, 904–05 (1961); State v. Rechtschaffer, 70 N.J. 395, 405, 60 A.2d 362 (1976); State v. Farmer, 48 N.J. 145, 170, 224 A.2d 481 Cite as: 164 N.J. 418, *436, 753 A.2d 1073, (1966), cert. denied, 386 U.S. 991, 87 S.Ct. 1305, 18 L.Ed.2d 335 (1967).

Under the standard enunciated in Perez, supra, a trial court has wide discretion in granting a mistrial. See, e.g., Illinois v. Somerville, 410 U.S. 58, 462, 93 S.Ct. 1066, 1069, 35 L.Ed.2d 425, 429 (1973). Where a trial court declares a mistrial because of a substantial concern that the trial's result may be tainted, "the trial judge's determination is entitled to special respect." Arizona v. Washington, supra, 434 U.S. at 510, 98 S.Ct. at 833, 54 L.Ed.2d at 731. "Where . . . the trial court acts sua sponte, over the objections of both parties, propriety of the mistrial depends upon the found exercise of the court's discretion." Rechtschaffer, supra, 70 N.J. at 406, 360 A.2d 362. In Rechtschaffer, we discussed substantial United States Supreme Court precedent that established pertinent standards to determine whether declaration of a mistrial was proper:

The common threads that run through the Supreme Court cases are centered about the propriety of the trial court's granting sua sponte the mistrial and its cause. Did the trial court properly exercise its discretion so that a mistrial was justified? Did it have a viable alternative? If justified, what circumstances created the situation? Was it due to prosecutorial or defense misconduct? Will a second trial accord with the ends of public justice and with proper judicial administration? Will the defendant be prejudiced by a second trial, and if so, to what extent? [Id. at 410–11, 360 A.2d 362.]

In that case, we concluded that neither manifest necessity nor the ends of public justice warranted the grant of the partial mistrial because the mistrial was not justified and the defendant was prejudiced by the mistrial declaration. Id. at 415, 360 A.2d 362.

In Arizona v. Washington, supra, the Supreme Court examined whether a mistrial as a manifest necessity where defendant's counsel made an improper and rejudicial comment during his opening statement. 434 U.S. at 498, 98 S.Ct. at 826, 54 L.Ed.2d at 723. The federal District Court had concluded that the trial court did not adequately consider alternatives to a mistrial and did not make a finding of manifest necessity; the Court of Appeals for the Ninth Circuit affirmed. The Supreme Court reversed the Ninth Circuit and concluded that the trial court exercised

sound discretion when it declared a mistrial because it was concerned about the possibility of a double jeopardy violation, and that the trial court did not act precipitously in response to the prosecutor's request for a mistrial. Similarly in Illinois v. Somerville, supra, the Supreme Court held that if a mistrial indicates a significant state policy and "aborts a proceeding that at best should have produced a verdict that could be upset by one of the parties," a defendant's interest may be outweighed by the "equally legitimate demand for public justice." 410 U.S. at 471, 93 S.Ct. at 1074, 35 L.Ed.2d at 435.

We balanced the defendant's and the State's interests in determining whether the defense of double jeopardy barred the retrial of defendant for murder: If some unexpected, untoward and undesigned incident or circumstance arises which does not bespeak bad faith, inexcusable neglect or inadvertence or oppressive conduct on the part of the State, but which in the considered judgment of the trial court creates an urgent need to discontinue the trial in order to safeguard the defendant against real or apparent prejudice stemming therefrom, the Federal and State Constitutions do not stand in the way of declaration of a mistrial. . . . Moreover, if an incident or circumstance of that nature moves the court to order a mistrial not only to safeguard the right of the defendant to a full and fair trial, but also to protect the right of society to have its trial processes applied fully and fairly in the due administration of the criminal law, there is even less basis for a claim of trespass upon the privilege against double jeopardy. Clearly the societal right to have the accused tried and punished if found guilty stands side by side with the right of the accused to be prosecuted fairly and not oppressively.

In this case, the trial court relied on Laganella when it denied defendant's motion for dismissal of the indictment prior to defendant's second trial. In Laganella, supra, the defendant's motion for a mistrial was granted by the trial court. 144 N.J.Super. at 277, 365 A.2d 224. The Appellate Division found that "the dismissal of the indictment below was a mistaken exercise of discretion." Id. at 283, 365 A.2d 224. In remanding the case for a new trial, the Appellate division held "that important interests other than those of defendant alone are involved in the trial of criminal cases." Id. at 287, 365 A.2d 224. The appellate Division rejected following a "hard and fast rule" or "ritualistic formula" and noted that "mere empanelment of a jury and commencement of a case does not automatically provide a criminal defendant with a bar to further prosecution." Id. at 286–87, 365 A.2d 224. Because the trial court and the state had acted in good faith, and the defendant would not be subjected to significant annoyance, harassment or expense, the judgment of dismissal was reversed. Id. at 288–90, 365 A.2d 224. The Appellate Division concluded that [t]o apply the bar of double jeopardy in the instant matter, absent compelling considerations of fairness to [the] defendant or for the purpose of protection against governmental action found by us not to be arbitrary, would disserve [the public interest], for there still has been no trial on the merits.

Against this jurisprudential backdrop we must determine whether defense counsel's prior representation of Sharonda Posey created an appearance of impropriety and whether the trial court properly declared a mistrial. In considering whether a lawyer's responsibility to a client is compromised by his representation of a former client and constitutes an appearance of impropriety, he address the issue from the perspective of "a reasonable and informed citizen." Opinion No. 653, supra, 132 N.J. at 132, 623 A.2d 241. We also consider whether the representation posed a "substantial risk of disserve either to the public interest or the interest of one of the clients." Dewey, supra, 109 N.J. at 216, 536 A.2d 243 (quoting RPC 1.7(c) (2)).

The trial court correctly found that Cucco's representation of defendant created an unacceptable appearance of impropriety. The trial court reasoned that Cucco may have obtained confidential information during his prior representation of Posey that he could now use to impeach her credibility on cross-examination. We note that Posey's prior conviction was drug-related and that defendant Loyal was charged with a murder that occurred during a drug transaction. Additionally, because of their prior relationship, the trial court may have been concerned that Cucco would cross-examine Posey less vigorously at the expense of defendant's interests. Moreover, Posey's decision to recant her statement implicating defendant enhanced the trial court's concerns. The prosecutor had contended that the jury would have to be notified of Cucco's prior representation of Posey in order to assess the proper weight to be given to both Posey's testimony and her statement to police. Both Posey's interest and defendant's interest may have been disserved by counsel's prior relationship with Posey.

Additionally, the public interest would have been disserved by Cucco's continued representation of defendant. The trial court noted that an independent observer might believe that "something is fishy" when a witness who was previously represented by defendant's counsel recants a prior statement that identified defendant as the shooter. As we stated in Garber: The public itself has the greatest stake in the propriety of the legal relationships that are created to properly administer criminal justice. . . . Clearly, the public interest in the administration of criminal justice in the circumstances of this case compelled the unbiased and unstinted representation of [the witness].

[Garber, supra, 95 N.J. at 614, 472 A.2d 566.]

In the context of this prosecution for a drug-related murder and other offenses, we are convinced that an appearance of impropriety existed where defendant's counsel previously had represented on drug charges a material recanting State's witness. Cucco's and Posey's failure to recall that prior representation or to recognize each other prior to trial is of no consequence.

Under those circumstances, we are persuaded that there was manifest necessity to declare a mistrial, considering the "ends of justice for the defendant and the State." Farmer, supra, 48 N.J. at 171, 224 A.2d 481. In our view, the trial court exercised sound discretion in declaring a mistrial and that decision is entitled to deference. Ibid. (noting that "appellate courts just realize that under our system the conduct of a trial is committed to the trial judge, and that in appraising the exercise of his discretionary action is a wise and tolerant restraint must be practiced if the separate levels of the judicial process are to be maintained.").

In United States v. Simonetti, 998 F.2d 39 (1st Cir. 1993), the Court of Appeals rejected defendant's double jeopardy challenge to his retrial on drug distribution charges and concluded that his counsel's conflict of interest that precluded his effective representation of defendant without a waiver from another client potentially implicated in the drug offenses justified the trial court's grant of a mistrial over defendant's objection. Finding that "manifest necessity" required the grant of a mistrial, the Court of Appeals observed that the "manifest necessity" standard protects not only a defendant's interests but also " 'the public's interest in fair trials designed to end in just judgments.' Id. at 41 (quoting Oregon v. Kennedy, 456 U.S. 667, 672, 102 S.Ct. 2083, 2087, 72 L.Ed.2d 416.

Precedents demonstrate that the primary basis for the trial court's declaration of a mistrial in this matter was the vindication of the public interest in a fair trial. Contrary to our dissenting colleague's view, post at 459–460, 753 A.2d at 1097, the mistrial was not mandated because counsel may have violated the appearance of impropriety standards. An ethical violation in a criminal trial ordinarily will not require a declaration of a mistrial. State v. Feaster, 156 N.J. 1, 85–87, 716 A.2d 395 (1998). As the cited cases demonstrate, however, in some circumstances a lawyer's conflict of interest may jeopardize not only the defendant's right to effective representation, but also "the institutional interest in the rendition of just verdicts in criminal cases," Wheat, supra, 486 U.S. at 160, 108 S.Ct. at 1698, 100 L.Ed.2d at 149.

We are fully persuaded that the trial court correctly concluded that defense counsel's prior representation of a material recanting witness posed a significant risk to the reliability of the outcome of defendant's trial. Additionally, the trial court found no evidence of misconduct, bad faith or unexcusable neglect on the part of the State. Defendant does not appear to have been prejudiced by the delay in the criminal proceedings. Based on the interests of the parties and the public in the proper administration of the criminal justice system, the trial court acted appropriately and within its wide range of discretion in declaring a mistrial over the objection of both the prosecution and defense counsel.

IV

The judgment of the Appellate Division is affirmed.[35]

Case Review Question: If both parties agreed to waive objection, why did the court still declare a mistrial?

4. The Sixth Amendment: Speedy Trial, Impartial Jury, Confrontation

In the past the Supreme Court has determined that a speedy trial is absolutely necessary to due process.[36] Therefore, a speedy trial must be included in the selective incorporation process of defining due process under the Fourteenth Amendment. However, the Court has just as adamantly refused to consider a standard test to determine whether a trial has or has not been provided quickly enough. The Court recognizes that different types of criminal cases require different amounts of preparation and investigation. Therefore, as long as the time for preparation is reasonable and trial is available, the Sixth Amendment right will have been honored.

The Court has established certain criteria for determining whether the Sixth Amendment right has been upheld. When it is alleged that the right to a speedy trial has been violated, the Supreme Court has provided a four-factor test that judges may employ to determine whether the allegation is true. The requirements to be considered are as follows:

- The actual time elapsed between arrest and trial
- The reasons the government has cited as the basis for the alleged delay
- Whether the defendant, at any time prior to trial, requested a speedy trial
- Whether the alleged delay in fact caused harm to the evidence or the defendant

The harm alleged can include problems for the defense, such as unavailability of witnesses after a long period of time, lengthened detention (deprivation of liberty) if the defendant was in custody, or any other detriment to the defendant that would have been avoided by a speedy trial.

The guarantee of a speedy trial takes effect only upon the actual indictment (formal charge) for a crime. Prior to this, the prosecution is free to investigate at length before determining that there is sufficient evidence to charge a defendant. There is no limit on how long a defendant may remain under suspicion and be the subject of a properly conducted investigation. Once the evidence has been accumulated, the prosecution must decide whether to prosecute. If the decision is made not to prosecute, the investigation may continue and charges may be brought later. It is required only that there be reasons for the delay other than to impair the defendant's ability to obtain evidence to be used in the defense.

Assignment 15.4

Examine the following situation and explain whether there was a violation of the right to a speedy trial.

George is a limousine driver, who, on his day off, is arrested for driving under the influence. George disputes the charges and requests a speedy trial. The date of the arrest is August 1 and the case is initially set for trial on September 10. However, George's attorney is tied up in another trial and the case is reset for October 1. On September 30 in the late evening, lightning strikes the courthouse and causes extensive damage. The case is rescheduled for November 15. On November 13, George suffers from appendicitis and has surgery. He requests a brief continuance but the judge is scheduled to be out of town for a conference. The case is reset for December 21. On December 18, the prosecution finds out that the arresting officer, who is the primary witness, is on vacation until December 26. The court is closed from December 24 through January 3, except for emergency hearings. The case is rescheduled for February 1. On February 1, the case goes to trial and George's attorney immediately makes a motion to dismiss the case for failure to grant a speedy trial. George was laid off from his job in mid-September because business was slow, although he had an excellent work record. However, he claims he has been unable to find employment due to the pending charges against him and their potential impact on his license to drive.

Also included in the Sixth Amendment, and in the definition of what constitutes due process under the Fourteenth Amendment, is the right to confront one's accusers. It is inherent in American law that before a person can be convicted on the basis of statements made by others, there must be the opportunity to face and challenge the statements of one's accusers. Because not every person accused of a crime can adequately and effectively confront or challenge his or her accuser, this has been determined to be a **critical stage** in the prosecution that requires assistance of counsel. This includes pretrial procedures, such as identification, and confrontation upon testimony at trial. The rationale is that the defendant should be given every opportunity to expose errors or irregularities in testimony of witnesses for the prosecution.

Subsequent to *Miranda*, the Court held that for the protection of several necessary rights (such as the right not to incriminate or assist in the prosecution against oneself), counsel must be available at all points in a prosecution where there is opportunity for unfairness or where untrustworthy evidence may be obtained. Later decisions have identified these stages of prosecution as interrogation or questioning, identification procedures, first court appearance where action may be taken against the defendant,

Critical Stage
Stage of a criminal proceeding in which the presumed innocence of the accused is in jeopardy so the accused is entitled to representation of counsel.

preliminary hearing or grand jury, arraignment, trial, sentencing, and probation revocation hearings. Various rights in addition to those in the Fifth Amendment have been interpreted to require this as part of the due process guarantee in the Fourteenth Amendment. The result has been that each state must follow these requirements in its own state laws and prosecutions.

Unless there are compelling circumstances, anyone who is accused is entitled to have an attorney present when a witness is asked to identify the accused as the one who committed a crime. Compelling circumstances would include situations that make it unreasonable to wait for an attorney to be present. Additionally, if a witness is shown only photographs of potential defendants, neither the defendant nor defendant's counsel has the right to be present. The right to assistance of counsel is considered to be necessary to aid the defendant in adequately responding to charges of a witness. Because there is little room for unfairness or prejudice in identifying a photograph, disallowing the presence of the defendant or counsel at this procedure is considered to do no harm to due process.

APPLICATION 15.5

A mugging crime was interrupted by a passerby who held the mugger until police arrived. In this type of situation, it is permissible for the witness and victim to make an identification at that time without benefit of counsel for the accused.

Point for Discussion: Why is availability of counsel not required at the crime scene identification if the perpetrator is in custody and not in danger of fleeing?

The Supreme Court has also found that the right to assistance of counsel occurs only after the defendant has been charged with a crime and the prosecution has commenced.[37] Therefore, if a person is asked to take part in a lineup or some other form of identification procedure prior to arrest, no right to assistance of counsel attaches. The point has been raised that most law enforcement agencies are encouraged to conduct identification procedures before charging the defendant and thus avoid the necessity of counsel. This is not seen as a particularly significant issue, however. First, the individual has the right to refuse to appear voluntarily in the lineup. Second, if the procedure is conducted in an unfair manner that unduly suggests the suspect to witnesses as the criminal, the suspect (subsequently the defendant) has the opportunity to allege this at trial. If proven, the evidence of the identification of the defendant will be inadmissible. Often, without a witness to identify the defendant as the one who committed the crime, a prosecution is unsuccessful. Therefore, police have the incentive to ensure that lineups are fairly conducted even before a defendant is formally charged with a crime.

5. The Eighth Amendment: Bail, Cruel and Unusual Punishment

The Eighth Amendment has also been expressly drawn into the Fourteenth Amendment definition of due process. The issues involve that of bail and freedom from cruel and unusual punishment. The Supreme Court addressed the issue of bail, the term used to describe release from custody during the time between arrest and the end of trial. Generally, the court asks for some guarantee or assurance that the defendant will not flee or commit other crimes if released. This assurance is the type or amount of bail that is required. The Eighth-Amendment guarantee against excessive bail has been integrated into the Fourteenth Amendment and applied to the states in an attempt to prevent the unwarranted detention and deprivation of liberty of accused persons prior to trial.

Many jurisdictions have predetermined amounts of bail for misdemeanors. In many states, if a person is charged with a traffic violation, the person's permanent driver's license will be accepted as bail. The license is then returned if the accused is found innocent or is given a different penalty upon conviction. If the charges are minor, a specific dollar amount may be posted with the police to obtain release until a hearing is conducted. In other cases, the persons charged must remain in custody until they have an opportunity to appear before a judge or magistrate. Usually, this is within a matter of hours or, at most, a few days. The judge will determine what an appropriate assurance is or, in some instances, may even release the persons on their word that they will reappear at the formal hearing on the charges against them. The latter is known as being released on one's own recognizance, or OR. In serious cases, and when there is reason to believe the accused will commit other crimes or flee the jurisdiction, the court may deny bail entirely and detain the person until trial.

The Eighth Amendment states that bail will not be excessive. A person is considered innocent until proven guilty at a trial in this country, so the rationale is that accused persons should be allowed to continue their lives, earn a living, and reside with their families. Just as the circumstances vary with every case, however, so do the considerations of what would be excessive bail. For minor offenses, it is relatively assured that most persons will appear at trial. Therefore, bail may be a predetermined amount for all persons charged with those offenses. For serious crimes, where the penalty for a finding of guilt may be severe, the temptation to avoid a trial and possible sentencing by fleeing the jurisdiction is much greater. Additionally, many of the accused in these cases have criminal backgrounds, so the likelihood that they will continue to commit crime while on bail is much greater.

The Supreme Court has reasoned that pretrial detention because bail is not allowed or because it is so excessive that it effectively prevents an accused person from posting it, could be a deprivation of liberty without due process of law—essentially, a sentence of imprisonment prior to a trial. Therefore, the factors that are considered in determining bail and the amount of bail required should be directly related.

The function of the courts in determining bail is to set an amount that will reasonably assure the appearance of the accused at trial. If the judge determines that this cannot be assured by a sum of money and that a person should not be released on bail, the judge must make a very clear statement in the court record of reasons that supports this decision. The presumption is that all persons should have an opportunity to be released on bail. Therefore, it can only be denied in compelling circumstances.

The courts must consider several factors when determining bail, including but not limited to the following:

- Past criminal history of the accused
- Past bail history of the accused
- Connections of the accused to the community, such as job, family, and home
- Danger posed to the community by the accused
- Likelihood the accused will flee from the jurisdiction

If enough of these factors or other considerations convince the court that the accused is likely to commit crimes or flee the jurisdiction, the court is justified in denying bail entirely. This does not constitute an improper violation of the individual right to due process, because the government interest in protecting the public is considered to be greater. This goes back to the traditional balance that courts try to achieve: the good of the individual versus the good of the people.

More often, the court is faced with a case that falls into a gray area. Although some factors are present that raise concern about the conduct of the accused on bail release, the evidence is not sufficient to warrant holding the accused in custody until trial. In such cases, the judicial officer must determine what amount of bail is reasonable to assure that the accused will not commit crimes or flee the jurisdiction. The court must also consider what amount the accused can reasonably be expected to post as assurance that he or she will appear for trial.

In questions of bail, there is a wide berth for judicial discretion. Decisions must be made on a case-by-case basis, and every individual accused presents a unique situation to the court. Therefore, for more serious crimes, there is generally no set rule for the amount of bail a court will require. The court must consider all the evidence before it on this question and exercise its best judgment. As long as a higher court can find that a determination of bail falls somewhere within a range of reasonableness, the initial determination of bail will not be altered.

The Eighth Amendment guarantees protection for all citizens from punishment deemed to be excessive or inappropriate for the crime committed, according to societal standards. What defines cruel and unusual has gone through dramatic changes in our nation's history consistent with changes in society.

Essentially, the Supreme Court has defined due process to include the protection of the Eighth Amendment with regard to the imposition of sentence. However, the Court has been somewhat reluctant to state specifics regarding what constitutes such punishment. The Court has gone so far as to prohibit barbaric punishment or punishment that is excessive for the crime committed. Further, it has upheld the death penalty, refusing to categorize it as cruel and unusual. Part of the rationale of the Court for its position on the death penalty is that the penalty has received approval by a significant majority of the states. This, in turn, supposedly reflects the belief of a majority of people that capital punishment is acceptable and appropriate. While the death penalty continues to be a topic of debate at state and federal levels of government, and the subject of frequent protests, until the laws are changed to reflect a changing society, it is unlikely that the Court will reverse its position.

6. Stages of Criminal Procedure

An understanding of the rights of accused persons in the criminal process allows a much clearer sense of the reasons for the various stages through which an accused must pass. These stages are all designed with the intent that every citizen shall have every available opportunity to have his or her conduct judged fairly without undue influence or unfair criticism. The following discussion of the actual stages of criminal procedure uses many of the examples already used in the discussion of the rights of the accused to illustrate the role these rights play in the criminal process.

Generally, before an arrest is made and a defendant is charged with a crime, the law enforcement agencies will attempt to obtain sufficient evidence to warrant the arrest and the conviction. In fact, a standard of all arrests is that the arresting officer had probable cause to believe the suspect had committed a crime. As a general rule, probable cause is established through the introduction of evidence that connects the accused to the crime.

Many times during or after the commission of a crime, the police look for evidence that will lead them to the person or persons who committed the crime. However, the constitutional rights guaranteed by the Fourth Amendment prevent the police from rampantly searching among members of the public and their belongings. Such searches would violate all rights of privacy and notions of fairness. The police are entitled to obtain whatever evidence exists publicly, but before they may delve into private property and dwellings, they must establish that there is probable cause to believe evidence of a crime exists there.

As indicated earlier in the chapter, items or occurrences in public view do not require probable cause, because it would be unreasonable for a person to consider such things private. This includes items that are on private property but can be viewed from outside the property. It is also permissible to use such items as binoculars, if the item only enhances the natural ability.

In addition, individuals do not have a right to privacy with regard to such matters as the phone numbers they have called. No one can reasonably expect the phone company not to be allowed to know and record numbers called since these records are necessary to the phone company's business. Since this is common knowledge to a third party, individuals should not expect that no other third party could obtain the information. Therefore, phone registers that record the numbers called from a private phone line require no showing of probable cause, nor do conversations made on public telephones since there can be no reasonable expectation of privacy when using a public facility.

Before the police may enter the private property of an individual, they must have probable cause to suspect a connection between the property and the crime committed. As stated earlier, they must have more than mere suspicion. They must have access to other evidence or testimony that would indicate the likelihood of criminal activity. For example, the police may have information from informants who have had contact with the person or persons suspected of criminal activity and who can provide specific information regarding their conduct (such as phone conversations about the crime) or the exact location of criminal evidence. If the police have conducted surveillance of the persons or property and have discovered highly suspicious activities taking place, a court may find probable cause.

If a court finds that there is probable cause to suspect that evidence of a crime exists in or on private property, it will issue an appropriate search warrant. Search warrants must be specific concerning the objective, location, and scope of the search. This prevents unreasonable invasions of privacy by some overzealous law enforcement officers.

If the police demonstrate to the court that there is enough criminal evidence to support a conviction, the court will issue an arrest warrant. When the warrant is issued, the police have the authority to take the defendant into custody and make initial criminal charges. At this point, the defendant's constitutional protection against being deprived of life or liberty without due process of law becomes a concern of law enforcement personnel.

In certain situations, no search or arrest warrant is required. In these special, otherwise known as exigent, circumstances, police have the authority to stop, search, and, if necessary, make an arrest. If there is probable cause to believe that individuals are committing a crime—or have in the immediate past committed a crime—the police have the authority to stop these individuals. When the individuals are stopped, the police can pat them down and search areas within their reach to determine whether anything is available that the individuals could use to harm the officers or effect an escape. The police then have the option of questioning the persons and releasing them or, if probable cause exists, the persons can be placed under arrest and the property in their immediate reach can be searched.

Another method used in federal, and some state, criminal prosecutions of serious crimes is the grand jury. This consists of 20 or more citizens who, for a period of several months, hear evidence of criminal activity in various cases presented by the prosecution. The duty of the grand jury is to determine whether there is enough evidence to prosecute someone for a crime. A grand jury proceeding often occurs even before an initial arrest has been made.

Much of the evidence the grand jury hears has been obtained through government investigation, the use of various search warrants, and the testimony of informants or other persons with relevant information. Suspects have no absolute right to appear at grand jury proceedings or to introduce evidence. The purpose of such proceedings is solely to determine whether enough evidence exists that a jury could find a person guilty of criminal conduct.

If the grand jury finds that sufficient evidence exists to formally charge an individual with a crime, it will issue an indictment that gives authority to arrest and charge the individual with the crime. An indictment operates much like an arrest warrant issued by a judge. After apprehension, the person is taken into custody and advised of his or her rights. At that point, the stages of actual prosecution begin.

a. Arrest and Interrogation   Persons who are initially arrested must be advised of their basic rights upon arrest under the *Miranda rule*. They must be informed of their right to remain silent and their right to counsel regardless of whether they can afford legal representation. Law enforcement agencies now commonly require all arrestees to sign a statement indicating that they have been notified of and understand their rights. These written statements have greatly reduced the number of arrestees who claim they were never advised of their rights or that the advisement came after they had incriminated themselves.

After an arrest, the law enforcement personnel and prosecutors may question (interrogate) the accused about the crime suspected and/or charged. Identification proceedings, such as lineups, where the victims or witnesses to the crime are asked to identify the alleged criminal from a group of persons, may also take place.

The arrestee has the right to have an attorney present to ensure that identification proceedings are not conducted in a way that would unduly influence the victims or witnesses to name the accused.[38] For example, if the police have information from a witness that the suspect was a particular race and they present a lineup of persons of other races except for the actual suspect, the witness would have no choice but to indicate the actual suspect as the criminal. Such an identification proceeding is unfair. Lineups must be conducted in such a way that they truly test the ability of the witness to identify the criminal.

Many law enforcement agencies avoid the necessity of providing attorneys for all those who are suspected of criminal activity. Instead, the police ask the individual prior to arrest to answer questions voluntarily or to take part in an identification proceeding. If the individual voluntarily complies, the police have complete consent and they do not have to advise the person of his or her rights or provide counsel. The individual does, however, have the right to obtain his or her own counsel or to refuse to cooperate. An exception occurs when a grand jury issues a subpoena to the individual. In that situation, the person is required to appear to be questioned but may avoid answering on the basis of the Fifth Amendment guarantee against self-incrimination.

A particular concern arises when an arrestee confesses to a crime. At this point, law enforcement personnel are under a particular duty to establish that the individual was not coerced in any way or misled into an involuntary confession. It must be established that the confession was given freely and without undue influence. Further, it must be shown that the individual understood the possible consequences of a confession. Increasingly, law enforcement agencies are establishing that a confession was made in fair circumstances by videotaping it. This relatively inexpensive tool is quite effective, and the court can actually observe from an objective view, the circumstances under which the confession was made. In this case, a defendant is much less likely to claim that it was unfairly obtained unless those circumstances truly existed. Similarly, law enforcement and prosecutors have much greater incentive to honor the rights of the accused and collect information in a fair and proper manner.

b. Pre-Trial Matters   Shortly after arrest, a preliminary hearing is scheduled for felony crimes and more serious misdemeanors. Other matters are simply scheduled for trial. At this time, the defendant and the prosecution appear before the judge for a decision as to whether sufficient admissible evidence exists to warrant further prosecution. The prosecution introduces evidence of the defendant's guilt. The defendant has the opportunity to challenge the admissibility of this evidence under the exclusionary rule. Generally, the defendant is not allowed to introduce evidence of defense. The burden is on the prosecutor to prove that a finding of guilt is possible. The purpose of the preliminary hearing is simply to determine whether there is enough admissible evidence to meet this burden. Since no conviction can result at this stage, there is no need for a defense at this point. In some cases, in which a significant amount of time will pass before a preliminary hearing, a brief hearing may be held to consider the issue of temporary bail.

If the court finds that insufficient evidence exists that would be admissible in court, the case will be dismissed and all charges dropped. In the event the court finds sufficient evidence to prosecute, the court will arrange for an **arraignment** and schedule the case for trial.

Arraignment
Stage of a criminal proceeding in which the accused is formally charged.

Arraignment follows the preliminary hearing. At this stage, the defendant is informed of the actual charge of which he or she is accused and for which he or she will be tried. Often, the charge is related to, but different from, the original charge for which the defendant was initially arrested. This occurs because some evidence may have been excluded by the court or because additional evidence has been accumulated since the time of arrest. Either of these developments may affect the ability of the prosecution to prove guilt on a particular charge. Therefore, the charge may be modified. Another possibility is that during the preliminary hearing the judge will determine that there is insufficient evidence for one charge but adequate evidence for another. In that event, the judge will order that the latter be the basis for prosecution.

During arraignment, the defendant is formally advised of the crime charged. Bail may also be reviewed by the court with respect to increase, decrease, or even withdrawal and remandment to custody. Most importantly, the defendant pleads on the issue of guilt at the arraignment.

Typically a defendant pleads in one of three ways. If the plea is guilty, the defendant is making an admission of responsibility for the crime committed. There is no need for a trial to prove guilt, and the procedure moves directly to sentencing. If the plea is not guilty, the court will schedule a trial date. At trial, the prosecution will attempt to prove the guilt of the defendant beyond a reasonable doubt. The third type of plea sometimes accepted by a court is nolo contendere, also known as no contest. This plea means that the defendant will not plead guilty, but will raise no defense. In essence the defendant is saying, "I will not admit guilt but I will also not challenge a prosecution or conviction."

As a result of a nolo contendre plea, the defendant has no recorded confession, but waives the right to a trial. Sentencing occurs after this plea just as it would upon a plea of guilty or a conviction after trial. Many times a defendant pleads nolo contendre when there is a possible related civil case and the defendant wishes no recorded admission of guilt that can be used to incur civil liability as well. It may also be used in a plea bargain where in exchange for a nolo contendre plea, the prosecution seeks a reduced sentence for the defendant and thereby avoids the time, expense, and potential risk associated with a jury trial.

c. Trial, Appeal, and Sentencing   The crucial stage of any prosecution is the trial. At this point, the trier of fact—usually the jury—will determine the guilt or innocence of the defendant based on the evidence of the prosecution. Guilt must be established beyond a reasonable doubt. In practical terms this means that one who considers the situation logically and rationally must have no doubt that the defendant committed the crime with which he or she is charged. Guilt cannot be based on prejudice or bias or pure circumstance. There must be no other reasonable explanation than that the accused committed the crime.

This burden of proof is quite severe to ensure that innocent individuals will not be convicted because of questionable circumstances. In the American legal system, individuals are considered innocent until proven guilty. Furthermore, they cannot be compelled to testify about information that might incriminate them. Some defendants, regardless of innocence, simply are not effective witnesses in a criminal prosecution because they do not communicate well, and would do their defense more harm than good by attempting to tell their story. A jury may not consider the failure to testify in one's own behalf as evidence of guilt. That evidence must be established by the prosecutor.

If the trier of fact determines that the prosecution has met the burden of proof, a conviction will result. If the burden is not met, the charges are dismissed, and the defendant is released from further proceedings. Upon dismissal, bail is returned to the defendant if the terms were not violated during the prosecution. Upon a conviction, bail may be returned, or it may be applied to a fine imposed as a penalty for the conviction.

After conviction, the court may sentence the defendant immediately, or sentencing may be scheduled for a later time. In some instances, a jury is asked to impose the sentence on the defendant. This usually occurs in very serious cases that require much thought and consideration of the circumstances of the crime, such as capital offenses where the sentence could even be death. The reasoning is that in such a serious matter, several of one's peers can determine just punishment as well as or better than a single judge. The prosecution and defense are both allowed to introduce evidence that will enable a fair sentence to be imposed based on all the relevant factors. This includes the state of mind of the defendant, such as malice or premeditation, and the extent of criminal conduct, such as extreme violence. Other facts such as intelligence, maturity, or likelihood of rehabilitation, and remorse may also affect sentencing.

If a defendant chooses to appeal, it is up to the trial court to determine whether the defendant will be released during the appeal. In more serious cases, the defendant is usually required to begin serving the sentence because appeals can take a very long time. Further, after conviction and sentencing, a defendant may be very tempted to flee the jurisdiction. If an appeal is successful and the conviction is overturned, the defendant is not entitled to any compensation for time served or inconvenience caused. In most of these cases, a new trial is ordered and the procedure starts over again. A defendant who is granted a new trial is treated as if the first trial never occurred. Therefore, the sentence in a new conviction can be greater or lesser.

CASE IN POINT

Noel v. State, 342 Ark. 35, 26 S.W. 3d 123 (2000).

DONALD L. CORBIN, Justice.

Appellant Riley Dobi Noel was convicted of three counts of capital murder and the count of attempted capital murder; he was sentenced to death by lethal injection and sixty years' imprisonment, respectively. This court affirmed his convictions and sentences in Noel v. State, 331 Ark. 79, 960 S.W.2d 639 (1998). Noel then filed a petition for postconviction relief pursuant to Ark. R.Crim. p. 37. The trial court denied the petition. On appeal, Noel alleges four instances in which his trial counsel was ineffective: (1) failing to present alibi testimony; (2) eliciting from Noel on direct examination that he was testifying against the advice of counsel; (3) failing to call witnesses to testify about Noel's demeanor and activities in the days prior to the murders; and (4) failing to request funds for an expert on eyewitness identification. Our jurisdiction of this appeal is pursuant to Rule 37 and Ark. Sup.Ct. R. 1–2 (a)(8). We find no error and affirm.

The trial record shows that on the evening of June 4, 1995, Noel and three other persons went to the home of Mary Hussian in Little Rock. Present in the home that night were Mrs. Hussian, three of her children, and Kyle Jones. The three children (Malak Hussian, age 10; Mustafa Hussian, age 12; and Marcel Young, age 17) were shot by Noel in the head as they lay on the living room floor. Meanwhile, a codefendant, Terry Carroll, attempted to shoot Mrs. Russian with a shotgun. The shotgun jammed, however, and Mrs. Hussian was eventually able to wrestle it away from Carroll. Jones escaped unharmed through the bathroom window. It was the State's theory that Noel committed the murders in retaliation for the death of his brother, which had occurred approximately one week earlier. Noel apparently

believed that his brother had been "set up" in a drive-by shooting by one of Mrs. Hussian's daughters.

In his petition for postconviction relief, Noel alleged nine instances in which his trial counsel was ineffective. To prevail on a claim of effective assistance of counsel, the petitioner must show first that counsel's performance was deficient. Jones v. State, 340 Ark. 1, 8 S.W.3d 482 (2000). This requires a showing that counsel made errors so serious that counsel was not functioning as the counsel" guaranteed by the Sixth Amendment. Petitioner must also show that the deficient performance prejudiced his defense; this requires a showing that counsel's errors were so serious as to deprive the petitioner of a fair trial. Id. Unless the petitioner makes both showings, it cannot be said that the conviction resulted from a breakdown in the adversarial process that renders the result unreliable. Chenowith v. State, 341 Ark. 722, 19 S.W.3d 612 (2000).

The reviewing court must indulge in a strong presumption that counsel's conduct falls within the wide range of reasonable professional assistance. To rebut this presumption, the petitioner must show that there is a reasonable probability that, but for counsel's errors, the factfinder would have had a reasonable doubt respecting guilt, i.e., that the decision reached could have been different absent the errors. A reasonable probability is there is sufficient to undermine confidence in the outcome of the trial. When making a determination on a claim of ineffectiveness, the totality of the evidence before the factfinder must be considered. Chenowith, 341 Ark. 722, 19 S.W.3d 612. This court will not reverse the denial of postconviction relief unless the trial court's findings are clearly erroneous or clearly against the correspondence of the evidence. Jones, 340 Ark. 1,

8 S.W.3d 482. With this standard in mind, we review the four allegations raised on appeal.

I.
Alleged Alibi Witnesses

Noel argues that trial counsel was ineffective for failing to present the testimony of alibi witnesses. The trial record reflects that an in-camera hearing was held, wherein defense counsel reported that Noel had given him the names of several witnesses who would provide an alibi for him. During the course of interviewing those witnesses, it was discovered that they could not provide a genuine alibi for Noel; however, the witnesses indicated that they were prepared to lie for him. Based on this knowledge, counsel advised that he could not present the false testimony, as it would violate the Model Rules of Professional Conduct.

During the postconviction hearing, Noel failed to call these alleged alibi witnesses to the stand. Moreover, he made no attempt to proffer the substance of the testimony that they would have provided at trial. This alone is sufficient reason to affirm. This court does not grant postconviction relief for ineffective assistance of counsel where the petitioner has failed to show that the omitted testimony was and how it could have changed the outcome. Pyle v. State, 340 Ark. 53, 8 S.W.3d 491 (2000).

Furthermore, the Supreme Court has recognized that as a matter of law, counsel 15 not ineffective for failing to present false testimony. In Nix v. Liteside, 475 U.S. 157, 106 S.Ct. 988, 89 L.Ed.2d 123 (1986), the defendant in murder trial had consistently told his attorney that he had acted in self-defense in stabbing the victim. He told his attorney that although he had not actually seen a gun in the victim's hand, he was convinced that the victim had a gun. Shortly before the trial, however, the defendant told his attorney that he had seen something metallic in the victim's hand. When questioned about this new information, the defendant stated: "If I don't say I saw a gun, I'm dead." Id. at 161, 106 S.Ct. 988. Defense counsel warned that if he testified falsely, it would be counsel's duty to advise the court that he felt the defendant was committing perjury, and that counsel would seek to withdraw from this case. At his trial, the defendant testified without making reference to seeing anything in the victim's hand, and he was convicted. Following his conviction, he claimed that he had received ineffective assistance of counsel. The Court disagreed, holding that counsel's conduct did not violate the reasonable

professional standards contemplated in Strickland v. Washington, 466 U.S. 668, 104 S.Ct. 2052, 80 L.Ed.2d 674 (1984). In reaching its decision, the court discussed the need to balance the Sixth Amendment right to effective counsel with the ethical obligations attorneys have as officers of the court. The Court explained that counsel's duty of loyalty and his duty to jealously advocate the defendant's cause are "limited to legitimate, lawful conduct compatible with the very nature of a trial as a search for truth." Nix, 175 U.S. at 166, 106 S.Ct. 988. Thus, "[a]lthough counsel must take all reasonable lawful means to attain the objectives of the client, counsel is precluded from taking steps or in any way assisting the client in presenting false evidence or otherwise violating the law." Id. The Court thus concluded that because there was no breach of any recognized professional duty, there was to deprivation of the right to effective assistance of counsel under Strickland. Finally, the Court held that "as a matter of law, counsel's conduct complained of here cannot establish the prejudice required for relief under the second strand of the Strickland inquiry." Id. at 175, 106 S.Ct. 988 (emphasis added). The only difference between this case and Nix is that, here, the false testimony was not being supplied by the defendant, but by his sympathizers. Counsel in this case acted properly by declining to present the false alibi testimony; to do otherwise would have been a violation of his ethical obligations. Rule 3.3(a) of the Model Rules of Professional Conduct provides: A lawyer shall not knowingly: . . . (4) offer evidence that the lawyer knows to be false." Subsection (c) provides: "A lawyer may refuse to offer evidence that the lawyer reasonably believes is false." Given these rules and the Supreme Court's recognition that a lawyer's duty of zealous representation extends only to legitimate, lawful conduct, we conclude that counsel was not ineffective for failing to present the false alibi testimony.

II.
Informing Jury that Noel Was Testifying Against Counsel's Advice

Noel contends that he was prejudiced when the jury was informed, during his direct examination, that he was testifying against the advice of counsel. The record reflects the following exchange between Noel and his trial counsel:

Q All right. Now, Riley, you're taking the stand here because you want to tell the jury your story. Is that correct?

Yes, sir.

And that's over my advice?

Yes, sir.

Against my advice?

A Yes, sir.

Noel urges that this was a comment on his credibility, or lack thereof, as a witness. He contends that by informing the jury that he was testifying against he advice of counsel, the jury could have concluded that even his own attorney and not believe he was telling the truth.

The State argues that this was a calculated trial tactic aimed at showing the jury that Noel was so insistent upon his innocence that he would risk taking the and, where his prior felony convictions would be revealed and he would likely undergo an exhausting cross-examination. Trial counsel testified that he chose reveal this information to show the jury how strongly Noel believed in his innocence. This strategy was further pursued by counsel in closing argument, herein he stated:

I told you in my opening that there were three witnesses that I anticipated would be presented, three main witnesses, for the State, and there were three main witnesses, testimony of witnesses against my client, Kyle Jones, Mary Russian, Curtis Cochran. . . . Now, we have two people that I told you would be very partisan witnesses, and they are. And I don't fault them at all. They have lost loved ones, and we feel sorry for them. It's a very tragic event. The third person is Curtis Cochran, and, you know, an admitted liar. Ladies and gentlemen, you have the Defendant, who took the stand in his own behalf, against the advice of his own attorney, and told you in his own way that he was not involved on June 4th, 1995. He told you his own story. He told you without any kind of deal from the State, no lighter sentence. He got it up, faced the music, and underwent a very grueling cross examination by the most experienced prosecutor on the prosecuting attorney's staff. . . . That, ladies and gentlemen, I think, rebuts a lot of the State's evidence[.] The trial court found that counsel was attempting to impress the jury with noel's sincerity in wanting to tell his side of the story, and that this was a matter of trial strategy. We cannot say that this ruling was clearly erroneous. Matters of trial strategy and tactics, even if arguably aprovident, fall within the realm of counsel's professional judgment and are not grounds for a finding of ineffective assistance of counsel. Chenowith, 341 Ark. 722, 19 S.W.3d 612; Weaver, 339 Ark. 97, 3 S.W.3d 323. Thus, even though another attorney may have chosen a different course,

trial strategy, even if it proves unsuccessful, is a matter of professional judgment. Fretwell v. State, 192 Ark. 96, 728 S.W.2d 180 (1987).

III.
Failing to Call Certain Witnesses

Noel argues that trial counsel was ineffective for failing to call several witnesses who would have testified as to his demeanor and activities during the days prior to the murders. The substance of their testimony was that Noel did not act like a person who was planning to murder these children in retaliation for his brother's death. While he acknowledges that the decision whether to call particular witnesses is a matter of trial strategy outside the purview of Rule 37, Noel argues that counsel's failure on this point coupled with the comment about his decision to testify against counsel's advice, cumulates into extreme prejudice and requires reversal under Strickland, 466 U.S. 668, 104 5 Ct. 2052, 80 L.Ed.2d 674. Inasmuch as Noel is making a cumulative-error argument, we do not address it because this court does not recognize cumulative error in allegations of ineffective assistance of counsel. See Huddleston v. State, 339 Ark. 266, 5 S.W.3d 46 (1999); Parks v. State, 301 Ark. 513, 785 S.W.2d 213 (1990).

In any event, Noel has failed to show that counsel's failure to call these witnesses was error. During the hearing on the petition, trial counsel stated that he did not recall having knowledge of any witnesses who could have testified that days before the murders, Noel was not acting like someone planning to kill. Counsel stated that he, co-counsel, and their investigator had interviewed every potential witness that Noel provided them, and there were no additional witnesses that could have been called on Noel's behalf. The trial court found that the admission of such demeanor testimony would not have altered the outcome of the trial and that, as a matter of law, the allegation is insufficient to warrant relief. We agree.

Whether or not counsel had known about such testimony, the failure to present it does not render counsel's performance ineffective. The decision whether to call particular witnesses is a matter of trial strategy that is outside the purview of Rule 37. Chenowith, 341 Ark. 722, 19 S.W.3d 612; Pillard, 338 Ark. 571, 998 S.W.2d 750. Trial counsel must use his or her best judgment to determine which witnesses will be beneficial to the client. Id. When assessing counsel's decision not to call a particular witness, we must take into account that the decision is largely a matter of professional judgment that experienced advocates could endlessly debate, and the fact that there was a witness or witnesses who could have offered beneficial testimony is not, in itself, proof of counsel's ineffectiveness. Id. Noel has not shown that counsel was deficient for not calling these particular witnesses or that his defense was prejudiced by the absence of their testimony. Accordingly, we affirm on this issue.

IV.
Funds for Expert Witness

Lastly, Noel argues that trial counsel was ineffective for failing to request funds to hire an expert witness to challenge the credibility of the eyewitness testimony of Mrs. Hussian and Kyle Jones. He contends that counsel's failure to do this prevented him from raising the issue on direct appeal. Noel acknowledges that this court's case law is not in his favor; however, he raises this issue to preserve it for federal review.

During the hearing below, trial counsel testified that he did not seek to retain an expert on eyewitness identification because he knew that Arkansas case law did not support the admissibility of such testimony. The trial court agreed, finding that the question of allowing an expert witness to testify regarding possible unreliability of eyewitness testimony had been addressed by this court and determined to be an invasion of the province of the jury. The trial court thus concluded that counsel was not ineffective for failing to request funds for such an expert. We agree with the trial court's analysis.

In Utley v. State, 308 Ark. 622, 626, 826 S.W.2d 268, 271 (1992), this court held that the admission of expert testimony regarding eyewitness identification would have hindered the jury's ability to judge impartially the credibility of the witnesses and the weight to be accorded their testimony. In arriving at this conclusion, this court observed that our appellate courts had long upheld the trial court's refusal to allow such expert testimony. For example, see Criglow v. State, 183 Ark. 407, 36 S.W.2d 400 (1931), this court explained: [T]he question whether these witnesses were mistaken in their identification, whether from fright or other cause, was one which the jury, and not an expert witness, should answer. This was a question upon which one man as well as another might form an opinion, and the function of passing upon the credibility and weight of testimony could not be taken from the jury. Id. at 409–10, 36 S.W.2d at 401–02.

Given the prior appellate holdings on this issue, it is not likely that counsel would have been successful in admitting such expert testimony to the jury. Thus, we cannot say that counsel's decision not to request funds for his purpose amounted to a denial of effective assistance of counsel. Counsel cannot be found ineffective for failing to make an argument that has no merit or has been previously rejected by this court. See Monts v. State, 312 Ark. 547, 51 S.W.2d 432 (1993); O'Rourke v. State, 298 Ark. 144, 765 S.W.2d 916 (1989) per curiam. Accordingly, Noel has failed to demonstrate both error and prejudice on this issue. Affirmed.[39]

Case Review Question: What should the defendant have done to strengthen his appeal?

> Prepare a flow chart showing the general progression of a criminal case from the time a crime is suspected, and the possible steps and outcomes.

Assignment 15.5

PARALEGALS IN THE WORKPLACE

In the 1980s and 1990s many jurisdictions, including the federal government, identified the paralegal as a qualified position. Paralegals can be quite effective in the criminal law arena in terms of preparation of what are largely form documents such as warrants, pleadings, and motions. Also, the paralegal can be effective at gathering information about the case, organizing and preparing trial documents, interviewing potential witnesses, and so forth. Paralegals may find employment not only in the offices of prosecutors but also in other governmental investigative agencies, courts, and court offices.

Chapter Summary

As this chapter has shown, the American legal system is committed to fairness to persons accused of criminal conduct, and every attempt is made to ensure that innocent persons are not convicted and punished. Much of the U.S. Constitution was written with this objective in mind, and it continues to be the basis for all aspects of criminal procedure.

Criminal procedure begins at the moment law enforcement authorities suspect criminal activity; often accused individuals are afforded constitutional protections before they are even aware that they are suspects. Criminal law provides very well-defined conditions of criminal conduct to avoid confusion by individuals as to whether their conduct may constitute a crime. After arrest, the Constitution continues to influence the proceedings through mandates regarding bail, right to counsel, specific charges of criminal conduct, and a speedy trial. The system, when properly applied, provides greater protection from improper convictions than perhaps any other legal system in the world.

Ethical Note

A common question asked of criminal defense lawyers is, "How can you represent someone that you know is guilty?" This seems to be a concept that the general public has great difficulty in reconciling as ethical behavior. However, representation of the accused is a cornerstone right guaranteed to all citizens under the U.S. Constitution. In the American system of justice, certain principles prevail. Everyone is innocent until proven guilty by evidence in a court of law. Not by the media, or speculation, or circumstance, or even the accused's own lawyer. Secondly, it is not the function of a criminal defense lawyer to judge the client. Rather, it is to see that the client's defense is heard in the best light possible and to take all necessary measures to achieve a fair trial for the client. The criminal defense lawyer is assisted in this endeavor by the Bill of Rights. Consequently, the answer to the earlier question is frequently not one of the ethics of the lawyer but one of the general public. It is important to view anyone accused of criminal conduct objectively until such time as the evidence is fully reviewed. This was the goal of the framers of the Constitution who sought primarily to reverse the standard of guilty until proven innocent.

Relevant Internet Sites

Criminal Law	www.aol.com/webcenters/legal/criminal.adp
Criminal Law	www.ncjrs.org
Criminal Procedure	www.nolo.com/encyclopedia/crim_ency.html

Internet Assignment 15.1

Locate the address and website, if any, for the local prosecutor in your jurisdiction.

Internet Assignment 15.2

Using Internet resources, find the statutory definition of a felony in your jurisdiction.

KEY TERMS

Actus Reus
Arraignment
Crime
Criminal Law
Critical Stage

Double Jeopardy
Due Process
Excusable
Felony
Justifiable

Mens Rea
Misdemeanor
Probable Cause

ENDNOTES

1. *Lord Fitzgerald Seaton v. Seaton*, L.R. 13 A.P.A.Ca. 78 (1888).
2. Model Penal Code Section 1.13(9).
3. *In Re Michael*, 423 A.2d 1180 (R.I. 1981).
4. *People v. Love*, 11 Cal.App.3d Supp. 1, 168 Cal.Rptr. 591 (1980).
5. Id.
6. 95 A.L.R.3d 248.
7. Model Penal Code Section 242.3: 2.06.
8. *Manner v. State*, 387 So.2d 1014 (Fla.App. 4th Dist. 1980).
9. Id.
10. *State v. Lora*, 213 Kan. 184, 515 P.2d 1086 (1973).
11. *Anderson v. State*, 61 Md. App. 436, 487 A.2d 294 (1985).
12. *Wilcox v. State*, 401 So.2d 789 (Ala.Crim.App. 1980).
13. *Dunn v. State*, 1612 Ind.App. 586, 316 N.E.2d 834 (1974).
14. *Callahan v. State*, 343 So.2d 551 (Ala.Crim.App. 1977).
15. *Commonwealth v. Hart*, 403 Pa. 652, 170 A.2d 850 (1961).
16. Model Penal Code Section 210.2.
17. Model Penal Code Section 2.07.
18. *State v. Williams*, 545 S.2d 2d 342 (Mo.App. 1976).
19. Model Penal Code Section 3.09.
20. *Daniel M'Naughten's Case*, 10 Cl. & F.200, 8 Eng. Rep. 718 (H.L., 1843).
21. 18 U.S.C. Section 20.
22. Model Penal Code Section 402.
23. *Palko v. Connecticut*, 302 U.S. 319, 58 S.Ct. 149, 82 L.Ed. 288 (1937).
24. *Mapp v. Ohio*, 267 U.S. 643 (1961).
25. *Wolf v. Colorado*, 338 U.S. 25 (1949).
26. Supra, Note 27.
27. 468 U.S. 897 (1984).
28. *Katz v. United States*, 389 U.S. 347 (1967).
29. Id.
30. *Vale v. Louisiana*, 399 U.S. 30 (1970).
31. See note 10.
32. *New York v. Belton*, 453 U.S. 454 (1981).
33. *Terry v. Ohio*, 392 U.S. 1 (1968).
34. 384 U.S. 436 (1966).
35. *State v. Loyal*, 164 N.J. 418, 753 A.2d 1073 (2000).
36. *Brewer v. Williams*, 430 U.S. 387 (1977).
37. *Barker v. Wingo*, 407 U.S. 514 (1972).
38. *Terry v. Ohio*, 392 U.S. 1 (1968).
39. *Noel v. Ark.*, 342 Ark. 35, 26 S.W.3d 123 (2000).

The Constitution of the United States

PREAMBLE

We the People of the United States, in Order to form a more perfect Union, establish Justice, insure domestic Tranquility, provide for the common defence, promote the general Welfare, and secure the Blessings of Liberty to ourselves and our Posterity, do ordain and establish this Constitution for the United States of America.

ARTICLE I

Section 1.   All legislative Powers herein granted shall be vested in a Congress of the United States, which shall consist of a Senate and House of Representatives.

Section 2.   The House of Representatives shall be composed of Members chosen every second Year by the People of the several States, and the Electors in each State shall have the Qualifications requisite for Electors of the most numerous Branch of the State Legislature.

No Person shall be a Representative who shall not have attained to the Age of twenty five Years, and been seven Years a Citizen of the United States, and who shall not, when elected, be an Inhabitant of that State in which he shall be chosen.

Representatives and direct Taxes shall be apportioned among the several States which may be included within this Union, according to their respective Numbers, which shall be determined by adding to the whole Number of free Persons, including those bound to Service for a Term of Years, and excluding Indians not taxed, three fifths of all other Persons. The actual Enumeration shall be made within three years after the first Meeting of the Congress of the United States, and within every subsequent Term of ten Years, in such Manner as they shall by Law direct. The Number of Representatives shall not exceed one for every thirty Thousand, but each State shall have at Least one Representative; and until such enumeration shall be made, the State of New Hampshire shall be entitled to chuse three, Massachusetts eight, Rhode Island and Providence Plantations one, Connecticut five, New York six, New Jersey four, Pennsylvania eight, Delaware one, Maryland six, Virginia ten, North Carolina five, South Carolina five, and Georgia three.

When vacancies happen in the Representation from any State, the Executive Authority thereof shall issue Writs of Election to fill such Vacancies.

The House of Representatives shall chuse their Speaker and other Officers; and shall have the sole Power of Impeachment.

Section 3.   The Senate of the United States shall be composed of two Senators from each State, chosen by the Legislature thereof, for six Years; and each Senator shall have one Vote.

Immediately after they shall be assembled in Consequence of the first Election, they shall be divided as equally as may be into three Classes. The Seats of the Senators of the first Class shall be vacated at the Expiration of the second Year, of the second Class at the Expiration of the fourth Year, and of the third Class at the Expiration of the sixth Year, so that one third may be chosen every second Year; and if Vacancies happen by Resignation, or otherwise, during the Recess of the Legislature of any State, the Executive thereof may make temporary Appointments until the next Meeting of the Legislature, which shall then fill such Vacancies.

No Person shall be a Senator who shall not have attained to the Age of thirty Years, and been nine Years a Citizen of the United States, and who shall not, when elected, be an Inhabitant of that State for which he shall be chosen.

The Vice President of the United States shall be President of the Senate, but shall have no Vote, unless they be equally divided.

The Senate shall chuse their other Officers, and also a President pro tempore, in the Absence of the Vice President, or when he shall exercise the Office of President of the United States.

The Senate shall have the sole Power to try all Impeachments. When sitting for that Purpose, they shall be on Oath or Affirmation. When the President of the United States is tried, the Chief Justice shall preside: And no Person shall be convicted without the Concurrence of two thirds of the Members present.

Judgment in Cases of Impeachment shall not extend further than to removal from Office, and disqualification to hold and enjoy any Office of honor, Trust, or Profit under the United States: but the Party convicted shall nevertheless be liable and subject to Indictment, Trial, Judgment, and Punishment, according to Law.

Section 4. The Times, Places and Manner of holding Elections for Senators and Representatives, shall be prescribed in each State by the Legislature thereof; but the Congress may at any time by Law make or alter such Regulations, except as to the Places of chusing Senators.

The Congress shall assemble at least once in every Year, and such Meeting shall be on the first Monday in December, unless they shall by Law appoint a different Day.

Section 5. Each House shall be the Judge of the Elections, Returns, and Qualifications of its own Members, and a Majority of each shall constitute a Quorum to do Business; but a smaller Number may adjourn from day to day, and may be authorized to compel the Attendance of absent Members, in such Manner, and under such Penalties as each House may provide.

Each House may determine the Rules of its Proceedings, punish its Members for disorderly Behavior, and, with the Concurrence of two thirds, expel a Member.

Each House shall keep a Journal of its Proceedings, and from time to time publish the same, excepting such Parts as may in their Judgment require Secrecy; and the Yeas and Nays of the Members of either House on any question shall, at the Desire of one fifth of those Present, be entered on the Journal.

Neither House, during the Session of Congress, shall, without the Consent of the other, adjourn for more than three days, nor to any other Place than that in which the two Houses shall be sitting.

Section 6. The Senators and Representatives shall receive a Compensation for their Services, to be ascertained by Law, and paid out of the Treasury of the United States. They shall in all Cases, except Treason, Felony and Breach of the Peace, be privileged from Arrest during their Attendance at the Session of their respective Houses, and in going to and returning from the same; and for any Speech or Debate in either House, they shall not be questioned in any other Place.

No Senator or Representative shall, during the Time for which he was elected, be appointed to any civil Office under the Authority of the United States, which shall have been created, or the Emoluments whereof shall have been increased during such time; and no Person holding any Office under the United States, shall be a Member of either House during his Continuance in Office.

Section 7. All Bills for raising Revenue shall originate in the House of Representatives; but the Senate may propose or concur with Amendments as on other Bills.

Every Bill which shall have passed the House of Representatives and the Senate, shall, before it become a Law, be presented to the President of the United States; If he approve he shall sign it, but if not he shall return it, with his Objections to the House in which it shall have originated, who shall enter the Objections at large on their Journal, and proceed to reconsider it. If after such Reconsideration two thirds of that House shall agree to pass the Bill, it shall be sent together with the Objections, to the other House, by which it shall likewise be reconsidered, and if approved by two thirds of that House, it shall become a Law. But in all such Cases the Votes of both Houses shall be determined by Yeas and Nays, and the Names of the Persons voting for and against the Bill shall be entered on the Journal of each House respectively. If any Bill shall not be returned by the President within ten Days (Sundays excepted) after it shall have been presented to him, the Same shall be a Law, in like Manner as if he had signed it, unless the Congress by their Adjournment prevent its Return in which Case it shall not be a Law.

Every Order, Resolution, or Vote, to which the Concurrence of the Senate and House of Representatives may be necessary (except on a question of Adjournment) shall be presented to the President of the United States; and before the Same shall take Effect, shall be approved by him, or being disapproved by him, shall be repassed by two thirds of the Senate and House of Representatives, according to the Rules and Limitations prescribed in the Case of a Bill.

Section 8. The Congress shall have Power To lay and collect Taxes, Duties, Imposts and Excises, to pay the Debts and provide for the common Defence and general Welfare of the United States; but all Duties, Imposts and Excises shall be uniform throughout the United States;

To borrow Money on the credit of the United States;

To regulate Commerce with foreign Nations, and among the several States, and with the Indian Tribes;

To establish an uniform Rule of Naturalization, and uniform Laws on the subject of Bankruptcies throughout the United States;

To coin Money, regulate the Value thereof, and of foreign Coin, and fix the Standard of Weights and Measures;

To provide for the Punishment of counterfeiting the Securities and current Coin of the United States;

To establish Post Offices and post Roads;

To promote the Progress of Science and useful Arts, by securing for limited Times to Authors and Inventors the exclusive Right to their respective Writings and Discoveries;

To constitute Tribunals inferior to the supreme Court;

To define and punish Piracies and Felonies committed on the high Seas, and Offenses against the Law of Nations;

To declare War, grant Letters of Marque and Reprisal, and make Rules concerning Captures on Land and Water;

To raise and support Armies, but no Appropriation of Money to that Use shall be for a longer Term than two Years;

To provide and maintain a Navy;

To make Rules for the Government and Regulation of the land and naval Forces;

To provide for calling forth the Militia to execute the Laws of the Union, suppress Insurrections and repel Invasions;

To provide for organizing, arming, and disciplining, the Militia, and for governing such Part of them as may be employed in the Service of the United States, reserving to the States respectively, the Appointment of the Officers, and the Authority of training the Militia according to the discipline prescribed by Congress;

To exercise exclusive Legislation in all Cases whatsoever, over such District (not exceeding ten Miles square) as may, by Cession of particular States, and the Acceptance of Congress, become the Seat of the Government of the United States, and to exercise like Authority over all Places purchased by the Consent of the Legislature of the State in which the Same shall be, for the Erection of Forts, Magazines, Arsenals, dock-Yards, and other needful Buildings;—And

To make all Laws which shall be necessary and proper for carrying into Execution the foregoing Powers, and all other Powers vested by this Constitution in the Government of the United States, or in any Department or Officer thereof.

Section 9. The Migration or Importation of such Persons as any of the States now existing shall think proper to admit, shall not be prohibited by the Congress prior to the Year one thousand eight hundred and eight, but a Tax or duty may be imposed on such Importation, not exceeding ten dollars for each Person.

The privilege of the Writ of Habeas Corpus shall not be suspended, unless when in Cases of Rebellion or Invasion the public Safety may require it.

No Bill of Attainder or ex post facto Law shall be passed.

No Capitation, or other direct, Tax shall be laid, unless in Proportion to the Census or Enumeration herein before directed to be taken.

No Tax or Duty shall be laid on Articles exported from any State.

No Preference shall be given by any Regulation of Commerce or Revenue to the Ports of one State over those of another: nor shall Vessels bound to, or from, one State be obliged to enter, clear, or pay Duties in another.

No Money shall be drawn from the Treasury, but in Consequence of Appropriations made by Law; and a regular Statement and Account of the Receipts and Expenditures of all public Money shall be published from time to time.

No Title of Nobility shall be granted by the United States: And no Person holding any Office of

Profit or Trust under them, shall, without the Consent of the Congress, accept of any present, Emolument, Office, or Title, of any kind whatever, from any King, Prince, or foreign State.

Section 10. No State shall enter into any Treaty, Alliance, or Confederation; grant Letters of Marque and Reprisal; coin Money; emit Bills of Credit; make any Thing but gold and silver Coin a Tender in Payment of Debts; pass any Bill of Attainder, ex post facto Law, or Law impairing the Obligation of Contracts, or grant any Title of Nobility.

No State shall, without the Consent of the Congress, lay any Imposts or Duties on Imports or Exports, except what may be absolutely necessary for executing it's inspection Laws: and the net Produce of all Duties and Imposts, laid by any State on Imports or Exports, shall be for the Use of the Treasury of the United States, and all such Laws shall be subject to the Revision and Controul of the Congress.

No State shall, without the Consent of Congress, lay any Duty of Tonnage, keep Troops, or Ships of War in time of Peace, enter into any Agreement or Compact with another State, or with a foreign Power, or engage in War, unless actually invaded, or in such imminent Danger as will not admit of delay.

ARTICLE II

Section 1. The executive Power shall be vested in a President of the United States of America. He shall hold his Office during the Term of four Years, and, together with the Vice President, chosen for the same Term, be elected, as follows:

Each State shall appoint, in such Manner as the Legislature thereof may direct, a Number of Electors, equal to the whole Number of Senators and Representatives to which the State may be entitled in the Congress; but no Senator or Representative, or Person holding an Office of Trust or Profit under the United States, shall be appointed an Elector.

The Electors shall meet in their respective States, and vote by Ballot for two Persons, of whom one at least shall not be an Inhabitant of the same State with themselves. And they shall make a List of all the Persons voted for, and of the Number of Votes for each; which List they shall sign and certify, and transmit sealed to the Seat of the Government of the United States, directed to the President of the Senate. The President of the Senate shall, in the Presence of the Senate and House of Representatives, open all the Certificates, and the Votes shall then be counted. The Person having the greatest Number of Votes shall be the President, if such Number be a Majority of the whole Number of Electors appointed; and if there be more than one who have such Majority, and have an equal Number of Votes, then the House of Representatives shall immediately chuse by Ballot one of them for President; and if no Person have a Majority, then from the five highest on the List the said House shall in like Manner chuse the President. But in chusing the President, the Votes shall be taken by States, the Representation from each State having one Vote; A quorum for this Purpose shall consist of a Member or Members from two thirds of the States, and a Majority of all the States shall be necessary to a Choice. In every Case, after the Choice of the President, the Person having the greater Number of Votes of the Electors shall be the Vice President. But if there should remain two or more who have equal Votes, the Senate shall chuse from them by Ballot the Vice President.

The Congress may determine the Time of chusing the Electors, and the Day on which they shall give their Votes; which Day shall be the same throughout the United States.

No person except a natural born Citizen, or a Citizen of the United States, at the time of the Adoption of this Constitution, shall be eligible to the Office of President; neither shall any Person be eligible to that Office who shall not have attained to the Age of thirty five Years, and been fourteen Years a Resident within the United States.

In Case of the Removal of the President from Office, or of his Death, Resignation or Inability to discharge the Powers and Duties of the said Office, the same shall devolve on the Vice President, and the Congress may by Law provide for the Case of Removal, Death, Resignation or Inability, both of the President and Vice President, declaring what Officer shall then act as President, and such Officer shall act accordingly, until the Disability be removed, or a President shall be elected.

The President shall, at stated Times, receive for his Services, a Compensation, which shall neither be increased nor diminished during the Period for which he shall have been elected, and he shall not receive within that Period any other Emolument from the United States, or any of them.

Before he enter on the Execution of his Office, he shall take the following Oath or Affirmation: "I do solemnly swear (or affirm) that I will faithfully execute the Office of President of the United States, and will to the best of my Ability, preserve, protect and defend the Constitution of the United States."

Section 2. The President shall be Commander in Chief of the Army and Navy of the United States, and of the Militia of the several States, when called into the actual Service of the United States; he may require the Opinion, in writing, of the principal Officer in each of the executive Departments, upon any Subject relating to the Duties of their respective Offices, and he shall have Power to grant Reprieves and Pardons for Offenses against the United States, except in Cases of Impeachment.

He shall have Power, by and with the Advice and Consent of the Senate to make Treaties, provided two thirds of the Senators present concur; and he shall nominate, and by and with the Advice and Consent of the Senate, shall appoint Ambassadors, other public Ministers and Consuls, Judges of the supreme Court, and all other Officers of the United States, whose Appointments are not herein otherwise provided for, and which shall be established by Law; but the Congress may by Law vest the Appointment of such inferior Officers, as they think proper, in the President alone, in the Courts of Law, or in the Heads of Departments.

The President shall have Power to fill up all Vacancies that may happen during the Recess of the Senate, by granting Commissions which shall expire at the End of their next Session.

Section 3. He shall from time to time give to the Congress Information of the State of the Union, and recommend to their Consideration such Measures as he shall judge necessary and expedient; he may, on extraordinary Occasions, convene both Houses, or either of them, and in Case of Disagreement between them, with Respect to the Time of Adjournment, he may adjourn them to such Time as he shall think proper; he shall receive Ambassadors and other public Ministers; he shall take Care that the Laws be faithfully executed, and shall Commission all the Officers of the United States.

Section 4. The President, Vice President and all civil Officers of the United States, shall be removed from Office on Impeachment for, and Conviction of, Treason, Bribery, or other high Crimes and Misdemeanors.

ARTICLE III

Section 1. The judicial Power of the United States, shall be vested in one supreme Court, and in such inferior Courts as the Congress may from time to time ordain and establish. The Judges, both of the supreme and inferior Courts, shall hold their Offices during good Behaviour, and shall, at stated Times, receive for their Services a Compensation, which shall not be diminished during their Continuance in Office.

Section 2. The judicial Power shall extend to all Cases, in Law and Equity, arising under this Constitution, the Laws of the United States, and Treaties made, or which shall be made, under their Authority;—to all Cases affecting Ambassadors, other public Ministers and Consuls;—to all Cases of admiralty and maritime Jurisdiction;—to Controversies to which the United States shall be a Party;—to Controversies between two or more States;—between a State and Citizens of another State;—between Citizens of different States;—between Citizens of the same State claiming Lands under Grants of different States, and between a State, or the Citizens thereof, and foreign States, Citizens or Subjects.

In all Cases affecting Ambassadors, other public Ministers and Consuls, and those in which a State shall be a Party, the supreme Court shall have original Jurisdiction. In all the other Cases before mentioned, the supreme Court shall have appellate Jurisdiction, both as to Law and Fact, with such Exceptions, and under such Regulations as the Congress shall make.

The Trial of all Crimes, except in Cases of Impeachment, shall be by Jury; and such Trial shall be held in the State where the said Crimes shall have been committed; but when not committed within any State, the Trial shall be at such Place or Places as the Congress may by Law have directed.

Section 3. Treason against the United States, shall consist only in levying War against them, or, in adhering to their Enemies, giving them Aid and Comfort. No Person shall be convicted of Treason unless on the Testimony of two Witnesses to the same overt Act, or on Confession in open Court.

The Congress shall have Power to declare the Punishment of Treason, but no Attainder of Treason shall work Corruption of Blood, or Forfeiture except during the Life of the Person attained.

ARTICLE IV

Section 1. Full Faith and Credit shall be given in each State to the public Acts, Records, and judicial Proceedings of every other State. And the Congress may by general Laws prescribe the Manner in which such Acts, Records and Proceedings shall be proved, and the Effect thereof.

Section 2. The Citizens of each State shall be entitled to all Privileges and Immunities of Citizens in the several States.

A Person charged in any State with Treason, Felony, or other Crime, who shall flee from Justice, and be found in another State, shall on Demand of the executive Authority of the State from which he fled, be delivered up, to be removed to the State having Jurisdiction of the Crime.

No Person held to Service or Labour in one State, under the Laws thereof, escaping into another, shall, in Consequence of any Law or Regulation therein, be discharged from such Service or Labour, but shall be delivered up on Claim of the Party to whom such Service or Labour may be due.

Section 3. New States may be admitted by the Congress into this Union; but no new State shall be formed or erected within the Jurisdiction of any other State; nor any State be formed by the Junction of two or more States, or Parts of States, without the Consent of the Legislatures of the States concerned as well as of the Congress.

The Congress shall have Power to dispose of and make all needful Rules and Regulations respecting the Territory or other Property belonging to the United States; and nothing in this Constitution shall be so construed as to Prejudice any Claims of the United States, or of any particular State.

Section 4. The United States shall guarantee to every State in this Union a Republican Form of Government, and shall protect each of them against Invasion; and on Application of the Legislature, or of the Executive (when the Legislature cannot be convened) against domestic Violence.

ARTICLE V

The Congress, whenever two thirds of both Houses shall deem it necessary, shall propose Amendments to this Constitution, or, on the Application of the Legislatures of two thirds of the several States, shall call a Convention for proposing Amendments, which, in either Case, shall be valid to all Intents and Purposes, as part of this Constitution, when ratified by the Legislatures of three fourths of the several States, or by Conventions in three fourths thereof, as the one or the other Mode of Ratification may be proposed by the Congress; Provided that no Amendment which may be made prior to the Year One thousand eight hundred and eight shall in any Manner affect the first and fourth Clauses in the Ninth Section of the first Article; and that no State, without its Consent, shall be deprived of its equal Suffrage in the Senate.

ARTICLE VI

All Debts contracted and Engagements entered into, before the Adoption of this Constitution shall be as valid against the United States under this Constitution, as under the Confederation.

This Constitution, and the Laws of the United States which shall be made in Pursuance thereof; and all Treaties made, or which shall be made, under the Authority of the United States, shall be the supreme Law of the Land; and the Judges in every State shall be bound thereby, any Thing in the Constitution or Laws of any State to the Contrary notwithstanding.

The Senators and Representatives before mentioned, and the Members of the several State Legislatures, and all executive and judicial Officers, both of the United States and of the several States, shall be bound by Oath or Affirmation, to support this Constitution; but no religious Test shall ever be required as a Qualification to any Office or public Trust under the United States.

ARTICLE VII

The Ratification of the Conventions of nine States shall be sufficient for the Establishment of this Constitution between the States so ratifying the Same.

AMENDMENT I [1791]

Congress shall make no law respecting an establishment of religion, or prohibiting the free exercise thereof; or abridging the freedom of speech, or of the press; or the right of the people peaceably to assembly, and to petition the Government for a redress of grievances.

AMENDMENT II [1791]

A well regulated Militia, being necessary to the security of a free State, the right of the people to keep and bear Arms, shall not be infringed.

AMENDMENT III [1791]

No Soldier shall, in time of peace be quartered in any house, without the consent of the Owner, nor in time of war, but in a manner to be prescribed by law.

AMENDMENT IV [1791]

The right of the people to be secure in their persons, houses, papers, and effects, against unreasonable searches and seizures, shall not be violated, and no Warrants shall issue, but upon probable cause, supported by Oath or affirmation, and particularly describing the place to be searched, and the persons or things to be seized.

AMENDMENT V [1791]

No person shall be held to answer for a capital, or otherwise infamous crime, unless on a presentment or indictment of a Grand Jury, except in cases arising in the land or naval forces, or in the Militia, when in actual service in time of War or public danger; nor shall any person be subject for the same offence to be twice put in jeopardy of life or limb; nor shall be compelled in any criminal case to be a witness against himself, nor be deprived of life, liberty, or property, without due process of law; nor shall private property be taken for public use, without just compensation.

AMENDMENT VI [1791]

In all criminal prosecutions, the accused   shall enjoy the right to a speedy and public trial, by an impartial jury of the State and district wherein the crime shall have been committed, which district shall have been previously ascertained by law, and to be informed of the nature and cause of the accusation; to be confronted with the witnesses against him; to have compulsory process for obtaining witnesses in his favor, and to have the Assistance of Counsel for his defence.

AMENDMENT VII [1791]

In Suits at common law, where the value in controversy shall exceed twenty dollars, the right of trial by jury shall be preserved, and no fact tried by jury, shall be otherwise re-examined in any Court of the United States, than according to the rules of the common law.

AMENDMENT VIII [1791]

Excessive bail shall not be required, nor excessive fines imposed, nor cruel and unusual punishments inflicted.

AMENDMENT IX [1791]

The enumeration in the Constitution, of certain rights, shall not be construed to deny or disparage others retained by the people.

AMENDMENT X [1791]

The powers not delegated to the United States by the Constitution, nor prohibited by it to the States, are reserved to the States respectively, or to the people.

AMENDMENT XI [1798]

The Judicial power of the United States shall not be construed to extend to any suit in law or equity, commenced or prosecuted against one of the United States by Citizens of another State, or by Citizens or Subjects of any Foreign State.

AMENDMENT XII [1804]

The Electors shall meet in their respective states, and vote by ballot for President and Vice President, one of whom, at least, shall not be an inhabitant of the same state with themselves; they shall name in their ballots the person voted for as President, and in distinct ballots the person voted for as Vice President, and they shall make distinct lists of all persons voted for as President, and of all persons voted for as Vice President, and of the number of votes for each, which lists they shall sign and certify, and transmit sealed to the seat of the government of the United States, directed to the President of the Senate;—The President of the Senate shall, in the presence of the Senate and House of Representatives, open all the certificates and the votes shall then be counted;—The person having the greatest number of votes for President, shall be the President, if such number be a majority of the whole number of Electors appointed; and if no person have such majority, then from the persons having the highest numbers not exceeding three on the list of those voted for as President, the House of Representatives shall choose immediately, by ballot, the President. But in choosing the President, the votes shall be taken by states, the representation from each state having one vote; a quorum for this purpose shall consist of a member or members from two-thirds of the states, and a majority of all states shall be necessary to a choice. And if the House of Representatives shall not choose a President whenever the right of choice shall devolve upon them, before the fourth day of March next following, then the Vice President shall act as President, as in the case of the death or other constitutional disability of the President.—The person having the greatest number of votes as Vice President, shall be the Vice President, if such number be a majority of the whole number of Electors appointed, and if no person have a majority, then from the two highest numbers on the list, the Senate shall choose the Vice President; a quorum for the purpose shall consist of two-thirds of the whole number of Senators, and a majority of the whole number shall be necessary to a choice. But no person constitutionally ineligible to the office of President shall be eligible to that of Vice President of the United States.

AMENDMENT XIII [1865]

Section 1.   Neither slavery nor involuntary servitude, except as a punishment for crime whereof the party shall have been duly convicted, shall exist within the United States, or any place subject to their jurisdiction.

Section 2.   Congress shall have power to enforce this article by appropriate legislation.

AMENDMENT XIV [1868]

Section 1.   All persons born or naturalized in the United States, and subject to the jurisdiction thereof, are citizens of the United States and of the State wherein they reside. No State shall make or enforce any law which shall abridge the privileges or immunities of citizens of the United States; nor shall any State deprive any person of life, liberty, or property, without due process of law; nor deny to any person within its jurisdiction the equal protection of the laws.

Section 2.   Representatives shall be apportioned among the several States according to their respective numbers, counting the whole number of persons in each State, excluding Indians not taxed. But when the right to vote at any election for the choice of electors for President and Vice President of the United States, Representatives in Congress, the Executive and Judicial officers of a State, or the members of the Legislature thereof, is denied to any of the male inhabitants of such State, being twenty-one years of age, and citizens of the United States, or in any way abridged, except for participation in rebellion, or other crime, the basis of representation therein shall be reduced in the proportion which the number of such male citizens shall bear to the whole number of male citizens twenty-one years of age in such State.

Section 3.   No person shall be a Senator or Representative in Congress, or elector of President and Vice President, or hold any office, civil or military, under the United States, or under any State, who having previously taken an oath, as a member of Congress, or as an officer of the United States, or as a member of any State legislature, or as an executive or judicial officer of any State, to support the Constitution of the United States, shall have engaged in insurrection or rebellion against the same, or given aid or comfort to the enemies thereof. But Congress may by a vote of two-thirds of each House, remove such disability.

Section 4.   The validity of the public debt of the United States, authorized by law, including debts incurred for payment of pensions and bounties for services in suppressing insurrection or rebellion, shall not be questioned. But neither the United States nor any State shall assume or pay any debt or obligation incurred in aid of insurrection or rebellion against the United States, or any claim for the loss or emancipation of any slave; but all such debts, obligations and claims shall be held illegal and void.

Section 5.   The Congress shall have power to enforce, by appropriate legislation, the provisions of this article.

AMENDMENT XV [1870]

Section 1.   The right of citizens of the United States to vote shall not be denied or abridged by the United States or by any State on account of race, color, or previous condition of servitude.

Section 2.   The Congress shall have power to enforce this article by appropriate legislation.

AMENDMENT XVI [1913]

The Congress shall have power to lay and collect taxes on incomes, from whatever source derived, without apportionment among the several States, and without regard to any census or enumeration.

AMENDMENT XVII [1913]

[1] The Senate of the United States shall be composed of two Senators from each State, elected by the people thereof, for six years; and each Senator shall have one vote. The electors in each State shall have the qualifications requisite for electors of the most numerous branch of the State legislatures.

[2] When vacancies happen in the representation of any State in the Senate, the executive authority of such State shall issue writs of election to fill such vacancies: *Provided*, That the legislature of any State may empower the executive thereof to make temporary appointments until the people fill the vacancies by election as the legislature may direct.

[3] This amendment shall not be so construed as to affect the election or term of any Senator chosen before it becomes valid as part of the Constitution.

AMENDMENT XVIII [1919]

Section 1.   After one year from the ratification of this article the manufacture, sale, or transportation of intoxicating liquors within, the importation thereof into, or the exportation thereof from the United States and all territory subject to the jurisdiction thereof for beverage purposes is hereby prohibited.

Section 2.   The Congress and the several States shall have concurrent power to enforce this article by appropriate legislation.

Section 3.   This article shall be inoperative unless it shall have been ratified as an amendment to the Constitution by the legislatures of the several States, as provided in the Constitution, within seven years from the date of the submission hereof to the States by the Congress.

AMENDMENT XIX [1920]

[1] The right of citizens of the United States to vote shall not be denied or abridged by the United States or by any State on account of sex.

[2] Congress shall have power to enforce this article by appropriate legislation.

AMENDMENT XX [1933]

Section 1.   The terms of the President and Vice President shall end at noon on the 20th day of January, and the terms of Senators and Representatives at noon on the 3d day of January, of the years in which such terms would have ended if this article had not been ratified; and the terms of their successors shall then begin.

Section 2.   The Congress shall assemble at least once in every year, and such meeting shall begin at noon on the 3d day of January, unless they shall by law appoint a different day.

Section 3.   If, at the time fixed for the beginning of the term of the President, the President elect shall have died, the Vice President elect shall become President. If the President shall not have been chosen before the time fixed for the beginning of his term, or if the President elect shall have failed to qualify, then the Vice President elect shall act as President until a President shall have qualified; and the Congress may by law provide for the case wherein neither a President elect nor a Vice President elect shall have qualified, declaring who shall then act as President, or the manner in which one who is to act shall be selected, and such person shall act accordingly until a President or Vice President shall have qualified.

Section 4.   The Congress may by law provide for the case of the death of any of the persons from whom the House of Representatives may choose a President whenever the right of choice shall have devolved upon them, and for the case of the death of any of the persons from whom the Senate may choose a Vice President whenever the right of choice shall have devolved upon them.

Section 5.   Sections 1 and 2 shall take effect on the 15th day of October following the ratification of this article.

Section 6.   This article shall be inoperative unless it shall have been ratified as an amendment to the Constitution by the legislatures of three-fourths of the several States within seven years from the date of its submission.

AMENDMENT XXI [1933]

Section 1. The eighteenth article of amendment to the Constitution of the United States is hereby repealed.

Section 2. The transportation or importation into any State, Territory, or possession of the United States for delivery or use therein of intoxicating liquors, in violation of the laws thereof, is hereby prohibited.

Section 3. This article shall be inoperative unless it shall have been ratified as an amendment to the Constitution by conventions in the several States, as provided in the Constitution, within seven years from the date of the submission hereof to the States by the Congress.

AMENDMENT XXII [1951]

Section 1. No person shall be elected to the office of the President more than twice, and no person who has held the office of President, or acted as President, for more than two years of a term to which some other person was elected President shall be elected to the office of President more than once. But this Article shall not apply to any person holding the office of President when this Article was proposed by the Congress, and shall not prevent any person who may be holding the office of President, or acting as President, during the term within which this Article becomes operative from holding the office of President or acting as President during the remainder of such term.

Section 2. This article shall be inoperative unless it shall have been ratified as an amendment to the Constitution by the legislatures of three-fourths of the several States within seven years from the date of its submission to the States by the Congress.

AMENDMENT XXIII [1961]

Section 1. The District constituting the seat of Government of the United States shall appoint in such manner as the Congress may direct:

A number of electors of President and Vice President equal to the whole number of Senators and Representatives in Congress to which the District would be entitled if it were a State, but in no event more than the least populous state; they shall be in addition to those appointed by the states, but they shall be considered, for the purposes of the election of President and Vice President, to be electors appointed by a state; and they shall meet in the District and perform such duties as provided by the twelfth article of amendment.

Section 2. The Congress shall have power to enforce this article by appropriate legislation.

AMENDMENT XXIV [1964]

Section 1. The right of citizens of the United States to vote in any primary or other election for President or Vice President, for electors for President or Vice President, or for Senator or Representative in Congress, shall not be denied or abridged by the United States, or any State by reason of failure to pay any poll tax or other tax.

Section 2. The Congress shall have power to enforce this article by appropriate legislation.

AMENDMENT XXV [1967]

Section 1. In case of the removal of the President from office or of his death or resignation, the Vice President shall become President.

Section 2. Whenever there is a vacancy in the office of the Vice President, the President shall nominate a Vice President who shall take office upon confirmation by a majority vote of both Houses of Congress.

Section 3. Whenever the President transmits to the President pro tempore of the Senate and the Speaker of the House of Representatives his written declaration that he is unable to discharge the powers and duties of his office, and until he transmits to them a written declaration to the contrary, such powers and duties shall be discharged by the Vice President as Acting President.

Section 4. Whenever the Vice President and a majority of either the principal officers of the executive departments or of such other body as Congress may by law provide, transmit to the President pro tempore of the Senate and the Speaker of the House of Representatives their written declaration that the President is unable to discharge the powers and duties of his office, the Vice President shall immediately assume the powers and duties of the office as Acting President.

Thereafter, when the President transmits to the President pro tempore of the Senate and the Speaker of the House of Representatives his written declaration that no inability exists, he shall resume the powers and duties of his office unless the Vice President and a majority of either the principal officers of the executive department or of such other body as Congress may by law provide, transmit within four days to the President pro tempore of the Senate and the Speaker of the House of Representatives their written declaration and the President is unable to discharge the powers and duties of his office. Thereupon Congress shall decide the issue, assembling within forty-eight hours for that purpose if not in session. If the Congress, within twenty-one days after receipt of the latter written declaration, or, if Congress is not in session, within twenty-one days after Congress is required to assemble, determines by two-thirds vote of both Houses that the President is unable to discharge the powers and duties of his office, the Vice President shall continue to discharge the same as Acting President; otherwise, the President shall resume the powers and duties of his office.

AMENDMENT XXVI [1971]

Section 1.   The right of citizens of the United States, who are eighteen years of age or older, to vote shall not be denied or abridged by the United States or by any State on account of age.

Section 2.   The Congress shall have power to enforce this article by appropriate legislation.

The Model Business Corporation Act

§ 1. Short Title*

This Act shall be known and may be cited as the ". . . . . .† Business Corporation Act."

§ 2. Definitions

As used in this Act, unless the context otherwise requires, the term:

(a) "Corporation" or "domestic corporation" means a corporation for profit subject to the provisions of this Act, except a foreign corporation.

(b) "Foreign corporation" means a corporation for profit organized under laws other than the laws of this State for a purpose or purposes for which a corporation may be organized under this Act.

(c) "Articles of incorporation" means the original or restated articles of incorporation or articles of consolidation and all amendments thereto including articles of merger.

(d) "Shares" means the units into which the proprietary interests in a corporation are divided.

(e) "Subscriber" means one who subscribes for shares in a corporation, whether before or after incorporation.

(f) "Shareholder" means one who is a holder of record of shares in a corporation. If the articles of incorporation or the by-laws so provide, the board of directors may adopt by resolution a procedure whereby a shareholder of the corporation may certify in writing to the corporation that all or a portion of the shares registered in the name of such shareholder are held for the account of a specified person or persons. The resolution shall set forth (1) the classification of shareholder who may certify, (2) the purpose or purposes for which the certification may be made, (3) the form of certification and information to be contained therein, (4) if the certification is with respect to a record date or closing of the stock transfer books within which the certification must be received by the corporation and (5) such other provisions with respect to the procedure as are deemed necessary or desirable. Upon receipt by the corporation of a certification complying with the procedure, the persons specified in the certification shall be deemed, for the purpose or purposes set forth in the certification, to be the holders of record of the number of shares specified in place of the shareholder making the certification.

(g) "Authorized shares" means the shares of all classes which the corporation is authorized to issue.

(h) "Employee" includes officers but not directors. A director may accept duties which make him also an employee.

(i) "Distribution" means a direct or indirect transfer of money or other property (except its own shares) or incurrence of indebtedness, by a corporation to or for the benefit of any of its shareholders in respect of any of its shares, whether by dividend or

---

*[By the Editor] The Model Business Corporation Act prepared by the Committee on Corporate Laws (Section of Corporation, Banking and Business Law) of the American Bar Association was originally patterned after the Illinois Business Corporation Act of 1933. It was first published as a complete act in 1950. In subsequent years several revisions, addenda and optional or alternative provisions were added. The Act was substantially revised and renumbered in 1969.

This Act should be distinguished from the Model Business Corporation Act promulgated in 1928 by the Commissioners on Uniform State Laws under the name "Uniform Business Corporation Act" and renamed Model Business Corporation Act in 1943. This Uniform Act was withdrawn in 1957.

The Model Business Corporation Act has been influential in the codification of corporation statutes in more than 35 states. However, there is no state that has totally adopted it in its current form. Moreover, since the Model Act itself has been substantially modified from time to time, there is considerable variation among the statutes of the states that used this Act as a model.

†Insert name of State.

by purchase, redemption or other acquisition of its shares, or otherwise.

§ 3. Purposes

Corporations may be organized under this Act for any lawful purpose or purposes, except for the purpose of banking or insurance.

§ 4. General Powers

Each corporation shall have power:

(a) To have perpetual succession by its corporate name unless a limited period of duration is stated in its articles of incorporation.

(b) To sue and be sued, complain and defend, in its corporate name.

(c) To have a corporate seal which may be altered at pleasure, and to use the same by causing it, or a facsimile thereof, to be impressed or affixed or in any other manner reproduced.

(d) To purchase, take, receive, lease, or otherwise acquire, own, hold, improve, use and otherwise deal in and with, real or personal property, or any interest therein, wherever situated.

(e) To sell, convey, mortgage, pledge, lease, exchange, transfer and otherwise dispose of all or any part of its property and assets.

(f) To lend money and use its credit to assist its employees.

(g) To purchase, take, receive, subscribe for, or otherwise acquire, own, hold, vote, use, employ, sell, mortgage, lend, pledge, or otherwise dispose of, and otherwise use and deal in and with, shares or other interests in, or obligations of, other domestic or foreign corporations, associations, partnerships or individuals, or direct or indirect obligations of the United States or of any other government, state, territory, governmental district or municipality or of any instrumentality thereof.

(h) To make contracts and guarantees and incur liabilities, borrow money at such rates of interest as the corporation may determine, issue its notes, bonds, and other obligations, and secure any of its obligations by mortgage or pledge of all or any of its property, franchises and income.

(i) To lend money for its corporate purposes, invest and reinvest its funds, and take and hold real and personal property as security for the payment of funds so loaned or invested.

(j) To conduct its business, carry on its operations and have offices and exercise the powers granted by this Act, within or without this State.

(k) To elect or appoint officers and agents of the corporation, and define their duties and fix their compensation.

(l) To make and alter by-laws, not inconsistent with its articles of incorporation or with the laws of this State, for the administration and regulation of the affairs of the corporation.

(m) To make donations for the public welfare or for charitable, scientific or educational purposes.

(n) To transact any lawful business which the board of directors shall find will be in aid of governmental policy.

(o) To pay pensions and establish pension plans, pension trusts, profit sharing plans, stock bonus plans, stock option plans and other incentive plans for any or all of its directors, officers and employees.

(p) To be a promoter, partner, member, associate, or manager of any partnership, joint venture, trust or other enterprise.

(q) To have and exercise all powers necessary or convenient to effect its purposes.

§ 5. Indemnification of Directors and Officers

(a) As used in this section:

(1) "Director" means any person who is or was a director of the corporation and any person who, while a director of the corporation, is or was serving at the request of the corporation as a director, officer, partner, trustee, employee or agent of another foreign or domestic corporation, partnership, joint venture, trust, other enterprise or employee benefit plan.

(2) "Corporation" includes any domestic or foreign predecessor entity of the corporation in a merger, consolidation or other transaction in which the predecessor's existence ceased upon consummation of such transaction.

(3)   "Expenses" include attorneys' fees.

(4)   "Official capacity" means

> (A)   when used with respect to a director, the office of director in the corporation, and
>
> (B)   when used with respect to a person other than a director, as contemplated in subsection (i), the elective or appointive office in the corporation held by the officer or the employment or agency relationship undertaken by the employee or agent in behalf of the corporation,

but in each case does not include service for any other foreign or domestic corporation or any partnership, joint venture, trust, other enterprise, or employee benefit plan.

(5)   "Party" includes a person who was, is, or is threatened to be made, a named defendant or respondent in a proceeding.

(6)   "Proceeding" means any threatened, pending or completed action, suit or proceeding, whether civil, criminal, administrative or investigative.

(b) A corporation shall have power to indemnify any person made a party to any proceeding by reason of the fact that he is or was a director if

(1)   he conducted himself in good faith; and

(2)   he reasonably believed

> (A)   in the case of conduct in his official capacity with the corporation, that his conduct was in its best interests, and
>
> (B)   in all other cases, that his conduct was at least not opposed to its best interests; and

(3)   in the case of any criminal proceeding, he had no reasonable cause to believe his conduct was unlawful.

Indemnification may be made against judgments, penalties, fines, settlements and reasonable expenses, actually incurred by the person in connection with the proceeding; except that if the proceeding was by or in the right of the corporation, indemnification may be made only against such reasonable expenses and shall not be made in respect of any proceeding in which the person shall have been adjudged to be liable to the corporation. The termination of any proceeding by judgment, order, settlement, conviction, or upon a plea of nolo contendere or its equivalent, shall not, of itself, be determinative that the person did not meet the requisite standard of conduct set forth in this subsection (b).

(c)   A director shall not be indemnified under subsection (b) in respect of any proceeding charging improper personal benefit to him, whether or not involving action in his official capacity, in which he shall have been adjudged to be liable on the basis that personal benefit was improperly received by him.

(d)   Unless limited by the articles of incorporation,

(1)   a director who has been wholly successful, on the merits or otherwise, in the defense of any proceeding referred to in subsection (b) shall be indemnified against reasonable expenses incurred by him in connection with the proceeding; and

(2)   a court of appropriate jurisdiction, upon application of a director and such notice as the court shall require, shall have authority to order indemnification in the following circumstances:

> (A)   if it determines a director is entitled to reimbursement under clause (1), the court shall order indemnification, in which case the director shall also be entitled to recover the expenses of securing such reimbursement; or
>
> (B)   if it determines that the director is fairly and reasonably entitled to indemnification in view of all the relevant circumstances, whether or not he has met the standard of conduct set forth in subsection (b) or has been adjudged liable in the circumstances described in subsection (c), the court may order such indemnification as the court shall deem proper, except that indemnification with respect to any proceeding by or in the right of the corporation or in which liability shall have been adjudged in the circumstances described in subsection (c) shall be limited to expenses.

A court of appropriate jurisdiction may be the same court in which the proceeding involving the director's liability took place.

(e)   No indemnification under subsection (b) shall be made by the corporation unless authorized in the specific case after a determination has been made that indemnification of the director is permissible in the circumstances because he has met the standard of conduct set forth in subsection (b). Such determination shall be made:

(1)   by the board of directors by a majority vote of a quorum consisting of directors not at the time parties to the proceeding; or

(2)   if such a quorum cannot be obtained, then by a majority vote of a committee of the board, duly designated to act in the matter by a majority vote of the full board (in which designation directors who are parties may participate), consisting solely of two or more directors not at the time parties to the proceeding; or

(3)   by special legal counsel, selected by the board of directors or a committee thereof by vote as set forth in clauses (1) or (2) of this subsection (e), or, if the requisite quorum of the full board cannot be obtained therefor and such committee cannot be established, by a majority vote of the full board (in which selection directors who are parties may participate); or

(4)   by the shareholders.

Authorization of indemnification and determination as to reasonableness of expenses shall be made in the same manner as the determination that indemnification is permissible, except that if the determination that indemnification is permissible is made by special legal counsel, authorization of indemnification and determination as to reasonableness of expenses shall be made in a manner specified in clause (3) in the preceding sentence for the selection of such counsel. Shares held by directors who are parties to the proceeding shall not be voted on the subject matter under this subsection (e).

(f)   Reasonable expenses incurred by a director who is a party to a proceeding may be paid or reimbursed by the corporation in advance of the final disposition of such proceeding upon receipt by the corporation of

(1)   a written affirmation by the director of his good faith belief that he has met the standard of conduct necessary for indemnification by the corporation as authorized in this section, and

(2)   a written undertaking by or on behalf of the director to repay such amount if it shall ultimately be determined that he has not met such standard of conduct, and after a determination that the facts then known to those making the determination would not preclude indemnification under this section. The undertaking required by clause (2) shall be an unlimited general obligation of the

director but need not be secured and may be accepted without reference to financial ability to make repayment. Determinations and authorizations of payments under this subsection (f) shall be made in the manner specified in subsection (e).

(g)   No provision for the corporation to indemnify or to advance expenses to a director who is made a party to the proceeding, whether contained in the articles of incorporation, the by-laws, a resolution of shareholders or directors, an agreement or otherwise (except as contemplated by subsection (j)), shall be valid unless consistent with this section or, to the extent that indemnity hereunder is limited by the articles of incorporation, consistent therewith. Nothing contained in this section shall limit the corporation's power to pay or reimburse expenses incurred by a director in connection with his appearance as a witness in a proceeding at a time when he has not been made a named defendant or respondent in the proceeding.

(h)   For purposes of this section, the corporation shall be deemed to have requested a director to serve an employee benefit plan whenever the performance by him of his duties to the corporation also imposes duties on, or otherwise involves services by, him to the plan or participants or beneficiaries of the plan; excise taxes assessed on a director with respect to an employee benefit plan pursuant to applicable law shall be deemed "fines"; and action taken or omitted by him with respect to an employee benefit plan in the performance of his duties for a purpose reasonably believed by him to be in the interest of the participants and beneficiaries of the plan shall be deemed to be for a purpose which is not opposed to the best interests of the corporation.

(i)   Unless limited by the articles of incorporation,

(1)   an officer of the corporation shall be indemnified as and to the same extent provided in subsection (d) for a director and shall be entitled to the same extent as a director to seek indemnification pursuant to the provisions of subsection (d);

(2)   a corporation shall have the power to indemnify and to advance expenses to an officer, employee or agent of the corporation to the same extent that it may indemnify and advance expenses to directors pursuant to this section; and

(3)   a corporation, in addition, shall have the power to indemnify and to advance expenses to an officer, employee or agent who is not a director to such further extent, consistent with law, as may

be provided by its articles of incorporation, by-laws, general or specific action of its board of directors, or contract.

(j)   A corporation shall have power to purchase and maintain insurance on behalf of any person who is or was a director, officer, employee or agent of the corporation, or who, while a director, officer, employee or agent of the corporation, is or was serving at the request of the corporation as a director, officer, partner, trustee, employee or agent of another foreign or domestic corporation, partnership, joint venture, trust, other enterprise or employee benefit plan, against any liability asserted against him and incurred by him in any such capacity or arising out of his status as such, whether or not the corporation would have the power to indemnify him against such liability under the provisions of this section.

(k)   Any indemnification of, or advance of expenses to, a director in accordance with this section, if arising out of a proceeding by or in the right of the corporation, shall be reported in writing to the shareholders with or before the notice of the next shareholders' meeting.

§ 6. Power of Corporation to Acquire Its Own Shares

A corporation shall have the power to acquire its own shares. All of its own shares acquired by a corporation shall, upon acquisition, constitute authorized but unissued shares, unless the articles of incorporation provide that they shall not be reissued, in which case the authorized shares shall be reduced by the number of shares acquired.

If the number of authorized shares is reduced by an acquisition, the corporation shall, not later than the time it files its next annual report under this Act with the Secretary of State, file a statement of cancellation showing the reduction in the authorized shares. The statement of cancellation shall be executed in duplicate by the corporation by its president or a vice president and by its secretary or an assistant secretary, and verified by one of the officers signing such statement, and shall set forth:

(a)   The name of the corporation.

(b)   The number of acquired shares cancelled, itemized by classes and series.

(c)   The aggregate number of authorized shares, itemized by classes and series, after giving effect to such cancellation.

Duplicate originals of such statement shall be delivered to the Secretary of State. If the Secretary of State finds that such statement conforms to law, he shall, when all fees and franchise taxes have been paid as in this Act prescribed:

(1)   Endorse on each of such duplicate originals the word "Filed," and the month, day and year of the filing thereof.

(2)   File one of such duplicate originals in his office.

(3)   Return the other duplicate original to the corporation or its representative.

§ 7. Defense of Ultra Vires

No act of a corporation and no conveyance or transfer of real or personal property to or by a corporation shall be invalid by reason of the fact that the corporation was without capacity or power to do such act or to make or receive such conveyance or transfer, but such lack of capacity or power may be asserted:

(a)   In a proceeding by a shareholder against the corporation to enjoin the doing of any act or the transfer of real or personal property by or to the corporation. If the unauthorized act or transfer sought to be enjoined is being, or is to be, performed or made pursuant to a contract to which the corporation is a party, the court may, if all of the parties to the contract are parties to the proceeding and if it deems the same to be equitable, set aside and enjoin the performance of such contract, and in so doing may allow to the corporation or to the other parties to the contract, as the case may be, compensation for the loss or damage sustained by either of them which may result from the action of the court in setting aside and enjoining the performance of such contract, but anticipated profits to be derived from the performance of the contract shall not be awarded by the court as a loss or damage sustained.

(b)   In a proceeding by the corporation, whether acting directly or through a receiver, trustee, or other legal representative, or through shareholders in a representative suit, against the incumbent or former officers or directors of the corporation.

(c)   In a proceeding by the Attorney General, as provided in this Act, to dissolve the corporation, or in a proceeding by the Attorney General to enjoin the corporation from the transaction of unauthorized business.

§ 8. Corporate Name

The corporate name:

(a) Shall contain the word "corporation," "company," "incorporated" or "limited," or shall contain an abbreviation of one of such words.

(b) Shall not contain any word or phrase which indicates or implies that it is organized for any purpose other than one or more of the purposes contained in its articles of incorporation.

(c) Shall not be the same as, or deceptively similar to, the name of any domestic corporation existing under the laws of this State or any foreign corporation authorized to transact business in this State, or a name the exclusive right to which is, at the time, reserved in the manner provided in this Act, or the name of a corporation which has in effect a registration of its corporate name as provided in this Act, except that this provision shall not apply if the applicant files with the Secretary of State either of the following: (1) the written consent of such other corporation or holder of a reserved or registered name to use the same or deceptively similar name and one or more words are added to make such name distinguishable from such other name, or (2) a certified copy of a final decree of a court of competent jurisdiction establishing the prior right of the applicant to the use of such name in this State.

A corporation with which another corporation, domestic or foreign, is merged, or which is formed by the reorganization or consolidation of one or more domestic or foreign corporations or upon a sale, lease or other disposition to or exchange with, a domestic corporation of all or substantially all the assets of another corporation, domestic or foreign, including its name, may have the same name as that used in this State by any of such corporations if such other corporation was organized under the laws of, or is authorized to transact business in, this State.

§ 9. Reserved Name

The exclusive right to the use of a corporate name may be reserved by:

(a) Any person intending to organize a corporation under this Act.

(b) Any domestic corporation intending to change its name.

(c) Any foreign corporation intending to make application for a certificate of authority to transact business in this State.

(d) Any foreign corporation authorized to transact business in this State and intending to change its name.

(e) Any person intending to organize a foreign corporation and intending to have such corporation make application for a certificate of authority to transact business in this State.

The reservation shall be made by filing with the Secretary of State an application to reserve a specified corporate name, executed by the applicant. If the Secretary of State finds that the name is available for corporate use, he shall reserve the same for the exclusive use of the applicant for a period of one hundred and twenty days.

The right to the exclusive use of a specified corporate name so reserved may be transferred to any other person or corporation by filing in the office of the Secretary of State a notice of such transfer, executed by the applicant for whom the name was reserved, and specifying the name and address of the transferee.

§ 10. Registered Name

Any corporation organized and existing under the laws of any state or territory of the United States may register its corporate name under this Act, provided its corporate name is not the same as, or deceptively similar to, the name of any domestic corporation existing under the laws of this State, or the name of any foreign corporation authorized to transact business in this State, or any corporate name reserved or registered under this Act.

Such registration shall be made by:

(a) Filing with the Secretary of State (1) an application for registration executed by the corporation by an officer thereof, setting forth the name of the corporation, the state or territory under the laws of which it is incorporated, the date of its incorporation, a statement that it is carrying on or doing business, and a brief statement of the business in which it is engaged, and (2) a certificate setting forth that such corporation is in good standing under the laws of the state or territory wherein it is organized, executed by the Secretary of State of such state or territory or by such other official as may have custody of the records pertaining to corporations, and

(b)   Paying to the Secretary of State a registration fee in the amount of .... for each month, or fraction thereof, between the date of filing such application and December 31st of the calendar year in which such application is filed.

Such registration shall be effective until the close of the calendar year in which the application for registration is filed.

§ 11. Renewal of Registered Name

A corporation which has in effect a registration of its corporate name, may renew such registration from year to year by annually filing an application for renewal setting forth the facts required to be set forth in an original application for registration and a certificate of good standing as required for the original registration and by paying a fee of .... A renewal application may be filed between the first day of October and the thirty-first day of December in each year, and shall extend the registration for the following calendar year.

§ 12. Registered Office and Registered Agent

Each corporation shall have and continuously maintain in this State:

(a)   A registered office which may be, but need not be, the same as its place of business.

(b)   A registered agent, which agent may be either an individual resident in this State whose business office is identical with such registered office, or a domestic corporation, or a foreign corporation authorized to transact business in this State, having a business office identical with such registered office.

§ 13. Change of Registered Office or Registered Agent

A corporation may change its registered office or change its registered agent, or both, upon filing in the office of the Secretary of State a statement setting forth:

(a)   The name of the corporation.

(b)   The address of its then registered office.

(c)   If the address of its registered office is to be changed, the address to which the registered office is to be changed.

(d)   The name of its then registered agent.

(e)   If its registered agent is to be changed, the name of its successor registered agent.

(f)   That the address of its registered office and the address of the business office of its registered agent, as changed, will be identical.

(g)   That such change was authorized by resolution duly adopted by its board of directors.

Such statement shall be executed by the corporation by its president, or a vice president, and verified by him, and delivered to the Secretary of State. If the Secretary of State finds that such statement conforms to the provisions of this Act, he shall file such statement in his office, and upon such filing the change of address of the registered office, or the appointment of a new registered agent, or both, as the case may be, shall become effective.

Any registered agent of a corporation may resign as such agent upon filing a written notice thereof, executed in duplicate, with the Secretary of State, who shall forthwith mail a copy thereof to the corporation at its registered office. The appointment of such agent shall terminate upon the expiration of thirty days after receipt of such notice by the Secretary of State.

If a registered agent changes his or its business address to another place within the same .... ,* he or it may change such address and the address of the registered office of any corporation of which he or it is registered agent by filing a statement as required above except that it need be signed only by the registered agent and need not be responsive to (e) or (g) and must recite that a copy of the statement has been mailed to the corporation.

§ 14. Service of Process on Corporation

The registered agent so appointed by a corporation shall be an agent of such corporation upon whom any process, notice or demand required or permitted by law to be served upon the corporation may be served.

---

*Supply designation of jurisdiction, such as county, etc., in accordance with local practice.

Whenever a corporation shall fail to appoint or maintain a registered agent in this State, or whenever its registered agent cannot with reasonable diligence be found at the registered office, then the Secretary of State shall be an agent of such corporation upon whom any such process, notice, or demand may be served. Service on the Secretary of State of any such process, notice, or demand shall be made by delivering to and leaving with him, or with any clerk having charge of the corporation department of his office, duplicate copies of such process, notice or demand. In the event any such process, notice or demand is served on the Secretary of State, he shall immediately cause one of the copies thereof to be forwarded by registered mail, addressed to the corporation at its registered office. Any service so had on the Secretary of State shall be returnable in not less than thirty days.

The Secretary of State shall keep a record of all processes, notices and demands served upon him under this section, and shall record therein the time of such service and his action with reference thereto.

Nothing herein contained shall limit or affect the right to serve any process, notice or demand required or permitted by law to be served upon a corporation in any other manner now or hereafter permitted by law.

§ 15. Authorized Shares

Each corporation shall have power to create and issue the number of shares stated in its articles of incorporation. Such shares may be divided into one or more classes with such designations, preferences, limitations, and relative rights as shall be stated in the articles of incorporation. The articles of incorporation may limit or deny the voting rights of or provide special voting rights for the shares of any class to the extent not inconsistent with the provisions of this Act.

Without limiting the authority herein contained, a corporation, when so provided in its articles of incorporation, may issue shares of preferred or special classes:

(a)   Subject to the right of the corporation to redeem any of such shares at the price fixed by the articles of incorporation for the redemption thereof.

(b)   Entitling the holders thereof to cumulative, non-cumulative or partially cumulative dividends.

(c)   Having preference over any other class or classes of shares as to the payment of dividends.

(d)   Having preference in the assets of the corporation over any other class or classes of shares upon the voluntary or involuntary liquidation of the corporation.

(e)   Convertible into shares of any other class or into shares of any series of the same or any other class, except a class having prior or superior rights and preferences as to dividends or distribution of assets upon liquidation.

§ 16. Issuance of Shares of Preferred or Special Classes in Series

If the articles of incorporation so provide, the shares of any preferred or special class may be divided into and issued in series. If the shares of any such class are to be issued in series, then each series shall be so designated as to distinguish the shares thereof from the shares of all other series and classes. Any or all of the series of any such class and the variations in the relative rights and preferences as between different series may be fixed and determined by the articles of incorporation, but all shares of the same class shall be identical except as to the following relative rights and preferences, as to which there may be variations between different series:

(A)   The rate of dividend.

(B)   Whether shares may be redeemed and, if so, the redemption price and the terms and conditions of redemption.

(C)   The amount payable upon shares in the event of voluntary and involuntary liquidation.

(D)   Sinking fund provisions, if any, for the redemption or purchase of shares.

(E)   The terms and conditions, if any, on which shares may be converted.

(F)   Voting rights, if any.

If the articles of incorporation shall expressly vest authority in the board of directors, then, to the extent that the articles of incorporation shall not have established series and fixed and determined the variations in the relative rights and preferences as between series, the board of directors shall have authority to divide any or all of such classes into series and, within the limitations set forth in this section and in the articles of incorporation, fix and determine the relative rights and preferences of the shares of any series so established.

In order for the board of directors to establish a series, where authority so to do is contained in the articles of incorporation, the board of directors shall adopt a resolution setting forth the designation of the series and fixing and determining the relative rights and preferences thereof, or so much thereof as shall not be fixed and determined by the articles of incorporation.

Prior to the issue of any shares of a series established by the resolution adopted by the board of directors, the corporation shall file in the office of the Secretary of State a statement setting forth:

(a) The name of the corporation.

(b) A copy of the resolution establishing and designating the series, and fixing and determining the relative rights and preferences thereof.

(c) The date of adoption of such resolution.

(d) That such resolution was duly adopted by the board of directors.

Such statement shall be executed in duplicate by the corporation by its president or a vice president and by its secretary or an assistant secretary, and verified by one of the officers signing such statement, and shall be delivered to the Secretary of State. If the Secretary of State finds that such statement conforms to law, he shall, when all franchise taxes and fees have been paid as in this Act prescribed:

(1) Endorse on each of such duplicate originals the word "Filed," and the month, day, and year of the filing thereof.
(2) File one of such duplicate originals in his office.
(3) Return the other duplicate original to the corporation or its representative.

Upon the filing of such statement by the Secretary of State, the resolution establishing and designating the series and fixing and determining the relative rights and preferences thereof shall become effective and shall constitute an amendment of the articles of incorporation.

§ 17. Subscriptions for Shares

A subscription for shares of a corporation to be organized shall be irrevocable for a period of six months, unless otherwise provided by the terms of the subscription agreement or unless all of the subscribers consent to the revocation of such subscription.

Unless otherwise provided in the subscription agreement, subscriptions for shares, whether made before or after the organization of a corporation, shall be paid in full at such time, or in such installments and at such times, as shall be determined by the board of directors. Any call made by the board of directors for payment on subscriptions shall be uniform as to all shares of the same class or as to all shares of the same series, as the case may be. In case of default in the payment of any installment or call when such payment is due, the corporation may proceed to collect the amount due in the same manner as any debt due the corporation. The by-laws may prescribe other penalties for failure to pay installments or calls that may become due, but no penalty working a forfeiture of a subscription, or of the amounts paid thereon, shall be declared as against any subscriber unless the amount due thereon shall remain unpaid for a period of twenty days after written demand has been made therefor. If mailed, such written demand shall be deemed to be made when deposited in the United States mail in a sealed envelope addressed to the subscriber at his last post-office address known to the corporation, with postage thereon prepaid. In the event of the sale of any shares by reason of any forfeiture, the excess of proceeds realized over the amount due and unpaid on such shares shall be paid to the delinquent subscriber or to his legal representative.

§ 18. Issuance of Shares

Subject to any restrictions in the articles of incorporation:

(a) Shares may be issued for such consideration as shall be authorized by the board of directors establishing a price (in money or other consideration) or a minimum price or general formula or method by which the price will be determined; and

(b) Upon authorization by the board of directors, the corporation may issue its own shares in exchange for or in conversion of its outstanding shares, or distribute its own shares, pro rata to its shareholders or the shareholders of one or more classes or series, to effectuate stock dividends or splits, and any such transaction shall not require consideration; provided, that no such issuance of shares of any class or series shall be made to the holders of shares of any other class or series unless it is either expressly provided for in the articles of incorporation, or is authorized by an affirmative vote or the written consent of the holders of at least a majority of the outstanding shares of the class or series in which the distribution is to be made.

§ 19. Payment for Shares

The consideration for the issuance of shares may be paid, in whole or in part, in money, in other property, tangible or intangible, or in labor or services actually performed for the corporation. When payment of the consideration for which shares are to be issued shall have been received by the corporation, such shares shall be nonassessable.

Neither promissory notes nor future services shall constitute payment or part payment for the issuance of shares of a corporation.

In the absence of fraud in the transaction, the judgment of the board of directors or the shareholders, as the case may be, as to the value of the consideration received for shares shall be conclusive.

§ 20. Stock Rights and Options

Subject to any provisions in respect thereof set forth in its articles of incorporation, a corporation may create and issue, whether or not in connection with the issuance and sale of any of its shares or other securities, rights or options entitling the holders thereof to purchase from the corporation shares of any class or classes. Such rights or options shall be evidenced in such manner as the board of directors shall approve and, subject to the provisions of the articles of incorporation, shall set forth the terms upon which, the time or times within which and the price or prices at which such shares may be purchased from the corporation upon the exercise of any such right or option. If such rights or options are to be issued to directors, officers or employees as such of the corporation or of any subsidiary thereof, and not to the shareholders generally, their issuance shall be approved by the affirmative vote of the holders of a majority of the shares entitled to vote thereon or shall be authorized by and consistent with a plan approved or ratified by such a vote of shareholders. In the absence of fraud in the transaction, the judgment of the board of directors as to the adequacy of the consideration received for such rights or options shall be conclusive.

§ 21. Determination of Amount of Stated Capital
[Repealed in 1979].

§ 22. Expenses of Organization, Reorganization and Financing

The reasonable charges and expenses of organization or reorganization of a corporation, and the reasonable expenses of and compensation for the sale or underwriting of its shares, may be paid or allowed by such corporation out of the consideration received by it in payment for its shares without thereby rendering such shares assessable.

§ 23. Shares Represented by Certificates and Uncertified Shares

The shares of a corporation shall be represented by certificates or shall be uncertificated shares. Certificates shall be signed by the chairman or vice-chairman of the board of directors or the president or a vice president and by the treasurer or an assistant treasurer or the secretary or an assistant secretary of the corporation, and may be sealed with the seal of the corporation or a facsimile thereof. Any of or all the signatures upon a certificate may be a facsimile. In case any officer, transfer agent or registrar who has signed or whose facsimile signature has been placed upon such certificate shall have ceased to be such officer, transfer agent or registrar before such certificate is issued, it may be issued by the corporation with the same effect as if he were such officer, transfer agent or registrar at the date of its issue.

Every certificate representing shares issued by a corporation which is authorized to issue shares of more than one class shall set forth upon the face or back of the certificate, or shall state that the corporation will furnish to any shareholder upon request and without charge, a full statement of the designations, preferences, limitations, and relative rights of the shares of each class authorized to be issued, and if the corporation is authorized to issue any preferred or special class in series, the variations in the relative rights and preferences between the shares of each such series so far as the same have been fixed and determined and the authority of the board of directors to fix and determine the relative rights and preferences of subsequent series.

Each certificate representing shares shall state upon the face thereof:

(a)   That the corporation is organized under the laws of this State.

(b)   The name of the person to whom issued.

(c)   The number and class of shares, and the designation of the series, if any, which such certificate represents.

(d)   The par value of each share represented by such certificate, or a statement that the shares are without par value.

No certificate shall be issued for any share until such share is fully paid.

Unless otherwise provided by the articles of incorporation or by-laws, the board of directors of a corporation may provide by resolution that some or all of any or all classes and series of its shares shall be uncertificated shares, provided that such resolution shall not apply to shares represented by a certificate until such certificate is surrendered to the corporation. Without a reasonable time after the issuance or transfer of uncertificated shares, the corporation shall send to the registered owner thereof a written notice containing the information required to be set forth or stated on certificates pursuant to the second and third paragraphs of this section. Except as otherwise expressly provided by law, the rights and obligations of the holders of uncertificated shares and the rights and obligations of the holders of certificates representing shares of the same class and series shall be identical.

§ 24. Fractional Shares
A corporation may (1) issue fractions of a share, either represented by a certificate or uncertificated, (2) arrange for the disposition of fractional interests by those entitled thereto, (3) pay in money the fair value of fractions of a share as of a time when those entitled to receive such fractions are determined, or (4) issue scrip in registered or bearer form which shall entitle the holder to receive a certificate for a full share or an uncertificated full share upon the surrender of such scrip aggregating a full share. A certificate for a fractional share or an uncertificated fractional share shall, but scrip shall not unless otherwise provided therein, entitle the holder to exercise voting rights, to receive dividends thereon, and to participate in any of the assets of the corporation in the event of liquidation. The board of directors may cause scrip to be issued subject to the condition that it shall become void if not exchanged for certificates representing full shares or uncertificated full shares before a specified date, or subject to the condition that the shares for which scrip is exchangeable may be sold by the corporation and the proceeds thereof distributed to the holders of scrip, or subject to any other conditions which the board of directors may deem advisable.

§ 25. Liability of Subscribers and Shareholders
A holder of or subscriber to shares of a corporation shall be under no obligation to the corporation or its creditors with respect to such shares other than the obligation to pay to the corporation the full consideration for which such shares were issued or to be issued.

Any person becoming an assignee or transferee of shares or of a subscription for shares in good faith and without knowledge or notice that the full consideration therefor has not been paid shall not be personally liable to the corporation or its creditors for any unpaid portion of such consideration.

An executor, administrator, conservator, guardian, trustee, assignee for the benefit of creditors, or receiver shall not be personally liable to the corporation as a holder of or subscriber to shares of a corporation but the estate and funds in his hands shall be so liable.

No pledgee or other holder of shares as collateral security shall be personally liable as a shareholder.

§ 26. Shareholders' Preemptive Rights
The shareholders of a corporation shall have no preemptive right to acquire unissued shares of the corporation, or securities of the corporation convertible into or carrying a right to subscribe to or acquire shares, except to the extent, if any, that such right is provided in the articles of incorporation.

§ 26A. Shareholders' Preemptive Rights [Alternative]
Except to the extent limited or denied by this section or by the articles of incorporation, shareholders shall have a preemptive right to acquire unissued shares or securities convertible into such shares or carrying a right to subscribe to or acquire shares.

Unless otherwise provided in the articles of incorporation,

(a)   No preemptive right shall exist.

(1)   to acquire any shares issued to directors, officers or employees pursuant to approval by the affirmative

vote of the holders of a majority of the shares entitled to vote thereon or when authorized by and consistent with a plan theretofore approved by such a vote of shareholders; or

(2)   to acquire any shares sold otherwise than for money.

(b)   Holders of shares of any class that is preferred or limited as to dividends or assets shall not be entitled to any preemptive right.

(c)   Holders of shares of common stock shall not be entitled to any preemptive right to shares of any class that is preferred or limited as to dividends or assets or to any obligations, unless convertible into shares of common stock or carrying a right to subscribe to or acquire shares of common stock.

(d)   Holders of common stock without voting power shall have no preemptive right to shares of common stock with voting power.

(e)   The preemptive right shall be only an opportunity to acquire shares or other securities under such terms and conditions as the board of directors may fix for the purpose of providing a fair and reasonable opportunity for the exercise of such right.

§ 27. By-Laws

The initial by-laws of a corporation shall be adopted by its board of directors. The power to alter, amend or repeal the by-laws or adopt new by-laws, subject to repeal or change by action of the shareholders, shall be vested in the board of directors unless reserved to the shareholders by the articles of incorporation. The by-laws may contain any provisions for the regulation and management of the affairs of the corporation not inconsistent with law or the articles of incorporation.

§ 27A. By-Laws and Other Powers in Emergency [Optional]

The board of directors of any corporation may adopt emergency by-laws, subject to repeal or change by action of the shareholders, which shall, notwithstanding any different provision elsewhere in this Act or in the articles of incorporation or by-laws, be operative during any emergency in the conduct of the business of the corporation resulting from an attack on the United States or any nuclear or atomic disaster. The emergency by-laws may make any provision that may

be practical and necessary for the circumstances of the emergency, including provisions that:

(a)   A meeting of the board of directors may be called by any officer or director in such manner and under such conditions as shall be prescribed in the emergency by-laws;

(b)   The director or directors in attendance at the meeting, or any greater number fixed by the emergency by-laws, shall constitute a quorum; and

(c)   The officers or other persons designated on a list approved by the board of directors before the emergency, all in such order of priority and subject to such conditions, and for such period of time (not longer than reasonably necessary after the termination of the emergency) as may be provided in the emergency by-laws or in the resolution approving the list shall, to the extent required to provide a quorum at any meeting of the board of directors, be deemed directors for such meeting.

The board of directors, either before or during any such emergency, may provide, and from time to time modify, lines of succession in the event that during such an emergency any or all officers or agents of the corporation shall for any reason be rendered incapable of discharging their duties.

The board of directors, either before or during any such emergency, may, effective in the emergency, change the head office or designate several alternative head offices or regional offices, or authorize the officers so to do.

To the extent not inconsistent with any emergency by-laws so adopted, the by-laws of the corporation shall remain in effect during any such emergency and upon its termination the emergency by-laws shall cease to be operative.

Unless otherwise provided in emergency by-laws, notice of any meeting of the board of directors during any such emergency may be given only to such of the directors as it may be feasible to reach at the time and by such means as may be feasible at the time, including publication or radio.

To the extent required to constitute a quorum at any meeting of the board of directors during any such emergency, the officers of the corporation who are present shall, unless otherwise provided in emergency by-laws, be deemed, in order of rank and within the same rank in order of seniority, directors for such meeting.

No officer, director or employee acting in accordance with any emergency by-laws shall be liable except for willful misconduct. No officer, director or employee shall be liable for any action taken by him in good faith in such an emergency in furtherance of the ordinary business affairs of the corporation even though not authorized by the by-laws then in effect.

§ 28. Meetings of Shareholders

Meetings of shareholders may be held at such place within or without this State as may be stated in or fixed in accordance with the by-laws. If no other place is stated or so fixed, meetings shall be held at the registered office of the corporation.

An annual meeting of the shareholders shall be held at such time as may be stated in or fixed in accordance with the by-laws. If the annual meeting is not held within any thirteen-month period the Court of .... may, on the application of any shareholder, summarily order a meeting to be held.

Special meetings of the shareholders may be called by the board of directors, the holders of not less than one-tenth of all the shares entitled to vote at the meeting, or such other persons as may be authorized in the articles of incorporation or the by-laws.

§ 29. Notice of Shareholders' Meetings

Written notice stating the place, day and hour of the meeting and, in case of a special meeting, the purpose or purposes for which the meeting is called, shall be delivered not less than ten nor more than fifty days before the date of the meeting, either personally or by mail, by or at the direction of the president, the secretary, or the officer or persons calling the meeting, to each shareholder of record entitled to vote at such meeting. If mailed, such notice shall be deemed to be delivered when deposited in the United States mail addressed to the shareholder at his address as it appears on the stock transfer books of the corporation, with postage thereon prepaid.

§ 30. Closing of Transfer Books and Fixing Record Date

For the purpose of determining shareholders entitled to notice of or to vote at any meeting of shareholders or any adjournment thereof, or entitled to receive payment of any dividend, or in order to make a deter-mination of shareholders for any other proper purpose, the board of directors of a corporation may provide that the stock transfer books shall be closed for a stated period but not to exceed, in any case, fifty days. If the stock transfer books shall be closed for the purpose of determining shareholders entitled to notice of or to vote at a meeting of shareholders, such books shall be closed for at least ten days immediately preceding such meeting. In lieu of closing the stock transfer books, the by-laws, or in the absence of an applicable by-law the board of directors, may fix in advance a date as the record date for any such determination of shareholders, such date in any case to be not more than fifty days and, in case of a meeting of shareholders, not less than ten days prior to the date on which the particular action, requiring such determination of shareholders, is to be taken. If the stock transfer books are not closed and no record date is fixed for the determination of shareholders entitled to notice of or to vote at a meeting of shareholders, or shareholders entitled to receive payment of a dividend, the date on which notice of the meeting is mailed or the date on which the resolution of the board of directors declaring such dividend is adopted, as the case may be, shall be the record date for such determination of shareholders. When a determination of shareholders entitled to vote at any meeting of shareholders has been made as provided in this section, such determination shall apply to any adjournment thereof.

§ 31. Voting Record

The officer or agent having charge of the stock transfer books for shares of a corporation shall make a complete record of the shareholders entitled to vote at such meeting or any adjournment thereof, arranged in alphabetical order, with the address of and the number of shares held by each. Such record shall be produced and kept open at the time and place of the meeting and shall be subject to the inspection of any shareholder during the whole time of the meeting for the purposes thereof.

Failure to comply with the requirements of this section shall not affect the validity of any action taken at such meeting.

An officer or agent having charge of the stock transfer books who shall fail to prepare the record of shareholders, or produce and keep it open for inspection at the meeting, as provided in this section, shall be liable to any shareholder suffering damage on account of such failure, to the extent of such damage.

§ 32. Quorum of Shareholders

Unless otherwise provided in the articles of incorporation, a majority of the shares entitled to vote, represented in person or by proxy, shall constitute a quorum at a meeting of shareholders, but in no event shall a quorum consist of less than one-third of the shares entitled to vote at the meeting. If a quorum is present, the affirmative vote of the majority of the shares represented at the meeting and entitled to vote on the subject matter shall be the act of the shareholders, unless the vote of a greater number or voting by classes is required by this Act or the articles of incorporation or by-laws.

§ 33. Voting of Shares

Each outstanding share, regardless of class, shall be entitled to one vote on each matter submitted to a vote at a meeting of shareholders, except as may be otherwise provided in the articles of incorporation. If the articles of incorporation provide for more or less than one vote for any share, on any matter, every reference in this Act to a majority or other proportion of shares shall refer to such a majority or other proportion of votes entitled to be cast.

Shares held by another corporation if a majority of the shares entitled to vote for the election of directors of such other corporation is held by the corporation, shall not be voted at any meeting or counted in determining the total number of outstanding shares at any given time.

A shareholder may vote either in person or by proxy executed in writing by the shareholder or by his duly authorized attorney-in-fact. No proxy shall be valid after eleven months from the date of its execution, unless otherwise provided in the proxy.

[Either of the following prefatory phrases may be inserted here: "The articles of incorporation may provide that" or "Unless the articles of incorporation otherwise provide"] . . . at each election of directors every shareholder entitled to vote at such election shall have the right to vote, in person or by proxy, the number of shares owned by him for as many persons as there are directors to be elected and for whose election he has a right to vote, or to cumulate his votes by giving one candidate as many votes as the number of such directors multiplied by the number of his shares shall equal, or by distributing such votes on the same principle among any number of such candidates.

Shares standing in the name of another corporation, domestic or foreign, may be voted by such officer, agent or proxy as the by-laws of such other corporation may prescribe, or, in the absence of such provision, as the board of directors of such other corporation may determine.

Shares held by an administrator, executor, guardian or conservator may be voted by him, either in person or by proxy, without a transfer of such shares into his name. Shares standing in the name of a trustee may be voted by him, either in person or by proxy, but no trustee shall be entitled to vote shares held by him without a transfer of such shares into his name.

Shares standing in the name of a receiver may be voted by such receiver, and shares held by or under the control of a receiver may be voted by such receiver without the transfer thereof into his name if authority so to do be contained in an appropriate order of the court by which such receiver was appointed.

A shareholder whose shares are pledged shall be entitled to vote such shares until the shares have been transferred into the name of the pledgee, and thereafter the pledgee shall be entitled to vote the shares so transferred.

On and after the date on which written notice of redemption of redeemable shares has been mailed to the holders thereof and a sum sufficient to redeem such shares has been deposited with a bank or trust company with irrevocable instruction and authority to pay the redemption price to the holders thereof upon surrender of certificates therefor, such shares shall not be entitled to vote on any matter and shall not be deemed to be outstanding shares.

§ 34. Voting Trusts and Agreements Among Shareholders

Any number of shareholders of a corporation may create a voting trust for the purpose of conferring upon a trustee or trustees the right to vote or otherwise represent their shares, for a period of not to exceed ten years, by entering into a written voting trust agreement specifying the terms and conditions of the voting trust, by depositing a counterpart of the agreement with the corporation at its registered office, and by transferring their shares to such trustee or trustees for the purposes of the agreement. Such trustee or trustees shall keep a record of the holders of voting trust certificates evidencing a beneficial interest in the voting trust, giving the names and addresses of all such holders and the number and class of the shares in respect of which the voting trust certificates held by each are issued, and shall deposit a copy of such record with the corporation at its registered office. The counterpart of the voting trust agreement and the copy of such record so deposited with the corporation shall be subject to the same right of examination by a shareholder of the corporation, in person or by agent or attorney, as are the books and records of the corporation, and such counterpart and such copy of such record shall be subject to examination by any holder of record of voting trust certificates, either in person or by agent or attorney, at any reasonable time for any proper purpose.

Agreements among shareholders regarding the voting of their shares shall be valid and enforceable in accordance with their terms. Such agreements shall not be subject to the provisions of this section regarding voting trusts.

§ 35. Board of Directors

All corporate powers shall be exercised by or under authority of, and the business and affairs of a corporation shall be managed under the direction of, a board of directors except as may be otherwise provided in this Act or the articles of incorporation. If any such provision is made in the articles of incorporation, the powers and duties conferred or imposed upon the board of directors by this Act shall be exercised or performed to such extent and by such person or persons as shall be provided in the articles of incorporation. Directors need not be residents of this State or shareholders of the corporation unless the articles of incorporation or by-laws so require. The articles of incorporation or by-laws may prescribe other qualifications for directors. The board of directors shall have authority to fix the compensation of directors unless otherwise provided in the articles of incorporation.

A director shall perform his duties as a director, including his duties as a member of any committee of the board upon which he may serve, in good faith, in a manner he reasonably believes to be in the best interests of the corporation, and with such care as an ordinarily prudent person in a like position would use under similar circumstances. In performing his duties, a director shall be entitled to rely on information,

opinions, reports or statements, including financial statements and other financial data, in each case prepared or presented by:

(a)   one or more officers or employees of the corporation whom the director reasonably believes to be reliable and competent in the matters presented,

(b)   counsel, public accountants or other persons as to matters which the director reasonably believes to be within such person's professional or expert competence, or

(c)   a committee of the board upon which he does not serve, duly designated in accordance with a provision of the articles of incorporation or the by-laws, as to matters within its designated authority, which committee the director reasonably believes to merit confidence, but he shall not be considered to be acting in good faith if he has knowledge concerning the matter in question that would cause such reliance to be unwarranted. A person who so performs his duties shall have no liability by reason of being or having been a director of the corporation.

A director of a corporation who is present at a meeting of its board of directors at which action on any corporate matter is taken shall be presumed to have assented to the action taken unless his dissent shall be entered in the minutes of the meeting or unless he shall file his written dissent to such action with the secretary of the meeting before the adjournment thereof or shall forward such dissent by registered mail to the secretary of the corporation immediately after the adjournment of the meeting. Such right to dissent shall not apply to a director who voted in favor of such action.

§ 36. Number and Election of Directors

The board of directors of a corporation shall consist of one or more members. The number of directors shall be fixed by, or in the manner provided in, the articles of incorporation or the by-laws, except as to the number constituting the initial board of directors, which number shall be fixed by the articles of incorporation. The number of directors may be increased or decreased from time to time by amendment to, or in the manner provided in, the articles of incorporation or the by-laws, but no decrease shall have the effect of shortening the term of any incumbent director. In the absence of a by-law providing for the number of directors, the number shall be the same as that provided for in the articles of incorporation. The names and addresses of the members of the first board of directors shall be stated in the articles of incorporation. Such persons shall hold office until the first annual meeting of shareholders, and until their successors shall have been elected and qualified. At the first annual meeting of shareholders and at each annual meeting thereafter the shareholders shall elect directors to hold office until the next succeeding annual meeting, except in case of the classification of directors as permitted by this Act. Each director shall hold office for the term for which he is elected and until his successor shall have been elected and qualified.

§ 37. Classification of Directors

When the board of directors shall consist of nine or more members, in lieu of electing the whole number of directors annually, the articles of incorporation may provide that the directors be divided into either two or three classes, each class to be as nearly equal in number as possible, the term of office of directors of the first class to expire at the first annual meeting of shareholders after their election, that of the second class to expire at the second annual meeting after their election, and that of the third class, if any, to expire at the third annual meeting after their election. At each annual meeting after such classification the number of directors equal to the number of the class whose term expires at the time of such meeting shall be elected to hold office until the second succeeding annual meeting, if there be two classes, or until the third succeeding annual meeting, if there be three classes. No classification of directors shall be effective prior to the first annual meeting of shareholders.

§ 38. Vacancies

Any vacancy occurring in the board of directors may be filled by the affirmative vote of a majority of the remaining directors though less than a quorum of the board of directors. A director elected to fill a vacancy shall be elected for the unexpired term of his predecessor in office. Any directorship to be filled by reason of an increase in the number of directors may be filled by the board of directors for the term of office continuing only until the next election of directors by the shareholders.

§ 39. Removal of Directors

At a meeting of shareholders called expressly for that purpose, directors may be removed in the manner provided in this section. Any director or the entire board of directors may be removed, with or without cause, by a vote of the holders of a majority of the shares then entitled to vote at an election of directors.

In the case of a corporation having cumulative voting, if less than the entire board is to be removed, no one of the directors may be removed if the votes cast against his removal would be sufficient to elect him if then cumulatively voted at an election of the entire board of directors, or, if there be classes of directors, at an election of the class of directors of which he is a part.

Whenever the holders of the shares of any class are entitled to elect one or more directors by the provisions of the articles of incorporation, the provisions of this section shall apply, in respect to the removal of a director or directors so elected, to the vote of the holders of the outstanding shares of that class and not to the vote of the outstanding shares as a whole.

§ 40. Quorum of Directors

A majority of the number of directors fixed by or in the manner provided in the by-laws or in the absence of a by-law fixing or providing for the number of directors, then of the number stated in the articles of incorporation, shall constitute a quorum for the transaction of business unless a greater number is required by the articles of incorporation or the by-laws. The act of the majority of the directors present at a meeting at which a quorum is present shall be the act of the board of directors, unless the act of a greater number is required by the articles of incorporation or the by-laws.

§ 41. Director Conflicts of Interest

No contract or other transaction between a corporation and one or more of its directors or any other corporation, firm, association or entity in which one or more of its directors are directors or officers or are financially interested, shall be either void or voidable because of such relationship or interest or because such director or directors are present at the meeting of the board of directors or a committee thereof which authorizes, approves or ratifies such contract or transaction or because his or their votes are counted for such purpose, if:

(a) the fact of such relationship or interest is disclosed or known to the board of directors or committee which authorizes, approves or ratifies the contract or transaction by a vote or consent sufficient for the purpose without counting the votes or consents of such interested directors; or

(b) the fact of such relationship or interest is disclosed or known to the shareholders entitled to vote and they authorize, approve or ratify such contract or transaction by vote or written consent; or

(c) the contract or transaction is fair and reasonable to the corporation.

Common or interested directors may be counted in determining the presence of a quorum at a meeting of the board of directors or a committee thereof which authorizes, approves or ratifies such contract or transaction.

§ 42. Executive and Other Committees

If the articles of incorporation or the by-laws so provide, the board of directors, by resolution adopted by a majority of the full board of directors, may designate from among its members an executive committee and one or more other committees each of which, to the extent provided in such resolution or in the articles of incorporation or the by-laws of the corporation, shall have and may exercise all the authority of the board of directors, except that no such committee shall have authority to (i) authorize distributions, (ii) approve or recommend to shareholders actions or proposals required by this Act to be approved by shareholders, (iii) designate candidates for the office of director, for purposes of proxy solicitation or otherwise, or fill vacancies on the board of directors or any committee thereof, (iv) amend the by-laws, (v) approve a plan of merger not requiring shareholder approval, (vi) authorize or approve the reacquisition of shares unless pursuant to a general formula or method specified by the board of directors, or (vii) authorize or approve the issuance or sale of, or any contract to issue or sell, shares or designate the terms of a series of a class of shares, provided that the board of directors, having acted regarding general authorization for the issuance or sale of shares, or any contract therefor, and, in the case of a series, the designation thereof, may, pursuant to a general formula or method specified by the board by resolution or by adoption of a stock option or other plan, authorize a committee to fix the terms of any

contract for the sale of the shares and to fix the terms upon which such shares may be issued or sold, including, without limitation, the price, the dividend rate, provisions for redemption, sinking fund, conversion, voting or preferential rights, and provisions for other features of a class of shares, or a series of a class of shares, with full power in such committee to adopt any final resolution setting forth all the terms thereof and to authorize the statement of the terms of a series for filing with the Secretary of State under this Act.

Neither the designation of any such committee, the delegation thereto of authority, nor action by such committee pursuant to such authority shall alone constitute compliance by any member of the board of directors, not a member of the committee in question, with his responsibility to act in good faith, in a manner he reasonably believes to be in the best interests of the corporation, and with such care as an ordinarily prudent person in a like position would use under similar circumstances.

§ 43. Place and Notice of Directors' Meetings; Committee Meetings

Meetings of the board of directors, regular or special, may be held either within or without this State.

Regular meetings of the board of directors or any committee designated thereby may be held with or without notice as prescribed in the by-laws. Special meetings of the board of directors or any committee designated thereby shall be held upon such notice as is prescribed in the by-laws. Attendance of a director at a meeting shall constitute a waiver of notice of such meeting, except where a director attends a meeting for the express purpose of objecting to the transaction of any business because the meeting is not lawfully called or convened. Neither the business to be transacted at, nor the purpose of, any regular or special meeting of the board of directors or any committee designated thereby need be specified in the notice or waiver of notice of such meeting unless required by the by-laws.

Except as may be otherwise restricted by the articles of incorporation or by-laws, members of the board of directors or any committee designated thereby may participate in a meeting of such board or committee by means of a conference telephone or similar communications equipment by means of which all persons participating in the meeting can hear each other at the same time and participation by such means shall constitute presence in person at a meeting.

§ 44. Action by Directors Without a Meeting

Unless otherwise provided by the articles of incorporation or by-laws, any action required by this Act to be taken at a meeting of the directors of a corporation, or any action which may be taken at a meeting of the directors or of a committee, may be taken without a meeting if a consent in writing, setting forth the action so taken, shall be signed by all of the directors, or all of the members of the committee, as the case may be. Such consent shall have the same effect as a unanimous vote.

§ 45. Distributions to Shareholders

Subject to any restrictions in the articles of incorporation, the board of directors may authorize and the corporation may make distributions, except that no distribution may be made if, after giving effect thereto, either:

(a)   the corporation would be unable to pay its debts as they become due in the usual course of its business; or

(b)   the corporation's total assets would be less than the sum of its total liabilities and (unless the articles of incorporation otherwise permit) the maximum amount that then would be payable, in any liquidation, in respect of all outstanding shares having preferential rights in liquidation.

Determinations under subparagraph (b) may be based upon (i) financial statements prepared on the basis of accounting practices and principles that are reasonable in the circumstances, or (ii) a fair valuation or other method that is reasonable in the circumstances.

In the case of a purchase, redemption or other acquisition of a corporation's shares, the effect of a distribution shall be measured as of the date money or other property is transferred or debt is incurred by the corporation, or as of the date the shareholder ceases to be a shareholder of the corporation with respect to such shares, whichever is earlier. In all other cases, the effect of a distribution shall be measured as of the date of its authorization if payment occurs 120 days or less following the date of authorization, or as of the date of payment if payment occurs more than 120 days following the date of authorization.

Indebtedness of a corporation incurred or issued to a shareholder in a distribution in accordance with this Section shall be on a parity with the indebtedness of the corporation to its general unsecured creditors except to the extent subordinated by agreement.

§ 46. Distributions from Capital Surplus

[Repealed in 1979].

§ 47. Loans to Employees and Directors

A corporation shall not lend money to or use its credit to assist its directors without authorization in the particular case by its shareholders, but may lend money to and use its credit to assist any employee of the corporation or of a subsidiary, including any such employee who is a director of the corporation, if the board of directors decides that such loan or assistance may benefit the corporation.

§ 48. Liability of Directors in Certain Cases

In addition to any other liabilities, a director who votes for or assents to any distribution contrary to the provisions of this Act or contrary to any restrictions contained in the articles of incorporation, shall, unless he complies with the standard provided in this Act for the performance of the duties of directors, be liable to the corporation, jointly and severally with all other directors so voting or assenting, for the amount of such dividend which is paid or the value of such distribution in excess of the amount of such distribution which could have been made without a violation of the provisions of this Act or the restrictions in the articles of incorporation.

Any director against whom a claim shall be asserted under or pursuant to this section for the making of a distribution and who shall be held liable thereon, shall be entitled to contribution from the shareholders who accepted or received any such distribution, knowing such distribution to have been made in violation of this Act, in proportion to the amounts received by them.

Any director against whom a claim shall be asserted under or pursuant to this section shall be entitled to contribution from any other director who voted for or assented to the action upon which the claim is asserted and who did not comply with the standard provided in this Act for the performance of the duties of directors.

§ 49. Provisions Relating to Actions by Shareholders

No action shall be brought in this State by a shareholder in the right of a domestic or foreign corporation unless the plaintiff was a holder of record of shares or of voting trust certificates therefor at the time of the transaction of which he complains, or his shares or voting trust certificates thereafter devolved upon him by operation of law from a person who was a holder of record at such time.

In any action hereafter instituted in the right of any domestic or foreign corporation by the holder or holders of record of shares of such corporation or of voting trust certificates therefor, the court having jurisdiction, upon final judgment and a finding that the action was brought without reasonable cause, may require the plaintiff or plaintiffs to pay to the parties named as defendant the reasonable expenses, including fees of attorneys, incurred by them in the defense of such action.

In any action now pending or hereafter instituted or maintained in the right of any domestic or foreign corporation by the holder or holders of record of less than five per cent of the outstanding shares of any class of such corporation or of voting trust certificates therefor, unless the shares or voting trust certificates so held have a market value in excess of twenty-five thousand dollars, the corporation in whose right such action is brought shall be entitled at any time before final judgment to require the plaintiff or plaintiffs to give security for the reasonable expenses, including fees of attorneys, that may be incurred by it in connection with such action or may be incurred by other parties named as defendant for which it may become legally liable. Market value shall be determined as of the date that the plaintiff institutes the action or, in the case of an intervenor, as of the date that he becomes a party to the action. The amount of such security may from time to time be increased or decreased, in the discretion of the court, upon showing that the security provided has or may become inadequate or is excessive. The corporation shall have recourse to such security in such amount as the court having jurisdiction shall determine upon the termination of such action, whether or not the court finds the action was brought without reasonable cause.

§ 50. Officers

The officers of a corporation shall consist of a president, one or more vice presidents as may be prescribed by the by-laws, a secretary, and a treasurer, each of whom shall be elected by the board of directors at such time and in such manner as may be prescribed by the by-laws. Such other officers and assistant officers and agents as may be deemed necessary may be elected or appointed by the board of di-

rectors or chosen in such other manner as may be prescribed by the by-laws. Any two or more offices may be held by the same person, except the offices of president and secretary.

All officers and agents of the corporation, as between themselves and the corporation, shall have such authority and perform such duties in the management of the corporation as may be provided in the by-laws, or as may be determined by resolution of the board of directors not inconsistent with the by-laws.

§ 51. Removal of Officers

Any officer or agent may be removed by the board of directors whenever in its judgment the best interests of the corporation will be served thereby, but such removal shall be without prejudice to the contract rights, if any, of the person so removed. Election or appointment of an officer or agent shall not of itself create contract rights.

§ 52. Books and Records: Financial Reports to Shareholders; Examination of Records

Each corporation shall keep correct and complete books and records of account and shall keep minutes of the proceedings of its shareholders and board of directors and shall keep at its registered office or principal place of business, or at the office of its transfer agent or registrar, a record of its shareholders, giving the names and addresses of all shareholders and the number and class of the shares held by each. Any books, records and minutes may be in written form or in any other form capable of being converted into written form within a reasonable time.

Any person who shall have been a holder of record of shares or of voting trust certificates therefor at least six months immediately preceding his demand or shall be the holder of record of, or the holder of record of voting trust certificates for, at least five percent of all the outstanding shares of the corporation, upon written demand stating the purpose thereof, shall have the right to examine, in person, or by agent or attorney, at any reasonable time or times, for any proper purpose its relevant books and records of account, minutes, and record of shareholders and to make extracts therefrom.

Any officer or agent who, or a corporation which, shall refuse to allow any such shareholder or holder of voting trust certificates, or his agent or attorney, so to examine and make extracts from its books and records of account, minutes, and record of shareholders, for any proper purpose, shall be liable to such shareholder or holder of voting trust certificates in a penalty of ten percent of the value of the shares owned by such shareholder, or in respect of which such voting trust certificates are issued, in addition to any other damages or remedy afforded him by law. It shall be a defense to any action for penalties under this section that the person suing therefor has within two years sold or offered for sale any list of shareholders or of holders of voting trust certificates for shares of such corporation or any other corporation or has aided or abetted any person in procuring any list of shareholders or of holders of voting trust certificates for any such purpose, or has improperly used any information secured through any prior examination of the books and records of account, or minutes, or record of shareholders or of holders of voting trust certificates for shares of such corporation or any other corporation, or was not acting in good faith or for a proper purpose in making his demand.

Nothing herein contained shall impair the power of any court of competent jurisdiction, upon proof by a shareholder or holder of voting trust certificates of proper purpose, irrespective of the period of time during which such shareholder or holder of voting trust certificates shall have been a shareholder of record or a holder of record of voting trust certificates, and irrespective of the number of shares held by him or represented by voting trust certificates held by him, to compel the production for examination by such shareholder or holder of voting trust certificates of the books and records of account, minutes and record of shareholders of a corporation.

Each corporation shall furnish to its shareholders annual financial statements, including at least a balance sheet as of the end of each fiscal year and a statement of income for such fiscal year, which shall be prepared on the basis of generally accepted accounting principles, if the corporation prepares financial statements for such fiscal year on that basis for any purpose, and may be consolidated statements of the corporation and one or more of its subsidiaries. The financial statements shall be mailed by the corporation to each of its shareholders within 120 days after the close of each fiscal year and, after such mailing and upon written request, shall be mailed by the corporation to any shareholder (or holder of a voting trust certificate for its shares) to whom a copy of the most recent annual financial statements has not previously been mailed. In the case of statements audited by a public accountant, each copy shall be accompanied by

a report setting forth his opinion thereon; in other cases, each copy shall be accompanied by a statement of the president or the person in charge of the corporation's financial accounting records (1) stating his reasonable belief as to whether or not the financial statements were prepared in accordance with generally accepted accounting principles and, if not, describing the basis of presentation, and (2) describing any respects in which the financial statements were not prepared on a basis consistent with those prepared for the previous year.

§ 53. Incorporators

One or more persons, or a domestic or foreign corporation, may act as incorporator or incorporators of a corporation by signing and delivering in duplicate to the Secretary of State articles of incorporation for such corporation.

§ 54. Articles of Incorporation

The articles of incorporation shall set forth:

(a)   The name of the corporation.

(b)   The period of duration, which may be perpetual.

(c)   The purpose or purposes for which the corporation is organized which may be stated to be, or to include, the transaction of any or all lawful business for which corporations may be incorporated under this Act.

(d)   The aggregate number of shares which the corporation shall have authority to issue and, if such shares are to be divided into classes, the number of shares of each class.

(e)   If the shares are to be divided into classes, the designation of each class and a statement of the preferences, limitations and relative rights in respect of the shares of each class.

(f)   If the corporation is to issue the shares of any preferred or special class in series, then the designation of each series and a statement of the variations in the relative rights and preferences as between series insofar as the same are to be fixed in the articles of incorporation, and a statement of any authority to be vested in the board of directors to establish series and fix and determine the variations in the relative rights and preferences as between series.

(g)   If any preemptive right is to be granted to shareholders, the provisions therefor.

(h)   The address of its initial registered office, and the name of its initial registered agent at such address.

(i)   The number of directors constituting the initial board of directors and the names and addresses of the persons who are to serve as directors until the first annual meeting of shareholders or until their successors be elected and qualify.

(j)   The name and address of each incorporator.

In addition to provisions required therein, the articles of incorporation may also contain provisions not inconsistent with law regarding:

(1)   the direction of the management of the business and the regulation of the affairs of the corporation;
(2)   the definition, limitation and regulation of the powers of the corporation, the directors, and the shareholders, or any class of the shareholders, including restrictions on the transfer of shares;
(3)   the par value of any authorized shares or class of shares;
(4)   any provision which under this Act is required or permitted to be set forth in the by-laws.

It shall not be necessary to set forth in the articles of incorporation any of the corporate powers enumerated in this Act.

§ 55. Filing of Articles of Incorporation

Duplicate originals of the articles of incorporation shall be delivered to the Secretary of State. If the Secretary of State finds that the articles of incorporation conform to law, he shall, when all fees have been paid as in this Act prescribed:

(a)   Endorse on each of such duplicate originals the word "Filed," and the month, day and year of the filing thereof.

(b)   File one of such duplicate originals in his office.

(c)   Issue a certificate of incorporation to which he shall affix the other duplicate original.

The certificate of incorporation, together with the duplicate original of the articles of incorporation affixed thereto by the Secretary of State, shall be returned to the incorporators or their representative.

§ 56. Effect of Issuance of Certificate of Incorporation

Upon the issuance of the certificate of incorporation, the corporate existence shall begin, and such certificate of incorporation shall be conclusive evidence that all conditions precedent required to be performed by the incorporators have been complied with and that the corporation has been incorporated under this Act, except as against this State in a proceeding to cancel or revoke the certificate of incorporation or for involuntary dissolution of the corporation.

§ 57. Organization Meeting of Directors

After the issuance of the certificate of incorporation an organization meeting of the board of directors named in the articles of incorporation shall be held, either within or without this State, at the call of a majority of the directors named in the articles of incorporation, for the purpose of adopting by-laws, electing officers and transacting such other business as may come before the meeting. The directors calling the meeting shall give at least three days' notice thereof by mail to each director so named, stating the time and place of the meeting.

§ 58. Right to Amend Articles of Incorporation

A corporation may amend its articles of incorporation, from time to time, in any and as many respects as may be desired, so long as its articles of incorporation as amended contain only such provisions as might be lawfully contained in original articles of incorporation at the time of making such amendment, and, if a change in shares or the rights of shareholders, or an exchange, reclassification or cancellation of shares or rights of shareholders is to be made, such provisions as may be necessary to effect such change, exchange, reclassification or cancellation.

In particular, and without limitation upon such general power of amendment, a corporation may amend its articles of incorporation, from time to time, so as:

(a)   To change its corporate name.

(b)   To change its period of duration.

(c)   To change, enlarge or diminish its corporate purposes.

(d) To increase or decrease the aggregate number of shares, or shares of any class, which the corporation has authority to issue.

(e) To provide, change or eliminate any provision with respect to the par value of any shares or class of shares.

(f) To exchange, classify, reclassify or cancel all or any part of its shares, whether issued or unissued.

(g) To change the designation of all or any part of its shares, whether issued or unissued, and to change the preferences, limitations, and the relative rights in respect of all or any part of its shares, whether issued or unissued.

(h) To change the shares of any class, whether issued or unissued [sic] into a different number of shares of the same class or into the same or a different number of shares of other classes.

(i) To create new classes of shares having rights and preferences either prior and superior or subordinate and inferior to the shares of any class then authorized, whether issued or unissued.

(j) To cancel or otherwise affect the right of the holders of the shares of any class to receive dividends which have accrued but have not been declared.

(k) To divide any preferred or special class of shares, whether issued or unissued, into series and fix and determine the designations of such series and the variations in the relative rights and preferences as between the shares of such series.

(l) To authorize the board of directors to establish, out of authorized but unissued shares, series of any preferred or special class of shares and fix and determine the relative rights and preferences of the shares of any series so established.

(m) To authorize the board of directors to fix and determine the relative rights and preferences of the authorized but unissued shares of series theretofore established in respect of which either the relative rights and preferences have not been fixed and determined or the relative rights and preferences theretofore fixed and determined are to be changed.

(n) To revoke, diminish, or enlarge the authority of the board of directors to establish series out of authorized but unissued shares of any preferred or special

class and fix and determine the relative rights and preferences of the shares of any series so established.

(o) To limit, deny or grant to shareholders of any class the preemptive right to acquire additional shares of the corporation, whether then or thereafter authorized.

§ 59. Procedure to Amend Articles of Incorporation

Amendments to the articles of incorporation shall be made in the following manner:

(a) The board of directors shall adopt a resolution setting forth the proposed amendment and, if shares have been issued, directing that it be submitted to a vote at a meeting of shareholders, which may be either the annual or a special meeting. If no shares have been issued, the amendment shall be adopted by resolution of the board of directors and the provisions for adoption by shareholders shall not apply. If the corporation has only one class of shares outstanding, an amendment solely to change the number of authorized shares to effectuate a split of, or stock dividend in, the corporation's own shares, or solely to do so and to change the number of authorized shares in proportion thereto, may be adopted by the board of directors; and the provisions for adoption by shareholders shall not apply, unless otherwise provided by the articles of incorporation. The resolution may incorporate the proposed amendment in restated articles of incorporation which contain a statement that except for the designated amendment the restated articles of incorporation correctly set forth without change the corresponding provisions of the articles of incorporation as theretofore amended, and that the restated articles of incorporation together with the designated amendment supersede the original articles of incorporation and all amendments thereto.

(b) Written notice setting forth the proposed amendment or a summary of the changes to be effected thereby shall be given to each shareholder of record entitled to vote thereon within the time and in the manner provided in this Act for the giving of notice of meetings of shareholders. If the meeting be an annual meeting, the proposed amendment of such summary may be included in the notice of such annual meeting.

(c) At such meeting a vote of the shareholders entitled to vote thereon shall be taken on the proposed amendment. The proposed amendment shall be adopted upon receiving the affirmative vote of the holders of a majority of the shares entitled to vote thereon, unless any class of shares is entitled to vote thereon as a class, in which event the proposed amendment shall be adopted upon receiving the affirmative vote of the holders of a majority of the shares of each class of shares entitled to vote thereon as a class and of the total shares entitled to vote thereon.

Any number of amendments may be submitted to the shareholders, and voted upon by them, at one meeting.

§ 60. Class Voting on Amendments

The holders of the outstanding shares of a class shall be entitled to vote as a class upon a proposed amendment, whether or not entitled to vote thereon by the provisions of the articles of incorporation, if the amendment would:

(a) Increase or decrease the aggregate number of authorized shares of such class.

(b) Effect an exchange, reclassification or cancellation of all or part of the shares of such class.

(c) Effect an exchange, or create a right of exchange, of all or any part of the shares of another class into the shares of such class.

(d) Change the designations, preferences, limitations or relative rights of the shares of such class.

(e) Change the shares of such class into the same or a different number of shares of the same class or another class or classes.

(f) Create a new class of shares having rights and preferences prior and superior to the shares of such class, or increase the rights and preferences or the number of authorized shares, of any class having rights and preferences prior or superior to the shares of such class.

(g) In the case of a preferred or special class of shares, divide the shares of such class into series and fix and determine the designation of such series and the variations in the relative rights and preferences between the shares of such series, or authorize the board of directors to do so.

(h) Limit or deny any existing preemptive rights of the shares of such class.

(i) Cancel or otherwise affect dividends on the shares of such class which have accrued but have not been declared.

§ 61. Articles of Amendment

The articles of amendment shall be executed in duplicate by the corporation by its president or a vice president and by its secretary or an assistant secretary, and verified by one of the officers signing such articles, and shall set forth:

(a) The name of the corporation.

(b) The amendments so adopted.

(c) The date of the adoption of the amendment by the shareholders, or by the board of directors where no shares have been issued.

(d) The number of shares outstanding, and the number of shares entitled to vote thereon, and if the shares of any class are entitled to vote thereon as a class, the designation and number of outstanding shares entitled to vote thereon of each such class.

(e) The number of shares voted for and against such amendment, respectively, and, if the shares of any class are entitled to vote thereon as a class, the number of shares of each such class voted for and against such amendment, respectively, or if no shares have been issued, a statement to that effect.

(f) If such amendment provides for an exchange, reclassification or cancellation of issued shares, and if the manner in which the same shall be effected is not set forth in the amendment, then a statement of the manner in which the same shall be effected.

§ 62. Filing of Articles of Amendment

Duplicate originals of the articles of amendment shall be delivered to the Secretary of State. If the Secretary of State finds that the articles of amendment conform to law, he shall, when all fees and franchise taxes have been paid as in this Act prescribed:

(a) Endorse on each of such duplicate originals the word "Filed," and the month, day and year of the filing thereof.

(b)   File one of such duplicate originals in his office.

(c)   Issue a certificate of amendment to which he shall affix the other duplicate original.

The certificate of amendment, together with the duplicate original of the articles of amendment affixed thereto by the Secretary of State, shall be returned to the corporation or its representative.

§ 63. Effect of Certificate of Amendment

Upon the issuance of the certificate of amendment by the Secretary of State, the amendment shall become effective and the articles of incorporation shall be deemed to be amended accordingly.

No amendment shall affect any existing cause of action in favor of or against such corporation, or any pending suit to which such corporation shall be a party, or the existing rights of persons other than shareholders; and, in the event the corporate name shall be changed by amendment, no suit brought by or against such corporation under its former name shall abate for that reason.

§ 64. Restated Articles of Incorporation

A domestic corporation may at any time restate its articles of incorporation as theretofore amended, by a resolution adopted by the board of directors.

Upon the adoption of such resolution, restated articles of incorporation shall be executed in duplicate by the corporation by its president or a vice president and by its secretary or assistant secretary and verified by one of the officers signing such articles and shall set forth all of the operative provisions of the articles of incorporation as theretofore amended together with a statement that the restated articles of incorporation correctly set forth without change the corresponding provisions of the articles of incorporation as theretofore amended and that the restated articles of incorporation supersede the original articles of incorporation and all amendments thereto.

Duplicate originals of the restated articles of incorporation shall be delivered to the Secretary of State. If the Secretary of State finds that such restated articles of incorporation conform to law, he shall, when all fees and franchise taxes have been paid as in this Act prescribed:

(1)   Endorse on each of such duplicate originals the word "Filed," and the month, day and year of the filing thereof.

(2)   File one of such duplicate originals in his office.

(3)   Issue a restated certificate of incorporation, to which he shall affix the other duplicate original.

The restated certificate of incorporation, together with the duplicate original of the restated articles of incorporation affixed thereto by the Secretary of State, shall be returned to the corporation or its representative.

Upon the issuance of the restated certificate of incorporation by the Secretary of State, the restated articles of incorporation shall become effective and shall supersede the original articles of incorporation and all amendments thereto.

§ 65. Amendment of Articles of Incorporation in Reorganization Proceedings

Whenever a plan of reorganization of a corporation has been confirmed by decree or order of a court of competent jurisdiction in proceedings for the reorganization of such corporation, pursuant to the provisions of any applicable statute of the United States relating to reorganizations of corporations, the articles of incorporation of the corporation may be amended, in the manner provided in this section, in as many respects as may be necessary to carry out the plan and put it into effect, so long as the articles of incorporation as amended contain only such provisions as might be lawfully contained in original articles of incorporation at the time of making such amendment.

In particular and without limitation upon such general power of amendment, the articles of incorporation may be amended for such purpose so as to:

(A)   Change the corporate name, period of duration or corporate purposes of the corporation;

(B)   Repeal, alter or amend the by-laws of the corporation;

(C)   Change the aggregate number of shares or shares of any class, which the corporation has authority to issue;

(D)   Change the preferences, limitations and relative rights in respect of all or any part of the shares of the corporation, and classify, reclassify or cancel all or any part thereof, whether issued or unissued;

(E)   Authorize the issuance of bonds, debentures or other obligations of the corporation, whether or not convertible into shares of any class or bearing warrants or other evidences of optional rights to purchase or subscribe for shares of any class, and fix the terms and conditions thereof; and

(F)   Constitute or reconstitute and classify or reclassify the board of directors of the corporation, and appoint directors and officers in place of or in addition to all or any of the directors or officers then in office.

Amendments to the articles of incorporation pursuant to this section shall be made in the following manner:

(a)   Articles of amendment approved by decree or order of such court shall be executed and verified in duplicate by such person or persons as the court shall designate or appoint for the purpose, and shall set forth the name of the corporation, the amendments of the articles of incorporation approved by the court, the date of the decree or order approving the articles of amendment, the title of the proceedings in which the decree or order was entered, and a statement that such decree or order was entered by a court having jurisdiction of the proceedings for the reorganization of the corporation pursuant to the provisions of an applicable statute of the United States.

(b)   Duplicate originals of the articles of amendment shall be delivered to the Secretary of State. If the Secretary of State finds that the articles of amendment conform to law, he shall, when all fees and franchise taxes have been paid as in this Act prescribed:

> (1)   Endorse on each of such duplicate originals the word "Filed," and the month, day and year of the filing thereof.
> (2)   File one of such duplicate originals in his office.
> (3)   Issue a certificate of amendment to which he shall affix the other duplicate original.

The certificate of amendment, together with the duplicate original of the articles of amendment affixed thereto by the Secretary of State, shall be returned to the corporation or its representative.

Upon the issuance of the certificate of amendment by the Secretary of State, the amendment shall become effective and the articles of incorporation shall be deemed to be amended accordingly, without any action thereon by the directors or shareholders of the corporation and with the same effect as if the amendments had been adopted by unanimous action of the directors and shareholders of the corporation.

§ 66. Restriction on Redemption or Purchase of Redeemable Shares
[Repealed in 1979].

§ 67. Cancellation of Redeemable Shares by Redemption or Purchase
[Repealed in 1979].

§ 68. Cancellation of Other Reacquired Shares
[Repealed in 1979].

§ 69. Reduction of Stated Capital in Certain Cases
[Repealed in 1979].

§ 70. Special Provisions Relating to Surplus and Reserves
[Repealed in 1979].

§ 71. Procedure for Merger
Any two or more domestic corporations may merge into one of such corporations pursuant to a plan of merger approved in the manner provided in this Act.

The board of directors of each corporation shall, by resolution adopted by each such board, approve a plan of merger setting forth:

(a)   The names of the corporations proposing to merge, and the name of the corporation into which they propose to merge, which is hereinafter designated as the surviving corporation.

(b)   The terms and conditions of the proposed merger.

(c)   The manner and basis of converting the shares of each corporation into shares, obligations or other securities of the surviving corporation or of any other corporation or, in whole or in part, into cash or other property.

(d)   A statement of any changes in the articles of incorporation of the surviving corporation to be effected by such merger.

(e)   Such other provisions with respect to the proposed merger as are deemed necessary or desirable.

§ 72. Procedure for Consolidation

Any two or more domestic corporations may consolidate into a new corporation pursuant to a plan of consolidation approved in the manner provided in this Act.

The board of directors of each corporation shall, by a resolution adopted by each such board, approve a plan of consolidation setting forth:

(a)   The names of the corporations proposing to consolidate, and the name of the new corporation into which they propose to consolidate, which is hereinafter designated as the new corporation.

(b)   The terms and conditions of the proposed consolidation.

(c)   The manner and basis of converting the shares of each corporation into shares, obligations or other securities of the new corporation or of any other corporation or, in whole or in part, into cash or other property.

(d)   With respect to the new corporation, all of the statements required to be set forth in articles of incorporation for corporations organized under this Act.

(e)   Such other provisions with respect to the proposed consolidation as are deemed necessary or desirable.

§ 72A. Procedure for Share Exchange

All the issued or all the outstanding shares of one or more classes of any domestic corporation may be acquired through the exchange of all such shares of such class or classes by another domestic or foreign corporation pursuant to a plan of exchange approved in the manner provided in this Act.

The board of directors of each corporation shall, by resolution adopted by each such board, approve a plan of exchange setting forth:

(a)   The name of the corporation the shares of which are proposed to be acquired by exchange and the name of the corporation to acquire the shares of such corporation in the exchange, which is hereinafter designated as the acquiring corporation.

(b)   The terms and conditions of the proposed exchange.

(c)   The manner and basis of exchanging the shares to be acquired for shares, obligations or other securities of the acquiring corporation or any other corpo-

ration, or, in whole or in part, for cash or other property.

(d)   Such other provisions with respect to the proposed exchange as are deemed necessary or desirable.

The procedure authorized by this section shall not be deemed to limit the power of a corporation to acquire all or part of the shares of any class of classes of a corporation through a voluntary exchange or otherwise by agreement with the shareholders.

§ 73. Approval by Shareholders

(a)   The board of directors of each corporation in the case of a merger or consolidation, and the board of directors of the corporation the shares of which are to be acquired in the case of an exchange, upon approving such plan of merger, consolidation or exchange, shall, by resolution, direct that the plan be submitted to a vote at a meeting of its shareholders, which may be either an annual or a special meeting. Written notice shall be given to each shareholder of record, whether or not entitled to vote at such meeting, not less than twenty days before such meeting, in the manner provided in this Act for the giving of notice of meetings of shareholders, and, whether the meeting be an annual or a special meeting, shall state that the purpose or one of the purposes is to consider the proposed plan of merger, consolidation or exchange. A copy or a summary of the plan of merger, consolidation or exchange, as the case may be, shall be included in or enclosed with such notice.

(b)   At each such meeting, a vote of the shareholders shall be taken on the proposed plan. The plan shall be approved upon receiving the affirmative vote of the holders of a majority of the shares entitled to vote thereon of each such corporation, unless any class of shares of any such corporation is entitled to vote thereon as a class, in which event, as to such corporation, the plan shall be approved upon receiving the affirmative vote of the holders of a majority of the shares of each class of shares entitled to vote thereon as a class and of the total shares entitled to vote thereon. Any class of shares of any such corporation shall be entitled to vote as a class if any such plan contains any provision which, if contained in a proposed amendment to articles of incorporation, would entitle such class of shares to vote as a class and, in the case of an exchange, if the class is included in the exchange.

(c)   After such approval by a vote of the shareholders of each such corporation, and at any time prior to the filing of the articles of merger, consolidation or exchange, the merger, consolidation or exchange may be abandoned pursuant to provisions therefor, if any, set forth in the plan.

(d)   (1) Notwithstanding the provisions of subsections (a) and (b), submission of a plan of merger to a vote at a meeting of shareholders of a surviving corporation shall not be required if:

(i) the articles of incorporation of the surviving corporation do not differ except in name from those of the corporation before the merger,

(ii) each holder of shares of the surviving corporation which were outstanding immediately before the effective date of the merger is to hold the same number of shares with identical rights immediately after,

(iii) the number of voting shares outstanding immediately after the merger, plus the number of voting shares issuable on conversion of other securities issued by virtue of the terms of the merger and on exercise of rights and warrants so issued, will not exceed by more than 20 percent the number of voting shares outstanding immediately before the merger, and

(iv) the number of participating shares outstanding immediately after the merger, plus the number of participating shares issuable on conversion of other securities issued by virtue of the terms of the merger and on exercise of rights and warrants so issued, will not exceed by more than 20 percent the number of participating shares outstanding immediately before the merger.

(2) As used in this subsection:

(i) "voting shares" means shares which entitle their holders to vote unconditionally in elections of directors;

(ii) "participating shares" means shares which entitle their holders to participate without limitation in distribution of earnings or surplus.

§ 74. Articles of Merger, Consolidation or Exchange

(a) Upon receiving the approvals required by Sections 71, 72 and 73, articles of merger or articles of consolidation shall be executed in duplicate by each corporation by its president or a vice president and by

its secretary or an assistant secretary, and verified by one of the officers of each corporation signing such articles, and shall set forth:

(1)   The plan of merger or the plan of consolidation;
(2)   As to each corporation, either (i) the number of shares outstanding, and, if the shares of any class are entitled to vote as a class, the designation and number of outstanding shares of each such class, or (ii) a statement that the vote of shareholders is not required by virtue of subsection 73(d);
(3)   As to each corporation the approval of whose shareholders is required, the number of shares voted for and against such plan, respectively, and, if the shares of any class are entitled to vote as a class, the number of shares of each such class voted for and against such plan, respectively.

(b)   Duplicate originals of the articles of merger, consolidation or exchange shall be delivered to the Secretary of State. If the Secretary of State finds that such articles conform to law, he shall, when all fees and franchise taxes have been paid as in this Act prescribed:

(1)   Endorse on each of such duplicate originals the word "Filed," and the month, day and year of the filing thereof.
(2)   File one of such duplicate originals in his office.
(3)   Issue a certificate of merger, consolidation or exchange to which he shall affix the other duplicate original.

(c)   The certificate of merger, consolidation or exchange together with the duplicate original of the articles affixed thereto by the Secretary of State, shall be returned to the surviving, new or acquiring corporation, as the case may be, or its representative.

§ 75. Merger of Subsidiary Corporation

Any corporation owning at least ninety per cent of the outstanding shares of each class of another corporation may merge such other corporation into itself without approval by a vote of the shareholders of either corporation. Its board of directors shall, by resolution, approve a plan of merger setting forth:

(A)   The name of the subsidiary corporation and the name of the corporation owning at least ninety per cent of its shares, which is hereinafter designated as the surviving corporation.

(B)   The manner and basis of converting the shares of the subsidiary corporation into shares, obligations or other securities of the surviving corporation or of any other corporation or, in whole or in part, into cash or other property.

A copy of such plan of merger shall be mailed to each shareholder of record of the subsidiary corporation.

Articles of merger shall be executed in duplicate by the surviving corporation by its president or a vice president and by its secretary or an assistant secretary, and verified by one of its officers signing such articles, and shall set forth:

(a)   The plan of merger;

(b)   The number of outstanding shares of each class of the subsidiary corporation and the number of such shares of each class owned by the surviving corporation; and

(c)   The date of the mailing to shareholders of the subsidiary corporation of a copy of the plan of merger.

On and after the thirtieth day after the mailing of a copy of the plan of merger to shareholders of the subsidiary corporation or upon the waiver thereof by the holders of all outstanding shares duplicate originals of the articles of merger shall be delivered to the Secretary of State. If the Secretary of State finds that such articles conform to law, he shall, when all fees and franchise taxes have been paid as in this Act prescribed:

(1)   Endorse on each of such duplicate originals the word "Filed," and the month, day and year of the filing thereof,
(2)   File one of such duplicate originals in his office, and
(3)   Issue a certificate of merger to which he shall affix the other duplicate original.

The certificate of merger, together with the duplicate original of the articles of merger affixed thereto by the Secretary of State, shall be returned to the surviving corporation or its representative.

§ 76. Effect of Merger, Consolidation or Exchange
Upon the issuance of the certificate of merger or the certificate of consolidation by the Secretary of State, the merger or consolidation shall be effected.

When such merger or consolidation has been effective:

(a)   The several corporations parties to the plan of merger or consolidation shall be a single corporation, which, in the case of a merger, shall be that corporation designated in the plan of merger as the surviving corporation, and, in the case of a consolidation, shall be the new corporation provided for in the plan of consolidation.

(b)   The separate existence of all corporations parties to the plan of merger or consolidation, except the surviving or new corporation, shall cease.

(c)   Such surviving or new corporation shall have all the rights, privileges, immunities and powers and shall be subject to all the duties and liabilities of a corporation organized under this Act.

(d)   Such surviving or new corporation shall thereupon and thereafter possess all the rights, privileges, immunities, and franchises, of a public as well as of a private nature, of each of the merging or consolidating corporations; and all property, real, personal and mixed, and all debts due on whatever account, including subscriptions to shares, and all other choses in action, and all and every other interest of or belonging to or due to each of the corporations so merged or consolidated, shall be taken and deemed to be transferred to and vested in such single corporation without further act or deed; and the title to any real estate, or any interest therein, vested in any of such corporations shall not revert or be in any way impaired by reason of such merger or consolidation.

(e)   Such surviving or new corporation shall thenceforth be responsible and liable for all the liabilities and obligations of each of the corporations so merged or consolidated; and any claim existing or action or proceeding pending by or against any of such corporations may be prosecuted as if such merger or consolidation had not taken place, or such surviving or new corporation may be substituted in its place. Neither the rights of creditors nor any liens upon the property of any such corporation shall be impaired by such merger or consolidation.

(f)   In the case of a merger, the articles of incorporation of the surviving corporation shall be deemed to be amended to the extent, if any, that changes in its articles of incorporation are stated in the plan of merger; and, in the case of a consolidation, the statements set forth in the articles of consolidation and which are required or permitted to be set forth in the articles of incorporation of corporations organized under this Act shall be deemed to be the original articles of incorporation of the new corporation.

§ 77. Merger, Consolidation or Exchange of Shares Between Domestic and Foreign Corporations

One or more foreign corporations and one or more domestic corporations may be merged or consolidated in the following manner, if such merger or consolidation is permitted by the laws of the state under which each such foreign corporation is organized:

(a)　Each domestic corporation shall comply with the provisions of this Act with respect to the merger or consolidation, as the case may be, of domestic corporations and each foreign corporation shall comply with the applicable provisions of the laws of the state under which it is organized.

(b)　If the surviving or new corporation, as the case may be, is to be governed by the laws of any state other than this State, it shall comply with the provisions of this Act with respect to foreign corporations if it is to transact business in this State, and in every case it shall file with the Secretary of State of this State:

(1)　An agreement that it may be served with process in this State in any proceeding for the enforcement of any obligation of any domestic corporation which is a party to such merger or consolidation and in any proceeding for the enforcement of the rights of a dissenting shareholder of any such domestic corporation against the surviving or new corporation;

(2)　An irrevocable appointment of the Secretary of State of this State as its agent to accept service of process in any such proceeding; and

(3)　An agreement that it will promptly pay to the dissenting shareholders of any such domestic corporation the amount, if any, to which they shall be entitled under the provisions of this Act with respect to the rights of dissenting shareholders.

The effect of such merger or consolidation shall be the same as in the case of the merger or consolidation of domestic corporations, if the surviving or new corporation is to be governed by the laws of this State. If the surviving or new corporation is to be governed by the laws of any state other than this State, the effect of such merger or consolidation shall be the same as in the case of the merger or consolidation of domestic corporations except insofar as the laws of such other state provide otherwise.

At any time prior to the filing of the articles of merger or consolidation, the merger or consolidation may be abandoned pursuant to provisions therefor, if any, set forth in the plan of merger or consolidation.

§ 78. Sale of Assets in Regular Course of Business and Mortgage or Pledge of Assets

The sale, lease, exchange, or other disposition of all, or substantially all, the property and assets of a corporation in the usual and regular course of its business and the mortgage or pledge of any or all property and assets of a corporation whether or not in the usual and regular course of business may be made upon such terms and conditions and for such consideration, which may consist in whole or in part of cash or other property, including shares, obligations or other securities of any other corporation, domestic or foreign, as shall be authorized by its board of directors; and in any such case no authorization or consent of the shareholders shall be required.

§ 79. Sale of Assets Other Than in Regular Course of Business

A sale, lease, exchange, or other disposition of all, or substantially all, the property and assets, with or without the good will, of a corporation, if not in the usual and regular course of its business, may be made upon such terms and conditions and for such consideration, which may consist in whole or in part of cash or other property, including shares, obligations or other securities of any other corporation, domestic or foreign, as may be authorized in the following manner:

(a)　The board of directors shall adopt a resolution recommending such sale, lease, exchange, or other disposition and directing the submission thereof to a vote at a meeting of shareholders, which may be either an annual or a special meeting.

(b)   Written notice shall be given to each shareholder of record, whether or not entitled to vote at such meeting, not less than twenty days before such meeting, in the manner provided in this Act for the giving of notice of meetings of shareholders, and, whether the meeting be an annual or a special meeting, shall state that the purpose, or one of the purposes is to consider the proposed sale, lease, exchange, or other disposition.

(c)   At such meeting the shareholders may authorize such sale, lease, exchange, or other disposition and may fix, or may authorize the board of directors to fix, any or all of the terms and conditions thereof and the consideration to be received by the corporation therefor. Such authorization shall require the affirmative vote of the holders of a majority of the shares of the corporation entitled to vote thereon, unless any class of shares is entitled to vote thereon as a class, in which event such authorization shall require the affirmative vote of the holders of a majority of the shares of each class of shares entitled to vote as a class thereon and of the total shares entitled to vote thereon.

(d)   After such authorization by a vote of shareholders, the board of directors nevertheless, in its discretion, may abandon such sale, lease, exchange, or other disposition of assets, subject to the rights of third parties under any contracts relating thereto, without further action or approval by shareholders.

§ 80. Right of Shareholders to Dissent and Obtain Payment for Shares

(a)   Any shareholder of a corporation shall have the right to dissent from, and to obtain payment for his shares in the event of, any of the following corporate actions:

(1)   Any plan of merger or consolidation to which the corporation is a party, except as provided in subsection (c);
(2)   Any sale or exchange of all or substantially all of the property and assets of the corporation not made in the usual or regular course of its business, including a sale in dissolution, but not including a sale pursuant to an order of a court having jurisdiction in the premises or a sale for cash on terms requiring that all or substantially all of the net proceeds of sale be distributed to the

shareholders in accordance with their respective interests within one year after the date of sale;
(3)   Any plan of exchange to which the corporation is a party as the corporation the shares of which are to be acquired;
(4)   Any amendment of the articles of incorporation which materially and adversely affects the rights appurtenant to the shares of the dissenting shareholder in that it:

(i)   alters or abolishes a preferential right of such shares;
(ii)   creates, alters or abolishes a right in respect of the redemption of such shares, including a provision respecting a sinking fund for the redemption or repurchase of such shares;
(iii)   alters or abolishes a preemptive right of the holder of such shares to acquire shares or other securities;
(iv)   excludes or limits the right of the holder of such shares to vote on any matter, or to cumulate his votes, except as such right may be limited by dilution through the issuance of shares or other securities with similar voting rights; or

(5)   Any other corporate action taken pursuant to a shareholder vote with respect to which the articles of incorporation, the bylaws, or a resolution of the board of directors directs that dissenting shareholders shall have a right to obtain payment for their shares.

(b)   (1) A record holder of shares may assert dissenters' rights as to less than all of the shares registered in his name only if he dissents with respect to all the shares beneficially owned by any one person, and discloses the name and address of the person or persons on whose behalf he dissents. In that event, his rights shall be determined as if the shares as to which he has dissented and his other shares were registered in the names of different shareholders.

(2)   A beneficial owner of shares who is not the record holder may assert dissenters' rights with respect to shares held on his behalf, and shall be treated as a dissenting shareholder under the terms of this section and section 81 if he submits to the corporation at the time of or before the assertion of these rights a written consent of the record holder.

(c)   The right to obtain payment under this section shall not apply to the shareholders of the surviving corporation in a merger if a vote of the shareholders of such corporation is not necessary to authorize such merger.

(d) A shareholder of a corporation who has a right under this section to obtain payment for his shares shall have no right at law or in equity to attack the validity of the corporate action that gives rise to his right to obtain payment, nor to have the action set aside or rescinded, except when the corporate action is unlawful or fraudulent with regard to the complaining shareholder or to the corporation.

§ 81. Procedures for Protection of Dissenters' Rights

(a) As used in this section:

(1) "Dissenter" means a shareholder or beneficial owner who is entitled to and does assert dissenters' rights under section 80, and who has performed every act required up to the time involved for the assertion of such rights.

(2) "Corporation" means the issuer of the shares held by the dissenter before the corporate action, or the successor by merger or consolidation of that issuer.

(3) "Fair value" of shares means their value immediately before the effectuation of the corporate action to which the dissenter objects, excluding any appreciation or depreciation in anticipation of such corporate action unless such exclusion would be inequitable.

(4) "Interest" means interest from the effective date of the corporate action until the date of payment, at the average rate currently paid by the corporation on its principal bank loans, or, if none, at such rate as is fair and equitable under all the circumstances.

(b) If a proposed corporate action which would give rise to dissenters' rights under section 80(a) is submitted to a vote at a meeting of shareholders, the notice of meeting shall notify all shareholders that they have or may have a right to dissent and obtain payment for their shares by complying with the terms of this section, and shall be accompanied by a copy of sections 80 and 81 of this Act.

(c) If the proposed corporate action is submitted to a vote at a meeting of shareholders, any shareholder who wishes to dissent and obtain payment for his shares must file with the corporation, prior to the vote, a written notice of intention to demand that he be paid fair compensation for his shares if the proposed action is effectuated, and shall refrain from voting his shares in approval of such action. A shareholder who fails in either respect shall acquire no right to payment for his shares under this section or section 80.

(d) If the proposed corporate action is approved by the required vote at a meeting of shareholders, the corporation shall mail a further notice to all shareholders who gave due notice of intention to demand payment and who refrained from voting in favor of the proposed action. If the proposed corporate action is to be taken without a vote of shareholders, the corporation shall send to all shareholders who are entitled to dissent and demand payment for their shares a notice of the adoption of the plan of corporate action. The notice shall (1) state where and when a demand for payment must be sent and certificates of certificated shares must be deposited in order to obtain payment, (2) inform holders of uncertificated shares to what extent transfer of shares will be restricted from the time that demand for payment is received, (3) supply a form for demanding payment which includes a request for certification of the date on which the shareholder, or the person on whose behalf the shareholder dissents, acquired beneficial ownership of the shares, and (4) be accompanied by a copy of sections 80 and 81 of this Act. The time set for the demand and deposit shall be not less than 30 days from the mailing of the notice.

(e) A shareholder who fails to demand payment, or fails (in the case of certificated shares) to deposit certificates, as required by a notice pursuant to subsection (d) shall have no right under this section or section 80 to receive payment for his shares. If the shares are not represented by certificates, the corporation may restrict their transfer from the time of receipt of demand for payment until effectuation of the proposed corporate action, or the release of restrictions under the terms of subsection (f). The dissenter shall retain all other rights of a shareholder until these rights are modified by effectuation of the proposed corporate action.

(f) (1) Within 60 days after the date set for demanding payment and depositing certificates, if the corporation has not effectuated the proposed corporate action and remitted payment for shares pursuant to paragraph (3), it shall return any certificates that have been deposited, and release uncertificated shares from any transfer restrictions imposed by reason of the demand for payment.

(2)   When uncertificated shares have been released from transfer restrictions, and deposited certificates have been returned, the corporation may at any later time send a new notice conforming to the requirements of subsection (d), with like effect.

(3)   Immediately upon effectuation of the proposed corporate action, or upon receipt of demand for payment if the corporate action has already been effectuated, the corporation shall remit to dissenters who have made demand and (if their shares are certificated) have deposited their certificates the amount which the corporation estimates to be the fair value of the shares, with interest if any has accrued. The remittance shall be accompanied by:

> (i)   the corporation's closing balance sheet and statement of income for a fiscal year ending not more than 16 months before the date of remittance, together with the latest available interim financial statements;
>
> (ii)   a statement of the corporation's estimate of fair value of the shares; and
>
> (iii)   a notice of the dissenter's right to demand supplemental payment, accompanied by a copy of sections 80 and 81 of this Act.

(g)   (1) If the corporation fails to remit as required by subsection (f), or if the dissenter believes that the amount remitted is less than the fair value of his shares, or that the interest is not correctly determined, he may send the corporation his own estimate of the value of the shares or of the interest, and demand payment of the deficiency.

(2)   If the dissenter does not file such an estimate within 30 days after the corporation's mailing of its remittance, he shall be entitled to no more than the amount remitted.

(h)   (1) Within 60 days after receiving a demand for payment pursuant to subsection (g), if any such demands for payment remain unsettled, the corporation shall file in an appropriate court a petition requesting that the fair value of the shares and interest thereon be determined by the court.

(2)   An appropriate court shall be a court of competent jurisdiction in the county of this state where the registered office of the corporation is located. If, in the case of a merger or consolidation or exchange of shares, the corporation is a foreign corporation without a registered office in this state, the petition shall be filed in the county where the registered office of the domestic corporation was last located.

(3)   All dissenters, wherever residing, whose demands have not been settled shall be made parties to the proceeding as in an action against their shares. A copy of the petition shall be served on each such dissenter; if a dissenter is a nonresident, the copy may be served on him by registered or certified mail or by publication as provided by law.

(4)   The jurisdiction of the court shall be plenary and exclusive. The court may appoint one or more persons as appraisers to receive evidence and recommend a decision on the question of fair value. The appraisers shall have such power and authority as shall be specified in the order of their appointment or in any amendment thereof. The dissenters shall be entitled to discovery in the same manner as parties in other civil suits.

(5)   All dissenters who are made parties shall be entitled to judgment for the amount by which the fair value of their shares is found to exceed the amount previously remitted, with interest.

(6)   If the corporation fails to file a petition as provided in paragraph (1) of this subsection, each dissenter who made a demand and who has not already settled his claim against the corporation shall be paid by the corporation the amount demanded by him, with interest, and may sue therefor in an appropriate court.

(i)   (1) The costs and expenses of any proceeding under subsection (h), including the reasonable compensation and expenses of appraisers appointed by the court, shall be determined by the court and assessed against the corporation, except that any part of the costs and expenses may be apportioned and assessed as the court may deem equitable against all or some of the dissenters who are parties and whose action in demanding supplemental payment the court finds to be arbitrary, vexatious, or not in good faith.

(2)   Fees and expenses of counsel and of experts for the respective parties may be assessed as the

court may deem equitable against the corporation and in favor of any or all dissenters if the corporation failed to comply substantially with the requirements of this section, and may be assessed against either the corporation or a dissenter, in favor of any other party, if the court finds that the party against whom the fees and expenses are assessed acted arbitrarily, vexatiously, or not in good faith in respect to the rights provided by this Section and Section 80.

(3) If the court finds that the services of counsel for any dissenter were of substantial benefit to other dissenters similarly situated, and should not be assessed against the corporation, it may award to these counsel reasonable fees to be paid out of the amounts awarded to the dissenters who were benefitted.

(j) (1) Notwithstanding the foregoing provisions of this section, the corporation may elect to withhold the remittance required by subsection (f) from any dissenter with respect to shares of which the dissenter (or the person on whose behalf the dissenter acts) was not the beneficial owner on the date of the first announcement to news media or to shareholders of the terms of the proposed corporate action. With respect to such shares, the corporation shall, upon effectuating the corporate action, state to each dissenter its estimate of the fair value of the shares, state the rate of interest to be used (explaining the basis thereof), and offer to pay the resulting amounts on receiving the dissenter's agreement to accept them in full satisfaction.

(2) If the dissenter believes that the amount offered is less than the fair value of the shares and interest determined according to this section, he may within 30 days after the date of mailing of the corporation's offer, mail the corporation his own estimate of fair value and interest, and demand their payment. If the dissenter fails to do so, he shall be entitled to no more than the corporation's offer.

(3) If the dissenter makes a demand as provided in paragraph (2), the provisions of subsections (h) and (i) shall apply to further proceedings on the dissenter's demand.

§ 82. Voluntary Dissolution by Incorporators

A corporation which has not commenced business and which has not issued any shares, may be voluntarily dissolved by its incorporators at any time in the following manner:

(a) Articles of dissolution shall be executed in duplicate by a majority of the incorporators, and verified by them, and shall set forth:

(1) The name of the corporation.
(2) The date of issuance of its certificate of incorporation.
(3) That none of its shares has been issued.
(4) That the corporation has not commenced business.
(5) That the amount, if any, actually paid in on subscriptions for its shares, less any part thereof disbursed for necessary expenses, has been returned to those entitled thereto.
(6) That no debts of the corporation remain unpaid.
(7) That a majority of the incorporators elect that the corporation be dissolved.

(b) Duplicate originals of the articles of dissolution shall be delivered to the Secretary of State. If the Secretary of State finds that the articles of dissolution conform to law, he shall, when all fees and franchise taxes have been paid as in this Act prescribed:

(1) Endorse on each of such duplicate originals the word "Filed," and the month, day and year of the filing thereof.
(2) File one of such duplicate originals in his office.
(3) Issue a certificate of dissolution to which he shall affix the other duplicate original.

The certificate of dissolution, together with the duplicate original of the articles of dissolution affixed thereto by the Secretary of State, shall be returned to the incorporators or their representative. Upon the issuance of such certificate of dissolution by the Secretary of State, the existence of the corporation shall cease.

§ 83. Voluntary Dissolution by Consent of Shareholders

A corporation may be voluntarily dissolved by the written consent of all of its shareholders.

Upon the execution of such written consent, a statement of intent to dissolve shall be executed in duplicate by the corporation by its president or a vice president and by its secretary or an assistant secretary, and verified by one of the officers signing such statement, which statement shall set forth:

(a)   The name of the corporation.

(b)   The names and respective addresses of its officers.

(c)   The names and respective addresses of its directors.

(d)   A copy of the written consent signed by all shareholders of the corporation.

(e)   A statement that such written consent has been signed by all shareholders of the corporation or signed in their names by their attorneys thereunto duly authorized.

§ 84. Voluntary Dissolution by Act of Corporation

A corporation may be dissolved by the act of the corporation, when authorized in the following manner:

(a)   The board of directors shall adopt a resolution recommending that the corporation be dissolved, and directing that the question of such dissolution be submitted to a vote at a meeting of shareholders, which may be either an annual or a special meeting.

(b)   Written notice shall be given to each shareholder of record entitled to vote at such meeting within the time and in the manner provided in this Act for the giving of notice of meetings of shareholders, and, whether the meeting be an annual or special meeting, shall state that the purpose, or one of the purposes, of such meeting is to consider the advisability of dissolving the corporation.

(c)   At such meeting a vote of shareholders entitled to vote thereat shall be taken on a resolution to dissolve the corporation. Such resolution shall be adopted upon receiving the affirmative vote of the holders of a majority of the shares of the corporation entitled to vote thereon, unless any class of shares is entitled to vote thereon as a class, in which event the resolution shall be adopted upon receiving the affirmative vote of the holders of a majority of the shares of each class of shares entitled to vote thereon as a class and of the total shares entitled to vote thereon.

(d)   Upon the adoption of such resolution, a statement of intent to dissolve shall be executed in duplicate by the corporation by its president or a vice president and by its secretary or an assistant secretary, and verified by one of the officers signing such statement, which statement shall set forth:

(1)   The name of the corporation.
(2)   The names and respective addresses of its officers.
(3)   The names and respective addresses of its directors.
(4)   A copy of the resolution adopted by the shareholders authorizing the dissolution of the corporation.
(5)   The number of shares outstanding, and, if the shares of any class are entitled to vote as a class, the designation and number of outstanding shares of each such class.
(6)   The number of shares voted for and against the resolution, respectively, and, if the shares of any class are entitled to vote as a class, the number of shares of each such class voted for and against the resolution, respectively.

§ 85. Filing of Statement of Intent to Dissolve

Duplicate originals of the statement of intent to dissolve, whether by consent of shareholders or by act of the corporation, shall be delivered to the Secretary of State. If the Secretary of State finds that such statement conforms to law, he shall, when all fees and franchise taxes have been paid as in this Act prescribed:

(a)   Endorse on each of such duplicate originals the word "Filed," and the month, day and year of the filing thereof.

(b)   File one of such duplicate originals in his office.

(c)   Return the other duplicate original to the corporation or its representative.

§ 86. Effect of Statement of Intent to Dissolve

Upon the filing by the Secretary of State of a statement of intent to dissolve, whether by consent of shareholders or by act of the corporation, the corporation shall cease to carry on its business, except insofar as may be necessary for the winding up thereof, but its corporate existence shall continue until a certificate of dissolution has been issued by the Secretary of State or until a decree dissolving the corporation has been entered by a court of competent jurisdiction as in this Act provided.

§ 87. Procedure after Filing of Statement of Intent to Dissolve

After the filing by the Secretary of State of a statement of intent to dissolve:

(a) The corporation shall immediately cause notice thereof to be mailed to each known creditor of the corporation.

(b) The corporation shall proceed to collect its assets, convey and dispose of such of its properties as are not to be distributed in kind to its shareholders, pay, satisfy and discharge its liabilities and obligations and do all other acts required to liquidate its business and affairs, and, after paying or adequately providing for the payment of all its obligations, distribute the remainder of its assets, either in cash or in kind, among its shareholders according to their respective rights and interests.

(c) The corporation, at any time during the liquidation of its business and affairs, may make application to a court of competent jurisdiction within the state and judicial subdivision in which the registered office or principal place of business of the corporation is situated, to have the liquidation continued under the supervision of the court as provided in this Act.

§ 88. Revocation of Voluntary Dissolution Proceedings by Consent of Shareholders

By the written consent of all of its shareholders, a corporation may, at any time prior to the issuance of a certificate of dissolution by the Secretary of State, revoke voluntary dissolution proceedings theretofore taken, in the following manner:

Upon the execution of such written consent, a statement of revocation of voluntary dissolution proceedings shall be executed in duplicate by the corporation by its president or a vice president and by its secretary or an assistant secretary, and verified by one of the officers signing such statement, which statement shall set forth:

(a) The name of the corporation.

(b) The names and respective addresses of its officers.

(c) The names and respective addresses of its directors.

(d) A copy of the written consent signed by all shareholders of the corporation revoking such voluntary dissolution proceedings.

(e) That such written consent has been signed by all shareholders of the corporation or signed in their names by their attorneys thereunto duly authorized.

§ 89. Revocation of Voluntary Dissolution Proceedings by Act of Corporation

By the act of the corporation, a corporation may, at any time prior to the issuance of a certificate of dissolution by the Secretary of State, revoke voluntary dissolution proceedings theretofore taken, in the following manner:

(a) The board of directors shall adopt a resolution recommending that the voluntary dissolution proceedings be revoked, and directing that the question of such revocation be submitted to a vote at a special meeting of shareholders.

(b) Written notice, stating that the purpose or one of the purposes of such meeting is to consider the advisability of revoking the voluntary dissolution proceedings, shall be given to each shareholder of record entitled to vote at such meeting within the time and in the manner provided in this Act for the giving of notice of special meetings of shareholders.

(c) At such meeting a vote of the shareholders entitled to vote thereat shall be taken on a resolution to revoke the voluntary dissolution proceedings, which shall require for its adoption the affirmative vote of the holders of a majority of the shares entitled to vote thereon.

(d) Upon the adoption of such resolution, a statement of revocation of voluntary dissolution proceedings shall be executed in duplicate by the corporation by its president or a vice president and by its secretary or an assistant secretary, and verified by one of the officers signing such statement, which statement shall set forth:

(1) The name of the corporation.
(2) The names and respective addresses of its officers.
(3) The names and respective addresses of its directors.
(4) A copy of the resolution adopted by the shareholders revoking the voluntary dissolution proceedings.
(5) The number of shares outstanding.
(6) The number of shares voted for and against the resolution, respectively.

§ 90. Filing of Statement of Revocation of Voluntary Dissolution Proceedings

Duplicate originals of the statement of revocation of voluntary dissolution proceedings, whether by consent of shareholders or by act of the corporation, shall be delivered to the Secretary of State. If the Secretary of State finds that such statement conforms to law, he shall, when all fees and franchise taxes have been paid as in this Act prescribed:

(a)   Endorse on each of such duplicate originals the word "Filed," and the month, day and year of the filing thereof.

(b)   File one of such duplicate originals in his office.

(c)   Return the other duplicate original to the corporation or its representative.

§ 91. Effect of Statement of Revocation of Voluntary Dissolution Proceedings

Upon the filing by the Secretary of State of a statement of revocation of voluntary dissolution proceedings, whether by consent of shareholders or by act of the corporation, the revocation of the voluntary dissolution proceedings shall become effective and the corporation may again carry on its business.

§ 92. Articles of Dissolution

If voluntary dissolution proceedings have not been revoked, then when all debts, liabilities and obligations of the corporation have been paid and discharged, or adequate provision has been made therefor, and all of the remaining property and assets of the corporation have been distributed to its shareholders, articles of dissolution shall be executed in duplicate by the corporation by its president or a vice president and by its secretary or an assistant secretary, and verified by one of the officers signing such statement, which statement shall set forth:

(a)   The name of the corporation.

(b)   That the Secretary of State has theretofore filed a statement of intent to dissolve the corporation, and the date on which such statement was filed.

(c)   That all debts, obligations and liabilities of the corporation have been paid and discharged or that adequate provision has been made therefor.

(d)   That all the remaining property and assets of the corporation have been distributed among its shareholders in accordance with their respective rights and interests.

(e)   That there are no suits pending against the corporation in any court, or that adequate provision has been made for the satisfaction of any judgment, order or decree which may be entered against it in any pending suit.

§ 93. Filing of Articles of Dissolution

Duplicate originals of such articles of dissolution shall be delivered to the Secretary of State. If the Secretary of State finds that such articles of dissolution conform to law, he shall, when all fees and franchise taxes have been paid as in this Act prescribed:

(a)   Endorse on each of such duplicate originals the word "Filed," and the month, day and year of the filing thereof.

(b)   File one of such duplicate originals in his office.

(c)   Issue a certificate of dissolution to which he shall affix the other duplicate original.

The certificate of dissolution, together with the duplicate original of the articles of dissolution affixed thereto by the Secretary of State, shall be returned to the representative of the dissolved corporation. Upon the issuance of such certificate of dissolution the existence of the corporation shall cease, except for the purpose of suits, other proceedings and appropriate corporate action by shareholders, directors and officers as provided in this Act.

§ 94. Involuntary Dissolution

A corporation may be dissolved involuntarily by a decree of the .... court in an action filed by the Attorney General when it is established that:

(a)   The corporation has failed to file its annual report within the time required by this Act, or has failed to pay its franchise tax on or before the first day of August of the year in which such franchise tax becomes due and payable; or

(b)   The corporation procured its articles of incorporation through fraud; or

(c)   The corporation has continued to exceed or abuse the authority conferred upon it by law; or

(d)   The corporation has failed for thirty days to appoint and maintain a registered agent in this State; or

(e)   The corporation has failed for thirty days after change of its registered office or registered agent to file in the office of the Secretary of State a statement of such change.

§ 95. Notification to Attorney General

The Secretary of State, on or before the last day of December of each year, shall certify to the Attorney General the names of all corporations which have failed to file their annual reports or to pay franchise taxes in accordance with the provisions of this Act, together with the facts pertinent thereto. He shall also certify, from time to time, the names of all corporations which have given other cause for dissolution as provided in this Act, together with the facts pertinent thereto. Whenever the Secretary of State shall certify the name of a corporation to the Attorney General as having given any cause for dissolution, the Secretary of State shall concurrently mail to the corporation at its registered office a notice that such certification has been made. Upon the receipt of such certification, the Attorney General shall file an action in the name of the State against such corporation for its dissolution. Every such certificate from the Secretary of State to the Attorney General pertaining to the failure of a corporation to file an annual report or pay a franchise tax shall be taken and received in all courts as prima facie evidence of the facts therein stated. If, before action is filed, the corporation shall file its annual report or pay its franchise tax, together with all penalties thereon, or shall appoint or maintain a registered agent as provided in this Act, or shall file with the Secretary of State the required statement of change of registered office or registered agent, such fact shall be forthwith certified by the Secretary of State to the Attorney General and he shall not file an action against such corporation for such cause. If, after action is filed, the corporation shall file its annual report or pay its franchise tax, together with all penalties thereon, or shall appoint or maintain a registered agent as provided in this Act, or shall file with the Secretary of State the required statement of change of registered office or registered agent, and shall pay the costs of such action, the action for such cause shall abate.

§ 96. Venue and Process

Every action for the involuntary dissolution of a corporation shall be commenced by the Attorney General either in the .... court of the county in which the registered office of the corporation is situated, or in the .... court of .... county. Summons shall issue and be served as in other civil actions. If process is returned not found, the Attorney General shall cause publication to be made as in other civil cases in some newspaper published in the county where the registered office of the corporation is situated, containing a notice of the pendency of such action, the title of the court, the title of the action, and the date on or after which default may be entered. The Attorney General may include in one notice the names of any number of corporations against which actions are then pending in the same court. The Attorney General shall cause a copy of such notice to be mailed to the corporation at its registered office within ten days after the first publication thereof. The certificate of the Attorney General of the mailing of such notice shall be prima facie evidence thereof. Such notice shall be published at least once each week for two successive weeks, and the first publication thereof may begin at any time after the summons has been returned. Unless a corporation shall have been served with summons, no default shall be taken against it earlier than thirty days after the first publication of such notice.

§ 97. Jurisdiction of Court to Liquidate Assets and Business of Corporation

The .... courts shall have full power to liquidate the assets and business of a corporation:

(a)   In an action by a shareholder when it is established:

(1)   That the directors are deadlocked in the management of the corporate affairs and the shareholders are unable to break the deadlock, and that irreparable injury to the corporation is being suffered or is threatened by reason thereof; or
(2)   That the acts of the directors or those in control of the corporation are illegal, oppressive or fraudulent; or
(3)   That the shareholders are deadlocked in voting power, and have failed, for a period which includes at least two consecutive annual meeting dates, to elect successors to directors whose terms have expired or would have expired upon the election of their successors; or
(4)   That the corporate assets are being misapplied or wasted.

(b)   In an action by a creditor:

(1)   Then the claim of the creditor has been reduced to judgment and an execution thereon returned unsatisfied and it is established that the corporation is insolvent; or

(2)   When the corporation has admitted in writing that the claim of the creditor is due and owing and it is established that the corporation is insolvent.

(c)   Upon application by a corporation which has filed a statement of intent to dissolve, as provided in this Act, to have its liquidation continued under the supervision of the court.

(d)   When an action has been filed by the Attorney General to dissolve a corporation and it is established that liquidation of its business and affairs should precede the entry of a decree of dissolution.

Proceedings under clause (a), (b) or (c) of this section shall be brought in the county in which the registered office or the principal office of the corporation is situated.

It shall not be necessary to make shareholders parties to any such action or proceeding unless relief is sought against them personally.

§ 98. Procedure in Liquidation of Corporation by Court

In proceedings to liquidate the assets and business of a corporation the court shall have power to issue injunctions, to appoint a receiver or receivers pendente lite, with such powers and duties as the court, from time to time, may direct, and to take such other proceedings as may be requisite to preserve the corporate assets wherever situated, and carry on the business of the corporation until a full hearing can be had.

After a hearing had upon such notice as the court may direct to be given to all parties to the proceedings and to any other parties in interest designated by the court, the court may appoint a liquidating receiver or receivers with authority to collect the assets of the corporation, including all amounts owing to the corporation by subscribers on account of any unpaid portion of the consideration for the issuance of shares. Such liquidating receiver or receivers shall have authority, subject to the order of the court, to sell, convey and dispose of all or any part of the assets of the corporation wherever situated, either at public or private sale. The assets of

the corporation or the proceeds resulting from a sale, conveyance or other disposition thereof shall be applied to the expenses of such liquidation and to the payment of the liabilities and obligations of the corporation, and any remaining assets or proceeds shall be distributed among its shareholders according to their respective rights and interests. The order appointing such liquidating receiver or receivers shall state their powers and duties. Such powers and duties may be increased or diminished at any time during the proceedings.

The court shall have power to allow from time to time as expenses of the liquidation compensation to the receiver or receivers and to attorneys in the proceeding, and to direct the payment thereof out of the assets of the corporation or the proceeds of any sale or disposition of such assets.

A receiver of a corporation appointed under the provisions of this section shall have authority to sue and defend in all courts in his own name as receiver of such corporation. The court appointing such receiver shall have exclusive jurisdiction of the corporation and its property, wherever situated.

§ 99. Qualifications of Receivers

A receiver shall in all cases be a natural person or a corporation authorized to act as receiver, which corporation may be a domestic corporation or a foreign corporation authorized to transact business in this State, and shall in all cases give such bond as the court may direct with such sureties as the court may require.

§ 100. Filing of Claims in Liquidation Proceedings

In proceedings to liquidate the assets and business of a corporation the court may require all creditors of the corporation to file with the clerk of the court or with the receiver, in such form as the court may prescribe, proofs under oath of their respective claims. If the court requires the filing of claims it shall fix a date, which shall be not less than four months from the date of the order, as the last day for the filing of claims, and shall prescribe the notice that shall be given to creditors and claimants of the date so fixed. Prior to the date so fixed, the court may extend the time for the filing of claims. Creditors and claimants failing to file proofs of claim on or before the date so fixed may be barred, by order of court, from participating in the distribution of the assets of the corporation.

§ 101. Discontinuance of Liquidation Proceedings

The liquidation of the assets and business of a corporation may be discontinued at any time during the liquidation proceedings when it is established that cause for liquidation no longer exists. In such event the court shall dismiss the proceedings and direct the receiver to redeliver to the corporation all its remaining property and assets.

§ 102. Decree of Involuntary Dissolution

In proceedings to liquidate the assets and business of a corporation, when the costs and expenses of such proceedings and all debts, obligations and liabilities of the corporation shall have been paid and discharged and all of its remaining property and assets distributed to its shareholders, or in case its property and assets are not sufficient to satisfy and discharge such costs, expenses, debts and obligations, all the property and assets have been applied so far as they will go to their payment, the court shall enter a decree dissolving the corporation, whereupon the existence of the corporation shall cease.

§ 103. Filing of Decree of Dissolution

In case the court shall enter a decree dissolving a corporation, it shall be the duty of the clerk of such court to cause a certified copy of the decree to be filed with the Secretary of State. No fee shall be charged by the Secretary of State for the filing thereof.

§ 104. Deposit with State Treasurer of Amount Due Certain Shareholders

Upon the voluntary or involuntary dissolution of a corporation, the portion of the assets distributable to a creditor or shareholder who is unknown or cannot be found, or who is under disability and there is no person legally competent to receive such distributive portion, shall be reduced to cash and deposited with the State Treasurer and shall be paid over to such creditor or shareholder or to his legal representative upon proof satisfactory to the State Treasurer of his right thereto.

§ 105. Survival of Remedy after Dissolution

The dissolution of a corporation either (1) by the issuance of a certificate of dissolution by the Secretary of State, or (2) by a decree of court when the court has not liquidated the assets and business of the corporation as provided in this Act, or (3) by expiration of its period of duration, shall not take away or impair any remedy available to or against such corporation, its directors, officers, or shareholders, for any right or claim existing, or any liability incurred, prior to such dissolution if action or other proceeding thereon is commenced within two years after the date of such dissolution. Any such action or proceeding by or against the corporation may be prosecuted or defended by the corporation in its corporate name. The shareholders, directors and officers shall have power to take such corporate or other action as shall be appropriate to protect such remedy, right or claim. If such corporation was dissolved by the expiration of its period of duration, such corporation may amend its articles of incorporation at any time during such period of two years so as to extend its period of duration.

§ 106. Admission of Foreign Corporation

No foreign corporation shall have the right to transact business in this State until it shall have procured a certificate of authority so to do from the Secretary of State. No foreign corporation shall be entitled to procure a certificate of authority under this Act to transact in this State any business which a corporation organized under this Act is not permitted to transact. A foreign corporation shall not be denied a certificate of authority by reason of the fact that the laws of the state or country under which such corporation is organized governing its organization and internal affairs differ from the laws of this State, and nothing in this Act contained shall be construed to authorize this State to regulate the organization or the internal affairs of such corporation.

Without excluding other activities which may not constitute transacting business in this State, a foreign corporation shall not be considered to be transacting business in this State, for the purposes of this Act, by reason of carrying on in this State any one or more of the following activities:

(a) Maintaining or defending any action or suit or any administrative or arbitration proceeding, or effecting the settlement thereof or the settlement of claims or disputes.

(b) Holding meetings of its directors or shareholders or carrying on other activities concerning its internal affairs.

(c)   Maintaining bank accounts.

(d)   Maintaining offices or agencies for the transfer, exchange and registration of its securities, or appointing and maintaining trustees or depositaries with relation to its securities.

(e)   Effecting sales through independent contractors.

(f)   Soliciting or procuring orders, whether by mail or through employees or agents or otherwise, where such orders require acceptance without this State before becoming binding contracts.

(g)   Creating as borrower or lender, or acquiring, indebtedness or mortgages or other security interests in real or personal property.

(h)   Securing or collecting debts or enforcing any rights in property securing the same.

(i)   Transacting any business in interstate commerce.

(j)   Conducting an isolated transaction completed within a period of thirty days and not in the course of a number of repeated transactions of like nature.

§ 107. Powers of Foreign Corporation

A foreign corporation which shall have received a certificate of authority under this Act shall, until a certificate of revocation or of withdrawal shall have been issued as provided in this Act, enjoy the same, but no greater, rights and privileges as a domestic corporation organized for the purposes set forth in the application pursuant to which such certificate of authority is issued; and, except as in this Act otherwise provided, shall be subject to the same duties, restrictions, penalties and liabilities now or hereafter imposed upon a domestic corporation of like character.

§ 108. Corporate Name of Foreign Corporation

No certificate of authority shall be issued to a foreign corporation unless the corporate name of such corporation:

(a)   Shall contain the word "corporation," "company," "incorporated," or "limited," or shall contain an abbreviation of one of such words, or such corporation shall, for use in this State, add at the end of its name one of such words or an abbreviation thereof.

(b)   Shall not contain any word or phrase which indicates or implies that it is organized for any purpose other than one or more of the purposes contained in its articles of incorporation or that it is authorized or empowered to conduct the business of banking or insurance.

(c)   Shall not be the same as, or deceptively similar to, the name of any domestic corporation existing under the laws of this State or any foreign corporation authorized to transact business in this State, or a name the exclusive right to which is, at the time, reserved in the manner provided in this Act, or the name of a corporation which has in effect a registration of its name as provided in this Act except that this provision shall not apply if the foreign corporation applying for a certificate of authority files with the Secretary of State any one of the following:

> (1)   a resolution of its board of directors adopting a fictitious name for use in transacting business in this State which fictitious name is not deceptively similar to the name of any domestic corporation or of any foreign corporation authorized to transact business in this State or to any name reserved or registered as provided in this Act, or
>
> (2)   the written consent of such other corporation or holder of a reserved or registered name to use the same or deceptively similar name and one or more words are added to make such name distinguishable from such other name, or
>
> (3)   a certified copy of a final decree of a court of competent jurisdiction establishing the prior right of such foreign corporation to the use of such name in this State.

§ 109. Change of Name by Foreign Corporation

Whenever a foreign corporation which is authorized to transact business in this State shall change its name to one under which a certificate of authority would not be granted to it on application therefor, the certificate of authority of such corporation shall be suspended and it shall not thereafter transact any business in this State until it has changed its name to a name which is available to it under the laws of this State or has otherwise complied with the provisions of this Act.

§ 110. Application for Certificate of Authority

A foreign corporation, in order to procure a certificate of authority to transact business in this State, shall make application therefor to the Secretary of State, which application shall set forth:

(a)   The name of the corporation and the state or county under the laws of which it is incorporated.

(b)   If the name of the corporation does not contain the word "corporation," "company," "incorporated," or "limited," or does not contain an abbreviation of one of such words, then the name of the corporation with the word or abbreviation which it elects to add thereto for use in this State.

(c)   The date of incorporation and the period of duration of the corporation.

(d)   The address of the principal office of the corporation in the state or country under the laws of which it is incorporated.

(e)   The address of the proposed registered office of the corporation in this State, and the name of its proposed registered agent in this State at such address.

(f)   The purpose or purposes of the corporation which it proposes to pursue in the transaction of business in this State.

(g)   The names and respective addresses of the directors and officers of the corporation.

(h)   A statement of the aggregate number of shares which the corporation has authority to issue, itemized by classes and series, if any, within a class.

(i)   A statement of the aggregate number of issued shares, itemized by class and by series, if any, within each class.

(j)   An estimate, expressed in dollars, of the value of all property to be owned by the corporation for the following year, wherever located, and an estimate of the value of the property of the corporation to be located within the State during such year, and an estimate, expressed in dollars of the gross amount of business which will be transacted by the corporation during such year, and an estimate of the gross amount thereof which will be transacted by the corporation at or from places of business in this State during such year.

(k)   Such additional information as may be necessary or appropriate in order to enable the Secretary of State to determine whether such corporation is entitled to a certificate of authority to transact business in this State and to determine and assess the fees and franchise taxes payable as in this Act prescribed.

Such application shall be made on forms prescribed and furnished by the Secretary of State and shall be executed in duplicate by the corporation by its president or a vice president and by its secretary or an assistant secretary, and verified by one of the officers signing such application.

§ 111. Filing of Application for Certificate of Authority

Duplicate originals of the application of the corporation for a certificate of authority shall be delivered to the Secretary of State, together with a copy of its articles of incorporation and all amendments thereto, duly authenticated by the proper officer of the state or country under the laws of which it is incorporated.

If the Secretary of State finds that such application conforms to law, he shall, when all fees and franchise taxes have been paid as in this Act prescribed:

(a)   Endorse on each of such documents the word "Filed," and the month, day and year of the filing thereof.

(b)   File in his office one of such duplicate originals of the application and the copy of the articles of incorporation and amendments thereto.

(c)   Issue a certificate of authority to transact business in this State to which he shall affix the other duplicate original application.

The certificate of authority, together with the duplicate original of the application affixed thereto by the Secretary of State, shall be returned to the corporation or its representative.

§ 112. Effect of Certificate of Authority

Upon the issuance of a certificate of authority by the Secretary of State, the corporation shall be authorized to transact business in this State for those purposes set forth in its application, subject, however, to the right of this State to suspend or to revoke such authority as provided in this Act.

§ 113. Registered Office and Registered Agent of Foreign Corporation

Each foreign corporation authorized to transact business in this State shall have and continuously maintain in this State:

(a)   A registered office which may be, but need not be, the same as its place of business in this State.

(b)   A registered agent, which agent may be either an individual resident in this State whose business office is identical with such registered office, or a domestic corporation, or a foreign corporation authorized to transact business in this State, having a business office identical with such registered office.

§ 114. Change of Registered Office or Registered Agent of Foreign Corporation

A foreign corporation authorized to transact business in this State may change its registered office or change its registered agent, or both, upon filing in the office of the Secretary of State a statement setting forth:

(a)   The name of the corporation.

(b)   The address of its then registered office.

(c)   If the address of its registered office be changed, the address to which the registered office is to be changed.

(d)   The name of its then registered agent.

(e)   If its registered agent be changed, the name of its successor registered agent.

(f)   That the address of its registered office and the address of the business office of its registered agent, as changed, will be identical.

(g)   That such change was authorized by resolution duly adopted by its board of directors.

Such statement shall be executed by the corporation by its president or a vice president, and verified by him, and delivered to the Secretary of State. If the Secretary of State finds that such statement conforms to the provisions of this Act, he shall file such statement in his office, and upon such filing the change of address of the registered office, or the appointment of a new registered agent, or both, as the case may be, shall become effective.

Any registered agent of a foreign corporation may resign as such agent upon filing a written notice thereof, executed in duplicate, with the Secretary of State, who shall forthwith mail a copy thereof to the corporation at its principal office in the state or country under the laws of which it is incorporated. The appointment of such agent shall terminate upon the expiration of thirty days after receipt of such notice by the Secretary of State.

If a registered agent changes his or its business address to another place within the same .... *, he or it may change such address and the address of the registered office of any corporation of which he or it is registered agent by filing a statement as required above except that it need be signed only by the registered agent and need not be responsive to (e) or (g) and must recite that a copy of the statement has been mailed to the corporation.

§ 115. Service of Process on Foreign Corporation

The registered agent so appointed by a foreign corporation authorized to transact business in this State shall be an agent of such corporation upon whom any process, notice or demand required or permitted by law to be served upon the corporation may be served.

Whenever a foreign corporation authorized to transact business in this State shall fail to appoint or maintain a registered agent in this State, or whenever any such registered agent cannot with reasonable diligence be found at the registered office, or whenever the certificate of authority of a foreign corporation shall be suspended or revoked, then the Secretary of State shall be an agent of such corporation upon whom any such process, notice, or demand may be served. Service on the Secretary of State of any such process, notice or demand shall be made by delivering to and leaving with him, or with any clerk having charge of the corporation department of his office, duplicate copies of such process, notice or demand. In the event any such process, notice or demand is served on the Secretary of State, he shall immediately cause one of such copies thereof to be forwarded by registered mail, addressed to the corporation at its principal office in the state or country under the laws of which it is incorporated. Any service so had on the Secretary of State shall be returnable in not less than thirty days.

The Secretary of State shall keep a record of all processes, notices and demands served upon him under this section, and shall record therein the time of such service and his action with reference thereto.

Nothing herein contained shall limit or affect the right to serve any process, notice or demand, required

---

*Supply designation of jurisdiction, such as county, etc., in accordance with local practice.

or permitted by law to be served upon a foreign corporation in any other manner now or hereafter permitted by law.

§ 116. Amendment to Articles of Incorporation of Foreign Corporation

Whenever the articles of incorporation of a foreign corporation authorized to transact business in this State are amended, such foreign corporation shall, within thirty days after such amendment becomes effective, file in the office of the Secretary of State a copy of such amendment duly authenticated by the proper officer of the state or country under the laws of which it is incorporated; but the filing thereof shall not of itself enlarge or alter the purpose or purposes which such corporation is authorized to pursue in the transaction of business in this State, nor authorize such corporation to transact business in this State under any other name than the name set forth in its certificate of authority.

§ 117. Merger of Foreign Corporation Authorized to Transact Business in This State

Whenever a foreign corporation authorized to transact business in this State shall be a party to a statutory merger permitted by the laws of the state or country under the laws of which it is incorporated, and such corporation shall be the surviving corporation, it shall, within thirty days after such merger becomes effective, file with the Secretary of State a copy of the articles of merger duly authenticated by the proper officer of the state or country under the laws of which such statutory merger was effected; and it shall not be necessary for such corporation to procure either a new or amended certificate of authority to transact business in this State unless the name of such corporation be changed thereby or unless the corporation desires to pursue in this State other or additional purposes than those which it is then authorized to transact in this State.

§ 118. Amended Certificate of Authority

A foreign corporation authorized to transact business in this State shall procure an amended certificate of authority in the event it changes its corporate name, or desires to pursue in this State other or additional purposes than those set forth in its prior application

for a certificate of authority, by making application therefor to the Secretary of State.

The requirements in respect to the form and contents of such application, the manner of its execution, the filing of duplicate originals thereof with the Secretary of State, the issuance of an amended certificate of authority and the effect thereof, shall be the same as in the case of an original application for a certificate of authority.

§ 119. Withdrawal of Foreign Corporation

A foreign corporation authorized to transact business in this State may withdraw from this State upon procuring from the Secretary of State a certificate of withdrawal. In order to procure such certificate of withdrawal, such foreign corporation shall deliver to the Secretary of State an application for withdrawal, which shall set forth:

(a)   The name of the corporation and the state or country under the laws of which it is incorporated.

(b)   That the corporation is not transacting business in this State.

(c)   That the corporation surrenders its authority to transact business in this State.

(d)   That the corporation revokes the authority of its registered agent in this State to accept service of process and consents that service of process in any action, suit or proceeding based upon any cause of action arising in this State during the time the corporation was authorized to transact business in this State may thereafter be made on such corporation by service thereof on the Secretary of State.

(e)   A post-office address to which the Secretary of State may mail a copy of any process against the corporation that may be served on him.

(f)   A statement of the aggregate number of shares which the corporation has authority to issue, itemized by class and series, if any, within each class, as of the date of such application.

(g)   A statement of the aggregate number of issued shares, itemized by class and series, if any, within each class, as of the date of such application.

(h)   Such additional information as may be necessary or appropriate in order to enable the Secretary of

State to determine and assess any unpaid fees or franchise taxes payable by such foreign corporation as in this Act prescribed.

The application for withdrawal shall be made on forms prescribed and furnished by the Secretary of State and shall be executed by the corporation by its president or a vice president and by its secretary or an assistant secretary, and verified by one of the officers signing the application, or, if the corporation is in the hands of a receiver or trustee, shall be executed on behalf of the corporation by such receiver or trustee and verified by him.

§ 120. Filing of Application for Withdrawal

Duplicate originals of such application for withdrawal shall be delivered to the Secretary of State. If the Secretary of State finds that such application conforms to the provisions of this Act, he shall, when all fees and franchise taxes have been paid as in this Act prescribed:

(a)　Endorse on each of such duplicate originals the word "Filed," and the month, day and year of the filing thereof.

(b)　File one of such duplicate originals in his office.

(c)　Issue a certificate of withdrawal to which he shall affix the other duplicate original.

The certificate of withdrawal, together with the duplicate original of the application for withdrawal affixed thereto by the Secretary of State, shall be returned to the corporation or its representative. Upon the issuance of such certificate of withdrawal, the authority of the corporation to transact business in this State shall cease.

§ 121. Revocation of Certificate of Authority

The certificate of authority of a foreign corporation to transact business in this State may be revoked by the Secretary of State upon the conditions prescribed in this section when:

(a)　The corporation has failed to file its annual report within the time required by this Act, or has failed to pay any fees, franchise taxes or penalties prescribed by this Act when they have become due and payable; or

(b)　The corporation has failed to appoint and maintain a registered agent in this State as required by this Act; or

(c)　The corporation has failed, after change of its registered office or registered agent, to file in the office of the Secretary of State a statement of such change as required by this Act; or

(d)　The corporation has failed to file in the office of the Secretary of State any amendment to its articles of incorporation or any articles of merger within the time prescribed by this Act; or

(e)　A misrepresentation has been made of any material matter in any application, report, affidavit, or other document submitted by such corporation pursuant to this Act.

No certificate of authority of a foreign corporation shall be revoked by the Secretary of State unless (1) he shall have given the corporation not less than sixty days' notice thereof by mail addressed to its registered office in this State, and (2) the corporation shall fail prior to revocation to file such annual report, or pay such fees, franchise taxes or penalties, or file the required statement of change of registered agent or registered office, or file such articles of amendment or articles of merger, or correct such misrepresentation.

§ 122. Issuance of Certificate of Revocation

Upon revoking any such certificate of authority, the Secretary of State shall:

(a)　Issue a certificate of revocation in duplicate.

(b)　File one of such certificates in his office.

(c)　Mail to such corporation at its registered office in this State a notice of such revocation accompanied by one of such certificates.

Upon the issuance of such certificate of revocation, the authority of the corporation to transact business in this State shall cease.

§ 123. Application to Corporations Heretofore Authorized to Transact Business in This State

Foreign corporations which are duly authorized to transact business in this State at the time this Act takes effect, for a purpose or purposes for which a corporation might secure such authority under this Act, shall, subject to the limitations set forth in their respective certificates of authority, be entitled to all the rights and privileges applicable to foreign corporations procuring certificates of authority to transact business in this

State under this Act, and from the time this Act takes effect such corporations shall be subject to all the limitations, restrictions, liabilities, and duties prescribed herein for foreign corporations procuring certificates of authority to transact business in this State under this Act.

§ 124. Transacting Business Without Certificate of Authority

No foreign corporation transacting business in this State without a certificate of authority shall be permitted to maintain any action, suit or proceeding in any court of this State, until such corporation shall have obtained a certificate of authority. Nor shall any action, suit or proceeding be maintained in any court of this State by any successor or assignee of such corporation on any right, claim or demand arising out of the transaction of business by such corporation in this State, until a certificate of authority shall have been obtained by such corporation or by a corporation which has acquired all or substantially all of its assets.

The failure of a foreign corporation to obtain a certificate of authority to transact business in this State shall not impair the validity of any contract or act of such corporation, and shall not prevent such corporation from defending any action, suit or proceeding in any court of this State.

A foreign corporation which transacts business in this State without a certificate of authority shall be liable to this State, for the years or parts thereof during which it transacted business in this State without a certificate of authority, in an amount equal to all fees and franchise taxes which would have been imposed by this Act upon such corporation had it duly applied for and received a certificate of authority to transact business in this State as required by this Act and thereafter filed all reports required by this Act, plus all penalties imposed by this Act for failure to pay such fees and franchise taxes. The Attorney General shall bring proceedings to recover all amounts due this State under the provisions of this Section.

§ 125. Annual Report of Domestic and Foreign Corporations

Each domestic corporation, and each foreign corporation authorized to transact business in this State, shall file, within the time prescribed by this Act, an annual report setting forth:

(a)   The name of the corporation and the state or country under the laws of which it is incorporated.

(b)   The address of the registered office of the corporation in this State, and the name of its registered agent in this State at such address, and, in case of a foreign corporation, the address of its principal office in the state or country under the laws of which it is incorporated.

(c)   A brief statement of the character of the business in which the corporation is actually engaged in this State.

(d)   The names and respective addresses of the directors and officers of the corporation.

(e)   A statement of the aggregate number of shares which the corporation has authority to issue, itemized by class and series, if any, within each class.

(f)   A statement of the aggregate number of issued shares, itemized by class and series, if any, within each class.

(g)   A statement, expressed in dollars, of the value of all the property owned by the corporation, wherever located, and the value of the property of the corporation located within this State, and a statement, expressed in dollars, of the gross amount of business transacted by the corporation for the twelve months ended on the thirty-first day of December preceding the date herein provided for the filing of such report and the gross amount thereof transacted by the corporation at or from places of business in this State. If, on the thirty-first day of December preceding the time herein provided for the filing of such report, the corporation had not been in existence for a period of twelve months, or in the case of a foreign corporation had not been authorized to transact business in this State for a period of twelve months, the statement with respect to business transacted shall be furnished for the period between the date of incorporation or the date of its authorization to transact business in this State, as the case may be, and such thirty-first day of December. If all the property of the corporation is located in this State and all of its business is transacted at or from places of business in this State, then the information required by this subparagraph need not be set forth in such report.

(h)   Such additional information as may be necessary or appropriate in order to enable the Secretary of State to determine and assess the proper amount of franchise taxes payable by such corporation.

Such annual report shall be made on forms prescribed and furnished by the Secretary of State, and the information therein contained shall be given as of the date of the execution of the report, except as to the information required by subparagraphs (g) and (h) which shall be given as of the close of business on the thirty-first day of December next preceding the date herein provided for the filing of such report. It shall be executed by the corporation by its president, a vice president, secretary, an assistant secretary, or treasurer, and verified by the officer executing the report, or, if the corporation is in the hands of a receiver or trustee, it shall be executed on behalf of the corporation and verified by such receiver or trustee.

§ 126. Filing of Annual Report of Domestic and Foreign Corporations

Such annual report of a domestic or foreign corporation shall be delivered to the Secretary of State between the first day of January and the first day of March of each year, except that the first annual report of a domestic or foreign corporation shall be filed between the first day of January and the first day of March of the year next succeeding the calendar year in which its certificate of incorporation or its certificate of authority, as the case may be, was issued by the Secretary of State. Proof to the satisfaction of the Secretary of State that prior to the first day of March such report was deposited in the United States mail in a sealed envelope, properly addressed, with postage prepaid, shall be deemed a compliance with this requirement. If the Secretary of State finds that such report conforms to the requirements of this Act, he shall file the same. If he finds that it does not so conform, he shall promptly return the same to the corporation for any necessary corrections, in which event the penalties hereinafter prescribed for failure to file such report within the time hereinabove provided shall not apply, if such report is corrected to conform to the requirements of this Act and returned to the Secretary of State within thirty days from the date on which it was mailed to the corporation by the Secretary of State.

§ 127. Fees, Franchise Taxes and Charges to be Collected by Secretary of State

The Secretary of State shall charge and collect in accordance with the provisions of this Act:

(a)   Fees for filing documents and issuing certificates.

(b)   Miscellaneous charges.

(c)   License fees.

(d)   Franchise taxes.

§ 128. Fees for Filing Documents and Issuing Certificates

The Secretary of State shall charge and collect for:

(a)   Filing articles of incorporation and issuing a certificate of incorporation, ... dollars.

(b)   Filing articles of amendment and issuing a certificate of amendment, ... dollars.

(c)   Filing restated articles of incorporation, ... dollars.

(d)   Filing articles of merger or consolidation and issuing a certificate of merger or consolidation, ... dollars.

(e)   Filing an application to reserve a corporate name, ... dollars.

(f)   Filing a notice of transfer of a reserved corporate name, ... dollars.

(g)   Filing a statement of change of address of registered office or change of registered agent or both, ... dollars.

(h)   Filing a statement of the establishment of a series of shares, ... dollars.

(i)   Filing a statement of intent to dissolve, ... dollars.

(j)   Filing a statement of revocation of voluntary dissolution proceedings, ... dollars.

(k)   Filing articles of dissolution, ... dollars.

(l)   Filing an application of a foreign corporation for a certificate of authority to transact business in this State and issuing a certificate of authority, ... dollars.

(m)   Filing an application of a foreign corporation for an amended certificate of authority to transact business in this State and issuing an amended certificate of authority, ... dollars.

(n)   Filing a copy of an amendment to the articles of incorporation of a foreign corporation holding a certificate of authority to transact business in this State, ... dollars.

(o)   Filing a copy of articles of merger of a foreign corporation holding a certificate of authority to transact business in this State, ... dollars.

(p)   Filing an application for withdrawal of a foreign corporation and issuing a certificate of withdrawal, ... dollars.

(q)   Filing any other statement or report, except an annual report, of a domestic or foreign corporation, ... dollars.

§ 129. Miscellaneous Charges

The Secretary of State shall charge and collect:

(a)   For furnishing a certified copy of any document, instrument, or paper relating to a corporation, ... cents per page and .... dollars for the certificate and affixing the seal thereto.

(b)   At the time of any service of process on him as resident agent of a corporation, ... dollars, which amount may be recovered as taxable costs by the party to the suit or action causing such service to be made if such party prevails in the suit or action.

§ 130. License Fees Payable by Domestic Corporations

The Secretary of State shall charge and collect from each domestic corporation license fees, based upon the number of shares which it will have authority to issue or the increase in the number of shares which it will have authority to issue, at the time of:

(a)   Filing articles of incorporation;

(b)   Filing articles of amendment increasing the number of authorized shares; and

(c)   Filing articles of merger or consolidation increasing the number of authorized shares which the surviving or new corporation, if a domestic corporation, will have the authority to issue above the aggregate number of shares which the constituent domestic corporations and constituent foreign corporations authorized to transact business in this State had authority to issue.

The license fees shall be at the rate of .... cents per share up to and including the first 10,000 authorized shares, ... cents per share for each authorized share in excess of 10,000 shares up to and including 100,000

shares, and .... cents per share for each authorized share in excess of 100,000 shares.

The license fees payable on an increase in the number of authorized shares shall be imposed only on the increased number of shares, and the number of previously authorized shares shall be taken into account in determining the rate applicable to the increased number of authorized shares.

§ 131. License Fees Payable by Foreign Corporations

The Secretary of State shall charge and collect from each foreign corporation license fees, based upon the proportion represented in this State of the number of shares which it has authority to issue or the increase in the number of shares which it has authority to issue, at the time of:

(a)   Filing an application for a certificate of authority to transact business in this State;

(b)   Filing articles of amendment which increased the number of authorized shares; and

(c)   Filing articles of merger or consolidation which increased the number of authorized shares which the surviving or new corporation, if a foreign corporation, has authority to issue above the aggregate number of shares which the constituent domestic corporations and constituent foreign corporations authorized to transact business in this State had authority to issue.

The license fees shall be at the rate of .... cents per share up to and including the first 10,000 authorized shares represented in this State, ... cents per share for each authorized share in excess of 10,000 shares up to and including 100,000 shares represented in this State, and .... cents per share for each authorized share in excess of 100,000 shares represented in this State.

The license fees payable on an increase in the number of authorized shares shall be imposed only on the increased number of such shares represented in this State, and the number of previously authorized shares represented in this State shall be taken into account in determining the rate applicable to the increased number of authorized shares.

The number of authorized shares represented in this State shall be that proportion of its total authorized shares which the sum of the value of its property located in this State and the gross amount of business transacted by it at or from places of business in this State bears to the sum of the value of all of its property, wherever located, and the gross amount of its business, wherever transacted. Such proportion shall be determined from information contained in the application for a certificate of authority to transact business in this State until the filing of an annual report and thereafter from information contained in the latest annual report filed by the corporation.

§ 132. Franchise Taxes Payable by Domestic Corporations

The Secretary of State shall charge and collect from each domestic corporation an initial franchise tax at the time of filing its articles of incorporation at the rate of one-twelfth of one-half of the license fee payable by such corporation under the provisions of this Act at the time of filing its articles of incorporation, for each calendar month, or fraction thereof, between the date of the issuance of the certificate of incorporation by the Secretary of State and the first day of July of the next succeeding calendar year.

The Secretary of State shall charge and collect from each domestic corporation an annual franchise tax, payable in advance for the period from July 1 in each year to July 1 in the succeeding year, beginning July 1 in the calendar year in which such corporation is required to file its first annual report under this Act, (Alternative 1: at the rate of .... per cent of the amount represented in this State of the stated capital of the corporation, as determined in accordance with accounting practices and principles that are reasonable in the circumstances, as disclosed by the latest report filed by the corporation with the Secretary of State) (Alternative 2: at the rate of .... cents per share up to and including the first 10,000 issued and outstanding shares, and .... cents per share for each issued and outstanding share in excess of 10,000 shares up to and including 100,000 shares, and .... cents per share for each issued and outstanding share in excess of 100,000 shares).

[If Alternative 2 is enacted, the following paragraph should be deleted.]

The amount represented in this State of the stated capital of the corporation shall be that proportion of its stated capital which the sum of the value of its property located in this State and the gross amount of business transacted by it at or from places of busi-

ness in this State bears to the sum of the value of all of its property, wherever located, and the gross amount of its business, wherever transacted.

§ 133. Franchise Taxes Payable by Foreign Corporations

The Secretary of State shall charge and collect from each foreign corporation authorized to transact business in this State an initial franchise tax at the time of filing its application for a certificate of authority at the rate of one-twelfth of one-half of the license fee payable by such corporation under the provisions of this Act at the time of filing such application, for each month, or fraction thereof, between the date of the issuance of the certificate of authority by the Secretary of State and the first day of July of the next succeeding calendar year.

The Secretary of State shall charge and collect from each foreign corporation authorized to transact business in this State an annual franchise tax, payable in advance for the period from July 1 in each year to July 1 in the succeeding year, beginning July 1 in the calendar year in which such corporation is required to file its first annual report under this Act, (Alternative 1: at the rate of .... per cent of the amount represented in this State of the stated capital of the corporation, as determined in accordance with accounting practices and principles that are reasonable in the circumstances, as disclosed by the latest annual report filed by the corporation with the Secretary of State) (Alternative 2: at a rate of .... cents per share up to and including the first 10,000 issued and outstanding shares represented in this State, and .... cents per share for each issued and outstanding share in excess of 10,000 shares up to and including 100,000 shares represented in this State, and .... cents per share for each issued and outstanding share in excess of 100,000 shares represented in this State).

[If Alternative 2 is enacted, the following paragraph should be deleted.]

The amount represented in this State of the stated capital of the corporation shall be that proportion of its stated capital which the sum of the value of its property located in this State and the gross amount of business transacted by it at or from places of business in this State bears to the sum of the value of all of its property, wherever located, and the gross amount of its business, wherever transacted.

§ 134. Assessment and Collection of Annual Franchise Taxes

It shall be the duty of the Secretary of State to collect all annual franchise taxes and penalties imposed by, or assessed in accordance with, this Act.

Between the first day of March and the first day of June of each year, the Secretary of State shall assess against each corporation, domestic and foreign, required to file an annual report in such year, the franchise tax payable by it for the period from July 1 of such year to July 1 of the succeeding year in accordance with the provisions of this Act, and, if it has failed to file its annual report within the time prescribed by this Act, the penalty imposed by this Act upon such corporation for its failure so to do; and shall mail a written notice to each corporation against which such tax is assessed, addressed to such corporation at its registered office in this State, notifying the corporation (1) of the amount of franchise tax assessed against it for the ensuing year and the amount of penalty, if any, assessed against it for failure to file its annual report; (2) that objections, if any, to such assessment will be heard by the officer making the assessment on or before the fifteenth day of June of such year, upon receipt of a request from the corporation; and (3) that such tax and penalty shall be payable to the Secretary of State on the first day of July next succeeding the date of the notice. Failure to receive such notice shall not relieve the corporation of its obligation to pay the tax and any penalty assessed, or invalidate the assessment thereof.

The Secretary of State shall have power to hear and determine objections to any assessment of franchise tax at any time after such assessment and, after hearing, to change or modify any such assessment. In the event of any adjustment of franchise tax with respect to which a penalty has been assessed for failure to file an annual report, the penalty shall be adjusted in accordance with the provisions of this Act imposing such penalty.

All annual franchise taxes and all penalties for failure to file annual reports shall be due and payable on the first day of July of each year. If the annual franchise tax assessed against any corporation subject to the provisions of this Act, together with all penalties assessed thereon, shall not be paid to the Secretary of State on or before the thirty-first day of July of the year in which such tax is due and payable, the Secretary of State shall certify such fact to the Attorney General on or before the fifteenth day of

November of such year, whereupon the Attorney General may institute an action against such corporation in the name of this State, in any court of competent jurisdiction, for the recovery of the amount of such franchise tax and penalties, together with the cost of suit, and prosecute the same to final judgment.

For the purpose of enforcing collection, all annual franchise taxes assessed in accordance with this Act, and all penalties assessed thereon and all interest and costs that shall accrue in connection with the collection thereof, shall be a prior and first lien on the real and personal property of the corporation from and including the first day of July of the year when such franchise taxes become due and payable until such taxes, penalties, interest, and costs shall have been paid.

§ 135. Penalties Imposed Upon Corporations

Each corporation, domestic or foreign, that fails or refuses to file its annual report for any year within the time prescribed by this Act shall be subject to a penalty of ten per cent of the amount of the franchise tax assessed against it for the period beginning July 1 of the year in which such report should have been filed. Such penalty shall be assessed by the Secretary of State at the time of the assessment of the franchise tax. If the amount of the franchise tax as originally assessed against such corporation be thereafter adjusted in accordance with the provisions of this Act, the amount of the penalty shall be likewise adjusted to ten per cent of the amount of the adjusted franchise tax. The amount of the franchise tax and the amount of the penalty shall be separately stated in any notice to the corporation with respect thereto.

If the franchise tax assessed in accordance with the provisions of this Act shall not be paid on or before the thirty-first day of July, it shall be deemed to be delinquent, and there shall be added a penalty of one per cent for each month or part of month that the same is delinquent, commencing with the month of August.

Each corporation, domestic or foreign, that fails or refuses to answer truthfully and fully within the time prescribed by this Act interrogatories propounded by the Secretary of State in accordance with the provisions of this Act, shall be deemed to be guilty of a misdemeanor and upon conviction thereof may be fined in any amount not exceeding five hundred dollars.

§ 136. Penalties Imposed Upon Officers and Directors

Each officer and director of a corporation, domestic or foreign, who fails or refuses within the time prescribed by this Act to answer truthfully and fully interrogatories propounded to him by the Secretary of State in accordance with the provisions of this Act, or who signs any articles, statement, report, application or other document filed with the Secretary of State which is known to such officer or director to be false in any material respect, shall be deemed to be guilty of a misdemeanor, and upon conviction thereof may be fined in any amount not exceeding .... dollars.

§ 137. Interrogatories by Secretary of State

The Secretary of State may propound to any corporation, domestic or foreign, subject to the provisions of this Act, and to any officer or director thereof, such interrogatories as may be reasonably necessary and proper to enable him to ascertain whether such corporation has complied with all the provisions of this Act applicable to such corporation. Such interrogatories shall be answered within thirty days after the mailing thereof, or within such additional time as shall be fixed by the Secretary of State, and the answers thereto shall be full and complete and shall be made in writing and under oath. If such interrogatories be directed to an individual they shall be answered by him, and if directed to a corporation they shall be answered by the president, vice president, secretary or assistant secretary thereof. The Secretary of State need not file any document to which such interrogatories relate until such interrogatories be answered as herein provided, and not then if the answers thereto disclose that such document is not in conformity with the provisions of this Act. The Secretary of State shall certify to the Attorney General, for such action as the Attorney General may deem appropriate, all interrogatories and answers thereto which disclose a violation of any of the provisions of this Act.

§ 138. Information Disclosed by Interrogatories

Interrogatories propounded by the Secretary of State and the answers thereto shall not be open to public inspection nor shall the Secretary of State disclose any facts or information obtained therefrom except insofar as his official duty may require the same to be made public or in the event such interrogatories or the answers thereto are required for evidence in any criminal proceedings or in any other action by this State.

§ 139. Powers of Secretary of State

The Secretary of State shall have the power and authority reasonably necessary to enable him to administer this Act efficiently and to perform the duties therein imposed upon him.

§ 140. Appeal from Secretary of State

If the Secretary of State shall fail to approve any articles of incorporation, amendment, merger, consolidation or dissolution, or any other document required by this Act to be approved by the Secretary of State before the same shall be filed in his office, he shall, within ten days after the delivery thereof to him, give written notice of his disapproval to the person or corporation, domestic or foreign, delivering the same, specifying the reasons therefor. From such disapproval such person or corporation may appeal to the .... court of the county in which the registered office of such corporation is, or is proposed to be, situated by filing with the clerk of such court a petition setting forth a copy of the articles or other document sought to be filed and a copy of the written disapproval thereof by the Secretary of State; whereupon the matter shall be tried de novo by the court, and the court shall either sustain the action of the Secretary of State or direct him to take such action as the court may deem proper.

If the Secretary of State shall revoke the certificate of authority to transact business in this State of any foreign corporation, pursuant to the provisions of this Act, such foreign corporation may likewise appeal to the .... court of the county where the registered office of such corporation in this State is situated, by filing with the clerk of such court a petition setting forth a copy of its certificate of authority to transact business in this State and a copy of the notice of revocation given by the Secretary of State; whereupon the matter shall be tried de novo by the court, and the court shall either sustain the action of the Secretary of State or direct him to take such action as the court may deem proper.

Appeals from all final orders and judgments entered by the .... court under this section in review of any ruling or decision of the Secretary of State may be taken as in other civil actions.

§ 141. Certificates and Certified Copies to be Received in Evidence

All certificates issued by the Secretary of State in accordance with the provisions of this Act, and all copies of documents filed in his office in accordance with the provisions of this Act when certified by him, shall be taken and received in all courts, public offices, and official bodies as prima facie evidence of the facts therein stated. A certificate by the Secretary of State under the great seal of this State, as to the existence or non-existence of the facts relating to corporations shall be taken and received in all courts, public offices, and official bodies as prima facie evidence of the existence or non-existence of the facts therein stated.

§ 142. Forms to be Furnished by Secretary of State

All reports required by this Act to be filed in the office of the Secretary of State shall be made on forms which shall be prescribed and furnished by the Secretary of State. Forms for all other documents to be filed in the office of the Secretary of State shall be furnished by the Secretary of State on request therefor, but the use thereof, unless otherwise specifically prescribed in this Act, shall not be mandatory.

§ 143. Greater Voting Requirements

Whenever, with respect to any action to be taken by the shareholders of a corporation, the articles of incorporation require the vote or concurrence of the holders of a greater proportion of the shares, or of any class or series thereof, than required by this Act with respect to such action, the provisions of the articles of incorporation shall control.

§ 144. Waiver of Notice

Whenever any notice is required to be given to any shareholder or director of a corporation under the provisions of this Act or under the provisions of the articles of incorporation or by-laws of the corporation, a waiver thereof in writing signed by the person or persons entitled to such notice, whether before or after the time stated therein, shall be equivalent to the giving of such notice.

§ 145. Action by Shareholders Without a Meeting

Any action required by this Act to be taken at a meeting of the shareholders of a corporation, or any action which may be taken at a meeting of the shareholders, may be taken without a meeting if a consent in writing, setting forth the action so taken, shall be signed by all of the shareholders entitled to vote with respect to the subject matter thereof.

Such consent shall have the same effect as a unanimous vote of shareholders, and may be stated as such in any articles or document filed with the Secretary of State under this Act.

§ 146. Unauthorized Assumption of Corporate Powers

All persons who assume to act as a corporation without authority so to do shall be jointly and severally liable for all debts and liabilities incurred or arising as a result thereof.

§ 147. Application to Existing Corporations

The provisions of this Act shall apply to all existing corporations organized under any general act of this State providing for the organization of corporations for a purpose or purposes for which a corporation might be organized under this Act, where the power has been reserved to amend, repeal or modify the act under which such corporation was organized and where such act is repealed by this Act.

§ 148. Application to Foreign and Interstate Commerce

The provisions of this Act shall apply to commerce with foreign nations and among the several states only insofar as the same may be permitted under the provisions of the Constitution of the United States.

§ 149. Reservation of Power

The ....* shall at all times have power to prescribe such regulations, provisions and limitations as it may deem advisable, which regulations, provisions and limitations shall be binding upon any and all corporations subject to the provisions of this Act, and the ....* shall have power to amend, repeal or modify this Act at pleasure.

§ 150. Effect of Repeal of Prior Acts

The repeal of a prior act by this Act shall not affect any right accrued or established, or any liability or penalty incurred, under the provisions of such act, prior to the repeal thereof.

---

*Insert name of legislative body.

§ 151. Effect of Invalidity of Part of this Act

If a court of competent jurisdiction shall adjudge to be invalid or unconstitutional any clause, sentence, paragraph, section or part of this Act, such judgment or decree shall not affect, impair, invalidate or nullify the remainder of this Act, but the effect thereof shall be confined to the clause, sentence, paragraph, section or part of this Act so adjudged to be invalid or unconstitutional.

§ 152. Exclusivity of Certain Provisions [Optional]

In circumstances to which section 45 and related sections of this Act are applicable, such provisions supersede the applicability of any other statutes of this state with respect to the legality of distributions.

§ 153. Repeal of Prior Acts (Insert appropriate provisions) ....

SPECIAL COMMENTS—CLOSE CORPORATIONS

In view of the increasing importance of close corporations, both for the small family business and for the larger undertakings conducted by some small number of other corporations, this liberalizing trend has now been followed by the 1969 Amendments to the Model Act. The first sentence of section 35, providing that the business of the corporation shall be managed by a board of directors, was supplemented by a new clause "except as may be otherwise provided in the articles of incorporation." This permits the shareholders to take over and exercise the functions of the directors by appropriate provision to that effect in the articles, or to allocate functions between the directors and shareholders in such manner as may be desired. Taken with other provisions of the Model Act, which are here enumerated for convenience, this rounds out the adaptability of the Model Act for all the needs of a close corporation:

(1)   By section 4(*l*) the by-laws may make any provision for the regulation of the affairs of the corporation that is not inconsistent with the articles or the laws of the incorporating state.

(2)   By section 15 shares may be divided into several classes and the articles may limit or deny the voting rights of or provide special voting rights for the shares of any class to the extent not inconsistent with the Model Act. The narrow limits of this exception are revealed by section 33 which provides that each outstanding share, regardless of class, shall be entitled to one vote on each matter submitted to a vote at a meeting of the shareholders "except as may be otherwise provided in the articles of incorporation," thus expressly authorizing more than one vote per share or less than one vote per share, either generally or in respect to particular matters.

(3)   By section 16 item (F) the shares of any preferred or special class may be issued in series and there may be variations between different series in numerous respects, including specifically the matter of voting rights, if any.

(4)   By section 32 the articles may reduce a quorum of shareholders to not less than one-third of the shares entitled to vote, or leave the quorum at the standard of a majority or, as confirmed by section 143, increase the number to any desired point.

(5)   By section 34 agreements among shareholders regarding the voting of their shares are made valid and enforceable in accordance with their terms without limitation in time. These could relate to the election or compensation of directors or officers or the creation of various types of securities for new financing or the conduct of business of various kinds or dividend policy or mergers and consolidations or other transactions without limit.

(6)   The flexibility permitted by the revision of section 35 in the distribution or reallocation of authority among directors and stockholders has already been mentioned.

(7)   Under section 36 the number of directors may be fixed by the by-laws at one or such greater number as may best serve the interests of the shareholders and that number may be increased or decreased from time to time by amendment to, or in the manner provided in, the articles or the by-laws, subject to any limiting provision adopted pursuant to law, such as an agreed requirement for a unanimous vote by directors for any such change or a requirement that amendments to the by-laws be made by shareholder vote. Similarly, under section 53, the incorporation may be effected by a single incorporator or by more as may be desired.

(8)   By section 37 directors may be classified. While this relates to directors classified in such manner that the term of office of a specified proportion terminates in each year, the Model Act does not forbid the election of separate directors by separate classes of stock.

(9) Section 40 permits the articles or the by-laws to require more than a majority of the directors to constitute a quorum for the transaction of business and also permits the articles or by-laws to require the act of a greater number than a majority of those present at a meeting where a quorum is present before any specified business may be transacted. Or a unanimous vote of all directors may be required. This may be utilized to confer a right of veto on any designated class in order to protect its special interests.

(10) By section 50 the authority and duties of the respective officers and agents of the corporation may be tailored and prescribed in the by-laws, or consistently with the by-laws, in such manner as the needs of the shareholders may indicate.

(11) By section 54 the articles may include any desired provision for the regulation of the internal affairs of the corporation, including, in particular, "any provision restricting the transfer of shares." This expressly validates agreements for prior offering of shares to the corporation or other shareholders. All such restrictions must, of course, be clearly shown on the stock certificate as required by the Uniform Commercial Code. A similarly broad provision for the contents of the by-laws is contained in section 27.

(12) By sections 60, 73 and 79, respectively, a class vote may be required for an amendment to the articles, for any merger or consolidation or for a sale of assets other than in the regular course of business.

(13) Section 143 permits the articles to require, for any particular action by the shareholders, the vote or concurrence of the holders of a greater proportion of the shares, or of any class or series thereof, than the Model Act itself requires.

(14) Section 44 permits action by directors without a meeting and section 145 permits the same for shareholders, while section 144 contains a broad provision on waiver of notice. Thus the formality of meetings may, where desired, be eliminated in whole or in part, except for the annual meeting required by section 28.

Under these provisions protection may be afforded for a great diversity of interests. By way of illustration, the shares may be divided into different classes with different voting rights and each class may be permitted to elect a different director. Or some classes may be permitted to vote on certain transactions, but not all. Even more drastically, some classes may be denied all voting rights whatever. Thus a family could provide for equal participation in the profits of the venture, but restrict the power of management to selected members. The advantages of having a known group of business associates may be safeguarded by restrictions on the transfer of shares. Most commonly this takes the form of a requirement for pro rata offering to the other shareholders before selling to an outsider. Or the other shareholders may be given an option, in the event of death or a proposed transfer, to buy the stock pro rata. The same option may be given to the corporation. The purchase price may be fixed by any agreed formula, such as adjusted book value or some multiple of recent earnings. Or stockholder agreements may be used to assure that, at least for a limited number of years, all shares will be voted for certain directors and officers, or in a certain way on other corporate matters. Cumulative voting may be provided for, by which each shareholder has a number of votes equal to the number of his shares multiplied by the number of directors to be elected, with the privilege of casting all of his votes for a single candidate, or dividing them as he may wish. This helps minorities obtain representation on the board of directors. Thus the holder of one-fourth of the shares voting, plus one share, is sure of electing one of three directors. The preemptive right is another important protection in the case of close corporations, since it assures each stockholder a right to maintain his proportionate interest. Still more definite protection is afforded by provisions in the articles that prohibit particular transactions except with the assent of a specified percentage of all outstanding shares or of each class of shares. Much the same protection can sometimes be obtained by requiring a specially large quorum for the election of directors, or a specially large vote, or even unanimous vote, by directors for the authorization of particular transactions. Quite the opposite situation exists if one of the participants is to be an inactive investor, for whom non-voting preferred stock, with its prior right to a return from earnings, may be sufficient. But even here he may require a veto power over major transactions, such as the issuance of debt, the issuance of additional preferred shares or mergers or consolidations. Or the preferred shareholders may be given as a class the right to elect one or more of the directors, particularly in the event that dividends should be in arrears.

These possibilities are listed merely as illustrations and not in any sense as exhausting the variations permissible under the Model Act.

The Uniform Partnership Act

(Adopted in 49 States [all of the states except Louisiana], the District of Columbia, the Virgin Islands, and Guam. The adoptions by Alabama and Nebraska do not follow the official text in every respect, but are substantially similar, with local variations.)

The Act consists of 7 Parts as follows:

I. Preliminary Provisions
II. Nature of Partnership
III. Relations of Partners to Persons Dealing with the Partnership
IV. Relations of Partners to One Another
V. Property Rights of a Partner
VI. Dissolution and Winding Up
VII. Miscellaneous Provisions

An Act to make uniform the Law of Partnerships
Be it enacted, etc.:

PART I
PRELIMINARY PROVISIONS

§ 1. Name of Act
This act may be cited as Uniform Partnership Act.

§ 2. Definition of Terms
In this act, "Court" includes every court and judge having jurisdiction in the case.

"Business" includes every trade, occupation, or profession.

"Person" includes individuals, partnerships, corporations, and other associations.

"Bankrupt" includes bankrupt under the Federal Bankruptcy Act or insolvent under any state insolvent act.

"Conveyance" includes every assignment, lease, mortgage, or encumbrance.

"Real property" includes land and any interest or estate in land.

§ 3. Interpretation of Knowledge and Notice
(1) A person has "knowledge" of a fact within the meaning of this act not only when he has actual knowledge thereof, but also when he has knowledge of such other facts as in the circumstances shows bad faith.

(2) A person has "notice" of a fact within the meaning of this act when the person who claims the benefit of the notice:
(a) States the fact to such person, or
(b) Delivers through the mail, or by other means of communication, a written statement of the fact to such person or to a proper person at his place of business or residence.

§ 4. Rules of Construction
(1) The rule that statutes in derogation of the common law are to be strictly construed shall have no application to this act.
(2) The law of estoppel shall apply under this act.
(3) The law of agency shall apply under this act.
(4) This act shall be so interpreted and construed as to effect its general purpose to make uniform the law of those states which enact it.
(5) This act shall not be construed so as to impair the obligations of any contract existing when the act goes into effect, nor to affect any action or proceedings begun or right accrued before this act takes effect.

§ 5. Rules for Cases Not Provided for in this Act.
In any case not provided for in this act the rules of law and equity, including the law merchant, shall govern.

PART II
NATURE OF PARTNERSHIP

§ 6. Partnership Defined
(1) A partnership is an association of two or more persons to carry on as co-owners a business for profit.
(2) But any association formed under any other statute of this state, or any statute adopted by authority, other than the authority of this state, is

not a partnership under this act, unless such association would have been a partnership in this state prior to the adoption of this act; but this act shall apply to limited partnerships except in so far as the statutes relating to such partnerships are inconsistent herewith.

§ 7. Rules for Determining the Existence of a Partnership

In determining whether a partnership exists, these rules shall apply:

(1) Except as provided by Section 16 persons who are not partners as to each other are not partners as to third persons.

(2) Joint tenancy, tenancy in common, tenancy by the entireties, joint property, common property, or part ownership does not of itself establish a partnership, whether such co-owners do or do not share any profits made by the use of the property.

(3) The sharing of gross returns does not of itself establish a partnership, whether or not the persons sharing them have a joint or common right or interest in any property from which the returns are derived.

(4) The receipt by a person of a share of the profits of a business is prima facie evidence that he is a partner in the business, but no such inference shall be drawn if such profits were received in payment:

   (a) As a debt by installments or otherwise,

   (b) As wages of an employee or rent to a landlord,

   (c) As an annuity to a widow or representative of a deceased partner,

   (d) As interest on a loan, though the amount of payment varies with the profits of the business.

   (e) As the consideration for the sale of a good-will of a business or other property by installments or otherwise.

§ 8. Partnership Property

(1) All property originally brought into the partnership stock or subsequently acquired by purchase or otherwise, on account of the partnership, is partnership property.

(2) Unless the contrary intention appears, property acquired with partnership funds is partnership property.

(3) Any estate in real property may be acquired in the partnership name. Title so acquired can be conveyed only in the partnership name.

(4) A conveyance to a partnership in the partnership name, though without words of inheritance, passes the entire estate of the grantor unless a contrary intent appears.

PART III

RELATIONS OF PARTNERS TO PERSONS DEALING WITH THE PARTNERSHIP

§ 9. Partner Agent of Partnership as to Partnership Business

(1) Every partner is an agent of the partnership for the purpose of its business, and the act of every partner, including the execution in the partnership name of any instrument, for apparently carrying on in the usual way the business of the partnership of which he is a member binds the partnership, unless the partner so acting has in fact no authority to act for the partnership in the particular matter, and the person with whom he is dealing has knowledge of the fact that he has no such authority.

(2) An act of a partner which is not apparently for the carrying on of the business of the partnership in the usual way does not bind the partnership unless authorized by the other partners.

(3) Unless authorized by the other partners or unless they have abandoned the business, one or more but less than all the partners have no authority to:

   (a) Assign the partnership property in trust for creditors or on the assignee's promise to pay the debts of the partnership,

   (b) Dispose of the good-will of the business,

   (c) Do any other act which would make it impossible to carry on the ordinary business of a partnership,

   (d) Confess a judgment,

   (e) Submit a partnership claim or liability to arbitration or reference.

(4) No act of a partner in contravention of a restriction on authority shall bind the partnership to persons having knowledge of the restriction.

§ 10. Conveyance of Real Property of the Partnership

(1) Where title to real property is in the partnership name, any partner may convey title to such property by a conveyance executed in the partnership

name; but the partnership may recover such property unless the partner's act binds the partnership under the provisions of paragraph (1) of section 9, or unless such property has been conveyed by the grantee or a person claiming through such grantee to a holder for value without knowledge that the partner, in making the conveyance, has exceeded his authority.

(2) Where title to real property is in the name of the partnership, a conveyance executed by a partner, in his own name, passes the equitable interest of the partnership, provided the act is one within the authority of the partner under the provisions of paragraph (1) of section 9.

(3) Where title to real property is in the name of one or more but not all the partners, and the record does not disclose the right of the partnership, the partners in whose name the title stands may convey title to such property, but the partnership may recover such property if the partners' act does not bind the partnership under the provisions of paragraph (1) of section 9, unless the purchaser or his assignee, is a holder for value, without knowledge.

(4) Where the title to real property is in the name of one or more or all the partners, or in a third person in trust for the partnership, a conveyance executed by a partner in the partnership name, or in his own name, passes the equitable interest of the partnership, provided the act is one within the authority of the partner under the provisions of paragraph (1) of section 9.

(5) Where the title to real property is in the names of all the partners a conveyance executed by all the partners passes all their rights in such property.

§ 11. Partnership Bound by Admission of Partner

An admission or representation made by any partner concerning partnership affairs within the scope of his authority as conferred by this act is evidence against the partnership.

§ 12. Partnership Charged with Knowledge of or Notice to Partner

Notice to any partner of any matter relating to partnership affairs, and the knowledge of the partner acting in the particular matter, acquired while a partner or then present to his mind, and the knowledge of any other partner who reasonably could and should have communicated it to the acting partner, operate as notice to or knowledge of the partnership, except in the case of a fraud on the partnership committed by or with the consent of that partner.

§ 13. Partnership Bound by Partner's Wrongful Act

Where, by any wrongful act or omission of any partner acting in the ordinary course of the business of the partnership or with the authority of his co-partners, loss or injury is caused to any person, not being a partner in the partnership, or any penalty is incurred, the partnership is liable therefor to the same extent as the partner so acting or omitting to act.

§ 14. Partnership Bound by Partner's Breach of Trust

The partnership is bound to make good the loss:

(a) Where one partner acting within the scope of his apparent authority receives money or property of a third person and misapplies it; and

(b) Where the partnership in the course of its business receives money or property of a third person and the money or property so received is misapplied by any partner while it is in the custody of the partnership.

§ 15. Nature of Partner's Liability

All partners are liable

(a) Jointly and severally for everything chargeable to the partnership under sections 13 and 14.

(b) Jointly for all other debts and obligations of the partnership; but any partner may enter into a separate obligation to perform a partnership contract.

§ 16. Partner by Estoppel

(1) When a person, by words spoken or written or by conduct, represents himself, or consents to another representing him to any one, as a partner in an existing partnership or with one or more persons not actual partners, he is liable to any such person to whom such representation has been made, who has, on the faith of such representation, given credit to the actual or apparent partnership, and if he has made such representation or consented to its being made in a public manner he is liable to such person, whether the representation has or has not been made or communicated to such person so giving credit by or with the knowledge of the apparent

partner making the representation or consenting to its being made.

    (a) When a partnership liability results, he is liable as though he were an actual member of the partnership.

    (b) When no partnership liability results, he is liable jointly with the other persons, if any, so consenting to the contract or representation as to incur liability, otherwise separately.

(2) When a person has been thus represented to be a partner in an existing partnership, or with one or more persons not actual partners, he is an agent of the persons consenting to such representation to bind them to the same extent and in the same manner as though he were a partner in fact, with respect to persons who rely upon the representation. Where all the members of the existing partnership consent to the representation, a partnership act or obligation results; but in all other cases it is the joint act or obligation of the person acting and the persons consenting to the representation.

§ 17. Liability of Incoming Partner
A person admitted as a partner into an existing partnership is liable for all the obligations of the partnership arising before his admission as though he had been a partner when such obligations were incurred, except that this liability shall be satisfied only out of partnership property.

PART IV
RELATIONS OF PARTNERS TO ONE ANOTHER
§ 18. Rules Determining Rights and Duties of Partners
The rights and duties of the partners in relation to the partnership shall be determined, subject to any agreement between them, by the following rules:

(a) Each partner shall be repaid his contributions, whether by way of capital or advances to the partnership property and share equally in the profits and surplus remaining after all liabilities, including those to partners, are satisfied; and must contribute towards the losses, whether of capital or otherwise, sustained by the partnership according to his share in the profits.

(b) The partnership must indemnify every partner in respect of payments made and personal liabilities reasonably incurred by him in the ordinary and proper conduct of its business, or for the preservation of its business or property.

(c) A partner, who in aid of the partnership makes any payment or advance beyond the amount of capital which he agreed to contribute, shall be paid interest from the date of the payment or advance.

(d) A partner shall receive interest on the capital contributed by him only from the date when repayment should be made.

(e) All partners have equal rights in the management and conduct of the partnership business.

(f) No partner is entitled to remuneration for acting in the partnership business, except that a surviving partner is entitled to reasonable compensation for his services in winding up the partnership affairs.

(g) No person can become a member of a partnership without the consent of all the partners.

(h) Any difference arising as to ordinary matters connected with the partnership business may be decided by a majority of the partners; but no act in contravention of any agreement between the partners may be done rightfully without the consent of all the partners.

§ 19. Partnership Books
The partnership books shall be kept, subject to any agreement between the partners, at the principal place of business of the partnership, and every partner shall at all times have access to and may inspect and copy any of them.

§ 20. Duty of Partners to Render Information
Partners shall render on demand true and full information of all things affecting the partnership to any partner or the legal representative of any deceased partner or partner under legal disability.

§ 21. Partner Accountable as a Fiduciary
(1) Every partner must account to the partnership for any benefit, and hold as trustee for it any profits derived by him without the consent of the other partners from any transaction connected with the formation, conduct, or liquidation of the partnership or from any use by him of its property.

(2) This section applies also to the representatives of a deceased partner engaged in the liquidation of

the affairs of the partnership as the personal representatives of the last surviving partner.

§ 22. Right to an Account

Any partner shall have the right to a formal account as to partnership affairs:

(a) If he is wrongfully excluded from the partnership business or possession of its property by his co-partners,

(b) If the right exists under the terms of any agreement,

(c) As provided by section 21,

(d) Whenever other circumstances render it just and reasonable.

§ 23. Continuation of Partnership Beyond Fixed Term

(1) When a partnership for a fixed term or particular undertaking is continued after the termination of such term or particular undertaking without any express agreement, the rights and duties of the partners remain the same as they were at such termination, so far as is consistent with a partnership at will.

(2) A continuation of the business by the partners or such of them as habitually acted therein during the term, without any settlement or liquidation of the partnership affairs, is prima facie evidence of a continuation of the partnership.

PART V
PROPERTY RIGHTS OF A PARTNER

§ 24. Extent of Property Rights of a Partner

The property rights of a partner are (1) his rights in specific partnership property, (2) his interest in the partnership, and (3) his right to participate in the management.

§ 25. Nature of a Partner's Right in Specific Partnership Property

(1) A partner is co-owner with his partners of specific partnership property holding as a tenant in partnership.

(2) The incidents of this tenancy are such that:

(a) A partner, subject to the provisions of this act and to any agreement between the partners, has an equal right with his partners to possess specific partnership property for partnership purposes; but he has no right to possess such property for any other purpose without the consent of his partners.

(b) A partner's right in specific partnership property is not assignable except in connection with the assignment of rights of all the partners in the same property.

(c) A partner's right in specific partnership property is not subject to attachment or execution, except on a claim against the partnership. When partnership property is attached for a partnership debt the partners, or any of them, or the representatives of a deceased partner, cannot claim any right under the homestead or exemption laws.

(d) On the death of a partner his right in specific partnership property vests in the surviving partner or partners, except where the deceased was the last surviving partner, when his right in such property vests in his legal representative. Such surviving partner or partners, or the legal representative of the last surviving partner, has no right to possess the partnership property for any but a partnership purpose.

(e) A partner's right in specific partnership property is not subject to dower, curtesy, or allowances to widows, heirs, or next of kin.

§ 26. Nature of Partner's Interest in the Partnership

A partner's interest in the partnership is his share of the profits and surplus, and the same is personal property.

§ 27. Assignment of Partner's Interest

(1) A conveyance by a partner of his interest in the partnership does not of itself dissolve the partnership, nor, as against the other partners in the absence of agreement, entitle the assignee, during the continuance of the partnership, to interfere in the management or administration of the partnership business or affairs, or to require any information or account of partnership transactions, or to inspect the partnership books; but it merely entitles the assignee to receive in accordance with his contract the profits to which the assigning partner would otherwise be entitled.

(2) In case of a dissolution of the partnership, the assignee is entitled to receive his assignor's interest and may require an account from the date only of the last account agreed to by all the partners.

§ 28. Partner's Interest Subject to Charging Order

(1) On due application to a competent court by any judgment creditor of a partner, the court which entered the judgment, order, or decree, or any other court, may charge the interest of the debtor partner with payment of the unsatisfied amount of such judgment debt with interest thereon; and may then or later appoint a receiver of his share of the profits, and of any other money due or to fall due to him in respect of the partnership, and make all other orders, directions, accounts and inquiries which the debtor partner might have made, or which the circumstances of the case may require.

(2) The interest charged may be redeemed at any time before foreclosure, or in case of a sale being directed by the court may be purchased without thereby causing a dissolution:

    (a) With separate property, by any one or more of the partners, or

    (b) With partnership property, by any one or more of the partners with the consent of all the partners whose interests are not so charged or sold.

(3) Nothing in this act shall be held to deprive a partner of his right, if any, under the exemption laws, as regards his interest in the partnership.

PART VI
DISSOLUTION AND WINDING UP
§ 29. Dissolution Defined

The dissolution of a partnership is the change in the relation of the partners caused by any partner ceasing to be associated in the carrying on as distinguished from the winding up of the business.

§ 30. Partnership not Terminated by Dissolution

On dissolution the partnership is not terminated, but continues until the winding up of partnership affairs is completed.

§ 31. Causes of Dissolution

Dissolution is caused:

(1) Without violation of the agreement between the partners,

    (a) By the termination of the definite term or particular undertaking specified in the agreement,

    (b) By the express will of any partner when no definite term or particular undertaking is specified,

    (c) By the express will of all the partners who have not assigned their interests or suffered them to be charged for their separate debts, either before or after the termination of any specified term or particular undertaking,

    (d) By the expulsion of any partner from the business bona fide in accordance with such a power conferred by the agreement between the partners;

(2) In contravention of the agreement between the partners, where the circumstances do not permit a dissolution under any other provision of this section, by the express will of any partner at any time;

(3) By any event which makes it unlawful for the business of the partnership to be carried on or for the members to carry it on in partnership;

(4) By the death of any partner;

(5) By the bankruptcy of any partner or the partnership;

(6) By decree of court under section 32.

§ 32. Dissolution by Decree of Court

(1) On application by or for a partner the court shall decree a dissolution whenever:

    (a) A partner has been declared a lunatic in any judicial proceeding or is shown to be of unsound mind,

    (b) A partner becomes in any other way incapable of performing his part of the partnership contract,

    (c) A partner has been guilty of such conduct as tends to affect prejudicially the carrying on of the business,

    (d) A partner wilfully or persistently commits a breach of the partnership agreement, or otherwise so conducts himself in matters relating to the partnership business that it is not reasonably practicable to carry on the business in partnership with him,

    (e) The business of the partnership can only be carried on at a loss,

    (f) Other circumstances render a dissolution equitable.

(2) On the application of the purchaser of a partner's interest under sections 28 or 29 [should read 27 or 28];

(a) After the termination of the specified term or particular undertaking,

(b) At any time if the partnership was a partnership at will when the interest was assigned or when the charging order was issued.

§ 33. General Effect of Dissolution on Authority of Partner

Except so far as may be necessary to wind up partnership affairs or to complete transactions begun but not then finished, dissolution terminates all authority of any partner to act for the partnership,

(1) With respect to the partners,

(a) When the dissolution is not by the act, bankruptcy or death of a partner; or

(b) When the dissolution is by such act, bankruptcy or death of a partner, in cases where section 34 so requires.

(2) With respect to persons not partners, as declared in section 35.

§ 34. Rights of Partner to Contribution from Co-partners After Dissolution

Where the dissolution is caused by the act, death or bankruptcy of a partner, each partner is liable to his co-partners for his share of any liability created by any partner acting for the partnership as if the partnership had not been dissolved unless

(a) The dissolution being by act of any partner, the partner acting for the partnership had knowledge of the dissolution, or

(b) The dissolution being by the death or bankruptcy of a partner, the partner acting for the partnership had knowledge or notice of the death or bankruptcy.

§ 35. Power of Partner to Bind Partnership to Third Persons After Dissolution

(1) After dissolution a partner can bind the partnership except as provided in Paragraph (3).

(a) By any act appropriate for winding up partnership affairs or completing transactions unfinished at dissolution;

(b) By any transaction which would bind the partnership if dissolution had not taken place, provided the other party to the transaction

(I) Had extended credit to the partnership prior to dissolution and had no knowledge or notice of the dissolution; or

(II) Though he had not so extended credit, had nevertheless known of the partnership prior to dissolution, and, having no knowledge or notice of dissolution, the fact of dissolution had not been advertised in a newspaper of general circulation in the place (or in each place if more than one) at which the partnership business was regularly carried on.

(2) The liability of a partner under paragraph (1b) shall be satisfied out of partnership assets alone when such partner had been prior to dissolution

(a) Unknown as a partner to the person with whom the contract is made; and

(b) So far unknown and inactive in partnership affairs that the business reputation of the partnership could not be said to have been in any degree due to his connection with it.

(3) The partnership is in no case bound by any act of a partner after dissolution

(a) Where the partnership is dissolved because it is unlawful to carry on the business, unless the act is appropriate for winding up partnership affairs; or

(b) Where the partner has become bankrupt; or

(c) Where the partner has no authority to wind up partnership affairs; except by a transaction with one who

(I) Had extended credit to the partnership prior to dissolution and had no knowledge or notice of his want of authority; or

(II) Had not extended credit to the partnership prior to dissolution, and, having no knowledge or notice of his want of authority, the fact of his want of authority has not been advertised in the manner provided for advertising the fact of dissolution in paragraph (1bII).

(4) Nothing in this section shall affect the liability under Section 16 of any person who after dissolution represents himself or consents to another representing him as a partner in a partnership engaged in carrying on business.

§ 36. Effect of Dissolution on Partner's Existing Liability

(1) The dissolution of the partnership does not of itself discharge the existing liability of any partner.

(2) A partner is discharged from any existing liability upon dissolution of the partnership by an agreement to that effect between himself, the partnership creditor and the person or partnership continuing the business; and such agreement may be inferred from the course of dealing between the creditor having knowledge of the dissolution and the person or partnership continuing the business.

(3) Where a person agrees to assume the existing obligations of a dissolved partnership, the partners whose obligations have been assumed shall be discharged from any liability to any creditor of the partnership who, knowing of the agreement, consents to a material alteration in the nature or time of payment of such obligations.

(4) The individual property of a deceased partner shall be liable for all obligations of the partnership incurred while he was a partner but subject to the prior payment of his separate debts.

§ 37. Right to Wind Up

Unless otherwise agreed the partners who have not wrongfully dissolved the partnership or the legal representative of the last surviving partner, not bankrupt, has the right to wind up the partnership affairs; provided, however, that any partner, his legal representative or his assignee, upon cause shown, may obtain winding up by the court.

§ 38. Rights of Partners to Application of Partnership Property

(1) When dissolution is caused in any way, except in contravention of the partnership agreement, each partner, as against his co-partners and all persons claiming through them in respect of their interests in the partnership, unless otherwise agreed, may have the partnership property applied to discharge its liabilities, and the surplus applied to pay in cash the net amount owing to the respective partners. But if dissolution is caused by expulsion of a partner, bona fide under the partnership agreement and if the expelled partner is discharged from all partnership liabilities, either by payment or agreement under section 36(2), he shall receive in cash only the net amount due him from the partnership.

(2) When dissolution is caused in contravention of the partnership agreement the rights of the partners shall be as follows:

(a) Each partner who has not caused dissolution wrongfully shall have,

    (I) All the rights specified in paragraph (1) of this section, and

    (II) The right, as against each partner who has caused the dissolution wrongfully, to damages for breach of the agreement.

(b) The partners who have not caused the dissolution wrongfully, if they all desire to continue the business in the same name, either by themselves or jointly with others, may do so, during the agreed term for the partnership and for that purpose may possess the partnership property, provided they secure the payment by bond approved by the court, or pay to any partner who has caused the dissolution wrongfully, the value of his interest in the partnership at the dissolution, less any damages recoverable under clause (2a II) of the section, and in like manner indemnify him against all present or future partnership liabilities.

(c) A partner who has caused the dissolution wrongfully shall have:

    (I) If the business is not continued under the provisions of paragraph (2b) all the rights of a partner under paragraph (1), subject to clause (2aII), of this section,

    (II) If the business is continued under paragraph (2b) of this section the right as against his co-partners and all claiming through them in respect of their interests in the partnership, to have the value of his interest in the partnership, less any damages caused to his co-partners by the dissolution, ascertained and paid to him in cash, or the payment secured by bond approved by the court, and to be released from all existing liabilities of the partnership; but in ascertaining the value of the partner's interest the value of the good-will of the business shall not be considered.

§ 39. Rights Where Partnership is Dissolved for Fraud or Misrepresentation

Where a partnership contract is rescinded on the ground of the fraud or misrepresentation of one of the parties thereto, the party entitled to rescind is, without prejudice to any other right, entitled,

(a) To a lien on, or right of retention of, the surplus of the partnership property after satisfying the partnership liabilities to third persons for any sum of money paid by him for the purchase of an interest in the partnership and for any capital or advances contributed by him; and

(b) To stand, after all liabilities to third persons have been satisfied, in the place of the creditors of the partnership for any payments made by him in respect of the partnership liabilities; and

(c) To be indemnified by the person guilty of the fraud or making the representation against all debts and liabilities of the partnership.

§ 40. Rules for Distribution

In settling accounts between the partners after dissolution, the following rules shall be observed, subject to any agreement to the contrary:

(a) The assets of the partnership are:

   (I) The partnership property,
   (II) The contributions of the partners necessary for the payment of all the liabilities specified in clause (b) of this paragraph.

(b) The liabilities of the partnership shall rank in order of payment, as follows:

   (I) Those owing to creditors other than partners,
   (II) Those owing to partners other than for capital and profits,
   (III) Those owing to partners in respect of capital,
   (IV) Those owing to partners in respect of profits.

(c) The assets shall be applied in the order of their declaration in clause (a) of this paragraph to the satisfaction of the liabilities.

(d) The partners shall contribute, as provided by section 18(a) the amount necessary to satisfy the lia-

bilities; but if any, but not all, of the partners are insolvent, or, not being subject to process, refuse to contribute, the other partners shall contribute their share of the liabilities, and, in the relative proportions in which they share the profits, the additional amount necessary to pay the liabilities.

(e) An assignee for the benefit of creditors or any person appointed by the court shall have the right to enforce the contributions specified in clause (d) of this paragraph.

(f) Any partner or his legal representative shall have the right to enforce the contributions specified in clause (d) of this paragraph, to the extent of the amount which he has paid in excess of his share of the liability.

(g) The individual property of a deceased partner shall be liable for the contributions specified in clause (d) of this paragraph.

(h) When partnership property and the individual properties of the partners are in possession of a court for distribution, partnership creditors shall have priority on partnership property and separate creditors on individual property, saving the rights of lien or secured creditors as heretofore.

(i) Where a partner has become bankrupt or his estate is insolvent the claims against his separate property shall rank in the following order:

   (I) Those owing to separate creditors,
   (III) Those owing to partnership creditors,
   (III) Those owing to partners by way of contribution.

§ 41. Liability of Persons Continuing the Business in Certain Cases

(1) When any new partner is admitted into an existing partnership, or when any partner retires and assigns (or the representative of the deceased partner assigns) his rights in partnership property to two or more of the partners, or to one or more of the partners and one or more third persons, if the business is continued without liquidation of the partnership affairs, creditors of the first or dissolved partnership are also creditors of the partnership so continuing the business.

(2) When all but one partner retire and assign (or the representative of a deceased partner assigns) their rights in partnership property to the remaining partner, who continues the business

without liquidation of partnership affairs, either alone or with others, creditors of the dissolved partnership are also creditors of the person or partnership so continuing the business.

(3) When any partner retires or dies and the business of the dissolved partnership is continued as set forth in paragraphs (1) and (2) of this section, with the consent of the retired partners or the representative of the deceased partner, but without any assignment of his right in partnership property, rights of creditors of the dissolved partnership and of the creditors of the person or partnership continuing the business shall be as if such assignment had been made.

(4) When all the partners or their representatives assign their rights in partnership property to one or more third persons who promise to pay the debts and who continue the business of the dissolved partnership, creditors of the dissolved partnership are also creditors of the person or partnership continuing the business.

(5) When any partner wrongfully causes a dissolution and the remaining partners continue the business under the provisions of section 38(2b), either alone or with others, and without liquidation of the partnership affairs, creditors of the dissolved partnership are also creditors of the person or partnership continuing the business.

(6) When a partner is expelled and the remaining partners continue the business either alone or with others, without liquidation of the partnership affairs, creditors of the dissolved partnership are also creditors of the person or partnership continuing the business.

(7) The liability of a third person becoming a partner in the partnership continuing the business, under this section, to the creditors of the dissolved partnership shall be satisfied out of partnership property only.

(8) When the business of a partnership after dissolution is continued under any conditions set forth in this section the creditors of the dissolved partnership, as against the separate creditors of the retiring or deceased partner or the representative of the deceased partner, have a prior right to any claim of the retired partner or the representative of the deceased partner against the person or partnership continuing the business, on account of the retired or deceased partner's interest in the dissolved partnership or on account of any consideration promised for such interest or for his right in partnership property.

(9) Nothing in this section shall be held to modify any right of creditors to set aside any assignment on the ground of fraud.

(10) The use by the person or partnership continuing the business of the partnership name, or the name of a deceased partner as part thereof, shall not of itself make the individual property of the deceased partner liable for any debts contracted by such person or partnership.

§ 42. Rights of Retiring or Estate of Deceased Partner When the Business is Continued

When any partner retires or dies, and the business is continued under any of the conditions set forth in section 41 (1, 2, 3, 5, 6), or section 38(2b) without any settlement of accounts as between him or his estate and the person or partnership continuing the business, unless otherwise agreed, he or his legal representative as against such persons or partnership may have the value of his interest at the date of dissolution ascertained, and shall receive as an ordinary creditor an amount equal to the value of his interest in the dissolved partnership with interest, or, at his option or at the option of his legal representative, in lieu of interest, the profits attributable to the use of his right in the property of the dissolved partnership; provided that the creditors of the dissolved partnership as against the separate creditors, or the representative of the retired or deceased partner, shall have priority on any claim arising under this section, as provided by section 41(8) of this act.

§ 43. Accrual of Actions

The right to an account of his interest shall accrue to any partner, or his legal representative, as against the winding up partners or the surviving partners or the person or partnership continuing the business, at the date of dissolution, in the absence of any agreement to the contrary.

PART VII
MISCELLANEOUS PROVISIONS
§ 44. When Act Takes Effect
This act shall take effect on the _____ day of _____ one thousand nine hundred and _____ .

§ 45. Legislation Repealed
All acts or parts of acts inconsistent with this act are hereby repealed.

The Uniform Limited Partnership Act

*(Adopted August 5, 1976, by the National Conference of Commissioners on Uniform State Laws, it is intended to replace the existing Uniform Limited Partnership Act (Appendix D). It has been adopted in 36 States: Alabama, Arizona, Arkansas, California, Colorado, Connecticut, Delaware, Florida, Idaho, Illinois, Iowa, Kansas, Maryland, Massachusetts, Michigan, Minnesota, Mississippi, Missouri, Montana, Nebraska, Nevada, New Jersey, North Carolina, North Dakota, Ohio, Oklahoma, Oregon, Rhode Island, South Carolina, South Dakota, Texas, Virginia, Washington, West Virginia, Wisconsin, and Wyoming.

The Act consists of 11 Articles as follows:

1. General Provisions
2. Formation; Certificate of Limited Partnership
3. Limited Partners
4. General Partners
5. Finance
6. Distributions and Withdrawal
7. Assignment of Partnership Interests
8. Dissolution
9. Foreign Limited Partnership
10. Derivative Actions
11. Miscellaneous

ARTICLE **1**
GENERAL PROVISIONS
§ 101. Definitions
As used in this Act, unless the context otherwise requires:

(1) "Certificate of limited partnership" means the certificate referred to in Section 201, and the certificate as amended or restated.

---

*At its annual conference in August 1985, the National Conference of Commissioners on Uniform State Laws approved amendments to the "Revised Uniform Partnership Act." This printing includes these amendments.

(2) "Contribution" means any cash, property, services rendered, or a promissory note or other binding obligation to contribute cash or property or to perform services, which a partner contributes to a limited partnership in his capacity as a partner.

(3) "Event of withdrawal of a general partner" means an event that causes a person to cease to be a general partner as provided in Section 402.

(4) "Foreign limited partnership" means a partnership formed under the laws of any state other than this State and having as partners one or more general partners and one or more limited partners.

(5) "General partner" means a person who has been admitted to a limited partnership as a general partner in accordance with the partnership agreement and named in the certificate of limited partnership as a general partner.

(6) "Limited partner" means a person who has been admitted to a limited partnership as a limited partner in accordance with the partnership agreement.

(7) "Limited partnership" and "domestic limited partnership" mean a partnership formed by two or more persons under the laws of this State and having one or more general partners and one or more limited partners.

(8) "Partner" means a limited or general partner.

(9) "Partnership agreement" means any valid agreement, written or oral, of the partners as to the affairs of a limited partnership and the conduct of its business.

(10) "Partnership interest" means a partner's share of the profits and losses of a limited partnership and the right to receive distributions of partnership assets.

(11) "Person" means a natural person, partnership, limited partnership (domestic or foreign), trust, estate, association, or corporation.

(12) "State" means a state, territory, or possession of the United States, the District of Columbia, or the Commonwealth of Puerto Rico.

§ 102. Name

The name of each limited partnership as set forth in its certificate of limited partnership:

(1) shall contain without abbreviation the words "limited partnership";

(2) may not contain the name of a limited partner unless (i) it is also the name of a general partner or the corporate name of a corporate general partner, or (ii) the business of the limited partnership had been carried on under that name before the admission of that limited partner;

(3) may not be the same as, or deceptively similar to, the name of any corporation or limited partnership organized under the laws of this State or licensed or registered as a foreign corporation or limited partnership in this State; and

(4) may not contain the following words [here insert prohibited words].

§ 103. Reservation of Name

(a) The exclusive right to the use of a name may be reserved by:

(1) any person intending to organize a limited partnership under this Act and to adopt that name;

(2) any domestic limited partnership or any foreign limited partnership registered in this State which, in either case, intends to adopt that name;

(3) any foreign limited partnership intending to register in this State and adopt that name; and

(4) any person intending to organize a foreign limited partnership and intending to have it register in this State and adopt that name.

(b) The reservation shall be made by filing with the Secretary of State an application, executed by the applicant, to reserve a specified name. If the Secretary of State finds that the name is available for use by a domestic or foreign limited partnership, he [or she] shall reserve the name for the exclusive use of the applicant for a period of 120 days.

Once having so reserved a name, the same applicant may not again reserve the same name until more than 60 days after the expiration of the last 120-day period for which that applicant reserved that name. The right to the exclusive use of a reserved name may be transferred to any other person by filing in the office of the Secretary of State a notice of the transfer, executed by the applicant for whom the name was reserved and specifying the name and address of the transferee.

§ 104. Specified Office and Agent

Each limited partnership shall continuously maintain in this State:

(1) an office, which may but need not be a place of its business in this State, at which shall be kept the records required by Section 105 to be maintained; and

(2) an agent for service of process on the limited partnership, which agent must be an individual resident of this State, a domestic corporation, or a foreign corporation authorized to do business in this State.

§ 105. Records to be Kept

(a) Each limited partnership shall keep at the office referred to in Section 104(1) the following:

(1) a current list of the full name and last known business address of each partner separately identifying the general partners (in alphabetical order) and the limited partners (in alphabetical order);

(2) a copy of the certificate of limited partnership and all certificates of amendment thereto, together with executed copies of any powers of attorney pursuant to which any certificate has been executed;

(3) copies of the limited partnership's federal, state and local income tax returns and reports, if any, for the three most recent years;

(4) copies of any then effective written partnership agreements and of any financial statements of the limited partnership for the three most recent years; and

(5) unless contained in a written partnership agreement, a writing setting out:

(i) the amount of cash and a description and statement of the agreed value of the other property or services contributed by each partner and which each partner has agreed to contribute;

   (ii) the times at which or events on the happening of which any additional contributions agreed to be made by each partner are to be made;

   (iii) any right of a partner to receive, or of a general partner to make, distributions to a partner which include a return of all or any part of the partner's contribution; and

   (iv) any events upon the happening of which the limited partnership is to be dissolved and its affairs wound up.

(b) Records kept under this section are subject to inspection and copying at the reasonable request at the expense of any partner during ordinary business hours.

§ 106. Nature of Business

A limited partnership may carry on any business that a partnership without limited partners may carry on except [here designate prohibited activities].

§ 107. Business Transactions of Partner with Partnership

Except as provided in the partnership agreement, a partner may lend money to and transact other business with the limited partnership and, subject to other applicable law, has the same rights and obligations with respect thereto as a person who is not a partner.

ARTICLE **2**
FORMATION; CERTIFICATE OF LIMITED PARTNERSHIP

§ 201. Certificate of Limited Partnership

(a) In order to form a limited partnership, a certificate of limited partnership must be executed and filed in the office of the Secretary of State. The certificate shall set forth:

   (1) the name of the limited partnership;

   (2) the address of the office and the name and address of the agent for service of process required to be maintained by Section 104;

   (3) the name and the business address of each general partner;

   (4) the latest date upon which the limited partnership is to dissolve; and

   (5) any other matters the general partners determine to include therein.

(b) A limited partnership is formed at the time of the filing of the certificate of limited partnership in the office of the Secretary of State or at any later time specified in the certificate of limited partnership if, in either case, there has been substantial compliance with the require-ments of this section.

§ 202. Amendment to Certificate

(a) A certificate of limited partnership is amended by filing a certificate of amendment thereto in the office of the Secretary of State. The certificate shall set forth:

   (1) the name of the limited partnership;

   (2) the date of filing the certificate; and

   (3) the amendment to the certificate.

(b) Within 30 days after the happening of any of the following events, an amendment to a certificate of limited partnership reflecting the occurrence of the event or events shall be filed:

   (1) the admission of a new general partner;

   (2) the withdrawal of a general partner; or

   (3) the continuation of the business under Section 801 after an event of withdrawal of a general partner.

(c) A general partner who becomes aware that any statement in a certificate of limited partnership was false when made or that any arrangements or other facts described have changed, making the certificate inaccurate in any respect, shall promptly amend the certificate.

(d) A certificate of limited partnership may be amended at any time for any other proper purpose the general partners determine.

(e) No person has any liability because an amendment to a certificate of limited partnership has not been filed to reflect the occurrence of any event referred to in subsection (b) of this section if the amendment is filed within the 30-day period specified in subsection (b).

(f) A restated certificate of limited partnership may be executed and filed in the same manner as a certificate of amendment.

§ 203. Cancellation of Certificate

A certificate of limited partnership shall be cancelled upon the dissolution and the commencement of winding up of the partnership or at any other time there are no limited partners. A certificate of cancellation shall be filed in the office of the Secretary of State and set forth:

(1) the name of the limited partnership;
(2) the date of filing of its certificate of limited partnership;
(3) the reason for filing the certificate of cancellation;
(4) the effective date (which shall be a date certain) of cancellation if it is not to be effective upon the filing of the certificate; and
(5) any other information the general partners filing the certificate determine.

§ 204. Execution of Certificates

(a) Each certificate required by this Article to be filed in the office of the Secretary of State shall be executed in the following manner:

   (1) an original certificate of limited partnership must be signed by all general partners,
   (2) a certificate of amendment must be signed by at least one general partner and by each other general partner designated in the certificate as a new general partner; and
   (3) a certificate of cancellation must be signed by all general partners.

(b) Any person may sign a certificate by an attorney-in-fact, but a power of attorney to sign a certificate relating to the admission of a general partner must specifically describe the admission.

(c) The execution of a certificate by a general partner constitutes an affirmation under the penalties of perjury that the facts stated therein are true.

§ 205. Execution by Judicial Act

If a person required by Section 204 to execute any certificate fails or refuses to do so, any other person who is adversely affected by the failure or refusal, may petition the [designate the appropriate court] to direct the execution of the certificate. If the court finds that it is proper for the certificate to be executed and that any person so designated has failed or refused to execute the certificate, it shall order the Secretary of State to record an appropriate certificate.

§ 206. Filing in Office of Secretary of State

(a) Two signed copies of the certificate of limited partnership and of any certificates of amendment or cancellation (or of any judicial decree of amendment or cancellation) shall be delivered to the Secretary of State. A person who executes a certificate as an agent or fiduciary need not exhibit evidence of his [or her] authority as a prerequisite to filing. Unless the Secretary of State finds that any certificate does not conform to law, upon receipt of all filing fees required by law he [or she] shall:

(1) endorse on each duplicate original the word "Filed" and the day, month, and year of the filing thereof;
(2) file one duplicate original in his [or her] office; and
(3) return the other duplicate original to the person who filed it or his [or her] representative.

(b) Upon the filing of a certificate of amendment (or judicial decree of amendment) in the office of the Secretary of State, the certificate of limited partnership shall be amended as set forth therein, and upon the effective date of a certificate of cancellation (or a judicial decree thereof), the certificate of limited partnership is cancelled.

§ 207. Liability for False Statement in Certificate

If any certificate of limited partnership or certificate of amendment or cancellation contains a false statement, one who suffers loss by reliance on the statement may recover damages for the loss from:

(1) any person who executes the certificate, or causes another to execute it on his behalf, and knew, and any general partner who knew or should have known, the statement to be false at the time the certificate was executed; and
(2) any general partner who thereafter knows or should have known that any arrangement or other fact described in the certificate has changed, making the statement inaccurate in any respect within a sufficient time before the statement was relied upon reasonably to have enabled that general partner to cancel or amend the certificate, or to file a petition for its cancellation or amendment under Section 205.

§ 208. Scope of Notice

The fact that a certificate of limited partnership is on file in the office of the Secretary of State is notice that the partnership is a limited partnership and the persons designated therein as general partners are general partners, but it is not notice of any other fact.

ARTICLE 3
LIMITED PARTNERS

§ 301. Admission of Additional Limited Partners

(a) A person becomes a limited partner:

    (1) at the time the limited partnership is formed; or

    (2) at any later time specified in the records of the limited partnership for becoming a limited partner.

(b) After the filing of a limited partnership's original certificate of limited partnership, a person may be admitted as an additional limited partner:

    (1) in the case of a person acquiring a partnership interest directly from the limited partnership, upon compliance with the partnership agreement or, if the partnership agreement does not so provide, upon the written consent of all partners; and

    (2) in the case of an assignee of a partnership interest of a partner who has the power, as provided in Section 704, to grant the assignee the right to become a limited partner, upon the exercise of that power and compliance with any conditions limiting the grant or exercise of the power.

§ 302. Voting

Subject to Section 303, the partnership agreement may grant to all or to a specified group of the limited partners the right to vote (on a per capita or any other basis) upon any matter.

§ 303. Liability to Third Parties

(a) Except as provided in subsection (d), a limited partner is not liable for the obligations of a limited partnership unless he [or she] is also a general partner or, in addition to the exercise of his [or her] rights and powers as a limited partner, he [or she] participates in the control of the business. However, if the limited partner participates in the control of the business, he [or she] is liable only to persons who transact business with the limited partnership reasonably believing, based upon the limited partner's conduct, that the limited partner is a general partner.

(b) A limited partner does not participate in the control of the business within the meaning of subsection (a) solely by doing one or more of the following:

    (1) being a contractor for or an agent or employee of the limited partnership or of a general partner or being an officer, director, or shareholder of a general partner that is a corporation;

    (2) consulting with and advising a general partner with respect to the business of the limited partnership;

    (3) acting as surety for the limited partnership or guaranteeing or assuming one or more specific obligations of the limited partnership;

    (4) taking any action required or permitted by law to bring or pursue a derivative action in the right of the limited partnership;

    (5) requesting or attending a meeting of partners;

    (6) proposing, approving, or disapproving, by voting or otherwise, one or more of the following matters:

        (i) the dissolution and winding up of the limited partnership;

        (ii) the sale, exchange, lease, mortgage, pledge, or other transfer of all or substantially all of the assets of the limited partnership;

        (iii) the incurrence of indebtedness by the limited partnership other than in the ordinary course of its business;

        (iv) a change in the nature of the business;

        (v) the admission or removal of a general partner;

        (vi) the admission or removal of a limited partner;

        (vii) a transaction involving an actual or potential conflict of interest between a general partner and the limited partnership or the limited partners;

        (viii) an amendment to the partnership agreement or certificate of limited partnership; or

        (ix) matters related to the business of the limited partnership not otherwise enumerated in this subsection (b), which the partnership agreement states in writing may be subject to the approval or disapproval of limited partners;

(7) winding up the limited partnership pursuant to Section 803; or

(8) exercising any right or power permitted to limited partners under this Act and not specifically enumerated in this subsection (b).

(c) The enumeration in subsection (b) does not mean that the possession or exercise of any other powers by a limited partner constitutes participation by him [or her] in the business of the limited partnership.

(d) A limited partner who knowingly permits his [or her] name to be used in the name of the limited partnership, except under circumstances permitted by Section 102(2), is liable to creditors who extend credit to the limited partnership without actual knowledge that the limited partner is not a general partner.

§ 304. Person Erroneously Believing Himself [or Herself] Limited Partner

(a) Except as provided in subsection (b), a person who makes a contribution to a business enterprise and erroneously but in good faith believes that he [or she] has become a limited partner in the enterprise is not a general partner in the enterprise and is not bound by its obligations by reason of making the contribution, receiving distributions from the enterprise, or exercising any rights of a limited partner, if, on ascertaining the mistake, he [or she]:

(1) causes an appropriate certificate of limited partnership or a certificate of amendment to be executed and filed; or

(2) withdraws from future equity participation in the enterprise by executing and filing in the office of the Secretary of State a certificate declaring withdrawal under this section.

(b) A person who makes a contribution of the kind described in subsection (a) is liable as a general partner to any third party who transacts business with the enterprise (i) before the person withdraws and an appropriate certificate is filed to show withdrawal, or (ii) before an appropriate certificate is filed to show that he [or she] is not a general partner, but in either case only if the third party actually believed in good faith that the person was a general partner at the time of the transaction.

§ 305. Information

Each limited partner has the right to:

(1) inspect and copy any of the partnership records required to be maintained by Section 105; and

(2) obtain from the general partners from time to time upon reasonable demand (i) true and full information regarding the state of the business and financial condition of the limited partnership, (ii) promptly after becoming available, a copy of the limited partnership's federal, state, and local income tax returns for each year, and (iii) other information regarding the affairs of the limited partnership as is just and reasonable.

ARTICLE 4
GENERAL PARTNERS

§ 401. Admission of Additional General Partners

After the filing of a limited partnership's original certificate of limited partnership, additional general partners may be admitted as provided in writing in the partnership agreement or, if the partnership agreement does not provide in writing for the admission of additional general partners, with the written consent of all partners.

§ 402. Events of Withdrawal

Except as approved by the specific written consent of all partners at the time, a person ceases to be a general partner of a limited partnership upon the happening of any of the following events:

(1) the general partner withdraws from the limited partnership as provided in Section 602;

(2) the general partner ceases to be a member of the limited partnership as provided in Section 702;

(3) the general partner is removed as a general partner in accordance with the partnership agreement;

(4) unless otherwise provided in writing in the partnership agreement, the general partner: (i) makes an assignment for the benefit of creditors; (ii) files a voluntary petition in bankruptcy; (iii) is adjudicated a bankrupt or insolvent; (iv) files a petition or answer seeking for himself [or herself] any reorganization, arrangement, composition, readjustment, liquidation, dissolution or similar relief under any statute, law, or regulation; (v) files an answer or other pleading admitting or failing to contest the material alle-

gations of a petition filed against him [or her] in any proceeding of this nature; or (vi) seeks, consents to, or acquiesces in the appointment of a trustee, receiver, or liquidator of the general partner or of all or any substantial part of his [or her] properties;

(5) unless otherwise provided in writing in the partnership agreement, [120] days after the commencement of any proceeding against the general partner seeking reorganization, arrangement, composition, readjustment, liquidation, dissolution or similar relief under any statute, law, or regulation, the proceeding has not been dismissed, or if within [90] days after the appointment without his [or her] consent or acquiescence of a trustee, receiver, or liquidator of the general partner or of all or any substantial part of his [or her] properties, the appointment is not vacated or stayed or within [90] days after the expiration of any such stay, the appointment is not vacated;

(6) in the case of a general partner who is a natural person,
    (i) his [or her] death; or
    (ii) the entry of an order by a court of competent jurisdiction adjudicating him [or her] incompetent to manage his [or her] person or his [or her] estate;

(7) in the case of a general partner who is acting as a general partner by virtue of being a trustee of a trust, the termination of the trust (but not merely the substitution of a new trustee);

(8) in the case of a general partner that is a separate partnership, the dissolution and commencement of winding up of the separate partnership;

(9) in the case of a general partner that is a corporation, the filing of a certificate of dissolution, or its equivalent, for the corporation or the revocation of its charter; or

(10) in the case of an estate, the distribution by the fiduciary of the estate's entire interest in the partnership.

§ 403. General Powers and Liabilities

(a) Except as provided in this Act or in the partnership agreement, a general partner of a limited partnership has the rights and powers and is subject to the restrictions of a partner in a partnership without limited partners.

(b) Except as provided in this Act, a general partner of a limited partnership has the liabilities of a partner in a partnership without limited partners to persons other than the partnership and the other partners. Except as provided in this Act or in the partnership agreement, a general partner of a limited partnership has the liabilities of a partner in a partnership without limited partners to the partnership and to the other partners.

§ 404. Contributions by General Partner

A general partner of a limited partnership may make contributions to the partnership and share in the profits and losses of, and in distributions from, the limited partnership as a general partner. A general partner also may make contributions to and share in profits, losses, and distributions as a limited partner. A person who is both a general partner and a limited partner has the rights and powers, and is subject to the restrictions and liabilities, of a general partner and, except as provided in the partnership agreement, also has the powers, and is subject to the restrictions, of a limited partner to the extent of his [or her] participation in the partnership as a limited partner.

§ 405. Voting

The partnership agreement may grant to all or certain identified general partners the right to vote (on a per capita or any other basis), separately or with all or any class of the limited partners, on any matter.

ARTICLE **5**
FINANCE
§ 501. Form of Contribution

The contribution of a partner may be in cash, property, or services rendered, or a promissory note or other obligation to contribute cash or property or to perform services.

§ 502. Liability for Contribution

(a) A promise by a limited partner to contribute to the limited partnership is not enforceable unless set out in a writing signed by the limited partner.

(b) Except as provided in the partnership agreement, a partner is obligated to the limited partnership to perform any enforceable promise to contribute cash or property or to perform services, even if he [or she] is unable to perform because of death, disability, or any other reason. If a partner does not make the required contribution of property or services, he [or she] is obligated at the option of the limited partnership to contribute cash equal to that portion of the value, as stated in the partnership records required to be kept pursuant to Section 105, of the stated contribution which has not been made.

(c) Unless otherwise provided in the partnership agreement, the obligation of a partner to make a contribution or return money or other property paid or distributed in violation of this Act may be compromised only by consent of all partners. Notwithstanding the compromise, a creditor of a limited partnership who extends credit, or otherwise acts in reliance on that obligation after the partner signs a writing which, reflects the obligation, and before the amendment or cancellation thereof to reflect the compromise, may enforce the original obligation.

§ 503. Sharing of Profits and Losses

The profits and losses of a limited partnership shall be allocated among the partners, and among classes of partners, in the manner provided in writing in the partnership agreement. If the partnership agreement does not so provide in writing, profits and losses shall be allocated on the basis of the value, as stated in the partnership records required to be kept pursuant to Section 105, of the contributions made by each partner to the extent they have been received by the partnership and have not been returned.

§ 504. Sharing of Distributions

Distributions of cash or other assets of a limited partnership shall be allocated among the partners and among classes of partners in the manner provided in writing in the partnership agreement. If the partnership agreement does not so provide in writing, distributions shall be made on the basis of the value, as stated in the partnership records required to be kept pursuant to Section 105, of the contributions made by each partner to the extent they have been received by the partnership and have not been returned.

ARTICLE 6
DISTRIBUTIONS AND WITHDRAWAL
§ 601. Interim Distributions

Except as provided in this Article, a partner is entitled to receive distributions from a limited partnership before his [or her] withdrawal from the limited partner-

ship and before the dissolution and winding up thereof to the extent and at the times or upon the happening of the events specified in the partnership agreement.

§ 602. Withdrawal of General Partner

A general partner may withdraw from a limited partnership at any time by giving written notice to the other partners, but if the withdrawal violates the partnership agreement, the limited partnership may recover from the withdrawing general partner damages for breach of the partnership agreement and offset the damages against the amount otherwise distributable to him [or her].

§ 603. Withdrawal of Limited Partner

A limited partner may withdraw from a limited partnership at the time or upon the happening of events specified in writing in the partnership agreement. If the agreement does not specify in writing the time or the events upon the happening of which a limited partner may withdraw or a definite time for the dissolution and winding up of the limited partnership, a limited partner may withdraw upon not less than six months' prior written notice to each general partner at his [or her] address on the books of the limited partnership at its office in this State.

§ 604. Distribution Upon Withdrawal

Except as provided in this Article, upon withdrawal any withdrawing partner is entitled to receive any distribution to which he [or she] is entitled under the partnership agreement and, if not otherwise provided in the agreement, he [or she] is entitled to receive, within a reasonable time after withdrawal, the fair value of his [or her] interest in the limited partnership as of the date of withdrawal based upon his [or her] right to share in distributions from the limited partnership.

§ 605. Distribution in Kind

Except as provided in the partnership agreement, a partner, regardless of the nature of his [or her] contribution, has no right to demand and receive any distribution from a limited partnership in any form other than cash. Except as provided in writing in the partnership agreement, a partner may not be compelled to accept a distribution of any asset in kind from a limited partnership to the extent that the percentage of the asset distributed to him [or her] exceeds a percentage of the asset which is equal to the percentage in which he [or she] shares in distributions from the limited partnership.

§ 606. Right to Distribution

At the time a partner becomes entitled to receive a distribution, he [or she] has the status of, and is entitled to all remedies available to, a creditor of the limited partnership with respect to the distribution.

§ 607. Limitations on Distribution

A partner may not receive a distribution from a limited partnership to the extent that, after giving effect to the distribution, all liabilities of the limited partnership, other than liabilities to partners on account of their partnership interests, exceed the fair value of the partnership assets.

§ 608. Liability Upon Return of Contribution

(a) If a partner has received the return of any part of his [or her] contribution without violation of the partnership agreement or this Act, he [or she] is liable to the limited partnership for a period of one year thereafter for the amount of the returned contribution, but only to the extent necessary to discharge the limited partnership's liabilities to creditors who extended credit to the limited partnership during the period the contribution was held by the partnership.

(b) If a partner has received the return of any part of his [or her] contribution in violation of the partnership agreement or this Act, he [or she] is liable to the limited partnership for a period of six years thereafter for the amount of the contribution wrongfully returned.

(c) A partner receives a return of his [or her] contribution to the extent that a distribution to him [or her] reduces his [or her] share of the fair value of the net assets of the limited partnership below the value, as set forth in the partnership records required to be kept pursuant to Section 105, of his contribution which has not been distributed to him [or her].

ARTICLE 7

ASSIGNMENT OF PARTNERSHIP INTERESTS

§ 701. Nature of Partnership Interest

A partnership interest is personal property.

§ 702. Assignment of Partnership Interest

Except as provided in the partnership agreement, a partnership interest is assignable in whole or in part. An assignment of a partnership interest does not dissolve a limited partnership or entitle the assignee to become or to exercise any rights of a partner. An assignment entitles the assignee to receive, to the extent assigned, only the distribution to which the assignor would be entitled. Except as provided in the partnership agreement, a partner ceases to be a partner upon assignment of all his [or her] partnership interest.

§ 703. Rights of Creditor

On application to a court of competent jurisdiction by any judgment creditor of a partner, the court may charge the partnership interest of the partner with payment of the unsatisfied amount of the judgment with interest. To the extent so charged, the judgment creditor has only the rights of an assignee of the partnership interest. This Act does not deprive any partner of the benefit of any exemption laws applicable to his [or her] partnership interest.

§ 704. Right of Assignee to Become Limited Partner

(a) An assignee of a partnership interest, including an assignee of a general partner, may become a limited partner if and to the extent that (i) the assignor gives the assignee that right in accordance with authority described in the partnership agreement, or (ii) all other partners consent.

(b) An assignee who has become a limited partner has, to the extent assigned, the rights and powers, and is subject to the restrictions and liabilities, of a limited partner under the partnership agreement and this Act. An assignee who becomes a limited partner also is liable for the obligations of his [or her] assignor to make and return contributions as provided in Articles 5 and 6. However, the assignee is not obligated for liabilities unknown to the assignee at the time he [or she] became a limited partner.

(c) If an assignee of a partnership interest becomes a limited partner, the assignor is not released from his [or her] liability to the limited partnership under Sections 207 and 502.

§ 705. Power of Estate of Deceased or Incompetent Partner

If a partner who is an individual dies or a court of competent jurisdiction adjudges him [or her] to be incompetent to manage his [or her] person or his [or her] property, the partner's executor, administrator, guardian, conservator, or other legal representative may exercise all the partner's rights for the purpose of settling his [or her] estate or administering his [or her] property, including any power the partner had to give an assignee the right to become a limited partner. If a partner is a corporation, trust, or other entity and is dissolved or terminated, the powers of that partner may be exercised by its legal representative or successor.

ARTICLE 8
DISSOLUTION

§ 801. Nonjudicial Dissolution
A limited partnership is dissolved and its affairs shall be wound up upon the happening of the first to occur of the following:

(1) at the time specified in the certificate of limited partnership;

(2) upon the happening of events specified in writing in the partnership agreement;

(3) written consent of all partners;

(4) an event of withdrawal of a general partner unless at the time there is at least one other general partner and the written provisions of the partnership agreement permit the business of the limited partnership to be carried on by the remaining general partner and that partner does so, but the limited partnership is not dissolved and is not required to be wound up by reason of any event of withdrawal, if, within 90 days after the withdrawal, all partners agree in writing to continue the business of the limited partnership and to the appointment of one or more additional general partners if necessary or desired; or

(5) entry of a decree of judicial dissolution under Section 802.

§ 802. Judicial Dissolution
On application by or for a partner the [designate the appropriate court] court may decree dissolution of a limited partnership whenever it is not reasonably practicable to carry on the business in conformity with the partnership agreement.

§ 803. Winding Up
Except as provided in the partnership agreement, the general partners who have not wrongfully dissolved a limited partnership or, if none, the limited partners, may wind up the limited partnership's affairs; but the [designate the appropriate court] court may wind up the limited partnership's affairs upon application of any partner, his [or her] legal representative, or assignee.

§ 804. Distribution of Assets
Upon the winding up of a limited partnership, the assets shall be distributed as follows:

(1) to creditors, including partners who are creditors, to the extent permitted by law, in satisfaction of liabilities of the limited partnership other than liabilities for distributions to partners under Section 601 or 604;

(2) except as provided in the partnership agreement, to partners and former partners in satisfaction of liabilities for distributions under Section 601 or 604; and

(3) except as provided in the partnership agreement, to partners first for the return of their contributions and secondly respecting their partnership interests, in the proportions in which the partners share in distributions.

ARTICLE 9
FOREIGN LIMITED PARTNERSHIPS

§ 901. Law Governing
Subject to the Constitution of this State, (i) the laws of the state under which a foreign limited partnership is organized govern its organization and internal affairs and the liability of its limited partners, and (ii) a foreign limited partnership may not be denied registration by reason of any difference between those laws and the laws of this State.

§ 902. Registration
Before transacting business in this State, a foreign limited partnership shall register with the Secretary of State. In order to register, a foreign limited partnership shall submit to the Secretary of State, in duplicate, an application for registration as a foreign limited partnership, signed and sworn to by a general partner and setting forth:

(1) the name of the foreign limited partnership and, if different, the name under which it proposes to register and transact business in this State;

(2) the State and date of its formation;

(3) the name and address of any agent for service of process on the foreign limited partnership whom

the foreign limited partnership elects to appoint; the agent must be an individual resident of this State, a domestic corporation, or a foreign corporation having a place of business in, and authorized to do business in, this State;

(4) a statement that the Secretary of State is appointed the agent of the foreign limited partnership for service of process if no agent has been appointed under paragraph (3) or, if appointed, the agent's authority has been revoked or if the agent cannot be found or served with the exercise of reasonable diligence;

(5) the address of the office required to be maintained in the state of its organization by the laws of that state or, if not so required, of the principal office of the foreign limited partnership;

(6) the name and business address of each general partner; and

(7) the address of the office at which is kept a list of the names and addresses of the limited partners and their capital contributions, together with an undertaking by the foreign limited partnership to keep those records until the foreign limited partnership's registration in this State is cancelled or withdrawn.

§ 903. Issuance of Registration

(a) If the Secretary of State finds that an application for registration conforms to law and all requisite fees have been paid, he [or she] shall:

(1) endorse on the application the word "Filed," and the month, day and year of the filing thereof;

(2) file in his [or her] office a duplicate original of the application; and

(3) issue a certificate of registration to transact business in this State.

(b) The certificate of registration, together with a duplicate original of the application, shall be returned to the person who filed the application or his [or her] representative.

§ 904. Name

A foreign limited partnership may register with the Secretary of State under any name, whether or not it is the name under which it is registered in its state of organization, that includes without abbreviation the words "limited partnership" and that could be registered by a domestic limited partnership.

§ 905. Changes and Amendments

If any statement in the application for registration of a foreign limited partnership was false when made or any arrangements or other facts described have changed, making the application inaccurate in any respect, the foreign limited partnership shall promptly file in the office of the Secretary of State a certificate, signed and sworn to by a general partner, correcting such statement.

§ 906. Cancellation of Registration

A foreign limited partnership may cancel its registration by filing with the Secretary of State a certificate of cancellation signed and sworn to by a general partner. A cancellation does not terminate the authority of the Secretary of State to accept service of process on the foreign limited partnership with respect to [claims for relief] [causes of action] arising out of the transactions of business in this State.

§ 907. Transaction of Business Without Registration

(a) A foreign limited partnership transacting business in this State may not maintain any action, suit, or proceeding in any court of this State until it has registered in this State.

(b) The failure of a foreign limited partnership to register in this State does not impair the validity of any contract or act of the foreign limited partnership or prevent the foreign limited partnership from defending any action, suit, or proceeding in any court of this State.

(c) A limited partner of a foreign limited partnership is not liable as a general partner of the foreign limited partnership solely by reason of having transacted business in this State without registration.

(d) A foreign limited partnership, by transacting business in this State without registration, appoints the Secretary of State as its agent for service of process with respect to [claims for relief] [causes of action] arising out of the transaction of business in this State.

§ 908. Action by [Appropriate Official]

The [designate the appropriate official] may bring an action to restrain a foreign limited partnership from transacting business in this State in violation of this Article.

ARTICLE 10
DERIVATIVE ACTIONS
§ 1001. Right of Action
A limited partner may bring an action in the right of a limited partnership to recover a judgment in its favor if general partners with authority to do so have refused to bring the action or if an effort to cause those general partners to bring the action is not likely to succeed.

§ 1002. Proper Plaintiff
In a derivative action, the plaintiff must be a partner at the time of bringing the action and (i) must have been a partner at the time of the transaction of which he [or she] complains or (ii) his [or her] status as a partner must have devolved upon him [or her] by operation of law or pursuant to the terms of the partnership agreement from a person who was a partner at the time of the transaction.

§ 1003. Pleading
In a derivative action, the complaint shall set forth with particularity the effort of the plaintiff to secure initiation of the action by a general partner or the reasons for not making the effort.

§ 1004. Expenses
If a derivative action is successful, in whole or in part, or if anything is received by the plaintiff as a result of a judgment, compromise or settlement of an action or claim, the court may award the plaintiff reasonable expenses, including reasonable attorney's fees, and shall direct him [or her] to remit to the limited partnership the remainder of those proceeds received by him [or her].

ARTICLE 11
MISCELLANEOUS
§ 1101. Construction and Application
This Act shall be so applied and construed to effectuate its general purpose to make uniform the law with respect to the subject of this Act among states enacting it.

§ 1102. Short Title
This Act may be cited as the Uniform Limited Partnership Act.

§ 1103. Severability
If any provision of this Act or its application to any person or circumstance is held invalid, the invalidity does not affect other provisions or applications of the Act which can be given effect without the invalid provision or application, and to this end the provisions of this Act are severable.

§ 1104. Effective Date, Extended Effective Date and Repeal
Except as set forth below, the effective date of this Act is _____ and the following acts [list existing limited partnership acts] are hereby repealed:

(1) The existing provisions for execution and filing of certificates of limited partnerships and amendments thereunder and cancellations thereof continue in effect until [specify time required to create central filing system], the extended effective date, and Sections 102, 103, 104, 105, 201, 202, 203, 204 and 206 are not effective until the extended effective date.

(2) Section 402, specifying the conditions under which a general partner ceases to be a member of a limited partnership, is not effective until the extended effective date, and the applicable provisions of existing law continue to govern until the extended effective date.

(3) Sections 501, 502 and 608 apply only to contributions and distributions made after the effective date of this Act.

(4) Section 704 applies only to assignments made after the effective date of this Act.

(5) Article 9, dealing with registration of foreign limited partnerships, is not effective until the extended effective date.

(6) Unless otherwise agreed by the partners, the applicable provisions of existing law governing allocation of profits and losses (rather than the provisions of Section 503), distributions to a withdrawing partner (rather than the provisions of Section 604), and distribution of assets upon the winding up of a limited partnership (rather than the provisions of Section 804) govern limited partnerships formed before the effective date of this Act.

§ 1105. Rules for Cases Not Provided for in This Act

In any case not provided for in this Act the provisions of the Uniform Partnership Act govern.

§ 1106. Savings Clause

The repeal of any statutory provision by this Act does not impair, or otherwise affect, the organization or the continued existence of a limited partnership existing at the effective date of this Act, nor does the repeal of any existing statutory provision by this Act impair any contract or affect any right accrued before the effective date of this Act.

GLOSSARY

Abandoned property   Personal property that has been deliberately left in a location without the intention to retrieve it.

Acceptance   Final step necessary to form a legal contract. A demonstration of agreement to all of the terms of the contract that has been offered.

Actus reus   Element of physical conduct necessary to commit a crime.

Administrative agency   Government office enabled by the legislature and overseen by the executive branch. The purpose of such agencies is to apply certain specified laws created by the legislature.

Administrative branch   Administrative agencies created pursuant to legislation and overseen by the executive branch to administer and define statutes.

Administrative Law   Regulations and decisions issued by administrative agencies that explain and detail statutes.

Administrative law judge   Judicial officer assigned to preside over cases between individuals or entities and government administrative agencies.

Administrative Procedures Act   Congressional enactment applied to all federal administrative agencies requiring them to follow certain procedures in the issuance of administrative law.

Adverse possession   When title to real property is acquired without purchase or voluntary transfer of title. Ordinarily, one who obtains title by adverse possession must openly and continuously exercise possession and control over the entire property inconsistent with the interest of the current owner and all others who claim rights to the property for a period of time specified by statute.

Affirm approve.   When an appellate court affirms the result in the original court, that result is approved and can be enforced without delay unless there is the opportunity to appeal to an even higher level court.

Affirmative defenses   Allegation by a defendant that conduct by the plaintiff legally precludes plaintiff from recovery.

Agency   Relationship in which one party, known as the agent, acts on behalf of another party, known as the principal. In a valid agency relationship, the agent can legally bind the principal; for example, an agent can enter into a contract on behalf of a principal.

Ancillary jurisdiction   Authority of a court over issues in a case subject to the court's authority on grounds unrelated to the issues.

Annulment   Legal relationship declared invalid in which the parties to the relationship are treated as if the relationship never existed, for example, marriage.

Antenuptial agreements   Agreement between parties prior to a marriage that states the terms for distribution of assets and liabilities in the event the marriage relationship ends.

Appellate jurisdiction   Authority of one court to review the actions in another court for the purpose of identifying an abuse of discretion. See Discretion.

Arraignment   Stage of a criminal proceeding in which the accused is formally charged.

Articles of incorporation   Document filed with the state at the time of incorporation to state the purpose of the corporation and define the corporate structure.

Assignment   A grant of rights to a third party, that an original party is entitled to under a contract.

Assumption of risk   Defense to negligence on the basis that the plaintiff knew of, appreciated, and voluntarily encountered the danger of the defendant's conduct.

Attorney   Individual who has completed the necessary requirements of education and training to apply for a license to practice law in a jurisdiction.

Bailment   Temporary relinquishment of control over one's personal property to a third party.

Bench trial   Trial in which the judge determines which law will be applicable and applies the law to the facts of the case.

Bilateral contract   An agreement between two or more persons in which each party promises to deliver a performance in exchange for the performance of the other.

Bill   Proposed law presented to the legislature for consideration.

Burden (Standard) of proof   Extent of evidence required for plaintiff to prevail in trial of an action.

Bylaws   Document of a corporation that details the methods of operation, such as officers and duties, chain of command, and general corporate procedures.

Case analysis   Function of evaluating and synthesizing a judicial opinion.

Case brief   Synopsis of a judicial opinion that identifies pivotal facts, primary issues, applicable legal standards, and rationale for decision.

Case law   Law that is created judicially when a legal principle of common law is extended to a similar situation in a courts ruling.

Cases   Judicial opinions that are common law or case law and that interpret statutory and administrative law.

Citation   Identifying information with regard to the source and specific location of a legal principle.

Civil Law   Law that governs the private rights of individuals, legal entities, and government. See Criminal law.

Code   Published collection of statutes within a jurisdiction.

Code of Federal Regulations (CFR)   Publication that contains all current U.S. administrative regulations.

Codicil   Amendment to a will. A codicil incorporates by reference non-conflicting terms of the will and republishes the date of the entire will.

Codification   Process of incorporating newly passed legislation into existing publication of statutes.

Common Law   Judicially created legal principles or standards. The judiciary has the authority to create law in situations where no applicable law exists.

Comparative negligence   Degree of plaintiff's own negligent conduct that was responsible for the plaintiff's injury.

Compensatory damages   Award of money payable to the injured party for the reasonable cost of the injuries.

Complaint   Document that apprises the court and the defendant of the nature of the cause of legal action by the plaintiff against defendant. Also known as a Petition.

Concurrent jurisdiction   When more than one court has authority to hear a case.

Consideration   That which one party provides to another party as inducement to enter into a contractual agreement. The benefit a party receives as the result of entering a contract with another party.

Constructive knowledge   That which one knew or should have known under the circumstances.

Contract   A legally binding agreement that obligates two or more parties to do something they were not already obligated to do or to refrain from doing something to which they were legally entitled.

Contractual Agreement   A promise or set of promises for the breach of which the law provides a remedy and the performance of which the law recognizes a duty.

Contractual capacity   Ability to enter into and be bound by a legal contract, which ability has not been diminished by age of minority or adjudicated incompetence.

Contributory negligence   Doctrine that maintains that a plaintiff who in any way contributes to his or her injury cannot recover from a negligent defendant.

Corporation   Entity legally recognized as independent of its owners, known as shareholders. A corporation can sue or be sued in its own name regarding its own rights and liabilities.

Criminal law   Law created and enforced by the government for the health, welfare, safety, and general good of the public.

Criminal procedure   Law created to assist in the fair and efficient enforcement of criminal law.

Critical stage   Stage of a criminal proceeding in which the presumed innocence of the accused is in jeopardy and so the accused is entitled to representation of counsel.

Custody   Legal right for primary care, education, and parenting of minor children.

Damage   Financial, physical, or emotional injury.

Defendant   Party against whom a lawsuit is instituted.

Delegation   Transfer of one's contractual obligations to a third person.

Delegation doctrine   Policy that Congress does not have the power to delegate or assign its original law making authority to any other body of government, nor may any other government entity assume such authority.

Deposition   Written or oral questions submitted to a party or witness in a lawsuit in which the answers are given orally and under oath, then transcribed into writing.

Direct question   Open-ended question that seeks a narrative answer.

Discovery   Court-supervised exchange of evidence and other relevant information between parties to a lawsuit.

Discretion   Limits of authority. Abuse of discretion occurs when one's authority is exceeded or improperly used; for example, abuse of discretion by a judge or jury is grounds for appeal.

Dissolution of marriage   End of a marriage relationship.

Diversity of citizenship   Method of achieving federal jurisdiction over a matter. It is necessary that all parties be diverse in domicile; that is, no plaintiff and defendant may be domiciled in the same state.

Domicile   The intended permanent place of residence of an individual. Corporations are domiciled in the state of incorporation and where the nerve center of corporate operations are located.

Double jeopardy   Being placed in jeopardy of loss of life or liberty by trial for the same alleged crime more than once.

Due process   That which is necessary to fundamental fairness in the American system of justice.

Easement   Legal right of one to interfere with property use by owner or one in legal possession of property due to a superseding interest.

Enabling act   Congressional enactment that creates the authority in the executive to organize and oversee an administrative agency.

Equity   Functional legal remedy sought when money damages would be inadequate as a method of compensating the injured party. Actions in equity nonperformance of certain acts.

Estate   All material assets of an individual or legal entity, including liquid assets (cash or items that can readily be converted to cash) and nonliquid assets.

Ethical   Legitimate, proper, above board, correct, unimpeachable, principled, honorable, decent, upright, respectable.

Ethical standards   Defined course of conduct imposed to satisfy ethical requirements.

Ethics   Principles, moral principles, code of conduct, right and wrong, values, conscience, moral philosophy, mores, criteria.

Evidence   Testimony, documentation, or tangible items admissible in court to support a party's claims or defenses in a lawsuit.

Exclusive jurisdiction   Authority of a court to hear a case that is superior to all other courts.

Excusable behavior   Behavior by one who, under the color of authority is considered to be innocent of otherwise criminal behavior.

Exhaustion of remedies   Requirement that anyone having a dispute with an administrative agency must first follow all available procedures to resolve the dispute within the agency before taking the issue before the judiciary.

External memorandum   Document of subjective tone prepared in support of a legal position and intended for members outside the legal team, for example, the court or opposing counsel.

Federal court   A court that is part of the U.S. courts.

Federal question   Method of achieving jurisdiction of the federal courts over a dispute between parties. It is necessary that a significant part of the dispute arise from the Constitution or a federal law.

Fee simple   Absolute ownership of property in American law.

Felony   Serious crime punishable by imprisonment in excess of one year and/or other significant penalties.

Fiduciary   Person or institution that manages money or property for another, someone in whom another has a right to place great trust and to expect great loyalty.

Fixture   Item of personal property that has been so affixed to real property that it cannot be removed without damage to the real property. A fixture is personal property that essentially becomes part of the real property.

Forced share   Legal right of a surviving spouse to receive a certain percentage of the estate of the deceased spouse, superior to the terms of a will or other rights of inheritance by heirs.

Foreseeable   Those facts of which a party was or should have been aware under the circumstances.

Forum non conveniens   (inconvenient forum) Applied when a court within a jurisdiction over a matter decreases that another court, which also has jurisdiction, would be the much more appropriate forum based on a test of several factors.

Freehold estate   Interest in real property that involves certain rights of ownership. See Nonfreehold estate.

Grand jury   A number of individuals, usually more than 20, who review the evidence to determine whether a defendant could be convicted of a crime if charged and tried based on the evidence thus far collected.

Guardianship   Legally appointed individual to manage the estate of one who has been declared legally incompetent.

Hostile witness   One who is predisposed to the opposition or who is an unwilling participant in a legal action.

In personam jurisdiction   Authority of a court over an individual and all of his or her assets.

Injunctive relief   Court-ordered action or nonaction to legally limit or enforce specific conduct.

In rem jurisdiction   Authority of a court over a person's real or personal property.

Intentional tort   Act that the actor knows or should know with substantial certainty will cause harm to another.

Internal memorandum   Document of objective tone prepared to communicate information about a client, case, or issue to other members of the legal team.

Interrogatories   Questions submitted by one party in a lawsuit to the opposing party. Said questions must pertain to the dispute between the parties and must be answered within a specific time and under oath. A method of discovery.

Intestate   Dying without a valid will.

Intestate succession   Method of distributing the estate of one who died without a valid will.

Joint tenancy   Form of multiple-property ownership in which the property owners have fee simple and share four unities. Each owner shares in the unity of right of survivorship.

Judge/jurist   Judicial officer who presides over cases in litigation within a court system.

Judicial opinion   Legal document stating the finding and rationale for an order of court.

Judiciary   Appointed or elected officials (judges, magistrates, justices of the peace) who preside in the courts over disputes among citizens and the government.

Jurisdiction   (1) Authority of a court over parties and subject of a dispute. (2) Geographical boundaries of the area and citizens over which a court has authority.

Jurisdiction in personam   See inpersonam jurisdiction.

Jurist   See Judge.

Justifiable behavior   Behavior by one who, under the circumstances, is considered to be innocent of otherwise criminal behavior.

Law clerk   Lawyer, law student, or paralegal who conducts legal research, writing, and various other duties but who does not represent individual clients or otherwise engage in the practice of law.

Lawyer   See attorney.

Leading question   Closed question that implies a specific answer.

Legal analysis   Process of examining precedent in detail to predict its effect on future similar circumstances.

Legal assistant   See Paralegal.

Legal separation   Legal document that establishes the property rights of the parties without effecting a dissolution of the marriage relationship.

Legal standard   Law created by one of the three sources of government: the legislature, executive branch, or the judiciary.

Legislative branch   Members of a congress elected by the citizens of a jurisdiction to represent their interests, for example, a senator or representative.

Liability   Legal responsibility resulting from an act or failure to act when there was a legal obligation to do so.

Life estate   Right to possess and use real property for the duration of one's life with limited ownership rights.

Limited partnership   Partnership of two or more persons in which the limited partner can be held liable for partnership debts only to the extent of his or her investment and cannot take part in general management and operation of the partnership business.

Lobbyist   Individual representing interested parties, who meets with legislators about proposed laws.

Long-arm jurisdiction   Authority of the government of one jurisdiction to reach into another jurisdiction for the purpose of exercising control over a particular citizen.

Lost property   Property unintentionally left by the owner in a place no longer known to the owner.

Maintenance   Financial assistance from a divorced spouse to the other divorced spouse to be used for necessary living expenses and income.

Mandatory authority   A legal standard that the court is required to follow.

Material   Necessary to a fair and informed decision. See Material evidence.

Material evidence   Evidence necessary to a fair and informed decision by the trier of fact.

Memorandum of law   Document containing legal analysis of issues. May be objectively (internal memorandum) or subjectively (external memorandum) written, depending upon the purpose of the document.

Mens rea   Mental state required as an element necessary to commit a criminal act.

Misdemeanor   Criminal offense punishable by a fine or imprisonment of less than one year.

Mislaid property   Property that was intentionally placed by the owner and later forgotten.

Modern balance   Goal of lawmaking authorities to balance the need for consistency and stability against the need for a flexible and adaptive government.

Motion   Formal request by a party to a lawsuit for court-ordered action or nonaction.

Naturalist theory   Philosophy that all persons know inherently the difference between right and wrong.

Negligence   Act or failure to act toward another when (1) a duty was owed to the other person, (2) the act or failure to act was less than a reasonable person would have done under the circumstances, (3) the act or failure to act was the direct cause of injury to the other person, and (4) the injury caused measurable financial, physical or written with words that indicate whether the document is payable to a stated person (bearer), and (6) that no additional acts are to be performed before payment.

Negotiable instrument   Document recognized by law as an exchange for legal tender and that meets all legal requirements, including that the document be (1) written, (2) signed, (3) for a specified amount, (4) payable on a certain date or on demand, (5) emotional damage to the other person.

Nonfreehold estate   Interest in real property that is limited in duration and involves the right of possession but not ownership. See Freehold estate.

Note   Negotiable instrument that involves two parties: the payor promises to pay an amount to the payee on a specified date.

Offer   A party presents an agreement for acceptance or rejection by a second party, which includes all necessary requirements and elements of a legal contract.

Original jurisdiction   Authority of a court to rule in a lawsuit from commencement through the conclusion of trial.

Overrule   Judicial action that states a legal standard previously recognized is no longer effective as law. Distinguished from reversal.

Par value   Legal value of stock (percentages of ownership) in corporation. Par value is determined by the board of directors of the corporation.

Paralegal/legal assistant   One who has legal training and education and performs tasks in the law office that have traditionally been performed by the attorney, with the exception of client advocacy and giving of legal advice. In some geographicical areas these terms are used interchangeably, while others they imply distinct levels of professional ability.

Partnership   Agreement of two or more parties to engage in business or enterprise, with profits and losses shared among all parties.

Pendent jurisdiction   Occurs when a case involves multiple issues and the court in which the case is filed has actual authority over some, but not all, of the issues in which case the court has the option to exercise authority over those issues it could not ordinarily decide, thus exercising a pendant jurisdiction.

Per capita   Distribution in equal shares, with each person representing one share.

Per stirpes   Distribution in equal shares to one level or class of persons; if a member of this level or class is deceased, the member's heirs divide the share.

Permanent injunction   Court order that permanently orders a party to act or refrain from acting in a particular manner.

Personal (in personam) jurisdiction   Authority of a court over an individual and all of his/her assets. See inpersonam jurisdiction.

Personal property   Movable items that are not land or permanently affixed to land. Personal property includes tangible (physical) and intangible items, such as rights of ownership in property held by others, such as bank accounts or rights of ownership in legal entities, for example, stock. It does not include rights to bring legal action against others, commonly known as a chose in action.

Persuasive authority   Relevant legal principle or secondary authority that is not legally binding/controlling.

Pleadings   Initial documents in a lawsuit that apprise the parties and the court of the legal position of plaintiff and defendant. Typically these are the complaint/petition and answer/response.

Positivist theory   Doctrine that there should be one government entity which is not subject to question and which is responsible for the final resolution of all disputes.

Precedent   Existing legal standards that courts look to for guidance when making a determination of a legal issue.

Preliminary injunctions   Court order that orders a party to act or refrain from acting in a particular manner for a specified period of time.

Primary authority   Legal authority that may or may not be binding/controlling, depending on the source and the application.

Probable cause   Legal concept of suspicion supported by facts necessary before a search or arrest can be conducted by law enforcement officers.

Probate   Process of paying creditors and distributing the estate of one who is deceased. Probate courts also often administer the estates of living persons who are incapable of managing their own affairs.

Procedural law   Law used to guide parties fairly and efficiently through the legal system.

Promoter   One who is hired as a fiduciary to recruit investors in a proposed corporation.

Property settlement   Agreement as to the property rights and obligations of co-owners and co-debtors, such as parties to a marriage.

Proximate cause   Direct cause sufficient to produce a result. No other intervening force can occur independently and prior to the result that is also sufficient to produce the result.

Punitive damages   Award of money payable to the injured party as punishment and act as a deterrent to the defendant and others for wanton and reckless conduct. Also referred to as exemplary damages.

Quasi in rem jurisdiction   Authority of a court to alter a person's interest and/or ownership in real or personal property.

Real property   Land or anything permanently affixed to land and no longer movable.

Reasonable conduct   Action or nonaction that is appropriate under the circumstances when all risks and benefits are taken into account.

Reasonable man   One similar in age, intelligence, and experience to the party alleged to be at fault who perceives and appreciates all dangers and benefits of action or nonaction and who acts in the more careful manner.

Recession   Legal termination of a contract prior to its completion. Cancellation.

Relevant evidence   Tends to establish an essential fact in a dispute.

Remand   Action of one court that returns a case to the court where it originated, such as following a reversal or improper transfer.

Removal   Transfer of a case to federal court that was originally filed in state court.

Reporter   Chronological publication of case law.

Request for production   Written request from one party in a lawsuit to the opposing party that seeks to copy and/or inspect documentary evidence relevant to the dispute. A method of discovery.

Res ipsa loquitur   "The thing speaks for itself." Method of proving negligence when (1) the injury would not ordinarily have occurred without negligence, (2) the instrument causing injury was in the exclusive control of the defendant, and (3) the plaintiff in no way contributed to the injury.

Respondeat superior   Liability of an employer for the acts of an employee who caused damage to a third party while acting within the scope of employment.

Reverse   The action of an appellate court used to invalidate a decision by a court of original jurisdiction. The parties to the lawsuit are affected accordingly.

Right of survivorship   Characteristic associated with multiple property ownership in which the ownership interest transfers automatically to co-owners upon death.

Secondary authority   Discussion of relevant principles issued by a private source.

Session law   Published statutes passed during a specific session of the legislature.

Shareholder   One who owns stock representing an ownership interest in a corporation.

Slip law   Individual statute not yet published with other statutes.

Slip opinion   Individual court opinion that is not yet published with other opinions.

Sociological theory   Doctrine that follows the principle that government should adapt laws to reflect the current needs and beliefs of society.

Sole proprietorship   Individual ownership of a business entity. The individual is personally liable for debts of the business.

Specific performance   Court order to complete the performance as stated in a contract. Allowed in certain cases of equity where the performance is unique and cannot be imitated or compensated by the payment of money.

Stare decisis   "Let the decision stand." Method used by the judiciary when applying precedent to current situations.

Statute of frauds   Statutory law that specifies what contracts must be in writing before they will be enforced.

Statutory analysis   Function of evaluating and synthesizing statutory law.

Statutory law   A statute. Law that is created by the legislature.

Strict liability   Liability without fault. Applied in situations where the intention or neglect of the party is immaterial. The mere performance of the act or omission will result in liability.

Subject matter jurisdiction   Authority of a court to determine the actual issue between the parties.

Substantive law   Law that creates and resolves the issue between the parties. Legal standard that guides conduct and is applied to determine whether or not conduct was legally appropriate.

Summary judgment   Determination prior to trial of the rights and obligations of the parties. This is granted only when there is no significant fact left to be decided on the basis of the evidence. The greatest weight of the evidence supports only one result.

Temporary restraining orders   Court order that requires a party to act or refrain from acting in a particular manner for a short time until the court has the opportunity to consider a more permanent ruling.

Tenancy by entirety   Form of multiple ownership of property between spouses that includes a right of survivorship.

Tenancy in common   Form of multiple ownership of property in which each tenant (owner) shares with the other(s) an undivided interest in the property.

Testate   Status of a person who leaves a valid will.

Testate succession   Method of distributing the estate of a deceased person in accordance with the terms of a valid will.

Testate   Method of distributing the estate of a deceased person in accordance with the terms of a valid will.

Third-party beneficiary   One who, as the result of gift or collateral agreement, is entitled to the contractual performance owed another.

Tort   Civil wrong by a party, other than breach of contract, that results in injury to the private rights or interests of another party.

Traditional balance   Goal of the judiciary to allow maximum personal freedom without detracting from the welfare of the general public.

Trial court   Court of original jurisdiction, with authority to hear evidence of parties and render a verdict.

Unauthorized practice of law   One who provides advocacy to third parties or gives legal advice or representation to others without proper jurisdictional licensure/certification.

Unilateral contract   A contractual agreement in which one party makes a promise to perform upon the actual performance of the other party.

Venue   Proper individual court within a jurisdiction to determine a dispute between parties.

Veto   Presidential power to invalidate law passed by a majority of Congress. A 2/3 majority of each house needed to override.

Voir dire   Process of selecting jurors for trial of an action.

INDEX